SEXUALITY NOW

EMBRACING DIVERSITY

First
Canadian
Edition

JANELL L. CARROLL
University of Hartford

EVELYN FIELD
Mount Royal University

DAVID AVELINE
Mount Royal University

NELSON
EDUCATION

NELSON EDUCATION

Sexuality Now: Embracing Diversity, First Canadian Edition

by Janell L. Carroll, Evelyn Field, and David Aveline

VP, Product and Partnership Solutions:
Anne Williams

Publisher, Digital and Print Content:
Lenore Taylor-Atkins

Marketing Manager:
Ann Byford

Content Development Manager:
Lisa Berland

Photo and Permissions Researcher:
Carrie McGregor

Production Project Manager:
Jennifer Hare

Production Service:
MPS Limited

Copy Editor:
Valerie Adams

Proofreader:
MPS Limited

Indexer:
MPS Limited

Design Director:
Ken Phipps

Managing Designer:
Franca Amore

Interior Design:
Diane Beasley

Cover Design:
Courtney Hellam

Cover Image:
© Robyn Graham Photography

Compositor:
MPS Limited

Library and Archives Canada Cataloguing in Publication Data

Carroll, Janell L., author
    Sexuality now : embracing diversity / Janell L. Carroll (University of Hartford), Evelyn Field (Mount Royal University), David Aveline (Mount Royal University).—First Canadian edition.

Includes bibliographical references and index.
ISBN 978-0-17-656136-9 (paperback)

    1. Sex instruction. 2. Sex instruction for youth. 3. Sex customs. 4. Sexual orientation. I. Aveline, David Timothy, 1951–, author II. Field, Evelyn, 1968–, author III. Title.

HQ35.2.C37 2016
613.9071   C2015-907541-6

ISBN-13: 978-0-17-656136-9
ISBN-10: 0-17-656136-6

About the Authors

Dr. Janell L. Carroll received her Ph.D. in human sexuality education from the University of Pennsylvania. A certified sexuality educator with the American Association of Sexuality Educators, Counselors, and Therapists, Dr. Carroll is a dynamic educator, speaker, and author, who has published many articles, authored a syndicated sexuality column, and appeared on numerous television talk shows. Dr. Carroll has travelled throughout the world exploring sexuality—from Japan's love hotels to Egypt's sex clinics—and has been actively involved in the development of several television pilots exploring sexuality. She has lectured extensively; has appeared on and has been quoted in several national publications, Internet news media outlets, and cyberpress articles; and has hosted sexuality-related radio talk shows. She is also the author of a popular press book for young girls about menstruation titled *The Day Aunt Flo Comes to Visit*.

On a personal level, Dr. Carroll feels it is her mission to educate students and the public at large about sexuality—to help people think and feel through the issues for themselves. Dr. Carroll's success as a teacher comes from the fact that she loves her students as much as she loves what she teaches. She sees students' questions about sex as the foundation for her course and has brought that attitude, together with her enthusiasm for helping them find answers, to *Sexuality Now*.

Dr. Carroll has won several teaching awards, including University of Hartford's Gordon Clark Ramsey Award for Creative Excellence, for sustained excellence and creativity in the classroom, and Planned Parenthood's Sexuality Educator of the Year. Before teaching at University of Hartford, Dr. Carroll was a tenured psychology professor at Baker University, where she was honoured with awards for Professor of the Year and Most Outstanding Person on Campus. Dr. Carroll's website (http://www.drjanellcarroll.com) is a popular site for people to learn about sexuality and ask questions.

Dr. Evelyn Field has published over 20 scientific articles in the area of sexual differences and development, co-authored several book chapters, and co-written a book titled *Sex Differences: Summarizing More than a Century of Scientific Research*. She has received awards from the National Science and Engineering Research Council (NSERC), the Alberta Foundation for Medical Research (Alberta Innovates), and the Canadian Institute for Health Research, and received the Governor General's Gold Academic Medal for her research.

Dr. Field has also received numerous recognitions for her teaching and research presentations, including a Student Champion Award from the Students Association at Mount Royal University. She is currently an Associate Professor and Chair for the Department of Psychology at Mount Royal University, where she teaches the third year Psychology of Sexuality Course.

Dr. David Aveline was born in London, England, came to Canada at age four, and was brought up in Quebec. He had a number of jobs before attending university, including underground miner in northern Manitoba, ditch digger, race track groom, youth counsellor, shoe salesman, and hotel manager. He received his Bachelor and Master's degrees in sociology from Concordia University in Montreal and his doctorate in sociology from Indiana University in the United States. Dr. Aveline has long had an interest in human sexuality. His mentors were Dr. Frances M. Shaver at Concordia, who has long studied sex workers, and Dr. Martin S. Weinberg and Dr. Collin J. Williams at Indiana University, who had previously been researchers at the Kinsey Institute. Dr. Aveline's interests in sexuality focus on identity construction, gender fluidity, historical states, and sexual negotiation. He has been a sociologist at Mount Royal University in Calgary for 12 years. He teaches sociology of the body, sociology of religion, and sexualities, and he divides his time between home life with his husband of 24 years and the classroom. He is currently working on a book on sexual negotiations between men from the post-war period to the present.

Brief Contents

Contents

Chapter 1

Exploring Human Sexuality: Past and Present   2

Chapter 2

Understanding Human Sexuality: Theory and Research   26

© Janell Carroll

Chapter 3

Female Sexual Anatomy, Development, and Health 54

© Shawn Pecor/Shutterstock

Chapter 4

Male Sexual Anatomy, Development, and Health   90

© Anthony Hatley/Alamy

Chapter 5
The Biology of Sex, Pregnancy, and Childbirth   112

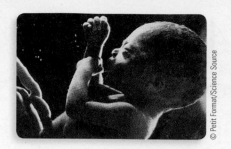

© Petit Format/Science Source

Chapter 6

Contraception and Abortion 152

Chapter 7

Sexually Transmitted Infections and HIV/AIDS   190

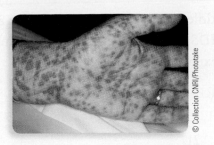

Chapter 8

Gender Development, Gender Roles, and Gender Identity   218

© Monkey Business Images/Shutterstock

Chapter 9

Sexual Orientation 238

Chapter 10
Childhood and Adolescent Sexuality   268

© Pressmaster/Shutterstock

Chapter 11
Communication and Sexuality   294

Chapter 12
Love and Intimacy   314

Chapter 13
Adult Sexual Relationships 336

© Beau Lark/Corbis

Chapter 14

Variations of Sexual Expression   360

© Leslie Sponseller/Getty Images

Chapter 15

Challenges to Sexual Functioning   388

© Roy McMahon/Corbis

Chapter 16

Harmful and Antisocial Sexual Expression   416

© Rainer Elstermann/Corbis

What Is "Abnormal" Sexual Expression?   418

   Judging Sexual Behaviour   419

Paraphilic Disorders   421

   Theories about Paraphilic Disorders   421

Chapter 17
Power and Sexual Coercion 442

© Mel Curtis/Getty Images

Chapter 18
Sexual Imagery and Selling Sex   474

© Frédéric Neema/Sygma/Corbis

Preface

Even though human beings have been having sex since the dawn of their appearance on the planet, sexuality has only been a topic of legitimate inquiry for the past 150 years. Beginning with the early sexologists of the 19th century and continuing today, there has been a gradual realization that sex overlaps with many key areas of human life beyond mere reproduction. Even during this time, for most of the earlier decades, sexual inquiry was legitimate only for physicians and other scientists and not for the general population.

French philosopher and historian Michel Foucault, in his well-known book *The History of Sexuality* published in 1978, made the following observation:

> If sex is repressed, that is, condemned to prohibition, non-existence, and silence, then the mere fact that one is speaking about it has the appearance of a transgression.... for decades now, we have found it difficult to speak on the subject without striking a different pose: we are conscious of defying established power, our tone of voice shows that we know we are being subversive, and we ardently conjure away the present and appeal to the future, whose day will be hastened by the contribution we believe we are making.

Today we realize the significance of sexuality in human life. It is intricately woven with conceptualizations of gender, the politics of gender and identity, family life, the law, religion, and the very fabric of society. Given past prohibitions, students who take courses in human sexuality join a group that has been allowed to delve into the topic only recently. They have high levels of interest and curiosity and their levels of knowledge vary. They also come from a variety of backgrounds in terms of experience, family structure, age, sexual and gender orientation, national origin, race, and ethnicity. It is therefore important to have a textbook that is comprehensive in its coverage, accurate in its presentation, and understandable in its dialogue with students who attempt to learn about the breadth of sexuality. This first Canadian edition attempts to do all of these things. It has up-to-date information, it is student friendly, and it presents the topics of human sexuality in a simple and direct manner. The three authors of this book—Dr. Evelyn Field, Dr. David Aveline, and Dr. Janell Carroll—welcome you to the study of human sexuality.

The New Canadian Edition

Even though there are many similarities between Canada and the United States, there are also profound differences in culture. Canada is almost a century younger as a nation, it has a different political system, it has recognized marriage equality for a decade, it has two national languages, and its ethnic make-up reflects its different immigration history. It is thus essential that a textbook on human sexuality accurately reflects the Canadian population and its place in the world.

This first Canadian edition of *Sexuality Now: Embracing Diversity* builds on the success of previous American editions to bring students a fresh look at sexuality as it emerges in its many forms in Canadian culture. It has a multicultural and multiethnic focus and it is updated with Canadian research, Canadian statistics, and Canadian citations. Differences between American and Canadian culture include major areas of sexuality such as attitudes toward sexual and gender orientation and laws pertaining to contraception. There are also many similarities in terms of challenges to sexual functioning, sexually transmitted infections, and coercive sexuality. This Canadian edition thus looks at areas of human sexuality that are particular to Canadian social life and global in terms of shared experiences across borders.

Real Research

The Canadian edition presents up-to-date research on sexuality with a Canadian focus in the "Real Research" feature. In each chapter, students will find several boxes that briefly highlight what Canadian researchers have looked at pertaining to the subjects at hand. The following are examples:

- The impact of sex education programs on the behaviour of Canadian high school students (Chapter 1, "Exploring Human Sexuality: Past and Present").

- A five-year study of the health and well-being of Canadian sex workers headed by Francis M. Shaver of Concordia University in Montreal and funded by the Social Science and Humanities Research Council of Canada (Chapter 2, "Understanding Human Sexuality: Theory and Research").

- A large-scale study on the sexual health of Chinese-Canadian seniors (Chapter 8, "Gender Development, Gender Roles, and Gender Identity").

- Research involving university students in Windsor, Ontario, finding that negative communication patterns significantly affect perceptions of relationship quality (Chapter 11, "Communication and Sexuality").

- Toronto psychologists' findings that the capacity to love may be influenced by whether people come from individualistic or collectivist cultures (Chapter 12, "Love and Intimacy").

- New Brunswick psychologists' findings that among a sample of college students, the majority of vaginal intercourse occurs within committed relationships (Chapter 13, "Adult Sexual Relationships").

- An analysis of Hindi cinema finding that independent films tend to treat sexual minorities in more dignifying ways (Chapter 18, "Sexual Imagery and Selling Sex").

On Your Mind

Often, when students attend lectures on human sexuality, they attempt to understand the material by relating it to their own lives or the things they have heard from friends, on television, or elsewhere. For this reason, boxes entitled "On Your Mind" are included in this book. These boxes attempt to get at some of the questions that students have in terms of the specific topics covered.

Janell Carroll has collected thousands of questions that students have about sexuality. She has visited colleges and universities all over the world to better understand what today's college and university students want to know about sexuality and how it differs among cultures. Student questions are helpful in understanding what information students want. Each "On Your Mind" feature answers a student question related to the nearby chapter content. Examples include:

- Why do men so often wake up with erections?

- Can a woman be raped by an ex-boyfriend?

- How can two people stay together their entire lives and not get bored?

- Is discomfort with same-sex public displays of affection homophobic?

- Is It harmful if sperm does not regularly exit the body?

- Is it damaging to children to see their parents naked?

- Why do women who live together experience menstruation at the same time?

- Can a woman breast-feed if her nipples are pierced?

- I have uterine fibroids? Will I ever be able to have a baby?

These types of questions are important because they reflect what is on students' minds.

Animal Variations

Because human beings are also animals, many chapters include a feature called "Animal Variations," which examines sexual behaviour among other species. The similarities human beings have with other species are at times quite remarkable. The following are examples:

- Similarities among human, chimpanzee, and bonobo monkey females in experiencing orgasm.

- Hermaphrodites in the animal kingdom.

- The ways in which male stickleback fish attract females.

- Intimacy among animals compared to that among humans.

- Sexual coercion in animals.

Sex in Real Life

In the "Sex in Real Life" features, we present information about sexuality that is relevant to everyday life. These features explore a variety of topics such as sex toys, polyamory, social networking, environmental toxins and sperm production, microbicides, Internet sexual behaviour, and media use by teenagers. The following are some examples:

- "Topfreedom" in Canada.

- The foundation of the Canadian Sex Research Forum.

- How people might be attracted to others who speak other languages.

- The annual Feminist Porn Awards in Toronto.

- HIV/AIDS risk levels of specific sexual behaviours.

- The "Bad Trick List" for sex workers in Montreal.

Sexual Diversity in Our World

One way students can challenge their taken-for-granted assumptions about sexuality is by learning how attitudes and practices vary across and within cultures both in Canada and around the world. In addition to cross-cultural and multicultural information within the chapters, "Sexual Diversity in Our World" features present specific topics that highlight sexual diversity. The following are examples:

- Chinese foot binding.

- Transsexuality and persecution of gays and lesbians in Iran.

- AIDS orphans in Africa.

- The concept of "virginity."

- Qualities of good same-sex marriages.

Timelines

Visual representations in textbooks can often make material easier for students to conceptualize and understand. With this in mind, there are several timelines of historical events in the appendix at the back of the book. The timelines in the Canadian edition include:

- Human Sexuality: Past and Present

- A History of Sex on Television

- Important Developments in the History of Sex Research

- The History of Contraception

- The History of Assisted Human Reproduction

- Canadian Gay and Lesbian History

- Same-Sex Unions around the Globe

Other Important Features

Throughout each chapter, there are highlighted definitions of important terms in the margin to improve students' memories about the material. "Review Questions" conclude each major section so that students can test their retention of the material, and a "Chapter Review" section appears at the end of each chapter. Also at the very end of each chapter is a list of websites where one can explore relevant issues further.

Distinctive Content by Chapter

Chapter 1: Exploring Human Sexuality: Past and Present

This chapter contains:

- An opening section on **what makes Canada** unique in its approach to human sexuality as well as some differences between Canada and the United States.

- A section on the **history of sexuality** from the ancient Mediterranean area to Medieval times to the 19th century. There are also sections on the **histories of sexuality of India, China, and Japan.**

- A separate section on the **history of sexuality in Canada** from the times when only **First Nations** people existed to the settlement of **New France** (now Quebec) to the 20th century.

- A section on **gay rights in Canada.**

- A section on the **history of sexuality in the United States.**

Chapter 2: Understanding Human Sexuality: Theory and Research

This chapter contains:

- A review of some major **biological, psychological, and sociological theories of sexuality.**

- A review of the **major sexologists of the 19th century** from Richard von Krafft-Ebing to Magnus Hirschfeld.

- A review of **20th-century sex researchers** from Alfred C. Kinsey to Martin S. Weinberg.

- A review of **sex research in Canada and the United States.**

- A review of **research methods** typically used in sex research.

Chapter 3: Female Sexual Anatomy, Development, and Health

This chapter contains:

- Tables of **variations in female sexual development.**

- Recommendations for **pelvic examinations** from the Canadian College of Obstetricians and Gynecologists, including the importance of regular Pap testing.

- A section on **menstrual suppression** with long-term birth control pills and an exploration of safety issues related to menstrual suppression.

- A section on **polycystic ovarian syndrome, pelvic inflammatory disease, and vaccines to prevent urinary tract infections.**

- A section on **breast, endometrial, and cervical cancers** with data from the Canadian Cancer Society and Statistics Canada. Included is research on various risk factors including smoking and oral contraceptive use.

- A review of the use of **mammography.**

- A review of the most recent updates from the DSM-5 on **premenstrual dysphoric disorder.**

- A section on the use of **hormone replacement therapy** in menopause.

Chapter 4: Male Sexual Anatomy, Development, and Health

This chapter contains:

- Tables of **variations of male sexual development.**

- A section on **environmental and dietary causes of decreasing sperm counts,** including stress, laptop computers, cell phones, biking, smoking, and alcohol use on sperm production.

- A section on **anabolic-androgenic steroid use** and adverse effects associated with its use.

- A section on **breast, penile, testicular, and prostate cancers in men,** with statistics from the Canadian Cancer Society and Statistics Canada. This includes new research on various risk factors.

- A section on **male circumcision,** including cross-cultural research.

Chapter 5: The Biology of Sex, Pregnancy, and Childbirth

This chapter contains:

- Statistics of **birth rates by age of mother** and **cesarean birth rates.**

- A section on **problems during pregnancy,** including ectopic pregnancy, diagnostic blood tests for Down syndrome, and genetic risk for breech birth.

- A section on assisted reproductive technologies, including new information on **global regulations of sperm donation** and information on **embryo and ova cryopreservation, pre-implantation genetic diagnosis,** and the use of **assisted reproductive techniques in LGB couples.**

Chapter 6: Contraception and Abortion

This chapter contains:

- Statistics on **contraceptive use in Canada,** median ages at reproductive events and **factors associated with unintended pregnancy, global contraceptive use** from the United Nations, and the use of **emergency contraception** in Canada.

- Discussions on **contraceptive use and abortion, with Canadian data.**

- A section on **medications and herbs that may interact with hormonal contraception,** including alcohol and certain antibiotics and antidepressants.

- Information and review of controversies surrounding **NuvaRing.**

- A discussion on the **relationship between oral contraceptives and breast and cervical cancers.**

- A section on **emergency contraception (EC),** including over-the-counter status and controversies about the use of EC in women with high BMIs.

- A section on **future directions in contraceptive research,** including injectable implants along with contraceptive vaccines for men and women.

- A section on **surgical and medical abortion procedures,** including abortion statistics in Canada and advantages and disadvantages of various procedures.

Chapter 7: Sexually Transmitted Infections and HIV/AIDS

This chapter contains:

- A history of sexually transmitted infection (STI) **prevalence and control in Canada.**

- A list of sex acts and their levels of risk from the **Canadian AIDS Society.**

- A section on **birth control, pregnancy, and STIs.**

- Sections on **ectoparasitic infections, bacterial infections,** and **viral infections.**

- A major section on **HIV/AIDS,** its incidence in **Canada,** and its diagnosis and treatment.

- A major section of the **global aspects,** incidence, and prevention efforts toward **HIV/AIDS.**

Chapter 8: Gender Development, Gender Roles, and Gender Identity

This chapter contains:

- A section on **intersexuality,** including a feature box dedicated to specific issues involved in the birth of an intersex child.

- A section on **disorders of sex development,** including clarifications about the revised DSM-5 and a review of chromosomal and hormonal conditions.

- A section on the **gender spectrum** that explores the **gender binary** and the richness of gender diversity.

- A section on **transgender rights** in Canada.

- A section on **Two-Spirit** people of First Nations cultures in Canada.

- A section on transgender people in other cultures, such as the **Hijra** of India, the **Khanith** of Oman, and the **Fa'afafine** of Samoa.

- A section on transsexualism and **medical and surgical gender transitions,** including metoidioplasty.

- **Photographs** of male-to-female and female-to-male sex reassignment surgery.

Chapter 9: Sexual Orientation

This chapter contains:

- A section on **theories of sexual orientation,** including those from biology, developmental psychology, and sociology.

- A section on the **legacy of psychiatric and medical definitions of deviance and illness** on the lives of gay, lesbian, and bisexual people.

- A section on **homosexuality in history** from ancient Greece and Rome to the 20th century.

- A section on **gay and lesbian lives in other cultures,** including those of South America, the Middle East, Africa, Asia, and the Pacific.

- A section on **gays, lesbians, and bisexuals through the life cycle.**

- A section on **homophobia** and hate crimes.

- A section on **gays and lesbians from visible minorities.**

Chapter 10: Childhood and Adolescent Sexuality

This chapter contains:

- A section with data from the most recent **governmental studies on childhood sexuality.**

- Statistics on **teenage sexual behaviour,** including masturbation, oral sex, anal and vaginal intercourse and same-sex sexual behaviour. This section also includes data on teenage contraceptive use, pregnancy, and abortion.

- Canadian data on **teenage sexual activity, timing of first sexual intercourse in teenagers,** and **contraceptive use in teenagers.**

Chapter 11: Communication and Sexuality

This chapter contains:

- A section on communication differences with respect to **gender, culture,** and **sexual orientation.**

- A section on **computer-mediated communication** and **social networks** and the **impact of this technology on communication patterns,** expectations, challenges, and misunderstandings involved with their use.

- A discussion of **online infidelity,** including common profiles and reactions from those involved.

- A section on **the importance of sexual communication,** including the challenges and obstacles associated with it, verbal and non-verbal sexual communication, and its reciprocal nature and important components.

Chapter 12: Love and Intimacy

This chapter contains:

- A section on the **forms and measures of love,** including Canadian sociologist John Alan Lee's **Colours of Love** and the theories of Robert Sternberg.

- A section on **neuroscience**, the **major histocompatibility complex**, pheromones, brain imaging, and the role these factors play in the development of love.
- A section on love among **children and teenagers**.
- A section on the **nature of attraction**.
- A section on love and **sexual orientation**.
- A section on love and intimacy in **other cultures**.
- A section on **relationship breakups** and vulnerability to self-blame, loss of self-esteem, and distrust of others.

Chapter 13: Adult Sexual Relationships

This chapter contains:
- A section on the **history** of dating in Canada.
- A section on **interracial and intercultural dating** in Canada.
- Sections on **non-marital** sexual activity, **cohabitation**, **common-law** relationships, and **marriage**.
- A section on **endogamous** and **exogamous** marriages.
- Sections on **marital satisfaction** and sexual activity during marriage as well as outside of marriage.
- A section on **non-exclusive relationships and marriages**.
- Discussions on **same-sex sexual activity** and **relationships** as well as **same-sex marriage in Canada**.
- Sections on **arranged marriages, polygamous marriages**, and **consanguineous** marriages in Canada.

Chapter 14: Variations of Sexual Expression

This chapter contains:
- A section on **celibacy, abstinence**, and **asexuality**.
- A section on **sexual fantasies**, their history, and gender differences among them.
- A section on the history of **masturbation**, frequencies among men and women, attitudes toward it, and sex toys used to enhance masturbation.
- A section on **cybersex**, teledildonics, and Bluedildonics.
- Sections on **oral sex, vaginal intercourse, anal intercourse**, and **BDSM and other fetishistic sexual activities**.

Chapter 15: Challenges to Sexual Functioning

This chapter contains:
- A discussion about **DSM-5 diagnostic revisions** for all categories of DSM sexual dysfunction.
- A section exploring **differences between desire problems and asexuality**.
- A section on **treatments for sexual dysfunction**.
- A section with **recommendations for the use of testosterone in erectile disorder**.
- A section on **vulvodynia** and **vulvar vestibulitis syndrome**.

- A revised and updated section on the effects of **cancer diagnosis** and **treatments** on sexual functioning and satisfaction.

Chapter 16: Harmful and Antisocial Sexual Expression

This chapter contains:
- A section on theories of paraphilic disorders according to the new **DSM-5**.
- A section on the types of paraphilic disorders, including, **courtship paraphilic disorders, algolagnic paraphilic disorders,** and ones involving **anomalous target** preferences.
- A section on the controversies surrounding the **concept of sexual addiction**.
- A section on **sex scandals**, including those within the **Catholic Church**, the **Canadian residential school system**, and several historic scandals in **Canada**.

Chapter 17: Power and Sexual Coercion

This chapter contains:
- A section on **rape and sexual assault on college campuses**.
- A discussion of the **Calgary Sexual Health Centre's WiseGuyz program**, which aims to reduce **rape and sexual assault**.
- A section on the link between **sexual assault and alcohol use on college campuses**.
- A section on **marital sexual assault**.
- A section on **intimate partner violence, intimate partner homicide**, stalking, and sexual harassment.

Chapter 18: Sexual Imagery and Selling Sex

This chapter contains:
- A discussion of the **history of erotic depictions** from prehistoric times to the age of European colonialism, including depictions of **India, China**, and **Japan**.
- A discussion of 19th-century and early 20th-century **erotic literature and attempts to censor it**.
- A discussion of **pulp novels and magazines**.
- A discussion of **erotic magazines** for both **heterosexual and gay men**.
- A discussion of the **"porn chic"** era of the early 1970s.
- A discussion of **sex in films and television shows** as well as gay, lesbian, and transgender representation.
- A discussion of definitions of obscenity and **censorship in Canada**.
- A discussion of **feminist pornography**.
- A section on **sex workers in Canadian history**.
- Sections on the **clients of sex workers; male, female, and transgender sex workers;** and **sex workers' efforts to organize** locally, nationally, and globally.

Instructor Resources

The **Nelson Education Teaching Advantage (NETA)** program delivers research-based instructor resources that promote student engagement and higher-order thinking to enable the success of Canadian students and educators. Visit Nelson Education's **Inspired Instruction** website at http://www.nelson.com/inspired/ to find out more about NETA.

The following instructor resources have been created for *Sexuality Now: Embracing Diversity,* First Canadian Edition. Access these ultimate tools for customizing lectures and presentations at www.nelson.com/instructor.

NETA Test Bank

This resource was written by Carolyn Ensley, Wilfrid Laurier University. It includes over 900 multiple-choice questions written according to NETA guidelines for effective construction and development of higher-order questions. Also included are 270 true/false questions and 180 short-answer questions.

The NETA Test Bank is available in a new, cloud-based platform. **Nelson Testing Powered by Cognero®** is a secure online testing system that allows instructors to author, edit, and manage test bank content from anywhere Internet access is available. No special installations or downloads are needed, and the desktop-inspired interface, with its drop-down menus and familiar, intuitive tools, allows instructors to create and manage tests with ease. Multiple test versions can be created in an instant, and content can be imported or exported into other systems. Tests can be delivered from a learning management system, the classroom, or wherever an instructor chooses. Testing Powered by Cognero for *Sexuality Now: Embracing Diversity* can also be accessed through http://www.nelson.com/instructor.

NETA PowerPoint

Microsoft® PowerPoint® lecture slides for every chapter have been created by Anastasia Bake, St. Clair College. There is an average of 40 slides per chapter, many featuring key figures, tables, and photographs from *Sexuality Now*. NETA principles of clear design and engaging content have been incorporated throughout, making it simple for instructors to customize the deck for their courses.

Image Library

This resource consists of digital copies of figures, short tables, and photographs used in the book. Instructors may use these jpegs to customize the NETA PowerPoint or create their own PowerPoint presentations.

MindTap®

MindTap for *Sexuality Now: Embracing Diversity*

MindTap for *Sexuality Now: Embracing Diversity* engages and empowers students to produce their best work—consistently. By seamlessly integrating course material with videos, activities, apps, and much more, MindTap creates a unique learning path that fosters increased comprehension and efficiency.

For students:

- MindTap delivers real-world relevance with activities and assignments that help students build critical thinking and analytic skills that will transfer to other courses and their professional lives.

- MindTap helps students stay organized and efficient with a single destination that reflects what's important to the instructor, along with the tools students need to master the content.

- MindTap empowers and motivates students with information that shows where they stand at all times—both individually and compared to the highest performers in class.

Additionally, for instructors, MindTap allows you to:

- Control what content students see and when they see it with a learning path that can be used as-is or matched to your syllabus exactly.

- Create a unique learning path of relevant readings and multimedia and activities that move students up the learning taxonomy from basic knowledge and comprehension to analysis, application, and critical thinking.

- Integrate your own content into the MindTap Reader using your own documents or pulling from sources like RSS feeds, YouTube videos, websites, Google Docs, and more.

- Use powerful analytics and reports that provide a snapshot of class progress, time in course, engagement, and completion.

In addition to the benefits of the platform, MindTap for *Sexuality Now:*

- Integrates videos and animations into the chapter-specific readings to fully engage students and reinforce important concepts.

- Features "From Dr. Carroll's Notebook," which helps set the tone for student learning.

- Includes "Speak Your Mind" videos that allow students to view and respond to intriguing questions about sex, compare their answers with their classmates, and view Dr. Carroll's responses.

- Enhances content with gradable matching activities and chapter-ending tests.

- The digital environment also allows the students to answer questions on key topics and discuss issues with classmates through the LAMS app.

Acknowledgments

This edition of *Sexuality Now* would not have been possible without the insightful reviews of this book or its previous edition of these colleagues. Our thanks to these reviewers for their contributions:

Anastasia Bake, *St. Clair College*
Kelly Brown, *Memorial University—Grenfell Campus*
Corey Isaacs, *Western University*
Stacey Jacobs, *University of Waterloo*
Scott Robert Mattson, *University of Windsor*
David Reagan, *Camosun College*

David Aveline would like to thank his husband, Miguel Angel Vazquez, for his support during the writing of this book, as well as colleague Shane Gannon for the many conversations about the material.

Evelyn Field would like to thank her colleague Dr. Scharie Tavcer for her contributions to this book. She also thanks her husband, Bart Farkas, daughter Emilie Field, and her family for their support during the writing of this book.

The authors also thank the Nelson team: Lenore Taylor-Atkins, publisher; Ann Byford, marketing manager; Lisa Berland, content development manager; Jennifer Hare, production project manager; Valerie Adams, copy editor; Carrie McGregor, photo researcher and permissions coordinator; and Manoj Kumar, project manager.

Note to the Student

As you read through the book, if you have any questions, thoughts, or opinions you'd like to share with us, we would love to hear from you. You may email us and ask for clarifications, suggest additions or changes, or just share your thoughts about this book. You can email either of the two Canadian authors, Dr. Evelyn Field (efield@mtroyal.ca) and Dr. David Aveline (daveline@mtroyal.ca), or you can write to them at the following addresses: Dr. Evelyn Field, Mount Royal University, 4825 Mount Royal Gate SW, Department of Psychology, Calgary, Alberta T3E 6K6, and Dr. David Aveline, Mount Royal University, 4825 Mount Royal Gate SW, Department of Sociology & Anthropology, Calgary, Alberta T3E 6K6. You may also email Dr. Janell Carroll (jcarroll@hartford.edu), the author and originator of the American editions of this book, or write to her at Dr. Janell L. Carroll, University of Hartford, Department of Psychology, 200 Bloomfield Avenue, West Hartford, CT, U.S.A. 06117.

We hope you find this book useful and enjoy learning about the many aspects of human sexuality.

Evelyn Field
David Aveline
Janell Carroll

1

Exploring Human Sexuality: Past and Present

We the Canadian authors are proud to bring you the first edition of Janelle Carroll's highly successful book, adapted for Canadian students of sexuality. As Dr. Carroll said in her last American edition,

I've travelled extensively throughout the United States and around the world, consulting with sexuality teachers, experts, and researchers and interviewing ordinary people about their sexuality. What I've gained through these experiences has been invaluable. All my education, training, and research about the interplay of biology, society, and

culture gave me knowledge, but experiencing other societies and cultures gave me understanding.

In keeping with this theme, we not only bring you Dr. Carroll's unique experience but we adapt her research to the Canadian ethos. While Canada and the United States are similar in some ways, they have different histories, different political systems, different crime rates, and different cultures. Such differences have a strong impact upon the ways in which sexuality is experienced and expressed. We hope that students who read this book will learn a great deal about sexuality and apply their new knowledge positively in their daily lives. ||

Welcome to the study of human sexuality. Many students believe they already know everything they need to know about human sexuality. The truth is that everyone has different levels of knowledge. Some students have parents who were open and honest about **sexuality**, while others had parents who never spoke a word about sex. Some students have had comprehensive levels of sex education in school, while others have had none and may bring knowledge about sex gained only from years of watching Internet pornography. In the end, it doesn't really matter what knowledge level you bring into this class. We guarantee that you will learn plenty more.

Canada has a broad range of values toward sexuality ranging from the marriage-principled Hutterites of Alberta to the polygamous beliefs and practices of Mormon Fundamentalists in Bountiful, British Columbia, to the hedonistic beliefs about recreational sex emerging from the nightclubs of Montreal, Toronto, and Vancouver. Perhaps what distinguishes Canada from many other nations is its strong commitment to equality, as might be indicated by it being the fourth country in the world to legalize same-sex marriage on July 20, 2005. Canadian marriages may now be between any two people, and there are no differences in rights and privileges under the law. Canada also recognizes the sexual rights of young people and does not criminalize sexual relationships between people 16 years old or older where there is full consent and, if one partner is under 18, where the older partner is not in a position of authority over the younger. At the same time, Canada is strongly committed to the promotion of sexual health, believing that sexual decision making by any individual should be informed by accurate information on birth control and **sexually transmitted infections (STIs)**, sound reasoning, and full self-efficacy. Ideally, decisions of whether to engage in sex, with whom, and how, should involve all of these things. According to the Sex Information and Education Council of Canada (SIECCAN), "Access to effective, broadly based sexual health education is an important contributing factor to the health and well-being of Canadian youth" (SIECCAN, 2010, p. 2). This outlook differs markedly from that of the United States, where there is strong support for "abstinence-only" instruction. Canada's approach has paid off well. The teenage pregnancy rate dropped by 40.8 percent between 1990 and 2010 and remains significantly lower than that of the United States, as well as England and Wales (McKay, 2012). In fact, it is also likely that Canadian woman on the whole enjoy greater sexual health than women in the United States because of universal health care.

One of the strongest influences in shaping our values, opinions, and attitudes toward human sexuality is our family, which might consist of our parents, stepparents, grandparents, or other caregivers. In this primary environment, we learn how to communicate, show affection, deal with emotions, and many more things that contribute to who we are today. We then go on to form families of our own and pass along that learning to the next generation. We will discuss this further in the upcoming chapters.

High school students receive a full and comprehensive sex education in Canada.

We also learn about sexuality from our friends and romantic partners in our daily lives, as well as the culture in which we live. Our exposure to issues of sexuality is augmented by the fact that we live in a sex-saturated society that uses sex to sell everything from cologne to cars. However, we also live in a time when people are reluctant to speak openly about human sexuality. Some people believe that providing sexuality information can cause problems—including increased teenage sexual activity and adolescent pregnancy rates. Others believe that learning about sexuality can empower people to make healthy decisions both today and in the future.

Recent events have profoundly affected the way we view sexuality. From the legalization of same-sex marriage to the advent of continuous birth control pills that eliminate menstrual periods to the continued fight against STIs, the media are filled with stories relating to our sexuality and relationships with others. These stories tell us much about how our culture understands, expresses, and limits our sexuality.

In this opening chapter, we define sexuality, examine sexual images in culture, and explore the effects of sexual imagery in the media. An historical exploration of sexuality follows in which we review the early evolution of human sexuality beginning with the impact of walking erect and ending with important ancient civilizations. Following this, we look at how sexuality was influenced by religion from the Early Christian Era to the Reformation. Finally, we take a look at modern developments and influences in Canada and the world from the 18th to the 21st century.

---

sexuality
A general term for the feelings and behaviours of human beings concerning sex.

sexually transmitted infections (STIs)
Infections transmitted from one person to another through sexual contact. They used to be called sexually transmitted diseases (STDs) and venereal diseases (VD).

REAL Research Smylie et al. (2008) looked at the impact of a sex education intervention program on 240 Grade 9 students in Canada. The students were asked to complete an anonymous self-report questionnaire a month after they attended this program and the questionnaires were compared to those of a control group. The intervention group showed positive changes in knowledge, sex-role attitudes, and the perception that birth control is important.

Some people choose not to have sex until they are deeply in love with someone or after they have married. Such people have decided to remain celibate until that time. When one becomes sexual, where, under what circumstances, and with whom involves a decision-making process, and such decisions are informed by a variety of factors within and around the person. For some people, religious beliefs are key factors—they firmly believe in the tenets of their faith, which permit sex only within marriage. People's behaviour might be similarly regulated by cultural expectations where marriage is a strong standard and celibacy is expected until that time. A third factor is a person's own sense of morality, whether it has its basis in religion or otherwise. Sex might be thought of as accept-able under one set of circumstances such as a steady relationship but not under another set. Whether or not to have sex is thus informed by a variety of personal and societal factors.

Human sexual behaviour differs from that of other animals in part because of moral, religious, legal, and interpersonal values. How simple it seems for animals that mate without caring about marriage, pregnancy, or hurting their partner's feel-ings! Human beings are not (typically) so casual about mating. Every culture has developed elaborate rituals, rules, laws, and moral principles that structure sexual relations. The very earliest legal and moral codes that archeologists have uncovered discuss sexual behaviour at great length, and rules surrounding it make up much of the legal and ethical codes of the world's cultures.

Sexuality is a basic drive and it is one of the few that involves intimate one-on-one interaction with another person's basic needs. Conflicts may arise when one's own needs, feelings, fears, and concerns are not the same as one's partner's. People can be hurt, used, and taken advantage of sexually, or they can be victims of honest miscommunication, especially because sex is so difficult for many people to discuss.

Sexuality is also closely related to the formation of love bonds and to procre-ation. Every society has a stake in procre-ation in that without adequate numbers of people, a society can languish, while with too many people, it can be overwhelmed.

Sexuality Today

Human sexuality is grounded in biological functioning, emerging in each of us as we develop, and is expressed within cultures through rules about sexual contact, attitudes about moral and immoral sexuality, habits of sexual behaviour, patterns of relations between the sexes, and more. In this section we look at how sexuality is defined and discuss how it is affected by the media and changing technologies.

Only Human: What Is Sexuality?

The sexual nature of human beings is unique in the animal kingdom. Although many of our fellow creatures also display complex sexual behaviours, only human beings have gone beyond instinctual mating rituals to create ideas, laws, customs, fantasies, and art around the sexual act. In other words, although sexual intercourse is common in the animal kingdom, sexuality is a uniquely human trait.

Sexuality is studied by **sexologists** who specialize in under-standing our sexuality, but also by biologists, psychologists, physicians, anthropologists, historians, sociologists, political scientists, public health specialists, and many other people in scholarly disciplines. For example, political scientists may study how sexuality reflects social power. Notably, powerful groups may have more access to sex partners or use their legislative power to restrict the sexual behaviours of less powerful groups.

Few areas of human life seem as contradictory and confusing as sexuality. North American societies are often considered sexu-ally repressed, yet images of sexuality are everywhere. We tend to think that everyone else is "doing it," yet we are often uncomfort-able talking about sex. Some feel that we should all be free to explore our sexuality, while others believe that there should be strong restrictions. To some, only sex between a man and a woman is natural and acceptable, while others believe that all kinds of sexual expression are equally valid. Many people find it puzzling that others find sexual excitement by being humiliated or spanked, exposing themselves in public, or wearing rubber. Although parents teach their children about safe driving, fire safety, and safety around strangers, many are profoundly uncom-fortable instructing their children on safe sexual practices. Such contradictions in culture serve to show that human sexuality is multifaceted.

Sex Sells: The Impact of the Media

Visual media are common in our daily lives. Magazines, newspa-pers, book covers, CD and DVD packaging, cereal boxes, and other products are adorned with pictures of people, scenes, or

sexologist
A person who engages in the scientific study of sexual behaviour. Sexologists can be from a variety of clinical or academic disciplines.

products. Advertisements peer at us from billboards, buses, cell phones, iPods, iPads, the Internet, and anywhere else that advertisers can buy space. Television, movies, computers, and other moving visual images are also common and we will only depend on them more as information technology continues to develop. We live in a visual culture with images we simply cannot escape.

Many of these images are subtly or explicitly sexual. Barely clothed males and females are so common in ads that we scarcely notice them anymore. Although we may not immediately recognize it, many of the advertisements we are exposed to use Photoshop to digitally alter the models' bodies and faces—raising beauty standards to unattainable levels. Various countries have proposed legislation that would require warning labels on photos that have been retouched (Myslewski, 2009).

Sex is all over television today. The majority of movies—even some of those directed at children—have sexual scenes that would not have been permitted in movie theatres a century ago.

Television shows such as *Jersey Shore* and *Gossip Girl* highlight sexual issues, whereas shows such as *16 and Pregnant* and *Teen Mom* explore teenage pregnancy, showcasing the real lives of teenage mothers. Critics argue that such shows "glamorize" teenage pregnancy and have led to its greater acceptance (Bates, 2010).

The Internet has also changed patterns of social communication and relationships (Gutkin, 2010; Niedzviecki, 2009; Lever et al., 2008). Social networking sites such as Facebook or Nexopia, together with email, texting, instant messaging, Skyping, and iChat, have changed the way people communicate with one another. Now one can communicate through tweets, blogs, uploads, updates, posts, or chats. You can text a breakup message, let the world know you're dating someone with the click of a button, and get an "app" for just about anything.

Countless websites are also available that offer information and advice and provide visitors with answers to their most personal questions. Vibrators and other sex toys, pornographic pictures and videos, and access to a variety of personal webcam sites can be purchased online, and a variety of blogs cater to just about any conceivable fantasy. The Internet allows for

In Ottawa in 1896, a 47-second film of Canadian actress May Irwin kissing a man caused an uproar in newspapers, which denounced it as lurid and vulgar, even though they only touched lips and no tongues were involved. Today, such uproar seems laughable.

anonymity and provides the freedom to ask questions and talk to others about sexual issues.

All of this information has not been lost on today's teenagers, who rate the media as some of their leading sources of sex information (Strasburger & The Council on Communications and Media, 2010; Strasburger, 2005). On average, teenagers spend more than seven hours a day with a variety of media filled with sexual messages and images (Rideout et al., 2010). Yet, much this media information is not educational. Although 70 percent of teen shows contain sexual content, less than 10 percent of them contain information on risks associated with sexual activity (Strasburger & The Council on Communications and Media, 2010). Even so, many young people accept these sexual portrayals as realistic, even though they are often inaccurate and misleading.

We now turn our attention to the history of human sexuality from prehistoric times to the present. Of course, in the space of one chapter, we cannot begin to cover the variety and richness of human sexual experience of the past. However, this overview will give an idea of how varied human cultures are, while also showing that human beings throughout history have had to grapple with some of the same sexual issues that confront us today. As we begin our review history, pay attention to how at some points in history attitudes about sexuality were conservative, whereas at other times they were more liberal. The pendulum continues to swing back and forth today as we w debate issues of human sexuality such as sex education and birth control.

REAL Research In a survey of 1216 teenagers living in Toronto, 65 percent were born in Canada and the rest were born elsewhere. Those not born in Canada were significantly less likely to have received sexual health education than the rest (Salehi & Flicker, 2010).

Review Questions

1 What are the benefits of comprehensive sexual health education for Canadian youth as opposed to abstinence-only education?

2 How might the media affect perceptions of sexuality?

3 How might television shows affect people's perceptions of sexuality in society? Give some examples.

The Early Evolution of Human Sexuality

Our ancestors began walking upright more than 3 million years ago according to recent fossil records. Before that, our ancestors were mostly **quadrupeds** who stood only for brief moments as baboons do now to survey the terrain. The evolution of an upright posture changed forever the way the human species engaged in sexual intercourse (Tannahill, 1980).

Stand Up and Look Around: Walking Erect

In an upright posture, the male genitals are rotated to the front of the body so that merely approaching someone involves displaying them. Because male confrontation often involved acts of aggression, the **phallus**—the male symbol of sex and potency—became associated with displays of aggression. In other words, an upright posture may have also contributed to a new tie between sexuality and aggression (Rancour-Laferriere, 1985).

The upright posture of the female emphasized not only her genitals but her breasts and hips, and the rotation of the female pelvis forward (the vagina faces the rear in most quadrupeds) enabled the possibility of face-to-face intercourse. Because more body area is in contact in face-to-face intercourse than in rear entry, the entire sensual aspect of intercourse was enhanced, manipulation of the breasts became possible and the clitoris was more easily stimulated. Only in human females does orgasm seem to be a common part of sexual contact.

Greek cups, plates, and other pottery often depicted erotic scenes, such as this one from the fifth century B.C.E.

© Scala/Art Resource, NY

Animal Variations	Do Non-human Female Primates Experience Orgasm?

Yes, some do, although it is relatively rare compared to human females. Other female primates rarely masturbate, although occasionally they stimulate themselves manually during intercourse. Bonobos (pygmy chimpanzees) have face-to-face intercourse on occasion and may reach orgasm. However, most chimpanzees engage in rear-entry intercourse, a position that does not favour female orgasm (Margulis & Sagan, 1991).

Sexuality in the Ancient Mediterranean

It may seem that ancient civilizations were different from ours, yet some had surprisingly progressive attitudes toward sex. Although the Egyptians condemned adultery, especially among women, it may still have been fairly common. A woman in Egypt had the right to divorce her husband, a privilege that was not given to Hebrew women. The Egyptians also left behind thousands of pictures, carvings, and even cartoons of erotic scenes (Doyle, 2005). All told, ancient Egyptians had sex lives that do not seem all that different from what we have today.

From writings and art, we know a bit about ancient accounts of STIs (some ancient medical texts discuss cures), menstruation (there were a variety of laws surrounding menstruation), circumcision (which was performed in Egypt and other parts of Africa), and contraception (Egyptian women inserted sponges or other objects in the vagina). Because a great value was put on having as many children as possible—especially sons for inheritance as well as military purposes—abortion was usually forbidden. Prostitution was common and **temple prostitutes** often had sex with worshippers to provide funds for the temples' upkeep or to worship the gods.

It is important to remember that throughout history, men dominated public life and women's voices were effectively silenced. We know far more about what men thought, how men lived, and even how men loved than we do about the lives and thoughts of women. In fact, it was only relatively recently in human history that women's voices have begun to be heard on a par with men's in literature, politics, art, and other parts of public life.

Of all the ancient civilizations, modern Western society owes the most to the interaction of three ancient cultures: Hebraic (Hebrews), Hellenistic (Greek), and Roman. Each made a contribution to our views of sexuality, so it is worthwhile to examine each culture briefly. At the beginning of each section, we give a date as to when these effects began.

---

quadruped
Any animal that walks on four legs.

phallus
Symbol of male power and aggression.

temple prostitutes
Women and sometimes men in ancient cultures who would have sex with worshippers in temples.

Exploring Human Sexuality: Past and Present

The Epic of Gilgamesh: A Mesopotamian Male-Male Love Story?

The Epic of Gilgamesh is a tale of the exploits of a King in Mesopotamia and is generally accepted as one of the oldest works of literature known, predating the Bible by a more than a thousand years. It was discovered by Assyrian archaeologist Hormuzd Rassam in the 1850s and the first translation appeared in 1870.

As the story goes, Gilgamesh was the king of the city of Uruk and he was a third human and two-thirds god. He treated his people very poorly. One of his habits was that he practised the *droits du seigneur* or the divine right to have sex with all women of Uruk on their wedding nights. The people pleaded with the gods to intervene, who then created a primitive man, Enkido, to distract Gilgamesh. Enkido lived in the wilds and caused havoc. Gilgamesh then sent a temple prostitute, Shamhat, to tame him. Shamhat found Enkido and the two had sex for several days—enough to tame Enkido and bring him back to Uruk. Meanwhile, Gilgamesh was about to

sleep with yet another woman on her wedding night, which greatly angered Enkido, and the two began to fight fiercely. Gilgamesh won, Enkido acknowledged his superiority, and they became close friends. Later, they went to the Cedar Forest to kill Hambaba, a monster and guardian of the forest. They managed to subdue him and, later on, Enkido died. Gilgamesh was stricken with grief over the loss of his beloved friend.

Were Gilgamesh and Enkido lovers? This is a matter of speculation as well as interpretation. While there are no passages that reveal that the two had sex together, there are descriptions of the love and emotion that Gilgamesh felt for his friend. For example, when he touches Enkido's chest and sees that there is no longer a heartbeat, he weeps and holds on to his body for six days and seven nights (Horner, 1978, p. 19). While it is likely that the friendship could be called "homosexual," one must be cautious not to impose modern constructions on a

© Universal Images Group/Getty

story that is 4000 years old. Ackerman (2005) believes that the relationship of Gilgamesh and Enkido is better understood through the ways in which gender was constructed at the time (active male, passive female). In other words, even though the two were both male, Gilgamesh was clearly the active partner, whether sexual or otherwise.

The Hebrews (1000–200 B.C.E.)

The Hebrew Bible, which was written sometime between 800 B.C.E. and 200 B.C.E, contains explicit rules about sexual behaviour, such as forbidding adultery, sex between men, sex with animals, and sex with various family members or their spouses. At the same time, there are tales of marital love and some texts were highly erotic and celebrative of sex. Here is one example:

> How beautiful are thy feet with shoes, O prince's daughter! The joints of thy thighs are like jewels, the work of the hands of a cunning workman.
> Thy navel is like a round goblet, which wanteth not liquor: thy belly is like an heap of wheat set about with lilies.
> Thy two breasts are like two young roes that are twins....
> This thy stature is like a palm tree, and thy breasts to clusters of grapes. (Song of Solomon 7: 1-3, 7, KJV)

The legacy of the Hebrew attitude toward sexuality has been profound. The focus on marital sexuality and procreation and the

negative attitudes toward homosexuality were adopted by Christianity and formed the basis of sexual attitudes for centuries thereafter. What was written thousands of years ago is still used today to judge and condemn gays, lesbians, and transgender people.

The Greeks (1000–200 B.C.E.)

The Greeks were more sexually permissive than the Hebrews. Their stories and myths are full of sexual exploits, incest, rape, and even **bestiality**, as when Zeus, the chief god, took the form of a swan to rape Leda. The Greeks clearly distinguished between love and sex in their tales, even giving each a separate god: Aphrodite was the goddess of sexual intercourse; Eros (her son) was the god of love.

Greece was one of the few major civilizations in Western history to institutionalize homosexuality successfully. In Greek **pederasty** (ped-er-AST-ee), an older man would befriend a postpubescent boy who had finished his formal education and, with the permission of his father, he would offer to mentor the boy and continue to educate him. Typically, the boy would have sex with his mentor as well. Sexual activity was channelled into specific roles where the mentor would be lustful and aggressive while the boy would be receptive and affectionate. While it is commonly thought that their sexual activity involved anal intercourse, this was probably rare. Moreover, intercourse took

bestiality
The act of having intercourse with an animal.

pederasty
Sexual contact between adult men and (usually) postpubescent boys.

place **interfemorally**, or between the thighs (Robson, 2013, p. 43). This man–boy relationship formed the basis of upper-class education and, rather than being secretive, it was publically acknowledged and celebrated. Socrates, for example, enjoyed the sexual attentions of his students (all male), and his students expressed jealousy when he paid too much physical attention to one or another.

In Greece, men and the male form were idealized. When the ancient Greek philosophers spoke of love, they did so almost exclusively in **homoerotic** terms. Men's non-sexual love for a postpubescent boys was seen as the ideal love, superior to the sexual love for women. Plato discussed such an ideal love and so we also now call friendships without a sexual element "**platonic**."

The Romans (500 B.C.E.–700 C.E.)

Rome had few restrictions about sexuality until late in the history of the empire, so early Romans had permissive attitudes toward homosexual behaviour, which was legal until the sixth century C.E. (Boswell, 1980). Marriage and sexual relations were viewed as means to improve one's economic and social standing. Passionate love almost never appears in the written accounts of the time. Bride and groom need not love each other for that kind of relationship would grow over the life of the marriage. More important was fair treatment, respect, and mutual consideration. Wives even encouraged their husbands to have slaves (of either gender) for the purposes of sexual release.

In Rome as in Greece, adult males who took the receptive position in anal intercourse were viewed with scorn while the same behaviour by youths, foreigners, slaves, or women was seen as an acceptable means to please a person who could improve one's place in society. Long-term homosexual unions also existed.

Sexuality in Ancient Asia

Chinese, Indian, and Japanese civilizations also had particular views of sexuality. In Indian culture, Hinduism and rebirth give life direction. In Chinese culture, people work to live in harmony with the Tao, which is made up of **yin and yang**. In Japan, the people followed Shintoism, or "the way of the gods." Each religion or philosophy had its influence upon sexual practices.

India (Beginning about 400 B.C.E.)

Hinduism, the religion of India for most of its history, concentrates on an individual's cycle of birth and rebirth, or **karma**. Karma involves a belief that a person's unjust deeds in this life are punished by suffering in a future life, and suffering in this life is undoubtedly punishment for wrongs committed in previous incarnations. The goal, then, is to live a just life now to avoid suffering in the future. One of the responsibilities in this life is to marry and procreate, and because sex is an important part of those responsibilities, it was generally viewed as a positive pursuit and even a source of power and magic.

There are legends about great women rulers early in India's history, and women had important roles in ceremonies and sacrifices. Still, India's social system, like others we have mentioned, was basically **patriarchal** (PAY-tree-arc-al), and Indian writers (again, mostly male) shared many of the negative views of women that were characteristic of other civilizations. Being born female was seen as a punishment for wrongdoings committed in previous lives. In fact, murdering a woman was not seen as a particularly serious crime, and **female infanticide** (in-FAN-teh-side) was not uncommon (V.L. Bullough, 1973).

By about 400 B.C.E., the first and most famous of India's sex manuals, the *Kama Sutra*, appeared. India is justifiably famous for this amazing book, which is a guide for living that includes sexual instruction. The *Kama Sutra* discusses not just sex but the nature of love, how to make a good home and family, and moral guidance in sex and love. It is obsessive about naming and classifying things. In fact, it categorizes men by the size of their penis (hare, bull, or horse man) and women by the size of their vagina (deer, mare, or cow-elephant woman). A good match in genital size was preferred between male and female partners but, barring that, a tight fit was better than a loose one (Tannahill, 1980). The *Kama Sutra* recommends that women learn how to please their husbands and it provides instructions on sexual techniques and illustrations of many sexual positions, some of which are virtually impossible for people who cannot twist their body like a pretzel. The *Kama Sutra* proposes that heterosexual intercourse should be a passionate activity that includes scratching, biting, and blows to the back accompanied by a variety of animal noises.

In India, marriage was an economic and religious obligation; families tried to arrange good marriages by betrothing their children at young ages, although they did not live with or have sex with their future spouses until after puberty. Because childbearing began when women were still young, they were often able to assert themselves in the household over elderly husbands. However, when a husband died, his wife was forbidden to remarry. They had to live simply, wear plain clothes, sleep on the ground, and devote their days to prayer and rituals that ensured their remarriage to the same husbands in future lives. Many women chose (or were forced) to end their lives as widows by the ritual act of *sati*, where women threw themselves on their husbands' burning funeral pyres to die after them (Jamanadas, 2008).

---

interfemoral intercourse
Sexual activity where a man would place his penis between his partner's thighs.

homoerotic
The erotic representation of same-sex love or desire.

platonic
Named after Plato's description of a deep loving friendship devoid of sexual contact or desire.

yin and yang
According to a Chinese belief, the universe is run by the interaction of two fundamental principles: yin, which is negative, passive, weak, yielding, and female; and yang, which is positive, assertive, active, strong, and male.

karma
The belief that a person's actions in one life determines his or her fate in future lives.

patriarchal
A society ruled by the male as the figure of authority, symbolized by the father's absolute authority in the home.

female infanticide
The killing of female infants; practised in some cultures that value males more than females.

Kama Sutra
An ancient Indian guide for living that includes sexual instruction.

Exploring Human Sexuality: Past and Present

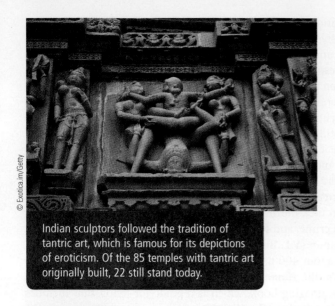

Indian sculptors followed the tradition of tantric art, which is famous for its depictions of eroticism. Of the 85 temples with tantric art originally built, 22 still stand today.

REAL Research Minna and Arundhati (2014) conducted four focus groups upon sexual health issues with unmarried rural men in India. Even though there is no physiological basis to their concerns, they found semen loss through masturbation or nocturnal emissions ("wet dreams") to be a major health concern for the men. Some men even sought out marriage specifically to avoid this "health problem." Because ages of first marriage are getting older, single life is getting longer. The researchers see sex education as a necessary solution.

China (Beginning about 200 B.C.E.)

Ancient Chinese civilization emphasized the interdependence of all things, unified in the Tao, which represents the basic unity of the universe. The Tao itself is made up of two principles, yin and yang, which represent the opposites of the world: yin is feminine, passive, and receptive; yang is masculine, active, and assertive. Sexuality in Chinese thought is not a matter of moral or allowable behaviour but, rather, is a natural procreative process, a joining of the yin and yang, the masculine and feminine principles.

Because sex itself was part of the basic process of following the Tao, sexual instruction and sex manuals were common and openly available in early Chinese society. These texts were explicit, with pictures of sexual positions and instructions on how to stimulate partners, and were often given to brides before their weddings.

Because women's essence, yin, is inexhaustible, whereas men's essence, yang (embodied in semen), is limited, men should feed their yang through prolonged contact with yin. In other words, heterosexual intercourse should be prolonged as long as possible, without ejaculation to release all the woman's accumulated yin energy. The man may experience orgasm without ejaculation, and techniques were developed to teach men how to do so. Men should try to have sex with many women to prevent the yin energy of any single woman from becoming depleted. It was also important for a man to experience a woman's orgasm when yin is at its peak to maximize his

contact with yin energy. The ancient Chinese were atypical for their time in stressing the importance of female orgasm (Margolis, 2004).

Same-sex relations were not discouraged, but because semen was seen as precious and primarily for impregnation, male homosexuality was viewed as a wasteful use of sperm (we discuss Chinese views of homosexuality further in Chapter 11). Aphrodisiacs were developed as well as drugs for all kinds of sexual problems. Also common were sexual devices to increase pleasure such as penis rings to maintain erection, balls and bells that were grafted under the skin of the head of the penis to increase its size, and *ben-wa* balls (usually two or three) containing mercury and other substances that were inserted in the vagina and bounced against each other to bring sexual pleasure.

Taoists believed that yin and yang were equally necessary complements of all existence. Yet, because yin is the passive, inferior principle, women were seen as subservient to men throughout their lives: first to their fathers, then to their husbands, and finally to their sons when their husbands died. **Polygamy** (pah-LIG-ah-mee) was practised until late in Chinese history and many middle-class men had between three and a dozen wives and concubines while those in nobility having 30 or more.

Japan

Japan was a feudal society until the 19th century when, beginning with the Meiji period, it gradually transformed to a world power. For much of its history, order was kept by military elite known as the samurai, who were loyal to their nobility and devoted their entire lives to perfecting their fighting skills. It was also a patriarchal society where men enjoyed conquests of both sexes. One early novel, *The Tale of Genji*, written in the 11th century, tells of the sexual exploits of Prince Genji, who had sex with many women and, at one point, when he could not find one of his favourites, slept with her younger brother instead.

Homosexuality was both common and acceptable in Japan and had close parallels to the ancient Greek system of pederasty. In monasteries and among the samurai, an adult male would take on a boy either at puberty or in his teens as an apprentice and at the same time have sex with him. The boy typically would recite a vow of not only love but fidelity and devotion. These relationships closely resembled marriages and would be dissolved once the boy came of age. Like the Greeks, Japanese males were open about their male partners and celebrated them (Saikaku, 1990).

Japan also had the system of the geisha, where women (and sometimes boys) entertained men as an art form in pleasure centres for the purpose. Wives were considered household managers and bearers of children and in terms of pleasure they were of secondary importance to concubines. Love was considered secondary to pleasure. Although the tradition of entertaining men sexually and otherwise took many forms throughout history, geishas did not appear until the 18th century. They were professional entertainers—accomplished singers, dancers, and musicians—and were also adept at proper manners and sexual pleasure.

polygamy
The practice of men or women marrying more than one person of the other sex.

Sexual Diversity in Our World — *Beauty, Status, and Chinese Foot Binding*

It is sometimes difficult to imagine how sexuality and gender are viewed in non-Western cultures. Yet, to those other cultures it may seem strange that some men and women in Western cultures undergo nose jobs, breast implants, liposuction, tattooing, piercing, waxing, or other procedures to look and feel more beautiful. Throughout history, cultures have searched for unique ways to achieve beauty, especially for women. At one point, exceptionally small waists on women were considered beautiful, and many women wore tight-fitting corsets.

Those who did so often underwent tremendous pain with broken ribs or damaged internal organs. More disturbing than corsets, however, was the Chinese practice of foot binding, which began in the tenth century and lasted for 1000 years (Ko, 2007).

Foot binding originated out of men's desire for women with small feminine feet. When it came time for a young girl to marry, a matchmaker would find suitable males who would then visit the girl's home to simply look at her feet. If her feet were considered too big, the man would refuse her as a marital partner. One 70-year-old woman who had her feet bound as a child said, "Men would choose or reject you as a prospective wife based on the size of your feet. There was a well-known saying, 'If you don't bind, you don't marry . . .'" (Rupp, 2007).

Foot binding was also sexual in nature—women with bound feet had a sway in their walk that was often viewed as erotic. However, they couldn't walk far, which is why foot binding literally kept women in their place.

The ideal foot length was three inches (about 7.5 centimetre), which was referred to as a *Golden Lotus* (*Golden Lotus* feet were often adorned with beautiful silk shoes). Feet that were three to four inches (about 7.5–10 centimetres) long were called *Silver Lotuses*. It is estimated that 40–50 percent of Chinese women had their feet bound in the 19th century, although in the upper classes, the percentages were closer to 100 percent (W.A. Rossi, 1993).

Foot binding was typically done on girls as young as four or five years

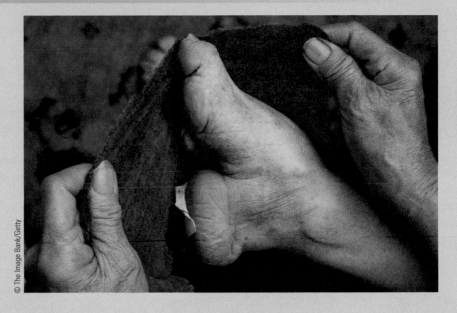
© The Image Bank/Getty

because the bones were still flexible. To bind feet, the mother or grandmother would first soak a girl's feet in warm water. She would then cut the toenails very short, massage the feet, and break the four small toes on each foot. These toes would be folded under, leaving the big toe intact. Silk bandages were wrapped tightly around the toes, and the bandages pulled each broken toe closer to the heel. These bandages were changed and tightened every couple of days so that the foot would not be allowed to grow normally. Typically, this process went on for ten or more years. It was immensely painful, and most girls could not walk for long distances. Most mothers would start the foot-binding process in the winter months so that the cold would help to numb the pain.

In the beginning, only wealthy families bound their daughters' feet because they could afford not to have their children work in the fields. By the 17th and 18th centuries, peasants and women from the countryside began foot binding when they realized that doing so might attract more wealthy suitors for marriage.

Foot binding had several long-term consequences. Many women had difficulties balancing, walking, standing, and squatting (using the toilet was especially

difficult). Muscular atrophy and infections were common, and many girls developed a terrible foot smell from the practice. Older women typically developed severe hip and spinal problems.

The practice of foot binding was outlawed in the latter part of the Qing Dynasty (1644–1911), when women were told to unwrap their feet or face heavy fines. Even so, the practice continued for years, and it wasn't until the formation of the People's Republic of China in 1949 that a strict prohibition was placed on foot binding. This prohibition continues today.

Although it's disturbing to read about this practice, it is interesting to look at how far societies will go for beauty. Foot binding became an integral part of the culture and was much more than a beauty statement. Women whose feet were bound were viewed as more desirable and of a higher social status, making it more likely they would find a husband to provide for them.

SOURCE: *Splendid Slippers: A Thousand Years of an Erotic Tradition* (B. Jackson, 1998); *In Every Step a Lotus: Shoes for Bound Feet* (Ko, 2001); *Cinderella's Sisters: A Revisionist History of Footbinding* (Ko, 2007); *Aching for Beauty: Footbinding in China* (Ping, 2002); and *The Sex Life of the Foot and Shoe* (W.A. Rossi, 1993).

Review Questions

1 How did prehistoric changes in human posture influence human sexuality?

2 What sources provide information on sexuality in early cultures?

3 Explain how the sexual standards of past civilizations influence our own judgments about events today.

Sexuality from Saint Paul to Martin Luther

Religion has influenced views about sexuality throughout history. Perhaps no single system of thought had as much impact on the Western world as Christianity, especially in its views of sexuality (Stark, 1996). Next we look at early Christianity and the Middle Ages, the influence of Islam and, and the views of sexuality that developed during the Renaissance.

Early Christianity: Chastity Becomes a Virtue (Beginning about 50 C.E.)

Christianity began as a small sect following the teachings of Jesus. It was formalized into a religious philosophy by St. Paul and other early leaders who were influenced by the Roman legal structure. Within a few hundred years after the death of Jesus, this sect would become the predominant religion of the Western world, which has influenced the attitudes of people toward sexuality to the present day.

Jesus said little on issues such as homosexuality and premarital sex. He was born Jewish and many of his attitudes were compatible with mainstream Jewish thought of the time. However, he was liberal in his thinking about sexuality, preaching, for example, that men should be held to the same standards as women on issues of adultery, divorce, and remarriage (V.L. Bullough, 1973). He was also liberal in his recommendations for punishing sexual misadventurers. According to one story, when confronted with a woman who had committed adultery, a sin for which the Hebrew Bible had mandated stoning, he famously said, "Let he who is without sin cast the first stone."

It was St. Paul and later followers, such as St. Jerome and St. Augustine, who established the Christian view of sexuality that was to dominate Western thought for nearly 2000 years. St. Paul's view of sex was that one should ideally not have it. He regarded celibacy as the highest form of living and emphasized control over one's own body. For those who are unable to control themselves, he suggested marriage as a lesser alternative, saying, "But if they cannot contain, let them marry; for it is better to marry than to burn" (I Corinthians, 7: 9 KJV). Therefore, the ideal situation was **celibacy** (SEH-luh-buh-see). **Chastity** became a virtue in that abstaining from sexual intercourse became a sign of holiness (Bergmann, 1987).

The legacy of early Christianity was a general association of sexuality with sin. All non-procreative sex was strictly forbidden, as were contraception, masturbation, and sex for pleasure's sake, typically leading to Christians feeling guilty about sex (Stark, 1996). The Christian view of sex has been one of the harshest of any major religious or cultural traditions. One can see how such religious views can influence one's views of sexuality. It is not uncommon for people to experience **cognitive dissonance** over their disparate views about sexuality and religion.

The Middle Ages: Eve the Temptress and Mary the Virgin (500–1400)

In the early Middle Ages, the Church's influence increased. Christianity had become the state religion of Rome, and although the Church did not have much formal power, its teachings had an influence on law. For example, homosexuality and even same-sex marriages had been legal for the first 200 years after Christianity became the state religion of Rome, but eventually the Church became less tolerant. A thriving homosexual subculture disappeared in the 13th century when the Church cracked down on a variety of groups—including Jews and Muslims (Boswell, 1980).

In 1215, the Church instituted **confession** and soon guides appeared that taught priests about the various sins the **penitents** (PENN-it-tents) might have committed. These guides concentrated strongly on sexual transgressions and used sexual sins more than any other kind to illustrate their points (Payer, 1991). All sex

---

celibacy
The state of remaining unmarried; often used today to mean abstaining from sex.

chastity
The state of being sexually pure, either through abstaining from intercourse or by adhering to strict rules of sexuality.

cognitive dissonance
Uncomfortable tension that comes from holding two conflicting thoughts at the same time.

confession
The Catholic practice of revealing one's sins to a priest.

penitents
Those who come to confess sins (thus the term "repent").

outside of marriage was considered sinful and some sex acts were forbidden even in marriage.

European women in the early Middle Ages were only slightly better off than they had been in ancient Greece and Rome. By the late Middle Ages, however, new ideas about women were brought back by the Crusaders from Islamic lands (see the section on Islam that follows) and women were elevated to a place of purity (Tannahill, 1980). Women were no longer temptresses but models of virtue. The idea of romantic love emerged at this time and spread through popular culture as balladeers and troubadours travelled from place to place singing songs of pure spiritual love untroubled by sex.

At the same time, women were said to be the holders of the secrets of sexuality (Thomasset, 1992). Before marriage, many men would employ the services of an **entremetteuse** to teach them how to have sex. These old women procured prostitutes for the men and were said to know the secrets of restoring potency and virginity and concocting potions.

Perhaps no person from the Middle Ages had a stronger impact on subsequent attitudes toward sexuality than Thomas Aquinas (1225–1274). Aquinas established the views of morality and correct sexual behaviour that form the basis of the Catholic Church's attitudes toward sexuality even today (Halsall, 1996). He drew from the idea of "natural law" to suggest that there were "natural" and "unnatural" sex acts. He argued that the sex organs were naturally intended for procreation and any other use of them was unnatural. He also argued that semen was intended only to impregnate and any other purpose was immoral. Aquinas's strong condemnation of homosexuality, which he called the worst of all sexual sins, set the tone for Christian attitudes toward same-sex relationships for many centuries.

Islam: A New Religion (about 500 C.E.)

Before Islam, the Arabic world was largely tribal and nomadic, where dessert dwellers were distant from each other and divided even further by blood feuds. The Prophet Muhammad was born in 570 C.E. and, at the age of 40, said that he received divine revelations, which were written down by scribes and became the holy book of the **Qur'an** (koe-RAN). Islam began in the year 622, which was year one of the Islamic calendar. As a new religion, Islam spread like a tidal wave throughout the Middle East, into Asia, and upward through Europe where the Moors occupied Spain for several centuries. Islamic society was the most advanced in the world, with a newly developed system of mathematics (Arabic numbers) to replace the Roman system, and had the world's most sophisticated techniques of medicine, warfare, and science (Wuthnow, 1998).

Many Islamic societies have strong rules of *satr al-'awra*, or modesty, which involve covering parts of the body considered private (which for women often means almost the entire body). Muhammad tried to preserve the rights of women. There are examples in the Qur'an of female saints and intellectuals,

and women who had power over their husbands and male children.

Under Sharia law, sex is legal only when a couple is married (Coulson, 1979). Sexual intercourse in marriage is a good religious deed for a Muslim male and the Qur'an likens wives to fields that men should cultivate frequently (Shafaat, 2004).

In traditional Islamic communities, women who were married to wealthy men usually lived in secluded areas in their husbands' homes, called **harems.** Harems were not the dens of sex and sensuality that are sometimes portrayed in films but self-contained enclaves where women learned to become self-sufficient in the absence of men. Among the middle and lower classes, men had less wealth to offer potential wives, which gave women more power.

> ### On Your Mind
> How extensive are honour crimes?

The United Nations estimates that about 5000 honour killings take place in the world every year, although it's impossible to know the exact number (Gill, 2009). Honour crimes occur most frequently in places where female chastity is of utmost importance, including countries in the Middle East and South Asia. These types of crimes target women whose actions— actual or suspected—violate the honour of her family. Crimes might include speaking to someone with whom one should not associate, loss of virginity, wearing inappropriate clothing, premarital or extramarital affairs, speaking out about various issues, and even being raped, where a woman is blamed for her plight. Recent reports suggest that some women in these parts of the world have been raped in an attempt to force them to reclaim their honour by serving as suicide bombers (Mandelbaum, 2010; Navai, 2009; McCracken, 2006). In Chapter 17, we explore other forms of gender-based violence, including domestic violence and sex trafficking.

The sultans of the Ottoman Empire, who ruled most of the Islamic world from the 15th to 20th centuries, had between 300 and 1200 concubines, mostly captured or bought as slaves. A sultan's mother ruled the harem and sometimes even ruled the empire itself if she was strong and her son was weak (Tan-nahill, 1980). Because each woman might sleep with the sultan once or twice a year at most, **eunuchs** (YOU-niks) guarded the women. Eunuchs were not able to have sex with the women because their testicles or penises (or both) were removed.

entremetteuse
Historically, a woman who procures sex partners for men or one who taught men about how to have sex.

Qur'an
The holy book of Islam. Also spelled Q'ran or Koran.

harem
Abbreviation of the Turkish word *harêmlik* (*harâm* in Arabic), meaning "women's quarters" or "sanctuary."

eunuch
Castrated male who guarded a harem.

Orientalist depictions of the Middle East were common in 19th-century art.

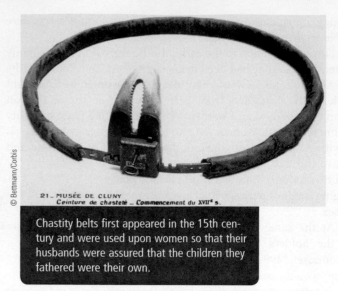

Chastity belts first appeared in the 15th century and were used upon women so that their husbands were assured that the children they fathered were their own.

The Renaissance: The Pursuit of Knowledge (Beginning about 1300)

The Renaissance, which began in Italy in the late 1300s, may be summed up as a time when intellectual and artistic thought turned from a focus on religion to a focus on human beings and their place in the world; from the sober and serious theology of the Middle Ages to a renewed sense of joy in life; from **asceticism** (ah-SET-ah-siz-um) to sensuality (New, 1969). Part of this cultural shift was new views of sexuality and, to some degree, the roles of women in society.

During the Renaissance, women made great strides in education and became more prominent in political affairs (Bornstein, 1979). Lively debates about the worth and value of women took place and, in 1532, it was argued that each creation mentioned in the book of Genesis was superior to the one before. Because women were the last thing created, they must be the most perfect creation. However, as seems to happen so often in history when women make modest gains, there was a backlash. By the 17th century, witchcraft trials appeared in Europe and the New World, which illustrated the fears that men still held of women's sexuality. Thousands of women were killed and the image of the evil witch became the symbol of men's fear of women for centuries to come.

asceticism
The practice of a lifestyle that rejects sensual pleasures such as drinking alcohol, eating rich food, or engaging in sex.

The Reformation: The Protestant Marital Partnership (Beginning about 1500)

In Western Europe in the early 16th century, Martin Luther challenged papal power, which began a movement known as Protestantism. Instead of valuing celibacy, Luther saw in the Bible the obligation to reproduce. He also saw marital love as blessed and considered sexuality a natural function. John Calvin, another important Protestant reformer, suggested that women were not just reproductive vessels but men's partners in all things.

To Luther, marriage was sacred, and sexual contact was sinful only when it occurred out of wedlock, just as any indulgence was sinful (V.L. Bullough, 1973). Because marriage was so important, a bad marriage should not continue, and so Luther broke away from the belief of the Catholic Church and allowed divorce.

Though sexuality was permissible only within marriage, it had other justifications besides reproduction such as a reduction of stress and an increase intimacy—a very different perspective on sex than that of the Catholic Church. Calvin saw the marital union as primarily a social and sexual relationship. Although procreation was important, companionship was the main goal of marriage.

Luther did accept the general subjugation of women to men in household affairs and felt that women were weaker than men and should humble themselves before their fathers and husbands. He excluded women from the clergy because of standards of "decency" and because of what he believed were women's inferior aptitudes for ministry.

Review Questions

1 How did the Christian view of sexuality change from the time of St. Paul to the time of Martin Luther and John Calvin?

2 How did views of sexuality change from the Reformation through the Renaissance?

3 Explain how religious beliefs can lead to cognitive dissonance.

The Enlightenment and the Victorian Era

The Enlightenment, an intellectual movement of the 18th century, influenced most of Europe. It favoured rational thought over traditional authority and suggested that human nature could be understood through psychology. Enlightenment writers argued that human drives and instincts are natural, so one must acknowledge the basic wisdom of human urges rather than deny them (Porter, 1982).

The Enlightenment (Beginning about 1700)

During the Enlightenment, sexual pleasure was considered natural and desirable. Some enlightenment thinkers even praised it as supreme. Sexuality had become so free that there was an unprecedented rise in premarital pregnancy and births to single mothers. About a fifth of all brides in the late 17th century were pregnant when they got married (Trumbach, 1990).

Even though it was a liberal era, some sexual activities such as homosexuality were condemned and those who practised it were persecuted. For example, between 1630 and 1732, there was a "sodomite panic" in the Netherlands where hundreds of men accused of homosexual acts were executed and hundreds more fled the country. France burned homosexuals long after it stopped burning witches. There were also times of relative tolerance. Napoleon Bonaparte relaxed the laws against homosexuality so that by 1860 it was tolerated and male prostitutes became common in France (Tannahill, 1980).

The Victorian Era (Early 1800s)

The Victorian era, which refers to Queen Victoria's rule, began in 1837 and lasted until early 1901. It was a time of great prosperity for England. Propriety and public behaviour became more important, especially to the upper class, and sexual attitudes became more conservative. Sex was not spoken of in polite company and sexual activity was restricted to the marital bed. It was also believed that any preoccupation with sex interfered with higher achievements. Privately, Victorian England was not as conservative as it had been portrayed and pornography, extramarital affairs, and prostitution were common. Still, the most important aspect of Victorian society was public propriety. Conservative values were often preached if not always practised.

The idea of male chivalry returned and women were expected to be virtuous, refined, delicate, fragile, vulnerable, aloof, and entirely devoid of any sexual desire. The prudery of the Victorian era sometimes went to extremes. Many Victorian women were too embarrassed to talk to a physician about their "female problems" and so would point out areas of discomfort on dolls (Hellerstein et al., 1981; see Sex in Real Life for more information about women who shared their gynecological concerns with their physicians). It was acceptable for women to play musical instruments but not the flute because pursing the lips was unladylike, not the cello because it had to be held between the legs, not brass instruments because they were too difficult for the delicate lungs of women, and not the violin because it forced a woman's neck into an uncomfortable position. Therefore, only keyboard instruments were considered "ladylike" (V.L. Bullough, 1973).

Sexuality was repressed in many ways. Physicians and writers of the time often argued that semen was precious and should be conserved. Sylvester Graham, a Presbyterian minister and founder of the American Vegetarian Society, recommended sex only 12 times a year. He argued that sexual indulgence led to all sorts of ailments and infirmities such as depression, faintness, headaches, and blindness.

The Victorian era had a great influence on sexuality in England and the British Empire. Some conservative attitudes that still exist today have origins in Victorian standards.

Review Questions

1 Explain how sexuality was viewed during the Enlightenment.

2 How did the Victorian era influence the view of sexuality?

3 Explain how sexuality was repressed during the Victorian era.

SEX
in Real Life
The History of Vibrators

Vibrators date back to the late 19th century. At this time, many women began voicing complaints to their physicians (who were mostly male) about their gynecological problems. Their symptoms typically included fainting, fluid congestion, insomnia, nervousness, abdominal heaviness, loss of appetite for food or sex, and a tendency to cause trouble for others, especially family members (Maines, 1999). Physicians concluded that these gynecological complaints were due to "pelvic hyperemia," otherwise known as genital congestion (Maines, 1999). This condition was diagnosed as "hysteria," a common and chronic complaint from women at the time. In fact, it was not until 1952 that the American Psychiatric Association dropped hysteria as a diagnosis (Slavney, 1990).

To relieve the symptoms of hysteria, physicians recommended "intercourse on the marriage bed" or vulvar massage by a physician or midwife (Maines, 1999). It was thought that rates of hysteria were higher in virgins and unmarried or widowed women because they did not engage in sexual intercourse. Hysteria was thus considered a condition resulting from lack of male attention.

Vulvar massage to induce paroxysm (orgasm) was typically painstaking and time-consuming for a physician, often requiring up to an hour for each woman. Because religious mandates prohibited self-masturbation, vulvar massage was defined as a purely medical procedure and, thus, the only acceptable solution for women without husbands.

The vibrator appeared in the late 1800s in response to physician demands for more rapid ways to treat hysteria. By the early 1900s, several types of vibrators were available from low-priced foot-powered models to expensive battery operated or electric models. Advertisements began to appear in women's magazines such as *Needlecraft, Woman's Home Companion,* and *Modern Women* (Maines, 1999). They were directed toward women and, to a lesser extent, men, with claims that vibrators make good gifts because they could give women a healthy glow with "bright eyes" and "pink cheeks" (Maines, 1999).

Social awareness of vibrators arose by the 1920s when the devices made their way into pornographic films (Maines, 1999). In fact, they were the 15th household appliance to be electrified after the sewing machine, fan, tea kettle, and

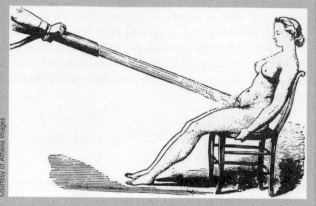

Courtesy of Athena Images

toaster (Maines, 1999). By the 1960s, because of changing sexual attitudes, vibrators were sold openly as aids to improve sexual functioning and satisfaction.

Marketers of vibrators are aware that sexual mores vary considerably and sales strategies vary as a result. In stores and on websites and in magazines devoted to sex products, there is little pretense about their purpose and they are sold directly as devices to induce orgasms. Other strategies are more subtle. According to one study in the *Canadian Review of Sociology & Anthropology*, vibrators and other sexual paraphernalia have often been sold at "naughty lady parties," which resemble Tupperware parties in people's homes (Baumann, 1991). The salesperson will bring out vibrators in the spirit of "fun" and she will also mention that they make great neck massagers for tired husbands. In so doing, they obscure the sexual purpose of the devices and make any purchase of them ambiguous. A woman may thus buy a vibrator, but she does not declare her purpose in so doing.

© Kurt Rogers/San Francisco Chronicle/Corbis

© Elyse D'Estout

Sexuality in Canada— Past and Present

Although evidence conflicts, it is estimated that Aboriginal (or Native) people have been in what is now Canada for at least 25 000 years and Europeans since 1000 C.E., when the Norse people touched on Newfoundland. John Cabot came five centuries later, exploring the east coast in 1497, and Jacques Cartier in 1534, sailing up the St. Lawrence River. Canada has been a nation since its confederation in 1867. In this section, we look at the history of sexuality in Canada, beginning with Aboriginal people and ending with the present.

Aboriginal Life and Sexuality

When Europeans came to North America, they found major differences between themselves and the people who lived there. First, family structures were different. The Native peoples of Quebec and Ontario commonly followed what anthropologists call the Iroquois kinship system which, unlike Europeans, distinguishes between parallel cousins (children of the father's brother and the mother's sister), who are considered siblings, and cross cousins (children of the mother's brother and the father's sister), who are considered merely cousins. Marrying parallel cousins was not an option, but cross cousins would be prime candidates, having grown up together (Trigger, 1969). European missionaries saw this practice as incestuous and discouraged it either by force or threat of eternal damnation.

Second, although Native men and women had different roles, they were matrilineal—the line of descent was traced through the mother and not the father. Among the Iroquois, women had real political power and the ability to appoint leaders. Again, this custom did not sit well with the missionaries, who firmly believed in women's subordinate roles.

Third and most striking, Native people had a three- and sometimes four-gender system. There were males and females, and there were also Two-Spirited people, who could be either biological males or females. Early anthropologists called these people *Berdache*, but this term is now generally considered offensive and has been replaced by **Two-Spirited**, meaning androgynous or possessing the spirits of both male and female. Male Two-Spirited people had special roles within their groups, often dressed in women's clothing, and usually married other men. They were also highly respected. According to Blackwood (1983), female Two-Spirited people were less common and existed mostly in western groups including the Kaska people of the Yukon. They had the skills of men, having shown an interest at an early age, and often married other women. Most data are on male Two-Spirited people, and to the early missionaries intent on Christianizing Native people, they were despised as sodomites destined for Hell. As Williams (1986, p. 181) put it, "everything Western was sanctioned as the will of God, while everything belonging to the indigenous culture was evil." Today, especially among the LGBTQ communities of Canada, there is better recognition of the uniqueness of the Two-Spirited tradition.

Two-Spirited people were misunderstood and condemned by early Christian missionaries.

Native culture slowly eroded over the years due to the interests of Europeans, particularly in the fur-trading enterprise. The Hudson Bay Company traded with Aboriginal people and eventually weakened their culture through corruption, the introduction of alcohol, and the appropriation of their labour. European women were prohibited from entering the fur-trading areas, which allowed men to take Native women as "country wives"—a relationship many saw as temporary (Kinsman, 1987, p. 72).

By the 19th century, there were efforts by the Canadian government and Catholic and Anglican Churches to assimilate Native people entirely through a residential school system. Children, by the age of about seven, were taken from their parents and placed in schools run by these churches, which were sometimes thousands of kilometres away. They were forbidden

Two-Spirited
Third and fourth genders among Aboriginal people, where they are said to have the spirits of both male and female.

to speak their own language, forced to pray in the chapels, and usually severely abused whether physically, mentally, or sexually. Boys as well as girls were raped by priests, nuns, and ministers, and many died from either neglect or exposure to disease. Much of these abuses have been documented by ex-minister Kevin Annett on his website "Hidden from History" (http://canadiangenocide.nativeweb.org/). In total, more than 150 000 Aboriginal children were sent to residential schools. On June 11, 2008, Prime Minister Stephen Harper issued an official apology to Native people for the Canadian government's part in this tragedy.

The King's Daughters, Naked Marches, and Polygamists

When the French settled in New France, few women and many single men came over, leaving the men's chances of marriage and family slim. Between 1663 and 1673, in an initiative by King Louis XIV to increase the population in the colonies and strengthen the French presence, about 800 young women were sent to Canada to marry the settlers and have families. They became known as *les filles du roi,* or the King's Daughters. Most of them did find husbands and, within a decade, the population of New France more than doubled. One of the King's Daughters, Catherine Guichelin, became the colony's first woman to be charged with prostitution, which she engaged in after her husband abandoned her. She was found guilty and banished from Quebec City.

Also by the 1660s, intermarriages between French colonists and Native women became common. The Catholic Church had hoped that once the women were Christianized they would lose interest in their culture. This "Frenchification" became an early assimilationist policy, which rather backfired. First, the Native women became important dignitaries between the two cultures for the fur trade; second, with their superior knowledge of the environment, French men became more interested in Native culture (Berkowitz, 2012, pp. 244–245). The ancestors of these unions developed a unique Native identity and became the Métis of which nearly a half million survive today.

Women were subordinate to their husbands by law and were expected to have children as early as possible, often marrying as young as 14 or 15 years old. They were also fiercely independent by necessity since their husbands were often absent for months in the fur trade, which made a society that was once mainly male to one where women became the majority. The influence of the Catholic Church would make the already difficult lives of women worse in its mandate to "go forth and multiply," leading them to spend much of their lives pregnant while dealing with the hardships of a frontier society (Errington, 1988).

The West eventually was opened up by the fur trade, bringing mainly British settlers in what is now the prairie provinces. Eventually, large populations of Germans, Russians, and Ukrainians came to settle and bear the harsh winters. One Russian group, the Doukhobors were a fiercely independent group who resented any government interference in their way of life. In protest, in the early 20th century, they would march through town naked, leading the Canadian government to outlaw public nudity entirely.

The Sons of Freedom, a group of Doukhobors in Western Canada, would stage naked marches as protests in the early 20th century against such things as compulsory education and government land appropriation.

Another group reaching Canada by way of the border of Alberta were Mormons, who now make up a sizable proportion of the province. The Mormons of Utah had long practised polygamy, but this was a barrier to statehood and, thus, recognition by the government of the United States. Utah gave up polygamy and received statehood in 1896, which prompted the remaining polygamist Mormons to move to Canada. They eventually gave up polygamy as well, prompting yet another faction to move westward to avoid government scrutiny. Today, fundamentalist Mormons live principally in Bountiful, British Columbia, and continue their polygamous marriages.

The Struggle to Legalize Abortion

Abortion had been banned entirely in Canada soon after Confederation in 1867, although numerous abortions had been carried out, usually crudely and under less-than-sanitary conditions. The first major reform occurred in 1969 when the Criminal Law Amendment Act allowed for "therapeutic abortions" if the mother's life was in danger and after a three-doctor panel had reviewed each case. Prior to this amendment, performing an abortion would lead to life imprisonment.

In his decision to challenge the law, Montreal physician and Holocaust survivor Henry Morgentaler began to challenge the law's restrictions by performing abortions without the three-doctor panel requirement. After being arrested, tried, and acquitted several times, he took his challenge to Canada's Supreme Court, which in 1988 led to the law being struck down entirely as contrary to the rights and freedoms of women.

Today, abortions are legal all over Canada and paid for through Medicare. Even so, Canadians remain divided on the issue. A third believe abortion should be legal under all

"Topfreedom" in Canada

Men in Canada have enjoyed taking off their shirts on hot days since the days of Jacques Cartier. Women, unless they are far into the woods, had rarely been able to do so. Because they have breasts, and because breasts are considered sexually provocative, the law had imposed restrictions on one sex and not the other. One hot day in 1991 in Guelph, Ontario, Gwen Jacobs took off her top and walked barebreasted in the streets. She was eventually arrested and convicted as having violated the community standards of decency. After a long struggle, the Ontario Court of Appeal overturned her conviction, reasoning that any harm she was doing to the community was "highly speculative" and that no one who was offended was forced

to continue looking at her. While there was no subsequent federal law to proclaim equality, the Jacobs case had become a powerful legal precedent reasoning that simple toplessness without a sexual context is not in and of itself offensive. In 2011, on the 20th anniversary of Jacob's arrest, some students staged a celebratory topless march.

The Topfreedom movement is not only Canadian but worldwide in its belief in total gender equality and considers any laws disallowing women the same freedom as men to be sex discrimination. The Canadian Topfree Equal Rights Association (http://tera.ca) also fights discrimination for breast-feeding, although this is mostly protected as a right in Canada.

© Moira Welsh/Getty

Gwen Jacobs of Guelph, Ontario, challenged the laws on toplessness in Canada and won.

circumstances, half believe there should be some restrictions, and the remainder either have no opinion or believe it should be illegal. In the United States, opinions are far more polarized, where about half believe it should be legal and half illegal.

Gay Rights in Canada

Homosexuality had been treated as "crimes against nature" in the early years and through much of history, given the stance of the French Catholic and English Protestant churches. Laws were formalized in the Criminal Code of Canada and by 1892 homosexuality was considered an "offence against morality" and stood as such until 1969. Curiously, the law seemed to omit lesbians, reflecting the belief of the time that women had little or no sexual desire and that such a crime did not exist. In fact, it was not until 1955 that a criminal trial involving lesbianism occurred, when Willimae Moore was charged with indecently assaulting a coworker in a government building in Yellowknife. The indecent assault in question was an attempted kiss (Blackhouse, 2008).

While homosexuality continued to be a crime, it also became defined as an illness by the burgeoning efforts of European and American psychiatrists. Gays and lesbians were "sick" and "criminal" and had to live within the shadows of society and were often restricted to furtive anonymous encounters. If they were not anonymous, gays and lesbians ran the risk of blackmail, and even if they were anonymous, a man could approach an undercover police officer and his life and reputation would be ruined (Warner, 2002).

Despite such obstacles, gay and lesbian communities thrived all over Canada, particularly after World War II, when young men flocked toward the cities. Gay men lived in rooming houses or similar types of housing, since large apartments and houses were reserved for families or people who fit the heterosexual model

(Kinsman, 1987, p. 145). One ethnographic work by Maurice Leznoff in Montreal from 1954 entitled "The Homosexual in Urban Society" gives a rare glimpse into the lives of gay men at the time. The gay community of Montreal in the 1950s was like an ecosystem. There were gay bars, city streets and parks known for cruising, some restaurants where gay men gathered, and even a YMCA where further cruising took place. Men would do their rounds and hope to meet someone to bring home with them. Typically, no names were exchanged nor any other identifying information (Leznoff, 1954). If they were caught, they would be put in jail, lose their jobs, and their names and addresses would be published in newspapers. Around any corner they could encounter a police officer, a gay basher, or a blackmailer. Heterosexuality in contrast was fully endorsed by society and men and women had the privilege of meeting each other in any public place and forming relationships openly. Furtive sex for gay men, as well as closely guarding their identities, was an adaption to oppression.

The tide began to change in Canada with the 1960s, when a young generation of baby boomers began to challenge the status quo. Legislation to decriminalize homosexuality between consenting adults was introduced in 1967, and it passed in 1969. That same year, in the United States, gays, lesbians, and drag queens rioted in the streets of New York after police had raided the Stonewall Inn—an event that catalyzed the "gay liberation" movement at the time.

Today, even though some old prejudices linger, gays and lesbians enjoy total equality under the law. They are protected in employment and housing, they may serve in the military, and they have full equality in marriage. While opponents of same-sex marriage warned of the erosion and even destruction of society a decade ago, this has not happened. And on February 11, 2013, an openly lesbian woman, Kathleen Wynne, who married her partner in 2005, became premier of Ontario.

Sexuality in American History

Canada's neighbour to the south had its own history of ideas about sexuality, which were tempered by the contributions of millions of immigrants from Europe, especially England. The following is a brief overview of American events and developments.

The 15th to 18th Centuries: The Puritan Ethic and Slavery

The Puritans were a Protestant group who came to the New World in the 15th century to set up a strict religious society. They imposed severe sanctions for sexual transgressions including the death penalty for sodomy, adultery, and rape (D'Emilio & Freedman, 1988). At the same time, they saw sex within marriage in a positive light and considered it a husband's duty to have intercourse with his wife. Today, the "Puritan ethic" is a term meaning excessively strict views of sexuality.

As in Canada, women came to the New World with the promise of greater independence and, because their husbands were away either hunting or at sea for months at a time, they achieved this independence by necessity. The women of the whaling colony of Nantucket, for example, successfully took over the island's businesses (V.L. Bullough, 1973).

Slavery was a fact of life in the New World for centuries until the emancipation of 1865. White slave owners would often visit their slave quarters and have intercourse with the women, who had little choice since their bodies were the property of their masters. As a result, many biracial children were born and lighter-skinned slaves became common. By the 18th century, for example, a fifth of children born out of wedlock in Virginia were biracial (D'Emilio & Freedman, 1988). Even though sex (forced or otherwise) had always taken place between White men and Black women, interracial marriages were not legally recognized until 1967, when the United States Supreme Court struck down all **anti-miscegenation laws** that prohibited them. Once slaves were free, a continued fear that Black men would rape White women provided a justification for continued segregation, even though it was more likely that White men would rape Black women. Despite the condemnation of Blacks as promiscuous, their premarital activity was likely not that much different from that of poor White (Clinton & Gillespie, 1997).

Meanwhile, the 17th century saw a lessening of the power of the Church and, as a result, a utilitarian philosophy that included the celebration of sexuality. This new found freedom of expression also led to an increase in prostitution as well as the use of contraception and concoctions to induce abortions. Not surprisingly, the birth rate dropped and the abortion rate increased (Gamson, 1990).

Sexuality Movements of the 19th Century

The 19th century witnessed the rise of several social movements pertaining to sexuality. First, the **free love movement** beginning in the 1820s centred on the idea that love should be the main prerequisite to sexual activity and that marriage is a form of sexual slavery for women.

Second, around mid-century, the Mormons headed west and formed communities in the Utah Territory where they practised what they called "plural marriage"—a form of polygamy where men had two or more wives. This practice was suspended by church leaders in 1890, which improved relations with the United States Government and eventually led to Utah's statehood in 1896. Polygamous marriages continued in secret and do so to the present day.

A number of other groups began alternative forms of marriage at the time. The Oneida community of New York State formed a group marriage system where all men in the community were married to all women. In contrast, the Shakers, who came from England, were a communal society of religious believers who practised celibacy and forbade any procreation (Hildebrand, 2008).

By the end of the century, the medical model of sexuality emerged and Americans became obsessed with what was considered sexual health. Physicians and reformers advocated self-restraint, abstention from masturbation, and the eating of simple rather than "stimulating" foods. They also believed that women were ruled by their wombs and many had their ovaries surgically removed to "correct" masturbation or sexual passion. An influential group of physicians even argued that women were biologically designed for procreation and thus too delicate to work or undergo the rigours of higher education. These theories completely ignored the fact that lower-class women and woman of colour often did hard work 12 to 15 hours a day. Male sexuality was viewed as normative.

Homosexual relationships took place covertly, although there were some open same-sex relationships that may or may not have been sexual. Two women who had never married, for example, might live together as "companions." These were known as "Boston marriages" and they rarely drew undue attention (Faderman, 1981). There were also men who wrote of intimate and loving relationships with other men without mentioning sexual contact. Gay poet Walt Whitman sometimes confirmed his attraction to men and at other times denied it. In accordance with the developing medical model of sexuality, physicians began to argue that homosexuality was an illness rather than a sin, a view that lasted until the 1970s (D'Emilio, 1998).

Movements for more open sexual relationships were countered by strong voices arguing for a return to a more religious and

---

anti-miscegenation laws
Laws prohibiting sex, marriage, or procreation between members of different races.

free love movement
A movement of the early 19th century maintaining that love should be the factor that determines whether one should have sex (not to be confused with the free love movement of the 1960s).

chaste morality, an argument that continues in the United States today. In the 1870s, dry goods salesman Anthony Comstock lobbied the legislature to outlaw obscenity. The resulting Comstock Act of 1873 prohibited the mailing of obscene, lewd, lascivious, and indecent writing or advertisements, including articles about contraception or abortion. Comstock himself was the act's most vigorous enforcer, and he reported hundreds of people to the authorities, even for such things as selling reprints of famous artwork containing nudity or famous books that mentioned prostitution (M.A. Blanchard & Semoncho, 2006). Thousands of books, sexual objects, and contraceptive devices were destroyed, denying many people contraceptive devices or information (D'Emilio & Freedman, 1988). It wasn't until 1965 that the United States Supreme Court struck down these laws.

The 20th Century: Sexual Crusaders and Sexologists

Even though the Comstock laws were in effect, one study of 1000 women found that 74 percent used some form of contraception, most had sex at least once a week, and 40 percent admitted masturbating during childhood or adolescence (D'Emilio & Freedman, 1988). These statistics reflect the freedom women gradually began to find as they moved to the cities, lived on their own, and worked outside the home (Irvine, 1990). Even so, the majority of women still considered reproduction the primary goal of sex.

The STI rate of the early 20th century was high, prompting physician Prince Morrow to begin a movement that involved a curious mixture of both liberal and traditional attitudes. This social hygiene movement convinced legislators that many women were catching STIs from husbands who frequented prostitutes and so laws were passed mandating blood tests before marriage. Police crackdowns on prostitution also occurred. Reformers were against premarital sex as well and saw masturbation as dangerous to one's health. They were also early (if unsuccessful) advocates for sex education in schools (D'Emilio & Freedman, 1988).

Pioneers of sex research advanced the understanding of sexuality rejecting religious teaching about how people should behave. We introduce them here and discuss them at length in the next chapter. Alfred Kinsey published his massive research on sexual behaviour in two volumes in 1948 and 1953 and both became bestsellers. Based on thousands of interviews, Kinsey's findings shocked the American people. His findings revealed that sex was much more important to peoples' lives than originally thought. Masturbation, homosexuality, and premarital and extramarital sex were common, and women had more sexual interest and desire than people thought (Kimmel & Plante, 2007). Later, William Masters and Virginia Johnson studied the physiology of sexual response. Their research yielded two important books (Masters & Johnson, 1966, 1970) that were also bestsellers. The work of these sexologists helped demystify sex and make it easier for people to discuss. Much of this work was condemned by moral crusaders, who criticized its lack of connection to traditional standards of morality (Irvine, 1990).

Two **sexual revolutions**, a term coined by Austrian psychoanalyst Wilhelm Reich, who strongly believed in a sexually liberated society (Allyn, 2000), took place in the 1920s and 1960s. At both times, traditional values and behaviours were challenged in favour of sexual freedom. The 1920s, for example, saw "flappers"—women with short bob hairstyles and short skirts and who were open about sexuality (Gourley, 2007).

The sexual revolution of the 1960s began in San Francisco, where thousands of young people or "hippies" proclaimed the power of love and sex, and where people went from "No sex before marriage" to "If it feels good, do it." Hippies and others rebelled against the moral code of American society (Lipton, 2003) and this included a Black Civil Rights movement and the growing student protests against the Vietnam War.

The 1960s also saw the reformulation of male gender roles and an examination of the double standard of sexuality (Escoffier, 2003). Furthermore, television, radio, and other mass media began to broadcast more liberal ideas about sexuality, and pornography became more acceptable. In 1953, Hugh Hefner began publishing *Playboy* magazine, and Helen Gurley Brown's *Sex and the Single Girl* (1962), Joan Garrity's *The Sensuous Woman* (1969), and David Reuben's *Everything You Always Wanted to Know About Sex (But Were Afraid to Ask)* (1969) flooded the book market.

The first contraceptive pill also liberated female sexuality in the early 1960s. For the first time, women were free to engage in intercourse without fear of becoming pregnant. Fashions also changed, emphasizing women's bodies and showing more skin. Women wore miniskirts, plunging necklines, and see-through blouses, further emphasizing their sexuality. Some women even publicly burned their bras in an act of defiance against male domination.

The Feminist Movement

There have always been women who protested against the patriarchy of their day. The most successful feminist movement of the 20th century was the **women's suffrage** movement, which placed women's

sexual revolutions
Changes in morality and sexual behaviour occurring in Western societies in the 1920s and the 1960s.

women's suffrage
A movement to grant women the right to vote.

issues on the national agenda. Margaret Sanger, a homemaker, profoundly influenced women's sexuality in the first half of the 20th century. After her grandmother died at age 50 after 18 pregnancies, she was determined to help women with birth control.

In 1917, Sanger met Katharine Dexter McCormick, who had graduated with a degree in biology from the Massachusetts Institute of Technology (she was the second woman to do so). In the next few years, Sanger worked with McCormick to build the Birth Control League. She brought her passion and energy, while McCormick provided the knowledge and capital. During the Depression of the 1930s, their movement gained momentum because many people were desperate to limit the size of their families. The number of birth control clinics in the United States grew from 55 in 1930 to over 800 in 1942 (Gibbs, 2010). In 1942, the Birth Control League changed its name to the Planned Parenthood Federation of America.

The modern feminist movement may be captured in the books of three women (Ferree & Hess, 1985): Simone de Beauvoir's *The Second Sex* (1949) highlighted men's treatment of women as sex objects, Betty Friedan's *The Feminine Mystique* (1963) looked at how educated women felt trapped in the roles of housewives, and Kate Millet's *Sexual Politics* (1969) argued that patriarchy led to violence and forced men to renounce all that is feminine in them. According to Millett, rape was an act against controlling women and men saw homosexuality as a failure of patriarchy and thus repressed it.

Feminists argued that they were entitled to sexual satisfaction, that relationships between the sexes were exploitative, and that women had a right to control their lives and their bodies. Some more radical feminists saw lesbian relationships as the only ones not based on male power. Part of the freedom women wanted was a right to choose when to be mothers, so abortion rights became a firm part of the feminist platform. Feminism has made great cultural and political strides and changed the nature of society and sexual behaviour. Still, men are paid more than women for the same work, poverty is increasing among single mothers, and rape and spousal abuse are major social problems (Lips, 2008). Thus, there is still much work to be done.

Gay Rights

During the Cold War of the 1950s and 1960s, American Senator Joseph McCarthy became famous for trying to purge the United States of communists. He also relentlessly hunted gays and lesbians, portraying them as perverts lurking in schools and on street corners, ready to pounce on unsuspecting youth. As a result, many were fired from their jobs or imprisoned in jails and mental hospitals. The news media participated in this view, as in a 1949 *Newsweek* article that identified all gays as "sex murderers." Psychiatrists tried a number of "cures," including lobotomies and castration. Churches were either silent or encouraged the persecution of gays and lesbians, and the Hollywood film industry purged itself of positive references to homosexuality. Many laws initiated during this period, such as immigration restrictions for gays and lesbians and policies banning gays from the military, continued for years afterward (Adam, 1987).

In 1951, the Mattachine Society, a gay rights organization, was founded in the United States by Harry Hay, and the Daughters of

After homosexuality was removed from the *Diagnostic and Statistical Manual* in 1973, it was no longer considered a psychiatric disorder.

Bilitis, a lesbian organization, was founded by four lesbian couples in San Francisco in 1955. Although these groups began with radical intentions, anti-gay sentiments of American authorities forced them to lay low throughout the 1950s. Although gay activism increased with protests throughout the 1960s, the modern gay rights movement is usually traced to the night in 1969 when police raided a New York City gay bar called Stonewall. For the first time, the gay community resisted violently and the police were greeted with a hail of debris thrown by the patrons of the bar. There had been previous acts of resistance but the Stonewall riot became a symbolic warning to police that gays and lesbians would no longer passively accept arrest and brutality.

Following the Stonewall riots, gay activists campaigned strongly against prejudice and discrimination nationwide. Groups and businesses hostile to gays were picketed, legislators were lobbied, committees and self-help groups were founded, legal agencies were formed, and educational groups tried to change the image of gays and lesbians. In 1973, strong gay lobbying caused the American Psychiatric Association to remove homosexuality from the *Diagnostic and Statistical Manual of Mental Disorders* (DSM), the official reference of psychiatric disorders. After this, it was no longer a "disease." This change removed the last scientific justification for treating gays and lesbians differently from other citizens. Soon the gay rights movement became a powerful presence in the United States, Canada, Australia, and Western Europe (Adam, 1987).

The 1970s was a time of unprecedented freedom for gays and lesbians. Bathhouses and bars became open centres of gay social life, and gay theatre groups, newspapers, and magazines appeared. In 1979, the National March on Washington for Lesbian and Gay Rights was a symbolic step forward for the gay movement (Ghaziani, 2005). The 1980s, however, was difficult. The AIDS epidemic in the United States and Europe doused the excitement of the 1970s as thousands of gay men died of complications from the disease (see Chapter 15). Historically, when such fearsome epidemics arise, people have been quick to find a minority group to blame for the disease, and gays and lesbians were quickly blamed for AIDS (Perrow & Guillén, 1990; Shilts, 2000).

In the 1990s, queer theory developed from gay and lesbian studies (we discuss queer theory in more detail in Chapter 2) and the gay rights movement did much to change sexual attitudes not only by pressing for recognition of sexual orientation but by arguing that all sexual minorities have a right to happiness.

Today, gays and lesbians continue to lobby for same-sex marriage. Although a handful of states allow gay couples to register as domestic partners and have certain health and death benefits, it is still controversial in American society. As of June 26, 2013, the United States Supreme Court struck down the laws barring federal recognition of same-sex marriage.

We are the sum total of our history. Our attitudes and beliefs reflect our historical influences from the ancient Hebrews and Greeks to the modern feminist and gay rights movements. Most of us have a hard time recognizing that our own constellation of beliefs, feelings, and moral positions about sex are products of our particular time and place and are in a constant state of evolution. It is important to keep this in mind as we explore the sexual behaviours of other people and cultures throughout this book.

In 2011, U.S. President Obama announced that his administration would no longer defend the Defense of Marriage Act (DOMA) that defined marriage as only between a man and a woman.

© Jari Hindstroem/Shutterstock

Review Questions

1 Explain how the Puritans viewed sex. Whom did they believe was responsible for upholding morality?

2 Explain some of the influences that led to the liberalization of sex in the 1700s.

3 What are the two most important movements that changed sexuality in the latter part of the 20th century? What did each contribute?

Chapter Review

Summary Points

1 Human sexuality is grounded in biological functioning, emerges as we develop, and is expressed by cultures through rules about sexual contact, attitudes about moral and immoral sexuality, and habits of sexual behaviour and patterns of relations between the sexes.

2 The sexual nature of human beings is unique in the animal kingdom. Humans have created ideas, laws, customs, fantasies, and art around the sexual act.

3 The media use sexuality frequently to sell products. However, sexuality is one of the most difficult topics to express and explore.

4 Evolution to an upright posture changed forever the way human beings engage in sexual intercourse.

5 Men dominated public life in early history and we know far more about men's thoughts than women's. The Hebrew Bible contains explicit rules about sexual behaviour. The focus on marital sexuality and procreation formed the basis of sexual attitudes in the West for centuries.

6 The Greeks were more sexually permissive than the Hebrews. In Greek culture, pederasty was considered a natural form of sexuality. Rome had few restrictions about sexuality until late in the history of the empire.

7 The Chinese belief in yin and yang taught people how to maximize their sexuality. A woman's essence, or yin, was viewed as inexhaustible, whereas a man's essence, yang, embodied in semen, was limited. Hinduism concentrates on an individual's cycle of birth and rebirth, also known as karma. India's most famous sex manual, the *Kama Sutra*, appeared sometime during the third or fourth century.

8 Perhaps no single system of thought has had as much impact on the Western world as Christianity. According to early forms of the belief system, sexuality itself was not sinful when performed as part of the marital union, but the ideal situation was celibacy. In fact,

Exploring Human Sexuality: Past and Present

with the advent of Christianity, chastity became a virtue for the first time in history.

9 In the early Middle Ages, the influence of the Church increased. Its teachings began to influence laws, which became more strict. Perhaps no person from the Middle Ages had a stronger impact on attitudes toward sexuality than Thomas Aquinas.

10 Muhammad began to preach a religion called Islam in the seventh century. Many Muslim societies have strong rules of modesty for women that involve covering private parts of their bodies. According to the Qur'an, marital sexual intercourse was a good religious deed and men were encouraged to do so frequently.

11 The Renaissance witnessed a new view of sexuality and of the roles of women in society. Women made great strides in education and became more prominent in political affairs. Pro-female tracts began to circulate, and lively debates about the value of women ensued. However, by the 17th century, witchcraft trials appeared, symbolizing the fear that men held of women's sexuality.

12 In the early 16th century, Martin Luther started Protestantism. He saw in the Bible the obligation to reproduce, considered marital love blessed, and considered sexuality a natural function. Sexuality was permissible only in the marital union and it had other justifications besides reproduction.

13 The Enlightenment (early 1700s) prized rational thought over traditional authority and suggested that human nature was to be understood through a study of human psychology. Sexual pleasure was considered natural and desirable.

14 During the Victorian era, conservative values were often preached although not always practised. The idea of male chivalry returned and women were considered to be virtuous, refined, delicate, fragile, vulnerable, and remote. Sexuality was repressed in many ways.

15 In Canada, Native people had different family structures that Christian missionaries found immoral. They were also matrilineal, and women had power. Two-Spirited people were also misunderstood by missionaries, although they had important roles in Native cultures.

16 The King's Daughters were women sent from France to Quebec to marry French colonists. While women were subordinate to their husbands, they became fiercely independent because their husbands were often away hunting.

17 Abortion became fully legal in Canada in 1988 and homosexuality was decriminalized in 1969.

18 During the 19th century, the free love movement preached that only love should be the prerequisite to sexual relations. However, by the end of the 19th century, the medical model of sexuality emerged and physicians and reformers advocated self-restraint, abstention from masturbation, and consumption of "non-stimulating" foods. The Comstock Act of 1873 prohibited the mailing of "obscene" material, including articles about contraception or abortion.

19 In the early 20th century, pioneers of sex research began their work, rejecting the religious and moral teachings about how people should behave.

20 The sexual revolutions brought changes in values and attitudes about sexuality. Society became more permissive and accepting of sexual freedom. Flappers and hippies helped bring more liberal attitudes about sexuality.

21 Feminism and the modern gay rights movement, beginning with the Stonewall riots of 1969, also affected society's attitudes about sexuality. The American Psychiatric Association removed homosexuality from the DSM.

Critical Thinking Questions

1 In what ways does Canada differ from the United States in terms of sexual behaviour and attitudes?

2 Why do you think "sex sells" when our culture traditionally has had a problem openly talking about sexuality?

3 Christianity has had a profound impact on people's attitudes toward sexuality. Do you think that it is still influential? How so?

4 How are China's and India's attitudes toward sexuality different from Western ones?

5 Provide two examples of how cultural images of beauty affect how men and women feel about themselves.

6 Explain how the sexual revolution of the 1960s shaped the cultural view of sexuality.

7 Compare and contrast the views of sexuality in Canadian society and in Islam.

Websites

World Health Organization (WHO)   The WHO is the coordinating health organization within the United Nations system and among its duties is to promote sexual and reproductive health worldwide. (http://www.who.int/)

The Sex Information and Education Council of Canada (SEICCAN)   SEICCAN is an organization that promotes comprehensive education about sexuality as well as individuals' rights to make responsible and informed choices about their own sexual behaviour. (http://www.sieccan.org/)

The Canadian Federation for Sexual Health (CFSH)   The CFSH is a charitable organization dedicated to the promotion of sexual health both in Canada and internationally. (http://www.cfsh.ca/)

Canadian Lesbian and Gay Archives (CLGA)   The CLGA is the largest independent LGBTQ+ archives in the world. With a focus on Canadian content, it acquires, preserves, and provides public access to information and archival materials in any medium. (http://www.clga.ca/)

The Kinsey Institute   This official website for the Kinsey Institute is one of only a handful of centres in the world that conducts interdisciplinary research exclusively on sex and has a large library that includes books, films, video, fine art, artifacts, photography, archives, and a large collection of pornographic images for scholarly study. (http://www.kinseyinstitute.org/)

The Journal of the History of Sexuality   This journal has a cross-cultural and cross-disciplinary focus that brings together original articles and critical reviews from historians, social scientists, and humanities scholars worldwide. (http://utpress.utexas.edu/index.php/journals/journal-of-the-history-of-sexuality)

2

Understanding Human Sexuality: Theory and Research

Valerie, a 20-year-old college student, took a human sexuality course her senior year and was excited when her professor assigned a project that required her to develop a research project exploring human sexuality. She needed to design a study, collect the data, and analyze the results. After much thought, she decided to explore the various places where college students have sex. Wanting to be creative and have fun with the assignment, she came up with the "Bikini Sex Project." She would wear a bikini around campus and interview students, asking them the locations of some of the craziest places they had engaged in sex. Then she asked the students to write the strangest place on her body. She liked the idea of interviews because they would help her establish rapport with students and explain the nature of her project. She hoped her unique approach would entice more students to participate in her study.

"I was really excited as I walked out of my dorm in my bikini. I began to stop students who were walking across campus and explained that I was doing a research study for my human sexuality class. I asked students where the craziest place they ever had sex was and told them they could write their answer anywhere on my body. The males were to write their answers in blue or black markers, while the females were to use the red or orange markers. This way I would be able to compare male and female answers, and look for any gender differences. Students who were virgins could write a large V on my body. It was interesting to see their reactions to my research design and even more interesting to see their responses to my question. College students have had sex in some really crazy places! All In all, it was a lot of fun to do. The only downside to my research study was that it took me WEEKS to wash the Sharpie marks off!" ▌▌

What would you have done if Valerie had approached you in her bikini, handed you a Sharpie, and asked you to write on her body the craziest place you'd ever had sex? Would you do it? Do you think most students would? Why or why not? In the end, do you think the responses she obtained were representative of all students at her university? These are good questions to ask, and they give us a great introduction into the study of human sexuality.

Sex studies seem to appear everywhere today—in magazines, newspapers, and on television. But how do you know whether the research is reliable and has been carried out properly? In this chapter, we explore both the major theories and the research methods that underlie the study of sexuality. We also examine some of the most influential sexuality studies that have been done. Theoretical development and ongoing research combine to provide a foundation on which to build further understanding of sexuality.

Before we start, you might wonder why reviewing theory and research in a sexuality textbook is important. Because theories guide our understanding of sexuality, and research helps answer our many questions, learning how theories are formulated and research is pursued will give you insight into the information that is provided in the chapters to come. Let's examine the various theories of sexuality and some of the important sex researchers.

Sigmund Freud (1856–1939), the father of psychoanalysis, set the stage for all psychological theories that followed.

© Hulton Archive/Getty Images

A **theory** is a set of assumptions, principles, or methods that help a researcher understand the nature of the phenomenon being studied. A theory provides an intellectual structure to help conceptualize, implement, and interpret a topic, such as human sexuality. The majority of researchers begin with theories about human behaviour that guide the kind of questions they ask about sexuality. For example, suppose researchers subscribe to the theory that sexuality is innate and biologically determined; they would probably design studies to examine such things as how the hypothalamus in the brain or the monthly cycle of hormones influences our sexual behaviour. It is unlikely they would be interested in studying the societal influences on sexuality. A person who believes sexuality is determined by environmental influences, in contrast, would be more likely to study how the media influences sexuality rather than genetic patterns of sexual behaviour.

Several theories—often clashing—guide much of our thinking about sexuality. These include psychological, biological, sociological, and evolutionary theoretical views of human sexuality. In addition, over the last few years, feminist and queer theories have also become important models for exploring and explaining sexual behaviour. We first explore each of these and look at how they influence sex research. While we do, however, it is important to remember that many theorists borrow from multiple theoretical perspectives, and that these categories often overlap and learn from each other.

Theories about Sexuality

The study of sexuality is multidisciplinary. Psychologists, sexologists, biologists, theologians, physicians, sociologists, anthropologists, and philosophers all perform sex research. The questions each discipline asks and how its practitioners transform those questions into research projects can differ greatly. However, the insights of these disciplines complement each other, and no single approach to the study of sexuality is better than another.

theory
A set of assumptions, principles, or methods that helps a researcher understand the nature of a phenomenon being studied.

libido
According to Freud, the energy generated by the sexual instinct.

thanatos
According to Freud, the self-destructive instinct, often turned outward in the form of aggression.

id
The collection of unconscious urges and desires that continually seek expression.

ego
The part of the personality that mediates between environmental demands (reality), conscience (superego), and instinctual needs (id).

superego
The social and parental standards an individual has internalized; the conscience.

Psychoanalytic Theory

Sigmund Freud (1856–1939) was the founder of the psychoanalytic theory. He believed that the sex drive was one of the most important forces in life, and he spent a considerable amount of time studying sexuality. According to Freud, human behaviour is motivated by instincts and drives. The two most powerful drives are **libido** (la-BEED-oh), which is sexual motivation, and **thanatos** (THAN-uh-toes), which is aggressiveness motivation. Of these two, the libido is the more powerful. Two of Freud's most controversial concepts include personality formation and psychosexual development.

Freud believed the personality contained the **id**, **ego**, and **superego**. At birth, a child has only the id portion of the personality, which functions as the pleasure centre. If the id were the only part of the personality that developed, we would always be seeking pleasure and fulfillment with little concern for others; in other words, we would operate in the way most animals do. As humans get older, however, the id balances its desires with other parts of the personality.

By the second year of life, the ego develops as the child begins to interact with his or her environment. The ego keeps the id in check by being realistic about what the child can and cannot have.

Because the majority of the id's desires may be socially unaccept-able, the ego works to restrain it.

Freud also believed that the last portion of the personality, the superego, develops by the age of five years. It contains both societal and parental values, and puts more restrictions on what a person can and cannot do. It acts as our conscience, and its most effective weapon is guilt. For example, let's say that a woman was raised in a very religious family, and she wants to wait until she's married to have sex. One night she starts hooking up with her boyfriend (an id action). It feels good, and the id is being fulfilled. Soon, reality kicks in (the ego), and she realizes that she is about to have sex in the backseat of a car! This causes her to re-evaluate the situation, and because she has been taught that premarital sex is wrong, she feels guilty (a superego action). Throughout our lives, the id, ego, and superego are in a constant struggle with each other, but it is the ego, or the realistic portion of our personality, that keeps the other two parts balanced.

If the ego does not keep things in balance, the superego could take over, and a person could be paralyzed by guilt. The id could also take over, forcing the person to search constantly for pleasure with little concern for others. Freud believed that the only way to bring these conditions into balance was for the person to undergo psychoanalysis.

Freud's most controversial idea was his theory of psychosexual development. He believed that one's basic personality was formed by events that happened in the first six years of life. During each stage of development, Freud identified a different erogenous (uh-RAJ-uh-nus) zone in which libidinal energy was directed. If the stage was not successfully completed, the libidinal energy was tied up in that zone, and the child could experience a fixation. Psychosexual development includes the oral, anal, phallic, and genital stages.

The first stage of psychosexual development, known as the oral stage, lasts through the first 18 months of life. According to Freud's theory, problems during this stage could result in an oral fixation, leading to behaviours such as cigarette smoking, over-eating, fingernail chewing, or alcohol abuse. The next stage, the anal stage begins when a child starts toilet training. Problems during this stage could lead to traits such as stubbornness, orderli-ness, or cleanliness.

According to Freud, the most important stage is the next one, the phallic stage, which occurs between the ages of three and six years. Freud believed that during the phallic stage, boys go through the Oedipus (ED-uh-puss) complex. Freud thought girls go through an Electra complex and develop penis envy. Freud believed that the Electra stage is never fully resolved, and because of this, women are less psychologically mature than men. At the end of this stage, boys and girls will typically identify with the same-sex parent and adopt masculine or feminine characteristics. The superego begins to develop during this time as well, and most children adopt their parents' values.

Before puberty (between the ages of 6 and 12), the child passes through the latency stage, and sexual interest goes underground. During this stage, little boys often think little girls have "cooties" (and vice versa), and childhood play primarily exists in same-sex groups. Puberty marks the genital stage, which is the final stage of psychosexual development. During this stage, sexuality becomes less internally directed and more directed at others as erotic objects.

Freud's ideas were controversial in the Victorian period in which he lived. His claims that children were sexual from birth and lusted for the other-sex parent caused tremendous shock in the conservative community of Vienna. Remember that at the time when Freud came up with his ideas, there was a strong cultural repression of sexuality. Doctors and ministers believed that masturbation was physically harmful and conversations about sex were unheard of. Among modern psychologists, Freud and the psychoanalytic theory have received a consider-able amount of criticism. The predominant criticism is that his theory is unscientific and does not lend itself to testing (Robinson, 1993). How could a researcher study the existence of the phallic stage? If it is indeed unconscious, then it would be impossible to hand out surveys to see when a child was in each stage. Because Freud based his theories on his patients, he has been accused of creating his theories around people who were sick; consequently, they may not apply to healthy people (we discuss this further in the section "Case Studies" on research methodology). Finally, Freud has also been heavily criticized because of his unflattering psychological portrait of women (Robinson, 1993).

psychoanalysis
System of psychotherapy developed by Freud that focuses on uncovering the unconscious material responsible for a patient's disorder.

psychosexual development
The childhood stages of development during which the id's pleasure-seeking energies focus on distinct erogenous zones.

erogenous zones
Areas of the body that are particularly sensitive to touch and are associated with sexual pleasure.

fixation
The tying up of psychic energy at a particular psychosexual stage, resulting in adult behaviours characteristic of the stage.

oral stage
A psychosexual stage in which the mouth, lips, and tongue are the primary erogenous zone.

anal stage
A psychosexual stage in which the anal area is the primary erogenous zone.

phallic stage
A psychosexual stage in which the genital region is the primary erogenous zone and in which the Oedipus or Electra complex develops.

Oedipus complex
A male child's sexual attraction for his mother and the consequent conflicts.

Electra complex
The incestuous desire of a daughter for her father.

latency stage
A psychosexual stage in which libido and sexual interest are repressed.

genital stage
Final psychosexual stage in which a person develops the ability to engage in adult sexual behaviour.

repression
A coping strategy by which unwanted thoughts or prohibited desires are forced out of consciousness and into the uncon-scious mind.

unconscious
All the ideas, thoughts, and feelings to which we have no conscious access.

Understanding Human Sexuality: Theory and Research

Behavioural Theory

Behaviourists believe that it is necessary to observe and measure behaviour to understand it. Psychological states, emotions, the unconscious, and feelings are not measurable and, therefore, are not valid for study. Only overt behaviour can be measured, observed, and controlled by scientists. Radical behaviourists (those who believe that we do not actually choose how we behave), such as B.F. Skinner (1953), claim that environmental rewards and punishments determine the types of behaviours in which we engage. This is referred to as **operant conditioning**.

We learn certain behaviours, including most sexual behaviours, through reinforcement and punishment. Reinforcements encourage a person to engage in a behaviour by associating it with pleasurable stimuli, whereas punishments make it less likely that a behaviour will be repeated, because the behaviour becomes associated with unpleasant stimuli. For instance, if a man decided to engage in extramarital sex with a colleague at work, it may be because of the positive reinforcements he receives, such as the excitement of going to work. If, in contrast, a man experiences an erection problem the first time he has sexual intercourse outside of his marriage, it may make it less likely he will try the behaviour again anytime soon. The negative experience reduces the likelihood that he will engage in the behaviour again.

To help change unwanted behaviour, behaviourists use **behaviour modification**. For example, if a man wants to rid himself of sexual fantasies about young boys, a behavioural therapist might use **aversion therapy**. To do so, the therapist might show the man slides of young boys; when he responds with an erection, an electrical shock is administered to his penis. If this is repeated several times, behaviourists believe the man will no longer respond with an erection. The punishment will have changed the behaviour. Contrast this form of therapy with that of a psychoanalytic therapist, who would probably want to study what happened to this man in the first six years of his life. A behaviour therapist would primarily be concerned with changing the behaviour and less concerned with its origins. Much of modern sex therapy uses the techniques developed by behaviourists (MacKenzie, 2011).

Social Learning Theory

Social learning theory actually grew out of behaviourism. Scientists began to question whether behaviourism was too limited in its explanation of human behaviour. Many believed that thoughts and feelings had more influence on behaviours than the behaviourists claimed. A noted social learning theorist, Albert Bandura (1969), argued that both external and internal events influence our behaviour. By this, he meant that external events, such as rewards and punishments, influence behaviour, but so do internal events, such as feelings, thoughts, and beliefs. Bandura began to bridge the gap between behaviourism and cognitive theory, which we discuss next.

Social learning theorists believe that imitation and identification are also important in the development of sexuality. For example, we identify with our same-sex parent and begin to imitate him or her, which helps us develop our own gender identity. In turn, we are praised and reinforced for these behaviours. Think for a moment about a young boy who identifies with his mother and begins to dress and act like her. He will probably be ridiculed or even punished, which may lead him to turn his attention to a socially acceptable figure, most likely his father. Peer pressure also influences our sexuality. We want to be liked; therefore, we may engage in certain behaviours because our peers encourage it. We also learn what is expected of us from television, our families, and even from music.

Cognitive Theory

So far, the theories we have discussed emphasize that either internal conflicts or external events control the development of personality. Unlike these, **cognitive theory** holds that people differ in how they process information, and this creates personality differences. We feel what we think we feel, and our thoughts also affect our behaviour. Our behaviour does not come from early experiences in childhood or from rewards or punishments; rather, it is a result of how we perceive and conceptualize what is happening around us.

As far as sexuality is concerned, cognitive theorists believe that the biggest sexual organ is between the ears (Walen & Roth, 1987). What sexually arouses us is what we think sexually arouses us. We pay attention to our physical sensations and label these reactions. For example, if a woman does not have an orgasm during sex with a partner, she could perceive this in one of two

---

On Your Mind

When scientists come up with new theories, how do they know they are true?

They don't. Theories begin as ideas to explain observed phenomena, but they must undergo testing and evaluation. Many early theories of sexuality were developed out of work with patients, such as Sigmund Freud's work, whereas others base their theories on behaviours they observe or the results of experiments they conduct. However, researchers never really know whether their theories are true. Some scientists become so biased by their own theories that they have trouble seeing explanations other than their own for certain behaviours. This is why scientific findings or ideas should always be tested and confirmed by other scientists.

---

behaviourists
Theorists who believe that behaviour is learned and can be altered.

operant conditioning
Learning resulting from the reinforcing response a person receives after a certain behaviour.

behaviour modification
Therapy based on operant conditioning and classical conditioning principles used to change behaviours.

aversion therapy
A technique that reduces the frequency of maladaptive behaviour by associating it with aversive stimuli.

cognitive theory
A theory proposing that our thoughts are responsible for our behaviours.

ways: She might think that having an orgasm is not really all that important and maybe next time she will have one; or, she could think that she is a failure because she did not have an orgasm and feel depressed as a result. What has caused the depression, however, is not the lack of an orgasm but her perception of it.

Humanistic Theory

Humanistic (or person-centred) psychologists believe that we all strive to develop ourselves to the best of our abilities and to achieve self-actualization (Raskin & Rogers, 1989). This is easier to do if we are raised with **unconditional positive regard,** which involves accepting and caring about another person without any stipulations or conditions. In other words, there are no rules a person must follow to be loved. An example of unconditional positive regard would be a child being caught playing sexual games with her friends and her parents explaining that they loved her but disapproved of her behaviour. If, on the other hand, the parents responded by yelling at the child and sending her to her room, she learns that when she does something wrong, her parents will withdraw their love. This is referred to as **conditional love.** The parents make it clear that they will love their child only when she acts properly.

Children who grow up with unconditional positive regard learn to accept their faults and weaknesses, whereas children who have experienced conditional love may try to ignore those traits because they know others would not approve. Accepting our faults and weaknesses leads us toward self-actualization.

Self-actualization occurs as we learn our own potential in life. We want to do things that make us feel good about ourselves. For many of us, casual sex with someone we don't know would not make us feel good; therefore, it does not contribute to our own growth. Sexual intimacy in a loving and committed relationship does feel good and helps contribute to our own self-actualization.

Biological Theory

The biological theory of human sexuality emphasizes that sexual behaviour is primarily a biological process. Sexual functioning, hormonal release, ovulation, ejaculation, conception, pregnancy, and birth are controlled physiologically. Those who advocate this theory also point out that human sexual behaviour, including gender roles and sexual orientation, are primarily due to inborn, genetic patterns and are not functions of social or psychological forces. Sexual problems are believed to be caused by physiological factors, and intervention often includes medications or surgery.

Evolutionary Theory

Unlike biological theory, which focuses on individual physiology, **evolutionary theory** looks more broadly at the physiological

changes of an entire species over time. To understand sexual behaviour in humans, evolutionary theorists study animal sexual patterns and look for evolutionary trends. They believe that sexuality exists for the purpose of reproducing the species, and individual sexuality is designed to maximize the chances of passing on one's genes. According to evolutionary theorists, the winners in the game of life are those who are most successful at transmitting their genes to the next generation.

Think about the qualities you look for in a partner. Students often say that they are looking for someone who is physically attractive, monogamous, has a sense of humour, and is intelligent, honest, extroverted, fun, and sensitive. An evolutionary theorist would argue that these qualities have evolved to ensure that a person would be able to provide healthy offspring and care for them well. A physically attractive person is more likely to be fit and healthy. Could this be important to us because of their reproductive capabilities? Evolutionary theorists would say so. They would also argue that qualities such as monogamy, honesty, and sensitivity would help ensure that a partner will be reliable and help raise the offspring.

Some sexual activities have evolved to ensure the survival of the species. For example, evolutionary theorists believe that orgasms have evolved to make sexual intercourse pleasurable; this, in turn, increases the frequency that people engage in it, and the possibility for reproduction is increased. Differences between the sexes in sexual desire and behaviour are also thought to have evolved. The double standard, which states that men are free to have casual sex, whereas women are not, exists because men produce millions of sperm per day and women produce only one viable ovum per month. Males try to "spread their seed" to ensure the reproduction of their family line, whereas females need to protect the one ovum they produce each month.

> ### On Your Mind
>
> I am a healthy female college student, but lately I've been having trouble reaching orgasm. How would the biological theory explain this?

A person who adopts a biological theory would explain differences in sexuality as resulting from anatomy, hormones, neurochemicals, or other physical explanations. Therefore, a biological theorist would suggest that trouble reaching orgasm would be because of physical reasons, such as hormonal or neurological causes. Treatment might involve a physical workup and blood work to evaluate hormone levels. However, other theoretical approaches would disagree with this assessment and would look at a variety of other issues, such as stress, internal thought processes, or social pressures.

self-actualization
Fulfillment of an individual's potentialities, including aptitudes, talents, and the like.

conditional love
Conditional acceptance of another, with restrictions on their behaviours or thoughts.

unconditional positive regard
Acceptance of another without restrictions on their behaviours or thoughts.

evolutionary theory
A theory that incorporates both evolution and sociology, and looks for trends in behaviours.

Understanding Human Sexuality: Theory and Research

When women become pregnant, they have a nine-month biological commitment ahead of them (and some would argue a lifelong commitment as well).

Evolutionary theory has received a considerable amount of criticism, however, particularly because evolutionary theorists tend to ignore the influence of both prior learning and societal influences on sexuality.

Sociological Theory

Sociologists are interested in how society influences sexual behaviour and, in turn, how sexual behaviour influences society. Even though the basic capacity to be sexual might be biologically inherent, how it is expressed is greatly influenced by social forces at play. In other words, much of what we think and how we behave sexually depends upon how large institutions such as the government, the church, medicine, and the law construct sexual identities and expressions and, as a result, how they produce the ways in which they are regarded. For example, decades ago people's views of homosexuality were strongly shaped by the definitions put upon it by medicine and psychiatry rendering gays and lesbians as "sick." Today, especially in the United States with its strong conservative presence, views of homosexuality are influenced by the dissemination of religious dogma, which depicts it as sinful and wrong. Canadian society now treats gays and lesbians as equal under the law and, as a result, definitions of sickness and sin have been largely abandoned in favour of a commitment to human rights. Sociologists not only look at what definitions are present in society, but how they are constructed and how they change over time. Society is both the producer and product of our identities, attitudes, and behaviours.

The family is a strong factor that influences sexual behaviour and desire. As we discussed in Chapter 1, families provide strong messages about what is acceptable and unacceptable. At the same time, religion, medicine, the economy, and other overriding factors influence how the family thinks and behaves. In turn,

Social influences such as religion affect people's attitudes about various sexual behaviours including sex outside of marriage, homosexuality, and abortion.

© Colorblind/Getty Images

religions have strong tenets on such matters as premarital sex, marriage, and gender roles within marriage, which are not only expressed but taught within the family. The strongly conservative views of Hutterite communities in Alberta and Mennonite communities in Ontario, for example, follow strict religious principles, which are taught and passed on through the family and shape sexual behaviour as something that is private and procreative only (Epp, 1958; Hofer, 1962). This leaves no room for homosexual behaviour at all, and any gays or lesbians who emerge must leave their communities for good (Braun, 2008; Mennonites also face gay issue, 2000).

The economy also influences the societal view of sexuality (DeLamater, 1987). Canada thrives under a system of capitalism, which involves an exchange of services for money. This influences the availability of sex-related services such as prostitution, pornography, and sex shops, which operate because they are profitable. Shifts in the economy, therefore, have repercussions not only for such services but also for matters such as childbearing. It was typical, for example, for families in farm communities in the early 1900s to have many children, since they provided labour for the farm and helped it thrive. Today, most Canadians live in cities and children have become expensive, resulting in far fewer births per couple. Morency and LaPlante (2010) found that Canadian couples' projected assessments of their financial situation after they had their first child strongly influenced decisions about if and when to have more children.

Sociologists therefore look at the connections between overriding social forces, how they play off of and influence one another, and how these relationships affect sexual behaviour and identities. Religion influences medical definitions of normality and mental illness, which influence public policy, which influences how laws are formed and changed, which influences the family, and so on. All social forces influence all other social forces, which play upon the individual and shape the ways in which sexual behaviours are carried out and regarded.

Anthropological Research

Anthropology is the broad study of human beings, concentrating on physical origins, linguistics, culture, and archeology. Cultural anthropologists typically do ethnographic research, meaning that they immerse themselves in a particular culture and describe it fully. One of anthropology's greatest contributions to the study of human sexuality is its cross-cultural perspective, which often reveals that behaviours thought to be universal actually vary from culture to culture. For example, D.S. Marshall (1971) carried out an ethnographic study upon the island of Mangaia in the South Pacific, and found the women to be sexually assertive—so much so that they often initiated sexual activity. However, on Inis Beag, a small island off the west coast of Ireland, sexuality is strongly repressed. It is considered appropriate only for procreation, menstruation is treated with disgust, and even breastfeeding is strongly discouraged (Messenger, 1993). Homosexuality is not tolerated, and heterosexual couples typically engage in sexual intercourse fully clothed, with only their genitals exposed. There is thus tremendous variation in the ways sexuality is viewed and expressed throughout the world.

Many Canadian anthropologists have devoted their time to the study of sexual activity and expression among First Nations groups and new immigrant communities. To name a few, Wynne and Currie (2011) looked at the effects of social exclusion from Canadian society upon the rates of sexually transmitted infections among Aboriginal populations, McKay (1999) looked at how partner selection among Aboriginals on Canadian reserves affects HIV transmission, and Sethi (2007) looked at the sex trafficking of Aboriginal girls in Canada. The broad-based anthropological perspective contributes to the knowledge of sexuality and is well respected in the social sciences.

Feminist Theory

Feminist theory argues that a patriarchal society has a strong influence on our ideas about sexuality as they pertain to gender and gender roles. Many feminist theorists believe that sexology as a discipline has been dominated by White, middle-class, hetero-sexist attitudes that influence what is focused upon in research and how the research is carried out (Ericksen, 1999; Irvine, 1990). A feminist perspective, in contrast, offers different views of sexuality that go beyond such biases (Ericksen, 1999; Tiefer, 2004). Several feminist researchers have been leaders in the effort to redefine sexual functioning and remove the medical and biological aspects that permeate sexuality today. Leonore Tiefer has written extensively about the medicalization of sexuality and suggests that there may not be any biological basis to sex drives at all. Instead, it may be that our culture influences sexual desire most of all (Kaschak & Tiefer, 2001; Tiefer, 2001).

Dorothy Smith, born in 1926, has been a sociology and women's studies professor at the University of British Columbia and the Ontario Institute for Studies in Education. She is widely recognized as the founder of feminist standpoint theory, which emphasizes that the views that women have are shaped and dictated by their particular standpoints—that is, women have particular experiences that men do not, and it is these experiences that shape the ways in which they interact with the world. This is not to say that all women share the same standpoint since they differ considerably by race, class, sexual orientation, and personal experience. It is, however, to say that being locked into gender tends to render particular experiences that are common throughout. It is through women's everyday lives that they shape and change their views of the world (Smith, 1987).

> **REAL Research** Olivier et al. (2006) analyzed the content of one of Canada's first electronic discussion lists—PAR-L (Policy, Action, Research List)—and found that while members had feminist concerns in common, differences among them pertaining to gender, age, race, language, and professional affiliation influence the interactions online. While these differences did create tensions, members enjoyed the benefits of feeling connected with feminist issues.

Typically, feminist theory has a number of variations, with some more liberal and others more radical. Overall, however, feminist scholars believe that the social construction of sexuality is based on power, which has been primarily in the hands of men for centuries (Collins, 1998). They further believe that there is gender inequality that, for the most part, places women in submissive and subordinate positions (Collins, 2000). This power that men have over women is often maintained through acts of sexual aggression such as rape, sexual abuse, sexual harassment, pornography, and prostitution (M. Jackson, 1984; MacKinnon, 1986). In addition, feminists argue that the patriarchal view of sexuality consistently views sex as penetrative, involving only a penis in a vagina. Sex begins with penetration and ends with ejaculation. Catharine MacKinnon (1987) suggests that male-dominated views of sexuality have resulted in a society that believes that "what is sexual gives a man an erection" (p. 75). All of this has led to the repression of female sexuality and, as a result, the lack of attention to female orgasms and same-sex sexual desire among women.

Feminist researchers also believe that there is much to be gained from collaborative or group research, which uses interviews to gain rich qualitative data (diMauro, 1995). Controlled laboratory experiments, which have been viewed as more masculine in structure because of their rigid nature, remove subjects from their social contexts, which affect the outcome of a study (Peplau & Conrad, 1989). We discuss this further later in the chapter.

Queer Theory

Growing out of lesbian and gay studies, queer theory developed in the 1990s. It shares a common political interest with feminist theory—a concern for women's and gay, lesbian, bisexual, and transgender rights. It goes beyond these categories, however, in that it problematizes heteronormativity or the tendency to see the world in terms of binaries such as male/female, husband/wife, and gay/straight. For example, heterosexuality is seen as a binary relation between male and female and is often wrongly imposed upon same-sex relationships, which have no such binary. Queer theory focuses primarily on the relationships among desire, language, and identity.

For desire, queer theorists seek to examine taken-for-granted categories of normal and abnormal and challenge them, seeing it instead as multifaceted rather than as a binary. For language, queer theorists point out that words that describe things are not only value laden but limited in their ability to capture entire realities. For identity, queer theory does not see such things as "gay" or "straight" as innate to individuals but products of the environments in which they are situated (Ravelli & Webber, 2010). The word "gay," for example, did not come to mean homosexually inclined until the 20th century.

sexology
The scientific study of sexuality.

heteronormativity
The tendency to view social life in terms of non-overlapping binaries such as male/female, husband/wife, and gay/straight.

Queer theory also proposes that domination and its characteristics such as heterosexism and homophobia should be resisted (Isaiah Green, 2007; Schlichter, 2004). Researchers need to examine how a variety of sexualities are constructed and to abandon traditional categories such as homosexual/heterosexual in so doing (Rudy, 2000). Categories are cultural constructions that limit and restrain. Overall, queer theorists and some feminists believe that meaningful societal change can come about only through radical change and cannot be introduced into a society in a piecemeal way (Turner, 2000).

We now turn our attention to some important sexologists and sexuality studies that have been done over the past two centuries.

Review Questions

1 What is a theory?

2 How might a theory help guide research?

3 Describe the influence of Sigmund Freud's theories of sexuality.

4 Compare and contrast behavioural, social learning, cognitive, humanistic, biological, evolutionary, and sociological theories.

5 Explain how feminist and queer theories have asked a different set of questions from other perspectives of sexuality.

Sex Research: Philosophers, Physicians, and Sexologists

The ancient Greeks, through physicians such as Hippocrates and philosophers such as Aristotle and Plato, may actually be the legitimate forefathers of sex research in that they were the first to develop theories regarding sexual responses and dysfunctions, sex legislation, reproduction and contraception, and sexual ethics. It was not until the 19th century, however, that a renewed discussion of sexual ethics took place. As Charles Darwin put forth his theory of evolution, and the disciplines of psychology and sociology began, the first programs sex education were established and classifications of sexual behaviour took shape.

Early Sex Research

In the 19th century, researchers from a variety of backgrounds, such as Charles Darwin, Heinrich Kaan, and Jean-Martin Charcot, laid the foundations of sex research in the modern sense. It was during this time that the study of sex began to concentrate more on what was considered to be bizarre, dangerous, and unhealthy. In 1843, Heinrich Kaan, a Russian physician, wrote *Psychopathia Sexualis*, which presented a classification of what he termed *sexual mental diseases*. This system was greatly expanded and refined about 40 years later by Richard von Krafft-Ebing in another book of the same title. Sex research during this time almost exclusively focused on people believed to be sick.

Much research upon sexuality at the time was thwarted. For their efforts, some researchers lost their professional status, others were accused of having the very sexual disorders they studied, and still others were thought to be motivated solely by lust, greed, or fame. However, as interest in medicine in general grew, researchers began to explore ways to improve health and peoples' lives. This included looking at human sexuality.

Physicians were the primary sex researchers in the late 19th century (keep in mind that at that time nearly all physicians were male). Because they were experts in biology and the human body, they were also thought to be experts in sexuality (V. Bullough, 1994). Interestingly, although most had little or no specialized knowledge of sexual topics, they still spoke with authority upon the subject.

Most early sexuality studies were done in Europe, primarily in Germany (V. Bullough, 1994). At the time, sex research was protected because it was considered part of medical research, even though holding a medical degree did not always offer protection. Some researchers used pseudonyms to publish their work, some were verbally attacked, and some had their data destroyed.

At the turn of the 20th century, the pioneering work of Sigmund Freud, Havelock Ellis, and Iwan Bloch established the study of sexual problems as a legitimate scientific pursuit in its own right. It is interesting to note that the overwhelming majority of sexology pioneers were Jewish (Haeberle, 1982), which made this new discipline controversial once the Nazis took power in pre-World War II Germany. As a result of the persecution of Jews, research upon sexuality moved from Germany to the United States. In 1921, several prominent European physicians attempted to set up an organization called the Committee for Research in Problems of Sex. After much hard work, the organization established itself but had low membership rates and a lack of research and publishing support. However, because of strong beliefs and persistence by the founders, the group continued.

Systematic research into sexuality in the United States began in the early 1920s, motivated by pressures from the social hygiene movement, which was concerned about sexually transmitted infections and their impact upon marriage and children.

In 1969, a group of individuals from several disciplines at the University of Calgary began conversations about human sexuality, and soon endeavoured to bring other professionals across Canada into the discussions. Their first official meeting took place in Calgary and then alternated between Banff, Alberta, and Niagara-on-the-Lake, Ontario. The Canadian Sex Research Forum (CSRF) has grown considerably over the years and recently had its 40th meeting in Kingston, Ontario. It now devotes itself to interdisciplinary, theoretical, and applied research upon human sexuality, and promoting sexual science, as well as the health of all Canadians (Canadian Sex Research Forum, n.d.; Lamont, 1977).

American society was generally conservative and many people viewed the "sex impulse" as a potential threat to societal stability. Funding for sex research was thus minimal. It took philanthropy from the fortunes of men such as John D. Rockefeller and Andrew Carnegie for researchers to afford to implement large-scale interdisciplinary projects that examined sexual issues.

Obstacles to Sex Research

There is considerable distrust of and opposition to sex research today, with many people believing that the mysteries surrounding sexuality will be taken away by increasing scientific knowledge. Many conservative and religious organizations believe that research done on topics such as adolescent sexuality only encourages young people to have sex. Sex researchers are accustomed to pressure from conservative groups that oppose their work. In fact, after Alfred Kinsey published his two large studies about male and female sexuality, which were funded by the Rockefeller Foundation, the United States Congress pressured the foundation to withdraw its financial support entirely, which it did (J.H. Jones, 1997).

Sex research has also become fragmented over the last few decades, with researchers coming from several different disciplines, including psychology, sociology, medicine, social work, and public health. Typically, sex researchers are unaware of what is being published by other disciplines. Journal articles are often inaccessible to a general audience or to researchers outside the discipline from which the research originated (diMauro, 1995). What tends to happen, therefore, is that people get information about sex research and its findings from the popular media, where reporters often pick and choose what they believe will be interesting, and distort or sensationalize the findings.

Researchers, educators, and clinicians who specialize in sexuality are scientists who engage in sophisticated research projects and publish their work in scientific journals. Because of the sensitive nature of sexuality as a topic, they are sometimes ridiculed, not viewed as "real" scientists, or accused of studying sexuality because of their own voyeuristic sexual desires. Geer and O'Donohue (1987) point out that, unlike other areas of science, sex research is often evaluated as either moral or immoral.

There are also obstacles in implementing the actual research projects. Researchers are often encouraged not to look at sexual relationships because of their intimate nature, and they face additional obstacles when looking at particular populations such as teenagers. When people are asked to participate in a project—for example, in a telephone survey or in filling out a questionnaire—they are often distrustful or they refuse outright, citing moral reasons. Methodological problems also have made it difficult to study human sexuality. We discuss these issues in more detail later in this chapter.

Regardless of the present obstacles, sex research has begun remove the stigma and ignorance associated with discussing human sexual behaviour as a serious topic. Ignorance and fear can contribute to irresponsible behaviour and factual information helps to prevent it. Today, understanding sexuality has become increasingly important to the work of psychologists, physicians, and educators.

Politics and Sex Research

In Chapter 1, we discussed how the changing political climate affects attitudes toward sexuality. Sex research is affected by those same changes in political climate. When Kinsey's work was published in the 1940s and 1950s, several politicians claimed that asking people about their sex lives, even in a non-judgmental fashion like Kinsey did, promoted immorality (Bancroft, 2004). Such negative attitudes affect the public's perception of sex research and persist to this day. For example, one ultra-conservative group in the United States, Focus on the Family, put out an information bulletin in 2005 that denounced Kinsey's research entirely and blamed such problems as alcohol and drug abuse, suicide, and pregnancy among teenagers upon the dissemination of his research (Focus on the Family, 2005).

Despite such claims, Kinsey's work helped lead to many social changes associated with sexuality. The changing roles of women and the development of birth control pills, for example, led to less acceptance for a double standard of sexuality and better lives for young women (Bancroft, 2004). In fact, after the publication of Kinsey's second book, American Law Institute lawyers and judges recommended decriminalizing many forms of sexual behaviour, including adultery, cohabitation, and homosexual relationships (Allyn, 1996). As a result, some states revised their laws about certain sexual practices (Bancroft, 2004).

The HIV/AIDS crisis, which began in the 1980s, provided a new opportunity for sex research, leading to one large-scale American sexuality study titled the National Health and Social

Frances M. Shaver, a sex researcher at Concordia University in Montreal, has studied people working in the sex industry since 1990. She is co-investigator of a five-year study funded by the Social Science and Humanities Research Council of Canada to examine the impact of public policy on the health and well-being of sex workers in two major Canadian cities. Shaver points out a number of methodological obstacles to studying sex workers. Notably, the boundaries of a sex worker population are generally unknown, making it difficult to get a representative sample, and because of their illegal activities, maintaining privacy and confidentiality can be very challenging (Shaver, 2005).

Louise Morgan/Concordia University. Used with permission of Louise Morgan and Dr. Shaver.

Frances M. Shaver

is one of the most comprehensive studies on sexual behaviour ever done. We discuss these studies in more detail later in this chapter.

In sum, while there is a need for increased understanding of human sexuality, there is much popular and political resistance to sex research (Bancroft, 2004). As a result, federal funding for sex research will continue to be problematic, so sex researchers have approached private foundations for funding. Many pharmaceutical companies have provided funding for studies of sexual problems and dysfunctions, but this has been controversial because they have a vested interest in the studies they fund. In fact, some pharmaceutical companies have been accused of creating and promoting certain dysfunctions to medicalize the conditions, thus creating a need for medication (Tiefer, 2006). Contraceptive manufacturers have also funded various research studies and their participation in these studies is sometimes also viewed with skepticism.

Life Survey (NHSLS) by the National Opinion Research Center at the University of Chicago in the early 1990s (Kimmel & Plante, 2007). This study was to include 20 000 participants, but it was cancelled because of mounting political pressure. Funding was acquired from private sources instead, reducing the number of participants to 3500 (Bancroft, 2004). Luckily, another large-scale study of sexual behaviour, the National Survey of Sexual Health and Behavior (NSSHB) managed to get funding from the manufacturer of Trojan condoms and was published in 2010. It

Review Questions

1 Describe the beginnings of sex research and explain how it has progressed.

2 Explain how sex research has been problem driven and give two examples.

3 Explain the controversies surrounding Kinsey's research.

4 Explain how politics can influence sex research.

Sex Researchers

The sex researchers discussed in this section along with their publications helped give credibility to the study of sexuality. Some adopted Freud's psychoanalytic theory while others developed their own ideas entirely. Although they had introduced new scientific principles into the study of sexuality, their influence was mostly limited to the field of medicine.

Early Promoters of Sexology

Several people were responsible for the early promotion of sexology, including Iwan Bloch, Magnus Hirschfeld, Albert Moll,

Richard von Krafft-Ebing, Havelock Ellis, Katharine Bement Davis, Clelia Mosher, Alfred Kinsey, Alan Bell, Martin Weinberg, Morton Hunt, William Masters, and Virginia Johnson. All of these researchers made a tremendous contribution to the study of sexology.

Iwan Bloch: Journal of Sexology

Iwan Bloch (1872–1922), a German dermatologist, believed that the medical view of sexual behaviour was short-sighted and that both historical and anthropological research could help broaden it. He hoped that sexual science would one day have the same structure and objectivity as other sciences. He also published the Marquis de Sade's novel about sexual violence, *The 120 Days of*

Sodom, under a pseudonym in 1904. Along with Magnus Hirschfeld, Bloch and several other physicians formed a medical society for sexology research in Berlin. It was the first of its kind and it exercised considerable influence (we discuss this society later). Beginning in 1914, Bloch published the *Journal of Sexology* and for almost two decades this journal collected and published important research in the growing field. Bloch planned to write a series of sexological studies but he died at age 50 and never did.

Magnus Hirschfeld: The Institute for Sexology

Magnus Hirschfeld (1868–1935) was a German physician whose work with patients inspired him and convinced him that negative attitudes toward homosexual men and women were inhumane and unfounded. Because Hirschfeld was independently wealthy, he was able to support his research with his own funds (V. Bullough, 1994).

Using a pseudonym, Hirschfeld wrote his first article on sexology in 1896. He argued that sexuality was the result of certain genetic patterns that resulted in a person being homosexual, bisexual, or heterosexual. He fought for a repeal of the laws that made homosexuality and bisexuality punishable by prison terms and heavy fines. This law, known as *Paragraph 175,* had been around since 1871 and was not actually repealed until 1994. In 1899, he began to write the *Yearbook for Sexual Intermediate Stages,* which he published for the purpose of educating the public about homosexuality and other sexual "deviations."

Thousands of people came to him for his help and advice about sexual problems and, in 1900, Hirschfeld began distributing questionnaires on sexuality. By this time, he had also become an expert upon sexual variations and even testified as an expert witness in the court cases of sexual offenders. Hirschfeld used only a small amount of his data in the books he published because he hoped to write a comprehensive study of sexuality at a later date. Unfortunately, his data were destroyed by the Nazis before they could be published.

In 1919, Hirschfeld produced a movie he titled *Anders als die Andern (Different From the Others),* which dramatized the plight of homosexual men who live in secret because of Paragraph 175. Hirschfeld appears prominently in this film as himself and explains that homosexuality is not a threat to society. This film was the first of its kind and has been restored from fragments that survived the Nazi purge. It is currently available in its full length on YouTube.

That same year, Hirschfeld founded the *Institut für Sexualwissenschaft* (Institute for Sexology), which contained his libraries, laboratory, and lecture halls. The institute grew in size and influence over the next few years but, as the political climate in Berlin heated up, Hirschfeld was forced to flee Germany in 1933. The Nazis publicly burned the institute and those who were

© ullstein bild/Getty

Magnus Hirschfeld (1868–1935) worked hard to establish sexuality as a legitimate field of study.

working there were sent to concentration camps. Hirschfeld never returned to Germany and lived in France until his death in 1935.

Hirschfeld's only failing was that he did not distinguish between homosexual and transgender individuals, seeing them as only variations of homosexuality. Today we know that transgender issues have nothing to do with sexual orientation and are instead about gender. Hirschfeld, however, was a tireless pioneer of both sexual science and sexual rights and was one of the first to try to make sense of a variety of sex and gender variations.

Albert Moll: Investigations Concerning the Libido Sexualis

Albert Moll (1862–1939), a German psychiatrist, was a pioneer of hypnotism, a debunker of the occult, and another promoter of *sexualwissenschaft* (sexology). He was however a conservative man who disliked both Freud and Hirschfeld, disagreeing with both of their standpoints. He saw Freud as misguided in his concentration on the unconscious mind, believing instead that behaviour is better explained by the conscious and the real. Freud retaliated and called him a "beast" and a "pettifogger." His objection to Hirschfeld was that he believed sexual science must be neutral and thus criticized him for his campaign for human rights at the time. Once the Nazis took power, he denounced Hirschfeld entirely (Sigusch, 2012).

In 1912, Moll's work on childhood sexuality—*The Sexual Life of the Child*—was published. Not only did he say that masturbation in children was not a sign of any pathology but he suggested two stages of sexuality. While children do have sexual feelings, they are generally amorphous and undifferentiated and neither homosexual nor heterosexual. It is not until the onset of puberty that they become focused (Sauerteig, 2012). Moll formed the International Society for Sex Research in 1913 to counter Hirschfeld's Medical Society of Sexology. He also organized an International Congress of Sex Research in Berlin in 1926.

Moll wrote several other books on sexology, including *Investigations Concerning the Libido Sexualis* in 1897. Unfortunately, it was probably Moll's disagreements with Freud that led to his being ignored by the majority of English-speaking sex researchers because Freud's ideas were so prominent during the first half of the 20th century (V. Bullough, 1994).

Richard von Krafft-Ebing: Psychopathia Sexualis

Richard von Krafft-Ebing (1840–1902) was one of the most significant medical writers on sexology in the late 19th century (V. Bullough, 1994). His work represented a shift at the time from looking at sexual variations as sinful and criminal to physically and psychologically produced. He, Moll, and others introduced tremendous sexual diversity to the scientific community, although at the time this was understood solely through the limited 19th century lenses of pathology and perversion. As Krafft-Ebing and others collected files of sexual variations, newly coined terms emerged such as *voyeurism, exhibitionism, masochism, sadism,* and *fetishism.* Krafft-Ebing himself coined the term *sadism* after the sexually violent activities of the notorious French Marquis de Sade.

In 1886, he published an update of a book titled *Psychopathia Sexualis,* which explored approximately 200 case histories of individuals who had experienced what were at the time considered to be sexual aberrations. French intellectual Michel Foucault described this era as a time of "medical colonization," where definitions of sickness and perversion were imposed on virtually any sexual desire or behaviour that did not involve reproduction (Oosterhuis, 2012).

Havelock Ellis (1859–1939) was a key figure in the early study of sexuality.

Havelock Ellis: Studies in the Psychology of Sex

Havelock Ellis (1859–1939) was an English subject who grew up in Victorian society but rebelled against the secrecy surrounding sexuality. In 1875, when he was 16 years old, he decided to make sexuality his life's work. In fact, it is reported that Ellis sought a medical degree primarily so he could legitimately and safely study sexuality (V. Bullough, 1994). On publication of his famous six-volume *Studies in the Psychology of Sex* (1897–1910; H. Ellis, 1910), Ellis established himself as an objective and non-judgmental researcher. In his collection of case histories from volunteers, he asserted that homosexuality and masturbation were not abnormal and should not be labelled as such (Reiss, 1982). In 1901, *The Lancet,* a prestigious English medical journal, reviewed his early volumes with the following:

> *[Studies in the Psychology of Sex] must not be sold to the public, for the reading and discussion of such topics are dangerous. The young and the weak would not be fortified in their purity by the knowledge that they would gain from these studies, while they certainly might be more open to temptation after the perusal of more than one of the chapters. (Grosskurth, 1980, p. 222)*

This passage, even in a medical journal, well reflects the sentiments of the time where it was thought that the less one knows about sex the better, lest people be corrupted by ideas. For this reason, many manuscripts from the early sexologists used Latin terms to describe sex acts or body parts so that they may be understood only by the educated.

The rise of behaviourism in the 1920s added new dimensions to sex research. The idea of studying specific sexual behaviours became more acceptable and the formulation of more sophisticated scientific research techniques provided researchers with more precise methods for doing so. Many researchers attempted to compile data on sexual behaviour, but the results were inconsistent and the data were poorly organized. This led Alfred Kinsey, an American researcher, to undertake a large-scale study of human sexuality as will be discussed in the next section.

Sex Research Moves to the United States

Although Alfred Kinsey was mainly responsible for developing sex research as a legitimate field of inquiry in the United States, other American researchers laid the foundation for his doing so. They include Clelia Mosher and Katharine Bement Davis. Other researchers continued to build on the work of these early researchers, including Evelyn Hooker, Alan Bell, Martin Weinberg, Morton Hunt, William Masters, and Virginia Johnson. Here we review their work and contributions to the field.

Clelia Mosher: Important Questions for Women

Not surprisingly, the overwhelming majority of early sex researchers were men. Male sexuality was viewed as normative and female sexuality was approached through the lens of male bias. Clelia Mosher (1863–1940), who became a professor of personal hygiene in 1910, was ahead of her time in asking questions about sexuality that were different from those of her male predecessors (Ericksen, 1999).

In 1892, while Mosher was a student at the University of Wisconsin, she began a research project that was to last 28 years. She asked upper-middle-class women how often they engaged in sexual intercourse, how often they wanted to engage in it, and whether they enjoyed it (Ma-Hood & Wenburg, 1980). Her main motivation was to help married women have more satisfying sex lives. Another question she asked the women in her study was, "What do you believe to be the true purpose of intercourse"? (Ericksen, 1999). Although the majority of women said that intercourse was for both sexual pleasure and procreation, many reported feeling guilty for wanting or needing sexual pleasure. Unfortunately, much of Mosher's work was never published and never became part of the knowledge of sexuality that circulated during her time (Ericksen, 1999). Her manuscripts, rich with data upon the sex lives of women (most of them born before 1870), were discovered only in 1973 in the archives of Stanford University, where she taught (Platoni, 2010).

Katharine Bement Davis: Defending Homosexuality

Katharine Davis (1861–1935) began her sex research along a different path. She was highly accomplished, being the first woman to earn a Ph.D. in political science-economics at Chicago University in 1901. She became head of the Correction

Commission in 1914 and the head of the Bureau of Social Hygiene in 1914. While superintendent of the New York State Reformatory for Women at Bedford, she became interested in prostitution and sexually transmitted infections. Her survey and analysis were the largest and most comprehensive of her time (Ellison, 2006; Ericksen, 1999).

Davis defended homosexuality as no different from heterosexuality and believed that lesbianism was not pathological. This idea was considered a threat in the early 1900s because it implied that women had sexual desires independent of men's bringing them out (Ellison, 2006; Faderman, 1981). Her ideas about lesbianism were mostly ignored.

Her ideas on prostitution were that it was caused by family and personal weakness. While this idea was predominant at the time and for a long time afterward, it received some criticism in that she did not consider economic circumstances—that is, the realities of poverty and need (Bowler et al., 2013).

Katharine Bement Davis (1861–1935) conducted some of the largest and most comprehensive sexuality studies of her time.

Alfred Kinsey: Large-Scale Sex Research Begins in the United States

Alfred Kinsey (1894–1956) was probably the most influential sex researcher of the 20th century. His work effectively changed many of the existing attitudes about sexuality. In 1938, while a professor of zoology at Indiana University, he was asked to coordinate a new course on marriage and the family, open only to graduate students or married students. Before courses like this appeared on college campuses, human sexuality had been discussed only within hygiene courses where the focus was primarily on the dangers of sexually transmitted infections and masturbation (Bullough, 1998).

Soon after the course began, students came to Kinsey with sexuality questions for which he did not have answers, and the existing literature was of little help. This encouraged him to begin collecting data on his students' sexual histories. His study grew and before long included students who were not in his classes, faculty members, friends, and non-faculty employees of Indiana University. Soon, he was able to obtain grant money that enabled him to hire research assistants.

The breadth and ingenuity of Kinsey's work was unprecedented at the time. He devised a coding system for responses during his interviews, which guaranteed anonymity for his

Alfred Kinsey (1894–1956) implemented the first large-scale survey of adult sexual behaviour in the United States.

subjects. He and his associates Wardell Pomeroy and Clyde Martin then went on to interview 18 000 men and women, asking them 350 to 500 or more questions each, which amounts to millions of bits of information. He was meticulous in covering virtually everything, even asking men how large their penis was when erect and flaccid, if it angled to the left or right, and its angle at erection (Kinsey et al., 1948). Eventually, he published *Sexual Behavior in the Human Male* in 1948 and *Sexual Behavior in the Human Female* in 1953. The reactions were like explosions. As it was said, Kinsey held a mirror up to the American people and they flinched.

In his early work, Kinsey claimed to be **atheoretical**. He believed that because sex research was so new, it was impossible to construct theories and hypotheses without first having a large body of information on which to base them. Kinsey's procedure involved collecting information on each participant's sexual life history, with an emphasis on specific sexual behaviours. His prime interest was therefore to count—to see how many engaged in various behaviours. Kinsey chose to interview participants rather than have them fill out questionnaires because he believed that questionnaires would not provide accurate responses. He was also unsure about whether participants would lie during an interview so he built checks to detect false information. For example, he would ask a question, get a response, and then ask a similar question to see if the response was the same. Also, data collected from husbands and wives were compared for consistency and the same interview was done two to four years later to see if the answers remained the same.

Kinsey was also worried about **interviewer bias** (interviewer opinions and attitudes that can influence information collected in the interview). To counter this, only Kinsey and three colleagues conducted the interviews. Of the total 18 000 interviews, Kinsey himself conducted 8000 (Pomeroy, 1972). Participants were asked a minimum of 350 questions and interviewers memorized each question so that they could more easily build rapport with participants without continually having to consult a paper questionnaire. Interviewers used appropriate terminology that participants would understand during the interview—for example, "penis" for educated people and "cock" for others. Interviews typically lasted several hours.

The sampling procedures Kinsey used were also strengths of his research. He believed that he would have a high refusal rate if he used **probability sampling**. Because of this, he used what he called "quota sampling accompanied by opportunistic collection"

atheoretical
Research that is not influenced by a particular theory.

interviewer bias
The bias of researchers caused by their own apparent opinions, thoughts, and attitudes about the research.

probability sampling
A research strategy that involves acquiring a random sample for inclusion in a study.

Understanding Human Sexuality: Theory and Research **39**

(Gebhard & Johnson, 1979, p. 26). In other words, if he saw that a particular group—such as young married women—was not well represented in his sample, he would find organizations with a high percentage of these participants and add them.

He obtained participants from colleges and universities, hospitals, prisons, mental hospitals, institutions for young delinquents, churches and synagogues, groups for people with sexual problems, settlement houses, homosexual groups, and members of various other groups such as the YMCA and YWCA. Within these groups, every member was strongly encouraged to participate in the project to minimize **volunteer bias**. Kinsey referred to this procedure as **100 percent sampling**.

Kinsey's research found that many practices that had previously been seen as perverse or rare, such as homosexuality, masturbation, and oral sex, were widely practised. These findings were highly controversial and led to strong reactions from conservative groups and religious organizations. Eventually, continued controversy about Kinsey's work resulted in the termination of several research grants.

The legacy of Kinsey's research was not only that it was the largest and most comprehensive sex survey ever conducted at the time, but it challenged many of the assumptions about sexuality in the United States and the world. In this sense, Kinsey was truly a pioneer in the field (V.L. Bullough, 1998).

Evelyn Hooker: Comparing Gay and Straight Men

Evelyn Hooker (1907–1996), a psychologist, was another important researcher. Her most notable study was on male homosexuality. Previous research on homosexuality had relied upon case histories from the files of psychiatrists who, not surprisingly, found that they had a variety of psychological problems (Bayer, 1981). Hooker had the idea of comparing gay men who had not sought psychiatric help to heterosexual men. She matched each group for age, level of education, and IQ. She then collected information about their life histories, personality profiles, and psychological evaluations, and asked other professionals to try to distinguish between the two groups on the basis of their profiles

| Table 2.1 | What Did Kinsey Find in His Early Research? |

Kinsey's groundbreaking research and the publication of his 1948 and 1953 books revealed many new findings about sexuality. What follows are a few of these findings. Keep in mind that these statistics are based on people's lives in the middle of the 20th century. For more information, visit the Kinsey Institute online at http://www.kinseyinstitute.org:

- Close to 50 percent of American men reported engaging in both heterosexual and homosexual activities, or having had "reacted to" persons of both sexes in the course of their adult life.
- Whereas about 25 percent of males had sexual intercourse by the age of 16, only 6 percent of females had done the same.
- Married couples reported engaging in sexual intercourse 2.8 times per week in their late teens and only once per week by the age of 50.
- The majority of couples reported only having sex in the missionary position (man on top, woman on bottom).
- By far the majority of men and women reported preferring sex with the lights out, while those who like the lights on were more likely to be men.
- About 50 percent of married men reported having sex outside of marriage, while about 25 percent of married women reported doing the same.
- The majority of men and women reported having masturbated.
- The majority of men and women reached their first orgasm during masturbation.
- Close to 70 percent of White heterosexual males reported at least one sexual experience with a prostitute. Most however reported doing so only once.

SOURCES: Kinsey, A., Pomeroy, W.B., & Martin, C.E. (1948). Sexual Behavior in the Human Male. Philadelphia: Saunders; Kinsey, A.C., Pomeroy, W., Martin, C.E., & Gebhard, P. (1953). Sexual Behavior in the Human Female. Philadelphia: Saunders.

and evaluations. They could not do so, demonstrating that there was little fundamental psychological difference between gay and heterosexual men. Hooker's research thus helped challenge the widely held view that homosexuality was a mental illness.

Morton Hunt: Playboy Updates Dr. Kinsey

Twenty-five years after Kinsey, science writer Morton Hunt (1920–) began a large-scale sexuality study in the 1970s. Hunt gathered his sample through random selection from telephone books in 24 American cities and believed it was comparable to Kinsey's research population. A total of 982 males and 1044 females were included in the study and were given self-administered questionnaires. In addition, Hunt interviewed an additional 200 males and females for qualitative data.

Although Hunt's sampling technique was thought to be an improvement over Kinsey's techniques, there were also drawbacks. People without listed phone numbers such as college students or institutionalized persons were left out of the study. Furthermore, even though each person in Hunt's sample was called and asked to participate in a group discussion about sexuality, only 20 percent agreed to do so. Because his sample was such a small percentage of those he contacted, volunteer bias (which we discuss in more detail later in this chapter) prevented his results from being **generalizable** to the population as a whole.

Despite the methodological drawbacks, Hunt's findings were consistent with Kinsey's—premarital sex was common as was the frequency of other sexual behaviours, such as oral and anal sex. Hunt published his research in *Sexual Behavior in the 1970s*

volunteer bias
A slanting of research data caused by the characteristics of participants who volunteer to participate.

100 percent sampling
A research strategy in which all members of a particular group are included in the sample.

generalizable
A statistical conclusion that the finding from a random sample within a population will be the same at that entire population.

(Hunt, 1974). In addition, he reviewed his findings in a series of articles in *Playboy* magazine.

Alan Bell, Martin Weinberg and Colin Williams: Homosexualities

Continuing the research on sexual orientation, two colleagues from the Kinsey Institute, Alan Bell (1932–2002) and Martin Weinberg (1939–), began a large-scale study in 1968 on the influences of homosexuality. Bell and Weinberg surveyed thousands of gay and heterosexual men and women to evaluate their mental health and if there were any social influences that might have influenced their sexual orientation. Their research supported Evelyn Hooker's previous findings—gays and lesbians were psychologically well-adjusted and satisfied with their intimate relationships. Bell and Weinberg believed that their research supported the biological basis for homosexuality, refuting the idea that it was learned or the result of negative experiences (McCoubrey, 2002). Their research was published in two books, *Homosexualities* (1978) and *Sexual Preference* (1981). Weinberg continued his research with his colleague Colin J. Williams and the two have co-authored several other books and articles based on his research on sexual orientation, including *Dual Attraction* (1994).

Weinberg and Williams have collaborated for several decades and have done research on numerous areas of non-traditional sexual behaviour, including gay bathhouse behaviour, prostitution, foot fetishism, and BDSM (bondage-discipline-sadism-masochism) communities.

Martin Weinberg (1939–), a professor of sociology at Indiana University, continues to be active in sex research and has explored sexual minorities, premarital sex, and sex work in the United States, Canada, Sweden, and New Zealand.

William Masters and Virginia Johnson: Measuring Sex in the Laboratory

William Masters (1915–2001), a gynecologist, and Virginia Johnson (1925–2013), a psychology researcher, began their sex research in 1954. They were the first modern scientists to observe and measure the act of sexual intercourse between men and women in a laboratory. They were primarily interested in the anatomy and physiology of the sexual response and later also explored sexual dysfunction. Masters and Johnson were a dual sex therapy team, representing both male and

Virginia Johnson (1925–2013) and William Masters (1915–2001) were the first to bring sex research into a laboratory.

female opinions, which reduced the chance for **gender bias**. Much of the work done by Masters and Johnson was supported by grants, the income from their books, and individual and couples therapy.

Masters and Johnson's first study, published in 1966, was titled *Human Sexual Response*. In an attempt to understand the physiological process that occurs during sexual intercourse, they brought 700 men and women into the laboratory to have their physiological reactions studied during sexual intercourse. The volunteers participated for financial reasons (participants were paid for participation), personal reasons, and even for the release of sexual tension. Masters and Johnson both stated that they believed some volunteers were looking for legitimate and safe sexual outlets. Because they were studying behaviours they believed were normative (i.e., they were practised by most people), they did not feel they needed to recruit a **random sample**.

When volunteers were accepted as participants in the study, they were first encouraged to engage in sexual activity in the laboratory without the investigators present. It was hoped that this would make them feel more comfortable with the new surroundings. Many reported that after a while they did not notice that they were being watched. During the study, they were monitored for any physiological changes with an electrocardiograph, which measured changes in the heart, and an electromyograph, which measured muscular changes. Measurements were taken of penile erection and vaginal lubrication with **penile strain gauges** and **photoplethysmographs** (FOH-toh-pleth-iss-mo-grafs).

Through their research, Masters and Johnson discovered several interesting aspects of sexual response, including women's potential for multiple orgasms and the fact that sexual responses do not disappear in old age. They also proposed a four-stage model for sexual response which we discuss in more detail in Chapter 5.

In 1970, Masters and Johnson published another important book, *Human Sexual Inadequacy*, which explored sexual dysfunction. Again they brought couples into the laboratory, but this time only those who were experiencing sexual problems. They evaluated the couples physiologically and psychologically and taught them exercises to improve their sexual functioning. Frequent follow-ups

gender bias
The bias of a researcher caused by his or her gender.

random sample
A group of people selected from an entire population in such a way as to ensure that any one person has as

much chance of being selected as another.

penile strain gauge
A device used to measure penile engorgement.

photoplethysmograph
A device used to measure vaginal lubrication.

were done to measure the therapeutic results. Some participants were even contacted five years after the study was completed.

Masters and Johnson found that there is often dual sexual dysfunction in couples (i.e., males who are experiencing erectile problems often have partners who are also experiencing sexual problems). Their studies also refuted Freud's theory that women are capable of both vaginal and clitoral orgasms and that only vaginal orgasms result from intercourse. According to their findings, all female orgasms result from direct or indirect clitoral stimulation.

It is important to point out that Masters and Johnson's books were written from a medical and not a psychological perspective. They also used clinical language, and many professionals speculate this was a tactic to avoid censorship of the books. However, even with this scientific and medical base, their work was not without controversy. Many people at the time viewed Masters and Johnson's work as both unethical and immoral in that they observed sexual intercourse as it was taking place.

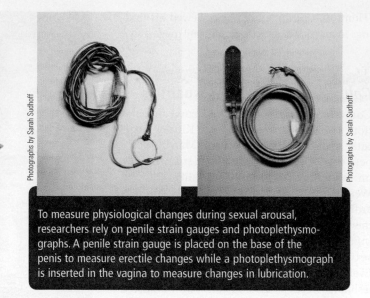

To measure physiological changes during sexual arousal, researchers rely on penile strain gauges and photoplethysmographs. A penile strain gauge is placed on the base of the penis to measure erectile changes while a photoplethysmograph is inserted in the vagina to measure changes in lubrication.

Review Questions

1 Explain the importance of the early pioneers of sexology.

2 What are the reasons why there were so few women engaged in the study of human sexuality?

3 Compare Alfred Kinsey's work to that of Masters and Johnson. What did these researchers contribute to the understanding of human sexuality?

Recent Sex Research in the United States

A variety of large studies have contributed to our knowledge of sexual behaviour. Two of the largest ones are the National Health and Social Life Survey (NHSLS) and the National Survey of Sexual Health and Behavior (NSSHB). Both were funded by private organizations in the United States. In this section, we discuss these two studies and their contributions to sex research.

National Health and Social Life Survey

In 1987, several years after the AIDS outbreak, the United States Department of Health and Human Services called for researchers to study the sexual attitudes and practices of American adults. A group of researchers from the University of Chicago—Edward Laumann, John Gagnon, Robert Michael, and Stuart Michaels—were selected to coordinate this study of more than 20 000 people. However, legislation to eliminate federal funding for sex research

was passed in 1991 and this eliminated most of the budget. Eventually, private funding was acquired from various foundations and it reduced the sample size to 3432 people between the ages of 18 and 59. The respondents were interviewed face-to-face and given brief questionnaires. The NHSLS was the most comprehensive study of sexual attitudes and behaviours since Kinsey, and because the researchers used more up-to-date sampling procedures, it was considered more reliable.

The results of the study showed that people were less sexually active than previously thought. The majority reported only having sex a few times a month or less, and sexual choices that people make were restricted by their social networks and, thus, localized. Among the findings of the NHSLS were the following:

- The median number of sex partners since age 18 was six for men and two for women.

- 75 percent of married men and 80 percent of married women reported not engaging in extramarital sex.

- 2.8 percent of men and 1.4 percent of women described themselves as homosexual or bisexual.

- 75 percent of men claimed to have consistent orgasms with their partners while only 29 percent of women reported the same.

- More than one in five women said they had been forced by a man to do something sexual against their will.

National Survey of Sexual Health and Behavior

By the time the National Survey of Sexual Health and Behavior (NSSHB) was published in late 2010, it had been 18 years since the previous large study. Several major social changes had taken place in the meantime, all with potential to influence sexual behaviour. (Reece et al., 2010b). For example, there were policy changes in sex education mandating abstinence-only programs and new medications for sexual dysfunctions came on the market.

The NSSHB was conducted by a team of sex researchers from the Center for Sexual Health Promotion at Indiana University and was funded by the manufacturer of Trojan condoms. This time online polling was used and participants were asked to fill out questionnaires. One statistician remarked that this "allowed researchers to ask about sex without ever personally asking anyone about sex" (Bialik, 2010a). The NSSHB study polled 5865 people ages 14 to 94.

The researchers found that people engaged in a wide variety of sexual behaviours. Young teenagers were found to be less sexually active than it was thought. For example, fewer than 25 percent had engaged in vaginal intercourse, although participation in sexual activities was found to gradually increase as teenagers matured (Rabin, 2010a). Some of the other notable findings are as follows:

- Masturbation is common throughout the life span and more common than partnered sexual behaviour during adolescence and old age.

- 30 percent of women and 5 percent of men reported experiencing pain during sexual intercourse.

- 23 percent of men and 13 percent of women older than 50 years reported their most recent sex was with a "friend" or "new acquaintance."

- 80 percent of sexually active boys between the ages of 14 and 17 reported using condoms the last time they engaged in sexual behaviour.

Review Questions

1 Compare and contrast the methods used for the two American studies. What were the advantages and disadvantages of each?

2 What were some of the major findings of the two studies? Where they similar?

Sex Research in Canada

It is not known whether the sexual behaviour of Canadians is similar to that of Americans because there have been no surveys with the same size and breadth of coverage as those in the United States. One may speculate, however, that because of differences in geography, culture, demographics, and public policy, there would be some variations. For example, Canadian sex education has not followed the abstinence-only model of the United States and Canada does not have such a strong religious conservative presence. These two factors alone would suggest that Canadians might be better informed about matters of sexual health and more open about sexual activity. Furthermore, Canadian lesbians and gays enjoy equal protection under the law including the right to marry, serve in the military, and sponsor their same-sex partners in immigration. This would suggest less secrecy and less homophobic attitudes. On the other hand, Canada has sizable populations of newly immigrated groups who have brought with them the sexual values of their own cultures. This would suggest pockets of sexual conservatism when compared to mainstream Canadians. Given the newness of these groups as well as the newness of same-sex marriage, research upon such matters has only just begun.

In this section, we look at several surveys relevant to Canadian sexual health and highlight some topical research pertaining to Canadian sexual behaviour.

National Surveys

Two national surveys of note are the National Longitudinal Survey of Children and Youth (NLSCY) and the Canadian Community Health Survey (CCHS). Although these studies survey large enough samples, they are not sexual behaviour surveys per se but rather include some questions on the topic. We look at each separately.

National Longitudinal Survey of Children and Youth

This national survey has been conducted every two years since 1994 and looks at such matters as children's overall health, family life, and education. It asks several questions about sexual activity such as whether respondents has had sexual intercourse and about their exposure to sexually transmitted infections. According to a summary report (Mitchell, 2009), the following tends were found among Canadian youth:

Understanding Human Sexuality: Theory and Research

- 39.9 percent of Canadian teenagers 14 to 19 have had consensual sexual intercourse. When broken down by gender, the figures are 41.6 percent for girls and 38.1 percent for boys.

- Teenagers were more likely to be sexually active in Quebec and the Maritime provinces.

- Parents' smoking and drinking behaviour had a strong impact upon whether teenagers choose to be sexually active. The children of parents who did not drink alcohol were 18 percent less likely to be sexually active, while children of parents who drank to excess were 24 percent more likely to be sexually active. This was especially true for girls whose parents drank to excess in that they were 38 percent more likely to be sexually active as teenagers.

- Children who attended church regularly were less likely to be sexually active although not dramatically so, since the proportion fell only to 30 percent.*

Canadian Community Health Survey

This survey is conducted every two years and targets Canadians 12 years old or older. Each respondent is interviewed for about 45 minutes with a battery of questions, several of which pertain to sexual activity. Among the findings as of February 2013 are the following:

- 43.5 percent of Canadian teenagers 15 to 19 have had sexual intercourse.

- 24.3 percent had their first sexual intercourse at age 15 or younger, 43.8 percent at 16 or 17, and 31.6 at 18 or 19.

- Of all Canadians aged 16 to 59, only 13 percent had two or more partners in the past 12 months. Of those 13 percent, 54.0 percent reported always using condoms and 24.4 percent reported never using them.

Canadian Sexual Health Indicators Survey

Currently, the Canadian Sexual Health Indicators Survey is at its beginning stages and data are available only for the pilot test and validation phase. There are a number of strengths to this survey. First, it concentrates upon indicators of sexual health as recommended by the World Health Organization, such as sexual self-efficacy, sexual satisfaction, and access to health services. Second, with the inclusion of focus groups, the pilot study was

*SOURCE: Institute of Marriage and Family Canada, "Rated PG: How Parental Influence Impacts Teen Sexual Activity." Retrieved October 4, 2015, from http://www.imfcanada.org/sites/default/files/Rated_PG_Part_1.pdf.

case study
A research methodology that involves an in-depth examination of one participant or a small number of participants.

validity
The property of a device measuring what it is intended to measure.

reliability
The dependability of a test as reflected in the consistency of its scores on repeated measurements of the same group.

successful in its efforts to reach sexual minorities as opposed to simply mainstream Canadians. In 2010, data were gathered from 1185 participants ages 16 to 24. Those defining as heterosexual amounted to only 76.2 percent while the rest defined as gay, lesbian, genderqueer, intersexed, and otherwise. Twenty-four transgender individuals were also included.

In terms of race or ethnic identity, only 71.7 percent defined themselves as White, which is a lesser proportion than the Canadian population as a whole. Others defined themselves as Chinese, Black, First Nations, Métis, and other. About 20 percent also reported speaking a language other than French or English at home.

This inclusion of sexual and racial minorities is progressive in overcoming obstacles in traditional surveys, which have been biased toward heterosexuality. For example, when the term "sexual intercourse" is used, it generally means penis in vagina. Gay men and lesbians have not known how to answer questions about this since they engage in other types of activities that may also be defined as intercourse. Similarly, lesbians have not known how to respond to questions such as "did you use a condom the last time you had sex" or "did you use any birth control methods." Answering that they did not suggests sexual irresponsibility even though such things are irrelevant to lesbian couples.

Sex Research Methods and Considerations

Now that we have explored some of the findings of studies in sexuality, let us look at the specifics of how these studies are conducted. Each study that we have discussed in this chapter was scientific, yet researchers used different experimental methods depending on the kind of information they were trying to gather. For example, Freud relied on a case study methodology, whereas Kinsey used interviews to gather data. There are other ways that researchers collect information, such as questionnaires, laboratory experiments, direct observation, participant observation, correlations, and Internet-based research methods.

Whatever techniques they use, researchers must be certain that their experiment passes standards of validity, reliability, and generalizability. Tests of validity determine whether a question or other method actually measures what it is designed to measure. For example, the people who read the question need to interpret it the same way as the researcher who wrote it. Reliability refers to the consistency of the measure. If we ask a question today, we would hope to get a similar answer if we ask it again in two months. Finally, generalizability refers to the ability of samples in a study to have wide applicability to the general population. A study can be generalized only if a random sample is used. All of the methods we review here must fit these three criteria.

Case Studies

When researchers describe a case study, they attempt to explore individual cases to formulate general hypotheses. Freud was famous for his use of this methodology. He would study hysteria in only one patient, because he didn't have several patients with similar complaints. Using this method, however, does not allow researchers to generalize to the wider public because the sample is small. Even so, the case study method may generate hypotheses that can lead to larger, generalizable studies.

Interviews

We began this chapter with an exploration of Valerie's "Bikini Sex Project," in which she used interviews to collect data about locations for sex. Interviews can be useful research tools because they allow the researcher to establish a rapport with each participant and emphasize the importance of honesty in the study. In addition, the researcher can vary the order of questions and skip questions that are irrelevant. However, they can be time-consuming and expensive.

Questionnaires and Surveys

Questionnaire or survey research is generally used to identify the attitudes, knowledge, or behaviour of large samples. For instance, Kinsey used this method to obtain information about his many participants, although questions have since been raised about Kinsey's validity and reliability. Kinsey recognized these problems and tried to increase the validity by using interviews to supplement the questionnaires.

Some researchers believe that questionnaires provide more honesty than interviews because the participant may be embarrassed to admit things to another person that he or she would be more likely to share with the anonymity of a questionnaire. Research has revealed that when people answer sexuality questionnaires, they are likely to leave out the questions that cause the most anxiety, especially questions about masturbation (Catania et al., 1986). We discuss using online questionnaires later in this section.

Direct Observation

Masters and Johnson used direct observation for their research on sexual response and physiology. This method is the least frequently used because it is difficult to find participants who are willing to come into the laboratory to have sex while researchers monitor their bodily functions. However, if direct observation can be done, it does provide information that cannot be obtained elsewhere. Researchers can monitor behaviour as it happens, giving the results more credibility. For example, a man may exaggerate the number of erections per sexual episode in a self-report, but he cannot exaggerate in a laboratory.

Direct observation is expensive and may not be as generalizable, because it would be impossible to gather a random sample. In addition, direct observation focuses on behaviours and, as a result, ignores feelings, attitudes, or personal history.

Participant Observation

Participant observation research involves researchers going into an environment and monitoring what is happening

naturally. For instance, a researcher who wants to explore the impact of alcohol on male and female flirting patterns might monitor interactions between and among men and women in bars. This would entail several visits and specific note taking on all that occurs. However, it is difficult to generalize from this type of research because the researcher could subtly, or not so subtly, influence the research findings. Also, this method has limited use in the area of sex research because much of sexual behaviour occurs in private.

Experimental Methods

Experiments are the only research method that allows us to isolate cause and effect. This is because in an experiment, strict control is maintained over all variables so that one variable can be isolated and examined.

For example, let's say you want to teach high-school students about AIDS, but you don't know which teaching methodology would be most beneficial. You could design an experiment to examine this more closely. First, you choose a high school and randomly assign all the students to one of three groups. You might start by giving them a questionnaire about AIDS to establish baseline data about what they know or believe. Group 1 then listens to a lecture about AIDS, Group 2 is shown a video, and Group 3 listens to people with AIDS talk about their experiences. Strict care is taken to make sure that all of the information that is presented in these classes is identical. The only thing that differs is the teaching method. In scientific terms, the type of teaching method is the **independent variable**, which is manipulated by the researcher. After each class, the students are given a test to determine what knowledge they have gained about AIDS. This measurement is to determine the effect of the independent variable on the **dependent variable**, which in this case is knowledge about AIDS. If one group shows more learning after one particular method was used, we might be able to attribute the learning to the type of methodology that was used.

Experiments can be more costly than any of the other methods discussed, in terms of both finances and time commitment. It is also possible that in an attempt to control the experiments, a researcher may cause the study to become too sterile or artificial (nothing like it would be outside of the laboratory), and the results may be faulty or inapplicable to the real world. Finally, experiments are not always possible in certain areas of research, especially in the field of sexuality. For instance, what if we wanted to examine whether early sexual abuse contributed to adult difficulties with intimate relationships? It would be entirely unethical to abuse children sexually to examine whether they develop these problems later in life.

participant observation
A research methodology that involves actual participation in the event being researched.

independent variable
The variable controlled by the experimenter and applied to the participant to determine its effect on the participant's reaction.

dependent variable
The measured results of an experiment that are believed to be a function of the independent variable.

Correlational Methods

Correlations are often used when it is not possible to do an experiment. For example, because it is unethical to do a controlled experiment in a sexual abuse study, we would study a given population to see whether there is any correlation between past sexual abuse and later difficulties with intimate relationships. The limitation of a correlational study is that it does not provide any information about cause. We would not learn whether past sexual abuse causes intimacy difficulties, even though we may learn that these factors are related. The intimacy difficulties could occur for several other reasons, including factors such as low self-esteem or a personality disorder.

Internet-Based Research Methods

Over the last few years, sex researchers have been relying on the Internet for data collection in many of their studies. The accessibility of the Web has given sex researchers access to a wider group of diverse participants. For example, the use of computer-assisted personal interviewing and audio computer-assisted self-interviewing, both of which are Internet-based research techniques, allows us to gather data from large samples easily and anonymously.

There are disadvantages and risks to Internet-based sex research (Mustanski, 2001). As in other research methods, participants can lie and sabotage research. Because surveys are anonymous, participants could submit multiple responses. To reduce the possibility of this happening, researchers could collect email addresses to check for multiple submissions, but this would negate participants' anonymity. One study that checked for multiple submissions found that participants rarely submitted more than one response (Reips, 2000).

More than 83 percent of Canadian households used the Internet in 2012 (Statistics Canada, 2013), but these Internet users may not be representative of all Canadians. In the United States, a

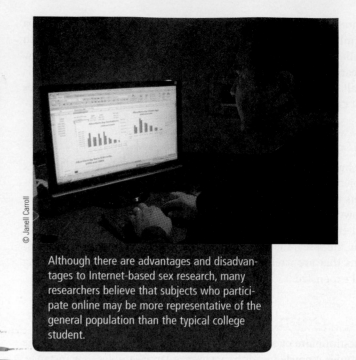

© Janell Carroll

Although there are advantages and disadvantages to Internet-based sex research, many researchers believe that subjects who participate online may be more representative of the general population than the typical college student.

variety of minorities are not well represented, and neither are those with low socio-economic status or education (National Telecommunications and Information Administration & U.S. Department of Commerce, 1999). Wealthier, White, and better-educated individuals are well represented on the Internet, and this can bias research results. However, even though these differences exist, some researchers claim that the participant pool available online may be more representative of the general population than a group of typical college students—who are the most common research participants (Mustanski, 2001; Reips & Bachtiger, 2000). One more concern about Internet-based sex research is that minors may have access to the studies. However, researchers must ask for informed consent, and participants must agree that they are older than 18 years before participating.

correlation
A statistical measure of the relationship between two variables.

correlational study
A type of research that examines the relationship between two or more variables.

Review Questions

1 Differentiate between validity and reliability, and give one example of each.

2 What makes a study generalizable?

3 Identify the advantages and disadvantages of using interviews and questionnaires.

4 Explain how direct observation and participant observation are used in research studies.

5 Explain how the Internet can be used in sex research. What are some of the benefits and drawbacks of this method?

Problems and Issues in Sex Research

Many problems in sex research are more difficult to contend with than they are in other types of research (see accompanying Sex in Real Life feature). These include ethical issues, volunteer bias, sampling problems, and reliability.

Ethical Issues

Ethical issues affect all social science—and sex research in particular. Before people participate in a study of sexuality, researchers must obtain their informed consent. This is especially important in an area such as sexuality because it is such a personal subject. Informed consent means that the subjects know what to expect from the questions and procedures, how the information will be used, that their confidentiality will be assured, and to whom they can address questions. Some things that people reveal in a study, such as their acknowledgment of an affair or a sexual dysfunction, can cause harm or embarrassment if researchers are careless enough to let others find out. Another ethical question that has generated controversy is whether children should be asked questions about sexuality. Overall, it is standard procedure in sex research to maintain confidentiality and obtain informed consent from all participants, regardless of age.

Volunteer Bias

Think back to Valerie's "Bikini Sex Project," which we discussed at the beginning of this chapter. Do you think that the students who walked by Valerie and ignored her request for information were different from those who stopped to write on her body? Or, do you believe her results are generalizable to students at all universities? If the volunteers could differ from non-volunteers, then there is a volunteer bias at work. Volunteer bias prevents the results of her study from being generalizable to the population as a whole.

As early as 1969, Rosenthal and Rosnow (1975) claimed that those who volunteer for psychological studies often have a special interest in the studies in which they participate. Studies that have examined volunteer bias in sex research conducted with college students generally support the finding that volunteers differ from non-volunteers (Catania et al., 1995; Gaither et al., 2003). Volunteers have been found to be more sexually liberal, more sexually experienced, and more interested in sexual variety, and they report less traditional sexual attitudes than non-volunteers (Bogaert, 1996; Gaither, 2000; Plaud et al., 1999; Wiederman, 1999). Research has also found that, overall, men are more likely than women to volunteer for sexuality studies (Gaither et al., 2003).

You might be wondering how researchers would know whether their volunteer sample is different from the non-volunteer sample. After all, how can researchers know anything about the non-volunteers who are not in the study? Researchers have designed ways to overcome this problem. Before asking for volunteers to take part in a sexuality study, researchers ask all participants to fill out a questionnaire that contains personality measures and sexuality questions. Participants are then asked whether they would volunteer for a sexuality study. Because the researchers already have information from both volunteers and non-volunteers, they simply compare these data.

Because volunteers appear to differ from non-volunteers, it is impossible to generalize the findings of a study that used a volunteer sample. The Kinsey studies attempted to decrease volunteer bias by obtaining full participation from each member of the groups they studied.

Sampling Problems

Sexuality studies routinely involve the use of college-age populations. Brecher and Brecher (1986) refer to these populations as samples of convenience, because the participants used are convenient for researchers who tend to work at universities. Kinsey used such samples in his initial research at Indiana University. The question is, can these studies be generalized to the rest of the population? Are college students similar to people of the same age who are not college students, or people who are older or younger? Probably not. These samples also underrepresent certain groups, such as minorities and the disabled.

On Your Mind

How do researchers know that what people tell them is true?

The fact is that they don't know, and they hope that people are being honest. Sometimes researchers build into studies little tricks that can catch someone who is lying, such as asking the same questions in different wording again later in a survey. Researchers also anticipate that participants will understand the questions asked and be able to provide the answers. In actuality, researchers may take many things for granted.

Reliability

How reliable is sex research? Couldn't it be that those who are sexually satisfied overestimate their frequency of sexual behaviour, whereas those who are dissatisfied underreport it? Both participant comfort in discussing sexuality and their memory

---

informed consent
Informing participants about what will be expected of them before they agree to participate in a research study.

confidentiality
Assurance that all materials collected in a research study will be kept private and confidential.

samples of convenience
A research methodology that involves using samples that are easy to collect and acquire.

SEX
What Questions Would They Ask?

Because theorists from different perspectives are interested in different areas of study, they ask different questions. What follows are examples of what might be asked within those perspectives.

Psychoanalytic: How are sexual problems later in life related to early childhood experiences? How do children resolve the Oedipal and Electra complexes? Does an overactive superego cause people to feel guilty about sexual behaviour?

Behavioural: What reinforces a person's attraction to various types of partners? What reinforcements work best in encouraging people to use contraception? What reasons are most prominent in the decision to lose one's virginity?

Social Learning: How does peer group pressure influence people's sexuality? What effects do the media have on our sexuality? How are children influenced by sexual messages on television?

Cognitive: What is the decision-making process related to contraceptive choice? What is the level of children's understanding of sexuality? How do men deal with erectile dysfunction?

Humanist: How do negative parental reactions to a first sexual experience affect teenagers? How does self-actualization affect sexuality?

Biological: How do genetics influence sexuality? What are the effects of hormone levels on sexual desire? How does menstruation affect sexual desire in women?

Evolutionary: What types of changes have occurred within human beings that ensure their survival? How do mating rituals ensure survival?

Sociological: How does religion influence sexuality? How does the threat of HIV/AIDS affect society? How have the norms surrounding particular sexual behaviours developed over time?

Feminist: How does patriarchy repress female sexuality? How do the media reinforce a male view of sexuality?

Queer Theory: What types of factors are involved in the formation of a lesbian or gay identity? How are same-sex and heterosexual desires interrelated?

---

about sexual behaviours have been found to affect the reliability of the study.

Some critics claim that changes in frequency of sexual behaviour over time may be due more to changes in the reporting of behaviour than to actual changes in frequency (Kaats & Davis, 1971). For instance, if we had done a study in 1995 about the number of college students who engaged in premarital sex and compared this with data collected in 1963, we would undoubtedly find more people reporting having had premarital sex in 1995. However, it could be that these higher numbers are due, in part, to the fact that more people felt comfortable talking about premarital sex in 1995 than they did in 1963. It is necessary to take

into account the time period of the study when evaluating the results, to ensure that we know the increase in numbers is actually due to an increase in behaviour.

Another problem that affects reliability involves the participant's memory. Because many sex researchers ask questions about behaviors that might have happened in one's adolescence, people may not always remember information accurately. For instance, if we were to ask a 52-year-old man the age at which he first masturbated, chances are good that he would not remember exactly how old he was. He would probably estimate the age at which he first masturbated. Estimates are not always precise enough for scientific study.

Review Questions

1 Define informed consent and explain the importance of confidentiality.

2 What differences have been found between those who volunteer and

those who don't volunteer for sex research?

3 Define a "sample of convenience" and explain how it is used.

4 How do satisfaction and memory issues potentially affect sex research?

Sex Research across Cultures

Many studies examine sexuality in cultures outside Canada and the United States. Some have been general studies that examine knowledge levels and attitudes in different populations; others have evaluated specific areas such as pregnancy, rape, homosexuality, or sex education. Many times these studies are done by researchers in other countries, but some have also been done by Canadian researchers.

Of all the topics that have been studied cross-culturally, we have probably learned the most about how societies' values and culture influence sexuality. Every culture develops its own rules about which sexual behaviours are encouraged and which will not be tolerated. In 1971, Donald Marshall and Robert Suggs published a classic anthropological study, *Human Sexual Behavior*, which examined how sexuality was expressed in several different cultures. This study remains one of the largest cultural studies ever done on sexuality, and some of its interesting findings include:

- Masturbation is rare in preliterate cultures (those without a written language).
- Foreplay is usually initiated by males in heterosexual couples.
- Heterosexuals engage in sexual intercourse most commonly at night before falling asleep.
- Female orgasmic ability varies greatly from culture to culture.

More recent studies on cross-cultural sexuality have yielded other interesting results. In 2002, Pfizer Pharmaceuticals undertook a comprehensive global study of sexuality. The Global Study of Sexual Attitudes and Behaviors surveyed more than 26 000 men and women in 28 countries. This study was the first global survey to assess behaviours, attitudes, beliefs, and sexual satisfaction. Surveys assessed the importance of sex and intimacy in relationships, attitudes and beliefs about sexual health, and treatment-seeking behaviours for sexual dysfunctions. This survey provided an international baseline regarding sexual attitudes to compare various countries and also monitor cultural changes over time. In 2007, Durex undertook another global study to explore sexual attitudes and behaviours in 41 countries. The study included 26 000 people who responded to a web survey (see the Sexual Diversity in Our World feature for more information about both of these studies).

On Your Mind

How could an entire culture's attitudes about sex differ from those of another culture?

It makes more sense when you think about two very different types of cultures. A collectivist culture (e.g., India, Pakistan, Thailand, or the Philippines) emphasizes the cultural group as a whole and thinks less about the individuals within that society. In contrast, an individualistic culture (e.g., Canada, the United States, Australia, or England) stresses the goals of individuals over the cultural group as a whole. This cultural difference can affect the way that sexuality is viewed. For example, a culture such as India may value marriage because it is good for the social standing of members of the society, whereas a marriage in Canada is valued because the two people love each other and want to spend their lives together.

Societal influences affect all aspects of sexuality. Throughout this book, we explore more details from cross-cultural studies on sexuality and examine how cultures vary from each other.

Review Questions

1 Of all the cross-cultural topics that have been studied, what have we learned the most about?

2 Identify two findings from Marshall and Suggs's large-scale cross-cultural study of sexuality.

3 Identify some of the findings from the Pfizer and Durex sex studies.

Understanding Human Sexuality: Theory and Research

A few global studies have shed some light on cross-cultural sexuality. Global studies are expensive to conduct, and because of this, usually pharmaceutical or contraceptive companies fund them.

The Global Study of Sexual Attitudes and Behaviors (GSSAB) was the first large, multi-country survey to study sexual attitudes, beliefs, and health in middle-age and older adults (Laumann et al., 2005). The study was funded by Pfizer Pharmaceuticals (the maker of Viagra). Interviews and surveys were conducted in 29 countries representing all world regions (Africa/Middle East, Asia, Australasia, Europe, Latin America, and North America). A total of 13 882 women and 13 618 men, aged 40 to 80 years old were included in the study.

Various countries required specific data collection methods. For example, random-digit telephone dialing was used in Europe, Israel, North America, Brazil, Australia, and New Zealand, and interviews were conducted by phone. However, a bias against telephone interviews in certain populations in Mexico required using in-person interviews. Mail surveys were used in Japan, but in other Asian countries, questionnaires were handed out in public locations. Finally, door-to-door methods using questionnaires were used in the Middle East and South Africa (Laumann et al., 2005). Cross-cultural research requires flexibility in the use of data collection methods.

Despite wide cultural variations, there are several predictors of sexual well-being—such as physical and mental health and relationship satisfaction—that are consistent throughout the regions of the world. In addition, ratings of sexual satisfaction throughout the world are correlated with overall happiness in both men and women (Laumann et al., 2006). However, there were some limitations to this study. First of all, there was a relatively low response rate of 19 percent, which means that those who did agree to participate may have been more interested or comfortable in discussing sexual issues (Laumann et al., 2005). In addition, since a variety of data collection methods were used, the results may not be generalizable in those countries where the data collection didn't enable researchers to collect a random sample, such as the Middle East, South Africa, and certain Asian countries.

Another global study of sexuality, the Durex Sexual Wellbeing Global Survey, was conducted in 2011–2012 and was financed by Reckitt Benckiser (the maker of Durex). The study included more than 29 000 adults in 37 countries (Durex, 2012). Internet-based research methodologies were used in every country except Nigeria, where face-to-face interviews were done because of low Internet usage. The Durex study found that the frequency of sexual activity varies by country (see Figure 2.1). Although 83 percent of respondents said that sex is an enjoyable part of their lives, only 45 percent said they were fully satisfied with their sex lives.

The study also found the average age for engaging in first vaginal intercourse worldwide is 19.3 (Durex, 2012). The age at first vaginal intercourse was 17.3 (youngest) in Brazil and 23.7 (oldest) in Malaysia. Finally, the study also reported that heterosexual couples in Colombia are the most sexually active, whereas heterosexual couples in Japan are the least active. Data from the Durex study have been used in a variety of studies, which we will talk about in upcoming chapters.

The London School of Hygiene also conducted a global study and used meta-analysis to analyze 200 studies on demographic sexual behaviours published between 1996 and 2006 from 59 countries (Wellings et al., 2006). This was an interesting idea for a study that compared data on published articles around the world instead of collecting new data. The study found that a shift toward later marriage around the world has led to an increase in premarital sexuality. It also revealed that monogamy is the dominant sexual pattern, and that around the world, men report more sexual partners than women.

There have also been some global studies on specific sexual issues. For example, one study evaluated contraceptive use in adolescents from 24 European and North American countries (Godeau et al., 2008).

Sex Research in the Future: Technology, Immigration, and Human Rights

First it must be said that, when considering all life, even though sexual behaviour in one form or another has been around over a billion years, the study of it has been around only about 150 years, and even during this short time, there have been numerous roadblocks to knowledge held up by politicians, the clergy, and moral entrepreneurs such as Anthony Comstock (discussed in Chapter 1). While humanity has made great strides in other areas, sexology is still a bold frontier with much territory to explore. This is ironic considering that sexuality is a topic so often discussed and yet still so little examined. We know so much about sex, and yet so little at the same time. We have found ways to discuss it without discussing it at all. Some people even deem it unworthy of study, believing that science has limits to what it should examine.

What is in store for Canadians in the future in terms of sex research? To answer this question we must turn to what is newly emergent in society in general. In this respect, first and foremost are the fledgling technologies that have changed the ways that

A total of 34 000 15-year-old students completed self-report questionnaires. The percentages of students reporting engaging in sexual intercourse ranged from 14 percent in Croatia to 38 percent in England. Condom use in Greece was close to 90 percent, whereas in Sweden it was closer to 53 percent (Godeau et al., 2008).

The Center for Health Promotion at Indiana University, which authored the National Survey of Sexual Behavior and Health study, has also been actively collecting data on global studies of sexuality, and many of these should be available within the next few years. Global studies can help us learn more about societal and cultural factors that influence sexuality. Unfortunately, these studies are expensive, and funding can be difficult to come by. To reduce cost, many global studies rely on Internet data collection and self-reporting, which also raise several reliability and validity concerns.

Percentage of Respondents who Report Engaging in Sex at Least Once a Week

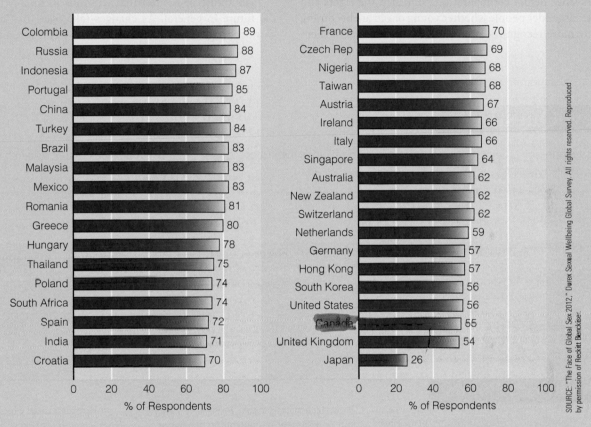

FIGURE **2.1** Frequency of having sex varies considerably by country.

people relate to one another. From the 1970s to the present, we have gone from wall-tethered telephones to pocket-size mobile phones, from electric typewriters to laptops, and from videocassette recorders to TiVo, YouTube, and Netflix. We have also gone from meeting potential partners in schools, cafés, and bars to sifting through hundreds of profiles on websites such as *Plenty-ofFish* and *Manhunt*. Research into the ways that human sexual desires and behaviours interface with such technology as well as emergent robotics is only beginning. How will such advancements in technology affect our sexual behaviour? How will they shape sexual desire? What will be the moral issues we face? Technology is advancing at a heightened rate and new ethical issues will emerge along with it.

Second, we must look at the recent changes that have occurred in terms of human rights and immigration in Canada and elsewhere. First Nations people in Canada have had their cultures decimated by colonialism and we are only now beginning to examine the consequences. For example, Inuit cultures had lasted thousands of years untouched by other cultures but are now losing their traditions to technology and mainstream Canadian influence. How have such changes affected their sexual lives, and how have such influences affected First Nations groups in general?

Canada is also a nation of immigrants, mostly French and English but with large populations of East and South Asians, Africans, South Americans, and those from the Middle East, as

Understanding Human Sexuality: Theory and Research

well as Europeans of Italian, German, and Scandinavian origin. How will the norms and values surrounding sexuality that they bring from their nations of origin interact with one another and change the face of Canadian sexuality in general? How will different religious affiliations—from Christian, to Muslim, to Hindu, to no affiliation at all—interact in areas of sexuality?

Furthermore, within a few decades, lesbians and gays have gone from social pariahs to legitimate minorities with full federal recognition of human rights and equalities. Notably, same-sex marriage is only a decade old and there is much research to be done on the ways gays and lesbians adapt to an institution enjoyed by all others since before confederation. Similarly, the rights and realities of transgender people whether young or old are becoming progressively more recognized. How will the definitions of them change and how will they integrate into a society that has traditionally seen sex and gender as fixed and innate?

Perhaps the most important question is how will the world change in terms of sexual behaviours and identities as we enter an era of advanced technology, rapid transport from one country to another, world trade, and globalization? The world is no longer a collection of separate and isolated cultures. It has become inextricably linked by technology, economy, and trade, where major changes in one culture have ripple effects upon all others. Sexuality, being an integral part of each of those cultures, will feel those ripples along with all other areas.

The future of sex research will thus inevitably be dictated by the future in general. As changes take place in Canada and the world, changes in the focus of research upon sexuality will follow.

Review Questions

1 How has technology changed directions in future sex research?

2 How do religious institutions often impede sex research?

3 What types of sex research have taken place in Canada?

Chapter Review

Summary Points

1 A theory is a set of assumptions, principles, or methods that help a researcher understand the nature of a phenomenon being studied. The psychoanalytic theory was developed by Sigmund Freud. He believed the sex drive was one of the most important forces in life. Two of Freud's most controversial concepts included personality formation (the development of the id, ego, and superego) and psychosexual development (oral, anal, phallic, latency, and genital stages).

2 Behavioural theory argues that only overt behaviour can be measured, observed, and controlled by scientists. Behaviourists use rewards and punishments to control behaviour. A treatment method called *behaviour modification* is used to help change unwanted behaviours.

3 Social learning theory looks at reward and punishment in controlling behaviour but also believes that internal events, such as feelings, thoughts, and beliefs, can also influence behaviour. Another theory, cognitive theory, holds that people differ in how they process information, and this creates personality differences. Our behaviour is a result of how we perceive and conceptualize what is happening around us.

4 Humanistic theory purports that we all strive to develop ourselves to the best of our abilities and to become self-actualized. Biological theory claims that sexual behaviour is primarily a biological process, whereas evolutionary theory incorporates both evolution and sociology to understand sexual behaviour. Sociological theorists are interested in how society influences sexual behaviour.

5 Feminist theory looks at how the social construction of sexuality is based on power and the view that women are submissive and subordinate to men. Queer theory asserts that domination, such as heterosexism and homophobia, should be resisted.

6 The legitimate forefathers of sex research may be Aristotle and Plato because they were the first to develop theories regarding sexual responses and dysfunctions, sex legislation, reproduction, contraception, and sexual ethics. The majority of the early sex research was done in Europe, primarily in Germany. It wasn't until the 1900s that sex research moved to the United States, which has led the way ever since.

7 Sex research has become fragmented with researchers coming from several disciplines. Many are unaware of the work being done by others.

8 The changing political climate affects attitudes about sexuality as well as sex research. Negative attitudes can affect the public perception of sex research. Politics also can influence what research gets funded.

9 The most influential early promoters of sexology were Iwan Bloch, Magnus Hirschfeld, Albert Moll, Richard von Krafft-Ebing, and Havelock Ellis. Clelia Mosher did a great deal of research in the late 1800s but most of her work was never published. Katharine Bement Davis believed that gays were no different from heterosexuals, but her work was largely ignored.

10 Alfred Kinsey was probably the most influential sex researcher of the 20th century. He was the first to take the study of sexuality away from the medical model. Kinsey established the Institute for Sex Research at Indiana University. Morton Hunt updated Kinsey's earlier work.

11 William Masters and Virginia Johnson were the first scientists to observe and measure sex acts in a laboratory. They discovered several interesting aspects of sexuality and developed a model called the *sexual response cycle*.

12 Allen Bell, Martin Weinberg, and Colin Williams conducted research upon sexual orientation as well as other areas of sexuality such as fetishism, BDSM communities, and prostitution.

13 Researchers can use several methods to study sexuality, including case study, questionnaire, interview, participant observation, experimental methods, and correlations.

14 Researchers must be certain that their experiment passes standards of validity, reliability, and generalizability. Several problems can affect sex research, such as ethical issues, volunteer bias, sampling, and reliability problems. Of all the topics that have been studied cross-culturally, we have learned the most about how societies' values and culture influence sexuality.

15 Sex research in the future will likely look at the interface between sexual relationships and technology.

Critical Thinking Questions

1 Is sex research as valid and reliable as other areas of research? Explain.

2 Do you think that people would be more honest about their sex lives if they were filling out an anonymous questionnaire or if they were being interviewed by a researcher? Which method of research do you think yields the highest degree of honesty?

3 What factors led sex research to move from Europe to the United States?

4 If you could study sexuality, what area would you choose? What methods of data collection would you use? Why?

Websites

The Sex Information and Education Council of Canada (SIECAN) This organization provides sexual health and education information to all individuals involved in sexual health education in Canada. (http://sieccan.org/wp/)

American Association of Sexuality Educators, Counselors, and Therapists (AASECT) This organization has numerous programs and certifications for those interested in becoming a certified sex educator or therapist. (http://www.aasect.org/)

Electronic Journal of Human Sexuality Disseminates knowledge to the international community and includes peer-reviewed research articles and dissertations on sexuality. (http://www.ejhs.org/)

Society for the Scientific Study of Sexuality (SSSS) SSSS is an interdisciplinary, international organization for sex researchers, clinicians, educators, and other professionals in related fields. (http://www.sexscience.org/)

3
Female Sexual Anatomy, Development, and Health

Many years ago I lost a good friend, Anne, to breast cancer. Prior to her diagnosis I didn't know too much about breast cancer. Anne was a mom with three young children at home. She fought hard for her life but in the end the cancer won. The main issue that worked against her was the fact that the cancer was not discovered until it was at a very advanced stage. From this painful experience I learned about the importance of breast self-examination (BSE) in the detection of early stage breast cancer. I have always recommended it to my students. It's important to familiarize yourself with your breasts so that you know how things normally look. This will enable you to more readily detect any change, such as a lump, dimpling, or skin irritation. However, the truth is that it wasn't until I met Stef Woods in the fall of 2010 that I realized just how important BSE really is. Stef had been diagnosed with breast cancer only seven months before I met her and she had already been through countless rounds of chemotherapy.

What makes Stef's story so important for you to hear is that she found the first lump in her breast when she was 25 years old. Stef had always been vigilant about breast self-exams, mostly because her mother had died of cancer 13 years earlier. Thankfully, the lump she found the first time was not cancerous. A few years later she found another lump and once again, it was not cancerous. However, the third time she found a lump she knew her luck might not hold out. Her doctor called to share her test results when she was getting a haircut. As she put the phone to her ear, she was keenly aware of her heart racing:

When I answered the phone, my first thought was that it was weird that my doctor didn't say everything was fine right off the bat. Instead, she asked how I was. Holding the phone was difficult because I was shaking so badly. "Your test is positive. You have breast cancer," she said. I talked to her for a few more moments, got up from the chair, walked to the

© Samuel Borges Photography/Shutterstock.

back room of the salon, and began to cry. In some ways, I had known something was seriously wrong before she told me. Of course I had found the lump, but in addition to that, my dog, Flake, had recently begun sleeping by my right breast. This was strange since she always slept at my feet. They say dogs can sense cancer. Over the next seven months, I learned many important lessons about life—I was forced to find strength I never knew I had, but I also realized the incredible power of friendship.

When I interviewed Stef, she was receiving her last round of chemotherapy before beginning radiation the following week. I think you will find our conversation both enlightening and encouraging. ▐▌

For many years, only physicians were thought to be privileged enough to know about the human body. Considering the number of sex manuals and guides that today line the shelves of Canadian bookstores, it may seem surprising that the majority of questions that students ask about human sexuality are fundamental, biological questions. Many parents are still uncomfortable discussing sexual biology with their children, and people of all ages often do not know whom to approach or are embarrassed about the questions they have regarding the workings of their own bodies. Questions about sexual biology are natural and given the complexity of the reproductive systems in men and women there are probably more myths and misinformation about sexual biology than for any other single aspect of human anatomy and physiology.

Children are naturally curious about their genitals and spend a good deal of time touching and exploring them. Some children however, are taught that this exploration is something to be ashamed of and is unacceptable. Because girls' genitals are difficult to view without a mirror, girls tend to be less familiar with their genitals than are boys.

In this chapter, we explore female anatomy and physiology in adulthood followed by an overview of female development, puberty, menopause, and common reproductive health issues. Although there are similarities during development and adulthood in individual female and male and intersexed anatomy and physiology, there are also differences. Unlike males, females have fluctuating hormone levels, monthly menstruation cycles that begin during puberty, and experience menopause. The material describing female sexual biology in this chapter and male sexual biology in Chapter 4, including the material on differences in sexual development in both chapters, will set the stage for exploring gender development, identity, and roles in Chapter 8, and the larger, fascinating world of human sexuality that makes up the remainder of this book.

The Female Sexual and Reproductive System

It is important for women, men, and intersexed individuals to understand the structure of the human reproductive systems. Women who have not done a thorough genital self-examination should do so, not only because it is an important part of the body to learn to appreciate but because any changes in genital appearance over the lifespan should be brought to the attention of a **gynecologist** or other health care provider. See the accompanying Sex in Real Life for instructions on performing a genital self-examination.

External Genitalia
The Vulva

Although many people refer to the female's external sex organs collectively as the "vagina," this is technically incorrect; the more accurate term for the whole region is **vulva.** The vulva is made up of the mons veneris, the labia majora and labia minora, the vestibule, the perineum, and the clitoris (see Figure 3.1). Although the

gynecologist
A physician who specializes in the study and treatment of disorders of the female reproductive system.

vulva
The collective designation for the external genitalia of the female.

All of the women in these photos have "normal" bodies. Individual differences in weight and size and shape of hips, breasts, and thighs, and even pubic hair are normal.

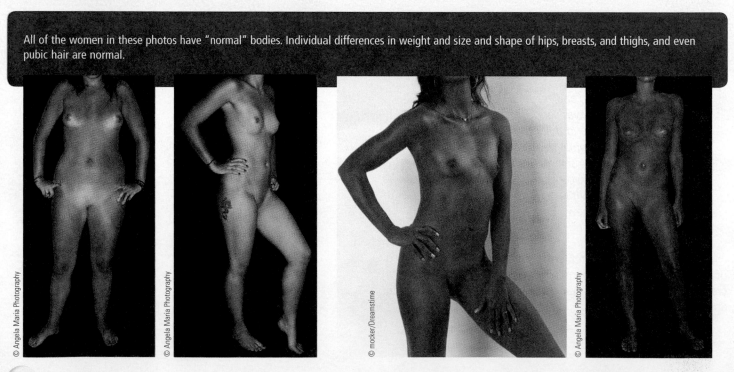

© Angela Maria Photography

© Angela Maria Photography

© mocker/Dreamstime

© Angela Maria Photography

SEX
in Real Life

Female Genital Self-Examination

Many female health problems can be identified when changes are detected in the internal or external sexual organs; therefore, self-examination has an important health and self-education function. If you are female, it will serve you well to follow this simple procedure once a month. If you are male, understanding this procedure will help you better understand why it is so important for females to examine their genitals regularly.

Begin by examining the outside of your genitals; using a hand mirror will help. Using your fingers to spread open the labia majora, try to identify the other external structures—the labia minora, the prepuce, the introitus (opening) of the vagina, and the urethral opening. Look at the way your genitals look while sitting, lying down, standing up, or squatting. Feel the different textures of each part of the vagina, and look carefully at the colouration and size of the tissues you can see. Both colouration and size can change with sexual arousal either through masturbation or sexual activity with a partner. Such changes are temporary, however, and

the genitals should return to normal within a couple of hours after sexual activity. Any changes over time in colour, firmness, or shape of the genitals should be brought to the attention of a health professional.

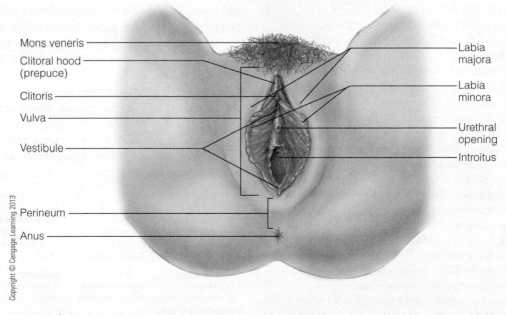

© Thomas Michael Corcoran/PhotoEdit

Genital self-examination can help a woman become more comfortable with her own body.

If it is not uncomfortable, you may want to move back the prepuce, or hood, over the clitoris and try to see the clitoral glans. Although the clitoris is easier to see when erect, note how it fits beneath the prepuce. Note also whether there is any

whitish material beneath the prepuce; fluids can accumulate and solidify in this area and you should gently clean beneath the prepuce regularly.

If you place a finger inside your vagina, you should be able to feel the pubic bone in the front inside part of your vagina. It is slightly behind the pubic bone that the G-spot is reported to be, but it is difficult for most women to stimulate the G-spot (assuming they have one) with their own fingers. Squat and press down with your stomach muscles as you push your fingers deeply in the vagina, and at the top of the vagina you may be able to feel your cervix, which feels a little like the tip of your nose. Note how it feels to touch the cervix (some women have a slightly uncomfortable feeling when their cervix is touched). Feeling comfortable inserting your fingers into your vagina will help you if you choose a barrier method of birth control, such as the contraceptive sponge or cervical cap, all of which must be inserted deep within the vagina at the cervix (see Chapter 13).

Mons veneris

Clitoral hood (prepuce)

Clitoris

Vulva

Vestibule

Perineum

Anus

Labia majora

Labia minora

Urethral opening

Introitus

Copyright © Cengage Learning 2013

FIGURE **3.1** The external genital structures of the mature female.

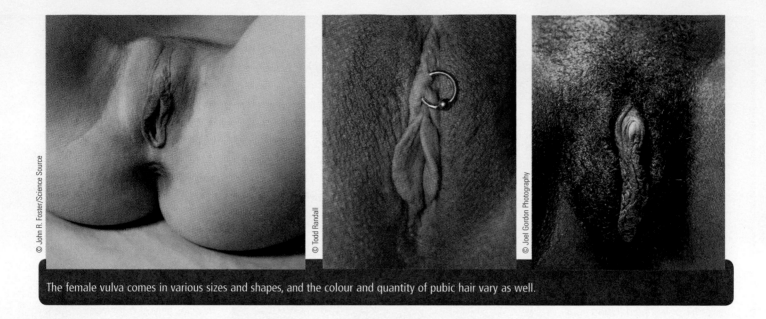

The female vulva comes in various sizes and shapes, and the colour and quantity of pubic hair vary as well.

vagina does open into the vulva, it is mainly an internal sex organ and is discussed in the next section.

The Mons Veneris

The fatty cushion resting over the front surface of the pubic bone is called the **mons veneris** or **mons pubis.** The mons veneris becomes covered with pubic hair during puberty, and although it is considered a stimulating place to caress during lovemaking, it serves largely as a protective cushion for the genitals, especially during sexual activity.

On Your Mind

I've always been worried about the size and shape of my vaginal lips. They just seem too big and floppy. At this point, I'm so embarrassed about them that I can't imagine ever being comfortable showing them to anyone. Is there anything I can do to fix them?

The size, length, shape, colour, texture, and symmetry of the labia and clitoris vary greatly among women (Lloyd, Crouch, Minto, Liao, & Creighton, 2005). Some women have long labial lips, whereas others have shorter ones. With the introduction of smaller swimsuits, bikini waxes, and exposure to various pornographic images, many women today are feeling increased pressure to undergo genital plastic surgery in search of a "designer vagina" (Goodman, 2009; Goodman et al., 2010; Liao & Creighton, 2007). However, there are several potential risks to these procedures, including pain, decreased sensitivity, and changes in sexual pleasure (Liao et al., 2010). Our cultural fixation with perfection has also led some women to undergo G-spot enhancement (injecting collagen into the area to increase sensitivity) and even anal bleaching (using bleach to restore the anus to a pinkish hue). A recent policy statement by the Obstetricians and Gynecologist Society of Canada (2013, p. E2) states that "There is little evidence to support any of the female genital cosmetic surgeries in terms of improvement to sexual satisfaction or self-image."

The Labia Majora

The **labia majora** (LAY-bee-uh muh-JOR-uh) (outer lips) are two longitudinal folds of fatty tissue that extend from the mons, frame the rest of the female genitalia, and meet at the perineum (the tissue between the vagina and the anus). The skin of the outer labia majora is pigmented and covered with hair, whereas the inner surface is hairless and contains sebaceous (oil) glands. During sexual excitement, the labia majora fill with blood and engorge, making the entire pubic region appear to swell.

The Labia Minora

The **labia minora** (LAY-bee-uh muh-NOR-uh) (inner lips) are two smaller pink skin folds situated inside the labia majora. They are generally more delicate, and thinner than the labia majora and join at the clitoris to form the **prepuce** (PREE-peus), the "hood" over the clitoris. The labia minora are varied in size and shape, and in some women may extend past the labia majora. The labia minora contain no hair follicles, although they are rich in sebaceous glands, blood vessels and nerve endings. They also contain some erectile tissue and serve to protect the vagina and urethra. During sexual arousal, the labia minora may darken, although the appearance can differ considerably among women.

mons veneris or mons pubis
The mound of fatty tissue over the female pubic bone, also referred to as mons pubis, meaning "pubic mound."

labia majora
Two longitudinal folds of skin extending downward and backward from the mons pubis of the female.

labia minora
Two small folds of mucous membrane lying within the labia majora of the female.

prepuce
A loose fold of skin that covers the clitoris.

The Clitoris

For a long time, people believed that the **clitoris** (KLIT-uh-rus) was only a small pocket of erectile tissue located under the prepuce. The invisibility of the clitoris led many to believe that this was the case. In 1991, a group of researchers developed a new description of the clitoris that encompasses all of the clitoral structures (see Figure 3.2) (Federation of Feminist Women's Health Centers, 1991). This more expansive definition of the clitoris was confirmed in 2005 with magnetic resonance imaging (O'Connell & DeLancey, 2005). In addition to the clitoral glans and shaft, which are part of the external genitalia, the clitoris is composed of a pair of crura (legs) that are internal extensions of the clitoris. The crura wrap around the urethra. There is also a pair of vestibular bulbs of the clitoris that lie under the labia minora and majora. These vestibular bulbs, crura, shaft, and glans of the clitoris form an erectile tissue cluster that fills with blood during sexual arousal.

Homologous to the penis (see Table 4.1 in Chapter 4 for a list of structures that are homologous between males and females), the clitoris is richly supplied with blood vessels, as well as nerve endings. The clitoral glans is a particularly sensitive to tactile stimulation. The glans, shaft, crura and vestibular bulbs, enlarge and engorge with blood in much the same way as the penis does during physical arousal. In addition, the clitoris is the only human organ for which the sole known function is to bring sexual pleasure (we discuss the clitoris and sexual pleasure in more detail in Chapter 14).

The clitoral glans is difficult to see in many women unless the prepuce is pulled back, although in some women the glans may swell enough during sexual excitement to emerge from under the prepuce (see the Sex in Real Life feature). It is easy to feel the clitoral glans, however, by gently grasping the prepuce and rolling it between the fingers. Some women do not enjoy direct stimulation of the glans and prefer stimulation through the prepuce. It is important to clean under the prepuce, for secretions can accumulate underneath and if left uncleaned, may produce an unpleasant odour.

In some cultures, the clitoris is removed surgically in a ritual **circumcision,** often referred to as a **clitorectomy.** Other parts of the vulva can also be removed in a procedure known as **infibulation** (in-fib-you-LAY-shun) (see accompanying Sexual Diversity in Our World feature).

Animal Variations — The Hyena and the Clitoris

In humans the clitoris is small relative to the male penis. In a curious twist on development however, in female hyenas the clitoris looks almost as large as the male penis! This enlargement of the clitoris in female hyenas is due to an abundance of androgen exposure early in development (Frank, 1997). For more on the effects of testosterone exposure effects on human female development see the section on CAH girls later in this chapter.

© Anup Shah/Visuals Unlimited, Inc.

In this photo the structure that looks like a penis is a clitoris on a female hyena.

REAL Research

The glans of the clitoris, although much smaller than the penis, has two to three times more sensory nerve endings than the glans of the penis (Shih, Cold, & Yang, 2013). The density of nerve endings in the glans clitoris may constitute the highest concentration of nerve endings anywhere in the human body, including the tongue or fingertips.

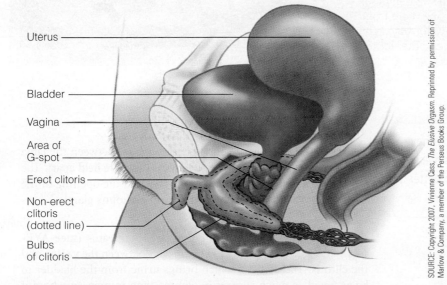

Uterus

Bladder

Vagina

Area of G-spot

Erect clitoris

Non-erect clitoris (dotted line)

Bulbs of clitoris

SOURCE: Copyright 2007, Vivienne Cass, *The Elusive Orgasm*. Reprinted by permission of Marlow & Company, a member of the Perseus Books Group.

FIGURE **3.2** Side inner view of the erect clitoris.

---

clitoris
An erectile organ of the female located under the prepuce and the labia; an organ of sexual pleasure.

circumcision
Surgical removal of the clitoris in women; also referred to as clitorectomy.

clitorectomy
Surgical removal of the clitoris; also referred to as circumcision.

infibulation
The ritual removal of the clitoris, prepuce, and labia, and the sewing together of the vestibule. Although this is practised in many African societies, today many are working to eliminate the practice.

Female Genital Mutilation

Female genital mutilation (FGM) involves partial or total removal of the external female genitalia for non-medical reasons (World Health Organization, 2008). Throughout history, FGM has been performed to distinguish "respectable" women and to ensure and preserve a girl's virginity (Gruenbaum, 2006; O'Connor, 2008). These procedures are also thought to make the female genitals "clean" and "beautiful" by eliminating masculine parts, such as the clitoris (Johansen, 2007). The most common reason given for undergoing such procedures is culture and tradition (Carcopino et al., 2004; Dare et al., 2004).

The World Health Organization has proposed four classifications of FGM:

- Type I: Partial or total removal of the clitoris and/or prepuce (clitorectomy)

- Type II: Partial or total removal of the clitoris and the labia minora with or without excision of the labia majora

- Type III: Narrowing of the vaginal orifice by cutting the labia minora and labia majora with or without excision of clitoris (infibulation)

- Type IV: All other harmful procedures to female genitalia for non-medical purposes including piercing, pricking, scraping, and cauterization*

*SOURCE: Printed from World Health Organization, "Classification of female genital mutilation." Retrieved October 4, 2015 from http://www.who.int/reproductivehealth/topics/fgm/overview/en/.

It is estimated that 130 million women around the world have experienced FGM, and another 2 million girls and young women undergo FGM procedures each year (Dattijo et al., 2010). Although FGM occurs all over the world, it is most prevalent in the eastern, northeastern, and western regions of Africa, some countries in Asia and the Middle East, and among certain immigrant communities in North America and Europe (World Health Organization, 2008).

FGM procedures are usually done on girls between the ages of four and eight; although in some cultures, it is performed later (Dare et al., 2004). Procedures are often done without anesthesia or antiseptic, and the majority of procedures are performed by medically untrained personnel (Dare et al., 2004). The most severe type of circumcision involves the complete removal of the clitoris and labia minora, and also the scraping of the labia majora with knives, broken bottles, or razor blades (Carcopino et al., 2004). The remaining tissue is sewn together, leaving a matchstick-sized hole to allow for the passing of urine and menstrual blood. The young girl's legs are then bound together with rope, and she is immobilized for anywhere from 14 to 40 days for the circumcision to heal. The tighter the

girl's infibulation, the higher the bride price will be for her.

FGM can cause extreme pain, urinary complications or dysfunction, shock, hemorrhage, infection, scarring, recurrent urinary infections, retention of menses at menarche, vulval cysts, and pelvic inflammatory disease (Nour, 2004; World Health Organization, 2008). Of these symptoms, severe pain and bleeding are most common (Dare et al., 2004).

There is ongoing controversy about what Canadians and others should do to try to discourage this practice (Dattijo et al., 2010; O'Connor, 2008). The United States has been strongly opposed to the practice of FGM and has worked hard to help reduce the practice. In 2008, the World Health Organization and other United Nations agencies launched a new Interagency Statement on Eliminating Female Genital Mutilation. They hope to see a worldwide end to the practice of FGM within the next decade.

© Ulrike Koternann/epa/Corbis

REAL Research Elite female athletes have been found to have better clitoral blood flow than non-athletes, which has been found to contribute to better sexual health and functioning (Karatas et al., 2010).

vestibule
The entire region between the labia minora, including the urethra and introitus.

The Vestibule

The **vestibule** is the name for the entire region between the labia minora and can be clearly seen when the labia are held apart. The vestibule contains the opening of the urethra, the opening of the vagina, also called the introitus, and the Bartholin's glands.

THE URETHRAL MEATUS The opening, or meatus (mee-AYE-tuss), to the urethra (yoo-REE-thruh) lies between the vagina and the clitoris. The urethra, which brings urine from the bladder to be excreted, is much shorter in women than in men, in whom it goes through the penis. A shorter urethra allows bacteria greater access into the urinary tract, making women much more susceptible to **urinary tract infections (UTIs)** (Azam, 2000; Kunin, 1997). One in five women will develop a UTI in her lifetime, and 20 percent of these women will experience a recurrence of the UTI after treatment (Hooton, 2003). Common symptoms for UTI include pain or burning in the urethra or bladder and an increased urge to urinate. Over-the-counter medication can help decrease pain, but antibiotics are necessary to cure the infection. Consuming cranberry products (i.e., drinks, breads) may be effective in decreasing UTI recurrence (Epp et al., 2010), although a recent meta-analysis suggests that cranberry juice and cranberry products are minimal in their effectiveness (Freire, 2013). Scientists are also working on a vaccine to prevent UTIs (Serino et al., 2010).

THE INTROITUS AND THE HYMEN   The entrance, or **introitus** (in-TROID-us), of the vagina also lies in the vestibule. The introitus is usually covered at birth by a fold of tissue known as the **hymen** (HIGH-men). The hymen is a highly variable structure in thickness and extent, and is sometimes absent). The centre of the hymen is usually perforated, and it is through this perforation that menstrual flow leaves the vagina and that a tampon may be inserted. If the hymen is intact, it will usually rupture easily and tear the first time a woman has sexual intercourse. This tearing of the hymen is often accompanied by a small amount of bleeding. If the woman is sexually aroused and well lubricated, the rupture of the hymen usually does not cause more than a brief moment's discomfort. In rare cases, a woman has an **imperforate hymen,** which is usually detected during puberty because her menstrual flow is blocked. A simple surgical procedure can open the imperforate hymen.

An intact hymen has been a symbol of "purity" throughout history, a sign that a woman has not engaged in sexual intercourse. In reality, many activities can tear the hymen, including vigorous exercise, horseback or bike riding, masturbation, or the insertion of tampons or other objects into the vagina (Cook & Dickens, 2009). Still, in many cultures during many historical eras, the absence of bloodstained sheets on the wedding night was enough to condemn a woman as "wanton" (promiscuous), and some knowing mothers encouraged their newlywed daughters to have a little vial of blood from a chicken or other animal to pour on the sheet of their bridal bed, just in case. Although virginity "testing" (to check for an intact hymen) is against the law in many parts of the world, including Turkey, Indonesia, and parts of South Africa, illegal virginity tests are still performed. In North America a recent survey of pediatricians and parents found a large disparity in what is known about hymen physiology between the two groups. Additionally, the majority of pediatricians surveyed

did not feel comfortable educating parents about the hymen (Brown, Lamb, Perkins, Naim, & Starling, 2014). Reconstructive surgery to repair a ruptured hymen, called *hymenoplasty,* is available in many countries, with high demand from Middle Eastern, Korean, and Latina women (Krikorian, 2004). However, many physicians are afraid to perform these surgeries because of fear of repercussions (Essen et al., 2010; O'Connor, 2008).

BARTHOLIN'S GLANDS   Bartholin's (BAR-tha-lenz) **glands,** are bean-shaped glands with ducts that empty into the vestibule in the middle of the labia minora. Historically, Bartholin's glands have been presumed to provide some vaginal lubrication during sexual arousal; however, research by Masters and Johnson (see Chapter 2) found that lubrication of the vagina is a result of vaginal transudation. Ultimately, the purpose of the Bartholin's glands during sexual intercourse remains unclear. These glands can become infected and form a cyst or abscess, causing pain and swelling in the labial and vaginal areas. Bartholin's gland cysts are most common in women of reproductive age and are typically treated with antibiotics and/or surgery (Bhide et al., 2010).

The Anus and Perineum

The anus is the external opening of the rectum through which feces is expelled. The area of tissue between the vagina and the anus is called the **perineum** (pear-uh-NEE-um), and research has found this area to be approximately twice as long in male versus female children at birth (Thankamony, Ong, Dunger, Acerini, & Hughes, 2009). This difference is likely due to the prenatal (in utero) exposure of males to androgens. The perineum is rich with nerve endings, and some men and women like to have this area stroked during sexual behaviour.

Internal Sex Organs

Now that we've covered the female external genitalia, let's explore the internal sex organs. The internal female sex organs include the vagina, uterus, cervix, Fallopian tubes, and ovaries (see Figure 3.3).

The Vagina

The **vagina** is a thin-walled tube extending from the cervix of the uterus to the external genitalia; it serves as the main female organ of intercourse, a passageway for arriving sperm, and a canal through which menstrual fluid and babies can pass from the uterus. It is tilted toward the back in most women and thus forms a 90-degree angle with the uterus, which is commonly tilted

---

urinary tract infection (UTI)
Infection of the urinary tract, often resulting in a frequent urge to urinate, painful burning in the bladder or urethra during urination, and fatigue.

introitus
Entrance to the vagina.

hymen
A thin fold of vascularized mucous membrane at the vaginal opening.

imperforate hymen
An abnormally closed hymen that usually does not allow the exit of menstrual fluid.

Bartholin's glands
A pair of glands on either side of the vaginal opening that open by a duct into the space between the hymen and the labia minora; also referred to as the greater vestibular glands.

perineum
Area between the vagina and the anus.

vagina
A thin-walled muscular tube that leads from the uterus to the vestibule and is used for sexual intercourse and as a passageway for menstrual fluid, sperm, and a newborn baby.

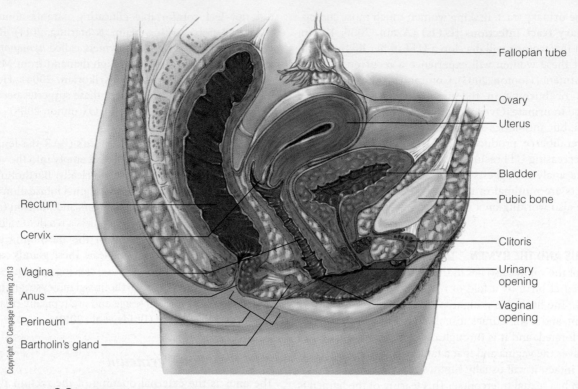

Fallopian tube
Ovary
Uterus
Bladder
Pubic bone
Clitoris
Urinary opening
Vaginal opening

Rectum
Cervix
Vagina
Anus
Perineum
Bartholin's gland

Copyright © Cengage Learning 2013

FIGURE 3.3 The female internal reproductive system (side view).

forward. The vagina is approximately 10 centimetres (4 inches) in length when relaxed but contains numerous folds that help it expand somewhat like an accordion. The vagina can expand to accommodate a penis during intercourse and can stretch four to five times its normal width during childbirth. The vagina does not contain glands per se but is lubricated via small openings on the vaginal walls during engorgement (almost as if the vagina is sweating) and by mucus produced from glands on the cervix. These vaginal secretions are important for lubricating the vagina during sex and also for maintaining the internal health of the vagina. Within the vagina are bacteria that keep the vaginal environment slightly acidic, which prevents the growth of unwanted bacteria that can cause odour or irritation. It is important to let the vagina clean itself and maintain its own health without the use of douching or feminine cleansing products (Cottrell, 2010; Farage, Lennon, & Ajavi, 2011).

A spot about the size of a dime or quarter in the lower third of the front part of the vagina, the **Gräfenberg spot (G-spot),** was first described by Ernest Gräfenberg in 1950. The G-spot is found about 5–8 centimetres up the anterior (front or stomach) side of the vagina, just past the pubic bone (see Figure 3.4; Whipple,

2000). The existence of the G-spot has been a controversial issue in the field of human sexuality for many years (Buisson et al., 2010). Although some women report pleasurable sensations when this area is stimulated (Foldes & Buisson, 2009; Jannini et al., 2010), there has never been any scientific proof of the existence of the G-spot (Pastor, 2010). Today, growing research on clitoral structures indicates that increased sensitivity in the G-spot area may actually be caused by stimulation of the crura and/or vestibular bulbs of the clitoris (Foldes & Buisson, 2009).

The Uterus

The **uterus** is a thick-walled, hollow, muscular organ in the pelvis sandwiched between the bladder in front and the rectum behind. It is approximately the shape of an inverted pear, with a dome-shaped top (fundus), a hollow body, and the doughnut-shaped cervix at the bottom. The uterus has several functions: It undergoes a cycle of change every month that leads to menstruation, and it provides a path for sperm to reach the **ovum** via the Fallopian tubes, which returns to the uterus after it is fertilized and implants itself in the uterine wall. The uterus also nourishes and protects the developing fetus during gestation and provides the contractions for expulsion of the mature fetus during labour. The uterus is about 8 centimetres (3 inches) long and flares to about 5 centimetres (2 inches) wide, but it increases greatly in size and weight during and after a pregnancy (see Chapter 5), and atrophies after menopause.

The uterine wall is about 2.5 centimetres (1 inch) thick and made up of three layers (see Figure 3.4). The outer layer, or **perimetrium,** is part of the tissue that covers most abdominal organs. The muscular layer of the uterus, the **myometrium,** contracts to expel menstrual fluid and to push the fetus out of the womb during delivery.

Gräfenberg spot (G-spot)
A structure that is said to lie on the anterior (front) wall of the vagina and is reputed to be a seat of sexual pleasure when stimulated.

uterus
The hollow muscular organ in females that is the site of menstruation, implantation of the fertilized ovum, and labour; also referred to as the womb.

ovum
The female reproductive cell or gamete; plural is ova. In common parlance the ovum is often referred to as an egg.

perimetrium
The outer wall of the uterus.

myometrium
The smooth muscle layer of the uterus.

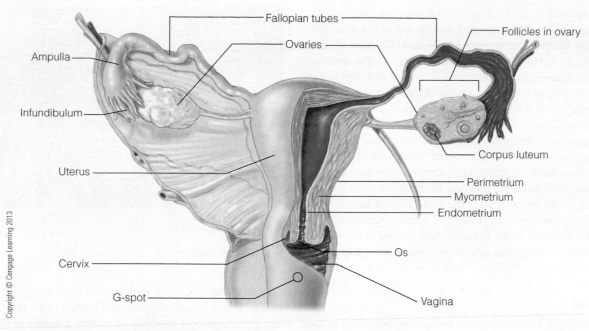

FIGURE **3.4** The female internal reproductive system (front view).

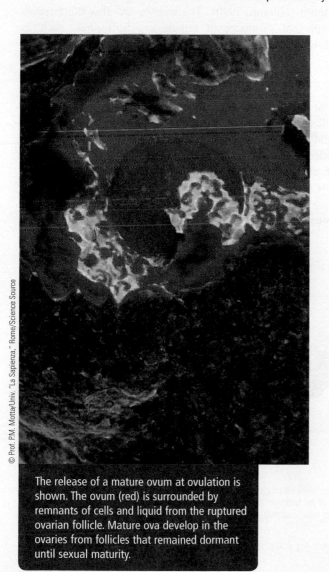

The release of a mature ovum at ovulation is shown. The ovum (red) is surrounded by remnants of cells and liquid from the ruptured ovarian follicle. Mature ova develop in the ovaries from follicles that remained dormant until sexual maturity.

The inner layer of the uterus, the **endometrium,** responds to fluctuating hormone levels, and the rich vascularised layer that builds up on the endometrial wall each month is shed during menstruation.

The Cervix

The **cervix** (SERV-ix) is the lower portion of the uterus that contains the opening, or **os,** leading into the uterine cavity. It is through the os that menstrual fluid flows out of the uterus and that sperm gain entrance. Glands of the cervix secrete mucus with varying properties during the monthly cycle. During **ovulation,** the mucus helps sperm transport through the os, and during infertile periods, it can block the sperm from entering. During childbirth, the cervix softens and the os dilates to allow the baby to pass through. The cervix can be seen with a mirror during a pelvic examination, and women should not hesitate to ask their gynecologist or other medical professional to show it to them. The cervix can also be felt at the top end of the vagina.

The Fallopian Tubes

Fallopian (fuh-LOH-pee-un) **tubes,** also called **oviducts,** are 10-centimetre-long, trumpet-shaped tubes that extend laterally from the sides of the uterus. From the side of the uterus, the tube expands

endometrium
The mucous membrane lining the uterus.

cervix
The doughnut-shaped bottom part of the uterus that protrudes into the top of the vagina.

os
The opening of the cervix that allows passage between the vagina and the uterus.

ovulation
The phase of the menstrual cycle in which an ovum is released.

Fallopian tubes
Two ducts that transport ova from the ovary to the uterus; also referred to as oviducts.

oviducts
Another name for the Fallopian tubes.

Female Sexual Anatomy, Development, and Health   **63**

into an ampulla, which curves around to a trumpet-shaped end, the **infundibulum** (in-fun-DIB-bue-lum). At the end of the infundibulum are finger-like projections called **fimbriae** (FIM-bree-ee) that curl around but do not touch the ovary (see Figure 3.4). The fimbriae sense a chemical messages released from the ovary that signals the release of the ovum and they begin a series of muscular contractions to help move the ovum down the Fallopian tube.

The inner surfaces of the Fallopian tubes are covered by cilia (hair-like projections); the constant beating action of the cilia creates a current along which the ovum is moved toward the uterus. The entire transit time from ovulation until arrival inside the uterus is normally about three days. Fertilization of the ovum usually takes place in the ampulla because, after the first 12 to 24 hours, post-ovulation fertilization is no longer likely to occur. Occasionally, the fertilized ovum implants in the Fallopian tube instead of the uterus, causing a potentially dangerous ectopic pregnancy (see Chapter 5).

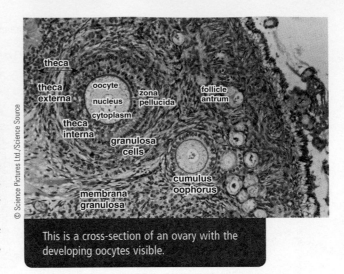

This is a cross-section of an ovary with the developing oocytes visible.

The Ovaries

The mature ovary is a structure most commonly described as the size and shape of a large almond shell. With age, the ovaries become smaller and firmer, and after menopause, they may become difficult for gynecologists to feel during an examination. The ovaries have dual responsibilities: to produce ova and to secrete hormones.

The ovary is the repository of **oocytes** (OH-oh-sites), also known as ova, or eggs, in the female. A woman is born with approximately 250 000 ova in each ovary, each sitting in its own primary follicle (Rome, 1998). A small fraction of these oocytes will develop into mature eggs during a woman's reproductive years (Macklon & Fauser, 2000). The primary follicle contains an immature ovum surrounded by a thin layer of follicular cells. At ovulation, the follicle bursts, and the ovum begins its journey down the Fallopian tube. The surface of a mature ovary is thus usually pitted and dimpled at sites of previous ovulations.

Ovulation can occur each month from either the right or left ovary. No one knows why one or the other ovary releases an ovum any given month; it seems to be mostly a matter of chance. If one ovary is removed, however, the other ovary will often ovulate every month (Nilsson, 1990). The ovaries are also the female's most important producer of female sex hormones, such as estrogen, which we discuss later in this chapter.

The Breasts

Breasts, or mammary glands, are modified sweat glands that produce milk to nourish a newborn child. The breasts contain fatty tissue and milk-producing glands, and are capped by a **nipple** surrounded by a round, pigmented area called the **areola** (ah-REE-oh-luh). Each breast contains between 15 and 20 lobes, made up of a number of compartments that contain **alveoli** (al-VEE-o-lie), the milk-secreting glands. Alveoli empty into **lactiferous** (lak-TIF-er-ous) **ducts**, which, in turn, pass the milk

The female breast is mostly fatty tissue and can take various shapes and sizes.

infundibulum
The funnel- or trumpet-shaped widening of the Fallopian tubes just before the fimbria.

fimbriae
The finger-like projections at each end of the Fallopian tubes that transport ovum from the ovary into the Fallopian tube. Singular is fimbria.

oocyte
A cell from which an ovum develops.

nipple
A pigmented, wrinkled protuberance on the surface of the breast that contains ducts for the release of milk.

areola
The pigmented ring around the nipple of the breast.

alveoli
Small cavities in the breast where milk is produced. Singular is alveolus.

lactiferous ducts
Small tubes (ducts) that connect the alveoli to the nipple and allow milk to be stored for secretion.

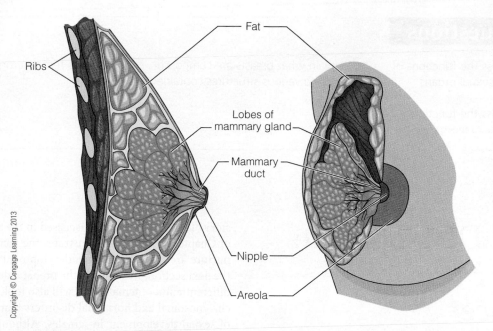

Copyright © Cengage Learning 2013

FIGURE 3.5 The female breast.

Labels: Fat · Ribs · Lobes of mammary gland · Mammary duct · Nipple · Areola

into the lactiferous sinuses, where the milk is stored until the **lactiferous sinuses** release it from the nipple (Figure 3.5). When **lactation** begins, infant suckling stimulates the posterior pituitary gland to release **prolactin,** a hormone that signals milk synthesis. **Oxytocin** is a hormone that signals to the breast to release milk from the alveoli into the lactiferous ducts then to the lactiferous sinuses for milk to be ejected. Milk ejection can occur when the breast is compressed either by a babies suckling, by a hand or by a breast pump.

Most people see the breasts as an erogenous zone and include stimulation of the breasts in sexual activity. Some women can even experience orgasm from breast and nipple stimulation alone. However, many women are uncomfortable about the size and shape of their breasts. Because breasts are a constant source of attention in our society and are considered an important part of a woman's attractiveness, women may worry that their breasts are unattractive, too small, or too large. According to a recent article in *Elevate Magazine* (Van De Geyn, 2013), more women in Canada would rather have their breasts enhanced than have liposuction. In an interview, Dr. William Andrade, FRCSC, of Newmarket, Ontario, stated that breast augmentation is often requested for the following reasons:

Some of the most common reasons include patients who have breast shape concerns (those who have a significant difference in the size and shape of their breasts); patients who want to

On Your Mind

I had my nipples pierced, but now I'm wondering whether I'll be able to breast-feed later on. Is there any research on nipple piercing and breast-feeding?

restore their previous breast shape (after childbirth or normal age-related changes); as well as women whose breasts appear normal, but are small in proportion to their other body features —they want a result that is in proportion to their body frame.

Body art, including nipple and genital piercing, is more popular today than ever (Bosello et al., 2010; Kapsimalakou et al., 2010; Kluger, 2010; Oultram, 2009). If you are going to have your nipples pierced, it is important to seek out a reputable technician to do the piercing and be sure to maintain good after-care to minimize the risk for infection. Most nipple piercings are done horizontally, which decreases the risk for scarring. An improperly pierced nipple, or frequent re-piercings, can lead to blocked milk ducts (Garbin et al., 2009). Because each nipple has several milk ducts, if there were scarring in one area of the nipple, it is possible that other milk ducts will still be functional. Even so, a small percentage of women with breast piercings experience problems breast-feeding, including duct obstruction and/or impaired lactation (Garbin et al, 2009; Gollapalli et al., 2010; Kapsimalakou et al., 2010; Kluger, 2010; Meltzer, 2005). Nipple jewellery should be removed before breast-feeding because it can be a choking hazard.

lactiferous sinuses	**lactation**	**prolactin**	**oxytocin**
The final storage spot for milk prior to its release from the breast via the nipple.	The collective name for milk creation, secretion, and ejection from the nipple.	A hormone secreted by the pituitary gland that initiates and maintains milk secretion.	A hormone secreted by the hypothalamus that stimulates contraction of both the uterus for delivery of the newborn and the mammary gland ducts for lactation.

Review Questions

1 Identify and discuss the functions of the external female sexual organs.

2 Identify and discuss the functions of the internal female sexual organs.

3 Explain what breasts are composed of and the various structures contained in them.

4 Discuss female erogenous zones.

Prenatal Development: X and Y Make the Difference

Before we go any further in our overview of female reproductive anatomy and female development, the synonymous use of the words *sex* and *gender* needs to be clarified. Researchers usually use the word **sex** to refer to the biological aspects of being male, female or intersexed, and **gender** to refer to the behavioural, psychological, and social characteristics of men and women (Pryzgoda & Chrisler, 2000).

When a baby is born, new parents are eager to hear whether "It's a girl!" or "It's a boy!" Some newborn babies however have ambiguous genitalia, and it is impossible to tell whether the sex of the newborn is a boy or a girl. A child with a variation of sexual development, such as a child with **gonads** (testes or ovaries) of one sex but ambiguous external genitalia, is often referred to as an **intersexed** individual (Lee et al., 2006; Marino, 2010). Assigning a new term for children born with ambiguous genitalia has helped to improve our understanding about this condition as a congenital disorder (Aaronson & Aaronson).

For many years, scientists have debated whether gender is more genetics and biology ("nature") or social environment and upbringing ("nurture"). Or is it a combination of the two? The story of Bruce and Brenda discussed in the Sex in Real Life feature of Chapter 8 (see p. 221) illustrates the fact that both nature and nurture are important in the development of sex and gender. In the next section, we focus on the prenatal development and sexual differentiation of females. We will also look at several examples of chromosomal and hormonal disorders that can lead to variations of sexual development in females. Although these variations of female sexual development are not common, their existence has helped us learn a great deal about how differences in the development of a person's sex and/or the development of their gender come to exist. Gender development, roles, and identity will be discussed at length in Chapter 8.

Sexual Reproduction

The majority of human beings have a biological urge to reproduce and pass on their genetic material to subsequent offspring. Any species that does not have functional reproductive equipment and a desire to use it will not last very long. Some organisms, such as baker's yeast, simply split in two, creating new yeast offspring that are genetically identical to the parent yeast. More complex organisms, however, reproduce through **sexual reproduction,** in which two parents each donate a **gamete** (GAM-ate), or **germ cell,** the two of which combine to create a new organism.

The germ cells from the male (sperm) and the much larger but also microscopic germ cell from the female (egg, or ovum) each contain half of the new person's genes and determine his or her sex, hair and eye colour, general body shape, and literally millions of other aspects of the developing fetus's physiology, development, and emotional nature. For this to occur, your body must take the blueprint of your genes provide and build **proteins**. These proteins are what your body uses to construct your tissue and bones, as well as your genitals and reproductive organs. Gene expression, however, does not stop once a human body has been built. The proteins that genes code for are constantly made throughout a person's lifetime and protein production or cessation is important for many of the life events that relate to human sexuality, including the advent of puberty and female **menopause.**

The cells in the human body, with the exception of sperm and ovum, contain 23 chromosomal pairs. One half of each pair is inherited from the mother and the other half of the pair is inherited from the father. Twenty-two of the pairs look almost identical

sex
The biological aspects of being male or female.

gender
The behavioural, psychological and social characteristics of being male or female.

gonads
The male and female sex glands—ovaries and testes.

intersexed
A child with gonads (testes or ovaries) of one sex but ambiguous external genitalia. May also be referred to as a difference in sexual development.

sexual reproduction
The production of offspring from the union of two parents.

gamete
A male or female reproductive cell—the spermatozoon in males or ovum in females; also referred to as a germ cell.

germ cell
A male or female reproductive cell—the spermatozoon or ovum; also referred to as a gamete.

proteins
The building blocks the human body uses to construct itself.

menopause
The cessation of menstruation.

and are referred to as **autosomes;** the exception is the 23rd pair, the **sex chromosomes.** The two sex chromosomes, which determine whether a person is male or female, are made up of an X chromosome donated by the mother through the ovum and either an X or a Y chromosome donated by the father's sperm. In normal development, if the male contributes an X chromosome, the child will be female (XX); if he contributes a Y chromosome, the child will be male (XY).

All the cells of the body (somatic cells), except gametes, contain 23 pairs of chromosomes (46 total) and called *diploid* (meaning "double"). However, if a merging sperm and egg also had 23 pairs each, they would create a child with 46 pairs of chromosomes. For children that have too many chromosomes and thus too many genes, the amount of protein production in cells changes and biological development is altered. This is what occurs in females who are XO or XXX. We will return to these two genetic syndromes in a few pages. So gametes are *haploid,* meaning they contain half the number of chromosomes (23) of a somatic cell (46). During **fertilization,** a haploid sperm and a haploid egg join to produce a diploid **zygote** (ZIE-goat) containing 23 chromosomal pairs, with half of each pair coming from each parent. The fertilized ovum (zygote) can now undergo **mitosis,** reproducing its 23 chromosomal pairs as it grows.

Whether the zygote (fertilized ovum) is a genetic male or female is determined at the moment of conception. As this zygote develops and becomes a multicellular organism or **embryo,** differentiation of an embryo's sexual characteristics also occur. If sexual differentiation proceeds without a problem, the embryo will develop into a **fetus** with male-typical or female-typical sexual characteristics.

Sexual Differentiation in Utero

A human baby normally undergoes around nine months of **gestation.** At about four to six weeks, the first tissues that will become the embryo's gonads begin to develop. Sexual differentiation begins a week or two later and is initiated by the sex chromosomes, which control at least four important aspects of sexual development: (1) the internal sexual organs (e.g., whether the fetus develops ovaries or testes); (2) the external sex organs (such

as the penis or clitoris); (3) the hormonal environment of the embryo; and (4) the sexual differentiation of the brain (Wilson & Davies, 2007; Savic et al., 2010).

Internal Sex Organs

In the first few weeks of development, XX (female) and XY (male) embryos are anatomically identical, however, around the fifth to sixth week, the undifferentiated gonads begin to develop into primitive gonads. In most females, the primitive gonads, due to the influence of estrogens from the mother, begin to differentiate into ovaries (rather than **testes**) by the 10th or 11th week. The primitive duct systems, the **Müllerian** (myul-EAR-ee-an) **duct** (female), **Wolffian** (wolf–EE-an) **duct** (male) also develops during this time (Krone et al., 2007). In female embryos, the lack of androgen exposure results in the disappearance of the Wolffian ducts, and the Müllerian ducts develop and fuse to form the uterus and upper third of the vagina. The unfused portion of the duct remains and develops into the two oviducts or Fallopian tubes (see Figure 3.6).

On Your Mind

Does the father's sperm really determine the sex of the child?

Yes, it is the sperm that determines the sex of the child. Some have proposed that Xs are heavier and swim slower but live longer and Ys are faster but die more quickly, or that a woman's vaginal environment or ovulation cycle may favour the survival of X or Y sperm These ideas, while popular, are not well supported by scientific research (Grant, 2006). However, the sex of the child does depend on whether an X-chromosome sperm or a Y-chromosome sperm, donated by the father, joins with the ovum (which is always an X). The irony is that for many years, in many cultures, men routinely blamed and even divorced women who did not produce a child of a certain sex (usually a boy), when, in fact, the man's sperm is the factor that determines a zygote's genetic sex as male or female.

External Genitalia

Female external genitalia follows a pattern of development similar to that of internal reproductive organs, Male and female external genitalia begin from the same prenatal tissue. Until the

---

autosome
Any chromosome that is not a sex chromosome.

sex chromosomes
Rod-shaped bodies found in the cell nucleus, X and Y chromosomes in humans, that contain information about whether the fetus will become male or female.

fertilization
The union of two gametes, which occurs when a haploid sperm and a haploid egg join to produce a diploid zygote,

containing 46 chromosomes or 23 chromosomal pairs.

zygote
The single cell resulting from the union of sperm and egg cells.

mitosis
The division of the nucleus of a cell into two new cells such that each new daughter cell has the same number and kind of chromosomes as the original parent.

embryo
The multicellular stage of development that occurs after a zygote is formed. In

humans this stage consists of the first ten weeks post the last menstrual period of the mother. During this time, all of the organs and basic body plan of baby is formed.

fetus
The name for a baby after the embryonic stage of development and prior to birth.

gestation
The period of intrauterine fetal development.

testes
Male gonads inside the scrotum that produce testosterone.

Müllerian duct
One of a pair of tubes in the embryo that will develop, in female embryos, into the fallopian tubes, uterus, and upper part of the vagina.

Wolffian duct
One of a pair of tubes in the embryo that will develop, in XY embryos, into the male reproductive tract.

Female Sexual Anatomy, Development, and Health

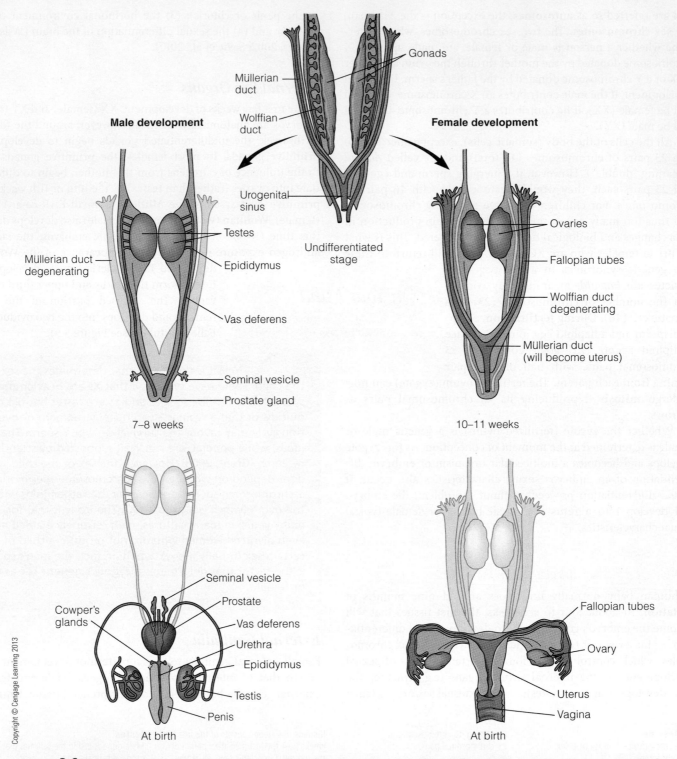

Male development

Gonads

Müllerian duct

Wolffian duct

Female development

Urogenital sinus

Undifferentiated stage

Testes

Müllerian duct degenerating

Epididymus

Vas deferens

Seminal vesicle

Prostate gland

7–8 weeks

Ovaries

Fallopian tubes

Wolffian duct degenerating

Müllerian duct (will become uterus)

10–11 weeks

Cowper's glands

Seminal vesicle

Prostate

Vas deferens

Urethra

Epididymus

Testis

Penis

At birth

Fallopian tubes

Ovary

Uterus

Vagina

At birth

FIGURE **3.6** Development of the male and female internal reproductive systems from the undifferentiated stage. We discuss the details of the development of the male reproductive system in Chapter 4.

eighth week, the undifferentiated tissue from which the genitalia will develop exists as a mound of skin, or tubercle, beneath the umbilical cord. In females, the external genitalia also begins to develop under the influence of female hormones produced by the placenta and by the mother in addition to the lack of influence from the Y chromosome. The genital tubercle develops into the clitoris, the labia minora, the vestibule, and the labia majora (see Figure 3.7).

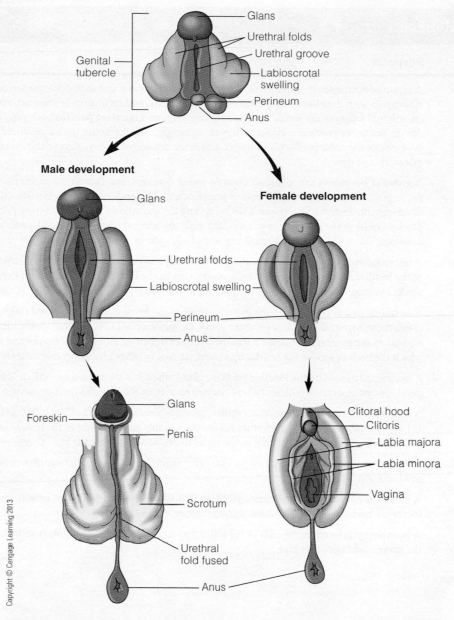

FIGURE **3.7** Development of the female and male external genitalia from the undifferentiated genital tubercle. We discuss the details of the development of the male reproductive system in Chapter 4.

Hormonal Development and Influences

Hormones play an important role in human development. Table 3.1 lists the various sex hormones and the roles they play. **Endocrine glands,** such as the gonads, secrete hormones directly into the bloodstream to be carried to the target organs. The ovaries, for example, produce the two major female hormones, estrogen and progesterone. **Estrogen** is an important influence in the development of female sexual characteristics throughout fetal development and later life, whereas **progesterone** regulates the menstrual cycle and prepares the uterus for pregnancy. In females the adrenal glands and ovaries also produce androgens such as **testosterone,** which is the precursor molecule necessary for the production of estrogens in females.

Brain Differentiation

Most hormonal secretions are regulated by the brain—in particular, by the hypothalamus, which is the body's single most important control centre. Yet, hormones also affect the development

endocrine gland
A gland that secretes hormones into the blood.

estrogen
A hormone that produces female secondary sex characteristics and affects the menstrual cycle.

progesterone
A hormone that is produced by the ovaries and helps to regulate the menstrual cycle.

testosterone
A hormone made in higher concentrations in males than females that is important for the masculinization of males. It is also the precursor molecule necessary for the production of estrogen.

Female Sexual Anatomy, Development, and Health

Table 3.1 The Sex Hormones

Hormone	Purposes
Androgens	A group of hormones that influences male sexual development and includes testosterone and androsterone. Androgens stimulate the development of male sex organs and secondary sex characteristics such as beard growth and a deepening voice. Testosterone also plays an important part (in both sexes) in stimulating sexual desire. The testes produce androgens in men, although a small amount is also produced by the adrenal glands. Women's ovaries also produce androgens, which are converted to estrogens in the ovary to stimulate the maturation of ova.
Estrogens	A group of hormones that influences female sexual development. Estrogen controls development of the female sex organs, the menstrual cycle, parts of pregnancy, and secondary sex characteristics such as breast development. They are also responsible for ending the growth of limb bones during puberty. The ovaries produce most of the estrogen in women, although the adrenal glands and the placenta also produce small amounts. Testes also produce a small amount of estrogen in men.
Progesterone	A hormone secreted by the ovaries. Progesterone helps to prepare the lining of the uterus for the implantation of the fertilized ovum, to stimulate milk production in the breasts, and to maintain the placenta. Progesterone works in conjunction with estrogen to prepare the female reproductive system for pregnancy.
Gonadotropin-releasing hormone (GnRH)	A hormone that is produced in the hypothalamus of the brain and is transported through the portal veins that connect the hypothalamus and pituitary gland. Gonadotropin means "gonad stimulating" and GnRH stimulates the pituitary to release hormones, such as follicle-stimulating hormone and luteinizing hormone, which themselves induce the ovaries and testes (as well as other glands) to secrete their hormones.
Follicle-stimulating hormone (FSH)	A hormone released by the anterior pituitary gland when it is stimulated by GnRH. FSH stimulates the development of ovarian follicles (where oocytes reside), in females and the formation of sperm in males.
Luteinizing hormone (LH)	A hormone released by the anterior pituitary gland when it is stimulated by GnRH. LH stimulates ovulation. LH also stimulates the release of other hormones, notably progesterone in the female and testosterone in the male. Finally, it stimulates the cells in the testes to produce testosterone.
Prolactin	A hormone released by the anterior pituitary that stimulates milk production after childbirth and also the production of progesterone.
Oxytocin	A hormone released by the posterior pituitary that stimulates the ejection of milk from the breasts and causes increased contractions of the uterus during labour.
Inhibin	A hormone produced by the cells of the testes that signals the anterior pituitary to decrease FSH production if the sperm count gets too high.

Copyright © Cengage Learning 2013

of the brain itself, both in the uterus and after birth (Savic et al., 2010). Male and female brains control different reproductive behaviours and thus undergo different development. For example, female brains control menstruation and, therefore, must signal the release of hormones in a monthly cycle, whereas male brains signal release continuously. With the brain, as with sexual organs, the presence of androgens during the appropriate critical stage of development may be the factor that programs the central nervous system to develop male sexual behaviours (Bocklandt & Vilain, 2007; Garcia-Falgueras & Swaab, 2010; Juntti et al., 2010). As we discussed earlier, sexual differentiation of the genitals begins early in a pregnancy, whereas sexual differentiation of the brain occurs much later in pregnancy (Savic et al., 2010).

Review Questions

1 Differentiate between sex and gender.

2 Describe sexual reproduction at the level of chromosomes, and explain what happens after a sperm fertilizes an ovum.

3 Be able to describe the roles of the hormones listed in Table 3.1 in the development and sexual function of the female body.

4 Describe sexual differentiation in a developing female fetus.

Atypical Sexual Development in Females

Prenatal development of children depends on carefully orchestrated developmental stages. At any stage, sex chromosome or hormone conditions can lead to variations of sexual development. The result can be a child born with ambiguous genitals or with the external genitals of one sex and the genetic makeup of the other sex. One of the rarest disorders in sexual development is **hermaphroditism** (her-MAFF-fro-dit-ism) (Krstic et al., 2000). In this condition, a child is born with fully formed ovaries and fully formed testes. Table 3.2 provides an overview of variations of sex development that are most common in XX female embryos.

Chromosomal Syndromes—Turner and Triple X

Variations of sex development can also occur due to several chromosomal conditions. Although researchers have identified more than 70 such conditions, we discuss here the two most common in females.

Turner syndrome is a chromosomal condition that occurs in approximately one of every 2500 live female births. Turner syndrome results from an ovum without any sex chromosome being fertilized by an X sperm (designated XO), which gives the child only 45 chromosomes altogether (if an ovum without a chromosome is fertilized by a Y sperm, and thus contains no X sex chromosome, it will not survive). The median age at which a young girl is diagnosed with Turner syndrome is about six to seven years old, although some are not diagnosed until much later (Massa et al., 2005).

Table 3.2 Atypical Sexual Development in Females

Syndrome	Chromosomal Pattern	External Genitals	Internal Structures	Description	Treatment
CHROMOSOMAL					
Turner syndrome	45, XO	Female	Uterus and oviducts	There is no menstruation or breast development; a broad chest with widely spaced nipples, loose skin around the neck, non-functioning ovaries, and infertility.	Androgens during puberty can help increase height, and estrogen and progesterone can help promote breast development and menstruation.
Triple X syndrome	47, XXX	Female	Female	There is likelihood of slight intellectual disability and decreased fertility or infertility.	None.
HORMONAL					
Congenital adrenal hyperplasia (CAH)	46, XX	Some male and some female traits	Internal organs are consistent with biological gender	Female infants may have clitoral enlargement and labial fusing due to prenatal exposure to androgens.	Surgery can correct external genitals if desired by the CAH individual.

Copyright © Cengage Learning 2013

hermaphroditism
A condition in which a child is born with fully formed ovaries and fully formed testes. May also be referred to as a disorder of sexual development.

Turner syndrome
A genetic variation in females in which there is only one X sex chromosome instead of two, characterized by lack of internal female sex organs, infertility, short stature, and intellectual disability.

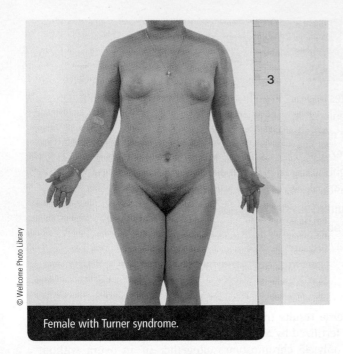

Female with Turner syndrome.

Although the external genitalia develop to look like a normal female's, the woman's ovaries do not develop fully, causing **amenorrhea** (aye-men-uh-REE-uh) and probable infertility. In addition, Turner syndrome is characterized by short stature, a relatively high-pitched voice, immature breast development, and abnormalities of certain internal organs (Menke et al., 2010; Moreno-Garcia et al., 2005). Early diagnosis is important because therapeutic administration of estrogen and progesterone during puberty can help enhance secondary sex characteristics and slightly increase height (Sheaffer el al., 2008). Although the majority of girls with Turner syndrome will never undergo puberty, those who do may be capable of pregnancy. However, pregnancies in women with Turner syndrome have a high risk for chromosomal abnormalities and fetal loss (Bouchlariotou et al., 2011). In adulthood, many women with Turner syndrome may experience hypertension, bone thinning, and/or thyroid problems (Conway et al., 2010).

Triple X syndrome (XXX) is a rare condition. As the name implies, this condition occurs when a normal ovum (which has an X chromosome) is fertilized by a sperm that has two X chromosomes, or when an ovum with two X chromosomes is fertilized by a normal X sperm. The XXX individual may grow up as a relatively normal female who is slightly taller than average, may exhibit slight intellectual disability, and may have decreased

fertility. Since their impairments are often very mild, their unusual genetic status may not be detected.

Hormonal Syndrome—CAH

Variations in sexual development can also be caused by hormonal conditions. In this section, we discuss the most common hormonal disorder of sex development in females, **congenital adrenal hyperplasia (CAH).**

CAH occurs when a child lacks an enzyme in the adrenal gland, forcing the body to produce higher amounts of androgen. It is estimated that approximately one in 15 000 infants are born with CAH, and today almost all newborns are screened for it (Johannsen et al., 2010; Roan, 2010). The excess androgens often have little effect on a developing male fetus and may have only a small effect on a developing female fetus, such as an enlarged clitoris (Johannsen et al., 2010; Roan, 2010). Although CAH girls have female internal gonads (uterus and ovaries), in severe cases, these girls may be born with masculinized external genitalia, as well as menstrual irregularities, early body hair, and/or a deepening of the voice (Johannsen et al., 2010). A similar syndrome can also develop if the mother takes androgens or drugs with effects that mimic male hormones (a number of pregnant women were prescribed such drugs in the 1950s, resulting in a group of CAH infants born during that time). Because newborn screening for CAH is common today, most CAH females are diagnosed at birth (Johannsen et al., 2010). Corrective surgery, if desired, can be done to form female genitalia, and drugs can be prescribed to control adrenal output (Warne et al., 2005). Because the internal organs are unaffected, even pregnancy is possible in many CAH females.

Early androgen concentrations in CAH girls may also affect childhood play and adult sexual orientation. Research has shown that CAH girls choose more male-typical toys and have higher rates of bisexuality and homosexuality than non-CAH girls (Meyer-Bahlburg et al., 2008; Pasterski et al., 2005, 2007). In 2010, a controversy began over the use of prenatal steroids to decrease the risk for CAH in female fetuses. Although the use of such hormones was thought to decrease the development of masculinized external genitalia in female fetuses and increase stereotypically

amenorrhea
The absence of menstruation.

triple X syndrome
A genetic abnormality in which a female has an extra X sex chromosome; characterized by decreased fertility, some genital abnormality, and slight intellectual disability.

congenital adrenal hyperplasia (CAH)
A disorder involving overproduction of androgen in the adrenal glands that can affect males and females. Females born with this condition frequently have masculinized genitals because of excess prenatal androgen exposure, whereas males typically experience early pubertal changes.

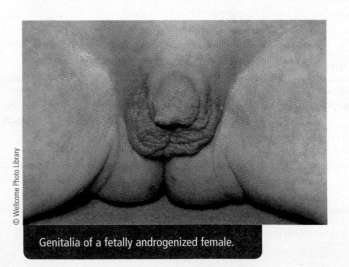

Genitalia of a fetally androgenized female.

feminine behaviours, these drugs also were found to potentially decrease the chances that the fetuses would be lesbian (Begley, 2010; Dreger et al., 2010; Roan, 2010). Critics believed that the use of prenatal steroids for CAH girls was "engineering for sexual orientation" (Roan, 2010).

Review Questions

1 What is hermaphroditism?

2 Compare and contrast Turner syndrome, triple X syndrome and CAH in female embryos.

The Female Maturation Cycle

Now that we've discussed the female sexual and reproductive system and female development, let's explore female maturation. The female reproductive system undergoes cyclic hormonal events that lead to pubertal changes, menstruation, and eventually, menopause.

Female Puberty

After birth, the female's sexual development progresses slowly until puberty. In the past, the first stirrings of puberty began somewhere between 10 and 14 years old, but research has found that girls are beginning puberty earlier than ever before (Biro et al., 2010). The proportion of girls who experience the physical changes of puberty (such as breast and pubic hair development) at ages seven and eight years old is greater today than was reported on girls born 10 to 30 years ago. Experts are looking at a number of factors that may be contributing to this trend, including diet, obesity, and/or exposure to environmental chemicals.

No one really knows how the body senses it is time for puberty to begin. The onset of puberty is often related to weight—a girl typically must have a certain body weight and appropriate fat-to-muscle ratio (Loucks & Nattiv, 2005; Warren et al., 2002). Girls who are overweight typically begin puberty earlier than those who are average or underweight (Blell et al., 2008; Kaplowitz, 2008). The onset of puberty can also vary with race and ethnicity. By the age of eight years old, 43 percent of Black, non-Hispanic, 31 percent of Hispanic, and 18 percent of White girls have breast development indicating early puberty (Biro et al., 2010). These racial and ethnic differences may be related to height and weight differences (Adair & Gordon-Larsen, 2001; Freedman et al., 2002). Other factors, such as genetic mutations (Teles et al., 2008), stressful home environments (Ellis & Essex, 2007; K. Kim & Smith, 1999; Ravert & Martin, 1997), and insecure maternal attachments in early childhood (Belsky et al., 2010) have also been found to contribute to early puberty in girls. More research is needed to explore these possible links.

When puberty begins, a girl's body signals the adrenal glands to begin to produce testosterone, which stimulates the appearance of pubic and underarm hair. During this time the hypothalamus in the brain also begins to secrete **gonadotropin-releasing hormone** (GnRH). This stimulates the pituitary gland to begin secreting the hormones **follicle-stimulating hormone** (FSH) and **lutenizing hormone** (LH). FSH and LH stimulate the ovaries to produce estrogen. As puberty continues, the ovaries, in response to stimulation by the pituitary gland, begin to release more and more estrogen into the circulatory system. Under the influence of estrogen, the Fallopian tubes, uterus, and vagina all mature and increase in size. The breasts also begin to develop, as fat deposits increase and the elaborate duct system develops. The pelvis broadens and changes from a narrow, funnel-like outlet to a broad oval outlet, flaring the hips. The skin remains soft and smooth under estrogen's influence, and fat cells increase in number in the buttocks and thighs.

The changes that accompany puberty prepare the woman for mature sexuality, pregnancy, and childbirth. At some point during puberty, usually at about the age of 11 or 12, a girl will begin to ovulate. Most women are unable to feel any internal signs during ovulation. In a few women, however, a slight pain or sensation, referred to as **mittelschmerz,** accompanies ovulation. The pain

gonadotropin-releasing hormone (GnRH)
A hormone produced in the hypothalamus that triggers the onset of puberty and sexual development, and is responsible for the release of FSH and LH from the pituitary.

follicle-stimulating hormone (FSH)
Released from the pituitary to stimulate the maturation of oocytes.

lutenizing hormone (LH)
Released from the pituitary to stimulate the release of an oocyte at ovulation

mittelschmerz
German for "middle pain." A pain in the abdomen or pelvis that some women feel at ovulation.

may result from a transitory internal irritation caused by the small amount of blood and fluid released at the site of the ruptured follicle.

For most girls, the beginning of ovulation often closely corresponds to **menarche** (MEN-are-kee), the first menstrual period. However, some may begin menstruating a few months before their first ovulation, whereas others may ovulate a few times before their first full menstrual cycle. In the first year after menarche, 80 percent of menstrual cycles are anovulatory (do not involve ovulation; Oriel & Schrager, 1999).

With minor variations, the average age of menarche in most developed countries is 12 to 13 years, but the age of menarche has been gradually decreasing. One hundred years ago, the average age of first menstruation was about 16 years (Patton & Viner, 2007; Remsberg et al., 2005). On average, menarche age is significantly earlier in Black, non-Hispanic girls than White or Hispanic girls (Chumlea et al., 2003; Freedman et al., 2002; Kaplowitz et al., 2001) and significantly later in Asian girls (Adair & Gordon-Larsen, 2001). In less-developed countries, the age of menarche is later. For example, in rural Chile, the average age of menarche is close to 14 years old (Dittmar, 2000). Environmental factors, such as high altitudes and poor nutrition, can delay the age at which a girl begins menstruating. There is also a heritability component to the age at which a woman begins menstruating—many girls reach menarche at approximately the same age as their biological mothers (Towne et al., 2005). An earlier age of menarche in biological mothers has been found to be related to increased risk of obesity in male and female offspring (see Figure 3.8).

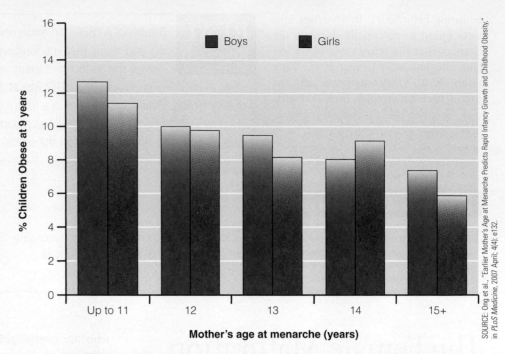

SOURCE: Ong et al., "Earlier Mother's Age at Menarche Predicts Rapid Infancy Growth and Childhood Obesity," in *PLoS Medicine*, 2007 April; 44): e132.

FIGURE **3.8** Prevalence of obesity in children at age nine, by mother's age at menarche (Ong et al., 2007).

In some cultures in the past, as soon as a girl reached menarche, she was considered ready to marry and begin bearing children. In North American culture, most people believe that there is a difference between being physiologically capable of bearing children and being psychologically ready for sexual intercourse and childbearing. In Chapter 10, we will discuss the psychological and emotional changes of female puberty.

Menstruation

Menstruation (also referred to as a "period") is the name for the monthly bleeding that the majority of healthy women of reproductive age experience. The menstrual cycle lasts from 24 to 35 days, but the average is 28 (meaning there are 28 days from the first day of bleeding to the next first day of bleeding). During the cycle, the lining of the uterus builds up and prepares for a pregnancy. When there is no pregnancy, menstruation occurs, and the lining of the uterus is shed in the form of blood and tissue. A cycle of hormones controls the buildup and the release. The biological purpose of the menstrual cycle is to prepare a woman's uterus for pregnancy.

The menstrual cycle can be divided into four general phases: follicular, ovulatory, luteal, and menstrual (see Figure 3.9). The **follicular phase** begins after the last menstruation has been completed and lasts anywhere from 6 to 13 days. Only a thin layer of endometrial cells remains from the last menstruation. As the follicles in the ovaries begin to ripen with the next cycle's ova, estrogen released by the ovaries stimulates regrowth of the endometrium's outer layer, to about 2 to 5 millimetres thick.

During the **ovulatory phase,** an ovum is released, usually about the 14th day of the cycle. The particulars of ovulation were described in the preceding section on the ovaries and Fallopian tubes. The third phase is the **luteal phase.** Immediately after

---

REAL Research Studies evaluating voice changes in women throughout the menstrual cycle have found that a woman's voice is rated by men as significantly more attractive when she is ovulating (Pipitone & Gallup, 2007). This may be because of the fact that the sound of a woman's voice serves as a subconscious sign of her fitness and fertility. No differences in ratings of voice attractiveness were found for women who were using birth control pills.

---

menarche
The start of menstrual cycling, usually during early puberty.

follicular phase
First phase of the menstrual cycle that begins after the last menstruation has been completed.

ovulatory phase
The second stage of the general menstrual cycle, when the ovum is released.

luteal phase
Third phase of the menstrual cycle, following ovulation, when the corpus luteum forms.

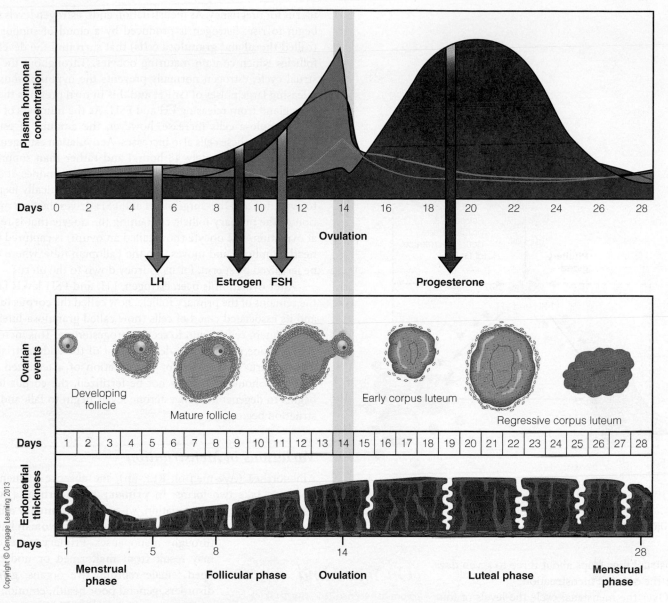

Plasma hormonal concentration

Days 0 2 4 6 8 10 12 14 16 18 20 22 24 26 28

Ovulation

LH   Estrogen FSH   Progesterone

Ovarian events

Developing follicle

Mature follicle

Early corpus luteum

Regressive corpus luteum

Days 1 2 3 4 5 6 7 8 9 10 11 12 13 14 15 16 17 18 19 20 21 22 23 24 25 26 27 28

Endometrial thickness

Days 1 5 8 14 28

Menstrual phase   Follicular phase   Ovulation   Luteal phase   Menstrual phase

Copyright © Cengage Learning 2013

FIGURE **3.9** The ovarian and menstrual cycles.

ovulation, a small, pouchlike gland, the **corpus luteum,** forms on the ovary. The corpus luteum secretes additional progesterone and estrogen for 10 to 12 days, which causes further growth of the cells in the endometrium and increases the blood supply to the lining of the uterus. The endometrium reaches a thickness of 4 to 6 millimetres during this stage (about a quarter of an inch) in preparation to receive and nourish a fertilized egg. If fertilization does not occur, however, the high levels of progesterone and estrogen

signal the hypothalamus to decrease LH and other hormone production. The corpus luteum begins to degenerate as LH levels decline. Approximately two days before the end of the normal cycle, the secretion of estrogen and progesterone decreases sharply as the corpus luteum becomes inactive, and the menstrual phase begins. Figure 3.10 illustrates the cycle of female hormones.

In the **menstrual phase,** the endometrial cells shrink and slough off (this flow is referred to as **menses** [MEN-seez]). The uterus begins to contract in an effort to expel the dead tissue along with a small quantity of blood. (It is these contractions that cause menstrual cramps, which can be painful in some women). During menstruation, approximately 35 millilitres of blood, 35 millilitres of fluid, some mucus, and the lining of the uterus (about 2 to 4 tablespoons of fluid in all) are expelled from the uterine cavity through the cervical os and ultimately the vagina. (If a woman is using oral contraceptives, the amount may be significantly smaller; see Chapter 6.) Some women lose too much blood during their menstruation and may develop **anemia.** For most women,

corpus luteum
A yellowish endocrine gland in the ovary formed when a follicle has discharged its secondary oocyte.

menstrual phase
Final stage of the general menstrual cycle, when the endometrial cells shrink and slough off.

menses
The blood and tissue discharged from the uterus during menstruation.

anemia
A deficiency in the oxygen carrying material of the blood, often causing symptoms of fatigue, irritability, dizziness, memory problems, shortness of breath, and headaches.

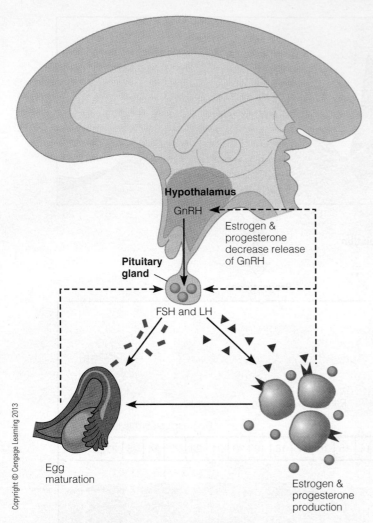

Hypothalamus

GnRH

Estrogen & progesterone decrease release of GnRH

Pituitary gland

FSH and LH

Egg maturation

Estrogen & progesterone production

FIGURE **3.10** The cycle of female hormones.

uterus for pregnancy. As menstruation ends, estrogen levels slowly begin to rise. Estrogen is produced by a cloud of support cells (called **thecal** and **granulosa cells**) that surround the developing follicles which contain maturing oocytes. Throughout the menstrual cycle, estrogen normally prevents the hypothalamus from releasing large pulses of GnRH and this in turn prevents the pituitary gland from releasing LH and FSH. As the numbers of thecal and granulosa cells increase, however, the amount of estrogen produced by these cells also increases. At ovulation estrogen levels peak (for approximately 48 hours) and rather than suppressing the hypothalamus and pituitary secretion of hormones, it stimulates their release. LH and FSH levels rise dramatically just prior to ovulation and this surge of LH and FSH drives the final maturation of the primary follicle containing the oocyte that is released at ovulation. The oocyte (now called an ovum) is captured by the nearby fimbriae and moves into the Fallopian tube, where it may be fertilized by sperm, for its journey down to the uterus.

After ovulation is over, estrogen, LH, and FSH levels fall and the remains of the primary follicle, now called the **corpus luteum**, and its associated cloud of cells (now called granulosa-lutein and thecal-lutein cells) begin to secrete progesterone. This increase in progesterone supports the development of the endometrial layer of the uterus to prepare for implantation of a fertilized ovum (zygote). Should the ovum not be fertilized, the corpus luteum begins to degenerate, progesterone levels begin to fall, and menstruation begins.

Variations in Menstruation

Amenorrhea (Aye-men-oh-REE-uh), the absence of menstruation, can take two forms. In **primary amenorrhea,** a woman never even begins menstruation, whereas in **secondary amenorrhea,** previously normal menses stop before the woman has gone through menopause. Primary amenorrhea may result from malformed or underdeveloped female reproductive organs, glandular disorders, general poor health, emotional factors, or excessive exercise. The most common cause of secondary amenorrhea is pregnancy, although it can also occur with emotional factors, certain diseases, surgical removal of the ovaries or uterus, hormonal imbalance caused naturally or through the ingestion of steroids, excessive exercise, or eating disorders. For example, almost all women with anorexia nervosa will experience amenorrhea (Pinheiro et al., 2007). When women suffering from anorexia

menstrual flow stops about three to seven days after the onset of menstruation.

Over the menstrual cycle the levels of four hormones: estrogen, progesterone, LH and FSH fluctuate to control ovulation and to stimulate the preparation of the endometrial layer of the

On Your Mind

Someone once told me that women who live together often experience menstruation at the same time. Is this true, and if it is, why does it happen?

Menstrual synchronicity, as this phenomenon is called, is thought to be common, and women who live in the same apartment or house may begin to cycle together (this does not happen if the women are using hormonal forms of birth control). This effect has also been referred to as the Wellesley effect after the name of the college where it was initially studied (McClintock, 1971). Controversy about menstrual synchronicity exists however since researchers have failed to find menstrual synchronicity in cohabitating lesbian couples (Weller & Weller, 1998) or in the Dogon of West Africa, where menstruating women share a hut during menstruation (Strassman, 1999). At this point scientists are not convinced that menstrual synchronicity is a reliable phenomenon.

thecal cells
Support cells for maturing oocytes that take cholesterol from the blood stream and convert it to androgens. These androgens are taken in by neighbouring granulosa cells.

granulosa cells
Support cells for maturing oocytes that take the androgens secreted from neighbouring thecal cells and convert them to a type of estrogen.

corpus luteum
The remains of the follicle that released an ovum during ovulation. The corpus luteum is responsible for the rise of progesterone that occurs during the luteal phase of the menstrual cycle.

primary amenorrhea
The lifelong absence of menstruation.

secondary amenorrhea
The absence of menstruation after a period of normal menses.

While regular exercise is a good thing, it's important for female athletes to maintain a healthy weight. Females who significantly reduce their body fat may stop menstruating.

exercise; relaxation; warm baths; yoga; and gentle massage of the lower back sometimes help, as do prostaglandin blocking pain relievers, such as ibuprofen.

Dysfunctional uterine bleeding includes irregular periods or unusually heavy periods and is a common complaint among women (Maness et al., 2010). Dysfunctional uterine bleeding is most common in women at both ends of the age spectrum (younger and older women) and typically occurs when the body does not respond to key hormones, such as estrogen and progesterone, resulting in anovulatory cycles. Causes include stress, excessive exercise, significant weight loss, vaginal injury, hormonal imbalances, and/or chronic illness (Estephan & Sinert, 2010).

Dysfunctional uterine bleeding can affect a woman's quality of life and can lead to both medical and social complications (Frick et al., 2009). Some women suffer from excessive menstrual flow, known as **menorrhagia** (men-or-RAY-gee-uh). Common complaints include feelings of sadness, irritability, restlessness, and sleep problems (including trouble falling asleep and also excessive sleepiness; Strine et al., 2005). Oral contraceptives may be prescribed to make menses lighter and more regular (Read, 2010). Later in this chapter, we discuss some newer options that women have to avoid menstruation altogether (Shulman, 2010).

Premenstrual Syndrome and Premenstrual Dysphoric Disorder

The term **premenstrual syndrome (PMS)** refers to physical or emotional symptoms that appear in some women during the latter half of the menstrual cycle. Estimates of the numbers of women who experience PMS vary widely depending on how it is defined, but only a small number of women find it debilitating. Researchers have found that the majority of women experience emotional, behavioural, or physical premenstrual symptoms (Boyle et al., 1987).

Interestingly, although there are no overall ethnic differences in the prevalence of premenstrual symptoms, research has found some differences in the types of symptoms that women experience. For example, Black women have been found to experience more food cravings during the premenstrual week than White women (Stout et al., 1986), whereas White women are more likely to report premenstrual mood changes and weight gain (Woods et al., 1982). Hispanic women report more severe symptoms associated with premenstrual times, whereas Asian women report less (Sternfeld et al., 2002). Keep in mind, however, that we don't know if these data are more reflective of variations in subjects' comfort in reporting symptoms or symptom severity.

nervosa regain weight, amenorrhea may persist and a physician should be consulted.

Menstrual cramps are caused by prostaglandins, which stimulate the uterus to contract and expel the endometrial lining during menstruation. The uterine muscles are powerful (remember that the muscles help push an infant out at birth), and menstrual contractions can be strong and sometimes quite painful. Although the majority of women experience mild-to-moderate cramping during menstruation, some experience **dysmenorrhea** (dis-men-uh-REE-uh), or extremely painful menstruation. Dysmenorrhea may be caused by a variety of inflammations, constipation, or even psychological stress. Poor eating habits, an increase in stress, alcohol use, insufficient sleep, and a lack of exercise can aggravate the problem. Reducing salt, sugar, and caffeine intake; moderate

dysmenorrhea
Painful menstruation.

dysfunctional uterine bleeding
Menstrual bleeding for long periods of time or intermittent bleeding throughout a cycle.

menorrhagia
Excessive menstrual flow.

premenstrual syndrome (PMS)
A group of physiological and psychological symptoms related to the post-ovulation phase of the menstrual cycle.

REAL Research In women who are not on hormonal contraception, cravings for foods high in carbohydrates and fat are common two weeks before their period starts, during the luteal phase of the menstrual cycle (Davidsen et al. 2007).

Female Sexual Anatomy, Development, and Health **77**

The existence of PMS has been controversial (Knaapen & Weisz, 2008). The term became well-known in the early 1980s when two separate British courts reduced the sentences of women who had killed their husbands on the grounds that severe PMS reduced their capacity to control their behaviour (Rittenhouse, 1991). Although this defence never succeeded in a U.S. or Canadian trial, publicity over the British trials led to much discussion about this syndrome. Some women objected to the idea of PMS, suggesting that it would reinforce the idea that women were "out of control" once a month and were slaves to their biology, whereas others supported it as an important biological justification of the symptoms they were experiencing each month. The extreme views of PMS have been tempered somewhat, and women who suffer from it can now find sympathetic physicians and a number of suggestions for coping strategies.

In 1994, the American Psychiatric Association introduced the diagnosis of **premenstrual dysphoric disorder (PMDD),** used to identify the most debilitating cases of PMS (Rapkin & Winer, 2008). PMDD is listed in the *DSM*-5, the latest guide to accepted psychiatric disorders of the American Psychiatric Association. It is estimated that approximately 3 percent to 8 percent of women meet the criteria for PMDD (Breech & Braverman, 2010; Rapkin et al., 2011).

There are four main groups of PMDD symptoms—mood, behavioural, somatic, and cognitive. Mood symptoms include depression, irritability, mood swings, sadness, and hostility. Behavioural symptoms include becoming argumentative, increased eating, and a decreased interest in activities. Somatic symptoms include abdominal bloating, fatigue, headaches, **hot flashes,** insomnia, backache, constipation, breast tenderness, and a craving for carbohydrates (Yen et al., 2010). Cognitive symptoms include confusion and poor concentration. PMDD symptoms seem to have both biological and lifestyle components, and so both medication and lifestyle changes can help.

Although the exact causes for PMDD remain unclear, it is often blamed on physiological factors, such as hormones, neurotransmitters, and brain mechanisms (Shulman, 2010). Hormonal fluctuations are related to mood disorders associated with PMDD, such as depression and hopelessness (Zukov et al., 2010). Researchers have also found that women with PMDD differentially express irritability, anger, depression, and have specific food cravings (Rapkin & Winer, 2008; Reed, Levin, & Evans,

2008). Once documented, the first treatment for PMS or PMDD usually involves lifestyle changes. Stress management, increased regular exercise, improved coping strategies, and drug therapy may help (Shulman, 2010).

Women who have a history of major depression, **post-traumatic stress disorder,** or sexual abuse, or those who smoke cigarettes, tend to be more at risk for development of PMS or PMDD (L.S. Cohen et al., 2002; Koci, 2004; Wittchen et al., 2002). One of the most promising pharmacological treatments has been the selective serotonin reuptake inhibitors, such as fluoxetine (Prozac) (Clayton, 2008; Rendas-Baum et al., 2010). Fluoxetine has yielded some promising results in the treatment of PMDD, although it can cause adverse effects, such as sexual dysfunction (Carr & Ensom, 2002).

Menstrual Manipulation and Suppression

Many years ago, women had fewer periods than they do today. Because of poorer health and nutrition, shorter life spans, more pregnancies, and longer periods spent breast-feeding, women had 50 to 150 periods during their lifetime (Ginty, 2005; Thomas & Ellertson, 2000), whereas today many women may have up to 450 periods over the lifespan. Many women today wish they could schedule their periods around certain events in their lives (e.g., athletic events, dates, or vacations).

Over the last few years, **menstrual manipulation** has become more popular, and in the future it is likely that **menstrual suppression** will make periods optional (Hicks & Rome, 2010). Birth control pills have been used to reduce menstrual bleeding and to delay the onset of menstruation. Some physicians prescribe continuous birth control pills (in which a woman takes birth control pills with no break), progesterone **intrauterine devices**, and injections to suppress menstrual periods.

Seasonale, an extended-use oral contraceptive, has been available in Canada since 2007 (*Calgary Herald*, 2007). It is taken for 84 consecutive days instead of the usual 21-day birth control regimen. Another similar extended-use pill, Seasonique, was approved for use in Canada in 2011 (Paladin Labs, 2011). Users of Seasonale and Seasonique experience only four periods a year, compared with the usual 13. Many women are excited about the option of reducing the number of menstrual periods; one study found that given a choice of having a period or not, 90 percent of women would choose not to have periods (Sulak et al., 2002). Lybrel, the first continuous-use birth control pill, was also available to women in the mid 2000s. Lybrel is taken for 365 days without placebos, allowing a woman to stop menstruating altogether. We will discuss these forms of birth control in more detail in Chapter 6.

Methods such as taking Seasonale, Seasonique, and Lybrel suppress the growth of the uterine lining, leaving little or nothing to be expelled during menstruation. This treatment has been used for years to treat a menstrual condition known as **endometriosis** (en-doe-mee-tree-OH-sus), which can cause severe menstrual cramping and irregular periods. Overall, there is no medical evidence that women need to have a monthly menstrual period, and studies conclude that continuous use of pills to stop periods is a

---

premenstrual dysphoric disorder (PMDD)
The most debilitating and severe cases of premenstrual syndrome.

hot flashes
A symptom of menopause in which a woman feels sudden heat, often accompanied by a flush.

post-traumatic stress disorder
A stress disorder that follows a traumatic event, causing flashbacks, heightened anxiety, and sleeplessness.

menstrual manipulation
The ability to plan and schedule the arrival of menstruation.

menstrual suppression
The elimination of menstrual periods.

intrauterine devices
Devices that are inserted into the uterus for contraception. Progesterone IUDs often inhibit menstruation.

endometriosis
The growth of endometrial tissue outside the uterus.

The Diva Cup is a silicone menstrual cup that can be used as an alternative to disposable menstrual products such as tampons.

safe and effective option for preventing pregnancy and reducing menstrual-related symptoms (Anderson et al., 2006; Merki-Feld et al., 2008; A.L. Nelson, 2007; Stacey, 2008).

Women with painful periods, intense cramps, and heavy menses may benefit from menstrual suppression (Anderson et al., 2006; Freeman, 2008; Merki-Feld et al., 2008; A.L. Nelson, 2007; Stacey, 2008). Some experts suggest that amenorrhea may be healthier than monthly periods because menstrual suppression also avoids the sharp hormonal changes that occur throughout the menstrual cycle.

Originally, birth control pills were designed to mimic the normal menstrual cycle, which is why they allowed a period of time for a woman to bleed. This bleeding, called *withdrawal bleeding,* is a result of stopping birth control pills or taking placebo pills for one week each month (Stacey, 2008). Withdrawal bleeding itself bears little biological resemblance to a menstrual period because there is little built-up endometrium to be shed (Thomas & Ellertson, 2000). Abnormal bleeding (spotting or clotting) or an absence of bleeding that occurs without the use of menstrual suppressing medication is an important event that should be reported to a health care provider promptly.

Menstruation and Sexual Behaviour

Many cultures have taboos about engaging in sexual intercourse, or any sexual behaviours, during menstruation. Although many heterosexual couples report avoiding sexual intercourse during menstruation (Hensel et al., 2004), research has found that this might have to do more with personal comfort than anything else. Heterosexual couples who are more comfortable with their sexuality report higher levels of sexual intercourse during menstruation than couples who are less comfortable (Rempel & Baumgartner, 2003).

Heterosexual and lesbian couples should discuss these issues and decide what they are comfortable with. As mentioned earlier, however, the advent of pharmaceuticals to induce menstrual suppression might make this question obsolete.

Menopause

The term *menopause* refers to a woman's final menstrual period but is often (incorrectly) used as a synonym for the **climacteric.** This term refers to the time in a woman's life in which the ovaries become less responsive to hormonal stimulation from the anterior pituitary, resulting in decreased hormone production. Decreased hormone production can lead to irregular cycles or a lack of menstruation. Amenorrhea may occur for two or three months, followed by a menstrual flow. Women may begin to experience these symptoms during **perimenopause** (pear-ee-MEN-oh-pawz), which occurs anywhere from two to eight years before menopause (Huang, 2007; Twiss et al., 2007). In most cases, menstruation does not stop suddenly. Periods become irregular and intervals between periods become longer. Once menopause has occurred and a woman has not had a period in one year, she is considered *postmenopausal* and is no longer considered at risk for pregnancy. Menopause typically occurs sometime between the ages of 40 and 58, although women whose mother gave birth after the age of 35 tend to experience menopause at a later age (Steiner et al., 2010).

Decreasing estrogen can lead to several possible adverse effects, including hot flashes, forgetfulness, mood swings, sleep disorders, bone loss, menstrual irregularities, vaginal dryness, decreased sexual interest, and joint aches (H.D. Nelson, 2008; Pinkerton & Stovall, 2010; Soares, 2010; Timur & Sahin, 2010; Tom et al., 2010). Changes in estrogen can also lead to atrophy of the primary sexual glands. The clitoris and labia become smaller, and vaginal atrophy, dryness, and bleeding during sexual activity can occur. Recent research, however, has shown that an ultra-low dose of locally applied estrogen, via a tablet inserted into the vagina, can help ameliorate these symptoms (Simon & Maamari, 2013). At the same time, the ovaries and uterus also begin to shrink. Other possible physiological changes include thinning of head hair, growth of hair on the upper lip and chin, drooping of the breasts and wrinkling of skin because of loss of elasticity, and **osteoporosis** (ah-stee-oh-po-ROW-sus), resulting in brittle bones.

It is estimated that 70 percent of women over age 80 will experience osteoporosis (Pinkerton & Stovall, 2010; Stanford, 2002). Incidentally, osteopenia (a thinning of the bones) also can occur in younger women and is a precursor to osteoporosis. If you smoke, use Depo Provera (see Chapter 6), or have an eating disorder or a family history of osteoporosis, consider asking your doctor for a bone density test. Beginning in their 20s, women are advised to ingest at least 1000 milligrams of calcium each day and

climacteric
The combination of physiological and psychological changes that develop at the end of a woman's reproductive life; usually includes menopause.

perimenopause
Transition period in a woman's life, just before menopause.

osteoporosis
An age-related disorder characterized by decreased bone mass and increased susceptibility to fractures as a result of decreased levels of estrogens.

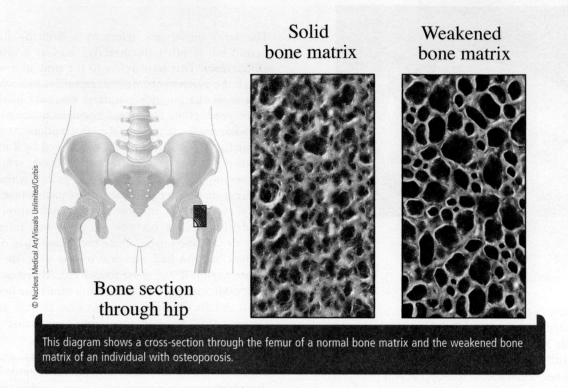

Solid bone matrix

Weakened bone matrix

Bone section through hip

© Nucleus Medical Art/Visuals Unlimited/Corbis

This diagram shows a cross-section through the femur of a normal bone matrix and the weakened bone matrix of an individual with osteoporosis.

to engage in frequent exercise to maintain bone strength (Lloyd et al., 2004; Manson, 2004).

Women who have undergone certain surgeries, such as removal of the ovaries, may experience a surgically induced menopause because of estrogen deprivation (Francucci et al., 2010). For this reason, estrogen treatment may be suggested for these women to decrease the potential menopausal symptoms.

REAL Research Female beer drinkers have been found to have greater bone density compared with non-beer and/or wine drinkers (Pedrera-Zamarano et al., 2009). The scientists who conducted this research suggested this may be a result of the *phytoestrogen* content (plant-based chemicals that are structurally similar to estrogen) in beer, which can contribute to increased bone density.

Most Canadian women go through menopause with few problems and many find it to be a liberating time, signalling the end of their childbearing years and a newfound freedom from contraception. In fact, the most prevalent sexual problems of

older women are not the classic complaints but rather the lack of tenderness and sexual contact with a partner (von Sydow, 2000). For many menopausal women, life satisfaction is more closely related to relationship with a partner, stress, and lifestyle than menopause status, hormone levels, or **hormone replacement therapy (HRT)** (Dennerstein et al., 2000). Keep in mind, however, that a woman's experience of menopause is also shaped by the culture in which she lives (Pitkin, 2010). Cultural issues have an enormous impact on our attitudes about aging, fertility, health, and sexuality.

Hormone Replacement Therapy

In the past, HRT was used to help maintain vaginal elasticity and lubrication, restore regular sleep patterns, and reduce hot flashes and depression. It was also helpful in decreasing the risks for development of osteoporosis, cardiovascular disease, and colorectal and lung cancers (Brinton & Schairer, 1997; Mahabir et al., 2008; Parry, 2008). However, in 2002, after the publication of results from the Women's Health Initiative that linked HRT to an increased rate of breast cancer, the use of HRT declined significantly.

Today, the use of HRT remains controversial (Pluchino et al., 2011; Yang & Reckelhoff, 2011). Although some health care providers continue to prescribe it for some patients, others have stopped prescribing it altogether; and some prescribe hormone replacement only for those women with severe menopausal symptoms (Mueck & Seeger, 2008; Tsai et al., 2011; Zanetti-Dallenbach et al., 2008). Newer therapies containing lower levels of hormones have recently become available, and an increasing number of

hormone replacement therapy (HRT)
Medication containing one or more female hormones, often used to treat symptoms of menopause.

physicians and health care providers are prescribing these newer options to their menopausal patients (Gardiner et al., 2011; Leite et al., 2010; Nappi et al., 2010; Tsai et al., 2011).

Menopausal women need to weigh the risks and benefits of menopausal treatments and HRT. It is important to discuss these issues with a trusted health care provider. No single treatment option is best for all women.

Review Questions

1 Identify and explain the physiological changes that signal the onset of puberty.

2 Identify and explain the four phases of the menstrual cycle.

3 Explain what is known about the existence of PMS/PMDD. What treatments are available?

4 Differentiate between menstrual manipulation and menstrual suppression.

5 Explain what causes the physical and emotional changes of perimenopause and menopause.

6 Explain the benefits and risks of HRT.

Female Reproductive and Sexual Health

It is a good idea for every woman to examine and explore her own sexual anatomy. A genital self-examination (see the Sex in Real Life section at the beginning of this chapter) can help increase a woman's comfort with her genitals. In addition, to maintain reproductive health, all women should undergo routine gynecological examinations with Papanicolaou (Pap) smears beginning within three years after first sexual intercourse or at age 21 (E.R. Tuller, 2010).

Routine gynecological examinations include a general medical history and a general checkup, a pelvic examination, and a breast examination. During the pelvic examination, the health care provider inspects the genitals, both internally and externally, and manually examines the internal organs.

In a pelvic exam, the health professional will often use a **speculum** to hold open the vagina to examine the cervix (although there is a sense of stretching, this is not generally painful). During a pelvic exam, a **Papanicolaou (Pap) smear** is taken from the cervix (see the discussion on cervical cancer that follows). The practitioner will then insert two fingers in the vagina and press down on the lower abdomen to feel the ovaries and uterus for abnormal lumps or pain. A rectovaginal exam may also be performed, in which the practitioner inserts one finger into the rectum and one into the vagina to feel the membranes in between.

It is important to choose a gynecologist or nurse practitioner with care, for this person should be a resource for sexual and birth control information as well as for routine reproductive health concerns. Referrals from friends or family members, college health services, women's health centers, and local sexual health centres can direct you to competent professionals. Do not be afraid to change health practitioners if you are not completely comfortable with the individual you currently use.

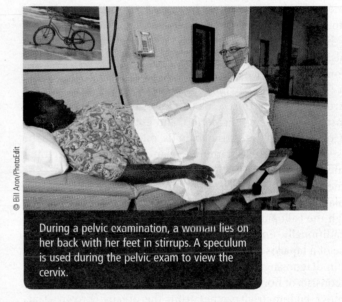

© Bill Aron/PhotoEdit

During a pelvic examination, a woman lies on her back with her feet in stirrups. A speculum is used during the pelvic exam to view the cervix.

Gynecological Health Concerns

Several conditions can interfere with gynecological health. We discuss some of the most prevalent, including endometriosis, toxic shock syndrome, polycystic ovarian syndrome (PCOS), uterine fibroids, vulvodynia, and vaginal infections.

Endometriosis

Endometriosis is a common gynecological condition that occurs when endometrial cells begin to migrate to places other than the uterus (Brown et al., 2010). Endometrial cells may implant on any of the reproductive organs or other abdominal organs and then

speculum	**Papanicolaou (Pap) smear**
An instrument for dilating the vagina to examine the cervix and other internal structures.	A microscopic examination of cells scraped from the cervix. Named after its inventor.

engorge and atrophy every month with the menstrual cycle, just like the endometrium does within the uterus. The disease ranges from mild to severe, and women may experience a range of symptoms or none at all.

Endometriosis is most common in women aged between 25 and 40 years who have never had children. Women who have not had children and those who experience short and heavy menstrual cycles have been found to be more at risk for endometriosis (Vigano et al., 2004). Among women of childbearing age, the estimated prevalence rate of endometriosis is as high as 10 percent; among infertile women, between 20 percent and 40 percent (Frackiewicz, 2000; Vigano et al., 2004). If you or someone you know has had symptoms of endometriosis, it is important that complaints are taken seriously by your health care providers.

The cause of endometriosis is still unknown, although some have suggested that it is due to retrograde menstrual flow (a process in which parts of the uterine lining are carried backward during the menstrual period into the Fallopian tubes and abdomen; Frackiewicz, 2000; Leyendecker et al., 2004). The symptoms of endometriosis depend on where the endometrial tissue has invaded but commonly include painful menstrual periods, pelvic or lower back pain, and pain during penetrative sex. Some women have also reported experiencing pain on defecation (Prentice, 2001). Symptoms often wax and wane with the menstrual cycle, starting a day or two before menstruation, becoming worse during the period, and gradually decreasing for a day or two afterward. The pain is often sharp and can be mistaken for menstrual cramping. Many women discover their endometriosis when they have trouble becoming pregnant. The endometrial cells can affect fertility by infiltrating the ovaries or Fallopian tubes and interfering with ovulation or ovum transport through the Fallopian tubes.

Traditionally, endometriosis is diagnosed through biopsy or the use of a **laparoscope**. Researchers are working on a urine test to aid in diagnosing endometriosis (Tokushige et al., 2011). Treatment consists of hormone therapy, surgery, or laser therapy to try to remove endometrial patches from the organs (Brown et al., 2010). Endometriosis declines during pregnancy and disappears after menopause in many but not all women (Morotti, Remoroida, Venturini, & Ferrero, 2012).

Menstrual Toxic Shock Syndrome

Menstrual toxic shock syndrome (mTSS) is an acute inflammatory disease that develops when *Staphylococcus aureus* bacteria are allowed to grow in the vagina. It is most commonly associated with the use of high-absorbency tampons and forgetting to remove a tampon, which becomes a breeding ground for bacteria.

mTSS is a fast-developing disease that can cause multiple organ failure. Symptoms of mTSS usually include fever, sore throat, diarrhea, vomiting, muscle aches, and a scarlet-coloured rash. It may progress rapidly from dizziness or fainting to respiratory distress, kidney failure, shock, and heart failure, and can be fatal if medical attention is not received immediately.

Despite the risks, it is estimated that more than 70 percent of women in the United States, Canada, and much of Western Europe use tampons during their periods (Parsonnet et al., 2005). Although any woman who uses tampons is at risk for development of mTSS, regularly removing tampons and using less absorbent tampons or using only pads reduces the risk for development of mTSS. Researchers are also evaluating whether adding glycerol monolaurate to tampons can decrease the risk for development of mTSS (Strandberg et al., 2009).

Polycystic Ovarian Syndrome

Polycystic ovarian syndrome (PCOS) is an endocrine disorder that affects approximately 7 percent of premenopausal women worldwide (Diamanti-Kandarakis, 2007). PCOS causes cyst formation on the ovaries during puberty, which causes estrogen levels to decrease and androgen levels (including testosterone) to increase. A girl with PCOS typically experiences irregular or absent menstruation; a lack of ovulation; excessive body and facial hair or hair loss; obesity; acne, oily skin, or dandruff; infertility; or any combination of these. Many women with PCOS experience fertility issues, and research is ongoing to find ways to help them achieve successful pregnancies (Nader, 2010).

Because many of the symptoms, including increased body and facial hair, acne, and weight gain, affect a woman's sense of self, many young women with PCOS experience emotional side effects, including mild depression or self-esteem issues. Getting adequate medical care, education, and support are crucial factors in managing PCOS. There are many possible long-term health concerns associated with PCOS, such as an increased risk for diabetes, high blood pressure, and increased cholesterol levels (Chen & Shi, 2010). A variety of treatment options are available, including oral contraception to regulate the menstrual period and inhibit testosterone production. Many women find that some of the symptoms associated with PCOS decrease with weight loss (A.M. Clark et al., 1995).

Uterine Fibroids

Uterine fibroids (leiomyomata) are non-cancerous growths that occur in the myometrium layer of the uterus (see Figure 3.3). It is estimated that three of four women have uterine fibroids, but because of the lack of symptoms, many women are unaware of them. If there are symptoms, a woman might experience pelvic pain and pressure, constipation, abdominal tenderness or bloating, frequent urination, heavy cramping, prolonged or heavy bleeding, and/or painful penetrative sex. Of all of these symptoms, excessive menstrual bleeding is the most common

laparoscope
A small instrument through which structures within the abdomen and pelvis can be viewed.

menstrual toxic shock syndrome (mTSS)
A bacteria-caused illness, associated with tampon use, that can lead to high fever, vomiting, diarrhea, sore throat and shock, loss of limbs, and death if left untreated.

polycystic ovarian syndrome (PCOS)
An endocrine disorder that can affect a woman's menstrual cycle, fertility, hormones, appearance, and long-term health.

uterine fibroid
A (usually non-cancerous) tumour of muscle and connective tissue that develops within, or is attached to, the uterine wall.

complaint. It is important to point out that the majority of uterine fibroids are not cancerous and do not cause any problems.

Women who are overweight are at greater risk for development of uterine fibroids (Pandey & Bhattacharyta, 2010), as are women who have a genetic risk in their family (i.e., a mother or sister with fibroids). Researchers have found an association of early life hormonal exposure (such as being fed soy formula during infancy), having a mother with pre-pregnancy diabetes, or being born at least one month early may be related to the development of uterine fibroids later in life (D'Aloisio et al., 2010). More research is needed to explore these putative lifestyle links with the advent of uterine fibroids.

Various treatments are used to treat uterine fibroids, including hormone, intrauterine devices (Maruo et al., 2010) or drug therapy to decrease endometrial buildup (Nieman et al., 2011), laser therapy, and/or surgery (Rabinovici et al., 2010). For many years, hysterectomy, the surgical removal of the uterus, was the leading treatment for uterine fibroids, although this is no longer the case today (Laughlin et al., 2010). Today, hysterectomy is used only in extreme cases in which the fibroids are very large.

Vulvodynia

At the beginning of the 21st century, many physicians were unaware that a condition known as **vulvodynia** (vull-voe-DY-nia) existed. Vulvodynia refers to chronic vulval pain and soreness, and it is estimated that 16 percent of women experience such pain (Danby & Margesson, 2010). Although a burning sensation is the most common symptom, women also report itching, burning, rawness, stinging, or stabbing vaginal/vulval pain (Danby & Margesson, 2010; Goldstein & Burrows, 2008). Pain can be either intermittent or constant and can range from mildly disturbing to completely disabling. Over the years, many women with vulvodynia were undiagnosed and left untreated because of a lack of understanding about the condition (Groysman, 2010). Because of this, women who suffer from vulvodynia experienced high levels of psychological distress and depression (Danby & Margesson, 2010; Jelovsek et al., 2008; Plante & Kamm, 2008).

No one really knows what causes vulvodynia, but there have been several suggestions including injury or irritation of the vulval nerves, hypersensitivity to vaginal yeast, allergic reaction to environmental irritants, or pelvic floor muscle spasms (Bohm-Starke, 2010; Murina et al., 2008, 2010; Tommola et al., 2010). Treatment options have included biofeedback, diet modification, drug therapy, oral and topical medications, nerve blocks, vulvar injections, surgery, and pelvic floor muscle strengthening (Groysman, 2010; Murina et al., 2010; Tommola et al., 2010). Treatment plans for women experiencing vulvodynia should be individualized, and care needs to be taken to address each individual woman's symptoms and function (Groysman, 2010).

Infections

URINARY TRACT AND BARTHOLIN'S GLANDS Numerous kinds of infections can afflict the female genital system. Some are sexually transmitted; these are discussed in Chapter 7. However, some infections of the female reproductive tract are not sexually transmitted. For example, as we discussed earlier in this chapter, the Bartholin's glands and the urinary tract can become infected, just as any area of the body can become infected when bacteria get inside and multiply. These infections may happen because of certain hygiene practices and are more frequent in those who engage in frequent sexual intercourse. When infected, the glands can swell and cause pressure and discomfort, and can interfere with walking, sitting, or sexual intercourse. Usually, a physician will need to drain the infected glands with a catheter and will prescribe a course of antibiotics (H. Blumstein, 2001).

On Your Mind

My gynecologist told me I have uterine fibroids and I'm scared to death. Could fibroids turn into cancer? Will I ever be able to have a baby?

The majority of fibroids are benign. It is rare for a uterine fibroid to turn into a cancer. Cancerous growths in the uterus called uterine *leiomyosarcomas* are rare and are not caused by the presence of uterine fibroids. The majority of women who have uterine fibroids have normal pregnancies and deliveries. However, in some cases, there may be some issues related to delivery, especially if the fibroids are large when it is time to deliver. If so, a Caesarean section may be indicated. Finding a health care provider you trust and educating yourself about uterine fibroids will lessen your fears.

BACTERIAL VAGINOSIS Concern about vaginal odour and cleanliness is typically what drives women to use a variety of feminine hygiene products. However, not all of these products are safe. For example, **douching** (mentioned previously when discussing the anatomy of the vagina) may put a woman at risk for vaginal infections because it changes the vagina's pH levels and can destroy healthy bacteria necessary to maintain proper pH balance and vaginal health (Cottrell, 2010; Farage et al., 2011). **Bacterial vaginosis (BV)** can occur when the balance of "vagina friendly" bacteria is upset, often by douching or sex (Larsson, et al. 2005). BV may go unnoticed in many women; however, some women will become aware of its presence by an unpleasant odour often referred to as a "fishy" smell. If you suspect you have BV, you should visit your health care provider to confirm this diagnosis. A vaginal swab will be taken to look for the presence of unwanted bacteria and to test for atypical pH levels. Vaginal secretions may also be examined for a yellowish, smelly discharge. Confirmation of BV will likely lead to your health care provider suggesting an antibiotic treatment in order to decrease the levels of unwanted bacterial flora within the vagina.

vulvodynia
Chronic vulvar pain and soreness.

douching
A method of vaginal rinsing or cleaning that involves squirting water or other solutions into the vagina.

bacterial vaginosis (BV)
A bacterial infection of the vagina caused by an imbalance of the bacteria normally residing in the vagina.

VAGINAL CANDIDIASIS Vaginal candidiasis (commonly referred to as a yeast or fungal infection) is caused by the yeast *Candida albicans*. Women generally suspect a yeast infection when they notice smelly, white, cottage cheese-like vaginal discharge over several days. This discharge is often irritating to the surrounding skin of the vulva. It can be diagnosed by a health care provider and treated with antifungal medications. For both bacterial vaginosis and yeast infections, recommendations for prevention include wearing cotton underwear and loose clothing to minimize the presence of moisture in the vulval area and make the environment less conducive to bacterial and fungal growth, wiping front to back, no douching as mentioned previously, no perfumed feminine cleansing/deodorizing products, using only a mild soap during bathing (Teitelman, 2010).

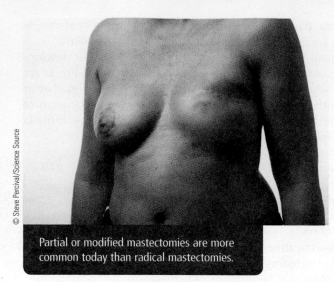

Partial or modified mastectomies are more common today than radical mastectomies.

Cancer of the Female Reproductive Organs

Cancer is a disease in which certain cells in the body do not function properly—they divide too quickly or produce excessive tissue that forms a tumour (or both). A number of cancers can affect the female reproductive organs. In this section, we discuss breast, uterine, cervical, endometrial, and ovarian cancers. We will also review preventive measures for detecting or avoiding common female health problems. In Chapter 15, we will discuss how these illnesses affect women's lives and sexuality.

Breast Cancer

We opened this chapter with a story about Stef, who has been battling breast cancer. Breast cancer is the most common cancer in women in Canada. In 2014, approximately 24 400 women were diagnosed with breast cancer, and 5000 died from the disease. On average 67 Canadian women will be diagnosed with breast cancer every day (Canadian Cancer Society, 2015a). There is no known way to prevent breast cancer; however, as Stef's story shows, early detection improves the chances that it can be treated successfully. So it is extremely important to detect it as early as possible. Every woman should regularly perform breast self-examinations (see the accompanying Sex in Real Life). Women should also have their breasts examined during routine gynecological checkups, which is a good time to ask for instruction on self-examination if you have any questions about the technique.

Another important preventive measure is **mammography.** In Canada, breast cancer rates rose in the 1990s and this rise has been attributed to mammography screening and better detection of breast cancer (Canadian Cancer Society, 2015a). Mammography can detect cancer at early stages when treatment is more effective and cures are more likely (Narod, Sun, Wall, Bains, & Miller, 2014). The Canadian Cancer Society advises women to have regular mammograms taken, beginning at the age of 50. You should discuss with your health care provider whether mammography is appropriate for you, and if so, how often.

The earliest sign of breast cancer is often an abnormality seen on a mammogram before a woman or her health care provider can feel it. However, sometimes there are symptoms, including nipple discharge, changes in nipple shape, and skin dimpling. It should be noted here that the discovery of a lump or mass in your breast does not mean you have cancer; most masses are **benign,** and many do not even need treatment. If it is **malignant** and left untreated, however, breast cancer usually spreads throughout the body, which is why it is important that any lump be immediately brought to the attention of your physician or other medical practitioner.

TREATMENT In the past, women with breast cancer usually had a **radical mastectomy.** Today, few women need such drastic surgery. More often, if necessary, a partial or modified mastectomy is performed, which leaves many of the underlying muscles and lymph nodes in place (see photo accompanying this section). If the breast must be removed, many women choose to undergo breast reconstruction, in which a new breast is formed from existing skin and fat or breast implants (Bellino et al., 2010).

If it appears that the tumour has not spread, a **lumpectomy** may be considered. A lumpectomy involves the removal of the tumour, together with some surrounding tissue, but the breast is left intact. Survival rates for women with breast cancer depend on several factors, including age, genetic susceptibility, tumour stage, and lymph node involvement (Canadian Cancer Society, 2015a).

mammography
A procedure for internal imaging of the breasts to evaluate breast disease or screen for breast cancer.

benign
A non-malignant, mild case of a disease that is favourable for recovery.

malignant
A cancerous growth that tends to spread into nearby normal tissue and travel to other parts of the body.

radical mastectomy
A surgical procedure that involves removal of the breast, its surrounding tissue, the muscles supporting the breast, and underarm lymph nodes.

lumpectomy
A modern surgical procedure for breast cancer in which only the tumorous lump and a small amount of surrounding tissue are removed.

radiation
A procedure that uses high-energy radiation to kill cancer cells by damaging their DNA.

chemotherapy
A procedure that uses chemicals to kill rapidly dividing cancer cells.

A breast self-examination (BSE), together with mammography and a clinical breast examination from a health care provider, can help reduce breast cancer in women. Recall that in the chapter opening story, Stef found a lump through a routine breast self-examination she was doing. Beginning in their 20s, women should become familiar with the shape and feel of their breasts so they can report any breast changes to a health care provider. If a woman does detect a thickening or a lump, however, she should make sure to inform her health care provider. After age 50, mammography, clinical breast exams, and even magnetic resonance imaging become more useful, although a monthly BSE may still be recommended (Saslow et al., 2007). Women with breast implants are also encouraged to perform BSEs (Tang & Gui, 2011).

Because the breasts are often less tender after menstruation, it is best to perform a BSE about a week after your period ends (see the photo below for more information about a BSE).

In the Mirror

The first step of a BSE is inspection. Look at your breasts in a mirror to learn their natural contours. With arms relaxed, note any elevation of the level of the nipple, bulging, or dimpling. Compare the size and shape of the breasts, remembering that one (usually the left) is normally slightly larger. Next, press your hands down firmly on your hips to tense the pectoral muscles, then raise your arms over your head looking for a shift in relative position of the two nipples. These manoeuvres also bring out any dimpling or bulging. After doing BSEs over time, any changes will become obvious, which is why it is best to begin BSEs earlier rather than later in life.

In the Shower

The shower is a good place to do a breast palpation (pressing)—fingers glide well over wet or soapy skin. Press the breast against the chest wall with the flat of the hand, testing the surface for warmth and moving the hand to test mobility. Pay close attention to increased heat or redness of the overlying skin, tenderness, dilated superficial veins, and retraction (dimpling, asymmetry, decreased mobility). Feel the tissue carefully in all four quadrants of the breast, being sure to include the tissue that extends up toward the armpit, and examine the armpit itself for any lymph node enlargement (see accompanying photo). Finally, gently squeeze the nipple inward and upward to determine whether there is any discharge.

Lying Down

Finally, lie down and put a folded towel or a pillow under your left shoulder. Placing your left hand behind your head and use your right hand to press firmly in small, circular motions all around the left breast, much as you did in the shower. As the figure below illustrates, there are a variety of techniques used in BSE, including the circle, line, and wedge methods. In the circle method, a woman moves her fingers in a circular pattern around the breast to feel for abnormal breast tissue. In the line method, a woman begins in the underarm area and uses an up-and-down motion to explore the breast. Finally, in the wedge method, a woman works her way toward the nipple, exploring one wedge section at a time. It is also important to check the nipples for any sign of discharge. Irregularities, lumps, or discharge should be reported to your health care provider immediately.

SOURCE: American Cancer Society, 2007a.

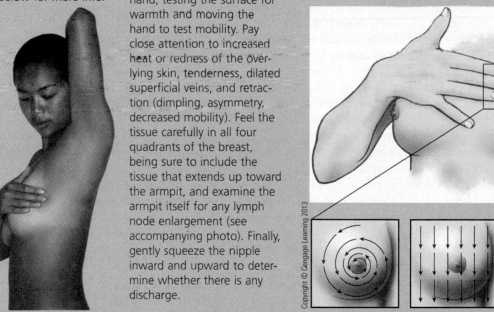

Radiation, chemotherapy, or both are often used in conjunction with the surgeries used to treat breast cancer.

RISK FACTORS Several factors may put a woman at greater risk for development of breast cancer. A woman's chance of acquiring breast cancer increases significantly as she ages. In fact, 77 percent of breast cancers appear in women who are 50 years or older, whereas less than 5 percent appear in women younger than 40 years (Jemal et al., 2005). An early onset of puberty and menarche may increase the chances of developing breast cancer, probably because of prolonged estrogen exposure (American Cancer Society, 2010). However, obesity, low levels of physical activity, and consuming one or more alcoholic drinks per day may have more to do with the development of breast cancer than do early onset of puberty or menarche (Li et al., 2010a; Verkasalo et al., 2001). Decreased risks have been found in women who exercise. In fact, in women with breast cancer, those who are physically active are less likely to die than those who are inactive (American Cancer Society, 2010). Breast-feeding has also been found to reduce a woman's lifetime risk for development of breast cancer (Eisinger & Burke, 2002).

Family history also may be a risk factor in breast cancer. No study however has been large enough to reliably show how the risk for breast cancer is influenced by familial patterns of breast cancer. Although women who have a first-degree relative with breast cancer may have an increased risk for the disease, most of these women will never experience the development of breast cancer (Collaborative Group on Hormonal Factors in Breast Cancer, 2001).

Genetic mutations (BRCA1 and BRCA2) associated with breast cancer have been found to lead to high risk for both breast and ovarian cancer. Although these mutations are rare, they are more common in women with relatives who have been diagnosed with breast or ovarian cancer or who have ethnicity or racial factors. Some women who have been found to have a high risk for development of breast cancer choose to undergo prophylactic (preventive) mastectomies before breast cancer can develop (Harmon, 2007; D.A. Levine & Gemignani, 2003; Sakorafas, 2005).

There has been some controversy over the effect of oral contraceptives on breast cancer rates, with many contradictory studies; some studies found an increased risk, and others found no increased risk (Cabaret et al., 2003; Narod et al., 2002). Although there have been slightly more breast cancers found in women who use oral contraceptives, these cancers have been less advanced and less aggressive (Fraser, 2000). A comprehensive study conducted by the U.S. Food and Drug Administration (FDA) concluded that there is no concrete evidence that the pill causes or influences the development of breast cancer; however, the long-term effects of using oral contraception are not yet certain, and those with a family history of breast cancer might want to consider using other forms of contraception.

Finally, many rumours and myths about things that cause breast cancer circulate from time to time such as the idea that using antiperspirant, wearing bras, having breast implants, or suffering a physical injury to the breast increases a woman's risk for breast cancer. Currently, none of these factors has been associated with an increased risk for breast cancer (Canadian Cancer Society 2015a).

CERVICAL CANCER The Public Health Agency of Canada estimates that there were approximately 1450 new cases of cervical cancer in Canada in 2014 (Public Health Agency of Canada, 2014).

The rates of cervical cancer have decreased over the past several decades. A Pap smear (the recommendation in Canada is to begin having Pap tests at 21 years of age; Canadian Cancer Society, 2015b) taken during routine pelvic exams, can detect early changes in the cervical cells, which may indicate cervical cancer. Most cervical cancer occurs in women between the ages of 30 and 59. Early diagnosis can lead to more effective treatment and higher cure rates. During a Pap smear, a few cells are painlessly scraped from the cervix and are examined under a microscope for abnormalities. The majority of cervical cancers develop slowly, so if a woman has regular Pap tests, nearly all cases can be successfully treated. At present the five-year survival rate from cervical cancer is 74 percent (Public Health Agency of Canada, 2014).

The main cause of cervical cancer is an infection with certain types of human papillomavirus (HPV), which we will discuss further in Chapter 7. Women who begin having sex at a young age or who have multiple sex partners are at an increased risk for HPV infection and cervical cancer. Long-term use of birth control pills and cigarette smoking are also associated with an increased risk for cervical cancer (Public Health Agency of Canada, 2014).

Unfortunately, few symptoms are associated with cervical cancer until the later stages of the disease. When the cervical cells become cancerous and invade nearby cells, a woman may experience abnormal bleeding during the month or after penetrative sex or a pelvic exam.

Cervical cancer has high cure rates because it starts as an easily identifiable lesion, called a **cervical intraepithelial neoplasia,** which usually progresses slowly into cervical cancer. Better early detection of cervical cancer has led to a sharp decrease in the numbers of serious cervical cancer cases. For many women abroad, routine pelvic examinations and Pap smears are not available. It is for this reason that approximately 80 percent of the 500 000 new cases of cervical cancer diagnosed every year are in poor countries such as sub-Saharan Africa and Latin America (Nebehay, 2004).

Cervical lesions can be treated with surgery, radiation, chemotherapy, or a combination of these treatments, which has resulted in cure rates up to 90 percent in early stage disease and a dramatic decline in mortality rate for cervical cancer. If the disease has progressed, treatment commonly includes a **hysterectomy** followed by radiation and chemotherapy. Health Canada has approved two vaccines for the prevention of most types of HPV that cause cervical cancer: Gardasil and Cervarix (Canadian Cancer Society, 2015c).

ENDOMETRIAL (UTERINE) CANCER The Canadian Cancer Society estimates that there were approximately 6000 new cases of uterine cancer in 2014 (Canadian Cancer Society, 2015d), most of which involved the endometrial lining. Incidence rates have been decreasing over the last few years. Symptoms include abnormal uterine bleeding or spotting and pain during urination or penetrative sex. Because a Pap smear is rarely effective in detecting early endometrial cancer, a **D&C (dilation and curettage)** is more reliable. Endometrial cancer is typically treated with surgery, radiation, hormones, and chemotherapy, depending on the stage of the disease.

---

cervical intraepithelial neoplasia
A change in the cells on the surface of the cervix that may signal early beginnings of cervical cancer; sometimes referred to as cervical dysplasia.

hysterectomy
The surgical removal of the uterus.

dilation and curettage (D&C)
The surgical scraping of the uterine wall with a spoon-shaped instrument.

Estrogen is a risk factor for endometrial cancer. Women who have been exposed to high levels of estrogen for hormone replacement therapies, and those who are overweight, experienced late menopause, never had children, or who have a history of PCOS are at increased risk for endometrial cancer (Canadian Cancer Society, 2015d). Because unexpected and heavy bleeding are possible indications of endometrial cancer, women who experience changes in menstrual bleeding should report this to their health care providers. If detected at an early stage, endometrial cancer has an 85 percent survival rate five years post-diagnosis (Canadian Cancer Society, 2015d).

OVARIAN CANCER   In 2013 it was estimated that 17 000 women in Canada were living with ovarian cancer, and approximately 2600 were diagnosed with ovarian cancer. Ovarian cancer is the fifth most common cancer for women in Canada and is the most fatal women's cancer (Ovarian Cancer Canada, 2014). Ovarian cancer is more common in northern European and North American countries than in Asia or developing countries. Overall rates of ovarian cancer have been decreasing over the last few years. Although not as common as uterine or breast cancer, ovarian cancer causes more deaths than any other cancer of the female reproductive system, because it invades the body silently, with few warning signs or symptoms until it reaches an advanced stage (Ovarian Cancer Canada, 2014). Because the ovary floats freely in the pelvic cavity, a tumour can grow undetected without producing many noticeable symptoms (i.e., there is little pressure on other organs; see Figure 3.4).

Although there are few symptoms of ovarian cancer, some women experience abdominal bloating, pelvic pain, difficulty eating or feeling full quickly, and an increased need to urinate (Canadian Cancer Society, 2015e). Because these symptoms are similar to other conditions (such as irritable bowel syndrome), it is important for a woman to check with her health care provider should she experience such symptoms for more than a week or two. The most important factor in the survival rate from ovarian cancer is early detection and diagnosis. It is estimated that two thirds of cases of ovarian cancer are diagnosed at a late stage of development (Mantica, 2005). A woman in whom an ovarian lump is detected should not panic. Most lumps turn out to be relatively harmless **ovarian cysts;** about 70 percent of all ovarian tumours are benign.

The cause of ovarian cancer is unknown. Like other cancers, an increased incidence is found in women who are childless, undergo early menopause, or eat a high-fat diet. Women who are lactose-intolerant or who use talc powder (especially on the vulva) have also been found to have higher rates of ovarian cancer. Women who take birth control pills, who were pregnant at an early age, or who had several pregnancies have particularly low rates of ovarian cancer. One study demonstrated that women who undergo tubal ligation (have their tubes tied to prevent pregnancy) also reduce the risk for ovarian cancer (Narod et al., 2001).

Although there is no 100 percent accurate test for ovarian cancer, health care providers can use blood tests, pelvic examinations, and ultrasound to screen for the cancer. Women who are at high risk for ovarian cancer may be given an ultrasound and pelvic exam, together with a CA-125 blood test. However, there is some controversy over the usefulness of these tests, because they have fairly high **false negatives** (Mantica, 2005; Rettenmaier et al., 2010; U.S. Preventive Services Task Force, 2005). This is why many women with ovarian cancer are diagnosed after the cancer has spread beyond the ovary.

Treatment for ovarian cancer is removal of the ovaries and possibly the Fallopian tubes and uterus. Chemotherapy may also be used. In women who have not yet had children, the uterus may be spared (Canadian Cancer Society, 2015e).

As you have learned throughout this chapter, understanding anatomy and physiology is an important piece in learning about human sexual behaviour. It is important to understand all of the physiological and hormonal influences and how they affect the female body before we can move on to the emotional and psychological issues involved in human sexuality. Anatomy and physiology, therefore, are really the foundations of any human sexuality class. We continue to lay this foundation in Chapter 4, "Male Sexual Anatomy, Development, and Health."

ovarian cysts	**false negatives**
Small, fluid-filled sacs, which can form on the ovary, that do not pose a health threat under most conditions.	Incorrect result of a medical test that wrongly shows the lack of a finding, condition, or disease.

Review Questions

1 Explain what is done in a yearly pelvic exam and why.

2 Name and explain three gynecological health concerns.

3 Identify and explain the risk factors that have been identified for breast cancer.

4 Explain how a vaccine for HPV can decrease the incidence of cervical cancer.

5 Identify and describe the two most common forms of reproductive organ cancer.

6 Explain why ovarian cancer is the most deadly gynecologic cancer.

Female Sexual Anatomy, Development, and Health   **87**

Chapter Review

Summary Points

1 The women's external sex organs, collectively called the vulva, include a number of separate structures, including the mons veneris, labia majora, and labia minora. The clitoris is composed of a glans, body, and paired crura (legs). It is richly supplied with both blood vessels and nerve endings and becomes erect during sexual excitement. The opening of the vagina is also referred to as the introitus.

2 The female's internal sexual organs include the vagina, uterus, Fallopian tubes, and ovaries. The vagina serves as the female organ of intercourse and the passageway to and from the uterus.

3 The uterus is a thick-walled, hollow, muscular organ that provides a path for sperm to reach the ovum and provides a home for the developing fetus. On the sides of the uterus lie two Fallopian tubes, and their job is to bring the ovum from the ovary into the uterus. The mature ovaries contain a woman's oocytes and are the major producers of female reproductive hormones.

4 The breasts are modified sweat glands that contain fatty tissue and produce milk to nourish a newborn. Milk creation, secretion, and ejection from the nipple are referred to as breast-feeding, or lactation.

5 Human beings use sexual reproduction to combine 23 chromosomes in the mother's gamete with the 23 in the father's. The zygote then begins to undergo cell differentiation. If the 23rd chromosome pair is XY, the fetus will develop typically female sexual characteristics.

6 Female genitalia develop from the Müllerian duct, whereas male genitalia develop from the Wolffian duct. Both male and female external genitalia develop from the same tubercle, so many male and female genital structures are homologous.

7 Endocrine glands secrete hormones directly into the bloodstream to be carried to the target organs. The ovaries primarily produce estrogen and progesterone, and the testicles produce androgens. The hypothalamus and pituitary gland are the body's central control centre for hormone secretions.

8 Disorders of sex development in females include sex chromosome and hormone disorders. Chromosomal syndromes are Turner and triple X syndromes, whereas the primary hormonal syndrome is congenital adrenal hyperplasia (CAH).

9 Female puberty occurs when the ovaries begin to release estrogen, which stimulates growth of the woman's sexual organs and menstruation. Menstruation can be divided into four general phases: the follicular phase, the ovulatory phase, the luteal phase, and the menstrual phase.

10 A number of menstrual problems are possible, including amenorrhea, which involves a lack of menstruation; menorrhagia, which involves excessive menstrual flow; and dysmenorrhea, which is painful menstruation. The physical and emotional symptoms that may occur late in the menstrual cycle are called premenstrual syndrome (PMS). The most debilitating and severe cases of PMS are referred to as premenstrual dysphoric disorder (PMDD).

11 Menstrual manipulation, the ability to schedule menstrual periods, and menstrual suppression, the ability to completely eliminate menses, are becoming more popular. There are cultural taboos against sexual intercourse during menstruation. However, engaging in sexual intercourse during menstruation is a personal decision; although there is no medical reason to avoid intimacy during this time, couples need to talk about what they are comfortable doing.

12 As women age, hormone or estrogen production wanes, leading to perimenopause and then menopause, or the cessation of menstruation. Some women use nutritional therapy to help lessen menopausal symptoms, whereas others use hormone replacement therapy (HRT), which has its advantages and disadvantages.

13 There are several gynecological health concerns. Endometriosis is a condition in which the uterine cells begin to migrate to places other than the uterus. Menstrual toxic shock syndrome (mTSS) is an infection, usually caused by the use of tampons. Symptoms of mTSS include high fever, vomiting, diarrhea, and sore throat. If left untreated, it can result in death.

14 Uterine fibroids are hard tissue masses in the uterus, and symptoms include pelvic pain, heavy cramping, and prolonged bleeding. Regular gynecological examination is recommended for all women to help detect uterine, ovarian, and cervical cancers. Genital self-examination is also an important part of women's health behaviour.

15 The most prevalent cancer in the world is breast cancer. Breast self-examination and mammography can help detect breast cancer early. The most common forms of uterine cancer are cervical and endometrial. The most deadly of all gynecologic cancers is ovarian.

Critical Thinking Questions

1 What were the early messages that you received (as a man or a woman) about menstruation? Did you receive any information about it when you were growing up? What do you wish would have been done differently?

2 Do you think that PMS really exists? Provide a rationale for your answer.

3 If you are heterosexual or a lesbian, how would you feel about engaging in sex during menstruation? Why do you think you feel this way? Trace how these feelings may have developed.

4 If you are a woman, have you ever practised a breast self-exam? If so, what made you decide to perform one? If you have never performed one, why not? If you are a man, do you encourage the women in your life to perform breast self-exams? Why or why not?

Websites

Museum of Menstruation & Women's Health (MUM)   An online museum that illustrates the rich history of menstruation and women's health. It contains information on menstruation's history and various aspects of menstruation. (http://www.mum.org/)

The Society of Obstetricians and Gynaecologists of Canada (SOGC)   The SOGC is the nation's leading group of professionals providing health care for women. This site contains information on recent news releases relevant to women's health, educational materials, and links to various other health-related websites. (http://sogc.org/)

National Women's Health Information Center (NWHIC)   This website, operated by the Department of Health and Human Services in the United States, provides a gateway to women's health information services. Information is available on pregnancy, cancers, nutrition, menopause, and HRT, as well as many other health-related areas. (http://www.healthywomen.org/)

National Vulvodynia Association (NVA)   The National Vulvodynia Association (NVA) is a non-profit organization created to educate and provide support. NVA coordinates a central source of information and encourages further research. (https://www.nva.org/)

Cancer.net   This site contains material for health professionals, including cancer treatments, prevention, and CANCERLIT, a bibliographic database. (http://www.cancer.net)

Canadian Cancer Society   This site contains material for health professionals, including cancer diagnosis, statistics, treatments, prevention and myths. (http://cancer.ca)

FORWARD (Foundation for Women's Health Research and Development)   FORWARD is a non-profit organization that works to eliminate female genital mutilation (FGM) and provide support services for those young girls and women who are victims of FGM. (http://www.forwarduk.org.uk/)

4

Male Sexual Anatomy, Development, and Health

Over the years, I've given many lectures on sexual anatomy and physiology. Students are always interested in learning more about both male and female reproductive anatomy. I usually ask students to submit anonymous questions about anatomy and then have a class discussion about these issues. One particular topic always gets a lot of questions: *penises*. Students are often very curious about them—how big are they, how men feel about them, do guys check out other guys' penises, and whether guys are intimidated by the size of men's penises in pornography. While I've had lots of conversations with groups of students about how men feel about penises in general, I have not had many opportunities to sit down with one man and talk about how he came to know his penis. What did he remember thinking about it when he was young? How did he feel he compared to other boys and men? Was there pressure to compare oneself with others? Lucky for me, I met Vic, a

very funny and interesting man who just so happened to want to talk about his penis. He grew up in a neighbourhood surrounded by older kids, which is why he knew more about sex and anatomy than most kids his age. But being the youngest also had its problems. One early memory involved being *pantsed* at the age of four.

The kids who pantsed me were a good ten years older than me. We had been hanging out with a big group of older kids, both girls and guys. I don't know why they did it. I bet the boys just wanted to make the girls laugh. All in all, I learned a ton from hanging out with older kids. I remember looking at Playboy magazines all the time at one kid's house. I was really active in sports and I also learned a lot in the locker room. It's funny because in high school, locker rooms were pretty reserved. No one showered and everyone tried to hide his junk. But, then came college and there were

naked swinging penises everywhere! While most guys were fairly modest and didn't just throw it around, some felt the need to show their penis to everyone! And it wasn't always the biggest guys, either. I often shied away from this because I felt I was kind of on the smaller side, but at some point it's inevitable that everyone sees it. I don't care what anyone says, but EVERY guy checks out each other's junk. The funny thing is that I always imagined that the huge soft penises in the locker room got enormous when they were hard. But since I didn't ever see them hard, I didn't know. Then one night I had an interesting experience that proved to me if a guy is huge when he's soft, he probably doesn't get much bigger when he's hard. ‖

In this chapter, we explore male anatomy and physiology. In the previous chapter, we discussed female anatomy, development, and reproductive health, and although there are many similarities between the two sexes, there are also many differences. One obvious difference is the fact that the male genitalia (the testes and penis) lie well outside of the body, whereas the female genitalia (vagina and clitoris) are located within the vestibule and are difficult to see without a mirror. Because of the location of the male genitalia, boys are often more comfortable and familiar with their genitalia compared with girls. In this chapter, we explore the male reproductive system, development, maturation, and sexual health issues.

Male Sexual and Reproductive System

Most men are fairly familiar with their penis and scrotum. Boys learn to hold their penises while urinating and notice them when their penis becomes erect. Yet, the male reproductive system is a complex series of glands and ducts, and few men have a full understanding of how the system is biologically organized and operates.

REAL Research

It is well known that in animals the penis is used to deliver sperm to the female reproductive tract in an attempt to fertilize an ovum. Sperm competition occurs when the sperm of two or more males is present in the Fallopian tubes, swimming to fertilize the ovum. Researchers, using artificial vaginas and dildos, have shown that dildos with a coronal ridge displaced more artificial semen from the vagina than dildos without a coronal ridge. This suggests that the shape of the human penis may have evolved to remove semen from the vagina of a woman who has had prior (recent) copulations to prevent pregnancy from previous matings (Gallup et al., 2003; Shackelford & Goetz, 2007).

External Genitalia

The external genitalia of the male include the penis (which consists of the glans and root) and the scrotum. In this section, we discuss the anatomy of the external male genitalia and the process of penile erection.

The Penis

The **penis** carries urine and **semen** to the outside of the body. The penis has the ability to engorge with blood and stiffen, which allows for penetration of the vagina. Although there is no bone and little muscle in the human penis, the root of the penis is attached to a number of muscles in the pelvis that are important for erectile function, and that assist ejaculation and allow men to move their penis slightly when erect. Throughout history, men have experienced anxiety about penis size. In the accompanying Sex in Real Life, we discuss this anxiety.

The penis is composed of three structures that are important for erectile function. Each of these structures contain erectile tissue called sinusoids—spongelike tissue that fills with blood to cause **erection**. Two lateral **corpora cavernosa** (CORE-purr-uh cav-er-NO-suh) lie on the upper sides of the penis, and the central **corpus spongiosum** (CORE-pus spon-gee-OH-sum) lies on the bottom and contains the urethra. Each of these erectile structures are surrounded by smooth muscle that are bound together with connective tissue and covered with skin.

THE GLANS PENIS   The penis ends in a conelike expansion called the **glans penis**. The glans penis is made up of the **corona**, the **frenulum** (FREN-yu-lum), the **urethral opening**, or **meatus** (mee-ATE-us) (see Figures 4.1 and 4.2). The glans is very sensitive to stimulation, and some males find direct or continuous stimulation of the glans irritating.

The prepuce of the glans penis is a circular fold of skin usually called the **foreskin**. The foreskin is a continuation of the loose skin that covers the penis as a whole to allow it to grow during erection. The foreskin can cover part or all of the glans and retracts back below the corona when the penis is erect. In many cultures, the foreskin is removed surgically through a procedure called a circumcision (sir-kum-SI-zhun; see the Sexual Diversity in Our World feature later in this chapter for more information about circumcision).

---

penis
The male copulatory and urinary organ, used both to urinate and move spermatozoa out of the urethra through ejaculation; it is the major organ of male sexual pleasure and is homologous to the female clitoris.

semen
A thick, whitish secretion of the male reproductive organs, containing spermatozoa and secretions from the seminal vesicles, prostate, and bulbourethral glands.

erection
The hardening of the penis caused by blood engorging the erectile tissue.

corpora cavernosa
Plural of corpus cavernosum (cavernous body); areas in the penis that fill with blood during erection.

corpus spongiosum
Meaning "spongy body," the erectile tissue in the penis that contains the urethra.

glans penis
The flaring, enlarged region at the end of the penis.

corona
The ridge of the glans penis.

frenulum
Fold of skin just below the glans and at the top of the shaft on the underside of the penis.

urethral opening or meatus
The opening of the penis through which urine and semen are expelled.

foreskin
The fold of skin that covers the glans penis; also called the *prepuce*.

SEX in Real Life *Penis Size and Male Anxiety*

The penis has been defined as the symbol of male sexuality throughout history. Men have often been plagued by concerns about penis function and size. As Vic discussed in the chapter opening story, many men worry about the size of their penis. Some men assume there is a correlation between penis size and masculinity, or sexual prowess, and many men assume that their partners prefer a large penis. Others worry about their size and fear that they are not "normal." Although there may be a psychological preference for large penises among some partners (just as some partners desire women with large breasts), penis size has no correlation with the ability to excite a partner sexually during sex.

The average flaccid penis is between 7.5 and 10 centimetres (3 and 4 inches)

long, and the average erect penis is about 15 centimetres (6 inches). Gary Griffen, author of *Penis Size and Enlargement* (1995), states that only 15 percent of men have an erect penis measuring more than 17.8 centimetres (7 inches), and fewer than 5000 erect penises worldwide measure 30 centimetres (12 inches). The opinion most men have that the average penis size is greater than it really is comes from pornographic films (which tend to use the largest men they can find), from men's perspective on their own penis (which, from the top, looks smaller than from the sides), and from overestimates of actual penis size (researchers consistently find that people's estimation of the size of penises they have just seen is larger than the actual penis size (Shamloul, 2005).

It is erroneous views such as these that cause some men to be anxious about their penis size. Some succumb to the advertisements for devices promising to enlarge their penises without surgery. Men who purchase these devices are bound to be disappointed, for there is no non-surgical way to enlarge the penis, and many of these techniques (most of which use suction) can do significant damage to penile tissue (D. Bagley, 2005). Other men with size anxiety may refrain from sex altogether, fearing they cannot please a partner or will be laughed at when their partner sees them naked. Yet, the vast majority of women and men report that penis size is not a significant factor in the quality of a sex partner.

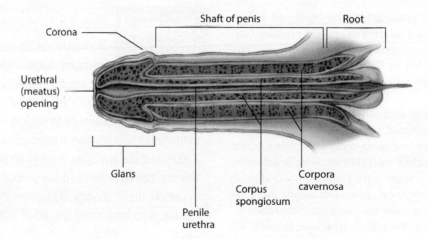

(a)

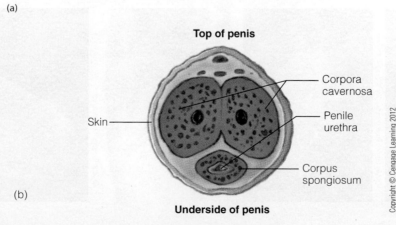

(b)

FIGURE **4.1** The internal structure of the penis.

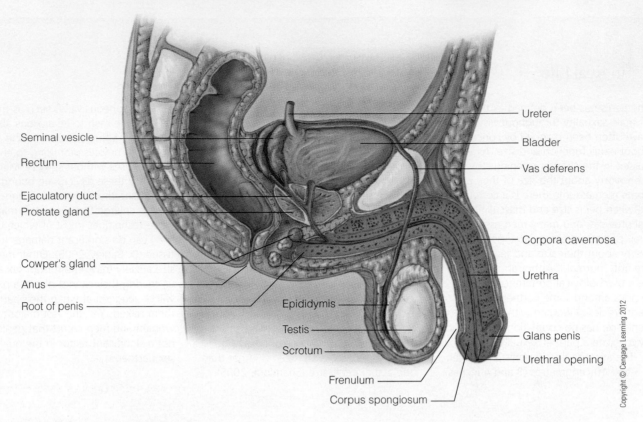

FIGURE **4.2** The male reproductive organs.

THE ROOT   The root of the penis enters the body just below the pubic bone and is attached to internal pelvic muscles (see Figure 4.2). The root of the penis goes farther into the body than most men realize; it can be felt in the perineum (between the scrotum and anus), particularly when the penis is erect.

ERECTION   Erections can occur with any form of stimulation the individual perceives as sexual—visual, tactile, auditory, olfactory, or cognitive. In addition, involuntary sleep-related erections occur several times each night in healthy men (Hirshkowitz & Schmidt, 2005). During an erection, the arteries of the penis allow blood to fill the sinusoidal spaces in the corpora cavernosa and corpus spongiosum. The veins that drain blood from the penis are compressed to prevent the blood from escaping. The erectile structures thus will fill

Animal Variations — The Male Baculum

Human males do not have a penis bone or baculum. Surprisingly, penis bones are found in many mammalian species, including gorillas, chimpanzees, bears, raccoons, and your pet dog. At present, no one has come up with scientific evidence to explain why the males of many mammalian species have a penis bone (Lariviere & Ferguson, 2002). Just like any other bone in an animal's body, however, this one can be broken! To see several examples of these bones in person, the Phallological Museum in Iceland (www.phallus.is) has baculum from many species of animals.

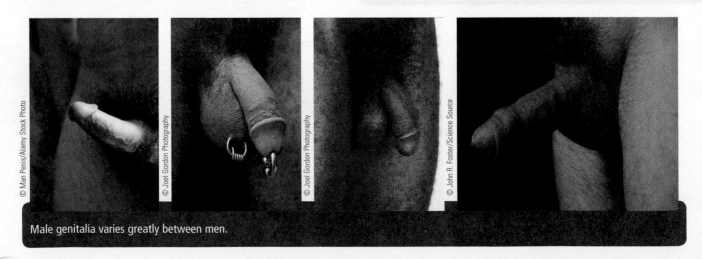

Male genitalia varies greatly between men.

Ethnicity, Religion, and Circumcision

Male circumcision is practised in many parts of the world. The World Health Organization estimates that more than 664 million males—or 30 percent—are circumcised (Malone & Steinbrecher, 2007). Reasons for circumcision vary around the world but include religious, cultural, social, and/or medical reasons. Non-religious circumcision became popular in the 1870s because it was thought to promote hygiene, reduce "unnatural" sexual behaviours, prevent syphilis and gonorrhea, and reduce masturbation (G. Kaplan, 1977; Wallerstein, 1980). An article published in 1947 supporting circumcision reported that cancer was more common in laboratory mice who were not circumcised (Plaut & Kohn-Speyer, 1947). All of these medical reports and social considerations have influenced the incidence of male circumcision.

Circumcision can be done at any age, but infant circumcision is commonly done in the United States, Canada, Australia, New Zealand, the Middle East, Central Asia, and West Africa. Many parents cite hygiene and health reasons for circumcising their infants at birth. In other areas of the world, such as East and southern Africa, male circumcisions are done in the mid-teens to early 20s and are viewed as rites of passage for boys and a transition from child to man (Crowley & Kesner, 1990). Other cultures believe that circumcision makes a boy a man because the foreskin is viewed as feminine (Silverman, 2004).

Various ethnic groups have different preferences concerning circumcising their male children. If circumcision is common in a particular ethnic group, parents may be inclined to circumcise their male children so their sons will look like other boys (Centers for Disease Control and Prevention, 2008h). In addition, fathers who are circumcised often have their sons circumcised (Goldman, 1999). These social considerations have been found to outweigh the medical facts when parents are deciding whether to circumcise their sons (M.S. Brown & Brown, 1987). Medical reasons for circumcision are rare, and it is mainly practised for religious and cultural reasons today (Malone & Steinbrecher, 2007).

The practice of male circumcision has elicited more controversy than any other surgical procedure in history (Alanis & Lucidi, 2004; Fox & Thomson, 2010; Hinchley, 2007; Patrick, 2007). Most of the controversy revolves around the risks and potential benefits of circumcision. Studies conducted in Africa show that male circumcision offers protection from HIV infection (M.S. Cohen et al., 2008d; Drain et al., 2006; Morris, 2007; Thomson et al., 2007). Male circumcision has been found to reduce risk for HIV in men by 60 percent (Smith et al., 2010; Weiss et al., 2010). Circumcision offered protection to both men who had sex with women and men who had sex with men (Dinh et al., 2011; Fox & Thomson, 2010).

Circumcised men have also been found to have lower rates of infant urinary tract infections (Simforoosh et al., 2012) and sexually transmitted infections, such as herpes and human papillomavirus (see Chapter 7; Weiss et al., 2010). Female partners of circumcised men also have lower rates of certain types of vaginal infections and cervical cancer (Alanis & Lucidi, 2004; Drain et al., 2006; Morris, 2007; Weiss et al., 2010). In 2012, the American Academy of Pediatrics Task Force on Circumcision supported the use of circumcision. In Canada the Paediatric Society of Canada's position statement was last updated in 1996. The society is currently revisiting the issue of circumcision with a new more neutral statement than the previous statement, which did not support circumcision (Kirkey, 2013). While there may be some medical benefits to circumcision, some experts believe these benefits are not strong enough for health care providers to recommend routine circumcision (Kinkade & Meadows, 2005; Tobian et al., 2010). Ultimately, it will be up to parents, in consultation with their health care provider, to determine whether circumcision is the best course of action for their male children.

© Nigel Pavitt/Getty Images

A Samburu youth is circumcised in Kenya while his sponsors attend to him—one holding his leg, while the other turns his face away from the circumciser. Boys are not allowed to show any signs of fear or pain during the procedure. Even the blink of an eyelid is frowned upon.

with blood, causing the penis to become erect. The penis returns to its flaccid state when the arteries constrict, the pressure closing off the veins is released, and the sequestered blood is allowed to drain.

Erection is basically a spinal reflex, and men who have spinal injuries can sometimes achieve reflex erections, in which their penis becomes erect even though they can feel no sensation there. These erections generally occur without cognitive or emotional excitement. In Chapter 15 we will return to this topic.

The Scrotum

The **scrotum** (SKROH-tum) is a loose, wrinkled pouch beneath the penis, covered with sparse pubic hair. The scrotum contains

scrotum
External pouch of skin that contains the testicles.

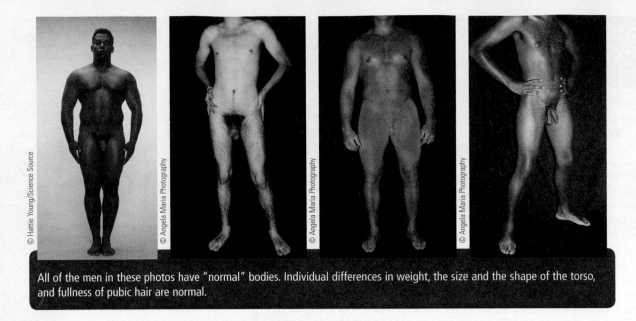

All of the men in these photos have "normal" bodies. Individual differences in weight, the size and the shape of the torso, and fullness of pubic hair are normal.

the testicles, each in a sac, separated by a thin layer of tissue. The testicles sit outside the body since sperm survival is optimal at a temperature 4-7°C lower than the body's temperature.

On Your Mind
Why do men so often wake up with erections?

Men's penises (and women's clitoral glans) become erect during a part of sleep known as the REM (rapid eye movement) cycle. Some physiologists have suggested that nighttime erections help keep the cells of the penis supplied with blood (Montorsi & Oettel, 2005). Both men and women typically enter REM sleep many times each night, and often we are in a REM cycle right before we wake up, which is why men often wake with an erection. Some men believe that having a full bladder makes the morning erection firmer and longer lasting, although there is little medical evidence to support this. Because men have no control over nighttime erections, physicians often ask men who have problems getting erections if they experience erections in their sleep, which can indicate whether their erectile problem is physiological or psychological. We discuss this further in Chapter 15.

When the testicles become too hot, sperm production is halted; in fact, soaking the testicles in hot water has been used as a form of birth control. (Of course, such a technique is highly unreliable, and it takes only a few hardy sperm to undo an hour of uncomfortable soaking). For example, it has been shown that there is a correlation between spending several hours a day seated in a vehicle (which keeps the testicles at a higher temperature than normal) and having a lower sperm count (Thonneau et al., 1998). In the accompanying

cremaster muscle
The "suspender" muscle that raises and lowers the scrotum to control scrotal temperature.

Sex in Real Life feature, we explore factors that have been found to decrease sperm concentrations and quality.

The scrotum is designed to regulate testicular temperature using two mechanisms. First, the skin overlying the scrotum contains many sweat glands and sweats freely, which cools the testicles when they become too warm. Second, the **cremaster muscle** of the scrotum contracts and expands: When the testicles become too cool, they are drawn closer to the body to increase their temperature; when they become too warm, they are lowered away from the body to reduce

REAL Research
Stress can affect sperm production—semen samples from male college students during exam periods found lower concentrations of sperm than samples collected at the beginning of the semester (Lampiao, 2009).

When a man jumps into a cold swimming pool, muscles in the scrotum pull the testicles up closer to the body in an attempt to maintain the correct temperature.

Sperm, Toxins, Cell Phones, and Tofu: What's the Relationship?

Spermatogenesis, or the production of sperm, begins at puberty. Sperm morphology (sperm form and structure) and motility (sperm's ability to swim), together with semen volume, begins to change and decline in a man's 20s and this continues over the lifespan (Eskenazi et al., 2003). Researchers have been evaluating changes in total sperm counts, quality, morphology, and motility, and have found evidence that sperm counts have been declining in men throughout the world (Dindyal, 2004; Huang et al., 2010; Muratori et al., 2011; Povey & Stocks, 2010). Although declines in sperm counts and quality are a normal function of aging, researchers have also begun to look at the effects of occupational, environmental, and lifestyle factors, such as radiation, heat, cigarette smoke, pollutants, sexually transmitted infections, cell phone usage, diet, and obesity on sperm counts and quality (Pacey, 2010; Povey & Stocks, 2010).

Environmental toxins, such as dioxins, bisphenol A, and phthalates, have been shown to reduce sperm health (Galloway et al., 2010; Li et al., 2011; Mocarelli et al., 2008; Taioli et al., 2005; Toppari et al., 2010). Dioxins are petroleum-derived chemicals that are in herbicides, pesticides, and industrial waste, but they are also commonly found in fish and cow milk products (Taioli et al., 2005). A U.S. study comparing semen quality in various geographic areas found reduced semen quality in areas where pesticides are commonly used (Swan, 2006). Phthalates, which are found in certain types of plastic, have also been found to decrease sperm counts and quality (Stahlhut et al., 2007; Voiland, 2008).

Cell phones have also been identified as possible factors affecting sperm health. Cell phones emit radiofrequency electromagnetic waves, which have been found to affect sperm quality. In a study of men at a clinic for infertility, a positive correlation was found between lower sperm quality and the time spent daily talking on

Cell phones emit radiofrequency electromagnetic waves, which may affect sperm quality.

a cell phone. Other studies, however, claim that cell phone usage may not be harmful to sperm (Deepinder et al., 2007; Erogul et al., 2006; Wdowiak et al., 2007). (For a recent review of the animal and human literature on sperm health and EM radiation see Sandro La Vignera et al., 2012.)

Several other lifestyle factors have been correlated with changes in sperm production and health, such as stress, laptop computer use (Sheynkin et al., 2005; Avendano et al., 2011), biking five or more hours a week (Wise et al., 2011), and smoking cigarettes and drinking alcohol (Kalyani et al., 2007). Researchers have also explored whether there is a relationship between soy intake and sperm concentrations, and have found conflicting results (Cederroth et al., 2010; Chavarro et al., 2008; Messina, 2010). Soy products contain high levels of isoflavones, which mimic estrogens in the body. Researchers in all these areas of inquiry will continue to explore the effects of lifestyle choices on sperm production and quality.

Decreasing sperm counts and quality may contribute to male infertility—in fact, 7 percent of infertility cases are due to defects in the quality, concentration, and/or motility of sperm (Muratori et al., 2011). There are no known treatments to help a man produce more or healthier sperm (Barratt et al., 2011). We will discuss male infertility in more detail in Chapter 5.

---

their temperature. Men often experience the phenomenon of having the scrotum relax and hang low when taking a warm shower, only to tighten up when cold air hits it after exiting the shower.

Internal Sex Organs

The internal sex organs of the male include the testes (testicles), epididymis, vas deferens, seminal vesicles, prostate gland, and bulbourethral glands (Cowper's glands). All of these organs play important roles in spermatogenesis, testosterone production, and the process of ejaculation.

The Testicles

The testicles (also referred to as the testes [TEST-eez]) are egg-shaped glands that rest in the scrotum, each about 5 centimetres (2 inches) long and 2.5 centimetres (1 inch) in diameter. Typically in adult men, one testicle hangs lower and one is slightly larger. The testicles are

connected to the body and the internal reproductive organs via the **spermatic cord**. The testicles serve two main functions: **spermatogenesis** and testosterone production (see Figures 4.3 and 4.4).

SPERMATOGENESIS   Sperm are produced and stored in microscopic tubes located in the testes, known as **seminiferous** (sem-uh-NIF-uh-rus) **tubules**. Figure 4.3 shows the development of the **spermatozoon** in the seminiferous tubules. First, a **spermatogonium** (sper-MAT-oh-go-nee-um) develops in the cells lining the outer

spermatic cord The internal structure that connects the testicles to the internal reproductive organs.	**seminiferous tubules** The tightly coiled ducts located in the testes where spermatozoa are produced.
spermatogenesis The production of sperm in the testes.	**spermatozoon** A mature sperm cell.
	spermatogonium An immature sperm cell that will develop into a spermatocyte.

Male Sexual Anatomy, Development, and Health

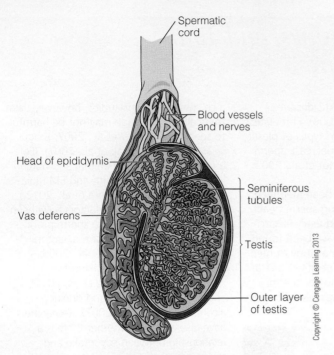

FIGURE **4.3** The internal structure of the testicle.

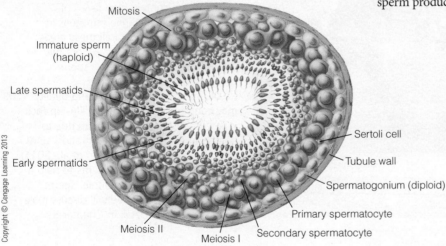

FIGURE **4.4** Spermatogenesis is continually taking place with various levels of sperm development throughout the testis.

wall of the seminiferous tubules and progressively moves toward the center of the tubules. Sertoli cells located in the seminiferous tubules secrete nutritional substances for the developing sperm.

As the spermatogonium grows, it becomes a primary **spermatocyte** (sper-MAT-oh-site) and then divides to form two secondary spermatocytes. As the developing sperm approach the centre

Coloured scan of seminiferous tubules, each containing a swirl of forming sperm cells (in blue).

of the seminiferous tubules, the secondary spermatocytes divide into two **spermatids**. The spermatid then reorganizes its nucleus to form a compact head, topped by an acrosome, which contains enzymes to help the sperm penetrate the ovum. The sperm also develops a midpiece, which generates energy, and a **flagellum** (flah-GEL-lum), which propels the mature spermatozoon. The production of sperm requires between 65 and 72 days to complete and the human male produces about 300 million sperm per day. (For more information on sperm production, see the accompanying Sex in Real Life feature).

TESTOSTERONE PRODUCTION Testosterone is produced in the testicles in **interstitial** (in-ter-STIH-shul) or **Leydig** (LIE-dig) **cells**. Testosterone is the primary androgen necessary for the physical development of males and for the development of sperm.

The Epididymis

Once formed, immature sperm enter the seminiferous tubule and migrate to the **epididymis** (ep-uh-DID-uh-mus; see Figure 4.3), where they mature for about 10 to 14 days; faulty or old sperm are reabsorbed here. The epididymis is a comma-shaped organ that sits atop the testicle and can be easily felt if the testicle is gently rolled between the fingers. If uncoiled, the epididymis would be about 60 metres (20 feet) in length. After sperm have matured, they can be held for several months in the epididymis and the vas deferens.

The Ejaculatory Pathway

The **vas deferens** (vass DEH-fuh-renz) is a tube that carries sperm from the testicles, mixes it with fluids from other glands, and propels the sperm toward the urethra during ejaculation

spermatocyte The intermediate stage in the growth of a spermatozoon.	**flagellum** The tail-like end of a spermatozoon that propels it forward.	**Leydig cells** The cells in the testes that produce testosterone; also referred to as interstitial cells.	**vas deferens** One of two long tubes that convey the sperm from the testes and in which other fluids are mixed to create semen.
spermatids The cells that make up the final intermediate stage in the production of sperm.	**interstitial cells** Cells responsible for the production of testosterone; also referred to as Leydig cells.	**epididymis** A comma-shaped organ that sits atop the testicle and holds sperm during maturation.	

(see Figure 4.2). **Ejaculation** is the physiological process whereby the seminal fluid is forcefully ejected from the penis. During ejaculation, sperm pass successively through the epididymis, the vas deferens, the ejaculatory duct, and the urethra, picking up fluid along the way from three glands—the seminal vesicles, the prostate gland, and the bulbourethral glands.

THE SEMINAL VESICLES The vas deferens hooks up over the ureter of the bladder and ends in an **ampulla**. Adjacent to the ampulla are the **seminal vesicles**. The seminal vesicles contribute various compounds necessary for the health of sperm and this fluid, containing fructose (sugar), vitamin C, and other proteins, makes up about 60 percent to 70 percent of the volume of the ejaculate. The vas deferens and the duct from the seminal vesicles merge into a common **ejaculatory duct**, a short straight tube that passes into the prostate gland and opens into the urethra.

THE PROSTATE GLAND The **prostate** (PROSS-tayt) **gland**, a walnut-sized gland at the base of the bladder, produces several substances, including simple sugars and zinc that are necessary for sperm health and survival. The vagina maintains an acidic pH to protect against bacteria, yet an acidic environment slows down and eventually kills sperm. Prostatic secretions, which comprise about 25 percent to 30 percent of the ejaculate, combined with the secretions from the seminal vesicles are alkaline and thought to neutralize the acidity of the vagina to allow sperm survival as they swim towards the cervix and ultimately the Fallopian tubes.

The prostate is close to the rectum, so a doctor can feel the prostate during a rectal examination. The prostate gland can cause a number of physical problems in men, especially older men, including prostate enlargement, which pushes up on the bladder and may constrict the urethra making urination difficult,

On Your Mind

I've heard people say that what a man eats can influence the taste of his semen. Is this really true?

It is common folklore that semen taste is affected by what a man eats prior to ejaculation. "Former porn actress, Annie Sprinkle, who tasted hundreds of men's semen, says vegetarians taste best, that eating fruit and drinking fruit juices a few hours before sex improves the taste, and that smoking, alcohol, meats, and asparagus make semen less palatable" (Castleman, 2009). In reality, however, no scientific studies have been done to study the influence of diet on the flavour of ejaculate. While not impossible, getting ethics approval to do this type of research, and the effort it would take to do this type of research well, would be difficult.

On Your Mind

If a man's testicles produce so much sperm every day, is it harmful if the sperm do not regularly exit the body? Can sperm build up and cause a problem?

and the development of prostate cancer (see the section entitled "Male Reproductive and Sexual Health" later in this chapter). In Canada, annual prostate examinations are recommended for men older than 40 years (Prostate Cancer Canada, 2015).

THE BULBOURETHRAL (COWPER'S) GLANDS The **bulbourethral** (bul-bow-you-REE-thral) or **Cowper's glands** are two pea-sized glands that flank the urethra just beneath the prostate gland. The glands have ducts that open right into the urethra and produce a fluid that cleans and lubricates the urethra for the passage of sperm, neutralizing any acidic urine that may remain in the urethra (Chughtai et al., 2005). The drop or more of pre-ejaculatory fluid that many men experience during arousal is the fluid from the bulbourethral glands. Although in the past researchers believed there was no sperm in the pre-ejaculatory fluid, newer research has found that the fluid may contain live sperm, so heterosexual men should use condoms if pregnancy is not desired (Killick et al., 2010).

Sperm are so tiny that even 300 million of them would form a mere drop or two of fluid; most male ejaculate is fluid from other glands. Sperm are regularly reabsorbed by the body as they sit in the epididymis and vas deferens. Many men go days, weeks, months, perhaps even years without ejaculating at all and do not suffer any physiological damage.

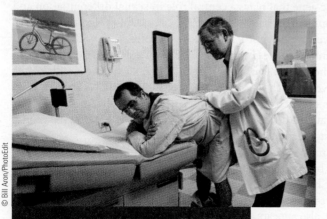

At some point in their lives men will be offered a prostate exam to help detect prostate cancer in its early stages. A man may be asked to either lean over or lie on his side while the health care provider inserts a gloved finger into a man's rectum to check the size of the prostate gland.

ejaculation
The reflex ejection or expulsion of semen from the penis.

ampulla
Base of the vas deferens, where the vas hooks up over the ureter of the bladder.

seminal vesicles
The pair of pouchlike structures lying next to the urinary bladder that secrete a component of semen into the ejaculatory ducts.

ejaculatory duct
A tube that transports spermatozoa from the vas deferens to the urethra.

prostate gland
A doughnut-shaped gland that wraps around the urethra as it comes out of the bladder, contributing fluid that contributes to semen composition.

bulbourethral or Cowper's gland
One of a pair of glands located under the prostate gland on either side of the urethra that secretes a fluid into the urethra.

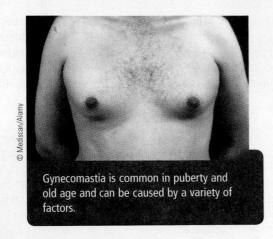

Gynecomastia is common in puberty and old age and can be caused by a variety of factors.

© Mediscan/Alamy

The Breasts

Men's breasts are mostly muscle, and although they do have nipples and areolae, they serve no functional purpose. Transsexual males, who want to change their sex (see Chapter 8), can enlarge their breasts to mimic the female breast by taking estrogen. Some men experience sexual pleasure from having their nipples stimulated, especially during periods of high excitement, whereas others do not.

Breast cancer does affect men, although it is rare and accounts for less than 1 percent of all cases (Reis et al., 2011). We will discuss breast cancer further later in this chapter. Another breast disorder that occurs in men is gynecomastia, or breast enlargement. Gynecomastia is common in all stages of a man's life; in fact, the prevalence rate is 60 percent to 90 percent in newborns, 50 percent to 60 percent in adolescents, and up to 70 percent in men aged 50 to 69 years old (Carlson, 2011; Johnson & Murad, 2009). It may be caused by hormonal issues, such as increased estrogen or decreased testosterone, the use of various medications, excessive weight, marijuana use, and/or certain diseases (Johnson & Murad, 2009). Certain environmental toxins have also been found to be related to the development of gynecomastia (Durmaz et al., 2010).

Although gynecomastia can make men feel self-conscious, most cases resolve without treatment within about one year (Johnson & Murad, 2009). It is typically a benign condition, but if there is pain or psychological distress, treatment options include pharmacological intervention and surgery, including liposuction (Cigna et al., 2011).

Review Questions

1 Identify the external male sex organs and discuss the functions of each.

2 Explain why the male gonads are located outside of the body.

3 Identify and discuss the functions of the internal male sexual organs.

4 Identify the internal male sex organs and discuss the functions of each.

5 Describe the path taken by a sperm from the moment it is a spermatogonium until it is ejaculated. What internal male organs contribute to semen production?

Prenatal Development: X and Y Make the Difference (Continued)

As stated in Chapter 3, XX embryos develop into females and XY embryos develop into male embryos. As in females, however, several things can happen during the first few months of development that will influence the sex-typical development of males. In the next section, we will describe the development of male embryos and the several common chromosomal and hormonal syndromes and physiological conditions that can alter male development.

testes
Male gonads inside the scrotum that produce testosterone.

testosterone
A male sex hormone that is secreted by the Leydig cells of mature testes and stimulates the development of sex characteristics in men.

Müllerian inhibiting factor
A hormone secreted in male embryos that prevents the Müllerian duct from developing into female reproductive organs.

The SRY Gene

The SRY (sex-determining region of the Y) is a Y chromosome–specific gene that plays a central role in sexual differentiation and development in males (DiNapoli & Capel, 2008; Ngun et al., 2011). However, it may not be only **testosterone** or the SRY gene that differentiates males from females. How males and females develop from the initial development of an XX or XY zygote is still an area of active research (DiNapoli & Capel, 2008). What is known, however, is that activation of the SRY gene turns on other genes that stimulate the development of the undifferentiated, internal genital ridges to become **testes** and secret **testosterone**.

In most males, the testes begin to differentiate from the primitive gonad by the seventh to eighth week after conception. If you recall from Chapter 3 (see Figure 3.6 on page 68), the **Müllerian** (myul-EAR-ee-an) **duct** (female) or the **Wolffian** (WOOL-fee-an) **duct** (male), also appears at this time (Krone et al., 2007). In the presence of a Y chromosome (and SRY and SOX9 gene), the gonads develop into testes, which soon begin producing **Müllerian inhibiting factor** and testosterone. Müllerian inhibiting factor causes the Müllerian ducts to disappear during the third month of gestation, and testosterone stimulates the Wolffian duct to develop into the structures surrounding the testicles. The body converts some testosterone into

Table 4.1   Homologous Tissues

Male and female organs that began from the same prenatal tissue are called homologous. Below are some of the homologous tissues.

Female	Male
Clitoral glans	Glans penis
Clitoral hood	Foreskin
Labia minora	Penile shaft
Labia majora	Scrotum
Ovaries	Testes

Copyright © Cengage Learning 2013

another **androgen**, called *dihydrotestosterone* (DHT), to stimulate the development of the male external sex organs.

External Sex Organs

External genitals follow a pattern similar to that of internal organs, and male and female genitalia all develop from the same tissue. Male and female organs that begin from the same prenatal tissue are called **homologous** (HOE-mol-lig-gus; see Table 4.1 for an overview of homologous tissues). Until the eighth week, the undifferentiated tissue from which the genitalia will develop exists as a mound of skin, or tubercle, beneath the umbilical cord (see Figure 3.7 on page 69). In males, by the eighth or ninth week, the

androgen
A hormone that promotes the development of male genitals and secondary sex characteristics. It is produced by the testes in men and by the adrenal glands in both men and women.

homologous
Corresponding in structure, position, or origin but not necessarily in function.

Klinefelter syndrome
A genetic disorder in men in which there are three sex chromosomes, XXY, instead of two; characterized by small testes, low sperm production, breast enlargement, and absence of facial and body hair.

testosterone therapy
The use of testosterone to replace missing hormones in males with hormone disorders.

secondary sexual characteristics
The physical characteristics, other than the genitalia, that distinguish male from female.

XYY syndrome
A genetic abnormality in which a male has an extra Y sex chromosome; it may

be characterized by decreased fertility, some genital abnormality, and slight intellectual disability.

congenital adrenal hyperplasia (CAH)
A disorder involving overproduction of androgen in the adrenal glands that can affect males and females. Males typically experience earlier than normal pubertal changes.

androgen-insensitivity syndrome (AIS)
A condition in which a genetic male's cells are insensitive to androgens, resulting in the development of female external genitalia (but no internal reproductive organs).

5-alpha reductase deficiency
A condition where a genetic male child does not have the enzyme necessary to convert testosterone to the more potent androgen dihydrotestosterone. These children they often appear as female or intersexed at birth but at puberty, with the increase in testosterone, they often become more masculinized.

testes begin androgen secretion, which begins to stimulate the development of male genitalia. The genital tubercle elongates to form the penis, in which lies the urethra, culminating in an external opening called the *urethral meatus*. Part of the tubercle also fuses together to form the scrotum, where the testicles will ultimately rest when they descend.

Variations of Sexual Development

Chromosomal Conditions

Variations of sex development in XY individuals can be caused by chromosomal conditions. Although researchers have identified many such conditions, we discuss here the most common ones that occur in embryos that have a Y chromosome present (see Table 4.2).

Klinefelter syndrome occurs when an ovum containing an extra X chromosome is fertilized by a Y sperm (designated XXY), giving a child 47 chromosomes all together (Giltay & Maiburg, 2010). Klinefelter syndrome prevalence rates are roughly one in 750 live male births (Forti et al., 2010; Giltay & Maiburg, 2010). In Klinefelter syndrome, the Y chromosome triggers the development of male genitalia, but the extra X prevents them from developing fully. As adults, men with Klinefelter syndrome typically have feminized body contours, small testes, low levels of testosterone, gynecomastia, and possible verbal deficits (Forti et al., 2010; Giltay & Maiburg, 2010). **Testosterone therapy**, especially if it is begun during adolescence, can enhance the development of **secondary sexual characteristics**. Although two thirds of men with Klinefelter syndrome are never diagnosed, those who are diagnosed are typically identified during an evaluation for infertility (Forti et al., 2010). Men with Klinefelter syndrome may still be able to father children through sperm retrieval. (We will discuss assisted reproductive techniques in more detail in Chapter 6; Forti et al., 2010).

XYY syndrome is a rare condition. This condition occurs when a normal ovum is fertilized by a sperm that has two Y chromosomes. The XYY individual may grow up as a normal male and often their unusual genetic status is not detected. Individuals with XYY however may have a slightly lower intelligence and low fertility (Kim et al., 2013).

Hormonal Conditions

Disorders of sex development can also be caused by hormonal conditions. In this section, we discuss three hormonal disorders of sex development in males, **congenital adrenal hyperplasia (CAH)** and **androgen-insensitivity syndrome (AIS)** and **5-alpha reductase deficiency**.

Congenital adrenal hyperplasia (CAH) occurs when a child lacks an enzyme in the adrenal gland, forcing the body to produce higher amounts of androgen. It is estimated that approximately one in 15 000 infants are born with CAH, and today almost all newborns are screened for it (Johannsen et al., 2010; Roan, 2010). The excess androgens often have little effect on a developing male fetus.

Table 4.2 Disorders of Sex Development

Syndrome	Chromosomal Pattern	External Genitals	Internal Structures	Description	Treatment
CHROMOSOMAL					
Klinefelter syndrome	47, XXY	Male	Male	Testes are small; breasts may develop; low testosterone levels, erectile dysfunction, and intellectual disability are common; people with this disorder have unusual body proportions and are usually infertile.	Testosterone during adolescence may help improve body shape and sex drive.
XYY syndrome	47, XYY	Male	Male	There is likelihood of slight intellectual disability, some genital irregularities, and decreased fertility or infertility.	None.
HORMONAL					
Congenital adrenal hyperplasia (CAH)	46, XX, XY	Some male and some female traits	Internal organs are consistent with biological gender	Whereas external male genitals are often normal, female infants may have clitoral enlargement and labial fusing.	Surgery can correct external genitals.
Androgen-insensitivity syndrome (AIS)	46, XY	Female	Male gonads in the abdomen	Usually AIS children are raised female. Breasts develop at puberty, but menstruation does not begin. Such a person has a shortened vagina, no internal sexual organs, and is sterile.	Surgery can lengthen vagina to accommodate a penis for intercourse if necessary.
5-alpha reductase deficiency	46, XY	Female or ambiguous at birth but male-like at puberty		Generally, raised as female until puberty, when exposure to high levels of testosterone stimulate penis development. They may be able to reproduce as males in adulthood.	In areas where 5-alpha reductase deficiency is common, typically no surgical changes to the genitalia occur.

Copyright © Cengage Learning 2013

Androgen Insensitivity Syndrome

Androgen-insensitivity syndrome (AIS), another hormonal condition, is often first detected when a seemingly normal teenage girl fails to menstruate and chromosomal analysis discovers that she is XY, a genetic male. Approximately one in 20 000 boys are born each year with AIS (Oakes et al., 2008). In this syndrome, although the gonads develop into testes and produce testosterone normally, the AIS individual's receptor (receptors are specialized proteins that provide a place for testosterone to bind to a cell and affect its function) for testosterone is not built properly and cannot bind testosterone. This prevents testosterone from masculinizing the body and the body develops externally as female. Because the Wolffian ducts did not respond to testosterone during the sexual differentiation phase, no male-typical internal reproductive organs develop except the testicles. However, because the gonads, which are male, did produce Müllerian inhibiting factor, the Müllerian ducts also did not develop into normal female internal organs. The AIS individual ends up with no internal reproductive organs except two testes, which remain in the abdomen producing testosterone.

The AIS infant has external female genitalia, but because the Müllerian ducts also form the last third of the vagina, the infant has only a very shallow vagina. Usually the syndrome is undetected at birth, and the child is brought up female. Because males do produce a small amount of estrogen, the breasts do develop, so it is only when the teen fails to menstruate that AIS is usually diagnosed. Surgery can then be initiated to lengthen the vagina to accommodate a penis for intercourse, although without any female internal reproductive organs, the individual remains infertile. Even though they are genetically male, most AIS individuals seem to be fully feminized and live as females.

5 Alpha Reductase Deficiency Syndrome

In 1974 a researcher from Cornell University, Julianne Imperato-McGinley, and her colleagues reported on several genetic males who had the inability to convert testosterone to a more potent androgen called dihydrotestosterone (Cai et al., 1996; Imperato-McGinley et al., 1974). The testicles of these males still produce testosterone and anti-Müllerian hormone so the internal reproductive system develops primarily as male. The external genitalia at birth often appear feminized or intersexed, however, since dihydrotestosterone is important for masculinizing the external genitalia; these children are often raised as girls. At puberty the dramatic increase in testosterone can often accomplish what did not occur at birth. The external genitalia begins to look more masculine and the phallus (penis) may enlarge. The body also changes in the male direction, with the absence of breast development, increased muscle mass, and a deepening voice. Children born with this syndrome may elect to have gender reassignment surgery to the male sex in adulthood. While fertility in adulthood is a challenge for these men, due to low semen quality, it may be possible (Atta et al., 2014).

Other Types of Atypical Development in Males

Hypospadias

In male children born with **hypospadias** (hyp-O-SPAY-di-as) the urethra, rather than opening at the top of the glans penis, opens on the underside of the glans penis or the penile shaft. It is more common in males with low birth weight and/or mothers who suffered from pre-eclampsia or maternal hypertension (see Chapter 5). The cause of this disorder is unknown and likely due to a complex interplay of genetic and environmental factors (Kalfa, Philibert, & Sultan, 2009; van der Zanden et al., 2012).

Micropenis

The term *micropenis* is used to refer to the penis of a newborn male that is less than 2 centimetres in stretched length (Tsang, 2010). Males who are born with a micropenis may choose to have phalloplasty done in adulthood to lengthen their penis. The efficacy of this treatment to alleviate distress over penile length is not known and more research is needed (Callens et al., 2013).

Cryptorchidism

Cryptorchidism (krip-TOR-kuh-diz-um), or undescended testes, is the most common genital disorder in boys (Mathers et al., 2011). One third of male infants who are born prematurely have cryptorchidism, whereas 2 percent to 5 percent of full-term male infants have at least one undescended testicle (Mathers et al., 2011). The testicles of a male fetus begin high in the abdomen near the kidneys and, during fetal development, descend into the scrotum through the inguinal canal (Hutson et al., 1994). See Figure 4.5.

There are no clear reasons why cryptorchidism occurs, although researchers have explored several contributing factors, including genetics, hormones (Massart & Saggese, 2010; Robin et al., 2010), placental abnormalities (Thorup et al., 2010), and maternal smoking during pregnancy (Lacerda et al., 2010). Recently, researchers have found geographic variations and increasing levels of cryptorchidism in several countries, which may indicate environmental effects and exposure to certain chemicals (Robin et al., 2010; Sharpe & Skakkebaek, 2008; Toppari et al., 2010). Research in these areas is ongoing.

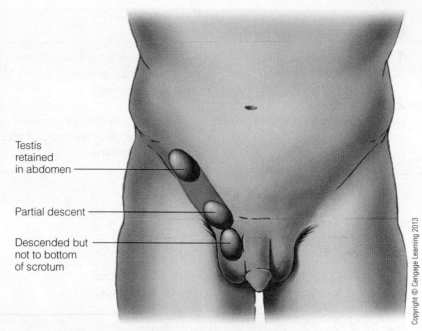

Testis retained in abdomen

Partial descent

Descended but not to bottom of scrotum

Copyright © Cengage Learning 2013

FIGURE 4.5 Although the testicles of a fetus begin high in the abdomen, they must descend into the scrotum during fetal development. This testicular descent is due to a structure called the gubernaculum, which is attached to the testicle. The gubernaculum does not change in size as the fetus grows and thus the testes are pulled down into the abdomen as the gubernaculums shortens relative to torso growth. If the testicles do not descend, the male may become infertile.

Newborn boys with cryptorchidism may be given testosterone to help with testicular descent. However, if the testes have not descended by six months of age, surgery is often required to relocate the undescended testis to the scrotum (Hack et al., 2003; Hutson & Hasthorpe, 2005). It is estimated that 90 percent of untreated men with cryptorchidism will be infertile, because excessive heat in the abdomen impairs the ability to produce viable sperm (AbouZeid et al., 2011; Mathers et al., 2011). Men with a history of cryptorchid testes also have an increased risk for testicular cancer (Robin et al., 2010; Thorup et al., 2010; Toppari et al., 2010).

> **Animal Variations** | **Disorders of Sexual Development in Animals**
>
> Anomalies of sexual development of the reproductive organs and genitalia are not restricted to humans. Androgen insensitivity syndrome has been documented in several species of animals, including dogs (A. Smith et al., 1983), horses (Howden, 2004), and cats (Meyers-Wallen et al., 1989). Hypospadias and disorders of sexual development can also be found in several breeds of domesticated dogs (Meyers-Wallen 2012; Switonski et al., 2012).

cryptorchidism
A condition in which the testes fail to descend into the scrotum.

Male Sexual Anatomy, Development, and Health

1 Describe the role of the SRY gene in male-typical development.

2 Describe the sexual differentiation process of a developing male embryo and fetus.

3 Identify the chromosomal conditions that may result in disorders of sexual development.

4 Identify the hormonal conditions that may result in disorders of sexual development.

5 What other developmental conditions can affect the sex-typical development of male embryos?

Male Maturation Cycle

At this point we have covered basic male reproductive physiology in adulthood and have explored typical and atypical sexual development. In the following section, we will cover the physical changes that accompany male puberty. Many of these changes are controlled by hormonal changes that occur and contribute to physical changes in a young boy's body. In Chapter 10, we discuss the psychosexual changes of male puberty.

Male Puberty

During a boy's early life, the two major functions of the testes—to produce male sex hormones and to produce sperm—remain dormant. Around ten years of age, the hypothalamus begins releasing gonadotropin-releasing hormone (GnRH), which stimulates the anterior pituitary gland to release follicle-stimulating hormone (FSH) and luteinizing hormone into the circulatory system.

These hormones flow through the circulatory system to the testes, where LH stimulates the production of the male sex hormone, testosterone, which, together with FSH, stimulates sperm production. A negative feedback system regulates hormone production; when the concentration of testosterone in the blood increases to a certain level, GnRH release from the hypothalamus is inhibited, causing inhibition of LH production and resulting in decreased testosterone production (see Figure 4.6 for more information about the negative-feedback loop). Alternately, when testosterone levels decrease below a certain level, GnRH production by the hypothalamus increases, which in turn increases the pituitary's LH production and testosterone production goes up. This negative feedback loop leads to the increase and subsequent decrease of testosterone in the circulatory system several times throughout the day.

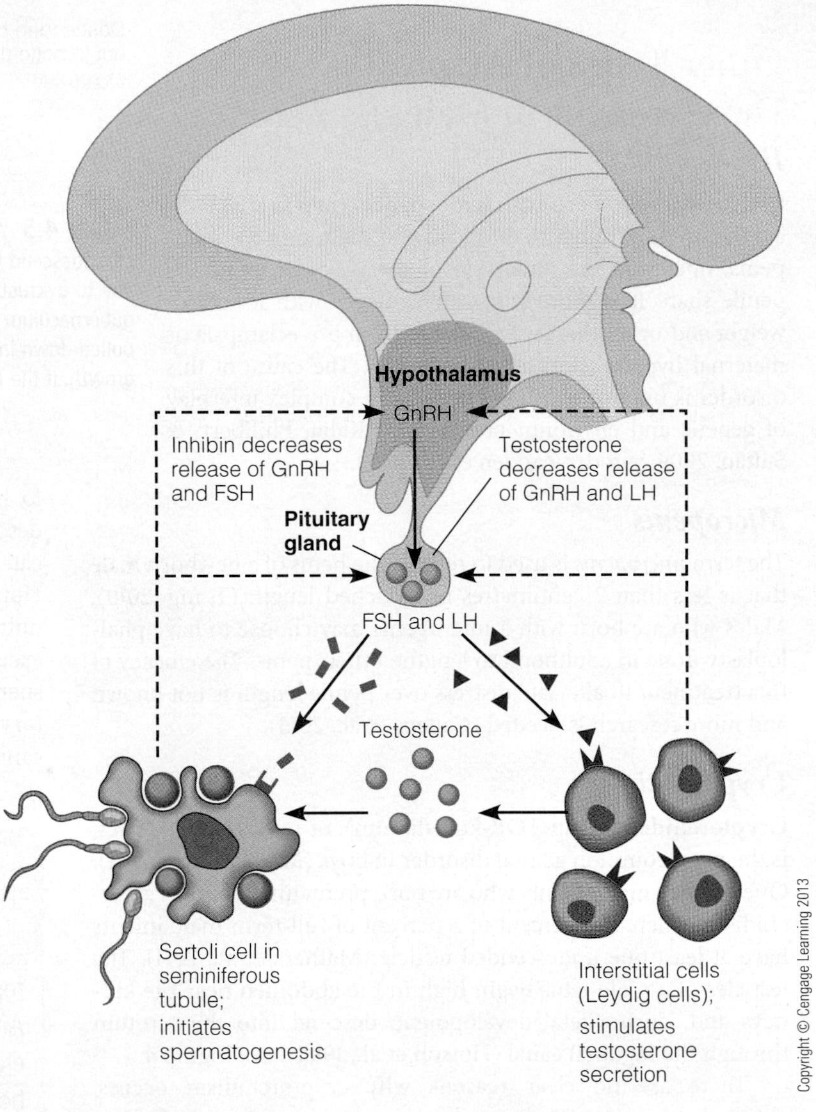

As puberty progresses, the testicles and penis enlarge. The epididymis, prostate, seminal vesicles, and bulbourethral glands also grow over the next several years. Increased testosterone levels stimulates an overall growth spurt in puberty. This spurt can be dramatic; teenage boys can grow 8-10 centimetres (3 or 4 inches) within a few months. The elevation of

FIGURE **4.6** The cycle of male hormones.

testosterone affects a number of male traits: The boy develops longer and heavier bones, larger muscles, thicker and tougher skin, a deepening voice because of growth of the voice box, pubic hair, facial and chest hair, increased sex drive, and increased metabolism.

Spermatogenesis begins at about 12 years of age, but ejaculation of mature sperm usually does not occur for about another 12 to 18 months. At puberty, FSH begins to stimulate sperm production in the seminiferous tubules, and the increased testosterone production by the Leydig cells induces the testes to mature and support spermatogenesis. The development of spermatogenesis and the sexual fluid glands correlates with the experience of nocturnal emissions in males.

EJACULATION Earlier in this chapter, we discussed erection as a spinal reflex. Ejaculation, which begins in puberty, like erection, also begins in the spinal column; however, unlike erection, there is seldom a "partial" ejaculation. Once the stimulation builds to the threshold, ejaculation usually continues until its conclusion. When the threshold is reached, the first stage of ejaculation begins: the epididymis, seminal vesicles, and prostate all empty their contents into the urethral bulb, which swells up to accommodate the semen. The bladder is closed off by an internal sphincter so that no urine is expelled with the semen. Once these stages begin, some males report feeling that ejaculation is imminent, that they are going to ejaculate and nothing can stop it; however, others report that this feeling of inevitability can be stopped by immediately ceasing all sensation. If stimulation continues, strong, rhythmic contractions of the muscles at the base of the penis squeeze the urethral bulb, and the ejaculate is propelled from the body, usually accompanied by the pleasurable sensation of orgasm. Most men have between 5 and 15 contractions during orgasm.

Once orgasm subsides, the arteries supplying the blood to the penis narrow, the veins taking the blood out enlarge, and the penis usually becomes limp. Depending on the level of excitement, the person's age, the length of time since the previous ejaculation, and his individual physiology, a new erection can occur anywhere from immediately to an hour or so later. In older men, however, a second erection can take hours or even a day or so (we will discuss aging and sexual function further in Chapter 15).

EJACULATE The male ejaculate, or semen, averages about 2 to 5 millilitres—about 1 or 2 teaspoons. Semen normally contains secretions from the seminal vesicles and the prostate gland and about 50 to 150 million sperm per millilitre. If there are fewer than 20 million sperm per millilitre, the male is likely to be infertile. Sperm is required in such large numbers because during procreation only a small fraction ever reach the ovum. Also, the sperm work together to achieve fertilization; for example, many die to

> **REAL Research** Men whose mothers smoked more than 19 cigarettes while they were in the womb have 19 percent lower semen volume and 38 percent lower total sperm count compared with men with non-smoking mothers (Ramlau-Hansen et al., 2007).

plug up the os of the cervix for the other sperm, and the combined enzyme production of all sperm is necessary for a single spermatozoon to fertilize the ovum.

Directly after ejaculation, the semen initially coagulates into a thick, mucous-like liquid. After 5 to 20 minutes, the prostatic enzymes contained in the semen cause it to thin out and liquefy. If it does not liquefy, coagulated semen in heterosexual men may be unable to complete its movement through the cervix and into the uterus.

On Your Mind

Can a male have an orgasm without an ejaculation?

Yes. Before puberty, boys may be capable of orgasm without ejaculation. In adulthood, some men report feeling several small orgasms before a larger one that includes ejaculation, whereas other men report that if they have sex a second or third time, there is orgasm without ejaculatory fluid. There are also some Eastern sexual disciplines, such as Tantra, that try to teach men to achieve orgasm without ejaculation because they believe that retaining semen is important for men.

Andropause

As men age, their blood testosterone concentrations decrease. Hormone levels in men have been found to decrease by about 1 percent each year after age 40 (Daw, 2002). Men do not go through an obvious set of stages, as menopausal women do, but some experience a less well-defined set of symptoms in their 70s or 80s called andropause (Makrantonaki et al., 2010). It is estimated that 2 percent of elderly men experience symptoms related to andropause (Pines, 2011). Although men's ability to ejaculate viable sperm is often retained past age 80 or 90, spermatogenesis does decrease, the ejaculate becomes thinner, and ejaculatory pressure decreases. The reduction in testosterone production results in decreased muscle strength, decreased libido, easy fatigue, and mood fluctuations (Bassil & Morley, 2010; Seidman, 2007). Men can also experience osteoporosis and anemia as they age (Bain, 2001).

Androgen Replacement Therapy

The use of androgen replacement therapy is controversial due to possible risks and limited long-term studies of its use (Basaria et al., 2010; Cunningham & Toma, 2011; Morales, 2004; Pines, 2011; Wu et al., 2010). Benefits to androgen replacement therapy (in men with lower than average testosterone levels) include increased sexual interest and functioning, increased bone density and muscle mass, and improved mood (Bassil & Morley, 2010). Even with these benefits there are several risks of androgen replacement therapy that have been reported, including (1) the possibility of an increased risk for prostate cancer, although there has been no conclusive evidence to support this risk (Bassil & Morley, 2010), and (2) the increased risk of cardiovascular disease. The use of androgen replacement therapy is most commonly prescribed to Canadian males aged 45–59, with males over 65 being the second most prescribed group (Health Canada, 2014).

Male Sexual Anatomy, Development, and Health **105**

Review Questions

1 Describe the two major functions of the testes, and explain the negative feedback loop between the testes, hypothalamus, and pituitary in males.

2 Identify the age at which spermatogenesis typically begins. What cells in the testes are necessary for sperm production?

3 Identify the organs that contribute to semen production?

4 What events occur during puberty to complete the male maturation process?

5 What effect do decreasing levels of testosterone have on men? How has androgen replacement therapy been found to help?

Male Reproductive and Sexual Health

It is a good idea for every man to examine and explore his own sexual anatomy. A regular genital self-examination can help increase a man's comfort with his genitals (see the accompanying Sex in Real Life feature). It can also help a man know what his testicles feel like in the event of a change in their physiology. We will first discuss various disorders that may affect the male reproductive organs; then we turn to cancer of the male reproductive organs, its diagnosis, and its treatment.

Disorders of the Male Reproductive Organs

Several conditions can affect the male external genitalia. It is important for both men and women to have a good understanding of what these conditions are and what symptoms they might cause.

Testicular Torsion

Testicular torsion refers to a twisting of a testis on its spermatic cord. Usually, it occurs when there is abnormal development of the spermatic cord or the membrane that covers the testicle (Wampler & Llanes, 2010). It is most common in men from puberty to the age of 25, and approximately one in 4000 men are affected by testicular torsion each year (Ringdahl & Teague, 2006). Testicular torsion can occur after exercise, sexual behaviour, or even while sleeping.

Acute scrotal pain and swelling are two of the most common symptoms, although there can also be abdominal pain, nausea,

and vomiting (Kapoor, 2008). Testicular torsion is a medical emergency, and any man who experiences a rapid onset of scrotal pain should have this pain checked by a health care provider immediately. An ultrasound is often used to help diagnose this condition, but because the twisted cord can cut off blood supply to the testicle and cause testicular damage, the condition must be diagnosed quickly (Cokkinos et al., 2011; Mongiat-Artus, 2004; Kapoor 2008; Ringdahl & Teague, 2006). Although we don't know exactly what causes testicular torsion, one group of scientists have reported that testicular torsion was more common in men with a family history of the condition (Shteynshlyuger & Freyle, 2011).

Inguinal Hernia

An **inguinal hernia** (ING-gwuh-nul HER-nee-uh) is caused when the intestine pushes through the opening in the abdominal wall into the **inguinal canal** (the inguinal canal was originally used by the testes when they descended into the scrotum shortly before birth). This can happen during heavy lifting or straining. When it does occur, the intestine pushes down onto the testicles and causes a bulge or lump in the scrotum. Other symptoms include abdominal pain and possible blockage of the intestine. Depending on the size and the pain associated with the bulge, surgery may be necessary to push the protruding intestines back into the abdomen (Hussain et al., 2010).

Hydrocele

A **hydrocele** (HI-druh-seal) is a condition in which there is an excessive accumulation of fluid within the tissue surrounding the testicle, which causes a scrotal mass (making the scrotum look and feel like a water balloon). This accumulation could be caused by an overproduction of fluid or poor reabsorption of the fluid, and it can also be caused by a leak through the inguinal canal. Hydroceles are common in newborn males and typically go away on their own after a few months. Although they are relatively painless, some men experience pain and swelling within the testicle. Health care providers often use ultrasound to diagnose a hydrocele, and treatment involves removing the built-up fluid through needle aspiration (Palmer, 2013).

Disorders of the Penis

PRIAPISM Priapism (PRY-uh-pizm) is an abnormally prolonged and painful erection that is not associated with sexual

---

testicular torsion
The twisting of a testis on its spermatic cord, which can cause severe pain and swelling.

inguinal hernia
A condition in which the intestines bulge through a hole in the abdominal muscles of the groin.

inguinal canal
Canal through which the testes descend into the scrotum.

hydrocele
A condition in which there is an excessive accumulation of fluid within the tissue surrounding the testicle, which causes a scrotal mass.

priapism
A condition in which erections are long-lasting and often painful.

Testicular Self-Examination

© Joel Gordon Photography

There are no obvious symptoms of testicular cancer; however, when detected early, it is treatable. The only early detection system for testicular cancer is testicular self-examination. A representative sample of American men found that only 2 percent to 10 percent of men perform monthly testicular self-examinations, and that various factors, such as gender roles and norms, may inhibit a man from performing a testicular self-examination (Reece et al., 2010a). Just like breast self-examinations in women, men should examine their testicles at least monthly. This will enable them to have an understanding of what things feel like under normal conditions, which will help them to find any lumps or abnormal growths, should they appear.

To do a testicular examination, compare both testicles simultaneously by grasping one with each hand, using thumb and forefinger. This may be best done while taking a warm shower, which causes the scrotum to relax and the testicles to hang lower. Explore their size, shape, and sensitivity to pressure.

As you get to know the exact shape and feel of your testicles, you will be able to notice any swelling, lumps, or unusual pain. While most lumps are benign and nothing to worry about any lumps should be reported to your health care provider.

---

desire or excitement (Cakin-Memik et al., 2010; Mi et al., 2008; Vander Horst et al., 2003). It is primarily a vascular condition that causes blood to become trapped in the erectile tissue of the penis. Although researchers don't know exactly what causes priapism, men with certain conditions, such as sickle cell disease, leukemia, and/or spinal cord injuries, are at greater risk for development of priapism (Mi et al., 2008). In some cases, drug use (erection drugs, cocaine, marijuana, or anticoagulants) is to blame. Researchers have been using penile tissue from various animals, such as dogs, cats, rabbits, and mice, to study priapism, how it occurs, and what can be done to ameliorate this condition (Dong et al., 2011).

Like testicular torsion, priapism is considered a medical emergency because it can damage erectile tissue if left untreated (Mi et al., 2008). Treatment may involve pharmaceutical agents to reduce blood flow or stents to remove the blood from the corpora cavernosa and corpus spongiosum. If there is a neurological or other physiological cause for the priapism, anesthesia and surgery may be necessary (Shrewsberry et al., 2010).

PEYRONIE'S DISEASE   Every male has individual curves to his penis when it becomes erect. In approximately 1 percent of men, however, this curvature makes penetration impossible, leading to a diagnosis of a condition known as **Peyronie's** (pay-row-NEEZ) **disease** (C.J. Smith et al., 2005; Perovic & Djinovic, 2010).

Peyronie's disease occurs in the connective tissue of the penis, and although some cases are asymptomatic, others experience development of plaques or areas of hardened tissue, which can cause severe erectile pain (Gelbard, 1988). No one knows what causes Peyronie's disease. It is possible that fibrous tissue buildup, excessive calcium, or trauma to the penis may contribute to this disorder (Gelbard, 1988). Typically, this happens between the ages of 45 and 60, although younger and older men can also experience

Peyronie's disease. This disease lasts approximately two years and may go away just as suddenly as it appears. It is treated in a variety of ways, including medication, surgery, or both, and many men find they are able to engage in penetrative sex again after treatment (Austoni et al., 2005; Heidari et al., 2010; Perovic & Djinovic, 2010; Seveso et al., 2010).

REAL Research   During vigorous vaginal or anal penetration, it is possible for the penis to slide out of the vagina (or anus) and slam into the perineum, resulting in a penile bruising (Bar-Yosef et al., 2007). Researchers have found that injuries such as these can lead to pain during erection, curvature of the penis, and potential hardening of the penile arteries. Seeking immediate medical attention may be necessary, especially if the pain increases.

BALANITIS   In some men, more common in those who are uncircumcised, inflammation of the glans penis can occur. Generally, balanitis (bal-an-IT-is) is due to poor hygiene and/or infection. This inflammation is often seen in early puberty and adulthood. It generally responds well to topically applied steroidal creams (Vincent & Mackinnon, 2005); however, confirmation of a diagnosis and treatment used should be confirmed by a health care provider.

Peyronie's disease
Abnormal calcifications or fibrous tissue in the penis, which may cause painful curvature, often making sexual intercourse impossible.

PHIMOSIS AND PARAPHIMOSIS Both of these medical problems occur in uncircumcised males and may lead to balanitis if not properly managed. Phimosis (FIM-O-sis) is the inability to retract the foreskin and expose the glans penis. This is most common in young babies and may persist into puberty. Unless there is difficulty with urination, it generally does not require medical intervention. Paraphimosis occurs when the foreskin is retracted below the corona of the penis and is stuck in that position. It is a serious condition that can constrict the glans penis and reduce blood flow to the glans. In the event of paraphimosis occurring, a health care provider should be seen immediately. Treatment options may include drugs to reduce swelling, or slitting of the foreskin. Circumcision may be recommended after the initial resolution of the condition (Little & White, 2005).

Anabolic-Androgenic Steroid Abuse

Since the early 2000s, steroids have become a controversial topic as more and more male athletes disclose past steroid use. In 2005, congressional hearings in the United States began to evaluate steroid abuse in Major League Baseball. Anabolic-androgenic steroids (AAS), also known as synthetic testosterone, have been used by elite athletes since the 1950s, but it wasn't until the 1980s that these types of drugs were abused by non-athletes as well (Kanayama et al., 2010).

There are steroids that occur naturally in the body, and they are known as androgens. During puberty in males, the release of androgens increases weight and muscle size, and can also increase endurance and aggressiveness. We know that millions of boys and men, primarily in Western countries, use AAS to enhance their appearance or athletic performance (Brennan et al., 2011; Kanayama et al., 2010). Women have also been found to abuse these drugs, although at lower levels than men (Gruber & Pope, 2000). The actual number of people who abuse AAS is unknown.

AAS use comes at a high price. The best documented effects are damage to the liver and the reproductive system, including shrinkage of the testicles (and menstrual cycle changes in women; Bonetti et al., 2007; Kanayama et al., 2010; Sato et al., 2008). Testicular shrinkage is primarily due to a disruption of the hypothalamic,

pituitary, gonadal axis. As mentioned previously, high testosterone levels signal to the hypothalamus to decrease the release of GnRH. This decrease in GnRH leads to a decrease in the release of LH and FSH from the pituitary gland. Ultimately, the decrease of LH from the pituitary leaves the testicles without a signal to make testosterone and over time this loss of testicular testosterone production by the testes leads to cell loss in the testes and a decrease in testicular size that may be irreversible. Other health concerns with AAS include cerebrovascular accidents (strokes), prostate gland changes, and impaired immune function (Wysoczanski et al., 2008). In athletes still in puberty, steroids can cause early fusion of the bone-growth plates, resulting in permanently shortened stature. Use of AAS has also been associated with changes in mood and behaviour, including increases in irritability, hostility, anger, aggression, depression, hypomania, psychotic episodes, and guilt (Kanayama et al., 2010; Venâncio et al., 2008). AAS users have also been found to be at greater risk for illicit drug use, particularly opioid use (Kanayama et al., 2010).

Cancers of the Male Reproductive Organs

Cancer is a disease in which certain cells in the body do not function properly—they divide too fast or produce excessive tissue that forms a tumor, or both. A number of cancers can affect the male reproductive organs. Let's now look at breast, penile, testicular, and prostatic cancers. In this section, we also review preventive measures for detecting or avoiding common male health problems. In Chapter 15, we will discuss how these illnesses affect men's lives and sexuality.

Male Breast Cancer

The Canadian Cancer Society estimated there were approximately 190 cases of breast cancer diagnosed in men in 2011, with approximately 55 of these cases resulting in death. Most of these cases occur in men over 60 (Canadian Cancer Society, 2015f). Even though breast cancer is rare in men, it has a higher mortality rate in men than in women, mainly because it is often diagnosed at a more advanced stage in men compared with women (Al-Saleh, 2011; Rosa & Masood, 2012).

Risk factors for breast cancer in men are similar to some of the risk factors for women, including heredity, obesity, hormonal issues, and physical inactivity. Newer research has found that a history of a bone fracture is a risk for breast cancer in men probably because of the association with osteoporosis (Brinton et al., 2008). Exposure to environmental toxins may also increase a man's risk for breast cancer (Maffini et al., 2006).

In Chapter 3, we reviewed the research on cancer and the *BRCA* genes. The presence of these genes in men can also lead to a higher risk for the development of both breast and prostate cancer (Stromsvik et al., 2010). The presence of these genes doubles the normal risk for prostate cancer and increases the risk for breast cancer by seven times (Tai et al., 2007). Research has found that, like women, men experience strong emotional reactions to positive test results for the *BRCA* genes. However, few disclose this information to others (Stromsvik et al., 2010). If they do talk to friends about it, most men report females as their main source of support and find it difficult to talk to other men about their diagnosis.

Major League Baseball player Barry Bonds. He was accused of using steroid like substances to enhance his performance.

Treatment for breast cancer for men involves radiation or chemotherapy, and if the cancer has spread to other parts of the body, surgical removal of the breasts may be necessary to eliminate the hormones that could support the growth of the cancer.

Penile Cancer

A wide variety of cancers involving the skin and soft tissues of the penis can occur, although cancer of the penis is rare (Mosconi et al., 2005). Any lesion on the penis must be examined by a physician, for benign and malignant conditions can be very similar in appearance, and sexually transmitted infections can appear as lesions. Even though most men handle and observe their penis daily, there is often significant delay between a person's recognition of a lesion and seeking medical attention. Fear and embarrassment may contribute most to this problem, yet almost all of these lesions are treatable if caught early.

Testicular Cancer

The Canadian Cancer Society estimates that there will be 1000 new cases of testicular cancer diagnosed each year. In 2010 40 men in Canada died from testicular cancer (Canadian Cancer Society, 2015g). Testicular cancer is the most common malignancy in men aged 25 to 34 (Garner et al., 2008). There are few symptoms until the cancer is advanced, which is why early detection is so important. Most men first develop testicular cancer as a painless testicular mass or a harder consistency of the testes. If there is pain or a sudden increase in testicular size this could be indicative of a tumour. Sometimes lower back pain, gynecomastia, shortness of breath, or urethral obstruction may also occur with tumor growth.

Risk factors for testicular cancer include a family history, cryptorchidism, increased height, body size, age at puberty, and dairy consumption (McGlynn et al., 2007). In addition, researchers have found that the incidence of testicular cancer is correlated to heat exposure, heavy metals, agricultural work, pesticides, certain chemicals, and frequent marijuana use (Trabert et al., 2011; McGlynn & Trabert, 2012).

Although the incidence of testicular cancer has continuously increased during the last few decades, cure rates have significantly improved. In fact, testicular cancer is one of the most curable forms of the disease (Canadian Cancer Society, 2015g). Treatment may involve radiation, chemotherapy, or the removal of the testicle. If removal of the testicle is necessary, many men opt to get a prosthetic testicle implanted, which gives the appearance of having two normal testicles. Finding testicular cancer early is important for the best prognosis. As mentioned in the Sex in Real Life feature, testicular self-examination and reporting any anomalies to your health care provider is essential for early cancer detection.

Prostate Cancer

As men age, their prostate glands enlarge. In most cases, this natural occurrence, **benign prostatic hypertrophy (BPH)**, causes few problems. Because of its anatomical position surrounding the urethra, BPH may block urination, and surgeons may need to remove the prostate if the condition becomes bad enough. Of far more concern than BPH is prostate cancer, which is the most frequently diagnosed cancer in men besides skin cancer. The Canadian Cancer Society estimates that approximately 23 600 men will be diagnosed and about 4000 men will die of prostate cancer each year in Canada (Canadian Cancer Society, 2015h).

Although men of all ages can experience development of prostate cancer, it is found most often in men older than 50 years. In fact, risk for prostate cancer increases in men up until the age of 70 and then begins to decline (American Cancer Society, 2011).

Worldwide, the incidence of prostate cancer varies, with the majority of cases diagnosed in economically developed countries (American Cancer Society, 2011).

On Your Mind

Can a man who has been treated for testicular cancer still have children?

Many men with testicular cancer also have fertility problems. Cancer treatments can cause scarring or ejaculation problems that will interfere with later fertility. During radiation or chemotherapy, sperm production does decline significantly, and some men have no sperm in their semen. However, for the majority of men, sperm production generally returns to normal within two to three years. Because many men with testicular cancer are in their reproductive prime, waiting two or more years might not be an option. For this reason, many health care providers recommend sperm banking before cancer treatment (Molnar et al., 2014).

The exact causes of prostate cancer are unknown, however we do know that several risk factors have been linked to prostate cancer. Men with a first-degree relative, such as a father or brother, are more likely to experience development of prostate cancer. In addition, men with the *BRCA* gene are also at increased risk for development of prostate cancer. Other risk factors include race/ethnicity, age, and a diet high in fat. Studies have shown that men whose diets include high levels of calcium and consumption of red and processed meats have higher risks (Canadian Cancer Society, 2015h).

Early signs of prostate cancer may include lower back, pelvic, or upper thigh pain; inability to urinate; loss of force in the urinary stream; urinary dribbling; pain or burning during urination; and frequent urination, especially at night. Many deaths from prostate cancer are preventable, because a simple five- or ten-second rectal examination by a physician, to detect hard lumps on the prostate, detects more than 50 percent of cases at a curable stage. Digital rectal examinations are recommended for men each year beginning at the age of 50 (Canadian Cancer Society, 2015h).

The **prostate-specific antigen (PSA)** blood test measures levels of PSA (a protein only produced by the prostate gland) that are overproduced by prostate cancer cells. This enables physicians

benign prostatic hypertrophy (BPH)	**prostate-specific antigen (PSA)**
The common enlargement of the prostate that occurs in most men after about age 50.	Blood test that measures levels of molecules that are overproduced by prostate cancer cells, enabling physicians to identify prostate cancer early.

Male Sexual Anatomy, Development, and Health

to identify prostate cancer and is recommended yearly for men older than 50 (although Black men and those with a first-degree relative with prostate cancer are often advised to begin screening earlier). The PSA test has been one of the most important advances in the area of prostate cancer (Lakhey et al., 2010; Madan & Gulley, 2010). Although not all tumours will show up on a PSA test, a high reading does indicate that something (such as a tumour) is releasing prostatic material into the blood, and a biopsy or further examination by a health care provider is warranted.

There are many treatments for prostate cancer and some argue that, in older men especially, the best thing is "watchful waiting" in which the cancer is simply left alone, because this type of cancer is slow growing and most men will die of other causes before the prostate cancer becomes life-threatening. Men who have a history of poor health, are older than 80 years, or are living in a geographically undesirable location for medical treatment often opt for watchful waiting (Harlan et al., 2001).

Others choose **radical prostatectomy** or radiation treatment, or **cryosurgery**, which uses a probe to freeze parts of the prostate (J.K. Cohen et al., 2008c). Two of the most common surgical adverse effects of prostate cancer treatment include erectile dysfunction and the inability to hold one's urine. However, the likelihood of these problems depends on several things, including the extent and severity

radical prostatectomy	cryosurgery
The surgical removal of the prostate.	Surgery that uses freezing techniques to destroy part of an organ.

of the cancer and a man's age at the time of surgery (H. Stewart et al., 2005). Although younger men who experienced satisfactory erections before any prostate cancer treatments have fewer erectile problems after surgery, for most men, erections will improve over time. Difficulty holding urine or urinary leakage may also occur; however, treatments are available to lessen these symptoms.

Newer treatments include drugs that attack only cells with cancer, unlike radiation and chemotherapy, which both kill healthy cells in addition to cells with cancer. Research has found that these drugs hold much promise in the treatment of prostate cancer (Plosker, 2011; C.J. Ryan & Small, 2005). Research into vaccines for prostate cancer also continues. In 2010, the U.S. Food and Drug Administration approved Provenge, the first vaccine for prostate cancer (Madan & Gulley, 2011). This vaccine uses a patient's own white blood cells to attack cancer cells. Questions have been raised however about research design flaws in the initial studies used to demonstrate the efficacy of the Provenge vaccine (Begley, 2012) and further research into the use of vaccines for prostate cancer is needed.

As you have learned throughout this chapter and Chapter 3, understanding anatomy and physiology is an important part of the knowledge required to understand human sexual behaviour. We must understand all of the physiological and hormonal influences, and how they affect both the female and male body, before we can move on to the emotional and psychological issues involved in human sexuality. Anatomy and physiology, therefore, are really the foundations of any human sexuality class. Now we can turn our attention to other important aspects of human sexuality.

Review Questions

1 Differentiate between cryptorchidism, testicular torsion, hydroceles, priapism, balanitis, phimosis, paraphimosis and Peyronie's disease. Explain what these conditions are and what symptoms they might cause. What are some treatments for these conditions?

2 Explain the adverse effects of anabolic androgenic steroid use.

3 Identify the most common cancers in men and describe their symptoms and treatment.

Chapter Review

Summary Points

1 Because the male genitalia sit outside the body, unlike female gonads, boys are often more comfortable with their genitalia. The external male sex organs include the penis and the scrotum.

2 The penis has the ability to fill with blood during sexual arousal. It contains the urethra and three cylinders—two corpora cavernosa

and one corpus spongiosum. These cylinders are bound together with connective tissue.

3 In many cultures, the foreskin of the penis is removed during circumcision. Although it is an extremely common surgical procedure, medical professionals are still mixed in their perspectives on the health value of circumcision.

4 An erection is a spinal reflex, and many types of sexual stimulation can lead to this response. When stimulation stops, the penis returns to its unaroused state. Most men have regular erections during their sleeping cycle and often wake up with an erection.

5 The scrotum sits outside the man's body and contains the testicles. Sperm survival requires a temperature that is a few degrees lower than the body's temperature. The cremaster muscle is responsible for the scrotum's positioning. When it is too hot, the muscle allows the scrotum to hang farther away from the body. When it is too cold, the muscle elevates the scrotum so that it is closer to the body.

6 The internal male sex organs include the testes, epididymis, vas deferens, seminal vesicles, prostate gland, and bulbourethral glands. All of these organs play important roles in spermatogenesis, testosterone production, and the process of ejaculation.

7 The testicles have two main functions: spermatogenesis and testosterone production. One testicle usually hangs lower (or higher) than the other so that they do not hit each other when compressed. Testosterone is produced in the Leydig cells.

8 Gynecomastia, or abnormal breast development, is common during male puberty and again in older age. It can be caused by drug therapy, drug abuse, hormonal imbalance, and certain diseases. It will often disappear on its own without surgical intervention. Some men do get breast cancer, and because it is rare, men who are diagnosed are often in advanced stages before their diagnoses.

9 Male internal reproductive organs develop from the Wolffian duct. Both male and female external genitalia develop from the same tubercle, so many male and female genital structures are homologous. In males the presence of androgens stimulates the development of male-typical external genitalia.

10 Disorders of sex development include sex chromosome and hormone disorders. Chromosomal conditions include Klinefelter and XYY syndromes, whereas hormonal conditions include congenital adrenal hyperplasia (CAH), androgen-insensitivity syndrome (AIS), and 5-alpha reductase deficiency. Atypical development in males also includes micropenis and hypospadias.

11 At about the age of ten, a boy enters the first stages of puberty. A negative feedback system regulates hormone production. As puberty progresses, the testicles increase in size, and the penis begins to grow. Increased testosterone stimulates an overall growth spurt in puberty, and the bones and muscles grow rapidly. Spermatogenesis usually begins about the age of 12, but it takes another year or so for an ejaculation to contain mature sperm.

12 Ejaculation is the physiological process whereby the seminal fluid is ejected from the penis. The vas deferens, seminal vesicles, prostate, and Cowper's glands all work together during ejaculation. Most men experience between 5 and 15 contractions during orgasm. After orgasm, the blood that has been trapped in the penis is released, and the penis becomes flaccid.

13 Blood testosterone levels decrease as a man ages, and although it is not as defined as menopause, men experience a condition known as andropause. During this time, sperm production slows down, the ejaculate becomes thinner, and ejaculatory pressure decreases.

14 There are several diseases of the male reproductive organs, including cryptorchidism, testicular torsion, priapism, balanitis, phimosis, paraphimosis, Peyronie's disease, inguinal hernia, and hydrocele. Fortunately, all of these are treatable conditions.

15 Athletes' use of steroids has increased notably since the late 1980s, even though it had been associated with several damaging changes in the body. Steroid use can cause liver and prostate gland changes, testicular shrinkage, and impaired immune function. Research has also found an increased risk for cerebrovascular accidents and, for young people, early fusion of bone growth plates.

16 Men who are diagnosed with breast cancer often do not tell anyone. Penile cancer is relatively uncommon, but it usually appears as a lesion on the penis. Testicular cancer is difficult to catch early because there are few symptoms. It is one of the most curable forms of the disease. Prostate cancer is more common in men older than 50 and is the most common cause of cancer deaths among men older than 60.

Critical Thinking Questions

1 Why is detailed knowledge of the sexual functioning of men important for the understanding of human sexuality?

2 If you have a baby boy in the future, would you have him circumcised? Why or why not?

3 Why do you think men are uncomfortable talking about their own body image issues? Why aren't men encouraged to explore these issues?

Websites

Testicular Cancer Resource Center The Testicular Cancer Resource Center provides accurate information about testicular self-examination and the diagnosis and treatment of testicular cancer. Links are also provided for other cancers and additional websites. (http://tcrc.acor.org/)

MedlinePlus Health Information: Men's Health Topics MedlinePlus contains information on issues such as prostate cancer, circumcision, reproductive health concerns, gay and bisexual health, and male genital disorders. (https://www.nlm.nih.gov/medlineplus/men.html)

National Organization of Circumcision Information Resource Centers (NOCIRC) NOCIRC is the first national clearinghouse for information about circumcision. It claims that it owns one of the largest collections of information about circumcision in the world. (http://www.nocirc.org/)

The Canadian Cancer Society This organization provides information on all the cancers that are common in Canadian men. This information includes risk factors, diagnosis, treatment options, and prognosis. (http://www.cancer.ca/)

Health Canada Current information about sexual health issues, recent drug approvals, and safety issues can be found at this website. (http://www.hc-sc.gc.ca/index-eng.php)

The Biology of Sex, Pregnancy, and Childbirth

Laura and Ozlem, a lesbian couple, have been together for almost 18 years, but from the very beginning of their relationship they knew they wanted to have children. Unlike fertile heterosexual couples, they were faced with the decision of *how* to have children. After years of discussions about their options, they finally decided on a "known" donor because they wanted their children to know who their father was and have a relationship with him. Since Ozlem was a few years older, she was artificially inseminated first, and in 2001, Deniz was born. Laura was artificially inseminated a few years later, and in 2005 Isabelle was born.

Besides our love, shared values, common interests, and commitment to each other, the fact that we wanted children to be in our lives has always been a part of our relationship. The specifics on how to make that happen were long discussed and well planned. We are fortunate to have a large circle of lesbian couples and friends who were also making similar decisions, and we all shared our experiences with each other. We decided to use sperm from a friend who agreed to relinquish all parental decision-making and responsibility to us. Our donor is a carpenter by trade with tremendous visual-spatial skills, athletic ability, and intelligence. He is kind and thoughtful and understood that we would be the parents but that he would

© Thomas Northcut/Getty Images

get to have the experience of knowing these children and having a relationship with them. He has no other children, so this would be his first and perhaps only opportunity to be a father. He also needed to make a commitment to help us have more than one child. Our children, aged ten and six years old, know their dad and call him by his first name. They see him about once a month, and he is thrilled that they are in his life.

Deniz and Isabelle were both excited to tell me about their two-mom family. They talked about what they do for fun, other two-mom families, and what they do when someone at school asks them about their family. Laura put it best: *"We're just like any other family. In fact, our similarities are far greater than our differences."* ▌▌

NEL

Studying Sexual Response

The development of the male typical and female typical body culminates in mid to late adolescence around the time that many individuals become sexually active. This sexual activity is driven by many factors, including hormones and neurotransmitters. In this chapter, we will discuss the biological model of the sexual response cycle, pregnancy, and childbirth.

Hormones and Neurotransmitters

Hormones and **neurotransmitters** both have powerful effects on our bodies. In most animals, the brain controls and regulates sexual behaviour, chiefly through hormones and neurotransmitters, and these have an enormous effect on sexual behaviour in humans as well (Krüger et al., 2006). We discussed hormones in Chapters 3 and 4 and reviewed the various endocrine glands that secrete hormones into the bloodstream, carrying them throughout the body. Sexologists believe that testosterone is the most influential hormone in the sexual behaviour of both men and women. Estrogen also plays a role in regulating the sexual behaviour of both sexes. Both men and women produce these hormones, although in differing quantities. For example, in men, testosterone is produced in the testes and adrenal glands, and in women, testosterone is produced in the adrenal glands and ovaries. Even so, men produce much more testosterone than women: Men produce 260 to 1000 nanograms per decilitre (ng/dL) of blood plasma (a nanogram is one billionth of a gram), whereas women produce about 15 to 70 ng/dL. The amount also varies and decreases with age.

Women's estrogen levels decline during menopause, which can lead to slower growth in the vaginal cells, resulting in thinner vaginal walls, vaginal dryness, and decreased vaginal sensitivity. Despite this decrease in estrogen, testosterone levels often remain constant, which may result in an increase in sexual desire even though the physical changes of menopause can negatively affect sexual functioning. In men, decreases in testosterone can lead to lessening sexual desire and decreases in the quality and quantity of erections. We discuss aging and sexuality in more detail in Chapter 15.

Neurotransmitters, chemical messengers in the body that transmit messages from one nerve cell to another, also have a powerful effect on our bodies. Various neurotransmitters, including oxytocin, serotonin, dopamine, and vasopressin, have been found to affect sexual desire, arousal, orgasm, and our desire to couple with certain partners (Ishak et al., 2008; Kosfeld et al., 2005; Lim & Young, 2006; Walch et al., 2001; K.A. Young et al., 2008; L.J. Young & Wang, 2004). Directly after orgasm, levels of serotonin, oxytocin, and vasopressin increase, which can lead to feelings of pleasure, relaxation, and attachment (Fisher, 2004). Researchers have also explored using various neurotransmitters to eliminate sexual urges and desires in sexual offenders (Saleh & Berlin, 2003).

In many male–female couples, one of the reasons for having intercourse, the insertion of the penis into the vagina, is to inseminate the female and create a baby. William Masters and Virginia Johnson, whom you met in Chapter 2, were the first scientists to try to objectively measure the various aspects of heterosexual sex. The series of physiological and psychological changes that occur in the body during sexual behaviour, are referred to collectively as our **sexual response**. Over the years, several models of these changes have been proposed to explain the exact progression and nature of the human sexual response. The best-known biological model is the Masters and Johnson's sexual response cycle. This model is beneficial in helping physicians and therapists identify how dysfunction, disease, illness, and disability affect sexual functioning (see also Chapter 15).

Masters and Johnson's Sexual Response Cycle

Based on their laboratory work, Masters and Johnson proposed a four-phase model of physiological arousal known as the **sexual response cycle** (see Figure 5.1). This cycle occurs during all sexual behaviours in which a person progresses from excitement to orgasm, whether it is through oral or anal sex, masturbation, or vaginal intercourse. These physiological processes are similar for all sexual relationships, whether they are between heterosexual or homosexual partners.

The four phases of the sexual response cycle are **excitement**, **plateau**, **orgasm**, and **resolution**. The two primary physical changes that occur during the sexual response cycle are **vasocongestion** (VAZ-oh-conn-jest-shun) and **myotonia** (my-uh-TONE-ee-uh), which we will discuss in greater detail shortly.

Sexual Response Cycle in Women

Sexual response patterns vary among women (and in the same woman depending on her menstrual cycle). These variations can be attributed to the amount of time spent in each phase. For

---

neurotransmitters
Specialized chemical messengers in the body that transmit messages from one nerve cell to another.

sexual response
Series of physiological and psychological changes that occur in the body during sexual behaviour.

sexual response cycle
Four-stage model of sexual arousal proposed by Masters and Johnson.

excitement
The first stage of the sexual response cycle, in which an erection occurs in males and vaginal lubrication occurs in females.

plateau
The second stage of the sexual response cycle, occurring before orgasm, in which vasocongestion builds up.

orgasm
The third stage of the sexual response cycle, which involves an intense sensation during the peak of sexual arousal and results in a release of sexual tension.

resolution
The fourth stage of the sexual response cycle, in which the body returns to the pre-aroused state.

vasocongestion
An increase in the blood concentrated in the male and female genitals, as well as in the female breasts, during sexual activity.

myotonia
Involuntary contractions of the muscles.

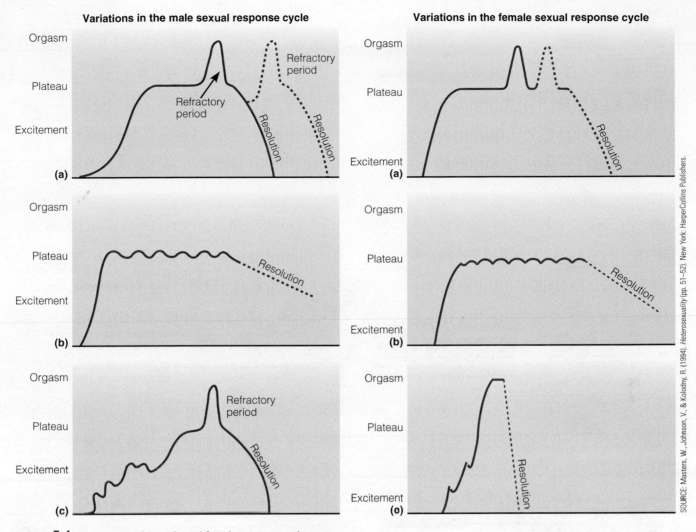

Variations in the male sexual response cycle

(a)

(b)

(c)

Variations in the female sexual response cycle

(a)

(b)

(o)

SOURCE: Masters, W., Johnson, V., & Kolodny, R. (1994). *Heterosexuality* (pp. 51–52). New York: HarperCollins Publishers.

FIGURE **5.1** Variations within male and female response cycles.

example, more time spent during the arousal phase may result in a greater orgasmic response. The intensity of the response may also be affected by factors such as menstrual cycle and previous childbearing. However, even with these differences, the basic physical response is always similar.

EXCITEMENT PHASE The first phase, excitement, begins with vasocongestion, an increase in the blood concentrated in the genitals, breasts, or both. Vasocongestion is the principal physical component of sexual arousal (Frohlich & Meston, 2000). Many circumstances can induce excitement, including hearing your partner's voice, seeing an erotic picture, having a fantasy, or being touched a certain way. Within 30 seconds, vasocongestion causes the vaginal walls to begin lubricating, a process called **transudation** (trans-SUE-day-shun). During the excitement phase, the walls of the vagina, which usually lie flat together, expand. This has been called the **tenting effect** (see Figure 5.2).

During sexual arousal in women who have not had children, the labia majora thin out and become flattened, and may pull slightly away from the introitus. The labia minora often turn bright pink and begin to increase in size. The increase in size of

the vaginal lips adds an average of 1.25–2.5 centimetres (0.5 to 1 inch) of length to the vaginal canal.

The breasts also experience changes during this phase. Nipple erections may occur in one or both breasts, and the areolas and the breasts enlarge (Figure 5.3).

Because of the increased vascularity (blood flow) to the genitals during pregnancy and childbirth, women who have had children have a more rapid increase in vasocongestion and enlargement of both the labia majora and minora, which may become two to three times larger by the end of the excitement phase. Vasocongestion may also cause the clitoral glans to become erect, depending on the type and intensity of stimulation. Generally, the more direct the stimulation, the

transudation
The lubrication of the vagina during sexual arousal.

tenting effect
During sexual arousal in females, the cervix and uterus pull up, and the

upper third of the vagina balloons open, making a larger opening in the cervix.

Excitement phase

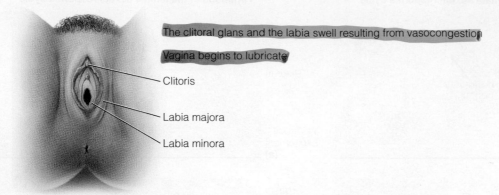

The clitoral glans and the labia swell resulting from vasocongestion

Vagina begins to lubricate

— Clitoris

— Labia majora

— Labia minora

Plateau phase

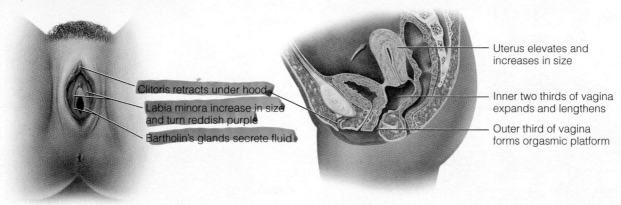

Clitoris retracts under hood

Labia minora increase in size
and turn reddish purple

Bartholin's glands secrete fluid

Uterus elevates and
increases in size

Inner two thirds of vagina
expands and lengthens

Outer third of vagina
forms orgasmic platform

Orgasmic phase

Uterus contracts

Orgasmic platform contracts
Rectal sphincter contracts

Resolution phase

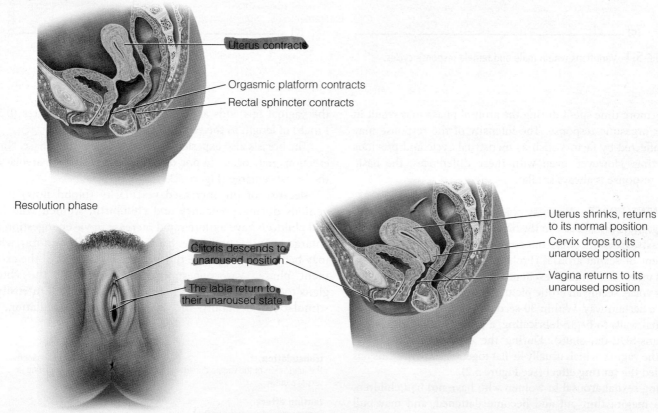

Clitoris descends to
unaroused position

The labia return to
their unaroused state

Uterus shrinks, returns
to its normal position
Cervix drops to its
unaroused position
Vagina returns to its
unaroused position

FIGURE **5.2** Internal and external changes in the female sexual response cycle.

SOURCE: Masters, W., Johnson, V., & Kolodny, R. (1994). *Heterosexuality* (p. 58). New York: HarperCollins Publishers.

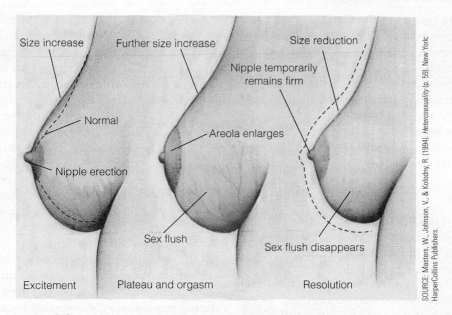

FIGURE **5.3** Breast changes in the female sexual response cycle.

SOURCE: Masters, W., Johnson, V., & Kolodny, R. (1994). *Heterosexuality* (p. 59). New York: HarperCollins Publishers.

more engorged the entire clitoral organ will become. Sexual arousal may also be facilitated by the neurotransmitter serotonin, which we discussed earlier in this chapter (Frohlich & Meston, 2000).

The excitement phase can last anywhere from a few minutes to hours. Toward the end of the excitement phase, a woman may experience a **sex flush**, which resembles a rash. This usually begins on the chest and, during the plateau stage, spreads from the breasts to the neck and face, shoulders, arms, abdomen, thighs, buttocks, and back. Women report varied sensations during the excitement phase, which are often felt all over the body, rather than being concentrated in one area.

PLATEAU PHASE Women often need more time than men to reach the plateau phase, because they have a larger and more vascular pelvic area, requiring more intense vasocongestion. Once they reach this stage, breast size continues to increase, and the nipples may remain erect. The clitoral glans retracts behind the clitoral hood anywhere from one to three minutes before orgasm, and just before orgasm, the clitoris may not be visible at all. Masters and Johnson claim that it is the clitoral hood rubbing and pulling over the clitoris that is responsible for the orgasm during sexual intercourse.

ORGASM PHASE At the end of the plateau phase, vasocongestion in the pelvis creates an **orgasmic platform** in the lower third of the vagina (see Figure 5.2). When this pressure reaches a certain point, a reflex in the surrounding muscles is set off, causing vigorous contractions. These contractions expel the blood that is trapped in the surrounding tissues and, in doing so, cause pleasurable orgasmic sensations. Myotonia of the pelvic muscles is primarily responsible for these contractions; without these muscles

(as in the case of a woman who has had a hysterectomy, the surgical removal of the uterus), the orgasmic response may be significantly reduced.

Muscular contractions occur about every 0.8 second during orgasm. In total, there are about 8 to 15 contractions, and the first 5 or 6 are felt most strongly. In women, contractions last longer than in men. A possible explanation for this is that vasocongestion occurs in the entire pelvic region in women (the internal clitoral organ fills the pelvic region), whereas it is very localized in men (mainly in the penis and testicles).

During orgasm, there is a release of vasocongestion and muscle tension. The body may shudder, jerk uncontrollably, or spasm. In addition, orgasms may involve facial grimacing, groans, spasms in the hands and feet, contractions of the gluteal and abdominal muscles, and contractions of the orgasmic platform. Peaks in blood pressure and respiration patterns have been found during both male and female orgasms.

REAL Research Although orgasms experienced during masturbation are more physiologically intense than orgasms during partner sex, orgasms during masturbation provide less overall sexual satisfaction than orgasms experienced during partner sex (Levin, 2007; Mah & Binik, 2005).

sex flush
A temporary reddish colour change of the skin that sometimes develops during sexual excitement.

orgasmic platform
The thickening of the walls of the lower third of the vagina.

The Biology of Sex, Pregnancy, and Childbirth **117**

Kinsey reported that 14 percent of women regularly experienced **multiple orgasms**, and although Masters and Johnson believed all women were capable of such orgasms, the majority of women they studied did not experience them. Multiple orgasms are more likely to occur from direct stimulation of the clitoris, rather than from penile thrusting during vaginal intercourse. Research into the female G-spot suggests that some women may have an area inside the vagina that, when stimulated, causes intense orgasms (see Chapter 3).

On Your Mind

I've heard that many women fake orgasm. Why would they do that?

It might surprise you, but both men and women report having faked orgasms at some point in their lives (Knox et al., 2008; Muehlenhard & Shippee, 2010). As for female faking, the U.S. National Survey on Sexual Health and Behavior found that although 85 percent of men said their female partner reached orgasm the last time they had sex, only 64 percent of women said they did (Herbenick et al., 2010). Although there are several potential reasons for this difference, it is possible that some of the partners of the men who responded to the survey were faking. Women fake orgasm for several reasons, including not knowing what type of physical stimulation would lead to orgasm, wanting to end a sexual encounter, or to avoid hurting a partner's feelings (because we live in a culture that often expects men to provide women's orgasms, a woman might fake to minimize any negative feelings in her partner; Muehlenhard & Shippee, 2010). Men have also been known to fake orgasms, and although the majority report doing so during vaginal intercourse, some men report faking orgasm during oral sex, manual stimulation, and/or phone sex (Muehlenhard & Shippee, 2010). Men's reasons for faking are similar to women's, but common reasons are because they are tired or don't feel that orgasm is possible. In all of these instances, partners are giving false information, and even though they are probably doing it under the guise of good intentions, open, honest communication about sexual needs and feelings is a far better strategy.

RESOLUTION PHASE During the last phase of the sexual response cycle, resolution, the body returns to pre-excitement conditions. The extra blood leaves the genitals, erections disappear, muscles relax, and heart and breathing rates return to normal.

multiple orgasms
More than one orgasm experienced within a short period.

tumescence
The swelling of the penis because of vasocongestion, causing an erection.

detumescence
The return of an erect penis to the flaccid state.

After orgasm, the skin is often sweaty, and the sex flush slowly disappears. The breasts begin to decrease in size, usually within five to ten minutes. Many women appear to have nipple erections after an orgasm because the breast as a whole quickly decreases in size while the areolae are still engorged. The clitoris returns to its original size but remains extremely sensitive for several minutes. Many women do not like the clitoris to be touched during this time because of the increased sensitivity.

Earlier we mentioned that a woman's menstrual cycle may influence her sexual responsiveness. Research has found that sexual excitement occurs more frequently during the last 14 days of a woman's menstrual cycle (Sherfey, 1972). During this time, more lubrication is produced during the excitement phase, which may be because of the increased vasocongestion. Orgasms can be very helpful in reducing cramps during menstruation, presumably because they help to relieve the buildup of pelvic vasocongestion that may occur as a side effect of menstruation (Ellison, 2000).

Sexual Response Cycle in Men

The sexual response cycle in males is similar to that of females, with vasocongestion and myotonia leading to physiological changes in the body (see Figure 5.4). However, in men, the four phases are less well defined.

EXCITEMENT PHASE During the excitement phase, the penis, like the clitoris in women, begins to fill with blood and become erect. Erection, or **tumescence** (too-MESS-cents), begins quickly during excitement, generally within three to five seconds (although the speed of this response lengthens with age). The excitement phase of the sexual response cycle in men is often very short, unless a man uses deliberate attempts to lengthen it. Often this causes **detumescence** (dee-too-MESS-cents), a gradual loss of tumescence. Distractions during the excitement phase (such as the telephone ringing) may also cause detumescence. However, once the plateau stage is reached, an erection is often more stable and less sensitive to outside influences.

During the excitement phase, the testicles also increase in size, becoming up to 50 percent larger. This is both a vasocongestive and myotonic response. The cremaster muscle pulls the testicles closer to the body to avoid injury during thrusting (see Chapter 4 for more information about this muscle).

PLATEAU PHASE All of these physical changes continue during the plateau phase. Some men may experience a sex flush, which is identical to the sex flush women experience. In addition, it is not uncommon for men to have nipple erections. Just before orgasm, the glans penis becomes engorged (this is comparable with the

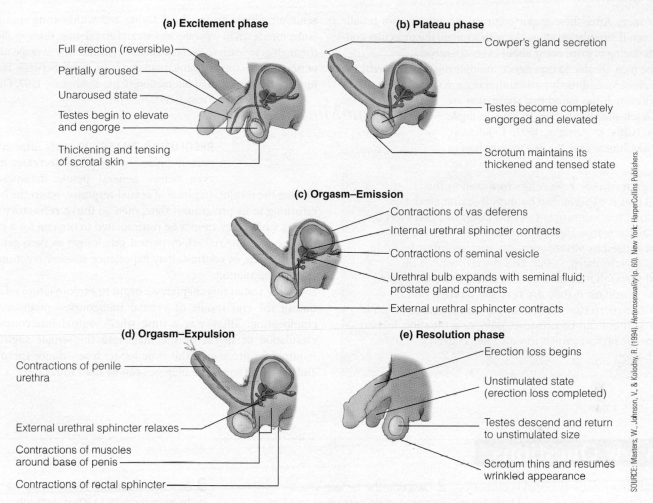

(a) Excitement phase

Full erection (reversible)

Partially aroused

Unaroused state

Testes begin to elevate and engorge

Thickening and tensing of scrotal skin

(b) Plateau phase

Cowper's gland secretion

Testes become completely engorged and elevated

Scrotum maintains its thickened and tensed state

(c) Orgasm–Emission

Contractions of vas deferens

Internal urethral sphincter contracts

Contractions of seminal vesicle

Urethral bulb expands with seminal fluid; prostate gland contracts

External urethral sphincter contracts

(d) Orgasm–Expulsion

Contractions of penile urethra

External urethral sphincter relaxes

Contractions of muscles around base of penis

Contractions of rectal sphincter

(e) Resolution phase

Erection loss begins

Unstimulated state (erection loss completed)

Testes descend and return to unstimulated size

Scrotum thins and resumes wrinkled appearance

SOURCE: Masters, W., Johnson, V., & Kolodny, R. (1994). *Heterosexuality* (p. 60). New York: HarperCollins Publishers.

FIGURE **5.4** External and internal changes in the male sexual response cycle.

engorgement of the clitoral glans in women). At this point, a few drops of pre-ejaculatory fluid from the Cowper's gland may appear on the glans of the penis.

ORGASM PHASE Orgasm and ejaculation do not always occur together (see Figure 5.4). In fact, there are men who are able to have orgasms without ejaculating and can have several orgasms before ejaculating. Although it is rare, some men are capable of anywhere from 2 to 16 orgasms before ejaculation, although the ability to have them decreases with age (Chia & Abrams, 1997; J. Johnson, 2001).

If orgasm and ejaculation occur at the same time, ejaculation can occur in two stages. During the first stage, which lasts only a few seconds, there are contractions in the vas deferens, seminal vesicles, and prostate gland. These contractions lead to **ejaculatory inevitability**, whereby just before orgasm there is a feeling that ejaculation can no longer be controlled. In the second stage, the semen is forced out of the urethra by muscle contractions (the same set of muscles that contract in female orgasm).

REAL Research Male ejaculation has been found to have physiological benefits for women, as well as for men. In men, regular ejaculations help keep sperm morphology (form and structure) and semen volume within normal ranges, and the deposit of sperm in the vaginal canal has been found to regulate ovulatory cycles, enhance mood, and reduce vaginal atrophy (a decrease in tissue firmness) in aging women (Levin, 2007).

The first three or four contractions are the most pleasurable and tend to be the most forceful (various herbal and drug products have recently appeared on the market claiming to increase male orgasmic contractions). The force of the ejaculation can propel semen up to 60 centimetres (24 inches), although this distance is considerably shorter

ejaculatory inevitability
A feeling that ejaculation can no longer be controlled.

The Biology of Sex, Pregnancy, and Childbirth   **119**

in older men. After these major contractions, minor ones usually follow, even if stimulation stops. As with women, the muscular contractions during orgasm occur about every 0.8 second.

Some men are able to experience multiple orgasms, whereby the orgasm phase leads directly into another orgasm without a refractory period. Research has found that some men are able to teach themselves how to have multiple orgasms (Chia & Abrams, 1997; J. Johnson, 2001). The Chinese were the first to learn how to

The concept of blue balls refers to a pain in the testicles that is experienced by men if sexual arousal is maintained for a significant period but is not followed by an orgasm. It is true that the pressure felt in the genitals, which is caused by vasocongestion, can be uncomfortable (Chalett & Nerenberg, 2000). This discomfort can be relieved through masturbation. Women also experience a similar condition if they are sexually aroused and do not reach orgasm (some people refer to such pain as "pink ovaries"). There can be pressure, pain, or a bloating feeling in the pelvic region, which can also be relieved through masturbation.

achieve multiple orgasm by delaying and withholding ejaculation. Some men learn to separate orgasm and ejaculation, thereby allowing themselves to learn to become multi-orgasmic. The average number of orgasms a multi-orgasmic man can have varies between two and nine orgasms per sexual interaction (Chia & Abrams, 1997; Dunn & Trost, 1989).

RESOLUTION PHASE Directly after ejaculation, the glans of the penis decreases in size, even before general penile detumescence. During the resolution phase of sexual response, when the body is returning to its pre-arousal state, men go into a **refractory stage**, during which they cannot be restimulated to orgasm for a certain time period. The refractory period gets longer as men get older. Younger men, in contrast, may experience another erection soon after an ejaculation.

In the rest of this chapter, we begin to explore issues related to one of the end results of vaginal intercourse—pregnancy and childbearing. There was a time when vaginal intercourse and ejaculation of sperm by the male into the female vagina was required for pregnancy, this is no longer true—donor sperm, ova, embryos, and surrogate uteruses can be used today.

Review Questions

1 Identify the most influential hormones and neurotransmitters in sexual behaviour and explain their roles in sexual behaviour.

2 Describe the female sexual response cycle according to Masters and Johnson.

3 Describe the male sexual response cycle according to Masters and Johnson.

4 Compare and contrast the female and male sexual response cycles.

Fertility

Most parents, sooner or later, must confront the moment when their child asks, "Where did I come from?" The answer they give depends on the parent, the child, the situation, and the culture. Every culture has its own traditional explanations for where babies come from. The Australian Aborigines, for example, believe that babies are created by the mother earth and, therefore, are products of the land. The spirits of children rest in certain areas of the land, and these spirits enter a young woman as she passes by (Dunham et al., 1992). Women who do not want to become pregnant either avoid these areas or dress up like old

women to fool the spirits. In Malaysia, the Malay people believe that because man is the more rational of the two sexes, babies come from men. Babies are formulated in the man's brain for 40 days before moving down to his penis for eventual ejaculation into a woman's womb. In Canada and the majority of the world, it is understood that ejaculation of sperm from the penis into the vagina, in the absence of birth control or sterility, or IVF procedures are the most common ways for a pregnancy to begin.

Statistics and Current Trends

In Canada the greatest number of births are in Ontario, followed by Quebec, Alberta, and British Columbia. In Canada in 2007, 2009, and 2011, there were 367 864, 380 863, and 377 636 births, respectively (see Figure 5.5). The majority of births are to mothers between 30 and 34 years of age (see Figure 5.6). Around the world, women's ages at first birth have been increasing (see Figure 5.7).

refractory stage
The period after an ejaculation in which men cannot be stimulated to another orgasm.

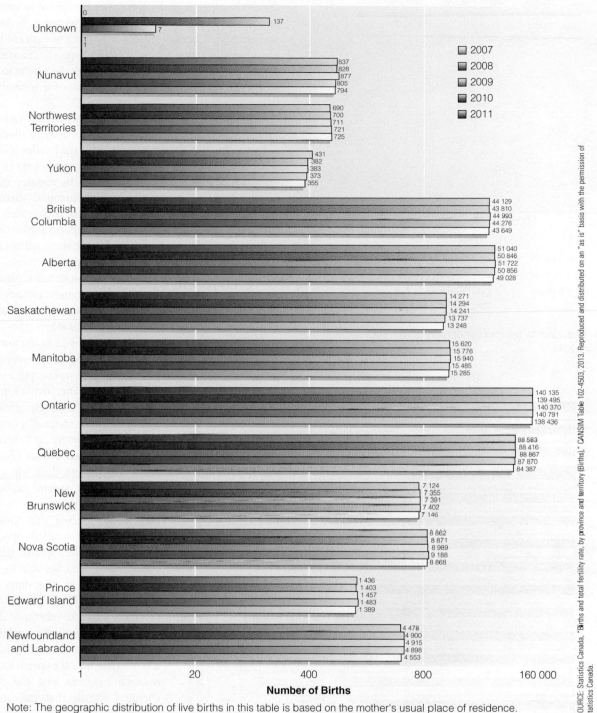

SOURCE: Statistics Canada, "Births and total fertility rate, by province and territory (Births)," CANSIM Table 102-4503, 2013. Reproduced and distributed on an "as is" basis with the permission of Statistics Canada.

Note: The geographic distribution of live births in this table is based on the mother's usual place of residence.

FIGURE **5.5** Number of live births in the provinces and territories between 2007 and 2011.

In 2006, average ages ranged from 25 (United States) to 29.4 (Switzerland). The average number of children born to Canadian mothers has dropped slightly between 2007 (1.66 children per mother) and 2011 (1.61 children per mother). The birth rate per mother in 2011 was highest in Nunavut (2.97 children per mother) and lowest in British Columbia (1.42 children per mother) (see Figure 5.8). Currently, there are more people in Canada over the age of 65 than under the age of 14, and it is predicted that by the year 2030 more people in Canada will die than will be born (Statistics Canada, 2015).

Conception

Our bodies are biologically programmed in many ways to help pregnancy occur. For instance, a woman's sexual desire is usually at its peak during ovulation until just before her menstruation (Bullivant et al., 2004). During ovulation, a **mucus plug** in the

mucus plug
A collection of thick mucus in the cervix that prevents bacteria from entering the uterus.

The Biology of Sex, Pregnancy, and Childbirth

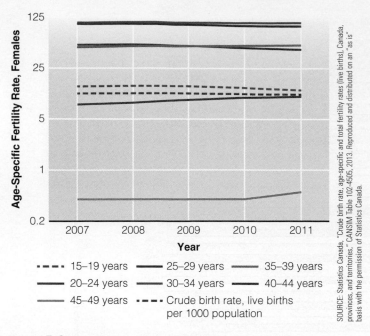

SOURCE: Statistics Canada, "Crude birth rate, age-specific and total fertility rates (live births), Canada, provinces, and territories," CANSIM Table 102-4505, 2013. Reproduced and distributed on an "as is" basis with the permission of Statistics Canada.

FIGURE 5.6 Birth rates by selected age of mother: final 2007–2010 and preliminary 2011.

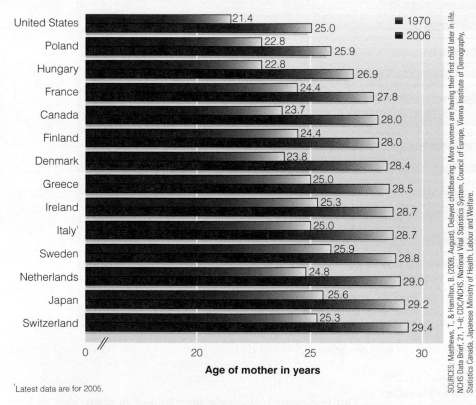

Latest data are for 2005.

SOURCES: Matthews, T., & Hamilton, B. (2009, August). Delayed childbearing: More women are having their first child later in life. NCHS Data Brief, 21, 1–8; CDC/NCHS, National Vital Statistics System, Council of Europe, Vienna Institute of Demography, Statistics Canada, Japanese Ministry of Health, Labour and Welfare.

FIGURE 5.7 Average age of mother at first birth in selected countries, 1970–2006.

spontaneous abortion
A natural process through which the body expels a developing embryo.

miscarriage
A pregnancy that terminates on its own; also referred to as a *spontaneous abortion*.

cervix disappears, making it easier for sperm to enter the uterus, and the cervical mucus changes in consistency, becoming thinner and stretchy. Cervical mucus may filter out sperm that has poor morphology (shape) and motility (speed) (Saurez and Pacey, 2006). Once sperm has passed through the cervix to the uterus, it will make its way to the fallopian tubes for insemination of the ovum.

The process of getting pregnant may appear rather easy; however, this is not always the case. Parental age can affect the health of sperm and ovum. Sperm from middle-aged males is less motile and is more likely to have alterations to its morphology (Johnson, Dunleavy, Gemmell, & Nakagawa, 2015). In females the number of oocytes and the support cells that surround them decrease in number and vitality (Coccia & Rizzello, 2008). Men and women's reproductive systems may contain antisperm antibodies (Bohring & Krause, 2005). Depending on the study, these antisperm antibodies may occur in up to 36 percent of infertile couples (Naz, 2004). When a fertile woman engages in unprotected vaginal intercourse, 30 percent of the time she becomes pregnant, although a significant number of these pregnancies end in **spontaneous abortion** (also called a **miscarriage**) (Zinaman et al., 1996).

Because the ovum can live for up to 24 hours and the majority of sperm can live up to 72 hours in the female reproductive tract, pregnancy may occur if intercourse takes place either a few days before or after ovulation (A.J. Wilcox et al., 1995). Although most sperm die within 72 hours, a small number, less than 1 percent, can survive up to seven days in the female reproductive tract (Ferreira-Poblete, 1997). Throughout their trip into the Fallopian tubes, the sperm haphazardly swim around, bumping into various structures and each other. During this time sperm also undergo a process called capacitation where the head of the sperm (the acrosome) changes and becomes able to attach to and penetrate through the outer layer of the ovum (Okabe, 2013). When (and if) sperm reach the jelly-like substance that surrounds the ovum called the zona pellucida, they are hyperactivated and swim quickly. Although it is not clear how the sperm locate the ovum, research indicates that the ovum releases chemical signals that indicate its location (Okabe, 2013).

Several sperm may reach the ovum, but only one will usually fertilize it. It is possible for multiple sperm to inseminate the egg (called polyspermy), but these fertilized ova do not survive. Once a sperm cell has fertilized the egg, the outer layer of the ovum immediately undergoes a physical change, making it impossible for any other sperm to enter. This entire process takes about 24 hours. Fertilization usually occurs in the ampulla (the funnel-shaped open end of the Fallopian tube; Figure 5.9); after fertilization, the fertilized ovum is referred to as a zygote.

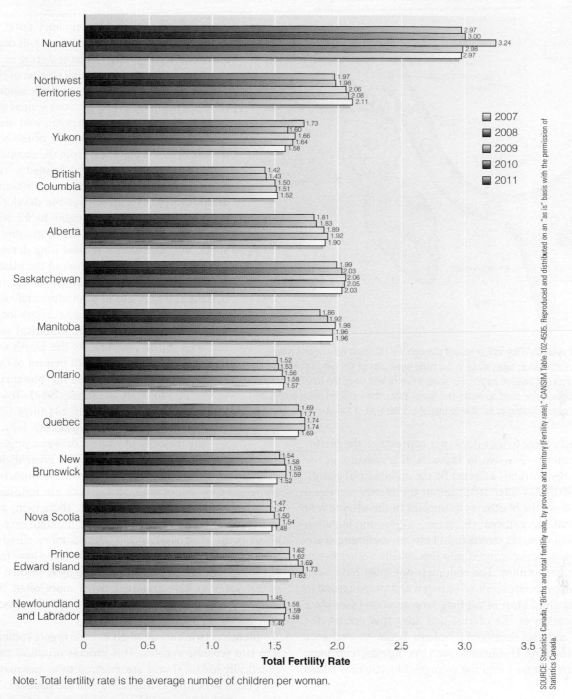

Fertility rate chart by province and territory, 2007 to 2011:

Nunavut
- 2007: 2.97
- 2008: 3.00
- 2009: 3.24
- 2010: 2.98
- 2011: 2.97

Northwest Territories
- 2007: 1.97
- 2008: 1.98
- 2009: 2.06
- 2010: 2.08
- 2011: 2.11

Yukon
- 2007: 1.73
- 2008: 1.60
- 2009: 1.66
- 2010: 1.64
- 2011: 1.58

British Columbia
- 2007: 1.42
- 2008: 1.43
- 2009: 1.50
- 2010: 1.51
- 2011: 1.52

Alberta
- 2007: 1.81
- 2008: 1.83
- 2009: 1.89
- 2010: 1.92
- 2011: 1.90

Saskatchewan
- 2007: 1.99
- 2008: 2.03
- 2009: 2.06
- 2010: 2.05
- 2011: 2.03

Manitoba
- 2007: 1.86
- 2008: 1.92
- 2009: 1.98
- 2010: 1.96
- 2011: 1.96

Ontario
- 2007: 1.52
- 2008: 1.53
- 2009: 1.56
- 2010: 1.58
- 2011: 1.57

Quebec
- 2007: 1.69
- 2008: 1.71
- 2009: 1.74
- 2010: 1.74
- 2011: 1.69

New Brunswick
- 2007: 1.54
- 2008: 1.58
- 2009: 1.59
- 2010: 1.59
- 2011: 1.52

Nova Scotia
- 2007: 1.47
- 2008: 1.47
- 2009: 1.50
- 2010: 1.54
- 2011: 1.48

Prince Edward Island
- 2007: 1.62
- 2008: 1.62
- 2009: 1.69
- 2010: 1.73
- 2011: 1.63

Newfoundland and Labrador
- 2007: 1.45
- 2008: 1.58
- 2009: 1.59
- 2010: 1.58
- 2011: 1.46

Legend: 2007, 2008, 2009, 2010, 2011

X-axis: **Total Fertility Rate** (0, 0.5, 1.0, 1.5, 2.0, 2.5, 3.0, 3.5)

SOURCE: Statistics Canada, "Births and total fertility rate, by province and territory (fertility rate)," CANSIM Table 102-4505. Reproduced and distributed on an "as is" basis with the permission of Statistics Canada.

Note: Total fertility rate is the average number of children per woman.

FIGURE 5.8 Fertility rates by province and territory from 2007 to 2011.

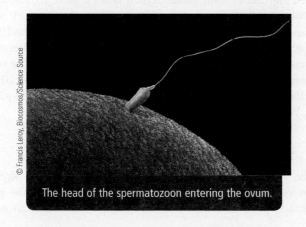

© Francis Leroy, Biocosmos/Science Source

The head of the spermatozoon entering the ovum.

Approximately 12 hours after the genetic material from the sperm and ovum join together, the first cell division begins. At this point, the collection of cells is referred to as a **blastocyst**. The blastocyst will divide in two every 12 to 15 hours, doubling in size. As this goes on, the cilia in the Fallopian tube gently push the blastocyst toward the uterus. Fallopian tube muscles also help to move the blastocyst by occasionally contracting.

blastocyst
The hollow ball of embryonic cells that enters the uterus from the Fallopian tube and eventually implants.

The Biology of Sex, Pregnancy, and Childbirth

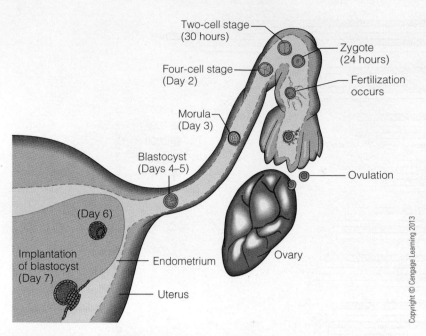

Two-cell stage
(30 hours)

Zygote
(24 hours)

Four-cell stage
(Day 2)

Fertilization
occurs

Morula
(Day 3)

Blastocyst
(Days 4–5)

Ovulation

(Day 6)

Implantation
of blastocyst
(Day 7)

Endometrium

Ovary

Uterus

Copyright © Cengage Learning 2013

FIGURE 5.9 After ovulation, the follicle moves through the Fallopian tube until it meets the spermatozoon. Fertilization takes place in the wide outer part of the tube. Approximately 24 hours later, the first cell division begins. For some three or four days, the fertilized ovum remains in the Fallopian tube, dividing again and again. When the fertilized ovum enters the uterus, it sheds its outer covering to be able to implant in the wall of the uterus.

Approximately three to four days after conception, the blastocyst enters the uterus. For two to three days, it remains in the uterus and absorbs nutrients secreted by the endometrial glands. On about the sixth day after fertilization, the uterus secretes a chemical that allows the blastocyst to implant in the uterine wall and develop into an embryo (R. Jones, 1984). Implantation involves a series of complex interactions between the lining of the uterus and the developing embryo, and this usually occurs five to eight days after fertilization. The endometrium must have been exposed to the appropriate levels of estrogen and progesterone to facilitate implantation. Most of the time, implantation takes place in the upper portion of the uterus, and after this occurs, the woman's body and the developing embryo begin to exchange chemical information. Hormones, such as human chorionic gonadotropin, are released into the woman's bloodstream (these

can be detected through pregnancy tests). If implantation does not occur, the blastocyst will degenerate and shed with the endometrial layer during menstruation.

After implantation, a small section of the blastocyst divides into three layers of cells—the ectoderm (which develops into the central nervous system and skin), the mesoderm (muscles and bones), and the endoderm (internal organs). The remainder of the blastocyst will develop into the placenta. From the second through the eighth weeks, the developing human is referred to as an **embryo** (EMM-bree-oh). A membrane called the **amnion** begins to grow over the developing embryo, and the amniotic cavity begins to fill with amniotic fluid. This fluid supports the fetus, protects it from shock, and also assists in fetal lung development. The **placenta**, which is the portion of the blastocyst that is grows into the uterine wall, supplies nutrients to the developing fetus, aids in respiratory and excretory functions, and secretes hormones necessary for the continuation of the pregnancy. The **umbilical cord** connects the fetus to the placenta. By the fourth week of pregnancy, the placenta covers 20 percent of the wall of the uterus, and at five months, the placenta covers half of the uterine wall (R. Jones, 1984). Toward the end of pregnancy, approximately 284 litres (75 gallons) of blood will pass through the placenta daily.

The majority of women deliver a single fetus. However, in approximately two of every 100 pregnancies there is a multiple birth. This can happen in two ways. Sometimes two ova are released by the ovaries, and if both are fertilized by sperm, **fraternal twins** (non-identical) result. These twins are **dizygotic**, and they can be either of the same or different sexes. Two thirds of all twins are fraternal and are no more closely genetically related than any two siblings. The tendency to have fraternal twins may be inherited from the mother, and older women (over the age of 30) seem to have fraternal twins more often than younger women (because of erratic ovulation and an increased possibility of releasing more than one ovum).

Identical twins occur when a single zygote completely divides into two separate zygotes. This process produces twins who are genetically identical and are referred to as **monozygotic** twins. They often look alike and are always of the same sex. In rare cases, the zygote fails to divide completely, and two babies may be joined together at some point in their bodies; these are known as **conjoined twins**, once referred to as Siamese twins. In some instances, many ova are released and fertilized, and triplets (three offspring) or quadruplets (four offspring) may result. Recently, the number of multiple births has been increasing as more older women become pregnant and fertility drug use, which can stimulate the release of ova, becomes widespread (Brandes et al., 2010; V.C. Wright et al., 2008).

Early Signs of Pregnancy

If the zygote does implant, most women experience physical signs very early that alert them to their pregnancy. The most common early indicator is missing a period, although some

embryo
The developing organism from the second to the eighth week of gestation.

amnion
A thin, tough, membranous sac that encloses the embryo or fetus.

placenta
The structure through which the exchange of materials between fetal and maternal circulations occurs.

umbilical cord
The long, ropelike structure that connects the fetus to the placenta.

fraternal twins
Two offspring developed from two separate ova fertilized by different spermatozoa.

dizygotic
Pertaining to or derived from two separate zygotes.

identical twins
Two offspring developed from a single zygote that completely divides into two separate, genetically identical zygotes.

monozygotic
Pertaining to or derived from one zygote.

conjoined twins
Twins who are born physically joined together.

Table 5.1 Pregnancy Signs

Physical Sign	Time of Appearance	Other Possible Reasons
Period late/absent	2–4 weeks after conception	Excessive weight gain or loss, fatigue, hormonal problems, stress, breast-feeding, going off birth control pills
Breast tenderness	1–2 weeks after conception	Use of birth control pills, hormonal imbalance, period onset
Increased fatigue	1–6 weeks after conception	Stress, depression, thyroid disorder, cold or flu
Morning sickness	2–8 weeks after conception	Stress, stomach disorders, food poisoning
Increased urination	6–8 weeks after conception	Urinary tract infection, excessive use of diuretics, diabetes
Fetal heartbeat	10–20 weeks and then throughout entire pregnancy	None
Backaches	Entire pregnancy	Back problems
Frequent headaches	May be entire pregnancy	Caffeine withdrawal, dehydration, eyestrain, birth control pills
Food cravings	Entire pregnancy	Poor diet, stress, depression, period onset
Darkening of nipples	Entire pregnancy	Hormonal imbalance
Fetal movement	16–22 weeks after conception	Bowel contractions, gas

women notice some "spotting" that occurs during the pregnancy (anything more than this is often referred to as irregular bleeding and may indicate a possible miscarriage). Other physical signs include breast tenderness, frequent urination, and **morning sickness** (see Table 5.1).

It is estimated that between 50 percent and 80 percent of all pregnant women experience some form of nausea, vomiting, or both, during pregnancy (Atanackovic et al., 2001; Matthews et al., 2010). This sickness may be due to the increase in estrogen and progesterone during pregnancy, but its cause is still uncertain (Verberg, Gillott, Al-Fardan, & Grudzinskas, 2005). It is often worse in the morning because there is no food in the stomach to counter its effects, although it can happen at any point during the day. Researchers believe that morning sickness may protect the fetus from food-borne illness and chemicals in certain foods during the first trimester, which is the most critical time in development (Boyd, 2000). The lowest rates of morning sickness are found in cultures without animal products as a food staple. Some women also develop food aversions, the most common of which are to meat, fish, poultry, and eggs—all foods that can carry harmful bacteria.

In rare cases, **pseudocyesis** (sue-doe-sigh-EE-sis), or false pregnancy, occurs. This is a condition in which a woman believes she is pregnant when she is not. Her belief is so strong that she begins to experience several of the signs of pregnancy (Svoboda, 2006). She may miss her period, experience morning sickness, and gain weight.

Pseudocyesis generally has a psychological basis but may have a physical cause. For instance, a tumour on the pituitary gland may cause an oversecretion of prolactin, which, in turn, can cause symptoms such as breast fullness and morning sickness.

Pseudocyesis has been found to be more common in women who believe childbearing is central to their identity, have a history of infertility or depression (or both), or have had a miscarriage (Whelan & Stewart, 1990). Although rare, there have been a few cases in which men experienced pseudocyesis, although this is typically due to psychological impairment (Shutty & Leadbetter, 1993). Male and female partners of pregnant women may

On Your Mind

Will guys ever be able to become "pregnant"?

As of 2015, there have not been any documented pregnancies in a biological man. However, it is possible that newer techniques will enable a biological man to carry a pregnancy to term in the future. An embryo would have to be implanted into a man's abdomen with the placenta and attached to an internal organ. Hormonal treatment would be necessary to sustain the pregnancy. In addition, the father would have to undergo a **cesarean section (C-section)** birth. There may not be many men standing in line to carry a pregnancy, however, because the hormones needed to maintain the pregnancy can cause breast enlargement and penile shrinkage.

morning sickness
The nausea and vomiting that some women have when they become pregnant; typically caused by the increase in hormones. Can occur at any point in the day.

pseudocyesis
A condition in which a woman experiences signs of pregnancy, even though she is not pregnant.

cesarean section (C-section)
A surgical procedure in which the woman's abdomen and uterus are surgically opened and a child is removed.

The Biology of Sex, Pregnancy, and Childbirth

experience a related condition called **couvade** (coo-VAHD). Partners with this condition experience the symptoms of their pregnant partners, including nausea, vomiting, increased or decreased appetite, diarrhea, or abdominal bloating (Brennan et al., 2007).

Pregnancy Testing

If you have had vaginal intercourse without using birth control or have experienced any of the signs of pregnancy, it is a good idea to take a pregnancy test. Over-the-counter pregnancy tests can be purchased in drugstores, but sometimes tests are less expensive or even free in university health centres.

On Your Mind

I have missed my period now for two months in a row. Does this mean that I am pregnant? What should I do?

If you have been engaging in vaginal intercourse, there is certainly a chance that you are pregnant. However, there are several other reasons for missing your period, including stress, losing weight, active participation in sports, or changes in eating patterns, as well as certain diseases. In any case, it is a good idea to complete a pregnancy test or make an appointment to consult with your health care provider.

Pregnancy tests measure for a hormone in the blood called **human chorionic gonadotropin** (**hCG;** corr-ee-ON-ick go-nadoh-TRO-pin), which is produced during pregnancy. The hormone hCG is manufactured by the cells in the developing placenta and can be identified in the blood or urine eight to nine days after ovulation. The presence of hCG helps build and maintain a thick endometrial layer, and thus prevents menstruation. Peak levels of hCG are reached in the second and third months of pregnancy and then drop off.

REAL Research Research on morning sickness has found that it may offer protection from breast cancer. One study found that women who experienced morning sickness during pregnancy had a 30 percent lower chance of development of breast cancer later in life, compared with women who did not experience morning sickness (and women who experienced severe morning sickness had an even lower risk; Jaworowicz, 2007). Researchers suggest that changing levels of hCG may be responsible for the nausea, and that these levels seem to offer protection from breast cancer.

Home pregnancy tests can be inaccurate if taken too soon after conception, and some women who postpone pregnancy tests until after the 12th week may have a false-negative pregnancy test because the hCG levels are too low to be detected by the test. If you are using an at-home test, be sure you know how soon after ovulation it can be used. Many tests today can detect hCG levels before a period is late. **False-positive** test results may occur in the presence of a kidney disease or infection, an overactive thyroid gland, or large doses of aspirin, tranquilizers, antidepressants, or anticonvulsant medications (Hatcher et al., 2007).

Of all pregnancy tests, **radioimmunoassay** (**RIA;** ray-dee-ohm-mue-noh-ASS-say) **blood tests** are the most accurate. RIA tests can detect hCG within a few days after conception and are also useful for monitoring the progress of a pregnancy that may be in jeopardy. The levels of hCG increase early in pregnancy, and if a woman's hormones do not follow this pattern, a spontaneous abortion or an **ectopic pregnancy** may have occurred. We will discuss both of these later in this chapter.

If a woman plans on continuing the pregnancy, her health care provider helps her to calculate a **due date**. Most physicians date the pregnancy from the first day of the last menstrual period rather than the day of ovulation or fertilization. The standard for due date calculation is called the **Naegele's** (nay-GEL-lays) **rule**—subtract three months from the first day of the last period and add seven days for a single birth (Mittendorf et al., 1990; for example, if the last period began on August 1, subtract three months and add seven days, which means that the due date would be May 8). This rule works most effectively with women who have standard 28-day menstrual cycles.

Sex Selection: Myth and Modern Methods

Throughout time, many couples have searched for ways to choose the sex of their child. A variety of techniques have been proposed by different cultures at different times. Aristotle believed that if a couple had sexual intercourse in the north wind, they would have a male child, and if intercourse took place in the south wind, they would have a female child. Hippocrates believed that males formed on the right side of the uterus and females on the left; so, to conceive a daughter, a woman was advised to lie on her left side directly after intercourse. The ancient Greeks thought that if a man cut or tied his left testicle, a couple would not have girls

couvade
A condition in which the male or female partner experiences the symptoms of the pregnant woman.

human chorionic gonadotropin (hCG)
The hormone that stimulates production of estrogen and progesterone to maintain pregnancy.

false positive
Incorrect result of a medical test or procedure that wrongly shows the presence of a finding.

radioimmunoassay (RIA) blood test
Blood pregnancy test.

ectopic pregnancy
The implantation of the fertilized egg outside the uterus, such as in the Fallopian tubes or abdomen.

due date
The projected birth date of a baby.

Naegele's rule
A means of figuring the due date by subtracting three months from the first day of the last menstrual period and adding seven days.

Is It a Boy or a Girl?

Throughout the world, people have relied on folk wisdom to predict the sex of their baby. Here are some examples:

It's a Girl!

- Baby sits on the left side of the womb (Nyinba, Nepal)

- Mother puts her left foot first crossing the threshold (Bihar, India)

- Baby sits low in the belly (Lepchas, Himalayas, and Bedouin tribes)

- Mother is grumpy with women (Dinka, Africa)

- Fetus moves slowly and gently (Dustin, North Borneo, and Egypt)

- Mother first feels the baby when she is outside (Serbia)

- Mother dreams of human skulls (Maori, New Zealand)

- Mother dreams of a head kerchief (Egypt)

- Mother craves spicy foods (Nyinba, Nepal)

- Mother's face has yellow spots (Poland)

- Baby "plays in stomach" before sixth month (Nyinba, Nepal)

It's a Boy!

- Baby sits on the right side of the womb (Nyinba, Nepal)

- Mother puts her right foot first crossing the threshold (Bihar, India)

- Baby sits high in the belly (Lepchas, Himalayas, and Bedouin tribes)

- Mother is grumpy with men (Dinka, Africa)

- Fetus moves fast and roughly (Dustin, North Borneo, and Egypt)

- Mother first feels baby move when at home (Serbia)

- Mother dreams of huia feathers (Maori, New Zealand)

- Mother dreams of a handkerchief (Egypt)

- Mother craves bland foods (Nyinba, Nepal)

- Mother looks well (Poland)

- Baby first "plays in stomach" after sixth month (Nyinba, Nepal)

SOURCE: Dunham, C., Myers, F., McDougall, A., & Barnden, N. (1992). *Mamatoto: A celebration of birth*. New York: Penguin Group.

because male sperm were thought to be produced in the right testicle (Dunham et al., 1992). Although some of these suggestions sound absurd today, people in many cultures still hold on to myths of how to choose and how to know the gender of their child (see accompanying Sexual Diversity in Our World).

Reasons for wanting to choose a child's sex vary; although some couples simply prefer a male or female child, others desire to choose the sex of their children for medical reasons. For example, certain inherited diseases are more likely to affect one sex (such as hemophilia a rare blood disorder, which affects more males).

Modern-day methods of gender selection were popularized by Shettles and Rorvik (1970) in their groundbreaking book *Your Baby's Sex: Now You Can Choose*. According to these authors, by taking into account the characteristics of the female (X) and male (Y) sperm, couples can use timing and pH-level adjustments to the vaginal environment (douches) to increase the concentration of X or Y sperm; there is no evidence, however, that this works.

Medical procedures for sex selection include "microsorting" (also known as "spinning"—separating the X and Y sperm followed by artificial insemination). Other tests that can be used to identify sex include genetic embryo testing and amniocentesis. When using these methods, the reported likelihood of conceiving a male is between 50 percent and 70 percent and a female is between 50 percent and 90 percent (Pozniak, 2002). Preimplantation genetic diagnosis (PGD) is a procedure typically used during assisted reproduction to determine where there are chromosomal or genetic abnormalities in an embryo. Some couples who prefer a child of a certain sex may also use PGD for this preference. As you can imagine, the use of PGD, because it has been used for sex selection, is controversial (Ehrlich et al., 2007; Gleicher et al., 2008; Kuliev & Verlinsky, 2008). Finally, an **amniocentesis** (am-nee-oh-sent-TEE-sis) can also determine, among other things, the chromosomal sex of the fetus. These tests raise many moral, sociological, and ethical issues about sex selection. For example, should parents be able to selectively abort a fetus on the basis of sex?

In several countries around the world, such as India, China, South Korea, and Taiwan, parents go to extremes to ensure the birth of a male baby. In some Indian states, for example, males are valued more than females because of their ability to care for and financially support aging parents. Female offspring, in contrast, move into a husband's home after marriage and are unavailable to help care for their parents. An old Indian saying claims that having a girl is like "watering your neighbour's lawn" (Sharma & Haub, 2008). The increasing availability of prenatal testing in India has been linked to an increase in the ratio of male to female births (Dubuc & Coleman, 2007; Jha et al., 2006; Sharma & Haub, 2008). Since 2001, however, male/female ratios have stabilized in India (Sharma & Haub, 2008).

amniocentesis
A procedure in which a small sample of amniotic fluid is analyzed to detect chromosomal abnormalities in the fetus or to determine the sex of the fetus.

Review Questions

1 Explain the process of conception, and describe how the human body is programmed to help pregnancy occur.

2 Identify four signs of pregnancy and explain why they occur.

3 Explain how pregnancy tests work.

4 Explain the methods for sex selection, and define and discuss infanticide.

Infertility

Infertility is defined as the inability to conceive (or impregnate) after one year of regular vaginal intercourse without the use of any form of birth control (if a woman is older than 35, usually infertility is diagnosed after six months of not being able to conceive). In Canada roughly one in six couples or 16 percent of couples experience infertility (Government of Canada, 2013).

We know that fertility rates naturally decline in men and women with increasing age, beginning as early as 30 and then decreasing more quickly after age 40—fewer than 10 percent of women in their early 20s have infertility issues, whereas 30 percent of women in their 40s do (Chavarro et al., 2007b). Sperm quality in men is also affected by aging (Girsh et al., 2008). In Chapter 4, we discussed the worldwide declines in sperm counts and quality because of occupational, environmental, and lifestyle factors. Studies have found that the health of male sperm in humans and other animals can be influenced by exposure to many environmental toxins, such as bisphenol A (BPA), mercury, paint solvents, lead, and possibly electronics (El-Helaly et al., 2010; Wong & Cheng, 2011). In addition, shift work and work-related stress can significantly increase the risk for male infertility (El-Helaly et al., 2010).

Infertility has a strong impact on a couple's well-being (Forti & Krausz, 1998). Emotional reactions to infertility can include depression, anxiety, anger, self-blame, guilt, frustration, and fear. Because the majority of people have no experience dealing with infertility, many of those who find out they are infertile isolate themselves. Overall, women tend to have more emotional reactions to infertility and are more willing to confide in someone about their infertility than are men (Hjelmstedt et al., 1999). Childbearing in North America is part of what defines being female, and so women who are infertile often feel less valued than fertile women. The term **motherhood mandate** refers to the idea that something is wrong with a woman if she does not play a central role in caregiving and child care (Riggs, 2005).

The most common causes of female infertility include ovulation disorders, blocked Fallopian tubes, endometriosis (see Chapter 3), structural uterine problems, or excessive uterine fibroids. The most common causes for male infertility include problems with sperm production (Lewis et al., 2008). Traditional semen analysis may not accurately identify fertility issues, and as a result, newer sperm tests are used today (Natali & Turek, 2011). Infertility can also be caused by past infections with gonorrhea, chlamydia, or pelvic inflammatory disease (Centers for Disease Control and Prevention, 2010a; Chavarro et al., 2007b; Eley & Pacey, 2010), which is one of the reasons college students are encouraged to have regular medical checkups and women are encouraged to have regular Pap smears. If a sexually transmitted infection is treated early, there is less chance that it will interfere with fertility. Infertility is also affected by age. Women and men who delay pregnancy may experience infertility because of the decreasing quality of their ova and sperm (Coccia & Rizzello, 2008; Girsh et al., 2008). For some men and women who experience reproductive problems, changing lifestyle patterns, reducing stress, and maintaining a recommended weight may restore fertility (Chavarro et al., 2007b). For other couples, new medical interventions offer new possibilities.

Fertility problems can be traced approximately 70 percent of the time to one of the partners (51 percent of the time to the female, and 19 percent of the time to the male). In 18 percent of cases, there is a combined problem, and in 18 percent the reason is unknown (Ontario Ministry of Children and Youth Services, 2013). Historically, women have been blamed for infertility problems, and until recently, men were not even considered a possible part of the problem.

Assisted Human Reproduction

Today, many couples—married, unmarried, straight, gay, lesbian, young, and old—use assisted human reproduction (AHR). Some couples use these techniques because they have infertility issues, whereas others use them to get pregnant without a partner or with a same-sex partner. Although in the past single women and gay, lesbian, and bisexual couples were denied access to AHR, this has been changing (Greenfeld, 2005; McManus et al., 2006; L.E. Ross et al., 2006b). In 2004 the Canadian Assisted Human Reproductive Act stated that people should not be denied access to AHR procedures on the basis of sexual orientation or marital status (S.C. 2004, c. 2 [AHRA], s. 2(e)). As of August 2012, trans human rights (gender identity) are protected under the human rights legislation of the Northwest Territories, Manitoba, and Ontario (Green, Tarasoff, & Epstien, 2012). Unique issues face gays, lesbians, and bisexuals who want to be pregnant. Lesbian and bisexual women

infertility	motherhood mandate
The inability to conceive (or impregnate).	The belief that something is wrong with a woman if she is not involved in caregiving or child care.

who use infertility services often find that because these centres primarily cater to infertile heterosexual women, they are required to undergo significant infertility workups (even though they are not "infertile") before any reproductive procedures (Mulligan & Heath, 2007; L. E. Ross et al., 2006a, 2006b). Gay men also face unique issues, as assisted reproduction is often more complicated and expensive because they need a surrogate to carry the pregnancy (C. Friedman, 2007). Although in the past, gay men sought out co-parenting arrangements with female friends, today many gay men use adoption and surrogacy (C. Friedman, 2007). Surrogacy raises additional issues for gay couples because they must choose whose sperm will be used. Some gay men mix their sperm so they don't know which one of them is the biological father.

In 2008, the average age of a woman using AHR was 35 years. Although many technologies are available to men and women today, deciding which treatment to use depends on factors such as cost, a woman's age, duration of infertility, and chances of conceiving without treatment. Many of these options are very time-consuming and expensive, and they do not guarantee success. In 2006 there were 25 fertility clinics in Canada—31.3 percent of AHR cycles led to a pregnancy, but only 24.6 percent resulted in a live birth (The Government of Canada, 2013).

Fertility Drugs

Some couples may use fertility drugs to help achieve a pregnancy. As we discussed in Chapters 3 and 4, ovulation and sperm production are a result of a well-balanced endocrine system (pituitary, hypothalamus, and gonads). Some women and men have hormonal irregularities that may interfere with the process of ovulation or sperm production. Although we do not always know why these hormonal problems develop, many problems can be treated with fertility drugs. For women fertility drugs primarily work by stimulating the pituitary gland to release more luteinizing and follicle stimulating hormone. These hormones stimulate follicle development and ultimately the release of more ova into the Fallopian tubes for possible insemination by sperm.

A major risk of the use of fertility drugs has been the development of **ovarian hyperstimulation syndrome** because the drugs stimulate the ovaries to produce more ova (Jakimiuk et al., 2007; Kwan et al., 2008; Van Voorhis, 2006; V.C. Wright et al., 2008). This has raised concern about the possible correlation between the use of fertility drugs and the development of breast or ovarian cancer. Whereas some studies have found a possible increased risk in women who have never been pregnant, older women, those with extensive fertility workups, and those with a history of cancer (Brinton, 2007; Pappo et al., 2008), other studies have found no increased risk (Hollander, 2000; Lerner-Geva et al., 2006). Fertility drugs also increase the likelihood of multiple births. Infants born through these techniques have been found to have lower birth weights, increased prematurity, and higher rates of birth defects and infant death (we will discuss birth defects more later in this chapter; see also Allen et al., 2008; Buckett et al., 2007; Centers for Disease Control and Prevention, 2007a; Kelly-Vance et al., 2004; Van Voorhis, 2006). Newer fertility drugs are less likely to stimulate release of multiple ova from the ovaries and have led to fewer multiple births (Check, 2010).

Surgery

Cervical, vaginal, or endometrial abnormalities that prevent conception may be corrected surgically. Scar tissue, cysts, tumours, or adhesions, as well as blockages inside the Fallopian tubes, may be surgically removed. The use of diagnostic techniques such as **laparoscopy** (la-puh-RAH-ske-pee) and **hysteroscopy** (hissstare-oh-OSK-coe-pee) are also common (Coccia et al., 2008). In men, surgery may be required to remove any blockage in the vas deferens or epididymis, or repair a **varicocele** (VA-ruh-coe-seal).

Artificial Insemination

Artificial insemination is the process of introducing sperm into a woman's reproductive tract without vaginal intercourse. This is a popular option for both heterosexual and same-sex couples. Ejaculated sperm, collected through masturbation, can come from a partner or from a sperm donor. Several samples may be collected from men with a low sperm count to increase the number of healthy sperm. Once the sperm is washed and assessed for viability, sperm can be deposited in the vagina, cervix, uterus (intrauterine), or Fallopian tubes (intratubal).

Men who decide to undergo sterilization or who may become sterile because of surgery or chemotherapy can collect sperm before the procedure. Sperm can be frozen for up to ten years in a **sperm bank**. Although the cost of donor sperm varies among sperm banks, typically donor sperm costs between $200 and $600 per insemination. Many sperm banks charge more for more information about the donor, such as a handwriting sample, photographs, or a video. Some couples buy several vials from the same donor so that offspring can have the same donor father. Recall that in the chapter opening story, Laura and Ozlem's children were conceived with sperm from the same known donor so they are genetically related to each other.

A donor may be found through one of the many sperm banks throughout Canada and abroad, usually from an online donor catalogue (see Websites at the end of this chapter for more information). After a donor is chosen, the sperm bank will typically send sperm to the physician who will be performing the insemination procedure, but in some cases, the sperm is sent directly to the buyer. Fertility drugs are often used in conjunction with artificial insemination to increase the chances that there will be healthy ova present when the sperm is introduced.

---

ovarian hyperstimulation syndrome
Adverse effects of excessive hormonal stimulation of the ovaries through fertility drugs, including abdominal bloating, nausea, diarrhea, weight gain, and abdominal, chest, and leg pain.

laparoscopy
A procedure that allows a direct view of all the pelvic organs, including the uterus, Fallopian tubes, and ovaries; also refers to a number of important surgeries (such as tubal ligation or gall bladder removal) involving a laparoscope.

hysteroscopy
Visual inspection of the uterine cavity with an endoscope.

varicocele
An unnatural swelling of the veins in the scrotum.

artificial insemination
Artificially introducing sperm into a woman's reproductive tract.

sperm bank
A storage facility that holds supplies of sperm for future use.

The Biology of Sex, Pregnancy, and Childbirth

In Vitro Fertilization

Another reproductive technology is **in vitro fertilization (IVF)**, or the creation of a test-tube baby. In 1978, Louise Brown, the first **test-tube baby**, was born in England. Since that time, thousands of babies have been conceived in this fashion. The name is a bit deceiving, however, because these babies are not born in a test tube; rather, they are *conceived* in a petri dish, which is a shallow circular dish with a loose-fitting cover. These fertilized eggs are then placed into the uterus of the female who will be carrying the baby to term. In 2010, Robert Edwards, a British scientist who developed IVF, won the Nobel Prize in medicine (Jha, 2010).

Heterosexual and lesbian women with infertility problems may use IVF because of blocked or damaged Fallopian tubes or endometriosis (see Chapter 3). Like other artificial reproductive technologies, fertility drugs are typically used before IVF to help stimulate the ovaries. When the ova have matured, four to six are retrieved with the use of microscopic needles inserted into the abdominal cavity. The ova are put into a petri dish and mixed with washed sperm. Once fertilization has occurred (usually anywhere from three to six days), the zygotes are either transferred to the woman's uterus or frozen for use at another time (we will discuss this further later in the chapter). Improved understanding of human reproduction has led to many improvements in IVF, such as increased success rates and decreased multiple births (Fechner & McGovern, 2011).

Earlier we discussed how PGD can be used on embryos to determine gender. However, this test is more commonly used to screen for chromosomal and genetic abnormalities. A PGD screening can cost between $3000 and $5000.

> **REAL Research** Researchers found that women who had a clown visit them while they were recovering from an IVF procedure were 16 percent more likely to become pregnant than women who did not have such a visit (Friedler et al., 2011). Experts believe that humour can have a beneficial effect on pregnancy.

Gamete and Zygote Intra–Fallopian Tube Transfer

Gamete intra–Fallopian tube transfer (GIFT) is similar to IVF in that ova and sperm are mixed in an artificial environment. However, after this occurs, both the ova and sperm are placed in the Fallopian tube, via a small incision, before fertilization. Fertilization is allowed to occur naturally rather than in an artificial environment. **Zygote intra–Fallopian tube transfer (ZIFT)** differs slightly from GIFT in that it allows ova and sperm to fertilize outside the body (similar to IVF). However, directly after fertilization, the embryo is placed in the woman's Fallopian tube (and not the uterus, like in IVF), which allows it to travel to the uterus and implant naturally. Although higher success rates were initially reported with these two procedures, they are more invasive than IVF, and today only a small percentage of couples use these procedures (Centers for Disease Control and Prevention, 2007a).

Intracellular Sperm Injections

Couples who experience sperm problems or ova that are resistant to fertilization may use **intracytoplasmic sperm injection (ICSI)**. ICSI involves injecting a single sperm into the centre of an ovum under a microscope. Usually, fresh, ejaculated sperm are used, but sperm can also be removed from the epididymis or the testes, or frozen sperm can be used (Balaban et al., in press; Kalsi et al., 2011; Yanagimachi, 2011).

Overall, ICSI results have been controversial—with some studies showing no adverse outcomes compared with natural conception (Knoester et al., 2008; Nauru et al., 2008) and other studies showing increased risks (J.L. Simpson & Lamb, 2001). Research indicates that ICSI may lead to an increased risk for genetic defect, which may be because ICSI eliminates many of the natural barriers to conception, increasing the transmission of abnormal genes (Al-Shawaf et al., 2005; Chemes & Rawe, 2010; Neri et al., 2008; Stanger et al., 2010; Terada et al., 2010). Scientists do not know why one sperm is successful over others for fertilization. Choosing a sperm randomly may not be appropriate, although physicians usually try to pick one that appears vigorous and healthy.

in vitro fertilization (IVF)
A procedure in which a woman's ova are removed from her body, fertilized with sperm in a laboratory, and then surgically implanted back into her uterus.

test-tube baby
A slang term for any zygote created by mixing sperm and egg outside a woman's body.

gamete intra–Fallopian tube transfer (GIFT)
A reproductive technique in which the sperm and ova are collected and injected into the Fallopian tube before fertilization.

zygote intra–Fallopian tube transfer (ZIFT)
A reproductive technique in which the sperm and ova are collected and fertilized outside the body, and the fertilized zygote is then placed into the Fallopian tube.

intracytoplasmic sperm injection (ICSI)
Fertility procedure that involves mechanically injecting a sperm into the centre of an ovum.

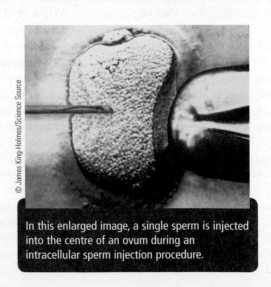

© James King-Holmes/Science Source

In this enlarged image, a single sperm is injected into the centre of an ovum during an intracellular sperm injection procedure.

Oocyte and Embryo Transplants

Women who are not able to produce healthy ova because of ovarian failure or age-related infertility and same-sex couples may use oocyte (egg) and embryo donation. Oocyte donation involves using a donor ova, whereas embryo donation can involve using frozen embryos donated by a couple or the creation of an embryo with a donated ova and sperm. Younger women are more likely to use their own ova, whereas 38 percent of 43- to 44-year-old women and 71 percent of 44-year-old and older women use donor ova (Centers for Disease Control and Prevention, 2010a). Women older than 40 have a higher chance of achieving pregnancy by using a donated ova than by using their own aged ova.

Surrogate Parenting

Surrogate parenting is a popular option for both heterosexual couples who cannot carry a pregnancy to term and same-sex couples. In this procedure, sperm and ovum are combined, and the zygote is implanted in another woman, called a **surrogate mother** or gestational carrier.

Surrogacy is legal in Canada; however, a surrogate mother, according to the Assisted Human Reproduction act passed in 2004, can only be reimbursed for out-of-pocket expenses. Outside of Canada, surrogacy continues to grow. For example, commercial surrogacy is growing in western India, where one clinic matches infertile U.S. couples with local women who are willing to serve as surrogates (Dolnick, 2007). These women are impregnated with embryos of couples who are unable to carry a pregnancy to term. These practices are available in many countries, although they raise many moral, ethical, and legal issues.

Other Options

Other options involve the freezing of embryos and sperm for later fertilization. It is estimated that 30 percent to 40 percent of all births from IVF were from frozen embryos (Borini et al., 2008).

This can be beneficial for men and women who are diagnosed with illnesses (such as cancer) whose treatment might interfere with their ability to manufacture healthy sperm or ova. The sperm can be collected from the testis, the epididymis, or an ejaculate, and can be frozen and stored in liquid nitrogen for many years through a process called **sperm cryopreservation**.

The effectiveness of the sperm, once thawed, is variable, and sometimes the sperm do not survive the thawing process. **Embryo cryopreservation** is also possible; but like sperm, not all embryos can survive the freezing and thawing process (Borini et al., 2008; Leibo, 2008; Youssry et al., 2008).

A growing number of women have been undergoing **ova cryopreservation** (also called *vitrification*), although this is still considered an experimental procedure (Scaravelli et al., 2010; Shufaro & Schenker, 2010). Typically, a woman uses fertility drugs to stimulate the ovulation of several ova, which are surgically extracted, frozen, and stored (Shellenbarger, 2008). Unlike sperm and embryos however, human eggs have a higher water concentration, which makes chromosomal damage more likely during the freezing and thawing processes (Martínez-Burgos et al., 2011).

On Your Mind

Do physicians ever mix up ova or embryos during embryo transplants? How do they know whose is whose?

Embryos are rarely mixed up because collection requirements are strictly followed. However, even using these methods, accidents can happen. When mistakes are made, clinics have a responsibility to inform patients about potential errors.

Ova cryopreservation can give women the opportunity to preserve their eggs for use later in life. It can also give women undergoing cancer radiation or chemotherapy an option to save ova for a later pregnancy (J.E. Roberts & Oktay, 2005; This, 2008). Newer research has evaluated the use of ovarian stimulation drugs and partial removal of ovarian tissue for cryobanking before cancer treatment (Huober-Zeeb et al., 2011). Ovarian tissue and ova cryopreservation are both areas of research that will continue to grow in the future.

surrogate parenting	**surrogate mother**	**sperm cryopreservation**	**ova cryopreservation**
Use of a woman who, through artificial insemination or in vitro fertilization, gestates a fetus for another woman or man.	A woman who is hired to carry a pregnancy for a couple who may not be able to do so.	The freezing of sperm for later use. **embryo cryopreservation** The freezing of embryos for later use.	The freezing of ova for later use.

Review Questions

1 Define infertility, and identify some of the most common causes of both male and female infertility.

2 Explain how same-sex couples, older women, and single women who seek assisted reproduction have been treated unfairly and identify some of the unique issues that confront these groups.

3 Identify and describe the various assisted reproductive options.

4 Differentiate between sperm, ova, and embryo cryopreservation. What are the risks associated with each?

A Healthy Pregnancy

Throughout pregnancy, important fetal development occurs as a pregnant woman's body changes and adjusts to these developments. We now explore these changes.

Prenatal Period

Pregnancy is divided into three periods called **trimesters**. Although you would think a trimester would be a three-month period, because pregnancies are dated from the woman's last menstrual period, a full-term pregnancy is actually 40 weeks; therefore, each trimester is approximately 12 to 15 weeks long. Throughout the pregnancy, physicians can use electronic monitoring and **sonography**, or **ultrasound**, to check on the status of the fetus. We now discuss the physical development of the typical, healthy mother and child in each of these trimesters.

First Trimester

The first 13 weeks of pregnancy constitute the first trimester of a human pregnancy. It is the trimester in which the most important embryonic development takes place. When a woman becomes pregnant, her entire system adjusts. Her heart pumps more blood, her weight increases, her lungs and digestive system work harder, and her thyroid gland grows.

PRENATAL DEVELOPMENT By the end of the first month of pregnancy, the fetal heart is formed and begins to pump blood. In fact, the circulatory system is the first organ system to function in the embryo (Rischer & Easton, 1992). Many of the other major systems develop, including the digestive system, beginnings of the brain, spinal cord, nervous system, muscles, reproductive system, arms, legs, eyes, fingers, and toes. By 14 weeks, the liver, kidneys, intestines, and lungs have also begun to develop and the circulatory and urinary systems are beginning to function. By the end of the first trimester, the fetus weighs about 15 grams (0.5 ounce) and is approximately 7.6 centimetres (3 inches) long.

CHANGES IN THE PREGNANT MOTHER During the first few weeks of pregnancy, a woman's body is exposed to increased levels of estrogen and progesterone. This can cause fatigue, breast tenderness, constipation, increased urination, and nausea or vomiting (see Table 5.1). Some women experience nausea and vomiting so severe during pregnancy that they must be hospitalized because of weight loss and malnutrition (Sheehan, 2007). Specific

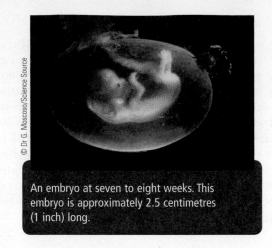

An embryo at seven to eight weeks. This embryo is approximately 2.5 centimetres (1 inch) long.

food cravings are normal, as is an increased sensitivity to smells and odours.

Since its introduction in 1950, ultrasound has become a useful tool in obstetrics. It can capture images of the embryo for measurement as early as 5.5 weeks into the pregnancy, and a heartbeat can be seen by six weeks. Fetal heartbeat can also be heard through a stethoscope at approximately nine to ten weeks. Ultrasounds help to confirm a pregnancy, rule out abnormalities, indicate gestational age, and confirm multiple pregnancies (we further discuss its use as a prenatal screening device later in this chapter). Newer three-dimensional and even four-dimensional ultrasounds allow parents to view almost lifelike fetal images, including yawns and facial expressions (see the nearby photo) (Handwerk, 2005).

Second Trimester

The second trimester consists of weeks 14–28 of pregnancy. The fetus looks more human and grows substantially during this trimester.

PRENATAL DEVELOPMENT The fetus around 33 centimetres (13 inches) long by the end of the second trimester. The fetus has developed tooth buds and reflexes, such as sucking and swallowing. Although the sex of the fetus is determined at conception, it is not immediately apparent during development. If the fetus is positioned correctly during ultrasound however, the sex may be determined as early as 16 weeks, although most of the time it is not possible until 20 to 22 weeks.

During the second trimester, soft hair, called **lanugo** (lan-NEW-go), and a waxy substance, known as **vernix**, cover the fetus's body. These may develop to protect the fetus from

---

trimester
Three periods of 12–15 weeks each; typically refers to the division of the nine months of pregnancy.

sonography
Electronic monitoring; also called *ultrasound*.

ultrasound
The use of ultrasonic waves to monitor a developing fetus; also called *sonography*.

lanugo
The downy covering of hair over a fetus.

vernix
Cheeselike substance that coats the fetus in the uterus.

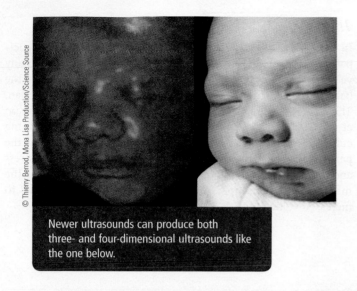

Newer ultrasounds can produce both three- and four-dimensional ultrasounds like the one below.

the constant exposure to the amniotic fluid. By the end of the second trimester, the fetus will weigh approximately 0.8 kilograms (1.75 pounds). If birth takes place at the end of the second trimester, the baby may be able to survive with intensive medical care.

CHANGES IN THE PREGNANT MOTHER During the second trimester, nausea begins to subside as the body adjusts to the increased levels of estrogen and progesterone. Breast sensitivity also tends to decrease. However, fatigue may continue, as well as an increase in appetite, heartburn, edema (ankle or leg swelling), and a noticeable vaginal discharge. Skin pigmentation changes can occur on the face. As the uterus grows larger and the blood circulation slows down, constipation and muscle cramps bother some women. Internally, the cervix turns a deep red, almost violet colour because of increased blood supply.

As the pregnancy progresses, the increasing size of the uterus and the restriction of the pelvic veins can cause more swelling of the ankles. Increased problems with varicose veins and hemorrhoids may also occur. Fetal movement is often felt in the second trimester, sometimes as early as the 16th week. For women in their second or subsequent pregnancies they may feel fetal movement prior to week 16 because of past experience during previous pregnancies (Office on Women's Health, U.S Department of Health and Human Services, 2010).

The second trimester of pregnancy is usually the most positive time psychologically for the mother. The early physiological signs of pregnancy such as morning sickness and fatigue lessen. As the developing fetus begins to move around, many women report that the movement of the developing fetus is comforting and that they feel better physically. Feeling better physically often leads to positive psychological feelings including excitement, happiness, and a sense of well-being. Many women report an increased sex drive during the second trimester, and for many couples, it is a period of high sexual satisfaction.

Third Trimester

The third trimester includes the final weeks of pregnancy (weeks 28–40) and ends with the birth of a child. The fetus gains both fat deposits and muscle mass during this period.

PRENATAL DEVELOPMENT By the end of the seventh month, the fetus begins to develop fat deposits. The fetus can react to pain, light, and sounds. Some fetuses develop occasional hiccups or begin to suck their thumb. If a baby is born at the end of the seventh month, there is a good chance of survival. In the eighth month, the majority of the organ systems are well developed, although the brain continues to grow. By the end of the eighth month, the fetus is about 38 centimetres (15 inches) long and weighs about 1.4 kilograms (3 pounds). During the third trimester, there is often stronger and more frequent fetal movement, which will slow down toward the ninth month (because the fetus has less room to move around). At birth, an infant, on average, weighs 3.4 kilograms (7.5 pounds) and is 50 centimetres (20 inches) long.

At five months, the fetus is becoming more active. It can turn its head, move its face, and make breathing movements. This five-month fetus is approximately 23 centimetres (9 inches) long.

CHANGES IN THE PREGNANT MOTHER Many of the symptoms from the second trimester continue into the third semester, with constipation and heartburn increasing in frequency. Backaches, leg cramps, increases in varicose veins, hemorrhoids, sleep problems, shortness of breath, and **Braxton–Hicks contractions** may occur. These contractions are scattered and relatively painless (the uterus hardens for a moment and then returns to normal). In the eighth and ninth months, the Braxton–Hicks contractions become stronger. A thin, yellowish liquid called **colostrum** (kuh-LAHS-trum) may be secreted from the nipples as the breasts prepare to produce milk for the baby. Toward the end of the third trimester, many women feel an increase in apprehension about labour and delivery; impatience and restlessness are common.

Braxton–Hicks contractions	**colostrum**
Intermittent contractions of the uterus after the third month of pregnancy.	A thin, yellowish fluid, high in protein and antibodies, secreted from the nipples at the end of pregnancy and during the first few days after delivery.

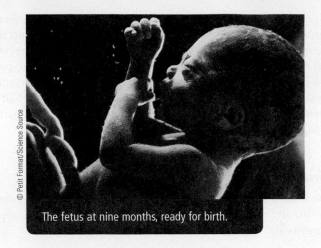

The fetus at nine months, ready for birth.

The Partner's Experience

In Canada today, partners are allowed and encouraged to participate in the birth. However, this was not always the case. For many years, fathers were told to go to the waiting room and sit until the baby was born. In some other cultures, such as in Bang Chan, Thailand, the father aids in the actual birth of his child (Dunham et al., 1992). The role of the father in pregnancy varies among cultures. Pregnancy can be a time of joy and anticipation for the partner of a pregnant woman, but it can also be a time of stress and anxiety. Feelings about parenting in combination with the many changes their partners are undergoing can all add to increased vulnerability.

Review Questions

1 How many weeks is a typical pregnancy, and how are trimesters determined?

2 Trace prenatal development and changes in the pregnant mother throughout the three trimesters of pregnancy.

3 Explain the changes in a pregnant mother, and identify the trimester in which a woman generally feels the most positive and explain why.

Health Care during Pregnancy

A pregnant woman can do many things to be healthy during her pregnancy, including participating in physical exercise, getting good nutrition, and avoiding drugs and alcohol. Women often maintain sexual interest during pregnancy, although it may begin to decrease during the third trimester.

Exercise and Nutrition

How much exercise should a woman get during pregnancy? Many physicians strongly advise light exercise during pregnancy; it has been found to result in a greater sense of well-being, enhanced mood, shorter labour, and fewer obstetric problems (Gavard & Artal, 2008; Polman et al., 2007). However, although participation in ongoing exercise throughout pregnancy can influence birth weight, severe exercise can result in a low-birth-weight baby (Pivarnik, 1998). Most health care providers agree that women should exercise during pregnancy. Pregnant women should discuss their exercise plans with their health care provider.

Although it is true that pregnant women are "cardiovascularly challenged" early in pregnancy, it is a myth that too much exercise may cause a miscarriage or harm the developing fetus. Hundreds of pregnant women learned this before the

legalization of abortion when they tried to exercise excessively or punch their abdomens in an unsuccessful attempt to dislodge the fertilized ovum.

Aquatic exercise may be the best choice for a pregnant woman because it is non-weight bearing, low impact, and reduces the risk for injury. In addition, aquatic exercise has been found to decrease maternal discomfort and improve body image (S.A. Smith & Michel, 2006). Physical stresses, such as prolonged standing, long work hours, and heavy lifting, can also affect a pregnancy. These stresses can, in rare cases, reduce blood flow to the uterus, resulting in lower birth weights and prematurity (Clapp, 1996). It is also important to drink lots of water during pregnancy because water is an essential nutrient and is important for all bodily functions.

Nutritional requirements during pregnancy call for extra protein, iron, calcium, folic acid, and vitamin B6 (found in foods such as milk, yogurt, beef, vegetables, beans, and dried fruits). In addition, it is important for a woman to increase her caloric intake during pregnancy. Pregnant women who do not follow nutritional requirements may have low-birth-weight babies, babies with birth defects, or an increased risk for miscarriage.

Research indicates that poor nutrition during pregnancy may also have long-term consequences for the infant's risk for cardiovascular disease, hypertension, and diabetes (Clapp & Lopez, 2007; Godfrey et al., 1996). Fetuses who are forced to adapt to a limited supply of nutrients may permanently "reprogram" their physiology and metabolism (Barker, 1997). Health Canada has nutritional guidelines for pregnant women on line at http://www.hc-sc.gc.ca/fn-an/nutrition/prenatal/index-eng.php.

During the second trimester, an average-weight woman is advised to increase her caloric intake by 300 calories per day. For vegetarians and vegans, it is necessary to increase consumption of vegetables, whole grains, nuts, and seeds, and also to include a protein supplement to ensure adequate protein intake. An increase in calcium is also necessary to help with bone calcification of the growing fetus. Because a woman's blood volume increases as much as 50 percent during pregnancy, iron may be diluted in the blood; thus, many pregnant women are advised to take prenatal vitamins, which include iron supplements.

Drugs and Alcohol

Physicians recommend avoiding several substances during pregnancy, including caffeine, nicotine, alcohol, marijuana, and other drugs. All of these substances are **teratogens** that can cross the placenta, enter into the developing fetus's bloodstream, and cause physical or mental deficiencies. One of the most famous teratogens is thalidomide, which was given to pregnant mothers in the early 1960s (Thalidomide Victims Association of Canada, 2015). Thalidomide was prescribed to pregnant mothers to help them sleep and combat morning sickness. It was not until babies were born with deformed arms and/or legs that it was realized that thalidomide could cross the placental barrier and alter the development of the baby. In addition to compounds a mother can take, other events such as viruses (influenza) and bacteria (STIs) can also adversely influence the healthy development of a baby.

Fetal alcohol spectrum disorder (FASD), a condition associated with alcohol intake, occurs when a woman drinks heavily during pregnancy, producing an infant with irreversible physical and mental disabilities. In one study of more than 12 000 U.S. women, 8 percent of the women reported consuming alcohol during the last three months of their pregnancy (Cheng et al., 2011). These physical and mental effects include below average height and weight at birth, a thin upper lip, a loss of the medial cleft or philtrum in the face between the upper lip and nose, and altered width between the eyes. At the level of the brain, infants often have a smaller brain and alterations to the cortex, cerebellum, and corpus callosum, which connects the two halves of the brain. Changes in brain anatomy are indicative of behavioural challenges in later life, including learning disabilities, problems with decision making or executive function, and memory deficits. Experts agree that there is no safe level of alcohol use during pregnancy (Sayal et al., 2007).

Smoking during pregnancy is also a risk factor for adversely altering the development of a healthy baby. Approximately 10 percent of women smoke cigarettes throughout their pregnancy (Weaver et al., 2008). Smoking during pregnancy has

On Your Mind

I've heard women say that if the average baby weighs about 3 kilograms (7 pounds), then they will gain no more than 4.5 kilograms (10 pounds) during pregnancy. Is that safe? How small a weight gain is considered healthy? What about anorexics and bulimics?

It is estimated that a pregnant woman of average size should gain between 7 and 18 kilograms (15 and 40 pounds) throughout a pregnancy, and weight loss or weight maintenance is not recommended (Bish et al., 2008). Pregnancy weight gain accounts for the fetus, amniotic fluid, placenta, and breast, muscle, and fat increases. Gaining less than this is not healthy for either the developing fetus or the mother—and may actually predispose a baby to obesity later in life (because fetuses learn to restrict calories in the womb, but when nutrition is readily available, overeating is likely; Barker, 1997). In addition, too little weight gain during pregnancy has also been found to be related to a higher blood pressure in offspring once they reach early childhood (P.M. Clark et al., 1998). Although women with eating disorders often experience an improvement in symptoms during a pregnancy (Crow et al., 2008), it's important that anyone with an eating disorder consult with her health care provider before getting pregnant to determine an appropriate weight gain.

been associated with spontaneous abortion, low birth weight, prematurity, and low iron levels (R P. Martin et al., 2005; Pandey et al., 2005). It has also been found to increase the risk for vascular damage to the developing fetus's brain and potentially interfere with a male's future ability to manufacture sperm (Storgaard et al., 2003). Children whose mothers smoked during pregnancy have been found to experience an accelerated aging of their lungs and a higher risk for lung damage later in life (Maritz, 2008). Second-hand smoke has negative effects, too, and partners, fathers, friends, relatives, and strangers who smoke around a pregnant woman jeopardize the future health of a developing baby.

REAL Research Research has found that marijuana use can negatively affect sperm development and production, leading to potential fertility problems (Badawy et al., 2008; Rossato et al., 2008). In addition, marijuana use in both men and women can negatively affect assisted reproduction procedures and contributes to lower infant birth rates (Klonoff-Cohen et al., 2006).

teratogens
A compound that a mother takes, or foreign agents, such as viruses or bacteria, that negatively alter the development of an embryo or fetus.

fetal alcohol spectrum disorder (FASD)
A disorder involving physical and mental deficiencies, nervous system damage, and facial abnormalities found in the offspring of mothers who consumed large quantities of alcohol during pregnancy.

Throughout this chapter we have been discussing trends in pregnancy and birth. Although birth rates have been decreasing overall, birth rates in single women older than 40 are increasing. Following is a story written by a woman who had a child on her own.

My life is not according to plan. I expected that after college, I would get a good job, find a great guy, fall in love, get married, and have three kids while establishing a rewarding career—all before the age of 30. In the real world, I have a successful career that I truly enjoy; I've been in love more than once but never married and never had children. At 43 years old, I was faced with the biggest decision of my life—having a child on my own. This is something I have discussed with friends and family over the years as a possibility but always hoped it wouldn't be necessary. Although I felt nervous, I also was really excited about my decision.

Anonymous sperm donation did not appeal to me. I really wanted to know the father: his personality, sense of humour, looks, intelligence, athleticism, and medical history. I did some research into sperm banks and sperm donation, and was actually pleasantly surprised at the amount of information each sperm bank provides (such as height, weight, hair colour, eye colour, ethnicity, education, occupation, family medical history). In many ways, it felt like an online dating service—but still wasn't the route I wanted to take.

Over the years, I have floated the idea of fathering a child for me to numerous male friends of mine. The man I chose has been a friend for a long time (we dated briefly many

years ago); he is married with children of his own and is a good father. We have agreed to keep his identity secret, and that he will not play a role in the child's life—emotionally or financially. We will remain good long-distance friends, and I will always be thankful for his generosity.

I went through a battery of fertility tests, and the test results were favourable for a woman my age. The entire process took about a year, and the year was full of excitement, as well as anguish and disappointment. I estimate that the treatments cost about $30 000 altogether, and my insurance company covered about half these costs, which is pretty good.

After a comprehensive workup, I started fertility drugs in preparation for in vitro fertilization (IVF). I was put on a series of drugs that produced several ova, and when the time was right, I was scheduled for ova retrieval. The doctor used a needle through my vagina to retrieve the four ova that were available. The lab took the ova and immediately attempted to fertilize them. Four embryos resulted, but only three survived to be frozen. I was unable to complete the transfer on that cycle, so we

decided to do a new full IVF cycle the following month.

The next month, everything seemed to be going perfectly—the ova retrieval and fertilization resulted in three embryos, and all three were transferred to my uterus (the transfer happened three days after the ova retrieval). I was sure I was pregnant, and when my period started again I was devastated. Afterward the doctor counselled me that it was highly unlikely my eggs would work and that I should consider egg donation or adoption unless I had unlimited funds and the stamina to keep trying. I said I would look into both options but wanted to transfer my frozen embryos as soon as possible.

The transfer took place that cycle. This time my optimism took a negative turn. In fact, I was so certain it failed that I didn't even bother with a home pregnancy test before going to the doctor for testing on the 12th day. To my surprise, while the nurse was drawing my blood, the urine test showed positive. My doctor said I was his oldest patient to get pregnant with her own eggs. As happy and relieved as I was, I tried to keep my joy in check—knowing that miscarriage and genetic abnormalities were not uncommon for someone my age. So I viewed each checkup and test as clearing a hurdle. Even so, the smile didn't leave my face for nine months.

After a 22-hour labour, I delivered a healthy baby girl. All in all, I feel like I hit the jackpot. Even though life is very different for me today, it is better than I could have ever imagined.

SOURCE: Author's files.

Pregnancy in Women Older than 30

Earlier in this chapter, we discussed how fertility decreases with age—both ova and sperm quality are affected by age (Coccia & Rizzello, 2008; Girsh et al., 2008; Lazarou & Morgentaler, 2008). Declines in fertility make it more difficult for older women to become pregnant. Today it is common for women to postpone their first pregnancies (Coccia & Rizzello, 2008). In the Canada, from 2007 to 2011, birth rates for women 15–19, 20–24, and 25–29 have decreased, while birth rates in mothers 30–34, 35–39, 40–44, and 45–49 have all increased (Statistics Canada, 2013).

Success rates for AHR in older women are low (Marinakis & Nikolaou, 2011). Although older women who do get pregnant are more likely to take better care of themselves and eat healthier than younger women, there are increased risks to the pregnancies, including spontaneous abortion, first-trimester bleeding, low birth weight, increased labour time and rate of C-section, and chromosomal abnormalities (see Table 5.2; Loke & Poon, 2011; Shelton et al., 2010).

REAL Research Women with declining fertility think more about sex and have higher levels of sexual interest than younger women (Easton et al., 2010). Researchers claim the "biological clock" ticking may be responsible for these shifts in sexual interest.

Sex during Pregnancy

In some cultures, sex during pregnancy is strongly recommended because it is believed that a father's semen is necessary for proper development of the fetus (Dunham et al., 1992). In an uncomplicated pregnancy, sexual behaviour and orgasm during pregnancy is safe throughout pregnancy unless your health care provider recommends otherwise. However, air should never be blown into the vagina of a pregnant woman because it could cause an air embolism, which could be fatal to both the mother and baby (Collins, Davis &, Lantz, 1994, Hill & Jones, 1993; Kaufman et al., 1987; Nicoll & Skupski, 2008; Sánchez et al., 2008).

Sexual interest and satisfaction usually begin to subside as the woman and fetus grow during the third trimester (Gokyildiz & Beji, 2005; Serati et al., 2010). The increasing size of the abdomen puts pressure on many of the internal organs and also may make certain sexual positions for vaginal intercourse difficult. Later in pregnancy, the side-by-side, rear-entry, and female-on-top positions are used more frequently because they take the weight and pressure off the uterus.

Table 5.2	Risk for Down Syndrome in Live Birth Infants Based on Maternal Age
Age of Mother	**Risk for Down Syndrome**
20	1 in 1527
25	1 in 1352
30	1 in 895
35	1 in 356
40	1 in 97
45	1 in 23
49	1 in 11

SOURCES: Hook, E.B. (1981). Rate of chromosome abnormalities at different maternal ages. *Obstetrics and Gynecology, 58*(3), 282–285; Newberger, D. (2000). Down syndrome: Prenatal risk assessment and diagnosis. *American Family Physician, 62*(4), 825–832.

Review Questions

1 Explain the benefits of exercise in pregnancy, and describe some of the issues that must be considered when exercising during pregnancy.

2 Explain the importance of avoiding drugs and alcohol during pregnancy.

3 Discuss the reasons women are delaying pregnancy more often these

days. What are the risks of delayed pregnancy?

4 Discuss the changes in women's sexual interest during pregnancy.

Problems during Pregnancy

The majority of women go through their pregnancy without any problems. However, understanding how complex the process of pregnancy is, it should not come as a surprise that occasionally things go wrong.

Ectopic Pregnancy

Most zygotes travel through the Fallopian tubes and end up in the uterus. In an ectopic pregnancy, the zygote implants outside of the uterus (Figure 5.10). Ninety-five percent of ectopic pregnancies occur when the fertilized ovum implants in the Fallopian tube (Hankins, 1995). These are called *tubal pregnancies*. The remaining 3 percent occur in the abdomen, cervix, or ovaries. The effects of

ectopic pregnancy can be serious because the Fallopian tubes, cervix, and abdomen cannot support a growing fetus. These organs can rupture, causing internal hemorrhaging and possibly death. Approximately 20 women a year die in Canada from complications due to ectopic pregnancy (Murray, Baakdah, Bardell, Tulandi, 2005). In the Keewatin District of the Canadian Central Arctic, ectopic pregnancy rates are 9.6 per 1000 pregnancies. In contrast, rates in southern Canada are 15.7 per 1000 percent. The reason for this difference is unclear but it may be related to differential rates of fertility between the two groups surveyed (Orr & Brown, 1998).

Possible symptoms include abdominal pain (usually on the side of the body that has the tubal pregnancy), cramping, pelvic pain, vaginal bleeding, nausea, dizziness, and fainting (Levine, 2007; Seeber & Barnhart, 2006; Tay et al., 2000). Future reproductive potential may also be affected by ectopic pregnancy. A woman who has experienced an ectopic pregnancy is at greater risk for development of another in future pregnancies (Sepilian & Wood, 2004).

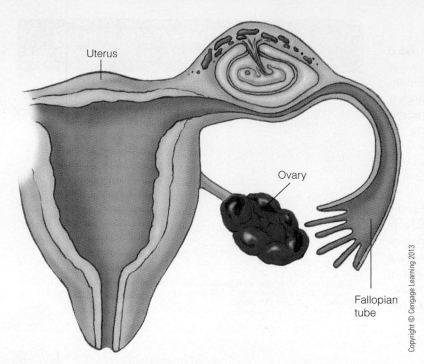

FIGURE **5.10** In an ectopic pregnancy, the fertilized ovum implants outside the uterus. In most cases, it remains in the Fallopian tube.

Today, physicians can monitor pregnancies through ultrasound and hCG levels, and many ectopic pregnancies can be treated without surgery (Seeber & Barnhart, 2006).

What contributes to the likelihood of an ectopic pregnancy? Although many women without risk factors can experience an ectopic pregnancy (Seeber & Barnhart, 2006), there are some factors that may put a woman at greater risk. Women who smoke and those who have had a sexually transmitted infection are at greater risk for an ectopic pregnancy (Ankum et al., 1996). Smoking cigarettes has been found to change the tubal contractions and muscular tone of the Fallopian tubes, which may lead to tubal inactivity, delayed ovum entry into the uterus, and changes in the tubes' ability to transport the ovum (Albers, 2007; Handler et al., 1989; Seeber & Barnhart, 2006).

Spontaneous Abortion

A spontaneous abortion, or miscarriage, is a natural termination of a pregnancy before the time that the fetus can live on its own. Approximately 15 percent to 20 percent of all diagnosed pregnancies end in miscarriage (Friebe & Arck, 2008). Miscarriages can occur at any time during a pregnancy, although the percentage declines dramatically after the first trimester.

chorionic villus sampling (CVS)	spina bifida
The sampling and testing of the chorion for fetal abnormalities.	A congenital defect of the vertebral column in which the halves of the neural arch of a vertebra fail to fuse in the midline.
maternal-serum alpha-fetoprotein screening (MSAFP)	
A blood test used during early pregnancy to determine neural tube defects such as spina bifida or anencephaly.	**anencephaly** Congenital absence of most of the brain and spinal cord.

In a significant number of miscarriages, there is some chromosomal abnormality (Christiansen, 1996; Vorsanova et al., 2010). In other cases, in which there are no chromosomal problems, the uterus may be too small, too weak, or abnormally shaped, or the miscarriage may be caused by maternal stress, nutritional deficiencies, drug exposure, or pelvic infection.

Common symptoms of miscarriage include vaginal bleeding, cramps, and lower back pain. Usually a normal menstrual period returns within three months after a miscarriage, and future pregnancies may be perfectly normal. However, some women experience repeated miscarriages, often caused by anatomic, endocrine, hormonal, genetic, or chromosomal abnormalities (Bick et al., 1998), as well as problems with defective sperm (Carrell et al., 2003).

A miscarriage can be emotionally difficult for both a woman and her partner, although research has found that male partners experience less intense emotional symptoms for a shorter period (Abboud & Liamputtong, 2003; Musters et al., 2011). Lesbian couples have been found to have an especially difficult time with miscarriage, probably because the complexity of planning and achieving a pregnancy are often much more difficult for lesbian couples (Wojnar, 2007).

Although historically health care providers have recommended women wait between 6 and 24 months before trying to get pregnant again after a miscarriage, newer research has found that shorter delays are associated with lower complication rates (Love et al., 2010). In addition, research on miscarriages after IVF has found that those who experience an early miscarriage have a greater likelihood of achieving a pregnancy that results in a live birth in their next IVF attempt (Kalu et al., 2011).

Birth Defects

It is estimated that one of every 33 babies is born with a birth defect (MMWR, 2008). There are many different types of birth defects that may be present at birth, and they range from minor to serious. Although many can be treated or cured, they are also the number one cause of death in the first year of life (Klausen, 2007). Prenatal diagnostic testing can be used to determine whether there are chromosomal or genetic abnormalities in the fetus. The most common tests include blood work, ultrasound, **chorionic villus sampling (CVS)**, **maternal-serum alpha-fetoprotein screening (MSAFP)**, amniocentesis, and cord blood sampling. Most of these tests are used by couples who have an increased risk for birth defects, although some couples may also use them to determine fetal sex. Because older women are more at risk for chromosomal and genetic abnormalities, these tests are often recommended for women older than 35. As we've already discussed, women who have undergone artificial reproductive technologies may choose to use PGD to identify any abnormalities in an embryo before implantation in the uterus (Kuliev & Verlinsky, 2008; Wang, 2007).

Genetic abnormalities include **spina bifida** (SPY-na BIF-id-uh), **anencephaly** (an-en-SEH-fuh-lee), sex chromosome abnormalities (such as Turner and Klinefelter syndromes; see Chapter 3), and many other diseases, such as cystic fibrosis or sickle cell disease.

Down syndrome, a chromosomal defect, can cause delayed mental and social development and the characteristics of slanted eyes and a flat face.

The most common chromosomal abnormality appears on the 21st chromosome and is known as **Down syndrome**.

Down syndrome occurs in one of every 691 live births (Parker et al., 2010; Irving et al., 2008). In Down syndrome, an extra chromosome has been added to the 21st chromosomal pair; although most of us have 46 chromosomes (23 from each parent), a person with Down syndrome has 47. A child with Down syndrome often exhibits low muscle tone, a flat facial profile, slanted eyes, delayed mental and social development, and an enlarged tongue. The Society for Obstetrics and Gynecology in Canada (2007) has recommended that "All pregnant women in Canada, regardless of age, should be offered, through an informed counselling process, the option of a prenatal screening test for the most common clinically significant fetal aneuploidies in addition to a second trimester ultrasound for dating, assessment of fetal anatomy, and detection of multiples." Screening can help determine whether a woman is at risk for having a child with Down syndrome and several other chromosomal abnormalities.

First-trimester screening typically involves a simple blood test combined with an ultrasound (Malone et al., 2005; Nicolaides et al., 2005; Orlandi et al., 2005). An ultrasound can evaluate the fetal neck thickness, which may indicate an increased risk for Down syndrome. In addition, ultrasound is often used to evaluate structural abnormalities in the fetus and to locate the fetus during other tests (Watson et al., 2008). Another more invasive test, a chorionic villus sampling (CVS), is available between the 10th and 12th weeks of pregnancy. In this procedure, a sliver of tissue from the chorion (the tissue that develops into the placenta) is removed and checked for abnormalities. CVS testing has more risks than ultrasound, including increased risk for miscarriage and potential limb reduction and deformities (Caughey et al., 2006).

Between the 15th and 20th week an amniocentesis may be used to detect either genetic or chromosomal abnormalities. In this procedure, **amniotic fluid** is extracted from the womb using a needle and is evaluated for genetic and chromosomal abnormalities. Amniocentesis increases the risk of miscarriage, cramping and vaginal bleeding, leaking amniotic fluid, and infection.

Another second trimester test, MSAFP, can be performed between the 16th and the 19th week. MSAFP is a simple blood test that evaluates levels of protein in the blood. High levels may indicate the presence of potential birth defects, including spinal bifida or anencephaly (Reynolds et al., 2008). The MSAFP can provide useful information that can help a woman decide whether she wants to undergo further testing. There are no risks to the MSAFP test besides the discomfort of drawing blood.

Finally, cordocentesis, or cord blood sampling, involves collecting blood from the umbilical cord anytime after the 18th week of pregnancy for a chromosome analysis (Berkow et al., 2000). Cordocentesis is an invasive test, and although it can slightly increase the risk for miscarriage, it is considered a safe and reliable procedure for prenatal diagnosis (Ghidini & Bocchi, 2007; Liao et al., 2006).

A diagnostic blood test for Down syndrome is available and can be performed early in a pregnancy. If the fetus of a pregnant woman has elevated levels of human chorionic gonadotrophin and PAPP-A (pregnancy associated plasma protein), the fetus may have Down syndrome (Edwards, 2010; BabyCenter, 2015). Keep in mind that if a woman does decide to undergo such testing, she, and her partner if appropriate, must decide what to do with the information these tests provide.

Rh Incompatibility

The Rh factor, an inherited trait, refers to a protein that naturally exists on some people's red blood cells. If your blood type is followed by " + ," you are "Rh positive," and if not, you are "Rh negative." A father or donor who is Rh positive often passes on his blood type to the baby. If the baby's mother is Rh negative, any of the fetal blood that comes into contact with hers (which happens during delivery, not pregnancy) will cause her to begin to manufacture antibodies against the fetal blood. This may be very dangerous for any future pregnancies. Because the mother has made antibodies to Rh-positive blood, she will reject the fetal Rh-positive blood, which can lead to fetal death in subsequent pregnancies. After an Rh-negative woman has delivered, she is given **RhoGAM** (row-GAM), which prevents Rh antibodies from forming and ensures that her future pregnancies will be healthy. RhoGAM is also given if an Rh-negative pregnant woman has an amniocentesis, miscarriage, or abortion.

Down syndrome
A problem occurring on the 21st chromosome of the developing fetus that can cause mental retardation and physical challenges.

amniotic fluid
The fluid in the amniotic cavity.

RhoGAM
Drug given to mothers whose Rh is incompatible with the fetus; prevents the formation of antibodies that can imperil future pregnancies.

Toxemia

In the last two to three months of pregnancy, 6 percent to 7 percent of women experience **toxemia** (tock-SEE-mee-uh), or **pre-eclampsia** (pre-ee-CLAMP-see-uh). Symptoms include rapid weight gain, fluid retention, an increase in blood pressure, and protein in the urine. If toxemia is allowed to progress, it can result in **eclampsia**, which involves convulsions, coma, and in approximately 15 percent of cases, death. Even though pre-eclampsia typically occurs at the end of pregnancy, research indicates that it may actually be caused by defective implantation or placental problems at the beginning of pregnancy (Urato & Norwitz, 2011).

Pre-eclampsia is a complication that occurs in approximately 3 percent of pregnancies (Hutcheon et al., 2011). Women whose mothers experienced pre-eclampsia are more likely to experience pre-eclampsia in their own pregnancies, and male offspring from mothers with pre-eclampsia are twice as likely to father children through a pre-eclampsia pregnancy as are men who were born from a normal pregnancy (Seppa, 2001; Urato & Norwitz, 2011). Screening tests for pre-eclampsia are being evaluated to identify women who might be at risk (Huppertz, 2011; Urato & Norwitz, 2011).

Review Questions

1 Define ectopic pregnancy and spontaneous abortion, and discuss what we know about these conditions.

2 Define prenatal diagnostic testing, identify some of the tests, and explain how they can be used to determine whether there are fetal abnormalities.

3 What are some examples of prenatal chromosomal abnormalities and what testing is available to detect it?

4 What is RhoGAM and why would a woman use it?

Childbirth

The average length of a pregnancy is nine months. Childbirth that occurs between three weeks before or two weeks after the due date is considered normal. It is estimated that only 4 percent of North American babies are born exactly on the due date predicted (Dunham et al., 1992). Early delivery may occur in cases in which the mother has exercised throughout the pregnancy, the fetus is female, or the mother has shorter menstrual cycles (R. Jones, 1984).

Animal Variations

The Length of Gestation Is . . .
Only mammals internally gestate their young. Human females carry their young internally for approximately nine months after conception; however, if you are a horse you will be pregnant for just under a year. Elephants and sperm whales have the longest gestation periods for mammals at almost two years. Not all animals carry their young for years—kangaroos, cats, and dogs all give birth within a couple of months of conception, and rabbits, mice, and rats are only pregnant for a few weeks.

No one knows why, but there is also a seasonal variation in human birth. More babies are conceived in the summer months and in late December (Macdowall et al., 2008). There are also more babies born between the hours of 1:00 and 7:00 A.M., and again this is thought to have evolved because of the increased protection and decreased chances of predator attacks (R. Jones, 1984).

Preparing for Birth

We do not know what starts the birth process. As the birth day comes closer, many women (and their partners!) become anxious, nervous, and excited about what is to come. Increasing knowledge and alleviating anxiety about the birth process are the main concepts behind childbirth classes. In these classes, women and their partners are taught what to expect during labour and delivery, and how to control the pain through breathing and massage. Tension and anxiety during labour have been found to increase pain, discomfort, and fatigue. Many couples feel more prepared and focused after taking these courses. However, some same-sex couples report feeling uncomfortable with childbirth classes that cater primarily to heterosexual couples (L.E. Ross et al., 2006a). Having other same-sex couples in the class often makes it a more positive experience.

A few weeks before delivery, the fetus usually moves into a "head-down" position in the uterus (Figure 5.11). This is referred

---

toxemia
A form of blood poisoning caused by kidney disturbances.

pre-eclampsia
A condition of hypertension during pregnancy, typically accompanied by leg swelling and other symptoms.

eclampsia
A progression of toxemia with similar, but worsening, conditions.

(Dunham et al., 1992). For low-risk pregnancies, home birth has been found to be as safe as a hospital delivery (K.C. Johnson & Daviss, 2005). Women need to make medically informed decisions about birthplace choices.

Currently in Canada, 98 percent of babies are born in hospitals. Most hospitals now offer the use of birthing centres, which include comfortable rooms with a bed for a woman's partner, music, a television, a shower, and perhaps even a Jacuzzi (to help ease labour pains). Many women in Canada, however, may decide to have their baby at home with the assistance of a midwife and/ or doula.

The majority of home births are done with the help of a **midwife** (Macdorman et al., 2011). In Canada there are about 900 midwives that are active, with about 100 graduates completing midwifery programs each year. All provinces and territories have practising midwives except New Brunswick, Prince Edward Island, Newfoundland and Labrador, and the Yukon. Currently, the cost of a home birth is covered by provincial health care in Ontario, British Columbia, Saskatchewan, Manitoba, Alberta, and Quebec (Picard, 2013).

Same-sex couples are more likely to use midwives in their birthing experience, even if they deliver in a hospital setting. This is primarily because many same-sex couples feel that midwives are more accepting of non-traditional families (L.E. Ross et al., 2006b).

In addition to a midwife, many women may elect to have a **doula** assist them through the birthing process. A doula cannot replace a midwife but can be of assistance to the pregnant mother and a midwife during a home birth. Doulas can also be present during a hospital delivery if allowed by hospital policy. During labour doulas provide support to pregnant mothers by helping them with breathing exercises, relaxation techniques, and with changing postures during labour amongst other tasks. Doulas can also be available to mothers during the postpartum period as they adjust to having a new baby in their lives. Doulas are available in some areas of Canada but not all. Doulas are not currently required to have any formal training, so it is important

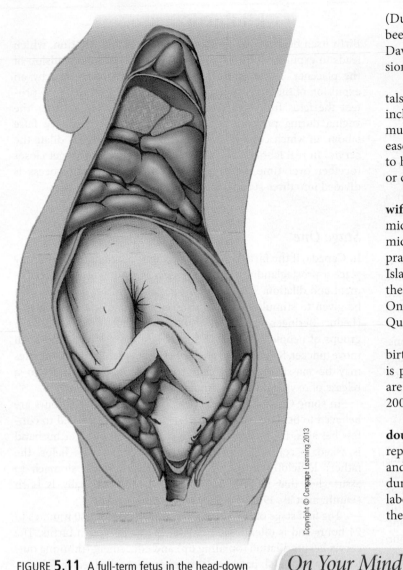

FIGURE 5.11 A full-term fetus in the head-down position in the uterus.

Copyright © Cengage Learning 2013

to as **engagement**. Ninety-seven percent of fetuses are in this position at birth (Nilsson, 1990). If a baby's feet or buttocks are first **(breech position)**, the physician may try either to rotate the baby before birth or recommend a C-section. We discuss C-sections this later in the chapter.

Birthplace Choices

In non-industrialized countries, nearly all babies are born at home; worldwide, approximately 80 percent of babies are

---

On Your Mind

What determines how long a woman will be in labour? Why do they say a woman's first baby is hardest?

Usually, first labours are the most difficult. Second and subsequent labours are usually easier and shorter because there is less resistance from the birth canal and the surrounding muscles. Overall, the biggest differences are in the amount of time it takes for the cervix to fully dilate and the amount of pushing necessary to move the baby from the birth canal. Typically, first labours are longer than subsequent labours. We do not know why some women have easier labours than others. It could be the result of diet or exercise during the pregnancy. Ethnic, racial, and maternal age differences have been found in the length of labour. Black women have been found to experience shorter second-stage labours than white, Asian, and Latina women (Greenberg et al., 2006). In addition, increasing maternal age is related to prolonged labour (Greenberg et al., 2007).

---

engagement
When the fetus moves down toward the birth canal before delivery.

breech position
An abnormal and often dangerous birthing position in which the baby's feet, knees, or buttocks emerge before the head.

midwife
A person who assists women during childbirth.

doula
a person who assists a women during the birthing process. They can assist but not replace a midwife.

to interview and check the references of the doula you are considering hire to assist you and/or your partner with the birth of your baby (BabyCenter, 2015).

Inducing the Birth

Inducing birth involves using techniques to start the birth process artificially. Usually this is in the form of drugs given in increasing doses to mimic the natural contractions of labour, although induced contractions can be more painful and prolonged than natural labour. Birth can occur anywhere from a few hours to several days after induction begins, depending on a woman's prior birth history. Since the early 1990s, there has been a tremendous increase in childbirth induction in Canada (Leduc, Beringer, Lee, & Dy, 2013).

Labour induction may be done in cases in which labour is slow to progress, pregnancy has lasted beyond 42 weeks, the baby is large, pre-eclampsia exists, or in cases of fetal death. Unless there is a medical reason, most women are advised to avoid labour induction (Amis, 2007; Durham et al., 2008). Some women elect to have inductions for non-medical reasons, including anything from wanting to avoid birth on a certain day (such as a holiday) or to accommodate a woman's or her partner's work schedule.

Birthing Positions

Although women can assume a variety of positions during childbirth, the dominant position in Westernized countries is the semi-reclined position with a woman's feet up in stirrups (DeJonge et al., 2008). Some feminist health professionals claim that this position is easier for the doctor than for the pregnant woman, and that it is the most ineffective and dangerous position for labour. Recently, women have been given more freedom in deciding how to position themselves for childbirth in Canada. A woman on her hands and knees or in the squatting position allows her pelvis and cervix to be at their widest. In addition, the force of gravity can be used to help in the birth process. Health care providers today recommend that women use whatever birthing position feels most comfortable for them (DeJonge et al., 2008; Gupta & Nikodem, 2000).

Positions for birth vary in different parts of the world. Rope midwives in rural areas of the Sudan hang a rope from the ceiling and have the mother grasp the rope and bear down in a squatting position. In Bang Chan, Thailand, a husband cradles his pregnant wife between his legs and digs his toes into her thighs. This toe pressure is thought to provide relief from her pain (Dunham et al., 1992).

cervical effacement	transition
The stretching and thinning of the cervix in preparation for birth.	The last period in labour, in which contractions are strongest and the periods in between contractions are the shortest.
dilation	
The expansion of the opening of the cervix in preparation for birth.	

Stages of Childbirth

Birth itself begins with **cervical effacement** and **dilation**, which leads to expulsion of the fetus and, soon afterward, expulsion of the placenta. The beginning of birth is usually marked by an expulsion of the mucus plug from the cervix. This plug may protect the fetus from any harmful bacteria that could enter the vagina during pregnancy. Sometimes women experience false labour, in which contractions are irregular and do not dilate the cervix. In real labour, contractions will be regular and get closer together over time. In a typical birth process, the process is divided into three stages.

Stage One

In Canada, if the birth process is taking too long, physicians may place a prostaglandin cream on the cervix to assist with effacement and dilation. The drugs misoprostol and oxytocin can also be given to stimulate uterine contractions and speed up labour (Leduc, Beringer, Lee, & Dy, 2013). In Bolivia, however, certain groups of people believe that nipple stimulation helps the birth move quicker. So if a birth is moving too slowly, a woman's nipples may be massaged. Biologically, nipple stimulation leads to a release of oxytocin which stimulates uterine contractions.

In some Guatemalan societies, long and difficult labours are believed to be due to a woman's sins, and so she is asked to confess her sins. If this does not help speed up labour, her husband is asked to confess. If neither of these confessions helps, the father's loincloth is wrapped around the woman's stomach to assure her that he will not leave her once the baby is born (Dunham et al., 1992).

The first stage of labour can last anywhere from 20 minutes to 24 hours and is often longer in first than subsequent births. The cervix begins dilation (opening up) and effacement (thinning out) to allow for fetal passage (this phase is called *early labour)*. Throughout the first stage of labour, the entrance to the cervix (the os) increases from 0 to 10 centimetres at the time of birth to allow for the passage of the fetus.

Toward the end of this stage, the amniotic sac usually ruptures (however, this may happen earlier or not at all in some women). Contractions may last for about 30 to 60 seconds at intervals of between 5 and 20 minutes, and the cervix usually dilates to 4 to 5 centimetres. Couples are advised to time the contractions and the interval between contractions and report these to their health care provider.

The contractions will eventually begin to last longer (one minute or more), become more intense, and increase in frequency (every one to three minutes). Dilation of the cervix continues from 4 to 8 centimetres (this phase is called *active labour*). The contractions that open the os can be very painful, and health care providers will usually monitor the progress of cervical dilation.

The last phase in stage one is called **transition**, which for most women is the most difficult part of the birth process. Contractions are very intense and long and have shorter periods in between, and the cervix dilates from 8 to 10 centimetres. The fetus moves into the base of the pelvis, creating an urge to push; however, the woman is advised not to push until her cervix is fully dilated.

The woman's body produces pain-reducing hormones called **endorphins**, which may dull the intensity of the contractions. Should a woman feel the need for more pain relief, she can also be given various pain medications. The most commonly used pain medications include analgesics (pain relievers) and anesthetics (which produce a loss of sensation). Which drug is used depends on the mother's preference, health history, and present condition and the baby's condition. An epidural block (an anesthetic) is very popular for the relief of severe labour pain. Although there has been an increased use of drugs to reduce the pain of labour in recent years, advances in medical technology today allow physicians to customize pain-relieving drugs for each woman (Leo & Sia, 2008; Moen & Irestedt, 2008).

In a hospital setting the fetus is often monitored for signs of distress, such as slowed heart rate or lack of oxygen. This is done either through the woman's abdomen with a sensor or by accessing the fetus's scalp through the cervix. Fetal monitoring can determine whether the fetus is in any danger that would require a quicker delivery or a C-section.

Stage Two

After the cervix has fully dilated, the second stage of birth, the expulsion of the fetus, begins. Contractions are somewhat less intense, lasting about 60 seconds and spaced at one- to three-minute intervals.

There is some controversy over whether lumbar tattoos can interfere with an epidural during labour. Whereas some studies claim they pose no risks (Douglas & Swenerton, 2002), others cite possible risks such as the potential for the epidural to push pigmented tissue into the spinal canal (Kuczkowski, 2006). If the tattoo is large, an anesthesiologist either needs to find a pigment-free area or make a small incision into the tattoo before administering the epidural.

© Seth Resnick/Superstock

Toward the end of this stage of labour, the doctor may perform an **episiotomy** (ee-pee-zee-AH-tuh-mee) to reduce the risk for a tearing of the tissue between the vaginal opening and anus as the fetus emerges. Currently, episiotomies are controversial, and the debate centres around several issues (Dahlen et al., in press). Those who support the practice argue that it can speed up labour, prevent tearing during a delivery, protect against future incontinence, and promote quicker healing. Those who argue against the practice claim that it increases infection, pain, and healing times, and may increase discomfort when penetrative sex is resumed (Chang et al., 2011; Hartmann et al., 2005; Radestad et al., 2008). In 2004 the Society of Obstetricians and Gynaecologists of Canada recommended against routine use of episiotomy and suggested its use only in limited cases (Cargill & MacKinnon, 2004).

On Your Mind

Is it safe to use drugs to lessen the pain of labour and birth?

Although some women believe in a "natural" childbirth (one without pain medications), other women want to use medication to lessen the pain. The search for a perfect drug to relieve pain, one that is safe for both the mother and her child, has been a long one. Every year, more and more progress is made. Medication is often recommended when labour is long and complicated, the pain is more than the mother can tolerate or interferes with her ability to push, forceps are required during the delivery, or when a mother is so restless and agitated that it inhibits labour progress. In all cases, the risks of drug use must be weighed against the benefits. How well a pain medication works depends on the mother, the dosage, and other factors. We do know that the use of some drugs, including epidurals, can increase labour time and may be associated with other risk factors. However, newer lower dosage epidurals have been found to produce fewer adverse effects and are better tolerated by women (Neruda, 2005).

As the woman pushes during contractions, the top of the head of the baby soon appears at the vagina, which is known as **crowning**. Once the face emerges, the mucus and fluid in the mouth and nostrils are removed by suction. The baby emerges and, after the first breath, usually lets out a cry. After the baby's first breath, the umbilical cord, which supplies the fetus with oxygen, is cut. Eye drops are put into the baby's eyes to prevent bacterial infection.

Directly after birth, many physicians and midwives place the newborn directly on the mother's chest to begin the bonding

endorphins
Neurotransmitters, concentrated in the pituitary gland and parts of the brain, that inhibit physical pain.

episiotomy
A cut made with surgical scissors to avoid tearing of the perineum at the end of the second stage of labour.

crowning
The emergence of a baby's head at the opening of the vagina at birth.

The Biology of Sex, Pregnancy, and Childbirth

process. However, sometimes the woman's partner may be the first to hold the child, or the nurses will perform an **Apgar test** (Finster & Wood, 2005). A newborn with a low Apgar score may require intensive care after delivery.

Stage Three

During the third stage of labour, the placenta (sometimes referred to as the "afterbirth") is expelled from the uterus. Strong contractions continue after the baby is born to push the placenta out of the uterus and through the vagina. Most women are not aware of this process because of the excitement of giving birth. The placenta must be checked to make sure all of it has been expelled. If there was any tearing or an episiotomy was performed, this will need to be sewn up after the placenta is removed. Usually this stage lasts about 30 minutes or so.

In parts of Kenya, the placenta of a female baby is buried under the fireplace, and the placenta of a male baby is buried by the stalls of baby camels. This practice is thought to forever connect the children's future to these locations. Some cultures bury their placentas, whereas others hang the placentas outside the home to show that a baby indeed arrived!

Review Questions

1 Describe the emotional and physical preparation necessary for the birth of a child, childbirth induction, and the various birthing positions.

2 Identify the three stages of birth and explain what happens at each stage. Generally, how long does each stage last?

3 Which phase of the birthing process is the most difficult for most women and why?

4 What is an episiotomy and why might it be used?

Problems during Birthing

For most women, the birth of a newborn baby proceeds without problems. However, a number of problems can arise including premature birth, breech birth, C-section delivery, and stillbirth. Earlier we discussed seasonal variations in birth, and research has found there are also seasonal variations in birthing problems around the world (Strand et al., 2011). Low birth weights, premature births, and stillbirths peak in the winter and summer. Experts believe this may be because of extreme temperature changes.

Premature Birth

The majority of babies are born late rather than early. Birth that takes place before the 37th week of pregnancy is considered **premature birth**. In 2010, 7.8 percent of babies born in Canada were premature. This is up from 1.01 percent in 1990 (QMI Agency, 2012). The incidence of premature birth has been rising, mostly due to the increased use of assisted reproductive technologies (Arpino et al., 2010).

Prematurity increases the risk for birth-related defects and infant mortality. Premature birth accounts for 28 percent of infant deaths worldwide (Menon, 2008). Pediatric research has led to tremendous improvements in the survival rates of premature infants. Infants born at 24 weeks' gestation have a greater than 50 percent chance of survival (Welty, 2005). Unfortunately, more than half of these infants who survive experience development of complications and long-term effects of being born premature.

Birth may occur prematurely for several reasons, including early labour or early rupture of the amniotic membranes or because of a maternal or fetal problem. It is common for women who have had one premature birth to have subsequent premature births. Approximately 50 percent of all twin births are premature, and delivery of multiple fetuses occurs about three weeks earlier, on average, than single births (Croft et al., 2010). In 2004, the world's smallest surviving premature baby was born, weighing in at 0.24 kilogram (8.6 ounces). Her twin sister weighed 0.51 kilogram (1 pound, 4 ounces; Huffstutter, 2004). These twins were delivered via C-section in the 26th week of pregnancy because of medical problems experienced by their mother. Other factors that may be related to premature birth include smoking during pregnancy, alcohol or drug use, inadequate weight gain or nutrition, heavy physical labour during the pregnancy, infections, and teenage pregnancy. Eating or drinking artificial sweeteners may also increase a woman's risk for premature birth. Pregnant women who drank one or more artificially sweetened soft drinks a day had higher rates of premature birth than women who either drank sugar-sweetened soft drinks or didn't drink soft drinks at all (Halldorsson et al., 2010).

Apgar test
Developed by Virginia Apgar, M.D., this system assesses the general physical condition of a newborn infant for five criteria: (A) activity/muscle tone, (P) pulse rate, (G) grimace and reflex irritability, (A) appearance/skin colour, and (R) respiration.

premature birth
Any infant born before the 37th week of pregnancy.

Breech Birth

In 97 percent of all births, the fetus emerges in the head-down position. However, in 3 percent to 4 percent of cases, the fetus is in the breech position, with the feet and buttocks against the cervix (Figure 5.12). Interestingly, about half of all fetuses are in this position before the seventh month of pregnancy, but most rotate before birth (R. Jones, 1984). Sometimes doctors are aware of the position of the fetus before delivery and can try to change the fetus's position for normal vaginal delivery. However, if this is not possible, or if it is discovered too late into delivery, labour may take an unusually long time. A skilled midwife or physician often can flip the baby or deliver it safely even in the breech position. However, in Canada today, a C-section will often be performed to ensure the health and well-being of both the mother and her child (Ghosh, 2005).

No one knows conclusively why some fetuses are born in the breech position. Researchers have found that there is an intergenerational recurrence of breech births: Fathers and mothers who were born breech have more than twice the risk for a breech delivery in their first births (Nordtveit et al., 2008). Another study found that breech births were twice as high in women who had a past C-section delivery (Vendittelli et al., 2008).

Cesarean-Section Delivery

The rate of C-section delivery continues to climb in Canada. The national C-section rate has increased from 17 percent of all births in 1995 to nearly 27 percent in 2010. In Alberta 28 percent of babies were born by C-section in 2009. In Ontario in 2011–12, nearly 29 percent of births were by C-section. C-sections cost more than vaginal births. This is due to a combination of factors, including operating room space, nurses, anesthesiologists, and a lengthier hospital stay. A 2006 Canadian Institute of Health Information report estimated that a vaginal birth costs approximately $2800 compared to $4600 for a C-section. Some researchers believe these increases are due to an increased number of women requesting C-sections or needing them for medical reasons, such as increased size of the fetus or chronic diseases in the mother (Addo, 2010; Born, Konklin, Tepper & Okun, 2014). The reasons for the increased number of C-sections in Canada are still inconclusive.

A C-section involves the delivery of the fetus through an incision in the abdominal wall. Some women choose a C-section birth to reduce possible pelvic floor trauma that can occur during vaginal delivery (Dietz, 2006; Herbruck, 2008). C-sections are medically necessary when the baby is too large for a woman to deliver vaginally, the woman is unable to push the baby out the birth canal, the placenta blocks the cervix (**placenta previa**), the cervix does not dilate to 10 centimeters, or the baby is in **fetal distress**. If a health care provider decides that a C-section is necessary, the woman is moved to an operating room and given either a general anesthetic or an epidural. The operation usually lasts between 20 and 90 minutes from start to finish (although the baby can be out within minutes if necessary).

In subsequent pregnancies, women who have had a C-section may be at greater risk for small fetal size, placental separation from the uterine wall, and uterine rupture (Daltveit et al., 2008). Even so, some women deliver their next babies vaginally after a C-section (referred to as a VBAC, or vaginal birth after C-section), whereas others choose another C-section for a variety of reasons, including to avoid the pain or the increased risks of vaginal labour.

Stillbirth

A fetus that dies after 20 weeks of pregnancy is called a **stillbirth** (before 20 weeks, it is called a *miscarriage*). There are many

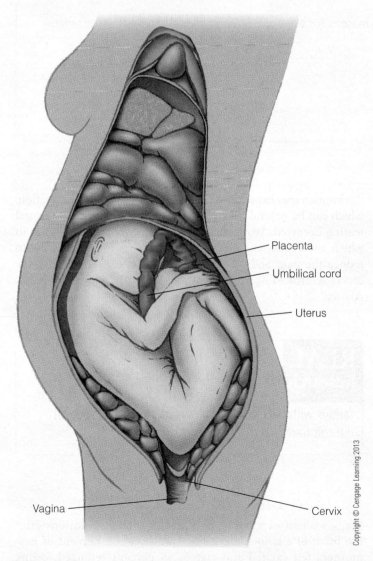

Placenta

Umbilical cord

Uterus

Vagina

Cervix

Copyright © Cengage Learning 2013

FIGURE **5.12** A full-term fetus in the breech position, with feet and buttocks against the cervix.

placenta previa
A condition in which the placenta is abnormally positioned in the uterus so that it partially or completely covers the opening of the cervix.

fetal distress
Condition in which a fetus has an abnormal heart rate or rhythm.

stillbirth
An infant who is born dead.

possible causes for a stillbirth, including umbilical cord accidents, problems with the placenta, birth defects, infections, and maternal diabetes or high blood pressure (Incerpi et al., 1998). Oftentimes the fetal loss is completely unexpected. Half of all stillbirths occur in pregnancies that appeared to be without problems (Pasupathy & Smith, 2005). Approximately 86 percent of fetal deaths occur before labour even begins, whereas 14 percent occur during labour and delivery (Fretts et al., 1992). In most cases, a woman goes into labour approximately two weeks after the fetus has died; if not, her labour will be induced. Some ethnic differences have been noted: Higher rates of stillbirth have been found in black and mixed-race couples (Getahun et al., 2005).

Improved treatments of certain maternal medical conditions have decreased the frequency of stillbirths in Canada. Many women are advised to do "kick checks" beginning in the 26th

week of pregnancy. If a woman notices that her fetus is kicking fewer than six times in an hour or has stopped moving or kicking, fetal monitoring can be performed to check on the status of the fetus. Research has shown that women who have experienced a stillbirth often have a live birth in their next pregnancy, even though they are often viewed as high-risk patients (Black et al., 2008).

In the 1970s, a perinatal bereavement movement began in the United States, which offered parents a way to deal with the death of a newborn (Banerjee, 2007). In Canada, the Canadian Paediatric Society has release a paper with guidelines for working with parents who have lost children during a pregnancy (Van Aerde, 2001). In addition many provinces, such as Ontario, have perinatal bereavement support services and groups (Ontario Funeral Home Association, 2011). These groups help families deal with issues related to stillbirth and infant death.

Review Questions

1 Define premature birth, and discuss some of the causes and risks associated with premature birth.

2 Define breech birth and identify some of the factors that have been associated with breech birth.

3 Explain some of the reasons for a C-section birth.

4 Differentiate between a miscarriage and a stillbirth.

Postpartum Parenthood

The majority of women and men are excited about being parents. However, many couples are not prepared for the many physical and emotional changes that occur after the child is born. They may also find changes in their sex lives because of the responsibility and exhaustion that often accompany parenthood.

More Physical Changes for the Mother

Many women report painful contractions for a few days after birth. These contractions are caused by the secretion of oxytocin, which is produced when a woman breast-feeds and is responsible for the shrinking of the uterus. The uterus returns to its original size about six weeks postpartum; in breast-feeding women, the uterus returns to its original size quicker than in non–breast-feeding women. A bloody discharge can persist for anywhere from a week to several weeks after delivery. After the bleeding stops, the discharge is often yellow–white and can last for a couple of weeks in mothers who breast-feed and up to a month or so in women who do not.

Women may experience an increase in frequency of urination, which can be painful if an episiotomy was performed or natural tearing occurred. Women may be advised to take sitz baths, in which the vagina and perineum are soaked in warm water to reduce the pain and to quicken the healing process. Until the cervix returns to its closed position, full baths are generally not advised.

REAL Research Attachment styles of new mothers and fathers have been found to affect adjustments to parenting (Talbot et al., 2009). Mothers and fathers with insecure attachments experienced the most difficult transitions.

Postpartum Psychological Changes

Many women experience an onset of intense emotions after the birth of a baby. One study found that 52 percent of new mothers felt excited and elated, 48 percent reported feeling like they did not need sleep, 37 percent reported feeling energetic, and 31 percent reported being more chatty (Heron et al., 2008). At the same time, many women report feeling overwhelmed and exhausted. Minor sadness is a common emotion after the birth of a baby (Howard et al., 2005). However, for some, it is a difficult time with endless crying spells and anxiety.

Researchers have found that one in eight women experience **postpartum depression** (Storm, 2011). Physical exhaustion, physiological changes, and an increased responsibility of childrearing all contribute to these feelings, coupled with postpartum hormonal changes (including a sudden decline in progesterone). Women with premature infants are at greater risk for postpartum depression because of the increased stress involved in these births (Storm, 2011).

Limited research on postpartum depression among lesbian and bisexual women has shown that it may be more common than in heterosexual women, but more research is needed in this area (L.E. Ross et al., 2007). Postpartum depression may also be higher among lesbian and bisexual women than in heterosexual women (L.E. Ross et al., 2007). A lack of social support and relationship problems can contribute to stress and depression after the birth of a baby in any couple (L.E. Ross et al., 2005). Male partners may also experience postpartum depression after the birth of a baby (Davé et al., 2010).

Partner violence has also been found to be related to postpartum depression (Ludermir et al., 2010). We discuss intimate partner violence in more detail in Chapter 17.

Partner support has been found to decrease postpartum depression in both heterosexual and same-sex couples (Misri et al., 2000; L.E. Ross, 2005; Storm, 2011). In the most severe cases, mental disturbances, called **postpartum psychosis**, occur; in rare cases, women have killed or neglected their babies after delivery (Rammouz et al., 2008).

Sexuality for New Parents

Although most physicians advise their heterosexual patients to wait six weeks postpartum before resuming intercourse, in an uncomplicated vaginal delivery (with no tears or episiotomy), intercourse can safely be engaged in two weeks after delivery. This period is usually necessary to ensure that no infection occurs and that the cervix has returned to its original position. If an episiotomy was performed, it may take up to three weeks for the stitches to dissolve. Health care providers generally advise women who have had a C-section birth to wait four to six weeks to resume sexual activity. In an uncomplicated delivery, 90 percent of women report resuming sexual activity by six months after the baby is born, although those with a complicated labour often wait longer to resume sexual activity (Brubaker et al., 2008). Immediately after delivery, many women report slower and less intense excitement stages of the sexual response cycle and a decrease in vaginal lubrication (Masters & Johnson, 1966). However, at three months postpartum, the majority of women return to their original levels of sexual desire and excitement.

Breast-Feeding the Baby

Within an hour after birth, the newborn baby usually begins a rooting reflex, which signals hunger. The baby's sucking triggers the flow of milk from the breast. This is done through receptors in the nipples, which signal the pituitary to produce prolactin, a chemical necessary for milk production. Another chemical, oxytocin, is also produced, which helps increase contractions in the uterus to shrink it to its original size. In the first few days of breast-feeding, the breasts release a fluid called *colostrum,* which is very important in strengthening the baby's immune system. This is one of the reasons that breast-feeding is recommended to new mothers.

In 2011–2012, 89 percent of Canadian mothers initiated breast-feeding soon after the birth of their child. This is up from 2003, when breast-feeding rates were at 85 percent (see Figure 5.13). Breast-feeding rates in 2011–12 ranged widely across Canada, with the lowest rates at 57 percent in Newfoundland and Labrador and

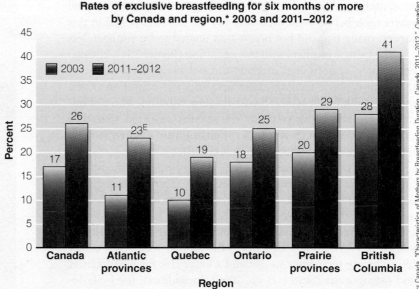

Rates of exclusive breastfeeding for six months or more by Canada and region,* 2003 and 2011–2012

SOURCE: Statistics Canada, "Characteristics of Mothers by Breastfeeding Duration, Canada, 2011–2012," *Canadian Community Health Survey, 2011–2012.* Reproduced and distributed on an "as is" basis with the permission of Statistics Canada.

* The territories were excluded as the difference between the 2003 and 2011–2012 estimates was not statistically significant. Due to small sample size, select provinces were grouped together to provide a difference that was statistically significant between the 2003 and 2011–2012 estimates.
E Use with caution (these data have a coefficient of variation from 16.6% to 33.3%).

FIGURE **5.13** Rates of breast-feeding in Canada, 2003 compared to 2011–12.

postpartum depression
A woman's clinical depression that occurs after childbirth.

postpartum psychosis
The rare occurrence of severe, debilitating depression or psychotic symptoms in the mother after childbirth.

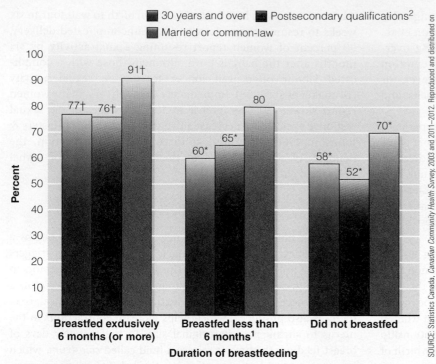

SOURCE: Statistics Canada, *Canadian Community Health Survey*, 2003 and 2011–2012. Reproduced and distributed on an "as is" basis with the permission of Statistics Canada.

Legend: 30 years and over; Postsecondary qualifications[2]; Married or common-law

Duration of breastfeeding	30 years and over	Postsecondary qualifications[2]	Married or common-law
Breastfed exclusively 6 months (or more)	77†	76†	91†
Breastfed less than 6 months[1]	60*	65*	80
Did not breastfed	58*	52*	70*

† Reference category.
* Significantly different from reference category.
1. Breastfed for less than 6 months refers to mothers who breastfed partially and exclusively.
2. Postsecondary qualifications include 'trades certificates,' 'college diplomas,' 'university certificates below bachelor level' and 'university degrees.'

FIGURE **5.14** Breast-feeding rates in Canada—influence of education, age and marital status

For some women, however, breast-feeding is not physically possible. Time constraints and work pressures may also prevent breast-feeding. It is estimated that a baby's primary caregiver loses between 450 and 700 hours of sleep in the first year of the baby's life, and overall, breast-feeding mothers lose the most sleep (Brizendine, 2006; Maas, 1998).

Some women who want to breast-feed but who also wish to return to work use a breast pump. This allows a woman to express milk from her breasts that can be given to her child through a bottle while she is away. Breast milk can be kept in the refrigerator or freezer, but it must be heated before feeding. Health Canada recommendations for breast-feeding are similar to the recommendations by the World Health Organization, with exclusive breast-feeding for the first four to six months of life and continued breast-feeding until at least age two before an infant is **weaned** (Health Canada, 2015).

Throughout this chapter, we have explored many issues related to fertility, infertility, pregnancy, and childbearing. In the next chapter, we begin to look at limiting fertility through contraception and abortion.

the highest rates in the Yukon and British Columbia at 96 percent. The Canadian Maternity Experiences Survey (2009) reports that most mothers receive some breast-feeding training in the hospital where their babies were delivered. For the mothers polled in this survey, many that did not breast-feed tended to be younger, less educated single mothers with less education (Figure 5.14). The two other main reasons that mothers did not breast-feed were that they found bottle-feeding easier or a medical condition of the mother or child prevented breast-feeding. Mothers who discontinued breast-feeding prior to six months reported that they stopped due to insufficient milk production or a move to solid foods for their child (Statistics Canada, 2013).

Benefits of breast-feeding include strengthening of the infant's immune system and correlation with age appropriate cognitive development (Caspi et al., 2007), and a reduction in infant allergies, asthma, diarrhea, tooth decay, and ear, urinary tract, and respiratory infections (Daniels & Adair, 2005; Duijts et al., 2010; Khadivzadeh & Parsai, 2005). Benefits to the mother include an earlier return to pre-pregnancy weight and a lower risk for breast cancer and osteoporosis (Stuebe et al., 2009). In addition, the body-to-body contact during breast-feeding has been found to decrease stress and improve mood for both mother and child (Groer, 2005).

weaned
To accustom a baby to take nourishment other than nursing from the breast.

Research has found that body contact during breast-feeding can decrease stress and improve mood for both the mother and her infant.

1 Describe the physical and emotional changes that women experience after the birth of a child.

2 Differentiate between postpartum depression and postpartum psychosis.

3 How might a woman's sexuality change after the birth of a baby?

4 Identify and explain some of the benefits of breast-feeding.

Chapter Review

Summary Points

1 Our hormones have a powerful effect on our bodies. The endocrine glands secrete hormones into the bloodstream. The most influential hormones in sexual behaviour are estrogen and testosterone. In most animals, the brain controls and regulates sexual behaviour chiefly through hormones, although in humans, learned experiences and social, cultural, and ethnic influences are also important. Hormone levels decrease as we age, and this can cause a variety of problems, such as vaginal dryness and decreased vaginal sensitivity in women, and slower and less frequent erections in men.

2 A series of physiological and psychological changes occur during sexual behaviour. Masters and Johnson's sexual response cycle involves four physiological phases, including excitement, plateau, orgasm, and resolution. During these phases, there are changes in both vasocongestion and myotonia. In men, there is a refractory period during resolution, and generally the stages are less well defined. In women, the menstrual cycle may affect the sexual response cycle.

3 The number of Canadian births has been changing slightly at all ages. The birth rate varies by province, with Ontario having the highest number of births, followed by Quebec, British Columbia, and Alberta. The highest number of births in Canada is to women in the 30–34 age group.

4 Pregnancy can happen when intercourse takes place a few days before or after ovulation, and the entire process of fertilization takes about 24 hours. The fertilized ovum is referred to as a *zygote*. After the first cell division, it is referred to as a *blastocyst*. From the second to the eighth week, the developing human is called an *embryo*.

5 Early signs of pregnancy include missing a period, breast tenderness, frequent urination, and morning sickness. Pregnancy tests measure for a hormone in the blood known as human chorionic gonadotropin (hCG). Pseudocyesis and couvade are rare conditions that can occur in both women and men.

6 Some couples try to choose the sex of their children by using sex-selection methods. During the 16th or 17th week of pregnancy, an amniocentesis can be performed to evaluate the fetus for chromosomal abnormalities, and it can also identify the sex of the fetus.

7 Many couples, including married, unmarried, straight, gay, lesbian, young, and older men and women, use assisted reproductive technologies. Although all couples use human assisted reproduction in hopes of achieving a pregnancy, same-sex couples and single women often use these methods to create a pregnancy.

8 Infertility is the inability to conceive (or impregnate) after one year of regular vaginal intercourse without the use of any form of birth control.

9 Couples interested in assisted reproduction have many options: fertility drugs; surgery to correct cervical, vaginal, or endometrial abnormalities and blockage in the vas deferens or epididymis; artificial insemination; in vitro fertilization (IVF); gamete intra–Fallopian tube transfer (GIFT); zygote intra–Fallopian tube transfer (ZIFT); zonal dissection; intracellular sperm injections; oocyte or embryo transplants; surrogate parenting; and cryopreservation.

10 Pregnancy is divided into three three-month periods called *trimesters*. In the first trimester, the most important embryonic development takes place. At this time, the fetus grows dramatically and is about 7.6 centimetres (3 inches) long by the end of this trimester.

11 The mother often feels the fetus moving around inside her uterus during the second trimester. By the end of this period, the fetus is approximately 33 centimetres (13 inches) long and weighs about 0.8 kilograms (1.75 pounds). The second trimester of pregnancy is usually the most positive time for the mother.

12 By the end of the eighth month, the fetus is about 38 centimetres (15 inches) long and weighs about 1.4 kilograms (3 pounds). Braxton–Hicks contractions begin, and colostrum may be secreted from the nipples.

13 A woman's exercise routine should not exceed pre-pregnancy levels. Exercise has been found to result in a greater sense of well-being, shorter labour, and fewer obstetric problems.

14 Drugs and alcohol can cross the placenta, enter into the developing fetus's bloodstream, and cause physical or mental deficiencies. Compounds that cross the placental barrier and alter the development of the baby are called terotogens. FASD occurs when a woman drinks during pregnancy, producing an infant with irreversible physical and mental disabilities.

15 Delaying pregnancy until later in life has some risks, including an increase in spontaneous abortion, first-trimester bleeding, low birth weight, increased labour time, increased rate of C-sections, and chromosomal abnormalities.

16 Sexual behaviour during pregnancy is safe for most mothers and the developing child up until the last several weeks of pregnancy, and possibly up to delivery; orgasm may occasionally cause painful uterine contractions.

17 In an ectopic pregnancy, the zygote implants outside the uterus, usually in the Fallopian tube. Although many women without risk factors can develop an ectopic pregnancy, some factors may put a woman at increased risk. These include smoking and a history of sexually transmitted infections.

18 The majority of miscarriages or spontaneous abortions occur during the first trimester of pregnancy. The most common reason for miscarriage is a fetal chromosomal abnormality. Prenatal diagnostic testing can be used to determine whether there are chromosomal or genetic abnormalities in the fetus.

19 One of every 33 babies is born with a birth defect. Prenatal diagnostic testing can be used to determine whether there are chromosomal or genetic abnormalities in the fetus. The risk for chromosomal abnormality increases as maternal age increases. The most common chromosomal abnormality is Down syndrome.

20 An Rh-negative woman must be given RhoGAM immediately after childbirth, abortion, or miscarriage so that she will not produce antibodies and to ensure that her future pregnancies are healthy. Toxemia is a form of blood poisoning that can develop in pregnant women; symptoms include weight gain, fluid retention, an increase in blood pressure, and protein in the urine.

21 Increasing knowledge and alleviating anxiety about the birth process are the main concepts behind childbirth classes. Worldwide, the majority of babies are born at home, although most Canadian babies are born in hospitals.

22 Birth itself takes place in three stages: cervical effacement and dilation, expulsion of the fetus, and expulsion of the placenta. The first stage of labour can last anywhere from 20 minutes to 24 hours and is longer in first births. Transition, the last part of stage one, is the most difficult part of the birth process. The second stage of birth involves the expulsion of the fetus. In the third stage of labour, strong contractions continue and push the placenta out of the uterus and through the vagina.

23 The majority of babies are born late, but if birth takes place before the 37th week of pregnancy, it is considered premature. Premature birth may occur early for several reasons, including early labour, early rupture of the amniotic membranes, or a maternal or fetal problem.

24 Problems during birthing include premature birth, breech birth, and stillbirth. A birth that takes place before the 37th week of pregnancy is considered premature and may occur for various reasons. The amniotic membranes may have ruptured, or there may be a maternal or fetal problem. Multiple births also occur earlier than single births. In a breech birth, the fetus has his or her feet and buttocks against the cervix, and either the baby is rotated or a C-section must be performed.

25 A C-section involves the delivery of the fetus through an incision in the abdominal

wall. C-sections are necessary when the baby is too large for a woman to deliver vaginally, the woman is unable to push the baby out the birth canal, there is placenta previa or placental separation from the baby before birth, or the baby is in fetal distress.

26 A fetus that dies after 20 weeks of pregnancy is called a *stillbirth*. The most common cause of stillbirth is a failure in the baby's oxygen supply, heart, or lungs.

27 After delivery, the uterus returns to its original size in about six weeks. Many women report painful contractions, caused by the hormone oxytocin, for a few days after birth. Uteruses of breast-feeding women return to the original size quicker than those of non–breast-feeding women.

28 The majority of women feel both excitement and exhaustion after the birth of a child. However, for some, it is a very difficult time of depression, crying spells, and anxiety. In severe cases, a woman might experience postpartum depression or postpartum psychosis.

29 Although most physicians advise their heterosexual patients to wait six weeks postpartum before resuming sexual intercourse, in an uncomplicated vaginal delivery (with no tears or episiotomy), intercourse may safely be engaged in two weeks after delivery. Many women report slower and less intense excitement stages of the sexual response cycle and a decrease in vaginal lubrication immediately after delivery; however, at three months' postpartum, most women return to their original levels of desire and excitement.

30 In the first few days of breast-feeding, the breasts release a fluid called *colostrum,* which is very important in strengthening the baby's immune system. Health Canada recommends breast-feeding exclusively for at least the first six months and sustained feeding for up to the first two years. The World Health Organization recommends breast-feeding for up to two years or longer.

Critical Thinking Questions

1 If sex pre-selection were possible, would you want to determine the sex of your children? Why or why not? If you did choose, what order would you choose? Why?

2 Do you think assisted reproductive techniques should be used in women older than 50? Older than 60? Do you think older moms can make good mothers? What about older dads?

3 If women can safely deliver at home, should they be encouraged to do so with the help of a midwife, or should they be encouraged to have children in the hospital? If you have children, where do you think you would want them to be born?

4 At what age do you think a child should be weaned? Should a woman breast-feed a child until he or she is six months old? Two years old? Four years old? How old?

5 In 2001, a woman ran an ad in a school newspaper at Stanford University offering $15 000 for a sperm donation from the right guy. She required the guy be intelligent, physically attractive, and over 1.83 metres (6 feet) tall. The year before, an ad ran in the same newspaper from a couple who offered $100 000 for eggs from an athletically gifted female student. Would you have answered either of these ads? Why or why not?

Websites

American Society for Reproductive Medicine (ASRM) The ASRM is an organization devoted to advancing knowledge and expertise in reproductive medicine, infertility, and ARTs. Links to a variety of helpful websites are available. (https://www.asrm.org/)

BirthStories This interesting website contains true birth stories from a variety of women, including first-time moms, veteran moms, and births after a pregnancy loss. It also has information on birthing, breast-feeding, and newborns. (http:// www.birthdiaries .com/)

International Council on Infertility Information Dissemination (INCIID) This website provides detailed information on the diagnosis and treatment of infertility, pregnancy loss, family-building options, and helpful fact sheets on various types of fertility treatments and assisted reproductive techniques. Information on adoption and child-free lifestyles is also included. (http://www.inciid.org/)

Resolve The National Infertility Association in the United States was established in 1974. It works to promote reproductive health, ensure equal access to fertility options for men and women experiencing infertility or other reproductive disorders, and provide support services and physician referral and education. (http:// www.resolve.org/)

StorkNet This website provides a week-by-week guide to a woman's pregnancy. For each of the 40 weeks of pregnancy, there is information about fetal development, what types of changes occur within the pregnant body, and suggested readings and links for more information. (http://www.storknet.com/)

6

Contraception and Abortion

Unintended pregnancy can be a reality for all women who are sexually active. Contraception exists to help women and men control their fertility. In this chapter, we'll explore various issues related to contraception and abortion. We begin with the story of Joan who experienced an unintended pregnancy in 1967 at the age of 18.

I knew I wasn't ready to have a baby. But I was terrified about my lack of options. I somehow found a doctor that would do illegal abortions in his office after hours. He told me that I needed to bring him $500 cash, come by myself, *and not tell ANYONE where I was going. I took the bus by myself to get to his office. I can still remember how blue the sky was that morning. I remember looking at it and thinking that today might be the day I die. But I still knew that I needed to go through with it. When I arrived at his office, no one was there except him. He told me to go to the examination room and take off all my clothes. When he came in the room, he sternly told me not to scream or make any noise during the procedure. Screaming would cause attention and no one could know what was going on. He said he gave me a drug to reduce the pain of the procedure*

but looking back now, I think it was a different drug because I felt everything. The procedure was incredibly painful. I just laid on the table and cried the whole time. When he finished he told me not to move. I was extremely uncomfortable because I was completely naked. He began telling me that I had a beautiful body and that he wanted to touch my breasts. I was shocked and feeling totally out of it. Thinking back now, I'm amazed that I did what he told me to but I honestly didn't know any better. A few years later, abortion was legalized in the United States and I underwent a second abortion. It was a totally different experience for me.

Today Joan works in women's health and is a firm supporter of woman's rights. No matter what your position on abortion, I hope you find her firsthand account as moving and powerful as I did. ▌

The typical North American woman spends about 30 years trying *not* to get pregnant and only a couple of years trying to become pregnant (see Figure 6.1; Boonstra et al., 2006). Contraceptive use has increased in the Canada over the last few years, and today more than 99 percent of sexually active women aged 15 to 44 years old have used at least one contraceptive method (Mosher & Jones, 2010). Condom use continues to increase (see Chapter 10), which has helped decrease sexually transmitted infections (STIs). Overall, the most popular contraceptive methods in North America are birth control pills (used by close to 11 million women) and female sterilization (used by approximately 10 million women; Mosher & Jones, 2010). Although contraceptive use has increased in the mid-2000s, many user characteristics interact with contraceptive use, such as age, ethnicity, race, marital status, past pregnancies, education, and income. Although unintended pregnancy can affect all women, research has found that several issues put women at greater risk for unintended pregnancies, such as being young, unmarried, or poor.

College and university students take risks when it comes to **contraception**, even though they are intelligent and educated about birth control. Many factors increase one's motivation to use contraception, including the ability to communicate with a partner, cost of the method, effectiveness rates, frequency of vaginal intercourse, motivation to avoid pregnancy, the contraceptive method's side effects, and one's openness about sexuality (Frost et al., 2008; Hatcher et al., 2011). Contraceptive use is further complicated by the fact that an ideal method for one person may not be an ideal method for another, and an ideal method for one person at one time in his or her life may not be an ideal method as that person enters into different life stages. Having a wide variety of choices available is important to allow couples to choose and change methods as their contraceptive needs change.

> **REAL Research** There is often a disconnect between which partner college and university students *think* should be responsible for birth control and which one is actually responsible (Brunner Huber & Ersek, 2011). Although close to 90 percent of college students report that the responsibility should be shared, it is shared in only about half of relationships.

---

contraception
The deliberate use of artificial methods or other techniques to prevent pregnancy as a consequence of vaginal intercourse.

As we begin our exploration into contraception and abortion, consider this: Have you thought about whether you ever want to have a child? Maybe you have an exact plan about when you'd like to experience a pregnancy in your life. Or perhaps you have already decided you won't have any children. For many couples, deciding how to plan, and also how to avoid, pregnancies are important issues in their lives. In this chapter, we explore the array of contraceptive methods available today, investigate their advantages and disadvantages, and also discuss emergency contraception and abortion.

Contraception: History and Method Considerations

Although many people believe that contraception is a modern invention, its origins actually extend back to ancient times. We now explore contraception throughout history, both within and outside of Canada.

Contraception in Ancient Times

People have always tried to invent ways to control fertility. The ancient Greeks used magic, superstition, herbs, and drugs to try and control their fertility. The Egyptians tried fumigating the female genitalia with certain mixtures, inserting a tampon into the vagina that had been soaked in herbal liquid and honey, and inserting a mixture of crocodile feces, sour milk, and honey (Dunham et al., 1992). Another strategy was to insert objects into the vagina that could entrap or block the sperm. Such objects include vegetable seed pods (South Africa), a cervical plug of grass (Africa), sponges soaked with alcohol (Persia), and empty pomegranate halves (Greece). These methods may sound far-fetched to us today, but they worked on many of the same principles as modern methods. In the accompanying Sexual Diversity in Our World feature, we discuss some of these methods.

Contraception in Canada: 1800s and Early 1900s?

In the early 1800s, there was a desire to discuss contraception as a way to control fertility to reduce poverty. However, contraception

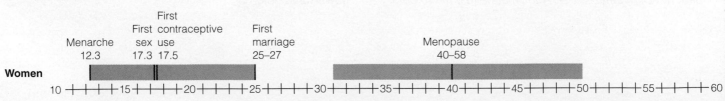

FIGURE **6.1** The Alan Guttmacher Institute has found that the average woman spends five years pregnant, postpartum, or trying to get pregnant, and 30 years avoiding pregnancy. Above is a timeline of reproductive events for the typical woman. The shaded areas represent when a typical woman is trying to avoid unintended pregnancy.

SOURCE: Based on data from Boonstra, H.D., Gold, R.B., Richards, C.L., & Finer, L.B. (2006). *Abortion in women's lives* (Figure 1.1, p. 7). New York: Guttmacher Institute.

Sexual Diversity in Our World

Herbal Lore and Contraception

In many places around the world, herbs are used as contraception. For example, American women in Appalachia drink tea made from Queen Anne's lace directly after sexual intercourse to prevent pregnancy (Rensberger, 1994). They are not alone. Many women from South Africa, Guatemala, Costa Rica, Haiti, China, and India rely on herbal contraceptives (L. Newman & Nyce, 1985). Newer hormonal methods of birth control have reduced fertility around the world, but non-hormonal methods such as natural family planning and herbal methods continue to be used. Some of the tested herbs have been found to have high success rates for contraceptive ability (Chaudhury, 1985).

A common herbal contraceptive in Paraguay is known as yuyos. Many types of yuyos are taken for fertility regulation (Bull & Melian, 1998). The herbs are usually soaked in water and drunk as tea. Older women teach younger women how to use these herbs, but problems sometimes occur when herbal methods are used improperly. Remember that this method works only when using a mix of herbs that have been found to offer contraceptive protection. Drinking herbal tea from the grocery store isn't going to protect you in the same way.

Failure rates from herbal contraceptives are higher than from more modern methods, but many do work better than using nothing at all. What is it that makes the herbal methods effective? We don't know, but perhaps some future contraceptive drugs may come from research into plant pharmaceuticals.

was considered a private affair, to be discussed only between partners in a relationship—even medical doctors were not allowed to provide information about contraception (although a few still did). Margaret Sanger, the founder of Planned Parenthood, was one of the first people to publicly advocate the importance of contraception in the United States. In Canada several important voices played a role in the legalization of contraception. The Canadian Birth Control League in British Columbia began the movement towards the legalization of birth control in Vancouver in the 1920s. However, it was Mary Hawkins in the Hamilton area and Dorothea Palmer (who was acquitted in 1937 for promoting birth control in the Ottawa region) in Ontario during the 1930s that broke open nationwide discussions on the legalization of birth control. Finally, in the 1960s Barbara and George Cadbury established the Planned Parenthood Association of Toronto and pushed forward the issue of legalized birth control in Canada, which became legal across the country in 1969.

Contraception Outside of Canada

Studies of contraceptive use throughout the world have found that social and economic issues, knowledge levels, religion, and gender roles affect contraceptive use (see Figure 6.2 for more information about unmet contraceptive needs throughout the world). A woman might not use contraception because she is uneducated about it or doesn't have access to methods. She may also worry about adverse effects, not understand she is at risk for pregnancy with sexual behaviour, or believe that she needs to be married to use contraception (Sedgh et al., 2007a). A country's religious views can also affect contraceptive use. In fact, many predominantly Catholic regions and countries, such as Ireland, Italy, Poland, and the Philippines, have limited contraceptive devices available. These countries often promote natural methods of contraception, such as withdrawal or natural family planning. In 2010, Catholic bishops in the Philippines led a massive national protest against the president of the Philippines, who supported artificial birth control (such as pills or other hormonal methods; France-Presse, 2010). In 2008, many Filipino bishops refused to give Holy Communion to politicians who approved of artificial birth control (Burke, 2008; Hoffman, 2008). Despite opposition from the Catholic Church, the Philippine government began providing family planning services in 2010.

It is also important to point out, however, that not all residents of Catholic countries agree with the Church's contraceptive views (de Freitas, 2004; Tomaso, 2008). In the Philippines, although more than 80 percent of the Philippine population is Catholic, the majority of people believe that couples should have legal assess to family planning (France-Presse, 2010). One study in Brazil, which contains one of the highest concentrations of Catholics, found that 88 percent of participants did not follow the Church's contraceptive teachings (in the United States, 75 percent of Catholics do the same; de Freitas, 2004; Tomaso, 2008). In 2008, 40 years after Pope Paul VI released *Humanae Vitae* (the document that prohibits Catholics from using artificial contraception), more than 50 Catholic groups from around the world joined forces to urge Pope Benedict XVI to lift the Catholic Church's ban on birth control (Tomaso, 2008); however, their efforts are still unsuccessful under the current Pope.

Gender roles and power differentials also contribute to a country's contraceptive use. Outside of Canada, many women may not be involved in contraceptive decision making, and contraceptive use is thought to reduce a man's masculinity. For example, in Israel, while Jewish law often opposes family planning, religious law often teaches that men should not "spill their seed." Contraceptive methods that can cause direct damage to sperm, such as vasectomy, withdrawal, condoms, or spermicides, are often not acceptable (Shtarkshall & Zemach, 2004). Contraceptive methods that do not harm sperm, such as oral contraceptives, are more acceptable.

Men are primarily responsible for birth control decisions in Japan. Japanese women express shock over the liberal views that

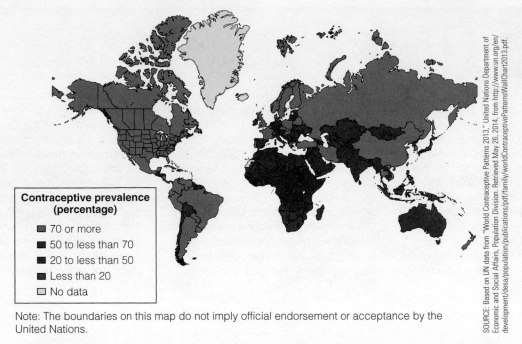

SOURCE: Based on UN data from "World Contraceptive Patterns 2013." United Nations Department of Economic and Social Affairs, Population Division. Retrieved May 26, 2014, from http://www.un.org/en/development/desa/population/publications/pdf/family/worldContraceptivePatternsWallChart2013.pdf.

Contraceptive prevalence (percentage)

- 70 or more
- 50 to less than 70
- 20 to less than 50
- Less than 20
- No data

Note: The boundaries on this map do not imply official endorsement or acceptance by the United Nations.

FIGURE **6.2** In 2007, a total of 721 million women worldwide were using a contraceptive method. Contraceptive use ranges from 3 percent in Chad to 88 percent in Norway, for a worldwide average of 63 percent.

many North American woman hold about birth control pill usage (Hatano & Shimazaki, 2004). In Kenya, married couples report low condom usage because condoms in marriage signify unfaithfulness on the part of the husband (Brockman, 2004).

Scandinavian countries are regarded as some of the most progressive with respect to contraceptive usage. In fact, Finland has been rated as a "model country" because a variety of contraceptive methods are easily available and students can obtain contraception from school health services (Kontula & Haavio-Mannila, 2004). In the Netherlands and Norway, oral contraceptive use is high, and many couples begin taking using contraceptives before becoming sexually active. In many of these countries, birth control is free and easily accessible.

REAL Research Motivations for contraceptive use are often influenced by cultural factors. In some areas of eastern Africa, condom use is extremely low because of the cultural significance of semen (Coast, 2007). Strongly held beliefs about wasting semen have led to low condom use, even when knowledge levels about contraception and STIs are high.

birth control
Another term for contraception.

Health Canada
Canadian government agency that has the power to approve or reject the use of new drugs.

Food and Drug Administration (FDA)
U.S. government agency that has the power to approve or reject the use of new drugs.

Contraception in Canada Today

Several methods of contraception, or **birth control**, are currently available. Before the availability of any contraceptive method in Canada, **Health Canada**, similar to the **U.S. Food and Drug Administration (FDA)** in the United States, must formally approve the method. Let's explore the approval process and individual lifestyle issues that may affect contraceptive method choice.

Contraception Approval Process

Health Canada is responsible for approving all prescription medications and medical devices in Canada. To get approval for a new drug, a pharmaceutical company must first submit a new drug application to the Health Products and Food Branch (HPFB) of Health Canada. To gain approval for a drug or new contraceptive method, the company who hopes to sell its product in Canada must do the following:

1. When a sponsor decides that it would like to market a drug in Canada, it files a "New Drug Submission" with the HPFB. This contains information and data about the drug's safety, effectiveness, and quality. It includes the results of the preclinical and clinical studies (whether done in Canada or elsewhere), details regarding the production of the drug, packaging and labelling details, and information regarding therapeutic claims and side effects.

2. The HPFB performs a thorough review of the submitted information, sometimes using external consultants and advisory committees.

3. The HPFB evaluates the safety, efficacy, and quality data to assess the potential benefits and risks of the drug.

4. The HPFB reviews the information that the sponsor proposes to provide to health care practitioners and consumers about the drug (e.g., the label, product brochure).

5. If, at the completion of the review, the conclusion is that the benefits outweigh the risks and that the risks can be mitigated, the drug is issued a Notice of Compliance (NOC), as well as a Drug Identification Number (DIN), which permits the sponsor to market the drug in Canada and indicates the drug's official approval in Canada (Health Canada, 2015).*

Like drugs, medical devices, such as intrauterine devices (IUDs) and diaphragms, are also subject to strict evaluation and regulation. It is estimated that it takes 10 to 14 years to develop a new contraceptive method (Hatcher et al., 2007; F.H. Stewart & Gabelnick, 2004).

Choosing a Method of Contraception

As we discussed earlier, no single method of birth control is best for everyone; the best one for you is one that you and your partner will use correctly every time you have vaginal intercourse.

Lifestyle Issues

Choosing a contraceptive method is an important decision and one that must be made with your lifestyle in mind. Important issues include your own personal health and health risks, the number of sexual partners you have, frequency of vaginal intercourse, your risk for acquiring an STI, how responsible you are, the cost of the method, and the method's advantages and disadvantages. Ultimately, the majority of women in Canada use some form of contraception. The most widely used methods are female sterilization, oral contraceptives, and condoms.

Unreliable Birth Control

Unfortunately, many men and women rely on myths and false information when it comes to contraception. They may keep their fingers crossed in hopes of not getting pregnant, have sex standing up to try and invoke gravity, or even jump up and down after sex in an attempt to dislodge sperm from swimming up the vagina. We know these techniques won't work, but for many years people thought they would. In the mid-1800s, physicians recommended douching as a contraceptive. Douching involves using a syringe-type instrument to inject a stream of water (which may be mixed with other chemicals) into the vagina. Today, health care providers strongly recommend against douching because it can increase the risk for pelvic infections and STIs. It is not an effective contraceptive method.

Another ineffective method is the **lactational amenorrhea method (LAM)**, which is based on the postpartum infertility that many women experience when they are breast-feeding (Hatcher et al., 2007). During breast-feeding, the cyclic ovarian hormones are typically suspended, which may inhibit ovulation. However, this is an ineffective contraceptive method because ovulation may still occur (Hatcher et al., 2011).

In the following sections, we will discuss effective methods of contraception, including barrier, hormonal, chemical, intrauterine, natural, permanent, and emergency contraception. For each of these methods, we will cover how they work, **effectiveness rates**, cost, advantages and disadvantages, and cross-cultural patterns of usage. Table 6.1 provides an overview of available contraceptive methods with their effectiveness in **typical use** (which includes user error) and **perfect use** (when a method is used without error).

---

lactational amenorrhea method (LAM)
A method of avoiding pregnancies based on the postpartum infertility that many women experience when they are breast-feeding.

effectiveness rates
Estimated rates of the number of women who do not become pregnant each year using each method of contraception.

typical use
Refers to the probability of contraceptive failure for less than perfect use of the method.

perfect use
Refers to the probability of contraceptive failure for use of the method without error.

Review Questions

1 Explain what we know about contraception in ancient times.

2 How was contraception viewed in Canada in the early 1900s?

3 What factors have been found to be related to contraceptive non use outside of Canada?

4 Identify two important lifestyle issues to consider when choosing a contraceptive method.

5 dentify and discuss ineffective contraceptive methods.

Table 6.1   Overview of Contraceptive Methods

Following is an overview of contraceptive methods, including effectiveness rates, prescription requirements, and non-contraceptive benefits. Even though both typical and perfect effectiveness rates are provided here, remember that a method's effectiveness depends on the user's ability to use the method correctly and to continue using it. For many methods, user failures are more common than method failures.

Method	Effectiveness Typical Use	Perfect Use	MD Visit?	Non-contraceptive Benefits	Male Involved?
Male sterilization	99%	99.9%	Yes	Possible reduction in prostate cancer risk	Yes
Female sterilization	99%	99.9%	Yes	Reduces risk for ovarian cancer	No
Implanon	99%	99%	Yes	Reduced menstrual flow and cramping; can be used while breast-feeding	No
Mirena IUD	99.2%	99.9%	Yes	Decreases menstrual flow and cramping; reduced risk for endometrial cancer	No
ParaGard IUD	99.2%	99.9%	Yes	Reduced risk for endometrial cancer	No
Depo-Provera	97%	99.7%	Yes	Reduced menstrual flow and cramping; decreased risk for pelvic inflammatory disease (PID) and ovarian and endometrial cancers; can be used while breast-feeding	No
NuvaRing	92%	99.7%	Yes	Decreases menstrual flow and cramping, premenstrual syndrome (PMS), acne, ovarian and endometrial cancers, the development of ovarian cysts, uterine and breast fibroids, and PID	No
Ortho Evra Patch	92%	99.7%	Yes	Decreases menstrual flow and cramping, PMS, acne, ovarian and endometrial cancers, the development of ovarian cysts, uterine and breast fibroids, and PID	No
Combination birth control pill	92%	99.7%	Yes	Decreases menstrual flow and cramping, PMS, acne, ovarian and endometrial cancers, the development of ovarian cysts, uterine and breast fibroids, and pelvic inflammatory disease	No
Progestin-only birth control pill	92%	99.7%	Yes	May have similar contraceptive benefits as combination pills	No
Extended-use birth control pill	98%	99.9%	Yes	Four periods or less per year and fewer menstrual-related problems; may reduce uterine fibroids and endometriosis symptoms	No
Male condom	85%	98%	No	Protects against sexually transmitted infections (STIs); delays premature ejaculation	Yes
Female condom	79%	95%	No	Protects against STIs	Possibly
Cervical barrier	84%	94%	Yes	Diaphragm may protect from cervical dysplasia	Possibly
Contraceptive sponge	68%	80%	No	None	Possibly
Fertility awareness methods	88%	97%	No	Can help a woman learn her cycle and eventually help in getting pregnant	Possibly
Withdrawal	73%	96%	No	None	Yes
Spermicide	71%	82%	No	Provides lubrication	Possibly
No method	15%	15%	No	n/a	n/a

SOURCES: Hatcher et al., 2011; Society for Obstetricians and Gynaecologists of Canada.

Barrier Methods

Barrier methods of contraception work by preventing the sperm from entering the uterus. These methods include condoms, cervical barriers, and the contraceptive sponge.

Male Condoms

Penile coverings have been used as a method of contraception since the beginning of recorded history. In 1350 B.C.E., Egyptian men wore decorative sheaths over their penises. Eventually, sheaths of linen and animal intestines were developed. In 1844, the Goodyear Company improved the strength and resiliency of rubber, and by 1850, rubber (latex) **condoms** were available in North America (McLaren, 1990). Polyurethane (paul-lee-YUR-ith-ain; non-latex) condoms were launched in the 1990s and can be used by those with latex allergies. However, if a person does not have a latex allergy, health care providers generally recommend using latex condoms because they have lower rates of slippage and breakage.

Male condoms are one of the most inexpensive and cost-effective contraceptive methods, providing not only high effectiveness rates but also added protection from STIs and HIV (Hatcher et al., 2011). Male condoms are made of either latex or plastic and typically cost about $1 each but may be free at health clinics, HIV agencies, Planned Parenthood centres and LGBTQ centres. See Figure 6.3 for more information about condom use by age and gender.

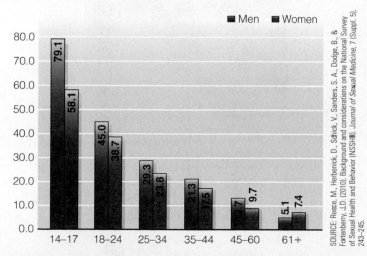

FIGURE **6.3** Condom use rates by age and gender.

SOURCE: Reece, M., Herbenick, D., Schick, V., Sanders, S. A., Dodge, B., & Fortenberry, J.D. (2010). Background and considerations on the National Survey of Sexual Health and Behavior (NSSHB). *Journal of Sexual Medicine, 7* (Suppl. 5), 243–245.

Table 6.2 **What to Use with Condoms**

Male condoms can be made out of latex or polyurethane. All types of lubricants, including oil-based lubricants, can be safely used with polyurethane condoms. However, latex condoms should be used with only a water-based lubricant. Following is a listing of products that can be used with all condoms and products that should never be used with latex condoms.

Use with All Condoms

- Water-based lubricants (including products such as AquaLube, AstroGlide, or K-Y Jelly)
- Glycerine
- Spermicides
- Saliva
- Water
- Silicone lubricant

Do Not Use with Latex Condoms

- Baby oil
- Cold creams
- Edible oils (such as olive, peanut, or canola oil)
- Massage oil
- Petroleum jelly
- Rubbing alcohol
- Suntan oil and lotions
- Vegetable or mineral oil
- Vaginal infection medications in cream or suppository form

SOURCE: Hatcher, R. A., Trussell, J., Nelson, A., Cates, W., Kowal, D., & Policar M. (2011). Contraceptive Technology (20th ed.). New York: Ardent Media.

How They Work

The male condom ("rubber" or "prophylactic") is placed on an erect penis before vaginal penetration (only use one—two are not necessary). Condoms must be put on before there is any vaginal contact by the penis because sperm may be present in the urethra. Some condom manufacturers recommend leaving space at the tip of the condom to allow room for the ejaculation, but others do not. To prevent tearing the condom, the vagina should be well lubricated. Although some condoms come prelubricated, if extra lubrication is needed, water, contraceptive jelly or cream, or a water-based lubricant such as K-Y Jelly should be used. Oil-based lubricants such as hand or body lotion, petroleum jelly (e.g., Vaseline), baby oil, massage oil, or creams for vaginal infections (e.g., Monistat and Vagisil) should not be used because they may damage the latex and cause the condom to break (polyurethane condoms are not damaged by these products; see Table 6.2).

To avoid the possibility of semen leaking out of the condom, withdrawal must take place immediately after ejaculation, while the penis is still erect, and the condom should be grasped firmly at the base to prevent its slipping off into the vagina during

condom
A latex, animal membrane, or polyurethane sheath that fits over the penis and is used for protection against pregnancy and sexually transmitted infections; female condoms made of either polyurethane or polymer, which protect the vaginal walls, are also available.

Over the years, public health experts have recommended using condoms that contain the spermicide nonoxynol-9 (N-9) to decrease the possibility of pregnancy. Although N-9 is an effective spermicide, several studies have raised concerns about its safety and protection effects for sexually transmitted infections (STIs). Frequent use of N-9 may increase HIV risk by creating rectal and vaginal ulceration. In addition to this, N-9 does not offer protection from gonorrhea, chlamydia, or HIV.

Concern over the use of N-9 has spurred development of new products, **microbicides**, which can reduce the risk for STIs. Ongoing trials are evaluating a variety of safer spermicides and/or microbicides (Baptista & Ramalho-Santos, 2009; Burke et al., 2010; Hughes et al., 2007; Ramjee et al., 2010; Saha et al., 2010).

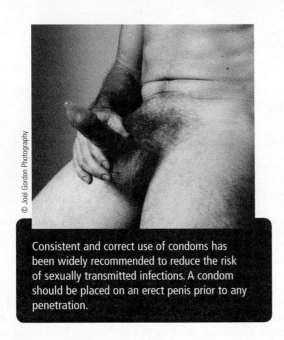

Consistent and correct use of condoms has been widely recommended to reduce the risk of sexually transmitted infections. A condom should be placed on an erect penis prior to any penetration.

Effectiveness

Effectiveness rates for male condoms range from 85 percent to 98 percent. Studies have demonstrated that when used correctly, the overall risk for condom breakage is very low (Hatcher et al., 2011). Using a condom after the expiration date is the leading cause of breakage.

Advantages

Male condoms allow couples to help prevent pregnancy, can be discreetly carried in a pocket or purse, offer some protection from many STIs, can be purchased without a prescription, are relatively inexpensive, have minimal adverse effects, may reduce the incidence of premature ejaculation, reduce **postcoital drip**, can be used in conjunction with other contraceptive methods, and can be used

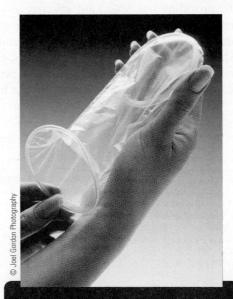

A female condom is inserted deep into the vagina prior to vaginal intercourse. The ring at the closed end holds the condom in the vagina, while the ring at the open end stays outside the vaginal opening during intercourse. The female condom can also be used during anal intercourse via insertion into the anus.

withdrawal. Condom users should always remember to check expiration dates before using condoms.

There are many types of male condoms on the market, including dry, lubricated, coloured, spermicidal, reservoir-tip, and ribbed-texture condoms. For protection from STIs, the most effective condoms are latex and polyurethane condoms. Spermicidal condoms are lubricated with a small amount of **nonoxynol-9**, but there are risks to using this **spermicide** (Hatcher et al., 2011; see the accompanying Sex in Real Life feature).

microbicide
Chemical that works by inhibiting sperm function; effective against HIV and other STIs, and not harmful to the vaginal or cervical cells.

nonoxynol-9
A spermicide that has been used to prevent pregnancy and protect against sexually transmitted infections.

spermicide
Chemical method of contraception, including creams, gels, foams, suppositories, and films, that works to reduce the survival of sperm in the vagina.

postcoital drip
A vaginal discharge (dripping) that occurs after sexual intercourse.

during oral or anal sex to reduce the risk for STIs (we discuss this further in Chapter 7). Polyurethane condoms are more resistant to damage than latex condoms, have a longer shelf life, and can be used with both oil- and water-based lubricants (Hatcher et al., 2011).

Disadvantages

The male condom decreases spontaneity, may pose sizing and erection problems, and may reduce male sensation. In one study, more than 75 percent of men and nearly 40 percent of women reported decreased sexual sensation with condom use (Crosby et al., 2008b). Condoms may not be comfortable for all men, and some who use polyurethane condoms report slipping or bunching up during use (Hollander, 2001). Finally, some men may feel uncomfortable interrupting foreplay to put one on.

Cross-Culture Use

Worldwide, male condoms are the fourth most popular contraceptive method (behind female sterilization, IUDs, and birth control pills), with 6 percent of couples reporting relying on

this method ("World Contraceptive Use 2009," 2009). Condoms are popular in more developed regions of the world, such as Europe and North America (Figure 6.4). Usage rates of between 20 percent and 40 percent have been reported in Argentina, Demark, Finland, Greece, Ireland, Jamaica, Singapore, Spain, Ukraine, the United Kingdom, and Uruguay.

In many other countries, however, male condoms are not widely used. This may be because of embarrassment, lack of availability, or religious prohibition. In Botswana, for example, many couples are embarrassed to purchase condoms (Mookodi et al., 2004), and a similar attitude is found in Brazil, especially among women (de Freitas, 2004). However, these attitudes are slowly changing because of increased condom availability. In Costa Rica, where religious prohibitions discourage condom use, men report not wanting to use condoms and prohibit their partners from using protection as well (Arroba, 2004).

> **On Your Mind**
>
> **Do some men have problems maintaining an erection when they use a condom?**

Some men do report that they have more difficulties maintaining an erection when they use a latex condom. Some couples complain that wearing a condom is like "taking a shower with a raincoat on," or that it decreases sensitivity during vaginal intercourse. Adding two or three drops of a lubricant, such as K-Y Jelly, into the condom before rolling it on to the penis can improve penile sensitivity. Many women also report that putting a small amount of a lubricant into their vagina before intercourse helps increase their pleasure and sensitivity while using a condom. Lubricated condoms may help maintain erections by increasing sensitivity, as will polyurethane condoms. It is also important to note that men who experience problems with premature ejaculation often find that condoms can help maintain erections.

REAL Research College students view condoms primarily as a means of preventing pregnancy, but few describe disease prevention as a main motivation for their use (O'Sullivan et al., 2010).

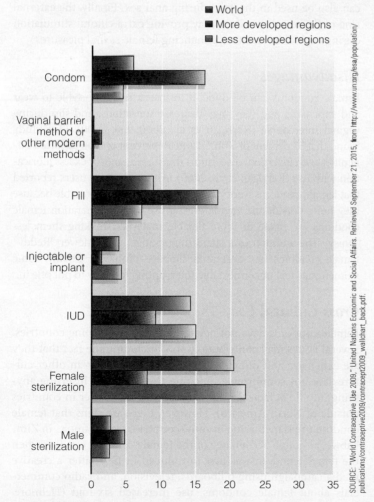

SOURCE: "World Contraceptive Use 2009," United Nations Economic and Social Affairs. Retrieved September 21, 2015, from http://www.un.org/esa/population/publications/contraceptive2009/contracept2009_wallchart_back.pdf.

FIGURE **6.4** Comparisons of worldwide contraceptive prevalence (by percentage) by level of economic development.

Female Condoms

The first female condom, the Reality Vaginal Pouch (often referred to as "FC"), became available in Canada in the 1990s. It is made of polyurethane and is about 17.8 centimetres (7 inches) long with two flexible polyurethane rings. The inner ring serves as an insertion device, and the outer ring stays on the outside of the vagina. In 2005, a newer female condom (the "FC2") made of a softer and more flexible material became available. Female condoms are more expensive than male condoms and cost approximately $3.00 each. Women in many countries in Africa have been known to wash and reuse FCs because of the high cost, although they are not made to be used this way (Potter et al., 2003).

Contraception and Abortion **161**

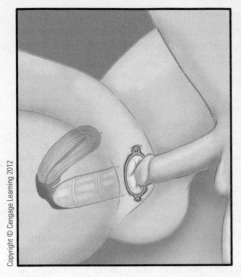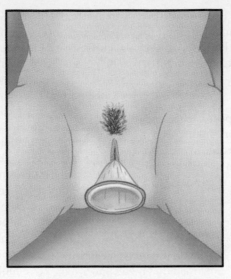

FIGURE 6.5 Female condoms are inserted into the vagina like a tampon. The inner ring is pushed up inside the vagina until it reaches the cervix, while the outer ring hangs about an inch outside of the vagina.

How They Work

A female condom is inserted into the vagina before penile penetration. The inner ring (or sponge, depending on which type of female condom used) is squeezed between the thumb and middle finger, making it long and thin, and then inserted into the vagina. Once this is done, an index finger inside the condom can push the inner ring/sponge up close to the cervix. The outer ring sits on the outside

Debra Messing, an ambassador with Population Services International (PSI), visits a beauty salon in Zimbabwe. PSI trains hairdressers as peer educators to talk to their clients about female condoms and HIV prevention. The hairdressers have helped to stop the rise of HIV and AIDS.

of the vulva (Figure 6.5). During intercourse, the penis is placed within the female condom, and care should be taken to make sure it does not slip between the condom and the vaginal wall. It is important that the vagina is well lubricated so that the female condom stays in place. Female and male condoms should never be used together, because they can adhere to each other and slip or break.

Effectiveness

Effectiveness rates for female condoms range from 79 percent to 95 percent.

Advantages

Like male condoms, female condoms can be discreetly carried in a purse, offer some STI protection, can be purchased without a prescription, reduce postcoital drip, can be used by those with latex allergies, can be used with oil-based lubricants, and have minimal adverse effects. Unlike male condoms, female condoms do not require a male erection to put on and will stay in place if a man loses his erection. Female condoms can also be used in the anus during anal sex. Finally, the external ring of the female condom may provide extra clitoral stimulation during vaginal intercourse, enhancing female sexual pleasure.

Disadvantages

Female condoms can be difficult to insert, uncomfortable to wear and expensive, and they may decrease sensations, and slip during vaginal intercourse (Kerrigan et al., 2000; Lie, 2000). One study found that 57 percent of women and 30 percent of men reported difficulties with insertion, discomfort during sex, and/or excess lubrication with use (Kerrigan et al., 2000). Although some users reported that female condoms were "noisy" to use and uncomfortable because they hung outside the vagina during use, newer generation female condoms are made of more flexible materials, making them less "noisy." The addition of a stabilizing sponge in the newer "Reddy" female condoms has decreased slippage problems. Finally, some women may feel uncomfortable interrupting foreplay to put one in.

Cross-Cultural Use

Female condoms have not been popular in developing countries. Several issues may contribute to this, including the fact that they are expensive and difficult to insert. Many women in other cultures are not comfortable touching the vagina or inserting anything into it (in fact, tampon use is also much lower in countries outside of North America). However, there are signs that female condom use is increasing in some countries. For example, in Zimbabwe, although acceptance of the female condom was low when the female condom was first introduced in 1997, after a creative media campaign using billboards, television, and radio commercials about female condoms, use increased six-fold (Helmore, 2010). The media campaign helped increase knowledge levels and broke down the stigma associated with female condoms.

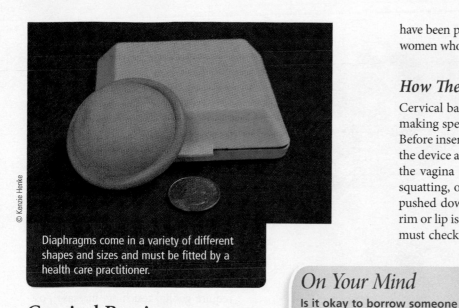

Diaphragms come in a variety of different shapes and sizes and must be fitted by a health care practitioner.

Cervical Barriers: Diaphragms and Cervical Caps

Cervical barriers include **diaphragms** (DIE-uh-fram) and **cervical caps**. These devices are inserted into the vagina before intercourse and fit over the cervix, creating a barrier so that sperm and ova cannot meet. We will discuss traditional diaphragms, Lea's Shield (not available in Canada), and the FemCap. Although these methods work in similar ways, they are designed and function a bit differently from each other.

The diaphragm is a dome-shaped cup, made of either latex or silicone, with a flexible rim. It comes in several sizes and shapes, and must be fitted by a health care provider. Like latex condoms, latex diaphragms should not be used with oil-based lubricants because these can damage the latex (see Table 6.2). Diaphragms range in cost from $15 to $75 and require spermicidal cream or jelly.

FemCap works like the other cervical barriers. Cervical caps are much smaller than diaphragms and are designed to sit more snugly on the cervix. They are made of silicone and come in three sizes—small for women who have never been pregnant, medium for women who have been pregnant but have not had a vaginal delivery, and large for women who have had a vaginal delivery of a full-term baby.

How They Work

Cervical barriers work by blocking the entrance to the uterus and making sperm inert through the use of spermicidal cream or jelly. Before insertion, spermicidal cream or jelly should be placed inside the device and rubbed on the rim. They are folded and inserted into the vagina while a woman is standing with one leg propped up, squatting, or lying on her back (Figure 6.6). The device should be pushed downward toward the back of the vagina, while the front rim or lip is tucked under the pubic bone. After insertion, a woman must check to see that the device is covering her cervix. Once in place, a woman should not be able to feel the device; if she does, it is improperly inserted.

These methods can be inserted before intercourse but should be left in place for at least eight hours after intercourse. Users of

On Your Mind

Is it okay to borrow someone else's diaphragm if I can't find mine?

Absolutely not. The diaphragm prevents sperm from entering the uterus by adhering to the cervix through suction. A health care provider must measure the cervix and prescribe the right size diaphragm for each individual woman to get this suction. If you use someone else's diaphragm, it may be the wrong size and thus ineffective. Also, because of the risk for acquiring an STI, it is not a good idea to share diaphragms.

cervical barrier
A plastic or rubber cover for the cervix that provides a contraceptive barrier to sperm.

diaphragm
A birth control device consisting of a latex dome on a flexible spring rim; used with spermicidal cream or jelly.

cervical cap
A birth control device similar to a diaphragm, but smaller.

FemCap
Reusable silicone barrier vaginal contraceptive that comes in three sizes.

(a)

(b)

The FemCap is a silicone cup shaped like a sailor's hat that fits securely over the cervix.

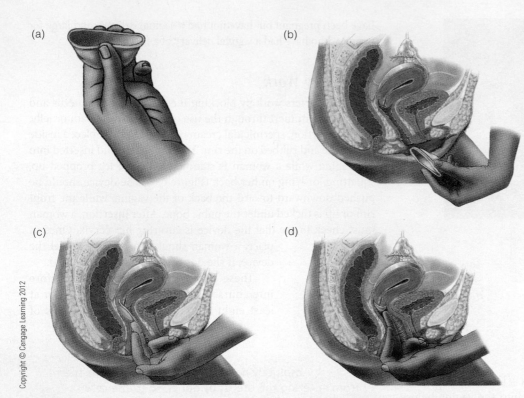

Advantages

Cervical barriers can be discreetly carried in a purse, are immediately effective, do not affect spontaneity or hormonal levels, and allow couples to engage in intercourse multiple times. Research has also found that diaphragm use may reduce the risk for cervical dysplasia and cancer (Hatcher et al., 2007).

Disadvantages

Cervical barriers require a prescription, do not offer protection from STIs, may be difficult to insert and/or remove, require genital touching, increase post-coital drip, may shift during vaginal intercourse, cannot be used during menstruation, and may develop a foul odour if left in place too long. In addition, some women experience allergic reactions to the spermicidal cream or jelly.

FIGURE **6.6** Insertion of diaphragm is folded in half, the cervix is covered by the diaphragm (and other cervical barriers): (a) after placing the spermicide, the rim to rim and (b) inserted into the vagina (c) as far as it will go, (d) check to feel diaphragm.

Cross-Cultural Use

Cervical barriers are widely used in England, and in some countries—including Germany, Austria, Switzerland, and the United States (Long, 2003). However, similar to cervical barriers, they are used infrequently in less-developed countries (see Figure 6.4). This is possibly related to a shortage of health care providers, limited availability of spermicidal cream or jelly, high cost, and required genital touching.

FemCap can have repeated intercourse without applying additional spermicidal cream or jelly, although health care providers recommend diaphragm users insert additional spermicide into the vagina without removing the device. The diaphragm should not be left in place for longer than 24 hours, and the FemCap can be left in for up to 48 hours. After use, all the devices should be washed with soap and water and allowed to air-dry.

With proper care, these devices can be used for approximately one year, depending on usage. If a woman loses or gains more than 4.5 kilograms (10 pounds) or experiences a pregnancy (regardless of how the pregnancy was resolved—through birth, miscarriage, or **abortion**), the diaphragm or FemCap must be refitted by her health care provider.

Effectiveness

Effectiveness rates for these devices range from 84 percent to 94 percent. Women who have not had children have higher effectiveness rates than women who have given birth.

abortion
Induced termination of a pregnancy before fetal viability.

The contraceptive sponge is a contraceptive device that prevents sperm from entering the uterus. It is made of polyurethane foam. Before sex, the contraceptive sponge is inserted deep into the vagina and held in place by vaginal muscles. The strap is used to remove the sponge.

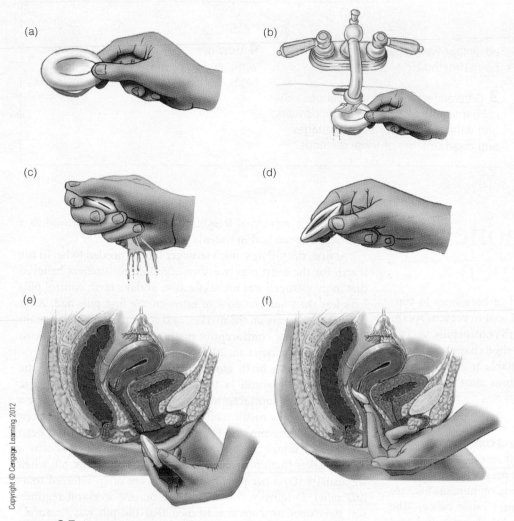

(a)

(b)

(c)

(d)

(e)

(f)

Copyright © Cengage Learning 2012

FIGURE **6.7** Insertion of a contraceptive sponge: (a) take it out of the packaging, (b) moisten with water, (c) wring out extra water, (d) fold in half, (e) insert the sponge into the vagina as far as it will go, (f) check to feel the cervix is covered by the sponge.

Contraceptive Sponge

The Today **contraceptive sponge** is a one-size-fits-all sponge that is a combination of a cervical barrier and spermicide. A box of three sponges can cost approximately $10 to $20, depending on where it is purchased.

How It Works

A contraceptive sponge works in three ways: as a barrier, blocking the entrance to the uterus; absorbing sperm; and deactivating sperm. Before vaginal insertion, the sponge is moistened with water, which activates the spermicide. It is then folded in half and inserted deep into the vagina (Figure 6.7). Like the diaphragm and cervical cap, the sponge must be checked to make sure it is covering the cervix. Intercourse can take place immediately after insertion or at any time during the next 24 hours and can occur as many times as desired without adding additional spermicidal jelly or cream. However, the sponge must be left in place for six hours

after intercourse. For removal, a cloth loop on the outside of the sponge is grasped to gently pull the sponge out of the vagina. Like the diaphragm, the sponge must be removed within 24 hours to reduce the risk for toxic shock syndrome.

Effectiveness

Effectiveness rates for the contraceptive sponge range from 68 percent to 80 percent. Women who have not had children have higher effectiveness rates than women who have given birth.

Advantages

Like cervical barriers, a contraceptive sponge can be discreetly carried in a purse, is immediately effective, does not affect spontaneity or hormonal levels, and allows couples to engage in intercourse multiple times during a 24-hour period. Unlike the cervical barriers, the contraceptive sponge can be purchased without a prescription.

Disadvantages

The contraceptive sponge does not offer protection from STIs, may be difficult to insert and/or remove, requires genital touching, increases postcoital drip, cannot be used during menstruation, may cause a foul odour if left in place too long, and may increase the risk for toxic shock syndrome and urinary tract infections (Hatcher et al., 2011). In addition, some women experience allergic reactions to the spermicidal cream or jelly.

Cross-Cultural Use

Contraceptive sponges have been fairly popular in European countries. In fact, women in France have used vaginal sponges dipped in various chemicals to avoid pregnancy for years. These sponges are washed and used over and over. This practice is not recommended, however, because of the risk for infection and toxic shock syndrome.

contraceptive sponge
Polyurethane sponge impregnated with spermicide, inserted into the vagina for contraception.

1 Explain how barrier methods of contraception work, and identify four barrier contraceptive methods in order of their effectiveness rates.

2 How do male and female condoms work, and what are some of the advantages and disadvantages of these barrier methods?

3 Differentiate between the various cervical barriers. How do these methods work, and what are some of the advantages and disadvantages of these methods?

4 How does the contraceptive sponge work, and what are some of the advantages and disadvantages of this method?

Combined Hormone Methods for Women

Combined hormone methods use a blend of hormones to suppress ovulation and thicken the cervical mucus to prevent sperm from joining the ovum. We will discuss birth control pills, vaginal rings, and patches. Combined hormone methods have been found to be effective, safe, reversible, and acceptable to most women. However, for protection against STIs, condoms must also be used.

Birth Control Pills

Margaret Sanger was the first to envision **oral contraceptives** (the birth control pill, or simply "the pill"). Many researchers had been working with chemical methods to inhibit pregnancy in animals, but they were reluctant to try these methods on humans because they feared that increasing hormones could cause cancer. The complexity of a woman's body chemistry and the expense involved in developing the pill inhibited its progress. While the birth control pill in Canada was available in the late 1950s as a prescription

oral contraceptive	combination birth control pill
The "pill"; a preparation of synthetic female hormones that blocks ovulation.	An oral contraceptive that contains synthetic estrogen and progesterone.

Many types of birth control pills are available, and a health care provider can prescribe the one that's best for you.

© Kenzie Henke

treatment for menstrual irregularities, it was not approved as a contraceptive method in Canada until 1969.

At first, the pill was much stronger than it needed to be. In the search for the most effective contraception, researchers believed that more estrogen was more effective. Today's birth control pills have less than half the dose of estrogen the first pills had. After more than 50 years on the market, oral contraceptives still remain the most popular contraceptive method around the world (Frost et al., 2008; Hatcher et al., 2011).

Combination birth control pills, which contain synthetic estrogen and progestin (a type of progesterone), are the most commonly used contraceptive method in Canada. They require a prescription and a medical office visit, and typically cost between $30 and $60 per month. Typical birth control pills have been designed to mimic an average menstrual cycle, which is why a woman takes them for 21 days and then has one week off, when she usually starts her period (these pills are often referred to as 21/7 pills). Originally, this three-week-on/one-week-off regimen was developed to convince women that the pill was "natural," which pill makers believed would make the product more acceptable to potential users and reassure them that they were not pregnant every month (Clarke & Miller, 2001; Thomas & Ellertson, 2000). The bleeding that women experience while on the pill is medically induced and has no known physiological benefit.

REAL Research Some brands of birth control pills may decrease sexual desire and vaginal lubrication, and these effects may last after a woman has stopped taking the pill (Graham et al., 2007; Hatcher et al., 2011). However, if a woman is less sensitive to hormonal changes, she may not notice these adverse effects. If she does, changing birth control pill brands may restore sexual desire.

Extended-cycle birth control pills became available in Canada in 2008 with the approval of Seasonale, which uses a continuous 84-day active pill with a seven-day placebo pill (an 84/7 pill). Seasonale enabled women to have only four periods per year. In 2011, Seasonique, a similar extended-cycle pill, was approved. The difference between Seasonale and Seasonique is in the placebo pills—although they are inactive in Seasonale, Seasonique placebo pills contain a low dose of estrogen that has been found to cause less spotting during the

Table 6.3 What to Do If You Forget

Many women who take birth control pills forget to take one at some time. As we've discussed throughout this chapter, the pill is most effective if taken every day at approximately the same time. If you miss a pill, it's a good idea to talk to your health care provider about what would be best to do. In many cases, it depends on several factors, including what kind of pill you are on, the dosage of the pill, how many pills you missed, and how soon into the pack you missed them. A seven-day backup method or emergency contraception may be needed. The following information is for women using a 21- or 28-day combination birth control pill.

Number of Pills Missed	When Pills Were Missed	What to Do	Use a Back up Method?
First 1–2 pills	Beginning of pack	Take a pill as soon as you remember. Take the next pill at usual time.	Yes
1–2 pills	Days 3–21	Take the pill as soon as you remember. Take the next pill at the usual time.	No
3 or more pills	First 2 weeks	Take the pill as soon as you remember. Take the next pill at the usual time.	Yes
3 or more pills	Third week	Do not finish pack. Start new pack.	Yes

SOURCE: Planned Parenthood Federation of America. (2007). What to do if you forget to take the pill. Retrieved May 26, 2014, from http://www.plannedparenthood.org/health-topics/birth-control/if-forget-takepill-19269.htm

2010; Shapiro & Dinger, 2010). It is important to talk to a health care provider to determine which pills are right for you.

How They Work

The hormones estrogen, progesterone, luteinizing hormone (LH), and follicle-stimulating hormone (FSH) fluctuate during a woman's menstrual cycle (see Figure 3.9 in Chapter 3). These fluctuations control the maturation of an ovum, ovulation, the development of the endometrium, and menstruation. The synthetic hormones replace a woman's own natural hormones but in different amounts. The increase in estrogen and progesterone prevent the pituitary gland from sending hormones to cause the ovaries to begin maturation of an ovum. Hormone levels while taking the pill are similar to when a woman is pregnant, and this is what interferes with ovulation. Birth control pills also work by thickening the cervical mucus (which inhibits the mobility of sperm) and by reducing the buildup of the endometrium.

active pills. Another continuous birth control pill that completely stops menstrual periods is Lybrel, which contains lower levels of estrogen than other pills but is taken daily for 365 days a year.

Continuous-use birth control pills are not new. In fact, before Health Canada approval of these methods, some health care providers were known to "bicycle" birth control pills (back-to-back use of two packs of active pills with placebo pills at the end of the second pack) or "tricycle" (back-to-back-back use of three packs of active pills with placebo pills at the end of the third pack; Hatcher et al., 2011). In addition, some health care providers have used short-term, continuous-use birth control pills for scheduling convenience (i.e., to eliminate the chance of having a period during an athletic event, vacation, or honeymoon; Hatcher et al., 2011). Birth control pills are also prescribed for non-contraceptive reasons, such as heavy or dysfunctional menstrual bleeding, irregular periods, recurrent ovarian cysts, polycystic ovary syndrome, or acne (Hatcher et al., 2011).

Today, dozens of brands of birth control pills are on the market. They vary with the amount of estrogen (low, regular, high, or varied levels) and the type of progestin (there are eight different types of progestin hormones). Recent studies have found that one type of progestin, *drospirenone,* may increase the risk for cardiovascular problems (Jick & Hernandez, 2011; Reid, 2010; Sehovic & Smith,

Combination birth control pills can either be **monophasic**, **biphasic**, or **triphasic** (try-FAY-sic). Monophasic pills contain the same amount of hormones in each pill, whereas biphasic and triphasic pills vary the hormonal amount. Biphasic pills change the level of hormones once during the menstrual cycle, whereas triphasic pills contain three sets of pills for each week during the cycle. Each week, the hormonal dosage is increased, rather than keeping the hormonal level consistent, as with monophasic pills. **Breakthrough bleeding** is more common in triphasic pills because of the fluctuating hormone levels.

Traditionally, birth control pills have been used on a monthly cycling plan that involved either a 21- or 28-day regimen and started on the first or fifth day of menstruation or on the first Sunday after menstruation. **Start days** vary depending on the pill manufacturer. The majority of manufacturers recommend a Sunday start day, which enables a woman to avoid menstruating during a weekend. Each pill must be taken every day at approximately the same time. This is important because they work by maintaining a certain hormonal level in the bloodstream. If this level drops, ovulation may occur (see the accompanying Table 6.3 for more information).

In most 28-day birth control pill packs, the last seven pills are **placebo pills**. The placebo pills do not contain hormones, and

monophasic pill
A type of oral contraceptive that contains one level of hormones in all the active pills.

biphasic pill
A type of oral contraceptive that contains two different doses of hormones in the active pills.

triphasic pill
A type of oral contraceptive that contains three different doses of hormones in the active pills.

breakthrough bleeding
Slight blood loss from the uterus that may occur when a woman is taking oral contraceptives.

start day
The actual day that the first pill is taken in a pack of oral contraceptives.

placebo pills
In a pack of 28-day oral contraceptives, the seven pills at the end; these pills are sugar pills and do not contain any hormones; they are used to help a woman remember to take a pill every day.

SEX
Drugs and Herbs That Interact with Oral Contraceptives

Many over-the-counter (non-prescription) drugs, prescription medications, and herbal supplements may reduce the effectiveness of the pill. Birth control pills may also increase or decrease another drug's effectiveness. When you take medications, you should always let your health care provider know that you are taking birth control pills.

Drugs that interact with oral contraceptives include the following:

Drug	Effect of Birth Control Pills on Drug
Acetaminophen (Tylenol)	Decreases effect of pain relief
Alcohol (beer, wine, mixed drinks, etc.)	increases effect of alcohol
Anticoagulants	Decreases anticoagulant effect (aspirin may be less effective when used with oral contraceptives)
Antibiotics (amoxicillin, tetracycline, ampicillin)	May decrease effectiveness of oral contraceptives
Antidepressants (Prozac, Paxil)	Increases blood levels of antidepressant
Antifungal medications (Grisactin)	Can cause breakthrough bleeding and spotting
Barbiturates (Seconal, Nembutal)	Decreases effectiveness of oral contraceptives
Vitamin C	May increase estrogen side effects in daily doses of 1000 mg or more
St. John's wort (Hypericum)	Decreases effectiveness of oral contraceptives

SOURCE: Hatcher, R.A., Trussell, J., Nelson, A., Cates, W., Steward, F., & Kowal, D. (2007). *Contraceptive Technology* (19th ed.). New York: Ardent Media.

because of this, a woman usually starts menstruating while taking them. In fact, some low-dose pill brands extended usage to 24 days with a reduced two- or four-day placebo pill regimen (a 24/2 or 24/4 pill; Hatcher et al., 2011). Women on these extended cycle regimens report higher levels of satisfaction than women on traditional 21/7 regimens (Caruso et al., 2011; Cremer et al., 2010; Davis et al., 2010; Dinger et al., 2011). Women who take birth control pills usually have lighter menstrual periods and decreased cramping because the pills decrease the buildup of the endometrium. Menstrual discomfort, such as cramping, is also reduced.

Before starting on birth control pills, a woman must have a full medical examination. Women with a history of circulatory problems, strokes, heart disease, breast or uterine cancer, hypertension, diabetes, and undiagnosed vaginal bleeding are generally advised not to take oral contraceptives (Hatcher et al., 2011). Although migraine headaches have typically been a reason for not using birth control pills, some women may experience fewer migraines while taking birth control pills, especially if used continuously without placebo pills (Hatcher et al., 2011). If a woman can use birth control pills, health care providers usually begin by prescribing a low-dose estrogen pill, and they increase the dosage if breakthrough bleeding or other symptoms occur.

There are several potential adverse effects to the use of birth control pills. Because the hormones in birth control pills are similar to those during pregnancy, many women experience signs of pregnancy. These may include nausea, increase in breast size, breast tenderness, water retention, increased appetite, fatigue, and high blood pressure (Hatcher et al., 2011; see Chapter 12). Symptoms usually disappear within a couple of months, after a woman's body becomes used to the hormonal levels. Other possible adverse effects include migraines, weight gain, depression, and decreases in sexual desire and bone density (Hatcher et al., 2011; Pitts & Emans, 2008). Possible serious adverse effects include blood clots, strokes, or heart attacks.

If a woman taking the pill experiences abdominal pain, chest pain, severe headaches, vision or eye problems, and severe leg or calf pain, she should contact her health care provider immediately. In addition, a woman who takes birth control pills should always inform her health care provider of her oral contraceptive use, especially if she is prescribed other medications or undergoes any type of surgery. Certain drugs may have negative interactions with oral contraceptives (see the accompanying Sex in Real Life feature). Women are advised not to smoke cigarettes while taking birth control pills, because smoking may increase the risk for cardiovascular disease (Bounhoure et al., 2008; Hatcher et al., 2011; Raval et al., 2011).

Finally, there has been debate in recent years about the relationship between oral contraceptive use and cancer. Although researchers have found that birth control pill use offers possible protection from breast and cervical cancers (Althuis et al., 2003; Deligeoroglou et al., 2003; Franceschi, 2005; Gaffield et al., 2009; Hatcher et al., 2007; Marchbanks et al., 2002; Moreno et al., 2002; Vessey et al., 2010), the research on other cancers has been less clear-cut. According to some studies, birth control pill use *increases* the risks for endometrial and ovarian cancers (Burkman et al., 2004; Emons et al., 2000; Greer et al., 2005; Modan et al., 2001; Schildkraut et al., 2002); however, more recent studies have found that use *decreases* the risks (Grimbizis & Tarlatzis, 2010; Ness et al., 2011; Schindler, 2010; Vessey et al., 2010). In fact, recent studies have found that the use of birth control pills may provide a significant protective effect from both ovarian and endometrial cancer, and protection may increase the longer birth control pills are taken (Cibula et al., 2010; Grimbizis & Tarlatzis, 2010; Mueck et al., 2010; Schindler, 2010). The risk for ovarian cancer decreased 20 percent for each five years of birth control use (Cibula et al., 2010). Experts believe that risks for cancer were higher in women who took oral contraceptives before 1975 because hormonal levels were much higher than the oral contraceptives available today (Gaffield et al., 2009). Women who have used oral contraceptives have a significantly lower rate of death from all cancers, compared with non-users (Geraghty, 2010; Hannaford et al., 2010).

Effectiveness

Effectiveness rates for oral contraceptives range from 92 percent to 99.7 percent (Hatcher et al., 2011). However, women who are significantly overweight may experience lower effectiveness rates using oral contraceptives (Brunner-Huber & Toth, 2007; Gardner, 2004; Hatcher et al., 2011).

Advantages

Oral contraceptives offer one of the highest effectiveness rates; do not interfere with spontaneity; increase menstrual regularity; and reduce the flow of menstruation, menstrual cramps, premenstrual syndrome, and facial acne (Hatcher et al., 2011). They also provide important degrees of protection against ovarian cysts, uterine and breast fibroids, certain cancers, and **pelvic inflammatory disease**. They may increase sexual enjoyment because fear of pregnancy is reduced, and they have rapid reversibility (the majority of women who stop taking the pill return to ovulation within two weeks; Hatcher et al., 2011).

Disadvantages

Oral contraceptives require a prescription, provide no protection from STIs, and have several potential adverse effects, including nausea, increase in breast size, headaches, and decreased sexual desire. In addition, oral contraceptives can be expensive, and a woman must remember to take them every day.

REAL Research Studies have found that the majority of adverse effects from birth control pill use, such as headaches, breast tenderness, or bloating, occur during the week when women take their placebo pills and not when they are taking their hormone pills (Hatcher et al., 2007; Sulak et al., 2000). This is one of the reasons pharmaceutical companies developed continuous-use birth control pills that reduce or eliminate menstrual periods.

Cross-Cultural Use

Worldwide, birth control pills are the third most popular contraceptive method (behind female sterilization and IUDs), with 9 percent of women relying on this method ("World Contraceptive Use 2009," 2009). However, usage is higher in more developed countries (see Figure 6.4). Contraceptive pill use is high in Europe but lower in Asian countries. For example, 60 percent of women use birth control pills in France (Schuberg, 2009), whereas approximately 1 percent of women in Japan use them (Hayashi, 2004). By comparison, approximately 31 percent of women in North America use birth control pills (Alan Guttmacher Institute, 2008a).

On Your Mind

I usually take my birth control pill at 7:00 a.m. each morning. When we switch to daylight savings time, what should I do? Should I continue to take my pill at 7:00 a.m. (the normal time I take it), or should I take it at 8:00 a.m. (what would have been 7:00 a.m.) now?

It is important to take birth control pills at about the same time each day. Making sure you pick a time that works for you and allows you to regularly remember is the most important thing. Typically, most pills have about a one- to two-hour window in which effectiveness is not compromised. Although an hour in each direction probably wouldn't matter, it's probably better to take it one hour earlier than later (especially if you are taking a low-dose pill). So, take the pill at your normal time when the clock springs forward (and you'll probably be fine taking it at the same time in the fall when the time changes back, but check with your health care provider to be sure).

Birth control pill use is high in Latin America, Belgium, France, Germany, Morocco, the Netherlands, Portugal, and Zimbabwe ("World Contraceptive Use 2009," 2009). In some countries, birth control pills are available without a prescription (Arroba, 2004; Ng & Ma, 2004).

Fears about safety and reliability issues in countries such as Japan and Russia reduce birth control pill use (Hayashi, 2004; Kon, 2004). Birth control pills were not approved for use in Japan until 1999. However, they have remained unpopular because of safety concerns,

pelvic inflammatory disease
Widespread infection of the female pelvic organs.

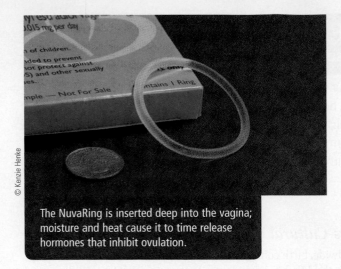

The NuvaRing is inserted deep into the vagina; moisture and heat cause it to time release hormones that inhibit ovulation.

negative side effects, required daily pill taking, countrywide conservatism, and lack of advertising (Hayashi, 2004).

Hormonal Ring

NuvaRing is a hormonal method of birth control that is a one-size-fits-all plastic ring that is inserted into the vagina once a month and releases a constant dose of estrogen and progestin. The amount of hormones released into the bloodstream with the NuvaRing is lower than in both oral contraceptives and the patch (we will talk more about the patch later in this chapter; Hatcher et al., 2011; van den Heuvel et al., 2005). The hormonal ring costs approximately $15 to $70 per month to use.

How It Works

Like birth control pills, NuvaRing works chiefly by inhibiting ovulation, but it is also likely to increase cervical mucus and changes the uterine lining (Hatcher et al., 2007). The ring is inserted deep inside the vagina, where the vaginal muscles hold it in place, and moisture and body heat activate the release of hormones. Each ring is left in place for three weeks and then taken out for one week, during which a woman typically has her period. The used ring is disposed of and a new ring is put back in after the week break.

Although rare, the NuvaRing may fall out of the vagina during a bowel movement, tampon use, or vaginal intercourse. If this happens and the ring has been out less than three hours, it should be washed and immediately be reinserted. If the ring falls out for more than three hours, a backup method of contraception should be used, because contraceptive effectiveness may be reduced.

Researchers continue to evaluate whether the NuvaRing can be used as continuous-use method, although it is not approved for this type of use at present (Hatcher et al., 2011; Mulders & Dieben, 2001). A longer-use vaginal ring that is continuously inserted after being removed for 1 week every month (unlike the shorter-use one that is disposed of after the one-week break) is currently available (Hatcher et al., 2011).

Effectiveness

Effectiveness rates for the NuvaRing range from 92 percent to 99.7 percent (Hatcher et al., 2011). Effectiveness rates may be lower when other medications are taken, when the unopened package is exposed to high temperatures or direct sunlight, or when the ring is left in the vagina for more than three weeks.

Advantages

The NuvaRing is highly effective, does not interfere with spontaneity, increases menstrual regularity, and reduces the flow of menstruation, menstrual cramps, and premenstrual syndrome (Hatcher et al., 2011). It is easy to use and provides lower levels of hormones than some of the other combined hormone methods. In addition, NuvaRing may also offer some protection from pelvic inflammatory disease and various cancers.

Disadvantages

A prescription is necessary to use NuvaRing, and it offers no protection against STIs. Health Canada has recently released new warnings for users of the NuvaRing. It is not recommended for women who smoke, are over the age of 35, have cardiovascular conditions, high blood pressure, migraines, or issues with diabetes or pancreatic function (Health Canada, 2014). In addition, it requires genital touching and may cause a variety of adverse effects, including breakthrough bleeding, weight gain or loss, breast tenderness, nausea, mood changes, headaches, decreased sexual desire, increased vaginal irritation and discharge, and a risk for toxic shock syndrome (Hatcher et al., 2011; Lopez et al., 2008; Health Canada, 2014). It may also take up to one to two months for a woman's period to return after she stops using the vaginal ring, and periods may not be regular for up to six months.

Cross-Cultural Use

NuvaRing was first approved in the Netherlands in 2001 and has since been approved by many other European countries. Australia approved the NuvaRing in 2007, which brought the total number of countries using NuvaRing to 32 ("NuvaRing Now Available for Australian Women," 2007). In some countries, usage levels may be low because the NuvaRing requires genital touching. Even so, cross-cultural research has found that the NuvaRing is highly effective, and users report high levels of satisfaction with this method (Brucker et al., 2008; Bruni et al., 2008; Merki-Feld & Hund, 2007; Novák et al., 2003).

Hormonal Patch

The **Ortho Evra patch** is a hormonal method of birth control that is approved for use in Canada. It is a thin, peach-coloured patch that sticks to the skin and time-releases hormones into the

NuvaRing	Ortho Evra patch
A small plastic contraceptive ring that is inserted into the vagina once a month and releases a constant dose of estrogen and progestin.	A thin, peach-coloured patch that sticks to the skin and time-releases synthetic estrogen and progestin into the bloodstream to inhibit ovulation, increase cervical mucus, and render the uterus inhospitable; also referred to as the "patch."

bloodstream. The hormonal patch costs approximately $15 to $75 per month to use.

How It Works

Like other hormonal methods, the Ortho Evra patch uses synthetic estrogen and progestin to inhibit ovulation, increase cervical mucus, and render the uterus inhospitable to implantation. The patch is placed on the buttock, stomach, upper arm, or torso (excluding the breast area) once a week for three weeks, followed by a patch-free week (break week), which usually causes a woman to have her period. A woman can maintain an active lifestyle with the patch in place—she can swim, shower, use saunas, and exercise without the patch falling off (Burkman, 2002; Zacur et al., 2002).

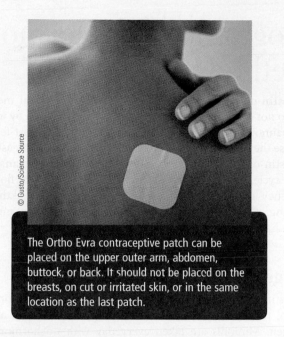
© Gusto/Science Source

The Ortho Evra contraceptive patch can be placed on the upper outer arm, abdomen, buttock, or back. It should not be placed on the breasts, on cut or irritated skin, or in the same location as the last patch.

REAL Research A study on the knowledge and beliefs about contraception in Latina women found that less than 50 percent of Latinas perceived birth control pills to be safe, and they had high levels of uncertainty and negative beliefs about the patch, IUDs, and hormonal injectables (Venkat et al., 2008). Compared with other ethnic groups, Latina women are more likely to overrate the risks associated with contraceptive use.

Effectiveness

Effectiveness rates for the Ortho Evra patch range from 92 percent to 99.7 percent (Hatcher et al., 2011). It may be less effective in women who are significantly overweight (Hatcher et al., 2011; Zieman et al., 2002), and as with other hormonal methods, certain medications can decrease effectiveness.

Advantages

The Ortho Evra patch is highly effective, does not interfere with spontaneity, increases menstrual regularity, and reduces menstrual flow, menstrual cramps, and premenstrual syndrome (Hatcher et al., 2011). Unlike other hormonal methods, the patch has a more than 90 percent perfect dosing level because it is applied directly to the skin (Burkman, 2002).

Disadvantages

The Ortho Evra patch has been found to expose women to higher levels of estrogen than typical birth control pills (Hitti, 2008; U.S. Food and Drug Administration, 2008), offers no protection from STIs, and may cause a variety of adverse effects, including breakthrough bleeding, breast tenderness, nausea, mood changes, changes in sexual desire, skin reactions, or headaches (Hatcher et al., 2011). Users of the hormonal patch may also be more at risk for the development of blood clots (Hitti, 2008; U.S. Food and Drug Administration, 2008). Beginning in 2005, lawsuits were filed against the patch's manufacturer, Ortho McNeil, claiming the device caused strokes and blood clots. Any woman with a history of or risk for blood clots should fully discuss her medical history with health care providers before using the Ortho Evra patch. Finally, because the patch is worn on the skin, it is nearly impossible to conceal, and it can collect fuzz and lint from the user's clothing. Because it is peach-coloured, it is also readily apparent on darker skin.

Cross-Cultural Use

We do not know a lot about Ortho Evra's use outside of North America because it is fairly new. However, early estimates have found that approximately 2 million women worldwide use the contraceptive patch (Bestic, 2005).

Review Questions

1 Explain how combination hormonal methods of contraception work.

2 Identify three combined hormonal contraceptive methods in order of their effectiveness rates.

3 What are extended-cycle birth control pills? How do they work?

4 How have health care providers been using regular birth control pills for extended-cycle use?

5 Identify the advantages and disadvantages of combined-hormonal contraceptive methods.

6 What do we know about the cross-cultural usage of combined-hormone contraceptive methods?

Progestin-Only Hormone Methods for Women

Progestin-only birth control methods are hormonal methods that do not contain estrogen. The methods can be used by women who cannot take estrogen or by women who are breast-feeding, because the hormones do not affect the production of breast milk. Progestin-only birth control works by changing a woman's menstrual cycle, which may result in changes in menstrual flow and frequency of periods, as well as an increase in breakthrough bleeding. Over time, many users of progestin-only methods report having no periods at all.

Progestin-Only Pills

Progestin-only pills (**minipills**) are similar to combination birth control pills, except they contain a progestin hormone and no estrogen. Minipills are taken every day with no hormone-free days (Hatcher et al., 2011).

How They Work

Similar to combination birth control pills, minipills work by inhibiting ovulation, thickening cervical mucus, and decreasing Fallopian tube cilia movement and the buildup of the endometrial lining.

Effectiveness

Effectiveness rates for minipills range from 92 percent to 99.7 percent (Hatcher et al., 2011).

Advantages

Minipills contain a lower overall hormone level than combination birth control pills and can be safely used by almost all women, including those who are older than 35, are overweight, smoke, have high blood pressure, have a history of blood clots, or women who are breast-feeding (Hatcher et al., 2011). They also reduce menstrual symptoms and may eliminate periods altogether. Once discontinued, fertility is quickly restored.

Disadvantages

Because minipills contain lower hormone levels, they require obsessive regularity in pill taking (Hatcher et al., 2011). They offer no protection from STIs and may cause several adverse effects, including menstrual cycle disturbances (such as breakthrough bleeding or spotting), headaches, nausea, weight gain or loss, breast tenderness, decreased sexual desire, and an increased risk for ovarian cysts (Hatcher et al., 2011). Because progestin affects cilia movement in the Fallopian tubes, women who get pregnant while taking minipills have a higher rate of ectopic pregnancy compared with women taking combination birth control pills (see Chapter 6 for more information about ectopic pregnancy). Finally, many pharmacies do not stock minipills, so they may be more difficult to find.

Subdermal Implants

Subdermal contraceptive implants involve surgically inserting under the skin a matchstick-sized rod that time-releases progestin. **Norplant** was the first such method introduced. However, because of multiple lawsuits and court battles, Norplant was withdrawn from the U.S. market in 2002. As of 2010, the only implant available in the United States is a system called Implanon. It is, however, not currently available in Canada. Several other versions are currently in development, both within and outside the United States. The cost of Implanon and the insertion ranges from $400 to $800. Removal ranges from $75 to $150.

How They Work

A subdermal contraceptive implant is inserted during the first five days of a woman's menstrual cycle (to ensure she is not pregnant). The implant time-releases progestin, and like other hormonal methods, it works by suppressing ovulation, thickening cervical mucus, and changing the endometrial lining. The Implanon implant can be left in place for three years. Once removed, ovulation usually returns within approximately six weeks (Makarainen et al., 1998).

Effectiveness

Effectiveness rates for Implanon are approximately 99 percent. Like other hormonal methods, effectiveness rates may be lower in women who are significantly overweight.

Advantages

Implanon is a highly effective, long-lasting, easily reversible contraceptive method with a rapid onset of protection (Hatcher et al., 2007). It can decrease menstrual flow, cramping, and risk for endometrial cancer, and can be used by women who are unable to take estrogen. In addition, Implanon can be left in place for up to three years but can be removed before this.

Disadvantages

Implanon requires a prescription and medical office visit. Possible adverse effects include irregular or heavy bleeding, especially

---

progestin-only birth control method	**minipills**	**subdermal contraceptive implant**
Contraceptive hormonal method that does not contain estrogen and works by changing a woman's menstrual cycle.	A type of birth control pill that contains only synthetic progesterone and no estrogen.	Contraceptive implant that time-releases a constant dose of progestin to inhibit ovulation.

within the first 6 to 12 months of usage. Other possible adverse effects include headaches, dizziness, nausea, weight gain, development of ovarian cysts, decreases in sexual desire, vaginal dryness, arm pain, and bleeding from the injection site (Hatcher et al., 2011). Removal may be difficult and generally takes longer than insertion. Researchers are working on a system that involves self-dissolving cylinders so that removal is unnecessary.

Cross-Cultural Use

Subdermal implants are more commonly used in less-developed regions of the world (see Figure 6.4). They are approved in more than 60 countries and have been used by more than 11 million women worldwide (Hatcher et al., 2011; Meirik et al., 2003). Norplant and Implanon have been used throughout Europe, Latin America, Australia, and Asia.

In the United Kingdom, health care providers have switched from Implanon to a new contraceptive implant, Nexplanon (Mansour, 2010; Rowlands et al., 2010). Nexplanon is easier to insert than Implanon, is good for three years, and has a rapid return to fertility after use.

Hormonal Injectables

The most commonly used hormonal injectable is depo-medroxyprogesterone acetate (DMPA, or **Depo-Provera**; DEP-poe PRO-vair-uh), which was approved by for contraceptive use in 2004 (Hatcher et al., 2007). Depo-Provera is injected once every three months, and each injection costs anywhere from $35 to $70 (an initial examination/visit may cost anywhere from $35 to $250, although subsequent visits will be less).

How It Works

Depo-Provera is a progestin injected into the muscle of a woman's arm or buttock. It begins working within 24 hours. Like other hormonal methods, it works by suppressing ovulation, thickening cervical mucus, and changing the endometrial lining.

Effectiveness

Effectiveness rates for Depo-Provera range from 97 percent to 99.7 percent (Hatcher et al., 2011).

Advantages

Depo-Provera is highly effective; does not interfere with spontaneity; reduces menstrual flow, cramping, and premenstrual syndrome; does not contain estrogen; lasts for three months; is only moderately expensive; and is reversible (Hatcher et al., 2011). In addition, users need only four shots per year.

Disadvantages

Women who use Depo-Provera must schedule office visits every three months for their injections, and they experience a range of adverse effects, including irregular bleeding and spotting, fatigue, dizzy spells, weakness, headaches or migraines, weight gain (it is estimated that a woman will gain an average of 2.4 kilograms [5.4 pounds] in the first year of Depo use), and a decrease in bone density (Hatcher et al., 2011; Pitts & Emans, 2008). More recent studies have found that bone loss is reversible after a woman stops using Depo-Provera (Kaunitz et al., 2008; Pitts & Emans, 2008). In addition, it may take a couple months to restore fertility after the last injection (Hatcher et al., 2011; Kaunitz, 2002).

Cross-Cultural Use

Like implants, injectable contraception is more commonly used in less-developed countries (see Figure 6.4). In some regions, such as Eastern and Southern Africa, injectable contraception is the most popular method, accounting for almost half of all contraceptive use. Depo-Provera has been approved for use in more than 80 countries, including Botswana, Denmark, Finland, Great Britain, France, Sweden, Mexico, Norway, Germany, New Zealand, South Africa, and Belgium (Francoeur & Noonan, 2004; Hatcher et al., 2004). In addition, another combination injectable, Lunelle, is popular cross-culturally but is not available within the United States or Canada.

Depo-Provera
Depo-medroxyprogesterone, an injectable contraceptive that prevents ovulation and thickens cervical mucus.

Review Questions

1 Explain how minipills differ from combined hormone birth control pills.

2 Explain how minipills, subdermal implants, and hormonal injectables work to prevent pregnancy.

3 Identify the advantages and disadvantages of each of the progestin-only hormone methods.

4 What do we know about the cross-cultural usage of progestin-only hormone methods?

Contraception and Abortion

Chemical Methods for Women

Spermicides come in a variety of forms, including creams, suppositories, gels, foams, foaming tablets, capsules, and films. Nonoxynol-9 is a spermicide that has been used for many years. It is available over the counter in many forms (creams, gels, suppositories, film, and condoms with spermicide) and can be used alone or in conjunction with another contraceptive method. However, as you saw from the earlier Sex in Real Life feature, there has been some controversy surrounding the use of nonoxynol-9. The cost for most spermicides ranges from $5 to $10.

How They Work

Spermicides contain two components: One is an inert base such as jelly, cream, foam, or film that holds the spermicide close to the cervix; the second is the spermicide itself. Foam, jelly, cream, and film are usually inserted into the vagina with either an applicator or a finger. **Vaginal contraceptive film** contains nonoxynol-9 and comes in a variety of package sizes. The film is wrapped around the index finger and inserted into the vagina.

Suppositories are inserted in the vagina 10 to 30 minutes before intercourse to allow time for the outer covering to melt. It is important to read manufacturer's directions for spermicide use carefully. Douching and tampon use should be avoided for six to eight hours after the use of spermicides because they interfere with effectiveness rates.

Effectiveness

Effectiveness rates for spermicides range from 71 percent to 82 percent. However, effectiveness depends on the type of spermicide and how consistently it is used. Overall, foam is more effective than jelly, cream, film, or suppositories.

vaginal contraceptive film
Spermicidal contraceptive film that is placed in the vagina.

© Janell Carroll

Safe, effective birth control you both can't feel!™

VCF
Dissolving
Vaginal Contraceptive Film
FOR PREVENTION OF PREGNANCY
• Begins to dissolve instantly
• No hormonal side effects
• Kills sperm on contact
• Sexually enhancing
Lasts up to 3 hours
9 SINGLE SEALED FILMS
Contains the Spermicide D

Vaginal contraceptive film is a paper-thin translucent film that dissolves in the vagina and releases spermicide.

Advantages

Spermicides do not require a prescription and can be easily purchased in drug stores, can be discreetly carried in a pocket or purse, do not interfere with a woman's hormones, can be inserted during foreplay, provide lubrication during intercourse, have minimal adverse effects, and can be used by a woman who is breast-feeding.

Disadvantages

Spermicides must be used each time a couple engages in vaginal intercourse, which may be expensive depending on frequency of intercourse. In addition, there is an increase in postcoital drip and some couples may be allergic or have adverse reactions. Spermicides often have an unpleasant taste, and they may cause vaginal skin irritations or an increase in urinary tract infections (Hatcher et al., 2011).

Cross-Cultural Use

Spermicides are widely used in some countries, including Argentina, Australia, Colombia, Costa Rica, Cuba, and many European and Scandinavian countries (Francoeur & Noonan, 2004). However, in many other countries, including Botswana, Brazil, Canada, China, Hong Kong, Japan, Kenya, and Puerto Rico, spermicides are not widely used, probably because of the relatively high cost or required genital touching.

Review Questions

1 Identify the various forms of spermicidal contraception.

2 What are some of the risks and controversies surrounding the use of nonoxynol-9 spermicide?

3 Explain how spermicides work and discuss effectiveness rates.

4 Identify the advantages and disadvantages of spermicidal contraceptive use.

Intrauterine Methods for Women

An IUD is a small device made of flexible plastic that is placed in the uterus to prevent pregnancy (Figure 6.8). The Dalkon Shield was a popular type of IUD up until 1975, when the A.H. Robins Company recommended that it be removed from all women who were using them. Users experienced severe pain, bleeding, and pelvic inflammatory disease, which led to sterility in some cases. The problems with the Dalkon Shield were primarily caused by the multifilament string that allowed bacteria to enter into the uterus through the cervix. Only two IUDs are currently available in Canada, the ParaGard and Mirena Intrauterine System.

Data from a 2009 Canadian National Survey found that 2.3 percent of women who use contraception use an IUD, with the highest use (5.8 percent) in women aged 30–39 (Black et al., 2009). Increases in use are due to many factors, including higher safety standards, more physicians and health care providers being trained in insertion and removal techniques, immigration from areas where IUDs are popular (e.g., Mexico), increased advertising, and positive word of mouth from other users (Hubacher et al., 2010).

The cost for an IUD, can range from $400 to $800. Typically, the Mirena IUD costs more than the ParaGard. These are not covered in Canada under general health care insurance, but they are often covered though private employee benefits.

How They Work

The ParaGard IUD is placed in the uterus and causes an increase in copper ions and enzymes, which impairs sperm function and prevents fertilization (Hatcher et al., 2011). It can be left in place for up to 12 years. The Mirena IUD time-releases progestin, which thickens the cervical mucus, inhibits sperm survival, and suppresses the endometrium (Hatcher et al., 2011). It can be left in place for up to five years. The IUD string hangs down from the cervix, and a woman can check the string to make sure the IUD is

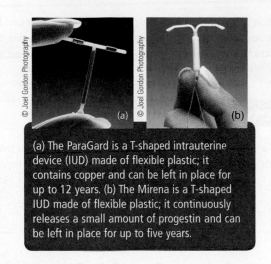

(a) The ParaGard is a T-shaped intrauterine device (IUD) made of flexible plastic; it contains copper and can be left in place for up to 12 years. (b) The Mirena is a T-shaped IUD made of flexible plastic; it continuously releases a small amount of progestin and can be left in place for up to five years.

still properly in place. Both IUDs may also interfere with the implantation of a fertilized ova.

Effectiveness

Effectiveness rates for IUDs range from 99.2 percent to 99.9 percent (Hatcher et al., 2011).

Advantages

IUDs are the least expensive method of contraception over time, and they do not interfere with spontaneity. In addition, they have long-lasting contraceptive effects. In addition, the Mirena IUS reduces or eliminates menstrual flow and cramping. IUDs can also be used as emergency contraception (we discuss emergency contraception later in this chapter). Once the IUD is removed, fertility is quickly restored. IUDs can be used during breast-feeding.

Disadvantages

IUDs require moderately painful insertion and removal procedures, may cause irregular bleeding patterns and spotting (and heavier periods if using the ParaGard IUD), offer no protection from STIs, and carry a small risk for uterine perforation. The IUD may also be felt by a sexual partner.

Cross-Cultural Use

Worldwide, IUDs are the second most popular contraceptive method (behind female sterilization), with 14 percent of women relying on this method ("World Contraceptive Use 2009," 2009). However, they are more popular in less developed regions of the world (see Figure 6.4). Whereas 2.3 percent of women in Canada and 5.5 percent of women in the United States use IUDs, 15 percent of women in Western Europe, 12 percent in Northern Europe, and 9 percent in Southern Europe use IUDs (Hubacher et al., 2010). The IUD has high usage rates in many Asian countries, Israel, Cuba, Egypt, and Estonia ("World Contraceptive Use 2009," 2009). The newer Mirena IUD has been available in Europe for

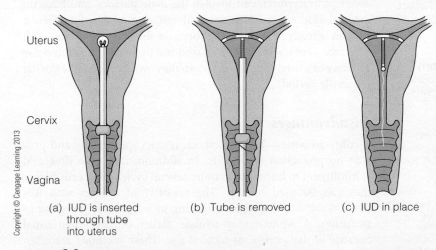

Uterus

Cervix

Vagina

Copyright © Cengage Learning 2013

(a) IUD is inserted through tube into uterus   (b) Tube is removed   (c) IUD in place

FIGURE 6.8 Insertion of an intrauterine device: (a) IUD is inserted through tube into the uterus, (b) tube is removed, (c) IUD is in place.

more than ten years, and it is estimated that millions of women have used it throughout the world. Overall, IUD usage rates vary depending on how much the devices are marketed and advertised.

GyneFix, an IUD containing a flexible row of copper beads instead of a rigid plastic frame like other IUDs, has been used for many years in countries such as Asia, Latin America, and Africa (Wildemeersch & Andrade, 2010).

Natural Methods for Women and Men

Natural methods of contraception do not alter any physiological function. They include natural family planning and **fertility awareness**, withdrawal, and abstinence.

Fertility Awareness–Based Methods

Fertility awareness–based methods involve identifying a woman's fertile period and either abstaining from vaginal intercourse or using another contraceptive method during this time. With the **rhythm method,** a couple simply keeps track of a woman's cycle; other, more intensive methods involve charting and recording physical fertility signs (such as monitoring daily **basal body temperature [BBT]** and checking cervical mucus; Hatcher et al., 2011). Typically, these intensive methods are referred to as **natural family planning**, or the **symptothermal method.**

How They Work

With the symptothermal method, a woman takes her BBT every morning before she gets out of bed and records it on a BBT chart. Changes in hormonal levels cause body temperature to increase 0.2°–0.4°C (0.4°–0.8°F) immediately before ovulation, and it remains elevated until menstruation begins. A woman using this method monitors her cervical mucus, which becomes thin and stretchy during ovulation to help transport sperm. At other times of the month, cervical mucus is thicker. After six months of consistent charting, a woman will be able to estimate the approximate time of ovulation, and she can then either abstain from vaginal intercourse or use contraception during her high-risk times (usually this period is between one and two weeks).

Effectiveness

Effectiveness rates for fertility awareness–based methods range from 88 percent to 97 percent (Hatcher et al., 2011). However, effectiveness rates depend on the accuracy of identifying a fertile period and a couple's ability to avoid intercourse (or use another contraceptive method) during this time.

Advantages

Fertility awareness–based methods are an acceptable form of birth control for those who cannot use another method for religious reasons. They can teach couples about the menstrual cycle, are inexpensive, may encourage couples to communicate more about contraception, can involve the male partner, and have no medical side effects. This method can also be helpful when a woman is ready to get pregnant because she may be familiar with when she is ovulating. Couples who use these methods often use a variety of sexual expressions when they avoid intercourse during the fertile period.

Disadvantages

Fertility awareness–based methods restrict spontaneity and provide no protection from STIs. In addition, they take time and commitment to learn, and require several cycles of records before they can be used reliably. The majority of failures with this method are due to couples engaging in intercourse too close to ovulation. A woman may ovulate earlier or later than usual because of diet, stress, or alcohol use. These methods are often best suited for those needing to space pregnancies, rather than for those who want to avoid pregnancy.

fertility awareness
Basal body temperature charting used in conjunction with another method of contraception.

fertility awareness–based methods
Contraceptive or family planning method that involves identifying a fertile period in a woman's cycle and either avoiding intercourse or using contraception during this time.

rhythm method
A contraceptive method that involves calculating the period of ovulation and avoiding sexual intercourse around this time.

basal body temperature (BBT)
The body's resting temperature used to calculate ovulation in the symptothermal method of contraception.

natural family planning
A contraceptive method that involves calculating ovulation and avoiding sexual intercourse during ovulation and at other unsafe times.

symptothermal method
A contraceptive method that involves monitoring both cervical mucus and basal body temperature to determine ovulation.

Cross-Cultural Use

Fertility awareness–based contraceptive methods are popular around the world. Mostly this is because they are inexpensive and do not require much assistance from health care providers. These methods are commonly used in parts of Africa, Western Asia, and Eastern Europe. These methods may be the only form of acceptable contraception in predominantly Catholic countries such as Ireland, Brazil, and the Philippines. In the Philippines, natural family planning and the rhythm method are thought to improve a couple's relationship because they need to work together to use the method (remember our earlier discussion about pressure from the Church against using modern methods of contraception in the Philippines; Leyson, 2004). Societal issues and marketing may also affect the use of this method. For example, cultural resistance to condom use has increased the popularity of these fertility awareness–based methods in Kenya, where they are the most commonly used contraceptive method (Brockman, 2004). Today, many women's groups from the United States travel to developing countries to teach fertility awareness–based methods.

Withdrawal

Withdrawal, or **coitus interruptus**, involves withdrawing the penis from the vagina before ejaculation. Although withdrawal is a popular contraceptive method, many couples use it because of convenience and dissatisfaction with other methods (Whittaker et al., 2010). When women in one study were asked about using withdrawal, 56 percent reported they had used it as a contraceptive method (Hatcher et al., 2007). However, many couples express anxiety about using it because it relies on the male to pull out in time. Withdrawal can be used alone or in conjunction with another contraceptive method.

How It Works

Withdrawal does not require any advance preparation. A couple engages in vaginal intercourse; before ejaculation, the male withdraws his penis away from the vaginal opening of the woman. The ejaculate does not enter the vagina.

Effectiveness

Effectiveness rates for withdrawal range from 73 percent to 96 percent (Hatcher et al., 2011).

Advantages

Withdrawal is an acceptable method of birth control for those who cannot use another method for religious reasons. It is free, does not require any devices or chemicals, and is better than using no method at all (Hatcher et al., 2011). In addition, it may be a good method for couples who don't have another method available.

Disadvantages

Withdrawal provides no protection from STIs, may contribute to ejaculatory problems, and can be difficult and stressful to use. Many men experience a mild to extreme "clouding of consciousness" just before orgasm when physical movements become involuntary (Hatcher et al., 2011). This method also requires trust from the female partner.

Cross-Cultural Use

Withdrawal is a popular contraceptive method throughout the world. It is one of the most frequently used methods in Austria, the Czech Republic, Greece, Ireland, and Italy (Francoeur & Noonan, 2004). In Azerbaijan, 64 percent of contraceptive users rely on withdrawal ("World Contraceptive Use 2009," 2009). Overall, it is a popular contraceptive method for couples with limited contraceptive choices or for those who are reluctant to use modern methods of contraception. In many countries, such as Iran, a lack of education and misconceptions about withdrawal has led to low usage rates (Rahnama et al., 2010). Many Iranian men and women believe that withdrawal does not work and will lead to multiple health problems, which it does not.

Abstinence

Abstinence (or not engaging in vaginal intercourse at all) is the only 100 percent effective contraceptive method (Hatcher et al., 2011). It has probably been the most important factor in controlling fertility throughout history. Abstinence may be primary (never having engaged in vaginal intercourse) or secondary (not currently engaging in vaginal intercourse). Couples may choose abstinence to prevent pregnancy, to protect against STIs, or for many other reasons.

---

coitus interruptus
A contraceptive method that involves withdrawal of the penis from the vagina before ejaculation.

Review Questions

1 Differentiate between the various types of fertility awareness–based methods. What factors influence the effectiveness rates of these methods?

2 Explain how changes in cervical mucus and body temperature provide information about ovulation.

3 Explain the use and effectiveness of withdrawal as a contraceptive method.

4 Identify the advantages and disadvantages of natural contraceptive methods.

5 Explain the cross-cultural use of natural contraceptive methods.

Permanent Contraceptive Methods

The primary difference between **sterilization** and other methods of contraception is that sterilization is typically considered irreversible. Although some people have been able to have their sterilizations reversed, this can be expensive and time-consuming (Peterson, 2008). The majority of people who request sterilization reversals do so because they have remarried and desire children with their new partners.

Female Sterilization

Female sterilization, or **tubal sterilization**, is the most widely used method of birth control in the world (Hatcher et al., 2011). In a tubal sterilization, a health care provider may close or block both Fallopian tubes so that the ovum and sperm cannot meet. Blocking the tubes can be done with **cauterization;** a ring, band, or clamp (which pinches the tube together); or **ligation** or non-surgical procedures that involve placing inserts to block the Fallopian tubes. In Canada, female sterilization procedures are generally done with the use of a laparoscope through a small incision either under the navel or lower in the abdomen. After the procedure, a woman continues to ovulate, but the ovum does not enter the uterus.

Another non-surgical sterilization method for women includes Essure, which was approved in 2001. Essure is a tiny, spring-like device that is threaded into the Fallopian tubes (Figure 6.9). Within three months, the body's own tissue grows around the device, blocking fertilization. A woman using this method must undergo testing to make sure that the Fallopian tubes are fully blocked. Essure is considered an irreversible method of female sterilization (Hatcher et al., 2011; Ledger, 2004).

Overall, the majority of women who choose permanent sterilization are content with their decision to do so (although the risk for regret is highest in women who undergo these procedures before age 30; Jamieson et al., 2002; Peterson, 2008). Interestingly, in Canada there are no current guidelines as to who may or may not receive sterilization. For many women who may wish to use sterilization as a permanent solution to birth control, they may have difficulty finding a physician willing to assist them (Papamarko, 2011). There are no hormonal changes, and ovaries continue to work and produce estrogen (Papamarko, 2011). Women maintain their levels of sexual interest and desire after permanent sterilization and report more positive than negative sexual side effects (Costello et al., 2002).

Male Sterilization

Male sterilization, or **vasectomy**, blocks the flow of sperm through the vas deferens (see Chapter 4). Typically, this procedure is simpler, less expensive, and has lower rates of complications than female sterilization (Shih et al., 2011). It is recommended that men wait for approximately three months post vasectomy before relying on its success as a permanent form of birth control. A "non-surgical" vasectomy is also an option, however; it is still done via a puncture of the scrotum, so that access to the vas deferens for ligation and cauterization is possible.

After a vasectomy, the testes continue to produce viable sperm cells, but with nowhere to go, they die and are absorbed by the body. Semen normally contains approximately 98 percent fluid and 2 percent sperm, and after a vasectomy, the man still ejaculates semen, but the semen contains no sperm (there is no overall change in volume or texture of the semen after a vasectomy). All other functions, such as the manufacturing of testosterone, erections, and urination, are unaffected by a vasectomy procedure.

The surgery for a vasectomy is performed as **outpatient surgery** with local anesthesia. Two small incisions about a 0.65–1.25 centimetres (one-fourth to one-half inch) long are made in the scrotum, and the vas deferens is clipped or cauterized, which usually takes approximately 20 minutes (Figure 6.10). Men are advised to use another form of contraception for 12 weeks after a vasectomy to ensure that there is no sperm left in the ejaculate (Hatcher et al., 2011). Typically, one or two repeat semen analyses are required to evaluate whether there is viable sperm in the sample. Semen samples can be collected during masturbation or through the use of a special condom during vaginal intercourse. In 2008, the U.S. FDA approved a post-vasectomy home sperm test called SpermCheck, which allows a man to test his semen sample at home rather than returning to a medical facility (Coppola et al., 2010). At present, this home sperm test is not available in Canada.

---

sterilization
Surgical contraceptive method that causes permanent infertility.

tubal sterilization
A surgical procedure in which the Fallopian tubes are cut, tied, or cauterized for permanent contraception.

cauterization
A sterilization procedure that involves burning or searing the Fallopian tubes or vas deferens for permanent sterilization.

ligation
A sterilization procedure that involves the tying or binding of the Fallopian tubes or vas deferens.

vasectomy
A surgical procedure in which each vas deferens is cut, tied, or cauterized for permanent contraception.

outpatient surgery
Surgery performed in the hospital or doctor's office, after which a patient is allowed to return home; inpatient surgery requires hospitalization.

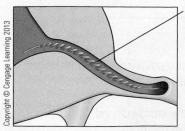

Essure is inserted into the Fallopian tube

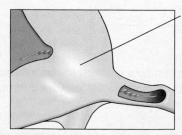

Body tissue grows into the Essure micro-insert, blocking the Fallopian tube

Copyright © Cengage Learning 2013

FIGURE 6.9 Essure, a permanent contraceptive method, is inserted into the Fallopian tubes in order to block the sperm from meeting the ovum.

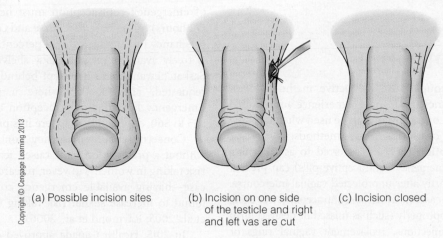

(a) Possible incision sites

(b) Incision on one side of the testicle and right and left vas are cut

(c) Incision closed

FIGURE **6.10** In a vasectomy, each vas deferens is clipped, cut, or cauterized.

After a vasectomy, a man may experience swelling, bleeding, bruising, or pain, but generally these subside within two weeks (Hatcher et al., 2011). The cost for the procedure varies widely, depending on where it is done. Overall, the cost for a vasectomy ranges from $300 to $1000 and is covered by provincial health insurance plans.

Effectiveness

Effectiveness for both male and female sterilization procedures ranges from 99 percent to 99.9 percent (Hatcher et al., 2011). Tubal sterilizations are effective immediately, whereas vasectomies require semen analysis for 12 weeks after the procedure to ensure no viable sperm remains.

Advantages

Sterilization is a highly effective permanent method of contraception. It offers a quick recovery, few long-term adverse effects, and once completed, does not interfere with spontaneity (Shih et al., 2011).

Disadvantages

Sterilization requires medical intervention and/or surgery, can be expensive, provides no protection from STIs, and is considered irreversible.

Cross-Cultural Use

Worldwide, female sterilization is used by more women than any other contraceptive method (see Figure 6.4). However, this procedure is more popular in less-developed regions of the world. Overall, female sterilizations are more popular than male, even though these procedures are often expensive and have more potential risks. In China, whereas 32 percent of women undergo sterilization, only 6 percent of men do (Wu, 2010).

In Brazil and India, nearly two fifths of women elect sterilizations, and most women do this early in their reproductive life (Brazilian women have the surgery at about 30 years old, whereas Indian women have it at about 26 years old; Leone & Padmadas, 2007). The Essure method has been used outside of Canada and the United States in many countries in Europe, as well as Mexico, Brazil, Venezuela, Chile, and Uruguay.

In countries where family planning clinics are sparse, many women travel long distances to be sterilized. In some countries, female sterilization procedures are outpatient procedures using local anesthesia (Hatcher et al., 2007). As we have discussed, access to and promotion of a certain method also contribute to its popularity. In addition, cultural acceptance of female sterilization has also led to higher rates of usage (Leone & Padmadas, 2007).

Review Questions

1 Identify the two main differences between sterilization and other contraceptive methods.

2 Explain some of the procedures used for female sterilization.

3 Explain some of the procedures used for male sterilization.

4 What are the advantages and disadvantages of sterilization as a contraceptive method?

5 Is sterilization a popular contraceptive method outside North America? Explain.

Emergency Contraception

Many individuals and couples use ineffective methods in an attempt to avoid pregnancy, and some experience unintended pregnancies. Emergency contraception can be used when a couple fails to use contraception or uses ineffective methods.

Emergency contraception (EC; also referred to as "morning after" contraception, or emergency contraceptive pills) can prevent pregnancy when taken shortly after unprotected vaginal intercourse. It is designed to be used in cases in which no contraception was used, contraception was used improperly (such as missed or delayed birth control pills, hormonal injections, replacement vaginal rings or patches), a male condom slipped or broke, a female condom or barrier device was improperly inserted or dislodged during intercourse, an IUD was expelled, or a sexual assault occurred (Hatcher et al., 2011). There are some misconceptions about emergency contraception. Although it is referred to as the "morning after pill," this is misleading because the pill can be used up to five days after unprotected intercourse and not just the morning after. In addition, it is important to point out that emergency contraception does *not* cause an abortion. Emergency contraception is birth control in that it works to *prevent* pregnancy (we will talk more about abortion later in this chapter).

There are several methods of emergency contraception, but the most familiar one in Canada is referred to as Plan B. It is a progestin-only method that works by inhibiting ovulation, thickening cervical mucus, and reducing endometrial buildup. Originally, Plan B involved taking two pills, 12 hours apart, but recently, Plan B One-Step became available, which requires taking only one pill. Plan B One-Step is gradually replacing the original Plan B. Another progestin-only emergency contraceptive method, Next Choice, is the generic equivalent to Plan B. All of these methods

> **emergency contraception**
> Contraception that is designed to prevent pregnancy after unprotected vaginal intercourse.

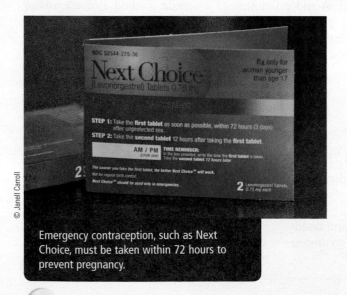

Emergency contraception, such as Next Choice, must be taken within 72 hours to prevent pregnancy.

© Janell Carroll

of emergency contraception must be taken within three days (72 hours) of vaginal intercourse and can reduce the likelihood of pregnancy by 81 percent to 90 percent. In most provinces Plan B is freely available on pharmacy shelves, with the exceptions of Saskatchewan where it is kept behind the counter and must be requested, and Quebec where a prescription is required. Emergency hormonal contraception costs vary anywhere from $35 to $60, depending on where it is purchased.

Concerns about emergency contraception being available without a prescription have raised fears about increased sexual risk taking in women. However, research has shown this is not the case—having available emergency contraception has not been found to increase sexual risk taking (M. Gold et al., 2004; Hu et al., 2005; Raymond et al., 2006).

In 2015, Health Canada approved ella, a new, non-hormonal form of emergency contraception. Ella is a single-dose pill that can prevent pregnancy up to five days after unprotected intercourse. The benefit of ella over Plan B is that it has a higher effectiveness rate (98 percent) and a longer window in which it can be used (five versus three days). Ella was approved in Europe in 2009, and today it is available in many countries around the world, including Austria, Belgium, Bulgaria, Czech Republic, Denmark, Finland, France, Germany, Greece, Guadeloupe, Hungary, Iceland, Lithuania, Monaco, Netherlands, Norway, Poland, Portugal, Romania, Spain, Sweden, and the United Kingdom.

Other options for emergency contraception include the use of ordinary combination and progestin-only birth control pills or the insertion of a copper-releasing IUD (Hatcher et al., 2011; Jensen, 2008). Birth control pills that contain estrogen and progestin work by inhibiting or delaying ovulation, making the endometrium less hospitable for implantation of an embryo, thickening the cervical mucus, altering the transportability of the Fallopian tubes, and inhibiting fertilization (Hatcher et al., 2011). Birth control pills that contain only progestin impair the ovulatory process but may also interfere with sperm functioning in the female reproductive tract (Hatcher et al., 2007). The IUD insertion method is used much less frequently than other methods of emergency contraception. Adverse effects for emergency insertion of a copper-releasing IUD include abdominal discomfort and vaginal bleeding or spotting (Hatcher et al., 2007).

Using birth control pills as emergency contraception can lead to nausea, vomiting, cramping, breast tenderness, headaches, abdominal pain, fatigue, and dizziness (Hatcher et al., 2011). The incidence of nausea and vomiting is significantly lower in women who use progestin-only pills, such as Plan B One-Step or Next Choice (Hatcher et al., 2007). Women who take emergency contraception may be advised to take anti-nausea medicine, such as dimenhydrinate (Dramamine), before taking their pills.

The typical user of emergency contraception in Canada is in women between the ages of 20 and 24, with the second highest use in women aged 15–19. Most women who use emergency contraception do so because of a failure of other contraceptive methods and do not use it on a regular basis. The availability of emergency contraception without the need for a prescription has increased its use in these age groups (Soon et al. 2005). One note of caution, however: Health Canada has recently issued a warning for a decrease of effectiveness of these types of contraceptives in women over 75 kilograms (165 pounds; Health Canada, 2014). Outside of Canada, emergency contraception is available in many countries throughout the world, including Australia, Belgium, China, Denmark, Finland, France, Greece, Iceland, India, Israel, Jamaica, Libya, New Zealand, the Netherlands, Norway, Portugal, Senegal, South Africa, Sri Lanka, Sweden, Switzerland, Tunisia, the United Kingdom, and many other countries. Emergency contraception is registered in 134 countries around the world, and in 63 of these countries, women have access to emergency contraception without a prescription (Wanja, 2010). It can be purchased without a prescription in countries such as France (since 1999), Norway (since 2000), Sweden (since 2001), the Netherlands (since 2004), and India (since 2005). In France, emergency contraception is free of charge.

Research on global users of emergency contraception found that 24- to 25-year-old Kenyan women are the major users of emergency contraception (Wanja, 2010). High usage was noted during weekends and holidays.

1 Identify the various types of emergency contraception available today.

2 Identify some of the reasons why a woman might use emergency contraception and explain how it works.

3 How soon does a woman need to take emergency contraception to have it be effective?

4 Identify some of the adverse effects of emergency contraception.

5 Who is the typical user of emergency contraception in Canada?

Contraception in the Future

Although many pregnancies occur because couples used no contraception, it is estimated that half of all unintended pregnancies occur because of contraceptive failures (Hatcher et al., 2011). Researchers and scientists today continue to look for effective contraceptive methods that are easy to use and have few or no side effects. A consistent concern has been finding a method that can offer high effectiveness rates along with STI protection (Hatcher et al., 2011).

What's Ahead for Men?

Historically, birth control has been considered a female's responsibility, and that may be why the condom and vasectomy are the only birth control methods available to men. Many feminists claim that the lack of research into male methods of birth control has to do with the fact that birth control research is done primarily by men. As a result, women are responsible for using birth control and must suffer through the potential adverse effects. Others claim that there are few male methods because it is easier to block the one ovum women produce each month than the millions of sperm in each ejaculation. Other arguments cite the fact that chemical contraception may decrease testosterone production, reduce the male sex drive, and harm future sperm production. We do know that many men express a willingness to share the burden of family planning (Mruk, 2008).

As of 2015, research into male contraception continued to explore chemical and hormonal contraception, reversible vasectomies, vas deferens plugs, herbal contraceptives, and vaccines. One of the most promising areas of research in male contraception is in the use of hormonal implants and injections for men. Subdermal implants are placed under the skin, and testosterone injections are used to suppress pituitary hormones responsible for spermatogenesis. The first large, placebo-controlled study using these methods found successful reductions in sperm production (Mommers et al., 2008). This method was well tolerated by the men in the study, and sperm production was back to normal levels within 15 weeks of discontinuing the method.

Research continues to explore another injectable implant, RISUG (reversible inhibition of sperm under guidance). RISUG is currently in advanced Phase III clinical trials in India (Jha et al., 2009; Kumar et al., 2008; Lohiya et al., 2010). It is injected into the vas deferens where it blocks the passage of sperm. Ongoing research will determine whether this will be a viable contraceptive option for men. Other implants, such as the Intra-Vas Device, are also being studied (Crawford, 2008; Sun et al., 2011).

Gossypol, a non-hormonal agent derived from cottonseed oil, has been used for years in China and reduces sperm production without changing testosterone levels (Chang et al., 2010; Hatcher et al., 2007; Li et al., 2010b; Song et al., 2006). Anti-cancer drugs, such as Lonidamine, are also being studied for their ability to reduce sperm production (Maranghi et al., 2005). Researchers continue to explore the development of a male pill that inhibits male ejaculation, causing an orgasm without ejaculation, or "dry orgasm" (Dawar, 2006; Hisasue et al., 2006).

Finally, scientists are evaluating contraceptive vaccines (called **immunocontraceptives**) that would suppress testicular function causing infertility until pregnancy is desired (Naz, 2009; Samuel & Naz, 2008; Wang et al., 2009). Anti-sperm contraceptive vaccines and genetically produced human antibodies inhibit sperm functions. Although there continues to be ongoing research into new contraception options for men, it is likely that no options will be available for several years at the earliest (Hatcher et al., 2007).

gossypol
An ingredient in cottonseed oil that, when injected or implanted, may inhibit sperm production.

immunocontraceptives
Vaccines designed to suppress testicular function and eliminate sperm and testosterone production.

What's Ahead for Women?

Women report that they want contraceptives that are simpler to use, have fewer adverse effects, and offer additional non-contraceptive benefits, such as STI protection, clearer skin, or less weight gain (Hatcher et al., 2007). Research is ongoing in an attempt to find a contraceptive method that addresses all these concerns.

Research continues to explore immunocontraceptives for women that would inhibit the function of human chorionic gonadotropin (see Chapter 3) and interrupt a woman's ability to become pregnant (Talwar et al., 2009). Other researchers are looking at vaccines that target sex hormones or gamete production (An et al., 2009; Naz, 2005; Wang et al., 2009). Unfortunately, vaccines often negatively affect other functions and do not offer adequate effectiveness yet. New IUDs, implants, injections, and permanent sterilization procedures are also being evaluated. Other research is evaluating longer-acting versions of existing methods, such as the contraceptive patch and hormonal ring.

Extended-use patches or rings may be options in the next few years. Finally, natural methods of contraception are also being studied. Saliva and urine tests can help natural planning by allowing a woman to determine whether she is ovulating. Fertility computers, which allow a woman to identify fertile periods, are currently undergoing clinical trials for FDA approval in the United States. Although we still have a long way to go in making better methods available for controlling whether pregnancy occurs, many improvements are in the works and may be available in the near future.

Financial factors, political pressure, and legal concerns hold back most of the contraceptive research today. Private funding is often difficult because such large amounts are necessary for most research. Unfortunately, the threat of lawsuits (such as the Dalkon Shield situation discussed earlier in the chapter) has effectively scared most big pharmaceutical companies away from contraceptive research (Hatcher et al., 2007; J.L. Schwartz & Gabelnick, 2002).

Review Questions

1 What do couples look for in new contraceptive methods?

2 Describe why there have been fewer birth control options for men and what the future holds for new male contraception.

3 Describe what the future holds for new female contraceptive methods.

Abortion

Because family planning involves controlling conception and birth, there are two main methods to achieve these goals—contraception and abortion (Leonard, 2006). Many believe that the ability to determine whether and when to have a child is a necessity today (Boonstra et al., 2006). At the beginning of this chapter, we pointed out that the typical North American woman spends at least 30 years trying *not* to get pregnant. Although the majority of women have used contraception, we know that many methods are difficult to use consistently and/or effectively, and no method is 100 percent effective. Unintended pregnancies do occur when a woman is using effective contraception, even though they are much more likely to occur when a woman uses no contraception. In fact, 52 percent of unintended pregnancies occur in the 11 percent of the women who use no contraception (Boonstra et al., 2006).

Certain groups of women have higher rates of unintended pregnancies, including those who are young, unmarried and/or poor. In order to decrease unintended pregnancies, it is essential to provide education to all children about their bodies, sex, sexuality and methods for the prevention of pregnancy. Unintended pregnancy is a stressful event for most women and has also been found to be related to high levels of intimate partner violence (Saftlas et al., 2010).

For women with stable relationships or the resources to raise a child, or both, an unintended pregnancy might not present much of a challenge. However, for many women, an unintended pregnancy can lead to serious consequences. In this section, we discuss the historical and legal perspectives of **induced abortion** in Canada, as well as statistics, abortion procedures, reactions to abortion, and cross-cultural research on abortion.

The Abortion Debate

Although some men and women are unsure about how they feel about abortion or feel somewhat in the middle, the majority of us fall on one side or the other of the abortion debate. **Pro-life supporters** believe that human life begins at conception, and thus an embryo, at any stage of development, is a person. Although some pro-life supporters believe that aborting a fetus is murder and that the government should make all abortions illegal, others believe that abortion should be available only for specific cases (such as rape or danger to a mother's life).

induced abortion
The intentional termination of a pregnancy.

pro-life supporter
Individual who believes that abortion should be illegal or strictly regulated by the government.

REAL Research Abortion is one of the most common medical interventions in women of reproductive age, and it is estimated that one in three women have an abortion by the age 45 (Jones et al., 2010).

On the other side of the issue, **pro-choice supporters** believe that a woman should have control over her fertility. Many people who are pro-choice believe there are a number of situations in which a woman may view abortion as a necessary option. Because not everyone agrees that life begins at conception, pro-choice supporters believe that it is a woman's choice whether to have an abortion, and they strongly believe that the government should not interfere with her decision.

The abortion debate often polarizes people into pro-life and pro-choice camps. In Canada three physicians who support the pro-choice perspective have been shot while at home. College and university students have generally been viewed as fairly liberal in their attitudes about abortion, but studies have found the same distribution of abortion attitudes as in other age groups (Carlton et al., 2000). A study published in 2001 by Reginald Bibby at the University of Lethbridge reported that 43 percent of adults and 55 percent of teenagers believe that abortion in Canada should be allowed for any reason. These numbers rise when people are asked about abortion after violent sexual assault (90 percent of and 84 percent of teenagers).

Table 6.4 Dr. Morgentaler—Highlights of His Life
1923—Henry Morgentaler born in Lodz, Poland.
1950—Moves to Canada after surviving Holocaust.
1955—Starts a family practice in Montreal.
1967—Urges Commons committee to reconsider abortion law.
1969—Opens Montreal abortion clinic.
1974—Acquitted by Quebec jury, later overturned by Quebec Court of Appeal. A jury later acquits Morgentaler a second time.
1983—Opens Toronto abortion clinic.
1984—Along with two other physicians he is acquitted by Ontario jury on abortion charges. The government appeals the decision.
1985—Raids on his Winnipeg clinics, the province of Manitoba charges him with seven counts of procuring a miscarriage.
1988—Celebrates the Supreme Court of Canada ruling striking down the abortion law as unconstitutional. It infringed upon a woman's right to "life, liberty and security of the person."
1994—Opens Fredericton abortion clinic—fought the New Brunswick government on its refusal to fund private abortion clinics, he won.
2005—University of Western Ontario in London grants him an honorary degree.
2008—the Canadian Labour Congress recognizes Dr. Morgentaler with its highest honour, the Award for Outstanding Service to Humanity.
2008—Named to the Order of Canada.
2013—Dies at the age of 90 years.

SOURCE: Abortion Rights Coalition of Canada, "The Morgentaler Decision." Retrieved March 17, 2015, from http://www.morgentaler25years.ca/about-henry-morgentaler.

Historical Perspectives

Abortion has been practised in many societies throughout history; in fact, there are few large-scale societies in which it has not been practised. Aristotle argued that abortion was necessary as a backup to contraception. He believed that a fetus was not alive until certain organs had been formed; for males, this occurred 40 days after conception, and for females, 90 days. In early Roman society, abortions were also allowed, but husbands had the power to determine whether their wives would undergo abortion.

Throughout most of Western history, religion determined general attitudes toward abortion, and both Judaism and Christianity have generally condemned abortion and punished those who used it. Still, throughout recorded history, abortions were performed. Many women died or were severely injured by illegal surgical abortions performed by semi-skilled practitioners.

Many women who could not have a legal abortion had the baby or underwent an illegal abortion (others may have used *self-induced abortion* methods, such as inserting sticks in the vagina, applying pressure to the abdomen, or drinking bleach). Illegal abortions, known as **back-alley abortions**, were very dangerous because they were often performed under unsanitary conditions and resulted in multiple complications, sometimes ending in death (recall the chapter opening story about a woman who underwent an illegal abortion).

In Canada individuals from the pro-life and from the pro-choice sides have heavily campaigned for their perspective to be the basis of Canadian law. In 1969, however, abortion law in Canada was changed, and women, under limited circumstances could have an abortion. Dr. Henry Morgentaler has been a strong advocate for the pro-choice movement in Canada and has been at the media forefront with regards to providing abortion services. Dr. Morgentaler began his work in the area of providing contraceptive services by performing vasectomies and providing IUDs and birth control to both married and unmarried people before he began providing abortions in 1969 at his first clinic in Montreal.

Dr. Morgentaler went on to become a leader in the pro-choice movement in Canada, opening abortion clinics across the country and coming face-to-face with many in the pro-life movement as he fought legal battles in several provinces for women to have the right to abortions (see Table 6.4). The culmination of this work came in 1988, when Canada's abortion law was overturned by the Supreme Court of Canada. The law was deemed unconstitutional and a violation of the Canadian Charter of Rights and Freedoms. To this day, abortion is legal in Canada and this service is provided to women across the country. However, many women in remote areas have difficulty accessing services and even those in urban areas are not given clear information

pro-choice supporter	**back-alley abortion**
Individual who believes that the abortion decision should be left up to the woman and not regulated by the government.	illegal abortion, which was all that was available before the legalization of abortion

Contraception and Abortion

Table 6.5 Rates of Induced Abortions in Hospitals versus Clinics by Province and Territory, 2010

	Hospitals	Clinics	Total
Newfoundland and Labrador	292	776	1 068
Prince Edward Island‡	0	0	0
Nova Scotia	2 125	0 §	2 125§
New Brunswick	471	627	1 098
Quebec	11 035	15 071	26 106**
Ontario	12 626	16 139**	28 765**
Manitoba	2 539	1 611	4 150
Saskatchewan	1 915	0 §	1 915§
Alberta	2 582	10 502	13 084
British Columbia	4 739	7 410†† (Clinic data is incomplete)	††
Yukon	147	0 §	147§
Northwest Territories	40	0 §	40§
Nunavut	100	0 §	100§
Total Reported	38 611	52 136††	90 747††

Induced abortion is defined as the medical termination of pregnancy. Equivalent terms include artificial abortion, therapeutic abortion, voluntary termination of pregnancy, elective termination of pregnancy and active termination of pregnancy.

† Figures include induced abortions performed in a hospital or clinic setting in Canada (numbers are presented by the province/territory in which the abortion was performed).

‡ Induced abortions are not performed in Prince Edward Island.

§ Induced abortions are not performed in clinics in Nova Scotia, Saskatchewan, Yukon, the Northwest Territories or Nunavut.

*** Ontario (clinic data only) and Quebec (clinic and hospital data) include only induced abortions covered by their respective provincial health insurance plans. Data from all other provinces/territories (including Ontario hospital data) includes all induced abortions, whether paid for by the patient or by a different health insurance plan. For example, patients with coverage under Quebec's health insurance plan receiving care in Manitoba are reported by Manitoba. However, patients with coverage under Manitoba's health insurance plan receiving care in Quebec are not reported (by either Quebec or Manitoba).*

†† Hospitals are mandated by their provincial/territorial ministry of health to report all hospital activity (not limited to abortions); therefore, coverage of abortions performed in Canadian hospitals can be considered complete. However, there is no such legislative requirement for clinics to report their activity (reporting is voluntary). For 2010, clinic data for British Columbia is incomplete.

SOURCE: "Number of Induced Abortions Reported in Canada in 2010, by Province/Territory of Hospital or Clinic," Canadian Institute for Health Information. Retrieved September 10, 2015, from https://www.cihi.ca/en/ta_10_alldatatables20120417_en.pdf.

from health care providers about how to access abortion services.

Who Has Abortions?

In Canada statistics on the frequency of induced abortions are not reliably reported and reporting may be inconsistent (Hudson-Sonnen, 2012).

Although many believe that young teenagers are the ones most likely to have abortions, the largest group of women having abortions are in their 20s, followed by women in their teens and 30s (Canadian Institute for Health Information, 2015). Data for the number of induced abortions in publicly funded hospitals and clinics versus private clinics in the provinces are depicted in Table 6.5. These numbers have declined slightly or remained stable over the last several decades.

Why Do Women Have Abortions?

Women choose abortion for many different reasons—an inability to care for a child, financial reasons, partner or relationship issues, as well as work, school, or family issues (Boonstra et al., 2006; Jones et al., 2010). There is no simple answer to the question of why a woman decides to have an abortion.

The majority of women—regardless of age, marital status, income, ethnicity, education, or number of children—cite a concern for others as a main factor in their decision to have an abortion (Boonstra et al., 2006). Many women consult with others when they are deciding what to do about an unintended pregnancy. In fact, 60 percent report talking to someone, most often their partner, when they make their decision (Finer et al., 2006).

Table 6.6 Early Abortion Options

Surgical Abortion	Medication Abortion
Highly effective	Highly effective
Relatively brief procedure	Procedure can take up to several days or more to complete
Involves invasive procedure	No invasive procedure (unless incomplete)
Allows local or general anesthesia	No anesthesia
Usually requires only one clinic or medical visit	Involves at least two clinic or medical visits
Bleeding is typically lighter after procedure	Bleeding is typically heavier after procedure
Occurs in medical setting	Can occur in privacy of own home

SOURCE: Hatcher et al. (2007).

Abortion Procedures

Today in Canada a woman can only obtain a surgical abortion, although medication induced abortions are available in other countries (see Table 6.6 for more information about early abortion options). There are two surgical procedures commonly used in Canada—**vacuum aspiration** and **dilation and evacuation (D&E)**. The most important factor in determining which procedure a woman should choose is the duration of a woman's pregnancy. A surgical abortion can be used in both the first and second trimesters.

In a first-trimester surgical abortion procedure, a woman is often offered some type of sedative. She lies on an examining table with her feet in stirrups, and a speculum is placed in her vagina to view the cervix. Local anesthesia is injected into the cervix, which numbs it slightly. **Dilation rods** are used to open the cervix and usually cause mild cramping of the uterus. After dilation, a **cannula** is inserted into the cervix and is attached to a **vacuum aspirator**, which empties the contents of the uterus. A first-trimester procedure usually takes between four and six minutes.

Second-trimester surgical abortions are those generally performed later than 16 weeks after a woman's last period. These procedures can be done in a private clinic, physician's office, or hospital. A woman may undergo a second-trimester procedure for several reasons, such as medical complications, fetal deformities that were not revealed earlier, divorce or marital problems, miscalculation of date of last menstrual period, financial or geographic problems (such as not living near a clinic that offers the procedure), or a denial of the pregnancy until the second trimester.

A dilation and evacuation (D&E) is often used in second-trimester procedures. The procedure is similar to a vacuum aspiration, but dilation may be done differently. Because the fetal tissue is larger, the cervix must be dilated more than it is in a first-trimester procedure. Dilators such as **laminaria** (lam-in-AIR-ree-uh) may be inserted into the cervix 12 to 24 hours before the procedure to help begin the dilation process. These dilators absorb fluid and slowly dilate the cervix. When a woman returns to the clinic or hospital, she will be given pain medication and numbing medication will be injected into the cervix. The dilators are removed, and the uterus is then emptied with suction and various instruments. A D&E usually takes about 15 to 20 minutes.

After a surgical abortion procedure, most women experience bleeding and cramping. Over-the-counter pain relievers, such as ibuprofen, will adequately reduce the pain and cramping. Although the heaviest bleeding might last only a few days, spotting can last for up to six weeks. Because these are medical procedures, potential risks are associated with these procedures, and these risks increase the longer a woman has been pregnant. Possible risks include an allergic reaction to medications, excessive bleeding, infection, injury to the cervix, uterine perforation, and/or an incomplete abortion. Health care providers advise women who are considering abortion to have an earlier procedure because the risks are lower in first-trimester procedures.

Most clinics and medical offices require a woman to stay a few hours after the procedure so that she can be monitored. If a woman is Rh-negative, she will be given RhoGAM after these procedures (see Chapter 3). Once home, she is advised to rest, not to lift heavy objects, to avoid vaginal intercourse, and not to use tampons for at least one week; all of these activities may increase the risk for infection. Typically, a woman's period will return within four to eight weeks. Most clinics advise a follow-up visit two to four weeks after the procedure.

Medication Abortion

A medication abortion involves the use of an "abortion pill" to end an early pregnancy. The abortion pill is actually a drug known as **mifepristone** (MYFE-priss-tone). Mifepristone was first approved for use in pregnancy termination in France in 1988, during which time it was referred to as RU-486. It was approved for use in the United States by the FDA in 2000. It is not currently

vacuum aspiration
The termination of a pregnancy by using suction to empty the contents of the uterus. Usually done only during the first trimester.

dilation and evacuation (D&E)
Surgical abortion that involves dilation of the cervix followed by suction and scraping of the uterine walls to ensure removal of all tissue. Usually done in the second trimester.

dilation rods
A series of graduated metal rods that are used to dilate the cervical opening during an abortion procedure.

cannula
A tube, used in an abortion procedure, through which the uterine contents are emptied.

vacuum aspirator
A vacuum pump that is used during abortion procedures.

second-trimester surgical abortion
Termination of pregnancy between the 14th and 21st weeks of pregnancy.

laminaria
Seaweed used in second-trimester abortion procedures to dilate the cervix. Used dried, it can swell three to five times its original diameter.

mifepristone
Drug used in medication abortion procedures; it blocks the development of progesterone, which causes a breakdown in the uterine lining. Referred to as RU-486 when it was in development.

available in Canada at this time but is under consideration for approval by Health Canada (Payton, 2015). In a medication abortion, mifepristone is used in conjunction with a second pill containing another drug, **misoprostol**.

Many clinics require a physical examination, blood work, and an ultrasound to determine the length of the pregnancy before prescribing the abortion pill. During this visit, medication abortion is explained and a woman is given antibiotics to reduce the possibility of infection. The actual medication abortion involves three steps.

The first step involves taking the abortion pill. A woman will usually begin bleeding within four to five hours after taking the pill. Mifepristone works by blocking the hormone progesterone, which is responsible for maintaining the buildup of the endometrium (see Chapter 3). Without it, however, the endometrial lining will break down and a pregnancy can no longer continue.

On Your Mind

If you had an abortion, could it make you infertile later on?

Women who undergo an abortion can become pregnant and give birth later on in their life without complications (Boonstra et al., 2006; Finer & Henshaw, 2006; Hatcher et al., 2007). However, there are rare cases of unexpected complications of abortion that can lead to infertility, such as uterine perforation or severe infection. Because medication abortion procedures are non-surgical, they have less risk for uterine perforation or infection.

The second step of a medication abortion involves taking another medication, misoprostol. This is usually taken within three days of the abortion pill. Misoprostol is a **prostaglandin**, and it causes the uterus to contract and expel the uterine contents. Many women experience heavy bleeding, cramping, nausea, diarrhea, abdominal pain, dizziness, or a minor fever and chills. This process may take four to five hours or more, and during this time a woman will experience an abortion. The bleeding will continue for up to four weeks after the medications are taken, and women can use pads or tampons during this time.

The third, and final, step involves a follow-up visit to the health care provider to make sure that the abortion is complete. A blood test, ultrasound, or both may be performed. Women who undergo a medication abortion must be prepared to have a surgical abortion if they experience an incomplete abortion. Because the drugs for medication abortion are known to cause birth defects, women are not advised to continue a pregnancy after using these drugs.

Medication abortion is a safe and effective procedure, and research indicates that it may be safer than surgical abortion procedures (Gan et al., 2008; M. Singh et al., 2008). Some women in Europe and the United States choose medication abortion over surgical abortion because it feels more "natural," offers privacy, can be done earlier, does not use anesthesia, and provides more control (see Table 6.6; F.H. Stewart et al., 2004). However, medication abortions often cause heavier bleeding and cramping than surgical abortions, and some women worry about being away from a medical facility (Lie et al., 2008). Finally, the length of time to expulsion (days compared with minutes) often makes medication abortion less appealing than a surgical abortion. In 2008, close to 60 percent of abortion providers in the United States offered medication abortion (Jones & Kooistra, 2011).

Reactions to Abortion

Although the decision to have an abortion is a difficult one, the physiological and psychological effects vary from person to person, and they depend on many factors. Here we'll explore the reactions of women, men, and teens.

Women's Reactions

The majority of evidence from research studies has found that legal abortion is safe and has few long-term physiological, psychological, or fertility-related problems later in life (Boonstra et al., 2006; Munk-Olsen et al., 2011; Warren et al., 2010). In Canada, Fisher and colleagues (2005) showed that women who have repeated abortions do not use this as a method of birth control; however, as stated earlier, these women may be more likely to suffer from partner abuse. Although we know less about reactions to medication abortion, preliminary research has found that women are pleased with this type of procedure because it allows them more control and privacy (Cameron et al., 2010).

After a first-trimester abortion, the most common physiological symptoms include cramping, heavy bleeding with possible clots, and nausea. These symptoms may persist for several days, but if any of these are severe, a health care provider should be seen for an evaluation. Severe complications are much more frequent in second-trimester procedures, as we discussed earlier. They include hemorrhaging, **cervical laceration**, **uterine perforation**, and infection (F.H. Stewart et al., 2004). Of these complications, uterine perforation is the most serious, although the risk for occurrence is small. Reviews of scientific literature have found that women who have abortions do not have an increased risk for breast cancer or long-term risks to future fertility (Finer & Henshaw, 2006; Hatcher et al., 2007; Richardson & Nash, 2006).

Although women experience a range of emotions after an abortion, the most prominent response is relief (Fergusson et al., 2009). Even though relief may be the immediate feeling, there are three categories of psychological reactions to abortion. Positive emotions include relief and happiness; socially based emotions include shame, guilt, and fear of disapproval; and internally based emotions include regret, anxiety, depression, doubt, and anger, which are based on the woman's feelings about the pregnancy (Thorp et al., 2003). A woman may cycle through each of these reactions—feeling relief one minute, depression or guilt the next. Other possible negative psychological symptoms include self-reproach, increased sadness, and a sense of loss.

misoprostol
A synthetic prostaglandin drug used for early abortion.

prostaglandin
Oral or injected drug taken to cause uterine contractions.

cervical laceration
Cuts or tears on the cervix.

uterine perforation
Tearing a hole in the uterus.

Certain conditions may put a woman more at risk for development of severe psychological symptoms. These include being young, not having family or partner support, being persuaded to have an abortion when she does not want one, having a difficult time making the decision to have an abortion, blaming the pregnancy on another person or on oneself, having a strong religious and moral background, having an abortion for medical or genetic reasons, having a history of psychiatric problems before the abortion, and having a late abortion procedure (Rue et al., 2004; Zolese & Blacker, 1992).

In most cases, although discovering an unintended pregnancy and deciding to abort are very stressful decisions, in the majority of cases, the emotional aftermath does not appear to be severe (Munk-Olsen et al., 2011; Warren et al., 2010). Still, it is very beneficial for a woman (and her partner) who is contemplating an abortion to discuss this with a counsellor or health care provider.

Men's Reactions

A woman's choice to have an abortion forces many couples to re-evaluate their relationship and ask themselves some difficult questions (Naziri, 2007). Do they both feel the same about each other? Is the relationship serious? Where is the relationship going? Keeping the lines of communication open during this time is very important. The male partner's involvement makes the abortion experience less traumatic for the woman; in fact, women whose partners support them and help them through the procedure show more positive responses after the abortion (Jones et al., 2011). Women who have no support from their partners or who make the decision themselves often experience greater emotional distress. In some cases, women have been found to conceal abortion decisions from their partners (Coker, 2007; Woo et al., 2005).

Although we know that an unintended pregnancy is difficult for many women, we often fail to acknowledge that men can also have a difficult time and may experience sadness, a sense of loss, and fear for their partner's well-being (Holmes, 2004). What makes it even more difficult for most men is that they often do not discuss the pregnancy with anyone other than their partner (Naziri, 2007).

Finally, earlier we mentioned the increased rate of intimate partner violence in couples with unintended pregnancies. Researchers have found that some men try to control their partner's abortion-related decisions (Hathaway et al., 2005; Miller et al., 2007). These behaviours are part of a larger pattern of behaviours involving forced sex, condom refusal, and contraceptive control. Abusive men have been found to be more involved in pregnancies ending in abortion than their non-abusive counterparts, especially in cases where there are repeat abortions (Silverman et al., 2010). This is an area of research that will continue to be explored in the future.

Teens and Abortion

Overall, Canadian teenagers are the second highest users of abortion services, after women in their early 20s (CIHI, 2015). Teenagers may be more vulnerable to post-abortion anxiety, depression, sleep problems, and substance use/abuse, mostly because of developmental limitations and a lack of emotional support from those around them (Coleman, 2006; Ely et al., 2010). As we discussed earlier, women who have no support often experience increased emotional distress after an abortion. However, most teens with adequate support do not experience negative post-abortion emotional reactions (Warren et al., 2010).

Cross-Cultural Aspects of Abortion

Worldwide, approximately 42 million abortions occur each year, and half of these involve illegal abortion procedures (Cohen, 2009). Abortion is legal throughout most of Europe, with the exception of Ireland and Poland, and it is widely available and safe (Cohen, 2009). Ironically, countries with liberal abortion laws have been found to have lower rates of abortion. For example, in the Netherlands, abortion is legal, free, and widely available, yet abortion rates are among the world's lowest (Boonstra et al., 2006). The Netherlands also has comprehensive sexuality education programs and liberal access to contraception, both of which contribute to low abortion rates (see Chapter 10 for more information about comprehensive sexuality education).

Many other countries have legalized abortion, including China (1957), Cuba (1965), Singapore (1970), India (1972), Zambia (1972), Vietnam (1975), Turkey (1983), Taiwan (1985), and South Africa (1996; Cohen, 2009). Since 1997, many more countries have legalized abortion, including Colombia, Ethiopia, Iran, Nepal, Portugal, and Thailand. During this same time, three countries, Poland, Nicaragua, and El Salvador, have decreased the availability of abortion by increasing various restrictions (Cohen, 2009). As of 2015, approximately 60 percent of women live in countries where abortion is legal. However, the remaining 40 percent of women live in areas where abortion is illegal or highly restricted. In countries where abortion is illegal, many women undergo dangerous procedures with no access to hospitals or medical care when complications occur (Boonstra et al., 2006). Illegal abortions are high in countries where abortion is prohibited, such as Bangladesh, Brazil, Colombia, the Dominican Republic, Nigeria, and Peru (Boonstra et al., 2006). Worldwide, an estimated 70 000 women die of unsafe abortion procedures each year (or seven women each hour; Cohen, 2009). In addition to this, more than 8 million women experience complications from unsafe abortions and are at risk for infertility (Cohen, 2009).

Researchers and experts are working to help legalize abortion around the world to help reduce the incidence of illegal abortions and post-abortion complications. However, this is only the first step to ensuring that women have adequate access to abortion services. In some countries where abortion is legal, safe services are unavailable to many women because of prohibitive prices or certain restrictions, such as the necessity of getting the consent of multiple physicians (as is the case in Zambia, where abortion has been legal since 1994; Cohen, 2009).

Abortion remains a controversial procedure in Canada, as well as in the rest of the world. In Canada, both sides of the issue battle from what they believe are basic principles: one side from a fetus's right to be born and the other from a woman's right to control her own body. The pendulum of this debate continues to swing back and forth. Although new developments like the availability of medication abortions in Canada may take the fight out of the abortion clinics and into women's homes, the only real certainty about the future of abortion is that it will remain a controversial area of Canadian life.

1 Trace the status of abortion throughout Canadian history.

2 Differentiate between first- and second-trimester surgical abortion procedures.

3 Differentiate between surgical and medication abortion, and explain how a woman might decide which procedure would be best for her.

4 Identify some physiological and psychological reactions to abortion, and discuss the research on men and abortion.

5 Describe what we know about abortion outside of Canada.

Chapter Review

Summary Points

1 Contraception is not a modern invention. The ancient Greeks and Egyptians used a variety of techniques to try to control their fertility. Several groups began to explore controlling fertility in the early 1800s, and Mary Hawkins and Dorothea Palmer were two of the first people to advocate the importance of birth control in Canada.

2 Contraception throughout the world has always been affected by social and economic issues, knowledge levels, religion, and gender roles. Outside of Canada, many women are not involved in contraceptive decision making, and contraceptive use is thought to reduce a man's masculinity. Scandinavian countries are regarded as some of the most progressive with respect to contraceptive usage. Finland has been rated as a model country in contraceptive use.

3 Health Canada has approved several methods of contraception, but no method is best for everyone. Health Canada is responsible for approving all prescription medicine in the Canada. A pharmaceutical company must submit proof that the drug is safe for human use. It is estimated that it takes 10 to 14 years to develop a new contraceptive method.

4 Issues that must be considered when choosing a contraceptive method include personal health, number of sexual partners, frequency of vaginal intercourse, risk for acquiring a sexually transmitted infection, responsibility of partners, method cost, and method advantages and disadvantages.

5 Barrier methods of birth control work by preventing the sperm from entering the uterus. Barrier methods include the male and female condoms, cervical barriers, and the contraceptive sponge. Male condoms can be made of latex, polyurethane, or lambskin. Female condoms are made of polyurethane.

6 Hormonal methods work by changing hormone levels to interrupt ovulation. Combined hormone methods include birth control pills, injections, vaginal rings, and patches. Combination birth control pills contain synthetic estrogen and a type of progestin. The increase in estrogen and progesterone prevents the pituitary gland from sending hormones to cause the ovaries to begin maturation of an ovum.

7 Other hormonal contraceptive options include a monthly injection of synthetic hormones, including estrogen and progestin; NuvaRing, a small plastic ring that releases a constant dose of estrogen and progestin, and is changed once a month; the Ortho Evra patch, which sticks to the skin and time-releases synthetic estrogen and progestin into the bloodstream. All of these work by inhibiting ovulation, increasing cervical mucus, and/or rendering the uterus inhospitable to implantation.

8 Progestin-based methods include subdermal implants, injectables, and minipills. Progestin-only methods include minipills, Implanon, and Depo-Provera. Implanon is a subdermal contraceptive implant, whereas Depo-Provera is a progestin-only injectable contraceptive that works by preventing ovulation and thickening cervical mucus. Chemical methods of contraception include spermicides such as creams, jellies, foams, suppositories, and films. Spermicides work by reducing the survival of sperm in the vagina.

9 IUDs are placed in the uterus and inhibit ovulation, whereas causing an increase in cervical mucus and endometrial buildup. The ParaGard IUD can be left in place for up to 12 years. The Mirena IUD also time-releases progestin into the lining of the uterus and can be left in place for up to five years.

10 Fertility awareness–based methods identify a woman's fertile period so she can abstain from vaginal intercourse or use another method of contraception. A more intensive method involves charting and recording physical fertility signs, such as monitoring daily body temperature.

11 Withdrawal, or coitus interruptus, is a method of contraception in which the man withdraws his penis from the vagina before ejaculation. This method can be used in conjunction with other contraceptive methods.

12 Tubal sterilization is the most widely used method of birth control in the world. In this procedure, a health care provider may sever or block both Fallopian tubes so that the ovum and sperm cannot meet. A vasectomy blocks the flow of sperm through the vas deferens, and although the testes will continue to produce viable sperm cells, the cells die and are reabsorbed by the body.

13 Emergency contraception prevents pregnancy when taken after unprotected vaginal intercourse. As of 2015, three brands have Health Canada approval, including Plan B One-Step, Next Choice, and ella. All are progestin-only methods and work by inhibiting ovulation. Emergency contraception should be started as soon as possible after unprotected intercourse to be effective. Birth control pills or an IUD may also be used as emergency contraception.

14 Contraception has long been thought to be a female's responsibility, and that may be why the condom and vasectomy are the only birth control methods available to men. Many feminists claim the lack of male methods is because most of those doing the contraceptive research are men, whereas others claim that most methods are for women because it is easier to interfere with one ovum a month than thousands of sperm a day.

15 Many new contraceptive methods are on the horizon, and many will be easier to use, longer acting, and have higher effectiveness rates. Immunocontraceptives are also being studied.

16 There are two methods of controlling conception: contraception and abortion. Although the majority of women use contraception, many methods are difficult to use effectively and/or consistently, and no method is 100 percent effective.

17 Certain groups of women are at greater risk for an unintended pregnancy, including those who are young, unmarried, poor or from low-income families.

18 In Canada, disagreements about abortion have been emotional and, at times, violent.

Whereas some are pro-life supporters, others are pro-choice supporters.

19 Abortion has been practised in many societies throughout history; in fact, there are few large-scale societies where it has not been practised. Before abortion was legalized, illegal abortions were common. Throughout most of Western history, religion determined general attitudes toward abortion.

20 In 1988, the Supreme Court of Canada struck down the law on abortion. Currently, in Canada there is no legal obstacle to abortion.

21 Legalization of abortion in Canada gave women the right to choose abortion, but also increased the safety of abortion. Experts believe the legality of abortion does not affect the incidence of unintended pregnancy, the real underlying cause of abortion.

22 Although women choose abortion for many different reasons, some of the most common include an inability to care for a child, financial reasons, partner or relationship issues, or work, school, or family commitments.

23 The decision to have an abortion is a difficult one, and physiological and psychological effects vary from person to person and depend on many factors. The most prominent reaction after an abortion is relief. Men may also experience difficulties, but the male partner's involvement makes the abortion experience less traumatic for the woman.

24 Intimate partner violence is higher in couples with unintended pregnancies. There are men who try and control their partner's abortion-related decisions. Abusive men are more involved in pregnancies ending in abortion, especially in cases where there are repeat abortions.

25 Teens may be more vulnerable to post-abortion anxiety, depression, sleep problems, and substance use and abuse, especially if there is a lack of emotional support from those around them.

26 Worldwide, 42 million abortions occur each year, and half of these involve illegal abortion procedures. Countries that have liberal abortion laws have been found to have lower rates of abortion.

Critical Thinking Questions

1 If you found out tomorrow that you (or your partner) were six weeks pregnant, what would your options be? Where would you go for help, and whom would you talk to? What would your biggest concerns be?

2 Suppose a good friend of yours, Sylvia, tells you that she is ten weeks pregnant, and she and her boyfriend have decided that she will have an abortion. She knows that you are taking the

sexuality course and asks you about her abortion options. What can you tell her?

3 What method of contraception do you think would work best for you at this time in your life? In five years? In ten years? Why?

4 Do you think permanent sterilization options (tubal ligation for women or vasectomies for

men) should be available to individuals in their 20s or 30s? Why or why not?

5 Do you think women who use herbal contraceptives should be taught about newer, more modern methods of birth control? What if the methods they are using are working for them?

Websites

Planned Parenthood Associations in Canada The following website lists resources across Canada for individuals looking for information about parenthood in Canada. (http://www.anac.on.ca/sourcebook/resource_planned.htm)

Planned Parenthood Federation of America Founded by Margaret Sanger in 1916 as America's first birth control clinic, This website offers information on birth control, emergency contraception, STIs, safer sex, pregnancy, abortion, and other health-related concerns. (http://www.plannedparenthood.org/)

Alan Guttmacher Institute The Alan Guttmacher Institute (AGI) is a non-profit

organization that focuses on sexual and reproductive health research, policy analysis, and public education. The institute's mission is to protect the reproductive choices of all women and men throughout the world. (https://www.guttmacher.org/)

The Morgentaler Decision A website dedicated to the history of one of Canada's most famous pro-choice advocates—Dr. Henry Morgentaler. (http://www.morgentaler25years.ca/about-henry-morgentaler/)

Birthcontrol.com This Canadian website sells innovative contraceptive products from around the world. Sponges, condoms, spermicides, and barrier methods of contraception

can be found, all at relatively inexpensive prices. (https://www.birthcontrol.com/)

National Abortion Federation The National Abortion Federation (NAF) is the professional association of abortion providers in the United States and Canada. NAF members provide the broadest spectrum of abortion expertise in North America. (http://prochoice.org/)

Abortion Rights Coalition of Canada This group is a nationwide pro-choice organization in Canada that was formed in 2005 to support education and women's rights regarding control over their reproductive choices. (http://www.arcc-cdac.ca/home.html)

7

Sexually Transmitted Infections and HIV/AIDS

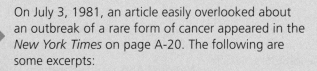

On July 3, 1981, an article easily overlooked about an outbreak of a rare form of cancer appeared in the *New York Times* on page A-20. The following are some excerpts:

Rare Cancer Seen in 41 Homosexuals
Doctors in New York and California have diagnosed among homosexual men 41 cases of a rare and often rapidly fatal form of cancer. Eight of the victims died less than 24 months after the diagnosis was made.

The cause of the outbreak is unknown, and there is as yet no evidence of contagion. But the doctors who have made the diagnoses, mostly in New York City and the San Francisco Bay area, are alerting other physicians who treat large numbers of homosexual men to the problem in an effort to help identify more cases and to reduce the delay in offering chemotherapy treatment. . . .

Doctors have been taught in the past that the cancer usually appeared first in spots on the legs and that the disease took a slow course of up to ten years. But these recent cases have shown that it appears in one or more violet-colored spots anywhere on the body. The spots generally do not itch or cause other symptoms, often can be mistaken for bruises, sometimes appear as lumps and can turn brown after a period of time. . . .

In the United States, it has primarily affected men older than 50 years. But in the recent cases, doctors at nine medical centers in New York and seven hospitals in California have been diagnosing the condition among younger men, all of whom said in the course of standard diagnostic interviews that they were homosexual. . . .

Nine of the 41 cases known to Dr. Friedman-Kien were diagnosed in California, and several of those victims reported that they had been in New York in the period preceding the

diagnosis. Dr. Friedman-Kien said that his colleagues were checking on reports of two victims diagnosed in Copenhagen, one of whom had visited New York.*

This rare form of cancer was known as *Kaposi's sarcoma* and had previously been extremely rare in North America, infecting only two people out of every 3 million. What was even more mysterious was that those who were infected all identified as either gay or bisexual. In less than a year, Kaposi's sarcoma, along with other opportunistic diseases such as

pneumocystis carinii pneumonia, became known as gay-related immune deficiency (GRID), acquired immunodeficiency disease (AID), and even "the gay cancer" (The Washington Blade, 1982). By September 1982, the name *acquired immune deficiency syndrome* or AIDS was chosen, and attitudes toward sexual behaviour changed forever (Morbidity and Mortality Weekly Report, 1982).

The history of sexually transmitted infections and AIDS has often been the history of blame—that of identifying groups of people and demonizing them for infecting the world. In reality, the transmission of such infections has nothing to do with the group to which one belongs or even the "lifestyle" one leads. Instead it has to do with behaviour—specifically, sexual behaviour. This chapter will not only emphasize this point but give the facts about sexually transmitted infections and HIV/AIDS. ▌▌

Sexually transmitted infections (STIs) is a blanket term for a number of infections gained through sexual activity, which include chlamydia, gonorrhea, syphilis, hepatitis B and C, human papillomavirus (genital warts), and even pubic lice and scabies. They are contacted through direct sexual contact with other people, particularly unprotected vaginal or anal intercourse and oral sex. Most STIs result from the exchange of semen, vaginal fluids, or blood. Syphilis and gonorrhea in particular used to be called *venereal diseases*—literally, the diseases of Venus, the Roman goddess of sexual pleasure—and then all STIs were referred to as *sexually transmitted diseases* (STDs). *Sexually transmitted infections* is now the preferred term for its broader scope and greater accuracy in that someone might still be able to infect other people without having an actual disease.

According to the Public Health Agency of Canada (PHAC, 2008), the rates of chlamydia, gonorrhea, and syphilis have been rising since 1997, with chlamydia being the most commonly reported STI. Measuring incidence by number of infected people per 100 000, chlamydia had risen from rates of 138.2 to 248.9 from 1999 to 2008—an increase of 80.2 percent. Women under 30 were most commonly affected and the highest rates were found in Nunavut, the Northwest Territories, and the Yukon.

In that same period, rates of gonorrhea more than doubled, rising from 16.6 to 38.2 per 100 000 people. Again, women under 30 were most commonly affected, and the highest rates were in the three territories once again, followed by Manitoba and Saskatchewan (PHAC, 2008).

The incidence of syphilis is far lower, although it has risen rapidly from 0.6 to 4.2 per 100 000, or by 568.2 percent. There was an increase in rates for men over 60, although the incidence remains low. Rates were highest among men 25 to 39 and women 20 to 24. The highest rates were in the Northwest Territories and Nova Scotia (PHAC, 2008). More details upon all three STIs appears later in this chapter.

As of 2008, the Canadian rates of all three infections fell between those of the United Kingdom and the United States—that is, they are lowest in the former and highest in the latter. When comparing the United States to Canada, the American rates are 62 percent higher for chlamydia, 292 percent higher for gonorrhea, and 5 percent higher for syphilis. For all three, women are more likely to be infected (PHAC, 2008).

Because of the stigma associated with STIs, people are often reluctant to seek treatment and, as a result, many cases go unreported and become even more detrimental to people's health. Because of this, people may be apprehensive about getting tested for STIs even when they are worried they might be infected. Some people even report that they would rather not know if they are infected at all (Barth et al., 2002). Many other people are unaware of the risk and consequences of STIs, and it is clear that lack of immediate treatment is a global health problem.

contagion
Disease transmission by direct or indirect contact.

Sexually Transmitted Infections

In this section we look at some of the social and psychological issues surrounding STIs. While they are essentially medical issues, their contraction is often a matter of lack of education, which, in turn, is affected by attitudes toward sexual behaviour as well as the distribution of health information. First we look at attitudes toward STIs; then we look at their intersections with gender, ethnicity, race, and sexual orientation; and then we look at education and prevention issues.

> **REAL Research** Ochoa and Sampalis (2014) conducted in-depth interviews with 25 Latina women in Montreal who had recently immigrated to Quebec. Their perceptions of their risk for contracting STIs and HIV/AIDS were dependent upon several factors, including language barriers, perceived access to health care facilities, and felt inequalities between the sexes.

A History of STIs in Canada

The sudden appearance of a new disease has always elicited concern about the nature of its **contagion**, especially when it concerned the military. In 1864 in the United Kingdom, such concern led to the passing of the Contagious Diseases Act, which empowered authorities to arrest prostitutes in army and navy towns and forcibly give them medical examinations. If they were found to be infected, they were put in locked hospitals for up to one year. Ironically, no such examinations or sanctions were given to their military clientele, reflecting the attitudes of the time that women were infectors of men rather than the other way around. Soon after, and because of a growing concern over the health of soldiers and sailors, this same policy was applied in Canada, and locked hospitals were set up in Toronto and Montreal (MacDougall, 1994).

Prior to World War I (1914–1918), Canadian society reflected the mores of the Victorian era, which saw women as wives and mothers in the private sphere of the home and men as the prime movers of economic life in the public sphere. Women who were not wives and mothers were therefore stigmatized as pariahs, and sexually transmitted infections were seen as the wages of sin. The "social purity" movement set out to eradicate STIs but, in so doing, it aimed its energies at perceived sexual vices such as prostitution, masturbation, and homosexuality, and its purpose was to preserve the "racial purity" of the Anglo-Saxon people (Kinsman, 1987). Medical treatment thus came with severe social judgment and many women resorted to home remedies, which ultimately failed.

It was not until World War I that Canada regarded STIs as a serious public health problem. Canadian soldiers who were on leave would typically have sex with prostitutes and the infection rates were said to have reached 28.5 percent. The Canadian, British, and Australian military set up "blue light depots" where soldiers could be examined after returning from leave (MacDougall, 1994).

Meanwhile, most provinces mobilized to combat incidences of syphilis, gonorrhea, and chancroid with educational campaigns and medical treatment. After the war, numerous clinics were set up across Canada to combat STIs, but moral attitudes proved counterproductive to the campaign to eradicate them in that few cases were reported and treatment often ceased after the patients felt better. To counteract this problem, educational campaigns involving films, lectures, pamphlets, and travelling exhibits served to bring STI infection into the open and treat it as purely a medical problem rather than a moral one. Nevertheless, it proved difficult to circumvent moral condemnation, and educational efforts were done with single-gender audiences.

During World War II (1939-1945), Canada once again turned its attention to the sexual health of the military. Blue light depots (now green) were established once again and posters with slogans such as "VINO + VENUS = VEEDEE" ("Wine plus sexual activity leads to venereal disease") appeared everywhere. Condoms were distributed to soldiers prior to leaves, which served to reduce the incidence of STIs. The infection rates of World War II had been only 92 per 1000—thus less than half that of World War I. Because of the attitudes of the time, education efforts were geared only toward male soldiers, while women in the armed forces received very little advice (MacDougall, 1994).

By the 1960s, the huge generation of post-war baby boomers had come of age and began to experiment with "free love" and casual sex. Sexually transmitted diseases once again became a problem and educational campaigns were stepped up—this time in a less judgmental manner. Free clinics cropped up everywhere and young people were encouraged to come if they thought they may be infected or simply to be tested. By the mid-1980s, HIV/AIDS had become a firm reality in Canada and educational efforts by provincial governments and grassroots organizations increased, encouraging condom use and changes of sexual behaviour.

STIs have historically been viewed as symbols of corrupt sexuality (Allen, 2000). When compared with other illnesses such as cancer or diabetes, attitudes have been considerably more negative and many believed that got what they deserved. This has been referred to as the "**punishment concept**" of disease. It was generally believed that to acquire an STI, one must break the silent moral code of sexual responsibility. Those who become infected therefore have done something bad, for which they are being punished.

Kopelman (1988) suggested that this conceptualization has endured because it serves as a defence mechanism. In believing that people are responsible for acquiring an STI because of their behaviour, others see themselves as safe by not engaging in that behaviour.

Safer Sex and Sexually Transmitted Infections

Much earlier rhetoric and research on STIs and HIV/AIDS discussed contagion in terms of "high-risk groups." For example, because young African Americans in the United States have a higher incidence of STIs than European Americans (Barrow et al., 2008), merely being a young African American was said to render one in a high risk group. While such a perspective does have merit in

epidemiology when calculating probabilities of infection, it can have negative repercussions in terms of prevention, politics, and prejudice. We have already discussed how prostitutes—and along with them, poor and disenfranchised women—were blamed for the spread of syphilis and gonorrhea during and after World War I, while the servicemen who engaged them were seen as mere victims.

In the 1980s (and beyond), Haitian Canadians, who made up a sizable minority in Quebec, were a named high-risk group for HIV/AIDS (Sabatier, 1988). They were even referred to indirectly in a Quebec-government-produced safer-sex pamphlet entitled "AIDS: Understanding AIDS" (1989), when it advised that it is "dangerous" to have sex "with a person who comes from a country with a high number of AIDS cases." As a result, this group and others were considered as people to avoid in any sexual or romantic pursuit.

Perhaps most prominently of all, however, were gay men, who were subject to much vitriolic rhetoric about their "immoral lifestyles" and how they were responsible for infecting the populations of their nations (Altman, 1987). As a result, African Americans, women, Haitians, Africans, gay men, and even lesbians (whose incidence of STIs and HIV has been very low) have been the victims of much prejudice.

Not only does the naming of risk groups have negative consequences for members within those groups, but it tends to distort the concept of "risk" for sexually active people. Disease transmission is dependent upon behaviour—that is, what one *does* sexually—and not on whether a partner is a member of a group. Having safer sex with any partner is a systematic way of avoiding infection in that the same behaviour is applied to all sexual activity regardless of circumstance. The careful selection of partners thought to be uninfected is not systematic (Aveline, 1995), nor is it accurate. Furthermore, while it might be a good idea to ask questions about another's sexual history, it is often the case that people do not know whether they are infected, misrepresent themselves, or lie outright (Cochran & Mays, 1990). Safer sex should thus be a matter of behaviour and not the interpretive selection of uninfected partners whether by sexual history or by group membership (see accompanying Sex in Real Life feature).

There are several factors associated with the decision to have safer sex, many of which have to do with self-efficacy. First, people are more likely to engage in unsafe sex after having drunk alcohol or used drugs (Dye & Upchurch, 2006; Rehm et al., 2012, Scott-Sheldon et al., 2009). If the sex is planned and condom use is intended, drunkenness may lead one to forget. If the sex is unplanned and spontaneous, people may also forget condoms or they may be unavailable.

Probably the best method of STI avoidance is the use of condoms during any penetrative sexual activity. There are, however, several obstacles to their use. First, they have historically been defined as birth-control devices rather than means of disease prevention. In one study of the sexual behaviour of Canadian university students, condom use was most likely when used to avoid pregnancy (Milhausen et al., 2013). As a result, many men and women might avoid them if the women were using other birth control methods.

punishment concept	**epidemiology**
The idea that people who had become infected with sexually transmitted infections did something wrong and are being punished.	The science of the incidence, prevalence, and distribution of disease in large populations.

The Canadian AIDS Society (CAS) assesses risk of HIV transmission on four levels— none, negligible, low, and high. Below is a selected list of sexual activities and the categories under which they fall. Note that these risk assessments are for HIV/AIDS only. One may, however, be at risk for other STIs. Note also that the CAS does not mention abstinence because it is not a sex act and thus irrelevant to protecting oneself during sexual activity.

Sex Act	Risk Category
Wet or dry kissing	None
Wet or dry kissing, exchange of blood (e.g., bleeding gums)	Low
Oral sex (fellatio) with a condom	Negligible
Oral sex (fellatio) without a condom	Low
Oral sex (cunnilingus) with a barrier	Negligible
Oral sex (cunnilingus) without a barrier	Low
Vaginal intercourse with a condom	Low
Vaginal intercourse without a condom	High
Anal intercourse with a condom	Low
Anal intercourse without a condom	High
Vaginal or anal fingering	Negligible
Masturbation by partner	None
Vulva-to-vulva rubbing	Negligible
Penetration by unshared sex toys (e.g., dildos)	None
Penetration by shared sex toys	High

SOURCE: Adapted from *HIV Transmission: Guidelines for Assessing Risk*. (2004). Canadian AIDS Society. Fifth Edition.

Second, condom use is directly related to levels of self-efficacy, or the ability to put into practice what one intends to put into practice. According to French and Holland (2013), who looked at a sample of American college students, low self-efficacy was directly related to the non-use of condoms while high self-efficacy was related to their use. Education and intervention techniques are thus necessary and have had a degree of success (Czuchry et al., 2009).

Finally, for condoms to be effective, they must be used correctly (Hollander, 1997). They must be stored at room temperature, opened carefully while avoiding sharp objects that may tear them such as jewellery, rolled on properly, and taken off properly. One must also use a water-based rather than oil-based lubricant. In one study of gay men who used condoms for anal intercourse, condom failure was most likely for those with little experience and decreased dramatically with greater experience (Thompson et al., 1993). As this and other studies strongly suggest, condom failures are matters of improper use rather than defects in manufacturing (Mindel & Sawleshwarkar, 2008).

Age, Race, Gender, Sexual Orientation, and Sexually Transmitted Infections

How do STIs intersect with age, race/ethnicity, gender, and the gender of sex partners? Because these variables may reflect different behaviours, outlooks, and experiences, higher rates have been found among young people, some minority populations, and men who have sex with men (MSM).

First, teenagers and young adults are disproportionately affected by STIs and the incidence among them continues to grow in Canada because many do not use condoms or do not use them consistently.

During vaginal intercourse, women are at high risk for long-term complications from STIs because the tissue of the vagina is much more fragile than penile skin. There is an additional risk in that semen often remains in the female reproductive tract for a period of time (Bolton et al., 2008). Women are also more likely to be **asymptomatic** and therefore would not know that they are infected. Some infections, such as herpes and HIV, also have properties of **latency**. A person can have the virus that causes the infection but not have symptoms, and tests may even show up negative. As a result, the person may be unaware that he or she is infecting others. This is why it is important to inform past sexual partners if you find yourself infected.

Some minority groups also have high rates of STIs. In Canada, rates of gonorrhea, syphilis, and chlamydia are far higher in the three territories as well as the northern sections of Ontario, Quebec, and the western provinces where the populations are mostly First Nations and Inuit groups (PHAC, 2008). Much of this pattern can be explained by limited access to health care and health education. On the whole, Aboriginal people have had STI rates up to four times higher than the general population (Calzavara et al., 1999).

It was originally thought that Aboriginal people on reserves were insulated from STIs because of their isolation and less interaction with other people. This however has never been the case. In one study (Calzavara et al., 1999), 651 Aboriginal men and women from 11 Ontario reserves were interviewed and 58 percent reported having sex in the last 12 months. Of this subgroup, 51 percent reported having sex partners inside their community, 27 percent reported partners from outside, and the remainder from both inside and out. Even though this last group was more likely to use condoms during sexual activity, a pathway into the communities was enabled from outside contacts.

In the United States, African Americans have higher rates of several STIs. Although they make up a minority of the population of the country, they accounted for 69 percent of gonorrhea cases, 47 percent of chlamydia cases, and 43 percent of syphilis cases in 2006 (Barrow et al., 2008). These elevated rates may be partially explained by the fact that African Americans are more likely to be treated in public clinics, which are more likely to report STIs (Arrington-Sanders et al., 2007). Other factors such as access to health care, the ability to seek help, poverty, and sexual behaviours are also responsible for some of the rate disparities (Centers for Disease Control and Prevention, 2010c).

Although it has historically been difficult to determine because of stigma, the rates of STIs among men who have sex with men (MSM) in Canada have recently been several times higher than those of men who have sex with women (MSW). In 2003, the Canadian Community Health Survey (CCHS), which included computer-based interviews of over 135 000 Canadians, included a question on sexual orientation for the first time. Thus, there are data on men identifying as gay or bisexual, but not all MSM.

According to Brennan et al. (2010), those men identifying as heterosexual were slightly older (with a mean age of 44.4 years), were more likely to be immigrants (21.9 percent), and were more likely to have less than a high school education (18.1 percent).

REAL Research Rotermann (2005) looked at a sample of 18 084 people 15 to 24 from the 2003 Canadian Community Health Survey and found that for both males and females the mean age of first sexual intercourse was 16.5. Those age 15 to 17 were most likely to have used a condom at their last sexual intercourse, while 20- to 24-year-olds were least likely. Rotermann explains this by suggesting that the older group was more likely to be in a relationship and thus saw condoms as less necessary. Of all sexually active respondents, 4 percent reported having had an STI.

When asked if they had ever been diagnosed with an STI, 5.4 percent of the heterosexual men, 9.4 of the bisexual men, and 26.6 percent of the gay men responded affirmatively. These figures however do not reflect current infection rates but historical ones in that the gay men (with a mean age of 39.9 years) were responding to whether they had *ever* been diagnosed, rather than their current health status. The reasons for the higher lifetime rates, however, may be that gay men have historically been more sexually active and more likely to have open relationships.

Although some health care providers believe that women who have sex with women (WSW) are at low risk for STIs, they can in fact acquire bacterial and viral STIs (Workowski & Berman, 2010). Transmission can occur with skin-to-skin contact, oral sex, and vaginal or anal penetration using hands, fingers, or shared sex toys. WSW are also at risk for various infections that can be transmitted during vulva-to-vulva contact. Because WSW often have fewer sex partners than heterosexual women and because they engage in less penetrative sex, their overall risk for STIs is reduced (VanderLaan & Vasey, 2008). However, WSW are less likely to undergo yearly pelvic examinations, putting them at greater risk for adverse complications of STIs (Bauer & Welles, 2001; Marrazzo, 2004; Tjepkema, 2008). Overall, the incidence of STIs is significantly greater among bisexual women than lesbians (Koh et al., 2005; Morrow & Allsworth, 2000; Tao, 2008).

Birth Control, Pregnancy, and Sexually Transmitted Infections

In Chapter 6, we discussed birth control methods and their varying levels of protection from STIs. Barrier methods such as condoms, diaphragms, or contraceptive sponges can decrease the risk for acquiring an STI. Although nonoxynol-9 (N-9) is an effective spermicide, frequent use can cause vaginal or anal irritation, which may increase the rate of genital ulceration, thus leading to higher risk for STI infection (Boonstra, 2005; Jain et al., 2005; B.A. Richardson, 2002; Wilkinson et al., 2002).

asymptomatic
Without recognizable symptoms.

latency
A period in which a person is infected with a sexually transmitted infection but does not test positive for it.

The role of oral contraceptives in preventing STIs is complicated. The increased hormone levels change the cervical mucus and the lining of the uterus, which can help prevent any infectious substance from moving up into the genital tract. In addition, the reduced buildup of the endometrium decreases the possibility of an infectious substance growing because there is less nutritive material for bacteria to survive. However, oral contraceptives may also cause the cervix to be more susceptible to infections because of changes in the vaginal discharge.

When a woman does become pregnant, untreated STIs can adversely affect her pregnancy. Syphilis, gonorrhea, chlamydia, herpes, hepatitis B, and HIV can cause miscarriages, stillbirths, early onset of labour, premature rupture of the amniotic sac, intellectual disability, and fetal or uterine infection (Kimberlin, 2007; Su et al., 2010). Syphilis can cross the placenta and infect a developing fetus, while other STIs such as gonorrhea, chlamydia, and herpes can infect newborn babies as they move through the vagina during delivery. HIV can also cross the placenta, infect a newborn at birth, or unlike other STIs, be transmitted during breast-feeding (Salazar-Gonzalez et al., 2011).

Bacterial STIs can be treated during pregnancy with antibiotics, and if treatment is begun immediately, there is less chance that the newborn will become infected. Antiviral medications can be given to pregnant women to lessen the symptoms of viral infections (Bardeguez et al., 2008; Kriebs, 2008). If there are active vaginal lesions or sores from an STI at the time of delivery, a health care provider may recommend a cesarean section.

In the following section, we will explore several categories of STIs, including ectoparasitic, bacterial, and viral, and then examine cross-cultural aspects of STIs.

Review Questions

1 Define the punishment concept of "disease and explain the consequences to people defined as members of "risk groups."

2 Name some sex acts and place them into the CAS's categories of "no risk" to "high risk."

3 How can STIs affect pregnancy and childbirth?

4 Discuss the role of birth control in decreasing STI risk.

Ectoparasitic Infections: Pubic Lice and Scabies

Ectoparasitic infections are caused by parasites that live on hair or the surface of the skin. The two that are sexually transmitted are pubic lice and scabies.

Pubic Lice

Pubic lice ("crabs") or *Pthirus pubis* are small wingless insects that attach themselves to pubic hair with their claws. They feed off blood vessels just beneath the skin and are difficult to detect because of their size. They may also attach themselves to other hair on the body, although they mainly infest pubic hair. When not attached to the human body, pubic lice cannot survive more than 24 hours. They reproduce rapidly and the female cements her eggs to the sides of pubic hair. These eggs hatch in seven to nine days and the newly hatched nits reproduce within 17 days. They live exclusively on human beings, although there are similar species that affect gorillas (Weiss, 2009).

Incidence

Pubic lice are common among sexually active people. It is difficult to know how many Canadians are affected because there are no mandatory reporting laws. The World Health Organization (WHO) lists pubic lice as one of the most common STIs worldwide (World Health Organization, 2006).

Symptoms

According to the Public Health Agency of Canada (PHAC, 2008), the most common symptom is a mild to unbearable itching, which is thought to be a result of an allergic reaction to the saliva that the lice secrete during their feeding. This itching as well as the lice bites may lead to skin irritation, and blue spots may appear where they have bitten. Constant scratching may in turn lead to secondary bacterial infection of the skin.

Diagnosis

A pubic lice infection is diagnosed by finding the parasites or eggs in the pubic hair. Although they can be seen with the naked eye, a magnifying lens can also be used.

Treatment

According to PHAC (2008), it is necessary to kill both the parasites and their eggs to treat pubic lice. In addition, the eggs must be destroyed on sheets, towels, and clothing. Over-the-counter creams or shampoos can be used and one may obtain more powerful ones through prescription if the over-the-counter methods do not work. All sheets, towels, and articles of clothing that have come into contact with the infected person prior to treatment should be machine washed in hot water 50 degrees Celsius or more and dried. Items that cannot be washed should

pubic lice
A parasitic sexually transmitted infection that infests the pubic hair and are transmitted through sexual contact; also called *crabs*.

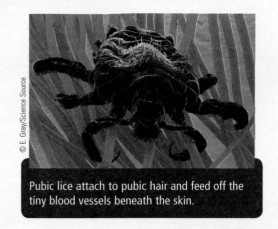

Pubic lice attach to pubic hair and feed off the tiny blood vessels beneath the skin.

be dry-cleaned or stored in a sealed plastic bag for two weeks. As with the other STIs, it is important to inform all sex partners within the previous month that they are at risk.

mostly affects children and the elderly. It is also common in Canada and affects many people who have contracted it through sexual contact.

Scabies

Scabies is an ectoparasitic infection of the skin by mites called *Sarcoptes scabiei*. It is spread during skin-to-skin contact both during sexual and nonsexual contact. It may also be transferred through objects. The mites burrow into the top layers of the skin where the female lays her eggs and can live for up to 48 hours on bed sheets and clothing. It can barely be seen with the naked eye.

Incidence

As with pubic lice, there are no mandatory reporting laws for scabies in Canada, but scabies affects millions of people worldwide. According to the WHO (2006), scabies is most common in hotter developing countries where there is much poverty and

Symptoms

Usually the first symptoms include a rash and intense itching. The first time a person is infected, the symptoms may take four to six weeks to develop. If a person has been infected with scabies previously, the symptoms usually develop more quickly.

Diagnosis

A diagnosis can usually be made on examination of the skin rash and a skin scraping can be done for confirmation. A delay in diagnosis can lead to a rapid spread of scabies, so immediate diagnosis and treatment are necessary (Tjioe & Vissers, 2008).

On Your Mind

Can public lice be spread through casual contact?

Yes. Although the principle means of transmission is through sexual contact, it is possible to become infested after sleeping in the bed of a person who was infected or by wearing the same clothes without washing them. It is also possible to become infested by sharing the same towels, combs and brushes, or toilet seats with a person who is infected.

Treatment

Prescription creams are available to treat scabies. All bed sheets, clothing, and towels must be washed in hot water and all sex partners should be treated. Usually itching continues for two to three weeks after treatment.

Review Questions

1 Identify the two ectoparasitic STIs and describe them.

2 Identify the most common symptoms associated with ectoparasitic STIs and explain what people should do if they experience any of those symptoms.

3 Identify the treatments for ectoparasitic STIs.

Bacterial Infections: Gonorrhea, Syphilis, Chlamydia, and Others

Some STIs are caused by bacteria. They include gonorrhea, syphilis, chlamydia, several vaginal infections, and pelvic inflammatory disease (PID). In this section, we explore the incidence, symptoms, diagnosis, and treatment for these infections.

Gonorrhea

Gonorrhea (the "clap") is caused by the bacterium *Neisseria gonorrhoeae*, which is found in the mucous membranes of the body, such as the cervix, urethra, mouth, throat, rectum, and eyes.

scabies	gonorrhea
A parasitic sexually transmitted infection that affects the skin and is spread during skin-to-skin contact both during sexual and non-sexual contact.	A bacterial sexually transmitted infection that causes a pus-like discharge and frequent urination in men. Many women are asymptomatic.

N. *gonorrhoeae* is fragile and can be destroyed by exposure to light, air, soap, water, or a change in temperature—thus, it is nearly impossible to transmit gonorrhea non-sexually. The only exception is the transmission of gonorrhea from a mother to her baby as the baby passes through the vagina during delivery. Transmission of gonorrhea occurs when mucous membranes come into contact with each other and this can occur during vaginal or anal intercourse, oral sex, and vulva-to-vulva contact.

Incidence

Of all bacterial STIs, gonorrhea is the second-most commonly reported in Canada, amounting to 12 723 cases in Canada in 2008. Between 1999 and 2008, rates increased from 22.0 to 42.9 per 100 000 people for men and from 12.2 to 33.5 per 100,000 for women (see Figure 7.1). Although the highest number of cases were in Ontario and Alberta, the highest rates were in Nunavut and the Northwest Territories. Women therefore had the greater increase at 151.5 percent. People under 20 years old accounted for nearly three-quarters of cases (71.5 percent) in 2008, and the highest rates for women were among 15- to 19-year-olds (PHAC, 2008).

Symptoms

Most men who are infected with gonorrhea experience symptoms alerting them of the infection. Because they do not appear

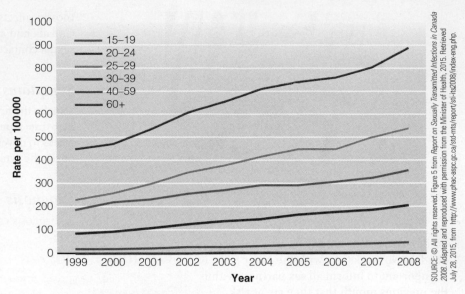

FIGURE **7.1** Reported rates of gonorrhea by sex and overall, 1999 to 2008, Canada.

immediately, they can unknowingly infect others beforehand (Workowski & Berman, 2010). Common symptoms in men are a urethral discharge, painful urination, an increase in the frequency and urgency of urination, and **epididymitis**, which is an inflammation epididymis found in the testicles. Symptoms usually appear between two and six days after infection.

Unlike men, most women do not experience symptoms until complications develop, such as pelvic inflammatory disease (discussed later in this chapter). If symptoms do develop, they typically begin within three to five days and include an increase in urinary frequency, abnormal uterine bleeding, and bleeding after vaginal penetration, which results from an irritation of the cervix. The cervical discharge can irritate the vaginal lining causing pain and discomfort. Urination can be difficult and painful. Gonorrhea is a major cause of PID in women.

Rectal gonorrhea, which can be transmitted to men and women during anal intercourse, may cause bloody stools and a pus-like discharge. If left untreated, gonorrhea can move throughout the body and settle in various areas including the joints and cause swelling, pain, and pus-filled infections.

Diagnosis

Testing for gonorrhea involves collecting a sample of the discharge from the cervix, urethra, anus, or throat with a cotton swab. The sample is incubated to allow the bacteria to multiply. It is then put on a slide and examined under a microscope for the presence of the **gonococcus bacterium**. Gonorrhea may also be detected in a urine sample.

Treatment

According to PHAC (2008), uncomplicated gonorrhea may be treated with a single done of oral or injectable antibiotics. Resistant strains however are more complicated and, as a result, antibiotics such as penicillin and tetracycline are no longer recommended in

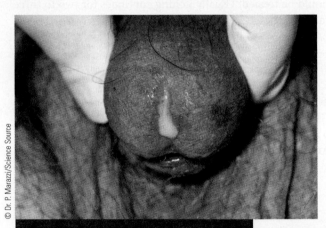

The majority of men infected with gonorrhea experience symptoms and will seek out treatment. Before diagnosis, they may have infected others unknowingly.

epididymitis
An inflammation of the epididymis found in the testicles of men, usually resulting from sexually transmitted infections.

gonococcus bacterium
The bacterium that causes gonorrhea (*Neisseria gonorrhoeae*).

Sexual Diversity in Our World

The Hassle Free Clinic, Toronto

The Hassle Free Clinic, one of Canada's largest sexual health clinics, has been a fixture in Toronto since the time it opened on Yonge Street in 1973. It formed in response to the needs of street people, gays and lesbians, and others seeking "hassle-free" medical treatment for STIs, advice on birth control, and other services. Since the 1980s it had been seen primarily as a gay health clinic because of the AIDS epidemic and the great number of men seeking testing and treatment. Once HIV testing became available in 1985, it immediately began offering anonymous testing even though this was illegal in Ontario at the time. It lobbied for several years for its legalization, which came about only in 1992. Throughout its history, it has been a major forerunner of frontline medical treatment. In June 2004, it moved to 66 Gerrard Street East in Toronto.

Canada. This has led the National Microbiology Laboratory at PHAC to constantly monitor other antibiotics, testing their resistance to various strains.

Because patients with gonorrhea are often co-infected with other STIs, such as chlamydia, dual treatment is possible (Workowski & Berman, 2010). If people are infected, their sex partners should also be tested, regardless of whether they are experiencing symptoms. Patients should be retested three months after treatment. Often, reinfection, after treatment is caused by the failure of sex partners to get tested or receive treatment.

Syphilis

Syphilis, according to one hypothesis, originated in North America and it was not until the time of Christopher Columbus that it was brought back to Europe (Rothschild, 2005). It is caused by infection of the bacterium *Treponema pallidum*, which enters the body through small tears in the skin and lives in the mucous membranes. Syphilis is transmitted during sexual contact and it usually first infects the cervix, penis, anus, or lips. **Congenital syphilis** may also be transmitted through the placenta during the first or second trimester of pregnancy.

Incidence

Like gonorrhea, syphilis has been legally notifiable in Canada since 1924. Rates were stable from 1993 to 2000 and then began to climb the next year, more so among men, who accounted for 86.1 percent of cases. In 2008, 1394 cases were reported to PHAC, or a rate of 4.2 per 100 000 people (see Figure 7.2). In that same year, and like gonorrhea, people under age 30 accounted for nearly three-quarters (73.6 percent) of cases. The highest rate was in the Northwest Territories, which skyrocketed at 122.4 per 100 000, compared to the next highest rate of 6.8 in Alberta. It should be noted, however, that because the populations of the territories are low (109 340 in all three territories in 2013) compared to the provinces, the rates may be skewed. The highest number of cases in 2008 was 444 in Ontario (PHAC, 2008).

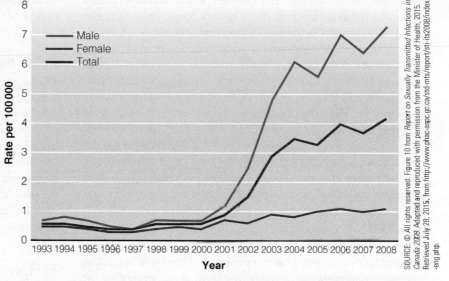

FIGURE 7.2 Reported rates of infectious syphilis by sex and overall, 1993 to 2008, Canada.

Symptoms

Infection with syphilis is divided into three stages. The first stage occurs from 10 to 90 days after infection and typically within two to six weeks. During this stage, there may be one or more small reddish-brown sores called **chancres**, which appear on the vulva, penis, vagina, cervix, anus, mouth, or lips. They are round sores with hard, raised edges and sunken centres. They are usually painless and do not itch. If left untreated, they will heal in three to eight weeks. Even so, a, person can still transmit the disease to sex partners.

---

syphilis
A bacterial sexually transmitted infection that progresses into primary, secondary, and tertiary stages.

congenital syphilis
A syphilis infection acquired by an infant from the mother during pregnancy.

chancre
A small, reddish brown sore that results from syphilis infection. This sore is the site at which the bacteria entered the body.

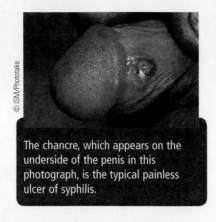
The chancre, which appears on the underside of the penis in this photograph, is the typical painless ulcer of syphilis.

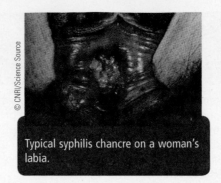
Typical syphilis chancre on a woman's labia.

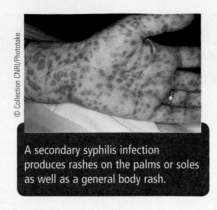
A secondary syphilis infection produces rashes on the palms or soles as well as a general body rash.

The secondary stage begins anywhere from three to six weeks after the chancre has healed. During this stage, syphilis invades the central nervous system. The infected person develops reddish patches on the skin that look like a rash or hives. There may also be wart-like growths in the area of infection (D.L. Brown & Frank, 2003). If the rash develops on the scalp, hair loss may occur. The lymph glands in the groin, armpits, neck, or other areas enlarge and become tender. Other symptoms at this stage include headaches, fever, and fatigue.

In the third stage, the disease goes into remission. The rash, fever, and other symptoms go away, and the infected person usually feels normal. The infected person, however, is still able to transmit the disease for about a year, after which he or she is no longer infectious. Left untreated, however, tertiary or late syphilis can cause neurological, sensory, muscular, and psychological difficulties and is eventually fatal.

Diagnosis

Anyone who develops a chancre should immediately go to a health care provider to be tested for the presence of the syphilis-causing bacteria. A diagnosis can be made by culturing and evaluating the lesion or through a blood test. Blood tests check for the presence of antibodies, which develop after a person is infected. During tertiary syphilis, blood tests may be negative or only weakly positive even if the infection exists (Singh et al., 2008). Sex partners should also be tested for syphilis even if they have no symptoms.

Treatment

In its early stages, syphilis is relatively easy to treat. If a person has been infected for less than a year, treatment typically involves a single injection of an antibiotic. Additional doses may be required if a person has been infected longer than a year (Workowski & Berman, 2010). However, if syphilis is allowed to progress to the later stages, it is no longer treatable and is often fatal.

Chlamydia

Chlamydia is the common name for infections caused by a bacterium called *Chlamydia trachomatis*. It can be transmitted during vaginal or anal intercourse or oral sex. Oral sex with an infected partner can lead to pharyngeal (throat) chlamydia infections as well (Karlsson et al., 2011). An infected woman can pass the infection to her newborn during childbirth.

Incidence

Unlike gonorrhea and syphilis, mandatory reporting of chlamydia cases have taken place in Canada only since 1991 and it is now the most frequently reported STI. In 2008, 82 919 cases were reported, or a rate of 248.9 per 100 000 people (see Figure 7.3). However, because many men and women are asymptomatic, the actual number of cases is likely much higher. People under age 30 accounted for 82.6 percent of cases. Rates were higher in women for people under 40 and higher in men for those over 40. Rates were highest in the Northwest Territories at 2010.0 per 100 000 or about one in 50 people (PHAC, 2008).

Symptoms

Chlamydia has been called a "silent disease" because many women and men are asymptomatic (Workowski & Berman, 2010). Those who do have symptoms usually develop them within one to three weeks after becoming infected. With or without symptoms, chlamydia is contagious, which explains why rates are increasing.

If there are symptoms, a woman might experience burning during urination, pain during penetration, and pain in the lower abdomen. In most women, the cervix is the site of infection with chlamydia and cervical bleeding or spotting may occur. Men may experience a penile discharge, burning sensations during urination, burning and itching around the opening of the urethra, and a pain or swelling in the testicles. The bacterium that causes chlamydia can also cause epididymitis and **non-gonococcal urethritis** in men.

In women, the bacteria can move from the uterus to the Fallopian tubes and ovaries, leading to PID and increasing the risk for infertility and ectopic pregnancies (Workowski & Berman, 2010). Chlamydia is considered one of the agents most responsible for the development of PID (Haggerty et al., 2010; Nair & Baguley, 2010; Soper, 2010). Women who are infected with cervical chlamydia and who undergo a surgical abortion or vaginal birth are also at increased risk for the development of PID (Boeke et al., 2005).

chlamydia	non-gonococcal urethritis
A bacterial sexually transmitted infection (STI), which is often asymptomatic. It is considered one of the most damaging of STIs.	Urethral infection in men that is usually caused by chlamydia.

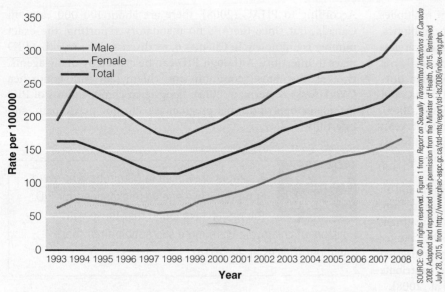

FIGURE 7.3 Reported rates of chlamydia by sex and overall, 1991 to 2008, Canada.

Diagnosis

Chlamydia is most often diagnosed through urine testing but also from cultures of the vagina, cervix, urethra, rectum, or mouth. Symptoms may also appear in the eye and swaps of the eyelids are necessary.

Treatment

The recommended treatment for chlamydia is antibiotics, typically azithromycin (one oral dose) or doxycycline twice a day for seven days (Workowski & Berman, 2010). Patients are advised to abstain from vaginal and anal intercourse as well as oral sex for seven days after beginning antibiotic treatment. All sex partners should also be tested even if they have no symptoms. Recurring chlamydia is usually due to the failure of sex partners to get tested or receive treatment. All men and women diagnosed with chlamydia should be retested within three months of treatment.

Vaginal Infections

Vaginal infections, characterized by a discharge, itching, and/or odour are most frequently caused by **bacterial vaginosis (BV)**, trichomoniasis, and candidiasis (Workowski & Berman, 2010).

BV is caused by an overgrowth of various types of bacteria in the vagina, which replace normal healthy bacteria. It is the most common cause of vaginal discharge, although many women might be asymptomatic (Workowski & Berman, 2010). If there are symptoms, they may include an increase in vaginal discharge (usually a thin, white discharge) accompanied by a strong fishy odour. Women who have sex with women may be at increased risk for BV because they have more exposure to vaginal secretions (Evans et al., 2007; Marrazzo et al., 2008, 2010).

Treatment involves the use of antibiotics and female sex partners should also be tested. Researchers are also evaluating the use of probiotics as a treatment of BV (Bolton et al., 2008; Marrazzo

et al., 2007). Probiotics such as the bacterium **Lactobacillus** are dietary supplements that help regulate bacteria and yeast in the body.

Trichomoniasis (trick-oh-mun-NYE-iss-sis; also called *trich*) is caused by *Trichomonas vaginalis* bacteria. Women can get it from an infected man or woman and a man usually gets it only from an infected woman. The trichomoniasis bacteria is acquired through male-female or female-female sexual behaviour and rarely through male-male sexual behaviour. Symptoms usually appear anywhere from three to 28 days after infection.

The most common symptom is an increase in vaginal discharge, which may be yellowish or greenish yellow, frothy, and foul smelling. It may cause a burning or itching sensation in the vagina. Some women are asymptomatic or have minimal symptoms (Workowski & Berman, 2010). In men, the most common site of infection is the urethra, and the infection is often asymptomatic. If there are symptoms, there may be a slight increase in burning on the tip of the penis, mild discharge, or slight burning after urination or ejaculation. Treatment for trichomoniasis involves the use of antibiotics and it is recommended that all partners should be treated and sex should be avoided until after treatment.

Vulvovaginal candidiasis (can-DID-i-asssis; yeast infections, also called *moniliasis* or *candidiasis*) is usually caused by *C. albicans*, but it can also be caused by other *Candida* (or yeast). Seventy-five percent of women will experience a **yeast infection** and about 40 percent to 45 percent will have two or more episodes in their lifetimes (C. Wilson, 2005;

On Your Mind

If a woman has a vaginal discharge that is yellowish white, itchy, and has no odour, should she use an over-the-counter cream?

Having a discharge does not mean that a woman definitely has a vaginal infection. Normal vaginal discharge can range from white to slightly yellow and it varies throughout the menstrual cycle. A yeast infection often causes vaginal itching and burning, pain during sex and urination, and a thick, white discharge. Researchers have found only one in four women who seek treatment for a yeast infection actually has one (Hoffstetter et al., 2008). Vaginal itching can also include inflammation and dry skin, and can be caused by STIs such as BV. Like a yeast infection, BV can sometimes be triggered by the use of antibiotics or the use of feminine hygiene products. Over-the-counter medications for yeast infections fight fungus, but they are ineffective against BV.

bacterial vaginosis (BV)
Bacterial infection that can cause vaginal discharge and odour but is often asymptomatic.

Lactobacillus
Bacteria in the vagina that helps maintain appropriate pH levels.

trichomoniasis
A vaginal infection that may result in discomfort, discharge, and inflammation.

vulvovaginal candidiasis
An infection of the vagina that involves an overgrowth of yeast known as candida. Also called a yeast infection.

Workowski & Berman, 2010). Typically the organism multiplies when the pH balance of the vagina is disturbed by antibiotics, douching, pregnancy, oral contraceptive use, diabetes, or careless wiping after defecation. Although yeast infections are usually not sexually transmitted during male-female sex, if a woman does experience multiple infections, her sex partners should be evaluated and treated with topical antifungal creams (C. Wilson, 2005). Although male sex partners are less likely to transmit yeast because the penis does not provide the right environment for its growth, female partners can transmit yeast infections during sexual activity (R. Bailey et al., 2008).

Symptoms of a yeast infection include burning, itching, and an increase in vaginal discharge. The discharge may be white, thin, and watery and may include thick white chunks. Treatment involves either an antifungal prescription or over-the-counter drugs, which are applied topically on the vulva and can be inserted into the vagina. Misuse of over-the-counter drugs can contribute to medication-resistant strains of yeast (Hoffstetter et al., 2008).

Like BV, probiotics have also been used in the treatment of yeast infections (Falagas et al., 2006; Watson & Calabretto, 2007). *Lactobacillus* is a type of beneficial bacteria found in the vagina of healthy women and also in yogurt. Eating one cup of yogurt daily may help reduce yeast infection recurrences (Falagas et al., 2006; Watson & Calabretto, 2007).

Pelvic Inflammatory Disease

PID is an infection of the female genital tract including the endometrium, Fallopian tubes, and the lining of the pelvic area.

According to PHAC (2008), there are about 100 000 cases in Canada, but since there is no mandatory reporting, the exact number is unknown. In Chapter 6, we discussed the role that PID plays in infertility. Although PID can be caused by many agents, two of the most common are chlamydia and gonorrhea (Workowski & Berman, 2010). Long-term complications of PID include ectopic and tubal pregnancies, chronic pelvic pain, and infertility.

> **REAL Research** A sample of women in Manitoba who were of reproductive age were examined for PID. The researchers found that those with a history of chlamydia were more susceptible than those without (Davies et al., 2014).

Symptoms of PID vary and there may be none at all or they may be severe. They may include acute pelvic pain, fever, painful urination, and abnormal vaginal bleeding or discharge. There are a variety of treatment approaches to PID, and treatment is usually dependent on the progression of the infection. For women with mildly to moderately severe PID, treatment is typically done with antibiotics. Women with acute cases may need intravenous treatments. Sex partners should be treated if they have had sexual contact with the woman 60 days before the onset of her symptoms.

Review Questions

1 Identify the bacterial STIs and describe their symptoms.

2 Explain how rates of bacterial STIs vary by age, gender, and geographic area.

3 Identify the common treatments for bacterial STIs.

4 Compare the common vaginal infections including trichomoniasis, BV, and vulvovaginal candidiasis.

5 Define pelvic inflammatory disease (PID) and identify causes, symptoms, and long-term risks.

Viral Infections: Herpes, Human Papillomavirus, and Hepatitis

STIs can also be caused by viruses. Once a virus invades a body cell, it is able to reproduce itself, so most of the time people will retain it for the rest of their lives. Viruses can live in the body even though people may not have any symptoms. We now discuss herpes, human papillomavirus (HPV), and hepatitis. Later in this chapter we will discuss HIV and AIDS.

Herpes

Herpes simplex 1 (HSV-1) and **herpes simplex 2 (HSV-2)** are members of the **herpes** virus family. HSV-1 is often transmitted through kissing or sharing eating utensils or drinking vessels and causes cold sores or blisters. Although HSV-1 can lead to genital herpes if an infected person performs oral sex on someone, the majority of cases of genital herpes are caused by an infection with HSV-2 (Workowski & Berman, 2010). When the virus infects a non-preferred site (i.e., HSV-1 infects the genitals or HSV-2 infects the mouth or lips), symptoms are often less severe.

herpes simplex 1 (HSV-1)
A viral infection usually transmitted through kissing or sharing eating utensils or drinking vessels and can cause cold sores or blisters on the face and mouth.

herpes simplex 2 (HSV-2)
A viral infection often sexually transmitted and responsible for genital ulcerations and blisters.

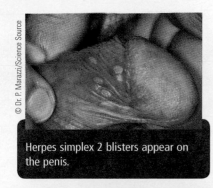

Herpes simplex 2 blisters appear on the penis.

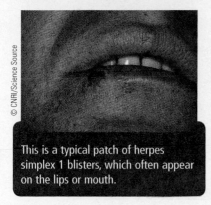

This is a typical patch of herpes simplex 1 blisters, which often appear on the lips or mouth.

HSV is highly contagious and may be released between outbreaks from the infected skin (often referred to as **viral shedding**). As a result, it is possible to transmit the virus even when the infected partner does not have any active symptoms (Mertz, 2008; Wald et al., 2000). Viral shedding is more common in genital HSV-2 infection than genital HSV-1 infection, especially during the first year after infection (Workowski & Berman, 2010). Infected people can also **autoinoculate** themselves by touching a cold sore or blister and then rubbing another part of their body.

Although HSV-2 is almost always sexually transmitted, HSV-1 is usually transmitted during childhood through non-sexual contact (Usatine & Tinitigan, 2010; Xu et al., 2006). In fact, studies suggest that by adolescence, 62 percent of people have been infected with HSV-1, and by the age of 60, 85 percent have been infected. Pregnant mothers can pass HSV-2 on to their infants while they are in the uterus, during delivery from exposure to active sores in the birth canal, or directly after birth (Corey & Handsfield, 2000).

Incidence

According to PHAC (2008), the incidence of genital herpes in Canada is not known, although in the United States about 2 million people become infected every year and they are more commonly women (Armstrong et al., 2001). However, because many men and women might have mild or unrecognizable infections, the majority of people with HSV-2 infections have never been diagnosed mainly because many do not experience blisters or ulcers (Workowski & Berman, 2010). Most people with genital herpes were infected by people who do not know they are infected themselves (Workowski & Berman, 2010).

Symptoms

Although many infected people do not experience the classic blisters associated with herpes, any symptoms usually appear within two to 12 days after infection. If blisters are present, the first episode is generally the most painful (Workowski & Berman, 2010).

At the onset, there is usually a tingling or burning sensation in the affected area, which can lead to itching and a red swollen appearance of the genitals. This period is called the **prodromal phase**. The sores usually last anywhere from eight to ten days and the level of pain they cause ranges from mild to severe. Urination also may be difficult. Small blisters may appear externally on the vagina or penis and are usually red and sometimes have a greyish centre. They will eventually burst and ooze a yellowish discharge. As they heal, a scab will form over them. Other symptoms of HSV include fever, headaches, pain, itching, vaginal or urethral discharge, and general fatigue. These symptoms peak within four days after the appearance of the blisters. Some patients with severe symptoms require hospitalization.

The frequency and severity of recurrent episodes of herpes depend on several factors including the amount of infectious agent (how much of the virus was contained in the original infecting fluids), the type of herpes, and the timing of treatment (Mark et al., 2008). People who experience symptoms during their first outbreak of genital HSV-2 infection will most likely experience recurrent episodes of blisters, but those infected with genital HSV-1 infections may not have recurrences at all (Workowski & Berman, 2010). The frequency of recurrent outbreaks diminishes over time. Certain triggers may increase the likelihood of an HSV outbreak, including exposure to sunlight (natural or tanning beds), lip trauma or chapping, sickness, menstruation, fatigue, and persistent anxiety and stress (F. Cohen et al., 1999). After several years, people may no longer experience outbreaks although they may still be contagious.

Psychological reactions to herpes outbreaks can include anxiety, guilt, anger, frustration, feelings of helplessness, a decrease in self-esteem, and depression (Dibble & Swanson, 2000). People with supportive partners and social relationships tend to do better psychologically. Those who receive psychological support services experience a greater reduction in recurrent episodes of herpes and an improvement in their emotional health (Swanson et al., 1999).

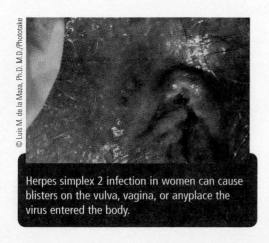

Herpes simplex 2 infection in women can cause blisters on the vulva, vagina, or anyplace the virus entered the body.

herpes
A highly contagious viral infection that causes eruptions of the skin or mucous membranes.

viral shedding
The release of viral infections between outbreaks from infected skin.

autoinoculate
To cause a secondary infection in the body from an already existing infection.

prodromal phase
The tingling or burning feeling that precedes the development of herpes blisters.

Diagnosis

During the first several weeks after infection, antibodies to HSV develop and they will remain in the body indefinitely. Blood tests are often used to diagnose HSV infection and to distinguish between HSV-1 and HSV-2. The presence of blisters caused by the herpes virus is often enough to diagnose the disease. Often, however, health care providers will take a scraping from the blisters to evaluate for the presence of HSV (Whitley & Roizman, 2001). No tests for the detection of HSV-1 or HSV-2 are entirely accurate because tests depend on the amount of infectious agent and the stage of the disease. Success rates for detecting HSV-2 antibodies vary from 80 percent to 98 percent and there are frequent false-negative results mainly because the tests are performed too early.

Treatment

The standard treatments for HSV infection today are oral antiviral drugs, which can be taken as needed to reduce an outbreak or as suppressive therapy to reduce recurrences (Workowski & Berman, 2010). These drugs also shorten the duration of outbreaks and prevent complications such as itching or scarring. They also reduce viral shedding. Suppressive therapy has been found to reduce the risk for infecting sex partners with genital HSV-2. Once a person stops taking these drugs, however, HSV symptoms will return.

Support groups, relaxation training, hypnosis, and individual therapy have also been found to reduce the stress associated with HSV infections, which can reduce the frequency and severity of outbreaks. Researchers continue to explore the development of a vaccine for HSV (Brans & Yao, 2010; Hu et al., 2011; Kask et al., 2010; Morello et al., 2011; Pouriayevali et al., 2011; Tirabassi et al., 2011). Other researchers have tested antiviral therapy to decrease viral shedding (Bernstein et al., 2011; Schiffer et al., 2010; Tan et al., 2011).

On Your Mind

Because herpes is not curable, can people still transmit it when they are asymptomatic?

Although rates of viral shedding have been found to decrease over time after the initial infection, it is possible to transmit the virus in the absence of active cold sores or lesions (Phipps et al., 2011). Health care providers recommend that people who have been infected with genital herpes always use condoms to decrease the risk of infecting their partners.

Human Papillomavirus

There are more than 40 types of HPVs that can infect the genitals, anus, mouth, and throat during vaginal and anal intercourse, oral sex, and vulva-to-vulva contact. Most people who are infected are unaware. Low-risk HPV (types 6 and 11) can cause **genital warts** (also called condyloma acuminata, venereal warts) which are different from regular warts. High-risk HPV (types 16 and 18) can cause abnormal Pap tests and increase cancer risk, especially cervical cancer in women (Grce & Davies, 2008; Tovar et al., 2008). Almost all cervical cancers can be attributed to HPV infection (Smith & Travis, 2011; Wattleworth, 2011). HPV is also a risk factor for several other types of cancer, including oral, penile, and anal cancer (Dietz & Nyberg, 2011). In fact, the incidence of anal cancer in MSM is greater than the incidence of cervical cancer among women (Chin-Hong et al., 2008; Dietz & Nyberg, 2011; Goodman et al., 2008; Palefsky, 2008).

According to research, one aspect of HPV infection that sets it apart from other viruses is that in more than 90 percent of cases, a person's immune system can clear HPV within two years (CDC, 2009c).

genital warts
Wart-like growths on the genitals, also called venereal warts, condylomata, or papilloma.

Warts that appear on the penis are usually flesh coloured and may have a bumpy appearance.

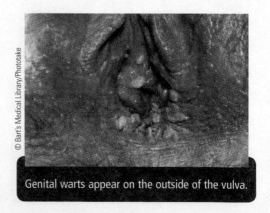

Genital warts appear on the outside of the vulva.

Incidence

According to PHAC (2008), HPV is common in Canada, although it is unmonitored and no population studies have occurred. According to studies in select populations, overall prevalence ranges from 10.8 percent to 29.0 percent and it is most common in adolescents and young adults under 25 years of age. In one study, prevalence varied by place of birth, finding that women from the western provinces, Ontario, and Europe were more likely to be affected. Higher rates were also seen in Nunavut.

Symptoms

Symptoms for HPV are dependent on the type of HPV infection. Although other types may cause genital warts, the most common ones to do so are types 6 and 11 (Workowski & Berman, 2010). These types may also cause warts in the throat, nose, and mouth. Warts are usually flesh coloured with bumpy surfaces. In some areas, they may grow together and have a cauliflower-like appearance. Warts develop in women on the vagina, vulva, introitus, or cervix, and in men on the penile shaft or under the foreskin (Workowski & Berman, 2010). They can also appear on the anus. Warts are generally asymptomatic and, unless they are large, many people do not notice them and unknowingly infect their sex partners. If warts grow in the throat (referred to as *recurrent respiratory papillomatosis*), they can potentially block the airway, causing breathing difficulties and/or a hoarse voice.

Typically, cervical cancer and other HPV-related cancers do not have symptoms until they are well advanced. Regular Pap smears will enable health care providers to monitor precancerous changes in the cervical cells (often referred to as **cervical dysplasia**). Identifying problems early can significantly reduce the risk of an infection developing into cancer.

Diagnosis

HPV may show up on Pap testing, but 80 percent to 90 percent of the time it does not (Kassler & Cates, 1992). Today, high-risk HPV DNA testing is available for women (Huang et al., in press). Cells are collected during a woman's Pap test and sent to a laboratory for analysis. Health care providers recommend that women who have more than one sex partner should ask their medical provider for an HPV DNA test. If genital warts are suspected, a health care provider may soak the infected area with acetic acid (white vinegar), which turns the warts white and makes them easier to see under magnification. An examination of the cervix under magnification (called *colposcopy*) can also be used. Biopsies may also performed to check for HPV.

Treatment

Because HPV infection can cause genital warts or abnormal changes in the cervical cells, it is important to seek treatment immediately if a person notices any genital warts. Genital warts can be treated in several ways and no treatment method is superior to another or best for all patients with HPV. Important factors for a health care provider to consider when deciding treatment options include the number and size of the warts, patient preference, convenience, and adverse effects.

Treatment alternatives include chemical topical solutions (to destroy external warts), cryotherapy (freezing the warts with liquid nitrogen), electrosurgical interventions (removal of warts using a mild electrical current), or high-intensity lasers to destroy the warts. It may be necessary to try several treatment methods and repeat applications are common.

> ### On Your Mind
>
> Could I get human papillomavirus (HPV) from the HPV vaccine? Can I get the vaccine if I've already had sex?

Both Gardasil and Cervarix contain inactivated virus-like particles from the HPV. Unlike most vaccines, they do not contain live viruses. The particles in the vaccine stimulate a woman's body to produce antibodies against HPV (FDA Office of Women's Health, 2006; Schlegel, 2007). Current recommendations are for women to have the vaccine before age 26, and ideally before becoming sexually active. However, if you are already sexually active but have not been exposed to HPV types 6, 11, 16, and 18, the vaccine will protect you from the types you have not already been exposed to. It is important to discuss these issues with your health care provider, but keep in mind that providers' opinions and attitudes about the vaccine influence whether they offer or promote the vaccine (Ishibashi et al., 2008).

An infected person should use condoms during sexual intercourse for at least six months after treatment (Lilley & Schaffer, 1990). Some couples use condoms regularly because of the possibility of transmitting the virus even when no warts are present. It is possible that a low-risk type infection may be cleared up by the immune system over time (Corneanu et al., 2011; Dunne, 2007). Women who have been diagnosed with a high-risk type of HPV may be encouraged to have pelvic examinations and Pap tests more frequently.

> ### Animal Variations
> **Do animals also have STIs?**
>
> Yes they do. While most humans will seek treatment, animals may go unchecked unless infections are detected by veterinarians or breeders. Many species live in groups where males come into sexual contact with large numbers of females. Any infections would thus spread rapidly. Cattle may become infected with trichomoniasis, papillomaviruses, and even chlamydia. One of the most common animal STIs is a parasite called *brucella*, which affects goats, sheep, cattle, swine, dogs, and occasionally humans (Oriel & Hayward, 1974).

cervical dysplasia
Disordered growth of cells in the cervix typically diagnosed with Pap testing.

Ideally, the HPV vaccine should be given before an individual is sexually active, although there is evidence that sexually active individuals may also benefit from the vaccine (National Cancer Institute, 2009). The vaccines can protect sexually active people from HPV types they have not been exposed to and may offer some protection from types to which they have already been exposed (National Cancer Institute, 2009). In addition to the reduced risk for cervical cancer in women and genital warts in both men and women, these vaccines may also reduce the risk for anal and mouth/throat cancers as well as cancer of the penis in men.

Because the vaccines are relatively new, the actual duration of immunity is unknown. Researchers continue to evaluate immunity duration but it appears that the vaccines are effective for at least four years (National Cancer Institute, 2009). Because the HPV vaccine does not protect against all types of HPV that can cause cancer, it is important that women continue to have regular Pap tests (Tovar et al., 2008).

For women, the negative side effects of the vaccine may include arm soreness, joint and muscle pain, and fatigue. In men, the most common negative side effect has been soreness at the site of the injection (Garnock-Jones & Giuliano, 2011). Some women have reported feeling light-headed after the injection (National Cancer Institute, 2009).

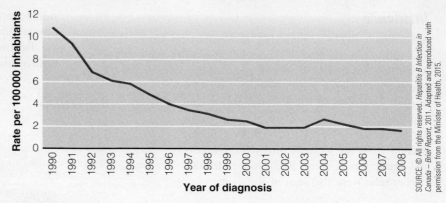

FIGURE **7.4** Reported rates of acute and indeterminate HBV infection cases by year in Canada, 1990–2008.

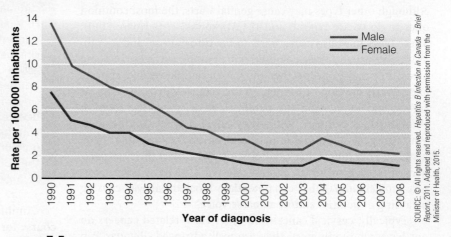

FIGURE **7.5** Reported rates of acute and indeterminate HBV infection cases by gender and year, 1990–2008.

Viral Hepatitis

Viral hepatitis is an infection that causes impaired liver function. The three main types of viral hepatitis include hepatitis A virus (HAV), hepatitis B virus (HBV), and hepatitis C virus (HCV). HAV is transmitted through anal–oral contact (analingus), HBV is predominantly spread through unprotected sexual behaviours, and although HCV can also be spread through sexual behaviour, it is mostly spread through illegal intravenous drug use or unscreened blood transfusions.

Incidence

HAV is most prevalent in developing countries with low levels of sanitation (Wasley et al., 2006) and is thus less common in Canada. HBV has been a reportable disease in Canada since 1969, and the rates have declined dramatically for both sexes from 1990 to 2008. During that period, the overall rate declined from 10.8 per 100 000 people to 1.7 per 100 000 people (see Figures 7.4 and 7.5). Globally, the World Health Organization estimates that 2 million people have evidence of past and present infection (WHO, 2008). In 2009, there were 11 357 reported cases (a rate of 33.7 per 100 000) of HCV in Canada, and this represented a

decline. The majority of cases are among intravenous drug users who are male and over age 30.

Symptoms

Symptoms of HAV usually occur within four weeks and include fatigue, abdominal pain, loss of appetite, and diarrhea. Symptoms of HBV usually occur within six weeks to six months after infection, although HBV is usually asymptomatic. Symptoms may include nausea, vomiting, jaundice, headaches, fever, a darkening of the urine, moderate liver enlargement, and fatigue. Most people infected with HCV are asymptomatic or have a mild illness that develops in eight or nine weeks. Between 60 percent and 70 percent of those infected with HCV will develop a chronic liver infection (Workowski & Berman, 2010).

Diagnosis

Blood tests are used to identify viral hepatitis infections.

Treatment

Antiviral therapies are available for the treatment and management of hepatitis. They are designed to reduce viral load by interfering with the life cycle of the virus and cause the body to generate an immune

viral hepatitis
A viral infection. The three main types of viral hepatitis are hepatitis A, B, and C.

response (Guha et al., 2003). Health care providers generally recommend bed rest and adequate fluid intake to avoid dehydration. Usually after a few weeks, an infected person feels better, although this can take longer in persons with severe and chronic infections.

Vaccines are available for the prevention of both HAV and HBV. Young children are often routinely vaccinated against both HAV and HBV. High-risk individuals include health care workers who may be exposed to blood products, intravenous drug users and their sex partners, people with multiple sex partners, people with chronic liver disease, MSM, and housemates of anyone with hepatitis. Researchers continue to seek a vaccine for HCV (Hwu et al., 2011; Ruhl et al., 2011).

1 Identify the viral STIs and describe them.

2 Explain how viral STIs vary by age, gender, and geographic area.

3 What are some typical treatments for viral STIs?

4 Identify the three types of hepatitis as well as their most common means of transmission.

HIV and AIDS

The first death from AIDS occurred in Canada in 1982 and the first organizations to raise awareness were gay-run grassroots organizations such as AIDS Vancouver and the AIDS Committee of Toronto. Since then, the government has become involved and there are now hundreds of groups involved composed of volunteers and professionals.

Although the **human immunodeficiency virus (HIV)** is a viral infection, several factors set it apart from other STIs and also shed some light on why the appearance of **acquired immune deficiency syndrome (AIDS)** in North America and Europe became so politically charged. HIV/AIDS first appeared in 1981, a time when modern medicine was believed to be well on its way to reducing epidemic diseases (D. Altman, 1986). In addition, AIDS was first identified among men who have sex with men (MSM) and intravenous drug users. Because of this early identification, the disease was linked with socially marginal groups and thought irrelevant to the general population (D. Altman, 1986; Kain, 1987). The media gave particular attention to the "lifestyles" of people with AIDS and implied that social deviance has a price. Politicians went even further and condemned people with AIDS outright as pariahs of society with no social conscience. Canadian sociologist Cindy Patton who has long specialized in the social aspects of HIV/AIDS, characterized these reactions in her book *Sex and Germs* (1985): "The new right's response to AIDS displays in blatant, ghastly terms what is latent in even the most sophisticated liberals. Old notions of sin, sickness, and criminality emerge in a full program aimed at suppressing difference." In other words, because AIDS affected gay men first in North America, it became fodder for those with religious objections to condemn them even further. Such notions have long been prevalent in the United States and elsewhere. One study found that in 1999, nearly one in five American adults said they "fear" a person with AIDS (Herek et al., 2002). We will discuss such attitudes later in this chapter.

AIDS is caused by a viral infection with HIV, which is primarily transmitted through body fluids including semen, vaginal fluid, breast milk, and blood. During unprotected vaginal or anal intercourse, this virus can enter the body through the vagina, penis, or rectum. Intravenous drug users can also transmit the virus to one another by sharing needles since HIV can exist outside the body for a short time. Oral sex may also transmit the virus, although the research has shown that the risk is low (Kohn et al., 2002; E.D. Robinson & Evans, 1999). Kissing has also been found to be low risk for transmitting HIV, especially when there are no open cuts or sores in the mouth or on the lips.

At present, HIV never goes away. It remains in the body for the rest of a person's life. However, unlike the herpes virus, an untreated HIV infection is often fatal. After a person is infected, the virus may remain dormant and cause no symptoms. As a result, people may not realize that they are infected. A blood test will reveal whether a person is HIV-positive. Once people become HIV-positive, they can transmit the virus to others immediately afterward.

What happens once someone becomes HIV-positive? HIV attacks the **T lymphocytes** (tee-LIM-foe-sites; **T helper cells**) in the blood, leaving fewer of them to fight off infection. When there is a foreign invader in the bloodstream, antibodies develop that are able to recognize the invader and destroy it. If they cannot do this or if there are too many viruses, a person becomes ill. These antibodies can be detected in the bloodstream anywhere from two weeks to six months after infection, which is how the screening

human immunodeficiency virus (HIV)
The retrovirus responsible for the development of AIDS

acquired immune deficiency syndrome (AIDS)
A condition of increased susceptibility to opportunistic diseases; results from an infection with HIV, which destroys the body's immune system.

T lymphocyte (T helper cell)
Type of white blood cell that helps to destroy harmful bacteria in the body.

REAL Research Of the 33.3 million people living with HIV in the world, 22.5 million live in sub-Saharan Africa (UNAIDS, 2010).

test for HIV works. The immune system also releases many white blood cells to help destroy invaders.

HIV attaches itself to the T helper cells and injects its infectious RNA into their fluid. This RNA contains an enzyme known as **reverse transcriptase** (trans-SCRIPT-ace), which is capable of changing the RNA into DNA. The new DNA then takes over the T helper cell and begins to manufacture more HIV.

In sum, the attack on the T helper cells causes the immune system to be less effective in its ability to fight disease opening the door for many **opportunistic diseases** that a HIV-negative person could easily fight off. Additionally, people with an STI are at greater risk of acquiring HIV (Gilson & Mindel, 2001; Hader et al., 2001; Pialoux et al., 2008).

Animal Variations — Where Did HIV and AIDS Come From?

The most accepted theory of origin is that the *simian immunodeficiency virus* (SIV) crossed over to humans from chimpanzees in western equatorial Africa and the sooty mangabey, another primate from sub-Saharan Africa. SIV does not normally cause the disease in host monkeys, so it has likely been around for a very long time. In central and sub-Saharan Africa, chimpanzees, sooty mangabeys, and other primates are often hunted, killed, and sold in city markets as "bushmeat." As a result, any event that might lead to a crossover is likely—cuts and open sores on hunters and butchers, the consumption of contaminated or uncooked meat, or otherwise. Researchers using molecular clock analysis of HIV sequence evolution have placed the crossover event at sometime before 1940. Once this happened, SIV mutated to HIV and then rapidly spread throughout the world (Sharp et al., 2001)

Incidence in Canada

PHAC collects data upon HIV/AIDS from a variety of sources, including the National HIV Surveillance System, immigration medical screening, and the Canadian Mortality Database. As of December 31, 2013, a total of 78 511 HIV cases have been reported, or between

reverse transcriptase
An enzyme capable of changing the RNA of HIV into DNA.

opportunistic disease
Disease that occurs when the immune system is weakened.

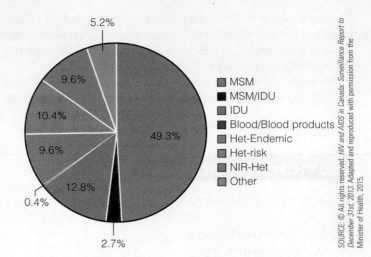

FIGURE 7.6 Proportion of HIV cases among Canadians over age 14 by exposure category.

2090 and 2729 per year since 1996. The number of cases has declined steadily since 2008, and the year 2013 had the lowest number for the past 18 years (PHAC, 2013). This amounts to a markedly lower rate than that of the United States where 1 170 989 people have been diagnosed with AIDS and there are about 50 000 new cases a year (CDC, 2014). The Centers for Disease Control and Prevention (CDC) in the United States also estimates that an additional 168 300 people are unaware that they are infected.

About three-quarters of people with HIV/AIDS in Canada are male. For the past ten years, the proportion of female cases has fluctuated between 21.9 percent and 26.8 percent. Females living with HIV/AIDS also tend to be younger, with 36.6 percent under age 30, compared to 25.0 percent of males (PHAC, 2013).

Figure 7.6 shows how people actually became HIV-positive, which is known in 66 percent of cases. Of this portion, MSM account for nearly half of cases, although this percentage represents a significant decrease from the early years of the epidemic, when more than 80 percent were of this category. Heterosexual contact accounts for nearly a third of cases (29.6 percent) and is further divided into three subcategories—contact with people born in a country where HIV is endemic (Het-Endemic), with a person at risk (Het-Risk), and with someone with no identified risk (NIR-Het). About one-eighth of cases are from intravenous drug use—that is, through sharing needles (IDU). When broken down by sex, MSM accounts for about two-thirds (62.7 percent) of male cases, while heterosexual contact accounts for about two-thirds (66.3 percent) of female cases. For heterosexual contact, there was a large difference in the Het-Endemic category—42.7 percent for females and only 22.9 percent for males (PHAC, 2013).

Racial and ethnic identity data were available in 2013 (see Figure 7.7) for only 59.9 percent of cases, so any figures are not representative of Canada by definition. Of this proportion, however, 49.4 percent identified as White, 17.3 percent as Black, and 16.9 percent as Aboriginal. Aboriginal people living with HIV/AIDS were more likely to be female, accounting for nearly a third (32.0 percent) of all reported female cases. The main exposure category for Aboriginal people was intravenous drug use, which accounted for 50.1 percent of cases.

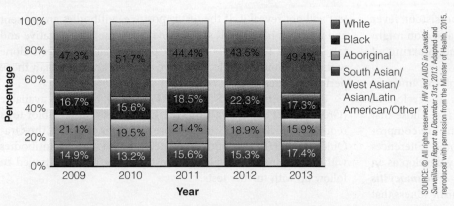

FIGURE **7.7** Proportion of reported HIV cases (all ages) by race/ethnicity—Canada, 2009–2013.

When Aboriginal Canadians suffer from depression, it is often because of racism, a history of foster care and adoption, and substance abuse. When they are also living with HIV and AIDS, they may have additional reasons. Seventy-two Aboriginal people with HIV/AIDS interviewed by Cain et al. (2011) also mention feelings of isolation from families, communities, and culture.

African, Caribbean, and Black (ACB) Canadians have been hit harder by HIV/AIDS than other groups, especially in Ontario where 57 percent live. According to the African and Caribbean Council on HIV/AIDS in Ontario (ACCHO), 12 percent of all people in 2003 were from such backgrounds (ACCHO, 2006) and 19 percent of all Ontarians by 2009 (ACCHO, 2013). One research project gave voice to 102 African and Caribbean Canadians in interviews and focus groups to assess the special issues of their communities. The participants discussed religious beliefs, denial of homosexuality, silence about sexuality, and access to treatment. Often, because of gossip in their communities, they were less likely to seek treatment or be tested. They were further discouraged by the racialization of HIV/ADS by the media, which they believed framed it as an African disease (ACCHO, 2006).

In the Ethnocultural Communities Facing AIDS Study (Singer et al., 1996), six ethnic cultures were examined in Montreal, Vancouver, and Toronto including, South Asians, Chinese, Arab, and Latinos. Cultural factors that increase the risk of HIV transmission such as dynamics involved in sex-role differences were remarkably similar. It was concluded that HIV-intervention efforts must consider sociocultural factors to be successful.

HIV/AIDS was not as prevalent as other STIs in the territories, the highest rate being in the Yukon at 2.7 per 100 000. Of the provinces, Saskatchewan had the highest rate at 11.4 and New Brunswick the lowest at 0.8.

Knowledge of AIDS and Sexual Behaviour

After more than three decades of the HIV/AIDS epidemic, it is likely that few Canadians do not know that HIV can be transmitted through sexual contact. Being knowledgeable, however, does not necessarily guarantee safer sexual behaviour (Bruce & Walker, 2001; Shapiro et al., 1999). It is, therefore, not sufficient to merely inform people about AIDS transmission—it is important to empower them to protect themselves as well. Educational programs must not only concentrate on knowledge levels but behavioural intervention (Fraser, 1997; Swenson et al., 1997).

According to Nova Scotian researchers Ross and Blum (2013), one group that tends to be ignored in AIDS education is older Canadians. To assess knowledge levels, they gave questionnaires to 186 heterosexual women aged 50 or older and found that they had low levels of knowledge of HIV/AIDS, correctly answering only half of questions on the average. There is thus a need for intervention among the aging.

Younger Canadians are also of concern. The Canadian Youth, Sexual Health, and HIV/AIDS Study (CYSHHAS) published in 2003 was based on large number of students in Grades 7, 9, and 11—11 074 adolescents in total. This study was driven by the World Health Organization's concepts of *sexual health* and *healthy sexuality*, which focus not only on behaviour and knowledge but the emotional, physical, cognitive, and social aspects of sexuality as well. When presented with the statement "I could not be a friend to someone who has HIV/AIDS," about a fifth of students strongly agreed or agreed in Grade 7, and less than 10 percent did so in Grade 11, thus reflecting growing empathy with maturity. Of those who were sexually active, 75 percent of Grade 9 boys and 60 percent of Grade 9 girls used a condom at last sexual intercourse, as did 73 percent of Grade 11 boys and 58 percent of Grade 11 girls. One of the main reasons for not doing so was that they did not expect to have sex. Another reason was the belief that condoms reduce sexual pleasure. There thus remains a significant need for ongoing intervention.

Symptoms

HIV infection results in a gradual deterioration of the immune system through the destruction of T helper lymphocytes (Friedman-Kien & Farthing, 1990). Once a person progresses from HIV seropositivity to full-blown AIDS, flu-like symptoms such as fever, sore throat, chronic swollen lymph nodes in the neck or armpits, headaches, and fatigue may appear. Later symptoms may include significant weight loss, severe diarrhea that persists for more than one month, night sweats, oral **candidiasis**, gingivitis, oral ulcers, and persistent fever (Friedman-Kien & Farthing, 1990). In addition, a person might experience persistent dizziness, confusion, and blurring of vision or hearing.

In an untreated person, the deterioration of the immune system makes it easier for opportunistic diseases to develop. In general, the incidences of opportunistic illnesses (i.e., those that can make people sick when their immune systems are compromised) are similar in men and women, with some differences based on anatomy. In women, cervical cancer may develop as an AIDS-defining condition (Hader et al., 2001). *Pneumocystis carinii* **pneumonia (PCP)** is one type of opportunistic illness that may develop in untreated men and women. This type of pneumonia was uncommon before 1981. Other opportunistic diseases include **toxoplasmosis**, **cryptococcosis**, **cytomegalovirus**, and **Kaposi's sarcoma (KS)**, which is a rare type of cancer that causes skin lesions. It was also rare before 1981. Without treatment, two thirds of men with AIDS will develop KS lesions on the head and neck (Alkhuja et al., 2001).

Diagnosis

Tests for HIV can either identify the virus in the blood or, more commonly, detect whether a person has developed antibodies to fight HIV. The most widely used test for antibodies is the **ELISA (enzyme-linked immunoabsorbent assay)**. If an ELISA test result is positive, a second test, known as the **Western blot**, is used to check for accuracy. These tests can determine the presence of HIV antibodies. If there are none, the test results are negative, indicating that the person is probably not infected with HIV. It takes some time for the body to develop antibodies. Thus there is a period in which a person may be infected with HIV but the test will not reveal it. If the test is positive, antibodies are present and a person has HIV. It should be noted that false-negative and false-positive test results are also possible although tests done within six months of infection have a higher accuracy than those performed later.

Since the mid-2000s, rapid HIV testing has been available (Greenwald et al., 2006). Both the ELISA and Western blot tests require as much as two weeks before a result is possible. The Ora-Quick Rapid HIV Antibody test detects the presence of antibodies within 20 minutes. People who test positive are encouraged to follow up with further tests.

Treatment

Since 1995, there has been a tremendous decrease in HIV- and AIDS-related deaths primarily because of the development of **highly active antiretroviral therapy** (**HAART**; Crum et al., 2006; M.H. Katz et al., 2002; Venkatesh et al., 2008). HAART is a combination of three or more HIV drugs, often referred to as "drug cocktails." This development in conjunction with **HIV RNA testing**, which allows health care providers to monitor the amount of virus in the bloodstream, has allowed for better control of HIV and has slowed the disease's progression.

HAART has also significantly increased the life expectancy of children infected with HIV at birth (Trends in HIV/AIDS Diagnoses, 2005). Today children infected with HIV are surviving longer than earlier in the epidemic because of HAART (Davies et al., 2008).

Before starting treatment for HIV infection, a person should be given both a viral load test and **CD41 T cell count**. These tests can determine how much HIV is in a person's system and also estimate the T helper white blood cell count, which can show how well a person's immune system is controlling the virus. A baseline CD41 cell count will also give a health care provider a starting measure to compare with later viral load estimates.

In the mid-1990s, HAART involved taking 20 to 30 or more pills with food restrictions. Some drugs needed to be taken on an empty stomach, while others had to be taken just after eating. This therapy often led to adverse effects, such as fatigue, nausea, and diarrhea. Newer drug regimens have used fewer pills and even only one pill combining all three antiretroviral drugs (Laurence, 2006; Sternberg, 2006).

Prevention of HIV/AIDS

The World Health Organization, the United Nations Programme on HIV/AIDS (UNAIDS), and the United Nations Population Fund (UNFPA) put out a joint position statement in July 2004 stating that "Condoms are an integral and essential part of comprehensive prevention and care programmes, and their promotion must be accelerated." They further stated that "The male latex condom is the single, most efficient, available technology to reduce the sexual transmission of HIV and other sexually transmitted infections." It seems logical as a result to promote condom use both nationally and globally, make them readily available, and empower men and women to use them (UNFPA, 2004).

---

oral candidiasis
An infection in the mouth caused by the excessive growth of a fungus that naturally occurs in the body.

***Pneumocystis carinii* pneumonia (PCP)**
A rare type of pneumonia and an opportunistic disease that often occurs in people with AIDS.

toxoplasmosis
A parasite that can cause headaches, sore throats, seizures, altered mental states, or comas.

cryptococcosis
An acute or chronic infection that can lead to pulmonary or central nervous system infection.

cytomegalovirus
A virus that can lead to diarrhea, weight loss, headache, fever, confusion, or blurred vision.

Kaposi's sarcoma (KS)
A form of cancer that often occurs in untreated men with AIDS.

ELISA (enzyme-linked immunoabsorbent assay)
The screening test used to detect HIV antibodies in blood samples.

Western blot
A test used to confirm a positive ELISA test and more accurate than the ELISA test but too expensive to be used as a primary screening device.

highly active antiretroviral therapy (HAART)
A combination of antiretroviral drugs for the treatment of infections by retroviruses, primarily HIV.

HIV RNA testing
A test that allows health care providers to monitor the amount of virus in the bloodstream.

CD41 T cell count
A test that can determine the T helper white blood cell count, which will show how well a person's immune system is controlling HIV.

Microbicides: New Barriers against HIV

Microbicides—compounds that are applied to the vagina or rectum to protect against STIs—are one of the most promising new developments in the fight against STIs (Neff et al., 2011). They will be especially important to women, many of whom do not have the social or economic power necessary to insist that their partners remain monogamous or use condoms. Microbicides come in several forms, such as creams, gels, and suppositories, and provide a physical barrier that keeps STIs from reaching certain cells by creating an acidic pH level to decrease infection or by preventing replication of the virus. As of mid-2011, there were more than 50 microbicide products in various stages of clinical development around the world. Phase III trials of Carraguard are ongoing in South Africa and Botswana, whereas Phase II and II trials of PRO 2000 and BufferGel were ongoing in India and South Africa.

Some microbicides offer contraceptive protection, whereas others offer only protection from diseases. Those that do not offer contraceptive protection can be used by women who have an STI (or a partner with an STI) but want children. Microbicides have been found to reduce HIV infection by 39 percent and HSV-2 infection by 51 percent (UNAIDS, 2010).

Aside from problems of self-efficacy regarding condom use mentioned earlier, there are still obstacles to the promotion, distribution, and even mentioning of condoms—among them, individuals, organizations, and even governments with moral objections to their use. The United States, for example, has long emphasized abstinence-only sex education, often to the exclusion of references to condoms, even though there is ample evidence that such programs are ineffective (SEICUS, 2007). Closely related are "virginity pledges," where teenagers pledge to remain abstinent until marriage. According to Bearman and Bruckner (2001, 2005) 88 percent of pledgers do indeed have vaginal intercourse before marriage, and they are significantly less likely to use condoms or contraceptives. Abstinence-only programs also ignore the lives of gay and lesbian teens who get no instruction whatsoever upon how to protect themselves.

At present, unless one is in a monogamous relationship where both partners have been tested for STIs and received negative results, condoms must be used for vaginal and anal intercourse to halt the progression of HIV/AIDS.

Review Questions

1 Explain how HIV is transmitted and how the virus affects the body.

2 Which groups in Canada have been more affected by HIV/AIDS?

3 Identify the various symptoms and opportunistic diseases that develop as a result of HIV and AIDS.

4 Explain how HAART works. What other factors are important in the treatment of HIV and AIDS?

5 What is the best way to protect oneself during sexual activity?

Global Aspects of AIDS

According to the WHO, HIV/AIDS has led to the deaths of over 39 million people between 1981 and 2013, and there were an additional 35 million living with HIV in 2013. Approximately 2.1 million people became newly infected that same year, which represents a decline from the 2.6 million in 2009. The majority of people living with HIV/AIDS are in sub-Saharan Africa (i.e., all countries and areas south of the Sahara Desert), with 24.7 million or 71 percent of all cases (WHO, 2014). HIV not only affects the quality of people's lives but their families and communities and the economic growth of nations. Fortunately, prevention efforts have improved despite obstacles, and there are now nearly 12 million people on antiretroviral therapy (ART).

Children under 16 are profoundly affected by the HIV/AIDS epidemic worldwide. It is estimated that every minute a child becomes infected with HIV and another child dies of an AIDS-related illness (UNAIDS, 2008). Most of these children live in sub-Saharan Africa and most were exposed to HIV by their mothers during pregnancy, childbirth, or breast-feeding.

Thailand: "No Condoms, No Sex"!

By 1993, the number of HIV/AIDS cases in Thailand had reached 1 million—97 percent of which were linked to transmission by sex workers. Dr Wiwat Rojanapithayakorn of the World Health Organization took on the challenge of reducing this number through the promotion of condoms. Because Thailand did not acknowledge the sex industry, this was at first challenging. Furthermore, customers did not want to use condoms, believing them to reduce pleasure. Rojanapithayakorn, however, worked with local authorities who threatened brothels with raids and closure if they were caught not using condoms. Soon, the "no condoms, no sex" message was everywhere. The goal was to bring about a 100 percent condom use policy. Efforts went even further. Soon, safer sex messages were broadcast every hour on Thailand's 488 radio stations and six television stations.

The results were remarkable. New cases of HIV/AIDS among sex workers fell from 13 percent to less than 1 percent in two months. Once the Thai government became involved in the distribution of free condoms, new HIV infections in Thailand dropped from 143 000 per year to less than 14 000. Similar campaigns were immediately put in place in Cambodia, China, the Philippines, Vietnam and other countries.

Caption: Thailand Prime Minister Mechai Viravaidya at the Cabbages and Condoms restaurant in Bangkok.

© Peter Charlesworth/Getty

Adapted from: Bulletin of the World Health Organization (2010). Thailand's new condom crusade, Volume 88, 6, 404–405.

In this section, we explore HIV/AIDS in Asia and the Pacific, Eastern Europe and Central Asia, sub-Saharan Africa, the Caribbean, Central and South America, and the Middle East and North Africa.

Asia and the Pacific

It is difficult to determine the number of HIV/AIDS cases in Asia because some countries such as China do not yet have sophisticated reporting systems and many people living with HIV/AIDS go unnoticed (Wu et al., 2011). There were however an estimated 5 million people in Asia living with HIV in 2009 and 360 000 people were newly infected with HIV that same year (UNAIDS, 2010). The countries with the highest burden are India with 2.1 million people living with HIV/AIDS, China with 780 000, and Indonesia with 610 000 (UNAIDS 2013a).

HIV rates have declined by more than 25 percent in India and Nepal, and levelled off in Malaysia and Sri Lanka between 2001 and 2009. Increased rates were found in Pakistan, Indonesia, and the Philippines. As of 2013, there has been a 26 percent reduction in new infections in Asia since 2001 (UNAIDS, 2013a). At the same time, infections among MSM are increasing due to the difficulties of implementing AIDS interventions among them.

The main mode of HIV transmission in Asian countries is unprotected male-female and male-male sex with intimate partners and paid sex workers (UNAIDS, 2010). High rates of HIV have also been found among injecting drug users. A large proportion of HIV infections occur in married women whose husbands frequent sex workers or inject drugs. Recently, there has been a push to increase condom use in sex workers, and this has been fairly successful in Cambodia and Thailand (UNAIDS, 2010).

One obstacle to the success of eradicating HIV/AIDS in Asia is the stigma associated with the disease. In one study, for example, 33 percent of HIV-positive Pakistanis and 20 percent of Thais were denied health services because of their status (UNAIDS, 2013b). Additionally, 37 countries criminalize some aspects of sex work and 18 criminalize same-sex sexual behaviour. This further increases stigma, creates fear, and exacerbates efforts to fight HIV infection. Gender inequality is another factor. Violence toward women and transgender people, or the threat of it, makes them far more susceptible to STIs and HIV infection (UNAIDS 2013b).

Condom use among sex workers and MSM varies considerably in Asia and the Pacific. In Bangladesh, only 26 percent of MSM reported using a condom during their last sexual intercourse as opposed to 60 percent in India and 86 percent in Thailand. Sex workers were more likely to have used condoms during their last encounter, although there was also considerable variation—41 percent in Pakistan, 60 percent in India, and 94 percent in Thailand (UNAIDS, 2013b). Thailand, for its zealous promotion of condoms, has had the most success (see the accompanying Sexual Diversity in Our World feature). India has also had some sex in reducing the number of new HIV cases with condom promotion, especially among female sex workers. Between 2003 and 2011, the prevalence among this group dropped from 54 percent to less than 10 percent (UNAIDS, 2014a).

Eastern Europe and Central Asia

The number of people living in Eastern Europe and Central Asia has nearly tripled since 2000, with a population of 361 million as of 2013. As of 2009, there was an estimated total of 1.4 million people living with HIV in this area (UNAIDS, 2010). The proportion of HIV cases are highest in the Russian Federation and the Ukraine, with 55 percent and 21 percent, respectively.

The number of cases in the Russian Federation is likely higher than reported. Although only 370 000 cases were reported in 2007, the actual number has been estimated at 1.4 million (UNAIDS, 2008a). Two-thirds of known cases were contracted through intravenous drug use and the other third through unprotected vaginal intercourse. Even though the reported MSM rates are negligible, they are likely much higher because of the country's anti-gay legislation and atmosphere of intense homophobia (Barsotti & Perelle, 2012; Dorf, 2013; Fenwick, 2014). Because homosexuality is illegal and gays are regularly harassed and beaten up, many who are HIV-positive will not seek out treatment for fear of violence and arrest.

Sub-Saharan Africa

The majority of the world's HIV-positive people live in sub-Saharan Africa. They make up close to 70 percent of the global number of 35 million (UNAIDS, 2013a). In 2013, an estimated 24.7 million people were living with HIV in sub-Saharan Africa, 58 percent of whom are women (UNAIDS, 2013b). The main mode of HIV transmission is vaginal intercourse, but intravenous drug users and MSM contribute to the total as well. The means of transmission, however, varies considerably from country to country, depending upon laws, policies, and culture. In Senegal, for example, MSM account for 21.8 percent of new cases, but the number is only 9.9 percent in South Africa. Sex workers account for 69.6 percent of cases in Swaziland but only 16.4 percent in Burkina Faso. Intravenous drug users account for 51.6 percent of new cases in Mauritius but only 4.2 percent in Nigeria (UNAIDS, 2013c). In 2013, there were about 1.5 million new cases and over a million people died that same year.

The HIV/AIDS epidemic in Africa has begun to abate. Between 2005 and 2013, the death toll dropped by 29 percent (UNAIDS, 2013b), and by 51 percent between 2005 and 2011 (UNAIDS, 2013c). Among the countries that have achieved a more than a 30 percent reduction are Cote D'Ivoire (Ivory Coast), Ethiopia, Kenya, and Zambia. Rwanda, Namibia, and Botswana report greater than 60 percent reductions (UNAIDS, 2013c).

Children are hard hit in sub-Saharan Africa, where an estimated 90 percent of all children 15 years or younger who are HIV-positive live (UNAIDS, 2010). In 2013, there were an estimated 210 000 children living with HIV/AIDS in the region (UNAIDS, 2014b). One study found that at one point, any 15-year-old in Botswana has an 80 percent chance of dying of AIDS (Piot, 2000). Botswana, however, was also the first African country to provide free services for preventing mother-to-child transmission. As of December 2012, 96 percent of all eligible people were receiving such treatment (UNAIDS, 2012a). Because sub-Saharan Africa has the world's largest population of HIV-positive children, South Africa's *Sesame Street* began to include an HIV-positive Muppet character in 2002—Kami, who is a five-year-old orphan whose parents died of AIDS. Kami's character was designed to help children in South Africa understand AIDS and teach them that it's all right to play with HIV-positive children. Aside from *Sesame Street*, Kami also appears at events sponsored by UNICEF.

Fewer new cases and fewer deaths are due to greater accessibility to antiretroviral therapy, greater awareness of HIV in general, and increased condom use. Condom use, however, has met with great resistance by religious organizations both in Africa and from the West. As one example, the Kenyan Midwives Project, which sought to distribute condoms to women in Kenya, met with considerable resistance to what was advertised as a family planning project (UNAIDS, 2000). In March 2009 on a visit to Africa, Pope Benedict XVI told reporters that the AIDS epidemic "cannot be overcome by the distribution of condoms: on the contrary, they increase it." This statement led to a fury of condemnation from the world's government leaders as well as major health organizations such as UNAIDS and the WHO. UNAIDS reiterated its statement that condoms are the most effective way or preventing infection and must be promoted (*The Lancet*, 2009). Others have said that condom use is a public health issue and not a spiritual one (Mukonyora, 2005; Muula, 2010). One thing is certain: Condom use has significantly reduced the number of new HIV cases in Africa and has tremendous support from the scientific and medical community.

© AP Photos/CP Images

In South Africa, an HIV-positive Muppet was added to the cast of *Sesame Street*. Her name is Kami, which is derived from the Tswana word for "acceptance."

Despite all the declines in HIV infection and increased access to treatments worldwide, the number of children who have lost their parents to AIDS has not declined (UNAIDS, 2010). In 2009, there were 16.6 million AIDS orphans and 90 percent of them lived in sub-Saharan Africa (UNAIDS, 2010). Although we typically think of an orphan as a child without parents, the word is used differently by those involved in the AIDS epidemic. A maternal orphan is a child who has lost a mother to AIDS, a paternal orphan has lost a father to AIDS, and a double orphan has lost both parents to AIDS (Fredriksson et al., 2008). AIDS orphans are often young—15 percent are newly born to four years old, 35 percent are five to nine years old, and 50 percent are 10 to 14 years old (Monasch & Boerma, 2004).

At the beginning of the AIDS epidemic in the 1980s, orphanages were set up in many African communities to help care for the children whose parents had died. Soon, the number of orphans quickly surpassed the amount of space available. Today, 90 percent of orphans in sub-Saharan Africa are cared for by extended family members (Heymann et al., 2007). In fact, more than a third of working adults in sub-Saharan Africa care for orphans in their households, but the majority of these families live in poverty and are unable to meet the essential caregiving needs of the orphans in their care (Heymann et al., 2007; Kidman et al., 2007; Roby & Shaw, 2006). Poverty in sub-Saharan Africa has forced some orphans into the labour market or the streets, where they may beg, steal, or prostitute themselves (Amanpour, 2006).

African orphans are at increased risk for many physical, socioeconomic, and psychological problems (Sherr et al., 2008). Many experience anxiety, depression, fear, anger, and guilt (Foster, 2006). Orphans also face social isolation, abuse, neglect, malnutrition, and homelessness. Many lose their opportunities for health care, future employment, and adequate education (Andrews et al., 2006; Cluver & Gardner, 2007; Foster, 2006; Li et al., 2008; Rivers et al., 2008). Because many extended families are unable to afford

© Friedrich Stark/Alamy

school and uniform fees, orphans are less likely to attend school than non-orphans (Kürzinger et al., 2008).

They are also at greater risk for negative sexual health outcomes compared with non-orphans. They are more likely to initiate sex early and have multiple sex partners, less likely to use condoms, and more likely to become pregnant (Birdthistle et al., 2008; Gregson et al., 2005). They are also at greater risk for forced sex and have a higher prevalence of herpes infections (Birdthistle et al., 2008).

As the HIV/AIDS rates continue to climb in many countries around the globe, it is imperative to find ways to reduce HIV/AIDS infections and increase access to antiretroviral treatment. Finding care and assistance for orphans also remains a priority. Local and global communities continue to reach out to AIDS orphans, ensuring adequate access to services and providing support for caregivers and families (Roby & Shaw, 2006; UNAIDS, 2008). Some groups provide psychological support, food, and/or clothing and offer resources to keep orphans in school (Foster, 2002). Many believe that finding ways to keep them in school may help in that education can increase self-esteem and ensure financial independence in the future (Fredriksson et al., 2008).

The Caribbean

The nations of the Caribbean are diverse in language (French, English, Dutch, and Spanish) and comprise about 36 million people. After Africa, the Caribbean has been hit hardest by HIV/AIDS, although it has had the largest decline (49 percent) in new infections since 2001 (UNAIDS, 2013a). One reason is that it now has the highest rate of condom use among sex workers and MSM. The HIV-prevalence rate in the area in 2012 was 1.0 percent of the adult population 15 to 49 years old, ranging from 3.3 percent in the Bahamas to less than 0.01 percent in Cuba (UNAIDS, 2013a).

Transmission modes are mainly through unprotected vaginal intercourse, especially during paid sex. Like sub-Saharan Africa, there are more women and girls living with HIV than men and boys (UNAIDS, 2010). Because of the strong stigma associated with male homosexuality, especially in Jamaica, MSM are far less likely to seek health care and treatment (Grew, 2008; West & Hewstone, 2012; White & Carr, 2005). The prevalence of HIV/AIDS in their communities thus remains unknown.

Central and South America

By 2013, Central and South America had a cumulative population of 564 million, with an estimated 1.5 million living with HIV/AIDS, a third of whom live in Brazil (UNAIDS, 2013a). Many cases are of MSM who, as in the Caribbean, are often reluctant to seek treatment or testing because of stigma. In Mexico as of 2007, more than half of HIV-positive people are MSM (UNAIDS, 2008b). High rates have also been found among female sex workers in Honduras, Guatemala, and El Salvador. In Uruguay, two-thirds of women had become infected through unprotected vaginal intercourse. Intravenous drug users account for only a small portion of cases in South and Central America (UNAIDS, 2008b).

The Middle East and Northern Africa

Although reliable data on HIV epidemics in some countries in the Middle East and North Africa are difficult to come by, available evidence has found that an estimated 460 000 people were living with HIV by the end of 2009, which was an increase from the 180 000 in 2001 (UNAIDS, 2010). The main mode of HIV transmission was vaginal intercourse with sex workers, MSM, and injecting drug use. In Iran, drug-related epidemics have contributed to increasing HIV rates. Although Sudan has increased efforts to educate the public about HIV and AIDS, one study found that only 5 percent of women knew that condom use could protect them, and more than two thirds of the women had never heard of a condom (UNAIDS, 2005).

In summary, recent research suggests that counselling and educational interventions are being increasingly recognized as important aspects of care for people with HIV and their families in developing countries. In addition, home-based health care is being established to remove some of the burden from the hospitals, increase quality health care, and reduce costs. On the other hand, cultural factors such as individual and institutionalized homophobia continue to exacerbate efforts.

HIV/AIDS Education and Popular Culture

To combat AIDS around the world, it is necessary to make people aware of its impact. Many local, national, and international organizations have done much in this respect with the distribution of information through posters, pamphlets, television and radio announcements, and the like. AIDS awareness has also been heightened through media within and arts and popular culture. One of the best-known African artists, Chari Samba, painted a whimsical scene called *Les Capotes Utilisées* (The Used Condoms) showing children catching condoms being thrown out of hotel windows by unseen lovers. Similarly, 130 women in South Africa made the *Keiskamma Altarpiece* of beadwork and embroidery as a message of hope for people living with HIV, which now tours the world (UNAIDS, 2014a). American artist Keith Haring has also painted many works which helped to raise awareness.

In 1987, AIDS and LGBT rights activist Cleve Jones conceived of the *NAMES Project*, which brought together individual quilts made by families and friends for people who had died of complications of AIDS. In the years that followed, it became the largest piece of folk art in the world, composed of more than 48 000 panels and weighing 49 tonnes. The panels include those for singer Freddie Mercury of Queen and movie star Rock Hudson, and pieces of it tour North America.

Hollywood as well as independent filmmakers have also done their part with movies made for theatres and television such as *The Dallas Buyers Club* (2013), *Philadelphia* (1993), *Parting Glances* (1986), and *An Early Frost* (1985). Among Canadian independent filmmakers, movies such as John Greyson's *Zero Patience* (1993) and Mike Hoolbloom's *Letters From Home* (1996) have also had an impact.

In many cities throughout the world, street art—whether in the form of quick streaks of a spray can or large murals—has provided a platform for the people to either raise awareness or communicate their frustrations and sentiments about government inaction. Such art has appeared in virtually every major city in the world and has done its part to fight AIDS and raise social awareness.

Safer Sexual Behaviour

People who are sexually active should not only ensure that they are tested regularly but do their best to encourage others to do so as well. It is also important to make sure one's partner has been tested as well. It is essential to get full testing for all STIs, including HIV (Johnson, 2005). Furthermore, it is important to use barrier methods, such as condoms, to reduce chances of acquiring an STI.

For people who already have an STI, early detection and management of the infection are important and can help lessen the possibility of infecting others. Those who are infected should also inform their sex partners as soon as a positive diagnosis is made to help reduce the chances that someone else will become infected. Many of the bacterial STIs can be treated with antibiotics. However, delaying treatment may result in more long-term consequences to one's health, such as PID or infertility.

Review Questions

1 Explain the global impact of the AIDS epidemic on children.

2 Identify the main mode of HIV transmission in Asian countries. What do you think could be done to decrease HIV infections in this area?

3 Identify the main mode of HIV transmission in Eastern Europe and Central Asian countries. What do you think could be done to decrease HIV infections in this area?

4 Identify the main mode of HIV transmission in sub-Saharan Africa. What efforts are currently being carried out to reduce HIV transmission?

5 Identify the main mode of HIV transmission in the Caribbean. How does homophobia exacerbate the epidemic?

6 Identify the main mode of HIV transmission in the Middle East. What do you think could be done to decrease HIV infections in this area?

Chapter Review

Summary Points

1 Sexually transmitted infections (STIs) have historically been viewed as symbols of corrupt sexuality, which is why there has been a "punishment concept" of disease.

2 The rates of syphilis, gonorrhea, and chlamydia have risen in Canada. They are higher than those of the United Kingdom but lower than those of the United States. Women are more likely to be infected with all three diseases. Many people are unaware that they are infected, and others are reluctant to seek treatment because of the stigma.

3 STI rates were high during World War I and much lower during World War II because of the distribution of condoms. Prostitutes were blamed for the spread of the diseases while their customers were thought to be the victims. In the United Kingdom, the Contagious Diseases Act of 1864 allowed police to round up and forcibly give medical examinations to all prostitutes and suspected women around military and naval bases.

4 Literature discussed contagion in terms of "high-risk groups," whereas the likelihood to become infected is a matter of high-risk behaviour. This led to much discrimination against minority groups such as gays, Haitians, and Aboriginal Canadians. Discourse in terms of groups, however, does have merit in epidemiological studies, which look at the distribution of a disease.

5 Condom use is an effective way to prevent contagion from STIs and HIV/AIDS. Many people still see them as a birth control device and might not use them if other birth control methods are involved. Condom use is also a matter of self-efficacy and education that empowers people to use condoms.

6 Untreated STIs can adversely affect pregnancy. Syphilis, gonorrhea, chlamydia, herpes, hepatitis B virus (HBV), and HIV can cause miscarriage, stillbirth, early onset of labour, premature rupture of the amniotic sac, intellectual disability of the child, and fetal or uterine infection.

7 Ectoparasitic infections are caused by parasites that live on the skin's surface and include pubic lice and scabies. First symptoms include a rash and intense itching. Treatment is done with topical creams to kill the parasites and their larvae.

8 The majority of women who are infected with gonorrhea are asymptomatic while men are symptomatic. Testing for gonorrhea involves collecting a sample of the discharge from the cervix, urethra, or another infected area with a cotton swab. Gonorrhea can be treated effectively with antibiotics.

9 Syphilis usually infects the cervix, penis, anus, or lips. It can also infect a baby during birth. Infection is divided into three stages: primary, secondary, and tertiary syphilis. Antibiotics are used for treatment.

10 Chlamydia infections are the most common bacterial STI in Canada. Most men and women with an infection are asymptomatic.

11 Vaginal infections, characterized by a discharge, itching, and/or odour, are most frequently associated with bacterial vaginosis (BV), trichomoniasis, and candidiasis. Most women have symptoms while most men are asymptomatic. Treatment includes oral antibiotics or vaginal suppositories.

12 BV is caused by an overgrowth of various types of bacteria in the vagina that replace normal healthy bacteria. It is the most common cause of vaginal discharge, and although many women are asymptomatic, it multiplies when the pH balance of the vagina is disturbed. Treatment includes either an antifungal prescription or over-the-counter drugs.

13 Pelvic inflammatory disease (PID) is an infection of the female genital tract including the endometrium, Fallopian tubes, and lining of the pelvic area. Long-term complications of PID include ectopic and tubal pregnancies, chronic pelvic pain, and infertility.

14 Viral infections include herpes simplex virus (HSV), human papillomavirus (HPV), viral hepatitis, and HIV. Herpes is caused by either HSV-1 or HSV-2. Once a person is infected, the symptoms can overlap. The virus can be transmitted even when a person does not have symptoms. Once infected, individuals will always carry the virus in their bodies. The standard therapy for HSV infection currently is antiviral drugs.

15 More than 40 types of HPV can infect the genitals, anus, mouth, and throat. Most people who are infected do not know they have it. Almost all cervical disease can be attributed to HPV infection. HPV is also a risk factor for oral, penile, and anal cancer. Sex partners of people with cervical warts usually experience development of warts within three or four months of contact. Genital warts can be treated in several ways. An HPV vaccine is now available and recommended for young girls and women.

16 Viral hepatitis is an infection that causes impaired liver function. There are three types: hepatitis A (HAV), hepatitis B (HBV), and hepatitis C (HCV). HAV infection is usually symptomatic while infections with HBV and HCV are asymptomatic. Blood tests are used to identify viral hepatitis infections. Vaccines are available for the prevention of both HAV and HBV, and research on a vaccine for HCV is in progress.

17 AIDS is caused by an infection with HIV and is primarily transmitted through body fluids, including semen, vaginal fluids, and blood. HIV attacks the T helper cells in the blood and antibodies can be detected in the bloodstream anywhere from two weeks to six months after infection. The attack on the T helper cells causes the immune system to be less effective in its ability to fight disease leading many infected people develop opportunistic diseases.

18 Tests for HIV can detect the virus itself or antibodies developed to fight HIV. Rapid HIV testing which detects the presence of antibodies to HIV is now possible.

19 Since 1995, there has been a significant decrease in AIDS-related deaths primarily because of the development of highly active antiretroviral therapy (HAART).

20 According to the WHO, HIV/AIDS has led to the deaths of over 39 million people between 1981 and 2013 and there were an additional 35 million living with HIV in 2013. Approximately 2.1 million people became newly infected that same year, which represents a decline from the 2.6 million in 2009. The majority of people living with HIV/AIDS are in sub-Saharan Africa. Prevention efforts have improved despite obstacles and there are now nearly 12 million people on antiretroviral therapy (ART).

21 It is difficult to determine the number of HIV/AIDS cases in some countries because of limited reporting systems, political issues, and the stigma of AIDS which discourages people from seeking testing of medical care. Asian countries with the highest burden of HIV/AIDS are India and China. Thailand has done much to control the epidemic by promoting condoms among sex workers and all others.

22 In Eastern Europe and Central Asia, HIV/AIDS is most prevalent in the Russian Federation and the Ukraine. Two-thirds of cases were acquired through intravenous drug use and sharing needles.

23 HIV/AIDS is most prevalent in sub-Saharan Africa, with about 70 percent of the world's cases. The principle mode of transmission is through vaginal intercourse. Because of antiretroviral therapy, the epidemic has begun to subside. Between 2005 and 2013, the death toll dropped by 29 percent. Children 15 years old and younger have been greatly affected by HIV/AIDS in Africa, with 210 000 HIV-positive individuals in 2013.

24 After Africa, the Caribbean has been hardest hit by the HIV/AIDS epidemic, although it declined dramatically by 49 percent from 2001 to 2013. HIV-positive MSM in Jamaica are reluctant to seek testing or treatment because of homophobia and violence toward gays. Brazil is the country most hard hit by the epidemic in South America.

25 One form of raising awareness and political protest regarding the HIV/AIDS epidemic has been through popular culture in the form of paintings, murals, movies, and street art. Among Canadian filmmakers, John Greyson's *Zero Patience* (1993) and Mike Hoolbloom's *Letters from Home* (1996) have also had an impact.

Critical Thinking Questions

1 For people who are sexually active, what is the best way for them to protect themselves from STIs and HIV/AIDS?

2 Condom failures are almost always a matter of improper use. What are some of the things to consider when using condoms properly?

3 HIV/AIDS transmission is not a matter of group membership but a matter of whether one practises safer sex. What do you think are some of the consequences for minorities when thinking in terms of high-risk groups? What are some of the consequences for individuals who define safer sex in terms of safer partners and not safer behaviour?

4 What are some of the ways people can raise awareness of STIs and HIV/AIDS on college campuses?

Websites

Public Health Agency of Canada (PHAC) This organization promotes the health and well-being of Canadians and includes a huge database of articles and fact sheets, including those for STIs and HIV/AIDS. (http://www.phac-aspc.gc.ca/index-eng.php)

AIDS Vancouver This organization has been around since 1983 and was the first to address the epidemic in Canada. Today, about 7000 people use its services each year. Its mission is to "alleviate individual and collective vulnerability to HIV and AIDS through support, public education and community based research." (http://www.aidsvancouver.org)

Centers for Disease Control and Prevention (CDC) This American agency has a division of STI prevention and provides information, including surveillance reports and disease facts. It also has an HIV/AIDS division that provides information including surveillance reports and facts about the infection. (http://www.cdc.gov/)

World Health Organization (WHO) An international organization that promotes health and well-being worldwide and contains a wealth of information, articles, reports, and fact sheets on STIs and AIDS. (http://www.who.int)

Joint United Nations Programme on HIV and AIDS (UNAIDS) UNAIDS provides monitoring and evaluation of AIDS research as well as access to various links and information on scenarios for the future, antiretroviral therapy, and HIV/AIDS in children and orphans. (http://www.UNAIDS.org)

LesbianSTDs This website provides information and resources regarding sexual health and STIs in women who have sex with women. (http://depts.washington.edu/wswstd/)

Canadian Aboriginal AIDS Network (CAAN) An organization devoted to providing up-to-date information on HIV/AIDS to Aboriginal Canadians. (http://caan.ca)

8

Gender Development, Gender Roles, and Gender Identity

If you're like most college students, you probably don't spend a great deal of time thinking about what gender you are. You wake up in the morning and when you catch your reflection in the mirror, you recognize yourself as a man or a woman. But what if when you made that morning trek to the mirror, the face looking back at you wasn't the gender you thought it should be? That's exactly what had been happening to Sophie. I met Sophie a few months before she graduated from the University of Nebraska. She was smart, beautiful, and passionate about life, hoping to one day find a job as a video game journalist. Twenty-two years ago when Sophie was born, she was assigned male, given a male name, and was raised as a boy. Despite her male body, she knew fairly early on that she wasn't a boy. Growing up in a small, mid-Western American town, Sophie couldn't easily put a finger on what didn't feel right as

a child, but she knew she was different. She didn't fit the idea of what was expected from boys and men in her hometown. There, boys were respected if they did tough, physical labour and showcased their aggression in sports such as football or wrestling. Sophie didn't play sports and wasn't aggressive. Instead, she loved to act and spent hours writing stories. After graduating from high school, Sophie was excited to begin a new chapter of life in college. During the summer after freshman year, Sophie began to undergo a medical transition so that her body would be in line with her mind.

My parents were very supportive of my decision to explore my gender issues. However, I think they would have preferred it if I waited to do it after college. They were worried about the process and what might happen to me while at college. When I did finally decide I was ready, I

came out to the whole campus. I got lots of hate mail, but there was more support overall than antagonism. I'd be lying if I said there weren't times where I was withdrawn and even clinically depressed. At this point, I'm happy to have had those harder moments because I know they helped me grow. When I look back I can honestly say I'm a better person now because of what I went through.

While many people might look at Sophie and get caught up in gender issues, the bottom line is that she is very much like any other college student—she likes Subway, video games, and drinks Coke. Talking with her made me realize how much many people take gender for granted. ▌▌

As we begin our discussion about gender, imagine that as you are reading this, an alien walks into the room. The alien tells you that "zee" (not he or she) is only on Earth for a short time and would like to learn as much as possible about life here during this visit. One of the things "zee" would like to learn about is **gender,** specifically, "What are a man and woman?" How would you answer such a question? You might try to explain how a man and woman look, act, think, or feel. But what is a man, and what is a woman?

As already discussed in Chapter 3 when a baby is born, new parents are eager to hear whether "It's a girl!" or "It's a boy!" but what if it was neither? What if a newborn had ambiguous genitalia, and it was impossible to tell whether it was a boy or a girl? A child with **gonads** (testes or ovaries) of one sex but ambiguous external genitalia has a condition known as **variations of sex development.** In the past, children with these conditions were often referred to as **intersexuals** or hermaphrodites (Lee et al., 2006; Marino, 2010). Assigning a new term for the condition has helped to improve our understanding about this condition as a congenital disorder (Aaronson & Aaronson, 2010).

Gender raises many issues. For example, if your college or university has on-campus housing, does it allow you to have a roommate who is the other gender? Beginning in 1970, many U.S. colleges began offering coeducational residential halls in addition to single-sex dorms—typically putting males and females on separate floors or wings (Gordon, 2010). Soon afterward, co-educational hallways were available. By 2008, gender-neutral housing, which allows students to share rooms regardless of gender, became available on a few campuses. Today, over 54 universities offered gender-neutral housing, including Dartmouth, Harvard, Princeton, University of Michigan, University of Pennsylvania, Yale, Stanford, Brown University, and Rutgers University (Branson, 2011; National Student GenderBlind, 2010).

Before we go any further, let's talk about how the words *sex* and *gender* are often used synonymously, even though they have different meanings. When you fill out a questionnaire that asks you "What is your sex?" how do you answer? When you apply for a driver's licence and are asked, "What gender are you?" how do you respond? Although your answers here might be the same, researchers usually use the word *sex* to refer to the biological aspects of being male or female, and *gender* to refer to the behavioural, psychological, and social characteristics of men and women (Pryzgoda & Chrisler, 2000).

You might wonder why exploring gender is important to our understanding of sexuality. How does gender affect sexuality? Gender stereotypes shape our opinions about how men and women act sexually. For example, if we believe that men are more aggressive than women, we might believe that these gender stereotypes carry over into the bedroom as well. Traditionally, men are viewed as the initiators in sexual activity, and they are the ones who are supposed to make all the "moves." Stereotypes about women, on the other hand, hold that women are more emotional and connected when it comes to sex—more into "making love" than "having sex." Do gender stereotypes really affect how we act and interact sexually? And how do gender stereotypes affect gay and lesbian couples? We explore the relationship between gender and sexuality later in this chapter.

REAL Research A comparison of television advertisements from Brazil, Canada, China, Germany, South Korea, Thailand, and the United States found that in all these countries women are more likely than men to be portrayed in gender-stereotypical ways (Paek et al., 2010).

So let's ask again, What is a man? A woman? For many years, scientists have debated whether gender is more genetics and biology ("nature") or social environment and upbringing ("nurture"). Or is it a combination of the two? The story of Bruce and Brenda discussed in the accompanying Sex in Real Life feature illustrates the fact that both nature and nurture are important in the development of gender. In Chapter 2, we discussed evolutionary theory, which argues that many behaviours in men and women have evolved in the survival of the species, and that gender differences between men and women may be at least partially a result of heredity.

In this chapter, we explore the nature via nurture debate as it relates to gender in hopes of finding answers to the questions "What is a man?" and "What is a woman?" We have already reviewed prenatal development and sexual differentiation in Chapters 3 and 4. We also looked at atypical sexual differentiation and chromosomal and hormonal disorders in those chapters. Although these disorders are not exceedingly common, their existence and how scientists have dealt with them help us learn more about gender. Our biological exploration of gender in Chapters 3 and 4 has set the foundation on which we can understand how complex gender really is. We also explore gender roles, theories about gender, and socialization throughout the life cycle.

Sexual Differentiation in the Womb

As discussed in Chapters 3 and 4, A human embryo normally undergoes about nine months of **gestation.** At about four to six weeks, the first tissues that will become the embryo's gonads begin to develop. Sexual differentiation begins a week or two later and is initiated by the sex chromosomes, which control at least four important aspects of sexual development: (1) the internal sexual

gender
The behavioural, psychological, and social characteristics associated with being biologically male or female.

gonads
The male and female sex glands—ovaries and testes.

variations of sex development
Medical term referring to conditions that can lead to atypical chromosomal,
gonadal, or anatomical sexual development.

intersexual
A child with gonads (testes or ovaries) of one sex but ambiguous external genitalia. May also be referred to as a disorder of sexual development.

gestation
The period of intrauterine fetal development.

SEX in Real Life — *A Case of a Boy Being Raised as a Girl*

In 1966, a young Canadian couple brought their two identical twin boys (Bruce and Brian) to the hospital for routine circumcisions; the boys were eight months old. A surgical mistake during one of the twin's circumcisions resulted in the destruction of his penis. The couple met with Dr. John Money, a well-known medical psychologist from Johns Hopkins University, who believed that gender was learned and could be changed through childrearing. He did not believe gender was contingent on chromosomes, genitals, or even sex hormones (Money, 1975). After meeting with Dr. Money and discussing their options, the couple decided to have their son, Bruce, undergo castration (removal of the testicles) and have surgery to transform his genitals into those of an anatomically correct female. Bruce became Brenda and was put on hormone treatment beginning in adolescence to maintain her feminine appearance. For many years, this Brenda/Bruce case stood as "proof" that children were psychosexually "neutral" at birth, and that gender could be assigned, no matter what the genetics or biology indicated.

This case had a profound effect on how children who were born with ambiguous genitalia or who had experienced genital trauma were raised (Colapinto, 2001).

However, even though Money paraded the Brenda/Bruce story as a success and around the globe intersexed children began sex reassignments, no one paid much attention to the fact that Brenda was struggling with her gender identity. In 1997, a study published by Milton Diamond, a reproductive biologist at the University of Hawaii, exposed the case and discussed how Brenda had struggled against her girlhood from the beginning (Diamond & Sigmundson, 1997). Once Brenda reached puberty, despite her hormone treatments, her misery increased. She became depressed and suicidal. She never felt that she was a girl, and she was relentlessly teased by peers. Her parents finally told her the truth, and at 15 years old, she stopped hormonal treatments and changed her name to David.

Soon afterward, David Reimer went public with his medical story in hopes of discouraging similar sex reassignment surgeries. In 2001, John Colapinto wrote the details of this real-life story in a book called *As Nature Made Him: The Boy Who Was Raised as a Girl* (Colapinto, 2001). This book, in conjunction with interviews with David, influenced medical understandings about the biology of gender. Today, the Intersex Society of North America opposes the use of sex reassignment surgery for non-consenting minors.

Although David Reimer eventually married and adopted children, his struggles with depression continued. In 2004, at age 38, Reimer took his own life (Burkeman & Younge, 2005).

organs (e.g., whether the fetus develops ovaries or testicles); (2) the external sex organs (such as the penis or clitoris); (3) the hormonal environment of the embryo; and (4) the sexual differentiation of the brain (which includes a cyclic or non-cyclic hormonal pattern) (Wilson & Davies, 2007). The timing of all these events varies, however. Although sexual differentiation of the genitals begins within the first two months of pregnancy, sexual differentiation of the brain, which is important for the development of gender, does not occur until sometime after the fifth month of pregnancy (Savic et al., 2010).

In Chapters 3 and 4 we discussed the various chromosomal and hormonal conditions that may affect gender. The more

Since male and female babies look so similar, many parents dress babies in blue or pink to identify their gender.

important question becomes, what can a parent do after a child is born with ambiguous genitals or the genitals of one sex and the genetic makeup of the other? For many years, parents of children with variations of sexual development have opted for immediate surgery to quickly assign their child's gender when he or she is born (Neergaard, 2005). However, medical experts today recommend waiting until a child is old enough to consent to treatment unless there is a medical emergency (Wiesemann et al., 2010).

Review Questions

1 What are some of the social issues that gender raises?

2 Differentiate between sex and gender, and explain how the Bruce/Brenda case shed light on the nature versus nurture debate.

Gender Roles and Gender Traits

Let's go back for a moment to that alien you met earlier in the chapter. When you describe what is male and female for the alien, chances are you will talk about stereotyped behaviour. You might say, "Men are strong, independent, and assertive, and often have a hard time showing emotion," or "Women are sensitive, nurturing, emotional, and soft." Descriptions like these are based on gender stereotypes. Gender stereotypes are fundamental to our ways of thinking, which makes it difficult to realize how thoroughly our conceptions of the world are shaped by gender issues. For example, when a baby is born, the very first question we ask is, "Is it a boy or a girl?" The parents proudly display a sign in their yard or send a card to friends, proclaiming, "It's a girl!" or "It's a boy!" as the sole identifying trait of the child. The card does not state, "It's a redhead!" From the moment of birth onward, the child is thought of first as male or female, and all other characteristics—whether the child is tall, bright, an artist, Irish, disabled, gay—are seen in light of the person's gender.

Overall, we expect men to act like men and women to act like women, and we may become confused and uncomfortable when we are denied knowledge of a person's gender. It is very difficult to know how to interact with someone whose gender we do not know because we are so programmed to react to people first according to their gender. If you walked into a party tonight and found yourself face-to-face with someone who you couldn't tell was male or female, how would you feel? Most likely you'd search for gender clues. Often our need to categorize people by gender is taken for granted. But why is it so important?

Even our language is constructed around gender. English has no neutral pronoun (neither do many other languages, including French, Spanish, German, and Italian), meaning that every time you refer to a person, you must write either "he" or "she." Therefore, nearly every sentence you write about a person reveals his or her gender, even if it reveals nothing else about that person.

Many of our basic assumptions about gender are open to dispute. Gender research has been growing explosively since the 1980s, and many of the results challenge long-held beliefs about gender differences. **Gender roles** are culturally defined behaviours that are seen as appropriate for males and females, including the attitudes, personality traits, emotions, and even postures and body language that are considered fundamental to being male or female in a culture. Gender roles also extend into social behaviours, such as the occupations we choose, how we dress and wear our hair, how we talk, and the ways in which we interact with others.

Note that by saying gender roles are culturally defined, we are suggesting that such differences are not primarily due to biological, physiological, or even psychological differences between men and women but, rather, to the ways in which we are taught to behave. Yet, many people believe that various gender differences in behaviour are biologically programmed. Who is correct?

Another way to ask the question is this: Which of our gender-specific behaviours are gender roles (i.e., culturally determined), and which are **gender traits** (innate or biologically determined)? If gender-specific behaviours are biologically determined, then they should remain constant in different societies; if they are social, then we should see very different gender roles in different societies. The majority of gender-specific behaviours, however, differ widely throughout the world and are determined primarily by culture.

Masculinity and Femininity

What is masculine? What is feminine? Not too long ago, the answers would have seemed quite obvious: Men naturally have masculine traits, meaning they are strong, stable, aggressive, competitive, self-reliant, and emotionally undemonstrative; women are naturally feminine, meaning they are intuitive, loving, nurturing, emotionally expressive, and gentle. Even today, many would agree that such traits describe the differences between the sexes. These gender stereotypes, however, are becoming less acceptable as our culture changes. **Masculinity** and **femininity** refer to the ideal cluster of traits that society attributes to each gender.

gender roles
Culturally defined ways of behaving seen as appropriate for males and females.

gender traits
Innate or biologically determined gender-specific behaviours.

masculinity
The ideal cluster of traits that society attributes to males.

femininity
The ideal cluster of traits that society attributes to females.

SEX in Real Life · *The Fear of Men?*

Over the years, many people have reacted with panic and fear to countless real and perceived threats to children. These threats include the fear of bullies, drugs, the Internet, and sexual predators (Radford, 2006). The media has helped to stir more fear in parents by pointing out that sexual predators could be lurking anywhere—near schools, churches, malls, or even movie theatres. By 2008, every state imposed notification laws so that communities would be alerted when a convicted sexual offender moved to town.

Although we talk more about sexual offender registries in Chapter 16, here let's explore how the rising panic in society about sexual predators has led to a fear of men.

Jeff Zaslow, a columnist with the *Wall Street Journal,* wrote an article in 2007 titled "Are We Teaching Our Children to Be Fearful of Men?" (Zaslow, 2007). In this article, Zaslow points out several ways in which society has contributed to rising fears about men. He discusses how when children get lost in a mall, they are often told to seek out a woman (preferably a "pregnant woman" or a "grandmother"), rather than a man. Or how airlines have changed their policies in seating unaccompanied minor children and now prefer to place them near female passengers. Could this fear of men have led to decreasing rates of male teachers and administrators in the elementary schools? Statistics show that the percentage of male elementary school teachers has declined from 18 percent to 9 percent in 2007 (Zaslow, 2007). More fear is instilled by John Walsh, host of *America's Most Wanted,* who advises parents not to hire male babysitters. A soccer club in Michigan requires one female parent on the sidelines at all times to protect children from any unwanted behaviours from men. In Pennsylvania, another soccer coach refrains from hugging his female players after a goal to make sure he's not sending the wrong message (Zaslow, 2007). Many experts today blame this fear of men on the media's image of men as a bad guy, especially when it comes to sexual crimes. John Walsh defended his position by comparing it with how we choose a dog: "What dog is more likely to bite and hurt you? A Doberman, not a poodle" (Zaslow, 2007).

Do you think that panic and fear about sexual predators have changed men's relationships with children? Do you believe that some men may be less likely to coach a female team because they are afraid of their behaviour being misinterpreted? These are all valid questions and point to the powerful nature of gender roles and attitudes in society. What do you think needs to be done?

Models of masculinity and femininity are changing rapidly in our society. It is not uncommon today to see female police officers on crime scenes or apprehending criminals, or women CEOs in the boardroom, nor is it uncommon to find stay-at-home dads at the park with kids or male librarians at the public library shelving books. Yet, gender role change can also result in confusion, fear, and even hostility in society. Gender roles exist, in part, because they allow comfortable interaction between the sexes. If you know exactly how you are supposed to behave and what personality traits you are supposed to assume in relation to the other sex, interactions between the sexes go more smoothly. When things change, determining correct behaviours becomes more difficult.

We also learn about masculinity and femininity from our ethnic group's cultural heritage (M. Crawford, 2006). In the United States, studies have documented less gender role stereotyping among Americans of African descent than among Americans of European descent. Overall, African Americans are less sex-role restricted than European Americans and believe that they possess both masculine and feminine traits (Carter et al., 2009; Dade & Sloan, 2000; Hill, 2002; Leaper, 2000). In fact, African Americans often view others through a lens of age and competency before gender.

Are Gender Roles Innate?

As gender stereotypes evolve, a trait may no longer be seen as the exclusive domain of a single gender. For example, many people have

> ### On Your Mind
> It seems that the majority of heterosexual women want a guy who is tough, and they don't give the nice guys a chance. Straight guys, on the other hand, tend to look for hot girls instead of thinking about how nice or intelligent the girls are. Why is this?
>
> Men and women always seem to wonder why people of the other sex behave the way they do. Yet, society itself supports those kinds of behaviours. Is it really any surprise that men often seem to pursue appearance over substance in women when advertising, television, and women's and men's magazines all emphasize women's appearance? Is it surprising, conversely, that some women pursue the "tough guys" when society teaches them to admire male power? In the end, it is society that determines the way we view gender relationships, and each of us is responsible to some degree for continuing those attitudes.

REAL Research Gender stereotyping is common on Indian television, where women are portrayed more often in home settings and less often as employed or as authority figures (Das, 2010).

been trying to change our current stereotypes of men as "unemotional" and women as "emotional." The constellation of traits that has been traditionally seen as masculine and feminine may be becoming less rigid. For many centuries, these types of gender traits were seen as innate, immutable, and part of the biological makeup of the sexes. Few scientists suggested that the differences between men and women were primarily social; most believed that women and men were fundamentally different.

Not only did scientists believe that the differences in the sexes were innate, but they also believed that men were superior—having developed past the "emotional" nature of women (Gould, 1981). While science has moved forward, these outdated attitudes still exist, both subtly in cultures like our own and overtly in cultures where women are allowed few of the rights granted to men.

How many of our gender behaviours are biological, and how many are socially transmitted? The truth is that the world may not split that cleanly into biological versus social causes of behaviour. Behaviours are complex and are almost always interactions between one's innate biological capacities and the environment in which one lives and acts. Behaviours that are considered innately "male" in one culture may be assumed to be innately "female" in another. Even when modern science suggests a certain gender trait that seems to be based on innate differences between the sexes, culture can contradict that trait or even deny it.

For example, most researchers accept the principle that males display more aggression than females; adult males certainly demonstrate this tendency, which is probably the result, in part, of higher levels of testosterone. When female bodybuilders, for example, take steroids, they often find themselves acquiring male traits, including losing breast tissue, growing more body hair, and becoming more aggressive. However, the difference is also demonstrated in early childhood, when boys are more aggressive in play, whereas girls tend to be more compliant and docile.

Yet, Margaret Mead's (1935/1988/2001) famous discussion of the Tchambuli tribe of New Guinea shows that such traits need not determine gender roles. Among the Tchambulis, the women performed the "aggressive" occupations such as fishing, commerce, and politics, whereas the men were more sedentary and artistic, and took more care of domestic life. The women assumed the dress appropriate for their activities—plain clothes and short hair—whereas the men dressed in bright colours. So even if we accept biological gender differences, societies such as the Tchambuli show that human culture can transcend biology.

Some gender differences are considered purely biological. Physically, males tend to be larger and stronger, with more of their body weight in muscle and less in body fat than females (Angier, 1999). Females, however, are born more neurologically advanced than males, and they mature faster. Females are also biologically heartier than males; more male fetuses miscarry, more males are stillborn, the male infant mortality rate is higher, males acquire more hereditary diseases and remain more susceptible to disease throughout life, and men die at younger ages than women. Males are also more likely to have developmental problems such as learning disabilities (Martin et al., 2008). It has long been believed that males are better at mathematics and spatial problems, whereas females are better at verbal tasks; for example, female children learn language skills earlier than males (Weatherall, 2002). Yet, many of these differences may be the result of socialization rather than biology (Hyde & Mertz, 2008).

Boys and girls do show some behavioural differences that appear to be universal. For example, in a study of six cultures, Whiting and her colleagues (Whiting & Edwards, 1988; Whiting & Whiting, 1975) discovered that certain traits seemed to characterize masculine and feminine behaviour in three- to six-year-olds. In almost all countries, boys engaged in more rough-and-tumble play, and boys "dominated egoistically" (tried to control the situation through commands), whereas girls more often sought or offered physical contact, sought help, and "suggested responsibly" (dominated socially by invoking rules or appealing to greater good).

Interestingly, although their strategies are different, both boys and girls often pursue the same ends; for example, rough-and-tumble play among boys and initiation of physical contact among girls are both strategies for touching and being touched. However, Whiting suggests that even these behaviours might be the result of different kinds of pressures put on boys and girls; for example, in their sample, older girls were expected to take care of young children more often than boys, and younger girls were given more responsibility than younger boys. These different expectations from each gender may explain later differences in their behaviours. So even gender behaviours that are spread across cultures may not prove to be innate differences.

There has always been evidence that men's and women's brains are different; autopsies have shown that men's brains are more asymmetrical than women's, and women seem to recover better from damage to the left hemisphere of the brain (as in strokes), where language is situated. Yet, it has always been unclear what facts such as these mean. Recently, newer techniques in brain imaging have provided evidence that women's and men's brains not only differ in size, but that women and men use their brains differently during certain activities (DeBellis et al., 2001; Hamberg, 2000; Menzler et al., 2011; Sánchez & Vilain, 2010; F. Schneider et al., 2000). Although it is too early to know what these differences mean, future studies may be able to provide clearer pictures of the different ways men and women think, and shed some light on the biological and social influences of these differences.

Aside from the behaviours and physical attributes just discussed, almost no differences between the sexes are universally accepted by researchers. This does not mean that there are not other biological gender differences; we simply do not know for sure. We must be careful not to move too far in the other direction and suggest that there are no innate differences between the sexes. Many of these differences remain controversial, such as relative levels of activity, curiosity, and facial recognition skills. These are relatively minor differences, however. Even if it turns out, for example, that female infants recognize faces earlier than males, as has been suggested, or that male children are more active than females, would that really account for the enormous gender role differences that have developed over time? Although biologists and other researchers still study innate differences between the sexes, today more attention is being paid to gender similarities.

Review Questions

1 Differentiate between gender roles and gender traits, and explain how cross-cultural research helps us identify each.

2 Compare *masculinity* and *femininity* and explain how our ethnic groups' cultural heritage may affect these concepts.

3 Which gender behaviours/traits are considered to be biologically based?

4 Are any gender differences universal?

Gender Role Theory

In Chapter 2, we reviewed general theories of sexuality, and the debates there centred on how much of human sexuality is programmed through our genes and physiology, and how much is influenced by culture and environment. Gender role theory struggles with the same issues, and different theorists take different positions. Social learning theorists believe that we learn gender roles almost entirely from our environment, whereas cognitive development theorists believe that children go through a set series of stages that correspond to certain beliefs and attitudes about gender. In this section, we talk about evolutionary, social learning, cognitive development, and gender schema theories.

When a baby is born, he or she possesses no knowledge and few instinctual behaviours. However, by the time the child is about age three or four years, he or she can usually talk, feed himself or herself, interact with adults, describe objects, and use correct facial expressions and body language. The child also typically exhibits a wide range of behaviours that are appropriate to his or her gender. The process whereby this infant who knows nothing becomes a preschooler who has the basic skills for functioning in society is called **socialization.**

Socialization occurs at every age and level of development, and the same is true of gender role socialization. Most boys dress and act like other boys and play with traditionally male toys (guns, trucks), whereas most girls insist on wearing dresses and express a desire to do traditionally "female" things, such as playing with dolls and toy kitchens. Is this behaviour innate, or are gender stereotypes still getting through to these children through television and in playing with their peers? The answer depends on which theory of gender role development you accept.

Evolutionary Theory: Adapting to Our Environment

Recently, we began to understand more about the biological differences between men and women through the field of evolutionary theory. Gender differences are seen as ways in which we have developed in our adaptation to our environment. For example, later in this book we explore how the double standard in sexual behaviour developed, in which a man with several partners was viewed as a "player," whereas a woman with several partners was viewed as a "slut." An evolutionary theorist would explain this gender difference in terms of the biological differences between men and women. A man can impregnate several women at any given time, but a woman, once pregnant, cannot become pregnant again until she gives birth. The time investment of these activities varies tremendously. If evolutionary success is determined by how many offspring we have, the men win hands down.

Social Learning Theory: Learning from Our Environment

Social learning theory suggests that we learn gender roles from our environment, from the same system of rewards and punishments that we learn our other social roles. For example, research shows that many parents commonly reward gender-appropriate behaviour and disapprove of (or even punish) gender-inappropriate behaviour. Telling a boy sternly not to cry "like a girl," approving a girl's use of makeup, taking a Barbie away from a boy and handing him Spider-Man, making girls help with cooking and cleaning and boys take out the trash—these little, everyday actions build into powerful messages about gender. Gender stereotypes can also influence our perceptions of a person's abilities. In one study, mothers were asked to guess how steep a slope their 11-month-old sons and daughters could crawl down. Although no gender differences were found in the abilities of the babies to climb the slopes, mothers were significantly more likely to underestimate the ability of their daughters (Eliot, 2009).

Children also learn to model their behaviour after the same-gender parent to win parental approval. They may learn about gender-appropriate behaviour from parents even if they are too young to perform the actions themselves; for example, they see that Mommy is more likely to make dinner, whereas Daddy is more likely to pay the bills. Children also see models of the "appropriate" ways for their genders to behave in their books, on television, and when interacting with others. Even the structure of our language conveys gender attitudes about things, such as the dominant position of the male; for example, the use of male words to include men and women (using "chairman" or "mankind" to refer to both men and women), or the differentiation between Miss and Mrs. to indicate whether a woman is married. However, people are trying to amend these inequalities today, as evidenced by the growing acceptance of words such as "chairperson" and "humankind," and the title "Ms."

REAL Research College males who play video games that "objectify" women are more likely to view women as sex objects and engage in inappropriate sexual advances toward women (Yao et al., 2010).

socialization
The process in which an infant is taught the basic skills for functioning in society.

Cognitive Development Theory: Age-Stage Learning

Cognitive development theory assumes that all children go through a universal pattern of development, and there really is not much parents can do to alter it. As children's brains mature and grow, they develop new abilities and concerns; at each stage, their understanding of gender changes in predictable ways. This theory follows the ideas of Piaget (1951), the child development theorist who suggested that social attitudes in children are mediated through their processes of cognitive development. In other words, children can process only a certain kind and amount of information at each developmental stage.

As children begin to be able to recognize the physical differences between girls and boys, and then to categorize themselves as one or the other, they look for information about their genders. Around the ages of two to five, they form strict stereotypes of gender based on their observed differences: Men are bigger and stronger and are seen in aggressive roles such as policeman and superhero; women tend to be associated with motherhood through their physicality (e.g., the child asks what the mother's breasts are and is told they are used to feed children) and through women's social roles of nurturing and emotional expressiveness. These "physicalistic" thought patterns are universal in young children and are organized around ideas of gender.

As children mature, they become more aware that gender roles are, to some degree, social and arbitrary, and cognitive development theory predicts, therefore, that rigid gender role behaviour should decrease after about the age of seven or eight. So cognitive development theory predicts what set of gender attitudes should appear at different ages; however, the research is still contradictory on whether its predictions are correct (see Albert & Porter, 1988).

Newer theories of gender role development try to combine social learning theory and cognitive development theory to address weaknesses in both. Cognitive development theory neglects social factors and differences in the ways different groups raise children. On the other hand, social learning theory neglects a child's age-related ability to understand and assimilate gender models, and portrays children as too passive; in social learning theory, children seem to accept whatever models of behaviour are offered without passing them through their own thought processes.

Gender Schema Theory: Our Cultural Maps

Sandra Bem's (1974, 1977, 1981) theory is a good example of a theory that tries to overcome the difficulties posed by the other theories. According to Bem, children (and, for that matter, all of us) think according to **schemas** (SKI-muz), which are cognitive mechanisms that organize our world. These schemas develop over time and are universal, like the stages in cognitive development theory; the difference lies in Bem's assertion that the contents of schemas are determined by the culture. Schemas are like maps in our heads that direct our thought processes.

Bem suggests that one schema we all have is a **gender schema,** which organizes our thinking about gender. From the moment we are born, information about gender is continuously presented to us by our parents, relatives, teachers, peers, television, movies, advertising, and the like. We absorb the more obvious information about sexual anatomy, "male" and "female" types of work and activities, and gender-linked personality traits. However, society also attributes gender to things as abstract as shapes (rounded, soft shapes are often described as "feminine," and sharp, angular shapes as "masculine") and even our drinks (champagne is seen as more feminine, whereas beer is seen as more masculine; Crawford et al., 2004).

Gender schemas are powerful in our culture. When we first meet a man, we immediately use our masculine gender schema and begin our relationship with an already established series of beliefs about him. For example, we may believe that men are strong or assertive. Our gender schema is more powerful than other schemas and is used more often, Bem argues, because our culture puts so much emphasis on gender and gender differences. This is where she parts company with cognitive development theorists, who argue that gender is important to children because of their naturally physicalistic ways of thinking.

The gender schema becomes so ingrained that we do not even realize its power. For example, some people so stereotype gender concepts that it would never occur to them to say, "My, how strong you are becoming!" to a little girl, whereas they say it easily to a little boy. Bem argues that "strong" as a feminine trait does not exist in the female schema for many people, so they rarely invoke the term *strong* to refer to women.

schema	gender schema
A cognitive mechanism that helps to organize information.	A cognitive mechanism that helps us to understand gender roles.

Review Questions

1 Explain how gender role socialization occurs in children.

2 Describe the differences among the evolutionary, social learning, and cognitive development theories.

3 Explain how one's development of a "gender schema" influences his or her view of gender. Give examples to support your answer.

Varieties of Gender

Culture and social structure interact to create **sex typing,** a way of thinking that has traditionally split the world into two basic categories—male and female—and that most behaviours, thoughts, actions, professions, emotions, and so on are more appropriate for one gender or the other (Eliot, 2009; Liben & Bigler, 2002; Maccoby, 2002). Although attitudes today have changed, sex typing is still prominent.

This way of thinking has been so ingrained in people that they do not realize the powerful hold they have over their conceptions of the world. Some cultures have even taken these ideas and created models of the universe based on masculine and feminine traits, such as the Chinese concept of yin and yang that we mentioned in Chapter 1.

Because gender is socially constructed, societies influence the ways in which it is defined. Williams and Best (1994) collected data upon conceptions of masculinity and femininity from 30 countries and found high agreement upon what is masculine and what is feminine. In another study of 37 countries, Buss (1994) found that women and men value different qualities in each other. In general, women tended to place a higher value on the qualities of being "good financial prospects" and "ambitious and industrious" for their mates while men tended to place a higher value on physical attractiveness.

Because of the pervasiveness of sex typing, it begins early in life and different behaviours may be observed even in young children. In one Canadian study (Moller et al., 1992), 86 Grade 2 children and 84 Grade 4 children were observed while at play. Boys tended to engage in more aggressive and rough-and-tumble play while girls tended to be more quieter and engage in more cooperative play. In another Canadian study of three- to seven-year-olds (Serbin & Sprafkin, 1986), it was found that the gender of another child was the most salient variable for forming friendships. Although children at this age knew little about sex roles, they still gravitated toward the same sex when seeking out others.

In Canada as well as the United States, people often see gender roles as mutually exclusive; that is, what is feminine is not masculine and what is masculine is not feminine (Spence, 1984). However, research has shown that many people have both masculine and feminine qualities (Bem, 1977; Spence, 1984). Bem (1974) suggests that this can lead to four types of personalities: high in masculinity and low in femininity, high in femininity and low in masculinity, low in both ("undifferentiated"), and high in both ("androgynous"). To see gender in such categories, or to conceptualize it as a continuum from one to the other challenges traditional assumptions about what is natural, or inherent, in human beings. Today, many scholars have come to realize that gender is more complicated than just splitting the world into male and female.

Masculinity: The Hunter

Virtually every society has different expectations of its males and females, and anthropological research, which emphasizes culture, has explored this issue extensively. In some cultures, boys must go through trials or rites of passage after which they earn their right to be men. Few cultures have comparable trials for girls. For example, the !Kung of the Kalahari desert in southern Africa have a "rite of first kill" that is performed twice—once after a boy kills his first large male animal and once after he kills his first large female animal (Collier & Rosaldo, 1981). During the ceremony, a gash is cut in the boy's chest and filled with what is thought to be a magical substance to keep him from becoming lazy. Hunting prowess is also ritually connected to marriage, where men acquire wives by demonstrating their ability to hunt (Lewin, 1988). A boy may not marry until he goes through the rite of first kill and, at the wedding, he must present to his bride's parents a large animal he has killed. Even the language of hunting and marriage is linked in that !Kung myths and games equate marriage with hunting and there is talk of men "chasing," "killing," and "eating" women as well.

In contrast, in Western societies, men may be judged by their prowess in business, where successful men are admired for their accomplishments. When success is linked to masculinity, it is often challenging for men to live up to such standards. Nevertheless, masculinity is still measured in a man's ability to provide for his family, be on top of every situation, and be stoic and direct.

Ironically, with greater complexities in society there are often contradictory roles: Men must be successful yet involved with their families, strong and stable yet not cut off from emotions, powerful yet sensitive, and sexually experienced yet faithful. In some cases, men learn to exaggerate the macho side of society's expectations and become **hypermasculine** males (Farr et al., 2004). To these men, violence is manly, danger is exciting, and sexuality must be pursued callously.

David Gilmore (1990) believes that there is an evolutionary purpose behind masculine socialization. In most societies, men are prepared for the role of safeguarding their groups' survival. They must be willing to give their lives in the hunt or in war to ensure their groups' future by protecting women's ability to reproduce. Men are not concerned with masculinity as an end in itself but with the welfare of society. In fact, Gilmore argues, men are just as nurturing as women. They are concerned with their groups' weaker and more helpless members and are often willing to risk their lives for the greater social good.

Although masculinity has its privileges, it has its downside, too. Men do not live as long as women partly because of the demands of the male role. They are more likely to die of stress-related illnesses such as lung cancer (men smoke more than women). They are also more likely to have motor vehicle accidents and more likely to commit suicide. Women attempt suicide more often, but men are more successful at actually killing themselves (Courtenay, 2000; D.R. Nicholas, 2000). It is likely, however, that this disparity is gradually changing. In contrast to the days when men worked in the public sphere and women stayed at home, the Canadian work force is slowly reaching equality, where women are also in stress-related occupations.

---

sex typing
A cognitive thinking pattern that divides the world into male and female categories and suggests appropriate behaviours, thoughts, actions, professions, and emotions for each.

hypermasculinity
Extreme masculinity in appearance, manner, behaviour, and worldview.

Today men are often judged by their success in their careers while women are often judged by their physical appearance.

Even with all the attention on how gender stereotypes harm women, men are equally the victims of society's expectations. Male gender roles tend to be narrower than those for women and men who conform to society's ideas of gender have less flexibility in their lives (Lips, 2008). For example, it is typically thought unacceptable for men to cry in public except in the most extreme circumstances. Boys are taught not to cry but this is difficult when they are emotionally moved. Some will therefore stop allowing themselves to be moved emotionally (Lombardo et al., 2001).

Femininity: The Nurturer

In keeping with heteronormativity, femininity has traditionally been defined as that which is not masculine—in other words, a separate sphere of behaviours, manners, and choices. Femininity is beautiful and not rugged, empathetic and not insensitive, weak and not strong. This becomes complicated in modern societies where women are in every profession from bus drivers to chief executives, engineers to soldiers, and physicians to firefighters. As society progresses toward equality, traditionally feminine traits become more and more incompatible with the demands of the labour market. For example, University of British Columbia professors Cherkowski and Bosetti (2014) have pointed out that the traditionally masculine structure of universities often leads academic women to tread a precarious path between their femininity and the demands of their careers.

For heterosexual men, there is also a strong association of femininity with sexual orientation, or at least the fear of being labelled as gay. Canadian psychologist Donald R. McCreary (1994) pointed out that such men typically avoid what is perceived as feminine because of its close association with homosexuality. It is

androgyny
Having both masculine and feminine characteristics.

likely, however, that such fears will slowly dissipate in Canada because gays and lesbians now typically enjoy equality and openness and many people now see such an association of femininity with sexual orientation as stereotypical.

Ideas of femininity have changed dramatically over the years. Rothman (1978) pointed out that there have been ever-changing conceptions of what "womanhood" (and, by extension, femininity) should be. In the 19th century, the "virtuous woman" was valued above all, and women instilled "morality" in society. Many women formed groups and fought against society's perceived social ills. The Women's Christian Temperance Union, for example, started a movement to ban alcohol. By the early 20th century, the concept of womanhood shifted to what Rothman calls "educated mother-hood," where women were supposed to learn all the new sophisti-cated theories of childrearing and shift their attention to the needs of children and family. Over the next few decades, women's roles were then redefined as "wife–companion," and they were supposed to redirect their energies toward being sexual companions for their husbands. Finally, Rothman argues, the 1960s began the era of "woman as person," when people began to see women as autono-mous, competent, and able to decide upon their own roles in life.

Among feminist scholars, ideological debates continue about the meaning of womanhood. For example, one belief has been that women who choose to stay at home and raise children are not fulfilling their potential and yet women who do work outside the home often report feelings of guilt about not being with their children (Crittenden, 2001; Lerner, 1998). Many argue that the idea of femininity itself is an attempt to mould women in ways that are determined by men. They maintain that the pressure upon women to stay young and thin is a reflection of male power (Wolf, 1991). The media reinforce the ideals of feminine beauty, and the pressures on women to conform to these ideals lead to eating disorders and a surge in cosmetic surgery (Wolf, 1991). As it happens, therefore, there is wide disagreement on what is feminine and how women should relate to their gender.

Androgyny: Feminine and Masculine

Androgyny (*andro* = male, *gyn* = female) is the idea that mascu-line and feminine traits may be present in the same person. The breakdown of traditional gender roles has focused attention on this concept. Bem (1977) suggested that people have different combinations of masculine and feminine traits. She defines people who have high scores for masculinity and femininity as androgy-nous. She believes that androgyny allows for greater flexibility in behaviour because people have a greater repertoire of possible reactions to a situation. Bem (1974, 1977, 1981) has tried to show that androgynous individuals can display "masculine" traits (such as independence) and "feminine" traits (such as gentleness) when situations call for either one.

Because of her research, some psychologists have suggested that androgyny is a desirable state and that androgynous attitudes are solutions to the tension between the sexes. On the other hand, later researchers have questioned whether the masculine and feminine traits that Bem used in her research are still valid decades later. Auster and Ohm (2000) believed that although 18 of 20 of Bem's feminine traits still qualified as feminine, only 8 of

Transsexuality in Iran

For many years, transgender men and women in Iran were considered homosexual. Because there are strict bans on homosexuality under Sharia law, transsexualism was not acknowledged. Today, Iran has the second-highest rate of sex reassignment surgery in the world. Years before, transsexuals were imprisoned, beaten, and even stoned to death. It took the bravery of one transgender woman to change things for the better.

For most of Maryann Khatoon Molkara's life, she knew she was a woman even though she was born a biological male. Maryann had experienced years of bullying and harassment, and she was fired from her job, injected with male hormones, and institutionalized. Knowing that the only way to change attitudes about transsexuals was for the Ayatollah Khomeini to issue a favourable statement, she began writing to him in 1975. She never received a response. Her luck changed during the mid-1980s when she was a volunteer caring for wounded soldiers during the Iran–Iraq war. One of her patients was a high-ranking government worker who helped her secure a meeting with top officials.

However, getting to Khomeini required her to break into a heavily guarded compound. She did this wearing a man's suit and carrying a copy of the Qur'an, but

was quickly surrounded by guards and severely beaten. Khomemni's brother, Hassan Pasandide, intervened and brought her to see him. The guards were fearful that Maryann was carrying explosives because they saw tape around her chest, but she removed the tape and revealed her breasts. After a long talk with the Ayatollah, a *fatwa* (a religious or legal decree) was issued in support of sex reassignment surgery. The *fatwa* gave her religious authorization to undergo sexual reassignment surgery.

Sex reassignment surgery has thus been legal in Iran since 1983. Today, many transsexuals travel to Iran from Eastern European and Middle Eastern countries for this purpose. Maryann continues her work fighting for transsexual rights and today she runs Iran's leading transsexual campaign group.

All is not ideal however. While sex reassignment surgery may be fitting for transsexuals, there is evidence showing that not everyone having such surgery is in fact a transsexual. According to a 2008 documentary film by Tanaz Eshaghian entitled *Be Like Others*, because gays and lesbians are so persecuted in Iran—even to the point of facing the death penalty—many will either claim to be transsexual or be pressured into sex

An Iranian male-to-female transsexual.

© Alexandra Boulat/VII/Corbis

reassignment surgery even though they are not transsexual at all. Eshaghian further suggests that this is especially the case for effeminate gay men. Because sex reassignment is considered better than a life of persecution and hiding, life in prison, or execution, an unknown number of gay men are virtually forced to change their sex and lead unhappy lives thereafter as a result.

SOURCE: The information in this feature was gathered from Barford (2008), Kamali (2010), McDowall and Kahn (2004), and Tait (2005).

20 of her masculine traits qualified as strictly masculine. (Traits originally associated with masculinity such as *analytical, individualistic, competitive, self-sufficient, risk taking,* and *defends own beliefs* are no longer viewed as distinctly masculine traits.) What this suggests is that masculinity and femininity are not objective qualities of human beings but rather dependent upon where one is located in time and space. What is masculine or feminine in one society may not be so in another and what is masculine or feminine in one historical time may not be so in another as well. Gender roles are thus changing constantly.

The Gender Spectrum

According to John Money (1955), the word "gender" was first used in the 1950s to refer to the feelings and behaviours that identify a person as masculine or feminine to distinguish it from "sex," which refers to chromosomes and genitals. A **gender binary** (an example of heteronormativity) divides people into two groups— male and female. Having a penis or vagina determines biological sex. However, some people are born with **ambiguous genitalia**,

meaning that their genitals have qualities of both. In such cases, a child is said to be **intersexed**.

Money (1955) suggested that most people are "gender congruent," meaning that their biological sex, gender identity, and gender expression all "match." For example, a person with a penis is a man, he considers himself to be a man, and he acts masculine. In other words, his physiology, gender identity, and gender expression are all in harmony with one another, creating a multidimensional **gender spectrum.** On the other hand, a person's gender spectrum may not be concordant. For example, a person might have the genitals of a woman but identify as a male

gender binary
A classification system that divides people into male and female or masculine and feminine.

ambiguous genitalia
Usually discovered at birth where a child has genitals that have qualities of both sexes.

intersexed
A person with ambiguous genitalia.

gender spectrum
The continuum of possibilities of biological gender, gender identity, and gender expression.

and act masculine. In such cases, a person is considered **gender diverse** or **transgender.** Although most transgender people feel confident and comfortable about their biological sex and gender identity, some experience **gender dysphoria** (dis-FOR-ee-uh) or confusion and/or discomfort with the feelings they have.

Transsexualism and Sex Reassignment Surgery

Transsexualism has profound implications for our conceptions of gender. Sex reassignment surgery began just after World War II when cosmetic surgeons began working on the genital reconstruction of wounded soldiers. In 1952, George Jorgensen, a retired Marine, went to Denmark to have his genitals surgically altered to resemble those of a female. He changed his name to Christine and became the first highly publicized case of a transsexual who underwent **sex reassignment surgery (SRS).** Jorgensen wanted to be a girl from an early age, avoided rough sports, and was a small, frail child with underdeveloped male genitals (Jorgensen, 1967). Her story is typical of other transsexuals who felt strongly from an early age that they were "born in the wrong body."

Billy Tipton, a well-known jazz musician, was discovered to be female when he died in 1989. He was married to a woman who was aware of his biological sex and he was the father of three adopted boys who did not learn of that he was female until after his death.

Transgender Rights in Canada

Historically, the struggle for transgender rights in Canada has been slow and difficult. Canadian historian Valerie Korinek (2012) looked at queer subcultures in Winnipeg from the 1930s to the 1960s and believed that transgendered lives witnessed a slight improvement after World War II once relaxed liquor laws and an expanding economy made Winnipeg a "queer capital" for the people of Manitoba, northern Ontario, and Saskatchewan. Canadian sociologist and Women's Studies professor Becki Ross (2012) interviewed three transsexual women about their past difficulties in the 1970s and 1980s, and among those difficulties was securing legitimate employment. For one thing, many transgender people were reluctant to fill out résumés of their employment before they changed gender. And more strikingly, because of their large hands, prominent Adam's apples, and deep voices, they were systematically rejected at every door. As a result, many went into sex work as a way to survive.

In 1996, Canadian professional downhill mountain biker Michelle Dumaresq underwent sex reassignment surgery, transforming from male to female. The International Olympic Committee had allowed transsexual people to compete professionally since 2004 provided that their reassignment surgery had occurred two years beforehand and that they had been on a regimen of hormones since then. This two-year period was to ensure that any residual advantage from testosterone would be neutralized. She has since won several important competitions.

In May, 2012, Canadian Jenna Talakova became the first transgender woman to compete in the Miss Universe pageant after she successfully challenged the rule that contestants must be "naturally born females." While she did not win, she was one of four contestants to be named Miss Congeniality.

These and other cases have slowly brought transgender issues to the forefront. In 2010, the Canadian Professional Association for Transgender Health (CPATH) issued a statement advising that gender variance and gender nonconforming behaviour should not be considered psychological disorders. It went on to say that Canadian legislation should be rewritten so as to guarantee gender variant individuals health care. This was realized two years later with the passing of Bill C-279, which officially names transgender persons as a protected class, or more specifically, it amends the Criminal Code of Canada to include "gender identity" as a distinguishing feature to be protected.

Medical and Surgical Gender Procedures

The World Professional Association for Transgender Health (2001) proposed standards of care that outline protocols and treatments for people seeking gender reassignment. These guidelines have helped those who identify as transgender around the world have access to safe health care and legal care. Without them, transgender people may sometimes resort to their own devices as has been shown in a large-scale study in Ontario. Khobzi Rotondi et al. (2013) looked at 433 participants from the Trans PULSE Project (see the Websites section at the end of this chapter) and found that of the 43 percent who were taking hormones, a quarter of them obtained them from non-medical sources (e.g., from friends). They also found cases of transgender people performing major surgeries on themselves as well. Easy access to proper health care is thus essential.

Secondary sex characteristics appear at puberty and their onset can have harmful emotional effects for teenagers who identify with the other gender. While such feelings often emerge in childhood, it is also possible that they may be resolved later. According to one study, 80 to 90 percent of children diagnosed with gender identity disorder no long have such feelings in adolescence (Public Health Agency of Canada, 2010).

---

gender diverse
An individual whose gender identity or gender expression lies outside of socially accepted gender norms.

transgender
A general term referring to a person or group of people who identify or express their gender in a variety of different ways, typically in opposition to their biological sex.

gender dysphoria
A condition in which a person feels confusion and/or discomfort with his or her biological sex and gender identity.

sex reassignment surgery (SRS)
A wide range of various surgical options to change genitalia on a transsexual.

Female-to-male transsexuals (FTM) are biological females, while male-to-female transsexuals (MTF) are biological males. A variety of medical and surgical options are available and sex reassignment surgery, which changes genitals to those of the other sex, is the last stage. Although some transsexuals go through this surgery, many do not. For a variety of reasons from financial to personal, they might stop short of sex reassignment surgery.

Treatment often begins with psychotherapy, which helps an individual explore options, establish realistic goals, and identify points of conflict that have been interfering with happiness. If they have not already done so, they may be encouraged to take the role of their desired gender by cross-dressing and with hair removal, body padding, vocal training, and so forth. This real-life test enables them to live as their desired gender and understand the effects that changing gender will have on their work, home, and personal relationships.

For some transsexuals, the next step typically involves cross-sex hormone therapy, where androgens are given to FTM transsexuals and estrogens (and sometimes testosterone-blockers) to MTF transsexuals. Taking these hormones significantly changes the physical appearance of a man or woman, typically within about two years.

Male-to-female transsexuals who take estrogens (and possibly testosterone blockers) develop breasts. There is also a redistribution of body fat, a decrease in upper body strength, a softening of the skin, a decrease in body hair, a slowing or stopping of hair loss in the scalp, a decrease in testicular size, and fewer erections (World Professional Organization for Transgender Health, 2001). Most of these effects are reversible if they stopped taking estrogen with the exception of the breast tissue. Female-to-male transsexuals who take testosterone will develop several permanent changes such as a deeper voice, clitoral enlargement, increased facial and body hair, and possible baldness. There are also reversible changes such as increased sexual desire, increased upper body strength, weight gain, and a redistribution of body fat (World Professional Organization for Transgender Health, 2001). For some transsexuals, the changes brought about by hormones are enough and they do not feel the need to undergo additional surgery.

Although hormonal therapy may produce adequate breast tissue in some MTF transsexuals, others may desire additional breast augmentation surgery. Female-to-male transsexuals often undergo mastectomies to remove their breasts entirely. Surgeries for MTF transsexuals include **penectomy, orchiectomy,** urethral rerouting, and **vaginoplasty.** Surgeries for FTM transsexuals include **hysterectomy,** urethral rerouting , **scrotoplasty, metoidioplasty,** and **phalloplasty.**

For FTM transsexuals, the most preferred option is a clitoral release procedure called metoidioplasty (Gibson, 2010; Perovic & Djordjevic, 2003). Testosterone therapy typically increases the size of the clitoris elongation to 2.5-7.5 centimetres (1-3 inches). A metoidioplasty releases the enlarged clitoris, allowing it to hang like a penis. Another surgical option, phalloplasty, involves constructing an artificial penis from abdominal skin. This is a difficult procedure and, as a result, is much less preferred. A penis made by phalloplasty cannot achieve a natural erection, so penile implants are usually used (we will discuss these implants in more detail in Chapter 15). Metoidioplasty has fewer complications, takes less time, and is less expensive. Over the years, sex reassignment surgery has been

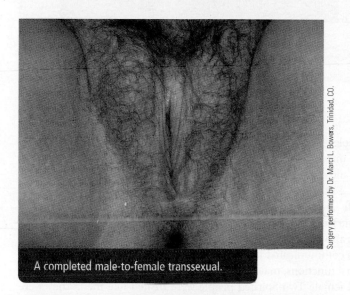

A completed male-to-female transsexual.

Surgery performed by Dr. Marci L. Bowers, Trinidad, CO.

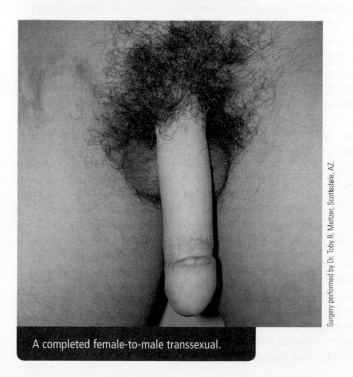

A completed female-to-male transsexual.

Surgery performed by Dr. Toby R. Meltzer, Scottsdale, AZ.

penectomy
Removal of the penis.

orchiectomy
Removal of the testes.

vaginoplasty
Surgical construction of the labia and vaginal canal.

hysterectomy
Surgical removal of all or part of the uterus.

scrotoplasty
Surgical construction of a scrotum. Silicone implants are placed in the scrotum.

metoidioplasty
enlarged surgical procedure where the clitoris is released from its position and moved forward to more closely resemble the position of a penis.

phalloplasty
Surgical construction of a penis.

Twelve-Year-Old Transgender Boy Gets New Birth Certificate

To truly enjoy an identity as the other gender, transgender people in Canada typically go through therapy, hormone treatment, and surgery. The journey does not end there, however, since one must also change the gender of one's driver's licence, passport, and birth certificate. Until recently, the province of Alberta would not change these documents until after surgery. In 2014, after his complaint to the Alberta Human Rights Commission, 12-year-old Wren Kauffman, a transgender boy who was born a biological female was issued a new birth certificate where the "F" was changed to "M." Not only is this landmark decision a victory for the rights of all transgender people in Alberta but it recognizes the importance of social validation for a person's true identity (Alberta grants new birth certificate to transgender boy, 2014).

© THE CANADIAN PRESS/Jason Franson

Wren Kauffman

controversial, with some cases of healthy postoperative functioning (DeCuypere et al., 2005; Johansson et al., 2010; Klein & Gorzalka, 2009; Lawrence, 2006) and other cases showing no alleviation of psychological suffering at all (Newfield et al., 2006; Olsson & Möller, 2006). Even so, some people seeking sex reassignment have longed for years to bring their bodies into line with their gender identities and sex reassignment surgery has been their ultimate goal.

Gender Diversity in Other Cultures

Some cultures challenge Western notions of gender and even have categories that may not only encompasses both aspects of gender but stand outside of them entirely. **Two-Spirited** people have been among First Nations cultures, and there are other third-gender categories in India, Thailand, and Samoa. It is important to understand these categories not through the eyes of our own culture but instead through the eyes of the cultures from which they emerge.

Two Spirited People of First Nations Cultures

Among First Nations people, the term "two-spirited" comes from the Ojibwa words *niizh manitoag* and refers to individuals possessing both masculine and feminine spirits. It was chosen at the Third Annual Intertribal Native American/First Nations Gay and Lesbian Conference in Winnipeg in 1990 to replace the term *berdache*, which was used for centuries to refer to them. During those times, berdache meant "male prostitute," which exemplified how European missionaries misunderstood their place among their

Two-Spirited
A term used by First Nations people and those of other parts of the world for a male or female who is thought to possess both masculine and feminine spirits.

people (Katz, 1976). A Two-Spirited person may be either a biological male or female who at an early age gravitated toward the other sex and eventually adopted the clothing and occupations of the other sex. First Nations cultures thus had a four-gender system—male, male Two-Spirited, female, and female Two-Spirited (Blackwood, 1994; Jacobs et al., 1997; W.L. Williams, 1986). Being Two-Spirited was also considered a vocation like being a hunter or warrior, which was communicated to certain boys in their first adult vision. In all social functions, male Two-Spirited people were treated like women and female Two-Spirited people were treated like men. They were respected, considered sacred, and believed to have special powers.

Female Two-Spirited people were initiated into puberty as men and, thereafter, they were essentially considered men. They hunted and trapped, fought in battle, and performed male ceremonial tasks. Among the Kaska people of the Yukon, they could marry a woman, although the unions remained childless, and the Two-Spirit would perform the appropriate rituals when her partner menstruated but would ignore her own menses. They were always prominent members of First Nations cultures. Sadly, as Aboriginal transsexual Saylesh Wesley said at the Transgender Archives Symposium at the University of Victoria in March 2014, much of the rich history of Two-Spirited people has been either distorted by the views of early missionaries or obliterated through colonialism (Wesley, 2014).

The Khanith of Oman

Oman, one of the Arab Emirates, has a class of biological males called the *Khanith* (Wikan, 1977), who often act as house servants. They dress in men's clothes but are feminine in appearance and manner. Their status in Islamic society is intermediate. They can move freely during the day as men but are restricted at night like women. They sit with women at weddings and may even see the bride's face but they pray with men. They have men's names and refer

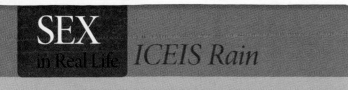
In 2014, ICEIS Rain (alias Massey Whiteknife) of Alberta and a member of the Mikisew Cree First Nation became the first Two-Spirited singer to perform at the Aboriginal People's Choice Music Awards (Kellaway, 2014).

Courtesy of Iceis Rain

ICEIS Rain

today being the *Hijra*. The Hijra are men who have traditionally undergone ritual castration in which all or part of their genitals are removed. Although this operation is still practised today, it is forbidden by law. As a result, not every Hijra is castrated. The Hijra are believed to have special powers to curse or bless male children at their births. They dress as women and their mannerisms are feminine (Nanda, 2001). Because they are often scorned in Indian society, many Hijra work as prostitutes in order to survive.

The Kathoey: Lady Boys of Thailand

Thailand has long had a third gender category of people known as the *Kathoey*, which translates to "a second kind of woman." The Kathoey are a collection of gender variant biological males who may be anywhere from post-operative or pre-operative transsexuals to merely feminine gay men. Collectively, they are known as "lady boys" and they are more accepted in Thailand than their counterparts in any other Asian culture, even to the point of having gender-neutral washrooms in universities. While some work as prostitutes, others have found places in the fashion industry or in cosmetics. Recently, singer and actress Bell Nuntita appeared on the talent show *Thailand's Got Talent* and became a YouTube sensation.

The Fa'afafine of Samoa

Fa'afafine literally means "in the manner of women" and describes a third-gender category of biological males who adopt the appearance and role of women. They have been accepted in Samoan cultures for centuries and have important family functions in the rearing of children. They have sex with men, but this is not considered homosexuality since two genders are involved. Persecution of them did not occur until Europeans who misunderstood their roles arrived and this continues today, particularly from a religious standpoint. As Canadian psychologists Vanderlaan and Vasey (2012) point out, because the Fa'afafine define themselves as a separate gender, they do not experience any gender dysphoria from their identities and their own bodies.

to themselves with masculine pronouns, but they carry with themselves the pride of women. The Khanith gender category, however, does seem to be fluid in that under particular circumstances they may lose their status as Khanith. For example, they are allowed to marry women and, if they do, they are considered men. They may also lose their status in old age once they have lost their feminine attractiveness. In general, however, the Khanith are a third gender and intermediate between men and women (Murray, 1997).

The Hijra of India

According to Gannon (2011), the Indian subcontinent has had several categories of other genders through its history, the most prominent

Other Third Genders

There are numerous other third-gender categories throughout the world, including the *Aikane* of native Hawaii, who were historically attached to the courts of chiefs and served sexual, social, and political functions (Morris, 1990); the *Muxes* of Mexico (Chinas, 1995); and the *Mahu* of Tahiti (Herdt & Stoller, 1990). The belief in these cultures that it is neither obvious nor natural that there are only two genders continues to challenge Western conceptualizations of the world.

Review Questions

1 Describe traditional views of masculinity and femininity. Explain how modern society has impacted upon these views, and identify the risk associated with these stereotypes.

2 What types of struggles have transgender people experienced in Canada?

3 Define androgyny and give several examples of androgynous behaviour.

4 What are the surgical options for gender reassignment?

Gender Role Socialization Throughout the Lifespan

Socialization is a life-long process of learning to be social, or learning to interact in the world in specific ways. Traditionally, males and females have received different forms of such training which determines their gender roles. In the first years of life, the primary socializing agents are one's parents. Later on, socialization continues in peer groups, in schools, in workplaces, and through other institutions. In this section we examine socialization into gender roles throughout life.

Childhood: Learning by Playing

From the moment they are born, children's lives are strongly defined by their gender. From their first names, to how they are dressed, to how their rooms are decorated, gender suffuses their lives. Not only do parents construct different environments for boys and girls from birth but they tend to treat them differently as well.

Parents also serve as gender role models. As early as age two, children begin to identify with their same-sex parent and by observing and imitating that parent's behaviour, they learn that

gender-identity disorder
A disorder in which a person has a strong and persistent identification with the other sex or the gender role of the other sex and is uncomfortable with his or her own biological sex or gender role.

homosocial play
Gender-segregated play.

Children learn much of their gender role behaviour from modelling.

objects and activities are associated with one gender or the other. The cognitive schema that children develop at this point are not flexible but universal. To the children, only women can wear skirts and only men can shave their faces. In fact, cross-gender humour can be funny to young children. A television program that shows a man wearing a dress or a woman with a mustache can elicit bursts of laughter. As children grow, they learn that there are often societal restrictions on acceptable behaviours for males and females.

Overall, boys are treated more harshly than girls when they adopt other gendered behaviours (Sandnabba & Ahlberg, 1999). Children who have a strong and persistent identification with the other sex or the gender role of the other sex and are uncomfortable with their own biological sex or gender role may be diagnosed with **gender-identity disorder.**

Early in childhood, gender segregation in play, also known as **homosocial play,** begins. Children tend to play with same-sex playmates as early as two years old (Maccoby & Jacklin, 1987). Researchers have tried rewarding children for playing with the other sex but, as soon as the reward is discontinued, play reverts back to same-sex groupings. This gender segregation may be because of the different playing styles of boys and girls, the attraction of children to others like themselves, or to learned social roles. Most probably it involves a combination of all these factors.

During the school years, gender roles become the measure by which children are judged by their peers. Children who violate sex-typed play are often rejected by their peers (Blakemore, 2003). This is especially true of boys who experience more rejection from their peers when they violate gender stereotypes than do girls. Interactions in classrooms can also reinforce gender stereotypes. Even though teachers believe they show equal attention to boys and girls, research shows that they spend more time with boys, give them more attention, praise and criticize them more often, direct more follow-up questions to them, and tolerate more bad behaviour among boys (Duffy et al., 2001). Also, teachers often stereotype the tasks they ask boys and girls to do. Boys may be asked to help move desks, while girls may be asked to erase the whiteboard.

Adolescence: Practice Being Female or Male

Gender roles are firmly established by adolescence and they guide teenagers through their exploration of peer relationships and different love styles with potential partners. Part of the task of adolescence is to figure out what it means to be a man or a woman and to try to adopt that role. Traditionally, boys learn that to be accepted they should be good at sports, express interest in sex and girls, not be overly emotional, and not display interests that are seen as

© Tony Freeman/PhotoEdit

feminine. Girls seem to have more latitude in their behaviour but are supposed to express interest in boys, be concerned with their appearance, and exercise some sexual restraint. When boys deviate from gender role behaviour, the consequences are more severe than for girls. However, when girls deviate from gender stereotypes of sexuality (by having multiple sex partners, for example), they experience more severe consequences.

Adolescence can be a particularly difficult time for transgender, gay, lesbian, or bisexual teenagers. There tends to be little tolerance for these behaviours in adolescence because they are viewed as the opposite of what teenagers are supposed to do. The lives of gay, lesbian, bisexual, and transgender teenagers may be fraught with tension. Many GLBT teenagers survive the adolescent years by limiting the sharing of their sexual orientations or gender identities. Many learn that if they do not, they may be subjected to violence or verbal harassment, which, according to one Canadian study, are particularly fuelled by religious conservatism (Hooghe, 2010). We further discuss such harassment in Chapter 9.

Teenage gender roles are constantly changing. In the 1930s and 1940s, teenage life was in many ways easier because gender roles were more rigid and everyone knew what was expected of them. Girls, for example, were taught never to call a boy and instead wait for boys to call them. While this amounted to a strong double standard, it was far less complicated. Today, teenage relationships seem fraught with greater ambiguity. For one thing, boys are no longer typically more sexually experienced than girls. For another, boys might be expected to take the lead in their dating relationships and yet acknowledge female equality at the same time. In contrast, teenage girls are taught to assert their independence but also be aware of existing social pressures that contribute to feelings of guilt and shame for girls who seek to fulfill their sexual needs. What this indicates is that gender roles are in flux and as a result less stable than in past decades.

Adulthood: Careers and Families

During World War II while men were fighting overseas, women took on jobs they had never had before. They worked in factories due to the necessities of war. Once the war was over, the men took over and middle-class women became housewives once again. This was a time of tremendous economic prosperity and one wage earner—the husband—was well able to support his entire family. In the 1960s, however, women entered the workforce once again and today there are an equal number of men and women earning salaries. In a typical middle-class Canadian family, both partners work outside the home.

This change led to a major shift in gender roles. Women are now professionals with careers; household duties such as childcare, laundry, meal preparation, and otherwise are ideally shared.

The Senior Years

Because Western cultures value youthfulness and hold many negative attitudes toward aging, life is often be difficult for seniors. For one thing, there is a double standard of aging, where older men might be viewed as "distinguished," while older women are viewed as simply "old" (Sontag, 1979; Teuscher & Teuscher, 2006).

Because women have historically been valued for their reproductive ability, they may be less valued once they lose their ability to reproduce. In contrast, men have been valued for their economic achievements and are not viewed as old until they are unable to work. Furthermore, although both men and women tend to value physical appearance, women tend to be more concerned about the effects of aging on how they look. (Slevin, 2010).

Media images foster negative attitudes toward seniors by pushing advertising for anti-aging products, such as creams, lotions, and cosmetic surgeries, to help seniors stay healthy and look younger (Gilleard & Higgs, 2000). One study even found that the majority of older women equated grey hair with ugliness and poorer health. Not surprisingly, the majority of women in the sample dyed their hair (Clarke & Korotchenko, 2010).

Attitudes about aging vary by race, ethnicity, and sexual orientation. Black and Latina women are more relaxed about aging than White women (Schuler et al., 2008), as are lesbians, who are also more positive (Slevin, 2010; Wolf, 1991). Gay men, on the other hand, tend to have more negative attitudes because gay culture places more emphasis on youthfulness (Slevin, 2010).

REAL Research Tsang et al. (2012) looked at health issues as they relate to sexual activity among a large sample (2272 participants) of Chinese-Canadian seniors. Health of the participants was related to frequency of sexual activity and sexual satisfaction for the men and only sexual satisfaction for the women.

Canada, like other Western nations, is an aging population, where a third of people are over the age of 55 and mean age hovering at about 40. Because women live longer, there are more women than men in later age groups. For people over 65, there are about 20 percent more women. What this means is that women are far more likely to experience the death of a partner than men and, thus, be alone in old age. Many Canadian seniors appear well adjusted, however, remaining vibrant and active into their old age. According to Bassett et al. (2007), the key to a healthy old age is to exercise and pay attention to nutrition, and have a positive attitude toward illness as opposed to letting it define oneself.

Toward Gender Equality

Can we create a society of total gender equality? Epstein (1986, 1988) believes that gender distinctions begin with dichotomous thinking—the splitting of the world into opposites such as good–bad, dark–light, soft–hard, male–female, and gay–straight. This is known as **heteronormativity**—where any phenomena are conceptualized as non-overlapping "opposites." Differences among things, including gender, are exaggerated and society invests a lot of energy in maintaining those distinctions.

heteronormativity
A tendency to divide phenomena into two non-overlapping categories, where the domain of one is separate from that of the other (e.g., male-female, masculine-feminine).

Many religious and cultural systems clearly define gender roles and some claim that differentiating gender roles means that one gender is subordinate to the other. Susan Rogers (1978) has argued that we cannot apply Western notions of gender equality to cultures with fundamentally different systems. She argues that equality can exist in a society only when women and men are seen as similar.

In Oman, for example, women are subject to strict rules that people in the West would see as subordination. Yet Rogers argues that women in Oman see themselves as different from men and are uninterested in the male role and male definitions of power. Is it appropriate for the West to impose its categories on their society and suggest that women in Oman are exploited and subordinate even though they themselves do not think so? Such questions go to the heart of the discussion of power in society.

The goal for many is not a society without gender distinctions. A world that denies differences in terms of race, religious beliefs, the type of genitalia people have, or sexual orientation is unjust. It is the content of gender and not its mere existence that societies can alter and this would provide each person an opportunity to live without being judged.

Review Questions

1 How are children and teenagers socialized into gender roles?

2 How are adults socialized into gender roles and how might this socialization affect career choice?

3 Describe the conflicting messages that women receive about career and family life.

4 How has the role of the husband/father in the family changed over the past few decades?

5 Explain how gender roles change as people enter later life.

Chapter Review

Summary Points

1 Gender roles are the culturally determined pattern of behaviours that societies prescribe to the sexes. Gender traits are the biologically determined characteristics of gender. Little agreement exists on which gender characteristics are innate and which are learned.

2 The terms *masculinity* and *femininity* are used in three ways in society: first, a masculine or feminine person is said to exemplify characteristics that differentiate the sexes; second, the terms refer to the extent to which adults adhere to socially prescribed gender roles; and third, masculinity and femininity refer to sexual characteristics.

3 Most people agree that males are larger, stronger, and more aggressive while females are neurologically more advanced than males, mature faster, and are biologically heartier. Some researchers also cite evidence that males have better spatial abilities while females have better verbal abilities.

4 Three types of theories about gender role development have been offered: social learning theories, which postulate that almost all gender knowledge is dependent on what children are taught; cognitive development theories, which suggest that children go through a universal set of stages during which they can learn only certain types of information about gender; and newer theories such as Bem's gender schema theory, which suggests that children do go through developmental stages and that the kinds of things they learn at each stage are mostly culturally determined.

5 Gender is socially constructed and societies determine how it is defined and what it means. In Western societies, masculinity and femininity are seen by many people as mutually exclusive. Masculine traits include being a good provider, strong, stable, unemotional, fearless, sexually experienced, and financially independent. Feminine traits include being beautiful, soft, empathetic, modest, and emotional.

6 Androgyny is defined as having high levels of both masculine and feminine characteristics. Some people advocate it as a way to transcend restrictive gender roles. Transsexuals believe their biological and psychological genders are incompatible, indicating that gender is more complex than simply determined from biological gender.

7 The gender binary divides people into two groups—male and female. We are typically put into either of these groups at birth. Societal expectations are that biological sex, gender identity, and gender expression are all concordant. However, all these variables interact to create a multidimensional gender spectrum. When behaviours fall outside of gender norms, they are gender diverse.

8 Gender dysphoria involves confusion and/or discomfort because people's biological gender does not match their psychological and social gender. Individuals who identify as genderqueer reject traditional gender roles and believe in the fluidity of gender.

9 Transsexuals are people whose feelings of gender do not match their biological sex. They often undergo sex reassignment surgery, which can transform someone from male to female or female to male.

10 There are a variety of medical and surgical options for gender reassignment. Some transsexuals undergo sex reassignment surgery (SRS) but many do not for a variety of reasons. The World Professional Association for Transgender Health has proposed standards of care that outline treatments for those seeking gender reassignment. Treatment usually begins with psychotherapy and then proceeds to medical and/or surgical procedures.

11 Some cultures challenge traditional notions of gender with categories that are neither male nor female. First Nations groups in North America have Two-Spirited people and the Hijra have been in India for centuries. There are numerous other third-gender categories, including those of Oman, Mexico, Samoa, and Thailand.

12 Infants are socialized into gender roles early through the way they are dressed and treated and through the environment in which they are brought up. Their behaviour is reinforced for appropriate gender activity. Adolescence is a time of forming adult gender roles and attitudes.

13 As men and women grow into adulthood, they tend to derive their gender identity from two realms—career and family. One of the biggest transformations in career and family life over the last few decades involves the movement of women out of the home and into paid employment.

14 Because Western cultures value youthfulness and hold many negative attitudes toward aging, growing older can be a difficult. Attitudes toward aging vary by race, ethnicity, and sexual orientation.

15 To build a society that avoids gender stereotyping and encourages gender equality, it is necessary to change dichotomous thinking and the splitting of the world into opposites such as good and bad. This is known as heteronormativity. Maintaining this way of thinking only exaggerates differences and invests energy into keeping things separate.

Critical Thinking Questions

1 Do you feel that gender is innate, socially learned, or a combination of both?

2 How are definitions of masculinity and femininity changing in society? Do traditional views still influence people's behaviours?

3 Why do you think some women consider the phrase "She's one of the guys" to be a compliment, while many men consider the phrase "He's one of the girls" to be an insult?

4 Which theory of gender development do you favour and why? What are the theory's strengths and weaknesses?

5 When looking at third-gender categories in other cultures, it is best to understand them through the lenses of those cultures and not our own. Please explain.

Websites

World Professional Association for Transgender Health (WPATH) Formerly known as the Harry Benjamin International Gender Dysphoria Association, WPATH is a professional organization devoted to the understanding and treatment of gender-identity disorders. The mission of WPATH is to promote care, education, research, advocacy, public policy, and respect in transgender health. (http://www.wpath.org)

Canadian Professional Association for Transgender Health (CPATH) A Canadian professional association devoted to the health and care of individuals with gender variant identities. (http://www.cpath.ca)

Camp fYrefly An educational and social centre located in Edmonton for young people 14 to 24 who have alternative gender and sexual identities. (http://www.fYrefly.ualberta.ca)

Transgender Archives: University of Victoria Library A special collection of documents, publications, and memorabilia from people and organizations that have worked for the rights of transsexuals in Canada. (http://transgenderarchives.ca/)

International Foundation for Gender Education (IFGE) A world organization promoting the acceptance of all types of transgender individuals. (http://ifge.org)

Trans PULSE Project A community-based research project that looks at the impact of discrimination on the health of transgender people in Ontario. (http://transpulseproject.ca)

Gender Development, Gender Roles, and Gender Identity **237**

9

Sexual Orientation

▶ After being arrested and jailed for "gross indecency" while living in Calgary, Everett George Klippert moved to Pine Point, a mining town in the Northwest Territories, just south of Great Slave Lake, to live the rest of his life in obscurity. Little did he know upon arrival that he would be instrumental in the reformation of Canada's Criminal Code that had long persecuted people like him and become a prominent figure in gay Canadian history.

Klippert was eventually hired as a mechanic's assistant. His boss knew of his past but hired him anyway. The RCMP also knew of his past and would often harass him by questioning him about crimes in the area. One day in 1965, they questioned him on a case of arson. They found that Klippert

had no part in it but, during the interrogation, he admitted to having consensual sex with four men. He was then charged with four counts of gross indecency once again, and sentenced to three years in jail.

While in custody, a court-ordered psychiatrist examined Klippert, found that the earlier arrest in Calgary failed to "turn him into a heterosexual," and pronounced him an "incurable homosexual." He was then labelled a dangerous sex offender and sentenced to "preventive detention" (meaning for an indefinite period of time). He appealed first to the Court of Appeal for the Northwest Territories and then to the Supreme Court of Canada. His case was denied both times.

Bud Orange, the Liberal Member of Parliament for the Northwest Territories, weighed in on the issue, saying, "I think

"There's no place for the state in the bedrooms of the nation."
—*Pierre Elliott Trudeau*

© Bob Peterson/Getty

that when two men engage in an act—which to me is a most repulsive act, but it is something they themselves consent to—I think it's their private business." He as well as New Democratic Party leader Tommy Douglas urged then-Justice Minister Pierre Elliot Trudeau to amend the law criminalizing homosexuality in Canada.

The Liberal Government acted swiftly. On December 21, 1967, it introduced Bill C-150, which would bring changes to the laws against homosexuality, as well as gambling and abortion. It was at that time that Trudeau made his historic statement to the press: "There's no place for the state in the bedrooms of the nation."

After a bitter political struggle where Trudeau was called "the beast of Sodom," Bill C-150 became law on May 14, 1969, thus legalizing consensual homosexuality between adults in private. Everett George Klippert had to wait two more years before he was released in 1971. He died in 1996 at the age of 70 (Freeman, 2010). ▐▌

Sexual orientation refers to the gender(s) to which a person is attracted emotionally, physically, sexually, and romantically. Heterosexuals are predominantly attracted to members of the other sex; gays and lesbians to members of the same sex; and bisexuals to both sexes. The word "homosexual" when used as a noun instead of an adjective is now considered offensive due to the historical use of it as oversexualizing gays and lesbians (Gibson, 1997; Nunn, 2011). In keeping with these sentiments, the terms "gays," "lesbians," "bisexuals," or "GLB people" are used in this discussion instead.

Although the classification of sexual orientation may seem simple, human sexual behaviour does not always fit on such a continuum. Today, many people use the abbreviation LGBT or, more completely, **GLBTTQQIAAP2S** to refer to people whose identity is gay, lesbian, bisexual, transsexual, transgender, questioning, queer, intersexed, allied, asexual, pansexual, and Two-Spirited. Others use the term **queer** as an all-encompassing label for minority sexual and gender orientations. This word was originally used as an epithet toward GLB people, but it has now been recaptured and turned into a positive label. Heterosexuals are informally referred to as "straight." Because we discussed transgender issues in Chapter 8 and will look at other orientations in Chapter 10, we focus on gay, lesbian, and bisexual issues in this chapter.

Before the 1970s, most research on homosexuality focused on the causes or on mental disorders presumed to be associated with it (homosexuality itself was classified as a mental disorder until 1973). In the 1990s, HIV and AIDS dominated the research studies (Boehmer, 2002). Today, the focus is upon the development of GLB identities, discrimination, community, history, coming-out issues, aging, and health care, to name a few areas. We discuss this research throughout this chapter.

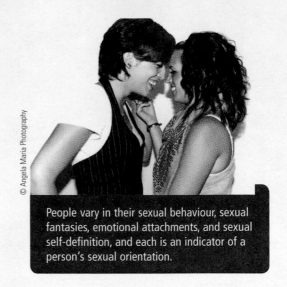

© Angela Maria Photography

People vary in their sexual behaviour, sexual fantasies, emotional attachments, and sexual self-definition, and each is an indicator of a person's sexual orientation.

Definitions of Sexual Orientation?

How should we conceptualize a person's **sexual orientation?** The simplest way might be through sexual behaviour—that is, whether someone has sex with men or women. Yet there are other factors to consider. What about a person's sexual fantasies? If a man sometimes fantasizes about sex with men even though he considers himself heterosexual and has sex only with women, what is his sexual orientation?

Romantic love may also determine a person's sexual orientation. If a married man has sex with men but loves his wife romantically and would never consider an emotional attachment to another man, is he bisexual or heterosexual?

People typically think of sexual orientation in discrete categories: People are either gay or lesbian, heterosexual, or occasionally bisexual. The full variety and richness of human sexual experience, however, cannot be easily captured in such restrictive categories. People can show enormous variety in their sexual behaviour, sexual fantasies, emotional attachments, and sexual self-definition, and each contributes to a person's sexual orientation.

In this chapter, we explore the nature of sexual orientation and the ways researchers and scholars think about it. Heterosexuality is a sexual orientation, and the question "Why is a person heterosexual?" is no less valid than "Why is a person gay, lesbian, or bisexual?" In this chapter, however, we focus our attention primarily on the research and writing about homosexuality and bisexuality.

Models of Sexual Orientation

Should sexual orientation be measured by behaviour (what one does), fantasy (what one would like to do), self-identification (what one considers oneself to be), or otherwise? Weinrich et al. (1993) observed that researchers who attempt to define sexual orientation are either "lumpers," who reduce such dimensions into as few categories as possible, or "splitters," who divide them into as many as possible to show variations of human experience.

GLBTTQQIAAP2S
Abbreviation for gay, lesbian, bisexual, transsexual, transgender, queer, questioning, intersexed, allied, asexual, pansexual, and Two-Spirited people. This is usually shortened to LGBT.

queer
An all-encompassing term for minority sexual and gender orientations.

sexual orientation
The gender(s) that a person is attracted to emotionally, physically, and romantically.

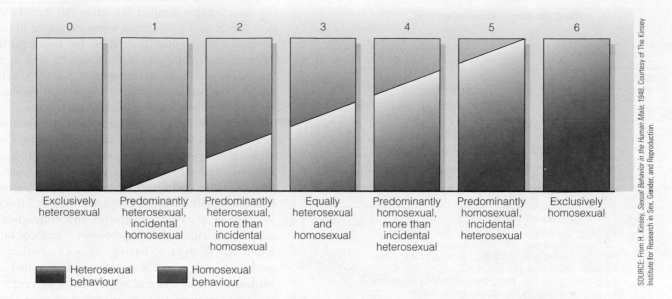

SOURCE: From H. Kinsey, *Sexual Behavior in the Human Male*, 1948. Courtesy of The Kinsey Institute for Research in Sex, Gender, and Reproduction.

FIGURE **9.1** The Kinsey continuum. The seven-point scale is based on behaviours ranging from exclusively heterosexual to exclusively homosexual.

Kinsey and his colleagues (1948) seemed to be the first type. They believed that relying on the categories "homosexual" and "heterosexual" to describe sexual orientation was inadequate. They also suggested that using a category such as "homosexual" was not as helpful as talking about homosexual behaviour (Gibson, 1997). In other words, it is more useful to compare degrees or types of homosexual behaviour.

With this in mind, Kinsey introduced a seven-point scale (Figure 9.1) ranging from exclusively heterosexual behaviour (0) to exclusively homosexual behaviour (6). This was the first scale to suggest that people engage in complex sexual behaviours that cannot be reduced simply to "homosexual" and "heterosexual." Sexual orientation in this respect is a continuous rather than a categorical variable. There are no natural cut-off points that would easily separate people into discrete categories (Berkey et al., 1990; Ellis et al., 1987).

The Kinsey scale has some limitations. First, Kinsey looked only at people's behaviour. Later researchers suggested that other factors such as emotional attachments and fantasies are far more important as determinants of sexual orientation (Bell et al., 1981; F. Klein, 1993; Storms, 1980, 1981). Second, the scale is vague about the number of sex partners versus the number of sexual encounters that place people at particular points on the scale. For example, if a man had sex with six men over a year and his wife once a week, is he a 5 (because he had sex with six men and only one woman) or a 2 (because he had 52 experiences with a woman, but only 6 with men) (Klein, 1990).

The Klein Sexual Orientation Grid (KSOG; Figure 9.2) falls into the splitter category. It takes the Kinsey continuum further by including seven dimensions—attraction, behaviour, fantasy,

emotional preference, social preference, self-identification, and "lifestyle" (Horowitz et al., 2001; Klein et al., 1985). Each of these dimensions is measured for the past, the present, and the ideal.

The advantage of the KSOG is that human experience may be seen as not simply following a single path but as a multidimensional phenomenon that leads to tremendous variation.

On Your Mind

If I played sex games with a friend of the same sex when I was 15, am I gay?

Sexual experimentation and sexual orientation are two different things. It is common for children and young teenagers to experiment with same-sex and other-sex contact. Whether one is gay, bisexual, or heterosexual, however, is a matter of romantic and erotic feelings toward one sex, the other, or both that continue beyond experimentation. In other words, sexual orientation is more than what one does sexually—it pertains more to feelings and desires.

Measuring Sexual Orientation: How Prevalent?

How prevalent are homosexuality and bisexuality in society? This question is impossible to answer for at least two reasons. First, before knowing how many there are, it is necessary to define what one is measuring. As we have seen, definitions of homosexuality vary considerably among scholars. More importantly, definitions vary among the people themselves. For example, Hencken (1984) describe several techniques by which men who have sex with men neutralize any definitions of themselves as gay or bisexual. Among

The Klein Sexual Orientation Grid

	Past	Present	Ideal
A. Sexual attraction			
B. Sexual behavior			
C. Sexual fantasies			
D. Emotional preference			
E. Social preference			
F. Self-identification			
G. Heterosexual/homosexual lifestyle			

0 = other sex only
1 = mostly other sex, incidental same sex
2 = mostly other sex, more than incidental same sex
3 = both sexes equally
4 = mostly same sex, more than incidental other sex
5 = mostly same sex, incidental other sex
6 = same sex only

SOURCE: From Fritz Klein, *Homosexuality/Heterosexuality*, p. 280. Courtesy of The Kinsey Institute for Research in Sex, Gender, and Reproduction.

FIGURE **9.2** The Klein Sexual Orientation Grid (KSOG) was designed to examine seven dimensions of an individual's sexual orientation to determine whether these dimensions have changed over time and to look at a person's fantasy of his or her "ideal" sexual orientation. The KSOG gives a set of numbers that can be compared to determine rates of different sexual orientations.

them are "I was drunk," "it's just physical," "I was just horny," and "I was experimenting." Earl (1990) and Doll et al. (1992) found similar techniques. Second, while it may be possible to obtain random samples of Liberal Party voters, physicians, or motorcycle riders, it is not possible to do so for marginalized or otherized groups such as gays, lesbians, and bisexuals. Many are **in the closet** and thus reluctant to tell their sexual orientation to anyone. As a result, there will always be an unknown number in any large population (McCormack, 2014).

We can however look at non-random samples for clues of prevalence. Kinsey and his colleagues (1948) found that 37 percent of men and 13 percent of women reported that they had had at least one adult sexual experience with a member of

in the closet
A phrase meaning that one hides one's sexual orientation.

the same sex that resulted in orgasm and that about 4 percent of men and 3 percent of women engaged in same-sex behaviour throughout their lives. He also reported that 10 percent of White men had sex mostly with men for at least three years between the ages of 16 and 55. This figure became the one most cited when estimating the prevalence of homosexuality in Western societies.

There continues to be efforts to determine how many gays, lesbians, or bisexuals there are today. Estimates range from 2 percent to 4 percent to more than 10 percent in males and 1 percent to 3 percent in females, while those for bisexuality are approximately 3 percent (M. Diamond, 1993; Hughes, 2006; Seidman & Rieder, 1994; Whitam et al., 1999). Laumann and colleagues (1994) found that although 5.5 percent of women said they found the thought of having sex with another woman appealing, only about 4 percent said they had had sex with one after age 18 and fewer than 2 percent had had sex with another woman in the past year. Similarly, although 9 percent of men said they had had sex with another male since puberty, a little more than 5 percent had had sex with a man since age 18 and only 2 percent had sex with a man in the past year. Overall, surveys indicate that the frequency of same-sex behaviour has remained fairly constant over the years despite changes in the political climates of nations (Pillard & Bailey, 1998).

There are additional problems with the studies just discussed. Many concentrate on same-sex behaviour—not attraction, fantasies, or desires. One study measured both same-sex attraction and behaviour and found that 16 percent to 20 percent of the adult population of the United States, United Kingdom, and France reported some same-sex attraction or behaviour since age 15 (Sell et al., 1995). The researchers claimed that these statistics were higher than past percentages because they included same-sex attraction. They also included people who were not sexually active but reported a history of same-sex behaviour in the past. Researchers often do not count people who are not sexually active as being gay or lesbian, even when they have a history of same-sex behaviour (Sell et al., 1995). Although there is much work to be done in determining the prevalence of homosexuality, scholars generally agree that between 3 percent and 4 percent of males are predominantly gay, 1.5 percent to 2 percent of women are predominantly lesbian, and about 2 percent to 5 percent of people are bisexual (Jenkins, 2010; Laumann et al., 1994).

Review Questions

1 Describe the difficulties involved in researchers' attempts to categorize sexual behaviour.

2 Outline the Kinsey model of sexual orientation and compare and contrast it with the KSOG.

3 Describe the research on the prevalence of GLB orientations. Explain why this research is difficult.

Why Are There Different Sexual Orientations?

There have been many erroneous studies on homosexuality. In the 1930s and 1940s, a group of scientists confused gender orientation with sexual orientation and tried to explain homosexuality by looking for "masculine" traits in lesbians and "feminine" traits in homosexual men. They claimed that gay men had broad shoulders and narrow hips (indicating "immature skeletal development") and lesbians had abnormal genitalia including larger-than-average vulvas, longer labia minora, a larger glans on the clitoris, and a smaller uterus (Terry, 1990). Modern research has failed to find any significant physiological differences between GLB people and heterosexuals, although attempts to determine physical differences continue.

There are numerous explanations of sexual orientation today. In this section we will look at four: biological, developmental, behavioural, and sociological. Biological explanations suggest that GLB people are physically different from heterosexuals. Developmental theories maintain that homosexuality develops in response to a person's upbringing and personal history and that GLB people are not physically different. Behavioural theories maintain that homosexuality is a learned behaviour, while sociological theories look at how social forces construct homosexuality in a society.

Scholars in different fields tend to take different approaches to explain why some people are gay, lesbian, or bisexual. Note, however, that almost all the researchers we will discuss treat sexual orientation as two exclusive, non-overlapping categories: homosexual and heterosexual. Most theories on sexual orientation ignore bisexuality or do not offer enough research to explain why bisexuality exists.

Note also that the search for the cause of homosexuality has historically not been a neutral endeavour. As mentioned, homosexuality was defined as a mental illness before 1973 and, thus, **etiology** was a matter of isolating factors that may point the way to a "cure." There has rarely if ever been any research on the cause of heterosexuality or for that matter on being a liberal, or a conservative, or a stamp collector. It is important, however, in the study of sexuality to be familiar with such theories not only for their results but as social indicators of historical concerns.

Biological Theories

Early biological theories implied that homosexuality is caused by abnormal physical development which contributed to the argument that homosexuality is a sickness. More recently, in an attempt to show that it is not a "choice" as numerous conservative politicians and religious leaders have claimed, have renewed the search for physiological difference in an attempt to determine whether homosexuality is a biologically based sexual variation. Biological theories claim that differing sexual orientations are due to differences in physiology. Explanations that have been offered pertain to genetics, hormones, birth order, or physiology.

Genetics

Genetic explanations generally come in the form of twin studies with the assumption that if twins are more likely to both be gay than regular siblings, homosexuality must be genetic. This explanation falls short, however, since twins are also more likely to be raised similarly and in similar home environments, thus making it difficult to rule out other factors. Three studies are of note: Franz Kallman in the early 1950s, Heston and Shield in the late 1960s, and Bailey and Pillard in the 1990s.

Franz Kallman (1953) was the first to search for a genetic component to homosexuality. He compared dizygotic (fraternal) twins with monozygotic (identical) twins and found an 11.5 percent concordance of homosexuality in the former and a 100 percent concordance in the latter. Because of sampling and other biases, however, his research is now disregarded.

Unlike Kallman, who got his subjects from the files of psychiatrists and correctional facilities, Heston and Shields (1968) looked at a hospital twin register. In their sample, dizygotic twins were 14 percent concordant for homosexuality and monozygotic twins were 43 percent concordant.

Bailey and Pillard's sample came from advertisements in gay publications. They report that in homosexual males, 52 percent of monozygotic twins, 22 percent of dizygotic twins, and 11 percent of adoptive brothers were also gay, showing that the more closely genetically related two siblings were, the more likely they were to share a sexual orientation (Bailey & Pillard, 1995). In a rare look at females, 48 percent of monozygotic twins, 16 percent of dizygotic twins, and 6 percent of adoptive siblings of lesbians were also lesbians (Bailey et al., 1995). As mentioned, however, twins share much more than genetics. They also share many more experiences than do other kinds of siblings. Because the studies cannot control for environmental factors, they cannot tell how much of the concordance is due to genetic factors. More recent research suggests that that sexual orientation is familial, or that it runs in the family (Francis, 2008; Schwartz et al., 2010).

Hamer and colleagues (1993) found in their sample that gay males tended to have more gay relatives on their mother's side. They traced this to a gene that they found in 33 of 40 gay brothers. This gene is inherited from the mother's side (Keller, 2005). Other research found that gay men also had more gay brothers than lesbian sisters, and lesbians had more lesbian sisters than gay brothers (Bogaert, 2005; Pattatucci, 1998). Still more research has found that male sexual orientation is inherited from the father's side (Schwartz et al., 2010). Genetic studies, although they are mostly consistent in their findings, are inconclusive and, as a result, further inquiry is needed.

---

etiology
The study of causation.

One thing must be kept in mind, according to evolutionary theory: If homosexuality were solely a genetic trait, it should have disappeared long ago. Because homosexual people have been less likely than heterosexuals to have children, each successive generation should have become smaller until genes for homosexuality disappeared entirely. Yet this has not been the case.

On Your Mind

At what age does sexual orientation begin?

This is difficult to answer because the presumption of heterosexuality begins at the moment of birth when cute little boys are called "future lady's men" and cute little girls are called "future heartbreakers." It is not simply taken for granted that they will grow up to be heterosexual; it is assumed that they already are (Davies, 1997; Peraldi, 1992). Prepubescent children are also socialized into heterosexual behaviour with dances at weddings, Valentine's Day cards to the other sex, and so forth. Any semblance of homosexual behaviour, on the other, hand is discouraged either gently or harshly, even when young children do not understand why. By the time they reach puberty, they are fully socialized into heterosexual rituals, rules, worldviews, and behaviours regardless of their true feelings, and rewarded for them either subtly or directly when they carry them out. Gays and lesbians often learn at very young ages that their feelings toward the same sex will be sanctioned, and they typically learn to be silent about them or hide them.

In reality, very young children do not have a sexual orientation. Even though they have been encouraged toward heterosexual behaviour and it is merely taken for granted that this is their interest, they have not become oriented consciously toward either sex. Those who ask when sexual orientation begins are often really asking when homosexuality begins. For that matter, numerous stories and testimonies of gay men and lesbians have included statements that they have been gay or lesbian or have had such feelings "as long as I can remember." Thus, we know that sexual orientation begins very early, but the extent to which such feelings are developed, defined, and handled is another question.

Hormones

Hormonal theories concentrate either on hormonal imbalances before birth or on hormone levels in adults. In this section, we examine both prenatal and adult hormonal levels. For more information about hormones, see Chapters 3 and 4.

When certain hormones are injected into pregnant rats or guinea pigs at critical periods of fetal development, the offspring can be made to exhibit homosexual behaviour (Dorner, 1983).

maternal immune hypothesis
Theory of sexual orientation that proposes that the fraternal birth order effect of gay brothers reflects the progressive immunization of some mothers to male-specific antigens by each succeeding male fetus.

Some researchers have found evidence that sexual orientation may be influenced by levels of prenatal hormones in human beings as well (Berenbaum & Snyder, 1995; Cohen-Bendahan et al., 2005; Jenkins, 2010; Rahman, 2005; Swaab, 2004). Hormonal levels can also be affected by stress during pregnancy, and other researchers have explored how this stress might influence later sexual orientation (Ellis, 1988; Hall & Schaeff, 2008).

Although many hormonal studies have focused on deficiencies in certain hormones, there is also research suggesting that excess hormonal exposure during prenatal development may be related to later sexual orientation. For example, females who were exposed to diethylstilbestrol (DES; synthetic estrogen) in the womb were more likely to identify as bisexual or lesbian compared with females who were not exposed (Meyer-Bahlburg et al., 1985).

Overall, the evidence for the effect of prenatal hormones on both male and female homosexuality is weak (Gooren, 2006; Hall & Schaeff, 2008; Whalen et al., 1990). In other words, even if prenatal hormones are a factor in sexual orientation, environmental factors may be equally important. The one area of research in prenatal hormones that has yielded the most interesting research has been on finger length, which we will discuss in the upcoming section on physiology.

REAL Research Studies have found that gay men are better at recognizing faces than both lesbians and heterosexual men (Brewster et al., 2010).

Other researchers have compared blood androgen levels in gay men with those in heterosexual men and most have found no significant differences (Green, 1988; Mbügua, 2006). Of five studies comparing hormone levels in lesbians and heterosexual women, three found no differences and two found higher levels of testosterone in lesbians (Dancey, 1990). Thus, studies find no evidence for the idea that sexual orientation is contingent upon hormone levels.

Birth Order

Blanchard and Klassen (1997) were curious about how birth order affects likelihood of being gay. They found that gay men have more older brothers than heterosexual men (Blanchard, 2008; McConaghy et al., 2006). They explained this phenomenon with the **maternal immune hypothesis,** which proposes that there is an antigen found only in male fetuses (the H-Y antigen), which causes an immune response in pregnant women, which becomes stronger with every successive male fetus. This antigen is thought to affect sexual orientation by affecting the brain in different ways in gay and heterosexual men. If this is the case, then the H-Y antigen would be stronger in older brothers and weaker in younger ones (Blanchard, 2008; Bogaert & Skorska, 2011; Schwartz et al., 2010; Valenzuela, 2010). Researchers have found that in families with multiple brothers, later-born brothers from the same mother are more likely to be gay (Blanchard, 2004; Bogaert & Skorska, 2011; Camperio-Ciani et al., 2004; Francis, 2008). In the samples studied, each older brother increases a man's chance of being gay by about 33 percent (Blanchard, 2008; Francis, 2008). Canadian researchers Cantor et al. (2002) found that the fraternal birth order effect accounts for the sexual orientation of one in seven gay men and that this would likely exceed all other causes for those with three or more older brothers. In contrast, it was found that the presence of older sisters from the same biological mother decreases the likelihood of homosexuality (Francis, 2008). Siblings from different mothers do not have an effect on sexual orientation (Blanchard, 1997).

There are a number of weaknesses to this hypothesis. First, it is unclear how the degree of H-Y antigen can affect something as complex as sexual orientation. Second, and more importantly, there are far more gay men in the world than can be accounted by mere birth order. Gay men are also likely to have younger brothers, have older sisters, or have no siblings at all. Furthermore, there are also younger or youngest brothers who are entirely heterosexual. Because the effect of the H-Y antigen is not universal, it must be looked at with caution.

Physiology

Two articles in the early 1990s reported differences between the brains of homosexual and heterosexual men (LeVay, 1991; Swaab & Hofman, 1990). Both studies found that certain areas of the hypothalamus, known to play a strong role in sexual urges, were either larger or smaller in gay men than heterosexual men.

There are four cell groups in the anterior hypothalamus known as the INAH 1, 2, 3, and 4. Simon LeVay (1991) examined these groups post-mortem in heterosexual men, heterosexual women, and gay men. While no differences appeared in the sizes of the INAH 1, 2, and 4, there were differences in the INAH 3, which was largest in heterosexual men, smaller in women, and smallest in gay men.

One weakness of studies of brain differences is that it has not yet been determined which came first. In other words, did the differences determine sexual orientation of did sexual orientation determine the differences? Were the differences there from birth or did they develop later in life (Kinnunen et al., 2004; Swaab, 2004)?

Researchers have also looked at differences between heterosexuals and GLB people among a variety of traits seeming to cover every part of the body. They have looked at amount of facial hair, size of external genitalia, ear structure, hair whorls on the back of the head, hearing, body shape, eye-blink startle responses, and spatial ability (Bailey & Hurd, 2005; Beaton & Mellor, 2007; Hall & Schaeff, 2008; Johnson et al., 2007; McFadden, 2011; Rahman & Koerting, 2008). Another study found that a samples of gay men and heterosexual women had similar spatial learning and memory abilities that differed from the sample of heterosexual men (Rahman & Koerting, 2008) and research on

handedness has found that gay men are more likely to be left-handed (Blanchard et al., 2006, 2008; Brewster et al., 2010; Martin et al., 2008; Schwartz et al., 2010; Valenzuela, 2008).

There has also been much research on finger lengths. The typical male-type finger pattern is a longer ring finger than index finger, while the typical female-type pattern is to have similar lengths. Several studies found that lesbians have a typical male-type finger length pattern and gay men are more likely to have a typical female-type finger length pattern (Galis et al., 2010; Grimbos et al., 2010; Hall & Schaeff, 2008; Martin et al., 2008; Schwartz et al., 2010). In addition, a sample of men with typical female-type finger length patterns were found to be more emotional than men with a typical male-type finger length (Rizman et al., 2007). Researchers have found that finger length is affected by prenatal testosterone and estrogen levels, especially in the right hand (Mc-Fadden et al., 2005; Rizwan et al., 2007; Schwartz et al., 2010).

In sum, although there have been some biological differences found among GLB people and heterosexuals, the findings are inconsistent and in many cases the evidence is weak. Given the complexity of biological factors, it is impossible to make accurate predications because of the randomness of neural connections during development (Pillard, 1998).

Developmental Theories

Developmental theories focus on a person's upbringing and history to find the origins of homosexuality. First, we discuss the most influential developmental theory—psychoanalytic theory, and then we examine gender-role non-conformity and peer-interaction theories.

Freud and the Psychoanalytic School

Sigmund Freud (1953) seemed to be of two minds about homosexuality. On the one hand, he believed that infants were "polymorphously perverse"—that is, having unfocused sex drives and, thus, potentially deriving sexual satisfaction from any object or body part. Because both males and females would potentially be arousing to infants according to Freud, everyone is inherently bisexual. He, therefore, did not see homosexuality as an illness.

On the other hand, Freud saw male heterosexuality as the result of normal maturation and male homosexuality as the result of an unresolved Oedipal complex (see Chapter 2 for a more complete discussion of this topic). An intense attachment to the mother coupled with a distant father could lead a boy to fear revenge by his father through castration. Female genitalia, lacking a penis, could then represent this castration and evoke fear throughout his life. After puberty, a boy might shift from desire for the mother to identification with her and begin to look for the love objects she would look for—men.

Like Freud's view of female sexuality in general, his theories on lesbianism were less coherent but he argued that young girls become angry when they discover that they lack a penis and

Homosexual Behaviour among Animals

Same-sex activity has been found in 450 species of birds and mammals (Bagemihl, 1999) and some scientists believe this number may be as high as 1500 (Moskowitz, 2008). In the summer months, killer whales spend some of their time engaging in homosexual activity (Mackay, 2000). Furthermore, many mammals engage in same-sex mounting behaviour. Males mount other males and females mount other females (although they rarely do it when a male is present). In some penguin species, males form lifelong same-sex partnerships (Bagemihl, 1999). Bonobo chimpanzees also engage in same-sex behaviour (Waal, 1995). Even so, there are no reliably reported cases in which individual animals display exclusively homosexual behaviour (Bagemihl, 1999).

blame their mothers (we discussed the Electra complex in Chapter 2). Unable to have their fathers, they defensively reject them, as well as all men, and minimize their anger at their mothers by eliminating the competition between them for male affection.

Freud also viewed homosexuality as partly narcissistic. By making love to a body like one's own, one is really making love to a mirror of oneself. Freud's generally tolerant attitude toward homosexuality was rejected by some later psychoanalysts, especially Sandor Rado (1949). Rado claimed that humans were not innately bisexual and that homosexuality was a mental illness. This view became standard for the psychiatric profession until at least the 1970s.

Another influential researcher who followed Rado's perspective was Irving Bieber. Bieber and colleagues (1962) studied 106 homosexual men and 100 heterosexual men who were in psychoanalysis. He claimed that all boys had an inherent erotic attraction to women. However, some had overly close and possessive mothers who were also overly intimate and sexually seductive. Their fathers, in contrast, were hostile or absent and this drove boys to the arms of their mothers, who inhibited their heterosexual development. Bieber thus blamed homosexuality on overly affectionate mothers who put the fear of heterosexuality in their sons.

REAL Research Toronto psychologists Hewitt and Moore (2002) surveyed 114 college students about what they believed causes homosexuality. Results were that explanations differed markedly by attitudes toward and degree of exposure gays and lesbians.

Legacy of the Psychoanalytic Model

Irving Bieber's work is now thoroughly discredited for its methodological flaws and other inherent biases. For one thing, the 106 gay men in his study were handpicked from the files of psychiatrists and, thus, had numerous psychological problems at the onset. He did not solicit any gay men who were well adjusted like those of his heterosexual sample. Nevertheless, the dominant-mother-absent-father model persists in popular beliefs even today.

After several years of struggle, the Board of Trustees of the American Psychiatric Association voted to remove homosexuality from its *Diagnostic and Statistical Manual of Psychiatric Disorders* (DSM). GLB people were no longer mentally ill by decree (Bayer, 1981). Prior to this vote, what seems to have been unique in any discourse on mental illness was that medical experts considered an entire group of people mentally ill by virtue of their behaviour while scores of those same people thought the opposite. Many disagreed that they were somehow mentally ill and lived productive lives despite the social obstacles (Chauncey, 1994). While some GLB people had internalized the definition of themselves as mentally ill and freely sought out psychiatrists (Duberman, 1991), many were forced by their families or legal authorities to undergo treatment. This treatment was often in the form of aversion therapy (Smith et al., 2004), vomit-inducing apomorphine therapy (Feldman, 1966), shock treatment, and worse.

The slow turn around began with the publication of the research of Evelyn Hooker, a clinical psychologist who challenged the psychoanalytic view that homosexuality was an illness. Hooker (1957) found two samples for her research—30 gay men and 30 heterosexual men. None of the men in either group had ever seen a psychiatrist. She then gave all of the men three psychological tests including the Rorschach Inkblot Test. Once she had her results, she removed all identifying information, gave them to several other psychiatrists, and challenged them to pick out the gay men. None of them were able to do so, and agreed that there were no discernible differences. Today, in Canada, Western Europe, and much of the world, psychiatric views of illness have long been left behind.

Gender-Role Non-conformity

Another group of researchers have looked at the connection between homosexuality and gender-role non-conformity, which is based on the assumption that children who behave in ways more characteristic of the other sex are more likely to grow up gay or lesbian. Alanko et al. (2010), for example, found that gay men tended to recall more feminine behaviour in childhood than did heterosexual men. Not only is there no causal connection, however, but because of the strong societal connection between femininity and homosexuality, the gay men would be more likely to recall feminine behaviour and the heterosexual men less likely.

Other studies (Bailey & Pillard, 1995; Lippa & Tan, 2001; Pillard, 1991) found that when gay men are given questionnaires on gender behaviour, they tend to score higher. Again given the strong societal association between femininity and male homosexuality, it is also likely that gay men may be more socially channelled toward femininity than anything else.

Well-known American sexologist Richard Green, for his book *The Sissy Boy Syndrome* (1987), did a prospective study comparing 66 pervasively feminine boys with 56 conventionally masculine boys over a 15-year period as they matured. Three quarters of the feminine boys grew up to be gay or bisexual and only one of the masculine boys became bisexual. The feminine boys had more psychological problems but they also tended to be harassed, rejected, and ignored more by their peers (Zucker, 1990). It is therefore most likely that these experiences led to the problems and not the feminine behaviour itself.

In Western societies, feminine boys are viewed more negatively than masculine girls (Sandnabba & Ahlberg, 1999). Feminine boys are also thought more often to be gay. It is therefore not only difficult to separate homosexuality and femininity, but no causal link can be made.

There are other explanations for femininity among gay men—for one, the performance of **camp,** which is a subcultural tradition of lampooning the serious, part of which involves the exaggeration of a stereotype (Dansky, 2013; Harvey, 2002; Hemmings, 2007; LaBruce, 2014). In other words, because gays are thought to be effeminate, feminine behaviour is a way of making fun of or minstrelizing that stereotype to discredit it. Minstrelization has also been observed among Aboriginal Canadians, who would exaggerate the negative stereotype against them for the same reason (Denton, 1975). Thus, while some gay men may be feminine and some lesbians masculine, much of the performativity of gender behaviour may be put on for its effect.

Behaviourist Theories

Behaviourists believe that homosexuality is brought about by the reinforcement of homosexual behaviour or the punishing of heterosexual behaviour (Masters & Johnson, 1979). For example, a person may have a same-sex encounter that is pleasurable and an encounter with the other sex that is frightening. That person may then focus on the same-sex encounter, reinforcing its pleasure with masturbation. Masters and Johnson (1979) believed that even in adulthood, some men and women move toward same-sex behaviours if they have bad heterosexual encounters and pleasant same-sex ones. This idea, however, is an assumption that has little basis in reality. It assumes that gay men and lesbians exist because they have somehow been scared off of heterosexuality as in the stereotype that women become lesbians because they either have been raped or hate men. It also misses the fact that gays and lesbians continue to exist even though the vast majority have had no painful heterosexual experiences. Finally, it misses the fact that many heterosexual people have had same-sex encounters that were not traumatic and simply decided that it was not for them. Homosexuality as an adaptive measure to traumatized sexuality is entirely unsubstantiated.

Sociological Theories

Sociological theories look at how social forces produce homosexuality in a society. They suggest that categories such as homosexuality, bisexuality, and heterosexuality are constructed through social and historical events and circumstances and lead people to fit themselves into them. In other words, people learn their cultures' ways of defining sexuality and they apply it to themselves.

The idea of "homosexuality" is a product of a particular culture at a particular time period and did not exist before 1868, when it was coined along with "heterosexuality" by sexologist Karoly Maria Kertbeny. Canadian sociologist Barry Adam (1987) argued that the use of the term *homosexuality* as a way to think about same-sex behaviour arose only after the Industrial Revolution freed people economically from the family unit and urbanization allowed them to choose new ways of living in the cities. Thus, the idea that people are either heterosexual, gay, lesbian, or bisexual is not a biological fact but simply a way of thinking that evolves as social definitions of reality change. In other societies, as we

> ## On Your Mind
> Is there any therapy that can change a person's sexual orientation?

Some people believe that gay people can change their sexual orientation through therapy or religious faith. Since the early 1980s, the "ex-gay" movement (people who once identified as gay or lesbian but now identify as heterosexual) has claimed that gays can be changed into heterosexuals through **reparative therapy** (also known as *conversion therapy*). These types of therapies are based on the premise that homosexuality is an illness that needs to be cured. GLB people who are subject to actual or expected negative family reactions to their sexual orientation and are raised in religious families are significantly more likely to seek out or be forced to participate in such therapy (Maccio, 2010).

Reparative therapy is condemned as ineffective and harmful by all reliable research, and the vast majority of professional organizations, including the Canadian Psychiatric Association, the American Psychiatric Association, the American Academy of Pediatrics, the Canadian Medical Association, and numerous others in Canada, the United States, and around the world (Cianciotto & Cahill, 2006; Cramer et al., 2008; Grace, 2005, 2008; Jenkins & Johnston, 2004). It can also cause harm to gay and lesbian people, especially teenagers; thus, it has been banned in some American states. Dr. Mirta Roses Periago, director of the Pan American Health Organization, said that practices known as "reparative therapy" or "conversion therapy" represent "a serious threat to the health and well-being—even the lives—of affected people" (PAHO, 2012). Such therapy is often carried out against the will of the patient, has been abusive, and has led to suicide among GLB teenagers.

camp
A lampooning of the serious, which may involve an exaggeration of a stereotype to discredit it.

reparative therapy
A discredited form of therapy considered harmful to gays and lesbians, which claims to change sexual orientation; also called *conversion therapy*.

note later, such terms are not used, and people's sexual behaviour is not defined by the sex of their partners.

Sexual desires are simply what they are, but once people act upon them, their activities and desires to engage in them are labelled with the available emergent categories of the time. Prior to the 19th century, people did not think of themselves in terms of a sexual orientation. People had no senses of themselves as heterosexual. Men who did have sex with men saw themselves only as acting upon their own desires. If they were caught, they were not exposed as gay but as having committed the sin of sodomy. The act was the only concern of the authorities and not any identification that went with it. Today, men who desire other men usually consider themselves "gay" and this is defined as a sexual orientation different from the rest. Any society's conceptualization of sexuality thus depends on existent categories available which are emergent over time.

Review Questions

1 Identify and describe the various areas of research within the biological theory of homosexuality.

2 Identify and describe the various developmental theories of homosexuality, as well as its critiques.

3 Explain the behavioural theory of homosexuality and its critiques.

4 Explain the sociological theory of homosexuality.

Homosexuality in Western History

Although it has been defined, regarded, and handled in many ways, homosexuality has existed among human beings since prehistoric times. There have been times when it has been fully accepted and times it has been punishable by death. The influence of the Church and the dissemination of its influence through colonialism has negatively affected societal tolerance and acceptance of homosexuality throughout the world for centuries.

The Classical Era

Male homosexuality was probably as common as heterosexuality in Ancient Greece and even celebrated in political and social life, and in art and literature. As discussed in Chapter 1, the relationship between a man and a boy, or the *erastes* and *eromenos*, was part of the educational system of the upper class of Athens and considered not only a civic duty for the man but a noble form of love for both. As is inferred in Plato's *Symposium*, the Greeks made no distinctions between homosexual and heterosexual behaviour, nor did they infer any traits or causes to go along with them. A beautiful boy and a beautiful woman were both worthy of admiration (Dover, 1978).

The men of Rome conceptualized same-sex sexual behaviour in terms of roles during sex. Men who penetrated other males during anal intercourse retained their masculinity while those whom they penetrated did not. Those who were penetrated were slaves, prostitutes, entertainers, captive soldiers, or favourites of Roman centurions. Free-born males were off limits (Williams, 2010). In Rome, prostitution was taxed by the state, and the writers of the time considered men loving men as natural as men loving women. Even after Rome became Christian, there was no legislation against same-sex sexual behaviour for more than 200 years.

Because the vast majority of writers of the time were men, same-sex sexual behaviour among women was given far less attention. The word *lesbian* derives from the island of Lesbos in Greece where the female poet Sappho lived about 600 B.C.E. While only fragments of her poetry survive today, some of her verses expressed a love and admiration toward women. Sex between women was rarely explicitly against the law in most

© Mimmo Jodice/Corbis

Archeological finds in many ancient societies indicate that same-sex behaviour was common.

ancient societies (in fact, two or more unmarried women living together was usually seen as proper; Bullough, 1979).

The Middle Ages

Up until the ninth century, there was no real recognition of homosexuality in Europe other than its existence as a sexual sin. In this sense, it was no different from any other sexual transgressions—bestiality, anal and oral intercourse, dorsal intercourse (man behind woman), interfemoral intercourse (penetration between the thighs), adultery, contraception, and abortion. Anyone caught having sex with the same sex was exposed as having committed a sexual sin and, thus, weak willed and having given into temptation (Hergemoller, 2006). The Church's indifference to homosexuality lasted well through the 13th century. In other words, for the first 1000 years of Christian domination, the Church showed little interest in homosexuality (Boswell, 1980; Kuefler, 2006; Siker, 1994). Male brothels existed, defences of same-sex relations began to appear in print, and homosexuality was a fairly accepted part of the general culture until the late Middle Ages.

By 1300, however, there was a new atmosphere of intolerance of differences, and homosexuality became a crime punishable by death almost everywhere (Boswell, 1980; Kuefler, 2006). This view of cardinal sin from the late Middle Ages has influenced the Western world's view of homosexuality ever since.

Oscar Wilde and Lord Alfred Douglas in the late 19th century.

Early Modern Europe

Although the word "lesbian" had been used since the tenth century in reference to the poet Sappho, there is no evidence that women described themselves as such and few people would have known of the term. Sex between women was thought impossible by most people up until the end of the 19th century. Sex between women if it did reach attention was never considered as grave a sin as that between men (Gowing, 2012).

According to Trumbach (1989), a shift took place in the way men who had sex with men were regarded around 1700. Whereas before, there was the idea of the sodomite "rake" (meaning a licentious male) whose conquests were boys as well as women, homosexual sex was now seen as the province of the deviant and the effeminate and, thus, sectioned off from "natural" sexual behaviour. This shift brought about the formation of a burgeoning "gay" subculture in Europe in the form of "Molly Houses," which were usually taverns with private rooms for men interested in other men, male prostitutes, and cross dressers. One of the most famous Molly Houses was Mother Clap's in London, which in 1726 was raided, and 40 men were arrested. Three men were executed, and the existence of such houses led to a growing atmosphere of homophobia in Europe (Azfar, 2012).

The Victorian Era

While the upper classes of England became increasingly repressive toward sexuality, this was in some ways more of an appearance than a reality. Successful men fathered many children, leaving their wives pregnant through much of their adult lives. In the meantime, it was common for men to visit the local brothels

for sexual satisfaction (Fisher, 1997). In this respect, male prostitution thrived. Gay men and bisexual men would frequently consort with soldiers, sailors, messengers, boys, and anyone else who was available for gifts, money, or favours (Weeks, 1989). There were also love affairs between men of the upper classes, as was exemplified by that between playwright Oscar Wilde and Lord Alfred Douglas. Wilde was unfortunately tried and found guilty of sodomy and imprisoned at Reading Gaol.

Love and sex between women continued to elude attention and was often hidden behind convention and propriety. In both Europe and North America, two "spinsters" would often set up house together in what became known as "Boston marriages," named after such an arrangement depicted in Henry James's novel The Bostonians. Historian Lillian Faderman (1981) did considerable research on women's correspondence and literature of the late 19th century and found many passionate verses between women who were probably lovers at the time. What is interesting, she notes, is that because there was so little discussion of lesbianism or sexual desire between women, many women were able to love each other innocently without the trappings of any negative definitions from society or psychiatry. Women's love affairs were also able to thrive since they lived in societies where it was thought natural and proper for women to be close with each other.

The 20th Century

One of the most liberated times for gay men of the 20th century was the 1920s and 1930s in Berlin. According to British novelist

Kathleen Wynne—25th Premier of Ontario

© Colin McConnell/Getty

Kathleen O'Day Wynne grew up in Richmond Hill, Ontario. She served as president of the Toronto Institute of Human Relations, she helped found MAD for Dancing, which donated funds to gay and lesbian youth, and served as Minister of Education, Minister of Transportation, and Minister of Municipal Affairs and Housing. Finally, she assumed the office of Premier of Ontario on January 26, 2013. As an open and married lesbian, her appointment stands as an example of Canada's commitment to gay and lesbian equality. During her campaign, her sexual orientation was barely mentioned—something that Canadian political observers noted as remarkable in that if she ran only a decade or two earlier it would have been a major topic of political attack ads (Loriggio, 2014). With Wynne's incumbency, the time for Canada to have a gay or lesbian prime minister is not far off.

Christopher Isherwood, he was able to enjoy gay life unfettered by any repression during his years in Berlin right up to the time the Nazi Party took power and began their campaign of repression. His experiences are described in his later novel *Christopher and His Kind* (1979). During the Nazi regime, many thousands of gay men and lesbians were put into concentration camps along with Jews and others and made to where a pink triangle for identification (Heger, 1980). The pink triangle became a symbol of gay liberation in the 1970s.

World War II (1940–1945) had done much for gay men and lesbians in that it allowed many Canadians and Americans to leave their farming communities and experience life in Europe. Once the war was over, single men and women flocked to North America's larger cities and fledgling gay communities emerged in Toronto, Montreal, Vancouver, and elsewhere. The 1950s, however, was a time for intense repression during the "red scare," where GLB people were seen as threats to national security since they could be blackmailed by foreign agents (Johnson, 2004).

In Canada, a similar witch hunt took place that also resulted in massive government firings. During this campaign, the Royal Canadian Mounted Police (RCMP) identified thousands of GLB people in the Ottawa area who were working as civil servants and in other satellite professions. They interrogated anyone they discovered and "encouraged" them to give names of others they knew to be gay as well. A homosexual orientation was in fact their only crime and the Canadian government's reasoning mirrored that of the United States: homosexual men were "practising criminals" by definition, thus subject to extortion and easy prey for blackmailing foreign agents (Beeby, 1992).

Ironically, the medical model's view of homosexuality as well as the persecution of GLB people changed the politics of homosexuality. Because physicians saw homosexuality not as just a behaviour but as maladaptive condition, this shaped the way people viewed GLB people (Risman & Schwartz, 1988). This led to the idea that "if homosexuality is something I am, not just something I do, then I should have a right to be 'who I am' just as Blacks, women, and other groups have a right to be who they are." The new view of homosexuality encouraged GLB people to band together and press for recognition of their civil rights as a minority group, which led to the modern gay and lesbian liberation movement.

Review Questions

1 Explain how our views on homosexuality have changed from ancient times through the Middle Ages.

2 Explain the historical differences for lesbians and gay men as well as what accounts for those differences.

3 Explain why it is inappropriate to use the term "gay" when referring to people in ancient times to the Middle Ages.

Homosexuality in Other Cultures

There is a tendency for many people to judge the world through the categories and values of their own culture. This is known as **ethnocentricity**. Yet what we call "homosexuality" may be viewed differently in other cultures. People may have same-sex sexual relations and yet not see themselves as different from other members of their culture. This can be minor as in Egypt, where men casually kiss and hold hands, or it can be fully sexual as in the ritualized homosexuality of Papua New Guinea, where young males have sexual contact exclusively with other males until they mature and marry, after which they have sexual contact only with women.

Same-sex behaviour is found in virtually every culture no matter how permissive or repressive that culture's attitude is toward it (Mihalik, 1988). The International Gay and Lesbian Human Rights Commission (IGLHRC) works to protect the rights of gays, lesbians, and bisexuals around the world. In many parts, GLB people experience discrimination, harassment, physical and emotional abuse, violence, and even execution. When a group of people worldwide are denied human rights, it is detrimental to their health in that it impedes their ability to secure food, shelter, and health care. In this section, we briefly explore such treatment as well as the general lives of GLB people in other cultures.

The United States

Although American GLB people made great strides in terms of gay rights in earlier decades, Canada's neighbour to the south still has tremendous opposition, much of which can be reduced to religious objections to homosexuality and the fear that any recognition of rights will lead to compromises in the freedom of religion. Whereas before, the gay rights struggle was against definitions of sickness and mental illness, it is now against those of religion and sin. For example, a legal amendment to the state constitution was proposed recently in Colorado by a right-wing religious group called Focus on the Family that would legalize discrimination against GLB people entirely. The "Religious Freedom Amendment" would allow any business owner (e.g., of a hotel or a restaurant) with a "sincerely held religious belief" to refuse service to GLB people, refuse to hire them, and even fire them outright (Ford, 2012). This amendment did not pass.

In the past decade, there have been a number of well-publicized cases of suicide by GLB teenagers because of school bullying. Nevertheless, proposals for anti-bullying laws, which would protect young boys and girls from harassment and violence in public schools, have met with strong resistance from religious groups and politicians who believe that such laws would prevent students, teachers, and school staff members from voicing "religious objections" to students because of their sexual orientation. One such law in Michigan, originally meant to protect teenagers from bullying, actually included a statement protecting the bullies as long as they were motivated by a "sincerely held religious belief or moral conviction" (Hall, 2012).

Even with such opposition, the United States does seem to be making progress. Same-sex marriage or civil unions are now recognized in the majority of the 50 states, as well as several counties of other states and Aboriginal groups such as the Cheyenne and Arapaho Nations. Same-sex sexual activity itself has been legal since 2003, and GLB people have been allowed to serve in the military since 2011. Still according to a 2013 world report by Human Rights Watch (HRW), only 21 states had laws prohibiting employment discrimination against GLB people as of 2012, and there was still no federal protection.

Latin America

As of January 2015, three South American countries have given legal recognition to same-sex marriage—Argentina (2010), Brazil (2013), and Uruguay (2013). Although many other Latin American countries may be open to same-sex relationships, political and public support for these relationships is not as strong. For example, many Costa Ricans support same-sex relationships and the legal recognition of these relationships, but the country has been strongly influenced by the Catholic Church, which sees homosexuality as an "intrinsic evil" (Harvey, 2007; Mayer, 2011).

In some Central and South American cultures, many people do not think in terms of homosexuality and heterosexuality but rather masculinity and femininity. Male gender roles, for example, may be defined by one's **machismo,** which, in terms of sexual behaviour, is determined by being the penetrator. Therefore, a man would not be considered gay for taking the penetrative role in anal and oral intercourse with other men. As long as he is penetrating, he is masculine.

According to Murray and Dynes (1999), this has been the case in Nicaragua, for example, where a penetrating partner is called *machista* or *hombre-hombre* ("manly man"), a term used for any masculine male. In fact, penetrating other men may even be seen as a sign of manliness and prestige, while being penetrated makes a man gay.

The implicit message of such definitions is that to mimic female behaviour is shameful for a male. Same-sex relationships, which are about sexual desire, are conflated with gender roles, which are about masculinity and femininity. This attitude reflects the general patriarchal nature of such cultures, where women often lack political and social power.

The Middle East and North Africa

There are currently no countries in the Middle East that recognize same-sex marriage, and many of them are highly oppressive toward GLB people. Iran imposes the death penalty for homosexual sex and people merely perceived to be gay are routinely arrested, tortured, and denied the right to a trial. Public GLB events are non-existent and private ones are routinely raided

---

ethnocentricity
To define other cultures using the categories and values of one's own.

machismo
Characterized or motivated by stereotypical masculine behaviour or actions.

Argentina was the first country in South America to allow same-sex marriage. Here, a man holds a sign reading "Yes, I want equality" during a 2010 demonstration in support.

(IGLHRC, 2011). Yemen is the same, if not worse. Under current law, men caught having sex with each other but who are not married (to women) will receive a flogging of 100 strokes for each partner and a year in jail. If they are married, they will be sentenced to death by stoning. Lesbians caught with each other face three years in jail (Almosawa, 2013).

In contrast, classic works of Arabic poetry often included homoerotic imagery and boys were often held up as the standard of beauty and sexuality in Arabic writing (Boswell, 1980). In some areas such as Egypt, it is common to see men holding hands or walking down the street arm in arm. Sexual relations in some areas of the Middle East are about power, which is defined through dominant and subordinate positions. In these areas, similar to some Latin American countries, being the penetrating partner with another man does not make a man gay (Sati, 1998).

Asian and the Pacific

There are no Asian countries at present that allow same-sex marriage or civil unions, although Taiwan has recently considered an amendment to enable it (PinkNews, 2014a).Only one Pacific country, New Zealand, allows same-sex marriage at present. Several Asian countries such as Bangladesh, India, Malaysia, Pakistan, and Sri Lanka have laws against same-sex behaviour (IGLHRC, 2010; Misra, 2009) and there is much harassment.

In 2001, the Chinese Psychiatric Association removed homosexuality from its list of mental disorders (Gallagher, 2001). This is a significant change for China, which as recently as 1994 openly opposed any gay or lesbian rights. Homosexuality was seen as a result of Western influences and it was considered a "Western social disease" (Ruan & Lau, 2004). Today, with modernization, attitudes are changing.

In India, although homosexual sex is still punishable by up to ten years in prison, several gay couples have made headlines by publicly revealing their marriages in attempts to overturn an existing law from 1861 (Predrag, 2005). As this law suggests, much of the negative attitudes in India as well as Sri Lanka are left over from British colonialism. Lesbians in India have made great strides in terms of organizing and raising consciousness about their place in society. Again with modernization, GLB people have begun to recognize themselves as a class and are fighting for their rights (Chatterjee, 2010). With this in mind, there seems to be much progress. Although less related to sexual orientation, India now has its first transgender major (Pink News, 2015).

Africa

So far, South Africa is the only African nation to allow same-sex marriage, which was legalized in 2006. African cultures and governments, however, are among the most homophobic in the world. More than two thirds of African countries have laws against homosexual behaviour (International Gay and Lesbian Human Rights Commission, 2010). As a result, there is a great deal of discrimination in terms of housing, employment, and health care and there is much fear and hiding. Uganda's Anti-Homosexuality Act, originally called the "kill the gays law" because it once proposed the death penalty, was signed into law in February 2014 and imposes life in prison for homosexual activity. It also imposes penalties to individuals for merely supporting LGBT organizations. Much of Uganda's information on homosexuality—which is entirely erroneous—comes from three American evangelists who conducted a two-day seminar on the "dangers" of gay sex. This misinformation was sufficient for Ugandan preachers to call for a "death to gays" bill, which was then amended to life in prison.

Ugandans whipped up to a frenzy call for death to gays and lesbians.

In some African countries, lesbians are victims of "corrective rape," where it is assumed that raping them will turn them into heterosexual women (Huff-Hannon, 2011). To call attention to the practice, a group in South Africa named *Luleki Sizwe* (after two South African women who died after corrective rape) posted photographs of women who had been beaten and raped, and circulated a petition to stop the practice. Within a few weeks, the group had more than 130 000 signatures from countries all over the world (Huff-Hannon, 2011). This got the attention of politicians and the national media, who supporters believe will be helpful in ending the practice.

What is interesting about this atmosphere of homophobia is that homosexuality had been practised in Africa for centuries without attracting much attention. For example, according to British anthropologist E. E. Evans-Pritchard (1970), the Azande people of Central Africa had a system whereby each male went through three stages: a "boy wife" of a warrior, a warrior with a "boy wife," and a husband of a woman. This system evolved as a way for the Azande to delay the age of marriage and, thus, control their population numbers. Negative attitudes toward homosexuality came only from the West during the days of colonialism and more recently from American anti-gay campaigners. In short, Africa's negative atmosphere toward homosexuality is a product of Western influence.

Gay and Lesbian Globalization

Homosexuality is found in virtually every culture in the world. How it is viewed depends on how it is defined from place to place. Whether in Africa, Asia, or South America, people who engage in same-sex sexual behaviour face a common struggle: they are discriminated against and this affects their health, well-being, and safety. Dennis Altman, an Australian political science professor, proposed the idea that while there are marked cultural differences among gays and lesbians around the world, there are cultural connections and, thus, an emergent global gay culture that supersedes culture. Chief among the changes are the tendencies of non-Western cultures to model their struggles for equality after Western struggles in Canada, the United States, Australia, and Europe. People who practise same-sex sexual activity are increasingly identifying with the Western identities of "gay" or "lesbian," which originally emerged from European and North American struggles. For example, while many countries saw homosexuality as a matter of roles where the penetrator is masculine and the penetrated is feminine, there is now a visibility of couples who are both masculine, may take either role, and do not vary in age, gender role, socio-economic level, or otherwise (Murray, 1999). While "gay" and "lesbian" are Western constructions, they are increasingly adopted as identities in the developing world as well.

Review Questions

1 In what ways does the denial of human rights to GLB people affect their health and well-being?

2 Explain how gender enters the definition of homosexuality in terms of roles in sexual behaviour.

Gays, Lesbians, and Bisexuals throughout the Life Cycle

Gays, lesbians, and bisexuals face particular issues that are not faced by heterosexuals. Some struggle with families and friends who reject them because of their sexual orientation as well as prejudice and discrimination in general society. Even so, with equal protection in Canada, many gays and lesbians enjoy equal treatment in their lives and live together happily. While their lives may differ because of culture, they have remarkable similarities to mainstream society. Even though Canada now recognizes same-sex marriage and affords full rights to gays and lesbians, such progression is only recent in history, and gays and lesbians still often face the same problems that are typical of the United States, which is less accepting. In this section, we examine the special issues that face gays, lesbians, and bisexuals.

Growing Up Gay, Lesbian, or Bisexual

Because gays and lesbians are an invisible minority, their differences are not recognized until they become apparent. This is not merely because they are a numerical minority; it is because society operates under a heterosexual presumption (Herdt, 1989; Peraldi, 1992). People conduct their daily lives under the assumption that everyone is heterosexual until proven otherwise. As a result, gay and lesbian teenagers are presented with a single model of sexual and romantic life. They are expected to be attracted to, go on dates with, and eventually to marry someone of the other sex.

This presumption and expectation of heterosexuality is everywhere. Parents assume that their children are heterosexual (Aveline, 2006), friends assume the same, teachers describe only a heterosexual world, and that world is all one sees on television, in movies, and in magazines, newspapers, and advertisements. With the gradual awareness that heterosexual feelings do not apply to them, teenagers begin to look for other models that fit with their feelings. Today, with the recognition of sexual diversity in Canada,

Positive portrayals of same-sex couples in advertising, such as this advertisement by Kenneth Cole, improves the images of gays and lesbians in society.

WE ALL WALK IN DIFFERENT SHOES.

GAY MARRIED COUPLE, JOANNA AND NICOLETTA TESSLER, WITH THEIR DAUGHTER, RUTHIE. KENNETHCOLE.COM 25 YEARS OF NON-UNIFORM THINKING.

there are at least some alternatives and role models, but for most of history, those alternatives did not exist and GLB teenagers often felt alone and isolated. Even today because of circumstances, some never get around to acknowledging their feelings or acting upon them for fear or repercussions. But because of their differences, they typically "come out," which is an acknowledgment and declaration of that difference. We discuss this practice in the next section.

Coming Out to Self and Others

One of the most important tasks of adolescence is to develop and integrate a positive adult identity. This poses an even greater challenge for gay and lesbian youths because they learn from a very young age the stigma of being different from the heterosexual norm (Ryan & Futterman, 2001). Special challenges often confront GLB people, including the need to establish a self-identity and communicate it to others. This is known as **coming out**. A number of models have been offered to explain how this process

coming out
Establishing both a personal and a public self-identity as gay, lesbian, or bisexual.

proceeds (Cass, 1979, 1984; E. Coleman, 1982; H. P. Martin, 1991; M. Schneider, 1989; Troiden, 1989).

Coming out refers first to acknowledging one's sexual identity to oneself and some GLB persons even have their own negative feelings about homosexuality to overcome. The often difficult and anxiety-ridden process of disclosing the truth to family, friends, and then becoming fully open comes later. Disclosure of identity plays an important role in identity development and psychological adjustment for GLB people.

Although first awareness of sexual orientation typically occurs between the ages of eight and nine, people vary in when they share this information with others. Some may come out early in their lives while others remain closeted into late adulthood (Savin-Williams & Diamond, 2000; H.E. Taylor, 2000) or for their entire lives. Coming out does not happen overnight; being gay or lesbian for some may mean a lifetime of disclosing different amounts of information to family, friends, and strangers in different contexts (Hofman, 2005). Deciding whether and how to tell friends and family are difficult decisions. To minimize the risk for rejection, many gay and lesbian adolescents choose whom they come out to very carefully (Vincke & van Heeringen, 2002).

Because the stigma against homosexuality is lessening over time, many teenagers are coming out earlier than in previous decades. Although in the 1970s many teenagers waited until adulthood to come out, in the 1980s and 1990s people began coming out in their teens (Ryan et al., 2009). Today in the 21st century, teenagers began coming out as early Grade 8 or 9 (Denizet-Lewis, 2009; Elias, 2007). A more accepting social climate and more enlightened parents facilitated these changes. In addition, increases in gay support groups high school and a more positive portrayal of gay role models in the popular media have also contributed to early ages in coming out (Elias, 2007). Years ago, many GLB people worked hard to hide their sexual orientation for fear of discrimination, harassment, and violence (Hudson, 2010). However, the changing social climate has also lessened the pressure to "fit in." Today, many more GLB people live openly.

Family Reactions to Coming Out

Some parents of GLB youths initially react with disappointment, shame, and shock when they learn about a son's or daughter's sexual orientation (D'Augelli, 2005; LaSala, 2000). They may feel responsible and believe they did something to "cause" their child's sexual orientation. In one study, more than 50 percent of gay and lesbian teens experienced a negative reaction from their parents when they came out (Martin et al., 2010; Ray, 2007). The family must go through its own "coming out," as parents and siblings slowly try to accept the idea and then tell their own friends. The importance of positive resolution in the family has prompted the formation of a the organization Parents, Families, and Friends of Lesbians and Gays (PFLAG), which helps parents learn to accept their children's sexual orientation and gain support from other families experiencing similar events.

A Model of Coming Out

A number of authors have created models of the process of coming out. For example, Vivienne Cass (1979, 1984) proposed one of the leading models which encompasses six stages of gay or lesbian identity formation.

Stage 1: Identity confusion. Individuals begin to believe that their behaviour may be defined as gay or lesbian. There may be a need to redefine their own concepts of gay and lesbian behaviour with all the biases and misinformation that most people have. They may accept that role and seek information, repress it and inhibit all gay and lesbian behaviours, or deny its relevance to their identities entirely.

Stage 2: Identity comparison. Individuals accept potential gay and lesbian identities. They reject the heterosexual model but have no substitute. They may feel different and even lost. If they are willing to consider a gay and lesbian self-definition, they may begin to look for appropriate models.

Stage 3: Identity tolerance. Individuals shift to the belief that they are probably gay or lesbian and begin to seek out gay communities for social, sexual, and emotional needs. Confusion declines but self-identity is still more tolerated than truly accepted. Usually, they still do not reveal their new identities to the heterosexual world and maintain a double life.

Stage 4: Identity acceptance. A positive view of self-identity is forged and a network of gay and lesbian friends is developed. Selective disclosure to friends and family is made and individuals often immerse themselves in gay culture.

Stage 5: Identity pride. Gay pride is developed and anger over treatment may lead to rejecting heterosexuality as bad. Individuals feel validated in their new life.

Stage 6: Identity synthesis. As individuals truly become comfortable with their sexual orientation and as heterosexual contacts increase, they realize the inaccuracy of dividing the world into "good gays and lesbians" and "bad heterosexuals." No longer is sexual orientation seen as the sole identity by which an individual can be characterized. Individuals live their lives openly so that disclosure is no longer an issue and they realize that there are many sides and aspects to personality of which sexual orientation is only one. The process of identity formation is complete.

While Cass's model is useful, it should be noted that it is not only from the 1970s—and thus about 40 years old—but based on the harsh anti-gay realities of American culture at the time. Today, with Canada's more accepting culture and major Western shifts in social justice, human rights recognition, and even technology, the process of coming out is likely quite different. This model should thus be viewed as a classic theory, which is contextual to its time and not necessarily a present path.

SOURCE: From Cass (1979, 1984).

Gay and lesbian youths who have positive coming-out experiences have higher self-confidence, lower rates of depression, and better psychological adjustment than those who have negative coming-out experiences (Needham & Austin, 2010; Ryan & Futterman, 2001).

On the other hand, parental rejection during the coming-out process can be a major health risk for GLB youth. Children who are rejected by their parents have been found to have increased levels of isolation, loneliness, depression, thoughts of suicide, sexually transmitted infections, and homelessness (Calzavara et al., 2011; D'Augelli, 2005; Needham & Austin, 2010; Ray, 2007; Ryan et al., 2009; Savin-Williams & Dube, 1998). Compared with GLB teenagers with no or low levels of family rejection, those who reported high levels of family rejection were:

- 8.4 times more likely to attempt suicide
- 6 times more likely to report high levels of depression
- 3.4 times more likely to use illegal drugs
- 3.4 times more likely to report engaging in unprotected sexual behaviour (Ryan et al., 2009)

At least half of gay and lesbian teenagers sampled in one research project experienced negative reactions from their parents when they came out and 26 percent were kicked out of their homes (Brown & Trevethan, 2010; Remafedi, 1987). In fact, the number one cause for homelessness for GLB teenagers is family conflict (Ray, 2006). In the United States, it is estimated that between 20 percent and 40 percent of homeless youths are gay, lesbian, or bisexual (Lockwood, 2008; Ray, 2006). Homeless GLB youths are also more likely to abuse drugs and alcohol and experience physical and sexual abuse (Chakraborty et al., 2011; Cochran et al., 2002; Gaetz, 2004; Needham & Austin, 2010; Ray, 2006).

REAL Research

David Aveline (one of the Canadian authors of this book) conducted 80 interviews with parents of gay men (Aveline, 2000). Because of reactions by co-workers and friends that are sometimes negative or patronizing, and because situations where they are asked if their sons are married yet or dating come up frequently in daily life, parents of gay people go through a coming out process similar to that of their children. In effect, they "come out" as parents of gay children.

According to Canadian sociologist David Aveline (2000), one of the main reasons parents react negatively to learning that their children are gay is that they believe they will have a miserable life—they will not be able to marry, they will not have children, and they will be alone in their old age. Today, with same-sex marriage and adoption as well as greater acceptance of GLB people in Canada, it is likely that such fears are becoming far less prevalent. A gay son or a lesbian daughter is now well able to marry, well able to adopt children, and has as much likelihood as anyone else in being long-partnered in their old age.

Effects of Stigma

Many gay and male bisexual youths report a history of feeling unattached and alienated—most probably because heterosexual dating was often a focal point in peer group bonds (Bauermeister et al., 2010; Herdt, 1989). The same is true of young lesbians and female bisexuals, although the pressure and alienation may be felt slightly later in life because same-sex affection and touching are more accepted for girls and because lesbians tend to determine their sexual orientation later than gay men. In general, GLB youths have been found to experience high levels of stigmatization and discrimination (Bauermeister et al., 2010; Chakraborty et al., 2011; Cox et al., 2010).

For many years, psychiatrists and other therapists argued that GLB people had greater psychopathology than heterosexuals. Their mistake, however, was to assume that this was because of their sexual orientation rather than society's negative reactions and persecution of them. Research in the United States has found GLB people are more likely to experience stress and tension and are more at risk for the development of chronic diseases and mental health issues (Conron et al., 2010). Furthermore, GLB youths have been found to have higher levels of depression and are more likely to think about and or commit suicide (Bauermeister et al., 2010; Chakraborty et al., 2011; Cox et al., 2010; A.R. D'Augelli et al., 2005b; Doty et al., 2010; Espelage et al., 2008; Hegna & Rossow, 2007; Newcomb & Mustanski, 2010). They also have been found to have higher rates of substance abuse and alcohol-related problems (Conron et al., 2010; Rivers & Noret, 2008; D.F. Roberts et al., 2005; Rosario et al., 2004; Ryan & Futterman, 2001), and higher rates of truancy, homelessness, and sexual abuse (D'Augelli et al., 2006; Taylor, 2000). Bisexual people have been found to be most likely to experience sadness, have thoughts of suicide, engage in binge drinking, and experience intimate partner violence (Conron et al., 2010; S.T. Russell et al., 2002).

These problems are the result of the enormous pressures of living in a society that discriminates against GLB people (Kertzner et al., 2009; Lock & Steiner, 1999; Roberts et al., 2010). Vulnerable and stigmatized groups in general have higher rates of these types of behaviours, which often result from coping with stigma-related stress. In addition, GLB people are particularly vulnerable to harassment and other forms of risk, further compounding their stress (Mishna et al., 2008).

Again in the United States, workplace discrimination also adds stress to the lives of GLB people. In one study, gay men were found to earn 23 percent less than married heterosexual men and 9 percent less than single heterosexual men who are living with a woman (Elmslie & Tebaldi, 2007). However, lesbians were not discriminated against when compared with heterosexual women.

They earn more than heterosexual women (Elmslie & Tebaldi, 2007; Peplau & Fingerhut, 2004).

In Canada, because of the strength of the Charter of Rights and Freedoms, the situation is quite different. According to federal law, it is illegal for any employer to pay an individual less (or more) merely on the basis of sexual orientation and illegal to consider this factor in hiring, promotion, or firing decisions. Furthermore, creating a hostile working environment for co-workers or employees is an actionable offence. According to a 2015 Angus Reid Public Opinion Poll (LGBT in the Workplace, 2015), such laws and regulations seem highly effective. Of 983 GLB adults surveyed, 93 percent described their employer's overall attitude toward GLB people as tolerant, 89 percent said the same of their co-workers, and 72 percent said that work conditions for GLB people have improved over the past five years. Additionally, most were out (of the closet) at work and of those who were not, about half said that probably nothing would happen to them if they were. The greater level of acceptance in Canada as well as the strong backing of the federal government has enabled GLB people to live healthier and more productive lives and as a result they experience far less stress than GLB people the United States.

Life Issues: Partnering, Parenthood, and Aging

After the teenage years, which are sometimes difficult, GLB people go through particular life stages. We now turn to three of them: same-sex coupling, parenting, and aging.

Looking for Partners

Because gays and lesbians live in a heterosexual world, meeting others for romantic or sexual pursuits can be difficult. For one thing, they need to recognize each other. Canadian sociologist Tracy Nielsen (2002) recognized this problem and sought to explore the ways in which lesbians identified each other in her ethnographic research in urban environments. Lesbians did this through the process of "gaydar" (gay radar), which draws upon atypical and even stereotypical appearances and actions of other women, which potentially identify their sexual orientation. For example, the lesbians interviewed by Nielsen mentioned such things as an "androgynous appearance," "lack of make-up," a "baseball cap backwards," and "multiple piercings," as indicators that someone might be lesbian. Thus, as Nielsen points out, stereotypes are a double-edged sword. They serve to exclude people from mainstream society, but they serve as markers of identification as well. Ironically, lesbians who do wish to be recognized can manipulate their appearances and actions toward the stereotypes for the purpose. This tactic of identification was also recognized by an earlier Canadian researcher, Maurice Leznoff (1954), who observed that gay men in Quebec would subtly manipulate their appearances through clothing and mannerisms to bring about recognition by other gay men.

The most efficient tactic for socializing, however, has been to create a space where a gay or lesbian orientation is understood by one's mere presence. For at least a century, this has been mainly in the form of a gay bar (Harry, 1974; Israelstam & Lambert, 1984;

Sexual activity by gay and lesbian couples can be an expression of deep love, affection, or lust.

Noel, 1978; Taub, 1982). If one woman sees another in a lesbian bar, she may safely assume that she is also lesbian. She may be wrong, but this is generally the exception to the rule and making such an assumption would not be considered socially unacceptable. Also, many schools and universities have clubs, support groups, and meeting areas for GLB students.

There are also gay sports clubs, gay religious groups, gay discussion groups, and many other groups. In addition, there are gay periodicals such as *Xtra!* that carry personal ads and ads for dating services, travel clubs, resorts, bed and breakfast inns, theatres, businesses, and other services to help gays and lesbians find partners. Toronto, for example publishes a comprehensive list of gay and gay-owned businesses every year. Finally, there are now widespread dating sites such as *Mandate* and *Adam4Adam* where GLB people can chat and meet.

Similar to heterosexual couples, GLB people in committed relationships, common-law relationships, or marriages have been found to experience less sadness, lower levels of stress, and an increased sense of well-being compared with GLB singles (Riggle et al., 2010).

Gay and Lesbian Parenting

Gay men and lesbian women can become parents in a variety of different ways including artificial insemination, adoption, or surrogacy (we discussed these options in Chapter 6). Over the last few years, gay and lesbian parenting has become more common and even popular gay and lesbian celebrities, such as Ricky

Martin, Rosie O'Donnell, Elton John, and Melissa Etheridge, have become parents. Many gay and lesbian couples become parents, and they cite most of the same reasons for wanting to be parents that heterosexual parents do (D'Augelli et al., 2006).

Gay and lesbian couples who wish to be parents may encounter problems that heterosexual couples do not face. Parenting is seldom an individual or couple decision for them and often involves several negotiations with others (Berkowitz & Marsiglio, 2007). Because of biology, female couples are more likely to have children. First, lesbians may already have children from previous heterosexual marriages and, second, women may be impregnated either by artificial insemination or by known other men. Members of male same-sex couples may also have children from previous marriages but it is more likely that the children will be living with their mothers. Surrogacy is also possible but it is also difficult and expensive. Adoption is frequently the only alternative.

In Canada, same-sex couples are now being approved for adoption in equal proportion to heterosexual couples (Sullivan & Harrington, 2009). Since 2002, legislative changes have increasingly broken down the barriers to same-sex adoption and parental rights. Among them are the recognition of same sex marriage, the granting of two mothers the rights to be named as parents on a child's birth certificate, the right of gays and lesbians to adopt jointly as couples, and the granting of a third person to be named as a parent (Dort, 2010).

After numerous studies, no significant differences have been found in the psychological adjustment and social relationships between the children of same-sex and heterosexual couples (Bos & Gartrell, 2010; Farr et al., 2010; Gartrell & Bos, 2010; Greenfeld, 2005; Hicks, 2005). All of the scientific evidence suggests that children who grow up with one or two gay or lesbian parents do as well emotionally, cognitively, and socially as children from heterosexual parents (American Psychological Association, 2005; Bos & Gartrell, 2010; Greenfeld, 2005; Perrin, 2002). Even so, some gay and lesbian couples find minimal support to parent children, and experience a social stigmatization of children that they do have (Pawelski et al., 2006).

Gay and Lesbian Seniors

Seniors today were young in times when homosexuality was considered deviant and immoral and they often remember unpleasant times and needed to be cautious. Many also entered heterosexual marriages hoping that this will "cure" them of their same-sex desires. They were also young when HIV/AIDS took the lives of their friends and intimate partners. Coming out before the senior years often helps older GLB people to feel more comfortable with their lives and sexual orientation. Gay and lesbian seniors who have not come out or come to terms with their sexual orientation may feel depressed or alone as they continue to age. In addition, they may experience depression and isolation from years of internalized homophobia (Altman, 2000; Gross, 2007). For some, hiding their sexual orientation even to the point where they are ready for a senior-care facility is their only choice. One gay man who had been in a relationship with his partner for more than 20 years said, "When I'm at the gate of the nursing home, the closet door is going to slam shut behind me" (Gross, 2007).

John Damien—Wrongfully Dismissed

John Damien, a former jockey and horse trainer, was at the top of his career in 1975 as one of the top three stewards for the Ontario Jockey Commission. His job was to act as judge during races and, among other tasks, declare the winners. These decisions were reached by the board of three and the majority ruled. On February 6, he was called into the office of the Ministry of Consumer and Commercial Relations of Ontario and handed a letter stating that he would not be reappointed for the next racing season. Furthermore, if he voluntarily resigned, he would receive a letter of recommendation and a cheque for $1200. When Damien insisted on the reason for his dismissal, he was told that "The Ontario Jockey Club

does not want you in the stands this year…We are concerned that you could be blackmailed…or that you could favour certain…people." In effect, he was fired because he was gay and for no other reason.

Damien refused to resign, was immediately dismissed and, with the help of the Gay Alliance toward Equality, filed a complaint with the Ontario Human Rights Commission. He was told that their mandate did not include sexual orientation and they could not hear his case. Meanwhile, his situation reached the front page of the *Globe and Mail*. Subsequently, Damien had great difficulty finding another job to survive, his money ran out, and he filed for bankruptcy in 1978.

In 1985, after years of lawsuits, countersuits and appeals, the Ontario Racing Commission finally agreed to pay Damien $50 000 for his wrongful dismissal. That same year, the Ontario government added sexual orientation to its human rights code. Damien, however, did not survive long enough to enjoy his victory, having died of pancreatic cancer only 22 days before.

John Damien is now mostly forgotten by Canadians. He is, however, a hero in that he paved the way for protection of all GLB people in Canada and many now owe their job security to his efforts. As he said of his struggle, "I'm a race tracker, you know. Once you come out of the gate, you'd better go all the way or you get trampled" (Rothon, 2007).

REAL Research Brotman et al. (2007) looked at issues concerning gay and lesbian seniors in Canada and the ways that caregivers related to them. They interviewed 17 caregivers in three cities and came up with a number of themes. Among the emergent themes were that gay and lesbian seniors felt that they might be discriminated against by caregivers because of their assumptions of heterosexuality.

Many issues confront aging gay and lesbian seniors. Studies have found that senior care facility staff often report intolerant or condemning attitudes toward GLB residents (Cahill et al., 2000; Gross, 2007; Röndahl et al., 2004). Because of Canada's aging population, the care of gay and lesbian seniors has become an increasingly important topic.

Gay, Lesbian, and Bisexual Organizations

Canada has gay and lesbian organizations of all kinds, from the local to the national level, and they serve a variety of needs. Egale

Canada Human Rights Trust works at the national level to combat homophobia and promote LGBT rights through education, research, political involvement, and community engagement. The Gay Alliance Toward Equality (GATE) was one of the first gay advocacy groups to form in Canada. It began in Vancouver and launched the first gay-related Supreme Court case when the *Vancouver Sun* refused to print an ad advertising their newspaper, *Gay Tide*. They also took on an advocacy role in the wrongful dismissal of John Damien (see the accompanying Sex in Real Life box).

There are also numerous community centres in major Canadian cities, such as the 519 Church Street Community Centre in Toronto and Qmunity in Vancouver. Other than that, there are groups and organizations for a wide variety of interests within gay communities, among them a gay rugby team in Ottawa, Integrity in Toronto for gay and lesbian Anglicans, and organizations serving the special situations of gay and lesbian Iranians, South Asians, and East Asians. For Canadians in isolated areas of the provinces and territories, there are also numerous online organizations and discussion groups. These groups serve to connect them to gays and lesbians in Canada and throughout the world.

Review Questions

1 Describe the need for GLB youths to establish a self-identity, and the task of coming out.

2 Explain some of the tasks involved in living a GLB life, including looking for partners, parenting, aging, and the specific problems they might encounter.

3 Describe some of the problems of aging specific to gay and lesbian seniors.

Homophobia, Heterosexism, and Hate Crimes

GLB people have long been stigmatized and, to a degree, this stigma still remains even in Canada. When homosexuality as an illness was removed from the *Diagnostic and Statistical Manual of Mental Disorders* in 1973, negative attitudes persisted. It was at this time that researchers turned the tables and bean to study these negative attitudes and behaviours. Homophobia, a term coined by American psychologist George Weinberg in 1972 in his book *Society and the Healthy Homosexual*, became the new pathology.

What Is Homophobia?

As Weinberg said in the opening lines of his book, "I would never consider a patient healthy unless he had overcome his prejudice toward homosexuality....his repugnance at homosexuality is certain to be harmful to him.... The person who belittles homosexuals with evident enjoyment is at the very least telling me that he wants to establish his own sense of importance through contrast with other people—a tenuous business" (1972). **Homophobia** is, therefore, an irrational fear of GLB people, which is often translated into discriminatory behaviour and, at times, violence.

Conventional wisdom suggests that those who protest the loudest have the most to hide. In other words, people who are loudest in their objections to homosexuality are themselves dealing with same-sex attraction. This hypothesis was tested by Adams et al. (1996), who divided men into homophobic and non-homophobic groups and then measured their penile tumescence while they watched gay erotic videos. The homophobic group experienced greater tumescence, suggesting that they harboured same-sex attractions of which they were unaware. According to Ontario psychologists MacInnis and Hodson (2013), however, the evidence for this conclusion is untestable beyond the tumescence and may be interpreted in a variety of ways.

Homophobia is also a matter of degree. Some people might accept homosexuality intellectually and yet still dislike being in the presence of GLB people, while others might object to homosexuality as a practice and yet have personal relationships with GLB people whom they accept (Forstein, 1988). When compared with people who hold positive views of GLB people, those with negative views are less likely to have had contact with them and more likely to be older and have fewer years of education. They are also more likely to be subscribe to a conservative religious ideology, have more traditional attitudes toward sex roles, be less permissive sexually, and be more authoritarian (Herek, 1984). Overall, heterosexual men compared with heterosexual women have been found to have significantly more negative attitudes toward gay men (Davies, 2004; Verweij et al., 2008).

It is important to point out that heterosexuals are not the only people to experience homophobia. GLB people who harbour negative feelings about homosexuality experience internalized homophobia. This is especially true in older generations who grew up in times where there was less acceptance of homosexuality. In some research, older gay men have been found to experience more internalized homophobia (or negative feelings based on sexual orientation directed at oneself) than lesbians (D'Augelli et al., 2001). GLB people with internalized homophobia have also been found to have decreased levels of self-esteem and increased levels of shame and psychological distress (D.J. Allen & Oleson, 1999; Szymanski et al., 2001).

A closely related problem for gay men and lesbians is **heterosexism,** which is the presumption of heterosexuality discussed earlier and the social power used to promote it (Neisen, 1990). Because heterosexual relationships are seen as "normal," a heterosexist person feels justified in suppressing or ignoring those who do not follow that model. But heterosexism is more than this. It is the systematic reinforcement of heterosexuality in society, which often excludes GLB people's lives and renders them invisible. It either places heterosexuality at the top in terms of importance or renders it as the only legitimate form of sexual expression.

Heterosexism begins in high schools where GLB people and their lives are typically not discussed, it continues in college classrooms where professors use only heterosexual examples to illustrate their points, and it continues in the work force where the presumption of heterosexuality permeates all activities. Julia Temple, a Newfoundland sociologist, looked at the extent of heterosexism through a content analysis of 20 francophone high school textbooks in Quebec aimed

On Your Mind

Is discomfort with same-sex public displays of affection homophobic?

Yes and no. If one sees two men or two women greeting each other with a kiss at a party or in the street and is uncomfortable when one might think nothing of it if the couple were a man and a woman, then one is making a distinction between acceptable and not acceptable that has no rational basis. If one sees two men or two women making out on a park bench and would be equally disturbed if it were a man and a woman, then one is not making a distinction. It must be kept in mind that it was not so long ago that people were disgusted when they saw mixed-race couples kissing on a park bench and would sometimes react violently. Today, this is a matter of course and usually raises no eyebrows at all. Others are disgusted when they see older couples kissing, or teenagers, or couples of significant age differences. The key here is to apply one's standards to all couples and not see it as acceptable for some but not others. The best advice, however, to anyone who is uncomfortable with two people kissing, regardless, is to simply look the other way.

homophobia
Irrational fear of GLB people and homosexuality.

heterosexism
The "presumption of heterosexuality" that has social implications.

at students aged 12 to 17. She found that 95 percent of pages mentioning sexuality made no references to same-sex sexual behaviour and of those pages that did, 80 percent of them referred to it in a negative manner. The heteronormativity she found exhibited itself in four ways: maintaining a clear dichotomy between homosexuality and heterosexuality, presenting heterosexuality as the only normal path, problematizing homosexuality as abnormal or unnatural, and maintaining strict boundaries of male/masculine and female/feminine. GLB teenagers who go through the school system are therefore rendered marginal, irrelevant, or invisible.

The greater awareness of sexual orientation has brought about changes to some of these assumptions, but heterosexism still dictates a large part of the way people consider the world. Heterosexism can lead to a lack of awareness of issues that can harm GLB individuals today.

Hate Crimes Against Gay, Lesbian, and Bisexual Individuals

Throughout history, persecution of minorities has been based on perspectives that portrayed those minorities as illegitimate, subhuman, or evil. Likewise, homophobia is not just a set of attitudes; it creates an atmosphere in which people feel they are permitted to harass, assault, and even kill GLB people. **Hate crimes** are those motivated by hatred of someone's religion, sex, race, sexual orientation, disability, gender identity, or ethnic group. They are known as "message crimes" because the offender believes that they send a message to the victim's affiliated group (American Psychiatric Association, 1998). Typically, hate crimes involve strong feelings of anger (Parrott & Peterson, 2008).

At times it is difficult to determine what constitutes a hate crime because the offender does not typically declare such motives. If a White person assaults a Black person, for example, it may just be that the two got into an argument and race was not a factor. Those who single out people, however, because they are members of minority groups are clearly attempting to send a message to that group. One might wonder why it is necessary to have hate crime legislation at all since assault is already illegal no matter who the victim is. The answer is that because GLB people (and other groups) have a disproportionate amount of crime against them, there must be an added deterrent.

According to Statistics Canada (2011), there were 1332 police-reported hate crimes in Canada in 2011, or 3.9 incidents per 100 000 population. About half (52 percent) of them were motivated by race or ethnicity, 25 percent by religion, and 18 percent by sexual orientation. Those motivated by sexual orientation were most likely to be violent. Eighty-eight percent of people accused of hate crimes were male and 60 percent were under age 25. It must be said that official statistics highlight only those crimes that reach the attention of the police. It is likely that far more hate crimes occur but they go unreported and, thus, unnoticed.

An even greater threat to minority groups comes in the form of hate organizations. While Canada does have small factions of White supremacist groups such as the Ku Klux Klan, it does not have large-scale, well-funded conservative organizations, such as the Family Research, Americans for the Truth About Homosexuality, and Focus on the Family, that regularly combat or spread misinformation about GLB people. These organizations and others are on the Southern Poverty Law Center's list of anti-LGBT hate groups for spreading known falsehoods and "demonizing propaganda" about LGBT people (Southern Poverty Law Center, 2015).

How Can One Combat Homophobia and Heterosexism?

Heterosexism is widespread and subtle and therefore difficult to combat. Adrienne Rich (1983), a prominent scholar of lesbian studies, uses the term *heterocentrism* to describe the neglect of GLB existence, even among feminists. Perhaps one can learn from the definition of a similar term: *ethnocentrism.* This refers to the

© George Pimentel/WireImage/Getty Images

In 2011, Lady Gaga, a prominent and long-time supporter of GLB rights, pulled the plug on a lucrative marketing deal with Target because of the company's inadequate support of GLB rights.

hate crime
A criminal offence, usually involving violence, intimidation, or vandalism, in which the victim is targeted because of his or her affiliation with a particular group.

Sexual Diversity in Our World: Gay-Themed Canadian Films

Year	Title	Location	Synopsis
1974	*Montreal Main*	Montreal	A photographer falls in love with a teenage boy.
1977	*Outrageous!*	Toronto	A female impersonator rooms with a pregnant schizophrenic and helps her cope with the world.
1993	*Zero Patience*	Toronto	The ghost of patient zero who first brought AIDS to Canada materializes and contacts old friends.
	Love & Human Remains	Montreal	A group of young people looking for love and meaning in the 1990s.
	The Hanging Garden	Cape Breton Island	A gay man returns to his family home after an absence of ten years.
1996	*Les Feluettes (Lilies)*	Montreal	A bishop goes to a prison to hear the confession of a boyhood friend jailed 40 years ago. The inmates force him to watch a play about what really happened.
	Flow	Various	Asian Canadian filmmaker Quentin Lee talks about his work and presents four short films.
2002	*Leaving Metropolis*	Winnipeg	A painter takes a job as a waiter in a couple's restaurant and falls for the husband.
2003	*Hey, Happy!*	Winnipeg	The relationship between a DJ and a UFO enthusiast. Filled with strange and characters and raves.
2004	*Wilby Wonderful*	Coast of Nova Scotia	Life on a small Maritime island with various characters including a suicidal man.
	Everyone	Vancouver	The perfect gay couple have a wedding in their back yard and begin to fight over…Everything!
	Prom Queen— The Marc Hall Story	Ottawa	The true story of a 17-year-old Ottawa boy at a Catholic high school who fought to take his boyfriend to the prom and whose case was heard by the Supreme Court.
	Sugar	Toronto	A troubled teenager hooks up with a hustler and the two hang out together.
	Denied	Oshawa, Ontario	A gay man is in love with his best friend.
2005	*Innocent*	Toronto	A gay Asian teenager emigrates from Hong Kong to Canada. He has a relationship with an older lawyer.
	Whole New Thing	Nova Scotia	Thirteen-year-old Emerson is raised by hippy parents. He develops a crush on his gay English teacher.
2007	*Half a Person*	Ontario	Two best friends take a road trip from Sudbury to Toronto.
	Breakfast with Scot	Toronto	A gay couple take custody of a young boy whose mother passed away.
2010	*Struggle*	Toronto	A young gay man goes to Toronto to "live, runs out of money, and falls in with a group of gay hustlers.

A scene from *Breakfast with Scot*.

© Capri Films/Courtesy Everett Collection

belief that all standards of correct behaviour are determined by one's own cultural background leading to racism, ethnic bigotry, and even sexism and heterosexism. Although ethnocentrism is still common, especially in Western societies, it is slowly being eroded by the passage of new laws, the media's spotlight on abuses, and improved education. Perhaps a similar strategy can be used to combat heterosexism.

Promoting Positive Change through the Media

Representations of GLB people are increasing in the media (Draganowski, 2004; Freymiller, 2005). Television shows such as *The L Word, Ellen, Gossip Girl, Queer as Folk,* and *Brothers and Sisters* have helped pave the way for GLB people, resulting in far less heterosexist programming than just a few years ago. Before this, homosexuality was portrayed only negatively, often with images of GLB people as psychopaths or murderers.

Another important development in the media is the explosion of music, fiction, non-fiction, plays, and movies that portray gay and lesbian life more realistically. Whereas once these types of media were shocking and hidden, now they appear on radio stations and in mainstream bookstores and movie theatres (see the Sexual Diversity in Our World feature).

Review Questions

1 Define homophobia and explain what factors have been found to be related to its development.

2 Define heterosexism and heterocentrism and give one example of each.

3 Explain how hate crimes are message crimes and give one example.

Lesbianism and Bisexuality

Many women do not fall neatly into regular sexual orientation categories. This might be because many people are less threatened by lesbian sexuality than by gay male sexuality. Some research on lesbianism suggests that women's sexual identity is more fluid than men's (Diamond, 2005; Gallo, 2000; Notman, 2002). For some women, an early lesbian relationship is temporarily or permanently replaced by a heterosexual one, or a heterosexual relationship may be replaced by a lesbian relationship later in life (Notman, 2002). Women have also been found to experience more attractions to both sexes than men (Hoburg et al., 2004). Overall, lesbian relationships have been reported as more satisfying, egalitarian, and empathic, and they have more effective conflict resolution than heterosexual relationships (Ussher & Perz, 2008).

Lesbian communities are vibrant ones. Bars, coffeehouses, bookstores, sports teams, political organizations, living cooperatives, media, and lesbian-run and -owned businesses often represent a political statement about the ways in which women can live and work together. A number of lesbian musicians—including k.d. lang, Melissa Etheridge, and Tracy Chapman—sing of issues important to the lesbian community and yet have strong crossover appeal to mainstream listeners. Many lesbian magazines are dedicated to fiction, erotica, current events, and photography.

Lesbians are more at risk for some health problems. They report higher levels of depression and antidepressant use than heterosexuals and they are more likely to be overweight, smoke cigarettes, and have high rates of alcohol consumption (Case et al., 2004; Struble et al., 2010). Some research suggests that much of this hinges on the amount of personal acceptance they receive from their parents. Lesbians who felt that their mothers were accepting of their sexual orientation had higher self-esteem and lower rates of smoking and alcohol consumption than those whose mothers were not accepting (LaSala, 2001). In addition, lesbians who feel supported and accepted have higher levels of self-esteem and well-being overall (Beals & Peplau, 2005). Lesbians have also been found to have lower rates of preventive care (yearly physical examinations) than heterosexual women (Herrick et al., 2010; Mays et al., 2002; Moegelin et al., 2010), yet they report high levels of optimism and excitement related to menopause (J.M. Kelly, 2005).

A recent study by the Zuna Institute, an American Advocacy group for African-American lesbians, found that Black lesbians are one of the most vulnerable groups, with an increased risk for physical and emotional health issues, shorter life expectancies, and poverty rates of 21 percent compared with poverty rates of 4 percent for White lesbians and 14 percent for gay Black men (Ramsey et al., 2010). As adults, they are more likely than White gay and lesbian couples to be parenting. Additionally, Black lesbians are less likely than other groups to seek out mental or physical health services (Ramsey et al., 2010).

Bisexuality has emerged recently as a separate identity from lesbian, gay, or heterosexual identities. Social and political bisexual groups began forming in the 1970s but it wasn't until the late 1980s that an organized bisexual movement became visible (Herek, 2002). Prior to this time, bisexual people typically experienced marginal lives in that they were thought unusual among gays and lesbians by their other interests and unusual among heterosexuals for the same reason.

Many people who identify as bisexual first identified as heterosexual and their self-labelling generally occurs later in life than either gay or lesbian self-labelling (Weinberg et al., 1994). Notably, for many years, few people noticed the absence of research on bisexuality, which stemmed from the fact that researchers believed that sexuality was composed of only two opposing forms of sexuality: heterosexuality and homosexuality (Herek, 2002; Rust, 2000).

Gays and lesbians have tended to see bisexuals either as on their way to becoming gay or lesbian or as people who want to be able to "play both sides of the fence." Similarly, heterosexuals have tended to lump bisexuals in with gays and lesbians. Some sexuality scholars have suggested that bisexuality is a myth, an attempt to deny one's homosexuality, identity confusion, or an attempt to be "trendy" (Rust, 2000; Carey, 2005; Rieger et al., 2005). Bisexuals themselves have begun to speak of **biphobia,** which they suggest exists among heterosexual people as well as gays and lesbians (Eliason, 1997; Galupo, 2006; Mulick & Wright, 2002; L. Wright et al., 2006). Like gays and lesbians, bisexuals experience hostility, discrimination, and violence in response to their sexual orientation (Herek, 2002). Some researchers suggest that bisexuals experience "double discrimination," because they may experience discrimination from both heterosexuals and gays and lesbians (Mulick & Wright, 2002). Compared with gays and lesbians, bisexuals have been found to have decreased social well-being, more barriers to health care, and increased sadness and suicidal thoughts (Conron et al., 2010; Kertzner et al., 2009).

Many bisexuals see themselves as having the best of both worlds. As one bisexual person put it, "The more I talk and think about it, and listen to people, I realize that there are no fences, no walls, no

heterosexuality or homosexuality. There are just people and the electricity between them" (quoted in Spolan, 1991). In our society, fear of intimacy is expressed through either homophobia by heterosexuals or **heterophobia** by gays and lesbians.

There are a number of patterns apparent in bisexual lives. In **sequential bisexuality,** a person has sex exclusively with someone of one gender followed by sex exclusively with someone of the other. **Contemporaneous bisexuality** refers to having male and female sex partners during the same period (J.P. Paul, 1984). Numbers are hard to come by because bisexuality itself is so hard to define. How many encounters with both sexes are needed for a person to be considered bisexual? One? Fifty? And what of fantasies? It is difficult to determine what percentage of people is bisexual because many who engage in bisexual behaviour do not self-identify as bisexual (Weinberg et al., 1994).

On Your Mind

Are bisexuals really equally attracted to both sexes?

Ebsworth and Lalumiere (2012), two Alberta psychologists, were interested in this question and conducted research to respond to it. They solicited subjects and divided them into groups dependent upon sexual orientation. There were 16 bisexual men, 19 bisexual women, 15 heterosexual men, 15 heterosexual women, 15 gay men, and 10 lesbians. Each group was shown pictures of males and females and the viewing times for each picture was recorded. The two bisexual groups had viewing times equal for pictures of both men and women, while the other groups had viewing times significantly longer for pictures of their preferred gender.

It is certainly possible for a bisexual person to prefer one gender over another, but the question of whether there is any fixed percentage differential (e.g., 70 percent women, 30 percent men) has not yet been examined.

Review Questions

1 Explain how women's sexual identity may be more fluid than men's sexual identity.

2 Some researchers claim that bisexuality does not exist. What does research tell us about bisexuality?

3 Differentiate between sequential and contemporaneous bisexuality.

Gays and Lesbians of Colour

Special concerns and problems confront GLB people who are members of racial and ethnic minorities. Homosexuality is less accepted by many ethnic groups and gay communities in Western societies often tend to render non-White members as invisible in their events, advertisements, and other media.

This leads to Black, Aboriginal, Asian, or Middle Eastern gay men and lesbians to feel marginalized by both sides. Minority

biphobia
Strongly negative attitudes toward bisexuals and bisexuality.

heterophobia
Strongly negative attitudes toward heterosexuals and heterosexuality.

sequential bisexuality
Having sex exclusively with someone of one gender followed by sex exclusively with someone of the other.

contemporaneous bisexuality
Having sex partners of both sexes during the same period.

GLB youths have been found to experience greater psychological distress than non-minority GLB youths (Diaz et al., 2001; McCabe et al., 2010).

Because Canada's main immigration groups are from East Asia and the Indian subcontinent, the presence of East and South Asians is well reflected in the gay and lesbian communities across the nation. Ontario social work professor Maurice Kwong-Lai Poon has done considerable research upon gay Asians (Poon, 2006; Poon & Ho, 2002, 2008; Poon et al., 2005), finding a number of commonalities in their experiences. Because of the emphasis upon White bodies, many feel marginalized and invisible in gay communities. They must also deal with stereotypes of passivity and weakness as is frequently the way Westerners view Asians (Said, 1978). As a result, they are ignored in gay bars, gay chat rooms, and elsewhere. According to Aveline (2010), who looked at the experiences of gay Asian men in British Columbia, many gay Asians resented the ways in which White gay men fetishized their racial features as "exotic" or based on stereotypes, preferring that they would like to be valued for their individuality rather than their race. At the same time, because of their sheer numbers as well as their efforts, gay Asians have become highly visible in Toronto and Vancouver gay communities and there are now a number of organizations that concentrate on their concerns.

Gays and lesbians of African or Caribbean descent have similar problems in terms of marginality in that they must constantly negotiate both their Black and their gay identities among other gays and other Black people (Husbands, et al., 2012). In one Toronto study (George, et al., 2012), Black gay men reflected on how their relationships emerged in the context of race and desire. Most subjects who were interviewed slept with other Black gay men as well as White men. With other Black men, they described a sense of comfort and fulfillment, while with White men they described the relationship either as purely sexual or inflected with racial objectification.

In the United States, gay African Americans can find their situation particularly troubling because they often have to deal with the heterosexism of the African-American community and the racism of other GLB people (Green, 2007; Tye, 2006). Some progress is being made, however. Books such as *Brother to Brother: New Writings by Black Gay Men* (Hemphill, 1991) have raised such issue in public. Many feminist and lesbian anthologies and most lesbian and feminist journals include writings explicitly by minority lesbians.

In sum, while gay communities are embracing of diversity, both gay Asians and gay Black men encounter experiences where they are racialized in terms of sexuality in daily life, in the search for partners, and in the general North American emphasis upon Whiteness in media and elsewhere. In addition, for recently immigrated ethnic minorities such as South Asians and Middle Eastern people, there is often tremendous parental pressure to marry and have children within their own communities. As a result, many are careful in revealing their gay or lesbian identities (Yates, 2012).

Review Questions

1 Identify and explain some common problems among gay Asian and gay Black men.

2 Describe some of the problems that confront GLB minority people in general.

Homosexuality in Religion and the Law

The Abrahamic religions (Judaism, Islam, and Christianity) have not only been historically sex negative but historically condemned same-sex sexual behaviour and been the prime movers in anti-gay teachings. As a result, there has been a great deal of negativity surrounding gays and lesbians in religion. In the United States, these negative views range from simple rejection to advocating punishment (PinkNews, 2014b).

Demographically, Canada is a more secular nation in that while 67 percent of the population identify as Christian, 24 percent identify as having "no religion affiliation" (Statistics Canada, 2013). This last group is the fastest-growing, having doubled in proportion from 1991 to 2011. As a result, Canadians have become far more accepting of GLB people to the point of mandating equality under the law.

Some Christian religions such as the United Church of Christ are more tolerant than others. This church and its members have welcomed GLB members, worked for equal rights, and even ordained GLB clergy. They do not view homosexuality as sinful. One of the most accepting denominations, the Metropolitan Community Churches, promotes itself as the world's largest organization with a primary affirming ministry to LGBT persons (Metropolitan Community Churches, 2005).

Other Christian denominations, such as Presbyterianism, Methodist, Lutheran, and Episcopalian, have more conflict over the issue of sexual orientation, resulting in both liberal and

Some Christian denominations have begun to promote a more liberal attitude toward GLB people, including ordination of gay and lesbian clergy.

conservative views. In recent years, a number of Christian denominations have voted to allow non-celibate gays to serve as clergy if they are in a committed relationship (Condon, 2010).

There is also controversy over sexual orientation in Jewish synagogues. Although Orthodox Jews believe that homosexuality is an abomination forbidden by the Torah, reform congregations are more likely to welcome GLB people. A Reform movement in 1990 allowed the ordaining of gay rabbis (Albert et al., 2001). In 2010, a Statement of Principles was signed and released by a group of Orthodox rabbis that supports the acceptance of GLB members (Nahshoni, 2010).

There is also no real consensus about gay and lesbian relationships among the various Buddhist sects. Buddhism differs from Christianity in that it views behaviours as helpful or not helpful (whereas Christianity views behaviours as good or evil) and looks at whether there was intent to help. As a result, Buddhism encourages relationships that are mutually loving and supportive.

Review Questions

1 What are the differences between Canada and the United States in terms of religion and GLB people.

2 Identify some of the more liberal and conservative religions and explain how each religion views GLB people.

Chapter Review

Summary Points

1 Sexual orientation refers to the sex(es) a person is attracted to emotionally, physically, sexually, and romantically. Heterosexuals are predominantly attracted to members of the other sex, gays and lesbians to members of the same sex, and bisexuals to both men and women.

2 Alfred Kinsey introduced a seven-point sexual orientation scale based mostly on people's sexual behaviour, while other researchers suggest that people's emotions and fantasies more than their behaviours are the most important determinants of sexual orientation. The Klein Sexual Orientation Grid (KSOG) includes the elements of time, fantasy, social behaviour, and self-identification.

3 The frequency of gay, lesbian, and bisexual behaviour has remained constant over the years. Scholars generally agree that between 3 percent and 4 percent of males are predominantly gay, 1.5 percent to 2 percent of women are predominantly lesbian, and about 2 percent to 5 percent of people are bisexual. However, many of these studies have methodological flaws and have not taken into account feelings of attraction or fantasies. Nor have they taken into account that many people are secretive because of stigma as well as the fact that definitions of homosexuality vary.

4 Several theories have been proposed to explain homosexuality. Among them are biological, developmental, behaviourist, and sociological theories.

5 Biological theories claim that differences in sexual orientation are caused by genetics, hormones, birth order, or simple physical traits. Developmental theories focus on a person's upbringing and personal history to find the origins of homosexuality. Behaviourist theories view homosexuality as a learned behaviour, and sociological theories explain how social forces serve to determine how homosexuality is defined and viewed.

6 Same-sex sexual activity was common throughout history and homosexuality was not treated with concern or much interest by early Jews or Christians. The Church's indifference to homosexuality lasted well through the 12th century. By 1300, however, the new intolerance of differences resulted in homosexuality being punishable by death almost everywhere in Europe. This view from the late Middle Ages has influenced the Western world's view of homosexuality for the past 700 years. In the 19th and early 20th centuries, physicians and scientists began to suggest that homosexuality was not a sin but an illness.

7 Same-sex sexual behaviour is found in virtually every culture. Many GLB people struggle with discrimination, prejudice, laws that do not recognize their unions, lack of benefits for their partners, and families who may reject them.

8 The coming out process is where GLB people acknowledge their sexual identities to themselves, then to particular others, and then to the public at large. Today's teenagers are coming out at earlier ages because of the lessening of stigma. However, there are still many GLB people who remain closeted, and some do so throughout their lives. Parental rejection during the coming-out process is a major health risk for GLB youths.

9 Because of social stigma, GLB youths are more likely to experience stress and tension and are at greater risk for the development of chronic diseases and mental health issues. They have higher rates of substance abuse, and higher rates of truancy, homelessness, sexual abuse, and suicide.

10 Children who grow up with one or two gay or lesbian parents do as well emotionally, cognitively, socially, and sexually as children with heterosexual parents.

11 Homophobia is an irrational fear of GLB people and homosexuality. Heterosexism is the presumption of heterosexuality and the social power used to promote it. Hate crimes, also known as message crimes, are motivated by hatred of someone's religion, sex, race, sexual orientation, disability, or ethnic group.

12 Bisexuals often identify first as heterosexuals and their self-labelling as bisexual generally occurs later in life than either gay or lesbian self-labelling. Biphobia is a fear of bisexuals.

13 Minority GLB youths have been found to experience greater psychological distress than non-minority GLB youths.

14 Religious intolerance of GLB people has led to strong rejection. There are some Christian and Jewish denominations that lean toward acceptance of GLB people.

Critical Thinking Questions

1 There seem to be quite a few explanations for the cause of homosexuality. Do you think that this search for the cause is politically motivated? For example, no one seems to search for the cause of heterosexuality, or for that matter, being left-handed. Why has there been so much attention to the cause of homosexuality?

2 The term "homosexual" when used as a noun (e.g., "He is a homosexual) is now considered offensive. Why do you think this is so? Consider in your answer the history of treatment of gays and lesbians in society.

3 Dennis Altman suggested that in spite of the strong cultural differences among GLB people in the world, there is such a thing as a "global gay." What does he mean by this and why would he believe it to be so?

4 Several nations in Africa—Uganda in particular—are markedly intolerant of GLB people. Where does this intolerance come from?

5 Explain the effects of heterosexism upon GLB lives. How can this situation be improved?

Websites

EGALE (Equality for Gays and Lesbians Everywhere) Canada A Canadian advocacy group for LGBT people that acts as a resource for lawmakers, intervenes in LGBT-related legal cases, and promotes education and awareness. (http://egale.ca)

IRQO (Iranian Queer Organization) An advocacy group offering support for LGBT people of Iranian background. Website is in Persian. (http://www.irqo.org/persian/)

Lambda Foundation A support organization and charity that creates scholarships and bursaries for LGBT people, and promotes research and the advancement of human rights. (http://www.lambdafoundation.com/)

Canadian Lesbian and Gay Archives A non-profit organization set up in 1975 that collects and stores historical documents and materials related to the history of gays and lesbians in Canada. (http://www.clga.ca/)

10 Childhood and Adolescent Sexuality

One of the primary goals of sex education should be to help teens develop a positive view of sexuality, provide them with adequate information to protect their sexual health, and help them to make good decisions. Around the world, the majority of teens do not get the information they need about sex to protect themselves. One place where this is definitely not the case is in the Netherlands, where comprehensive sex education is mandatory. I decided to take a trip to the Netherlands to learn more about their approach to sex education. I met with Ruud Winkel, a well-known biology/sex education teacher at Amsterdam Lyceum, a Dutch secondary school. Ruud teaches human sexuality to 13- to 18-year-olds.

Each child is required to take his class and no one is allowed to opt out. Ruud also told me many interesting facts about his class:

I spend the first five minutes of every class letting students ask me questions about sex. I've had the strangest questions but I'm glad they can ask me. Common questions are "How much sperm have you got?" "What does an orgasm feel like?" "What's a wet dream?" or "How long does it take to get a baby out?" I answer their questions and we have great discussions about them. Throughout the class, I teach them about sexually transmitted infections, orgasms, birth control, and masturbation. I think it's

important for them to know that masturbation is normal and that everyone does it. We also talk about sexual intercourse. In fact, we show students a video with a man and woman making love. We think it's important that they understand what making love is all about. How can we teach about making babies if we didn't teach them about making love? In the end, I want students to understand that sex is good and that they should enjoy it.

The Netherlands has the world's lowest rates of teenage pregnancy, birth, and abortion. While we can't say that comprehensive programs are directly responsible for these lower rates, we do know that the Dutch have a unique approach. My work in the Netherlands has helped me to understand the complexity of sexuality education. Dutch sex education focuses on responsibility, respect, and pleasure, and doesn't shy away from the tough questions. ▌▌

Today's adolescents are growing up with conflicting messages about sexuality. Nightly news stories focus on a variety of issues related to sexuality, including same-sex marriage, erectile drugs, vaccines for STIs, and increasing rates of HIV and AIDS around the world (Fortenberry et al., 2010; Kelly et al., 2009; Romer et al., 2009). Popular reality television shows such as *16 and Pregnant* and *Teen Mom* tell stories about teen pregnancy. Many adolescents also have unlimited exposure to sexual information and images through the Internet (Hennessy et al., 2009). All of these events and influences have shaped this generation of adolescents.

We think of children today as undergoing their own, exclusive stage of development. Children are not just "little adults," and though they can be sexual, children's sexuality is not adult sexuality

(Gordon & Schroeder, 1995). Children want love, appreciate sensuality, and engage in behaviours that set the stage for their adult sexuality. Nonetheless, we must be careful not to attribute adult motives to childhood behaviours. When a five-year-old boy and a five-year-old girl sharing a bath reach out to touch each others' genitals, the meaning that they ascribe to that action cannot be considered "sexual" as adults use the term. As Plummer (1991) notes, a little boy having an erection shows simply that his physiology functions normally; seeing the erection as "sexual" is to overlay an adult social meaning onto the physiology. The child is probably not even aware of the "sexual" nature of his erection and, indeed, may not even be aware that his penis is erect.

Sexual growth involves a host of factors—physical maturation of the sexual organs, psychological dynamics, familial relations, and peer relations, all within the social and cultural beliefs about gender roles and sexuality. In this chapter, we'll begin with the challenges faced by researchers who study childhood and adolescent sexuality. Then we'll take a look at sexuality from infancy through adolescence. Finally, we'll discuss sexuality education in Canada and the legal perspective on sexual behaviour in adolescents.

Throughout most of history, children were treated as miniature adults, and concepts such as "childhood" and "adolescence" did not exist (Aries, 1962). Most children worked, dressed, and were expected to behave (as much as they were capable) like adults.

Studying Childhood and Adolescent Sexuality

The study of childhood sexuality is challenging and the studies are limited. A recent review by de Graaf and Rademakers (2011) found only 14 articles addressing the issue of sexuality in childhood. The majority of these 14 studies do not focus on childhood behaviour; rather, they focus on questions asking what children know about sex. Many people oppose questioning children about sexuality, often believing that research on child sexuality will somehow encourage promiscuity. Others seem to believe that if we do not talk about children's sexuality, it will just go away.

Despite the opposition, researchers have been forging ahead in their study of children's sexual behaviour despite the opposition. We will discuss the research on child and adolescent sexuality throughout this chapter.

Sexuality research in children and adolescents is often problem driven. Many studies are aimed at decreasing "problems," such as STI rates or teenage pregnancy. In a recent review, Fortenberry (2013) stated that we need to expand our study of adolescent sexuality to look at issues such as sexual desire, sexual desire, sexual behaviours, and sexual function. Future research is also needed to understand the perspectives and behaviours of adolescents with regards to how differences in gender, ethnicity, race, religion, and social class influence the meaning of eroticism and sexuality in young people's lives.

Review Questions

1 Explain how today's adolescents are being exposed to sexuality in different ways than the generations before them.

2 Explain why there has been opposition to childhood sexuality research.

3 Give one example of how research into to childhood sexuality has been problem driven.

Beginnings: Birth to Age Two

We will begin by looking at the physical and psychosexual changes from birth to age two. Many of the behaviours children engage in during this developmental stage arise out of curiosity. We would not label any behaviours that young children engage in as sexual.

Physical Development

Ultrasound has given us pictures of male fetuses with erections in the uterus, and some infants develop erections shortly after birth, even before the umbilical cord is cut (Masters et al., 1982). Female infants are capable of vaginal lubrication from birth (Martinson, 1981). Infant girls produce some estrogen from the adrenal glands before puberty, whereas infant boys have small testes that produce very small amounts of testosterone. The production of these hormones is important for physiological development and function throughout the life span.

Male infants commonly have erections and may have erections during breast-feeding (which can be very disconcerting to the mother), and girls may have clitoral erections and lubrication (but this is unlikely to be noticed). Genital touching is common in infancy, and many infants touch their genitals as soon as their hands are coordinated enough to do so (Casteels et al., 2004). Some babies only occasionally or rarely touch themselves, whereas others do it more regularly. Genital touching is normal at this age, and parents should not be concerned about it.

Early childhood is a crucial period for physical development. Children of this age must learn to master the basic physical actions, such as eye–hand coordination, walking, talking, and generally learning to control their bodies. Think of all the new things a child must learn—all the rules of speaking and communicating; extremely complex physical skills such as self-feeding, walking, and running; how to interact with other children and adults; control of bodily wastes through toilet training; and handling all the frustrations of not being able to do most of the things they want to do when they want to do them. Although this period of childhood is not a particularly active one in terms of physical sexual development, children may learn more in the first few years of childhood about the nature of their bodies than they learn during the remainder of their lives.

Psychosexual Development: Bonding and Gender

Throughout this textbook we discuss the importance of relationships and the development of an attachment to a primary caregiver

Young girls and boys are curious about their bodies and bodily functions.

is very important for normal child development. Infants can develop many attachment styles, including secure, anxious/ambivalent, or avoidant. Infants are helpless creatures, incapable of obtaining nourishment or warmth or relieving pain or distress. The bond between a mother and child is more than psychological, a baby's crying actually helps stimulate the secretion of the hormone *oxytocin* in the mother, which releases her milk for breast-feeding (Rossi, 1978).

Equally important as the infant's need for nourishment is the need for holding, cuddling, and close contact with caregivers. An infant's need for warmth and contact was demonstrated in Harlow's (1959) famous experiment, in which rhesus monkeys were separated at birth from their mothers. When offered two surrogate mothers, one a wire figure of a monkey equipped with milk bottles and one a terry-cloth–covered figure, the monkeys clung to the terry-cloth figure for warmth and security, and ventured over to the wire figure only when desperate for nourishment. The need for a sense of warmth and security in infancy can overwhelm even the desire to eat.

In Chapter 8, we discussed how children begin to develop their gender identity (M. Lewis, 1987). After about age two, it becomes increasingly difficult to change the child's gender identity. It takes a little longer to achieve gender constancy, whereby young children come to understand that they will not become a member of the other sex sometime in the future. Most children develop **gender constancy** by about age six, and a strong identification with one gender typically develops and becomes a fundamental part of a child's self-concept (Warin, 2000).

> **gender constancy**
> The realization in the young child that one's gender does not normally change over the life span.

Review Questions

1 Explain how infants have functional sexual anatomy, perhaps even before birth.

2 Identify the single most important aspect of infant development, and explain the importance of warmth and contact with caregivers.

3 Differentiate between gender identity and gender constancy.

Early Childhood: Ages Two to Five

In early childhood children begin to understand what it means to be a boy or girl. Children in the majority of the Western world also learn that their genitals are private during these years, and they often begin to associate sexuality with privacy.

Physical Development: Mastering the Basics

Kinsey and his colleagues (1948, 1953) established that half of boys between the ages of three and four could achieve the urogenital muscle spasms of orgasm (although no fluid is ejaculated), and almost all boys could do it three to five years before puberty. Kinsey did not collect systematic data on the abilities of young girls to reach orgasm, although he did include some anecdotal stories on the subject.

Psychosexual Development: What It Means to Be a Girl or a Boy

In early childhood, children begin serious exploration of their bodies. It is usually during this period that children are toilet trained, and they go through a period of intense interest in their genitals and bodily wastes. They begin to ask the first, basic questions about sex, usually

On Your Mind

Is it damaging to children to see their parents naked? What about accidentally seeing them having sex?

For many years in Western society, it has been thought that children would be somehow traumatized by seeing their parents naked. In fact, nudity is natural and common in many cultures, such as European countries. Parents' casual nudity, openness to sexual questions, and willingness to let their children sleep at times in their beds has been correlated with generally positive overall effects on the well-being of children (Lewis & Janda, 1988; Okami et al., 1998). If children walk in on their parents having sex, the parents' best tactic is not to be upset, but to tell the children calmly that the parents are showing each other how much they love each other. Most children are scared when they walk in on their parents having sex and talking about it can help the children understand. More significant trauma can come from the parents' overreaction than from the sight of parents having sex.

about why boys and girls have different genitals and what they are for. They begin to explore what it means to be "boys" or "girls" and turn to their parents, siblings, or television for models of gender behaviour. Sometimes children at this age will appear flirtatious or engage in sexual behaviours such as kissing in an attempt to understand gender roles.

Sexual Behaviour: Curiosity and Responsibility

Toddlers are not yet aware of the idea of sexuality or genital sexual relations. Like infants, toddlers and young children engage in many behaviours that involve exploring their bodies and doing things that feel good. Both girls and boys at this age continue to engage in genital touching. More than 70 percent of mothers in one study reported that their children younger than six touched themselves (Okami et al., 1997), and in a study done to determine normative sexual behaviour in young children the researchers found that parents reported that over 60 percent of boys and over 40 percent of young girls between the ages of two and five touched their genitalia or breasts when at home (Friedrich, Fisher, Broughton, Houston & Shafran, 1998).

Genital touching is actually more common in early childhood than later childhood, although it picks up again after puberty (Friedrich et al., 1991). Boys at this age are capable of erection, and some proudly show it off to visitors. Parental reaction at this stage is important; strong disapproval may teach their children to hide the behaviour and to be secretive and even ashamed of their bodies, whereas parents who are tolerant of their children's emerging sexuality can teach them to respect and take pride in their bodies. It is perfectly appropriate to make rules about the times and places that such behaviour is acceptable, just as one makes rules about other childhood actions, such as the correct time and place to eat or to urinate.

Child sex play often begins with games exposing the genitals ("I'll show you mine if you show me yours...."), and by the age of four, may move on to undressing and touching, followed by asking questions about sex around age five. Sometimes young children will rub their bodies against each other, often with members of the same sex, which seems to provide general tactile pleasure (Friedrich, Fisher, Broughton, Houston & Shafran, 1998).

Sexual Knowledge and Attitudes

During this period of early childhood, children learn that the genitals are different from the rest of the body. They remain covered up, at least in public, and touching or playing with them is either discouraged or to be done only in private. This is the beginning of the sense of secrecy surrounding sexuality.

Children this age, especially girls, rarely learn the anatomically correct names for their genitals. Why is it that some parents teach their children the correct names for all the body parts except their genitalia? What message do you think it might send children when we use cute play words such as "vajayjay," "weiner," or "piddlewiddle" for their genital organs?

In our culture, boys are often taught about the penis, but girls rarely are taught about the vulva, vagina, or clitoris. Although girls are quite interested in boys' genitalia, boys tend to be relatively uninterested in girls' genitalia (Gundersen et al., 1981). This tends to discourage girls from learning more about their sexuality (Ogletree & Ginsburg, 2000). Learning the correct anatomical names for the genitalia, however, is important for all children. It is important to make it clear that these are respected parts of their anatomy—just like their arms and nose—and it is acceptable to talk about these parts, especially if they are ill or hurt in the genital area. Also, it helps to create trust with our children that we can talk openly about all of their physical issues and questions. It is also important for children to understand their anatomy and how it relates to boundaries with regards to acceptable behaviours in childhood with regards to physical contact. In Chapter 17 we will discuss how sexual abuse in children can lead to later sexual revictimization and unintended teenage pregnancy (Lalor & McElvaney, 2010).

Review Questions

1 Explain how curiosity is still the basis for sexuality in early childhood.

2 What does the research show about genital touching during this age range?

3 Explain how a lack of knowledge about proper anatomical terms for the genitals may affect girls.

4 What is the impact of learning in childhood that the genitals are different from the rest of the body? Explain.

Middle Childhood to Preteen: Ages 6 to 12

Between ages six and 12, the first outward signs of puberty often occur, and both boys and girls become more private about their bodies. Children begin building a larger knowledge base about sexual information and acquire information from many sources, including their parents/caregivers, peers, and siblings. During the middle childhood to preteen years, children often play in same-sex groups and may begin masturbating and/or engaging in sexual fantasy and/or sexual contact.

Young boys develop strong relationships with same-sex and other-sex friends and relatives, and these relationships set the stage for adult intimate relationships.

Physical Development: Preadolescence and Puberty

Puberty, together with prenatal sexual differentiation, are the two major stages of physiological sexual development. Puberty marks the transition from sexual immaturity to maturity and the start of reproductive ability. In Chapters 3 and 4, we discussed the physiological and hormonal changes that accompany puberty, so in this chapter we review only those physical changes that have an effect on the nature of adolescent sexuality.

Until a child's body starts the enormous changes involved in puberty, the sexual organs grow in size relative to general body growth. Although the body begins internal changes to prepare for puberty as early as age six or seven, the first outward signs of puberty typically begins at nine or ten. The physiological changes of puberty begin anywhere between the ages of eight and 13 in most girls and nine and 14 in most boys. As we discussed in Chapter 3, researchers have found that girls are beginning puberty earlier than ever before (Biro et al., 2010). See Figure 10.1 for more information about signs of puberty in boys and girls. Overall, girls' maturation is about 1.5 to two years ahead of boys' (Gemelli, 1996).

In girls, **breast buds** appear, and pubic hair growth may begin. In boys, pubic hair growth generally starts a couple of years later than in girls, and on average, girls experience menarche before boys experience their first ejaculation (often referred to as **semenarche**; SEM-min-ark). Preadolescent boys experience frequent erections,

breast buds
The first swelling of the area around the nipple that indicates the beginning of breast development.

semenarche
The experience of first ejaculation.

Childhood and Adolescent Sexuality **273**

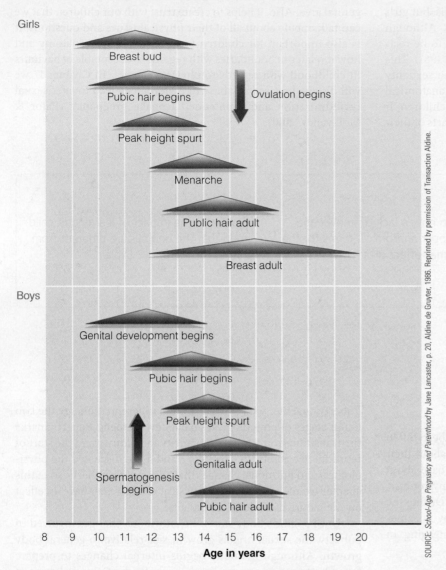

The Age Sequence of Pubertal Maturation in Boys and Girls

Girls
- Breast bud
- Pubic hair begins
- Peak height spurt
- Ovulation begins
- Menarche
- Public hair adult
- Breast adult

Boys
- Genital development begins
- Pubic hair begins
- Peak height spurt
- Spermatogenesis begins
- Genitalia adult
- Pubic hair adult

Age in years
8 9 10 11 12 13 14 15 16 17 18 19 20

SOURCE: *School-Age Pregnancy and Parenthood* by Jane Lancaster, p. 20, Aldine de Gruyter, 1986. Reprinted by permission of Transaction Aldine.

FIGURE **10.1** This graph illustrates the average ages when boys and girls go through the major bodily changes of puberty.

even to non-erotic stimuli. Common reactions to semenarche include surprise, curiosity, confusion, and pleasure; typically most boys don't tell anyone about this event (Frankel, 2002; J.H. Stein & Reiser, 1994).

During puberty, the time when attractiveness to others begins to become more important, the body starts growing in disproportionate ways. Fat can accumulate before muscles mature, feet can grow before the legs catch up, the nose may be the first part of the face to begin its growth spurt, and one side of the body may grow faster than the other (M. Diamond & Diamond, 1986). Add acne, a voice (in males) that squeaks at unexpected moments, and unfamiliarity with limbs that have suddenly grown much longer than one is accustomed to, and it is no wonder that adolescence is often a time of awkwardness and discomfort.

Psychosexual Development: Becoming More Private

As children mature, sexual behaviours, such as public genital touching or sex games, decrease. However, this may be because such behaviours are less tolerated by parents and adults as the child grows older. For example, although it may be acceptable for a three-year-old to put his hand down his pants, such behaviour would not be as acceptable for a nine-year-old.

Typically, children engage in more sexual exploration behaviour up until age five and then this behaviour decreases. One study found that two-year-old children of both sexes engaged in more natural sexual exploration than did children in the 10- to 12-year-old range (Friedrich, 1998). This may simply be because children get better at hiding such behaviours.

Sexual Behaviour: Learning about Sex and Sexuality

Children through the middle and late childhood years continue to engage in genital touching and may explore both same- and other-sex contact. Curiosity drives some to display their genitals and seek out the genitals of other children. Prepubescence is the age of sexual discovery; most children learn about adult sexual behaviours such as sexual intercourse at this age and assimilate cultural taboos and prejudices concerning unconventional sexual behavior. For example, it is at this age that children (especially boys) may begin to use sexual insults with each other, and may question their friends' desirability and sexuality. In 2010, a new campaign was launched in the United States called "Think B4 You Speak" to help children and adolescents understand the negativity of such phrases and the potential consequences of the words they use.

Masturbation

Generally, by the end of this period, most children are capable of stimulating themselves. Although orgasm may be possible, not all children in this age range engage in genital touching for the purpose of orgasm. Boys often learn masturbation from peers, and as they get older, they may masturbate in groups. Girls, on the other hand, typically discover masturbation by accident. When masturbation does begin, both boys and girls may stimulate themselves by rubbing their penis or vulva against soft objects like blankets, pillows, or stuffed animals. Many girls experience pleasure and even orgasm by rhythmically rubbing their legs together.

SEXUAL CONTACT Children from age six to puberty engage in a variety of same- and other-sex play. Sex games, such as "spin

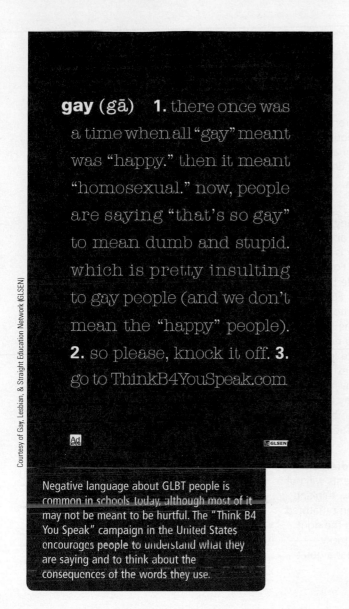

gay (gā) **1.** there once was a time when all "gay" meant was "happy." then it meant "homosexual." now, people are saying "that's so gay" to mean dumb and stupid. which is pretty insulting to gay people (and we don't mean the "happy" people). **2.** so please, knock it off. **3.** go to ThinkB4YouSpeak.com

Negative language about GLBT people is common in schools today, although most of it may not be meant to be hurtful. The "Think B4 You Speak" campaign in the United States encourages people to understand what they are saying and to think about the consequences of the words they use.

Animal Variations

Why Do We Play?

We all recognize play in children when we see it but why do we do it? The question of why humans and animals play is debated by play behaviour experts (Pellis, Field, Smith, & Pellis, 1997). Several theories exist suggesting that play is preparation for adult life and in particular for sexual behaviour. While we don't know for certain why humans play, we do know that play behaviour in rhesus macaques is serious work. During preadolescent and adolescent play, male and female rhesus macaques learn to foot clasp their fellow playmates. This foot clasp occurs when one animal jumps onto the back of the other animal and wraps it feet around the ankles of the animal underneath.

This behaviour is necessary for males to properly mount females in adulthood. If a male can't mount and clasp his feet around the ankles of the female, he will be too low to align the penis with the female's vagina. This would prevent the male from having successful sex and may decrease the number of offspring that he will have (Goy & Wallen, 1979).

the bottle" (spinning a bottle in a circle while asking a question such as, "Who is going to kiss Marie?" then the person whom the bottle points to must perform the task), are common and allow children to make sexual contact under the guise of a game. Play, in a sense, is the "work" of childhood, teaching interpersonal and physical skills that will be developed as we mature. Children at this age have some knowledge about sex and are curious about it, but they often have incomplete or erroneous ideas. Both boys and girls exhibit a range of same-sex sexual behaviours as they move through childhood, from casual rubbing and contact during horseplay to more focused attention on the genitals. Parents may get upset and confused when they discover that their child engages in sexual play. Sex play in children is perfectly normal, and parents should probably be more concerned if their children show no interest in their own or other children's bodies than if they want to find out what other children have "down there."

Rates of sexual contact among school-age children are difficult to come by, and most experts still cite Kinsey's data of 1948 and 1953. Kinsey found that 57 percent of men and 46 percent of women remembered engaging in some kind of sex play in the preadolescent years. However, the problem with research in this area is that many studies are retrospective (i.e., they asked older adults to remember what they did when they were young), and there are many reasons to think people's recollections of childhood sexuality may not be entirely accurate.

Sexuality and Relationships: What We Learn

Our parents, or the adults who raised us, are the very first teachers of love and intimacy. As we grow and find relationships of our own, we tend to relate to others in our love relationships much as we did when we were young. As we grow up, all of our experiences influence our sexuality in one way or another. We learn different aspects of sexuality from these varied influences; for example, we may learn values and taboos from our siblings, information from our peers, and sexual and relationship behaviour from the television and the Internet. As adolescents' bodies continue to change, they may feel anxious, and accurate knowledge about sex, from parents, friends, and/or teachers may lead to a more positive self-image and self-acceptance. We discuss the importance of and current state of sexuality education in Canada later in this chapter.

Relationships with Peers

As children age and try to determine how they will fare in the world outside the family, their peer groups increase in importance.

When parents think about talking to their children about sex, many report feeling very anxious and insecure about their ability to talk about it. Anxiety comes from many places, including the following:

- **Fear:** Many parents worry that something bad will happen to their children if they start talking to them about sex. Parents worry that they will wait too long, start too early, say the wrong thing, or give misinformation. They also may worry that talking about sexuality will take away their children's innocence, by making them grow up too fast or become overly interested in sexuality.

- **Lack of comfort:** Because most parents did not talk to their parents about sex, many feel uncomfortable in presenting it themselves. Those who did talk about it usually talked with their mothers. This causes many fathers to feel especially uncomfortable facing the prospect of educating their sons and daughters.

- **Lack of skills:** Parents often do not know how to say what they want to say. Some parents resort to a lecture about the "birds and bees," whereas others simply ask their children, "Do you have any questions?"

- **Misinformation:** Many parents do not have the necessary facts about sexuality. Many might not have information about sex and/or sexuality and be unsure about where to go to get it.

So what can a parent do?

- **Educate yourself:** For many people, the information they have about sexual development and sexuality is cobbled together from experience. For parents this experience is invaluable but it may not be a complete picture. For example, many people do not know that the proper term for the genital area in women is the *vulva* not the *vagina*. It is also valuable to learn what is current in the study of sexuality as your kids get older. The environment kids develop in and the way they are exposed to information can be very different from the environment many parents grew up in.

- **Start talking to your children early and anticipate:** Often parents will put off talking to kids about sex, thinking they are too young or haven't matured enough. While determining the right time to talk to your kids is tricky, remember that they will hear a great deal of information, often misinformation, from their peers. This may happen much earlier than parents anticipate. A great place to start is teaching young preschool kids the appropriate terms for their anatomy and then progressing to more complex information as they develop. For more resources to help you talk to your kids, see the list of websites at the end of this chapter.

- **Acknowledge diversity and discuss your values with your children:** Kids will always compare themselves to others and to the images they see online or in the media. Explain to them that breasts, penises, and vulvas come in all shapes and sizes and there is no single definition of normal. It is also important to have open conversations with your children (keeping in mind that they may not agree with you) about your values on issues such as when it is appropriate to start having sex, the use of birth control, and what love and marriage or committed relationships, with sex included, mean to you.

SOURCE: Wilson, P. (1994). Forming a partnership between parents and sexuality educators. *SIECUS Report, 22,* 1–5.

Friendships are an essential part of adolescent social development (Ojanen et al., 2010). Children learn acceptable attitudes and behaviours for common games, sports, and even the latest media trends from their friends.

In their relationships with each other, boys and girls in middle childhood often imitate adults.

© Pressmaster/Shutterstock

SAME-SEX PEERS During middle childhood, adolescents overwhelmingly prefer same-sex to other-sex friends (Hendrick & Hendrick, 2000; Mehta & Strough, 2010). Although other-sex friendships do develop, the majority of early play is done in same-sex groupings (Fabes et al., 2003). Early on, these friendships tend to be activity based (friends are made because of shared interests or proximity), but by early adolescence, affective qualities (such as trust, loyalty, honesty) replace the activity-based interests (Bigelow, 1977; Ojanen et al., 2010). As a result, friendships in adolescence become more stable, supportive, and intimate than they were before this time.

Peers are a major catalyst in the decision to partake in voluntary sexual experimentation with others. Often initial sexual experimentation takes place among preadolescents of the same sex. Same-sex experimentation is quite common in childhood, even among people who grow up to be predominantly heterosexual.

OTHER-SEX PEERS For most children, preadolescence is when they begin to be aware of their sexuality and to see peers as potential boyfriends or girlfriends. Although this does not happen until the very end of this period, children as young as

11 begin to develop interest in others and may begin pairing off within larger groups of friends or at parties. Preadolescence has traditionally been a time of early sexual contact, such as kissing and petting, but for many this does not occur until later.

SIBLINGS Another fairly common childhood experience is sexual contact with siblings or close relatives, such as cousins. Most of the time, this occurs in sex games or fondling, but it can also occur as abuse, with an older sibling or relative coercing a younger one into unwanted sexual activity. Greenwald and Leitenberg (1989) found that among a sample of college students, 17 percent reported having sibling sexual contact before age 13. Only a small percentage involved force or threat, and penetration was rare. Research on sexual contact between siblings suggests that it can be psychologically damaging when there is a large difference between the ages of siblings or coercive force is used (Finkelhor, 1980; Rudd & Herzberger, 1999).

Review Questions

1 Explain physical and psychosexual development in middle childhood through the preteen years.

2 Identify and discuss the types of sexual behaviours that are common in middle childhood through the preteen years.

3 Discuss the importance of relationships with parents, peers, and siblings in childhood through preadolescence.

Adolescence: Ages 12 to 18

Adolescence begins after the onset of puberty and ends when the person achieves "adulthood," signified by a sense of individual identity and an ability to cope independently with internal and external problems (Lovejoy & Estridge, 1987). People reach adulthood at different times; adolescence can end in the late teens, or it can stretch into a person's 20s. Most societies throughout history have developed rites of passage around puberty. For example, the Jewish Bar or Bat Mitzvah, Christian confirmation, and the Hispanic Quinceanera.

We know the most about this developmental period because of ongoing research studies on adolescent sexual behaviour (Fortenberry, 2013). Overall, we know there is no other time in the life cycle that so many things happen at once: the body undergoes rapid change; the individual begins a psychological separation from the parents; and peer relationships, dating, and sexuality increase in importance.

Physical Development: Big Changes

During early adolescence children can add 15 centimetres in height and gain 5–10 kilograms in less than a year. Boys may develop a lower voice and a more decidedly adult physique, whereas girls develop breasts and a more female physique. Biological changes take place in virtually every system of the body and include changes in cardiovascular status, energy levels, sexual desire, mood, and personality characteristics (Hamburg, 1986).

Because girls' growth spurts happen earlier than boys', there is a period when girls will be at least equal in height and often taller than boys. Girls who consider themselves to be "on time" with regards to their progression of adolescent development feel more attractive and positive about their bodies than those who consider themselves "early" or "late" (Hamburg, 1986). The combination of changing bodies, peer pressure, and the beginnings of sexual activity may influence some adolescents to have a negative **body image** (Brumberg, 1997).

Females

Menarche is the hallmark of female puberty and is often viewed as one of the most important events in a woman's life (Ersoy et al., 2005; we discussed the physiology of menarche in Chapter 3). Menstruation may be accompanied by cramps and discomfort, as well as embarrassment if the onset is at an inopportune time (such as in the middle of school). Some girls begin menstruation with little idea of what is happening or with myths about it being bad

© Miriam Reik/Alamy

Many cultures have rituals of passage that signify the entry of the child into adulthood. Here a young Jewish boy reads from the Torah at his Bar Mitzvah.

body image
A person's feelings and mental picture of his or her own body's beauty.

to bathe, swim, exercise, or engage in sexual activities during this time. Many girls are unfamiliar with their genital anatomy, making tasks such as inserting tampons difficult and frustrating (Carroll, 2009; M. Diamond & Diamond, 1986).

The beginning of menstruation can mean different things to an adolescent girl depending on her family and/or cultural context. Girls who are prepared for menstruation and who are recognized for their intellectual or creative capabilities are more likely to describe pleasurable reactions to the onset of menstruation than girls who are not prepared (Teitelman, 2004).

Males

For males the first sign of sexual maturity—ejaculation—is generally a pleasurable experience. Adolescent development in males differs in many ways from the development in girls. Boys' voices change more drastically than girls', and their growth spurts tend to be more extreme and dramatic, usually accompanied by an increase in appetite. Because boys' adolescent growth tends to be more uneven and sporadic than girls', adolescent males will often appear gangly or awkward. As boys continue to develop, the larynx enlarges, bones grow, and the frame takes on a more adult appearance. It is common for adolescent males to experience frequent spontaneous erections, nocturnal emissions, increased levels of masturbation, and the development of sexual desire for a partner.

Psychosexual Development: Emotional Self-Awareness

Adolescence is, by far, the most psychologically and socially difficult of the life cycle changes. Adolescents must achieve comfort with their bodies, develop an identity separate from their parents, try to prove their capacity to establish meaningful intimate and sexual relationships, begin to think abstractly and futuristically, and establish emotional self-awareness (Gemelli, 1996).

Adolescence (Ages 12 to 18)

In early adolescence, preteens begin to shift their role from child to adolescent, trying to forge an identity separate from their family by establishing stronger relationships with peers. Same-sex friendships are common by Grade 8 and may develop into first same-sex sexual contacts as well (L.M. Diamond, 2000). The importance of a best friend grows as an adolescent matures. In fact, by the end of high school, both girls and boys rated their relationship with their best friend as their most important relationship (B.B. Brown et al., 1997; see Figure 10.2).

Early adolescence, as most of us remember, is often filled with "cliques," as people look to peers for validation and standards of behaviour. Dating also often begins at this age, which drives many adolescents to become preoccupied with their bodily appearance and to experiment with different "looks." Young adolescents are often very concerned with body image at this time. Some young males and females, in an attempt to achieve the perfect figure, will endlessly diet, sometimes to the point of serious eating disorders, or will try drugs such as steroids to achieve the body they desire (Pisetsky et al., 2008).

© DreamPictures/Getty Images

In early and middle adolescence, teens try on different looks, from trendy to rebellious, as they develop an identity separate from their parents.

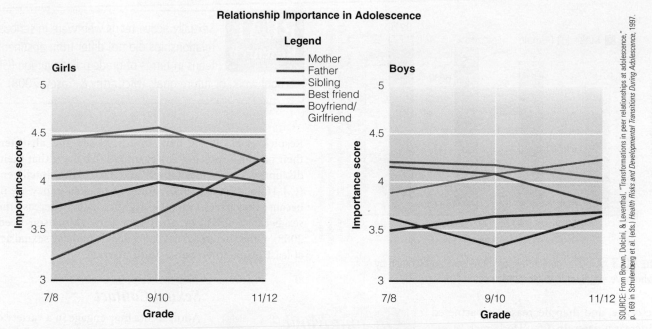

Relationship Importance in Adolescence

SOURCE: From Brown, Dolcini, & Leventhal, "Transformations in peer relationships at adolescence," p. 169 in Schulenberg et al. (eds.) *Health Risks and Developmental Transitions During Adolescence*, 1997.

FIGURE **10.2** This graph shows the age differences in mean ratings of the importance of each type of relationship to one's life during adolescence (1 = not at all important; 5 = extremely important).

By about age 14, most adolescents experience an increasing interest in intimate relationships. The social environment also helps build this interest through school-sponsored dances and private parties (B.B. Brown et al., 1997). Adolescents who have not yet reached puberty or those who feel they might be gay or lesbian may feel intense pressure to express interest in other-sex relationships at this time (K.M. Cohen & Savin-Williams, 1996). Many adolescents increase the frequency of dating as they try to integrate sexuality into their growing capacity for adult-to-adult intimacy.

For the average middle adolescent, dating consists of going to movies or spending time together after school or on weekends. Early dating is often quite informal, and going out in mixed groups is very popular. During this period, couples develop longer-term and more exclusive relationships, and early sexual experimentation (deep kissing, fondling) may also begin.

Oftentimes, the pattern for gay, lesbian, bisexual, or unsure/questioning adolescents may be quite different from that of their heterosexual counterparts. They might not fit into the heterosexual dating scene and may try to hide their disinterest in the discussions of the other sex (Faulkner & Cranston, 1998). Rates of depression, loneliness, drug and alcohol abuse, and suicide are significantly higher for gay, lesbian, bisexual, and unsure/questioning youth (Cochran et al., 2007; King et al., 2008; Marshal et al., 2009; McCabe et al., 2010; Needham & Austin, 2010; Zhao et al., 2010). Family reactions to a gay, lesbian, or bisexual identity and self-expectations may result in depression or confusion. Psychologists have found that gay, lesbian, and bisexual youths who have supportive families and high levels of family connectedness have better health outcomes than those without this family support (Doty et al., 2010; Needham & Austin, 2010; Ryan et al., 2009).

There is no clear line between adolescence and adulthood. Almost all cultures allow marriage and other adult privileges in late adolescence, although there still may be certain restrictions (such as needing parental permission to marry). Late adolescence was, until recently, the stage during which people in Western cultures were expected to begin their search for marital partners through serious dating. As we discuss in Chapter 13, many of today's adults wait longer to establish permanent relationships and perhaps marry.

Sexual Behaviour: Experimentation and Abstinence

Although many television reports and news headlines about adolescent sexual behaviour seem to imply that adolescents are reckless and becoming sexually active at young ages, the National Survey of Sexual Health and Behavior (NSSHB) in the United States found that today's adolescents are more likely to abstain or act responsibly about sexual behaviour (Fortenberry et al., 2010).

 REAL Research Whereas 31 percent of teens say their parents most influence their decisions about sex, 43 percent of parents say friends most influence their teens' decisions about sex (Albert, 2009).

Masturbation

As boys and girls enter adolescence, masturbation sharply increases, and the activity is more directed toward achieving orgasm than simply producing pleasurable sensations. Masturbation is common throughout the life span, increases during

Childhood and Adolescent Sexuality **279**

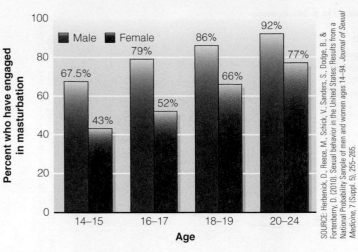

SOURCE: Herbenick, D., Reece, M., Schick, V., Sanders, S., Dodge, B., & Fortenberry, D. (2010). Sexual behavior in the United States: Results from a National Probability Sample of men and women ages 14–94. *Journal of Sexual Medicine, 7* (Suppl. 5), 255–265.

FIGURE 10.3 Average percentage of young men and women by age who have engaged in masturbation.

adolescence, and then decreases as partnered sex increases later in life (Herbenick et al., 2010a). Kinsey and his colleagues (1953) also found a sharp increase between the ages of 13 and 15 in boys, with 82 percent of boys having masturbated by age 15. The girls' pattern was more gradual, with 20 percent having masturbated by age 15 and no sharp increase at any point. Figure 10.3 outlines the rates of masturbation at various ages.

Masturbation rates in males are generally higher than in females (Herbenick et al., 2010a). This could be because of several things. First of all, women may underreport their masturbation in surveys because they are less comfortable discussing it. Boys tend to reinforce the social acceptability of masturbation by talking about it more freely among themselves. There may also be biophysical reasons for more frequent male masturbation, such as the obvious nature of the male erection and higher levels of testosterone.

The Onset of Sexual Behaviour

Adolescents often think about many factors when deciding to be sexual. Perceived family and peer attitudes about sexuality are key factors in the decision to become sexual (Akers et al., 2011). Heterosexual teens who delay sexual intercourse are more likely to live with both biological parents (Upchurch et al., 2001), feel a personal connection to their family (Meschke et al., 2000;

On Your Mind

I am 19 years old, and I masturbate at least twice a week, but not as much if I am having good sex with my girlfriend. But she tells me that she doesn't masturbate as much as I do. Why do teenage men masturbate so much more than teenage women?

abstinence
Refraining from intercourse and often other forms of sexual contact.

fellatio
The act of sexually stimulating the male genitals with the mouth.

cunnilingus
The act of sexually stimulating the female genitals with the mouth.

Resnick et al., 1997), have discussed sex and **abstinence** with their parents (Sprecher & Regan, 1996), believe that their mother disapproves of premarital sex, and have higher intelligence levels (C.J. Halpern et al., 2000). Some teens decide they are not ready because they haven't met the "right" person, whereas others delay sex because of STI or pregnancy fears (Morrison-Beedy et al., 2008). Other heterosexual teens decide to delay sexual activity, or at least sexual intercourse, until marriage.

Sexual Contact

Adolescents may engage in a variety of sexual behaviours, including kissing, oral sex, sexual intercourse, and anal sex. In Canada there are three major studies that have been conducted to collect information on sexual intercourse practices in Canadian youth. These studies include the B.C. Adolescent Health Survey (1992), sexualityandU.ca, 2012, and Health of Canada's Young People (2010).

KISSING AND PETTING Kissing and touching are the first sexual contact that most adolescents have with potential sexual partners. Coles and Stokes (1985) reported that 73 percent of 13-year-old girls and 60 percent of 13-year-old boys had kissed at least once. Because younger heterosexual girls tend to date older boys, they have higher rates of these kinds of activities at earlier ages than heterosexual boys do, but the differences diminish over time. For example, 20 percent of 13-year-old boys reported touching a girl's breast, whereas 35 percent of 13-year-old girls reported having had their breasts touched.

ORAL SEX Acceptance of oral sex has increased among young people. Kinsey and his colleagues (1948, 1953) reported that 17 percent of adolescents reported engaging in **fellatio** (fil-LAY-she-oh) and 11 percent in **cunnilingus** (kun-nah-LING-gus). The U.S. National Survey of Family Growth found that among teenagers between the ages of 15 and 19, 54 percent of girls and 55 percent of boys reported having engaged in oral sex (Flanigan et al., 2005; Lindberg et al., 2008). The more recent NSSHB found that oral sex has increased in all age groups (Herbenick et al., 2010a).

For many years, there has been a popular perception in the media that heterosexual teens engage in oral sex instead of sexual intercourse because it allows them to preserve their virginity and eliminates pregnancy risk (Stein, 2008; Wind, 2008). However, researchers have challenged this idea (Lindberg et al., 2008). An analysis of the sexual practices of 2271 15- to 19-year-olds found that oral sex was more common in adolescent couples who had already initiated sexual intercourse—87 percent of non-virgin teens reported engaging in oral sex, whereas only 27 percent of virgins reported engaging in oral sex (Lindberg et al., 2008). In fact, six months after first engaging in sexual intercourse, 82 percent of heterosexual teens have engaged in oral sex. The majority of heterosexual teens engage in oral sex after they have already engaged in sexual intercourse.

Other research on adolescent oral sex has found that heterosexual female adolescents are significantly more likely than heterosexual males to indicate they have given oral sex (Lindberg et al., 2008). Heterosexual teens from lower socioeconomic classes and those with more conservative attitudes about sexuality were significantly less likely to report engaging in oral sex, whereas heterosexual adolescents from higher socioeconomic classes and those with more liberal attitudes were more likely to report engaging in oral sex.

ANAL SEX Adolescents who had already engaged in penile-vaginal intercourse were more likely to have engaged in anal sex (Lindberg et al., 2008). For some gay adolescents, engaging in anal sex is their defining moment of "losing their virginity." One study of college students found that 80 percent of respondents believed that a man or woman could lose his or her virginity with a same-sex partner, whereas 10 percent believed that only a man could do so (Trotter & Alderson, 2007). More research is needed in this area.

HETEROSEXUAL INTERCOURSE It is important for teachers, adults, and youth to understand the legal perspective surrounding age of consent for sexual behaviour in Canada (SEICCAN, 2009). On May 1, 2008 the Tackling Violent Crime Act released its regulations regarding the legal age of sexual consent in Canada. The following regulations were created:

*The age of consent for sexual activity is **16 years**. It was raised from 14 years on May 1, 2008 by the Tackling Violent Crime Act. However, the age of consent is **18 years** where the sexual activity "exploits" the young person—when it involves prostitution, pornography or occurs in a relationship of authority, trust or dependency (e.g., with a teacher, coach or babysitter). Sexual activity can also be considered exploitative based on the nature and circumstances of the relationship, e.g., the young person's age, the age difference between the young person and their partner, how the relationship developed (quickly, secretly, or over the Internet) and how the partner may have controlled or influenced the young person.*

The Criminal Code provides "close in age" or "peer group" exceptions. For example, a 14 or 15 year old can consent to sexual activity with a partner as long as the partner is less than five years older and there is no relationship of trust, authority or dependency or any other exploitation of the young person. This means that if the partner is 5 years or older than the 14 or 15 year old, any sexual activity will be considered a criminal offence unless it occurs after they are married to each other (in accordance with the "solemnization" of marriage requirements that are established in each province and territory, governing how and when a marriage can be performed, including the minimum age at which someone may marry).

The Criminal Code protects all Canadians, including children, against sexual abuse and exploitation. For example, the Criminal Code contains offences that protect everyone against all forms of sexual assault (section 271); sexual assault with a weapon, threats to a third party or causing bodily harm (section 272); and aggravated sexual assault (section 273), voyeurism (section 162), obscenity (section 163) and trafficking in persons (section 279.01).

Children are also protected by child-specific offences in the Criminal Code. These offences include Sexual Interference (section 151), invitation to sexual touching (section 152), sexual exploitation (section 153), incest (section 155), child pornography (section 163.1), luring a child (section 172.1), exposure (subsection 173(2)), procuring (sections 170 and 171), child prostitution (subsections 286.1(2), 286.2(2) and 286.3(2)), bestiality (section 160) and child sex tourism (subsections 7(4.1)–7(4.3). In addition to these criminal laws against child sexual abuse and exploitation, each province and territory has its own laws to protect children against abuse, exploitation and neglect.*

We know that by Grade 9 close to 20 percent of girls and boys have had sexual intercourse (see Figure 10.4). Once adolescents have graduated from high school or are over 18, more than 65 percent report having had sexual intercourse (Eaton et al., 2006; Herbenick et al., 2010a; Smylie, Maticka-Tyndale & Boyd, 2008). Although the number of sexually active teens hasn't changed much in the last two decades, there has been a slight decline in the number of teens engaging in sexual intercourse since 1996 (Abma et al., 2010; see Figure 10.5).

In most of the developed world, the majority of heterosexual men and women engage in sexual intercourse during their teen years (Alan Guttmacher Institute, 2002). In fact, the age at which heterosexual teenagers become sexually active is similar across comparable developed countries, such as Canada, France, Sweden, and the United States.

However, males and females tend to react differently to their first sexual intercourse. The National Health and Social Life

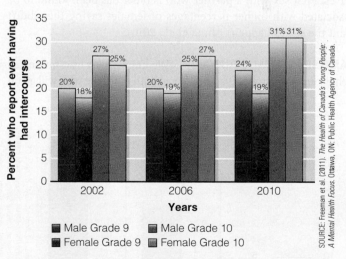

SOURCE: Freeman et al. (2011). *The Health of Canada's Young People: A Mental Health Focus*. Ottawa, ON: Public Health Agency of Canada.

FIGURE **10.4** Approximate percentages of Grade 9 and 10 males and females who report ever having had intercourse, 2002, 2006, 2010.

* SOURCE: *Age of Consent to Sexual Activity, Frequently Asked Questions*, Department of Justice Canada February 2015. Reproduced with the permission of the Department of Justice Canada, 2015.

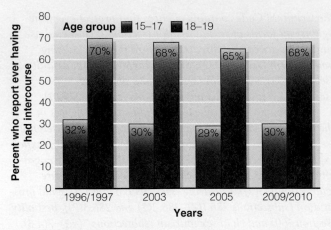

FIGURE **10.5** Percentage of Canadian youth aged 15–17, 18–19 reporting ever having sexual intercourse, 1996/1997, 2003, 2005, 2009/2010.

SOURCES: Rotermann, M. (2008). Trends in teen sexual behaviour and condom use. *Health Reports, 19,* (3), 1–5. Rotermann, M. (2012). Sexual behaviour and condom use of 15- to 24-year-olds in 2003 and 2009/2010. *Health Reports, 23,* (1), 1–5; The Society of Obstetricians and Gynaecologists of Canada, "Statistics on Sexual Intercourse Experience Among Canadian Teenagers." http://www.sexualityandu.ca/sexual-health/statistics1/statistics-on-sexual-intercourse-experience-among-canadian-teenagers. Reproduced and distributed on an "as is" basis with the permission of Statistics Canada.

Survey (1992) found that more than 90 percent of men said they wanted to have sexual intercourse the first time they did it; more than half were motivated by curiosity, whereas only a quarter said they had sexual intercourse out of affection for their partner. About 70 percent of women reported wanting to have sexual intercourse. Nearly half of the women said they had sex the first time out of affection for their partner, whereas a quarter cited curiosity as their primary motivation. In a U.S. survey, 62 percent of males in contrast to 43 percent of females said they wanted to have sexual intercourse the first time it happened (Abma et al. 2010; see Figure 10.6 for more information about gender differences in feelings about first sexual intercourse). For many teens, this experience contributes to the redefining of self and the reconfiguration of relationships with friends, family members, and sexual partners (Upchurch et al., 1998).

Although the majority of female teens have first sex partners who are one to three years older, 25 percent of female teens have first sex partners who are four or more years older than themselves. First sex with a partner who is older has been found to be associated with higher percentages of females saying they didn't want the sex to happen (Abma et al., 2010).

SAME-SEX SEXUAL BEHAVIOUR   We know that same-sex sexual behaviour is common in adolescence, both for those who will go on

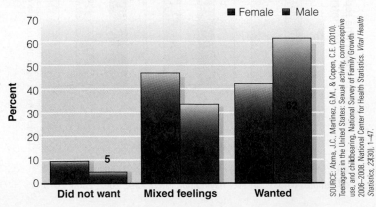

FIGURE **10.6**   How much first sex was wanted when it happened among females and males aged 18–24 who had their first sex before age 20: United States, 2006–2008.

SOURCE: Abma, J.C., Martinez, G.M., & Copen, C.E. (2010). Teenagers in the United States: Sexual activity, contraceptive use, and childbearing, National Survey of Family Growth 2006–2008. National Center for Health Statistics. *Vital Health Statistics, 23*(30), 1–47.

to have predominantly heterosexual relationships and those who will have predominantly homosexual relationships. Some gay and lesbian adolescents experience sexual intercourse during their teenage years, before they identify themselves as lesbian or gay (Saewyc et al., 1998).

It is difficult to determine actual figures for adolescent same-sex sexual behaviour. Studies of high-school students find that about 10 percent to 13 percent report being "unsure" about their sexual orientation, whereas 1 percent to 6 percent consider themselves homosexual or bisexual; still, anywhere from 8 percent to 12 percent report sexual contact with same-sex partners (Faulkner & Cranston, 1998). Such research, however, relies on self-reports; people may define homosexuality differently, or they may not be comfortable being open about their experiences because of homosexual stigma.

OTHER SEXUAL SITUATIONS   There are many other types of sexual situations that adolescents can experience. Some teenagers, especially runaways, both male and female, engage in prostitution. Others make money by becoming involved in child pornography, posing nude for pictures, or performing sexual acts. Although there are few comprehensive studies of the results of engaging in prostitution or pornography as an adolescent (or younger), there is every clinical indication that it results in many sexual and psychological difficulties later on (we discuss this subject more in Chapter 18).

Many of the sexual variations seen in adults, such as transvestism, exhibitionism, and voyeurism, may begin in adolescence, although it is more common for these desires to be expressed in early adulthood. We discuss these sexual variations in depth in Chapter 14.

Ethnic Differences in Sexual Activity

An adolescent's ethnicity, race, and culture affect his or her sexual attitudes, which sexual behaviours he or she engages in, and the frequency of these behaviours (Centers for Disease Control and Prevention, 2010g; Fortenberry et al., 2010; Zimmer-Gembeck & Helfand, 2008).

Several ethnic and racial differences have been found in participation of certain sexual behaviours, such as oral and anal sex, age of first sexual intercourse, and age differences between sexual partners (Eaton et al., 2006; Fortenberry et al., 2010; Frost & Driscoll, 2006; Herbenick et al., 2010a; Lindberg et al., 2008). Ethnic and racial differences have also been found in contraceptive use, teen pregnancy, birth rates, abortion, and rates of STIs (Buffardi et al., 2008; Forhan, 2008; Martin et al., 2007; Martinez et al., 2006; Mosher et al., 2004; Reece et al., 2010c; Ventura et al., 2007). Although work is being done in the area of ethnicity and sexuality in Canada (Maticka-Tyndale, Shirpak, & Chinichian, 2007; Shirpak, Maticka-Tyndale, & Chinichian, 2008) more research is needed in this area in Canada.

Influences: Peers, Family, and Religion

The decision to engage in sexual contact with another person is a personal one, yet it is influenced by many social factors, including peers, family, and religion. A number of other social factors influence sexual behaviour as well, and we discuss here a few of the more important ones.

Peer Influences

Peer pressure is often cited as the most important influence on teen sexual behaviour, and adolescence is certainly a time when the influence of one's friends and peers is at a peak (Busse et al., 2010). Many adolescents base their own self-worth on peer approval (Akers et al., 2011; Rudolph et al., 2005). Even among preadolescents, peer influences are strong; among Grade 6 youth who have engaged in sexual intercourse, students were more likely to initiate sexual intercourse if they thought that peers were engaging in it and that it would bring them some kind of social gain. Those who did not initiate sexual intercourse were more likely to believe that their behaviour would be stigmatized or disapproved of by their peers (Grunbaum et al., 2002).

A person's perception of what his or her peers are doing has a greater influence than peers' actual behaviour. Among those subject to, and applying peer pressure, many heterosexual adolescent males feel the need to "prove" their masculinity, leading to early sexual activity. Peer pressure is often rated as one of the top reasons that adolescents give for engaging in sexual intercourse.

Relationship with Parents

Good parental communication, an atmosphere of honesty and openness in the home, and reasonable rules about dating and relationships are among the most important factors associated with adolescents delaying their first sexual intercourse (Akers et al., 2011; Hahm et al., 2008; Lam et al., 2008; Regnerus & Luckies, 2006). Heterosexual children from these homes are also more likely to use contraception when they do engage in sexual intercourse (Halpern-Felsher et al., 2004; Zimmer-Gembeck & Helfand, 2008). This is the case among almost all races and ethnic groups (L.M. Baumeister et al., 1995; Brooks-Gunn & Furstenberg, 1989; Kotchick et al., 1999).

Researchers have found that many parents do not discuss sex before an adolescent's first sexual experience (Beckett et al., 2010). If a parent does talk about sex, it is generally the mother who tends to be the primary communicator about sexuality to children (L.M. Baumeister et al., 1995; Raffaelli & Green, 2003).

REAL Research Lesbian, gay, and bisexual men have lower levels of parental support than heterosexual men (Needham & Austin, 2010). Lower levels of parental support are related to depression, drug and alcohol use, and suicidal thoughts.

On Your Mind

Sometimes I feel I should have sex just to get it over with—being a virgin is embarrassing! It's pretty hard to resist when everybody else seems to be doing it.

The decision to have sex is an important one. Too often this step is taken without consideration of its consequences—for example, whether we feel psychologically or emotionally ready and whether our partner does. Sex should never be the result of pressure (by our partner, our friends, or ourselves). There may be many reasons that we want to delay sexual experimentation—including moral or religious reasons. Teens also often overestimate the numbers of their friends who are sexually active.

Typically mothers talk more to daughters about sexuality than sons (Martin & Luke, 2010).

In the U.S. National Longitudinal Study of Adolescent Health (2002), it was reported that there is a maternal influence on the timing of first sexual intercourse for heterosexual adolescents, especially for females. A mother's satisfaction with her relationship with her daughter and frequent communication about sex is related to a delay of first sexual intercourse (Lam et al., 2008; Tsui-Sui et al., 2010). Fathers are also important; girls who have a close relationship with their father are also more likely to delay sex (Day & Padilla-Walker, 2009; Regnerus & Luchies, 2006; Wilson et al., 2010).

Religion

Although the relationship between religiosity and sexual activity is complex, in general, heterosexual youths that identify as religious tend to delay first sexual intercourse, have fewer incidents of premarital sexual activity, and have fewer sexual partners (S. Hardy & Raffaelli, 2003; Hull et al., 2010; Nonnemaker et al., 2003). The correlation may be because young people who value religion in their lives are less sexually experienced overall (P. King & Boyatzis, 2004; S. D. White & DeBlassie, 1992). Not only do major Western religions and many other world religions discourage premarital sex, but religious adolescents also tend to develop friendships and relationships within their religious institutions, and thus have strong ties to people who are more likely to disapprove of early sexual activity. However, once teens begin engaging in sexual behaviours, religious affiliation and frequency of religious attendance have been found to have little impact on frequency of sexual behaviours (R. Jones et al., 2005).

Contraception, Pregnancy and Abortion: Complex Issues

Although we discuss pregnancy, contraception, and abortion more in Chapters 5 and 6, we touch on these concepts here. Approximately 70–75 percent of Canadian teens use a contraceptive method when they engage in sexual intercourse, and condoms are the most popular method (Abma et al., 2010; see Figure 10.7). Adolescents who are able to talk to their mothers

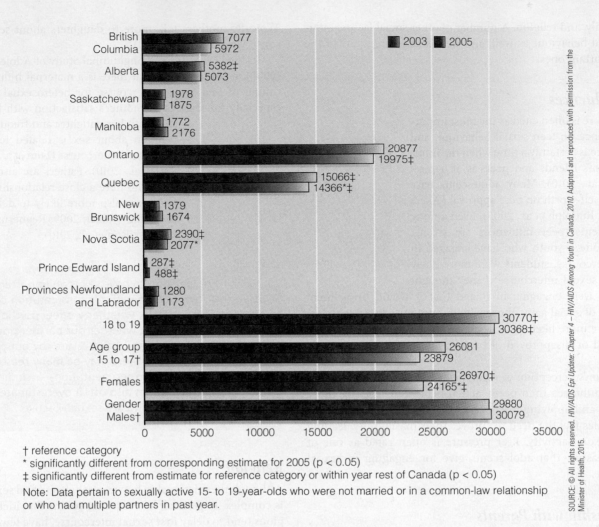

† reference category

* significantly different from corresponding estimate for 2005 (p < 0.05)

‡ significantly different from estimate for reference category or within year rest of Canada (p < 0.05)

Note: Data pertain to sexually active 15- to 19-year-olds who were not married or in a common-law relationship or who had multiple partners in past year.

FIGURE **10.7** Condom use in Canadian adolescents by sex and region.

about sexuality are more likely to use contraception than adolescents who cannot talk to their mothers (Lam et al., 2008; Meschke et al., 2000). In fact, condoms are the most frequently used contraceptive method among sexually active adolescents (Abma et al., 2010; Reece et al., 2010c). However, in the Sexual Health Toronto (2007) survey, it was found that kids who began having sex at an earlier age were more inconsistent in their condom use.

Of all the areas of adolescent sexual behaviour, we probably know the most about teenage pregnancy because of its many impacts on the life of the teenager, the teenager's family, and

> **REAL Research**
>
> A study of 24 industrialized countries found that the three most popular contraceptive methods used by teens were condoms, condoms along with birth control pills, and birth control pills alone (Godeau et al., 2008).

society as a whole. The teen birth rate in Canada (Statistics Canada, Teen Pregnancy, 2015) was 1.9/1000 in females under the age of 15 and 29.2/1000 in females between the ages of 15 and 19 in 2005. For comparison, the rate in 15- to 19-year-olds in the United States was 42.5 births per 1000 females in 2007, which was higher than many other countries around the world (Abma et al., 2010; Brugman et al., 2010). The long-term consequences of teenage pregnancy may be difficult for the mother, child, and extended family. Teenage mothers are more likely to drop out of school, have poorer physical and mental health, and be on welfare than their non-childbearing peers. Their children often have lower birth weights, poorer health and cognitive abilities, more behavioural problems, and fewer educational opportunities (Meschke et al., 2000). Teen parenting also has an impact on others, such as the parents of the teens (who may end up having to take care of their children's children), and on society in general, because these parents are more likely to need government assistance.

Teen pregnancies do not always preclude teen mothers from living healthy, fulfilling lives. Many teenagers who become pregnant raise healthy babies while pursuing their own interests. However,

Teen pregnancy can be a challenge for a mother. Those who cope the best with having a child receive strong support from their family and peers.

the problems a teenage mother faces are many, especially if there is no partner participating in the child's care. A teen who has support from her partner, family, and friends, and who is able to stay in school, has a better chance of living a fulfilling life.

In studies of teen pregnancy and birth, most of the focus has been on the mothers, who often bear the brunt of the emotional, personal, and financial costs of childbearing (Wei, 2000). Adolescent fathers are more difficult to study. Teenage fathers may not support their partners and become uninvolved soon after, and thus the problem of single mothers raising children can be traced, in part, to the lack of responsibility of teen fathers. Society asks little of the teenage male, and there are few social pressures on him to take responsibility for his offspring. Some adolescent fathers do accept their role in both pregnancy and parenthood, and realistically assess their responsibilities toward the mother and child. Ideally, teenage fathers should be integrated into the lives of their children and should be expected to take equal responsibility for them.

Sexually Transmitted Infections: Education and Prevention

Although we discuss STIs in great detail in Chapter 7, here we briefly discuss adolescent STI rates. Sexually active teens are at greater risk for acquiring some STIs for behavioural, cultural, and biological reasons (Abma et al., 2010). Rates of chlamydia and gonorrhea are rising among 15- to 19-year-olds more than any other age group (Abma et al., 2010). Although rates of other STIs are lower, they have been steadily increasing every year (Weinstock et al., 2004).

Although gay, lesbian, and bisexual youths may not need contraception for birth control purposes, they do need it for protection from STIs. Condom use is essential to protect against STIs such as chlamydia, gonorrhea, and HIV, which is found in all ethnic groups in Canada (see Figure 10.8). Researchers have found that gay men are less likely to use condoms than their straight counterparts (S.M. Blake et al., 2001; Saewyc et al., 1998). Increasing condom use in all teens, regardless of sexual orientation, is imperative in decreasing STIs.

Preventing STIs and teenage pregnancy are both important goals of sex education programs. In the following section, we discuss the importance of sexuality education and what is being taught in schools today.

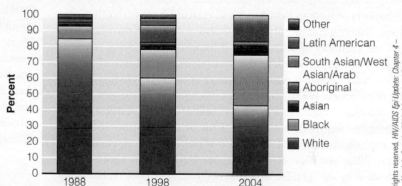

Note: Because of changes in the reporting of AIDS cases in Ontario, ethnicity/race was not available for cases reported after the second half of 2005.

FIGURE **10.8** Rate of HIV by ethnic origin.

Review Questions

1 Explain physical and psychosexual development in adolescence.

2 Explain what we know about the specific sexual behaviours that often occur during adolescence.

3 Identify and explain the influences on adolescent sexuality.

4 Identify and discuss the reasons that adolescents may be erratic users of contraception.

Childhood and Adolescent Sexuality

What Children Need to Know: Sexual Health Education

We opened this chapter with an interview with a Dutch sex educator. As we discussed, sexual health education inspires powerful emotions and a considerable amount of controversy. In fact, it may be one of the most heated topics in the field of sexuality, as different sides debate whether and how sexual health education programs should be implemented in Canadian schools.

Why Sexual Health Education Is Important

Although many people claim that knowledge about sexuality may be harmful, scientists have found that it is the lack of sexual health education, ignorance about sexual issues, or unresolved curiosity that is harmful (S. Gordon, 1986). Students who participate in comprehensive sexual health education programs are less permissive about premarital sex than students who do not take these courses. Accurate knowledge about sex may also lead to a more positive self-image and self-acceptance. Sexuality affects almost all aspects of human behaviour and relationships with other persons. Therefore, if we understand and accept our own sexuality and the sexuality of others, we will have more satisfying relationships. Some experts believe that not talking to children about sex before adolescence is a primary cause of sexual problems later in life (Calderone, 1983).

Another reason to support sexual health education in Canada is that children receive a lot of information about sex through the media, and much of it is not based on fact (Rideout et al., 2010; see Figure 10.9 for more information about media exposure by age, gender, and parents' education). A recent study

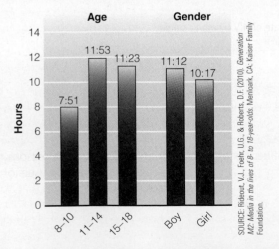

Average amount of total media exposure by:

SOURCE: Rideout, V.J., Foehr, U.G., & Roberts, D.F. (2010). *Generation M2: Media in the lives of 8- to 18-year-olds.* Menloark, CA: Kaiser Family Foundation.

FIGURE **10.9** Total media exposure by demographics, Kaiser Family Foundation, 2010.

in of Canadian youth reported that while the media and peers are often primary sources of information about sexuality, their preference is to first receive sexual health information from their school (80 percent), friends (76 percent), and parents (63 percent) (Byers et al., 2003; Frappier et al., 2008). Sex is present in the songs children listen to, the magazines they read, and the shows they watch on television and on the Internet. Although it is true that there is a growing number of educational sites on the Internet dedicated to sexuality (see the end of the Chapter for several Canadian based sites), there are also many poor sources of information on the Web.

> **REAL Research** Research on parent–adolescent communication has found that many adolescent boys receive little or no parental communication about sex (M. Epstein & Ward, 2008). Instead, boys learn about sex mostly from their peers and the media.

Proponents of sexual health education believe that sexual learning occurs even when there are no formalized sexual health education programs. When teachers or parents avoid children's questions or appear embarrassed or evasive, they reinforce children's ideas that sex is secret, mysterious, and bad (Walker & Milton, 2006). As adolescents approach puberty, they may feel anxious about their bodily changes or their relationships with other people. Many teenagers feel uncomfortable asking questions and may be pressured by their peers to engage in sexual activity when they do not feel ready. Giving adolescents information about sex can help them to deal with these changes. The majority of parents, teachers, and students want sexuality education to be taught in secondary schools and high schools and favour comprehensive sex education (Bleakley et al., 2006; Sex Information Council of Canada, 2010).

History of Sexual Education in Canada

People have always been curious about sex. However, it was only in the 20th century that the movement to develop formal and effective sexuality education programs began. Public discussion of sexuality was due, in part, to the moral purity movement of the late 19th century and the medicalization of sex movement in the early 20th century. Several developments in Canada and the United States set the stage for a push for sexual health education to be included in the school curriculum in Canada. Concern over skyrocketing rates of venereal diseases (what we now refer to as STIs) in the early 1900s, increasing rates of teenage pregnancy in the 1960s and 1970s, and the threat of HIV in the 1980s encouraged many school boards to push for the teaching of sexual health education in schools.

In Canada, as in the United States, the opposition to sexual health education has often been due to two attitudes: first, that sexuality is private, should be discouraged in children, and is best discussed in the context of a person's moral and religious beliefs; and second, that public schools are by their nature public, cannot discuss sex without giving children implicit permission to be sexual, and should not promote the moral or religious beliefs of any particular group. **Comprehensive sexual health education programs** are those that begin in kindergarten and continue through Grade 12; they include a wide variety of topics and help students to develop their own skills and learn factual information. **Abstinence-only programs** (primarily found in the United States) emphasize abstinence from all sexual behaviours, and they typically do not provide information about contraception or disease prevention. Interestingly, according to a recent survey of Canadian youth on what constitutes abstinence and/or sex (e.g., can oral sex still be considered abstinence from sex?), it is far from clear how abstinence is defined in our society (Byers, Henderson & Hobson, 2009; Randall and Byers, 2003).

Sexual Health Education Today

Sexual health education can have different goals. Knowledge acquisition, improving personal psychological adjustment, and improving relationships between partners are popular goals. Early sexual health education programs focused primarily on increasing knowledge levels and educating students about the risks of pregnancy (Kirby, 1992), believing that if knowledge levels were increased, then students would understand why it was important for them to avoid unprotected sexual intercourse. Soon sexual health education programs added values clarification and skills, including communication and decision-making skills. Our current sexual health education programs are based on the idea that if knowledge levels were increased and if students became more aware of their own values and had better decision-making skills, they would have an easier time talking to their partners and evaluating their own behavior.

The Public Health Agency of Canada (2008) published the third edition of the *Canadian Guidelines for Sexual Health Education*. This document was based on five principles for the development of sexual health education in Canada:

- *Accessibility*—Sexual health education should be accessible to all individuals, regardless of background.
- *Comprehensiveness*—Sexual health education should address diverse sexual health promotion and illness prevention objectives and should be a coordinated effort of individuals, organizations, agencies and governments.
- *Effectiveness of Educational Approaches and Methods*— Sexual health education should incorporate the key elements of knowledge acquisition and understanding, motivation and personal insight, skills that support sexual health and the critical awareness and skills needed to create environments conducive to sexual health.
- *Training and Administrative Support*—Sexual health education should be presented by confident, well-trained, knowledgeable and nonjudgmental individuals who receive strong administrative support from their agency or organization.*

- *Planning, Evaluation, Updating and Social Development*—Sexual health education achieves maximum impact when it is:
  - planned carefully in collaboration with intended audiences;
  - evaluated on program outcomes and participant feedback;
  - updated regularly; and
  - reinforced by environments that are conducive to sexual health education. (Public Health Agency of Canada, 2009)

In Canada sexual health education varies by province since education and curriculum development is determined at the provincial and territorial level. The provision of sexuality education in schools in Canada is still controversial. In 2010 in Ontario the government was forced to withdraw its revised sexual health curriculum for Grades 1–8 due to perceived opposition to the proposed curriculum revisions. A revised plan was released in 2015 and it will be interesting to follow the reactions to the new guidelines for sexual health education in Ontario (Young, 2015). However, according to a recent comparison of curriculum goals across the provinces, it appears that the new Ontario guidelines for sexual health education are similar to those in other provinces (see Table 10.1).

In the accompanying Sex in Real Life feature, we will provide an overview of what children want to know and what they are ready for. We recommend that you compare this information to the information in Table 10.1 describing at what ages children are exposed to various topics and concepts during sexual health education in schools across Canada.

Some of the abstinence-only programs use scare tactics to encourage abstinence, by claiming the consequences of premarital sexual behaviour to include:

[L]oss of reputation; limitations in dating/marriage choices; negative effects on sexual adjustment; negative effects on happiness (premarital sex, especially with more than one person, has been linked to the development of emotional illness [and the] loss of self-esteem); family conflict and possible premature separation from the family; confusion regarding personal value (e.g., "Am I loved because I am me, because of my personality and looks, or because I am a sex object?"); and loss of goals. (Kantor, 1992, p. 4)

Effects and Results of Sexuality Education Programs

The main way that researchers determine whether a sexual health program is successful is by measuring behavioural changes after a

---

comprehensive sexual health education programs
Programs that often begin in kindergarten and continue through Grade 12, presenting a wide variety of topics to help students develop their own skills while learning factual information.

abstinence-only programs
Sexual health education programs that emphasize abstinence from all sexual behaviours.

The grade at which children are expected to know the names of all body parts:

- Ontario: Grade 1
- B.C.: Kindergarten
- Alberta: Kindergarten
- Saskatchewan: Grade 5 (possibly earlier)
- Manitoba: Kindergarten
- Quebec: By 5 years old
- New Brunswick: Grade 6
- PEI: Grade 6
- Nova Scotia: Grade 3
- Newfoundland and Labrador: Grade 4

The grade at which children are told about STIs and their prevention:

- Ontario: Grade 7
- B.C.: Grade 6
- Alberta: Grade 6
- Saskatchewan: Grade 6
- Manitoba: Grade 7
- Quebec: Between 12 and 17 years old
- New Brunswick: Grades 9 and 10
- P.E.I: Grade 8 (expected to understand abstinence in Grade 7)
- Nova Scotia: Between Grades 5 and 7: HIV/AIDS mentioned in Grade 5, consequences of sex in Grade 6, contraceptive methods in Grade 7
- Newfoundland and Labrador: Grade 7 (HIV/AIDS mentioned in Grade 5)

The grade at which children are introduced to the concept of sexual orientation:

- Ontario: Grade 3
- B.C.: Grade 6
- Alberta: Unclear
- Saskatchewan: Grade 3
- Manitoba: Unclear
- Quebec: By 5 years old
- New Brunswick: Grade 8
- PEI: Grade 8
- Nova Scotia: Grade 3
- Newfoundland and Labrador: Grade 9 (may be mentioned earlier)

The grade at which children are told about Internet safety and/or sexting:

- Ontario: Grade 4
- B.C.: Grade 4
- Alberta: Unclear
- Saskatchewan: Grade 4
- Manitoba: Unclear
- Quebec: Unclear, but strong focus on safety/exploitation starting in kindergarten
- New Brunswick: Unclear
- PEI: Unclear
- Nova Scotia: Grade 8
- Newfoundland and Labrador: Unclear

The grade at which children are introduced to the concept of gender identity:

- Ontario: Grade 3
- B.C.: Grade 6
- Alberta: Unclear
- Saskatchewan: Grade 1
- Manitoba: Grade 5
- Quebec: Between 8 and 11 years old
- New Brunswick: Grade 6
- P.E.I.: Unclear
- Nova Scotia: Grade 4
- Newfoundland and Labrador: Unclear

The grade at which children are told about birth control:

- Ontario: Grade 7
- B.C.: Grade 6 (unclear)
- Alberta: Grade 8
- Saskatchewan: Grade 9
- Manitoba: Grade 7
- Quebec: Between 12 and 17 years old
- New Brunswick: Grades 9 and 10
- P.E.I.: Grade 8 (expected to understand abstinence in Grade 7)
- Nova Scotia: Grade 7
- Newfoundland and Labrador: Grade 8

The grade at which children are told about sexual abuse:

- Ontario: Grade 4
- B.C.: Kindergarten
- Alberta: Grade 8
- Saskatchewan: Grade 3
- Manitoba: Unclear
- Quebec: By 5 years old
- New Brunswick: Grade 8
- PEI: Grade 8
- Nova Scotia: Grade 5
- Newfoundland and Labrador: Grade 2

The grade at which children are expected to understand consent (healthy relationships in general are discussed earlier, or the two are blurred in many provinces):

- Ontario: Grade 7 (some mention in Grade 2)
- B.C.: Grade 8
- Alberta: Grade 8
- Saskatchewan: Grade 9
- Manitoba: Grade 5
- Quebec: Between 10 and 11 years old
- New Brunswick: Grade 7, emphasized in Grades 9 and 10
- P.E.I.: Grade 9
- Nova Scotia: Grade 7
- Newfoundland and Labrador: Grade 8

Note: Quebec does not have a formal dedicated sex education curriculum, opting instead to integrate this instruction into other subjects. This approach has resulted in some criticism.

SOURCE: Global News, "Sexual Education Compared Across Canada," (2015, February 24) by Leslie Young. Retrieved July 28, 2015, from http://globalnews.ca/news/1847912/sexual-education-compared-across-canada.

SEX in Real Life

What Do Children Want to Know and What Are They Ready For?

Because developmental differences influence children's ability to comprehend sexuality education, educators often evaluate what types of questions students ask to develop programs that can meet the needs of different age levels. Many proponents of sexual health education programs believe that these programs should be sequential (i.e., there should be a logical order in the curriculum) and comprehensive (i.e., they should include information on biological, psychological, social, and spiritual components). Following are some typical questions students ask at various ages and suggestions for what to include in sexuality education programs at these levels.

Age Range	Developmental Issues	Questions Children Might Ask	Focus of Sexuality Education
3 to 5 years	Shorter attention spans	*What is that?* (referring to specific body parts) *What do mommies do? What do daddies do? Where do babies come from?*	At this level, sexual health education can focus on the roles of family members, the development of a positive self-image, and an understanding that living things grow, reproduce, and die.
6 to 8 years	Very curious about how the body works	*Where was I before I was born? How does my mommy get a baby? Did I come from an egg?*	Sexual health education can include information on plant and animal reproduction, gender similarities and differences, growth and development, and self-esteem.
9 to 12 years	Curiosity about their bodies continues, and heterosexual children are often interested in the other sex and reproduction; gay, lesbian, and bisexual children may experience same-sex interests at this time	*How does the reproductive system work? Why do some girls have larger breasts than others? Do boys menstruate? Why don't some women have babies?*	Sexual health education can include focus on biological topics such as the endocrine system, menstruation, masturbation and wet dreams, sexual intercourse, birth control, abortion, self-esteem, and interpersonal relationships.
12 to 14 years	Preteens may be concerned or confused about the physical changes of puberty, including changes in body shape, body control, reproductive ability, menstruation, breast and penis development, and voice changes	*How can you keep yourself looking attractive? Should your parents know if you're going steady? Why are some people homosexual? Does a girl ever have a wet dream? Does sexual intercourse hurt? Why do people get married?*	Sexual health education can focus on increasing knowledge of contraception, intimate sexual behaviour (why people do what they do), dating, and variations in sexual behaviours (homosexuality, transvestism, transsexualism).
15 to 17 years	Increased interest in sexual topics and curiosity about relationships with others, families, reproduction, and various sexual activity patterns; many teenagers begin dating at this time	*What is prostitution? What do girls really want in a good date? How far should you go on a date? Is it good to have sexual intercourse before marriage? Why is sex considered a dirty word?*	Sexual health education can include more information on birth control, abortion, dating, premarital sexual behaviour, communication, marriage patterns, sexual myths, moral decisions, parenthood, sexuality research, sexual dysfunction, and the history of sexuality.

SOURCE: Based on Breuss, C.E., & Greenberg, S. (1981). *Sex education: Theory and practice*. Belmont, CA: Wadsworth, p. 223–231.

program has been presented. According to the Sex Information and Education Council of Canada, there are ten components to a successful sexual education program (see Table 10.2). The standard measures include sexual behaviour, pregnancy, and contraceptive use (Remez, 2000). If the rates of sexual behaviour increase after sexuality education, a program is judged to be ineffective. If these rates decrease, a program is successful. So what are the effects of sex education programs? Do sexual health education courses change people's actual sexual behaviour? It is difficult to measure and evaluate these behavioural changes after a sexuality education program, but it appears that there are some limited changes.

Comprehensive sexual health education programs have been found to be the most successful at helping adolescents delay their involvement in sexual intercourse and helping to protect adolescents from STIs and unintended pregnancies (Kirby, 2001, 2007; Kohler et al., 2008; Starkman & Rajani, 2002). In addition, sexual health education programs that teach contraception and communication skills have been found to delay the onset of sexual intercourse or reduce the frequency of sexual intercourse, reduce the number of sexual partners, and increase the use of contraception (Kirby, 2007; Kohler et al., 2008). Abstinence-only programs, in contrast, have not yielded successful results in delaying the onset

Childhood and Adolescent Sexuality

Table 10.2	10 Necessary Components for Sexual Health Education According to SIECCAN

1. To complete curriculum objectives enough class time must be available.

2. Train your teachers and administrative support for effective program delivery.

3. Use sound teaching methods and valid theoretical models such as the information, motivation and behavioural skills (IMB) model.

4. Take into account and tailor instruction to meet the needs of students with varying developmental stages, ethnocultural backgrounds and sexual orientation.

5. Target discussions to clarify what behaviours lead to negative outcomes such as STIs and unintended pregnancy.

6. Deliver information that will assist recipients to develop appropriate behaviours regarding condom or contraceptive use and personal limits for sexual behaviours.

7. Information or program activities addressing peer pressure, the individual environment and social context relating to adolescent sexuality.

8. Refusing sex and practising safer sex are necessary skills that can be developed by students with information, motivation, and behavioural skills training.

9. Students need the opportunity to practise communication skills, negotiation of contraceptive use, and the setting sexual limits to become active participants in their sexual health program.

10. For future program development, the evaluation of a program's strengths and weaknesses is beneficial.

SOURCE: Adapted from SIECCAN, Sexual Health Education in the Schools: Questions and Answers, *3rd edition*, table 1, p. 11. Used with permission.

of intercourse (Kirby, 2007; Weed, 2008), and a federally funded study of abstinence-only programs in the United States found that these programs had no effects on sexual abstinence (Trenholm et al., 2007). Overall, there have been no published reports of abstinence-based programs providing significant effects on delaying sexual intercourse (Kirby, 2007; Kohler et al., 2008; Weed, 2008).

Measuring attitudes or changes in attitudes and values is difficult at best. Overall, we do know that comprehensive sex education programs can increase knowledge levels, affect attitudes, and change behaviours (Kirby, 2007; Kohler et al., 2008). The most successful programs are those in which schools and parents worked together to develop the program. However, many effects of sexual health education programs may not be quantifiable. Programs may help students to feel more confident, be more responsible, improve their mental health, and increase their communication skills. We rarely measure these changes, and in an interview study of young adults in Nova Scotia and British Columbia, a common criticism of our current sexual health education curriculum was a lack of focus on the positive aspects of sex (Shoveller et al., 2004).

Sexual Health Education Today: What Is Still Needed

As mentioned, sexual health education programs that increase their focus on the development of positive skills such as improving

communication skills between adolescents are desired by adolescents. Sexual health education programs often focus on solving problems such as unintended teenage pregnancy or lack of contraceptive use. While important, developing positive sexual health skills around communication and self-worth are also necessary.

To foster the development of sexual health education and skill development in our youth, we must also train the teachers that deliver our programs. A study by Cohen et al. (2004) reported that two thirds of New Brunswick elementary and middle school teachers had not received training for the instruction of their sexual health education curriculum. In order to address this problem in part, Alberta teachers and health professionals have developed a website (http://www.teachingsexualhealth.ca) to help teachers develop lesson plans appropriate to the grade level of their students.

As part of our training of sexual health educators we also need to provide material and resources for our educators on topics such as working with sexual-minority youth and disabled youth, information about our multicultural society, and teaching adults about sexual health throughout their life span. A recent study of Canadian adults found that many physicians are not proactive when it comes to asking their patients about sexual health issues, and adult patients may be too uncomfortable to bring their issues to the attention of their physician (Wittenberg & Gerber, 2009).

Educational materials are being developed on the sexual health topics we have listed and programs for continuing education of professionals are also being developed. For example, the Canadian Teachers' Federation has published five publications

Sexuality Education around the World

In 2010, the World Health Organization (WHO) published the first detailed European guidelines to help develop curricula for sexuality education programs, entitled the *Standards for Sexuality Education in Europe: A Framework for Policy Makers, Educational and Health Authorities and Specialists* (World Health Organization, 2010). The guidelines were developed by a group of 20 experts from nine European countries, along with the WHO and the Federal Centre for Health Education in Germany. The focus of sexuality education in Europe has shifted from the risks associated with sex to a more holistic approach that asserts that children and teens need unbiased, scientifically correct information about sexuality in order to develop the skills necessary to protect themselves in the future (World Health Organization, 2010).

Around the world, the European countries have the longest history of sexuality education. Sweden made sexuality education a mandatory subject in schools in 1955. From there, it became mandatory in Germany (1968), Austria (1970), the Netherlands (1970), France, the United Kingdom, Portugal, Spain (2001), and Ireland (2003; World Health Organization, 2010). Today, Swedish children receive a portion of sexuality education in youth health centres in addition to schools, since this helps them to learn where to seek out services should they need them. As we discussed in the chapter opening story, the Netherlands has the world's lowest rates of teenage pregnancy, abortion, and childbearing. It is the best example of the value of high-quality sex education. The Dutch government supports a variety of sexuality organizations and finances mass-media campaigns aimed at educating the public about sexuality.

The majority of European sexuality education programs are "personal-growth" oriented, unlike the United States, which tends to be "prevention" oriented or "problem-solving" oriented (World Health Organization, 2010). In fact, educators point out that:

Dr. Carroll visits with students from Amsterdam's Lyceum, a Dutch secondary school.

In Western Europe, sexuality, as it emerges and develops during adolescence, is not primarily perceived as a problem and a threat, but as a valuable source of personal enrichment (World Health Organization, 2010, p. 15).

In many other countries around the world, the focus of sex education has also been "prevention" oriented, focusing specifically on HIV and AIDS education, especially in those countries that are significantly affected by HIV and AIDS (United Nations Scientific and Cultural Organization [UNESCO], 2008). In Japan, the Japanese Association for Sexuality Education was established in 1974 to help design comprehensive sexuality education in the schools, although abstinence education has always been very popular in Japan. In 1986, a new sexuality education curriculum was distributed to all middle and high schools in Japan (Kitazawa, 1994). This was again revised in 1992, and the Japanese Ministry of Education approved the discussion of secondary sex characteristics in coeducational Grade 5 classes and also mandated that sexuality education be taught in schools. Before this time, there was no discussion of sexuality in elementary schools (Hatano & Shimazaki, 2004).

We know that around the world, few young adults receive adequate sex education and, as a result, are at risk for negative consequences (UNESCO, 2009). Today, there is overwhelming evidence to support the need for sex education. Sex education can increase knowledge levels and reduce the risk for teen pregnancy and STIs. Yet, debates and controversies will continue throughout the world about the necessity of these programs; how best to implement the programs; who should teach them; and how success should be measured (UNESCO, 2009). Experts are hopeful that continued research on global sex education will increase support for global sex education.

supporting bisexual, gay, lesbian, transgender and two-spirited issues in education. Their most recent publication is called *Supporting Transgender and Transsexual Students in K-12 Schools: A Guide for Educators* (Wells, Roberts, & Allen, 2012). Stephanie Mitelman at McGill University, and a founding member of the executive board for the Sexual Health Network of Quebec, in collaboration with several colleagues, has created materials for sexual health education that are available via the Sexpressions website (http//www.sexpressions.ca/who-we-are.asp).

In Canada not all post-secondary institutions have courses on human sexuality and when they are offered the number of students that may have access to them are limited. Programs in sexuality are offered at the Université du Québec in Montreal, the University of Waterloo, York University, and the University of Toronto, with specialized training being offered at the University of Guelph via its Guelph Sexuality Conference and the biannual Western Canadian Sexual Health Conference.

In summary, childhood and adolescent sexuality is an evolving phenomenon. Sexual knowledge and sexual behaviour are common among children in today's society, in which sexuality is so much a part of our culture. However, knowledge does not necessarily mean that children must act on it. Encouraging children and teenagers to think carefully about sexuality and to advise them to be active in controlling their expression and acceptance of sexual behaviours with others is important for the development of a person's sense of self-worth and self.

What we do know is that a close and respectful parent–adolescent relationship that allows for open communication about sexuality has been found to decrease adolescent sexual behaviours and reduce the influence of peers with regard to sexual issues (Meschke et al., 2000). This is an important finding and it is partially responsible for delaying first intercourse, reducing the number of teenage pregnancies, and reducing numbers of sexual partners. Open communication about sexuality, along with good, solid sexuality education, encourages this kind of responsible sexual behaviour.

Review Questions

1 Explain both sides of the sexuality education debate.

2 Compare and contrast differences in sexual education curriculum across the provinces in Canada.

3 What are the key ingredients for effective sexual health education according to the Sex Information and Education Council of Canada?

4 Discuss research findings on the effects of sexuality education.

Chapter Review

Summary Points

1 Throughout most of history, children were treated as miniature adults, and concepts such as childhood did not exist. Children were considered presexual.

2 Sexual anatomy is functional even before we are born. Male infants are capable of erection, and female infants are capable of vaginal lubrication. The single most important aspect of infant development is children's relationship with their caretakers. Gender identity develops between the ages of one and two years. It takes a little longer to develop gender constancy, which is the realization that their gender will not change during their lifetime. Genital touching is common at this age.

3 In early childhood, physical development continues. In fact, children may learn more in the first few years of childhood about the nature of their bodies than they learn in the entire remainder of their lives. Child sex play is common at this age, and many parents or caregivers need to teach that this behaviour is private. Children learn that their genitals are private and must be covered up in public. Boys are often taught about the penis, yet it is rare for girls to be taught about the clitoris.

4 Sometime between the ages of six and 12, a child experiences the first outward signs of puberty. In girls, the first sign of puberty is the appearance of breast buds, and soon they will experience menarche. Preadolescent boys experience frequent erections, and soon they will experience semenarche or ejaculation. Typically boys do not tell anyone about this event. Prepubescence is the age of sexual discovery.

5 During preadolescence, genital touching continues, and both sexual fantasies and sex games may begin. All of our intimate relationships influence our sexuality. We learn a great deal about our sexuality from our parents and our peers.

6 Puberty prepares the body for adult sexuality and reproduction. Adolescence often includes our emotional and cognitive reactions to puberty. There are many physical, emotional, and cognitive changes during this time.

7 Some of the first signs of male puberty include body changes, increased body hair, a growth spurt, and voice deepening. For the most part, early development in boys is usually not as embarrassing as it is in girls.

8 The National Survey of Sexual Health and Behavior (NSSHB) explored several sexual behaviors in teens. Masturbation was found to increase during adolescence and then decrease as partnered sex increases later in life. Rates of anal sex were low for young teens, but for some gay teens anal sex may be the defining moment of losing their virginity.

9 Approximately half of all Canadian students in Grades 9 through 12 have engaged in sexual intercourse. First intercourse is usually unplanned but rarely spontaneous.

Today's adolescents have high condom contraceptive use.

10 Opposition to sexuality education has often been due to two attitudes: One says that sexuality is private, and the second says that public schools cannot discuss sex without giving children implicit permission to be sexual and should not promote certain values.

11 Comprehensive sexual health education programs include a wide variety of topics and help students to develop their own skills and learn factual information. Abstinence-only programs emphasize abstinence from all sexual behaviours, and they typically do not provide information about contraception or disease prevention.

12 Canada has comprehensive sexual health education programs that vary by province and territory. While there are differences between the various provinces and territories regarding

what age various topics are discussed, there are similarities in the educational material covered by the different provinces.

13 To find out if sex education programs are successful, researchers often measure behavioural changes after the program. The standard measures include sexual behaviour, pregnancy, and contraceptive use. Comprehensive sexuality programs have been found to be the most successful at helping adolescents delay their involvement in sexual intercourse, helping protect adolescents from STIs and unintended pregnancies, delaying the onset of sexual intercourse or reducing the frequency of sexual intercourse, reducing the number of sexual partners, and increasing the use of contraception. Abstinence-only programs have not yielded successful results in delaying the onset of intercourse. There have not been any published reports showing that abstinence-based programs can delay sexual intercourse.

Critical Thinking Questions

1 Should genital touching in young children be encouraged, ignored, or discouraged? What message do you think it sends to a child when parents encourage their child to discover and play with toes, ears, and fingers but pull the child's hands away when he or she discovers his or her genitals?

2 Young children often play sex games, such as "doctor," with each other. What age differences

do you think pose the biggest problems? Are sex games acceptable? Why or why not? How should a parent respond?

3 Where should children get their sexual knowledge? Is it better to learn about some things from a particular place? Explain.

4 Why do you think adolescence is a difficult time for many people? What can be done to

make the transition through adolescence easier?

5 People today are engaging in sex relatively early in life, often in their middle or early teens. Do you think this is a good time to experiment with sex, or do you think it is too early? What do you think is the "ideal" age to begin experimenting with sex?

Websites

Society of Obstetricians and Gynaecologists of Canada (SOGC) This society has developed a website called SexualityAndU.ca that emphasizes the importance of knowledge about sexual health and the behavioural skills that are required for having a healthy attitude towards sexual behaviour and sexuality. (http://sogc.org/)

Sex Information and Education Council of Canada (SIECCAN) This agency provides education resources to individuals across Canada including documents addressing questions about sexual health education in schools. (http://www.sieccan.org/)

Public Health Agency of Canada You will find the most recent documents on sexual health education in Canada as well as statistics related to STIs, teen pregnancy rates, and use of condoms by teens. (http://www.phac-aspc.gc.ca/publicat/cgshe-ldnemss/index-eng.php)

Canadian Teachers' Federation This organization has five publications supporting bisexual, gay, lesbian, transgender, and Two-Spirited issues in education. Their most recent publication is

Supporting Transgender and Transsexual Students in K-12 Schools: A Guide for Educators. (http://www.ctf-fce.ca/Documents/BGLTTSeries_OrderForm_EN_Web.pdf)

Teaching Sexual Health This website was created by Alberta teachers and health professionals to promote sexual health education. (http://www.teachingsexualhealth.ca)

Alan Guttmacher Institute The mission of the Alan Guttmacher Institute (AGI) is to provide information and services about issues of sexuality. The institute conducts important research on adolescent and child sexual issues. (http://www.guttmacher.org/)

Society for Research on Adolescence The Society for Research on Adolescence's goal is to promote the understanding of adolescence through research and dissemination. Members conduct theoretical studies, basic and applied research, and policy analyses to understand and enhance adolescent development. (http://www.s-r-a.org/)

11 Communication and Sexuality

Communication, or the exchange of information between people, is at the very core of social life. It has changed dramatically over the last century—from hand-written letters, which took weeks and sometimes months to deliver, to ever-progressing versions of the telephone, to the computer age, where distance is rendered irrelevant with the Internet and mobile telephones. Since its inception in 1867, Canada has faced unique challenges in communication—first, in terms of maintaining political and social unity in a country of nearly 10 million square kilometres that spans an entire continent from Vancouver Island to the east coast of Newfoundland, and second, with its two official languages and numerous other cultures. Figuring prominently in maintaining unity has been the Canadian Broadcasting Corporation (CBC), which, since 1936, has offered services in French and English, as well as eight Aboriginal languages, and today provides programs in Cantonese, Hindi, Tagalog, and other languages that serve communities prominent in Canada.

Today, with the Internet, communication may be face-to-face with such programs as Skype or take place instantly with the click of a send button. Additionally, as we will discuss, Canadians are among the most frequent Facebook users in the world, and most who use this social network site log in to their pages for the latest updates several times a day.

How has all of this affected human sexuality? For one thing, it has enabled partners to be in touch with each other at any point whether a few blocks away or across the continent. Second, with the proliferation of dating sites, it has allowed people who pursue relationships to greatly expand their searches to other cities, other provinces, and even other countries. We not only explore these phenomena in this chapter but we look closely at some of the dynamics of communication—particularly those pertaining to positive sexual relationships. It is our hope that in presenting the latest research that we may be useful in the maintenance of relationships, whether at their beginning or well into old age.

Communication has changed considerably over the last few decades. In the past, if one wanted to talk to people, one visited them, picked up the telephone, or wrote a letter. Today, many people rely upon texting, e-mail, instant messaging (IMing), Facebook, and Twitter to communicate with friends, families, and intimate partners (Christofides et al., 2009; Diamanduros et al., 2007). Although such technology has allowed more communication, it has also made that communication far more complex. Furthermore, while we have gained greater access when communicating with others, we have also sacrificed depth in the ways in which we do so. "How are you" has become "sup," "in my opinion" has become "imo," and a hearty laugh has become "lol."

In this chapter, we discuss the importance of communication, how we learn to do so, how people differ in the ways in which they communicate, changing technologies, and ways to improve inter-personal communication skills, including the ability to talk about sexual issues. Improving communication skills has been found to enrich personal sexuality. We discuss such topics as achieving a sense of self-worth as it pertains to sexual feelings and activities and how good communication can improve relationships. The information in this chapter may be helpful in years to come.

The Importance of Communication

Let us say that two people meet each other in a bar for the first time. Their eyes find each other across a room and slowly they make their way over to talk to each other. What might they say?

Partners who are able to talk freely to each other have a better chance of their relationship lasting.

How we communicate with someone initially often sets the tone for further communication.

What might they not say? How might they decide on what is appropriate? Typically, they would exchange greetings or make use of what Canadian social researcher Erving Goffman called "side involvements" and talk about such things as the quality of the music, how crowded it is, or otherwise (Goffman, 1967, p. 113). One unwritten rule about communication with a stranger is not to talk about anything too personal or reveal too much about oneself. Intimacy comes gradually with rapport.

In terms of intimacy and rapport, social psychologists have suggested the "onion theory of communication." We all are like onions with many layers and, when we first meet someone, we are careful about what we say. This initial stage is represented by the first layers of the onion. As more time goes by (which differs from couple to couple), we begin to peel back more layers. Initial topics such as the weather or what classes one finds most enjoyable are low risk because they do not involve much personal information. The next layers may include views upon politics or family relationships and are thus more personal. The typical sequence of the onion theory is that both parties reveal progressively more personal information about themselves. If one shares something personal, the other person is likely to do the same. Ultimately, more and more layers are peeled off and each person knows the other to a greater and greater extent. Once enough layers are stripped away, intimacy takes root.

Some people make the mistake of prematurely peeling back their layers. They might talk about personal issues very early in a relationship and this may make others feel uncomfortable or repel them entirely (Weisel & King, 2007). Even so, there are some variations upon this rule. For example, if two strangers are sitting together on a long flight from Vancouver to Halifax, they might quickly share personal information about themselves. Here, there is the assumption is that both will never see each other again so each perceives little or no risk in such sharing. Once they reach their destination, both go off in different directions. Another example may be seen with vacationers. If someone were to fly down to Acapulco or Cancun, Mexico, and be there only five days, he or she might very quickly share personal information with another person and initial intimacy might come much more

Recipes for Good Same-Sex Marriages: The Importance of Communication

When same-sex marriage became fully recognized, Canadian lawyer Kathleen A. Lahey and psychologist Kevin Alderson sought to explore the relationships of the women and men who had married, giving them opportunities to talk about the ways in which they communicate with their partners in their book, *Same-Sex Marriage* (Lahey & Alderson, 2004). One of their subjects, Patti, related the following anecdote when asked about the ways in which she communicates with her partner of eight years, Terrah:

Try to catch yourself when you're taking the other person for granted. The other day I was leaving the house and while locking the door, I began having really wonderful thoughts about Terrah and I thought, "I should really leave Terrah a really nice note," but I was outside and I thought, "No, I didn't take Terrah for granted." Take the effort, go back in the house, and leave her the nice note you're thinking about and then go to work. In any way you can, express the good thoughts and feelings that you may be having about one another. Don't assume that the other person knows, and even if they know,

who doesn't like to hear it over and over again. (p. 122)

Patti firmly believes that the quality of any marriage (and no doubt, any loving relationship) is a question of being open about positive thoughts and feelings and communicating them to one's partner. When this does not happen, a partner may sometimes feel taken for granted or begin to speculate about how his or her partner feels about being in their relationship. Simple but true: Good communication leads to good relationships.

quickly. Having only a short time before flying home and the motivation to reap the most enjoyment within a short time somehow accelerates the path to intimacy and even sexual encounters. In regular life though, the onion layers typically come off more slowly.

In any case, good communication is one of the most important factors in a satisfying relationship (Eaker et al., 2007; Ledermann et al., 2010; Moore, 2010; Rehman & Holtzworth-Munroe, 2007). Communication skills can be applied to all areas of life, such as improving family relationships, having better in friendships at school or work, developing a loving relationship, or even discussing sexual issues with a partner. For love and intimacy to grow, each partner should know how the other feels. It is communication that fosters mutual understanding, increases emotional intimacy, and helps deepen feelings of love.

Relationships are often fraught with difficulties. This may be compounded even more if two people live together. It is common to experience difficulties when sharing space with another person. Therapists typically emphasize the importance of communication skills, and communication self-help books are plentiful on bookstore shelves. Problems often occur when partners have poor communication skills, feel unable to self-disclose, or have trouble listening to each other. Anger and frustration are common reactions to poor communication and misunderstandings can lead to a downward spiral in which communication becomes less and less effective. Furthermore, poor communication skills can contribute to other serious relationship problems, including physical and emotional abuse (Cornelius et al., 2010). They may also interfere with enjoyable sexual intimacy, which is why we include communication as a topic in this book.

Not all relationship problems are caused by poor communication. Sometimes they emerge from a couple's lack of willingness to acknowledge an issue that needs to be worked out, such as one partner enjoying a particular sex act that the other does not. At other times, issues such as poor health or economic stress

can create problems that hinder communication and intimacy. Regardless of the issue, it is best solved with open and honest dialogue.

Overall, couples who know how to communicate are happier, more satisfied, and have more lasting relationships (Hahlweg et al., 2000; Moore, 2010; Rehman & Holtzworth-Munroe, 2007). Learning to communicate well, however, is not easy. Why do some people find it difficult to talk intimately with a partner? We keep this question in mind as we further explore the many facets of communication.

Learning to Communicate

Communication is a learned behaviour which begins in early childhood with the gradual awareness of cause and effect (e.g., crying communicates hunger to parents) and becomes ever more sophisticated as people grow. As children acquire language, they learn effective ways to communicate. Eventually, in adulthood, people have ideally learned the most efficient ways of communicating their thoughts, desires, needs, and emotions.

The journey toward mature styles of communication, however, is long and sometimes arduous. Canadian-born television host Art Linkletter hosted a show called *House Party* from 1945 to 1967, and at the end of the show, he interviewed groups of children around five or six years old (*"Kids Say the Darndest Things"*). The reason for the show's great success was that children of this age have not yet developed filters and tend to say exactly what is on their minds. The result was often amusing to adults who might have imagined the reactions of others if adults were equally as candid. Eventually, as we grow, we learn to organize and filter our thoughts before expressing them to others.

We typically learn these various filters—what is socially acceptable in conversation—as we grow up. As we learn to empathize with the feelings of others, we begin to worry about what they might think or feel. We might even feel selfish for asking for things we want and need. It is therefore essential that we learn to strike a balance between the needs and desires of others and those of our own.

Goals of Communication

According to Vanfossen (1996), when we communicate with others, we have three competing goals. The first is to "get the job done." We have something to say to someone and we want to say it. Second, we have a "relational goal." We want to maintain a relationship and not hurt or alienate the other person with what we want to say. Third, we have an "identity management goal." We want the ways we communicate our message to project a particular image of ourselves. Thus, we want to tell our partner something, not hurt the relationship in doing so, and yet maintain our image of ourselves. These three goals sometimes are at odds with one another, making the job of communicating our thoughts, needs, or desires difficult. Communication is thus more than the simple relay of a message but a consideration of its impact upon another person as well as a reflection of our own needs.

Families and Communication

In Chapter 1, we discussed the important influence that our family has on our personal development. Our ability to communicate and the strategies we use to do so are often learned through interactions with other family members (Schrodt, 2009), who typically inform, negotiate, and reinforce the values and beliefs we come to hold. They also share stories, exchange ideas, and discuss issues that emerge in daily life (Howe et al., 2010; Tannen et al., 2007). Along the way, interactions and experiences within our families may teach us important aspects of communication such as negotiation, conflict resolution, civil debate, and even interpersonal skills in romantic relationships (Ledbetter, 2010; Schrodt et al., 2009).

One large-scale Canadian study looked at how communication during family dinners impacted upon the mental well-being of 26 069 children aged 11 to 15. The researchers found that the quality and the ease of communication between parents and children had a positive impact upon their mental health (Elgar, et al., 2013). Good family communication helps children develop a social and emotional understanding of the world around them (Howe et al., 2010), and can affect their self-esteem, mental well-being (Schrodt & Ledbetter, 2007), and even potential for depression (Koerner & Fitzpatrick, 1997). In short, how a family communicates is a good indicator of the ways that its individual members communicate.

REAL Research With an interest in communication patterns, Arcuri (2014) recruited 113 heterosexual couples at the University of Windsor, (Ontario) and asked them to fill out a questionnaire about communication patterns and quality of relationship, among other variables. She found that negative communication patterns significantly affected perceived relationship quality.

If children learn positive ways of communicating, they will develop equally effective strategies for communicating with others. If they learn negative ways, however, they may encounter difficulties later in life.

Communication Differences and Similarities

There are numerous other influences on the ways that people communicate. Various aspects of who we are such as age, gender, sexual orientation, cultural background, level of education, health, language, and even mood can all have an impact upon communication strategies and skills (Knöfler & Imhof, 2007). We now explore the impact of gender, culture, sexual orientation, and language in greater depth.

Communication and Gender

Do men and women have different styles or ways of communicating? Are conversations among men different from conversations among women? Gender differences in communication have long been a topic of scientific interest (Burleson et al., 1996; Lakoff, 1975; Litosseliti, 2006; Tannen, 1990). There is some research supporting the theory that conversations between women and men may be more complex than those in same-sex groups (Athenstaedt et al., 2004; Edwards & Hamilton, 2004). Why might this be so? Is it a matter of differences in communication styles? We look at these questions.

Research on Gender Differences

Deborah Tannen (1990) has done a great deal of research on communication and gender differences. She has termed the fundamental differences between the ways men and women communicate as

© Fuse/Getty Images

One male mode of communication uses more report-talk, which imparts knowledge and helps to establish status.

genderlects (JEN-der-lecks). She and others found that women tend to use more "rapport-talk," which establishes relationships and connections, while men tend to use more "report-talk," which imparts knowledge (Eckstein & Goldman, 2001). Tannen (1990) also found that women tend to use conversations to establish and maintain intimacy, while men tend to do so to establish status.

Another of Tannen's findings was that women tend to be less assertive in their communication. For example, when stating an opinion, women might end a statement with a **tag question** (e.g., "It's really cold in here, *isn't it*?" or "That's an interesting idea, *isn't it*?") to invite discussion and minimize disagreements. They also tend to use **disclaimers** (e.g., "I may be wrong, but…"), **question statements** (e.g., "Am I off base here?") (Vanfossen, 1996), and **hedge words** (e.g., "sort of," "kind of," "aren't you," or "would you mind?"). All of these tend to decrease a speaker's perceived assertiveness as opposed to direct questions and statements.

There has been some criticism of Tannen's genderlect theory, the most prominent of which has focused on her unidimensional approach to gender differences in communication. To Tannen, gender is based on *biological* sex. Therefore, all women communicate one way and all men do so in another way. It could be that differences in the learning of communication skills rather than in biology account for communication differences. If the reasons for the differences were biologically based, then all men and all women would show the same communication patterns.

Communication researchers have identified two types of skills—affective and instrumental (Burleson, 2003; Burleson et al., 1996). Affective communication skills are comforting and involve a significant amount of listening, while instrumental skills are more persuasive and narrative. Both may be positive skills in that listening to others is important in understanding their wants and needs, and instrumental skills are important in communicating one's own wants and needs effectively.

© Blend Images/Getty

One female mode of communication uses more rapport-talk, which tends to establish relationships and maintain intimacy.

On Your Mind

Is it possible that through communication a couple can salvage a relationship after one person cheated on the other?

How might one go about doing so? This question was posed to Canadian advice columnist Ellie Tesher by one of her readers in her column of October 9, 2014:

Question:

My wife of 23 years had an intimate, secret, two-year affair with a man she knew years ago. I discovered it and was heartbroken and hurt. All of our friends and family found out. We separated for almost a year. We decided to try and work things out, initially progressing. Then I discovered they're going to the same gym where they originally met.

She says nothing's going on, but I don't believe her. I expressed my concerns, but she won't consider my feelings, won't stop going to "her" gym, and doesn't ask me to join her. I suspect that even if I did join her they'd pretend not to know each other. Her affair partner's married with his own family and still lives with them. She acts like nothing's going on, but there's no intimacy between us. She won't move out nor make any concessions for me. She wants to live her normal family life but do as she pleases. I feel I have no choice but to divorce her. What do I do?

Answer:

For a marriage to renew after an affair, there must be a sincere effort to regain trust, and mutual discussion of what was missing in the marriage that allowed this to happen. She's not trying to reassure you she can be trusted again. You're both not discussing the state of your union, i.e. acknowledging your feelings about the affair, and both being open about why it happened. Get to marital counselling together.

In this case, the husband is being honest and expressing his concerns, while the wife seems unwilling to discuss or acknowledge them. Should this continue, divorce seems imminent. In any relationship, one must not only listen to the other but acknowledge what he is she is feeling. Only then will both parties be able to reach a mutually agreeable solution (Tesher, 2014).

SOURCE: *Toronto Star*, October 9, 2014, "Both parties have to want to make it work," by Ellie Tesher. Retrieved July 29, 2015, from http://ellieadvice.com/both-parties-have-to-want-it-to-make-it-work.

Other researchers (e.g., Kunkel & Burleson, 1998) have similarly found that people value different types of communication skills in relationships with others. For example, when people need social support, they are

genderlects
Coined by Deborah Tannen, this term refers to the fundamental differences between the way men and women communicate.

tag question
A phrase that renounces or denies the validity of what one is saying by adding a question at the end of a statement.

disclaimer
A phrase that renounces or denies the validity of what one is saying with a negative statement.

question statement
A phrase that renounces or denies the validity of what one is saying by adding a question at the end of a statement.

hedge word
A word that renounces or denies the validity of what one is saying by using certain words to decrease perceived assertiveness.

more likely to prefer the company of friends with affectively oriented skills. If they want to discuss strategies or learn more about a particular topic, they are more likely to seek out people with instrumentally oriented skills. In general, women tend to value affectively oriented communication skills, while men tend to value instrumentally oriented skills (Burleson et al., 1996; Samter & Burleson, 2005). There are, of course, many exceptions.

Another interesting area of research involves speech quantity. It is often believed that women talk more than men. This has been supported by Brizendine (2006) whose female subjects used about 20 000 words per day, while the male subjects used only about 7000. As she stated, communication differences between the sexes are due to prenatal hormonal development, which results in greater growth in the communication and emotional processing centres of women's brains. This in turn leads women to be more verbally expressive. She added, however, that social identities of men and women are influenced by social power dynamics, which further lead to differing patterns of communication. Thus, there may be biological determinants of sex differences in communication, but social ones as well (Brizendine & Allen, 2010). There is, however, disagreement to the assertion that communication differences have any biological basis. When other researchers attempted to replicate Brizendine's study, however, they found that both the men and women in their study used about 16 000 words a day (Mehl et al., 2007). Furthermore, the subjects in this study were college students, which may have limited the results, but the researchers point out that if differences were biologically based, they would have appeared in this sample as well. There is even further disagreement in Canada that any biological basis for such speech differences exist. As University of Toronto linguistics researchers James and Drakich (1993) pointed out, it is also essential to examine the social, structural, and situational variables of conversations to make sense of any study on differential rates of speaking.

Another Canadian study (Fraccaro et al., 2013) looked at the effects of voice manipulation by men and women to increase their sexual attractiveness. Women tend to prefer men with lower-pitched voices, while men tend to prefer women with higher-pitched voices. Given that both men and women are capable of manipulating their pitch (lowering or raising it) depending upon the occasion, Fracarro and his associates looked at whether doing so affects perceived sexual attractiveness. While they found that voice manipulation does not necessarily after a speaker's attractiveness, a lower pitch in voice was associated with dominance. This finding suggests that lower pitch in men contributes to the perception of their dominance.

It is important to keep in mind that numerous studies of gender and communication have found that sex differences in many areas are small (Aries, 1996; Dindia & Canary, 2006). There are certainly other factors that contribute to people's ability to communicate, such as social philosophies, gender role socialization, dominance, power, and even the dynamics inherent in one's family of origin. Typically, studies of gender differences in communication have included only young, more educated, middle-class subjects (Mortenson, 2002), and it is not known whether these findings are generalizable to a larger population. It is also important to keep in mind that communication patterns and skills may vary among cultures.

Gender Differences as "Cross-Cultural" Socialization

Researchers often disagree about whether gender differences in communication exist, and those who do agree often disagree on the reasons. There may biological influences but also psychological and social ones as well. Social role theory explains the differences in terms of role expectations for masculinity and femininity, while societal development theories focus on male dominance and its effects, which may in turn affect communication patterns.

Animal Variations

Mimetic Courtship Signals

According to Searcy and Nowicki (2005), whether among fish, fowl, or mammals, males of inferior physical quality are markedly disadvantaged in their quests to mate with females. It is therefore to their advantage to send out *mimetic* or false courtship signals denoting superiority regardless of reality in hope that they attract mates. In other words, the males of many species are able to give out false information to females, which exaggerates their worthiness as mates. One striking example of a mimetic courtship signal is found among male sticklebacks, a type of fish found in the coastal waters off British Columbia. Red colourations on their bodies are a visual signal of superiority given off to attract females. The more the areas of red, the more attractive they are as potential mates. They are able to manipulate the size and number of these colourations, but not without cost in that doing so attracts aggression from other males. Thus, while male sticklebacks may be able to increase their red colourations—thus exaggerating their desirability to females—they are more likely to do so in the absence of other males (Candolin, 2000).

Gender differences may also be understood through a cross-cultural perspective (A.M. Johnson, 2001; Mulvaney, 1994). If two people from different cultures were in conversation and each had little or no experience with the culture of the other, there might be obstacles to understanding in that neither one would be familiar with the nuances and subtleties of t the other's culture. This may be generalized to "cultural" differences between men and woman, each of whom learn different styles of communication, which in certain situations may be unfamiliar to the other sex. Maltz and

Borker (1982) point out that men and women are raised within different "sociolinguistic subcultures" and therefore learn different communication rules. They interpret conversations and use language differently. Learning how to communicate begins with children in same-sex play groups, which often are organized differently. Most young girls play in small groups and have best friends. Reaching greater levels of intimacy is a typical goal and games such as playing house do not have winners and losers. Boys, on the other hand, learn to express dominance through speech and play in hierarchically organized groups that focus on directing and winning (Maltz & Borker, 1982). Boys often compete for status by telling jokes, showing off, or claiming they are the best at things. Boys and girls learn the communication styles of their respective genders and they retain such patterns throughout life. As adolescents, they begin to communicate in mixed-sex groups using the rules they learned through same-sex communication. This often leads to problems. For example, girls tend to nod their head when listening to other girls as cues that they understand. When a woman nods her head during a conversation with a man, he might think she agrees with him when in fact she may simply be showing him that she is listening. When a man does not nod his head similarly, a woman may think he is not listening. These differences may thus lead to misunderstandings. Understanding the differences in communication styles will not automatically prevent disagreements, but it does have the potential to reduce them.

Communication and Culture

As mentioned earlier, communication patterns vary considerably across culture. One important variation is the degree to which a culture encourages individual or collective needs (Cai et al., 2000). Individualistic cultures encourage individual goals and values and an independent sense of self (Matsumoto, 1996), while collectivist cultures encourage members to value group needs over individual ones. Canadian, American, and British cultures tend to be more individualistic, while Asian and Latin cultures tend to be more collectivistic (Adler et al., 2007). When an individualistic approach is predominant, people are more likely to be comfortable disclosing personal information to a variety of others (Gudykunst et al., 1996). In contrast, those in collectivistic cultures such as Japan or Korea are less likely to disclose personal information to those outside of their immediate family, believing it to be inappropriate (Chen & Danish, 2010; Gudykunst et al., 1996; Seki et al., 2002).

Communication patterns begin when children play in same-sex groups.

REAL Research Kral et al. (2011) were interested in factors associated with the mental well-being of Inuit youth in the Canadian territory Nunavut, which has a population of approximately 32 000 people. They found three factors to be most important: the family, talking/communication, and involvements in traditional Inuit cultural values and practices. The absence of these factors was conversely associated with unhappiness and suicide.

Furthermore, anthropologists have identified two distinct ways in which individuals from different cultures deliver messages to one another (Adler et al., 2007). In "low-context cultures" such as those of Germany, Switzerland, Sweden, and Canada, people use language to express thoughts, feelings, and ideas as directly as possible (Hall, 1976; Hall, 1990). Statements tend to be simple and direct. In "high-context" cultures such as those of Asia or the Middle East, there is greater reliance upon subtle and non-verbal cues (Am-bady et al., 1996; Hall, 1990). Here, communication is far less direct and a listener's understanding depends on the context of the conversation, an understanding of non-verbal behaviour, relationship history, and social norms.

Communication and Sexual Orientation

Gays and lesbians may be dating, in a common-law relationship, or married. While the majority of research of communication has not considered sexual orientation, there have been some studies of the patterns and strategies of gay and lesbian couples. However, as Canadian psychologist Brian MacDonald (1998) pointed out before the recognition of same-sex marriage, such research may not be accurate because it looks only at out-of-the-closet gay and lesbian couples. Older gay and lesbian couples, especially in the United States, are likely less involved with gay communities in their areas and fear losing friends, families, or livelihoods. Today, however, with full recognition of gay rights including marriage, it is likely that fewer and fewer couples live in secrecy. The field is thus ripe for researchers to tap.

Psychologists Lahey and Alderson (2004) serve as an example in their analysis of some of the first married same-sex couples across Canada. What is interesting here is that it becomes possible to look at communication within couples unfettered by the trappings of gender. However two women or two men communicate, the dynamics involved effectively rule out any such effects by definition. It must also be noted that even though same-sex marriage was not recognized until 2005, many gays and lesbians who did marry were not new couples. It is likely that many were already in committed relationships long beforehand. As Nova Scotian researcher Aine Humble (2013) points out, many such couples have had to incorporate the definition of "married" into their psyches. Such a shift may further affect the dynamics of their relationships.

How do gay and lesbian couples communicate? The data seem to indicate that there are very few differences compared to heterosexual couples. Canadian psychiatrist Robert Burgoyne (2001) administered a standardized relationship assessment questionnaire to two groups of gay couples: one composed of 32 male couples beginning couple therapy (the clinical group) and the other to a group of couples not in therapy (the non-clinical group). While the clinical group had generally low scores, the non-clinical group differed little in their functioning

When both parties in a couple are of the same sex, gender becomes irrelevant.

from heterosexual couples examined in previous research. As it seems, whether gay, lesbian, or heterosexual, good communication will likely lead to good relationships.

> **REAL Research** Canadian psychologist Uzma Rehman and associates (2011) hypothesized that relationship satisfaction among newlywed couples would differ as to whether a conflict was about a sexual or a non-sexual problem. After looking at a sample of 15 such couples, they found that while conflict about a non-sexual topic had no affect on relationship satisfaction, wives reported significantly less satisfaction with a sexual topic. These findings support the idea that sexual satisfaction is highly significant in marriage.

Communication and Language

Canada has two official languages—French and English. English is most widely spoken and French is spoken primarily in Quebec, as well as areas, including St. Boniface, Manitoba, and the Acadian areas of the Maritime provinces. Additionally, while most Canadians function well speaking French or English, other languages (e.g., Punjabi, Chinese/Cantonese, Spanish, German, Tagalog, and Arabic) are the first languages of sizable proportions of Canadians, and there are about a quarter million speakers of Cree, Inuktitut, and other Aboriginal languages. With such diversity, communication is often an obstacle, especially if one is not comfortable using a second language, and this may lead to limited communication (Baker & MacIntyre, 2003).

With this diversity, marriages and common-law relationships between people of different languages are inevitable, as is the case with the Métis (with French and Aboriginal heritages), Anglophones and Francophones of Quebec, and even Asian–English marriages in British Columbia. As Quebec researchers MacLeod et al. (2011) suggest, if children grow up in bilingual families of origin where both languages are used equally, then they are likely to become proficient in both languages simultaneously. If, however, there is more exposure to one language, then that one language will become predominant. Furthermore, people of different languages may fall in love and wish to commit themselves to each other. While they may intend to raise their children in a bilingual household, it is often the case that the majority language in the surrounding community will become predominant (V. de Klerk, 2001).

Regardless of language, when one party in a couple has less of a command of the words to communicate than the other, difficulties may arise in that both may find it difficult to express the nuances of their thoughts as well as understand those of the other. This may become less of a problem over time, however, in that not only will both become progressively more efficient in the language of the other, but they will become keenly attuned to the other ways in which they communicate, with facial expressions, tone of voice, and the like.

Australian linguistics professor Ingrid Piller recently wrote about a little-explored desire among some people where they are sexually attracted to people who speak other languages. Literature and popular culture are rife with examples of English speakers who find French, Spanish, Italian, and other "romance" language speakers sexy and thus pursue the men or women who speak them. Because Canada is a country with two official languages and numerous others spoken at home or in various communities, there is no doubt that what Piller has dubbed "language desire" has been a strong motivator of romance among many Canadians (Piller, 2002).

Types of Communication

There is more to communication than words alone. People also engage in **non-verbal communication** to get their messages across, and many individuals communicate with others online through e-mail or texting. These two methods raise important issues.

Non-verbal Communication

Most communication is verbal. Non-verbal cues, however, are also important in conveying messages to others (Guffey, 1999; Knapp & Hall, 2005). Although this includes facial expressions, hand and arm gestures, postures, and body positioning, it can also include speech rates, durations, and intensities (Boomer, 1963; Ekman & Friesen, 1969; Mehrabian, 2009; Sauter et al., 2010). Non-verbal communication can trigger emotional reactions in listeners. While listening to others, people often experience an *emotional contagion,* synchronizing their facial expressions with those of others (Tamiello et al., 2009). For example, watching the non-verbal cues from a friend who looks sad can often make people feel sad as well.

Although non-verbal cues become more clear as the intensity of emotional expressions increases, people originally learn to recognize them as they grow up. Young children can identify expressions of anger, fear, happiness, and sadness, and their ability to identify such emotions increases as they age (Montirosso et al., 2010). However, older adults begin to lose the ability to recognize basic emotions in facial, vocal, and bodily expressions. For example, Ruffman et al. (2009) found that approximately 75 percent of a sample of older adults can only identify emotional expressions at a level similar to young teenagers. Non-verbal communication may also differ by culture. Many negative emotions such as anger or disgust can be recognized across cultures, but some positive emotions such as joy and happiness are often communicated with culture-specific signals and thus may be difficult for people from other cultures to recognize (Sauter et al., 2010). Verbal and non-verbal communication may be either concordant or discordant. When they are concordant, what is said is harmonious with a person's actions. When they are discordant, however, a person might be saying one thing while non-verbally communicating something different. For example, if a woman says, "I really like you," with a deadpan expression on her face, we might conclude that she is being sarcastic. Non-verbal communication can thus change the meaning of verbal communication entirely. As humans, we are uniquely designed to read these non-verbal cues and respond accordingly. Interestingly, most children do not learn to identify sarcasm until later in childhood (Glenwright & Pexman, 2010).

How well can one read non-verbal cues of someone with whom one is interacting? Is it easier to read the non-verbal cues of someone we know well? The ability to do so is an important ingredient in successful interpersonal relationships. It might be easier to read someone once we know them well. Overall, women are typically better at decoding and translating non-verbal communication (DeLange, 1995). Furthermore, women's non-verbal communication techniques tend to include more eye contact and head nods, while men's techniques tend to have fewer non-verbal cues to let

© Mary Kate Denny/PhotoEdit

Looking at the non-verbal cues in this photo, what would you guess is going on with this couple and why?

non-verbal communication
Communication without words, including eye contact, head nodding, touching, and the like.

others know that they are listening (J.C. Pearson et al., 1991). Women have also been found to smile, lean forward, touch, and gaze more often than men in conversation (Wood, 1999).

Computer-Mediated Communication

Computer-mediated communication (CMC) includes communication tools for conveying written text via the Internet. This includes emailing, texting, tweeting, and communicating through Facebook. Internet communication has increased in popularity over the last few years, and most of today's college students use such CMC methods daily in their communication with their friends and family. There are some issues related to such communication for many couples. There are also questions about CMC exchanges. How does it compare with face-to-face communication? Are there differences in how women and men communicate online?

We will discuss meeting people online in more detail in Chapter 13. For now, we will only introduce the topic briefly. One of the advantages of communicating online is that it is possible to gather information from a person's profile such as a Facebook page before meeting face-to-face, or "in real life."

Surprisingly, researchers have found that information posted on people's Facebook pages can provide fairly accurate information about someone's personality (Back et al., 2010). Many people are skeptical about the probability of meeting a partner online given that conversations are reduced only typed words or video relays, but couples can often become acquainted easily.

Online communication can reduce the role that physical characteristics play in the development of attraction and, as a result,

As an undergraduate student, Mark Zuckerberg created *CourseMatch* in 2003 to help Harvard students find out what courses their friends were taking. Soon afterward he created *Facemash*, which allowed students to rate the attractiveness of two fellow students. In 2004, he launched *Thefacebook*, which eventually became *Facebook*. As of 2011, *Zuckerberg's* personal wealth was estimated at $13.5 billion.

© Bloomberg/Getty Images

On Your Mind

How private are Facebook pages?

Even though social networking services have privacy settings, there is no guarantee that posted information will not reach the wrong people or the public in general. In 2009, a Quebec woman was on paid leave from her employment due to clinical depression. Her employer then found pictures she posted of herself on Facebook having fun at the beach and at a bar featuring male strippers. Her sick leave benefits were immediately cut off (Fowler, 2012). Lyndon et al. (2011) surveyed 411 college students on whether and how they might stalk ex-partners on Facebook. They found that a significant number engaged in such behaviours as public harassment and venting. It is wise, therefore, to be cautious about the type of information you post on your Facebook page.

enhance rapport and self-disclosure. People who communicate online often have higher rates of self-disclosure and direct questioning than those who meet face-to-face (Antheunis et al., 2007; Gibbs et al., 2006). There may even be some advantages to meeting people online. For example, doing so can enhance personal communication by making it easier to stay in touch with people. Horrigan et al. (2001) found that more than half of Internet users reported increased communication with their families, and nearly 70 percent reported increased communication with friends.

Other researchers have found gender effects in online communication styles (Baron, 2004; Colley et al., 2010). For example, communicating with others online has been found to reduce gender roles that are often in place during face-to-face conversation and may constrain it. As a result, women often have an easier time making their voices heard online. They also tend to use **emoticons** (e-MOTE-ick-cons) more often than men do (B.P. Bailey et al., 2003; Baron, 2004). Emoticons serve to express emotions but they may also deflect from the seriousness of women's statements (Dresner & Herring, 2010; Riordan & Kreuz, 2010). In this respect, they are similar to tag questions during used during face-to-face conversation.

Many people now use dating sites to look for and initiate meaningful relationships. It is interesting to consider, however, that in textual chats non-verbal communication would not exist. This means of partner formation thus misses the rich nuances of body language, which may give clues as to another person's interest. One Canadian study (Kotlyar, & Ariely, 2013) examined the use of **avatars** (see Figure 11.1) as substitutes for non-verbal communication and found that participants rated

computer-mediated communication (CMC)
Communication through networked computers.

emoticons
Facial symbols used in online communication that represent emotions (e.g., ☺).

avatar
A computer user's online representation of himself or herself presented in two- or three-dimensional art.

their chats far more positively as a result. Avatars may be crude substitutes, but they do bring back some important variables in non-verbal communication.

There is also some research on the use of avatars in CMC (see Figure 11.1), which have increasingly been used to express emotions or feelings in online communication (Koda et al., 2009; Palomares & Lee, 2010). The online expression of emotion through emoticons or avatars may not be universally understood within all cultures. Studies have found that there are cultural differences in their interpretation (Koda et al., 2009). Generally, negative expressions (such as frowns or furrowed brows) have a wider cultural understanding, while positive expressions (such as smiling or winking) have more variations in interpretation (Koda et al., 2009).

It is important to point out that researchers who study online communication often have no way of knowing the gender of the people online because people may create "virtual identities" online that bare little or no resemblance to their own (McAdams, 1996; Vaast, 2007). A man might claim to be a woman or the reverse. However, one study found that by using linguistic gender markers, including references to emotion, insults, and compliments, it was possible to identify the gender of anonymous CMC users with 91.4 percent accuracy (Thomson & Murachver, 2001).

REAL Research What are the differences between people who use Facebook and people who do not? Canadian psychologists Ljepava et al. (2013) distributed questionnaires online to explore this question and found a number of significant differences. Non-users of Facebook were less likely to self-disclose and had higher covert narcissistic traits. Frequent users showed more overt narcissistic traits and reported more intimate friends.

© Laurel/Alamy

© mona redshine studio/Shutterstock

FIGURE **11.1** Avatars, which are often used in online communication, can be used to help users express emotions or feelings. What emotions do you think these avatars are expressing?

There is even evidence in Canada (and no doubt elsewhere) that children and teenagers go online posing as adults as a way of rehearsing for real-life encounters (Lynch, 2007), so it is wise to exercise caution.

Infidelity is the breach of a promise, whether explicitly stated through marriage vows or implied. If two people have agreed to be monogamous, and if one of them is not, that person has been unfaithful to the other by definition. When considering traditional infidelity, one can imagine a sliding scale of intimacy with someone outside of a relationship. People may flirt with others, kiss or grope, have intercourse once, have a long-term affair, or even be involved in secret bigamy (being in two marriages simultaneously), which is illegal under Canadian law. Some people might be tolerant of a little flirting by their partners, but the more intimate the contact, the more likely it would be defined as infidelity.

Where would having erotic chats with others online fit in? What if one partner finds such a chat on the other partner's computer or perhaps even catches him or her masturbating with someone on Skype? Again we might imagine a sliding scale. A person may be caught having cybersex with someone in the same city, thus enabling a real possibility of meeting in person in the future, or the other person may be half a world away, virtually precluding any future meeting. The former instance might be considered highly threatening since the other person might appear in the real world; the latter is less so since the other person would never appear. Some partners might not be threatened at all; others believe that if one's attention is on someone else in a sexual manner, then it is cheating, regardless of the possibility of it becoming real. Not only is there a sexual connection, but often an emotional one as well.

Research on such matters has been only recent. Guadagno and Sagarin (2010) gave questionnaires to 332 heterosexual undergraduates and found that while they considered online fidelity to be serious, it caused less emotional distress than in-person infidelity. Henline et al. (2007) found a similar pattern with 123 university students in that online infidelity was considered a less serious breach. There was a difference, however, in attitudes toward online activity that was purely sexual as opposed to sexual and emotional. Not only was an emotional connection considered more threatening, but it was believed that one would likely lead to the other and that this would make a future meeting in person more likely. Finally, Whitty and Quigley (2008), in their survey of undergraduates in Northern Ireland, found similar results in that while online infidelity was considered a transgression, it was far less serious than offline infidelity.

One thing seems certain: Online sexuality is such a new phenomenon (barely 30 years old) that it is difficult to grasp all of the ways it impacts social life. Online infidelity is thus something that most couples are likely experiencing for the first time. It might thus be wise to discuss such matters before they become an issue.

Over the past few years, online social networks have become popular. Social networks are structures made up of individuals who are tied together through institutions, friendships, dating, or special interests. Social relationships are viewed in terms of "nodes" (individuals) and "ties" (the connections between the individuals) forming a map of connections between people. They cater to a variety of interests such as music, gaming, politics, and travel. There are also networks for gay, lesbian, and bisexual people, as well as ethnic and racial groups.

Facebook is the most popular site in Canada, with 19 million people logging on to their pages at least once a month and 14 million doing so daily. This proportion of the population is higher than both the United States and the global average. Instagram is the second-most popular site, with a rapidly growing membership (*Maclean's*, 2013).

Since 2006, Facebook has been open to anyone over age 13. It is the most popular website for uploading photos—14 million are uploaded each day.

Researchers of social networks have found that the shape of a network affects its usefulness to a member. Smaller and tighter networks allow for less variety because people tend to have similar knowledge bases and attitudes. Larger networks often allow more creativity and open discussions about new ideas and topics.

Early research on social networks found that most people are able to form only a limited number of connections to other people. "Dunbar's number" is a concept that proposed that the typical size of a social network is 150 members (Bialik, 2007; Dunbar, 1998). This number was concluded from cross-cultural and evolutionary research that found a limit to how many friends a person can recognize and about whom he or she can track information.

Review Questions

1 Explain why good communication is vital to a healthy relationship. Give some examples of how poor communication might lead to problems in a relationship.

2 Describe the three competing goals for good communication. What might be the best way to merge these goals successfully?

3 How might non-verbal communication enhance intimacy when forming a relationship? How might the lack of it during textual chats inhibit intimacy?

4 What are some differences between individualistic and collectivistic cultures as well as high- and low-context cultures?

Describe how these differences can affect communication.

5 How might infidelity differ online compared to that in real life? What does research say?

Sexual Communication

The discussion so far has been about communicating with people in everyday life. What about communicating with intimate partners about sex? This is often more challenging because sexuality is a sensitive topic for many people. Despite how Canadian society has progressed over the decades, there are still social forces that instill a sense of shame about sexual thoughts and feelings and people are often taught at an early age not to talk about sex or to refer to it only with euphemisms. Approaching the subject for the first time in a relationship implies moving to a new level of intimacy. It also risks judgment and possible rejection. Some couples avoid conversations about sex altogether. It is therefore not surprising that when Hickman and Muehlenhard (1999) asked people how they showed their consent to engage in sex with a partner, the majority reported that they said nothing at all. There is strong evidence, however, that couples who are able to communicate with each other about sexual issues experience more relationship satisfaction (Faulkner & Lannutti, 2010).

Important Components in Sexual Communication

Several factors contribute to healthy sexual communication. They are a positive self-image, self-disclosure, trust, and listening. We discuss each separately.

Positive Self-Images and Feeling Good about Oneself

Healthy sexuality depends on feeling good about oneself. If people have negative self-images or do not like certain aspects of their bodies or personalities, they will likely have difficulties feeling attractive to intimate partners. Imagine a person who is

Good lovers are not mind readers. They learn what turns their partners on through listening and communication.

Self-Disclosure and Asking for What One Needs

Opening up and talking with a partner, or **self-disclosure**, helps deepen intimacy and sexual satisfaction (Macneil, 2004; Posey et al., 2010; Schiffrin et al., 2010). This is important in maintaining healthy and satisfying sexual relationships. Self-disclosure lets one's partner know what is wrong and how one feels about it. It also enables one to ask for specific changes (Fowers, 1998). When people open up and share, their partners are more likely to do the same (Posey et al., 2010).

Good lovers are not mind readers—they are simply able and willing to listen and communicate with their partners. Doing so helps ensure that both partners are on the same page when it comes to various sexual activities and behaviours. One example comes from a self-help book by Masterton (1987) entitled *How to Drive Your Woman Wild in Bed*. In the book, one man recounted an early sexual experience:

> I'll never forget the first time. She was lying on her parents' bed with the lamplight shining on her, naked and suntanned all over... I climbed on that bed and I lifted her up onto my thighs—she was so light I could always pick her right up—and I opened up her [vagina] with one hand and I rammed my [penis] up there like it was a Polaris missile. Do you know, she screamed out loud, and she dug her nails in my back, and without being too crude about it, I [screwed] her until she didn't know what the hell was happening.... She loved it. She screamed out loud every single time. I mean I was an active, aggressive lover. (Masterton, 1987, p. 70)

overly concerned about his or her body while in bed with a partner. For example, a woman might be worried that her partner will not be attracted to her body because of its size or shape. A man might be anxious about the size of his penis. Such fears interfere with people's ability to, relax, open up, and enjoy a sexual experience.

Talking about anxieties, concerns, or worries with partners can help them to understand, and this may even be the first step toward coming to terms with such issues. Furthermore, many people have parts of their bodies they wish they could change and many people are more critical of their own bodies than those of their partners. This is especially true for women. Rawana and Morgan (2014) looked at 4359 adolescents aged 12 to 21 using data from the Canadian-based National Longitudinal Survey of Children and Youth. They found that girls were far more likely to suffer from low self-esteem due to negative body images. This problem is so pervasive that there are now efforts to implement programs designed to increase self-esteem and body image in Canadian schools (Norwood et al., 2011).

Self-esteem has a powerful effect on how people communicate with others (Adler et al., 2007). People with positive self-esteem often expect to be accepted by their partners, while those with negative self-esteem might expect to be rejected (Hamachek, 1982). It is not difficult to see how negative self-image and fear of rejection can inhibit healthy sexual communication.

Learning to like one's own body may be difficult. In Chapter 1, we discussed the impact of advertisements in magazines and on television on people's insecurities with their portrayals of ideal bodies. The beauty images that the media present are typically impossible to achieve and leave many people feeling unattractive by comparison. To sell products, advertisers must first convince people that they are not okay the way they are—that they need to change their looks, smell, or habits. North American society puts a high value on physical attractiveness throughout the life cycle, and body image greatly affects how attractive one feels.

On Your Mind

Are there ways that people can make themselves more attractive to romantic partners?

Researchers at North Carolina State University have found evidence suggesting that when people reward partner interactions through communication, they will become more physically attractive to their partners (Albada et al., 2002). Couples in this research who communicated in positive ways such as giving compliments or expressing affection rated each other more physically attractive than those who did not. The bottom line is that good communication can enhance physical attractiveness.

His partner, however, viewed the sex differently:

> What did I think about it?... I don't know. I think the only word you could use would be "flabbergasted" He threw me on the bed as if he were Tarzan, and tugged off all of my clothes, and then he took off his own clothes so fast it was almost like he was trying to beat the world record.... He took hold of me and virtually lifted me right up in the air as if I were a child, and then he pushed himself right up me, with hardly any foreplay or any preliminaries or anything. (Masterton, 1987, p. 73)

self-disclosure
The process of sharing feelings.

Communication and Sexuality

Communication is vital here. While the man thought he was doing exactly what his partner wanted, the woman was wondering why he was behaving in such a way. Eventually, this couple's relationship ended because the two were unable to open up and talk about what they needed and wanted in their sexual relationship. This left both feeling confused and frustrated. If this couple would have self-disclosed more, they might have been able to work through their issues. Without doing so, however, the relationship was destined to fail.

Discussing sexual needs with a partner has been found to increase relationship satisfaction (Moore, 2010; Noland, 2010). This is not

On Your Mind

What are the best pick-up lines? Do they really work?

One can find many websites with long lists of pick-up lines and there is no doubt competition for the worst of them. Here are some contenders that would make anyone groan:

- "If I could rearrange the alphabet, I'd put U and I together."
- "Are you sitting on the F5 key? Your backside is refreshing."
- "If you were a booger I'd pick you first."
- "Do you have any raisons? No? Then how about a date"?
- "You must be tired because you've been running through my mind all night."

Social psychologists have actually looked at the use of pick-up lines (or opening lines) in order to measure their effectiveness. Senko and Fyffe (2010) saw three types of lines: flippant (e.g., "Do you have a sunburn or are you always this hot"?), direct (e.g., "I feel a little embarrassed about this but I'd like to meet you. What's your name?"), and Innocuous (e.g., "Do you have the time"?). To test them out, they asked 70 college women to imagine a male stranger approaching them with a flippant, innocuous, or direct line. The men were described as attractive or non-attractive, or they were not described at all. The women were then asked to rate whether they would be willing to engage in a long-term or a short-term relationship with the man. For long-term relationships, the women were more likely to favour direct or innocuous lines, since flippant ones signified a lack of trustworthiness. For short-term relationships, it did not matter what opening lines were used as long as the man was attractive. As this research suggests, the success of an opening line depends not so much on its content but upon a man's level of attractiveness and a woman's sexual goals.

Should one use flippant opening lines? Senko and Fyffe's research seems to say no, although they suggest that flippancy is also intended to show a sense of humour, which is a desirable trait in long-term relationships. The best advice, however, is probably to be genuine and, if that is not possible, be original!

always easy. Telling a partner what one wants during sexual activity can be difficult. Sexuality is an area where many people feel insecure. Many people wonder whether they are good in bed and worry that their partners might not think so. At the same time, they may be hesitant to make suggestions to improve their partners' techniques, thinking that they may feel insulted. Such anxieties do not foster a sense of open and mutual communication. Ultimately, not being open about one's likes or dislikes is self-defeating and may lead to resentment and unhappiness.

Trusting One's Partner

One of the most important ingredients in any happy and satisfying sexual relationship is trust (Simpson, 2007). Trusting one's partner leads to confidence in him or her and a feeling of security in a relationship. Earlier, we discussed the importance of the family of origin in learning to communicate. The family also contributes to one's ability to trust an intimate partner. Having more trusting relationships early in life lays the foundation for happier and healthier sexual relationships later on (Campbell et al., 2010). We also discussed the importance of self-disclosure. A key factor related to the ability to self-disclose in sexual relationships is trust (Ignatius & Kokkonen, 2007). With trust,, self-disclosure becomes easier.

Building trust, however, takes time. It is typically a process of *uncertainty reduction* (Holmes & Rempel, 1989). Prior relationships might influence the ability to trust, but the level of trust in any new sexual relationship depends in large part on various aspects of the partner (Campell et al., 2010). Being hurt by someone before, experiencing a loss, or being fearful about rejection can all interfere with the ability to trust an intimate partner but, over time, trust can be improved.

People who report being more trusting of their partners also tend to be more optimistic about their relationships and think more positive thoughts about their partner's negative behaviours (e.g., trusting partners are less likely to take things personally if their partners are late in meeting them; Simpson, 2007). On the other hand, non-trusting partners are more likely to have doubts and concerns and are more likely to think their partners do not love them enough.

Non-verbal Communication

As mentioned earlier, non-verbal communication can include facial expressions, hand and arm gestures, postures, body positioning, and other movements (Ekman & Friesen, 1969; Mehrabian, 2009; Sauter et al., 2010). It can be especially important in sexual relationships because of many people's reluctance to communicate verbally.

Although verbal communication about one's likes and needs is more effective than non-verbal communication, it is useful in expressing sexual desires and it also reinforces verbal messages. For example, if a woman would like her partner to touch her breasts more during sexual activity, she can show this by moving her body more when her partner is doing so. She can also move her partner's hand to her breasts or she can moan to communicate her pleasure. Keep in mind, however, that this can lead to misunderstandings, as demonstrated by a couple cited in Barbach's (1982) self-help book self-help book entitled *For Each Other: Sharing Sexual Intimacy:*

> One woman attempted to communicate her preference for being kissed on the ears by kissing her partner's ears. However, she found that the more she kissed her partner's ears, the less he seemed to kiss hers. Over a period of time her kissing of his ears continued to increase, while his kissing of her ears stopped altogether. Finally she asked him why he never kissed her ears anymore, only to discover that he hated having his ears kissed and was trying to communicate this by not kissing hers. After their discussion, he began to kiss her ears, she stopped kissing his, and both were happier for the exchange. (Barbach, 1982, p. 105)

Obstacles to Sexual Communication

Several factors can interfere with people's ability to talk about sex with their partners such as embarrassment or concerns about sexual terminology.

Although many couples avoid communication about sex, learning to communicate one's sexual desires and needs can strengthen a relationship.

Embarrassment

Earlier we discussed how many people are instilled with a sense of shame about sexuality as they grow up. Many have been taught that sex is dirty or bad and they feel uncomfortable talking about it. There are ways, however, to avoid embarrassment and feel more comfortable talking about sex.

For one thing, it is good to relax and take things slowly.

Researchers have found that many young adults are embarrassed when talking about sex (van Teijlingen et al., 2007), and this can inhibit one's ability to open up and talk with one's partners. People often worry that their partners will judge them or think differently about them if they do, but it is also likely that they will appreciate being told the truth.

Opening up to a partner gets easier over time. The more comfortable one becomes in a relationship, the less embarrassing talking about sex tends to be. For some, using humour and being able to laugh can help reduce tension, although this should be good natured. One Canadian study (Campbell et al., 2008) looked at the use of humour by 98 dating couples and found that when the humour was affiliative rather than aggressive, people reported being more satisfied with their dates.

Sexual Terminology

To have a meaningful conversation about sexuality with one's partner, one needs be familiar with sexual terms. This book provides many terms for sex organs, behaviours, and activities, but it is also a good idea to use terms with which one is most comfortable. Some people may be more comfortable with terms such as *vagina, penis,* and *sexual intercourse,* while others use sexual slang such as *pussy, cock,* and *fucking.* For some people, scientific terminology can be unromantic and awkward, while sexual slang may lead to discomfort in others. Talking about vocabulary issues with one's partner can help lessen anxiety and make one more comfortable with sexual communication.

Review Questions

1 Why is a positive self-image important in sexual relationships and how can it improve communication?

2 Explain how self-disclosure and trust can increase satisfaction in sexual relationships.

3 How can non-verbal communication help express sexual likes and dislikes?

4 Identify and explain some obstacles to sexual communication.

Listening, Expressing Criticism, and Non-constructive Communication

Some couples tend to criticize each other when it is best to listen and make positive comments (P. Coleman, 2002). Often, a person becomes defensive and angry when the other says something he or she doesn't want to hear. We now discuss the importance of listening, constructive communication, and verbal disagreements.

The Importance of Listening

Listening is an important communication skill (Adler et al., 2007). According to some research, adults spend nearly 70 percent of their waking time communicating and 45 percent of this time listening (Adler et al., 2007; Rankin, 1952). **Active listening** involves the use of non-verbal communication to let others know that one is attentive and present in a conversation. For example, while one person is talking, the other maintains eye contact to show that she or he is actively listening.

Another important skill is **non-defensive listening**, which involves focusing one's attention on what others are saying without being defensive (Gottman, 1994). This technique relies on self-restraint, which is sometimes absent in couples who have a difficult time listening to each other. It can be difficult to listen fully, but this skill reduces one's inclination to interrupt or to defend oneself.

Poor listeners often think that they understand what their partners are trying to say, but they often do not. They might also try to circumvent a discussion by talking about something else. It is difficult to really listen to someone when one is angry or defensive. Good listening allows people to understand and retain information while building and maintaining their relationships (Adler et al., 2007).

Becoming a More Effective Listener

A number of things interfere with people's ability to be a effective listeners, such as information overload, preoccupation with personal concerns, rapid thoughts, and noise (Golen, 1990; Hulbert, 1989). It is easy to reach information overload today because people hear so much during the course of a day that it can be difficult to listen carefully to everything. As a result, human beings tend to be selective in what they hear. A preoccupation with personal concerns may also interfere with the ability to listen. Listening is also affected by the brain actively processing information within the environment. Consider this: People are capable of understanding speech at rates of up to 600 words per minute, yet the average person speaks at a rate of 100 to 140 words per minute (Versfeld & Dreschler, 2002). This gives the brain time to think about other things at the same time one is listening. As a result, it may be hard to focus on what is being said. Finally, other conversations, music, and even traffic noise can all interfere with people's ability to listen. Listening to another person is therefore not an automatic process but something that takes practice as well as effort.

One Canadian study (Doell, 2011) found that improving on listening skills can increase the quality of a relationship. Doell looked at data from 14 married couples in therapy and found that as listening skills increased, the couples reported being more satisfied with their relationships and had a greater sense of "we-ness" or sense of being a couple as opposed to two separate people.

Being listened to can make people feel worthy, protected, and cared about. One strategy that may be helpful is to summarize what one's partner has said briefly once it has been said. This lets people know they have been heard and enables them to correct any misunderstandings. Similarly, it is important to validate people's statements with such phrases as "I can understand why you might feel that way" or "I know what you mean." In sum, good listening can only add to the intimacy of a relationship.

Message Interpretation

Imagine a situation where someone trips and falls while walking in the park one day. Someone else says, "Be careful!" How can that be interpreted? Does it mean that the person was moving too quickly? Does it mean that the other is genuinely concerned about possible injury? In any conversation, each person must interpret the meaning of the other's message (R. Edwards, 1998), and this is dependent on factors such as the nature of the relationship, one's mood at the time, or the situation one is in.

If people are angry, they might perceive more hostility in ambiguous or benign comments (Epps & Kendall, 1995). Being worried about something or preoccupied with an issue can also affect one's interpretation. For example, in one study, women who were preoccupied with their weight were more likely to interpret ambiguous sentences with negative meanings, while women who were not so preoccupied did not (Jackman et al., 1995). Because they were conscious of their weight, they assumed others might notice it as well. Because of such differential interpretation, misunderstandings sometimes arise. It is thus important that if one is unsure of what was said, one should attempt to clarify.

Negative Feelings and Criticism

Everyone becomes angry now and then and not all conversations have happy and peaceful endings. Because of this, it is important to manage any tension. When couples disagree, the start of such a conversation can indicate whether the two will become angry or quietly discuss the issue at hand (P. Coleman, 2002). If harsh words are used, chances are that a disagreement will emerge and

---

active listening
Communication and listening techniques where listeners use non-verbal communication such as nodding or eye contact to signal that they are attentive to a speaker.

non-defensive listening
A listening strategy in which listeners focus attention on what others are saying without being defensive.

tension will escalate. However, if softer words are used, there is a better chance that the disagreement can be resolved.

It is also important to gracefully accept criticism, which may be difficult. Everyone also becomes defensive at times. Although it might be impossible to eliminate all defensiveness, it is important to reduce it to resolve disagreements. This enables one to hear what the other is saying. Common defensive techniques are to deny criticism (e.g., "That is just not true"!), make excuses without taking any responsibility (e.g., "I was just exhausted"!), deflecting responsibility (e.g., "Me? What about your behaviour"?), and righteous indignation (e.g., "How could you possibly say such a hurtful thing"?) (P. Coleman, 2002). All of these techniques interfere with one's ability to understand what others are saying. Keeping defensiveness in check is another important aspect of good communication.

Unhappy couples tend to filter out positive comments even when they are not in conflict and even tend to interpret neutral ones negatively. In contrast, happy couples tend to interpret neutral comments positively (Nelson, 2005). This suggests that neutral comments are often interpreted on the basis of the quality of a relationship.

Non-constructive Communication: "Don't Yell at Me"!

Couples often make mistakes in their communication patterns, which can lead to arguments, misunderstandings, and conflicts. **Overgeneralizations**—such as making statements like "Why do you always…?" or "You never…."—generally exaggerate the frequency of an issue. This can lead to defensiveness and communication shutdown. It is best to be specific about complaints and tell others what is on one's mind. For example, if one member of a couple is frustrated by the amount of time the other member spends with friends, it is important to communicate this issue specifically without being defensive or overgeneralizing. When this is done, compromise of a resolution is more likely.

Name-calling may make any situation worse. Derogatory terms will not lead to healthy communication. Digging up the past is another non-constructive communication pattern that also adds to negativity. It is further important to stay away from old arguments and accusations. If a situation is resolved on the spot, there will likely be no past animosities to dwell on.

Another common mistake that couples make in conversations is to use **overkill**. When one is frustrated with one's partner and threatens the worst (e.g., "If you don't do that, I will leave you"), the results may backfire. It is important to focus on the issue at hand and not any extraneous factors.

It is also a good idea not to get overwhelmed and throw too many issues in the conversation at once. This makes it difficult to focus on resolving any one issue because there is too much happening. Also, avoid yelling or screaming, which can cause people to become defensive and angry as well as less likely attune themselves to what is being said. Even though it may not be easy at times, it is important to stay calm when confronting someone with one's frustrations.

Any of these communication patterns can interfere with the resolution of problems and concerns.

Fighting

Verbal disagreements are a common part of intimate relationships and are more likely during times of stress (Bodenmann et al., 2010). Couples may disagree about public issues, concerns outside of their relationship, or personal issues (Johnson, 2009). Generally, discussing public issues may be stimulating, while arguing about personal issues is may help to portray oneself in a more positive light (Johnson, 2009). Regardless of the type of argument, couples who disagree are usually happier than those who say, "We never fight!" It is important to point out, however, that verbal disagreements are different from physical violence. We will discuss domestic violence in Chapter 17.

Happy couples have been found to think more positive thoughts about each other during their disagreements while unhappy couples are inundated with negative thoughts about each other (P. Coleman, 2002). Even though a happy couple may disagree about an issue, the two partners still feel positively about each other. Forgiveness is another important aspect of healthy couples. Couples who positively rate their relationships are more likely to forgive their partners for transgressions, while those less invested in a relationship are more likely to withhold forgiveness (Guerrero & Bachman, 2010).

> **REAL Research** Schumann and Ross (2010), two psychologists from the University of Waterloo, were interested in why women tend to apologize more than men. They asked a sample of men and women to keep diaries where they recorded all offences they had committed or experienced and whether an apology was made by either themselves or the other parties. Women reported more apologies, but they also reported committing more offences. There were actually no gender differences in the number of apologies offered. The findings suggest that men apologize less frequently because they have a higher threshold of what amounts to behaviour that warrants an apology.

Some couples avoid conflict by ignoring problems or avoiding communicating about sensitive issues (Dillow et al., 2009). Women are especially more likely to say that this decreases their satisfaction in relationship (Afifi et al., 2009).

What happens after an argument? Generally, women are more likely to want a re-establishment of closeness, while men are more likely to withdraw (Noller, 1993). Taking a time-out and finishing a discussion later, learning to compromise, or validating each others' differences in opinions are some of the ways to resolve a disagreement. In many relationships, however, there may be issues

overgeneralization
Making statements that tend to exaggerate the frequency of a particular issue.

overkill
A common mistake that couples make during arguments where one person threatens the worst but does not mean what he or she says.

Communication and Sexuality **311**

that are unresolvable. It is important to know which issues can be worked out and which cannot.

Throughout this chapter, we have discussed the importance of communication and its role in the development of healthy and satisfying relationships. When it comes to sexual relationships, good communication skills are vital. By talking to one's partner, one can communicate sexual needs and desires and learn one's partner's sexual needs. This can strengthen a relationship. It is important to be honest and open and ask for what one needs.

REAL Research Vicki Deveau, a University of Calgary doctoral student in psychology, looked at issues of seeking revenge upon intimate partners. Among her findings were that couple members sometimes wanted revenge but did not seek revenge, believing that this was not the right thing to do (Deveau, 2006).

Review Questions

1 Why is listening one of the most important communication skills? What is non-defensive listening?

2 Explain how information overload, personal concerns, rapid thoughts, and noise interfere with people's ability to listen.

3 Describe two non-constructive communication strategies and explain why they might lead to a communication shutdown.

Chapter Review

Summary Points

1 Good communication skills are integral to all healthy relationships. Couples who know how to communicate are happier, more satisfied, and have a better chance of making their relationship last. Many relationship problems stem from poor communication.

2 Communication fosters mutual understanding, increases emotional intimacy, and helps deepen feelings of love and intimacy. A lack of communication skills often leads to trouble in relationships. Having poor communication skills, an inability to self-disclose, or trouble listening can all lead to communication problems.

3 The three goals of communication include getting the job done, maintaining the relationship, and managing one's identity. These goals compete with each other making communication difficult.

4 An ability to communicate and the strategies used to do so are learned through interactions within families. Some of these skills are negotiation, conflict avoidance, and arguing effectively. Children develop a social and emotional understanding of the world around them.

5 Deborah Tannen proposed that there are fundamental differences between the way men and women communicate. She called these differences *genderlects*. She found that women engage in more rapport-talk while men engage in more report-talk.

6 Two categories of communication skills have been proposed—affective and instrumental. Affectively oriented skills involve comforting and listening, while instrumentally oriented skills are more narrative and persuasive. Women are more likely to value the former, while men are more likely to value the latter.

7 Some theorists have attempted to explain gender differences in communication. Gender communication may be understood from a cross-cultural perspective. Researchers have suggested that men and women may come from different sociolinguistic subcultures and learn different rules of communication.

8 Individualistic cultures encourage their members to have individual goals and values and an independent sense of self. Collectivist cultures emphasize the needs of members over individuals. Communication patterns have been found to vary depending on cultural orientation. In addition, anthropologists have

identified low- and high-context cultures. The first type uses language to express thoughts and feelings directly while the second type relies more on subtle and non-verbal cues.

9 Most communication is non-verbal—such as using eye contact, smiling, or touching. Non-verbal communication can trigger an *emotional contagion* in listeners. As people get older, they get better at recognizing non-verbal cues, but at a certain age our abilities to recognize these cues begin to decrease. Researchers have found that women are better at decoding and translating non-verbal communication.

10 Computer-mediated communication (CMC) has become important in the last two decades. It can reduce the role that physical characteristics play and increase rapport and self-disclosure. It can also reduce the constraints that gender roles have upon communication. There is some research suggesting that women have an easier time making their voices heard online than in face-to-face communication.

11 Women are more likely to use emoticons online. Avatars may be used to express emotions or feelings as well. However, there are cultural differences in the interpretation of online avatars. Negative expressions have a wider cultural understanding, while positive ones have more variations.

12 Sex often magnifies communication that exists in any close relationship. Many people are taught that talking about sex is dirty and are therefore uncomfortable with it. Couples who communicate about sexual issues report more relationship satisfaction. Those with a positive self-esteem often expect their partners to accept them, while those with negative self-esteem often expect rejection. Although verbal communication about sex is preferable, non-verbal communication is also useful.

13 Self-disclosure is critical in maintaining healthy and satisfying sexual relationships. It helps partners know each other's needs. Trust is also important and it makes self-disclosure easier. Those who trust their sex partners feel better about their relationships. Both embarrassment and sexual terminology issues can interfere with people's ability to communicate about sex.

14 Some things can interfere with the ability to listen, such as information overload, personal concerns, rapid thoughts, and noise. Active and non-defensive listening are important.

15 When we express negative feelings, it is important not to use harsh words because tension may escalate. It is also important to learn to accept criticism without becoming defensive. Some mistakes in communication patterns are overgeneralizations, name-calling, and overkill. Verbal disagreements are a common part of intimate relationships and often occur during times of stress. Happy couples think more positive thoughts during disagreements than do unhappy ones.

Critical Thinking Questions

1 Researchers have found that couples who know how to communicate have a greater likelihood of making their relationship last. What do you believe is the key to a good relationship?

2 What does the research show about any communication differences between the genders? Where would men be at an advantage, and where would women be at an advantage?

3 Non-verbal communication is sometimes involuntary (where people give impressions unintentionally) and sometimes voluntary (where the movement is intentional). Give an example of both.

4 What are the advantages and disadvantages of social networking services? How have they changed the ways we communicate?

5 Identify some of the problems people might have in communicating with their partners about sexual issues? How might they be resolved?

6 How might the absence of gender variation in same-sex relationships affect gay and lesbian couples?

7 What are some of the obstacles to communication among couples of different languages? How might this affect a relationship?

8 Are there any differences in the ways that men and women communicate? What does the research say, and are there any disagreements over the findings?

Websites

The Journal of Communication   This is an interdisciplinary journal with an extensive online offering that focuses upon communication research, practice, policy, and theory, and includes the most up-to-date and important findings in the communication field. (http://onlinelibrary.wiley.com/journal/10.1111/(ISSN)1460-2466)

The Canadian Journal of Communication   This journal publishes Canadian research and scholarship upon communication. As its website states, "In pursuing this objective, particular attention is paid to research that has a distinctive Canadian flavour by virtue of choice of topic or by drawing on the legacy of Canadian theory and research. The purview of the journal is the entire field of communication studies as practiced in Canada or with relevance to Canada." (http://www.cjc-online.ca/)

12 Love and Intimacy

Dance Me to the End of Love

Dance me to your beauty with a burning violin
Dance me through the panic 'til I'm gathered safely in
Lift me like an olive branch and be my homeward dove
Dance me to the end of love

Oh let me see your beauty when the witnesses are gone
Let me feel you moving like they do in Babylon
Show me slowly what I only know the limits of
Dance me to the end of love

Dance me to the wedding now, dance me on and on
Dance me very tenderly and dance me very long
We're both of us beneath our love, we're both of
us above
Dance me to the end of love

Dance me to the children who are asking to be born
Dance me through the curtains that our kisses have
outworn
Raise a tent of shelter now, though every thread is torn
Dance me to the end of love

Dance me to your beauty with a burning violin
Dance me through the panic till I'm gathered safely in
Touch me with your naked hand or touch me with
your glove
Dance me to the end of love*

---

* SOURCE: Dance Me To The End Of Love
Words and Music by Leonard Cohen
Copyright © 1985 Sony/ATV Music Publishing LLC and Stranger
Music Inc.

Love and the ability to form intimate relationships with others are important for both our physical and emotional health. In his 1999 best-selling book *Love and Survival: The Scientific Basis for the Healing Power of Intimacy*, Dean Ornish (1999) discusses the importance of love and intimacy. He points to a variety of research studies that support the fact that physical health is strengthened when people feel loved and can open up and talk to each other. Many studies support Ornish's findings and have found that social support and love are related to stronger immune systems and lower levels of illnesses (Dodd, 2010; Goldman-Mellor et al., 2010; Maunder & Hunter, 2008). The following are two other findings from Ornish's (1999) longitudinal research:

- College students who had distant and non-emotional relationships with their parents had significantly higher rates of high blood pressure and heart disease years later than did students who reported close and emotionally connected relationships.

- Heart patients who felt loved had 50 percent less arterial damage than those who said they did not feel loved.

In this chapter, we talk about the forms and measures of love, where love comes from, love throughout the life cycle, and building intimate relationships.

What Is Love?

One of the great mysteries of humankind is the capacity to love, to make attachments with others that involve deep feeling, selflessness, and commitment. Throughout history, literature and art have portrayed the saving powers of love. There have been many songs written about its passion and many films have depicted its power to change people's lives. Yet after centuries of writers discussing love, philosophers musing over its hold on men and women, how much do we really know about love? Are there different kinds of love—friendship, passion, love of parents—or are they all simply variations on one fundamental emotion? Does love really "grow"? Is love different at age 15 than 50? What is the relationship between love and sexuality?

REAL Research Toronto psychologists Karen Dion and Kenneth Dion (1996) point out that the capacity for romantic love may be influenced by whether individuals come from individualistic or collectivist cultures. These factors at both the psychological and societal level have the potential to determine the perceived importance of romantic love in the selection of a partner for marriage.

When people love each other, they experience less stress in their lives, stronger immune systems, and better overall health.

People often wonder why they fall in love with the certain kinds of people. The mystery of love may be part of its attraction. People are surrounded with images of love in the media and are taught from the time they first listen to fairy tales that love is the answer to most of life's problems. Movies, music, and television inundate society with stories of love and these stories have a powerful impact (Griffin, 2006).

Love in Other Times and Places

The desire for love has been around since ancient times. The following poem from the late Egyptian empire written more than 3000 years ago serves as an example:

I found my lover on his bed, and my heart was sweet to excess.
I shall never be far away (from) you while my hand is in your hand,
and I shall stroll with you in every favourite place
How pleasant is this hour, may it extend for me to eternity
since I have lain with you, you have lifted high my heart.
In mourning or in rejoicing be not far from me.
(Quoted in Bergmann, 1987, p. 5)

The Hebrew Bible contains many passages of romantic love and erotic poetry as is evident in the imagery in the Song of Solomon as follows:

How fair and how pleasant art though, O love, for delights!
This thy stature is like to a palm tree, and thy breasts to cluster of grapes.
I said, I will go up to the palm tree, I will take hold of the boughs thereof;
Now also thy breasts shall be as clusters of the vine, and the smell of thy nose like apples.
And the roof of thy mouth like the best wine for my beloved, that goeth down sweetly
Causing the lips of those that are asleep to speak.
(Song of Solomon, 7:6–9, KJV)

The Hebrew Bible even contains stories of same-sex love, as is evident in the relationship between David and Jonathan in II Samuel 1:19-27 (KJV), which is described as "passing the love of women" (Horner, 1978). People of the Middle Ages also glorified **romantic love**, including loving from afar or loving those one could not have (**unrequited love**).

Not until the 19th century did people begin to believe that romantic love was the most desirable type of relationship. Through most of Western history, marriage was an economic union, usually arranged by parents. Once wed, husbands and wives were encouraged to learn to love one another. Today in Western cultures, people typically choose their own romantic partners. This creates a situation that is often difficult for new immigrants to Canada. For example, Nancy Netting (2006), a researcher in British Columbia, looked at the experiences of young Indo-Canadians, who basically live in two worlds. First, they are pressured by the traditional arranged marriage system of their families, and, second, they live in Canadian society where love is the main motivation for marriage. As a result, they are often torn between two worlds and negotiate between two decisions.

Review Questions

1 Discuss the effects of love and intimacy on physical health.

2 Explain how images of love in the media influence people's concept of love.

3 Explain how love today may be different from love that was experienced through most of Western history.

Forms and Measures of Love

Virtually everyone experiences feelings of love for another person, whether it be toward a romantic partner, a parent, a child, or a close friend. Philosophers, historians, psychologists, sociologists, and even poets and singers have all made attempts to untangle the intricacies of love. In this section we look at romantic love as well as other types of love people experience in their daily lives.

Romantic versus Companionate Love

Romantic love is the all-encompassing passionate love of songs and poetry and of tearjerker movies and romance novels and has become the prevailing model of relationships in the Western world. Romantic love may involve passion, infatuation, obsession, and even love-sickness, and with it comes a sense of ecstasy and anxiety, physical attraction, and sexual desire. People tend to idealize their romantic partners, ignoring their faults in the newfound joy of the attachment. Passionate love blooms in the initial euphoria of a new attachment to another person and it often seems as if we are swept away by it. This is why people say that they "fall" in love or even "fall head over heels" in love.

Few feelings are as joyous or exciting as romantic love. Emotions are often so intense that people talk about being unable to contain them. Romantic love feels as if it spills out of us onto everything we see. Some people joke that there is

© Hill Street Studios/Getty

Companionate love involves deep affection, trust, loyalty, attachment, and intimacy. Although passion is often present, companionate love lacks the high and low swings of romantic love.

romantic love
Idealized love based on romance and perfection.

unrequited love
Loving another when the love will never be returned.

1	"Up Where We Belong"	Buffy Sainte-Marie	Saskatchewan
2	"As Only a Heart Would Dare"	Susan Aglukark	Manitoba, Nunavut
3	"Native Puppy Love"	A Tribe Called Red	Ontario
4	"Love is the Only Thing"	Arthur Renwick	British Columbia
5	"Let Love Win"	Bonnie Couchie	Ontario
6	"Loving You"	The C-Weed Band	Manitoba
7	"Don't Say Goodbye"	Colette Trudeau	British Columbia
8	"Never Felt So Alone"	D'Aoust Brothers	Manitoba
9	"Lovesick Blues"	Derek Miller	Ontario
10	"Can't Have Me"	Desiree Dorion	Manitoba

nothing quite as intolerable as those in love. They are so annoyingly happy all the time. It is not surprising that such a powerful emotion is celebrated in poetry, story, and song. It is also not surprising that it seems as though it will last forever. This is at least what is taught when the couples in fairy tales "live happily ever after" and when couples in movies ride off into the sunset.

Unfortunately, perhaps, the passion of that intensity fades after a time. If the relationship is to continue, romantic love usually develops into **companionate love** or **conjugal love**. This type of love involves feelings of deep affection, attachment, intimacy, and ease with the partner as well as the development of trust, loyalty, acceptance, and a willingness to sacrifice (Critelli et al., 1986; Regan, 2006; Shaver & Hazan, 1987). Although companionate love does not have the high and low swings of romantic love, passion is certainly present for many people. Companionate love may even be a deeper more intimate love than romantic love.

It can be difficult for couples to switch from passionate love to the deeper and more mature companionate love (Peck, 1978). Because the model of love they see on television and in movies is a highly sexualized, swept-off-your-feet type of romantic love, some may see the mellowing of that passion as a loss of love rather than a development to another level. Yet the mutual commitment to develop a new, more mature kind of love is, in fact, what is meant by "true love." What follows are some major theories of love from the social sciences.

The Colours of Love: John Alan Lee

Canadian sociologist John Alan Lee (1974, 1988, 1998) suggests that in romantic relationships, there are more forms of love than just romantic and companionate love. Lee collected statements about love from hundreds of works of fiction and nonfiction, starting with the Hebrew Bible and progressing from ancient and modern authors. He gathered a panel of professionals in literature, philosophy, and the social sciences, and had them sort into categories the thousands of statements he found. Lee's research identified six basic ways to love, which he calls "colours of love" and gave each type Greek or Latin names. His categories are described in Table 12.1.

Lee's colours of love have generated a substantial body of research, much of which shows that his love styles are independent from one another and that each can be measured to some degree (Hendrick & Hendrick, 1989). He points out that two lovers with compatible styles are probably going to be happier and more content with each other than two with incompatible styles.

There is also evidence that different love styles sometimes take place in different spheres of our lives. One group of psychologists in Quebec (St-Yves et al., 1990) was interested in whether love of animals affected love of people. In other words, do people who love animals (agape) have a greater capacity for romantic love (eros)? After administering questionnaires to two groups of people, they did find that pet owners loved animals more than non-pet owners, but there were no differences in either group in their capacity for romantic love.

Couples who approach love differently often cannot understand why their partners react the way they do or how they can hurt their partners unintentionally. Imagine how bored an erotic lover would be with a pragmatic lover or how much a ludic lover would hurt a manic lover. In both cases, each would consider the other callous or even cruel, suggests Lee, and this is likely when people simply tend to love differently. Higher levels of manic and ludic love are associated with poorer psychological health, while higher levels of storge and eros love are associated with higher levels of psychological health (Blair, 2000).

companionate or conjugal love
An intimate form of love that involves friendly affection and deep attachment based on a familiarity with the loved one.

Table 12.1 Lee's Colours of Love

John Alan Lee, a professor emeritus of sociology at the University of Toronto, suggests that there are six types of love as follows:

1. **Eros: The Romantic Lover**	Eros is like romantic love. Erotic lovers speak of their immediate attraction to their lovers, to his or her eyes, skin, fragrance, or body. Most have the picture of an ideal partner in their mind which a real partner cannot fulfill; that is why purely erotic love does not last. In childhood, erotic lovers often had a secure attachment with their caregivers.
2. **Ludus (LOO-diss): The Game-Playing Lover**	Ludic lovers play the "game" of love, enjoying the act of seduction. Commitment, dependency, and intimacy are not valued, and ludic lovers will often juggle several relationships at the same time. In childhood, ludic lovers often had an avoidant attachment style with their caregivers.
3. **Storge (STOR-gay): The Quiet, Calm Lover**	Storgic love is a quiet, calm love that builds over time. It is similar to companionate love. Storgic lovers do not suddenly "fall in love" and do not dream of an idealized, romantic lover. Marriage, stability, and comfort within love are the goal. Should the relationship break up, storgic partners would probably remain friends, a status unthinkable to erotic lovers who have split.
4. **Mania: The Crazy Lover**	Manic lovers are possessive and dependent, consumed by thoughts of the beloved, and are often on a roller-coaster of highs and lows. Each encouraging sign from the lover brings joy; each little slight brings heartache. This makes their lives dramatic and painful. Manic lovers fear separation. They may sit by the telephone waiting for the beloved to call or they may call their beloved repeatedly. They tend to wonder why all their relationships ultimately fail. In childhood, manic lovers often had an anxious/ambivalent attachment style with their caregivers.
5. **Pragma: The Practical Lover**	Pragmatic lovers have a "shopping list" of qualities they are looking for in a relationship. They are practical about their relationship and lovers. They want a deep lasting love but believe the best way to get it is to assess their own qualities and make the best "deal" in the romantic marketplace. They tend to be planners—planning the best time to get married, have children, and even when to divorce.
6. **Agape (AH-ga-pay): The Selfless Lover**	Agapic love is altruistic, selfless, never demanding, patient, and true.. It is never jealous, does not need reciprocity, and tends to happen in brief episodes. Lee found very few long-term agapic lovers.

SOURCE: John Allan Lee, "The Styles of Loving," Psychology Today 8(5): 43–51. Reprinted with permission from Psychology Today Magazine. Copyright © 1974 by Sussex Publishers, Inc.

REAL Research Storm and Storm (1984) designed a questionnaire to assess Canadian university students' attitudes toward love, sex, and intimacy. Love and intimacy were both desirable and sex was thought undesirable unless the other two elements were present. Sex with the absence of love was also thought to reduce the chances of intimacy.

Love Triangles: Robert Sternberg

Robert Sternberg (1998, 1999) has suggested that different strategies of loving are really different ways of combining the basic building blocks of love. He has proposed that love is made up of three elements—passion, intimacy, and commitment—that can be combined in different ways. Sternberg refers to the absence of all three components as "non-love."

Passion is sparked by physical attraction and sexual desire and drives a person to pursue a romantic relationship. It instills a deep desire for union, and although it is often expressed sexually, self-esteem, nurturing, domination, submission, and self-actualization may also be involved in the experience. Passion is the element that identifies romantic forms of love. For example, it is absent in the love of a parent for a child. Passion fires up quickly in a romantic relationship and it is often the first element to fade (Ahmetoglu et al., 2010).

Intimacy involves feelings of closeness and connectedness in a loving relationship. It is the emotional investment one has in the relationship and includes such things as a desire to support and help the other, happiness, mutual understanding, emotional support, and communication. The intimacy component of love is experienced in many loving relationships such as those between parent and child, siblings, and friends.

Commitment in the short term is the willingness to love someone. In the long term it is the determination to maintain that love. This element can sustain a relationship that is temporarily (or even permanently) going through a period without passion or intimacy. A marriage ceremony, for example, is a public statement of a couple's commitment to each other. Unlike passion, which is quick to fire up and die out, commitment builds slowly and is often related to relationship length (Ahmetoglu et al., 2010).

Sternberg combines these elements into seven forms of love, which are described in Table 12.2. A person may experience different forms of love at different times; romantic love may give way to companionate love, or the infatuated lover may find a person to whom he or she is willing to commit and settle down. In the emotionally healthy person, as we shall see, love evolves and changes as we mature (Sternberg, 1998).

Can We Measure Love?

Is it possible to measure the strength and quality of love? One strategy is to create a scale that does this by measuring something strongly associated with love. Zick Rubin (1970, 1973) was one of the first researchers to try to scientifically measure love. He conceptualized love as a form of attachment to another person and created a "love scale" that measures what he believed to be the three components of attachment: degrees of needing

Table 12.2 Sternberg's Triangular Theory of Love

Robert Sternberg, a professor of psychology at Yale University in the United States, believes that love is made up of three elements: passion, intimacy, and commitment, each of which may be present in a relationship. The presence of these components produces eight triangles, seven of which involve at least one component and one without any components, referred to as non-love. Problems can occur in a relationship if one person's triangle differs significantly from that of the other. Following are the types of love proposed by Sternberg.

Non-love	In most of our casual daily relationships, there is no sense of intimacy, passion, or commitment.
Liking	When there is intimacy without (sexual) passion and without strong personal commitment, we are friends. Friends can sometimes separate for long periods and resume the relationship as if it had never ended.
Infatuation	Passion alone leads to infatuation, which refers to physiological arousal and a sexual desire for another person. Casual hookups and one-night stands would fall into this category. Typically, infatuation fades, often to be replaced with infatuation for someone else.
Empty love	Empty love involves only commitment such as by a couple who stays together even though their relationship lost its passion and intimacy long ago. Relationships can also begin with commitment alone and develop intimacy and passion.
Romantic love	Passion and intimacy lead to romantic love which is often the first phase of a relationship. Romantic love is often an intense and joyful experience.
Companionate love	Companionate love ranges from long-term, deeply committed friendships to long-term couples who have experienced a decrease in the passionate aspect of their love.
Fatuous (FAT-you-us) love	Love is fatuous (which means silly or foolish) when one does not really know the person to whom one is making a commitment. It has passion and commitment without intimacy. This occurs when a commitment is made after a whirlwind romance, but before couples have had time to truly connect with each other. Hollywood often portrays this type of relationship.
Consummate love	Consummate or complete love has all three elements in balance. It is the type of love that is thought to be ideal.

SOURCE: Robert J. Sternberg, "A Triangle Theory of Love," Psychological Review 93(2): 119–135. Reprinted by permission of the author.

("If I could never be with ___, I would feel miserable."), caring ("I would do almost anything for ___."), and trusting ("I feel very possessive about ___."). Rubin's scale proved to be an accurate tool to measure love. For example, how a couple scored on the "love scale" was correlated not only with their rating of the probability that they got married but how often they gazed at each other.

Others researchers develop their own scales. Davis and Latty-Mann (1987) created the Relationship Rating Scale (RRS), which measures various aspects of relationships such as intimacy, passion, and conflict. Hatfield and Sprecher (1986) created the Passionate Love Scale (PLS), which measures the degree of intense passion or "longing for union." These two scales have also been successful in measuring aspects of love.

There are some obstacles to measuring something as complex as love. Most love scales focus on romantic love and are not as good at measuring companionate love (Sternberg, 1987). Also, when researchers ask people questions about love, they can answer only with their conscious attitudes toward love. Some theorists suggest that people do not consciously know why they love, how they love, or even how much they love. Other theorists argue that people do not realize to what degree love is physiological (we will discuss physiological arousal theories later in this chapter). As a result, scales measuring love may only be tapping into how people believe they love.

On Your Mind
What is the difference between love and lust?

Each individual must struggle with these questions as he or she matures, particularly in the teenage and early adulthood years before gaining much experience with romantic love. There is no easy answer but there are some indications that a relationship may be infatuation rather than love when it involves a compulsion rather than a desire to be with the person, a feeling of lack of trust such as a need to check up on the partner, extreme emotions such as ecstatic highs followed by depressing lows, and a willingness to take abuse or behave in destructive ways that one would not have done before the relationship. Some questions to ask about one's love relationship are: Would I want this person as a friend if he or she were not my lover? Do my friends and family think he or she is not right for me? (Friends and family are often more level-headed judges of character than an infatuated individual.) Do I really know this person or am I merely fantasizing about how he or she is with little confirmation? In general, however, it is not always easy to tell the difference between infatuation and love. Many people have a hard time distinguishing between the two (Aloni & Bernieri, 2004).

Review Questions

1 What is the difference between romantic and companionate love?

2 Describe John Alan Lee's six colours of love.

3 Describe the three elements of love according to Robert Sternberg. Explain how these elements combine to make seven different types of relationships.

4 Is it possible to measure love? What problems have researchers run into when attempting to do so?

Origins of Love

Why do people love in the first place? What purpose does love serve? After all, animals mate successfully without experiencing love. Theories upon why people form emotional bonds can be grouped into five general categories: behavioural reinforcement, cognitive, evolutionary, physiological arousal, and biological. We look at each group separately in this section.

Behavioural Reinforcement Theories

The first group of theories suggests that people love because other people reinforce positive feelings in themselves. Lott and Lott (1961) suggested that a rewarding or positive feeling in the presence of another person makes someone like him or her, even when the reward has nothing to do with the other person. For example, they found that children who were rewarded continually by their teachers at school came to like their classmates more than children who were not equally rewarded. The opposite is also true. Griffitt and Veitch (1971) found that people tend to dislike others they meet in a hot crowded room no matter what those people's personalities are like. Behavioural reinforcement theories suggest that people like others they associate with feeling good and they love people if the association is very good. Love, therefore, develops through a series of mutually reinforcing activities and the greater the positive reinforcement, the more the likelihood of love.

Behaviour reinforcement theories suggest that people love other people they associate with feeling good. Love for other people grows out of doing things together that are mutually reinforcing.

Cognitive Theories

Cognitive theories of love are based on the premise that people's ways of thinking affect their behaviour. For example, if people find themselves doing things for certain people and enjoying the fact that they are doing so, they might conclude that they do them because they really like or even love those people. This theory suggests that action comes first and the interpretation of that action comes later (Tzeng, 1992). Studies have also found that when people think that certain people like them, they are more likely to be attracted to them (Ridge & Reber, 2002).

Evolutionary Theory

This next set of theories tries to understand the evolutionary advantages of human behaviours. In this respect, love developed as the human form of three basic instincts: the need to be protected from outside threats, the instinct of parents to protect their children, and the sexual drive. Love is thus an evolutionary strategy that helps people form the bonds they need to reproduce and pass their genes on to the next generation (Gonzaga & Haselton, 2008). People therefore love to propagate the species.

As Maestripieri (2012) puts it, as human ancestors developed, their brains became far more complex. This led to an increased period of dependency in infants and thus necessitated the participation of both parents in caring for them. The development of the emotion of love thus ensured that parents would stay together at least for that period.

This would explain why people tend to fall in love with others whom they think have positive traits. They want to pass those traits along to their children. In fact, evolutionary theorists argue that their perspective can explain why heterosexual men look for attractive women and heterosexual women look for successful men. The men want a healthy woman to carry their offspring and the women want a man with the resources to protect them and

help to care for the child in the long period they devote to reproduction. For most of history, this included nine months of pregnancy and more than a year of breast-feeding. Love creates the union that maximizes each partner's chance of passing on his or her genes to the next generation.

Anthropologist Helen Fisher (2006), who along with others studied the brain patters of people who were in love, believes that three factors developed to ensure the propagation of the human species: lust, attraction, and attachment. Lust evokes sexual desire, which ensures that reproduction will take place; attraction ensures that a relationship is ongoing; attachment ensures that it will last. While it might be logical to assume that they happen in sequence, Fisher maintains that a relationship can begin with any one of them. Some people begin with lust, which leads to attraction and then attachment, while others might begin with attachment, which leads to attraction and then lust. Some people have sex and then fall in love; others fall in love and then have sex. In any case, evolutionary theory maintains that these factors are "built in" to human beings to ensure that they will survive to the next generation.

Physiological Arousal Theory

How does love feel? Many people describe physiological sensations when they are in love: "I felt so excited I couldn't breathe"; "My throat choked up"; "I felt a tingling all over." What is interesting is that these statements could they also be descriptions of fear, anger, or excitement. Is there a difference between being in love and feeling the sensations one might have on a rollercoaster?

In a well-known experiment, Schachter and Singer (1962) gave students either a placebo or a shot of epinephrine (adrenaline), which causes general arousal and produces sweaty palms, increased heart rate, and increased breathing. They divided the students into four groups. The first group was told exactly what was happening and what to expect, the second group was told the wrong set of symptoms to expect (itching, numbness, and a slight headache), the third group was told nothing, and the fourth group got an injection of saline solution (the placebo) rather than epinephrine. Each group was put into a waiting room with a student who was a confederate and part of the study. In half the cases, the confederate students acted happy and in the other half they acted angry. When the students in the informed group felt aroused, they assumed that they were feeling the effects of the epinephrine. However, the uninformed groups tended to believe they were experiencing the same emotion as the other person in the room. They thought they were happy or they thought they were angry. Schachter and Singer (2001) concluded that an emotion happens when there is general physiological arousal and people attach a label to it, and that label might be any emotion. In other words, people tend to be vulnerable to experiencing love (or another emotion) when they are physiologically aroused. This might explain why the excitement people feel when they are having sex is often defined as love. More recent studies confirm physiological arousal theory (Aron et al., 2005; H. Fisher, 2004). For example, in one study, couples who met during a crisis (such as during an emergency plane landing) were found to be more likely to feel strongly about one another (Aron et al., 2005; Kluger, 2008). They often incorrectly attributed their high levels of arousal to feelings for the other people.

So is love just a label people give to a racing heart? Perhaps arousal has a stronger connection to initial attraction than to love. Maybe this is why lust is so often confused with love.

Other Biological Factors

Research has also shown that other biological factors influence who people fall in love with (Garver-Apgar et al., 2006; Rodriguez, 2004; Santos et al., 2005; Savic et al., 2005; Thorne & Amrein, 2003). For example, people register the smells of others through their pheromones, which are odourless chemicals secreted by humans and other animals (Rodriguez, 2004; Thorne & Amrein, 2003). These pheromones are processed in the hypothalamus and they influence the choice of a sex partner (Savic et al., 2005). Both men and women respond to pheromones. In one study, for example, women reported that their male partners were more loving and more jealous when they were ovulating (Hasleton et al., 2007).

Pheromones have also been found to influence attraction, mating, and bonding (Crawford et al., 2011; Wright, 1994), as well as promote the love bond between a mother and her young children (Kohl & Francoeur, 2002). Research on pheromones and sexual orientation has found that while heterosexual men do not have any hypothalamic responses to the testosterone-derived pheromone *androstadien-3-one*, both gay men and heterosexual women do. Because both are sexually oriented toward men and heterosexual men are not, such a response would be likely (Savic et al., 2005).

An earlier research project by Black and Biron (1982) from Quebec had different results. A male or female confederate emanating the odour of a pheromone or a synthetic musk or no odour at all was put in a room with groups of students of the other sex and told to interact briefly with each one. The students were then asked to rate the attractiveness of the confederates. Surprisingly, there were no differences among the groups.

People's odour preferences are influenced by their *major histocompatibility complex* (MHC), which is a group of genes that helps the body recognize invaders such as bacteria and viruses (Garver-Apgar et al., 2006; Herz, 2007; Santos et al., 2005). To pass a more complete MHC along to children and protect them with the broadest array of disease resistance, parents may be programmed to mate with a partner whose MHC differs from their own (Crawford et al., 2011; Roberts & Roiser, 2010). In other words, people are more likely to be attracted to and fall in love with someone whose MHC is different from their own (Garver-Apgar et al., 2006). Later research has even explored how the use of hormonal contraceptives such as birth control pills may alter the MHC and odour preferences in women (Crawford et al., 2011; Ferdenzi et al., 2009; Roberts & Roiser, 2010; Roberts et al., 2008).

Finally, researchers have looked for love in neurotransmitters and various areas of the brain. Using magnetic resonance imaging, some studies have found that certain areas of the brain are stimulated when couples are in love (Aron et al., 2005; Fisher et al., 2010; H. Fisher, 2004; Ortigue et al., 2010). In addition, when these areas are stimulated, neurotransmitters such as dopamine create motivation and desire to be with a particular partner (Fisher et al., 2010). So it appears that love is at least partially reducible to biological factors within the human body. Certainly more research is needed in these areas.

Review Questions

1 How does behavioural reinforcement theory explain love?

2 How do cognitive theories explain love?

3 How does evolutionary theory explain love?

4 How does the physiological arousal theory explain love?

5 What other biological factors influence love?

Love from Childhood to Maturity

People typically experience the love of others through their lives. First, there is love for one's parents or caregivers, and then siblings, friends, and romantic partners. At each stage of life, lessons are learned about love that help people mature into the next stage. In this section, we look at the different stages of individual development as well as the various ways love manifests itself at each stage.

Childhood

In infancy, the nature and quality of the bond with parents or caregivers can have profound effects on the ability of a person to form attachments throughout life (see Chapter 10). Our parents or the adults who raised us are our first teachers of love and intimacy. Loving, attentive caregivers tend to produce secure and happy

pheromones
Chemical substances secreted by humans and other animals that facilitate communication.

children (Rauer & Volling, 2007). Children are keenly aware of parental love and those who feel loved report feeling safe and protected (D'Cruz & Stagnitti, 2010).

When babies or young children feel sad, scared, or threatened, they often seek out their mother. From an evolutionary perspective, the desire for closeness with the mother increases an infant's chances of survival (Mofrad et al., 2010). Bowlby (1969) proposed that infants develop an attachment or an emotional bond with their mothers. Although Bowlby wrote about attachment as a mother–child bond, we know today that children can develop this bond with a mother, father, nanny, grandparent, or primary caregiver. However, it was the mother's response to her child that Bowlby believed was most important. If a mother responded in a sensitive, patient, and kind manner, her child was more likely to form a secure attachment (Prior & Glaser, 2006). However, if the mother responded in an inconsistent, angry, or dismissive manner, her child would form an insecure attachment. Throughout this time, an infant's brain responds to the facial expressions, touch, and scent of the primary caregiver (Hall, 2005). Consistent and sensitive caregiving makes a child feel protected and safe, which sets the foundation for regulating emotions later in life (Wellisch, 2010).

The administering of love and caring is particularly important for infants who are in foster care, as Marcellus (2008) of the Vancouver Island Health Authority in Victoria, British Columbia, points out. Foster parents of those who have been exposed to drugs or alcohol, for example, may face particular challenges in making up for possible neglect of love and attention in the past. As another British Colombian psychologist points out, without proper care, older children who are adopted or put in foster care may have attachment difficulties that will hinder their lives (Haegert, 1999).

Ainsworth and her colleagues (1978) built on Bowlby's research and suggested that infants form one of three types of attachment patterns that follow them throughout life. Secure infants tolerate caregivers being out of their sight because they believe the caregivers will respond if they cry out or need care. Inconsistent

A strong and secure bond with a caregiver can have profound effects on the ability of a person to form attachments throughout life.

caregiving results in anxious/ambivalent babies who cry more than secure babies and panic when the caregivers leave them. Avoidant babies often have caregivers who are uncomfortable with hugging and holding them and tend to force separation on the children at early ages. Researchers have also found that a child's attachment style is established by the age of nine months (Prior & Glaser, 2006).

Childhood attachment styles remain as people grow up and may influence the type of intimate relationships they form as adults (K. Burton, 2005; Mikulincer & Shaver, 2005). In fact, they tend to relate to others in their love relationships much as they did with their primary caregiver when they were young. Adults who had a secure attachment in childhood report more positive childhood experiences, higher levels of self-esteem (Feeney & Noller, 1990), better health (Maunder & Hunter, 2008), and even more advanced language development (Prior & Glaser, 2006). They further have less anxiety (Diamond & Fagundes, 2010; Gentzler et al., 2010), less shame, guilt, and loneliness (Akbag & Imamoglu, 2010), more positive views of themselves and others, and they have a fairly easy time trusting others and forming intimate relationships (Bartholomew & Horowitz, 1991; Neal & Frick-Horbury, 2001).

Adults who had anxious/ambivalent attachments with their caregivers often have negative views of others and difficult time trusting them. They may worry that their partners do not really love them or will leave them. Finally, those with an avoidant attachment pattern often have negative views of others and are uncomfortable with intimacy. If people grow up in families in which their caregiver was inconsistent or distant, they see love as emotionally risky. In fact, those who do not experience intimacy growing up may have a harder time establishing intimate relationships as adults (Brumbaugh & Fraley, 2010; Dorr, 2001). This does not mean that it is not possible to love others if they did not experience intimacy as children, but it can be more difficult for them.

Attachment styles can also be affected by parental divorce. Researchers have found that children of divorced parents have decreased psychological, social, and physical well-being after the divorce (Hetherington, 2003), are less trusting of their partners in intimate relationships (Coordt, 2005; Ensign et al., 1998; Jacquet & Surra, 2001), and are more likely to experience a divorce later in life (Amato & De-Boer, 2001). Interestingly, men whose parents have divorced are less likely to experience problems in their intimate relationships unless their female partner has divorced parents (Jacquet & Surra, 2001). In contrast, however, having divorced parents does not put children at an overall disadvantage in the development of love relationships (Coordt, 2005; Sprecher et al., 1998). The most important factor is the quality of the relationships with the parents before and after the divorce. If children have a good relationship with at least one parent, negative effects from the divorce may be reduced (Ensign et al., 1998).

Adolescence

There is something attractive about young love. This is perhaps why it is celebrated so prominently in novels and movies. The love relationship seems so important, so earnest, and so

Young love lays the groundwork for adult intimacy.

intimacy. Adolescents must learn to establish a strong personal identity separate from their families, and as a result, experimenting with different approaches to others is natural. Young people develop a **role repertoire** that follows them into adulthood. Similarly, they experiment with different intimacy styles (J. Johnson & Alford, 1987) and develop an **intimacy repertoire**, or a set of behaviours that they use to forge close relationships throughout their lives.

The process of establishing such a repertoire can be difficult, which explains why adolescent relationships can be so intense and fraught with jealousy, and why adolescents often are unable to see beyond their relationships (J. Johnson & Alford, 1987). The first relationships often take the form of a crush or infatuation and are often directed toward unattainable partners such as teachers or movie stars. Male and female movie stars even provide adolescents with safe outlets for developing romantic love before dating and sexual activity begin (Karniol, 2001).

Sometimes the first lessons of love are painful, as teenagers learn that love may not be returned or that feelings of passion fade. Yet managing such feelings helps them develop a mature love style. Several factors have been found to be associated with the ability to find romantic love in adolescence, such as marital status of one's parents, the quality of one's parental relationship, and comfort with one's own body (Cecchetti, 2007; Coordt, 2005; Seiffge-Krenke et al., 2001). In fact, as discussed earlier, difficulties with intimate relationships in adulthood may be related to the attachment styles that were created in childhood.

The emotions of young love are so powerful that adolescents may think that they are the only ones to have gone through such joy, pain, and confusion. They may gain some comfort in knowing that almost everyone goes through the same process to some degree. Confusion about love certainly does not end with adolescence.

passionate in the teenage years, and yet so innocent in retrospect. Why are the highs and lows of love so important at this stage of life? Adolescent love teaches people how to react to emotions and even handle the pain of love. It also lays the groundwork for adult

Review Questions

1 Explain how the nature and quality of young children's bond with caregivers can affect their ability to form relationships later in life.

2 Identify the various attachment styles.

3 What makes love relationships so difficult and unstable for many adolescents?

Why do those highs and lows decrease as we get older?

Adult Love and Intimacy

Love can last many years. As time goes by, it grows and changes, and maintaining a sense of stability and continuity while still allowing for change and growth may be challenging.

Intimacy is different from loving. People love animals, music, or great leaders, but intimacy requires reciprocity. It takes two. Intimacy is a dance of two souls, each of whom must reveal a little, risk a little, and try a lot. In some ways, true intimacy is more difficult to achieve than true love

because the emotion of love may be effortless while intimacy requires effort.

Does fate determine with whom people will fall in love or are there other factors at work? We now examine some factors that contribute to adult love and intimacy.

role repertoire
A set of behaviours that people use in their interactions with others. Once they find what works, they develop patterns of interacting with others.

intimacy repertoire
A set of behaviours that people use to forge intimate relationships throughout their lives.

Attraction

It is no accident that most people are attracted to others much like themselves. Most relationships tend to be between people who are of similar ages and socio-economic levels and the same religions, races, and ethnic backgrounds. Societies operate in such a way as to generate a **field of eligibles** (Kerckhoff, 1964) and, thus, restrict the pool of potential partners for each person. For example, if a couple is of vastly different ages, they may be ridiculed. If, however, people begin to date others thought to be acceptable, they will receive positive reinforcement from their families, friends, and society in general.

It is important to keep in mind, however, that in countries such as Canada, the United States, England, and Australia, such restrictions are changing rapidly. First, because people now live longer and healthier lives, age is less of a barrier than it was previously. Second, because of greater equality between the sexes, women with younger male partners are far less stigmatized. Third, and perhaps most importantly, racism and other forms of prejudice have become more and more unacceptable and, as a result, there is a greater proportion of interracial dating and marriage.

Statistics Canada looks at "mixed unions," which it defines as married or common-law couples living in the same household, where either one or both members is of a visible minority. Such couples have increased steadily: 2.6 percent in 1991, 3.1 percent in 2001, and 4.6 percent in 2011. The vast majority of these mixed unions live in large cities, with Vancouver having the greatest proportion, followed by Toronto, Victoria, and Calgary. Most of these couples tend to be new immigrants to Canada. Of all mixed union couples, 49.2 percent had one member born in another country, and an additional 19.4 percent had both members born in other countries. These couples also tend to be younger than Canadian couples in general, thus reflecting Canada's changing values (Statistics Canada, National Household Survey, 2011).

According to social psychologists, one of the most reliable predictors of attraction is **propinquity**, or the physical and psychological proximity between people. Although people might believe that they could meet a complete stranger in the streets and fall madly in love, this scenario is rare. Because of social boundaries between strangers in large cities and norms that dictate how people interact, people are far more likely to find partners among the people they know or meet through their social networks. They are much more likely to meet them at parties, workplaces, schools, or friends' houses. In short, contact between people and, thus, initial attraction is far more likely to occur in places where there is direct contact with others and fewer rules about interaction.

Propinquity is more than simple access to others. If people know that they are going to see someone regularly, they are more likely to emphasize that person's good points and minimize any bad points. They do this through an effort to exist within pleasant and manageable environments and, thus, have smooth interactions with others. Seeing someone regularly also enables people to observe this person in a variety of situations and potentially see a variety of emotions or problem-solving techniques. Propinquity therefore enables familiarity and familiarity enables attraction and intimacy.

Despite the increasing trend toward mixed couples in Canada, people still tend to be attracted to partners similar to themselves in ethnicity, race, social class, religion, education, and even in attitudes and personality (Byrne & Murnen, 1988; Hitsch et al., 2010). Although folklore tells us both that "birds of a feather flock together" and that "opposites attract," research supports only the first saying. People are also more likely to be attracted to others who have similar family histories and political views (Michael et al., 1994; Z. Rubin, 1973).

There is also the matter of physical attraction. The "matching hypothesis" claims that people are drawn to others with similar levels of attractiveness. When considering a romantic partner, both men and women may be willing to compromise on some qualities they are looking for in a partner, but they are less likely to do so with physical attractiveness (Sprecher & Regan, 2002). Often, physical attractiveness is related to body weight. In one Canadian study, Puhl and Boland (2001) asked a sample of 240 university students to rate the attractiveness of three computer altered female figures who were either underweight, normal weight, or overweight. Not surprisingly, those who were underweight were considered the most attractive by both males and females.

People considered physically attractive are assumed to have more socially desirable personalities and to be happier and more successful (Little et al., 2006; Swami & Furnham, 2008). There is some truth in this as well. As one indication of the power of physical attractiveness, Kaczorowski (1998) looked at physical attractiveness ratings from the Canadian Quality of Life Survey and found that people who rated themselves as above average in looks earned the highest wages, those rating themselves as below average earned the lowest wages, and those rating themselves as average falling into the middle wage category. Other factors that may influence attraction are openness, receptiveness, emotional stability, financial stability, and perhaps even a good sense of humour. In the past, research on gender and attraction found that heterosexual women were more likely to rate financial stability in a partner as more important than did heterosexual men (Buss, 1989). This was consistent across cultures. However, such gender differences have decreased and both heterosexual men and women are now more likely to report being attracted to partners with good financial resources (Buss et al., 2001; Sheldon, 2007).

What is it, finally, that people really look for in a partner? Although physical attractiveness is considered important, men and women around the world also report that mutual attraction, kindness, and reciprocal love are important factors as well (Buss et al., 2001; Pearce et al., 2010). In addition to this, people are in surprising agreement on what factors they want in an ideal partner. One study of college students in seven periods from 1939 to 1996 found that the same desired characteristics for both sexes were dependable character, emotional stability/maturity, pleasing disposition, and mutual attraction/love (Amador et al., 2005). Now that doesn't seem to be too much to ask, does it?

---

field of eligibles
The group of people from which it is socially acceptable to choose an intimate partner.

propinquity
The physical and psychological proximity between people.

This young girl is from a Longneck culture in Mae Hong Son, Thailand, where an elongated neck is considered physically attractive.

Attraction and Gender Inequity

Do men and women across the world look for the same traits? Buss (1989) carried out a series of surveys comparing the importance of, among other things, physical attractiveness, earning potential, and age difference to men and women in 37 cultures. He surveyed 4601 males and 5446 females ranging in age from 16 to 28 from 33 countries located on six continents and five islands. He found that in all 37 cultures, men valued physical attractiveness in a partner more than women, and women valued financial capacity more than men. Additionally, men preferred mates who were younger, and women preferred mates who were older.

These results reflect a global gender inequity more than anything else in that most of the world operates in such a way that women are more valued for their domestic potential while men are more valued for their ability to provide support for the family. In Canada, however, women are also valued for their financial capacity. Between 1967 and 1993, the proportion of couples who both worked outside the home rose from 33 percent to 60 percent. The traditional model of a working husband and a stay-at-home wife has now become a minority. In fact, the proportion of Canadian dual-wage-earner couples where the woman earns more than

the man rose from 11 percent to 25 percent in the same period. Of couples with only one wage earner, 20 percent, or one out of five, were composed of wives with stay-at-home husbands in 1993 (Crompton & Geran, 1995). These figures have risen even higher in the past two decades.

Intimate Relationships

The word *intimacy* is derived from the Latin *intimus,* meaning "inner" or "innermost" (Hatfield, 1988). Keeping one's innermost self hidden is easy; revealing deepest desires, longings, and insecurities is more difficult. As we discussed in Chapter 11, intimate partners reveal beliefs and ideas to each other, disclose personal facts, share opinions, and admit to their fears and hopes. In fact, self-disclosure is so important that early researchers believed it to be the very definition of intimacy (M.S. Clark & Reis, 1988). True self-disclosure is a two-way street in that it involves both partners sharing feelings, fears, and dreams, not simply facts and opinions. Individuals who can self-disclose have been found to have higher levels of self-esteem and rate their relationships as more satisfying (Macneil, 2004; Posey et al., 2010; Schiffrin et al., 2010; Sprecher & Hendrick, 2004).

Intimacy involves a sense of closeness, bondedness, and connectedness (Popovic, 2005; R.J. Sternberg, 1987). People who value intimacy tend to express greater trust in their friends, are more concerned for their well-being, tend to disclose more emotional, personal, and relational content, and have more positive thoughts about others. They also are thought to be likable and non-competitive by peers in that they smile, laugh, and make eye contact more often. They also report higher marital enjoyment (M.S. Clark & Reis, 1988).

Disclosure, however, can be risky. The other person may not understand or accept the information offered or may not reciprocate. Risk taking and trust are thus crucial to the development of intimacy. Because intimacy makes us vulnerable, however, it can also lead to betrayal, disappointment, anger, and jealousy.

Male and Female Styles of Intimacy

If any area of research in love and intimacy has yielded conflicting findings, it is the question of gender differences. Overall, research has found that heterosexual women tend to give more importance to the hope of having an intimate relationship in their future than heterosexual men (Oner, 2001). However, M.S. Clark and Reis (1988) suggest that the subject remains murky because many other variables are at work, such as culturally determined gender roles.

As one example, men and women equally report desiring and valuing intimacy but many men grow up with behavioural inhibitions to expressing it. From very young ages, boys are discouraged from displaying vulnerability. As one man's experience reveals in the accompanying Sex in Real Life feature, it is acceptable for men to talk about sex but talk of intimacy is often taboo. Although this man's experience may have been exaggerated by the all-male atmosphere of the locker room, such attitudes are communicated in subtle ways to many men. Men may thus remain silent about intimacy however strongly they may desire it. It could also be that men simply express intimacy differently— perhaps more through action than words (Gilmore, 1990).

SEX In the Men's Locker Room

The following is a story written by a man who was reflecting upon his experiences growing up as a young boy. It well reveals impact of gender roles on people's expressions of love and intimacy today.

I played organized sports for 15 years, and they were as much a part of my growing up as Cheerios, television, and homework. My sexuality unfolded within this all-male social world of sport, where sex was always a major focus. I remember, for example, when we as prepubertal boys used the old "buying baseball cards" routine as a cover to sneak peeks at Playboy and Swank magazines at the newsstand. We would talk endlessly after practices about "boobs" and what it must feel like to kiss and neck. Later, in junior high, we teased one another in the locker room about "jerking off" or being virgins, and there were endless interrogations about "how far" everybody was getting with their girlfriends.

Eventually, boyish anticipation spilled into real sexual relationships with girls, which, to my delight and confusion, turned out to be a lot more complex than I ever imagined. While sex (kissing, necking, and petting) got more exciting, it also got more difficult to figure out and talk about. Inside, most of the boys, like myself, needed to love and be loved. We were awkwardly reaching out for intimacy. Yet publicly, the message that got imparted was to "catch feels," be cool, and connect with girls but don't allow yourself to depend on them. Once when I was a high-school junior, the gang in the weight room accused me of being wrapped around my girlfriend's finger. Nothing could be further from the truth, I assured them; to prove it, I broke up with her. I felt miserable about this at the time, and I still feel bad about it.

Within the college jock subculture, men's public protests against intimacy sometimes became exaggerated and ugly. I remember two teammates, drunk and rowdy, ripping girls' blouses off at a mixer and crawling on their bellies across the dance floor to look up skirts. Then there were the Sunday morning late breakfasts in the dorm. We jocks would usually all sit at one table and be forced to listen to one braggart or another describe his sexual exploits of the night before. Although a lot of us were turned off by such kiss-and-tell, ego-boosting tactics, we never openly criticized them. Real or fabricated, displays of raunchy sex were also assumed to "win points."

When sexual relationships were "serious," that is, tempered by love and commitment, the unspoken rule was silence. It was rare when we young men shared our feelings about women, misgivings about sexual performance, or disdain for the crudeness and insensitivity of some of our teammates. I now see the tragic irony in this: We could talk about superficial sex and anything that used, trivialized, or debased women, but frank discussions about sexuality that unfolded within a loving relationship were taboo. Within the locker room subculture, sex and love were seldom allowed to mix. There was a terrible split between inner needs and outer appearances, between our desire for the love of women and our feigned indifference toward them.

SOURCE: Sabo, D.S., & Runfola, R. (1980). *Jock: Sports and male identity.* New York: Prentice Hall. Reprinted with permission.

Androgynous people, however, may have the advantage. Coleman and Ganong (1985) measured men and women on scales of masculinity and femininity and compared those who scored higher on one scale than the other with those who scored high on both scales. The androgynous people were more aware of their love feelings, more expressive, and more tolerant of their partners' faults than those who scored high on only the masculinity scale. They were also more cognitively aware, more willing to express faults, and more tolerant than those who scored high only on the femininity scale.

REAL Research Ontario psychologist S.W. Pyke (1985) tested the hypothesis that androgynous individuals are more flexible and more adaptable than people of other gender-role orientations by looking at 26 published studies that used the Bem Sex-Role Inventory. She found that androgynous people were more adaptable and had higher levels of psychological well-being than feminine or undifferentiated subjects but also found no difference between them and the masculine subjects.

With a society heading increasingly to the idea of gender equality, there is strong evidence indicating that the differences in attitudes between the genders are changing. Although in the past women were more comfortable with intimate encounters and men were more comfortable taking independent action, now a new, more androgynous breed of men and women are emerging who are comfortable with both roles (Choi, 2004).

Intimacy and Sexual Orientation

The word "homosexual" is far less used as a noun today because it suggests that gays and lesbians are only interested in sex—a belief that was pervasive for a century or more. How different is gay love? One Australian study (Brown et al., 2013) sought to answer this question in looking at the path gay men typically go through on the way to consummate love, which again is the integration of passion, intimacy, and commitment as defined by Sternberg (1998). After interviewing 12 gay men in depth, the researchers identified four stages toward consummate love. In the first stage, gay men needed to understand and become comfortable with their own sexual desires. In other words, because they are different from the mainstream, they needed intimacy with themselves before going on to others. In the second stage, they explored their sexual desires and, thus, experience with passion. For some of the subjects, this was seen as making up for lost time as teenagers

Intimacy in Animals

Do other animals share intimacy? The answer to this question depends upon how one defines intimacy. According to social psychologist Herbert Blumer (1969), humans differ from other animals in that they are able to reflect upon the past, present, and future. People are unique in that they are able to imagine themselves as they were or might have been in past situations and they are able to imagine what life will have in store for them in years to come. Indeed, in their minds, humans are able to have conversations with ancestors who are long dead as well as children who have not yet been born. Although animals do have memories of past events, they relate to them on a more instinctual level (e.g., a dog might be fearful of another dog because of its past behaviour). Animals generally react toward the "thereness" of their immediate environments, where what is present matters and what is not present does not exist. Among humans, intimacy is about opening up, which involves not only the sharing of past experiences and feelings in the present but a trust that those experiences and feelings will be respected in the future. Intimacy, therefore, brings in *past* experiences, *present* feelings, and *future* predictions. To this extent, intimacy in the way it is defined is not possible with animals because of their lack of ability to step outside of time. It is true, however, as Canadian biologist Jenny Christal and Whitehead (2001) suggests in her study of sperm whales, that some species of animals form strong attachments and these attachments may be defined more broadly as intimacy.

As discussed in Chapter 11, cultural differences in individual versus group needs can affect communication patterns (Cai et al., 2000). They can also affect patterns of intimacy. Passionate love is typically emphasized in individualistic cultures, but in collectivist cultures it is often viewed negatively because it may disrupt family traditions (Kim & Hatfield, 2004). For example, although Canadians often equate love with happiness, the Chinese often equate it with sadness and jealousy (Shaver et al., 1992), because people in collectivist cultures traditionally marry for reasons other than love. Passionate love dies and is not viewed as something stable enough upon which to base a marriage.

In a study of five cultures (Ting-Toomey et al., 1991), intimacy style was directly related to whether the culture was individualistic, collectivistic, or mixed, as well as the degree to which it adopted stereotypical views of gender roles (i.e., how much it tended to see men as assertive and women as nurturing). Japan with its collectivistic culture and traditional gender roles had lower scores in measures of attachment and commitment and was less likely to value self-disclosure than the people of France or the United States (Kito, 2005). Many Americans also adhere to traditional gender roles but, because of their highly individualistic culture, the United States tends to have high levels of confusion and ambivalence about relationships. France is also a culture with high individualism but also a strong group orientation. As a result, the French have a more balanced view of masculine and feminine gender roles and had the lowest degree of conflict in intimate relationships.

when they could not act upon their desires at all. Third, they needed to experiment with relationships by dating and having boyfriends, thus experimenting and becoming familiar with intimacy. In the final stage, they progressed to stable relationships and, thus, brought in the third element of commitment.

In short, after coming to terms with their sexual orientation, the gay men in the study began with passion, then integrated it with intimacy, and then integrated passion and intimacy with commitment. With the exception of coming to terms with sexual orientation, this seems little different from the typical heterosexual path to relationships. One begins to experiment sexually, then begins dating, and finally ends up in marriage or a common-law relationship.

It is interesting to note that gay men and lesbians live in a world that is defined solely in heterosexual terms and love as a perfect union of man and woman is just one facet. With rare exceptions, such as Shakespeare's sonnets (see the Sexual Diversity in Our World feature), literature and poetry deals only with heterosexual love, as do virtually all movies, television shows, and songs.

Intimacy in Different Cultures

Are human emotions expressed in the same way everywhere? Although there is evidence that the majority of cultures experience romantic love, it is also true that the influences of culture have a more powerful impact on love beliefs than gender (Sprecher & Toro-Morn, 2002). Culture affects how people define love, how easily they fall in love, with whom they fall in love, and how relationships proceed (Kim & Hatfield, 2004).

Culture also affects one's sense of self. For example, in China, people's sense of self is commonly felt in their relationships with others. "A Chinese man would often consider his roles as a son, brother, husband, or a father, before he would think of himself as an individual" (Dion & Dion, 2010). In China, love is typically thought of in terms of how a mate would be received by family and community and less so in terms of one's own sense of romance (Sprecher & Toro-Morn, 2002).

Finally, R. Levine et al. (1995) conducted surveys of college students from several Western as well as Asian nations and focused on the perceived significance of love for the building of a marriage. They found that love is given highest importance in Westernized nations, where people enter marriages based on love, and the lowest importance in the less developed Asian nations, where marriages are based on compatibility and are often arranged by families. Thus, culture plays a role in the importance given to love in the pursuit of a partner.

Sexual Diversity in Our World

"Come Live with Me and Be My Love"

The homoerotic content of classical literature dealing with love has often been disguised and, as a result, was easily overlooked. Many of William Shakespeare's 154 sonnets deal with love—whether about love lost, love never consummated, or love from afar. Although they lack any significant erotic content, most of them were written to a young man and not a female. Similarly, Elizabethan dramatist Christopher Marlowe's famous lament, "Come live with me and be my love," was shaped by the Roman poet Virgil's 2nd Eclogue written in 43 B.C.E. dealing with a shepherd's efforts to get a beloved boy to live with him (Woods, 1998).

Here is Marlowe's poem. Notice that it is genderless.

COME live with me and be my Love,
And we will all the pleasures prove
That hills and valleys, dale and field,
And all the craggy mountains yield.

There will we sit upon the rocks
And see the shepherds feed their flocks,
By shallow rivers, to whose falls
Melodious birds sing madrigals.

There will I make thee beds of roses
And a thousand fragrant posies
A cap of flowers, and a kirtle
Embroider'd all with leaves of myrtle.

A gown made of the finest wool
Which from our pretty lambs we pull,

Fair lined slippers for the cold,
With buckles of the purest gold.

A belt of straw and ivy buds
With coral clasps and amber studs:
And if these pleasures may thee move,
Come live with me and be my Love.

Thy silver dishes for thy meat
As precious as the gods do eat,
Shall on an ivory table be
Prepared each day for thee and me.

The shepherd swains shall dance and sing
For thy delight each May-morning:
If these delights thy mind may move,
Then live with me and be my Love.

SEX in Real Life

Love—It's All in the Head

What does the brain have to do with feelings of love and romance? New research into brain physiology has found that the brain is more involved than previously thought. Magnetic resonance imaging of brain functioning revealed that certain areas experience increases in blood flow when people who are newly in love look at photographs of their romantic partners (Aron et al., 2005; Ortigue et al., 2010). More than 2500 brain images from 17 men and women who rated themselves as "intensely in love" were analyzed using magnetic resonance imaging technology, which monitors increases in blood flow indicating neural activity. Strong activity was noted in the motivation areas of the brain where an overabundance of cells produces or receives the neurotransmitter dopamine (Aron et al., 2005). Other studies have found that when a person is in love, 12 areas of the brain are stimulated to release neurotransmitters, including dopamine, oxytocin, adrenaline, and vasopressin (Ortigue et al., 2010). All of these neurotransmitters contribute to feelings of euphoria and happiness.

Dopamine is also critical for motivation. For example, neuroscientists have found that people who gamble have increased dopamine levels when they are winning (Carey, 2005). All of this research suggests that romantic love serves as a motivation for a person to reach a goal. In this case, the goal is to spend time with the love interest.

The area of our brain responsible for sexual arousal was also stimulated in these newly in love participants but it was the motivation area that received the most stimulation. The researchers hypothesized that when the motivation area of the brain is stimulated, people are motivated toward their love interests above all else. This would seem logical. When people are hungry, thirsty, or tired, the motivation area of their brains are stimulated, motivating them to find food, water, or a place to sleep. When people are romantically in love, this same area motivates them to make connections and seek out their love interests.

This may also explain why new love often feels so powerful. Feelings of euphoria, sleeplessness, a preoccupation of thoughts of the love interest, and an inability to concentrate are all common when a person is newly in love. Some people describe new love as a "drug" and one that often leads them to do things they would not normally do.

Although more research is needed on neuroscience, brain activity, and emotions, it has been suggested that this research might help us understand why people with autism are often indifferent to romantic relationships (Carey, 2005). This could be because of the atypical development in the motivation areas of the brain, which is typical for people with autism. In addition, this research may also help people to understand why love changes as the years go by. The strength of activity in the motivation section of the brain often weakens as the length of the relationship increases (Carey, 2005).

SOURCE: Aron et al., 2005.

It is not that love stays with us; it is that we stay with love.

© Yagi Studio/Getty

Long-Term Love and Commitment

The ability to maintain love over time is one of the hallmarks of maturity. Many people regard love as something that happens to them, almost like catching a cold. In truth, it takes effort and commitment to maintain love. It is not that love stays with us; it is that we stay with love. Many long-term relationships end because the two people stopped working on them. In this sense, the old saying is true: The opposite of love is not hate, but indifference.

Robert J. Sternberg (1985), as mentioned earlier, claimed that passion, intimacy, and commitment are the three elements of love. In consummate love, all three are present. Research has found that age and relationship length are both positively related to intimacy and commitment. The older the couple and the longer the relationship, the stronger the intimacy and commitment (Ahmetoglu et al., 2010). Couples going through hard times can often persevere and build even stronger and more intimate relationships when their commitment reflects such a deep sense of trust.

Loss of Love

Popular songs are often about the loss of love. The blues and country and western music are well-known for songs lamenting about a love that they lost. For most people, a breakup can cause deep sadness and a profound sense of loss (Locker et al., 2010). Researchers have found that when people think another has rejected them, they experience physiological changes, which may even include a skip in their heartbeat (Moor et al., 2010).

After a breakup, many people are vulnerable to self-blame, loss of self-esteem, and distrust of others, and some of them might rush into another relationship to replace the lost partner (Locker et al., 2010; Timmreck, 1990). Researchers have found that a relationship breakup stimulates areas of the brain that are related to motivation, reward, and addiction, which might partially explain excessive alcohol consumption or drug abuse by those who have been rejected (Fisher et al., 2010).

As difficult as breakups can be, several factors may lower levels of distress. The first is high self-esteem, which can help people continue to feel hopeful and think more positive thoughts about themselves after a breakup (Svoboda, 2011). Those with low self-esteem often blame themselves and worry that no one will ever love them again. Second, people with secure attachment styles often have an easier time with breakups, while those with anxious attachment styles may have the most difficulty (Locker et al., 2010; Svoboda, 2011). They may even try desperately to hold onto their relationships, refusing to let go.

There is no easy way to decrease the pain of a breakup. Time can help a rejected partner feel better because as time goes by there is less activity in the area of the brain related to attachment (Fisher et al., 2010). We will discuss relationship breakups more in Chapter 13.

On Your Mind

How can two people stay together their entire lives and not get bored?

Although it might be hard to believe this is possible, it is important to remember that love grows and changes over time. People also grow and change with time. When both partners allow for this growth and development, they often have new experiences where they may express their love for one another. People get bored primarily when they lose interest, not because the other person has no mysteries left. Furthermore, it is common to become bored with the routines and realities of everyday life as they are. This does not mean, however, that life has become boring.

Review Questions

1 Why are people attracted to certain types of people? What factors might be involved?

2 What are some of the qualities that men and women may find attractive in other cultures? What does this say about perceptions of gender?

3 Explain the importance of self-disclosure on the development of intimacy.

4 Explain what researchers have found with respect to gender differences in intimacy styles.

Love, Sex, and How We Build Intimate Relationships

People have sex for a variety of reasons and at a variety of relationship stages. Some, because of religious convictions or cultural values, will only do so once they are married. Others may reach a level of comfort only when their relationships have progressed to a deep level of love and intimacy. Still others might do so as long as there is liking, strong rapport, and a reasonable assumption that they will be with their partners for some time in the future. Finally, many people have no problem having sex with relative strangers as long as there is mutual attraction and consent. The level at which people have sex thus depends a great deal upon their desires, intentions, values, and comfort level in doing so. While acknowledging that there are a variety of reasons for having sex, we restrict this section to people who are either on the way to or within committed relationships. First, we look at some factors that will likely enhance intimacy, and then we look at some negative behaviours within intimate relationships.

> **REAL Research** Canadian sex researcher Eleanor Maticka-Tyndale was interested in Canadian college students' intentions to have sex with others they meet on spring break (reading week). She and her associates gave questionnaires to 151 students before a trip to Daytona Beach, Florida, and 681 students following their return from spring break. The results shows that while more men intended to have sex on their vacations, a more or less equal number of men and women actually engaged in it (Maticka-Tyndale et al., 1998).

Enhancing Intimacy Skills

There are many ways to improve intimacy skills. Developing intimacy often begins with understanding and liking oneself—self-love. Other important skills we can develop to enhance the ability to form relationships include receptivity, listening, showing affection, and trust.

Self-Love

Self-love is different from conceit or narcissism. It is not a process of promoting oneself but of being at ease with one's positive qualities and forgiving oneself for any faults. If people are not willing to get to know themselves and to accept their own faults, why

self-love
Love for oneself; the instinct or desire to promote one's own well-being.

narcissism
Excessive admiration of oneself.

would others think they are any more interested in them or that they would judge them any less harshly? Many people look to others for indications of their own self-worth. It is first necessary to take responsibility to know oneself and then to accept oneself.

Receptivity

Many people think they are receptive to others when they are actually sending subtle signals that they do not want to be bothered. Receptivity can be communicated through eye contact and smiling. This allows other people to feel comfortable and that someone is approachable.

Listening

We discussed in Chapter 11 how true communication begins with listening. Nothing shows caring for another person quite as much as giving them full attention. It can be difficult to listen to people when they talk only of themselves or to people who see any comment made by another person in terms of how it relates to them. Learning to truly listen enhances intimacy.

Affection

What are the best ways to show affection for another person? In watching loving parents with their children, it is easy to see how affection is displayed. Parents attend to their children, smile at them, touch them in affectionate ways, look into their eyes, and hug and kiss them. Most people want the same things from their intimate partners. Affection shows a sense of warmth and security with one's partner.

Trust

Intimacy requires trust and this usually develops slowly as time progresses. Having such trust leads to more confidence that a relationship will last. When a couple trusts each other, each expects partner the other to care and respond to his or her needs (Zak et al., 1998).

Women from divorced families are often less able to trust their partners. Perhaps it is because these women have seen firsthand what happens in unsuccessful marriages and they believe that intimate relationships just do not work. Men may also be less able to trust their partners when they are ambivalent or cautious about trust. The important thing to remember is that often the longer a relationship lasts, the more trust is established (Jacquet & Surra, 2001).

The Dark Side of Love

Love evokes powerful emotions that can also be destructive to a relationship and may require effort to overcome. We now examine three aspects of the dark side of love—jealousy, compulsiveness, and possessiveness.

Jealousy: The Green-Eyed Monster

Jealousy is a common experience in intimate relationships (Knox et al., 2007). Imagine you are at a party with a person with whom

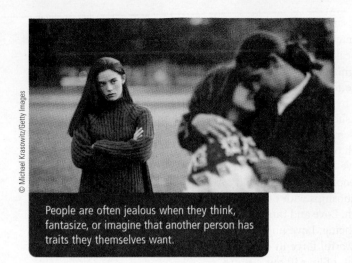

People are often jealous when they think, fantasize, or imagine that another person has traits they themselves want.

you have an exclusive sexual relationship. To be jealous is an emotional reaction to a relationship that one perceives as being threatened (Knox et al., 1999, 2007; Sharpsteen & Kirkpatrick, 1997). A threat is a matter of interpretation. People who fully trust their partners may not be able to imagine a situation in which the relationship is really threatened. People are most jealous when another person seen as a threat has traits they themselves would like to have. They might imagine that their partners will find that other person more desirable.

Heterosexual men and women experience similar levels of jealousy in intimate relationships, yet there is some disagreement over what triggers that jealousy (Fleischmann et al., 2005). Some researchers have found that men are more jealous when they believe that their partners have had sexual encounters with other men, while women are often more focused on the emotional or relationship aspects of infidelity (Buss, 2003; Schützwohl, 2008). This may have to do with whether a relationship is short term or long term (Penke & Asendorpf, 2008). In short-term relationships, both men and women are more threatened by sexual infidelity, while emotional infidelity is often more threatening in long-term relationships (Mathes, 2005). Other studies have found physiological responses, such as increased blood pressure, in both men and women when they imagined scenarios of their partners committing either emotional or sexual infidelity (DeSteno et al., 2002; C.R. Harris, 2003; Turner, 2000).

While less is known about jealousy among gay and lesbian couples because research has historically omitted their relationships (Blow & Hartnett, 2005), there is a growing body of research addressing this issue. Sheets and Wolf (2001) asked groups of heterosexual, gay, and lesbian subjects to imagine a scenario where their partners were unfaithful. Surprisingly, the group that suffered the least emotional distress were heterosexual men. Other research has found little difference in terms of jealousy and sexual orientation (Harris, 2002).

Regardless of sexual orientation, people who do not experience jealousy have been found to be more secure, and this security in intimate relationships tends to increase as relationships grow (Knox et al., 1999, 2007). Although it is thought that jealousy is an indication of strong love for a person, it is more about lack of trust.

There is also evidence that jealousy may be influenced by culture. One study on levels of distrust of men among women of different ethnic backgrounds found that Latina women had more distrust of men with whom they had intimate relationships than African-American or White women. Of the Latina women, levels of distrust were highest in Dominican women, followed by Puerto Rican and Mexican women (Estacion & Cherlin, 2010).

Jealousy often indicates lack of trust and low self-esteem (Knox et al., 2007; Puente & Cohen, 2003). It can also be a self-fulfilling prophecy. Jealous individuals can drive their partners away, which convinces them that they were right to be jealous in the first place. Communicating with a partner about jealous feelings can often help to maintain a relationship (Guerrero & Afifi, 1999). Opening up and talking about uncertainty or reassessing a relationship can help restore and strengthen it.

Compulsiveness: Addicted to Love

Being in love can produce a sense of ecstasy, euphoria, and a feeling of well-being, much like a powerful drug. In fact, when people are in love, their bodies release *phenylethylamine*, which produces those feelings (Sabelli et al., 1996). Phenylethylamine is also an ingredient in chocolate, which may be why some people love it so much. There are people who move from relationship to relationship as if they were addicted and trying to continually recreate that feeling. Or they may obsessively hang on to a love partner long after his or her interest has waned (see Table 12.1 on page 319).

 REAL Research Heterosexual men and women systematically overestimate the attractiveness of members of their own sex, and these overestimations may be because of biological programming to view others as potential threats to their love relationships (Hill, 2007).

Love addiction is reinforced by the popular media's portrayals (even as far back as Shakespeare's *Romeo and Juliet*) of passionate love as all-consuming. It fosters the belief that only one person is fated to be another's soul mate and that two people who have found each other will live "happily ever after." Some people feel the need to be in love because society teaches that only then are they really whole, happy, and fulfilled. Yet love based solely on need is rarely satisfactory. In Peele and Brodsky's (1991) book *Love and Addiction*, they argue that love addiction is more common than most believe and that it is based on a continuation of an adolescent view of love that is never replaced as people mature. Counselling or psychotherapy may help people come to terms with their addiction to love.

Possessiveness: Every Move You Make, I'll Be Watching You

Because love also entails dependency to some degree and a strong connection between people, there is always the danger that the strength of the bond can be used by one partner to manipulate the other. Abusive love relationships occur when one partner tries to increase his or her own sense of self-worth or to control the other's behaviour by withdrawing or manipulating love.

For intimacy to grow, partners must nurture each other. Controlling behaviour generally smothers a relationship. No one likes being manipulated, whether it is subtle through the use of guilt or overt through physical force. Part of love is the joy of seeing one's partner free to pursue his or her desires. Although every relationship has its boundaries, freedom within those agreed-on constraints is what encourages growth and maturation of both partners.

Possessiveness suggests a problem of self-esteem and personal boundaries and can even lead to **criminal harassment** or **stalking**. In Canada this consists of "repeated conduct that is carried out over a period of time and which causes you to reasonably fear for

your safety or the safety of someone known" (Royal Canadian Mounted Police, 2012). It may include following someone, repeatedly calling, or leaving messages or unwanted gifts. It has been recognized as a crime in Canada since 1993 and was first brought to the forefront when singer Anne Murray was relentlessly pursued by a Saskatchewan farmer. Thinking about another person with such a level of obsession is a sign of a serious psychological problem, one that should be brought to the attention of a mental health professional.

We started this chapter talking about the importance of love in people's lives. The ability to form loving, caring, and intimate relationships with others is important for emotional and physical health. Love and intimacy are two of the most powerful factors in well-being. Love might not always be easy to understand but it is a powerful force in one's life, and intimacy is an important component of love in our culture.

---

criminal harassment or stalking
Relentlessly pursuing someone or making threatening gestures or claims toward a person when a relationship is unwanted.

Review Questions

1 Why do people feel jealous, and how are jealousy and self-esteem related?

2 Compare and contrast compulsiveness and possessiveness.

3 What are some common types of criminal harassment?

Chapter Review

Summary Points

1 People go through life trying to come to terms with love and why they are attracted to certain types or why they fall in love with the wrong people. The mystery of love is part of its attraction.

2 Not until the 19th century did people begin to believe that romantic love was the most desirable form. Through most of Western history, marriage was an economic union arranged by the parents. Once wed, husbands and wives were encouraged to learn to love each other. This is still a major system in many non-Western cultures.

3 Romantic love comes with a sense of ecstasy and anxiety, physical attraction, and sexual

desire. People tend to idealize those whom they love, ignoring faults in the newfound joy of the attachment. Passionate love blooms in the initial euphoria of a new attachment to a sex partner. If a relationship is to continue, romantic love must develop into companionate love.

4 Romantic love is the passionate and highly sexual part of loving. Companionate love involves feelings of affection, intimacy, and attachment to another person. In many cultures, marriages are based on companionate love, assuming that passion will grow as the couple does.

5 Canadian sociologist John Alan Lee suggests that there are six basic types of love. Robert

Sternberg suggests that love is made up of three elements: passion, intimacy, and commitment, which can combine in different ways in relationships, creating seven basic ways to love and an eighth state called *non-love,* which is an absence of all three elements.

6 Behavioural reinforcement theories suggest that people love because the other person reinforces positive feelings in them that are attractive even when the reward has nothing to do with the other person.

7 Cognitive theories propose that people love because they think they love. This theory suggests that the action comes first and the interpretation comes later.

8 In physiological arousal theory, people are vulnerable to experiencing love (or another emotion) when they are physiologically aroused for whatever reason. An emotion happens when there is general physiological arousal for whatever reason and a label is attached to it. That label might be any emotion.

9 Evolutionary perspectives maintain that that love developed out of people's need to be protected from outside threats, to protect children, and from our sex drive. Love is an evolutionary strategy that helps form the bonds needed to pass genes on to the next generation.

10 Biological theories maintain that pheromones may contribute to feelings of love. Odour preferences are influenced by *major histocompatibility complex* (MHC). Neurotransmitters and the brain also have been found to affect feelings of love.

11 Love develops over the life cycle. In infancy, children develop attachments to their caregivers. Receiving love in return has an influence on the capacity to love later in life. In adolescence, people deal with issues of separation from parents and begin to explore adult ways of loving. Adolescents tend to experience romantic love. Attachment styles learned in infancy, such as secure, avoidant, and ambivalent styles, may last through life and influence the formation of adult attachments in adolescence.

12 As people mature and enter adulthood, forming intimate relationships becomes important. Developing intimacy is risky and men and women have different styles, but intimacy is seen as an important component of mature love in Western culture. As people grow older, commitment in love becomes more important, and passion may decrease in importance.

13 Relationships take effort and when a couple stops working on their relationship, both partners can become lonely, love can fade, and intimacy can evaporate. When love is lost, for whatever reason, it is often a time of pain and mourning. The support of family and friends can help people let go of the lost love and try to form new attachments.

14 Men and women may have different intimacy styles. For example, men may learn to suppress communication about intimacy as they grow, or they may learn to express it in different ways.

15 Developing intimacy begins with understanding and liking oneself. Receptivity, listening, showing affection, trusting in one's partner, and respecting him or her are important in the development of intimacy.

16 Love also has its negative side. Jealousy plagues many people in their love relationships, while others seem addicted to love and go in and out of love relationships. Some people also use love as a means to manipulate and control others.

17 Possessiveness indicates a problem of self-esteem, and personal boundaries and can eventually lead to criminal harassment. Canada has clear laws that enable the police to arrest a person who constantly pursues someone or makes threatening gestures.

Critical Thinking Questions

1 Consider John Alan Lee's six colours of love and imagine a relationship where each would be predominant. Which do you think would be hardest to deal with in a partner and why?

2 Consider Robert Sternberg's three elements of love. Think of a couple who has just met and progresses to consummate love. Which do you think comes first, and then second, and then third. Why?

3 One popular belief about pheromones is that they have a hypnotic quality and can generate sexual attraction, even though someone would not normally be aroused without them. Do you believe that there is any truth to this belief? Why or why not?

4 Marriages in many non-Western countries tend to be arranged by families, while people in Western societies usually base their marriages upon whether they love the other person. Are there advantages or disadvantages to having love as the main criterion? What are those advantages and disadvantages?

5 When people are attracted to another person, they often pursue that person romantically. At what point, however, does romantic pursuit turn into stalking or criminal harassment? This question might be easy if people said "not interested" immediately, but this is often not the case in that many people prefer to discourage someone gently.

Websites

Royal Canadian Mounted Police (RCMP) Criminal Harassment—Stalking   This site offers detailed advice for people who are being stalked. (http://www.rcmp-grc.gc.ca/cp-pc/crimhar-eng.htm)

13 Adult Sexual Relationships

Today in Canada, single people have numerous environments and methods to meet eligible others. A century ago, especially in the sparsely populated western provinces, this was difficult for both sexes.

Looking for love through newspapers and magazines has been around for several hundred years and, as long as the advertisers mentioned that they were looking for marriage partners ("object matrimony") in earlier times, few raised any objections. Historian Dan Azoulay (2000) of York University looked at many such letters in Canada's *Western Home Monthly* by both men and women from the Prairie provinces between 1905 and 1924. This was a time when young men were often isolated on farms or hunting camps and working from morning to night with little time to socialize, let alone

find eligible women. Women were also isolated with such jobs as school teachers and housekeepers in remote areas, and they would similarly come across few single men. With the loneliness that they must have felt, advertising in a journal that reached deep into Alberta, Saskatchewan, and Manitoba seemed like a good idea at the time. Typically, men or women would send in letters to be published, wait for replies, and begin corresponding with the most interesting or eligible of them. Here is an example of a promise from one man calling himself "a railroader" living in Crowfoot, Alberta in 1906:

Cooking is something every young girl or woman should be able to do. But as for feeding calves, pigs, and milking cows, as well as weeding the garden, etc., why all this

"A woman is not a horse."

work is simply out of the question and I cannot understand why any young man starting in life would have the nerve to expect his young wife to do such drudgery. He should remember that a woman is not a horse. If I ... get a wife I will never expect her to do as much as some of our Alberta bachelors expect a wife to do. (Azoulay, 2000, p. 134)

No doubt this sensitive young bachelor had no shortage of takers. After some correspondence, two people would agree to meet and often marry. Because Canada was vast and mail was slow, however, this process took quite some time. The *Western Home Monthly* not only brought the news of the time to early Canadians, but the loves of their lives as well (Azoulay, 2000). ▐▐

Throughout this book, we have discussed the importance of family upon people's feelings about love, intimacy, and relationships. We also know that other factors such as society, culture, ethnicity, race, religion, and age, influence connections with others. By late adolescence, the majority of adolescents have the ability to become involved in an intimate sexual relationship (Shulman et al., 2010). However, every society has rules to control the ways that people develop sexual bonds with other people. In many parts of the world (e.g., India), it is common for parents or other family members to arrange for their children to meet members of the other sex, marry them, and begin their sexual lives together. The expectation—like that in the West—was that couples would remain sexually faithful and that marital unions would end only in death. In such societies, adult sexual relationships are clearly defined, and deviating from the norm is viewed negatively.

In Canada, people engage in a variety of sexual relationships including same-sex, other-sex, premarital, marital, extramarital, casual, polygamous, and polyamorous relationships. In this chapter, we look at people's intimate sexual relationships.

Dating

In the 1800s, Canada was primarily rural and most people lived in small towns and cities or on farms. Teenagers did not date but instead spent time with each other under the watchful eyes of parents, grandparents, or older siblings. As Canadian historian Peter Ward (1990) pointed out in his study of courtship in the Maritime provinces of the 19th century, young people were not free to court and marry as they pleased because of an "interlocking web of tensions" or rules of regulations coming formally from the church and state on one side and informally from family and community on the other. As a result, there was little room for necessary privacy for couples to get to know each other before making any proposal and many would-be affairs were thwarted by such restrictions.

Privacy for young couples came only with the invention of the automobile where, by the 1920s, teenagers were able to get away from their families and be alone with each other. Dating by the 1950s still held a strong sense of formality and propriety. A boy would pick up a girl at her house, her father and mother would meet or chat with him, and then the two would go to a well-defined event such as a chaperoned school-sponsored dance or a movie. The girl would be brought home by the curfew her parents imposed (Benokraitis, 1993). Today, formal dating has given way to more casual dating, in part because of society's more permissive attitudes toward exploring romantic relationships. Teenagers still go to movies and dances but just as often they will get together at someone's house or a coffee shop. As has long been the custom, teenagers often use friend networks to find out if someone might be interested in them before asking him or her out.

It can be more difficult to meet potential partners as a person gets older. The Internet, however, has provided a new way to meet people through websites, chat rooms, and online dating services.

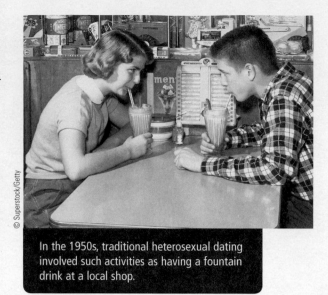
In the 1950s, traditional heterosexual dating involved such activities as having a fountain drink at a local shop.

REAL Research New Brunswick psychologists Sarah Vannier and Lucia O'Sullivan (2012) surveyed 431 young Canadians (mean age = 21.7 years; 72 percent female) about their most recent episode of heterosexual oral sex. The majority of episodes occurred within a committed relationship and included intercourse. Oral sex upon women was rare unless it was reciprocated by oral sex on men.

In Chapter 12, we discussed the physical benefits of love and intimacy. Dating has been found to provide similar benefits. Relationships provide companionship, emotional support, and even economic support. This may be partially dependent upon the kind of people in relationships. For example, people with a strong sense of self have been found to be more satisfied and happy with their dating relationships (Fruth, 2007; Fuller-Fricke, 2007), while those without have been found to experience more relationship conflict (Longua, 2010).

"Dating" has changed on college campuses over the years. Today it is common for groups of students to "hang out" rather

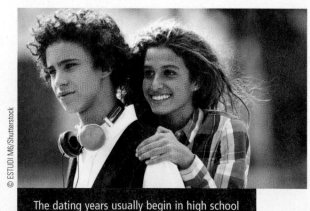
The dating years usually begin in high school in Canada.

The "half-age-plus-seven" rule, which has been around at least since the patriarchal Victorian times, is a rule about the acceptable age for a woman when a man marries her. A man divides his age in half and adds seven to arrive at the lowest socially acceptable age for his bride. In his 1903 book *Her Royal Highness—Woman*, French author Max O'Rell writes:

... at what age should a man marry? Well, at all events, never before he is quite prepared to provide for a wife, whatever her position may be. When

© Found Image Press/Corbis

this indispensable condition is satisfied, I shall say never, or seldom, before thirty. ... I heard the other day a very good piece of advice, which I should like to repeat here, as I endorse it thoroughly: A man should marry a woman half his age, plus seven. Try it at whatever age you like, and you will find it works very well. (O'Rell, 1903)

While men still tend to be older in couples today, there is far greater freedom for large age disparities for both sexes. The greater the disparity, however, the greater the social disapproval.

---

than go out on dates. Typically, men and women go out with groups of friends. Glenn and Marquardt (2002) found that half of female seniors reported being asked out by a man on six or more dates while at college and one third of both men and women said they had been on only one or two dates. Clearly, patterns are changing.

Why might there be less dating today? The sexual revolution has changed society's attitudes about sexuality, making **hook-ups** and **friends with benefits** more acceptable. Today, casual sex has become more common on college campuses than dating according to some evidence (Bradshaw et al., 2010; Littleton et al., 2009b).

These changes from the one-on-one pre-arranged date system may also reflect the fact that men and women are now able to be friends, while this was discouraged decades ago. Typically in the 1950s, the only way a man could have access to a woman's company was within the formalities of a date. Today, young men and women mix as equals freely and anyone is free to ask anyone out for coffee. Thus, if any romantic interest emerges, there is much room to express it. Thus, men are less likely to ask a woman out formally and both sexes are free to associate with each other informally. This also gives women far more freedom to pursue men.

Interracial and Intercultural Dating

Rapidly growing minority populations in Canada and the United States have led to increases in interracial, interfaith, and intercultural dating (Lewis & Ford-Robertson, 2010; Uskel, et al. 2007). Canada's immigration rate in 2008 was 7.3 new arrivals per 1000 people compared to 2.9 per 1000 in the United States. There

are now large populations from South and East Asia and the Middle East and a growing tendency among younger people to define their ethnic identity as simply "Canadian" (Statistics Canada, 2011a). High schools and universities, especially in Vancouver, Toronto, and Montreal, are now largely multicultural (Triadafilopoulos, 2012), and there is a tendency to broaden the curriculum so as to include global perspectives and, thus, demystify the differences among groups (Kulig, et al., 1999). In one study of 234 young Muslim Canadians, men were more likely open to dating outside of their group. The strongest predictor, however, was whether subjects identified more strongly with their Islamic communities or with mainstream Canada (Cila & Lalonde, 2014). The latter group was more open. Similarly, Uskel, et al. (2011) found that both South Asian and European Canadians were consistently more amenable to interracial dating when they identified more with Canada as a whole rather than their cultural group, and the same was found among young Jewish Canadians (Haji, et al., 2011).

Overall, those who are more open to dating someone from a different cultural group are younger (Tsunokai et al., 2009), more politically liberal, and less religious (Yancey, 2007). In the United States, African Americans are twice as likely as Whites to report being open to interracial dating (Knox et al., 2000; Rosenblatt et al., 1995). African-American and Latina women with greater education are also more likely to be involved in interracial

hook-up
A slang term meaning getting together for the purpose of sex when not in a relationship.

friends with benefits
An arrangement where two people get together occasionally or regularly solely for the purpose of sex.

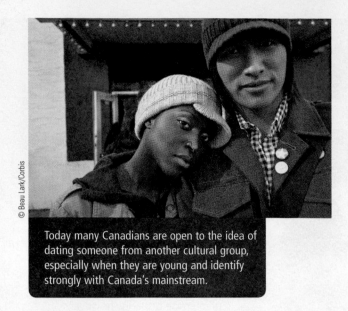

Today many Canadians are open to the idea of dating someone from another cultural group, especially when they are young and identify strongly with Canada's mainstream.

relationships, as are White women with less education (Fu, 2010). Finally, gays and lesbians tend to be more open to interracial relationships (Oswald & Clausell, 2005).

Non-marital Sexual Activity

Canadians usually begin dating around 15 or 16 years of age. The mean age of marriage, however, was 29.1 for women and 31.1 for men in 2008. This leaves about 15 years, much of which may be spent in relationships, prior to finding a permanent partner. As a result, it seems inevitable that sexual activity will be a part of unmarried people's lives. Compared to a century ago when young men and women got together primarily for the purpose of considering marriage, dating relationships now often involve sex. Busby et al. (2010) looked at the timing of sex in a relationship and found that couples who waited to have sex experience better relationship outcomes. To wait, however, is not necessarily a conscious or formal decision, since it may be that one member of a couple is waiting for the other to show signs of interest in sex, or both may be waiting for circumstances to be amenable. It may also be that one or both parties wish to concentrate more on getting to know each other rather than consciously setting a time frame for physical intimacy.

Over the past several decades, Canadians have become far more tolerant of non-marital sex. Those who considered it "not wrong at all" rose from 39 percent in 1975 to 57 percent in 1995. Those who consider it "always wrong" fell from 19 percent to 13 percent during that same period. Canadians who actually engaged in non-marital sex doubled between the 1960s and 1970s, and the gender gap narrowed from a 20 percent to an 8 percent difference, suggesting a greater acceptance of female autonomy (Roberts et al., 2005). As for the recent incidence of non-marital sex, the rate of 18- and 19-year-olds who report having had sexual intercourse has remained between 65 percent and 70 percent since 1996. There are far less data in Canada than the United States because there are no comprehensive surveys on sexual behaviour. Even so, because of the differences in culture between the two countries, one should be cautious about applying American statistics to Canadian life.

Alberta psychologists Gusarova et al. (2012) sought to examine satisfaction within friends-with-benefits relationships with questionnaires to 146 men and 135 women. The majority reported positive (38 percent) or neutral (37 percent) outcomes, and only 22 percent said that the arrangement ended because of emotional complications. On the other hand, 40 percent said that they would not engage in a friends-with-benefits relationship again, and women were more likely to enter into one hoping that it would turn into a dating relationship.

One's propensity to engage in sex before marriage depends upon a number of factors, with religiosity being one of the strongest. The Hutterites of Alberta and Mennonites of Ontario not only live in small isolated communities but any sex before marriage is forbidden within their belief system. Conservative Muslims would also have similar proscriptions. Generally, young people who do have sex before marriage are less religious and tend to be more liberal.

REAL Research In-depth interviews were conducted with nine Muslim-Canadian adolescents about sexuality education. They reported that they found some subjects in mainstream sexuality education problematic to their beliefs and preferred that their parents be their sexuality educators instead. Their parents, however, rarely discussed sex with them (Zain Al-Dien, 2010).

There is little information on the extent to which gay and lesbian young Canadians have sex. Same-sex dating is a relatively new phenomenon because of the lessening of stigma. In past decades, young gays and lesbians generally could not risk being seen together in public too often because of homophobic reactions and possible exposure. For example, they could not go to a school-sponsored dance, let alone dance together as couples. Today in Canada these reactions are far less common and in many places gays and lesbians are free even to show affection to each other. Although society is still structured around heterosexuality, it is slowly making room for alternative forms.

Breaking Up

How a person reacts to a breakup depends on several factors, such as who initiated the breakup, the amount of contact with the ex-boyfriend or girlfriend after the breakup, and how much social support a person has. Typically, the one who initiated the breakup feels less distress but more guilt (Locker et al., 2010). Those who did not initiate the breakup often feel rejected, and experience more depression and a loss of self-esteem (Perilloux & Buss, 2008). Some rejected partners become obsessive about their lost relationship and engage in stalking behaviours such as repeated texting or calling (Fisher et al., 2010). Having continued contact with an ex-boyfriend or girlfriend can make it more difficult to

Sexual Diversity in Our World

Virginity—A Troublesome Concept

Traditionally, the term "virginity" was used only for young women. It meant that they had never had penile-vaginal intercourse and that that their hymens were intact. It has therefore been a cultural status for women with important implications, especially in places past and present that value the "purity" of women before marriage. At first intercourse, the hymen usually breaks and there is pain and blood. If a woman did have intercourse in the past, no bleeding would occur and the "proof of virginity" many cultures saw as essential would be absent. For centuries, with the help of trusted others, women have often faked their virginity to save face. During the 13th century, they would insert dove's bladders filled with blood into their vaginas, which, if they were lucky, would break at just the right moment (Coyne Kelly & Leslie, 1999). From the 1920s to the 1950s in the United States (and no doubt in Canada), family doctors could be convinced to sew the "lover's knot," which consisted of several stitches into the labia of brides-to-be so that on their wedding night they would feel pain and bleed (Kelly, 2000). Today, faking virginity is a far simpler matter for it is possible to go online and purchase a "fake hymen" for as little as $29.95, which will ooze a blood-like substance upon contact with a penis.

Perhaps virginity is a concept that is best put to bed. Today, sex researchers have replaced this term with "first intercourse" or "first sexual experience" instead, which easily applies to both males and females. Virginity is further problematic when applied to gay men since the concept was never intended for first anal intercourse, whether insertive or receptive. Furthermore, lesbians may not be penetrated by their partners at all. One must also consider that when young women have their first intercourse they are said to have "lost" their virginity, while young men are said to have "gained" sexual experience. "First sexual experience" is not only more accurate but more egalitarian for all genders and all sexual orientations.

recover from a breakup. One of the most important factors in recovering is social support. Those who have friends to lean on and talk to have an easier time moving on.

Cohabitation

Cohabitation, or living together without being married, is more complex in definition than it seems. Today, Canada has common-law marriages where a couple lives together in a marriage-like relationship and, as such, is equal to marriage. This is possible in the United States as well, but only in a few areas. People also share lodgings who are merely roommates, whether same sex or other sex. Still further, same-sex couples in the United States have had no choice but to cohabitate without marriage because their unions are generally not recognized. We discuss common-law marriage later in this chapter. Here, we restrict our discussion to conjugal couples who live together casually or for long periods before common-law marriages were recognized.

In the United States, there were 3.2 million unmarried couples living together in 1990 and 7.5 million in 2010 (Bumpass & Lu, 2000; Pew Research Center, 2010). The main reason for this increase in cohabitation was having limited finances (Pew Research Center, 2010). The United States Census Bureau found a connection between partners' employment status and cohabitation. Since the beginning of the 21st century, the percentage of couples who moved in together in which only one was unemployed has increased, while the percentage of couples who were both employed has decreased (Pew Research Center, 2010).

Although the increase in cohabitation has led to a decrease in marriage (which we will discuss further later in this chapter), couples who live together have been found to transition to marriage within three years (Goodwin et al., 2010). Not all couples marry, however. Some people live together with one partner, break up, and live then with another. This is known as **serial cohabitation.** Overall, longer cohabitation has been found to be associated with higher likelihood of divorce (Cohan & Kleinbaum, 2002; Seltzer, 2000; Stevenson & Wolfers, 2007).

There are advantages and disadvantages to cohabitation. It allows couples to learn more about each other's habits and idiosyncrasies, share finances, and mature in their relationship. Yet, there are also problems. Parents and relatives may not support the union and governments tend not to recognize people who live together for purposes of spousal privileges or taxes. This has certainly been the case with gay and lesbian couples in the United States where both partners are forced to file income tax returns as single individuals and they are regarded as mere roommates. Couples who live together before marriage are more likely to get divorced once they do than those who do not live together (Guzzo, 2009; Rhoades et al., 2009). However, it may not be that living together itself increases the chance of divorce but that couples who choose to live together may have been more likely to divorce even if they did not live together first (Stevenson & Wolfers, 2007). They may also feel that they would not be happy in a marriage, they may be more accepting of divorce, they may be

serial cohabitation
A series of cohabitating relationships with a person living with one partner, breaking up, and living with a new partner.

less religious and less traditional, or they may be less committed in the beginning of the relationship. It is thus difficult to generalize any findings. A recent study found that 60 percent of couples in the sample cohabited to spend more time together, 19 percent did so for financial reasons, and 14 percent did so to test the relationship (Rhoades et al., 2009).

We do know that couples who are committed to each other (i.e., those who are planning to get married or are engaged) have a better chance of a successful marriage after living together (Guzzo, 2009; Rhoades et al., 2009). In fact, these committed couples have the same chance of divorce as those who marry without living together first (Goodwin et al., 2010).

Review Questions

1 Explain how dating has changed among young people today and why.

2 Identify some of the reasons why there have been increases in inter-group dating.

3 What factors are associated with an easier breakup?

4 What is responsible for current increases in cohabitation?

5 How has the denial of same-sex marriage in the United States affected same-sex couples?

Marriage

Since 2005, marriage in Canada has been defined as the union between any two people, whether a male and female, two males, or two females. Prior to 2005, only the union between a male and a female was recognized. Anyone 18 or 19 years of age and over may marry depending upon the province. Additionally, 16- and 17-year-olds may marry with their parents' permission. Marriages may be either religiously sanctioned when performed by a member of a clergy or civilly sanctioned by marriage commissioners, judges, justices of the peace, or court clerks.

In the mid-1960s, about 80 percent of people between 24 and 34 years of age were married. By the 1970s, issues such as an economic downturn, an increased number of women in higher education and the labour force, and increasing rates of cohabitation led to a decrease the in marriage rate. Today, many couples delay marriage or even avoid it entirely (Dougherty, 2010; Mather & Lavery, 2010).

In this section we look at marriage statistics and trends, common-law relationships, intercultural marriages, marriages in later life, marital satisfaction, and sex within and outside of marriage. We reserve the discussion of same-sex marriage to later in this chapter only because of its newness. Here we focus on male-female marriage.

Statistics and Current Trends in Marriage

The proportion of married people in Canada has fluctuated over the years depending upon economic trends and historical events. In the 1930s during the Depression, there were fewer marriages due to high unemployment and the economic burden of children. During World War II the proportion increased, partially because of men avoiding conscription (Milan, 2011). Once the sexual revolution of the 1970s was firmly in place, more young people entered college, the time for preparation for life became longer, and they were freer to have sexual relationships outside of marriage.

In 2011, 46.4 percent of the population 16 years of age and over were legally married, while the rest were never married, divorced, separated, or widowed. This stands in sharp contrast to the proportion 30 years earlier, in which 60.9 percent were married. The proportion in 2011 varied considerably by province, from 53.9 percent in Newfoundland and Labrador to 35.4 percent in Quebec. The older that people are, the less likely they are to have been never married (Milan, 2011).

The decreasing rate of marriage is related to a number of factors. First, the mean age of marriage is higher than it has ever been. Between 1972 and 2008, the average ages of first marriages rose from 22.5 to 29.1 for women and from 24.9 to 31.1 for men (Employment and Social Development Canada, 2015). This would indicate an increasing complexity in preparation for life, including a greater time spent in education. Among 25- to 29-year-olds, the proportion that were unmarried tripled, rising from 26.0 percent in 1981 to 73.1 percent in 2011. For people in their early 30s, the rates rose from 15.0 percent to 54.0 percent in the same period (Milan, 2011).

Second, more Canadians are choosing common-law relationships either before marriage as temporary states or as long-term alternatives. It used to be that living together without marriage had a stigma attached to it. Today that stigma has largely disappeared.

Common-Law Unions

When including common-law unions, the proportion of Canadians living with partners rises from 46.4 percent of those legally married to 57.7 percent of the population. A fifth of Canadian couples are thus in common-law unions. This figure has thus risen dramatically from 1981, when the proportion was at 6.3 percent. Although common-law unions are most common among people 25 to 29 years of age, they have also been increasing in older age cohorts. In contrast, the proportion of 20- to 24-year-olds in common-law unions has decreased, indicating again that preparation for life in terms of education and employment has become more complex (Statistics Canada, 2002).

Living Apart Together

Statistics Canada has traditionally defined a "couple" as either married or in a common-law relationship and living in the same household. This does not mean, however, that all other adults are single. Seven percent of Canadians or 1.9 million people are members of couples and may even be married, but they live apart. These relationships are called "living apart together" (LAT) and the couple may be in the same area, in different provinces, or even different countries. The reasons for living apart vary. Some prefer to do so while others cite educational or employment reasons. For example, two professionals may find it difficult to land acceptable jobs in the same city. Others have decided for various reasons that they cannot live together and are happier in different households (Turcotte, 2013).

In 2001 among women aged 50 to 69, the vast majority entered into coupledom through marriage, which is not surprising since common-law unions were not available to them. Younger generations, however, have taken advantage of common-law unions. Among 30- to 39-year-olds, 40 percent are expected to choose a common-law union and this figure rises to 53 percent for 20- to 29-year-olds (Statistics Canada, 2002).

Marriages seem to be more stable. The probability that the first common-law union will end in separation is twice as high as that of the first marriage, with a difference of 63 percent and 30 percent, respectively. This high breakup rate also increases the possibility that women will enter a second common-law union, which in turn increases the probability of a second breakup (Statistics Canada, 2002).

Endogamous and Exogamous Marriages

Endogamous marriages are ones where people marry within their group as in same culture or same religion, and **exogamous marriages** are ones where people marry outside of their groups. Exogamous marriages depend upon the pool of people available with the same backgrounds. For example, Protestants in Quebec are more likely to marry Catholics because only 5 percent of the province is Protestant and 83 percent are Catholic. Similarly, African Americans make up only 12 percent of the United States and are thus more likely to marry Whites. Most Canadian marriages and common-law unions are endogamous; here we look at a number of differences between couples who are exogamous or in "mixed unions."

Of the 14.1 million marriages and unions in 2001, only 3.2 percent were composed of a visible and a non-visible minority member. This figure, however, was up 35 percent from 1991, which reflects Canada's growing population of minority groups of which there are now more than ever before (Milan & Hamm, 2004). Unions may also be composed of two different visible minority members such as Chinese and Middle Eastern, although this is far less common, accounting for only 0.4 percent of all unions. In just over half (53 percent) of the mixed unions, the visible minority member was a man, and in just under half (47 percent) a woman. It is more common for a non-visible minority woman to marry a man who is Black, Middle Eastern, or South Asian, while non-visible minority men tended to marry women who are Chinese, Filipino, Hispanic, or Japanese.

In the United States, less than one in a 1000 new marriages were between a Black and a White spouse in 1961, but this number increased to one in 150 in 1980. By 2010, one in seven new marriages was between spouses of different races or ethnicities (Fincham & Beach, 2010; Lewis & Ford-Robertson, 2010; Saulny, 2010; Shibusawa, 2009). Of the almost 4 million American couples who married in 2008, 31 percent of Asians, 26 percent of Hispanics, 16 percent of Blacks, and 9 percent of Whites married someone whose race or ethnicity was different from their own (Passel et al., 2010).

Among Blacks and Asians, there were significant gender differences in exogamous marriages. Although 22 percent of Black male newlyweds in 2008 married outside their race, only 9 percent of Black females did the same (Passel et al., 2010). Gender differences were found in the opposite direction for Asians. While 40 percent of Asian female newlyweds married outside their race, only 20 percent of Asian males did the same.

As of 2001, 19 percent of Canada's 14.1 million couples were in interreligious unions. More than half of these unions were between Catholics and Protestants, representing nearly 10 percent of all couples. Interreligious unions are subject to definition. Statistics Canada considers a union interreligious if two partners are from different broad religious groups (e.g., a Hindu and a Muslim) but not if they are from two denominations within the same group (e.g., a Presbyterian and an Anglican). Couples may consider religious background a profound difference or, if the partners are more secular in their outlook, they may be indifferent to it. The higher the religiosity, however, the less likely one is to marry outside of one's religious group. Conservative Protestants, for example, are more likely to marry other conservative Protestants. Sikhs, Muslims, and Hindus are the least likely to be in interreligious unions.

Another growing trend in Canada is the rise of married couples with the same level of education. Traditionally, because a woman's education was considered less important in that she was typically expected to remain home as a housewife and mother, men tended to marry down in education while women tended to marry up. Today, because of the importance of both partners being

endogamous marriage	**exogamous marriage**
Marriage within one's group.	Marriages outside of one's group.

in the labour force, marriages among partners with the same level of education have increased. The rates of such marriages were 42 percent in 1971 and 54 percent in 2001. The majority of educational discrepancies are of couples with adjacent levels—that is, they have similar levels and not the same (Hou & Myles, 2007).

© Somos Images/Corbis

Most older married couples say their marriages have improved over time and that the later years are some of their happiest.

Most Canadian couples are composed of people who are close to each other in age. In 2001, 58 percent of those with other-sex partners were within three years of each other, while another 24 percent were four to six years apart. Of the remaining couples, 10 percent were seven to nine years apart, and 8 percent were 10 years or more apart. In the vast majority of age-discrepant couples, the man was older—36 percent, as opposed to 6 percent where the woman was older (Boyd and Li, 2003).

In past decades, psychological assessments of older–younger couples were not favourable, often concluding that they were formed because of father–daughter or mother–son issues. People were also quick to judge them in terms of power discrepancies, where the older partner had power over the younger one. The fact that older partners are generally men reflects a time of less egalitarian marriages where a man spent years establishing himself so he was able to provide for children, a home, and a wife who was not in the labour force. This is also a reflection of a double standard, where aging in women is seen as negative while older men are seen as experienced (Boyd & Li, 2003).

In general, the greater number of exogamous marriages, the lesser the social distance between individuals and groups. Given that Canada is becoming increasingly diverse and understanding of differences is increasingly emphasized, it is likely that exogamous marriages will continue to increase.

Marriage in Later Life

Between 2006 and 2011, the number of seniors in Canada increased by 14.1 percent, amounting to nearly 5 million people or 14.8 percent of the population who are 65 and older. This figure is higher than the United States (13.0 percent) but lower than Japan, France, and the United Kingdom. Interestingly, in 2011 Canada had 5825 people who had reached the age of 100 or more years (Statistics Canada, 2011b).

Marriage has a positive impact on the lives of both aging men and women. Older adults who are married are happier and have lower rates of disease than those who are not (Dupre & Meadows, 2007).

In 2007, men and women older than 65 were much more likely to be married than at any other time in history (Stevenson

& Wolfers, 2007). However, because women live longer than men, widowhood is more common for them. Seventy-nine percent of men between the ages of 65 to 74 were married in 2004 compared to only 57 percent of women in the same age group.

Many older adults who experience the death of a spouse will remarry. Older men are twice as likely to do so. Older women are less likely to remarry because they outnumber men, and older men often marry younger women (M. Coleman et al., 2000). Marriages that follow the death of a spouse tend to be more successful if the couple had the opportunity to get to know each other fairly well beforehand, if their children and peers approve of the marriage, and if they are in good health, are financially stable, and have adequate living conditions.

Marital Satisfaction

Marital satisfaction for men is related to the frequency of pleasurable activities that involve doing fun things together in the relationship while for women it is related to the frequency of pleasurable activities that focus on emotional closeness. Other important variables, including being able to talk to each other and self-disclose, physical and emotional intimacy, and personality similarities, are all instrumental in achieving greater relationship quality.

The quality of the friendship with one's spouse is the most important factor in marital satisfaction for both men and women (Gottman & Silver, 2000). He also found that a couple's ability to resolve conflict added to their marital stability. High rewards such as emotional support and a satisfying sex life and low costs such as arguing and financial burdens are also important in marital satisfaction (Impett et al., 2001). If a marriage has high costs but low rewards, a person might end a relationship or look outside a marriage for alternative rewards.

Overall, marriage provides fewer health benefits to women and more to men. For instance, although married men have better physical and mental health, more self-reported happiness, and experience fewer psychological problems than either divorced, single, or widowed men (Joung et al., 1995), married women do not receive these same health benefits (Hemstrom, 1996). This may be because women have multiple role responsibilities. For example, married women still tend to do the bulk of housework and disproportionately take care of children (Baxter & Hewitt, 2010). Many women report that their marriages are more unfair to them than their husbands (Forry et al., 2007). The good news is that since the early 2000s there has been a trend in the mental health benefits of marriage applying equally to men and women (R.W. Simon, 2002; K. Williams & Umberson, 2004), which may be a result of an increased equality in marriage (W.B. Wilcox & Nock, 2006).

People who are married tend to be happier and healthier and have longer lives than either widowed or divorced persons of the same age (Dush & Amato, 2005; Waldinger & Schulz, 2010). In one study, married couples had the highest level of well-being, followed by (in order) common-law couples, steady dating relationships, casual dating relationships, and individuals who dated infrequently or not at all (Dush & Amato, 2005). Marriage has also been found to reduce the impact of several potentially traumatic events, including job loss, retirement, and illness (Waldinger & Schulz, 2010). In traditional marriages among the middle class, the woman usually stayed home with her children while the man worked outside the home. Today, dual-wage-earner families are more typical, leading to increased equality (Stevenson & Isen, 2010). Such marriages have been found to be happier and more fulfilling than traditional marriages (Stevenson & Wolfers, 2008). Partners with more education report more happiness in their marriages as well (Stevenson & Isen, 2010).

Sex within Marriage

Sex is an essential part of most marriages and most married people report that it is integral to a good marriage. Additionally, men often report higher sexual needs than women (Elliott & Umberson, 2008). There is also a great deal of variation in who initiates sex, in what sexual behaviours a couple engages, and how often they engage in them. Overall, the majority of married couples report satisfaction with their marital sex (Sprecher, 2002).

In the United States, the National Survey of Sexual Health and Behavior found that the majority of married couples have sex weekly or a few times per month and that younger married couples engage in sex more frequently (Herbenick et al., 2010a). Laumann and his colleagues (1994) found that 40 percent of married couples have sexual intercourse two or more times a week, while 50 percent engage do so a few times a month. The frequency of sexual activity and satisfaction with a couple's sex life have been found to be positively correlated (Blumstein & Schwartz, 1983); that is, the more frequent the sexual activity, the greater the relationship satisfaction. However, it is not known whether increased frequency of sex causes more satisfaction or whether increased relationship satisfaction causes increased sexual activity.

As we discussed in Chapter 12, long-term relationships often start out high on passion and this decreases over time (Brewis & Meyer, 2005; Starling, 1999). Many couples report engaging in sex less often as their marriage progresses. This is consistent with cross-cultural studies, which found that a declining frequency of

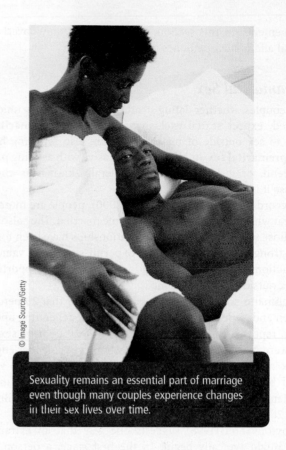

Sexuality remains an essential part of marriage even though many couples experience changes in their sex lives over time.

© Image Source/Getty

sexual activity over time is a common feature of human populations (Brewis & Meyer, 2005). Some marriages are **asexual relationships,** which means that the partners do not engage in sexual activity. This may be because one or both partners do not have sexual desire for each other anymore or it may be because of a mutual decision not to have sex (Donnelly & Burgess, 2008). In either case, most asexual married couples are in stable relationships and feel reluctant to leave (Donnelly & Burgess, 2008). What is essential here is whether such couples have other shared interests and an asexual marriage does not necessarily mean an unaffectionate one.

Sex Outside of Marriage

In all societies, marriage is a public declaration of sexual exclusivity between two people; however, traditionally, when women were regarded more as property, this applied only to the woman and not the man, who may have had mistresses and concubines. During traditional weddings in Western societies, both parties say their vows, which typically include a promise to be "faithful." Faithfulness here means sexual exclusivity, which, as is well known, not everyone follows. Sex outside of marriage, however, does not necessarily mean cheating or dishonesty. While most marital partners insist on exclusivity, others make more open

asexual relationship
A type of intimate relationship in which the partners do not engage in sexual activity.

arrangements. In this section, we explore not only covert extramarital affairs but open ones as well.

Extramarital Sex

Most couples, whether dating steadily, in common-law unions, or married, expect sexual exclusivity. Although **extramarital sex** refers to sex outside of marriage, we are also referring here to **extrapremarital sex**, or being non-exclusive with a dating partner, boyfriend, or girlfriend. This is generally known as **cheating** because it is done covertly.

According to Treas and Giesen (2000), people are more likely to cheat while living together than while married. They also found that those who cheat in intimate relationships have been found to have stronger sexual interests, more permissive sexual values, less satisfaction in their intimate relationship, and more opportunities for sex outside the relationship.

Laumann and his colleagues (1994) found that 20 percent of women and 15 percent to 35 percent of men, depending upon age group, reported that they had engaged in extramarital sex while they were married. Even for people who never consider engaging in sex outside of marriage, many often wonder about what it would be like. Typically, religiosity and church attendance are associated with lower incidences of extramarital affairs (Burdette et al., 2007).

Layton-Tholl (1998) suggests one way that an extramarital affair might typically begin. In the first stage, a person might become emotionally close to someone at school, work, a party, or even on the Internet. As he or she gets to know that person, there is chemistry and powerful attraction. This leads to the second stage in which the couple decides to keep the relationship secret. They do not tell anyone about their attraction and the fact that it is a secret adds fuel to the passion. In the third stage, the couple starts doing things together, even though they would not refer to it as dating. Each may still believe that their relationship is simply a friendship. Finally, in the fourth stage, the relationship becomes sexual, leading to an intense emotional and sexual affair.

Although many people think that sexual desire drives an extramarital affair, research has found that more than 90 percent of extramarital affairs occur because of unmet emotional needs within a marital relationship (Previti & Amato, 2004). Laumann and his colleagues (1994) found that couples are more likely to be faithful to each other as long as their marriage is intact and satisfying. A.P. Thompson (1984) suggested three types of extramarital affairs: sexual but not emotional, sexual and emotional, and emotional but not sexual. Twenty-one percent of respondents having extramarital sex were involved in predominantly sexual affairs; 19 percent in both sexual and emotional affairs; and 18 percent in affairs that were emotional but not sexual (the remaining affairs did not fit clearly into any of these categories). Affairs that are both emotional and sexual appear to affect a marital relationship the most, while affairs that are primarily sexual affect it the least.

Gender plays a role in both the type of extramarital affairs in which a person engages and a partner's acceptance of these affairs. Women are more likely to have emotional but not sexual affairs and men are more likely to have sexual affairs. When it comes to accepting a partner's extramarital affair, women experience more emotional distress about affairs than do men and they rate emotional affairs as more harmful than sexual affairs (Guerrero et al., 2004). Men, on the other hand, rate sexual affairs as more harmful than emotional affairs (see Chapter 12 for more information about gender differences in jealousy). Extramarital affairs lower marital happiness and increase the risk for divorce (Previti & Amato, 2004).

Non-exclusive Relationships and Marriages

Some married people open up their relationships and encourage their partners to have sex outside of the marriage, believing that sexual variety and experience enhance their own sex lives. Couples engage in **co-marital sex** (the consent of married couples to sexually exchange partners) and some of them may be referred to as **swingers** or **polyamorists**. Non-married couples can also be polyamorists and can have partners outside of their primary relationship.

In 1972, George and Nena O'Neill published a book entitled Open Marriage (O'Neill & O'Neill, 1972). In this book, they explained that "sexual adventuring" was fine as long as both spouses knew about it. In open marriages, each partner is free to seek sex partners outside of the marriage.

Swingers are people who have sex with others as a couple. They may visit swingers clubs and conventions, or they may simply seek out other couples through advertising and exchange partners. Many engage in "safe-sex circles" in which they have sex only with people who have tested negative for sexually transmitted infections. According to O'Bryne and Watts (2011), who surveyed swingers and directly observed two Canadian swinger's clubs, respondents reported unsafe sex practices frequently. Of 32 men and 40 women, 16 percent did not use condoms for vaginal intercourse and 31 percent did not do so for anal intercourse.

The majority of swingers are White, middle class, middle-aged, and churchgoing (Bergstrand & Williams, 2000). The North American Swing Club Association claims that there are organized swing clubs in Canada, the United States, Japan, England, Germany, and France (Berg-strand & Williams, 2000). In addition, SwingFest, an annual American swinger lifestyle convention, brings in thousands of swingers from around the world (Swingfest.com). Not surprisingly, the Internet is the main source of contact for swingers (R.H. Rubin, 2001). There are also several swingers clubs as well as websites in Canada that have thousands of members.

---

extramarital sex
Having sex with someone other than one's husband or wife.

extrapremarital sex
Having sex with someone other than one to whom one is committed but not married.

cheating
Having sex with someone other than one's partner even though there was a promise of fidelity.

co-marital sex
The consenting of married couples to exchange partners sexually.

swinger
A married man or woman who openly exchanges other sex partners.

polyamorist
A man or woman who has more than one relationship.

SEX in Real Life — *What Is Polyamory?*

We live in a society that expects monogamy from sex partners. Serial monogamy, where people have only one sex partner at any one time, is common on college campuses. Although the majority of men and women have more than one sexual partner in their lifetime, they are usually monogamous while in these relationships.

Researchers are just beginning to explore the concept of polyamory—"ethically non-monogamous" relationships in which people engage in loving sexual relationships with more than one person at a time (Bennett, 2009). Polyamorous

people have a consensual and agreed-on context to these intimate relationships outside of their primary partnerships (Weitzman, 1999). They can be old, young, gay, or heterosexual, and the key to the relationship is honesty. Polyamorous men and women openly discuss sexual behaviour outside their primary relationship. Unlike "swingers," the emphasis is on the relationships rather than the sex. Polyamorous relationships can take many forms, including:

1. **Primary-Plus:** One person in a primary relationship agrees to pursue outside relationships. New

partners are "secondary lovers" and the primary relationship remains the most important.

2. **Triad:** Three people involved in a committed intimate relationship. All three people are equal and there is no primary relationship.

3. **Individual with Multiple Primaries:** This type resembles a "V" in which one person has separate but equal relationships with two or more other people who have no relationship with one another (Davidson, 2002).

Most swingers have strict rules meant to protect the marriage and sex is seen as separate from the loving relations they have. The marriage is always viewed as the primary relationship and sex outside this relationship is thought only to strengthen it (deVisser & McDonald, 2007). In fact, swingers report happier marriages and a higher life satisfaction than non-swingers (Bergstrand & Williams, 2000). Research has found that jealousy increased sexual excitement and arousal in swinging couples, particularly in men (deVisser & McDonald, 2007). However, for some couples, jealousy can be detrimental to the relationship (Bergstrand & Williams, 2000).

Review Questions

1 Explain current trends in marriage.

2 Define "mixed marriage" and explain how it has changed over the years.

3 Explain what we know about marital happiness as it pertains to gender.

4 Explore the importance of sex in marriage.

5 What do we know about sex outside of marriage? Explain extramarital affairs, polyamory, and non-exclusive marriages.

Same-Sex Relationships

In some ways, gay and lesbian relationships have changed more than heterosexual ones over the last few decades. First, these relationships came "out of the closet" in 1970s, when the gay liberation movement led to the blossoming and acceptance of GLB people. Then, with the advent of HIV/AIDS in the 1980s, gay men began to have fewer sex partners and more long-term monogamous relationships. Today, with full equality across Canada, GLB people are able to live openly, enjoy full protection under the law, and suffer far less from the effects of stigma.

According to Statistics Canada (2014), there were 64 575 same-sex couples in Canada in 2011. This was up 42.4 percent from 2006 and continues to rise. Most were either living together on in common-law unions, with only 15.5 percent of

them married since July 2005. Same-sex couples made up less than 1 percent of all couples in Canada, as they did in Australia and the United Kingdom. This cannot be held as representative, however, since many GLB people are still reluctant to declare themselves. Same-sex couples were slightly more likely to be male (54.5 percent) than female (45.5 percent). Married couples were more likely to be younger 25.3 percent of them were between the ages of 15 and 34, compared to only 17.5 percent of mixed-sex couples. In contrast, only 6.2 percent were age 65 and over, compared to 17.8 percent of mixed-sex couples. Female same-sex couples were five times more likely to have children at home than were male same-sex couples. Finally, same-sex couples were more likely to be urban, with 45.6 percent living in or around Montreal, Toronto, and Vancouver, compared to only 33.4 percent of mixed-sex couples.

Differences between Same-Sex and Other-Sex Relationships

For many years, researchers suggested that same-sex relationships were less stable in adulthood because of negative early life experiences and the challenges of accepting one's sexual orientation (Savin-Williams, 2001). Others claimed that societal pressures on same-sex couples, such as the struggle to manage a gay or lesbian identity in a heterosexist culture, lead to weaker intimate relationships (Pachankis & Goldfried, 2004). Although it may be true that same-sex couples face more relationship challenges, these claims have not been supported by research (Herek, 2006; Roisman et al., 2008). The majority of gay men and lesbian women were found to be secure in both their sexual orientation and childhood experiences and they were able to connect fully in intimate relationships (Roisman et al., 2008). Partnered gay and lesbian men and women reported more happiness than those who are single (Wienke & Hill, 2008).

Same-sex couples are more likely to not follow gender role behaviour. They equally share household responsibilities and communicate more effectively than other-sex couples (Balsam et al., 2008; Boon & Alderson, 2009; Cohen et al., 2008; R.J. Green, 2008; Mock & Cornelius, 2007; Soloman et al., 2005; Wienke & Hill, 2009). They also have higher levels of relationship satisfaction; share more affection, humour, and joy in their relationships; have less conflict; and have less fear and negative feelings about their relationships (Gottman et al., 2003; Herek, 2006; Pachankis & Gold-fried, 2004; Roisman et al., 2008). Like heterosexual relationships, partners in gay and lesbian relationships with more resources or power have been found to perform fewer household chores (Sutphin, 2010). Many, however, report that they have more challenges dealing with societal discrimination and negative attitudes toward homosexuality.

Overall, same-sex couples may be more satisfied with their intimate relationships because they are forced to work harder at them (R.J. Green et al., 1996). They may not have as much family or societal support as heterosexual couples, which tends to put more focus on their intimate relationships. Lesbian relationships are often emotionally closer than gay male couples, who, in turn, have often been found to be emotionally closer than heterosexual married couples (R.J. Green, 2008; Mock & Cornelius, 2007). Lesbians have also been found to have more intimate communication in their relationships (Henderson et al., 2009).

Another interesting area of research has explored "benchmarks," or events that mark important dates in a relationship such as a first date, engagement, or wedding. Before the recognition of marriage, many same-sex couples lacked a unified definition for defining the beginning of their relationship. They may celebrate first meeting, first date, or first sex (Degges-White & Marszalek, 2008). In countries without same-sex marriage, commitment ceremonies, civil unions, and domestic partnerships have become important celebrations for many same-sex couples because they help establish a couple's relationship (R.J. Green & Mitchell, 2002).

civil union
A legal union of a same-sex couple, sanctioned by a civil authority.

Without the availability of formal relationship status, many same-sex couples experience boundary and commitment ambiguity (R.J. Green & Mitchell, 2002). Because there have been few role models, many same-sex couples do not know what their relationships should look like and must work together to form relationships that work for them. Although this gives them increased flexibility in defining roles, it also may present additional challenges to their relationships (Degges-White & Marszalek, 2008).

Sexuality in Same-Sex Relationships

Heterosexual couples have two people who are morphologically different and, thus, there is no ambiguity as to who does what to whom when having intercourse. As Peter Fisher pointed out in his classic book *The Gay Mystique* (1975), however, what two men or two women do is often a mystery to outsiders. In terms of penetrative acts such anal intercourse, vaginal intercourse with a strap-on dildo for lesbians, and oral sex, these are matters of preference. Three terms used among gays and lesbians are *top*, *bottom*, and *versatile*. Tops prefer the insertive role, bottoms the receptive role, and versatile ("vers") people either one.

Like heterosexual couples, gay men and lesbians report many positive aspects of sex in their relationships. Some of them are emotional and physical intimacy, feeling accepted and supported, increased communication, and a positive view of self (Cohen et al., 2008). Yet, to gain these benefits, they report that it is necessary to be vulnerable and take risks. The stigma of social and cultural attitudes about same-sex relationships in many countries can interfere with healthy sexual functioning (Cohen et al., 2008).

Gay men have sex more often than both lesbian and heterosexual couples (Kurdek, 2006). Lower rates of sexual behaviour in lesbian couples have been explained in several ways. It could be that the biological nature of the sex drive is lower in women, that females typically do not initiate sexual activity and may not be comfortable doing so, or that women are less likely than men to express their feelings through sex. Lesbians do consistently report that they have sex less often. However, according to one Canadian-American study, the time duration of their sexual activity lasts significantly longer. Thus, they have sex less, but have it longer at the same time (Blair & Pukall, 2014). Less, therefore, seems to be more.

As seen in the same-sex unions timeline in the Appendix, many countries have opted for same-sex **civil unions** instead of marriage, and these unions still carry all or most of the rights accorded to married couples.

Same-Sex Marriage in Canada

In 1967, Justice Minister Pierre Elliott Trudeau told the press that "there is no place for the state in the bedrooms of the nation." His sentiments and efforts were made into law when, two years later, homosexuality was removed from Criminal Code of Canada. Nearly four decades later, on February 1, 2005, the Civil Marriage Act (Bill C-38) was introduced in Parliament. It passed in the House of Commons and the Senate months later and became federal law when it received royal assent on July 20, 2005. The language of Bill C-38 is as follows:

This enactment extends the legal capacity for marriage for civil purposes to same-sex couples in order to reflect values of tolerance, respect and equality, consistent with the Canadian Charter of Rights and Freedoms. It also makes consequential amendments to other Acts to ensure equal access for same-sex couples to the civil effects of marriage and divorce.

Same-sex marriage had already become legal in eight out of ten provinces beginning with Ontario in 2003 but, as a nation, Canada became the third country in the world to legally recognize it after the Netherlands and Belgium. Full conjugal rights are accorded to any two people, regardless of sex, who marry. These rights include filing income tax returns as a couple (and not two single people as had been the case), the right to visit and make decisions for a partner in the hospital, the right to sponsor one's partner in immigration, survivor benefits, child custody rights, inheritance rights, and numerous other rights that were historically not available for same-sex couples. One argument against same-sex marriage was that gay and lesbian couples could have most or all of those rights in civil unions instead. The response was that by according marriage only to other-sex couples and civil unions to same-sex couples, one marginalizes the relationships of the latter. Instead Canada opted for full equality.

The official terms for married partners are "husband" and "wife." A man may thus refer to his husband and a woman may thus refer to her wife. However, given that there are several relationship options for any two people—boyfriend/girlfriend or boyfriends and girlfriends, living together, common-law marriages, and full marriages, many people regardless of relationship type or the sex of whom they are with now use the generic term "partner" instead. Heterosexual couples who do use this term typically believe that this creates equality for all types of relationships.

Now that same-sex marriage has been around for a decade, most Canadians fully support it. In a 2012 telephone survey of 2694 randomly selected Canadians, 55.4 percent approved of same-sex marriage, while the remainder disapproved or had no opinion. Those who disapproved tended to be male, older, in lower income brackets, Albertan, and Conservative Party supporters (Forum Research, 2012).

Same-Sex Marriage in the United States

The United States is not only a more religious country than Canada, but religious groups and entrepreneurs (e.g., Jerry, Falwell, Pat Robertson) have powerful lobby forums that

Same-sex marriages often have the same rituals as other-sex marriages, but with adjustments for gender such as "husband and husband" or "wife and wife" instead of "husband and wife."

influence political decision making. In 1996, the U.S. Congress enacted the Defense of Marriage Act, which prohibited federal recognition of civil unions, domestic partnerships, and same-sex marriages. Even though individual American states may have such options, the federal government will not recognize them. In addition, based on this act, each state can recognize or deny any relationship between same-sex couples and define marriage as a "legal union of one man and one woman as husband and wife." The Defense of Marriage Act also removed any federal spousal rights of civil unions, domestic partnerships, and same-sex marriages (Mason et al., 2001). Today there seems to be an increasing path to same-sex marriage. In 2010, President Barack Obama mandated that United States hospitals extend visitation rights to partners of gay and lesbians and also respect patients' choices about health care decisions (Shear, 2010). The Defense of Marriage Act was struck down in 2013.

In June 2015, the U.S. Supreme Court voted in a five-to-four decision to allow same-sex marriage in all 50 states, leading the United States to join the many other countries in Europe and elsewhere in recognizing marriages between two men and two women.

Review Questions

1 Explain why same-sex relationships may experience less power imbalance and greater equality and satisfaction than heterosexual relationships.

2 Explain the benefits of equal marriage in terms of civil rights and human rights.

Arranged Marriages in Canada

For mainstream Canadians the idea of arranged marriages might sound strange. Canada has long been a society where individuals search for their own life partners, as has been well portrayed in literature, television, and film. Once they find someone, they base their decision to marry upon love more than anything else and it is simply taken for granted that a newly wedded couple are deeply in love. Yet the romantic love that people feel while courting does not last forever and, when there is nothing to replace it such as mutual interests or goals, couples often divorce.

Arranged marriages are based on the premise that parents or older family members, who have lived longer and are thus wiser and more knowledgeable, select partners for their children based on compatibility. While there may be strong encouragement to marry a particular man or women, and even forced marriages, the children are typically free to refuse. A marriage is arranged ideally on the basis of compatibility in terms of socioeconomic level, caste, education, family connections, personality, reputation, job stability, and other factors, with the idea that love comes later because of similarity (Batabyal, 2001; Xiaohe & Whyte, 1990). For a woman, she is assured a husband who can provide for her and her children and who is compatible in all of the important ways.

Arranged marriages are common in India, Pakistan, Bangladesh, and Sri Lanka.

Sometimes a matchmaker might be consulted in finding a husband of wife for one's children, and this may extend across borders (Hung, 2006). An Indo-Canadian man might be told that there is a good match for him in India and the two might begin corresponding. Once an arrangement has been reached, the family will sponsor the woman to come to Canada and she will then marry the man. This practice serves to create many **transnational families,** where blood relations and constant communication takes place over two countries and sometimes more (Tse & Waters, 2013).

Such marriages were typical worldwide until the 18th century when individuals in growing industrialized nations became increasingly autonomous and love and romance became the prime motivator. They continue to be typical in North America among particular communities, such as the Orthodox Jews of Montreal and newly immigrated South Asians. In nations such as India, Pakistan, Nepal, and Bangladesh, arranged marriages are common (Moore, 1994).

Newly immigrated Canadians tend to bring the values, customs, and outlooks of their countries of origin and adhere to them. The second generation has typically grown up in families and communities with these values, and yet become acculturated to Canadian customs as well. As a result, they are often torn between the pressure of arranged marriages on one side and the freedom and expectation to choose their own life partner on the other. While there is pressure for new immigrants in Canada to conform, adhering to the arranged marriage system is tied closely to ethnic identity and loyalty to family and community (Samuel, 2010; Zaidi & Shuraydi, 2002). As a result, rejection of parents' choice is not a simple matter. Furthermore, as Jaspal (2014) points out, this is particularly difficult for gay men and lesbians, who are typically reluctant to reveal their sexual orientations to their parents. Many likely marry the women or men chosen for them simply to please their parents.

Arranged marriages are common in Canada and often involve one partner who is transnational.

transnational families
Families that have ties in two or more countries.

Forced Marriages

Forced marriage occurs when one or both parties are forced into a marriage against their will by threat of physical violence or psychological coercion. This differs from mere insistence or disappointment by parents, as may be the case in arranged marriages where there is no choice. It may also involve minors. Such a practice is against Canada's Charter of Rights and Freedoms, as well as the Universal Declaration of Human Rights adopted by the United Nations in 1948. Because this practice is not legal, there is an unknown number of cases in Canada.

According to an analysis by Quebec sociologist Naïma Bendriss (2008), there are several reasons why forced marriages may occur. First, families might feel that they need to protect their daughters. If they marry them off to a trusted family friend, they believe they will ensure them a good future and an assurance of honour. They also feel that they will contain their sexuality by giving them an outlet and preventing the dishonour of possible premarital sex. Second, parents may be fearful of their daughters marrying outsiders, especially those outside of their religion or culture, which would be defined by their community as dishonourable. A forced marriage is thus believed necessary to maintain family honour. Third, forcing marriages might be seen as preventing a family from exile. If a son or daughter marries someone from the home country, then ties with the communities of that country are maintained. Finally, and as has often been the case in Western society in the form of "shotgun weddings," a forced marriage might be because of an out-of-wedlock pregnancy.

Review Questions

1 What are the advantages and disadvantages of arranged marriages?

2 How might the custom of arranged marriages be particularly stressful for gays and lesbians?

3 What are some of the reasons that young people might be forced into marriages?

Polygamous Marriages in Canada

Polygamy is a marriage form where one of more people is married to two or more people of the other sex. It differs from monogamy where one person is married to only one other person. Other than the odd exception, the only form found in Canada is where one man has multiple wives. We now look at polygamous marriages, their forms, their history, and their qualities.

Types of Polygamy

There are four types of polygamy: polygyny, bigamy, polyandry, and polygynandry. The most common type is **polygyny,** where one man is married to two or more women. There are pockets of polygynist communities in Canada, the largest of which is in British Columbia. Polygyny is held up as the ideal form of marriage in many cultures (Murdock, 1967; Trevithick, 1997). In any culture, however, such marriages are always in the minority compared to monogamous ones for an obvious reason. Because any culture is likely to have a more or less equal number of males and females, only some men are able to have multiple wives. Roughly speaking, for every man with two wives, another man is likely to have none. A common form of polygyny is **sororal polygyny,** where one man is married to a group of sisters. This is thought to be ideal in that the wives know each other and are thus more likely to get along.

Furthermore, polygyny has been supported as a logical solution within a hunting or agrarian society with a high male death rate due to war. Polygyny tends to produce large families and, thus, more hands for labour, which are essential to survival. Within Islam, the Qur'an describes it as a way for widows and orphans of men who were killed in battle to be protected within the families of other men (Bala, 2009).

One form of polygamy is called *bigamy*, where one person is married to two others—usually, a man with two wives and often without one wife knowing about the other. It differs from polygyny in that one is unlawful cohabitation with two or more wives while the other, bigamy, is the crime of having two marriage licences. In contrast, polygynists usually have one marriage licence and then other "wives."

The second form of polygamy is uncommon in the world. **Polyandry** is where one woman has multiple husbands and, if fraternal polyandry, the husbands are brothers. Although it was said to occur in only four societies in the Himalayas of Asia, Starkweather and Hames (2012) found that it had occurred in 63 others throughout the world, including the Inuit, Blackfoot, and several other Aboriginal groups in Canada. The main reason for polyandry given by anthropologists is that if a set of brothers were to marry one woman, the land they stand to inherit would remain intact, while if each had a wife, it would be divided among them and too small to sustain their families. Among the Inuit, male absenteeism together with fear of wife abduction was the main reason according to Balikci (1963). If one husband were away on a hunting trip, another could stay home and protect the wife.

The third type, which is even more rare, is called **polygynandry,** where two or more men are married to two or more women. In 1846, an American clergyman named John Humphrey Noyes began the Oneida community in New York State consisting of 87 men and woman, where all men were married to all women (Klephart, 1976). By 1878, this number grew to 306. Members practised sexual countenance, where the man would not attempt

polygyny
A marriage form where one man is married to two or more women.

sororal polygyny
A marriage form where one man is married to a group of sisters.

polyandry
A marriage form where one woman is married to two or more men.

polygynandry
A marriage form where two or more men are married to two or more women.

to ejaculate into the woman, which seemed to work well since there were only 12 unplanned pregnancies (Van Wormer, 2006).

Closely related to polygynandry is the fourth type of polygamy—**polyfidelity**, where a group of people who may be gay, bisexual, or heterosexual agree to have sex only with other members of that group. Such an arrangement became increasingly popular in the 1980s (with the threat of HIV/AIDS) as a measure of safety in that if each member were tested for STIs prior to membership and each remains faithful, then sex can be enjoyed without worry. Such arrangements, however, were more temporary than the permanent arrangements of polygynandry.

Polygamy in Canada

Originally, the main polygamists in North America were the early Mormons of the United States who practised "plural marriage" from the 1840s to the 1890s when, after pressure from the American government, they put an official end to it. Most Mormons adjusted to monogamy, some continued polygyny and went into hiding, and others fled to Canada. Among those who did were polygynists Charles Ora Card who established Cardston, Alberta, and Thomas Rowel Leavitt, who established Leavitt, Alberta, nearby. The Canadian government similarly disallowed the practice and the Mormon polygynists fled once again. Most recently, some have settled in the town of Bountiful next to Creston, British Columbia. There are now approximately 1000 residents belonging to the Fundamentalist Church of Jesus Christ of Latter Day Saints (FLDS), most of whom are descended from a half dozen men. This group as well as some Canadian Muslims practise polygamy either in secret or in defiance of the law.

Polygamous marriages are illegal in Canada and have been so since 1892, with the arrival of the first polygamous Mormons. According to Section 293 of the Criminal Code, "Every one who practises or enters into or in any manner agrees or consents to

Monogamous couple and children.

practise or enter into … any form of polygamy, or … any kind of conjugal union with more than one person at the same time, … is guilty of an indictable offence and liable to imprisonment for a term not exceeding five years." The controversy lies not with having sex with more than one woman but in the living arrangements, which not only promote the inequality of women, but may be detrimental to child welfare. One practice in Bountiful is to expel many teenage boys and young men to ensure that a chosen few will have multiple wives (Armstrong, 2005). They are put out into the world with little education and skills and have difficulty surviving. Girls are prepared to be wives and submissive to their husbands. Girls who are sometimes underage are forced to marry men (Bala, 2009). Although the polygamy laws have been challenged on the basis of freedom of religion, the Supreme Court has upheld the law and it remains illegal.

Review Questions

1 What are the different types of polygamy and how do they differ?

2 Why is it not possible for all men to have multiple wives?

3 What are some of the arguments for and against polygamy in Canada?

Consanguineous Marriages

Consanguineous marriages are those between blood relatives, most commonly between cousins who would share 6.25 percent of the genes of a common ancestor. While there may be no consequences, the doubling up of any congenital defects increases

the chances that they will be passed down to children. In this section, we explore this phenomenon internationally, nationally, culturally, and historically.

International Incidence

Among prehistoric unions, it is likely that a great deal of reproductive activity took place between close relatives, for they existed in bands of 20 or 30 and often did not come across other humans in their short life spans. There is further no reason to believe that they had any concept of biological relatedness at all (Bittles & Black, 2010a).

polyfidelity
An arrangement by a group of gay, bisexual, or heterosexual people where	each member agrees to have sex only with members within the group.

Changing Inuit Marriages

The Inuit have occupied northern Canada for thousands of years. As of 2011, there were 50 115 Inuit, most of whom reside in the three northern territories (Aboriginal Affairs and Northern Development Canada, 2013). Historically, a girl would marry at around 14 years of age and marriages were typically arranged by parents. They sometimes arranged marriages for their children before they were born. To survive in a harsh environment, marriage was a partnership where husband and wife did their duties. The man hunted and made shelter and the woman made clothing, prepared food and water, and raised the children.

The Inuit had no real contact with Europeans or Canadians until World War II and the Cold War, which made the

Arctic strategically important. Many Inuit were converted to Christianity by missionaries, and marriages now more closely resemble those in the rest of Canada. Parents may attempt to suggest husbands or wives for their children but their advice can be disregarded. Sexual activity may also take place before marriage and it is not considered wrong by the majority. Marriages take place in local churches and a couple either moves into a house of their own or stays with one of their parents until a house becomes available (Pauktuutit Inuit Women of Canada, 2006).

Today, it is estimated that a billion people live in communities where consanguineous marriages are respected, most of whom are in West Asia, the Middle East, and North Africa. In these areas, marriages within families account for 20 percent to 50 percent of all marriages (Bittles & Black, 2010b). They may also be favoured in community pockets in Canada, the United States, Europe, and Australia, where the newly immigrated bring the customs of their cultures with them (Hamamy, 2011).

The reasons given for consanguineous marriages are social and economic rather than religious. If one were to marry within the family, there is an increased chance of amicable relations in that one's spouse is a family member who has been known for a long time. They would thus be more likely to get along. Such amicable relations would likely increase the power of women in that their in-laws are also family members with whom they have had a life-long relationship (Hamamy, 2011). Furthermore, family structure and property are maintained.

People considering consanguineous unions are generally aware that they increase the chances of congenital defects in their children and often seek medical counselling before they marry. In contrast, however, it is simultaneously considered a healthy thing to do in that if marriages occur among known individuals, they weed out unknown health factors.

The world's major religions have differing proscriptions against consanguineous marriages, ranging from forbiddance, to tolerance, to encouragement. The Roman Catholic Church will permit marriages between first cousins but only with permission on a case-by-case basis, while Protestant denominations permit them entirely. Aryan Hindus of northern India forbid all consanguineous unions going back five to seven generations, while the

Dravidian Hindus in the south encourage them. Muslim and Jewish proscriptions are similar, although uncle-niece marriages are permitted within Judaism. Finally, Buddhism permits marriage between first cousins, while Sikhs forbid them.

Aboriginal Kinship Systems

Today it is known that consanguineous marriages increase the chance of undesirable traits in children, but this was not always known and, among Aboriginal peoples, marriages depended upon kinship systems. Early American anthropologist Lewis Henry Morgan identified six main types and described them in 1871: Iroquois, Crow, Omaha, Eskimo, Hawaiian, and Sudanese. Under the Iroquois, Crow, and Omaha systems, cross cousins (offspring of parents' other-sex siblings) might be favoured for marriage, while parallel cousins (offspring of parents' same-sex siblings) would not. While the biological sharing of genes would be equal for both, they were defined as different under these systems.

Consanguineous Marriage in Canada

First-cousin marriages have never been unheard of in the Western hemisphere. Among those who did marry their cousins were Albert Einstein, Charles Darwin, Igor Stravinsky, Edgar Allen Poe, H.G., Wells, and Canada's first prime minister John A. Macdonald, who married his first cousin Isabella Clark. Furthermore, the Canadian Criminal Code does not prohibit first-cousin marriages, although they are discouraged because of genetics issues and are stigmatized as incest. Forbidden marriages are

Canada's first prime minister, Sir John A. Macdonald, married his first cousin, Isabella Clark.

under section 155 of the Criminal Code and include people "who, knowing that another person is by blood relationship his or her parent, child, brother, sister, grandparent or grandchild, as the case may be, has sexual intercourse with that person."

Parenthood—Same-Sex and Other-Sex Couples

Although we discuss pregnancy and childbirth in Chapter 5, here we'll examine the impact of parenting on adult relationships. We know that in heterosexual relationships, children can be conceived or born at any time regardless of whether a couple is hooking up, dating, living together, or married. Some couples decide to have children without a formal commitment, some get married and have children, and others get married because the woman is pregnant. Although pregnancies can be unplanned, ambivalence and uncertainty are common in couples making decisions about parenthood (Pinquart et al., 2008).

Same-sex couples also decide to become parents and do so in a variety of ways, including surrogacy, adoption, foster care, and private arrangements with friends or families. One or both partners may also already have children. Like heterosexual couples, same-sex couples may decide to have children while dating, living together, or married. In any case, the decision to have children is one that most people face at one time or another, and the timing of parenthood can affect a couple's relationship quality. Although some gay and lesbian couples expect to raise their own children, others adopt or become foster parents.

REAL Research Many new parents, regardless of sexual orientation, experience declines in their relationship quality after the first year of parenthood, with women reporting larger declines in love for their partners (Goldberg et al., 2010).

Parenting and Relationship Satisfaction

Longitudinal research has found the quality of intimate relationships declines for many couples once they become parents (Campos et al., 2009; Claxton & Perry-Jenkins, 2008; Goldberg et al., 2010). Parents often experience decreases in time for leisure or to be with each other and thus report lower relationship satisfaction than couples without children. Relationship satisfaction continues to decline as the number of children increases. It is higher before the children come, declines steadily until it hits a low when the children are in their teens, and then begins to increase once they leave the house (Papalia et al., 2002). Often this is because of disagreements about child-care.

REAL Research A sample of 57 Chinese-Canadian parents and 59 mainland Chinese parents were surveyed on parenting styles. The Chinese-Canadian parents tended to be firm with their children, while the Chinese parents were more likely to be strict and authoritarian (Chuang & Yanjie, 2009).

Many gay and lesbian parents also have to contend with societal attitudes about same-sex parenting. Couples who live in areas where there is little acceptance of gay families have higher levels of depression and negativity after becoming parents (Goldberg et al., 2010). Living in a gay-friendly area can make the transition to parenthood easier. After the legalization

Having children decreases a couple's quality time together and this can lower relationship satisfaction.

of same-sex marriage in July 2005, the number of people declaring themselves as gay or lesbian couples increased by 42 percent. Those who were raising children made up 9.4 percent of all same-sex couples, 89 percent of which were female and 20 percent of which were male (The Vanier Institute of the Family, 2013).

While there is ample evidence that children of same-sex couples are as well adjusted as others (see Chapter 10), many report discrimination and hostility toward them in schools because their parents are of the same sex. According to a comprehensive survey of homophobic discrimination in Canadian schools (Taylor et al., 2011), 37 percent reported verbal harassment and 27 percent reported physical harassment. Furthermore, about a fifth said that their teachers either "sometimes" or "frequently" made homophobic comments. Such discrimination not only affects the well-being of children but their families as well.

Review Questions

1 Identify one way in which having children affects adult relationships.

2 What types of discrimination do children of same-sex couples face?

3 Give two examples of how an intimate relationship might decline when a couple has children.

Divorce

There have been substantial changes in the institution of marriage since the 1960s. During most of history, a married couple was viewed as a single legal entity (M.A. Mason et al., 2001). Today, marriage is viewed more as a partnership. This shift in perception brought with it a shift in how marriage was dissolved. The liberalization of divorce laws made it easier to obtain a divorce and made it a less expensive process.

Since the Divorce Act of 1968, there has been **no-fault divorce,** which means neither partner needs to be found guilty of a transgression such as adultery to dissolve the marriage. Before this act, it was necessary for one partner to produce evidence of the other's wrongdoing for divorce to be granted. The Divorce Act has led to increased rates.

One might think that making divorce easier through a no-fault clause would lead couples to give up on otherwise salvageable marriages. It is more likely, however, that those already unhappy marriages became easier to dissolve. The sentiment of the Divorce Act was that while Canada as a nation has an interest in the stability of marriage, it cannot achieve that stability by forcing unhappy marriages to remain intact.

Statistics and Current Trends

In 2008, 70 226 couples were divorced, amounting to a rate of 21.1 per 10 000 population, and the rates have been stable since the 1990s. The highest rates occurred in the Yukon and Alberta and the lowest in Nunavut, the Northwest Territories, and Quebec.

On Your Mind

What is an annulment?

An annulment is both a legal and a religious term meaning that a marriage is voided—that is, it is said to have never taken place at all. It is quite rare in Canada because of its requirements and, thus, divorce is the most common way to end a marriage. If a marriage is a contract, then the contract may be voided if there was misrepresentation, force, or diminished mental capacity. For example, if one marries a person who is already married to someone else, that marriage is annulled. Other reasons might be that one of the parties was underage at the time, one party was unable to consummate the marriage due to impotence, or one party did not have the mental capacity to enter into a marriage due to drunkenness or mental disability (Canadian Divorce News, 2013).

The Catholic Church considers marriage as a union of a man and women in the eyes of God—in its language, they become one flesh. Once vows are declared, there must be sufficient reason to retract them. Those reasons are similar to secular annulments, but there are additional ones such as the marriage not being performed by a legitimate clergyman.

Under Sharia law, or Islamic religious law, a husband may divorce his wife easily. For a wife, however, it is far more difficult and annulment is one available option. With proper witnesses and documentation, she may be granted an annulment if her husband was not a Muslim before the marriage, if he abandoned Islam after the marriage, or, again, if the husband is physically unable to consummate the marriage (Esposito, 2002).

no-fault divorce
A divorce law that allows for the dissolution of a marriage without placing blame on either of the partners.

Adult Sexual Relationships

There is some evidence that suggests that unhappiness in many marriages begins in the seventh year (Dalton, 2000). This is known as the "seven-year itch."

Interestingly, the "seven-year itch" originally referred to an infection with scabies, an untreatable skin condition at the time that took seven years to go away. The phrase

was first used in reference to marriage in a play of the same name by George Axelrod in 1953, which was made into a movie starring Marilyn Monroe in 1955.

The increasing rates after the Divorce Act of 1968 have had less to do with unhappiness in marriage as with changes in laws. The Divorce Act allowed a couple to be divorced through "no fault" after three years of separation. In 1986, an amendment reduced this time to one year, and the divorce rate rose to 36.4 couples per 10 000 population. The mean ages of divorce in 2008 were 41.9 years for women and 44.5 years for men (Milan, 2011).

About a fifth of the divorces in 2008 were from marriages that lasted five years or less, another fifth from those five to nine years, and two fifths from those from 10 to 25 years. The average duration of all marriages that ended in divorce was 13.1 years. The reason given for almost all divorces as provided by law was separation for more than one year (93.5 percent). The remainder gave reasons of adultery, mental cruelty, and physical cruelty (Milan, 2011). Although mental or physical cruelty was cited in only 2.8 percent of cases, this is no indication of the rates of these behaviours, since they may have occurred among couples citing separation for more than a year as well.

In the United States, divorce rates increased sharply between 1970 and 1975 because of the liberalization of divorce laws (Kreider, 2005). Rates stabilized after this and began to decrease. By 2005, they were at the lowest level since 1970 (Stevenson & Wolfers, 2007). It is estimated that roughly 20 percent of adults have divorced and the United States Census Bureau reported that 50 percent of marriages end in divorce (Kreider, 2005; U.S. Census Bureau, 2007). However, research has found that marital stability has increased each decade. While 23 percent of couples in the 1970s split within 10 years, only 16 percent did so in the 1990s (Parker-Pope, 2010). In 2008, the median duration of a marriage in the United States was 18 years (Cohn, 2009).

Reasons for Divorce

What causes a couple to end their marriage? The question is complicated because not all unstable or unhappy marriages end in divorce. Couples stay together for a variety of reasons, such as for the sake of the children, because of lack of initiative, because of religious prohibitions against divorce, or for financial reasons. Similarly, couples with seemingly happy marriages separate and divorce, sometimes to the surprise of one of the partners, who did not even know that the other was unhappy.

A mutually shared decision to divorce is actually uncommon. Usually, one partner wants to terminate a relationship more than

the other, who is still strongly attached to the marriage and is more distraught at its termination. In fact, the declaration that a partner wants a divorce often comes as a shock to his or her spouse. When one partner is the initiator, it is usually the woman. One study found that women initiated two thirds of all divorces (Brinig & Allen, 2000). The partner who initiated the divorce has often completed the mourning of the relationship by the time the divorce is complete, unlike the partner whose mourning begins once the divorce is finalized.

Divorce rates are influenced by changes in legal, political, religious, and familial patterns. For example, as we mentioned earlier, no-fault divorce laws have made it easier for couples to dissolve a marriage. The growth of low-cost legal clinics and the overabundance of lawyers have made divorce cheaper and thus more accessible. In addition, the more equitable distribution of marital assets has made some people less apprehensive about losing everything to their spouses. Changing social issues, such as more women entering the workforce and earning advanced degrees, have also had an impact on divorce rates. Research has found that divorce is more common in couples in which the woman has a professional degree (Wilson, 2008).

Certain situations may predispose a couple to divorce. People who have been divorced before or whose parents have divorced have more accepting attitudes toward divorce than those who grew up in stable families (Amato & Hohmann-Marriott, 2007; Eldar-Avidan et al., 2009; Sassler et al., 2009; Wolfinger, 2000). Similarly, people who have divorced parents are more likely to report marital problems in their own relationships and tend to be more skeptical about marriage, feeling insecure about its permanence (Gähler et al., 2009; Jacquet & Surra, 2001; Weigel, 2007; Wolfinger, 2000).

Other factors that may contribute to divorce are marrying at a young age (S.P. Morgan & Rindfuss, 1985), marrying because of an unplanned pregnancy (G. Becker et al., 1977), alcohol or drug abuse (R.L. Collins et al., 2007), and having children quickly after getting married (S.P. Morgan & Rindfuss, 1985). The interval between marriage and the arrival of children is an important factor. Waiting longer promotes stability by giving couples time to get accustomed to being married beforehand and may also allow them to become more financially secure (S.P. Morgan & Rindfuss, 1985). Religion is also important. Catholics and Jews are less likely to divorce than Protestants, and divorce rates tend to be higher for marriages of mixed religions. Furthermore, the more religious people are, the more conservative the views they have toward divorce (Stokes & Ellison, 2010).

Finally, some people make poor assessments of their partners or believe that the little annoyances or character traits that they dislike in their potential spouses will disappear or change after marriage (Neff & Karney, 2005).

Adjusting to Divorce

How a person adjusts to a divorce depends on several factors, including who initiated the divorce, attitudes toward divorce, income levels, and the onset of an extramarital relationship (Wang & Amato, 2000). Social connectedness is also an important factor (Moller et al., 2003) in that having a support system helps a great deal. Although most divorces are emotionally painful for both partners, 80 percent of the women and 50 percent of the men said that their divorce was the right decision after a ten-year follow up (Faludi, 1991).

Depression and sadness can surface when divorced men and women find that they have less in common with married friends. Couples tend to make friends with other couples and, once people are single again, they are often dropped because friends may see them as threatening. Older individuals experience more psychological problems because there are fewer options for forming new relationships (H. Wang & Amato, 2000). Older divorced women are especially more likely to feel anger and loneliness than younger divorced women.

Another area that is affected after divorce is finances. Financial adjustment is often harder for women because their standard of living declines more than a man's (H. Wang & Amato, 2000). They typically end up with the children and alimony payments do not offset the costs. Children also restrict their freedom and they go out less often. Men's incomes increase by around one third, while women's falls more than a fifth (Jenkins, 2009). Many women who previously lived a middle-class life find themselves slipping below the poverty line after divorce.

Dating after a divorce can be difficult for some people. They may have been married for many years and find that dating has changed since they were younger. It is not uncommon for newly single people to feel frustrated or confused about how to go about dating.

The majority of divorced people remarry, and some remarry, divorce, and remarry again. Overall, 13 percent to 14 percent of people marry twice, 3 percent marry three or more times, and less than 1 percent marry four or more times (Kreider, 2005). Men remarry at higher rates (M. Coleman et al., 2000), and couples in second marriages report higher relationship satisfaction than do couples in first marriages (McCarthy & Ginsberg, 2007).

Review Questions

1 Explain the advantages of a no-fault divorce.

2 Identify some of the factors that might predispose a couple to divorce.

3 Explain how both men and women adjust to divorce.

Chapter Review

Summary Points

1 Intimate relationships are a fundamental part of human development. Overall, married men and women feel positive about their intimate relationships. Although same-sex couples face more relationship challenges than heterosexual couples, the majority of couples are secure and happy in their relationships.

2 Among young people, there have been some changes in dating practices. For one thing, they are more likely to get together in groups within which two people might pair off. This is enabled by the ability for men and women to be friends, which was uncommon before the 1960s. At that time, formal dating was the main way of gaining access to other-sex company.

3 In traditional dating, a boy would pick up a girl at her house, giving her father and mother time to meet with him and then they would go to a pre-arranged event. The most difficult part of dating is the initial invitation. Hooking up, or having a friend with benefits, has become more open. In one study, people either felt positive about the experience or they were neutral.

4 In recent years, living together outside of marriage or common-law unions have increased. Some advantages of cohabitation are that it allows couples to learn more about each other, share finances, and mature in their relationship. Cohabitating couples tend to either marry or separate after just a few years. About 50 percent of all couples who live together break up within a year or less and those who marry are at increased risk for divorce. Longer cohabitation has been found to be associated with higher likelihood of divorce.

5 The mean age for first marriage in 2013 was 29.1 for women and 31.1 for men. Marital satisfaction has been found to be related to the quality of a friendship, frequency of pleasurable activities, being able to talk to each other and offer self-disclosure, physical and emotional intimacy, and personality similarities.

6 Marital quality tends to peak in the first few years of a marriage, declines when children are in their teens, and then rises again. The majority of married couples report that their marriages are happy and satisfying. People who are married tend to be happier, healthier, and have longer lives than either widowed or divorced persons of the same age. Marriage has also been found to reduce the impact of several potentially traumatic events, including job loss, retirement, and illness. Overall, marriage provides more health benefits to men than women.

7 The higher the frequency of sexual activity in marriage, the greater the sexual satisfaction. During the early years, sex is more frequent and generally satisfying. During the next 15 or so years, other aspects of life take precedence over sex, and the couple may experience difficulty in maintaining sexual interest in each other. In the later years, men often report more satisfaction with marriage than do women.

8 Almost all couples, whether dating, living together, or married, expect sexual exclusivity. Those who cheat have stronger sexual interests, more permissive sexual values, less satisfaction in their intimate relationship, and more opportunities for sex outside the relationship. Studies of same-sex couples have found that gay men are more likely to cheat than lesbian women.

9 Women experience more emotional distress about infidelity than men. A woman is also more likely to be upset about emotional infidelity and a man is more likely to be upset about his partner's sexual infidelity. Some couples engage in co-marital sex such as swinging.

10 Compared to heterosexual couples, gay and lesbian couples have higher levels of relationship satisfaction, share more affection, humour, and joy; and have less fear and negative feelings about their relationships. These relationships are often more equal as well.

11 Arranged marriages have been common throughout history and still occur in many parts of the world. Typically, parents find spouses for their children based upon key factors of compatibility. Arranged marriages also occur among newly immigrated Canadians. Where this occurs, second-generation Canadians are often torn between the expectations of their parents and the norms of Canada. Arranged marriages are not to be confused with forced marriages, which also occur for such reasons as maintaining family honour.

12 There are four types of polygamy: polygyny, bigamy, polyandry, and polygynandry. Polygyny is the most common form and occurs mostly among fundamentalist Mormons in British Columbia. This is illegal in Canada because of concern for the equal treatment of women and welfare of children.

13 Consanguineous marriages occur mostly in the Middle East and North Africa, and are most commonly between cousins. They are often preferred because they strengthen ties within the family and ensure more amicable relations. Depending upon the kinship system, they also occurred among Aboriginal groups where cross-cousins were favoured for marriage. Cousin marriages are legal in Canada.

14 Today, marriage is seen as a partnership. This shift in perception of marriage has brought with it a shift in divorce. The liberalization of laws has made it easier and less expensive to obtain a divorce. The current divorce rate remains high compared with earlier times.

15 Certain factors increase the likelihood of divorce. These include marrying at a young age, marrying because of an unplanned pregnancy, communication problems, having divorced before, or having parents who have divorced. Women often have an increase in depression after a divorce, while men experience poorer physical and mental health. Men tend to have more disposable income after a divorce, while women who usually must care for the children have less.

Critical Thinking Questions

1 In the 1950s, dating was scripted where a boy picks a girl up at her house and the two go to a pre-arranged event. How has dating changed today? What is the more typical pattern among college students?

2 Today, many people either hook up with someone or have a friend with benefits and enjoy doing so. This stands in sharp contrast to the idea that any sex outside of marriage is harmful. How does this reflect the changing sexual attitudes of Western societies?

3 Mixed dating and marriages in terms of religion, race, and other factors are increasing in Canada as visible minority populations grow. How might this affect the differences among Canadians in terms of those factors?

4 Instead of the terms "husband" or "wife," many couples, whether gay, lesbian or heterosexual, choose the word "partner" when referring to the people to whom they are committed. What are the advantages and disadvantages of such a term?

5 It is often said that monogamy is unnatural. If this is so, how do open marriages, polyamorous relationships, and swinging affect relationships? Are they beneficial or are there disadvantages.

6 Gay and lesbian relations differ from heterosexual ones in that there is no gender differentiation. How might this lead to greater equality between people in such couples?

7 Arranged marriages have been typical for centuries and are still common today. What are the advantages of relying on one's parents to find a suitable marriage partner? What are the disadvantages? Is being in love a sufficient reason to choose a partner?

8 If a man and three women decide to live together in a polygynist relationship, all parties are of age, and there is no coercion or abuse of children, should Canadian law still render this illegal? Why?

Websites

Service Canada   This website contains all kinds of information for people undergoing life events, including getting married and how to obtain a licence, having children and parental leave rights, and getting a divorce. It also lists services for Aboriginal people, newly immigrated Canadians, people with disabilities, seniors, and students. (http://www.servicecanada.gc.ca)

Civil Marriage Act   This website by the government of Canada contains the Civil Marriage Act. It defines marriage as "the lawful union of two persons to the exclusion of all others" and does not mention the sex of those two persons. (http://laws-lois.justice .gc.ca/eng/acts/c-31.5/page-1.html)

14 Variations of Sexual Expression

> *My hands were running through her hair and playing tremblingly with the gleaming fur, which rose and fell like a moonlit wave upon her heaving bosom, and drove all my senses into confusion. And I kissed her. No, she kissed me savagely, pitilessly, as if she wanted to slay me with her kisses. I was as in a delirium, and had long since lost my reason, but now I, too, was breathless. I sought to free myself. (From* Venus in Furs, *by Leopold von Sacher-Masoch, 1870)*
>
> *My lips were parched, I gasped for breath; my joints were stiff, my veins were swollen, yet I sat still, like all the crowd around me. But suddenly a heavy hand seemed to be laid upon my lap, something was bent and clasped and grasped, which made me faint with lust. The hand was moved up and down, slowly at first, and then faster and faster it went in rhythm with the song. My brain began to reel as throughout every vein a burning lava coursed, and them, some drops even gushed out—I panted. (From* Teleny, *attributed to Oscar Wilde, 1897)*
>
> *I can feel his mouth O Lord I must stretch myself I wished he was here or somebody to let myself go with and come again like that I feel all fire inside me. (From* Ulysses, *by James Joyce, 1922)*
>
> *Yes, this was love, this ridiculous bouncing of the buttocks, and the wilting of the poor, insignificant, moist little penis. This was the divine love! After all, the moderns were right when they felt contempt for the performance; for it was a performance. (From* Lady Chatterley's Lover, *by D.H. Lawrence, 1928)*

I find myself wondering what it feels like, during intercourse, to be a woman—whether the pleasure is keener, etc. Try to imagine something penetrating my groin, but have only a vague sensation of pain. (From Tropic of Cancer, by Henry Miller, 1934)

The zipless fuck is absolutely pure. It is free of ulterior motives. There is no power game. The man is not "taking" and the woman is not "giving." No one is attempting to cuckold a husband or humiliate a wife. No one is trying to prove anything or get anything out of anyone. The zipless fuck is the purest thing there is. And it is rarer than the unicorn. And I have never had one. (From Fear of Flying, by Erica Jong, 1973)

When she closed her eyes she felt he had many hands, which touched her everywhere, and many mouths, which passed so swiftly over her, and with a wolflike sharpness, his teeth sank into her fleshiest parts. Naked now, he lay his full length over her. She enjoyed his weight on her, enjoyed being crushed under his body. She wanted him soldered to her, from mouth to feet. Shivers passed through her body. (From Delta of Venus, by Anaïs Nin, 1977)

If one thing is apparent, it is that sexual expression is as varied a part of human life as any other. What people do sexually can take many forms in terms of fantasies, activities, interests, and desires. Sex may be a private activity by individuals, an expression of love or desire between two partners, or the special interests of entire communities. In this chapter we are concerned with what people do sexually. We begin with an overview of the sexual behaviours of Canadian college students, then celibacy, abstinence, and asexuality. We then look at sexual fantasy, solitary sexual behaviour, sex between two people, and finally the interests of special communities, such as men and women who practise BDSM.

Sex and the Single Canadian College Student

In general, college students are over the age of 18 and, thus, at the beginning of adulthood. In the United States, religion professor Donna Freitas published a controversial book entitled *The End of Sex: How Hookup Culture Is Leaving a Generation Unhappy, Sexually Unfulfilled, and Confused about Intimacy* (Freitas, 2013). She maintains that hooking up is rampant on college campuses across the country and somehow compromises students' ability to find true intimacy in the future. Before going to college, young people get messages from parents that college is not a time to be "tied down" and, thus, they should concentrate on their studies instead of dating. This together with media messages making sex a commodity leads them to have hook-ups without commitment, which Freitas says leads to unhappiness, dissatisfaction, and confusion.

According to a yet-to-be-published study of a representative sample of 1500 Canadian college students 18- to 24-years-old surveyed by the Sexuality Information and Education Council of Canada (SIECCAN), this does not appear to be the case in Canada. Seventy-seven percent of women and 73 percent of men said that they had already had sex, which they defined as oral, vaginal, or anal. Ninety-six percent identified as heterosexual and 4 percent gay, lesbian, or other. Of those who were sexually active, the majority reported being "happy" or "very happy" with their sex lives and many were in committed relationships. The report looked at three types of sexual relationships:

- *Casual:* Hook-ups, one-night stands, booty calls, friends with benefits.
- *Dating:* A couple is dating exclusively but have not committed to each other.
- *Committed:* Living together, engaged, common-law, married, or have committed to each other.

When asked about their last sex partner, 60 percent of men and 70 percent of women said that it was either their spouse, fiancé, or a committed partner, and 30 percent of men and 25 percent of women said that it was with a casual partner. The most common type of casual partner was a friend with benefits (Schwartz, 2013). On the negative side, only about half of those who were sexually active reported using a condom during their last sexual encounter, and most defined condoms as a birth control measure rather than a means of protection from sexually transmitted infections (STIs).

In another nationally representative sample of 653 Canadian university students (Milhausen et al., 2013), results were similar. Forty-nine percent were in committed dating relationships and the others were not dating anyone (17.2 percent), casually dating (16.4 percent), or living together, engaged, or married (17.5 percent). Thus, two thirds were in committed relationships. Condom use was also low, with less than half (47.2 percent) of those sexually active reporting having used one during their last vaginal intercourse. The usage rates were higher for men (55.4 percent) than for women (43.3 percent). The strongest predictor of condom use was as a measure of contraception. In other words, if a couple were using other contraceptive methods, they were less likely to use condoms.

In short, low rates of condom use place Canadian university students at significant risk for STIs. It should also be emphasized that these surveys were only for college students in Canada. The first

The majority of Canadian college students report being happy with their sex lives.

study does not represent students who are older than 24 and both do not represent 18- to 24-year-olds or older who are not attending college.

Another survey gives clues to other segments of the younger population. Egan (2001) surveyed backpackers travelling in Canada in the summer of 2000. Twenty-six percent reported having sex with a casual partner on their trip. Most were male and reported a higher number of casual partners prior to their trip.

Sixty-four percent of them used a condom, which is higher than the reported rates by college students.

It must be emphasized at the onset of this chapter that unless one is in a committed relationship where both partners have been tested, condoms are necessary for protection from STIs. While about half of Canadian college students take adequate measures of protection, there is still a significantly large at-risk population.

Review Questions

1 What are the rates of condom use among college students?

2 How do the majority of Canadian college students view their sex lives?

Celibacy, Abstinence, and Asexuality

Before discussing the many ways in which people relate to each other and have sex, we begin with not having it. Although it is said that sexual activity is a basic human need, not everyone pursues it. Some people such as many Catholic priests lead **celibate** lives, others for various reasons choose to be **abstinent** until they find a worthwhile or permanent partner, and still others calling themselves **asexuals** have no interest in sex at all. The difference between celibacy and abstinence is that the former suggests a more or less permanent state while the latter suggests a temporary one as in abstinence until marriage. The difference between abstinence and asexuality is like the difference between ignoring hunger until a good meal comes along and not being hungry at all. One more term, *chastity*, refers more to the patriarchal concept of female purity (i.e., virginity) more than anything else. We discuss celibacy, abstinence, and asexuality separately.

Celibacy

When people are celibate, they have typically made a conscious decision or taken a solemn vow to do so, as do nuns and priests in the Catholic Church before the bestowal of Holy Orders. This does not mean that they have no interest in sex, only that they have promised to avoid it. Early church fathers such as St. Augustine and St. Paul taught that celibacy leads to the highest form of spiritual consciousness and that those who have the strength to do so should pursue it. Today the policy of celibacy among Catholic clerics has been sharply criticized if not blamed entirely for the flurry of child abuse uncovered in recent decades (Adams, 2003; Sipe, 2004). In Canada, there have been a number of scandals, most prominent among them the systematic abuse of

over 300 boys at the Mount Cashel Orphanage in St. John's, Newfoundland, by celibate members of the Christian Brothers of Ireland in Canada. While some clerics have little trouble adhering to their vows, others constantly struggle with them and burn out (Joseph, 2010).

Another celibate group are Side B Christians who are openly gay but believe that sex with other men is morally wrong (Creek, 2013). Side A Christians support the idea of gay relationships; Side B supports celibacy. Similarly, there are gay Mormons who have chosen to be open about their sexual orientation but live completely celibate lives (Thurston, 2007). Other gays and lesbians simply leave their religion behind or work within it toward change. Still others believe that religion plays no part in their lives.

A third reason people might choose celibacy is because they are HIV positive (Siegel & Raveis, 1993; Siegel & Schrimshaw, 2003). They do not feel sexual or they do not want to risk infecting others. Today, as people become progressively more knowledgeable about safer sex, and because effective drugs can prolong life indefinitely (see Chapter 7), it is likely that fewer and fewer people who are HIV-positive relegate their lives to this state.

A fourth reason to be celibate is that people may find themselves in marriages where their partners are unable or unwilling to have sex and they themselves are unwilling to end their marriages or have extramarital affairs (Donnelly & Burgess, 2008; Smith, 2007). In such cases, celibacy is an option not chosen but imposed.

---

celibacy
A more or less permanent commitment to not having sex.

abstinence
A temporary commitment to not having sex.

asexuality
A complete lack of interest in sex.

Variations of Sexual Expression

Catholic priests take vows of lifelong celibacy.

Asexuality

Asexuality is not celibacy, nor is it abstinence. It is a lack of sexual attraction either entirely or predominantly. One empirical sample concluded that approximately 1 percent of the population is asexual (Bogaert, 2004). It has been likened to hypoactive sexual desire disorder (HSDD) as introduced in the fourth edition of the *Diagnostic and Statistical Manual of Mental Disorders (DSM-IV)* in 1992 in that both refer to a lack of sexual attraction, but HSDD is usually accompanied by distress factors such as depression or difficulty relating to others (Chasin, 2013). Because asexuality does not necessarily lead to unhappiness, there is no rationale to pathologize it. Asexual people vary in terms of their involvement in sexuality. Some will actually have sex with others simply to please their partners or to have children, while others prefer only romantic or affectionate involvement such as hugging or kissing. Others are not involved in sex at all, preferring only friendships with others. Some asexuals will also masturbate but they typically do not consider this part of sexual activity in that it does not involve other people.

Because of the assumption that all people are sexual, there is currently much discussion on whether asexuality exists beyond a temporary or even disordered aversion to sex. Others see it as a bona fide sexual orientation along with homosexuality and heterosexuality and believe that it should be accepted as such (MacInnis & Hodson, 2013). Others such as Alberta scholar Ela Przybylo (2011) point out that it is defined as a reaction to living in a society inundated with sex, thus believing it to be more anti-sexual than asexual.

Ironically, many asexual people undergo a process of identity formation much like that of gays and lesbians. They begin

Abstinence

Abstinence, also called *countenance*, differs from celibacy in that in that it is a temporary state typically imposed or self-imposed because of religious, moral, or cultural proscriptions (Gardner, 2011). During the 1980s, abstinence became a politically charged issue with the rise of conservatism in the United States and a push toward abstinence-only education (see Chapter 1). Canada has rejected such programs in favour of full sex education (SIECCAN, 2010). As a result, the teenage pregnancy rate dropped by 40.8 percent between 1990 and 2010 and remains significantly lower than that of the United States, as well as England and Wales (McKay, 2012).

Among the problems inherent in abstinence education is that the term is often left undefined and is thus subject to definition. Abstinence programs tend to emphasize virginity, chastity, purity, and not having sex until marriage. It follows that many young people will define this as pertaining only to vaginal intercourse since traditionally at least, this is what virginity, chastity, and purity mean. Not only is this act irrelevant to gays and lesbians but it ignores all other sexual behaviours as well. In one sample of 454 university students, 50.1 percent believed that oral sex is consistent with abstinent behaviour and 90.4 percent believed that it maintains virginity. For anal intercourse, those figures were 9.5 percent and 39.4 percent, respectively (Hans & Kimberly, 2011). Bersamin et al. (1995) and Haglund (2003) found similar definitions in earlier surveys. While abstaining from vaginal intercourse effectively precludes pregnancy, it does not rule out sexually transmitted infections if other sexual behaviours are practised.

Asexual pride flag.

with an awareness of their difference among others, they explore the reasons for this difference, they consider medical definitions in wondering whether there is something wrong with them, they may even seek medical advice, and they eventually reach an understanding and acceptance of themselves (Carrigan, 2011). Furthermore, they may seek out others like themselves, which adds further salience to their identities as asexuals, and they form communities or get involved with those already present.

Asexual people have become well organized over the past decade to the level of community where there is a pride flag denoting asexuality as an orientation, gathering places, and websites. There is a main site—Asexual Visibility and Education Network—and there are also several blogs, local community sites, and personals sites such as Asexual Pals and Celibate Passions for people looking for non-sexual relationships. Asexuals have also marched in gay pride parades, and their voices are quickly joining the general discourse on sexuality.

Review Questions

1 What are the differences among asexuality, celibacy, and abstinence?

2 Why is asexuality now regarded by many academics as a sexual orientation?

3 What might be the reasons for celibacy and abstinence?

4 What steps might be typical in the "coming out process" of asexual people?

Sexual Fantasies

Sexual fantasies are common forms of sexual expression that many people act out in their minds (Frostino, 2007; Hicks & Leitenberg, 2001). Here are several findings from recent research. Overall, men have been found to have more **sexual cognitions** or thoughts about sex (Renaud & Byers, 1999). In fact, Laumann et al. (1994) in their large-scale survey of the American population found that 54 percent of men and 19 percent of women thought about sex at least once a day. Both sexes have been found to have sexual fantasies either sporadically, during masturbation, or when having sex with partners (Kahr, 2008; Leitenberg & Henning, 1995). Liberal attitudes toward sex as well as more sexual experience have been found to be associated with more explicit sexual fantasies (Kahr, 2008). Some people report never having sexual fantasies. According to Cado and Leitenberg (1990), people who do not have them have a greater likelihood of sexual dissatisfaction and sexual dysfunction. Finally, the sexual fantasies of gay, lesbian, bisexual, and heterosexual people have been found to be similar except for the sex of the fantasized partner (Leitenberg & Henning, 1995).

The Nature of Sexual Fantasies

What is a sexual fantasy? Is it a scripted sexual scenario that is acted out in the mind? Is it a recollection or alteration of a past sexual encounter or one that one would like to experience in the future? Or is it simply to have sexual thoughts about others real or imagined? Is it an imagined scenario where one is involved and playing a part or does it involve only other people? What if one is simply aroused by a stranger who is waiting for a bus or sitting in a bar? At what point does this arousal enter the realm of fantasy? What is the difference between a sexual fantasy and a sexual thought? When does a fantasy become an obsession? All of these questions are good ones since sexual fantasy is an often-used phrase but rarely defined in precise terms. For purposes of this discussion, we define sexual fantasy as cognitions about other people involving sexual desire or imagined activity. Those others may be real people or idealized versions of desired lovers.

Most sexual fantasies have three components. First are the characters, which may be current partners, past boyfriends or girlfriends, authority figures, classmates, neighbours, people seen in the streets that day, or idyllic lovers. Second are the contexts of the imagined encounters, which may involve seduction, conquest, chance meetings, summer vacations, forbidden love, paid sex, same-sex encounters, age-discordant encounters, or any type of scenario one can imagine. Third is the activity, which may be intercourse, oral sex, or any number of acts. The following is an example of a described sexual fantasy:

REAL Research British Columbia Psychologists Yule et al. (2014) surveyed a large sample of people identifying as asexual and compared their answers to those of control groups. They were significantly less likely to have masturbated in the past month and more likely to report never having had a sexual fantasy. Forty percent said that they never had a sexual fantasy and 11 percent said that their sexual fantasies did not involve other people.

---

sexual cognitions
Thoughts about sex.

She has black hair and I stop the car and motion her to get in. She walks quickly, with a slight attitude. She gets in with silence—her hands and eyes speak for her. I take her home, and she pulls me in. I undress her, and she is ready for me. Down on the bed she goes, and down on her I go. With legs spread, her clitoris is swollen and erect, hungry for my touch. I give her what she wants. She moans as orgasm courses through her body. (Author Janell Carroll's files)

In this case the characters are the fantasizer and a woman with black hair. The contexts are a chance meeting involving a stranger and sexual activity in the fantasizer's home. The sexual activity is oral sex upon the stranger, which arouses her to the point of orgasm. Next is a different fantasy:

My sexual fantasy is to be stranded on an island with beautiful women from different countries (all of them horny, of course). I'm the only male. I would make all of them have multiple orgasms, and I would like to have an everlasting erection so I could please them all nonstop. (Author Janell Carroll's files)

Here the characters are the fantasizer and some beautiful women from different countries, the context is that all are stranded on an island, and the activities are to give all the women multiple orgasms with a permanent erection. Not all sexual fantasies are so well scripted. They may simply be flashing thoughts of desired people or activities and they may rapidly change from one scene to another. What is interesting as well is that sexual fantasies need not be realistic or even obey the laws of physics. One may fantasize about sexy aliens from another planet, historical characters, flying through the air making love to a superhero, or otherwise. Finally, merely having a sexual fantasy is no indication of wanting it to occur in real life. Often, people have fantasies that they know are illegal, harmful, or antisocial if they were realized, such as sex with a best friend's partner or forced sex. In general, people know the difference between fantasy and reality and are well able to keep the two separate.

Sexual fantasies help enhance masturbation, increase sexual arousal, help one to reach orgasm, and allow a one to explore various sexual activities that one might find taboo or too threatening to act out. As people mature, they typically have a select number of fantasies that arouse them over and over again. In this respect, one might liken a repertoire of sexual fantasies to a CD collection. One plays an album that one enjoys until it gets repetitive. Then one selects another and plays that one.

A History of Attitudes toward Sexual Fantasies

Sexual fantasies have both delighted and plagued humanity for thousands of years. The early Christian fathers in the first several centuries c.e. saw them as sinful and synonymous with adultery itself, as is clearly mentioned in the New Testament book of Matthew (5:28 KJV): "But I say unto you, That whosoever looketh upon a woman to lust after her hath committed adultery with her already in his heart." Furthermore, Romans 8:6 (KJV) states that "to be carnally minded is death," and James 1:15 (KJV) warns that "when lust hath conceived, it bringeth forth sin." One early church father, Saint Jerome, had led a fully sexual life before celibacy and wrote that his mind had been plagued with remembered desire and his imagination had filled the room with "troupes of dancing girls" (Tannahill, 1980). He, Tertullian, Paul, Augustine, and others considered any lustful thoughts to be sinful and their views influenced Christian thought upon sexual fantasy for centuries.

In the Middle Ages, men who entertained sexual fantasies of particular women often thought themselves to be bewitched and sometimes accused them of witchcraft, which led to them being arrested and ultimately burned at the stake (Elliott, 1999). By the 12th century, both men and women complained that they would be visited at night by *incubi* (male demons) or *succubi* (female demons), who would copulate with them. If these encounters cannot be explained by masturbation, they can certainly be explained by intense sexual fantasies (Tannahill, 1980).

The Dream of the Fisherman's Wife by Japanese artist Hokusai in 1814 depicts the fantasy of a woman involving two octopi. The larger one performs cunnilingus upon her while the smaller one fondles her lips and nipple.

Early psychiatry, beginning with Sigmund Freud, looked upon sexual fantasies as symptomatic of psychological disturbance or sexual frustration. Freud believed that only sexually unsatisfied people fantasized about sex. While this view slowly softened as the 20th century progressed, this was only for heterosexuals and particularly males for whom it was believed that conquest-type sexual fantasies that asserted masculine dominance over women were healthy cognitions. For gay men, however, especially those who fantasized about dominant partners, it indicated feminine desires (Oversey, 1969). For decades, psychiatry had looked upon gay and lesbian sexual fantasies as symptomatic of an illness, and it was not until after the gay rights movement that such views were abandoned (Bayer, 1987).

Gender and Sexual Fantasies

In general, sexual fantasies tend to differ by gender. Women tend to have fantasies that are more emotional and more romantic, with lots of touching and kissing and lying in the arms of a lover. They also tend to be with familiar others rather than strangers. According to one study, the five most frequently reported sexual fantasies by a sample of women are sex with a current partner, reliving a past sexual experience, engaging in different sexual positions, having sex in rooms other than the bedroom, and sex on a carpeted floor (Maltz & Boss, 2001). Men's fantasies tend to be more assertive and impersonal with conquest themes, more attention to sex acts, and more scenes where the lover is an idyllic stranger (Hicks & Leitenberg, 2001; Zurbriggen & Yost, 2004). In a sample of men, the five most frequently reported sexual fantasies for men are engaging in different sexual positions, having an aggressive lover, getting oral sex, having sex with a new lover, and having sex on a beach (Maltz & Boss, 2001).

Although there has been little research upon the sexual fantasies of gay men and lesbians, it seems likely that gender is a stronger predictor than sexual orientation. Gay men are likely to have more impersonal fantasies, while lesbians are likely to have ones that are more emotional and romantic (Kahr, 2008). Because gay men are not restricted by gender however, it is possible that they are more flexible than heterosexual men in that they may be either the subject or the object in their own fantasies.

Despite what one might think, rape fantasies are common among women—between 31 percent and 60 percent of women have reported having them in research samples (Barner, 2003; Bivona & Critelli, 2009; Strassberg & Lockerd, 1998). This presents a puzzle of why women would choose forced sex in their fantasies rather than consensual sex. According to Bivona et al. (2012), there are three common explanations. The first is *sexual blame avoidance*. Because women are socialized to be chaste and not too interested in sex, fantasies where they are forced to have sex are ways to have sex free of guilt and blame, thus avoiding self-labels of "slut" or "tramp." The second explanation is *openness to sexual experience*. Women who have been more open about sex in their lives are more likely to have a variety of sexual fantasies including those involving rape. Third is the *sexual desirability* explanation. A woman imagines herself as so sexually desirable that men cannot control themselves in her presence. While these explanations conflict with one another, it may be that all three may apply depending upon the types of women. It is important to note here that having a rape fantasy in the safety of one's imagination is no indication that a woman wants this to be a reality.

On Your Mind

I sometimes fantasize about a sexual encounter I had in high school when I was 15 with another 15-year-old. Do I have pedophilic tendencies?

Before answering your question, it is important to point out that pedophiles are attracted to prepubescent children, not teenagers. Sexual fantasies may be scenarios with known others, strangers, or even fictitious characters. They may also be relived memories of past sexual encounters that aroused us at the time. When reliving this encounter in your mind, you are remembering how you were aroused as a 15-year-old just discovering your sexuality. This encounter was likely exciting to you and you are reliving that excitement. While this fantasy might be an indication of a desire to go back in time and feel that excitement again, it is not an indication that you would like to relive it as an adult. In short, you are recalling the way you felt when you were 15; you are not wishing to live it as an adult. Many people have fond memories of sexual dalliances that took place in adolescence, and wishing they could relive them does not mean that they want to relive them in the present as adults.

At the same time, a survey of the sexual fantasies of a sample of 162 men and women found that men fantasized about sexual dominance more than did women (Zurbriggen & Yost, 2004) and those who did tended to be more accepting of rape myths (e.g., "any healthy women can successfully resist a rape is she wants."). Still one must be cautious about connecting fantasy with reality. Another sample of college-aged males (Greenlinger & Byrne, 1987) showed strong contradictions between the two. While 53.9 percent responded "yes" to the item "I fantasize about forcing a woman to have sex," 89.6 percent responded the same to the item "I don't understand how a man could possibly rape a woman." What is played out in fantasy, therefore, seems far less likely to be played out in reality.

Review Questions

1 What are some common gender differences in sexual fantasy?

2 What are the three common explanations as to why rape fantasies are common among women?

3 What were the attitudes of the early Christian fathers toward sexual fantasies, and how were they explained?

Solitary Sexual Activity—Masturbation

Despite a long historical legacy upon the evils of "self-abuse," masturbation is harmless and has no detrimental effects upon one's health (Herbenick et al., 2010). It fulfills a variety of needs for people in that it decreases sexual tension and provides an outlet for sexual fantasy (see Figures 14.1 and 14.2). It also allows people to experiment with their bodies and learn what feels good, where and how they like to be touched, and the most efficient way to bring about their own orgasms. In this section we look at the incidence of masturbation, the social and psychological factors surrounding it, and the history of attitudes toward it.

Today, masturbation is often recommended as a strategy to improve sexual health, avoid unwanted pregnancy, and avoid sexually transmitted infections (Kaestle & Allen, 2011). It may even compensate for the lack of a partner or dissatisfaction with sex (Das, 2007).

> **REAL Research** Masturbation is not unique to humans. It is common in most other primates as well as mammals including dogs, cats, horses, rats, hamsters, deer, and whales (Levin, 2007).

John Harvey Kellogg, the inventor of Kellogg's Cornflakes, was a zealous anti-masturbation campaigner in the 19th century.

A History of Masturbation

The history of masturbation begins with the Biblical story of Onan (Genesis 38: 8-10). Under the *levirate* marital system of the ancient Hebrews, it was the duty of a man to impregnate his brother's wife if that brother died without giving her children. Onan was commanded to do so by his father and instead of doing his duty, he "spilled his seed upon the ground." This act as well as any wasting of semen came to be known as *onanism* and, centuries later, was exclusively associated with masturbation (Stengers & Van Neck, 2001).

By the 18th century, masturbation was not only associated with sin but with health, as with the publication of a pamphlet by Dutch theologian Balthazar Bekker in 1716 entitled *Onania, or the Heinous Sin of Self-Pollution, And All Its Frightful Consequences, In Both Sexes, Considered: With Spiritual and Physical Advice To Those Who Have Already Injured Themselves By This Abominable Practice*. Among the consequences listed were indigestion, back pain, pimples, epilepsy, ravenous hunger, vomiting, and attacks of rage. In 1760, Swiss physician Samuel-Auguste Tissot published a book entitled *L'Onanisme*, which cited case histories of young men suffering from the effects of masturbation. He asserted that semen was a life force and any loss of it was debilitating to health—so much so that masturbation would lead to death. The loss of one ounce of semen he said was equivalent to the loss of 40 ounces (1.18 litres) of blood (Braume, 2011).

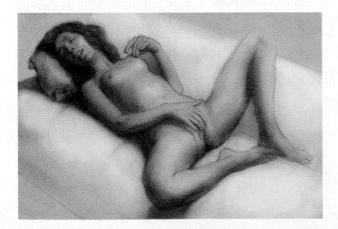

FIGURE **14.1** Female masturbation.

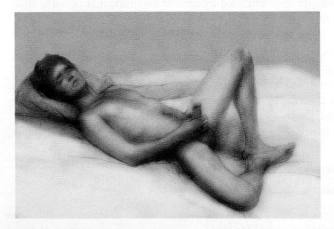

FIGURE **14.2** Male masturbation.

The late 19th and early 20th centuries was the backdrop of a vehement anti-masturbation campaign in the United States and Canada driven by the belief that it leads to severe physical and mental harm (Laqueur, 2003). By far, the most zealous campaigner against masturbation was John Harvey Kellogg (1852–1943), who, in his book *Plain Facts for Young and Old* (1881), recommended circumcision for boys and drops of carbolic acid on the clitoris for girls as prevention measures. He further believed that masturbation was the result of an unhealthy diet and, with his brother, invented the breakfast cereal that became known as Kellogg's Cornflakes as a remedy. American Christian pioneer Ellen G. White, in her book *A Solemn Appeal* (1870), wrote that the "solitary vice" is even more harmful to women since they are the weaker sex (Stengers & Van Neck, 2001).

As the 20th century progressed, attitudes slowly changed, in part because of Alfred C. Kinsey's research (see next section) showing that most people did indeed masturbate with no consequences at all. Today, masturbation is considered entirely harmless to mental and physical well-being.

Frequency of Masturbation

While there are no comprehensive surveys on sexual behaviour in Canada, we can glean frequencies from data in other countries. In Australia, a representative sample of 10 173 men and 9134 women aged 16 to 59 was surveyed on a variety of sexual behaviour, including masturbation (Richters et al. 2003). While incidences were higher than in the United States, they were still well below Kinsey's figures. Sixty-two percent of men and 35 percent of women reported masturbating in the past year, and 48 percent and 25 percent, respectively, had done so in the past four weeks.

In the United States, pioneering sex researcher Alfred C. Kinsey found that masturbation was common in both men and women (Kinsey et al., 1948; Kinsey et al., 1953). Among females, he found that 62 percent had masturbated and most of those to the point of orgasm. Among males, he found that 92 percent of the population masturbated, 68.4 percent of boys experienced their first orgasm through masturbation, and most of the rest through nocturnal emissions ("wet dreams"). For the vast majority, masturbation was done through manual stimulation and lasted only a few minutes. Others in his sample were more imaginative and included anal stimulation with fingers and even **auto-fellatio**.

Laumann et al. (1994) in their large survey of the American population decades after Kinsey's research found somewhat lower incidences. For men, 36.7 percent reported that they had not masturbated in the past 12 months, while only 26.7 percent reported that they did so at least once a week. These same figures for women were 58.3 percent and 7.6 percent, respectively. They explain this low incidence with a number of factors. Because the United States is highly religious in nature, masturbation is often considered a moral lapse. Caution should therefore be exercised when generalizing to Canada.

Research on the frequency of masturbation often looks at college students, who tend to masturbate less frequently than high school students. These reduced frequencies, however, are not matters of "maturity" but circumstance. College students often live in residence, where they have roommates and share the same washrooms. As a result, there is less opportunity for privacy than those who would still live with their parents and have private rooms. Furthermore, as men and women progress from being alone to being in a coupled relationship, masturbation frequency goes down.

Attitudes toward Masturbation

Because of religious proscriptions against masturbation as well as its historical legacy of negativity, masturbation produced considerable discomfort and guilt among many people (Patton, 1986). Focus on the Family, a conservative religious group in the United States, for example warns that "compulsive masturbation will lead to the inability to become intimate later in life" and cites serial killer Ted Bundy as an example (Aterburn, 1991). Misinformation from the days of Tissot and onanism still lingers as well. Lo Presto et al. (1985), for example, found guilt and false information to be common in a sample of high school students, and Sierra et al. (2010) found the same among a group of 610 Salvadorian teenagers.

To examine North American attitudes toward masturbation, Canadian psychologists Madanikia et al. (2013) looked at 44 popular films with masturbation scenes, including *The 40 Year Old Virgin* (2005) and *Borat* (2006). Male masturbation especially was portrayed negatively, often as a substitute for partnered sex, and with consequences such as getting caught.

Because religious and cultural proscriptions vary, frequency of masturbation also varies among groups. For example, in the United States, Asian-American women have been found to masturbate significantly less frequently than non-Asian women (Meston et al., 1996). The same was found among African-American women in another sample in that they report masturbating less frequently than White women (Shulman & Home, 2003). There is some evidence that gay men and lesbians have healthier attitudes toward masturbation (Califia, 1979), which would stand to reason in that in their lovemaking, they often masturbate their partners who by definition have the same genitalia. Furthermore, for gays and lesbians who live in isolated areas or are still in the closet, masturbation if often their only outlet.

Sex Toys and Masturbation

Sex toys or sexual enhancement products come in a variety of forms and may be used for partnered sex or privately for masturbation. There are dildos in every size as well as strap-on dildos, *ben-wa balls* for vaginal insertion, anal beads, "butt plugs," prostate massagers, nipple clamps, cock rings,

auto-fellatio
An act where a male performs oral sex upon himself.

A "butt plug" is used for anal stimulation.

penis sleeves, artificial vaginas, blow-up dolls, and electro-stimulators, to name a few. As it seems, every imaginable device to enhance orgasms has already been invented. This is not to mention a variety of lubricants with brand names such as *Play, Climax, AstroGlide, Babe Lube, Wet, Fist*, and *Ram*. Some are even flavoured so as to taste good during oral sex. They are banned entirely in some countries, such as Malaysia and India (Singh, 2007), and sold freely in others, such as Canada and the United States.

With the relaxing of the Comstock laws, which outlawed sending any sexual paraphernalia by mail in the United States, sex toys may be ordered online and shipped by mail or they may be sold directly in shops. A third way they are distributed is through sex-toy parties hosted at people's homes in much the same way that Tupperware was sold in the 1950s. The majority of such parties are for women—one person hosts, a distributor brings a variety of products, and the host invites as many friends as she can. The result is a relaxed atmosphere where women may purchase products safely and receive sex-positive education, which promotes knowledge and sexual health (Jozkowski et al., 2012; Schick et al., 2013).

Review Questions

1 Trace the history of attitudes toward masturbation from Biblical times to the present.

2 What is the overall frequency of masturbation in men and in women?

3 How can sex toys promote sexual health?

Disembodied Sexual Activity—Cybersex

In the 1993 movie *Demolition Man*, set in the mid-21st century, Sandra Bullock's character asks Sylvester Stallone's character if he would like to have sex. He readily agrees and, to his surprise, she brings out two helmets for them to put on that somehow simulate sex with each other in their minds as they sit motionless with their eyes closed facing each other. While we have not reached such technological sophistication yet, disembodied sex—or cybersex—has become multifaceted over the past decade. It lies in limbo somewhere in between masturbation and partnered sex—there is a remote partner but one is alone and there is no physical contact. It is in effect sex with another person without that person's presence.

The main forerunner to cybersex was telephone sex. Two people would describe erotic activities to each other over the telephone, which may involve scenes and actions they would like to take place or perhaps role playing where both take on a role in a sexual story and play out their parts. By the 1980s, telephone sex became sufficiently commercialized where companies would

advertise their services in erotic magazines or elsewhere and take calls from people who typically masturbated while on the telephone. Live operators or "fantasy artists" would take down credit card information and verify ages, and then they would engage in sexually explicit talk they believed suited the callers' desires. Some worked at call centres; others worked directly from their homes (Flowers, 1998). One Canadian company, TorontoPhoneSex, charges $3.29 per minute and the charges appear on the customer's next telephone bill. While such companies still exist, much of their business has now been overshadowed by Internet alternatives.

According to one Canadian study, cybersex is a common activity not only among university students, but people in general (Shaughnessy et al., 2013). It can involve solitary activity where a person simply masturbates to found erotic imagery, but it can also involve another person with text, voice, video relay, or all three at once contributing to increasing telepresence where individuals have the sense of being present in other locations. Erotic textual chats are little different from telephone sex where intimate sex acts are described in detail or two people might role play and act out their parts. In the latter form, one person begins a story, the other continues it, and so on back and forth as the two simultaneously create a narrative. Visual relay programs such as Skype allow

Cybersex allows people to live out fantasies in a safe environment.

attached to one's genitals on one end and a computer on the other. Control over genital stimulation may then be given to any other person, who will then be able to bring the user to orgasm from a remote distance (Goodman & Vertesi, 2012). *Bluedildonics* are similar devices that may be controlled through a Bluetooth connection. Such devices constitute a new era in sex toys where stimulation devices are merged with computer technology for enhanced *human-computer interaction* (HCI) experiences (Bardzell & Bardzell, 2011).

Sex with Dolls and Robots

How far can technology go? The next wave of HCI devices may well be robots designed to look and feel human as one might see on *Star Trek* and other science fiction series. Sex dolls, or life-size human imitations, have been around for a long time. They are more or less lifeless figures that must be carried everywhere and posed. Sex robots, on the other hand, are interactive by virtue of a simple artificial intelligence and can actually move. Although still relatively primitive, they are also around today. One example from TrueCompanion.com is Roxxxy who can be purchased online for about $7500. Her vagina is equipped with sensing devices that produce stimulating movements, she can move her arms, and she can be programmed with any of five different personalities such as "Wild Wendy," "S&M Susan," and "Mature Martha." TrueCompanions.com also offers a male sex robot named Rocky. While the technology for these devices has a long way to go, it has paved the way to a future where increasingly sophisticated robots may appear on the market within decades.

If sex with robots becomes common in the future, a number of interesting questions arise. First, if one considers that the only difference between a sex robot and a vibrator is the level of mechanical sophistication, sex with a robot is no different than a private act of masturbation using that vibrator (Levy, 2007). Yet it is not known how such changes will affect human relationships. For example, as Western societies slowly transformed over the

two (or more) people to face each other and perform sex acts for one another's enjoyment. Still further, one may join a fantasy site such as Red Light Center where, through an *avatar*, or graphic image representing oneself, one may have virtual sex with the avatars of others. Any member may choose any type of avatar—male or female, Black, Asian, or White, or with any number of other characteristics, allowing him or her to play out any fantasy imaginable.

How might one explain the popularity of cybersex? Young et al. (2000) see a number of factors. The first is anonymity. With the use of a screen name, people may engage in cybersex without fear of having their identities revealed and, because they use their personal computers, with little fear of being caught by anyone. Second, there is convenience. One may access erotic sites at any time and go in and out with little difficulty. Third, there is the opportunity for escape. People may sit at their computers, engage in a sexual dalliance that they feel has nothing to do with the rest of their lives, and then return to reality as quickly as they left it. These and other factors make cybersex an attractive venture for many people around the world, particularly those in remote areas. Cybersex in general is probably no substitute for the real thing, but through such sites it does allow long-distance lovers to be intimate and gives people the opportunity to play out their sexual fantasies in a safe environment. It must also be said, however, that it may also lead to socially and psychologically harmful behaviours where people spend more and more time in the world of cybersex and less and less time in the real world.

Teledildonics and Bluedildonics

One recent development in sexual enhancement technology is *teledildonics*, which involves a series of devices that may be

Life-like sex dolls that move and talk are now marketed in Canada and the United States.

Variations of Sexual Expression

past century from rural to urban, that is, from living in small intimate cooperative communities to huge cities, the need for independence and privacy has increased. If satisfactory sex can be achieved without human beings, will this lead to a decreased need for relationships with others? The likely answer is that it will not, since human relationships with all their complexities seem to have no substitute. Yet, with the increased sophistication of artificial intelligence, such lines may become blurred in the future.

Review Questions

1 Explain why cybersex falls somewhere between masturbation and partnered sexual activity as not quite one but not quite the other.

2 What are teledildonics? How do they work?

3 How will sex with robots, as it becomes common, affect human relations in the future?

Partnered Sexual Activity

Erotic activities with a partner may seem as if they may be reduced to several acts done in sequence culminating in orgasm but there is in fact a wide variety. They may also be penetrative or non-penetrative and they may concentrate upon the genitals or elsewhere. In this section we look at some of the main sex acts between two people, including oral sex and vaginal or anal intercourse. Depending upon genital combination, some acts may only be performed by male-female couples, while others may be performed by any two people regardless of gender. With the exception of vaginal intercourse, or unless specified, we make no assumptions about the gender of couples in our descriptions.

Foreplay

With the growing acceptance of gay and lesbian couples, and with the advent of HIV/AIDS, *foreplay* is becoming an outdated term. Traditionally, foreplay meant hugging, kissing, licking, caressing, and similar acts to get a woman sufficiently aroused for intercourse (Weiss & Brody, 2009). The implication was that intercourse is at the centre of sexual activity and that anything done beforehand is merely a warm-up. While this is still a common pattern, it ignores several things. First, hugging, kissing and caressing are sometimes ends in themselves. Couples enjoy them equally and may not even move on to any penetrative acts. There has been much emphasis on non-penetrative sex since HIV/AIDS came to the forefront in that it is considered part of safer sex. Second, the idea of foreplay where one person prepares the other for penetration ignores sex between two men or two women where penetration may not happen at all or where each may penetrate the other in sequence.

At the same time, as anthropologist Margaret Mead pointed out long ago, the mechanisms enabling female orgasm are not the same as that of the male and, if the men move immediately to penetration, women are far less likely to achieve orgasm as is often the case in highly patriarchal societies. If penetration is the intention, therefore, foreplay is a necessary step (Baily, 1968; Hunt & Curtis, 2006).

REAL Research Canadian psychologists Miller and Byers (2004) asked members of a sample of 152 male–female couples about their partners' ideal time duration of foreplay. Women consistently underestimated the durations desired by their partners, suggesting that they based their lovemaking on sexual stereotypes of men believing that they typically preferred less time in foreplay and more time in intercourse.

Caressing and snuggling are common during foreplay.

© Exactostock/SuperStock

Manual Sex and Mutual Masturbation

Manual sex, also referred to as a "hand job" or "jerking someone off" upon men and "fingering" upon women, is the manipulation of the genitals, which can be done by one partner to the other, or as **mutual masturbation**. Generally, people think of manual sex as something that happens before penetrative sex, but it has recently come to be regarded as a form of safer sex. For partners who want to avoid or are indifferent to intercourse, this is a common method of bringing the other to orgasm either consecutively or concurrently.

One of the advantages of having a same-sex partner is that both parties are familiar with the genitals of the other, know what feels good, and are able to relate to the pleasure that they are giving in their lovemaking. Still, both men and women vary considerably in what they enjoy, and partners must still learn what techniques feel good to the other. When men and women have sex, they are not familiar with genitals of their partners and they must learn as well. It is therefore important to communicate to the other what feels good and what is most efficient in producing pleasure.

Many people, especially men, do not know what to do with a clitoris or vagina and must therefore learn. Because each woman differs in how she likes her clitoris stroked or rubbed, it is important that partners communicate their preferences. A water-based lubricant such as K-Y Jelly can make manual sex more comfortable. Most women enjoy a light caressing of the shaft of the clitoris together with an occasional circling around it. Others enjoy penetration of the vagina with the fingers. Still other women prefer to have their clitoris rolled between the lips of the labia or the entire area of the vulva caressed. As a woman gets more aroused, she may breathe more deeply or moan and her muscles may become tense.

Many men like to have their penis stimulated with consistent strokes. At the beginning, however, many also enjoy soft stroking. The testicles can also be responsive to touch, although out of fear of hurting them, some people, especially women, avoid touching them at all. Generally, light stroking can be pleasurable.

When a man is fully erect, the foreskin of the penis may be fully retracted and resemble that of a circumcised male, it may still envelop the head of the penis, or it may cover the head only partially. Many men may dislike the head of their penis being touched too much due to sensitivity and prefer that it is rubbed up and down with the foreskin instead. Stimulation at the base may also help bring on orgasm in that it mimics deep thrusting. Switching positions, pressures, and techniques often can be pleasurable for a man as well in that a good hand job uses variety. To bring about orgasm, however, the most common technique uses quick up-and-down motions that are done without too much pressure.

One variation of manual sex is *brachioproctic* or *brachiovaginal* insertion, otherwise known as "fisting," "fist fucking," or "hand balling." Here, a hand or part of one is inserted into the rectum or vagina. As Gayle Rubin (2011) asserts, this is the only sex act invented in the 20th century. It was originally an exclusively gay practice and then it was adopted by heterosexuals.

On Your Mind
Why do people fake orgasms?

Although it is said to be highly pleasurable and can be performed with safety precautions such as the wearing of latex gloves, it can also cause lacerations and perforations in the rectum and vagina.

Fisting is performed by only a small minority of people, and the wearing of latex gloves has become more common since the advent of HIV/AIDS (Richters et al., 2003).

Both men and women report having faked orgasms at some point in their lives (Knox et al., 2008; Muehlenhard & Shippee, 2010). For women, Herbenick et al. (2010) found that although 85 percent of men said their female partner reached orgasm the last time they had sex, only 64 percent of women said they had done so. One reason women reported was not knowing what type of physical stimulation would lead to orgasm. In another research sample, some women said that they wanted to end a sexual encounter without hurting their partner's feelings (Muehlenhard & Shippee, 2010). Additionally some men in the same study reported faking orgasms during vaginal intercourse, oral sex, manual stimulation, and even telephone sex. Their most common reason was because they were tired or they did not feel that an orgasm is possible.

Oral Sex

Oral sex upon a woman is called **cunnilingus** and that upon a man is called **fellatio**. Common terms depending upon if it is done to a man or woman are "giving a blow job," "sucking off," "going down on" or "eating out" someone. There is also a third type called **anilingus,** where the anus is orally stimulated. Fellatio and cunnilingus may be done by one partner upon another or it may be done simultaneously (performing "sixty-nine"; see Figure 14.3). All are

mutual masturbation
Two people masturbating each other at the same time or one after the other.

cunnilingus
Oral sex upon a woman's vagina.

fellatio
Oral sex upon a man's penis.

anilingus
Oral stimulation of the anus.

FIGURE **14.3** The sixty-nine position.

Édouard-Henri Avril was an illustrator of erotic literature in the 19th century in France. Here he illustrates oral sex of a man upon a woman in Greek motif.

Ancient Times, plate XII of "De Figuris Veneris" by F.K. Forberg, engraved by the artist, 1900 (litho), Avril, Édouard-Henri (Paul) (1849–1928)/Private Collection/The Stapleton Collection/Bridgeman Images

commonly practised, although there have been taboos associated with oral sex. For some people, it may be against their religious beliefs or they may simply find it disgusting. For other people, it is an important part of lovemaking and something they enjoy receiving as well as giving.

A History of Oral Sex

Oral sex has been practised throughout history. Ancient Greek terra cotta vases, 10th-century temples in India, and 19th-century playing cards all portrayed couples engaging in it. For example, the Kama Sutra, an ancient South Asian text that includes instruction on sexual techniques, lists eight ways to perform fellatio.

REAL Research Canadian psychologists Vanier and Byers (2013) interviewed 50 women and 35 men ages 17 to 24 about their attitudes toward oral sex. Several themes emerged in their analysis, among them that oral sex is a symbol of love and commitment, that it is never discussed, and that it requires intense focus upon a partner.

According to Canadian sociologists Hunt and Curtis (2006), oral sex was the topic of shifting discourses throughout the 20th century, going from definitions of perversion to sexual liberalism to problematic behaviour once again by the 2000s with teenage sex. The late 19th and early 20th centuries saw many publications called "marriage manuals" with titles such as *The Sex Technique in Marriage* (Hutton, 1936) and *Ethical Sex Relations* (Whitehead &

Hoff, 1928) but there was no mention of oral sex. These books were written as medical manuals, were steeped in euphemism, and generally considered vaginal intercourse for procreation as the only legitimate form of sexual activity (Melody & Peterson, 1999).

Oral sex first entered marriage manuals later in the century with the suggestion of cunnilingus as a way to lubricate the vagina to get the woman ready for intercourse. Cunnilingus thus became a necessary part of foreplay to prepare women for penetration. Fellatio then entered discussions as a means of reciprocation to the male (Hunt & Curtis, 2006). By the sexual revolution of the 1960s, oral sex became a legitimate sex act in itself and a means of giving pleasure to one's partner. It had in effect become a legitimate form of lovemaking. By the late 1980s, it became a viable alternative to intercourse in that it is less likely to transmit HIV/AIDS. Sex manuals such as *The New Joy of Sex* (Comfort & Rubenstein, 1992) and *Dr. Ruth's Guide to Safer Sex* (Westheimer, 1992) continued to promote it as such (Hunt & Curtis, 2006). Finally, oral sex came fully out of the closet in the United States in January 1998 when President Bill Clinton was discovered to have received fellatio from White House intern Monica Lewinsky, and for the first time, it was mentioned in national news broadcasts.

Today, as Hunt and Curtis note, oral sex has become a legitimate part of adult lovemaking but has become a central focus of concern with sex and teenagers. As one example, "rainbow parties" have been discussed in the media recently where teenage girls wear different colours of lipstick and imprint them on the penises of boys so that the boy with the most colours wins. Such parties, however, seem more of an urban myth in that they are rare if not non-existent (Lewin, 2005). Thus, the history of definitions of oral sex has gone from silence and perversion, to legitimization as a part of lovemaking, to problematic once again.

Incidence of Oral Sex

While there are no comprehensive surveys in Canada, we are able to extrapolate from American data. Kinsey and his associates (Kinsey et al., 1948; Kinsey et al., 1953) found both fellatio and cunnilingus common among both men and women and commonly practised upon the same sex and the other sex, although they varied considerably among people with only an elementary school education (11 percent), only high school (20 percent), and a college education (60 percent). Today, according to Herbenick et al. (2010), most adults in all age groups have engaged in oral sex at some point and rates of oral sex tend to decrease with age. Although only 7 percent of women older than 70 years report giving oral sex to a man in the last year, 43 percent said they had done so at some point in their lives (Herbenick et al., 2010a). Also, men are more likely to have received oral sex (Brewster & Tillman, 2008). Men and women in better health engage in more oral sex than those in poor or failing health (Herbenick et al., 2010).

Among African Americans in the United States, rates of receiving oral sex from the other sex are greater than rates of

Do Couples Break Up over Sexual Incompatibilities?

Do couples break up over sexual incompatibilities? Kinsey and his associates (1948) had the following to say on the matter:

There is a not inconsiderable list of histories in which dissension over oral relations has caused serious disagreements in marriage, and a fair number of divorces have revolved around this question, although the contesting partners rarely disclose the real source of their difficulty when they come to court action. There are several instances of wives who have murdered their husbands because they insisted on mouth-genital contacts. Unfortunately, marriage counselors, clinical psychologists, and psychiatrists have not known enough about the basis biology of these contacts, nor enough about the actual frequencies of such behavior in the population, ..."

Here, Kinsey was referring to cases from the 1930s and 1940s when oral sex had a social shroud of silence surrounding it to the point where many people never though it existed before they married. In those days a request for oral sex by a husband would have often met with shock and abhorrence. Today with greater awareness and more comprehensive sex education, oral sex is considered a normative part of lovemaking.

---

giving it (Dodge et al., 2010). Although 44 percent of Black women have received oral sex from a man, only 37 percent have given it. Among Black men, 53 percent have received oral sex from a woman, but 43 percent have given it. Approximately 7 percent of Black men have given oral sex to men or received it, and 13 percent of Black women have done the same with other women (Dodge et al., 2010). Among Hispanics, 62 percent of men have given oral sex to a woman, 65 percent have received it from a woman, and about half of Hispanic women have given or received oral sex from a man. Rates of same-sex oral sex in Hispanic men and women are lower. Twelve percent of Hispanic women have given oral sex and 10 percent have received it from a woman (Dodge et al., 2010). Those figures are 11 percent and 13 percent respectively for men (Dodge et al., 2010).

Although same-sex oral sex was not commonly reported by women, it was most prevalent among 18- to 24-year-olds (Herbenick et al., 2010a). Five percent to 8 percent of 18- to 59-year-old men have received oral sex from a man in the past year (Herbenick et al., 2010). However, 14 percent of 40- to 49-year-old men and 15 percent of 50- to 59-year-old men have received oral sex from a man in their lifetimes. Between 4 percent and 8 percent of men have performed oral sex on a man in the past year, and more than 10 percent of 40- to 59-year-old men have done the same (see Figure 14.4).

Cunnilingus

Women have historically been inundated with negative messages about their vaginas. Many makers of feminine powders, douches, creams, jellies, and other scented items try to persuade them that their products will make the vagina smell better. As a result, many women express concern about cleanliness during cunnilingus. When their partners do so, fears and anxieties often prevent women from enjoying the experience. This, coupled with many women's lack of familiarity with their own vagina, contributes to strong discomfort with oral sex.

Many men and women find cunnilingus to be erotic. They report that the taste of the vaginal secretions is arousing to them and that they find the vulva beautiful and sexy, including its smell

and taste. For women receiving cunnilingus, they typically want it to begin slowly and they dislike an immediate concentration on the clitoris. A persistent rhythmic caressing of the tongue on the clitoris will cause many women to reach orgasm. Some women enjoy a finger inserted into their vagina or anus at the same time for extra stimulation. Because pregnant women have an increased vascularity of the vagina and uterus, care should be taken to not blow air into a woman's vagina. This can force air into her uterine veins, which can cause a fatal condition known as an air embolism in which an air bubble travels through the bloodstream and can obstruct the vessel (Hill & Jones, 1993; Kaufman et al., 1987; Nicoll & Skupski, 2008; Sánchez et al., 2008).

Although women in often worry that men may find their vaginas unappealing, this is less the case in woman-to-woman

FIGURE **14.4** Gay men use a variety of sexual techniques in their lovemaking.

FIGURE **14.5** Lesbians have been found to be more sexually responsive and more satisfied in their sexual relationships than the heterosexual women.

relationships (see Figure 14.5). As one woman said, "Gay women are very much into each other's genitals.... Not only accepting, but truly appreciative of women's genitals and bodies.... Lesbians are really into women's bodies, all parts" (Blumstein & Schwartz, 1983, p. 238).

Fellatio

Most men enjoy oral sex and many are disappointed if their partners do not like to perform fellatio (Blumstein & Schwartz, 1983). Like lesbian couples, the more oral sex that occurs in gay couples, the more sexually satisfied the couple (Blumstein & Schwartz, 1983).

Before fellatio, many men enjoy having their partners stroke and kiss various parts of their bodies, gradually getting closer to their penis and testicles. Some men like to have their testicles orally stimulated as well. They may also like to have the head of the penis gently licked and sucked while their partner's hand slowly moves up and down the shaft. When the foreskin still covers the head of the penis during erection, some men like to have it retracted before sucking while others do not. It is thus important to know one's partner's preferences. When performing fellatio, it is important to keep the teeth out of the way since this may cause discomfort. Some men like the sensation of being gently scratched with teeth during oral sex, but this must be done very carefully. Generally, a rhythmic up-and-down sucking motion is highly pleasurable and will lead to orgasm. Some men and women are able to take the entire penis into their mouths and throat which increases pleasure considerably. This is known as the *deep throat* technique. Many others are incapable of doing this, however, because of the gagging reflex.

Some men and women are concerned about having their partners ejaculate in their mouths during fellatio. If a person is free from all STIs, swallowing the ejaculate is harmless. Some people enjoy the taste, feel, and idea of tasting and swallowing ejaculate, while others do not. If swallowing is unacceptable, another option may be to spit out the ejaculate or withdraw before ejaculation.

The amount of semen a man ejaculates often depends upon age and on how long it has been since his last ejaculation. If a long period has gone by, generally the amount will be larger. An average ejaculation is approximately one to two teaspoons and consists mainly of fructose, enzymes, and different vitamins, and is about five calories. The taste of the ejaculate can vary depending on a man's use of drugs or alcohol, stress level, and diet (Tarkovsky, 2006).

Anilingus

Anilingus or "rimming" involves licking the anus or the surrounding area. It is a common practice among gay men, less common among heterosexuals, and even less so among lesbians (Diamant et al. 2000). Because the anus is highly sensitive, it can produce considerable pleasure. There are however health risks involved because of contact with human feces. For safer practice, it is wise to place a latex sheath or dental dam over the anal area before proceeding.

Vaginal Intercourse

When people think about sex, they think of vaginal intercourse (Sanders & Reinisch, 1999). Because of its procreational potential, it has long been placed at the centre of lovemaking. Laumann et al (1994) found that a third of survey respondents engaged in vaginal intercourse at least twice a week, another third a few times a month, and the remainder either a few times a year or not at all. Frequency depends on a number of factors such as age. In one sample, 18- to 29-year-olds engage in vaginal intercourse an average of 112 times a year, 30- to 39-year-olds do so an average of 86 times per year, and 40- to 49-year-olds do so an average of 69 times per year (Piccinino & Mosher, 1998). Still, the majority of 18- to 49-year-old men and women reported engaging in vaginal intercourse in the past 90 days (Herbenick et al., 2010a). Like other partnered sexual behaviours, men and women in better health were more likely to report engaging in vaginal intercourse.

During arousal, the vagina becomes lubricated, making penetration easier and providing more pleasure for both partners. It is important for couples to delay vaginal penetration until after lubrication has begun. Penetrating a dry vagina can be uncomfortable for both partners. If a woman is aroused but more lubrication is needed, a water-based lubricant should be used. Many women like a slower pace for intercourse. It can be intimate and erotic to do so slowly circling the hips and varying pressure and sensations.

Although many men try to delay ejaculation until their partners are satisfied with the length of time thrusting, a longer time does not always ensure female orgasm. If intercourse lasts for too long, the vagina may become dry and this can be uncomfortable. Corty and Guardiani (2008) reported that vaginal intercourse typically lasts between three and 13 minutes. Intercourse that lasts only one to two minutes was viewed as too short; more than 13 minutes was considered too long. They recommend that "adequate" vaginal intercourse lasts three to seven minutes and "desirable" intercourse lasts seven to 13 minutes.

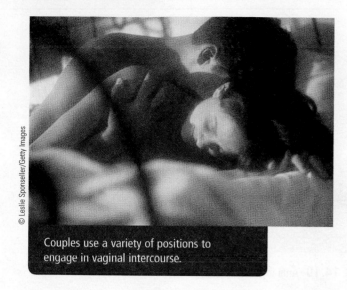

Couples use a variety of positions to engage in vaginal intercourse.

FIGURE **14.7** The female-on-top position.

Positions for Vaginal Intercourse

According to *The Complete Manual of Sexual Positions* (Stewart, 1990), there are 116 vaginal entry positions and in *The New Joy of Sex* (Comfort & Rubenstein, 1992) 112 positions are illustrated. We will limit this discussion to four positions: male-on-top, female-on-top, rear entry, and side by side. There are advantages and disadvantages to each and couples should choose the ones that are best for them.

The male-on-top position (Figure 14.6), also called the missionary position or male superior position, is one of the most common. The woman lies on her back and spreads her legs, often bending her knees to make penetration easier, and the man positions himself on top between her legs. Because his full weight is usually uncomfortable for the woman, the man supports himself on his arms or elbows and knees. This position allows the male to control the thrusting and permits deep penetration. It enables partners to look at each other, kiss, and hug as well. The woman can move her legs up around her partner or even put them on his shoulders. She can also use a pillow under her hips to change the thrusting angle and increase clitoral stimulation. This position may be the most effective for procreation because the penis can be thrust deep into the vagina, which allows the semen to be deposited as deeply as possible. Furthermore, because the woman is lying on her back, the semen does not leak out as easily.

There are some disadvantages to the male-on-top position. If either partner is overweight, or if the female is in the advanced stages of pregnancy, it can be uncomfortable. Also, the deep penetration may be uncomfortable for the woman, especially if her partner has a large penis, which can bump the cervix. It also makes clitoral stimulation difficult and may prevent the woman from moving her hips or controlling the strength or frequency of thrusting. Finally, it may be difficult for the man to support his weight, because his arms and knees may get tired.

For the female-on-top position (Figure 14.7), also called female superior position, the man lies on his back while his partner positions herself on top of him. She can put her knees on either side of him or lie between his legs. By leaning forward, she has greater control over the angle and degree of thrusting and can get more clitoral stimulation. Other variations of this position include the woman sitting astride the man facing his feet or the woman sitting on top of her partner while he sits in a chair. The man's hands are also free and he can caress the woman's body during intercourse. Because this position is face-to-face, the partners are able to see each other, kiss, and have eye contact. On the other hand, it puts the primary responsibility on the female and some women may not feel comfortable taking an active role in vaginal intercourse. Some men may feel uncomfortable letting their partners be on top and may not receive enough penile stimulation to maintain an erection.

The side-by-side position (Figure 14.8) takes the primary responsibility off both partners and allows them to relax during

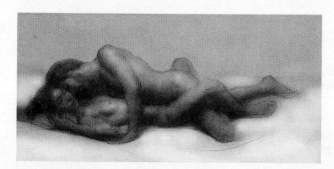

FIGURE **14.6** The male-on-top position.

FIGURE **14.8** The side-by-side position.

FIGURE **14.9** The side rear-entry position.

FIGURE **14.10** Anal intercourse.

vaginal intercourse. Partners lie on their sides and the woman lifts one leg to facilitate penile penetration. This is a good position for couples who want to take it slowly and extend their lovemaking. Both partners have their hands free and can caress each other's bodies. At times, however, couples in this position have difficulties with penetration. It may also be difficult to get a momentum going and achieve deep penetration. Women may also have a difficult time maintaining contact with the male's pubic bone during intercourse and this often decreases the chances of orgasm.

There are many variations to the rear-entry position of vaginal intercourse and the pace can vary with the method chosen. One variation involves a woman on her hands and knees ("doggie style"), while her partner is on his knees behind her. The female may also lie on her stomach with a pillow under her hips while the male enters her from behind. Still another variation is the side-by-side position where the male penetrates the woman from behind (Figure 14.9).

Rear-entry positions provide an opportunity for clitoral stimulation either by the male or the female. They may also provide direct stimulation of the G-spot and be good for women who are in the later stages of pregnancy or who are overweight.

Anal Intercourse

Anal intercourse (Figure 14.10) may be performed by two men, a man and a woman, or two women when one of them wears a strap-on dildo. A strap-on dildo also makes it possible for a women to play the insertive role with a man. Many gay men engage in anal intercourse, although many do not. Laumann et al. (1994) found that 80 percent reported doing so. Some have preferences for the insertive role, others the receptive role, and still other either one.

During anal intercourse, the penis enters his partner's rectum. There are many nerve endings in the anus, which is frequently involved in sexual response even if it is not directly stimulated. Additionally, because men have prostrates, they may be stimulated when they are entered, which may lead to intense pleasure. Many men and women experience orgasm during anal intercourse, especially with simultaneous penile or clitoral stimulation (Maynard et al., 2009). Laumann et al. (1994) found that only 10 percent of male–female couples engaged in anal intercourse, while Herbenick et al. (2010a) found that 10 percent to 14 percent of women aged 18 to 29 did so. For gay men, however, this is a common practice.

Because the rectum is not capable of producing lubrication and the tissue is fragile, it is important that water-based lubricants such as *K-Y Jelly* be used. Oil-based lubricants such as *Vaseline* must be avoided because they will damage latex condoms. Without lubrication, there may be pain, discomfort, and possibly tearing of the tissue in the anus. During anal intercourse, the sphincter muscle must be slowly relaxed or intercourse can be painful. It is thus important to go slowly.

Review Questions

1 Explain why mutual masturbation can be a form of safer sex.

2 Explain the shifts in the ways oral sex has been viewed in society of the years.

3 Describe the differences that have been found in how men and women view oral sex.

4 Identify any gender differences that have been found in the experience of vaginal intercourse.

5 Identify various positions for sexual intercourse. Describe the advantages and disadvantages of each.

Unconventional Sexual Behaviour

The previous sections dealt with mainstream sexual activities. Here, we deal with less conventional ones, which are often viewed negatively by society. We examine sexual activity practised either by a minority of people or by organized minorities in the form of subcultures. Such sexual activity is known collectively as **kink,** which is a colloquial term for unconventional sexual interests. For minority sexual activity, we look mainly at fetishes in masturbation and partnered activity. For subcultural activity, we look mainly at BDSM communities. We discuss fetishes in greater detail in Chapter 16 when we look at paraphilias. Meanwhile, in this section, we restrict our discussion to fetishistic behaviour and BDSM activities that are viewed positively and are not problematic or distressful to the individuals concerned. While some people view unconventional sexual activities as pathological or immoral, others firmly believe that they add richness and variety to their lives.

Fetishistic Sexual Activity

The term *fetish* was originally used in anthropology to describe objects believed to have supernatural powers. It was first applied to West African animistic religions (MacGaffey, 1994). By definition, however, one would have to regard certain objects in Western religions such as the Christian cross or the host in Catholic communions as fetishes as well. The idea of sexual fetishism was first described by French psychologist Alfred Binet, the developer of the IQ Test, in 1887. Richard von Krafft-Ebing described a number of fetishes in his late 19th-century work *Psychopathia Sexualis.*

Fetishes are sexual desires brought about either by parts of bodies or inanimate objects. One may have a fetish for shoes or feet, for lacy brassieres or nipples, or for tight jeans or navels. If the fetish is for a body part, it is more accurately called **partialism**. Because of the 19th-century legacy of pathologizing any sexual interests that deviate from vaginal intercourse, fetishes are often thought of as aberrant today and generally misunderstood. If, however, a fetish does not interfere with normal social or psychological functioning, and if it causes no harm to oneself or others, then there is little reason to consider it an illness. It is merely a variation in what some people find erotically appealing. Many people do bring fetishes into masturbation or sex with partners and, if the partners are amenable, they can enhance lovemaking.

Fetishes and Labelling

It may be argued that labelling something as a fetish is no more than a value judgment. Virtually all heterosexual men are aroused by women's breasts and they typically spend much time on them during lovemaking. There are also magazines devoted entirely to women's breasts. Even with the greatest of fascination and devotion, however, this is not considered a fetish since with breasts there is consensus that they are erotically appealing. With feet,

Canadian singer Justin Bieber promotes the sensuality of men's underwear.

however, there is no consensus and, as a result, liking them is marginalized and considered a fetish. The labelling of something as a fetish while ignoring more popular interests thus becomes a value judgment. The entire body of a man or woman is typically enjoyed by a partner; some people merely find some parts more appealing than others.

There is also consensus by heterosexual males on the erotic appeal of sexy underwear on women—so much so that companies such as *Victoria's Secret* have made fortunes selling lacy panties and bras, teddies, camisoles, and other products meant to arouse men. Other companies such as *Calvin Klein* have marketed men's underwear with pictures of them between the jeans and taut torsos of young models such as Mark Wahlberg and Justin Bieber, accentuating their erotic appeal. The idea is that these items of clothing are sexy to anyone, while there is no consensus on the erotic appeal of shoes and socks, handkerchiefs and tee-shirts, and suits and ties. Being turned on by a woman in a pair of black-lace stockings is considered normal, while liking a man in a pair of sweat socks is not. As a result, there seems little rational basis to label some interests fetishes while others not.

Incidence and Types of Fetishes

Because of the difficulties and subjectivities of definition, the extent to which people have fetishes is unknown. There have also

kink	**partialism**
A catch-all term meaning any unconventional sexual activity.	A fetish for a particular body part such as a foot or nipples.

Variations of Sexual Expression

been no comprehensive surveys to determine how many people have fetishes or what types they have. Kinsey et al. (1948) mentioned fetishes only in the context of men visiting prostitutes who are more likely to be tolerant of or fulfill their desires involving them. Clues to what might be more common can be found in a number of studies such as that by Chalkley and Powell (1983), who looked at a sample of 48 people with fetishes. Among those people, 83 percent of their fetishes involved items of clothing or footwear. Again, because of the way clothing is marketed in Western societies, it seems entirely likely that this would be the most common category. Similarly, Kyongseok et al. (2010) examined 200 videos on YouTube tagged "smoking fetish," where sexy young women are seen smoking. Once again, given the prevalence of such videos together with sexy smoking scenes in popular films such as *Basic Instinct* (1992), such a fetish seems media created as well.

It is also likely that people are far more likely in recent decades to acknowledge their fetishes since knowledge of sex since the days of Kinsey is more widespread. One article in *Contemporary Sexuality* (Once taboo, fetishes now flourishing, 2001) quotes American clinical psychologist Herb Samuels as saying that fetishes were "underground" until the advent of HIV/AIDS, which led people to look for new ways to maintain their sex lives and, thus, there became a greater interest in fetished activity and a lessening of stigma toward it.

Fetishes and Symbolic Representation

Why are some people aroused by high-heeled shoes, cowboy boots, garters, jockstraps, brassieres, and neckties? The answer lies in symbolic representation and association. High-heeled shoes for example are representations of a type of woman who would typically wear them. A person is therefore not aroused by the shoes themselves but their association with that type of woman. Similarly, lacy brassieres might represent another type of woman, a jockstrap might represent an athletic young man, and a cowboy boot might represent a cowboy. Many people have types of other people to whom they are attracted, whether blonde women, powerful women, rugged men, or athletes. The fetish object merely represents those types to the individual and the arousal comes from association. Much of this association is created by media imagery. Victoria's Secret and Calvin Klein, for example, market their products by putting them on sexy young women and men who are ideals that may be arousing to the viewer. That arousal becomes transferred to the products themselves and they may become fetishized. In this respect, this is little different from looking at a souvenir on one's kitchen counter and having a fond memory of the vacation where it was purchased. Objects, by association with their context, may evoke strong feelings and sexual arousal is merely one of them.

Fetish objects are often used in masturbation. A person may hold the fetish object, have it close to look at, or otherwise while masturbating. For that person, doing so can enhance orgasms. Sometimes fetish objects are used in lovemaking. A man may appreciate his wife or girlfriend wearing sexy lingerie, or a gay man might be turned on when his partner wears a jockstrap and sweat socks. Garters may also be arousing to heterosexual men in that they draw attention to women's legs. Although there are

probably a limited number of fetish objects that commonly lead to arousal, there is always a range of possibilities and fetish objects can take many forms.

Situational Erotica and Fetishes

Fetishes are not necessarily restricted to objects or body parts. Some people are also aroused by particular situations where sex occurs or where there has been previous arousal. For example, some men prefer to visit prostitutes because they have been previously excited by them (Monto, 2004). Other people might fantasize about or enjoy sex on a beach, sex in a cheap hotel room, sex in a parked car, an encounter with a perfect stranger, or otherwise. While being aroused by particular situations or scenarios is not necessarily to the level of fetishes, they can be fetishized when arousal is sufficiently enhanced by them. In most cases, however, it is likely that a situation will simply augment arousal.

Because situations and scenarios are arousing, there is an entire industry of hotels with specialized rooms and travel agencies with glossy pictures of people embracing on secluded beaches that suggests to the consumer that sexual activity will be ignited by such situations or that marriages will be rekindled by them. In

Hotel rooms often have rooms with seductive atmospheres which cater to people's sexual desires.

Fetish clubs are known throughout the world catering to men and women with special interests.

The Fursonas of Furries

Furries are people interested in anthropomorphized animal personas (or "fursonas"), some of whom enjoy dressing up in animal costumes. While the sexual aspect of furries is exaggerated by the media, there are those who do enjoy sex with other furries, whether online as cybersex or in real life.

Plante et al. (2011) conducted a large online survey of furries with almost 7000 respondents from 70 countries. The furries tended to be young (a mean age of 23 for those over age 18), and 84 percent were male. Additionally, 67 percent were from the United States and 10.2 percent were from Canada. About half were atheists of agnostics. Furries also seemed to be more fluid in terms of gender—62 percent had a fursona of the same gender, while 5 percent had one of the other gender.

The remainder were at least open to the idea of other-gendered fursonas. Their sexual orientations were also fluid—28 percent identified as exclusively heterosexual, while 20 percent identified as exclusively gay or lesbian. The remainder, a little more than half, were in between. About a third of furries say that sexual attraction is an important part of their participation in the subculture. Many were also in relationships with other furries. While a minority of furries do like to have sex or at least cuddle as their fursonas, it seems according to Plante et al. that most do not. While it might seem logical to classify furry fursonas as a fetish, it seems more in the spirit of whimsical fun than anything else.

© Richard Kalvar/Magnum Photos

Furries are people who enjoy dressing up in animal personas ("fursonas").

Japan there are many "love hotels," where couples can rent rooms for several hours or an entire night (Chaplin, 2007). Because Japanese homes are typically small and privacy is difficult, many Japanese couples say that they have difficulty getting in the mood for sex (Keasler, 2006). Love hotels offer privacy, and the sexual décor is meant to be arousing. Entrances are discreet, there is limited contact with hotel staff, and some hotels offer specific themes such as samurai, jungle, pirate, or BDSM. There may even be a costume rental option offering ones for maids, nurses, schoolgirls, or cheerleaders (Keasler, 2006). In sum, such hotels not only offer privacy for sex but the tools with which to create erotic situations as well.

Internet Communities

One of the drawbacks of having a fetish is that it may be difficult to find partners either tolerant of one's interests or amenable to them. Some people attempt to ignore their fetishes while others do their best to embrace them and turn to the Internet either for visual stimuli or as a way of finding a community of others with the same interests. Available websites may be general for people with a variety of fetishes or specific to one fetish only. *Fetlife* is a more general site launched in Montreal, Quebec, in 2008. On this site, anyone may start a discussion group surrounding any fetish and, as of 2015, there were over 3 million members. There are also blogs by such hosts as *Tumblr*, which cater to almost any fetish as well. Not only are there websites and blogs for clothing fetishes but those pertaining to rubber items, beards, plush toys, and many other interests.

Animal Variations **Animals' Fetishes**

Can animals have fetishes? Yes and no. In humans, a sexual fetish is a matter of an object symbolizing a sexually desired type of person or situation. Sexual arousal is therefore because of symbolic association. With animals there is no symbolizing process but instead a form of Pavlovian conditioning. Cetinkaya and Domjan (2006) conditioned male quail by pairing a terrycloth object with an opportunity to mate with a female. Eventually, half of the quail began to copulate with the object, thus developing a "fetish." Canadian researchers Pfaus et al. (2013) conducted a similar experiment with rats using a "rodent jacket," leading the rats to develop a "fetish" for the jacket. Thus, quail were aroused by terrycloth objects and rats were aroused by rodent jackets. This is not, however, symbolic association but instead a matter of classical conditioning.

The Divine Marquis and Leopold von Sacher-Masoch

The terms *sadism* and *masochism* were originally coined by Richard von Krafft-Ebing in his 19th century work *Psychopathia Sexualis* published in the 1870s—*sadism* for the French aristocrat the Marquis de Sade (1740–1814) and *masochism* for Austrian gothic writer Leopold von Sacher-Masoch (1836–1895).

The Marquis de Sade was a French aristocrat who became famous not only for his violent and blasphemous sexual escapades that transgressed the boundaries of the law, gender, and even age but his literary works as well. Troubles began in 1768 when he met an older prostitute named Rose Keller and brought her back to his chateau on the pretense of needing a housekeeper. He not only whipped her while he masturbated but made her

commit blasphemy toward a crucifix. She escaped out the window and went to the authorities who then arrested the Marquis. Four years later, during an orgy with prostitutes, he accidentally poisoned one of them, although she survived. He fled, but he was condemned to death in absentia not only for the poisoning but for

sodomy upon his manservant, Latour. Eventually, he was imprisoned and ultimately died in an insane asylum. At the age of 70, he had an affair with a jailer's daughter, which lasted until his death.

The Marquis is known not only for his sexual excesses but for his erotic writings, particularly *Justine, or the Misfortunes of Virtue, The 120 Days of Sodom,* and *Philosophy in the Bedroom.* Rather than being regarded as the desperate scrawlings of a madman, these novels came to be known as significant works of philosophy and erotic literature.

Leopold von Sacher-Masoch was the author of the 1869 novel *Venus in Furs* in which a man becomes captivated by a cruel woman wearing fur named Wanda and begs to be her slave. He lived this novel to an extent in his private life with his mistress Baroness Fanny Pistor with whom he signed a contract to be her slave for six months as long as she wore furs when she was in a cruel mood.

The legacy of these two men— one from the 18th century and one from the 19th century—was that they became the namesakes of an entire genre of sexuality and entered a vocabulary beyond sex where any cruel person is a sadist and anyone who welcomes abuse is a masochist.

© Universal Art Archive/Alamy Stock Photo

© INTERFOTO/Alamy Stock Photo

The namesakes of sadism and masochism—the Marquis de Sade and Leopold von Sacher-Masoch.

BDSM

As mentioned, **BDSM** is a set of overlapping acronyms for bondage and discipline (BD), dominance and submission (DS), and sadism and masochism (SM; Stiles & Clark, 2011). The first set refers to the use of restraints, the second to power and control, and the third to pleasure in one's own or another's pain (Hébert & Weaver, 2014). Activities can range from mild to extreme and BDSM practitioners usually refer to non-BDSM activities as "vanilla sex." For many people, BDSM is more than a mere sexual

interest; it is a sexual identity and a sense of belonging to an entire subculture of members who are male, female, and transgender as well as heterosexual, gay, and lesbian. They use the metaphor of "play" for their activities.

Because of the 19th century legacy of placing unconventional sex into medical categories, BDSM is still pathologized and there is a constant debate over whether such an interest is psychologically and socially problematic (Taylor & Ussher, 2001; Kleinplatz & Moser, 2004). Rather than being mentally ill, BDSM enthusiasts are generally highly responsible in their activities and do not suffer from any social or psychological adverse effects. Connolly (2006), for example, administered seven psychometric tests to 32 BDSM practitioners and found no psychopathological traits at all. They were in fact well-adjusted individuals. There is also evidence that interest in BDSM activities is more common than suspected, even

> **BDSM**
> An overlapping set of three acronyms:
> BD = bondage and discipline;
> DS = dominance and submission;
> SM = sadism and masochism.
> Altogether, BDSM.

though they may not be defined as such. Canadian researchers Renault and Byers (1999) gave questionnaires to a sample of university students and found that 65 percent had fantasies of being tied up while 63 percent fantasized about tying someone else up. Because of the proliferation of information on the Internet, it is likely that more and more people are exploring their interests as a result. While attitudes toward BDSM are still negative, more and more people are learning about it (Yost, 2010).

Weinberg et al. (1984) found that BDSM play consists of five social qualities. First is that it involves dominance and submission. One person dominates another and that other submits to the dominant one's authority and power. Second is role-play. Both parties know that they are playing a role outside of reality and each acts it out to varying degrees. When they are in their roles, they say and do things consistent with what might be expected of those roles. When out of them, they are equal partners. Sometimes the roles are highly scripted (e.g., slave owner/slave, mistress/schoolboy) and at other times they are loosely defined under the dominance and submission rubric.

Third and most important is consent. It is here that people who practise BDSM differ from psychopathy where someone might enjoy inflicting pain against another's will. Without consent it is no longer play but rape, sexual coercion, or violence. As an extra measure of safety, players often have a *safe word* (e.g., "banana") where if it is said, all play stops immediately. Fourth, there must be a sexual content to the play. Often, BDSM play does not involve actual sex but still has a sexual content to it whether there is penetration or otherwise. Fifth, players must define what they are doing as BDSM and, thus, have a mutual definition of what is taking place. Without this mutual definition, what is taking place is outside the BDSM rubric.

Some people prefer to play the dominant role ("doms"), while others prefer the submissive role ("subs"). There are also people called "switches," who may play either role depending upon the nature of the other or the situation. Most people, however, prefer one role or the other. If the players are male and female, the dom is often the female, which goes against the patriarchal legacy of men dominating women. A woman who specializes in being a dom is called a **dominatrix** (plural = dominatrices). Because many are sex workers, however, we discuss this more in Chapter 18.

Nordling et al. (2006) looked at a sample of 22 female and 162 male practitioners of BDSM and found significant differences between gay and heterosexual participants. The gay men had higher levels of education and came to BDSM later in life. They also showed a preference for the dominant role while heterosexual men tended to prefer the submissive one. BDSM communities also tended to be more accepting of bisexual people than the mainstream (Lenius, 2001).

Often, to practise BDSM regularly is to be a member of a BDSM community (Lenius, 2001). Doms and subs get to know each other by reputation or experience. BDSM communities tend to be highly organized locally, nationally, and even internationally, with events, contests such as Mr. Leather, gatherings such as the Folsom Street Fair in San Francisco, and conferences. In Canada there are numerous organizations as well as local Internet discussion groups and personal websites.

dominatrix
A woman who specializes in dominating others during BDSM play.

Review Questions

1 In what ways can fetishes be regarded as value judgments?

2 Explain the appeal of fetishes in terms of symbolic representation.

3 How can situations enhance sexual arousal and intimacy?

4 According to Weinberg et al., what are the five components of BDSM?

5 Explain the importance of consent in BDSM play.

Safer Sexual Behaviours

Now that we have explored some of the ways people come together sexually, it is beneficial to discuss ways to do so safely. For a fuller discussion of safer sex practices, see Chapter 7. In general, safer sex means avoiding the exchange of body fluids through barrier means such as condoms and dental damns. In so doing, one can avoid sexually transmitted infections (STIs) and unwanted pregnancies. It also means entering sexual situations with full self-efficacy, full information, and full awareness. Alcohol

and drug use impairs judgment and people may make decisions they later regret.

Because information on condom effectiveness varies, it is important to get information from legitimate and unbiased sources such as SIECCEN. It is also important to learn how to use condoms correctly (see the accompanying Sex in Real Life feature). Another measure of protection is a dental dam, which is a square piece of thin latex stretched across the vulva or anus to prevent the exchange of body fluids during oral sex. Dental dams are available in many drugstores and health clinics across Canada.

How to Use Male Condoms Correctly

1. Store condoms at room temperature and in places where they are not subject to pressure or abrasion such as wallets.

2. Use a new condom for every sex act and check the expiry date.

3. Tear open the package carefully. Do not use teeth or scissors.

4. Place the condom on the head of the penis making sure the rolled up ring is on the outside.

5. Squeeze the tip so that no air is trapped inside and roll the condom down to the base of the penis.

6. Use a water-based and not an oil-based lubricant.

7. After ejaculation, hold the condom in place and withdraw while still erect. Discard.

How to Use Female Condoms Correctly

1. Store condoms at room temperature and in places where they are not subject to pressure or abrasion.

2. Use a new condom for every sex act and check the expiry date.

3. Choose a position that is comfortable for insertion – squatting, raise one leg, lying or sitting down.

4. Make sure the condom is well lubricated; this will help the condom stay in place.

5. Squeeze the inner ring with your thumb and middle finger and insert the inner ring and sheath into the vaginal opening. Using your index finger push the inner ring as far as it will go. The outer ring should remain outside the vagina.

6. When having sex, the penis should be guided into the condom in order to ensure that it does not slip into the vagina outside the condom.

SOURCE: Trojan, "How to Use Condoms Correctly." Retrieved July 28, 2015, from http://trojanprofessional.ca/pdfs/HowtoUse CondomsCorrectly.pdf. © Church & Dwight Co., Inc. Use of C&D property is with the express written permission of Church & Dwight Co., Inc., Princeton, New Jersey.

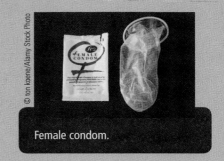

Female condom.

SOURCE: Resources developed by the BC Harm Reduction Strategies and Services Committee, "Female Condoms: Questions and Answers." Retrieved July 28, 2015, from http://www.bccdc.ca/NR/rdonlyres/ 6553335D-039E-4B61-B95D-92E9671464E2/ 0/FemaleCondomsQAAug10.pdf.

Male condom.

Review Questions

1 What are some guidelines for safer sex behaviour?

2 Explain how drinking may be linked to engaging in unsafe sexual behaviour.

Chapter Review

Summary Points

1 Most Canadian college students report being happy with their sex lives and most are in some form of committed relationship. This stands in sharp contrast to the United States where numerous studies report lack of happiness.

2 Celibacy, abstinence, and asexuality all refer to not having sex. Celibacy suggests a permanent state where a vow not to have sex is taken, abstinence suggests a temporary state where one is waiting for love or marriage, and asexuality is a lack of interest in sex. There is discussion in academia as to whether asexuality is a bona fide sexual orientation.

3 Many asexuals undergo a "coming out process" where they realize their difference, consider whether there is something wrong with them, eventually reach an understanding of themselves, and seek out a community of people like themselves.

4 Men generally think about sex more than women and people who have more liberal attitudes toward sex and more sexual experience generally have more explicit sexual fantasies. Most sexual fantasies have three parts: characters, contexts, and sexual activity. They can help enhance masturbation and explore sexual activities one might find taboo.

5 The early church fathers of Christianity stated that thoughts of sex are sinful and synonymous with adultery itself. This influenced Christian thought for centuries. Early psychiatry viewed sexual fantasies as symptomatic of mental disturbance and sexual frustration.

6 Women tend to have more emotional and romantic fantasies, while men tend to have more assertive and sexual ones. Women commonly have fantasies of being forced to have sex. Theories as to why this is so are as follows: (1) If they see themselves as forced, they avoid blame and guilt over sex; (2) they tend to be more open toward sex; (3) they wish to be so irresistible that men cannot control themselves. It is important to note that fantasies of forced sex in no way indicate a wish for it to be a reality.

7 Masturbation is a harmless activity practised by the majority of people. The Biblical story of Onan is often cited as the beginning of negative attitudes toward it, as it became known as onanism. By the 16th century, it was associated with numerous medical consequences, including back pains, epilepsy, and pimples. John Harvey Kellogg, the developer of breakfast cereals, was a vehement anti-masturbation campaigner and even recommended circumcision as a way to prevent it.

8 It was not until Kinsey's research in the 20th century that people began to view masturbation as harmless. There are still religious proscriptions against it. Masturbation can be augmented with sex toys such as dildos and vibrators which are sold either through mail order or during private functions at people's homes.

9 Cybersex lies in limbo somewhere between masturbation and partnered sex. Telephone sex became popular by the 1980s and commercialized, but such businesses have suffered greatly because of the Internet. Typically during cybersex, people engage in erotic chats often involving role playing, where each plays a part in an unfolding erotic story. Cybersex provides anonymity, convenience, and an opportunity to play out one's fantasies.

10 Teledildonics are devices that hook up to the body, and control of them may be given to remote others. There are now expensive life-like sex dolls, and robotic sex is at its primitive stages.

11 Foreplay used to be defined as activity necessary to get a woman sufficiently aroused for vaginal intercourse. Since the advent of HIV/AIDS, people have paid far more attention to non-penetrative sex acts as means to pleasure in themselves.

12 Manual sex (hand jobs or fingering) and mutual masturbation may be pleasurable to individuals and it is thus important to learn the ways in which one's partner enjoys being stimulated in this way. A small minority of individuals engage in fisting, which is the insertion of the fist into the vagina or rectum.

13 There are three types of oral sex: fellatio upon a man, cunnilingus upon a woman, and anilingus upon either sex. Oral sex may be done simultaneously as "sixty-nine." Definitions of oral sex have shifted from perversion in the early 20th century, to a legitimate form of lovemaking by the 1980s. National surveys in the United States have found oral sex to be common in both sexes.

14 Vaginal intercourse is the only act that can only be done by a male-female couple, although lesbians may also do so with a strap-on dildo. There are four main positions: male on top, female on top, side by side, and rear entry. Anal intercourse can be practised by male-female or male-male couples.

15 There is a wide variety of unconventional sexual behaviours such as fetishistic activities and BDSM. Where consent is involved and where there are no physical, social, or psychological ill effects, they may be enjoyed by anyone who finds them appealing.

16 There are several types of fetishes—those for inanimate objects, those for parts of bodies (partialism), and those for erotic situations. The labelling of something as a fetish is problematic and is often regarded as a value judgment. Fetishes are generally symbolic representations of types of people. High-heeled shoes, for example, may be erotically appealing by association with the type of woman one imagines wearing them.

17 BDSM involves bondage and discipline, dominance and submission, and sadism and masochism. People who practise these activities generally show no psychopathological effects and are highly conscientious about informed consent. There are five components to BDSM—dominance, role play, consent, a sexual context, and mutual definition. Many who practise BDSM are members of highly organized BDSM communities.

18 Condoms are important means of protection. People should know how to use them properly and avoid drinking alcohol if planning to have sex.

Critical Thinking Questions

1 Canadian college students seem to be far happier with their sex lives and seem more likely to be in committed relationships. Why do you think this is so?

2 Most people who identify as asexual say that they have no desire to have sex, nor do they think about it. Why are they often thought of as psychologically maladapted, and why does society have a hard time accepting them?

3 Men have more assertive and impersonal sexual fantasies, and women have more affectionate and romantic ones. What does this say about gender differences? Are the differences because of socialization or biology?

4 People often continue to masturbate after they are married. Is this indicative of a failed marriage or is it simply part of human sexual nature?

5 Two strangers are chatting with each other through text on line. One is in Canada, the other in New Zealand. They are having cybersex. Is this more masturbation or more partnered sexual activity?

6 When two men or two women have sex, each knows how the other's body responds and each can relate to what the other is feeling. When a man and woman have sex, this is not the case. Does this lack of familiarity detract from sexual intimacy or somehow enhance it?

7 How has oral sex transformed from problematic in the early 20th century to legitimate by the 1960s to problematic once again in the 1990s?

8 If a person has a fetish or is into BDSM and he or she finds a willing partner, is there anything wrong with these practices?

Websites

Asexual Visibility and Education Network (AVEN)   AVEN is a primary online resource for asexual people. It offers links to other sites, blogs, discussion groups, information and updates, and personal sites for people looking for non-sexual relationships. (http://www.sexuality.org)

Electronic Journal of Human Sexuality   This online publication of the Institute for Advanced Study of Human Sexuality in San Francisco disseminates information about all aspects of human sexuality. It offers a database of research articles, book reviews, and posters from various conference presentations. (http://www.ejhs.org)

The Sex Information and Education Council of Canada   SEICCAN is an organization that promotes comprehensive education about sexuality as well as individuals' rights to make responsible and informed choices about their own sexual behaviour. (http://sieccan.org)

Canadian Federation for Sexual Health   Formerly called Planned Parents Federation of Canada, the CFSH supports access to sexual health education and provides services within communities. (http://cfsh.ca)

15 Challenges to Sexual Functioning

Dr. Woet Gianotten, co-founder of the International Society in Sexuality and Cancer, is an expert in oncosexology, an area of medicine that focuses on the sexual and relational needs of patients with cancer, as well as their partners. As a physician and sexologist, he has spent many years exploring how disease, cancer, physical impairments, and medical interventions affect sexual functioning. Intrigued by the benefits of a satisfying sexual relationship, he began asking, "How can a good sex life affect physical health?" He strongly believes that an active and satisfying sex life can lead to better health and a greatly improved quality of life. I caught up with Dr. Gianotten in Utrecht, Holland, to learn more about his work.

Many doctors are hesitant to talk to patients about sex, and when they don't ask about it, many cancer patients feel anxious or embarrassed and think they shouldn't

have sexual needs. I have learned that patients are often afraid to talk to their doctors about sex, and that doctors are afraid to talk to their patients about sex. The funny thing is, I have also found that sex therapists are often afraid to talk to patients about cancer! When I ask patients if they would like it if their doctor asked them about their sex lives, all my patients say "Yes!" It would help them to feel recognized as a sexual being and would let them know they are still a member of the living tribe. Maintaining a regular and satisfying sex life helps them feel loved, secure, and more like a man or woman. In addition to this, orgasms release endorphins and can decrease pain and suffering. Even those in the end stages of their lives desire sex and orgasms. One woman told me that she had more sex during the last days of her husband's life because they were so afraid that each day would be his last.

Sexual expression and orgasm are important aspects of many people's lives. One 65-year-old woman I met was prescribed medication to help alleviate her depression after her husband died. Sometime later, she entered into a new relationship but found that she was unable to reach orgasm. She was one of those women who always enjoyed an active sex life—even when her husband was dying. But she was a plain woman, and when she went to her physician to talk about her problems reaching orgasm, he asked her if an orgasm was really that important to her. She told him, "If I can't get an orgasm, please give me pills to die." ▌▌

S exual health is important to our overall health and quality of life. Although many people might believe that satisfactory sexual functioning comes naturally, we know that many men and women experience challenges to their sexual functioning. In this chapter, we explore how physiological and psychological issues, together with chronic illnesses and disabilities, can create problems in sexual functioning, and we explore current treatments for these problems.

Challenges to Sexual Functioning

As we begin our exploration of challenges to sexual functioning, it is important to point out that sexual problems are quite common. Many people experience times when they do not feel sufficiently aroused, have a lower level of enthusiasm, or have trouble relaxing during sex. In fact, the majority of couples report periodic sexual problems (E. Frank et al., 1978). The majority of the time these problems do not interfere with overall sexual functioning and they go away on their own. However, for some people, the problems continue and may even get worse over time.

Defining a sexual problem can be difficult. If a woman can't reach orgasm during intercourse or a man can't get an erection one night, would you say they have a sexual problem? To help clarify definitions, some sex therapists in Canada and the United States use the *Diagnostic and Statistical Manual of Mental Disorders* (DSM), which provides diagnostic criteria for the most common sexual problems. It is occasionally updated, with the fifth edition published in 2013 (referred to as the DSM-5; American Psychiatric Association, 2013). Although the DSM has been an important tool in helping to diagnose and classify sexual problems, it has some limitations. First, the DSM has used a physiological framing of sexual problems, which fails to acknowledge the relational aspects of sexual behaviour (Basson, 2000; Tiefer, 1991). Although physiological functions, such as erection and lubrication, may be important aspects of sexual functioning, so too are relationship, culture, and gender issues, which are acknowledged but not dealt with directly in the DSM-5 section entitled "Sexual Dysfunction."

It is also important to point out that, although some individuals who experience sexual problems are not distressed by them, others do feel distressed and seek out therapy. When an individual does seek out sex therapy, it typically begins with a medical evaluation to explore any physiological issues that might be contributing to the sexual problem. This is not always an easy task because psychological and physiological factors can overlap. Let's take a look at some of these factors.

Psychological Challenges to Sexual Functioning

A variety of psychological factors can challenge sexual functioning, including unconscious fears, ongoing stress, anxiety, depression, guilt, anger, fear of intimacy, dependency, abandonment, and concern over loss of control (Reynaert et al., 2010). Anxiety can play an important role in developing and maintaining sexual problems (Figure 15.1). **Performance fears**, distractions, shifts in attention, or preoccupation during sexual arousal may interfere with the ability to respond sexually (Bancroft et al., 2005; Kaplan, 1974; Masters & Johnson, 1970). When anxiety levels are high, physiological arousal may be impossible. A lack of privacy or feeling rushed can also contribute to sexual problems.

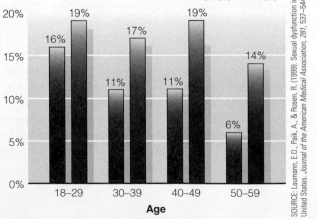

Although our sexual response changes as we age, many older couples still enjoy an active, satisfying sex life.

performance fears
The fear of not being able to perform during sexual behaviour.

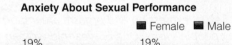

FIGURE **15.1** Percentage of self-reported anxiousness about performance during sex, by gender and age.

SOURCE: Laumann, E.O., Paik, A., & Rosen, R. (1999). Sexual dysfunction in the United States. *Journal of the American Medical Association, 281*, 537–544.

Throughout this textbook we discuss various components of healthy and successful relationships, including trust, respect, and the ability to communicate one's needs. Because sexual problems often occur within the context of intimate relationships, all of these issues can affect sexual functioning. Feeling unappreciated, anger, insecurity, resentment, conflict, or a lack of trust can lead to problems with sexual functioning.

Physiological Challenges to Sexual Functioning

Healthy sexuality depends on a fine interplay of vascular, hormonal, and neurological functioning. However, a variety of physiological factors can interfere with these functions including various injuries, disabilities, illnesses, and diseases. Treatments for various diseases, such as chemotherapy and radiation, can also contribute to sexual problems (Bessede et al., 2011; Ho et al., 2011; Ochsenkühn et al., 2011; Smith, 2010).

We also know that prescription drugs, such as **psychotropic medications** and birth control pills, can affect certain aspects of sexual functioning (see Chapter 6 for more information about birth control usage; Fava et al., 2011; Strohmaier et al., 2011; Yee, 2010). Non-prescription drugs such as tobacco, alcohol, marijuana, LSD, and cocaine may also affect sexual functioning.

Finally, the common physical changes of aging can affect sexual functioning. As men and women age, these physical changes contribute to an increased prevalence of sexual problems (Beaudreau et al., 2011; Camacho & Reyes-Ortiz, 2005; Yassin & Saad, 2008; Yee, 2010). We will discuss treatment for various physiological factors that affect sexual health and function later in this chapter.

Evaluating Sexual Problems

For a sex therapist or physician to formulate a treatment plan for a sexual problem, it is important that the therapist understand more about how the patient experiences the problem. For example, how long has it been going on? Has it always happened or is it fairly new? A **primary sexual problem** is one that has always existed, whereas a **secondary sexual problem** is one that develops after a period of adequate functioning.

Therapists also need to know the context of the sexual problem: Does it occur all the time or just some of the time? A **situational sexual problem** is a problem that occurs during certain sexual activities or with certain partners. A **generalizable sexual problem** is a problem that occurs in every situation, during every type of sexual activity, and with every sexual partner. It is important to clarify these differences, for they may affect treatment strategies. For instance, primary problems tend to have more biological or physiological causes, whereas secondary problems tend to have more psychological causes.

Treating Sexual Problems

In Canada, treatment of most sexual problems begins with a medical history and workup to identify any physiological causes. In addition to a medical history and examination, it is also important to evaluate any past sexual trauma or abuse that may cause or contribute to the problem. After identifying potential causes, the next step is to determine a plan of treatment. Such treatment may be **multimodal,** involving more than one type of therapy.

Much of the current clinical research today focuses on developing new drugs, like Viagra, to treat sexual problems (even though a number of problems may be caused by or worsened by other medications). There is also a brisk business in health supplements to aid in sexual functioning, including **aphrodisiacs** (see Sex in Real Life feature later in the chapter).

We will discuss illness, disability, and sexual functioning later in this chapter, but now let's turn to specific sexual problems and treatment options. Problems commonly occur with sexual desire or arousal, orgasm, or pain during sexual behaviour.

REAL Research Many men and women who experience sexual problems do not talk about their concerns with their health care providers, mostly because they feel embarrassed and/or lack the communication skills to do so (Kingsberg & Knudson, 2011).

psychotropic medications Medications prescribed for psychological disorders, such as depression.	**secondary sexual problem** A sexual problem that occurs after a period of normal sexual functioning.	**generalizable sexual problem** A sexual problem that occurs in every sexual situation.	**aphrodisiac** A substance that increases, or is believed to increase, a person's sexual desire.
primary sexual problem A sexual problem that has always existed.	**situational sexual problem** A sexual problem that occurs only in specific situations.	**multimodal** Using a variety of techniques.	

Review Questions

1 Identify and describe some of the psychological factors that have been found to interfere with sexual functioning.

2 Identify and describe some of the physiological factors that have been found to interfere with sexual functioning.

3 Explain how sexual problems are evaluated and how this might affect treatment strategies.

4 Explain the approach to treatment of sexual problems.

Challenges to Sexual Functioning **391**

Problems with Sexual Desire

Problems with sexual desire involve a deficient or absent desire for sexual activity. There may be a lack of sexual fantasies, a reduction of or absence in initiating sexual activity, or a decrease in self-stimulation.

The DSM-5 has two categories of sexual desire disorders: female sexual interest/arousal disorder and male hypoactive sexual desire disorder.

Female Sexual Interest/Arousal Disorder

In the DSM-5 (2013), **female sexual interest/arousal disorder** (p. 433) is defined as:

A. *Lack of, or significantly reduced, sexual interest/arousal, as manifested by at least three of the following:*

 1) *Absent/reduced interest in sexual activity*
 2) *Absent/reduced sexual/erotic thoughts or fantasies*
 3) *No/reduced initiation of sexual activity, and typically unreceptive to a partner's attempts to initiate.*
 4) *Absent/reduced sexual excitement/pleasure during sexual activity in almost all or all (approximately 75%–100%) sexual encounters (in identified situational contexts or, if generalized, in all contexts).*
 5) *Absent/reduced sexual excitement/pleasure in response to any internal or external sexual/erotic cues (e.g., written, verbal, visual)*
 6) *Absent/reduced genital or nongenital sensations during sexual activity in almost all or all (approximately 75%–100%) sexual encounters (in identified situational contexts or, if generalized, in all contexts).*

B. *The systems in Criterion A must have persisted for a minimum duration of approximately 6 months.*

C. *The symptoms in Criterion A must cause clinically significant distress in the individual.*

D. *The sexual dysfunction is not better explained by a nonsexual mental disorder or as a consequence of severe relationship distress or other significant stressors and is not attributable to the effects of a substance/medication or another medical condition.*

SOURCE: Reprinted with permission from the Diagnostic and Statistical Manual of Mental Disorders, Fifth Edition, (Copyright © 2013). American Psychiatric Association. All Rights Reserved.

Male Hypoactive Sexual Desire Disorder

In the DSM-5 (2013), **male hypoactive sexual disorder** (p. 440) is defined as:

A. *Persistently or recurrently deficient (or absent) sexual/erotic thoughts or fantasies and desire for sexual activity. The judgement of deficiency is made by the clinician, taking into account factors that affect sexual functioning, such as age and general and socio-cultural contexts of the individual's life.*

B. *The systems in Criterion A must have persisted for a minimum duration of approximately 6 months.*

C. *The symptoms in Criterion A must cause clinically significant distress in the individual.*

D. *The sexual dysfunction is not better explained by a nonsexual mental disorder or as a consequence of severe relationship distress or other significant stressors and is not attributable to the effects of a substance/medication or another medical condition.*

SOURCE: Reprinted with permission from the Diagnostic and Statistical Manual of Mental Disorders, Fifth Edition, (Copyright © 2013). American Psychiatric Association. All Rights Reserved.

When diagnosing either of these disorders (and the DSM-5 disorders discussed in the remainder of this chapter), trained professionals need to also determine (a) whether the disorder is lifelong or was acquired at some point during development or in adulthood, (b) whether the disorder is generalizable to all situations or only happens in certain contexts, and (c) specify the severity of the disorder as mild moderate or severe. See Figure 15.2 for more information on lack of interest in sex.

Psychological factors that may contribute to either of these disorders include a lack of attraction to one's partner, fear of intimacy or pregnancy, marital or relationship conflicts, religious concerns, depression, and other psychological disorders (Lai, 2011).

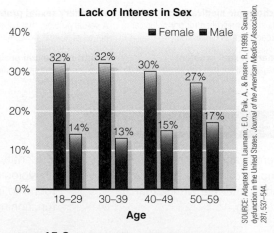

FIGURE **15.2** Percentage of self-reported lack of interest in sex, by gender, ethnicity, and age.

female sexual interest/arousal disorder	male hypoactive sexual desire disorder
Diminished or absent sexual interest or desire in females.	Diminished or absent sexual desire and a lack of sexual thoughts or fantasies.

Desire disorders can also result from negative messages about sexuality while growing up, treating sex as a chore, a concern over loss of control, or a negative body image (Heiman & LoPiccolo, 1992). In addition, eating disorders, sexual coercion, and sexual abuse have also been found to be associated with problems of desire (Carter et al., 2007; Gilmore et al., 2010; Pinheiro et al., 2010; Rellini et al., 2011). In one study of survivors of sexual assault, more than half had long-lasting problems with sexual desire (Campbell et al., 2006).

Physiological factors, such as hormonal problems, medication side effects, chronic use of alcohol, chronic illness, and treatment for various illnesses may also contribute to decreased sexual desire (Basson et al., 2010; Bessede et al., in press; Graziottin, 2007; Ho et al., 2011; Leiblum et al., 2006; Lutfey et al., 2008; Ochsenkühn et al., 2011; Smith, 2010).

Treating Arousal and Sexual Interest Disorders

Many therapists consider problems with arousal or sexual desire to be one of the most complicated sexual problems to treat. As we discussed previously, treatment first involves a medical workup to identify any physiological causes. A psychological evaluation will explore any past sexual trauma or abuse that may interfere with sexual desire or interest.

A variety of different treatment options are available. Cognitive–behavioural therapy, a form of psychotherapy that emphasizes the importance of how a person thinks and the effect these thoughts have on a person's feelings and behaviours, has offered promising results. These types of therapy are brief, highly instructional, and structured. The client may also be assigned homework exercises to help identify these motivations (Brotto, Basson, Carlson & Zhu, 2013; Brotto & Basson, 2014).

In 2000 the EROS therapy device was cleared by the FDA in the United States, and shortly after this became available in Canada as a prescription device for the treatment of female sexual arousal and desire problems (see nearby photo; Wilson et al.,

2001). The small, battery-powered device is designed to be used in the privacy of a woman's own home. It creates a gentle suction on the clitoris and genital area, which increases blood flow and leads to clitoral engorgement. The clitoral engorgement triggers responses in the vaginal nerves, which increases sexual stimulation and sensations and causes vaginal lubrication. Studies have found that the EROS device can help increase vaginal lubrication and vasocongestion.

Since the release of Viagra for men in 1998, there has been a rush of research trying to find the magic pill for women (Berman et al., 2003; Caruso et al., 2006; Feldhaus-Dahir, 2010). Although some studies have evaluated the use of Viagra in women, overall, it has been found to provide little benefit in the treatment of female sexual arousal and desire problems (Alexander et al., 2011; Basson et al., 2002; Basson, 2010; Snapes, Zborowski & Siems, 2010).

In the last several years, there was growing interest in a nasal spray inhaler dubbed PT-141 (bremelanotide) for treatment of female sexual arousal and desire problems, which showed some promise in increasing sexual interest and behaviours in women by stimulating the central nervous system (Diamond et al., 2006; Pfaus et al., 2007; Safarinejad, 2008; Shadiack et al., 2007). However, in 2008, the FDA reduced clinical trials of PT-141 because of safety concerns (Diamond et al., 2006; Perelman, 2007; Pfaus et al., 2007; Safarinejad, 2008; Shadiack et al., 2007). Limited ongoing trials continue to evaluate this drug and variations of the drug. Studies have also been conducted on a variety of **vasoactive agents** to reduce female sexual arousal and desire problems, including Vasomax, or phentolamine. Although testosterone has been used in women, this has been controversial (Hubayter & Simon, 2008; Talakoub et al., 2002). Because of safety concerns, approval of products for women that contain testosterone have not been granted (Fabre et al., 2011). As of 2015, the FDA, Health Canada and the U.S. Food and Drug Administration have not approved any medications for arousal and desire disorders in women, although a variety of medications have been proposed (Fabre et al., 2011; Feldhaus-Dahir, 2010).

As of 2015, no Health Canada–approved medications were available for the treatment of low sexual desire in women. Research continues to explore a variety of pharmacological treatments for women, including the drug Gepirone, other methods of testosterone administration, and medications that act on the central nervous system (Fabre et al., 2011; Palacios, 2011).

Pharmacological treatment has also been used in men with low sexual desire. Because testosterone is largely responsible for male sexual desire, men with low testosterone levels have historically been treated with testosterone injections. However, researchers have been unable to show a consistent and beneficial role of testosterone in increasing sexual desire in men (Allan et al., 2008; Isidori et al., 2005). Overall, the majority of men who experience low sexual desire have normal levels of testosterone (Wespes & Schulman, 2002).

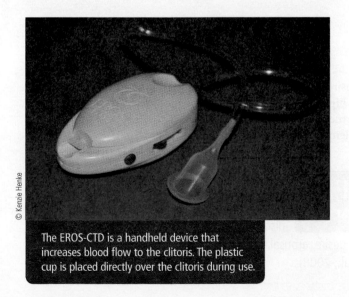

© Kenzie Henke

The EROS-CTD is a handheld device that increases blood flow to the clitoris. The plastic cup is placed directly over the clitoris during use.

vasoactive agent
Medication that causes dilation of the blood vessels.

What Is an Aphrodisiac?

Throughout history, people from primitive—and not so primitive—cultures have searched for the "ultimate" aphrodisiac to enhance sexual interest and performance. Oysters, for example, have been reported to increase sexual desire, although this has never been proved. The idea that oysters

In Bangkok, Thailand, a vendor is pushing cobra blood to improve sexual drive. Customers choose their own snake; then the snake is split open with a razor blade. An incision is made in the major artery of the snake, and all the blood is drained into a wineglass. The blood is then mixed with warm whiskey and a dash of honey. Users believe it helps their sex drive.

are an aphrodisiac may have originated from their resemblance to male testicles, or even to female ovaries. Ancient people believed that food with the shape or qualities of the genitals possessed aphrodisiac qualities; seeds of all kinds were associated with fertility and desire. Scientists have also reported that watermelon can increase sexual desire and interest (Santa Ana, 2008).

In various cultures, carrots, cucumbers, chili peppers, rhino horns, and various seafood, as well as eggs and poppy seeds, were thought to increase sexual desire. The market for so-called aphrodisiacs in some countries has added to the decline of some endangered species, such as the rhinoceros, valued for its horn.

There are no proven aphrodisiacs, but it is possible that if a person thinks something will increase his or her sexual desire, it just might do so (Shamloul, 2010). Simply believing something will increase desire may cause it to work. Here are some of the most popular substances that have been thought to increase sexual desire:

- *Alcohol.* Although some people believe that alcohol increases their sexual desire, in actuality, it merely decreases anxiety and inhibitions, and then only in low doses. In large amounts, alcohol can impair sexual functioning.

- *Amyl nitrate.* Amyl nitrate (also called "snappers" or "poppers") is thought to increase orgasmic sensations. It is

inhaled from capsules that are "popped" open for quick use. Amyl nitrate causes a rapid dilation of arteries that supply the heart and other organs with blood, which may cause warmth in the genitals. Amyl nitrate may dilate arteries in the brain, causing euphoria or giddiness, and relax the sphincter muscle to ease penetration during anal sex. Adverse effects include severe dizziness, migraine headaches, and fainting. (Amyl nitrate is used by cardiac patients to reduce heart pain.)

- *Ginseng.* Ginseng is an herb that has been thought to increase sexual desire. Preliminary research has found it may have some positive aphrodisiac properties, but more research is needed to confirm (Shamloul, 2010).

- *Marijuana.* Reduces inhibitions and may improve mood. No proven effect on sexual desire.

- *Spanish fly.* Consists of ground-up beetle wings (cantharides) from Europe and causes inflammation of the urinary tract and dilation of the blood vessels. Although some people find the burning sensation arousing, Spanish fly may cause death from its toxic side effects.

- *Yohimbine*: **Yohimbine** comes from the African Yohimbe tree. Preliminary research has found it may have some mild aphrodisiac properties, but this does not support its widespread use (Shamloul, 2010).

Sometimes it is not one partner's level of desire that is the problem but the **discrepancy in desire** between the partners. Many couples experience differences in their levels of desire—one partner may desire sex more often than the other. If Lisa wants to have sex once a week, but her partner wants sex every day, which partner do you think would be identified as having a problem? If you guessed Lisa, you're right. Often the partner with a lower level

of desire will show up at a therapist's office and not the partner with higher desire (R.C. Rosen & Leiblum, 1987). But if Lisa had a partner with a similar level of desire, there would be no sexual problems.

yohimbine
Produced from the bark of the African yohimbe tree; often used as an aphrodisiac.

discrepancy in desire
Differences in levels of sexual desire in a couple.

REAL Research Sexual problems are common in men and women who experience post-traumatic stress disorder, which can affect overall sexual activity, desire, arousal, orgasm, and satisfaction (Chudakov et al., 2008).

Treating Sexual Problems in Other Cultures

Sex therapy in Canada and the United States has been criticized for its adherence to Western sexual attitudes and values, with an almost total ignorance of cultural differences in sexual problems and therapy. Our view of sex tends to emphasize that activity is pleasurable (or at least natural), both partners are equally involved, couples need and want to be educated about sex, and communication is important to have good sexual relationships (Lavee, 1991; So & Cheung, 2005). It is important to recognize, however, that these ideas might not be shared outside North America or within different ethnic groups; therefore, Masters and Johnson's classic therapy model is much less acceptable to these groups. Sexual goals are different among cultural groups with an egalitarian ideology than among those without (Lau et al., 2005). An egalitarian ideology views mutual sexual pleasure and communication as important, whereas non-egalitarian ideologies view heterosexual intercourse as the goal and men's sexual pleasure as more important than women's (Reiss, 1986). Double standards of sexual pleasure are common, for example, in many Portuguese, Mexican, Puerto Rican, and Latino groups. Some Asian groups also often have strong cultural prohibitions about discussing sexuality. So North American values such as open communication, mutual satisfaction, and accommodation to a partner's sexuality may not be appropriate in working with people from these cultures.

In cultures in which low female sexual desire is not viewed as a problem, hypoactive sexual desire wouldn't be viewed as a sexual problem; it would be an acceptable part of female sexuality. In some Muslim groups, for example, the only problems that exist are those that interfere with men's sexual behaviour (Lavee, 1991).

Approaches to sexual problems also differ outside North America. Some cultures believe in supernatural causes of sexual disorders (such as the man being cursed by a powerful woman or being given the evil eye; So & Cheung, 2005). Malay and Chinese men who experience erectile disorders tend to blame their wives for the problem, whereas Indian men attribute their problem to fate (Low et al., 2002). However, Asian culture has also produced the Tantric ceremonial sexual ritual, which might be viewed as therapy for sexual disorders.

Tantric sex involves five exercises (Voigt, 1991). First, a couple begins by developing a private ritual to prepare them to share sexual expression: the lighting of candles; using perfume, lotions, music, a special bed or room; certain lighting patterns; massage; reciting poetry together; or meditating. Then they synchronize their breathing by lying together and "getting in touch" with each other. Direct eye contact is sustained throughout the ritual. (Couples often say that they feel uncomfortable using eye contact, but with practice it becomes very powerful.)

Next, "motionless intercourse" begins, in which the couple remains motionless at the peak of the sensual experience. For many couples, this may be during the time of initial penetration. Initially, this motionlessness may last only a few minutes, building up to increasingly longer periods. The final aspect of the Tantric ritual is to expand the sexual exchange without orgasm, resulting in an intensification of the sexual–spiritual energy (this is similar to Masters and Johnson's technique of delaying orgasm to enjoy the physical sensations of touching and caressing).

Review Questions

1 Differentiate the problems of desire that men and women may experience.

2 Explore some of the possible causes for the problems of sexual desire and interest.

3 Identify the strategies for treating desire and sexual interest problems.

Problems with Sexual Arousal

In men, **sexual arousal disorders** can lead to **erectile disorder (ED)**. These problems can occur even when a person reports adequate focus, intensity, and duration of sexual stimulation. Disorders can be primary or, more commonly, secondary, in that they only occur with a certain partner or specific sexual behaviour.

REAL Research Hair loss treatments, including Propecia and Minoxidil, have been found to cause various adverse sexual effects in men, such as reduced sexual interest and erection and orgasm problems, and these effects were found to last for up to 40 months after discontinuing the treatment (Irwig & Kolukula, 2011).

---

sexual arousal disorder
Diminished or absent response of sexual excitation to an arousing stimulus.

erectile disorder (ED)
Diminished or absent ability to attain or maintain, until completion of the sexual activity, an adequate erection.

Erectile Disorder

Normal erectile functioning involves neurological, endocrine, vascular, and muscular factors. Psychological factors including fear of failure and performance anxiety may also affect erectile functioning. Anxiety has been found to have a cyclical effect on erectile functioning: If a man experiences a problem getting an erection one night, the next time he engages in sexual behavior he remembers the failure and becomes anxious. This anxiety, in turn, interferes with his ability to have an erection.

REAL Research

A Finnish study found that regular vaginal intercourse in heterosexual men protects against the development of erectile disorders among men aged 55 to 75 years (Koskimäki et al., 2008).

On Your Mind

Is erectile disorder hereditary?

No, erectile disorder itself is not hereditary. However, certain diseases, such as diabetes, may have a heritable component and can lead to an erectile disorder or other sexual problems. It is important to catch these diseases early so that medical intervention can decrease any possible sexual adverse effects.

ED is defined as the persistent inability to obtain or maintain an erection sufficient for satisfactory sexual behavior. ED affects millions of men, and the incidence increases with age (Figure 15.3). Whereas 12 percent of men younger than 59 experience ED, 22 percent of men aged 60 to 69, and 30 percent of men older than 69 experience ED (Bacon et al., 2003; Costabile et al., 2008; Liu et al., 2010; Lue, 2000).

Approximately 70 percent of ED cases have a physical basis, with the major risk factors being diabetes, high cholesterol levels, or chronic medical illnesses (Fink et al., 2002; Yassin & Saad, 2008). In many cases, ED is due to a combination of factors. Unfortunately, when health care providers identify a physical problem (such as hypertension) in a patient suffering from ED, they might not continue to explore the psychological factors. Or if a psychological problem is found first (such as a recent divorce),

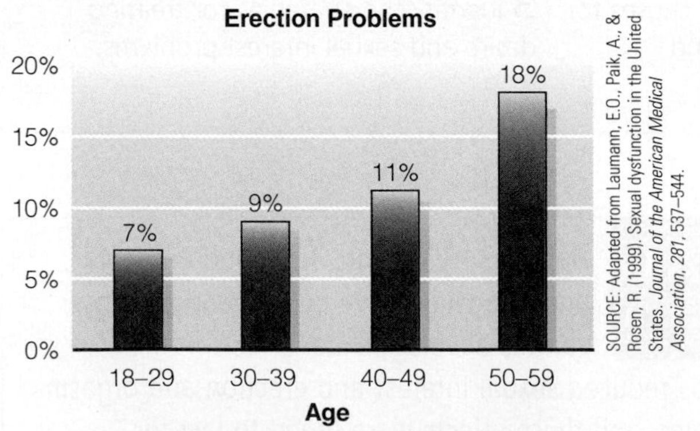

health care providers might not perform a medical evaluation. Overall, EDs in younger men (20–35 years old) are more likely to be psychologically based, whereas EDs in older men (60 and older), they are more likely to be due to physical factors (Lue, 2000).

To diagnose the causes of ED, health care providers and sex therapists may use tests such as the **nocturnal penile tumescence test** (Elhanbly et al., 2009). Men normally experience two or three erections a night during stages of rapid eye movement (REM) sleep. If these erections do not occur, it is a good indication that there is a physiological problem; if they do occur, erectile problems are more likely to have psychological causes. The nocturnal penile tumescence test requires a man to spend the night in a sleep laboratory hooked up to several machines, but newer devices allow him to monitor his sleep erections in the privacy of his own home. RigiScan, a portable diagnostic monitor, measures both rigidity and tumescence at the base and tip of the penis. Stamp tests and other at-home devices are also used (Elhanbly et al., 2009). A stamp test uses perforated bands resembling postage stamps, which are placed on the base of the penis before retiring for the night. In the morning, if the perforations have ripped, this indicates that the man had normal physiological functioning while sleeping.

Animal Variations

Erectile Dysfunction: Not Just for Humans

Often when we think about erectile dysfunction, we assume it is just a human problem; however, it can occur or be created in animals. For example, in one study, male New Zealand white rabbits were given a high-cholesterol diet that causes a buildup of fatty deposits in the arteries, leading to reduced blood flow. Ninety-three percent of the rabbits given the high-cholesterol diet developed erectile dysfunction (Azadzoi & Goldstein, 1992). In both rat and rabbit animal models of diabetes, erectile dysfunction has been documented (Zhang et al., 2006), and exposure to cigarette smoke in dogs can cause erectile dysfunction (Juenemann et al., 1987).

Erection Problems

SOURCE: Adapted from Laumann, E.O., Paik, A., & Rosen, R. (1999). Sexual dysfunction in the United States. *Journal of the American Medical Association, 281*, 537–544.

FIGURE **15.3** The prevalence of erection problems in men increases with age.

nocturnal penile tumescence test
A study performed to evaluate erections during sleep that helps clarify the causes of erectile disorder.

Treating Male Erectile Disorder

Of all the sexual disorders, there are more treatment options for male ED than for any other disorder. A tremendous amount of research has been dedicated to finding causes and treatment options for ED. Depending on the cause, treatment for ED includes psychological treatment, pharmacological treatment (drugs), hormonal and intracavernous injections, vascular surgery, vacuum constriction devices, and prosthesis implantation. The success rate for treating male ED ranges from 50 percent to 80 percent (Lue, 2000).

PSYCHOLOGICAL TREATMENT The primary psychological treatments for ED include **systematic desensitization** and sex therapy that includes education, **sensate focus**, and communication training (Heiman, 2002). These treatments can help reduce feelings of anxiety and can evaluate issues that are interfering with erectile response. Relationship therapy can also help explore issues in a relationship that might contribute to ED, such as unresolved anger, bitterness, or guilt.

PHARMACOLOGICAL TREATMENT The first oral medication for ED, Viagra (sildenafil citrate), was approved by the Health Canada in 2003, and in 2004 Levitra (vardenafil) and 2008 Cialis (tadalafil) and were approved. Several additional drugs are being tested for the treatment of ED (Limin et al., 2010). These drugs can be used in a variety of ED cases—those that are **psychogenic** (sike-oh-JEN-nick), illness related, or have physical causes. Today, more than 50 million men with ED worldwide have used one of these drugs, and they are considered the first line of treatment for ED (Eardley, 2010; Palit & Eardley, 2010).

All of these drugs produce muscle relaxation in the penis, dilation of the arteries supplying the penis, and an inflow of blood, which can lead to penile erection. They do not increase a man's sexual desire and will not produce an erection without adequate sexual stimulation. Typically, a man must take Viagra about one hour before he desires an erection, and Cialis and Levitra often work within 15 to 30 minutes. Erections can last up to four hours, although Cialis can aid in stimulating erections for up to 36 hours (which is why French media referred to it as "le weekend," because it can be taken on a Friday night and last until early Sunday; Japsen, 2003). Overall, studies have found that patients prefer Cialis over Viagra and Levitra, mainly because of its longer duration (Morales et al., 2011).

These medications have several adverse effects, including headaches, a flushing in the cheeks and neck, nasal congestion, and indigestion. Less common adverse effects include an increased risk for vision problems, including changes in colour vision and possible total vision loss, and ringing in the ears or total hearing loss (Mukherjee & Shivakumar, 2007; Wooltorton, 2006). Critics of pharmacological treatment for ED point out that drug use focuses solely on an erection and fails to take into account the multidimensional nature of male sexuality (B.W. McCarthy & Fucito, 2005).

HORMONAL TREATMENTS Hormonal treatments may help improve erections in men who have hormonal irregularities (such as too much prolactin or too little gonadal hormones; Lue, 2000). Excessive prolactin can interfere with adequate secretion of testosterone and can cause ED. A man with low testosterone levels can be prescribed testosterone therapy through injections, patches, gels, or creams. However, as we discussed earlier, research has been unable to show a consistent and beneficial role of testosterone in increasing sexual functioning in men (Allan et al., 2008; Isidori et al., 2005).

A testosterone patch or gel is applied directly to the scrotum, whereas gels and creams can be applied to other parts of the body such as the arms or stomach. AndroDerm, a testosterone patch, was approved for use in Canada in 2000 and AndroGel, a clear, colourless, odourless gel, was approved in 2002. AndroGel is applied daily and is absorbed into the skin. Some men prefer this type of application over a painful injection or patch. Adverse effects are rare but include headaches, acne, depression, gynecomastia, and hypertension. None of these testosterone preparations should be used by men with prostate cancer because they can exacerbate this condition.

On Your Mind

A couple of guys I know have some Viagra, and they have been trying to get me to take it. Is it safe to use this drug if you don't have ED?

Although recreational use of Viagra and other erectile drugs is not uncommon, it does not always live up to expectations (Crosby & Diclemente, 2004; Eloi-Stiven et al., 2007; Fisher et al., 2006; Musacchio et al., 2006). Men who use these drugs are often disappointed because it doesn't always lead to longer and firmer erections, and can often contribute to physical adverse effects, such as harmful changes in blood pressure (Crosby & Diclemente, 2004; D. Fisher et al., 2006). In addition, men who use these drugs recreationally are more likely to engage in unsafe sex compared with those not using these drugs, which puts them at greater risk for sexually transmitted infections (Swearingen & Klausner, 2005).

INTRACAVERNOUS INJECTIONS Also used to treat ED are **intracavernous** (in-truh-CAV-er-nuss) **injections** (Alexandre

systematic desensitization
A treatment method for sexual disorders that involves neutralizing the anxiety-producing aspects of sexual situations and behaviour by a process of gradual exposure.

sensate focus
A series of touching experiences that are assigned to couples in sex therapy to teach non-verbal communication and reduce anxiety.

psychogenic
Relating to psychological causes.

intracavernous injection
A treatment method for erectile disorder in which vasodilating drugs are injected into the penis for the purpose of creating an erection.

et al., 2007; Lue, 2000). Men and their partners are taught to self-inject these preparations directly into the corpora cavernosa (see Chapter 4) while the penis is gently stretched out. The injections cause the blood vessels to relax, which increases blood flow to the penis. The majority of patients report very minor pain from these injections. However, each time a man desires an erection, he must use this injection. The higher the dosage of medication, the longer the erection will last.

One possible adverse effect of treatment using intracavernosus injections is priapism. Other side effects are more related to the injection than to the drug itself and may include pain, bleeding, or bruising (Alexandre et al., 2007; Israilov et al., 2002). Prostaglandin pellets have also been used to increase blood flow to the penis. The pellets are inserted directly into the urethra, where they are absorbed. Erections with these methods will typically occur within 20 minutes and can last for an hour and a half.

VACUUM CONSTRICTION DEVICES In the past several years, **vacuum constriction devices**, which use suction to induce erections, have become more popular, in part because they are less invasive and safer than injections. These devices involve putting the flaccid penis into a vacuum cylinder and pumping it to draw blood into the corpora cavernosa (similar to the one Austin Powers was caught with in *Austin Powers: International Man of Mystery*). A constriction ring is rolled onto the base of

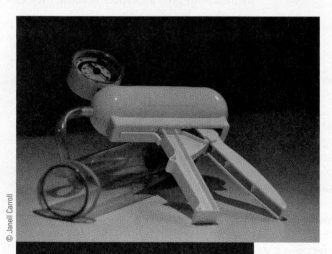

Vacuum constriction devices, such as the ErecAid, are often used in the treatment of erectile dysfunction. A man places his penis in the cylinder and vacuum suction increases blood flow to the penis, creating an erection.

© Janell Carroll

vacuum constriction device
Treatment device for erectile disorder used to pull blood into the penis.

revascularization
A procedure used in the treatment of vascular erectile disorder in which the vascular system is rerouted to ensure better blood flow to the penis.

prosthesis implantation
A treatment method for erectile disorder in which a prosthesis is surgically implanted into the penis.

semirigid rod
A flexible rod that is implanted into the penis during prosthetic surgery.

the penis after it is removed from the vacuum device to keep the blood in the penis. This ring is left on the penis until the erection is no longer desired. When it is removed, the man will lose his erection. Negative side effects include possible bruising and, in rare cases, testicular entrapment in the vacuum chamber (Lue, 2000). Overall, these devices can be expensive, bulky, and noisy, and they reduce spontaneity, which some couples find unappealing.

SURGICAL TREATMENTS Surgical intervention has increased as a treatment for ED. In some cases, physicians perform **revascularization** to improve erectile functioning; in other cases, **prosthesis** (pross-THEE-sis) **implantation** may be recommended. Acrylic implants for ED were first used in 1952, but they were replaced by silicone rubber in the 1960s and then by a variety of synthetic materials in the 1970s. Today there are two main types of implants: **semirigid rods**, which provide a permanent state of erection but can be bent up and down; and inflatable devices that become firm when the man pumps them up (Simmons & Montague, 2008). Penetrative sexual behaviours may safely be engaged in four to eight weeks after surgery. After prosthesis implantation, a man is still able to orgasm, ejaculate, and impregnate (Simmons & Montague, 2008). While these implants are generally considered safe, on rare occasions they can break (Bozkurt et al., 2014), or lead to penile deformity if the implants shift position in the penis (Akand, Ozayar, Yaman, & Demirel, 2007). In these cases, surgery will be necessary to correct the failure of the implant.

Sexual satisfaction after a prosthesis implantation has been found in men younger and older than 75 (Chung, Solomon, DeYoung, & Brock, 2014). Success of implants is to be related to several factors, such as a man's relationship with his partner and feelings about his own masculinity (Kempeneers et al., 2004). While many couples report increased sexual satisfaction after surgery (Bettocchi et al., 2010), between 10 percent and 20 percent of patients remain dissatisfied, dysfunctional, or sexually inactive

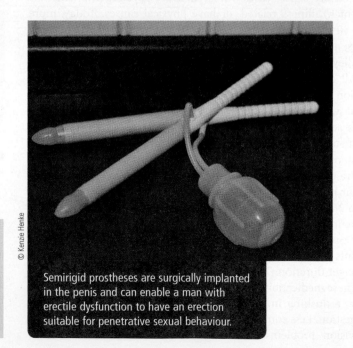

© Kenzie Henke

Semirigid prostheses are surgically implanted in the penis and can enable a man with erectile dysfunction to have an erection suitable for penetrative sexual behaviour.

(Minervini et al., 2006). If a man has psychological factors that contribute to his erectile difficulties, these issues are likely to resurface after a prosthesis is implanted.

Some studies have found greater success rates when using a combination of various therapies, such as a vacuum erectile device together with medications or injections, or various other combinations (Dhir et al., 2011).

Other Problems with Sexual Arousal

A sexual disorder category called **hypersexual disorder** was considered for as a new diagnostic category into the DSM-5 but ultimately was not included (Kafka, 2010; Reid et al., 2012; Toussaint & Pitchot, 2013; Walters, Knight, & Långström, 2011). This disorder involves recurrent and intense sexual fantasies, sexual urges, and sexual behaviour. Proponents of this disorder argue that it causes personal distress and can impair social, occupational, or other areas of functioning. Another disorder that has been explored in the research, **persistent sexual arousal syndrome**, is also not listed in the DSM-5 (Leiblum & Goldmeier, 2008; Leiblum & Seehuus, 2009; Levin & Wylie, 2010; Waldinger & Schweitzer, 2009). The opposite of an arousal problem, this generally occurs in women and consists of an excessive and unremitting arousal. Genital arousal can last for hours or days despite a lack of sexual desire or stimulation and can be distressing and worrisome to women, although many may be reluctant to discuss it with health care providers. More research is needed to shed more light on this disorder.

Review Questions

1 Identify and explain the problems with sexual arousal.

2 Identify possible treatment strategies for female sexual arousal disorder.

3 Define erectile disorder (ED) and identify some of the tests used to diagnose male ED.

4 Identify some of the pharmacological and hormonal treatments for ED.

5 Identify how intracavernous injections, vacuum constriction devices, and surgery are used in the treatment of ED.

Problems with Orgasm

Every individual reaches orgasm differently, and has different wants and needs to build sexual excitement. Some men and women need very little stimulation, others need a great deal of stimulation, and some never reach orgasm. The DSM-5 had three categories of orgasmic disorders: **female orgasmic disorder**, **delayed ejaculation**, and **early (premature) ejaculation**.

Female Orgasmic Disorder

Historically, this disorder was referred to as "frigidity," which had negative implications. As in other disorders of sexual functioning (such as premature ejaculation and delayed ejaculation), when clinicians assess an individual for this disorder, they are looking for whether it is situational or generalizable, how long it has been present during the life span and how severe it is. The DSM-5 (2013, pp. 429–430) defines female orgasmic disorder as:

A. *Presence of either of the following symptoms and experienced on almost all or all (approximately 75%–100% occasions of sexual activity (in identified situational contexts or, if generalized, in all contexts):*
  1. Marked delay in, marked infrequency of, or absence of orgasm.
  2. Markedly reduced intensity of orgasmic sensations.
B. *The symptoms in Criterion A have persisted for a minimum duration of approximately 6 months.*

C. *The symptoms in Criterion A cause clinically significant distress in the individual.*
D. *The sexual dysfunction is not better explained by a nonsexual mental disorder or as a consequence of severe relationship distress (e.g., partner violence) or other significant stressors and is not attributable to the effects of a substance/medication or another medical condition.*

SOURCE: Reprinted with permission from the Diagnostic and Statistical Manual of Mental Disorders, Fifth Edition, (Copyright © 2013). American Psychiatric Association. All Rights Reserved.

Scientists have found that approximately one quarter of women report orgasmic disorder (Ishak et al., 2010; Laumann et al., 1994; Meston et al., 2004). Researchers have found that educational levels are related to orgasmic problems. Those with higher levels of education report lower levels of orgasmic problems (Figure 15.4). Remember that the DSM definition does not

hypersexual disorder
Recurrent and intense sexual fantasies, sexual urges, and sexual behaviour.

persistent sexual arousal syndrome
An excessive and unremitting level of sexual arousal. May also be referred to as persistent genital arousal disorder.

female orgasmic disorder
A delay or absence of orgasm after a normal phase of sexual excitement.

delayed ejaculation
An orgasm disorder characterized by a delay, infrequent, or absence of ejaculation.

early (premature) ejaculation
a recurrent pattern of ejaculation in approximately one minute or less during partnered sexual activity.

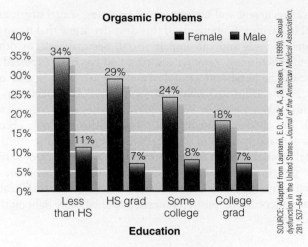

Orgasmic Problems

■ Female ■ Male

- Less than HS: 34% (Female), 11% (Male)
- HS grad: 29% (Female), 7% (Male)
- Some college: 24% (Female), 8% (Male)
- College grad: 18% (Female), 7% (Male)

Education

SOURCE: Adapted from Laumann, E.O., Paik, A., & Rosen, R. (1999). Sexual dysfunction in the United States. *Journal of the American Medical Association,* 281, 537–544.

FIGURE **15.4** Higher educational levels are negatively associated with sexual problems for both men and women.

indicate that orgasm must occur during vaginal intercourse. The majority of heterosexual women are unable to orgasm during vaginal intercourse. If a woman is unable to orgasm during all sexual activities after a normal phase of sexual excitement, she may be experiencing orgasmic disorder. Some women who take certain psychotropic drugs, including many types of antidepressants, may also experience delayed or absent orgasms (Labbate, 2008); these cases, however, would not fit the current DSM-5 category of female orgasmic disorder.

Lifelong orgasmic disorder describes a condition in which a woman has never had an orgasm. *Acquired orgasmic disorder* refers to a condition in which a woman was able to have orgasms previously but later has trouble reaching orgasm. *Situational orgasmic disorder* refers to a condition in which a woman can have orgasms only with one type of stimulation.

Women with orgasmic disorders, compared with orgasmic women, often report less relationship satisfaction and lower levels of emotional closeness (González et al., 2006). They also have more difficulties in asking their partners

On Your Mind

I seem to have problems achieving orgasm with my partner, yet I am able to with the help of a vibrator. Are there different levels of orgasm? Sometimes it is so deep and complete and emotional; other times it is very satisfying but not to the tips of my toes! Is this normal? I would love to be able to achieve the same satisfaction with my partner as I can by myself or with a vibrator.

Different levels of sexual satisfaction result from orgasms. Orgasms differ based on stress, emotions, thoughts, physical health, menstrual cycles, sexual position, and method of stimulation. However, Masters and Johnson did find that masturbation usually evoked more powerful orgasms than intercourse. To experience these orgasms with your partner, you might try masturbating together or using a vibrator with your partner.

bibliotherapy
Using books and educational material for the treatment of sexual disorders or other problems.

for direct clitoral stimulation, discussing how slow or fast they want to go, or how hard or soft stimulation should be. Some women worry about what their partners might think if they make sexual suggestions or feel uncomfortable receiving stimulation (such as cunnilingus or manual stimulation) without stimulating their partners at the same time. Distracting thoughts, such as "his hand must be falling asleep" or "he can't be enjoying this" can increase existing anxiety and interfere with orgasm (Birnbaum et al., 2001; M.P. Kelly et al., 1990).

REAL Research A nationally representative study of U.S. women found that although 40 percent of women reported experiencing low sexual desire, decreased sexual arousal, and/or problems reaching orgasm, only 12 percent indicated these issues were a source of personal distress (Shifren et al., 2008).

Treating Female Orgasmic Disorder

Today, the majority of treatment programs for orgasmic disorder involve a combination of different treatment approaches, such as homework assignments, sex education, communication skills training, cognitive restructuring, desensitization, and other techniques (Meston et al., 2004). The most effective treatment for female orgasmic disorder was developed by LoPiccolo and Lobitz (1972) and involves teaching a woman to masturbate to orgasm.

On a psychological level, masturbation also helps increase the pleasurable anticipation of sex. Education, self-exploration, communication training, and body awareness are also included in masturbation training for orgasmic problems. Masturbation exercises begin with a woman examining her body and vulva with mirrors. Then she is instructed to find which areas of her body feel the most pleasurable when touched and to stroke them. If this does not result in orgasm, a vibrator is used. As a woman progresses through these stages, she may involve her sexual partner so that the partner is able to learn which areas are more sensitive than others.

Although masturbation training is the most effective treatment for female orgasmic disorder, some therapists do not incorporate it into their treatment for a variety of reasons (including patient or therapist discomfort). Interestingly, improving orgasmic responses does not always increase sexual satisfaction. Heterosexual women may report increased pleasure with vaginal intercourse over masturbation because it provides more intimacy and closeness (Jayne, 1981), even though masturbation may be a better means of reaching orgasm (Dodson, 1993).

Two additional treatments involve systematic desensitization and **bibliotherapy**. Both of these have been found to be helpful in cases in which there is a great deal of sexual anxiety. In systematic desensitization, events that cause anxiety are recalled into imagination; then a relaxation technique is used to decrease the anxiety. With enough repetition and practice, eventually the anxiety-producing events lose the ability to create anxiety. Both masturbation training and systematic desensitization have been found to be effective; however, masturbation training has higher effectiveness rates (Heiman & Meston, 1997).

Bibliotherapy, which uses written works as therapy, has also been found to be helpful for not only orgasmic disorders but other sexual disorders as well. It can help a person regain some control and understand the problems she is experiencing. Although the results may be short-lived, bibliotherapy has been found to improve sexual functioning (van Lankveld et al., 2001).

Ejaculatory Disorders

The ejaculatory process is controlled by various endocrine factors, including testosterone, oxytocin, prolactin, and thyroid hormones (Corona et al., 2011). There is a wide spectrum of ejaculatory disorders, ranging from early to a delayed or absent ejaculation (Bettocchi et al., 2008). In the following subsections, we discuss premature (early) ejaculation, delayed ejaculation, and various other ejaculatory problems.

Premature (Early) Ejaculation

Premature (early) ejaculation is difficult to define. Does it depend on how many penile thrusts take place before orgasm, how many minutes elapse between actual penetration and orgasm, or whether a man reaches orgasm before his partner does? All of these definitions are problematic because they involve individual differences in sexual functioning. The time it takes to ejaculate may vary based on a man's age, sexual experience, health, and stress level. The DSM-5 (2013, p. 443) defines early (premature) ejaculation as:

A. persistent or recurrent pattern of ejaculation occurring during partnered sexual activity within approximately 1 minute following vaginal penetration and before the individual wishes it,

B. The systems in Criterion A must have been present for at least 6 months and must be experienced on almost all or all (approximately 75%–100%) occasions of sexual activity (in identified situational contexts or, if generalized, in all contexts)

C. The symptoms in Criterion A must cause clinically significant distress in the individual and,

D. The sexual dysfunction is not better explained by a nonsexual mental disorder or as a consequence of severe relationship distress or other significant stressors and is not attributable to the effects of a substance/medication or another medical condition.

SOURCE: Reprinted with permission from the Diagnostic and Statistical Manual of Mental Disorders, Fifth Edition, (Copyright © 2013). American Psychiatric Association. All Rights Reserved.

On Your Mind

Why do women fake orgasms rather than honestly telling their partners what they are doing wrong?

Faking orgasms often occurs as a result of a sexual problem. To a man or woman who experiences problems with orgasm or delayed ejaculation, faking an orgasm may seem the best way to end the sexual activity or to please the partner. However, such deceptions are not healthy in a committed relationship, and partners are generally advised to discuss any sexual problems they have instead of covering them up. Some women and men may have difficulties communicating sexual needs and desires. So instead of talking to their partners about what sexually excites them, they hope that their partners just know what to do. However, what feels best to person may not feel good to another, and what feels good may change over time. Many variables can also interfere with sexual pleasure, such as stress, fatigue, anxiety, or depression. It is important that couples communicate their desires so that their sex life is satisfying for both of them.

Early ejaculation is the most common sexual problem affecting men and it can affect men of all ages (Figure 15.5; Linton & Wylie, 2010; Renshaw, 2005; Rowland et al., 2010; Serefoglu et al., 2011; Vardi et al., 2008). The frequency of early ejaculation is constant as men age (Montorsi, 2005) and differs among cultures (Laumann et al., 2005). Men in the Middle East report a prevalence rate of 10-15 percent, while those in Europe have an approximate rate of 20 percent. Men in Asia and Central and North America report rates of early ejaculation between 25 and 32 percent. Early ejaculation can lead to decreases in sexual satisfaction and quality of life for both men and their partners.

Historically, early ejaculation has been considered a psychological disorder (Benson et al., 2009). Psychological factors that have been found to contribute include stress, anxiety, unresolved

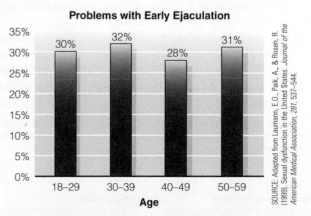

SOURCE: Adapted from Laumann, E.O., Paik, A. & Rosen, R. (1999). Sexual dysfunction in the United States. *Journal of the American Medical Association, 281*, 537–544.

FIGURE **15.5** Although early ejaculation is often associated with younger males, studies have found it can occur at any age.

conflict, guilt, shame, and performance pressures (i.e., wanting to satisfy a partner). Some evolutionary theorists claim that early ejaculation may provide a biological advantage in that a man who ejaculates quickly would be more likely to impregnate a partner than a man who requires prolonged stimulation. Masters and Johnson (1970) originally proposed that early ejaculation develops when a man's early sexual experiences are rushed because of the fear of being caught or discovered. These fears, they believed, could condition a man to ejaculate rapidly. Others have pointed out that early ejaculation occurs in men who are unable to accurately judge their own levels of sexual arousal, which would enable them to use self-control and avoid rapid ejaculation (H.S. Kaplan, 1974).

Potential physiological factors also might contribute to early ejaculation. Research has found that some men might have "hyperexcitability" or an "oversensitivity" of their penis, which prevents them from delaying orgasm. Nerves in the lumbar spine are related to ejaculation, and ultimately it may be the brain that is responsible. Differences in the serotonin system have been found between men with early ejaculatory responses in comparison to men with typical ejaculatory responses (Benson et al., 2009; Waldinger, 2002). Other physiological factors that may contribute to early ejaculation include hormones, infections and there is evidence that early ejaculation may have a genetic component, wherein a male has a higher chance of experiencing it if his father did (Jern et al., 2009).

Delayed Ejaculation

Delayed ejaculation is defined in the DSM-5 (APA, 2013, p. 424) as:

A. *Either of the following symptoms must be experienced on almost all or all occasions (approximately 75%–100%) of the partnered sexual activity (in identified situational contexts, or if generalized, in all contexts), and without the individual desiring delay:*
   1. *marked delay in ejaculation*
   2. *marked infrequency or absence of ejaculation*
B. *The systems in Criterion A must have persisted for a minimum duration of approximately 6 months.*
C. *The symptoms in Criterion A must cause clinically significant distress in the individual and,*
D. *The sexual dysfunction is not better explained by a nonsexual mental disorder or as a consequence of severe relationship distress or other significant stressors and is not attributable to the effects of a substance/medication or another medical condition.*

SOURCE: Reprinted with permission from the Diagnostic and Statistical Manual of Mental Disorders, Fifth Edition, (Copyright © 2013). American Psychiatric Association. All Rights Reserved.

retrograde ejaculation
A condition in which the male ejaculate is released into the bladder instead of being ejaculated outside the body through the urethra.

anejaculation
A sexual disorder that involves an absence of ejaculation.

Delayed ejaculation is relatively rare—less than 3 percent of men report experiencing it (Perelman & Rowland, 2006). However, those who do experience it often experience considerable anxiety and distress, and may also experience relationship problems related to the problem. Studies have found that many men with delayed ejaculation have a history of high masturbatory activity, lower levels of sexual satisfaction, and higher levels of anxiety and depression (Abdel-Hamid & Saleh, 2011).

Delayed ejaculation can be the result of both psychological and physiological factors. Psychological factors include stress, a lack of attraction to one's partner, a strict religious background, atypical masturbation patterns, or past traumatic events such as sexual abuse. Physiological factors include the use of certain drugs and various illnesses, nerve damage, and spinal cord injury (SCI).

Other Ejaculatory Disorders

A relatively uncommon ejaculatory disorder involves **retrograde ejaculation**, in which the ejaculate empties into the bladder instead of being ejaculated outside the body through the urethra. A man with retrograde ejaculation typically experiences orgasm with little or no ejaculation (also called a "dry orgasm"; Ohl et al., 2008; Rowland et al., 2010). Some experts refer to this condition as **anejaculation**. Although both of these conditions are not harmful, they can cause infertility (Aust & Lewis-Jones, 2004; Zhao et al., 2004). Although it is not considered a sexual problem, some men may experience painful ejaculation, which can be the result of infections or other medical issues (Lee et al., 2008; Schultheiss, 2008). Common causes for these conditions include chronic illnesses, surgeries, SCI, or prescription drug use (Bettocchi et al., 2008; Kaplan, 2009; Mufti et al., 2008; Nagai et al., 2008; Tsivian et al., 2009).

Treating Ejaculatory Disorders

Treatment for ejaculatory disorders often depends on the duration, context, and causes of the disorder. Lifelong ejaculatory problems are often treated with medications or topical anesthetics, whereas other cases might be treated with behavioural therapy, with or without medications (Rowland et al., 2010; Shindel et al., 2008).

Treating Early (Premature) Ejaculation

A variety of psychological, topical, and oral therapies have been used to treat early ejaculation, with varying levels of success (Hellstrom, 2006; Owen, 2009). A common treatment for early ejaculation has been the use of selective serotonin reuptake inhibitors (SSRIs), because a common side effect of these drugs is delayed ejaculation (Linton & Wylie, 2010; Rowland et al., 2010; Shindel et al., 2008). However, these medications need to be taken daily and have a slow onset of action (Owen, 2009). Although research continues to explore a variety of other drugs for the treatment of early ejaculation, one promising drug, *Dapoxetine*

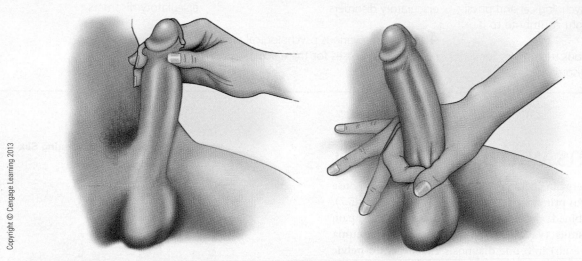

FIGURE **15.6** The squeeze technique is often recommended in the treatment of premature ejaculation. Pressure is applied either at the top or to the base of the penis for several seconds until the urge to ejaculate subsides.

(Priligy), has undergone several large trials in the United States and has been approved in more than 50 countries worldwide, including Italy, Spain, Portugal, Sweden and Germany (Buvat, Tesfayae, Rothman, Rivas, & Giuliano, 2009; Corona et al., 2011; Owen, 2009).

Treatment may also include the use of behavioural techniques known as the **squeeze** or **stop–start techniques** (Shindel et al., 2008). Both involve stimulating the penis to the point just before ejaculation. With the squeeze technique, sexual stimulation or masturbation is engaged in just short of orgasm; then stimulation is stopped. The man or his partner puts a thumb on the frenulum and the first and second fingers on the dorsal side of the penis (Figure 15.6). Pressure is applied for three to four seconds, until the urge to ejaculate subsides. With the stop–start technique, stimulation is simply stopped until the ejaculatory urge subsides. Stimulation is then repeated up until that point, and this process is repeated over and over. Using these methods, a man can usually gain some control over his erection within two to ten weeks and can have excellent control within several months. It is believed that these techniques may help a man get in touch with his arousal levels and sensations. Suggested effectiveness rates have been as high as 98 percent, although it is unclear how this effectiveness is being measured (Masters & Johnson, 1970). In addition, many studies fail to mention whether the treatment permanently solves the problem or if periodic repetition of the techniques is necessary.

Treating Delayed Ejaculation

Treatment for delayed ejaculation can include changing prescription medications, discontinuing the use of non-prescription drugs or alcohol, or sex therapy. Delayed ejaculation is often difficult to treat, and no evidence-based treatments have been proved to eliminate this disorder (Nelson et al., 2007; Richardson et al., 2006). A novel treatment uses penile vibratory stimulation, which involves increasing penile sensations during sexual activity with a small vibrator (Nelson et al., 2007). It has been found to be an effective treatment, although more research is needed. A variety of medications, are currently being evaluated for the treatment of delayed ejaculation (Abdel-Hamid & Saleh, 2011; Chan et al., 2008; Waldinger, 2005); however, nothing has been approved or is likely to be approved for many years (McMahon, 2014).

It can be challenging to treat delayed ejaculation caused by psychological factors. One 43-year-old man shared with me his lifelong problem in reaching orgasm with his partner. He had been sexually abused as a child for many years by an uncle who was a few years older than he. During this abuse, the uncle tried to make him reach orgasm. However, as a boy, he had learned to withhold the orgasmic response. Later on in life, this pattern continued even though he was not consciously trying to do so.

One psychological treatment involves instructing a man to use situations in which he is able to achieve ejaculation to help him during those in which he is not. For example, if a man can ejaculate during masturbation while fantasizing about being watched during sexual activity, he is told to use this fantasy while he is with his partner. Gradually, the man is asked to incorporate his partner into the sexual fantasy and to masturbate while with the partner.

squeeze technique
A technique in which the ejaculatory reflex is reconditioned using a firm grasp on the penis.

stop–start technique
A technique in which the ejaculatory reflex is reconditioned using intermittent pressure on the glans of the penis.

Review Questions

1 Define female orgasmic disorder, and explain possible psychological and physical factors that might contribute to it.

2 Identify the various treatments for female orgasmic disorder.

3 Identify and differentiate the various ejaculatory disorders.

4 Identify the various psychological and physiological causes for the ejaculatory disorders.

5 Identify the various treatments for the ejaculatory disorders.

Problems with Sexual Pain

Sexual pain disorders can occur at any stage of the sexual response cycle, and they occur primarily in women of all ages (Figure 15.7). The DSM-5 combined the two previous categories of pain disorders—**vaginismus** (vadg-ih-NISS-muss) and **dyspareunia** (diss-par-ROON-ee-uh) into one diagnosis called **genito-pelvic pain/penetration disorder**.

Genito-Pelvic Pain/Penetration Disorders

According to the DSM-5 (APA, 2013, p. 437), for a woman to be diagnosed with a genito-pelvic pain/penetration disorder, she must meet the following diagnostic criteria:

A. *Persistent or recurrent difficulties with one (or more) of the following:*
   1. *Vaginal penetration during intercourse.*
   2. *Marked vulvovaginal or pelvic pain during vaginal intercourse or penetration attempts.*
   3. *Marked fear or anxiety about vulvovaginal or pelvic pain in anticipation of, during, or as a result of vaginal penetration.*
   4. *Marked tensing or tightening of the pelvic floor muscles during attempted vaginal penetration*

B. *The systems in Criterion A must have been present for a minimum duration of approximately 6 months.*

C. *The symptoms in Criterion A must cause clinically significant distress in the individual.*

D. *The sexual dysfunction is not better explained by a nonsexual mental disorder or as a consequence of severe relationship distress or other significant stressors and is not attributable to the effects of a substance/medication or another medical condition.*

SOURCE: Reprinted with permission from the Diagnostic and Statistical Manual of Mental Disorders, Fifth Edition, (Copyright © 2013). American Psychiatric Association. All Rights Reserved.

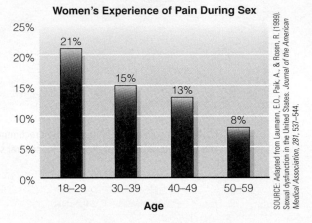

Women's Experience of Pain During Sex

SOURCE: Adapted from Laumann, E.O., Paik, A., & Rosen, R. (1999). Sexual dysfunction in the United States. *Journal of the American Medical Association, 281,* 537–544.

FIGURE 15.7 Although fewer women may be sexually active as they age, fewer older women self-report pain during sex.

The **pubococcygeus** (pub-oh-cock-SIGH-gee-us) **muscle** surrounds the entrance to the vagina and controls the vaginal opening. Involuntary spasms of this muscle can make penetration painful and virtually impossible (Lahaie et al., 2010; Oz-demir et al., 2008; Rosenbaum, 2011). Many women tolerate the sexual pain in order to meet their partners' needs or expectations (Boardman & Stockdale, 2009). These conditions may be situation-specific, meaning that a woman may be able to allow penetration under certain circumstances but not in others (e.g., during a pelvic examination but not during intercourse; LoPiccolo & Stock, 1986). It is estimated that between 4 percent and 42 percent of women have experienced involuntary spasms of the vaginal muscles (Hope et al., 2010), whereas approximately 15 percent of heterosexual women report experiencing pain during penetration (Laumann et al., 1999).

Sexual pain can occur before, during, or after sexual behaviour and may range from slight pain to severe. When severe, it can make sexual behaviour and penetration difficult, if not impossible. One woman had been in a relationship with her partner for more than three years, but they had never been able to engage in penile–vaginal

---

vaginismus
Involuntary spasms of the muscles around the vagina in response to attempts at penetration.

dyspareunia
Genital pain associated with sexual behaviour.

genito-pelvic pain/penetration disorders
A category of sexual problems that involve persistent or recurrent difficulties with penetrative sex, pelvic pain, and/or fear or anxiety about pelvic pain, which causes significant distress.

pubococcygeus muscle
A muscle that surrounds and supports the vagina.

intercourse because she felt as if her vagina "*was closed up*" (Author's files). Penetration of her vagina with her partner's fingers was possible and enjoyable, but once penile penetration was attempted, her vagina was impenetrable. She also shared that she had been forced to engage in sex with her stepfather for several years of her early life.

Unfortunately, few well-controlled studies exist on causes of sexual pain (Lahaie et al., 2010; van Lankveld et al., 2010). However, we know that a number of factors may contribute to sexual pain and fear of penetration (Lahaie et al., 2014), from physical problems to allergies or infections. Vulvodynia and **vulvar vestibulitis** (vess-tib-u-LI-TE-is) **syndrome**, a type of vulvodynia, are considered common causes of sexual pain today (Perrigouard et al., 2008).

Psychological problems can also contribute. Sexual pain and fear of penetration is more common in women who have been sexually abused or raped, and these problems often occur together with other sexual problems, such as desire or arousal problems (Weaver, 2009). In addition, women with conservative values and relatively strict sex-related moral standards have been found to be at greater risk for these disorders (Borg et al., 2011), as are women who report feelings of disgust when they think of sex (Borget al., 2010).

Treating Genito-Pelvic Pain/ Penetration Disorders

Although many women who experience sexual pain and fear of penetration do not seek treatment, medical evaluations and counseling can help isolate possible causes and solutions. It is important to consult with a health care provider. A physical examination can check for physiological problems that may be contributing to these disorders. It is also helpful for couples to become educated about these disorders to reduce their anxiety or tension. If a history of sexual abuse or rape exists, it is important to work through the trauma before beginning treatment specifically aimed at reducing the pain or fear associated with sexual behaviour.

Treatments can include physical therapy, prescription medications, and various psychological therapies. Cognitive–behavioural therapy has been found to reduce pain and increase comfort with penetration (Engman et al., 2010). After undergoing cognitive–behavioural therapy, 81 percent of women reported they were able to engage in penetrative sex and had experienced increases in self-esteem and self-worth as a sexual partner (Engman et al., 2010).

Other treatment options include biofeedback, surgery, and the use of Botox to reduce vaginal and pelvic pain (Butrick, 2009; Gunter, 2007; Pacik, 2009; Park & Paraiso, 2009). Some health care workers teach women experiencing pain and penetration disorders to use **dilators**, which can help to open and relax the vaginal muscles. If this is successful, penetration can be attempted. In some cases, however, it may be necessary to use a dilator on a regular basis just before penetration. It is estimated that between 75 percent and 100 percent of women who use this technique are able to experience penetrative sex by the end of treatment (Heiman, 2002).

Review Questions

1 Identify and differentiate among the various sexual pain disorders.

2 Explain how genito-pelvic pain and penetration disorders are treated.

Substance/Medication-Induced Sexual Dysfunction

The final major diagnostic criteria for sexual dysfunction in the DSM-5 is for those whose sexual difficulties stem from the use of drugs such as alcohol, opioids, sedative hypnotics, anxiolytics, antipsychotics, amphetamine or cocaine (stimulants), and other substances. For an individual to be diagnosed with a substance/medication-induced sexual dysfunction, he or she must meet the following criteria (APA, 2013, p. 446):

A. *A clinically significant disturbance in sexual function is predominant in the clinical picture.*

B. *There is evidence from the history, physical examination, or laboratory findings of both (1) and (2):*

1. *The symptoms in Criterion A developed during or soon after substance intoxication or withdrawal or after exposure to a medication*

2. *The involved substance/medication is capable of producing the symptoms in Criterion A.*

C. *The disturbance is not better explained by a sexual dysfunction that is not substance/ medication induced.*

D. *The disturbance does not occur exclusively during the course of a delirium*

E. *The disturbance causes clinically significant distress in the individual.*

SOURCE: Reprinted with permission from the Diagnostic and Statistical Manual of Mental Disorders, Fifth Edition, (Copyright © 2013). American Psychiatric Association. All Rights Reserved.

vulvar vestibulitis syndrome	**dilators**
Syndrome that causes pain and burning in the vaginal vestibule and often occurs during wearing tight pants.	A graduated series of metal rods used in the treatment of genito-pelvic pain/ penetration disorders.

For this classification of sexual dysfunction, a clinician also needs to look carefully at how well the sexual dysfunction onset or offset correlates with the onset or ending of the use of the drug in question and the severity of the disruption the drug has on sexual activity. There are many drugs, both legal and illegal, that can have an effect on sexual functioning; however, here we will briefly look at four categories of drugs with known sexual dysfunction effects—alcohol, opioids, stimulants, and antipsychotics.

Alcoholism

Alcohol dependence and alcohol abuse can both contribute to sexual problems. Ethyl alcohol is a general nervous system depressant that has both long- and short-term effects on sexual functioning, with sexual dysfunction rates of over 40 percent in males who drink regularly (Deihl et al., 2015; Glina, Sharlip & Hellstrom 2013; Grover, Mattoo, Pendharkar, & Kandappan, 2014). While the causal relationship between alcohol and sexual dysfunction is unclear (ZaaZaa, Bella, & Shamoul, 2013), alcohol does affect almost every bodily system. The damage it causes to the body with long-term use can lead to impairments in sexual function and these may be irreversible even with the cessation of alcohol use.

Alcoholism also has a dramatic impact on relationships. It often co-exists with anger, resentment, depression, and other familial and relationship problems. Some people become abusive when drunk, whereas others may withdraw and become non-communicative. Problem drinking may lead a person into a spiral of guilt, lowered self-esteem, and even thoughts of suicide. Recovery is a long, often difficult process that requires therapy and the support of family and friends (Kelley & Fals-Stewart, 2002).

Opioids

Opioids are pain-relieving medications available via prescription or illegally. The most familiar drugs in this class are morphine, heroin, oxycodone, and oxycontin. Naltrexone, methadone, and buprenorphine are used to treat opioid addiction, and these can also lead to problems with sexual function. The rate of sexual dysfunction is 34–85 percent in heroin addicts, 4–81 percent for those on a methadone maintenance program, 36–81 percent for those on a buprenorphine maintenance program, and up to 90 percent for those using naltrexone for treatment of their opioid addiction (Grover, Mattoo, Pendharkar, & Kandappan, 2014; Hallinan et al., 2008; Quaglio et al., 2008). For individuals taking opioids or using a treatment program, the most common sexual problems are erectile dysfunction, premature or delayed ejaculation and a reduction in their reported drive for sex, and treatment can lead to hypogonadism (Hallinan 2009). In women, vaginal dryness and sexual listlessness have been reported (Grover, Mattoo, Pendharkar, & Kandappan, 2014; Lia et al., 2013). As with recovery from

alcoholism, recovery from opioid addiction is a long and often difficult process that requires support from the medical establishment, therapists, friends, and family members.

Stimulants

Several stimulant drugs, such as cocaine, amphetamine and Methylenedioxymethamphetamine or MDMA (Ecstasy) can influence sexual function. Amphetamines and MDMA are perceived to increase sexual desire even though they have also been shown to decrease erectile ability and delay ejaculation (Bang-Ping, 2009). These drugs may also lead to an increase of risk-taking behaviour. For example, male-male anal sex without a condom is more likely with cocaine use (McNall & Remafedi, 1999). Stimulants in general may increase the frequency of sexual behaviour, sexual desire, and orgasmic sensations (Passie, Hartmann, Schneider, Emrich & Kruger, 2005; Zemishlany, Aizenberg & Wiesman, 2001); however, they are likely to impair physiological sexual ability, especially in males.

Antipsychotic Medications

Neuroleptics or antipsychotic drugs used for the treatment of schizophrenia (see section entitled "Mental Illness" later in the chapter) can cause increased or decreased desire for sex. Changes in sexual behaviour for individuals taking antipsychotic medication is one of the main reasons for non-compliance with drug treatment therapies (Bella & Shamloul, 2014). In men decreased sexual desire and erectile and ejaculatory problems are the most commonly reported effects of antipsychotic medications (Hummer et al., 1999; Mitchell & Popkin, 1982). For women, these drugs may affect their sexual arousal, lubrication, ability to orgasm, and overall levels of sexual desire (Schmidt et al., 2012). Conversely, for some individuals, drug treatment for schizophrenia can improve their perception of their sexuality (Kelly & Conley, 2004; 2006). For both men and women, antipsychotic medications increase prolactin levels, a hormone involved in the control of sexual function, and treating the increase in prolactin may ameliorate the sexual dysfunction seen with several antipsychotic medications (De Hert, Detraux & Peuskens, 2014; Nunes, Moreira, Razzouk, Nunes, & Mari Jde, 2012).

The effects of drugs on sexual function and sexual desire will be different for an individual depending on age, sex, and genetic background. Even drugs within a class of drugs, like the various types of opioids or antipsychotics, will not have the same effects on sexual function across individuals. One treatment strategy to ameliorate the effects of a drug on sexual function is to switch to a different drug within the class of drugs that is being used to treat a given disorder. For example, several antipsychotics are known to have less of an effect on sexual behaviour than others, and the switch to these drugs may lead to greater treatment compliance (Schmidt et al., 2012). To understand how a drug may be affecting your sexual desire, sexual function, or behaviour, it is always best to discuss your concerns with a family physician or health care provider.

neuroleptics
A class of antipsychotic drugs.

Review Questions

1 What are the criteria in the DSM-5 that must be met for a substance/medication-induced sexual dysfunction?

2 How do alcohol, opioids, stimulants, and antipsychotic medications affect sexual function?

Aging, Illness, Disability, and Sexual Functioning

We all need love, and we all need contact with others. Many illnesses and their treatments can interfere with a person's sexual desire, physiological functioning, or both. Sexual functioning involves a complex physiological process, which can be impaired by pain, immobility, changes in bodily functions, or increased use of prescription medications; many of these changes are correlated with aging. One of the most important things we can do as individuals to protect our sexual function is to take care of our health (see the accompanying Sex in Real Life feature). As people age, they inevitably experience changes in their physical health, some of which can affect normal sexual functioning (Table 15.1). Many of these changes in sexual functioning are exacerbated by sexual inactivity. In fact, research clearly indicates that older adults who have remained sexually active throughout their aging years have a greater potential for a more satisfying sex life later in life, see Figure 15.8 (Dimah & Dimah,

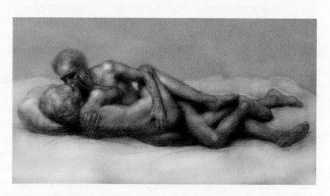

FIGURE **15.8** The majority of older adults maintain an interest in sex and sexual activity.

2004; Lindau & Gavrilova, 2010). Better knowledge of these changes would help older adults anticipate changes in their sexual activity.

Frequent complaints among older women are decreases in sexual desire and pain during vaginal intercourse (Schick et al., 2010). Older men are more likely to report problems with erectile functioning, and many turn to erectile drugs to enhance sexual functioning. Physical problems, such as arthritis, diabetes, and osteoporosis, can interfere with sexual functioning.

Often problems involve psychological issues as well. Sudden illness causes shock, anger, resentment, anxiety, and depression, all of which can adversely affect sexual desire and functioning. Many illnesses cause disfiguration and force a person to deal with radical changes in body image; after removal of a limb, breast, testicle, or the need to wear an external bag to collect bodily waste, many people wonder: How could anyone possibly find me sexually attractive?

Serious illness often puts strains on loving relationships. A partner may be forced to become nurse, cook, maid, and caretaker, as well as lover. The caretaker of an ill person may worry that the sick partner is too weak or fragile for sex or may be too concerned with his or her illness to want sexual contact. Still, many couples do enjoy loving, full relationships. Recall the chapter-opening interview with Dr. Woet Gianotten, who discussed that even terminally ill men and women desire sexual intimacy. Maintaining a healthy and satisfying sex life

Table 15.1 Physical Changes in Older Men and Women

In men:

- Delayed and less firm erection
- More direct stimulation needed for erection
- Extended refractory period (12–24 hours before re-arousal can occur)
- Reduced elevation of the testicles
- Reduced vasocongestive response to the testicles and scrotum
- Fewer expulsive contractions during orgasm
- Less forceful expulsion of seminal fluid and a reduced volume of ejaculate
- Rapid loss of erection after ejaculation
- Ability to maintain an erection for a longer period
- Less ejaculatory urgency
- Decrease in size and firmness of the testes, changes in testicle elevation, less sex flush, and decreased swelling and erection of the nipples

In women:

- Reduced or increased sexual interest
- Possible painful intercourse because of menopausal changes
- Decreased volume of vaginal lubrication
- Decreased expansive ability of the vagina
- Possible pain during orgasm because of less flexibility
- Thinning of the vaginal walls
- Shortening of vaginal width and length
- Decreased sex flush, reduced increase in breast volume, and longer post-orgasmic nipple erection

For many people in their teens, 20s, and 30s, the ability to perform sexually is often taken for granted. The lifestyle habits of many individuals during these years, such as smoking, drinking, stress, and not enough sleep can have a profound effect on sexual performance as we age. Optimizing your sexuality as you age requires paying attention to your current psychological and social situations in addition to taking care of your health (Kleinplatz, Menard & Wannamaker, 2014). Erectile dysfunction or a lack of sexual desire in one's 40s and 50s may occur due to years of not taking care of one's body—physically and/or psychologically.

Researchers have studied the effects of many lifestyle factors on sexual function and desire. Based on a review of the literature, several lifestyle choices haven been shown to increase sexual satisfaction and ability in men and women.

Exercise

Of all of the "therapies" one can choose to improve sexual desire and function, exercise may be the most effective and certainly the most cost effective. Exercise can improve all aspects of personal health and its benefits are not restricted to sex. In those with a decreased or lost sexual ability or desire, exercise has been shown to improve sexual function in men after heart disease (Ettala et al., 2014; Lange & Levine, 2014) and recovering from prostate cancer (Cormie, Newton, Taaffe, Spry & Galvão, 2013), and in women after vaginal reconstructive surgery (Pauls, Crisp, Novicki, Fellner & Kleeman 2013), during menopause (Stojanovska, Apostolopoulos, Polman & Borkoles, 2014), and after breast cancer (Juraskova et al., 2013).

Yoga, Mindfulness, and Meditation

Many men and women who struggle with sexual function can see improvements with mindfulness and meditation. Mindfulness practices can help women boost sexual desire and help them cope with vaginal pelvic pain (Brotto & Basson, 2014; Brotto, Basson, Carlson and Zhu, 2013). In peri- and postmenopausal women, hormone levels are falling as the ovaries begin to shut down and stop making estrogen. Women in menopause often have difficulty sleeping, may be irritable, and may feel a reduction in their sexual libido. Several studies have shown that exercise and more specifically yoga and/or meditation can help them ameliorate these distressing symptoms of menopause and lead to an improved perception of their quality of life (Kim, Ryu, Kim & Song, 2013; Nayak, Kamath, Kumar, & Rao, 2014; Stojanovska, Apostolopoulos, Polman, & Borkoles, 2014).

Sleep

Getting the appropriate amount of sleep for your age is also critical to maintaining good interpersonal and sexual relationships. Getting enough or good-quality sleep has been shown to improve sexual functioning in postmenopausal women (Eraslan, Ertekin, Ertekin & Oztürk, 2014) and improve erectile function in men with sleep apnea and individuals with schizophrenia who experience erectile dysfunction (Boin, Nozoe, Polesel, Andersen & Tufik, 2014; Gonçalves, Guilleminault, Ramos, Palha, & Paiva, 2005).

Diet and Nutrition

The last of the key elements of good health and ultimately good sexual function as you age is diet and nutrition. As mentioned earlier in the chapter, several drugs, such as alcohol and stimulants, can influence sexual behaviours. For both of these substances, less is more when it comes to sexual function. Cigarette smoking is also known to impair erectile ability in men (Harte, 2014). In order to protect or restore sexual function as we age, a diet that allows us to keep an appropriate weight for our height, as well as maintaining cardiovascular health, is essential for our ability to engage in the physical activities associated with sex (Esposito et al., 2008; Khoo et al., 2014).

© Lucky Business/Shutterstock

can increase personal happiness and satisfaction for those who are chronically ill or suffering from a variety of medical conditions.

As Dr. Gianotten discussed, the real questions that sick people and their partners have about their sexuality are too often ignored by medical professionals (Ivarsson et al., 2010). They may be questions of mechanics (e.g., "What positions can I get into now that I have lost a leg?"), questions of function (e.g., "Will my genitals still work now that I have a spinal cord injury?"), or questions of attractiveness (e.g., "Will my husband still want me now that I have lost a breast?"). Let's review a sample of physical and mental challenges that confront people, and also some of the sexual questions and problems that can arise.

Cardiovascular Illnesses

Heart disease, including **hypertension, angina,** and **myocardial infarction,** is the number two (cancer is number one) cause of

hypertension
Abnormally high blood pressure.

angina
Chest pains that accompany heart disease.

myocardial infarction
A cut-off of blood to the heart muscle, causing damage to the heart; also referred to as a heart attack.

death in Canada (Statistics Canada, 2014). A person with heart disease—even a person who has had a heart transplant—can return to a normal sex life shortly after recovery with the consent of their physician. Most cardiologists allow sexual behaviour as soon as the patient feels up to it, although they usually recommend that heart transplant patients wait from four to eight weeks to give the incision time to heal. However, researchers have found that the frequency of sexual behaviour after myocardial infarctions does decrease. In fact, only one in four couples returns to their previous levels of sexual behaviour (Ben-Zion & Shiber, 2006). Why does this occur?

One reason is fear. Many patients (or their partners) fear that their damaged (or new) heart is not up to the strain of sexual behaviour or orgasm (Eyada & Atwa, 2007; Kazemi-Saleh et al., 2007; McCall-Hosenfeld et al., 2008; Masoomi et al., 2010). This fear can be triggered by the fact that, when men and women become sexually excited, their heartbeat and respiration increases, and they may break out into a sweat (these are also signs of a heart attack). Some people with heart disease actually do experience some angina during sexual activity. Although not usually serious, these incidents may be frightening. Although sexual activity can trigger a myocardial infarction, this risk is extremely low (Baylin et al., 2007; Muller et al., 1996). In fact, except for patients with very serious heart conditions, sex puts no more strain on the heart than walking up a flight or two of stairs.

Some problems also involve physical factors. Because penile erection is a vascular process, involving the flow of blood into the penis, it is not surprising that ED is a common problem in male patients with cardiovascular problems (Hebert et al., 2008). Some heart medications also can dampen desire or cause erectile problems, or, less often, women may experience a decrease in lubrication. Sometimes adjusting medications can help couples who are experiencing such problems.

After a heart attack or other heart problems, it is not uncommon to have feelings of depression, inadequacy (especially among men), or loss of attractiveness (especially among women; Almeida et al., 2012; Duarte Freitas et al., 2011; Eyada & Atwa, 2007). In addition, in older patients, a partner often assumes the responsibility of enforcing the doctor's orders: "*Watch what you eat!*" "*Don't drink alcohol!*" "*Don't put so much salt on that!*" "*Get some exercise!*" This is hardly a role that leads to sexual desire. Any combination of these factors may lead one or both partners to avoid sex.

Strokes, also called cerebrovascular accidents, happen when blood is cut off from part of the brain, usually because a small blood vessel bursts. Although every stroke is different depending on what areas of the brain are damaged, some common results are **hemiplegia** (he-mi-PLEE-jee-uh), **aphasia** (uh-FAY-zhee-uh), and other cognitive, perceptual, and memory problems. As with other types of brain injury (such as those caused by automobile accidents), damage to the brain can affect sexuality in a number of ways.

In most cases of stroke, sexual functioning itself is not damaged, and many stroke victims do go on to resume sexual activity. After a stroke, the problems that confront a couple with normal functioning are similar to those with cardiovascular disease: fear of causing another stroke, worries about sexual attractiveness, and the stresses and anxieties of having to cope with a major illness. However, a stroke can also cause physiological changes that affect sexuality. Some men may experience priapism after a stroke,

because the nerves controlling the erectile tissue on one side of the penis are affected. Hemiplegia can result in spastic movements (jerking motions) and reduced sensation on one side of Paralysis can also contribute to a feeling of awkwardness or unattractiveness. In addition, aphasia can affect a person's ability to communicate or understand sexual cues.

Some stroke victims also go through periods of **disinhibition**, in which they exhibit behaviour that, before the stroke, they would have been able to suppress. This can include hypersexuality, in which the patient makes lewd comments, masturbates in public, disrobes publicly, or makes inappropriate sexual advances (Larkin, 1992). Others may experience **hyposexuality**, in which they show decreased sexual desire, or they may experience ED. Sexual intervention programs have been designed for use in rehabilitation hospitals, and they can be of great help in teaching couples how to deal with the difficulties of adjusting to life after a stroke.

Cancer

Cancer can involve almost any organ of the body and has a reputation of being invariably fatal. In Canada, it is the leading cause of death (Statistics Canada, 2014). However, cure rates have increased dramatically, and some cancers are now more than 90 percent curable. Still, cancer can kill, and a diagnosis of cancer is usually accompanied by shock, numbness, and gripping fear. Also, as in other illnesses, partners may need to become caretakers, and roles can change. Cancer treatments are likely to disrupt a patients' sexual functioning (Burns et al., 2007; Carpentier & Fortenberry, 2010; Li & Rew, 2010; Ofman, 2004; Reese, 2011). These disruptions may be temporary or long lasting.

For example, surgery is required for a number of cancers of the digestive system, and it can lead to **ostomies** (OST-stome-mees). People with cancer of the colon often need to have part or all of the large intestine removed; the rectum may be removed as well. A surgical opening, called a **stoma** (STOW-mah), is made in the abdomen to allow waste products to exit the body. This is collected in a bag, which, for many patients, must be worn at all times (others can take it off periodically). Ostomy bags are visually unpleasant and may emit an odour, and the adjustment to their presence can be difficult for some couples. Having a new opening in the body to eliminate bodily wastes is itself a hard thing to accept for many people, but most eventually adjust to it and, barring other problems related to their disease, go on to live healthy and sexually active lives.

stroke Occurs when blood is cut off from part of the brain, usually because a small blood vessel bursts.	**hyposexuality** Abnormal suppression of sexual desire and behaviour; the term usually refers to behaviour caused by some disturbance of the brain.
hemiplegia Paralysis of one side of the body.	**ostomies** Operations to remove part of the small or large intestine or the bladder, resulting in the need to create an artificial opening in the body for the elimination of bodily wastes.
aphasia Defects in the ability to express and/or understand speech, signs, or written communication, caused by damage to the speech centres of the brain.	
disinhibition The loss of normal control over behaviours such as expressing sexuality or taking one's clothes off in public.	**stoma** Surgical opening made in the abdomen to allow waste products to exit the body.

Cancer can affect sexual functioning in other ways as well. Physical scars, the loss of limbs or body parts, changes in skin texture when radiation therapy is used, the loss of hair, nausea, bloating, weight gain or loss, and acne are just some of the ways that cancer and its treatment can affect the body and one's body image. In addition, the psychological trauma and the fear of death can lead to depression, which can inhibit sexual relations. Perhaps the most drastic situations, however, occur when cancer affects the sexual organs themselves.

Breast Cancer

In North American society, breasts are a focal part of female sexual attractiveness, and women often invest much of their feminine self-image in their breasts. For many years, a diagnosis of breast cancer usually meant that a woman lost that breast; **mastectomy** was the preferred treatment. **Simple mastectomies** meant that the breast tissue alone was removed, whereas radical mastectomies involved the removal of the breast together with other tissues and lymph nodes. As we discussed in Chapter 3, the numbers of mastectomies have decreased today, and many women are opting for lumpectomies. These are often coupled with chemotherapy, radiation therapy, or both.

Breast cancer and cancer treatments can negatively affect several physiological, psychological, and interpersonal aspects of sexual functioning and satisfaction (Biglia et al., 2010; Davis et al., 2010b; Emilee et al., 2010; Manganiello et al., 2011; Melisko et al., 2010; Reese

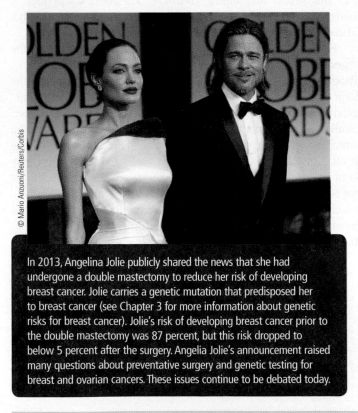

© Mario Anzuoni/Reuters/Corbis

In 2013, Angelina Jolie publicly shared the news that she had undergone a double mastectomy to reduce her risk of developing breast cancer. Jolie carries a genetic mutation that predisposed her to breast cancer (see Chapter 3 for more information about genetic risks for breast cancer). Jolie's risk of developing breast cancer prior to the double mastectomy was 87 percent, but this risk dropped to below 5 percent after the surgery. Angelia Jolie's announcement raised many questions about preventative surgery and genetic testing for breast and ovarian cancers. These issues continue to be debated today.

mastectomy
Surgical removal of a breast.

simple mastectomy
Surgical removal of the breast tissue.

oophorectomy
Surgical removal of the ovaries.

et al., 2010; Sadovsky et al., 2010). Chemotherapy and endocrine treatments have been found to create abrupt menopause in young women, leading to vaginal dryness, pain, discomfort, and significantly reduced levels of sexual desire (Carter et al., 2011; Ochsenkühn et al., 2011). Mastectomies have also been found to have a negative impact on women's sexuality and body images (Brandberg et al., 2008; Manganiello et al., 2011). A woman who loses a breast may worry that her partner will no longer find her attractive or desirable.

One study found that although 80 percent of women reported a satisfying sex life before breast cancer, 70 percent reported sexual problems after their treatment for breast cancer (Panjari et al., 2011). Sexual problems included decreased arousal and desire, problems with body image, as well as an increase in menopausal symptoms (i.e., hot flashes and night sweats). Educating women about these changes and providing them with information on how to cope with them can improve sexual functioning (Carter et al., 2011).

Pelvic Cancer and Hysterectomies

Cancer can also occur in a woman's vagina, uterus, cervix, or ovaries. Although women with vaginal and cervical cancers often experience more sexual problems than women without these cancers, rates of sexual activity and partnering are similar (Lindau et al., 2007). Negative changes in sexual functioning have been found in some studies, but not in others (Donovan et al., 2007; Gamel et al., 2000; Greenwald & McCorkle, 2008). Common sexual issues include insufficient vaginal lubrication, shortened vaginas, reduced vaginal elasticity, and sexual pain (Bergmark et al., 1999). Overall, a woman's feelings about her cancer treatment and her social support network are both important in sexual recovery from these treatments. Educating women about the sexual effects of cancer can help improve sexual functioning (Lindau et al., 2007).

Cancer of the reproductive organs may result in a hysterectomy. In a total hysterectomy, the uterus and cervix (which is part of the uterus) are removed; in a radical hysterectomy, the ovaries are also removed (**oophorectomy**; oh-uh-for-RECT-toe-mee), together with the Fallopian tubes and surrounding tissue. Hysterectomies are also performed for conditions other than cancer, such as fibroids, endometriosis, and uterine prolapse.

A hysterectomy may or may not affect sexual functioning, but many health care providers neglect to discuss the sexual implications of hysterectomy (Jongpipan & Charoenkwan, 2007). If the ovaries are removed with the uterus, a woman will experience hormonal imbalances that can lead to reduced vaginal lubrication, hot flashes, night sweats, insomnia, mood swings, and other bodily changes. Whether removal of the uterus decreases physical sexual response is controversial, with some studies finding that it does and others finding that it does not (Jongpipan & Charoenkwan, 2007; Maas et al., 2004; Srivastava et al., 2008). Women with a history of depression or sexual problems are often at increased risk for development of more of these symptoms after a hysterectomy (Shifren & Avis, 2007).

Prostate Cancer

As we discussed in Chapter 4, almost all men will experience a normal enlargement of the prostate gland if they live long enough. Prostate cancer is one of the most common cancers in men older than 50. In the past, when a man experienced an enlarged prostate or was diagnosed with prostate cancer, a **prostatectomy** (pross-tuh-TECK-toe-mee) may have been performed, sometimes along with a **cystectomy**. These procedures often involved cutting the nerves necessary for erection, resulting in ED. A possible adverse effect of prostatectomy may be **incontinence**, sometimes necessitating an **indwelling catheter**. Many couples fear that this means the end of their sex life because removing and reinserting the catheter can lead to infection. However, the catheter can be folded alongside the penis during sexual behaviour or held in place with a condom (Sandowski, 1989). For men who experience ED from the surgery, penile prostheses or intracavernous injections are possible.

Today, newer surgical techniques have resulted in less ED. Although improved prostate cancer screening has led to higher survival rates, the development of androgen deprivation therapy to decrease the development of prostate cancer has been found to contribute to sexual problems (Elliott et al., 2010). Because men begin this therapy earlier and stay on it longer, many experience decreases in sexual performance and satisfaction (Elliott et al., 2010). As in all surgeries of this kind, the man must also cope with the fear of disease, concern about his masculinity and body image, concern about the reactions of his sexual partner, and the new sensations or sexual functioning that can accompany prostate surgery.

When men are diagnosed with prostate cancer, many worry about sexual functioning after treatment (Knight & Latini, 2009). Overall, many men do experience declines in sexual functioning after prostate cancer treatment (Droupy, 2010; Howlett et al., 2010; Huyghe et al., 2009; Savareux & Droupy, 2009; Wittmann et al., 2011).

Testicular Cancer

Cancer of the penis or scrotum is rare, and cancer of the testes is only slightly more common (see Chapter 4). Still, the sexual problems that result from these diseases are similar to those from prostate cancer. Testicular cancer is most common in men who are in their most productive years. Researchers have found that although sexual issues, including ejaculatory problems, are common after treatment for testicular cancer (Dahl et al., 2007), there is considerable improvement one year after diagnosis (van Basten et al., 1999).

In Chapter 4, we discussed testicular cancer, and although the surgical removal of a testicle (orchiectomy) because of cancer usually does not affect the ability to reproduce (sperm can be banked, and the remaining testicle may produce enough sperm and adequate testosterone), some men do experience psychological difficulties. This is mainly because of feelings that they have lost part of their manhood or fears about the appearance of their scrotum. The appearance of the scrotum can be helped by inserting a testicular prosthesis that takes the place of the missing testicle. In some rare cases, cancer of the penis may necessitate a partial or total penectomy (pee-NECK-toe-mee). In a total penectomy, the man's urethra is redirected downward to a new opening that is created between the scrotum and anus. Even with a penectomy, some men can have orgasms by stimulating whatever tissue is left where the penis was, and the ejaculate leaves the body through the urethra (Schover & Jensen, 1988).

It is well documented that sexual problems can occur as a result of any type of cancer or cancer treatment (Ofman, 2004; Sheppard & Wylie, 2001). However, they may only be a temporary result of the stress associated with the situation (Ofman, 2004).

Diabetes

Diabetes is caused by the inability of the pancreas to produce insulin, which is used to process blood sugar into energy, or by the inability of the body to use the insulin produced. Diabetes may affect children (Type I diabetes), who must then depend on insulin injections for the rest of their lives, or it may appear later (Type II diabetes) and may then be controlled through diet or oral medication. Diabetes is a serious condition that can ultimately lead to blindness, renal failure, and other problems.

People with diabetes often experience multiple and complex sexual difficulties. In fact, sexual problems (especially difficulty in getting an erection for men) may be one of the first signs of diabetes. A large number of men in the later stages of diabetes have penile prostheses implanted (discussed earlier in this chapter). Although women with Type I diabetes may experience some problems with vaginal lubrication, the majority do not seem to have significantly more problems than non-diabetic women. However, women with Type II diabetes often experience loss of desire, difficulties in lubrication, decreased sexual satisfaction, and problems with orgasm (Esposito et al., 2010; Giraldi & Kristensen, 2010; Schover & Jensen, 1988).

Differentiating between how much of a person's sexual difficulty is due to underlying physiological problems and how much is due to psychological issues is often difficult. Depression, fear of ED, lack of sexual response, anxiety about the future, and the life changes that diabetes can bring can all dampen sexual desire. Sex therapy is often an important part of diabetes treatment.

Arthritis

One area of health that is often overlooked when discussing sexual health, sexual drive, and an individual's perception of him- or herself as a sexual being is arthritis (Hamilton, 1981). At present, there are 120 different diagnosable forms of arthritis (Newman, 2007). Arthritis is one of the most common chronic health conditions in Canada, and just under 20 percent of women and 13 percent of men 15 years of age or older in Canada will be diagnosed with arthritis in their lifetime. The highest rates of occurrence of this group of diseases are in individuals between 45 and 64 (44 percent) (Public Health Agency of Canada, 2011). This is at a time in life where many adults are at the prime of their sexual desire and sexual activity levels. Many individuals who suffer from arthritis worry about whether their sex lives as they know it will be over, whether they will have enough mobility to engage in sexual activity, and whether they will be able to withstand the pain that may be associated with moving joints that are stiff and suffering from inflammation (Palmer & El Meidany, 2011). Many individuals with arthritis are reluctant to discuss the impact their disease has on their levels of sexual desire and sexual activity.

prostatectomy	**incontinence**
The surgical removal of the prostate gland.	Lack of normal voluntary control of urinary functions.
cystectomy	**indwelling catheter**
Surgical removal of the bladder.	A permanent catheter, inserted in the bladder, to allow the removal of urine in those who are unable to urinate or are incontinent.

Challenges to Sexual Functioning **411**

Many individuals with arthritis are able and willing to fill out surveys addressing issues related to sexual activity and this can provide a gateway to discussions about treatments and alternative ways or positions for engaging in sexual activity (Palmer & El Meidany, 2011). Using supports such as triangular foam cushions to support the pelvis and limbs can alleviate the pressure on the joints that can occur during sex. Treatments such as pain relievers to reduce joint inflammation, hot and cold topical muscle relaxants, and exploring alternative forms of sexual expression can be useful for those with arthritis (Tristano, 2009). Psychological therapy can also be helpful for the partners in a sexual relationship in order for them to discuss their sexual needs and adjust their behaviours to accommodate the pain a person with arthritis may be experiencing.

Multiple Sclerosis

Multiple sclerosis (MS) involves a breakdown of the myelin sheath that wraps around large axons in the central nervous system. This sheath is important for making sure that the signals of the central nervous system reach your body. For example, if you wish to move your big toe, your brain has to send a signal to your spinal cord that is then routed to your toe. When the myelin sheath degrades, the signals from the brain to the periphery of the body become weaker and in severe cases do not make it to their destination. Multiple sclerosis can manifest in a variety of symptoms, such as dizziness, weakness, blurred or double vision, muscle spasms, spasticity, and loss of control of limbs and muscles. Symptoms can come and go without warning, but MS is progressive and may worsen over time. MS often strikes people between the ages of 20 and 50, at a time when they are establishing sexual relationships and families (M.P. McCabe, 2002).

MS can affect sexual functioning in many ways. Most commonly, men with MS experience ED (M.P. McCabe, 2002), whereas women with MS experience difficulties reaching orgasm (Tepavcevic et al., 2008; Tzortzis et al., 2008). Both men and women may become hypersensitive to touch, experiencing even light caresses as painful or unpleasant. Fatigue, muscle spasms, and loss of bladder and bowel function can also inhibit sexual contact. Sexual counselling, penile prostheses in men, and artificial lubrication in women can help overcome some of these difficulties.

Spinal Cord Injuries

The spinal cord brings impulses from the brain to the various parts of the body; damage to the cord can cut off those impulses in any areas served by nerves below the damaged section. SCIs can significantly affect sexual health and functioning (Borisoff et al., 2010; Cardoso et al., 2009). In Canada 85 556 people in 2010 were living with a spinal cord injury (Noonan et al., 2012). To assess potential problems with sexual activity, a physician must know exactly where on the spine the injury occurred and how extensively the cord has been damaged (Alexander et al., 2009; Benevento & Sipski, 2002). Although some return of sensation and movement can be achieved in many injuries, most people are left with permanent disabilities.

---

paraplegia
Paralysis of the legs and lower part of the body, affecting both sensation and motor response.

quadriplegia
Paralysis of all four limbs.

In more extreme cases, SCI can result in total or partial **paraplegia** (pah-ruh-PLEE-jee-uh) or total or partial **quadriplegia** (kwa-druh-PLEE-jee-uh). In these cases, the person is rendered extremely dependent on his or her partner or caretaker.

Men are four times more likely than women to experience SCI, and if the injury is above a certain vertebra, a man may still be able to have an erection through the body's reflex mechanism. However, it may be difficult to maintain an erection because there are reduced skin sensations in the penis. Injuries to the lower part of the spine are more likely to result in erectile difficulties in men, but they are also more likely to preserve some sensation in the genitals. Men without disabilities maintain erections, in part, through psychic arousal, such as sexual thoughts, feelings, and fantasies; however, with SCI, psychic arousal cannot provide continuing stimulation. Most men with SCIs who are capable of having erections are not able to climax or ejaculate, which involves a more complex mechanism than an erection (Benevento & Sipski, 2002). A number of men report experiencing orgasm without ejaculation (Sipski et al., 2006).

Women with SCI can lose sensation in the genitals, and with it the ability to lubricate during sexual activity, making penetrative sex difficult (Lombardi et al., 2009, 2010). However, many men and women with SCIs maintain orgasmic ability (M. Alexander & Rosen, 2008; Kreuter et al., 2011). "Phantom orgasm," a psychic sensation of having an orgasm without the corresponding physical reactions, is also common. Skin sensation in the areas unaffected by the injury can become greater, and new erogenous zones can appear (D.J. Brown et al., 2005; Ferreiro-Velasco et al., 2005).

Sexual problems develop over time as the full impact of their situation takes effect. Although men with SCI can resume sexual activity within a year of their injury, their frequency of sexual activity decreases after the injury (C.J. Alexander et al., 1993). Many men and women enjoy a variety of sexual activities after SCI, including kissing, hugging, and touching. A healthy sex life after SCI is possible if a man or woman can learn to overcome the physical and psychological obstacles of their injuries (Kreuter et al., 2008).

Rehabilitation from SCI can be a long, difficult process. Still, with a caring partner, meaningful sexual contact can be achieved. Men incapable of having an erection can still use their mouths and sometimes their hands. If penetrative sex is desired, couples can use "stuffing" techniques, in which the flaccid penis is pushed into the vagina or anus. Possible treatment methods include prosthesis implantation, vacuum erection devices, and the injection of vasoactive drugs. Prosthesis implantation in men with SCIs have shown high satisfaction and low complication rates (Kim et al., 2008). Research has found that various erectile drugs, including Viagra, can significantly improve erections in men with SCI (Fink et al., 2002; Lombardi et al., 2009, 2010).

Mental Illness

People with psychological disorders have sexual fantasies, needs, and feelings, and they have the same right to a fulfilling sexual life as others do. However, historically they have either been treated as asexual, or their sexuality has been viewed as illegitimate, warped, or needing external control (Apfel & Handel, 1993). Yet a sudden or drastic change in sexual habits may be a sign of mental illness or a sign that a mentally ill person is getting worse (or better, depending on the change).

People with **schizophrenia**, for example, can be among the most impaired and difficult psychiatric patients, and compliance with social norms can be challenging for these individuals. People with schizophrenia have been found to grapple with the same sexual questions and problems as other people. The same is true of people with **major depression** and other **affective disorders**. They may experience hyposexuality when depressed or hypersexuality in periods of mania. Both can also occur as a result of antidepressant medications. Otherwise, their sexual problems do not differ significantly from those of people without major psychiatric problems (Schover & Jensen, 1988).

Sexual issues among those with intellectual disabilities are often neglected in psychiatric training, and health care providers who treat these patients have often spent more time trying to control and limit patients' sexual behaviour than they have in treating sexual problems. For years, those with intellectual disabilities have been kept from learning about sexuality and having sexual relationships. It is as if an otherwise healthy adult is supposed to display no sexual interest or activity at all. Educators have designed special sexuality education programs for the intellectually and developmentally disabled to make sure that they express their sexuality in a socially approved manner (Monat-Haller, 1992). However, to deny people with psychiatric problems or disabilities the pleasure of a sexual life is cruel and unnecessary.

Many people with intellectual disabilities (and physical disabilities) must spend long periods of their lives—sometimes their entire lives—in institutions, which makes developing a sex life difficult. Institutions differ greatly in the amount of sexual contact they allow; some allow none whatsoever, whereas others allow mutually consenting sexual contact, with the staff carefully overseeing the patients' contraceptive and hygienic needs (Trudel & Desjardins, 1992).

Another aspect of institutional life involves the sexual exploitation of patients with mental illness or intellectual disabilities. This is well-known but seldom discussed by those who work in such institutions. About half of all women in psychiatric hospitals report having been abused as children or adolescents, and many are then abused in a hospital or other institutional setting. Children who grow up with developmental disabilities are between four and ten times more likely to be abused than children without those difficulties (Baladerian, 1991). Therefore, it is difficult to separate the sexual problems of mental illness, developmental disability, and psychiatric illness from histories of sexual abuse (Apfel & Handel, 1993; Monat-Haller, 1992).

Other Conditions

Many other conditions, such as chronic pain from illnesses such as migraine headaches and back pain can make sexual behaviour difficult or impossible at times. Respiratory illnesses, such as **chronic obstructive pulmonary disease (COPD)** and asthma (Goodell, 2007; Hackett, 2009), can also have a significant negative effect on sexual functioning. Not only do these diseases make physical exertion difficult, but they can also impair perceptual and motor skills. Millions of people who have COPD learn to take medicine before sexual activity and slow down their pace of sexual activity; their partners learn to use positions that allow the person with COPD to breathe comfortably.

Review Questions

1 Explain how physical illness and its treatment can interfere with sexual desire, physiological functioning, or both.

2 Explain why it is important for health care workers to ask patients about their sex lives.

3 Explain how cardiovascular illnesses can affect sexual functioning.

4 Explain how various cancers can affect sexual functioning.

5 Explain how diabetes, MS, SCIs, mental illness, arthritis, and aging can affect sexual functioning.

Getting Help

People who have substance abuse issues or are ill or disabled have the same sexual needs and desires as everyone else. In the past, these needs have too often been neglected not because the disabled individuals themselves were not interested in sexuality, but because health care providers and other health care professionals were uncomfortable learning about their sexual needs and discussing them with their patients. Fortunately, this has been changing, and now sexuality counselling is a normal part of the recuperation from many diseases and injuries in many hospitals.

If you are experiencing problems with sexual functioning, it is important to seek help as soon as possible. Often, when the problems are ignored, they lead to bigger problems down the road. If

schizophrenia
A condition that affects the individual's ability to think, behave, or perceive things normally.

major depression
A persistent, chronic state in which the person feels he or she has no worth, cannot function normally, and entertains thoughts of or attempts suicide.

affective disorders
A class of mental disorders that affect mood.

chronic obstructive pulmonary disease (COPD)
A disease of the lung that affects breathing.

you are in college and have a student counselling centre available to you, this may be a good place to start looking for help. Request a counsellor who has received training in sexuality or ask to be referred to one who has.

Review Questions

1 Explain how the sexual needs of people who are ill or disabled have been neglected over the years.

2 Explain why sexuality counselling is an important part of the recovery process.

3 Why might it be beneficial to seek help and not ignore a sexual problem?

Chapter Review

Summary Points

1 Healthy sexuality depends on good mental and physical functioning. Sexual problems are common and may occur when we don't feel sufficiently aroused, have a lower level of enthusiasm, or have trouble relaxing during sex. The majority of couples report periodic sexual problems, but most of the time these problems do not interfere with overall sexual functioning and they go away on their own.

2 Defining a sexual problem can be difficult. To help clarify definitions, many sex therapists use the *Diagnostic and Statistical Manual of Mental Disorders* (DSM-5), which provides diagnostic criteria for the most common sexual problems.

3 Psychological factors that can challenge sexual functioning include unconscious fears, stress, anxiety, depression, guilt, anger, fear of intimacy, dependency, abandonment, concern over loss of control, and performance fears. In addition, relationship issues can also contribute to sexual problems, such as feeling unappreciated, anger, insecurity, resentment, conflict, or a lack of trust.

4 Physiological factors that can challenge sexual functioning include various injuries, disabilities, illnesses, diseases, medications, street drugs, and aging. Treatments for various diseases, such as chemotherapy and radiation, can also contribute to sexual problems.

5 Sexual problems can be primary or secondary and situational or global. Research has found that primary problems have more biological or physiological causes, whereas secondary problems tend to have more psychological causes. Situational problems occur during certain sexual activities or with certain partners, whereas global problems

occur in every situation, during every type of sexual activity, and with every sexual partner.

6 The DSM-5 had two categories of sexual desire disorders, female sexual interest/arousal disorder and male hypoactive sexual desire disorder. Many therapists consider problems with sexual desire to be one of the most complicated sexual problems to treat. A variety of different treatment options are available. Cognitive–behavioural therapy, a form of psychotherapy that emphasizes the importance of how a person thinks and the effect these thoughts have on a person's feelings and behaviours, has offered promising results. Pharmacological treatments have also been used.

7 In men, sexual arousal disorders can lead to *erectile disorder (ED)*. Approximately 70 percent of EDs have a physical basis, with the major risk factors being diabetes, high cholesterol levels, or chronic medical illnesses. EDs in younger men are more likely to be psychologically based, whereas EDs in older men are more likely to be due to physical factors. Of all the sexual disorders, there are more treatment options for male ED than for any other sexual disorder.

8 Treatment options include psychological treatment (including systematic desensitization and sex therapy); psychopharmacological, hormonal, and intracavernous injections; vascular surgery; vacuum constriction devices; and prosthesis implantation. The treatment of ED has changed considerably since erectile drugs became available.

9 The DSM-5 had three categories of orgasmic disorders, including female orgasmic disorder, delayed ejaculation, and

early (premature) ejaculation. There are both physiological factors (such as chronic illness, diabetes, neurological problems, hormonal deficiencies, or alcoholism) and psychological factors (such as a lack of sex education, fear or anxiety, or psychological disorders) that may interfere with a woman's ability to reach orgasm. The majority of treatment programs for orgasmic disorder involve a combination of different treatment approaches, such as homework assignments, sex education, communication skills training, cognitive restructuring, desensitization, and other techniques.

10 The ejaculatory process is controlled by various endocrine factors, including testosterone, oxytocin, prolactin, and thyroid hormones. There is a wide spectrum of ejaculatory disorders, ranging from premature or early ejaculation to a delay or absence of ejaculation. Early ejaculation refers to a condition in which a man reaches orgasm just before, or immediately following, penetration. Early ejaculation is the most common sexual problem affecting men. Treatment methods include cognitive-behavioural therapy and pharmaceutical treatments. Two popular behavioural techniques include the stop–start and the squeeze techniques.

11 Delayed ejaculation involves a delayed, infrequent, or absent ejaculation that has occurred for six months or more and occurs on most occasions of sexual activity. Delayed ejaculation is relatively rare.

12 Other ejaculatory disorders include retrograde ejaculation, in which the ejaculate empties into the bladder instead of being ejaculated outside the body through the urethra. A man with retrograde ejaculation typically experiences orgasm with little or no ejaculation (also called a "dry orgasm" or anejaculation). Treatment for ejaculatory disorders often depends on the duration, context, and causes of the disorder. Lifelong ejaculatory problems are often treated with medications or topical anesthetics, whereas other cases might be treated with behavioural therapy, with or without medications.

13 The DSM-5 has one category of pain disorders associated with sex—genito-pelvic pain/penetration disorder. Treatment for genito-pelvic pain and penetration disorders can include physical therapy, prescription medications, and various therapies. Cognitive–behavioural therapy has been found to reduce pain and increase comfort with penetration. After treatment,

many women report being able to engage in penetrative sex, as well as increases in self-esteem and self-worth. Other treatment options include biofeedback, surgery, and the use of Botox to reduce vaginal and pelvic pain.

14 The final defined category of sexual dysfunction in the DSM-5 is the substance/medication-induced sexual dysfunction. The major classes of drugs that are addressed with regards to their effects on sexual function are alcohol, the opioids, sedative/hypnotic/anxiolytic drugs, and stimulants such as cocaine and amphetamine.

15 Physical illness and its treatment can interfere with a person's sexual desire, physiological functioning, or both. Cardiovascular problems, including hypertension, myocardial infarctions, strokes, and cancer, can all affect

sexual functioning. Cancer treatments can negatively affect several physiological, psychological, and interpersonal aspects of sexual functioning and satisfaction.

16 Chronic illnesses, such as diabetes, multiple sclerosis (MS), and arthritis can also negatively affect sexual functioning. Spinal cord injuries (SCIs), mental illness, and intellectual disabilities present specific challenges to sexual functioning. People who are ill or disabled have the same sexual needs and desires that healthy people do.

17 People who are experiencing sexual problems, illness, disease, or disability should seek treatment as soon as possible to avoid the development of further problems. When problems are ignored, they tend to lead to bigger problems down the road.

Critical Thinking Questions

1 Suppose that one night you discover that you are having trouble reaching orgasm with your partner. What do you do about it? When it happens several times, what do you do? Who would you feel comfortable talking to about this problem?

2 If you were suddenly disabled or developed a chronic illness that may be associated with aging such as arthritis, would you lose your desire to

love and be loved, to touch and be touched, and to be regarded by another as sexy and desirable? How could this loss of desire be prevented?

3 Do you think college students without ED should recreationally take erectile drugs? Why or why not?

4 Do you think that drug companies could convince us that a sexual problem exists when

there is none? Should researchers be doing more work to uncover the causes of female sexual problems, even if the pharmaceutical companies are paying for this research? Why or why not?

5 Although women may be diagnosed with persistent sexual arousal syndrome, there is no companion diagnosis for men. Why do you think this is? Do you think there should be such a diagnosis for men? Why or why not?

Websites

Dr. Elke Reissing, Human Sexuality Research Laboratory, University of Ottawa   Dr. Reissing has published several studies on vaginismus and sexual behaviour in men and women in Canada. Her website is an excellent resource for her work on sexual relationships in Canada and aspects of sexual dysfunction and their effects on sexual behaviour. (http://socialsciences.uottawa.ca/human-sexuality-research/)

Dr. Lori Brotto, UBC Sexual Health Laboratory   Dr. Brotto is a specialist in the psychophysiological aspects of women diagnosed with sexual dysfunction. (http://brottolab.com)

Dr. Rosemary Basson, Sexual Medicine Specialist at the University of British Columbia   This website provides free online education in several areas of sexual health. (http://thischangedmypractice.com/author/robasson/)

Board of Examiners of Sex Therapy and Counselling in Ontario (BESTCO)   This organization specializes in assisting therapists with sex therapy certification and continuing education. (http://www.bestco.info)

University of Guelph Intensive Sex Therapy Training Program   This program provides one-week intensive programs on sex therapy and counselling. (http://guelphsexualityconference.ca/intensive-sex-therapy-training-program/)

International Society for the Study of Women's Sexual Health (ISSWSH)   The ISSWSH is a multidisciplinary, academic, and scientific organization that works to provide opportunities for communication among scholars, researchers, and practitioners about women's sexual functioning, as well as to provide the public with accurate information about women's sexual health. (http://www.isswsh.org/)

Disability Resources   This website offers information on sexuality for people with disabilities and for parents of children with disabilities. General disability information can be found, as well as disability-specific information. (http://www.disabilityresources.org/SEX.html)

New View Campaign   Formed in 2000, this campaign challenges the medicalization of sex by the pharmaceutical companies. The website contains information, contacts, and media interviews. (http://www.newviewcampaign.org/)

Information for Men with Erectile Dysfunction—Mayo Clinic   This website provides basic information about erectile dysfunction and its treatments. (http://www.mayoclinic.org/diseases-conditions/erectile-dysfunction/basics/definition/con-20034244)

16 Harmful and Antisocial Sexual Expression

"Give me the whip."

I looked about the room.

"No," she exclaimed, "stay as you are, kneeling."
She went over to the fire-place, took the whip from the mantle-piece, and, watching me with a smile, let it hiss through the air; then she slowly rolled up the sleeve of her fur-jacket.

"Marvellous woman!" I exclaimed.

"Silence, slave!" She suddenly scowled, looked savage, and struck me with the whip. A moment later she threw her arm tenderly about me, and pityingly bent down to me. "Did I hurt you?" she asked, half-shyly, half-timidly.

"No," I replied, "and even if you had, pains that come through you are a joy. Strike again, if it gives you pleasure."

"But it doesn't give me pleasure."

Again I was seized with that strange intoxication.

"Whip me," I begged, "whip me without mercy."

Wanda swung the whip, and hit me twice. "Are you satisfied now?"

"No."

"Seriously, no?"

"Whip me, I beg you, it is a joy to me."

"Yes, because you know very well that it isn't serious," she replied, "because I haven't the heart to hurt you. This brutal game goes against my grain. Were I really the woman who beats her slaves you would be horrified."

"No, Wanda," I replied, "I love you more than myself; I am devoted to you for death and life. In all seriousness, you can do with me whatever you will, whatever your caprice suggests."

"Severin!"

"Tread me underfoot!" I exclaimed, and flung myself face to the floor before her.

"I hate all this play-acting," said Wanda impatiently.

"Well, then maltreat me seriously."

An uncanny pause.

"Severin, I warn you for the last time," began Wanda.

"If you love me, be cruel towards me," I pleaded with upraised eyes.

"If I love you," repeated Wanda. "Very well!" She stepped back and looked at me with a sombre smile. "Be then my slave, and know what it means to be delivered into the hands of a woman." And at the same moment she gave me a kick.

"How do you like that, slave?"

Then she flourished the whip.

"Get up!"

I was about to rise.

"Not that way," she commanded, "on your knees."

I obeyed, and she began to apply the lash.

The blows fell rapidly and powerfully on my back and arms. Each one cut into my flesh and burned there, but the pains enraptured me. They came from her whom I adored, and for whom I was ready at any hour to lay down my life.

She stopped. "I am beginning to enjoy it," she said, "but enough for to-day. I am beginning to feel a demonic curiosity to see how far your strength goes. I take a cruel joy in seeing you tremble and writhe beneath my whip, and in hearing your groans and wails; I want to go on whipping without pity until you beg for mercy, until you lose your senses. You have awakened dangerous elements in my being. But now get up."

I seized her hand to press it to my lips.

"What impudence."

She shoved me away with her foot.

"Out of my sight, slave!"

SOURCE: From *Venus in Furs*, by Leopold von Sacher-Masoch, 1869. ▮▮

There have been numerous terms to describe people whose sexuality is non-conformist over the past two centuries, among them *sexual inversion, sexual perversion, sexual deviation*, and *sexual psychopathy*. In the 19th century, sexual inversion referred mainly to homosexuality but under the umbrella of its amorphous definition it also covered transsexualism, transvestism, and anyone who did not conform to heterosexuality and gender norms. A gay man was an invert, and so were a pedophile, a drag queen, a male prostitute, and a masculine woman. Indeed, according to Richard von Krafft-Ebing in the late 19th century (see Chapter 2), female sexual inversion was "the masculine soul, heaving in the female bosom" (Taylor, 1998). Later on came the terms *pervert* and *deviant*, which were similarly murky in their definitions—so much so that to the public eye there existed generic male strangers, all of whom lurked in the shadows of suburbia and preyed upon innocent women and children (Chener, 2012). Even the *Motion Picture Production Code*, which imposed moral standards upon American films from 1930 to 1968, specified "no sexual perversion," without offering any definition. The "pervert" therefore was almost a folk figure who had no parameters.

Canada enacted "criminal sexual psychopath" laws in 1948 (Chenier, 2012) and they encompassed a variety of sexual behaviours—homosexuality and pedophilia among them. In this chapter, we do not look at "perverts" and deviants" but instead at specific sexual variations that usually harm individuals. We use the guidelines of the fifth edition of the *Diagnostic and Statistical Manual* (DSM-5; American Psychiatric Association, 2013). Unlike its predecessors, this edition distinguishes between unusual sexual behaviour and that which is harmful or "disordered." This distinction represents a significant shift in psychiatry that it now also distinguishes between merely having a paraphilic interest and that interest leading to stress or harm.

What Is "Abnormal" Sexual Expression?

What is abnormal sexual expression? Perhaps the need we feel to brand some sexual behaviours as perverse is summed up by Levine et al. (1990, p. 92) when they say that images of alternative sexualities "often involve arousal without the pretense of caring or human attachment." In other words, people tend to be uncomfortable with sex for its own sake in that it is separate from ideas of love, intimacy, or human attachment (Laws & O'Donohue, 2008). Human sexuality takes on many forms. Societies pay little attention to most differences in expression among individuals but they tend to draw distinct lines when it comes to sexuality. There is sexual behaviour that is celebrated, sexual behaviour that is tolerated, and sexual behaviour that is considered aberrant (Laws & Donohue, 2008). Undergraduate textbooks in human sexuality have often referred to particular forms of sexual expression as "abnormal" and these lines have varied considerably over time. In 1906, Richard von Krafft-Ebing defined virtually all forms of sexual expression that do not conform to the "purpose of nature" as aberrant (Brown, 1983, p. 227). In this respect, his views, medically informed as they supposedly were, differed little from early Christian fathers St. Augustine and St. Paul (see Chapter 1). With Krafft-Ebing, even oral sex would be indicative of mental illness.

> **REAL Research** Nova Scotian researchers Hébert and Weaver (2014) looked at the personality characteristics of 270 BDSM practitioners with online questionnaires. Dominants scores higher on life satisfaction and self-esteem while submissive scores higher on emotionality. There were no differences in empathy, altruism, and agreeableness.

Sigmund Freud also drew boundaries narrowly. He stated that the criterion of normalcy was love and that defences against "perversion" were the bedrock of civilization in that this is what trivializes or degrades love (Cooper, 1991). In other words, sex that does not involve love or at least intimacy is perverse. Given that Europe had one of the highest incidences of prostitution during his time and clients were often married men of the upper classes (Chesney, 1970), and given that men typically were sexually experienced before marriage, most people in Freud's view would have been perverse.

As Canadian sociologists Hunt and Curtis (2006) pointed out, oral sex has shifted from aberrant to normal to problematic once again. It was considered perverse during the early 20th century, became part of a healthy repertoire of lovemaking by the 1960s, and has been problematized once again in the 21st century when discussing adolescent sexual behaviour (Dake et al., 2011; Song & Halperin-Felsher, 2011).

Masturbation serves as another example. By the 16th century, it became associated with a host of ailments including pimples, epilepsy, circulatory problems, sore backs, and fatigue (Brame, 2011). There were vehement campaigns against it in the late 19th and early 20th centuries by such moral entrepreneurs as John Harvey Kellogg (see Chapter 14), and it was not until the publication of Kinsey's research (Kinsey et al., 1948; Kinsey et al., 1953) that it was dismissed as mentally and physically harmless. Prior to this, however, it was considered extremely harmful and indicative of mental illness.

Perhaps homosexuality serves as the best example of all. Men and women were persecuted for their differences since Biblical times, homosexual expression landed many people in prison or in mental hospitals where they often were given shock treatment against their will in the 20th century, and it was not until after the gay liberation movement in the late 1960s that attitudes began to change. Gays and lesbians transformed from mentally ill people to ordinary people in 1973 once the American Psychiatric Association removed it from their list of aberrations (Gardner, 1993). This transformation from sexual perversion to simple human variation came not from advances in psychiatry but from social and political efforts and education. Whether something is a mental illness

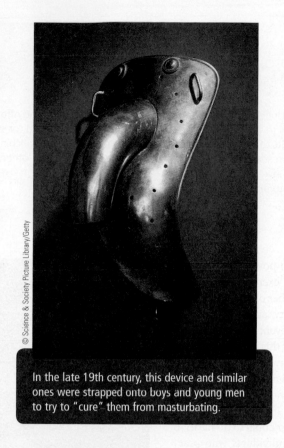

In the late 19th century, this device and similar ones were strapped onto boys and young men to try to "cure" them from masturbating.

People who practise BDSM often enjoy role playing and consider consent very important.

was not a matter of objective criteria but instead a vote. Today, gay and lesbian Canadians enjoy full equality under the law. However, the fact that homosexuality was defined as a mental illness until recently lends support to the idea that definitions of deviance, and thus normal sexual behaviour, are matters of powerful groups imposing their will upon less powerful groups. Were it not for the gay rights struggle from the 1960s to the 21st century, it is likely that gays and lesbians would still be defined as mentally ill. Freedom from such definitions today is the result of a long struggle involving education and a slow change of attitudes.

Even modern definitions of normalcy contain thinly veiled value judgments. As Gudjonsson (1986, p. 92) said, "The sexually variant individual typically exhibits sexual arousal or responses to inappropriate people ... objects ... or activities." "Appropriate" or "inappropriate" are value-laden terms and inappropriate people, objects, or activities of sexual attention vary by time, by culture, and among people. Despite the subjectivity of judgment, particular behaviours are considered the most common deviations from conventional heterosexual behaviour.

At the same time, even though the boundaries between normal and abnormal are subjective and shift between time, place, and person, boundaries must be drawn to live in a healthy, safe, and orderly society. Many people might say that fetishes or consensual BDSM are harmless but few would support pedophilia, necrophilia (sex with dead people), public exhibitionism, and voyeuristic activity (e.g., "peeping Toms"). Few would also support one person imposing his or her will on another. Such behaviour harms individuals, transgresses the rights of others, and invades privacy. Virtually all societies past and present have some boundaries concerning sexual normalcy, whether they are articulated or not (Reiss, 1986), and in many cases the main criteria have been the protection of others. Just as other forms of behaviour are limited by law and government for the protection of others, sexual behaviour has been as well.

Judging Sexual Behaviour

The classification of atypical sexual behaviour into pathological categories is controversial. Some psychiatrists such as Robert L. Stoller (1996) claim that terms such as "paraphilia" do not describe anything at all. He objected to the idea of trying to create psychological explanations that group people by their sexual habits. Doing so only reflects a society's value judgments about sexuality and nothing more. Swedish psychiatrists had just this sentiment in mind back in 2008 when they voted to remove transvestism, fetishism, and sadomasochism entirely from their official list of mental disorders (Krueger, 2009).

How then shall we judge sexual behaviour? There are several models from which to choose. The first is *sickness or sanity*. The word "sick" is typically used as an epithet for behaviour that disgusts others. All too often, it is a no more than a visceral reaction or moral judgment and, thus, meaningless. What one person finds disgusting another finds appealing. Furthermore, the medical profession has a long history of pathologizing behaviours on their own merit—that is, defining an activity as mentally ill and then using evidence of that activity to confirm mental illness. This is called a **tautology**, or circular reasoning. The logic of a tautological

tautology
Circular reasoning.

Sex Offender Information Registration Act

Canada has a law that compels sex offenders in all provinces and territories to register with the Royal Canadian Mounted Police (RCMP). This law, the Sex Offender Information Registration Act (SOIRA), requires that sex offenders register annually as well as every time they change their addresses or names. Unlike the laws of the United States, the public does not have access to this registry. It is for the purpose of the RCMP and other authorities to track known sex offenders and improve their ability to investigate crimes. Offenders are required to remain registered for 10 years, 20 years, or life depending upon the severity of the offence, and they may have been convicted for sexual interference, invitation to sexual touching, incest, bestiality, sexual assault, or otherwise.

SOURCE: Royal Canadian Mounted Police: http://rcmp.gc.ca.

argument goes like this: *Behaviour X* is a mental illness; therefore, people who do *Behaviour X* are mentally ill. As can easily be seen, the same logic would apply to knitting, drinking milk, and voting in an election. This same argument was used by the lawyers of cannibalistic serial killer Jeffrey Dahmer in 1992. As they claimed, Dahmer is insane because anyone who does what he did must be insane (*Wilmington Morning Star*, 1992). This defence was rejected by the courts, he was declared sane, and was sentenced to prison. If a behaviour is to be a mental illness, there must be symptoms independent of that behaviour to confirm any mental illness, such as depression, flights from reality, or otherwise. Historically, psychiatric assessments of mental illness regarding oral sex, masturbation, and homosexuality have been mere tautologies.

REAL Research Canadian sociologists Ricciardelli and Moir (2013) interviewed 56 men on parole regarding the treatment of sex offenders by other prisoners. They found that other prisoners stigmatized them greatly. While rapists are regarded as slightly higher than child molesters, both are treated as outcasts in prison communities.

The second model is whether an activity is *against the law*. While it is a simple matter to condemn behaviours that are illegal such as pedophilia, it is not so simple to accept all behaviours that are legal. Sometimes behaviours that break no laws may be physically or psychologically harmful to individuals and those with whom they associate. In reference to harm, British philosopher John Stewart Mill, in his book *On Liberty* (1859), said the following: "The only purpose for which power can be rightfully exercised over any member of a civilized community, against his will, is to prevent harm to others."

If this is accepted, then we have a strong criterion with which to judge sexual behaviour—the *harm principle*. If any behaviour has the potential to do harm to the individuals who practise it or to others, then there must be intervention either by legal authorities or the medical profession. The age-of-consent laws in Canada exist for this very reason. Society has a duty of protect its vulnerable members from harm. Second are privacy laws. The privacy of Canadian citizens must be protected and any behaviour that violates this right warrants intervention as well. Third and fourth are physical and mental harm. If sexual behaviour causes individuals sufficient stress, then interventions are further warranted.

As a result, we have some criteria with which to define abnormal sexual behaviour—that which causes distress or harm to the individual or other individuals, that which involves non-consenting individuals, and that which invades privacy. However, sexual behaviour where all parties are of age, where there is informed consent, and where there is no physical or mental harm to any parties concerned are matters of freedom of expression in Canadian society.

John Stewart Mill (1806–1873) asserted that individuals must be prevented from doing serious harm to themselves and others.

Review Questions

1 Explain how the medical profession has categorized sexual behaviour as aberrant through history and explain how this might affect public opinion.

2 Explain the "sickness and sin" model of abnormal sexual behaviour and give reasons why this is problematic.

3 Explain John Stewart Mill's harm principle and apply it to human sexuality.

4 What is the best definition of abnormal sexual behaviour and why?

Paraphilic Disorders

The word **paraphilia**, coined by Austrian folklorist and sexologist Friedrich Salomo Krauss (1859–1938), is derived from the Greek words *para* (beside) and *philia* (love or attraction). In other words, paraphilias are sexual behaviours that are beside or outside of the norm and, thus, unusual or different. The DSM has changed considerably over the years in its definition of paraphilias. The DSM-I (1952) and DSM-II (1968) used the term "sexual deviation" instead and simply offered a list including homosexuality, transvestism, sexual sadism, pedophilia, fetishism, and "other sexual deviation" (Laws & Donohue, 2008). Not surprisingly, this last example for which no definition was provided was subject to much bias and psychiatrists varied considerably in their opinions and treatments.

Paraphilias came into medical vocabulary with the DSM-III (1980) and by the publication of the DSM-5 (2013), the American Psychiatric Association (APA) specified that paraphilias in and of themselves are not psychiatric disorders and instead used the term *paraphilic disorder*. There are two criteria specified where either one qualifies a person as having such a disorder (APA, 2013b):

- Personal distress about one's interest not merely resulting from societal disapproval.
- A desire or behaviour that involves another person's psychological distress, injury, or death, or a desire involving unwilling individuals or those unable to give legal consent.

This change represents a significant shift in that it brings in the harm principle, provides diagnostic criteria with which to judge behaviours other than simply the behaviours themselves (thus avoiding tautological reasoning), and de-pathologizes people who merely have atypical sexual interests such as BDSM activities (Wright, 2010). The fact that society is uncomfortable with particular sexual behaviours or that many people find them disgusting are no longer sufficient criteria to label them as mental illnesses.

Many people find leather clothing sexually stimulating. This is an entirely harmless interest.

© Nico Hermann/Westend61/Corbis

Eight main paraphilias are listed in the DSM-5: voyeuristic disorder, exhibitionistic disorder, frotteuristic disorder, sexual masochism disorder, sexual sadism disorder, pedophilic disorder, fetishistic disorder, and transvestic disorder (APA, 2013). Others mentioned are telephone scatologia (making obscene telephone calls), necrophilia (sex with dead people), and zoophilia (sex with animals).

Most people who engage in paraphilic behaviours are male. Other than this, people with paraphilias come from every socioeconomic bracket, every ethnic and racial group, and from every sexual orientation (Seligman & Hardenburg, 2000). Although there are no classic profiles that fit all people with paraphilic disorders, certain factors appear to be related to their development. According to Seligman and Hardenburg (2000), people with some of the more serious paraphilic disorders have experienced significant family problems during childhood that contribute to poor social skills and distorted views of sexual intimacy. The intensity of these behaviours also ranges from paraphilic disordered sexual fantasies during masturbation to unacceptable sexual behaviour such as that with a child. Extreme cases of paraphilic disorders are similar to many impulse-control disorders such as those involving substance abuse, gambling, and eating disorders (Goodman, 1993). Many people may feel conflicted about their behaviour. They may repeatedly try to suppress their desires but be unable to do so (Seligman & Hardenburg, 2000). When this is the case, treatment is warranted.

As one example, many people find lingerie exciting. However, in extreme cases, the lingerie itself becomes the object of sexual attention and not a means of enhancing sexual activity with a partner. For this reason, some have suggested that the defining characteristic of a paraphilic disorder is that it replaces the whole with the part, allowing people to distance themselves from complex human sexual contact and replace it with the undemanding sexuality of an inanimate object, a scene, or a single action (Kaplan, 1991).

Motivations for paraphilic disordered behaviours vary. Some people claim that they provide meaning to their lives and give them a sense of self, while others say they relieve their depression and loneliness or help them express rage (Goodman, 1993; Levine et al., 1990). Some violent or criminally disordered paraphiliacs have little ability to feel empathy for their victims and may convince themselves that their victims enjoy the experiences even though they do not consent to them (Seligman & Hardenburg, 2000). These, however, are extreme cases and are thus atypical of people with any paraphilic interests.

Regardless of severity, the prime directives for treatment are now not the sexual interests themselves but discomfort with them beyond mere reaction to societal disapproval as well as the harm that they might do to individuals or the others they seek to involve. We keep this in mind throughout this chapter.

Theories about Paraphilic Disorders

It is difficult to generate explanations for the origins of paraphilic disorders since their origins are complex. Most people have sexual

paraphilia
Unusual sexual behaviour, often seen as symptomatic of a mental illness.

Harmful and Antisocial Sexual Expression

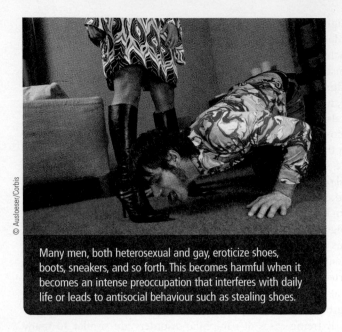

Many men, both heterosexual and gay, eroticize shoes, boots, sneakers, and so forth. This becomes harmful when it becomes an intense preoccupation that interferes with daily life or leads to antisocial behaviour such as stealing shoes.

interests of some kind but how they become channelled down one path or another is often a matter of conjecture. Nevertheless, most explanations fall into three categories: biological, psychological, and social. The answer may lay in any one of them or in all three combined.

Biological and Sociobiological Theories

Biological explanations are based on the premise that sexuality develops unfettered unless certain physical conditions channel it in other directions. Physical illnesses, disturbances in the brain structure or chemistry, higher levels of testosterone, and other factors can lead to unwanted sexual desires or behaviours (Giotakos et al., 2005; Rahman & Symeonides, 2008; Sartorius et al., 2008). This does not mean that all people with paraphilic disorders have such conditions. They are factors that may lead some people to develop paraphilic disorders but they do not explain the majority of them.

According to Gardner (1993), as well as Qunsey and Lalumiere (1995), the development of paraphilias (disordered or not) may be rooted in evolution to ensure species survival. According to evolutionary theory, male animals compete for females so that females are ensured a stronger superior male or one with superior genes for reproduction. This process was mirrored in past societies where men were hunters and fighters while women were child-bearers. Women who were chosen by hunters and fighters are assured protection from enemies and harsh elements, while those chosen by weaker males were not. The greater the sexual desire in males then, the more they will be motivated to seek out females and the greater the potential of species survival.

Paraphilias from the evolutionary perspective are thus *hypersexualization* within men, or the increasing of sexual desire, to ensure species survival. Put another way, they are exaggerations of sexual desire. For example, youth is valued in women because of its

connection to fertility. Pedophilic desires would thus be an exaggeration of the desire for fertility (even though, ironically, prepubescent children are not fertile). Voyeurism, exhibitionism, and frotteurism evoke situations where the possibility of sexual intercourse, thus species survival, is increased, and fetishism keeps sexual desire alive. This explanation, however, assumes that biology is fully behind social behaviour and does not take into consideration the mechanisms of mind and culture. While it might be true that sexual urges of one kind or another lead to the desire to have sex, the vast majority of human beings channel them within socially acceptable circumstances. These circumstances, in turn, are dictated by culture and an interpretation of what is appropriate.

Psychoanalytic Theory

Psychoanalysis maintains that paraphilic disorders can be traced back to the difficult time male infants have negotiating their way through the oedipal crisis and castration anxiety. This would explain why paraphilic disorders are far more common among men. Both boys and girls identify strongly with their mothers but girls continue that identification while boys must separate from their mothers to establish male identities.

American psychoanalyst Louise Kaplan suggests that paraphilic disorders involve issues of masculinity or femininity, believing that "Every male perversion entails a masquerade or impersonation of masculinity and every female perversion entails a masquerade or impersonation of femininity" (Kaplan, 1991, p. 249). For example, a man who exposes himself in public may be coping with castration anxiety by evoking a reaction to his penis from women. He feels validated when his penis inspires fear, which may be why exhibitionists disproportionately choose young girls because they are more likely to be afraid of such actions (Kline, 1987). This confirms to an exhibitionist the power of his masculinity.

Similarly, voyeurs who are excited by spying on others while nude or having sex may be fixated on the experience that evoked their castration anxieties as children—the sight of genitals and sexuality (Kline, 1987). Spying allows a person to gain power over the fearful and hidden world of sexuality while safe from the possibility of contact. The visual component of castration anxiety occurs when a boy sees the power and size of his father's penis and the lack of one on his mother or sisters. The act of looking initiates castration anxiety and, for the voyeur, the looking has never ceased. Yet looking itself cannot really relieve the anxiety permanently and so the voyeur is compelled to spy on others again and again.

The problem with psychoanalysis is that its explanations are circular and, thus, not provable. In other words, castration anxiety and an Oedipal complex are not empirically observable. As a result, such theories are not falsifiable and must be accepted on faith. A number of scholars, British psychologist Hans Eysenck (1993) and American psychiatrist Thomas Szasz (1974) among them, have made such critiques. For example, it is possible that exhibitionists have a need to feel masculine, but the link to the Oedipus complex is untestable and, thus, a tautology. The same would be true for all paraphilias and paraphilic disorders.

Developmental Theories

Developmental theories focus on the development of a paraphilic disorder and attempt to trace it back to its origin. Freud suggested that children are *polymorphously perverse*, meaning that they have an unspecified and amorphous erotic potential that can be attached to almost anyone or anything. People learn from early ages which objects society deems appropriate to desire, but with polymorphous perversity this desire can be channelled anywhere where there is attraction. For example, clothing companies often sexualize their products as might be seen in shoe advertisements that accentuate the long sexy legs of models while focusing on the shoes they wear. The shoes come to symbolically represent the sexy women who wear them and some boys may develop a fetish as a result. In other words, it is assumed that paraphilic desires have their origins in events taking place at early ages and they become rooted in a person's mind. While this may explain fetishes, however, it does not explain fetishistic disorders.

A theory that builds on similar ideas is John Money's (1984, 1986, 1990) **lovemaps**. Money suggests that the auditory, tactile, and visual stimuli people experience during childhood sex play form a template in their brains that defines their ideal lovers and ideal sexual situations. If this sex play remains undisturbed, development of the lovemaps continues undisturbed as well. If, however, the child is punished for normal sexual curiosity or if there are traumas during this stage such as sexual abuse, development of the lovemap can be disrupted and, thus, channelled in different ways.

Money posits three types of disruptions, the first of which is **hypophilia**. Negative stimuli prevent the development of certain aspects of sexuality and the genitals may be prevented from fully functioning. Females are more likely to experience hypophilia resulting in an inability to have an orgasm, vaginal pain, or lubrication problems later in life. Second is **hyperphilia**. A person defies any negative sexual stimuli and becomes overly sexually active, often to the point of being compulsively sexual. Third, a lovemap can be disrupted when there is a substitution of new elements and a paraphilia can develop. Because sexual curiosity has been discouraged or made painful, the child redirects erotic energy toward other objects that are not forbidden, such as shoes, rubber, or otherwise. A child may also turn his or her erotic energy inward and become excited by pain or humiliation. At times, this interest can reach the level of a paraphilic disorder.

Once a lovemap is set, it becomes stable and change is difficult. Money (1984) suggested that sexual arousal to particular objects may arise when parents make a child feel shame about interest in those objects. For example, a boy may be caught with his mother's brassiere in the normal course of curiosity about a woman's body but, when he is severely chastised, the brassiere becomes forbidden, dirty, and promising of sexual secrets. The boy may begin to seek them out as a result and develop a fetish for them.

Canadian sexologist Kurt Freund explains paraphilic disorders as "courtship disorders" (Freund & Blanchard, 1986; Freund et al., 1983, 1984). As a rule, people go through four stages of courtship—the search phase (looking for a partner), the pre-tactile interaction phase (talking or flirting), the tactile interaction stage

Sexologist John Money (1921–2006) developed the concept of "lovemaps" in which people develop templates of ideal lovers and sexual situations as they grow and mature.

© Diana Walker/Getty

(touching, kissing, etc.), and the genital union stage (intercourse). Paraphilias come from distortions of the first three phases. Voyeurism is a distortion of the first stage, while exhibitionism is a distortion of the second stage. Once again, however, such theories can only be accepted on faith since they are not falsifiable and, thus, cannot be supported by any empirical research.

Behavioural Theories

Behaviourists suggest that paraphilic disorders develop because some behaviour becomes associated with sexual pleasure through conditioning (Wilson, 1987). For example, if a boy were to get a spanking and has an erection at the same time either by coincidence or because he is aroused, the spanking becomes reinforcement to the pleasure of the erection. He may masturbate to this memory, which further reinforces the association. In effect, he becomes conditioned to associate spanking with sexual pleasure. Thus, if non-sexual objects, situations, or activities become associated with sexual pleasure, then sexual pleasure from them may occur later on (Berner & Briken, 2012). In this respect, paraphilic behaviour is a matter of conditioning and, once it leads to distress, it becomes a disorder.

---

lovemap
A term coined by John Money to refer to the templates of ideal lovers and sexual situations people develop as they grow up.

hypophilia
Lack of full functioning of the sex organs because of negative stimuli.

hyperphilia
Compulsive sexuality caused by overcompensating for negative reactions to childhood sexuality.

Sociological Theories

Sociologists approach paraphilias in general from a number of perspectives, among them the ways in which a particular behaviour comes to be labelled as deviant. For example, homosexuality is a simple behaviour where people of the same sex have sex with each other. The reactions to it, however, by the church, the legal system, and the medical profession had made it into a moral evil that had real consequences for gays and lesbians and such reactions continue even today. The same might be said for people who have fetishes or those who practise sadomasochism (see BDSM, Chapter 14), who are often labelled as dangerous and psychopathic. In this respect, it is not the behaviour that is under scrutiny but the societal reactions and institutional policies toward it that lead to its definition. Paraphilias, in effect, are behaviours in conflict with current social standards (Wright, 2010). This is not to say that these standards are not justified, especially when concerning the protection of people from harm and exploitation. It is to say that social standards change over time and, thus, so does the labelling.

A second concern of sociologists is how gender interacts with sexuality in the creation of fetishes. Most people with paraphilias are men, which is no accident in a society that has historically been patriarchal. Because women have been made into sex objects for the male gaze, it is inevitable that objects symbolizing femininity and womanhood have been fetishized. Furthermore, women's fear of male sexuality might also become eroticized, which would lead to exhibitionism. Interestingly, with the legitimization of gay men as sexual citizens in society and with the rise of feminist consciousness, men's bodies and the objects that surround them (e.g., jockstraps, boots) have become increasingly fetishized as a result. Fetishization may thus be influenced considerably by gender power in society.

Closely related to this perspective are the ways in which male and female sexualities are defined and regarded. For example, if a man undresses in front of a window at night, he may be regarded as an exhibitionist. If a woman does the same, the men who see her through her window might be regarded as voyeurs. Similarly, male strippers in nightclubs are often thought of as showing off, while female strippers are portrayed as victims of male domination. Because male sexuality is portrayed as aggressive and female sexuality as submissive, perceptions of aberrant sexuality may be channelled in similarly gendered ways.

A third area of interest is the emergence of new fetishes or sexual behaviours and the gradual disappearance of old ones. For example, no one would have a shoe fetish in a culture where people did not wear shoes. Shoe fetishes are therefore dependent not only

© Hulton Archive/Getty

Fetishes for various clothing are dependent upon their existence, use, and presentation in society. Because "bustles" are out of fashion in the 21st century, it is unlikely that fetishes for them still exist.

upon people wearing them but how they are regarded and presented. As mentioned, high-heeled shoes for women are often marketed in glossy advertisements in ways that accentuate the sexiness of women's legs. The message to women is that they too can be sexy by wearing such shoes and the message to men is that women who do wear them are sexy (Collins, 2005). Such ads lead to sexual fantasies involving the shoes and the fantasies lead to fetishes. There are also many ads with shirtless young men with visible name-brand underwear worn several centimetres above their jeans, which further evokes fantasies and fetishes. Fetishes in this respect are therefore created by marketing. Conversely, as fashion changes and styles become outdated, the fetishes surrounding them die out with a generation of people that can only remember them. For example, it is unlikely that anyone has a fetish for petticoats or bustles anymore since they have not been in fashion for more than a century.

Review Questions

1 How have the definitions of paraphilias changed over the last century?

2 What are the two criteria for diagnosing paraphilic disorders according to the DSM-5?

3 How are paraphilias explained by evolutionary theory?

4 What are the main weaknesses of the psychoanalytic perspective?

5 How is simply defining a behaviour as mentally ill on its own merits a tautology?

6 How does John Money's concept of lovemaps explain paraphilic disorders?

7 According to sociology, how does gender enter into the definitions of paraphilias?

Types of Paraphilic Disorders

According to the DSM-5 (APA, 2013), a paraphilia is an "intense and persistent sexual interest other than sexual interest in genital stimulation or preparatory fondling with phenotypically normal, physically mature, consenting human partners." In other words, it is any interest in sexual activities that do not involve stimulation of the penis or vagina of consenting adults or preparation in so doing." Dozens of paraphilic interests have been identified and each has been given a specific name. *Gynandromorphophilia* is an interest in transsexual women, *olfactophilia* is an interest in smells, *sthenolagnia* is an interest in muscles or displays of strength, and *agalmatophilia* is an interest in statues or immobility. The majority of paraphilias are innocuous, harmless, and merely part of human sexual diversity. A paraphilic disorder on the other hand is "a paraphilia that is currently causing distress or impairment to the individual or a paraphilia whose satisfaction has entailed personal harm, or risk of harm, to others" (APA, 2013).

There are eight paraphilic disorders detailed in the DSM-5 chosen for their common occurrence along with two more categories called "other specified paraphilic disorder" and "unspecified paraphilic disorder." The eight listed ones are either courtship disorders (voyeuristic disorder, exhibitionistic disorder, frotteurism), algolagnic disorders involving pain and suffering (sexual sadism disorder and sexual masochism disorder), and anomalous target preferences (pedophilic disorder, fetishistic disorder, transvestic disorder). We discuss them in this order in this section.

Courtship Paraphilic Disorders

Voyeuristic disorder, exhibitionistic disorder, and **frotteuristic disorder** are collectively known as "courtship disorders" in that they all pertain to ways of approaching another person sexually. Many people have enjoyed voyeurism or exhibitionism or both at some point. Much of sexual arousal is based on visual stimuli and, if no one were aroused by the bodies of other people or presented their bodies in sexual manners, there would probably be far less sexual activity in the world. A century ago when most Canadians lived in rural communities, the sight of any naked bodies was restricted mostly to one's husband or wife, children, or same-sex siblings. Today in Western societies, images of barely dressed bodies or nudity are everywhere. Aside from advertising images, nude scenes in popular films and adult magazines. There are millions of naked bodies on the Internet, whether in advertisements, on pornographic websites, websites with personal ads, or otherwise. When people do put up Internet personal ads, they typically include pictures, some of which may be nude and some of which may be of only parts of their naked bodies such as genitals, breasts, or buttocks. Most of these pictures are taken at home where one can see beyond the bodies into the people's living rooms or bedrooms, which add a further voyeuristic component to the images. Such websites vicariously provide opportunities for exhibitionism as well as fodder for voyeurs.

With advances in technology, people with voyeuristic paraphilic disorder have greater opportunities to spy on people without their knowledge. This presents new challenges for police.

Voyeuristic disorder and exhibitionistic disorder, however, have little to do with the explosion of naked imagery over the last few decades or the desire to see them. Simple exhibitionism and voyeurism by consenting parties (i.e., one wants to show and the other wants to look) virtually cancel each other out through their complementarity. Disorders come when looking at naked people or people having sex, or being seen naked or engaging in sex, becomes the primary means of sexual arousal and when they lead to antisocial behaviour and stress in individuals or others (Langevin & Lang, 1987).

Voyeuristic Disorder

Voyeuristic disorder involves individuals whose prime means of sexual gratification is watching unsuspecting people undressing, naked, or having sex. "Peeping Toms" are almost always male and typically heterosexual (Lavin, 2008). Although voyeuristic disorder is almost always restricted to peeping, there have been a few cases where it has led to rape (Holmes, 1991). Voyeurs are typically not charged with sex crimes but with trespassing or sometimes breaking and entering instead (Lavin, 2008). As a result, it is difficult to know how many peeping Toms exist. One estimate, however, is that over the lifetime voyeuristic disorder occurs in 12 percent of males and 4 percent of females (Långström & Seto, 2006). This does not mean, however, that they invade people's privacy regularly. Many might do so only once or twice out of curiosity.

Voyeuristic disorders typically begin in adolescence. However, according to the DSM-5 criteria, no one is diagnosed as such until the age of 18, so as to separate the disorder from natural adolescent

voyeuristic disorder
Recurrent and intense arousal from observing unsuspecting people undressing or engaging in sex acts.

exhibitionistic disorder
Recurrent and intense arousal from exposing one's genitals to unsuspecting strangers.

frotteuristic disorder
Recurrent and intense sexual arousal from rubbing the genitals against a non-consenting person in a crowded place.

Harmful and Antisocial Sexual Expression

curiosity. There is also a difference between looking in windows as one passes by and going out of one's way to spy on others.

It is likely that much voyeuristic disorder has been subsumed by the availability of pornography or adult personal websites on the Internet. Still, for many, this may be unsatisfying in that much of the excitement comes from people not knowing or approving of a voyeur seeing them. In this respect, there are also websites that capture unsuspecting sexual activity or nudity such as in locker rooms (Griffiths, 2000).

With the increasing sophistication of technology, new types of voyeurs who photograph or videotape women in compromising ways have emerged. The popularity of the miniskirt in the 1960s brought about such viewing and photographing *en masse*. "Upskirt" and "downblouse" photographs are often uploaded onto websites featuring such images. Similarly, hidden cameras may also be taken into locker rooms or public washrooms where unsuspected people undressing may be photographed as well.

Closely related to voyeurism and voyeuristic disorder is **troilism,** which involves a situation where two people have sex while a third person watches. This is different from a simple "threesome" or *ménage à trois* where three people all have sex together. Troilism may involve aspects of voyeurism, exhibitionism, and sometimes even latent homosexual desires. For example, a man who is aroused by watching his wife fellate another man may be consciously or subconsciously putting himself in her place. The voyeuristic component, however, is different from that of peeping Toms in that the two people having sex know that they are being watched and typically enjoy it.

More recently, troilism has become eroticized as a *cuckold* situation where the observer is humiliated by the two having sex. A cuckold generally refers to a husband whose wife cheats on him or who invests energy raising children who are not his own. The term comes from the female cuckoo bird who would sometimes lay her eggs in the nests of other birds. There are a number of reasons for wanting a cuckold situation, among them a desire to be humiliated, an effort to re-enact a perfect love scene, and a desire to live vicariously through a superior lover. Again, this is not a disorder unless it leads to stress or unwanted situations.

Exhibitionism, both male and female, is common at festivals such as Mardi Gras and Southern Decadence in New Orleans, Louisiana.

© Mario Tama/Getty

REAL Research University of Waterloo psychologists Rye and Meaney (2007) asked a sample of college students if they would hypothetically watch two attractive people have sex. More males than females said they would but only if the chances of being caught were minimal.

troilism
A situation where two people have sex while another observes.

Exhibitionistic Disorder

Exhibitionistic disorder usually involves a man (a "flasher") who experiences recurrent and intense arousal from exposing his genitals to unsuspecting women or girls (Murphy & Page, 2008). An exhibitionist is usually excited by the lack of consent of the women as expressed in their shock or fearful reactions. The man may also masturbate either while flashing or later when thinking about the reactions of his victims. Flashing may also escalate in times of stress or disappointment (Murphy & Page, 2008; Seligman & Hardenburg, 2000). According to therapists, it is difficult to stop such behaviour (Rabinowitz et al., 2002).

Exhibitionism is legally classified as "indecent exposure" and accounts for up to a third of all sex convictions in Canada, the United States, and Europe (Bogaerts et al., 2006; Langevin & Lang, 1987; Murphy & Page, 2008). This category inflates the rates because not all indecent exposure is exhibitionism. People may also be charged with indecent exposure if caught urinating in public, streaking, or otherwise. Unlike peeping Toms, however, exhibitionists have witnesses to their crimes and, as such, there is a higher likelihood of being caught. Although it is not known how many exhibitionists there are, it is known that many women are flashed. In some samples of college women, 40 percent to 60 percent of females reported having been flashed at some point in their lives (Murphy & Page, 2008).

Exhibitionistic disorder in women is rare (Grob, 1985; Rhoads & Boekelheide, 1985). Female exhibitionists may need to feel feminine and appreciated and seeing men admire their exposed bodies reinforces their sense of sexual value and femininity. However, exhibitionism in women might be more hidden since women have legitimate opportunities to expose themselves such as wearing low-cut dresses that reveal cleavage. As such, this may be enough for female exhibitionists.

Streaking, which is the act of running naked through a public place, is done either as a prank or as a form of political protest. As protest, the phenomenon emerged from the counterculture of the 1960s as a defiant snub against the perceived hypocrisy of the establishment (Carrington & McDonald, 1997). Because it was seen as fun, however, it failed as a political tool for protest (Kirkpatrick, 2010). As a prank, it has also been common on college campuses since the 1960s and football games have often had streakers run across the fields. There were also streakers at the Olympic Games in Montreal in 1976, and one man streaked across the stage during the Academy Awards ceremony in 1974 after which actor David Niven famously quipped, "But isn't it fascinating to think that probably the only laugh that man will ever get in

his life is by stripping off and showing his shortcomings?"

Similarly "mooning" is the act of dropping one's trousers to display bare buttocks and is done to express contempt or scorn.

While usually done on an individual basis, there have occasionally been mass moonings. In London, England, in 2000, a crowd of anti-monarchist protesters gathered outside Buckingham Palace and several of them dropped their pants in an attempt to bring about a "2000 bum salute" to the Queen. They were quickly arrested by the police (BBC News, 2000).

Nudity is not a new form of protest. In 1899, about 7000 Doukhobors emigrated from Russia to Saskatchewan to escape religious persecution. They objected, however, to government restrictions upon their lives such as mandatory education of children, military service, and swearing an oath of allegiance to Canada. They protested by doing such things as burning their own money or burning their own homes, and a group of them known as the Sons of Freedom would stage naked marches through the towns, a practice that continued into the 1960s.

Although female exhibitionism is rare, it is interesting how much more acceptable it is for a woman to expose her body in North American society. Rihanna wore a see-through sparkly gown at a recent award ceremony and various media sources called her a fashion icon.

Frotteuristic Disorder

Frotteuristic disorder involves one person, typically a man, rubbing his genitals against another person, typically a woman, in a crowded place where he can claim it was an accident and get away quickly. Because it can be excused as a mistake or clumsiness in most cases, unless there are witnesses to clear cases of violation, frotteurism is difficult to prosecute. Consequently, it offers sexual gratification with little investment or risk. There is little data on female frotteurs for a number of reasons. First, men are more likely to excuse women who rub up against them and even welcome it. Second, there has been little attention to frotteurism in general and it only appeared for the first time in the third edition of the DSM published in 1980 (Långström, 2010).

Closely related is **toucheurism,** which is the compulsive desire to touch strangers in public with one's hands for sexual arousal. Frotteurism and toucheurism come from the French terms for "rubbing" (*frotter*) and "touching" (*toucher*), respectively. It has been estimated that 10 percent to 14 percent of men seen in clinical outpatient settings have committed one, the other, or both. Typically, these acts occur on buses and subway cars, in shopping malls, at crowded concerts, or any place where people are in close quarters. There have also been cases of frotteurism or toucheurism by physicians and dentists who rub against or touch their patients (Langevin & Lang, 1987).

toucheurism
Recurrent and intense sexual arousal from touching strangers.

Problems with groping and frotteurism on public transportation have led to the establishment of women-only passenger cars in Japan and South Korea.

as a *bona fide* mental illness (Balon, 2012; Knight et al., 2013). The decision was not to include it in the DSM-5, which was supported by many psychiatrists and psychologists. The arguments for including PCD were that many men who have raped have been diagnosed with sexual sadism (Krueger, 2009) and that rape itself is an act of violence. Whether committing rape, however, is a sufficient criterion to diagnose mental illness lacks precision, as Université de Montréal psychologists Agaleryan and Rouleau (2014) assert. Many have also said that rapists are criminals first and foremost and that to give them a label of illness might somehow detract from the personal responsibility for their behaviour as such. It is likely that this debate will continue, and whether PCD will be included in subsequent versions of the DSM remains to be seen.

Paraphilic Disorders Involving Anomalous Target Preferences

Using the language of the DSM-5, a target preference is a matter of to whom or to what one is attracted. When the target is non-human, fetishes are usually involved (discussed in detail in Chapter 14) and included in the DSM-5 discussions are **fetishistic disorder** and **transvestic disorder**. When the target is an inappropriate human (i.e., a child) **pedophilic disorder** is involved.

Pedophilic Disorder

Pedophilia is often misunderstood to mean any adult who desires or has sex with someone under the age of consent. American television shows such as *Law and Order: Special Victims Unit* constantly make this mistake with plots about adult men having sex with 16- and 17-year-olds (the age of consent in the United States varies by state; it is 16 in Canada). In reality, a pedophile is someone, usually male, who is erotically attracted to prepubescent children. Once children develop secondary sex characteristics (e.g., formation of hips, growth of penis, pubic hair), a pedophile's interest wanes. Erotic attraction to adolescents is more accurately called *hebephilia* (early adolescence) and *ephebophilia* (mid- to late adolescence) (Money, 1986). On the other end of the continuum, attraction to the elderly is called *gerontophilia*.

The DSM-5 uses the term "pedophilic disorder" rather than pedophilia. Unlike other paraphilias, however, it is not useful to make a distinction between pedophiles who might not suffer stress or anxiety because of their interests and those who do not. The "well-adjusted pedophile" is irrelevant in that children are vulnerable, not capable of informed consent by virtue of their age, and must be protected. Pedophilia is thus illegal in every nation in the world (O'Grady, 2001).

Girls are twice as likely as boys to be victims of pedophiliac behaviour (Murray, 2000). In one study, 44 percent of pedophiles preferred only girls, 33 percent only boys, and 23 percent both boys and girls (Murray, 2000). Boys are less likely to reject sexual advances or report them to authorities (Brongersma, 1990). Not everyone with pedophilic desires acts upon them. Some only look at children and never contact them, while others go further.

Algolagnic Paraphilic Disorders

Sexual masochism disorder and **sexual sadism disorder** are collectively known as "algolagnic paraphilic disorders" because they involve pain and humiliation. In Chapter 14 we discussed BDSM play where two (or more) people take on either dominant or submissive roles and act out sexual scenarios. Within BDSM communities, consent is very important and the general rule is that the dominant person does not go beyond what is expected or agreed upon. People who practise BDSM are typically not disordered in any way and enjoy their activities with their partners (Connolly, 2006). Historically, the psychiatric profession has failed to make the distinction between consensual play and psychopathy, assuming that all BDSM activities are either sadism or masochism disorders, which is why the separation of paraphilias from their disorders represents a significant shift in thought as well as human rights.

Sexual sadism disorder occurs when the need to hurt or humiliate goes outside of the realm of consensual play or when individuals cannot control their urges as such. In extreme cases where psychopathy is involved, significant harm can be done to other individuals. It may also be associated with borderline personality disorder or antisocial personality disorder. Sexual masochism disorder occurs when the desire for suffering, hurt, or humiliation reaches the level of physical or psychological trauma.

At present, there exists a controversy as to whether "paraphilic coercive disorder" (PCD) should have been included in the DSM

sexual masochism disorder
Distress from masochism—often to the point of needing to do so for any sexual arousal.

sexual sadism disorder
Distress from sadism—often to the point of needing to do so for any sexual arousal.

fetishistic disorder
Distress from fetishes—often to the point of needing the fetish for any sexual arousal.

transvestic disorder
Distress from cross dressing—often to the point of needing to do so for any sexual arousal.

pedophilic disorder
Recurrent and intense sexual arousal from prepubescent to pubescent children.

The Dutch Pedophilia Party

In 2006, a new Dutch political party, known as the Party for Neighbourly Love, Freedom, and Diversity (PNVD) emerged in the Netherlands and was led by three pedophiles—Ad van den Berg, Martin Uittenbogaard, and Nobert de Jonge. It became known as Pedopartij (pedo party) because two issues on their platform were lowering the age of consent for sexual activity to 12 and legalizing child pornography. The Netherlands courts allowed this party, believing that in a free society it has the same right to existence as any other party and that it is up to the voters to judge its merit (BBC News, 2006). Although the three founders likely knew that they would get few if any votes, they formed the party to give a voice to pedophiles, many of whom felt they had been ignored and silenced over the years.

© Petra Lambert

One of the authors of this book, Janell Carroll, met with Ad van den Berg and Martin Uittenbogaard while in The Netherlands and talked with them informally. Mr. Uittenbogaard said that it is difficult being open about his interests. He received numerous death threats and rocks were thrown through his windows.

He believes that society is against pedophilia because it is taboo. Mr. van den Berg said that it was difficult to explain why he was attracted to boys. He remembered his attraction began when he was young but he did not act on it until he was 32 years old. He had never been attracted to adult men or women. He also mentioned several platonic and sexual relationships he had with boys, most of whom were 11 to 13 years old. He did not see himself as a predator. When boys tell him they do not want to be touched, he respects this. In 2010, the party disbanded due to a lack of public support.

Contrary to what might be thought, the most common sexual behaviour is simple fondling and exhibitionism rather than penetration (Murray, 2000). Female pedophiles do exist, although they often abuse children in concert with another person, usually their male partner. They may be attempting to please their partners rather than satisfy their own desires. They have also been found to have a higher incidence of psychiatric disorders (Chow & Choy, 2002). We discuss this in more detail later in this chapter.

According to a report on crime statistics in Canada (Statistics Canada, 2011), there were more than 3822 cases of sex crimes against children in 2011, including invitation to sexual touching, sexual exploitation, and luring a child via computer. These crimes were most common in Quebec with 27.3 percent, followed by Ontario with 23.7 percent, and British Columbia with 19.6 percent. The rates per 100 000 population, however, were highest in Nunavut (150) and the Northwest Territories (37) and lowest in Ontario (6) and Alberta (9).

A number of pedophile organizations in Western countries such the now-defunct Party for Neighbourly Love, Freedom, and Diversity in the Netherlands (see the Sexual Diversity in Our World feature) argue that adult-child sexual relations should be legalized under the platform of "the sexual rights of children and adolescents" (Okami, 1990). The North American Man–Boy Love Association (NAMBLA) supports the abolition of age-of-consent laws and believes that there is a difference between those who simply want to use children for sexual release and those who develop long-lasting, often exclusive, and even loving relationships. These ideas, however, have little public support.

Being a victim of sexual abuse in childhood is one of the most frequently reported risk factors for developing pedophilic desires later on (Glasser et al., 2001; Långström et al., 2000; Seto, 2004). It is estimated that 35 percent of pedophiles have experienced such abuse (Keegan, 2001). There is also evidence that the choice of gender and age of victims often reflects a pattern of past sexual abuse in a pedophile's life (Pollock & Hashmall, 1991). However, although past sexual abuse is a risk factor, the majority of male victims of child sexual abuse do not become pedophiles (Salter et al., 2003).

© AP Photo/MGM Entertainment/Newscom

Toys such as Bratz dolls sexualize girls and can encourage them to think of and treat their bodies as sex objects.

Fetishistic Disorder

A fetishistic disorder involves distress from a recurrent and intense sexual arousal from fantasies, urges, or behaviours surrounding non-living objects such as shoes or brassieres or body parts such as feet or hands. Most people with fetishes are male (Darcangelo, 2008) and, thus, most with the associated disorder are male as well. The strength of a preference for an object varies from thinking about it or holding it during masturbation to a desire to include it in all sexual activity.

Many people have fetishes and even include them in their lovemaking without becoming dependent on them for arousal. A fetishistic disorder occurs when there is distress about a fetish or when a person needs the presence of the fantasy of it to become aroused. Some fetishists integrate the objects of their desire into their sex lives and their partners may even share the enjoyment. Others might have a secret fetish with collections of shoes, underwear, or even photographs of body parts over which they might masturbate. Some are even fearful of discovery, which leads to distress. When a fetish becomes so predominant that it interferes with regular lovemaking, or when an individual is compelled toward antisocial acts (e.g., stealing women's panties from launderettes), it has reached the level of disorder.

On Your Mind

I like to make love to my girlfriend while she wears a blonde wig. Do I have a fetish?

Whether something is a fetish is a matter of degree. If the blonde wig merely enhances lovemaking and increases its erotic quality, and if your girlfriend does not mind wearing it, then there is little reason not to include it. If, however, you are incapable of becoming aroused without the blonde wig, then it has reached the level of a fetish that interferes with sexual functioning. Furthermore, if your girlfriend objects to wearing the wig and you pressure her into putting it on before you make love, or if you have had a series of break-ups because other women have refused to wear it, then significant life stress is present and it may have reached the level of a fetishistic disorder. In general, however, many people bring objects into their lovemaking and, as long as both parties are amenable, there is little reason to worry.

A person with a foot or shoe fetish often spends much time on shoes during sexual activity.

Transvestic Disorder

The word "transvestite" was coined by Magnus Hirschfeld (see Chapter 1) and incorporates the Latin terms *trans* meaning "across" and *vestitus* meaning "dressed." The prime concern here is therefore cross-dressing, which is different from transsexualism, gender queers, and even drag queens, who impersonate women for entertainment purposes. Transvestism, in contrast, involves the wearing of clothing of the other gender for sexual arousal and, in most cases, of men cross-dressing in women's clothing. Most transvestites are also heterosexual. While there are women who might become aroused by wearing men's clothing, this is rare. Among the reasons for this disparity is that women in Western societies have far more freedom in their choice of clothing than men do. Most obviously, while pants have long been acceptable for women, dresses are still not acceptable for men. A woman wanting to dress as a man would thus need to wear the most stereotypically masculine outfits, while a man wanting to dress as a woman would have many clothes from which to choose.

Transvestism in and of itself is usually harmless and can even provide comfort to individuals in providing temporary respites from the pressures of everyday life. Most transvestites feel that they have no need of therapy to stop their behaviour (Newring et al., 2008). Often treatment is sought only when a transvestite's partner is upset over the cross-dressing and it causes stress in a relationship. Many female partners of male transvestites do not understand their need to dress in women's clothing even though they may tolerate it (Dzelme & Jones, 2001; Newring et al., 2008). Once stress occurs, it reaches the level of a transvestic disorder. The stress, however, must be more than that brought about by circumstance.

Transvestism is usually so firmly fixed in a man's psyche that eradication is neither possible nor desirable. The goal of therapy is to relieve the anxieties and guilt of transvestites and the way they relate personally and sexually to their partners, families, or society (Newring et al., 2008). Transvestite support groups have been organized in many large cities in Canada and may offer comfort. There are also numerous websites that offer support to online communities.

Other Specified Paraphilic Disorders

The DSM-5 describes other specified paraphilic disorders as "presentations in which symptoms characteristic of a paraphilic disorder that cause clinically significant distress or impairment in social, occupational, or other important areas of functioning predominate but do not meet the full criteria for any of the disorders in the paraphilic disorders diagnostic class." We examine several such disorders here.

The Feederism Community

Feederism is a fetished sexual activity where "feeders" or "encouragers," who are usually male, are aroused by feeding or encouraging eating and weight gaining by "gainers" or feedees," who are usually female. The erotic component comes from the act of participating in another's weight gain and the feeding may progress to the point of immobility for the female. Because this is a fetish that has only recently attracted attention through Internet websites, there is little academic research on it. One Canadian study, however, figures prominently. Bestard (2008) conducted interviews with 17 men and 13 women within

A subplot in the film *City Island* (2009) involved teenage Ezra Miller becoming aroused by watching an obese neighbour eat.

© CINESON ENTERTAINMENT/MEDICI ENTERTAINMENT/ Album/Newscom

the online feederism community (e.g., fantasyfeeder.com) and suggested a sliding scale or continuum between mere fantasy and feeding to the point of immobility. First, there are people who merely fantasize about feeding or being fed, then there are encouragers who cook food and encourage eating, then there are actual feeders, and finally feeders to the point of ill health and immobility. This last behaviour, however, is uncommon and those who engage in it are considered within the community to be on the fringe. Feederism has figured prominently as side plots in at least two popular films—*In & Out* (1997) and *City Island* (2009).

Telephone Scatalophilia

With advanced telecommunications technology and call display options, it is surprising that obscene telephone calls still occur. Although the incidence has gradually lessened, they are still around. Obscene telephone calls have been a widespread problem probably as long as household telephones have been common. Smith and Morra (1994) looked at a 1992 survey of 1990 women on sexual harassment in Canada and found that 83.2 percent had received obscene or threatening telephone calls. Those who were divorced, separated, younger, or living in a major city were most likely to be victims of such calls. The typical obscene caller was an unknown male. Few women actually reported the calls to police and those who did tended to say that the responses were not helpful. Most of the women surveyed also said that the calls affected them emotionally.

Telephone scatolophilia occurs when people, almost always male, call women or children and become excited when they react to their suggestions. Most obscene callers masturbate either during the call or afterward. Like exhibitionism, telephone scatolophilia is non-consensual and the caller is aroused by reactions of fear, disgust, or outrage. Many obscene callers have problems with their primary relationships and suffer from feelings of isolation and inadequacy (Holmes, 1991). Many also have co-existing paraphilic disorders such as voyeurism and exhibitionism (Price et al. 2002).

Obscene callers may describe sex acts they will perform on their victims or attempt to entice them into revealing aspects of their own sex lives or masturbate while they listen. Others threaten harm if they do not do what they ask. Some will even get women's telephone numbers while observing them writing cheques at supermarkets or elsewhere (Matek, 1988). The police's advice to anyone who receives such calls has long been to hang up immediately without any verbal reactions at all. In so doing, obscene callers will receive no stimulation or satisfaction and likely move on.

It is interesting to note that changes in technology have led to changes in behaviour. With the invention of e-mail and other means of communication, spammers from many countries have sent out mass sex-related messages advertising prostitution, pornographic websites, Viagra sales, and similar subject matter. Filters exist for spammers, however, and those messages that do get through are easily ignored or deleted.

Zoophilia

Zoophilia and **bestiality** are often confused as terms. In general, the former refers to an erotic attraction to animals while the latter is the actual behaviour of having sex with animals. Closely related according to Krafft-Ebing in his *Psychopathia Sexualis* (1886) is "zoophilia erotica," where the principle attraction is to animal skin, fur or hide. There is also animal voyeurism known as "faunoiphilia," where a person is aroused by watching animals mate.

Not every zoophiliac has sex with animals and not everyone who commits bestiality is erotically attracted to them (Ranger & Fedoroff, 2014). Probably most teenage boys and men who have sex with animals are simply using the animals as convenient

---

telephone scatolophilia
Sexual arousal from making obscene telephone calls.

zoophilia
Recurrent and intense sexual arousal from fantasies or behaviours involving animals.

bestiality
The act of having intercourse with an animal.

masturbation devices more than anything else. Similarly, men have been known to cut a hole in a watermelon, warm it in the sun, and use it for masturbation as well.

Kinsey and his colleagues (1948, 1953) found that about 8 percent of men and 3.6 percent of women have engaged in bestiality. When controlling for location, however, the rates rose to between 40 percent and 50 percent for rural areas (Laws & O'Donohue, 2008). It is likely that people who have had sex with animals are those who have greater access to them. It therefore follows that as Canada and the United States transformed from mostly rural to mostly urban nations over the past century, such access has been considerably reduced. At the same time, however, there are numerous websites specializing in bestiality videos and discussions, which may have increased interest as well.

Necrophilia

Evidence of **necrophilia**, or having sex with corpses, has been found in ancient civilizations. Greek historian Herodotus observed around 440 B.C.E. that among the Egyptians, the remains of wives of noble men were not turned over to embalmers until three or four days after death for fear that they would sexually violate them. Today necrophilic scenes appear occasionally in literature and films, such as the Canadian film *Kissed* (1996) about a woman a young woman who has long been fascinated with corpses and gets a job as an embalmer in a funeral home.

Rosman and Resnick (1989) looked at 34 cases of necrophilia and found that in 68 percent of them, the desire for an unresisting and non-rejecting partner was the main motivation. They identified three types of necrophilia: *necrophilic fantasy* in which a person has persistent fantasies about sex with dead bodies without actually engaging in such behaviour; *regular necrophilia*, which involves the use of dead bodies for sexual pleasure; and *necrophilic homicide*, where a person commits murder to obtain a corpse for sexual pleasure. Necrophilia itself is extremely rare and the third type is the least common among all cases (Milner et al., 2008).

Infantilism

Infantilism is not a disorder per se but rather a fetished activity that involves role-playing where a person intentionally regresses to a baby-like state within a role-play situation. This may involve baby talk by another person, being fed with a bottle, wearing diapers, and even having them changed. While there is very little psychological or sociological research on infantilism, the appeal seems to be the tranquil state that one feels when regressing to an infant stage. There is direct attention from another person, nurturing, and one does not have to make any decisions, which may be appealing to people who need to do so constantly in their jobs.

Infantilists previously communicated through newsletters such as the *Diaper Pail Fraternity*, which began in 1979 (Bass, 2013). Today there are several online communities where members can contact others with the same interest. *Daily Diapers*, for example, allows members to view other members' photographs of themselves in diapers and put in personal ads to meet others, as well as share experiences with other members. It has thousands of members from all over the world.

Review Questions

1 What is the difference between a paraphilia and a paraphilic disorder?

2 Female exhibitionism seems less common, or less commonly identified, than male exhibitionism. Why is this?

3 What is the difference between BDSM as discussed in Chapter 14 and sadism and masochism paraphilic disorders?

4 What are the differences among pedophilia, hebephilia, and ephebophilia?

5 In what ways are necrophilia and bestiality opportunistic?

6 What is the main appeal of infantilism?

Sexual Addiction

Sexual addition, otherwise known as **hypersexuality**, is a compulsive desire to have sex despite the probability of negative consequences. As such, a sexual encounter provides a temporary "fix" from stress felt in everyday life much like that of alcohol or drugs. The perils of sexual addiction began to appear in popular media as early as the 1970s with films such as *Looking for Mr. Goodbar* (1977) and *Fatal Attraction* (1987), with underlying messages that sex without commitment has dire consequences. Out-of-control sexual behaviour as a mental illness appeared in the first edition of the DSM (published in 1952) with terms such as *nymphomania* for women who had frequent sex without commitment and *Don Juanism* for men who did the same (Levine & Troiden, 1988). Because the former quickly became an epithet while the latter became complimentary in popular culture, these names amounted to a thinly disguised double standard.

Because sexual desire is inherent in human beings, sexual addiction is a highly contested concept. While some psychologists believe that it is as real as alcoholism and drug addiction,

necrophilia
Recurrent and intense sexual arousal from fantasies or behaviours involving dead bodies.

hypersexuality
A compulsive desire to have sex despite the probability of negative consequences.

Sexual addiction is a much contested concept. While some consider it a legitimate mental illness, others consider it a mere value judgment. The DSM-5 does not include it.

addiction can lead to emotional suffering and problems in one's occupational functioning and marital and family relationships (Bird, 2006; Miner et al., 2007).

Carnes's model of sexual addiction is based on ten criteria, beginning with a loss of control leading to compulsive sexual behaviour. Efforts to stop fail, leading to significant amounts of time spent either doing the behaviour or recovering from it. A person becomes preoccupied with sexual activity, which leads to an inability to fulfill obligations of work, family, and social life. Eventually, despite financial, social, or legal problems caused by the sexual behaviour, a person still does not stop. Stopping causes anxiety, stress, irritability, and even physical discomfort and so the behaviour continues (Carnes, 2001). Recommendations for therapy include individual counselling, group therapy, and going through a 12-step program.

Many have criticized the idea of sexual addiction, suggesting that it is no more than an ideological construct arising from a shift toward conservatism brought about by the HIV/AIDS epidemic and the rise of the Christian Right in the United States in the 1980s. This shift stands in sharp contrast to the sexual revolution of the 1960s, where "free love" was seen as positive and liberating. Levine and Troiden (1988) pointed out that there are three competing social scripts surrounding sexual activity in Western societies—*procreational, relational*, and *recreational*. The first defines sexual activity within marriage and for procreation as the only legitimate reason to have sex while all else is illegitimate. The second widens the net seeing legitimate sex as that within a committed relationship for the purposes of enhancing feelings of closeness. The third is the most permissive, seeing all sex between willing and consenting adults—even among strangers—as legitimate.

The procreational script took precedence in the post-war era of the 1950s where the average middle-class woman was a housewife and sex outside of marriage was thought deviant. Masturbation, oral sex, and "promiscuity" were all symptoms of mental illness according to the DSM-I in 1952. The recreational script then took precedence in the 1960s and 1970s and, after the advent of HIV/AIDS in the 1980s, the relational script arose. As Levine and Troiden (1988) point out, the concept of sexual addiction emerged in an era when concern over HIV transmission and teenage pregnancy became paramount.

For some, sexual addiction is a contested topic. Many psychologists and sociologists believe it to be a value judgment fuelled by conservative politics and religious dogma (Ley, 2012). For example, many "treatment centres," such as the Millennium Counseling Center in the United States, are religiously based, and the Alcoholics Anonymous-based 12-step program also has strong religious components. Nevertheless, even though there is no mention of it in the DSM-5, the treatment of sexual addiction has become a growing industry for therapists, many of whom now make their living treating people for what they see as addictive behaviour. There are also a number of self-help groups, such as *Sexaholics Anonymous, Sex Addicts Anonymous, Sex and Love Addicts Anonymous*, and *Co-Dependents of Sexual Addicts*. Some scholars suggest that there has been an attempt to return to a pathological model of sexuality using the concept of addiction as a springboard (Irvine, 1995).

others believe it to be a concept created within a sex-negative culture. In other words, to label someone who has sex recreationally with a variety of partners an "addict," even when doing so can be unfulfilling, amounts to a moral or religious judgment masquerading as science. Sexual addiction was not included in the DSM-5 as a legitimate mental disorder because "there is insufficient peer-reviewed evidence to establish the diagnostic criteria and course descriptions needed to identify these behaviors as mental disorders" (APA, 2013). Despite this lack of inclusion, others believe that if an addiction involves an uncontrollable craving for a specific object or activity, the need for repeated sexual encounters, which may likely be unfulfilling, fits well with this model (Bancroft & Vukadinovic, 2004; G.H. Golden, 2001).

One of the main proponents of sexual addiction is Patrick Carnes (2001), who, in his book *Out of the Shadows: Understanding Sexual Addiction*, laid the groundwork for diagnosis and treatment of "sex addicts." He pointed out the parallels between sexual addiction and compulsive gambling, both of which involve obsessive and compulsive behaviour. According to Carnes, "sex addicts" go through four cycles repeatedly: (1) a preoccupation with sex, (2) ritualization of preparation for sex (such as primping oneself in a bathroom mirror and going to singles bars), (3) compulsive sexual behaviour over which individuals believe that they have no control, and (4) despair as the realization hits that they have again repeated a destructive sequence of events. Just like alcohol or gambling addiction, according to Carnes, sexual

Review Questions

1 According to Patrick Carnes, what is the typical cycle of sexual addiction?

2 What are the objections to the concept of sexual addiction?

3 What are the three social scripts surrounding sexual activity and how do they differ?

4 How has religion and morality intermingled with the concept of sexual addiction?

Assessment and Treatment of Sex Offenders

While dozens of paraphilic interests have been identified, it is presently not possible to know their distribution in society. In a sex-negative society, many people feel uncomfortable talking about their sexual practices, especially if they are socially stigmatized (Laws & O'Donahue, 2008). As a result, no surveys can be done that will generate accurate rates of how many do this or that and who is interested in what.

The majority of people with paraphilias function well in life and do not believe that they need any counselling. They are content with their sexual selves. Others seek treatment because of the stress they feel over the stigma toward their sexual interests, much like gay men and lesbians did in the past. According to the DSM-5, however, stress felt by stigma is not sufficient reason for the diagnosing of a disordered state. Still others seek treatment because their sexual interests lead to significant distress and interfere with their functioning in daily life. In such cases, disorders are thought to be present and treatment is recommended.

Many people with antisocial paraphilias such as pedophilia or voyeuristic disorder are referred to clinicians by legal authorities. In such cases, assessment is often done through self-report, behavioural observation, physiological tests, or personality inventories (Seligman & Hardenburg, 2000). Self-reports may not be reliable, however, in that people under court order to receive treatment may be highly motivated to report that their interests have ceased. Other people may truly believe they have overcome their interests when in fact they have not. In such cases, physiological tests may be used for assessment.

The most reliable technique for men is **penile plethysmography**, which may be used for male sex offenders. (See Chapter 2 for a photo of a plethysmograph.) For example, a pedophile can be shown films depicting naked or near-naked children and the plethysmograph attached to his penis will record his penile blood volume, and thus the level of arousal. If he is aroused by the

penile plethysmography
A test performed by measuring the amount of blood that enters the penis in response to a stimulus which indicates level of arousal.

pictures, it is an indication that pedophilic desires are still present. A similar test is also available to test the sexual response of female offenders (Laws & O'Donahue, 2008; Seligman & Hardenburg, 2000).

Personality inventories such as the *Minnesota Multiphasic Personality Inventory* (MMPI) can help establish personality patterns and determine whether there are additional psychological disorders (Seligman & Hardenburg, 2000). Other psychological inventories for depression and anxiety may also be used.

As is shown in Table 16.1, treatment of sex offenders is multi-faceted and may include group, individual, and family therapy; medication; education; and self-help groups (Laws & O'Donahue, 2008; Seligman & Hardenburg, 2000). It is aimed at the reduction or elimination of the offending behaviours, relapse prevention, and increasing victim empathy (d'Amora & Hobson, 2003). If the behaviours can be changed even when fantasies and inner emotional life are not altered, individuals are less likely to harm others or themselves. Behaviour-modification techniques have been most commonly used and are most successful.

Therapy to resolve any early childhood trauma or experiences that help maintain the offending behaviours may also be helpful (Kaplan et al., 1994). It can increase self-esteem and social skills, which are often lacking in sex offenders. Positive behaviours can be encouraged by teaching social skills, which allow people under therapy to meet more people as potential legitimate sex partners. Counselling, modelling (taking after a positive role model), or feedback to change emotions and thoughts may change a person's attitudes toward a sex object. In empathy training, people are taught to increase their compassion by putting themselves in the same situations as their victims. Incarcerated sex offenders may be exposed to relapse-prevention therapies, which focus on controlling a cycle of troubling emotions, distorted thinking, and fantasies that accompany their activities (Goleman, 1992). These techniques are used in group psychotherapy or individual counselling sessions. Group therapy has been found to be an important tool in reducing isolation, improving social skills, and reducing shame and secrecy (Seligman & Hardenburg, 2000).

Many sex offenders find their desires difficult to suppress. In such cases, aversion therapy, where an unwanted behaviour is linked to an unpleasant stimulus, has been a common method of treatment (Laws & O'Donahue, 2008; Seligman & Hardenburg, 2000). For example, a pedophile might be shown pictures of children or asked to fantasize about them while exposing him to an unpleasant odour, a drug that causes nausea, or an electric shock. These techniques have had some success, although their

Table 16.1 Treatment Options for Sex Offenders

Treatment for sex offenders may involve several approaches. The goals of treatment are to reduce or eliminate an offending behaviour and increase feelings of self-esteem and victim empathy. Many sex offenders are ordered by courts to undergo therapy. Others seek out therapy on their own and tend to be more motivated toward change. There is thus more success in their treatment. Some will reduce their antisocial behaviour after treatment and some may not. The following are various treatment options.

Type of Therapy	Therapeutic Methods
Individual	One-on-one therapy with a psychologist or counsellor to improve self-esteem and social skills. It often uses modelling, empathy, and social-skills training, controlling the cycle of troubling emotions, distorted thinking, and the fantasies that accompany activities.
Group	A form of psychotherapy in which a therapist works with a group of sex offenders. Interactions between group members are analyzed and considered therapeutic.
Family	Treatment of more than one member of a family in the same session. Family relationships and processes are explored and evaluated for their potential role in a sex offender's behaviour.
Cognitive-behavioural	A combination of cognitive and behaviour therapy to weaken connections between certain situations and emotional/physical reactions to them including depression and self-defeating or self-damaging behaviours. It also looks at how thinking patterns help contribute to the unwanted behaviour and emphasizes relaxation and improving emotional health.
Systematic desensitization	A technique used in behaviour therapy to treat problems of anxiety. Clients are exposed to threatening situations under relaxed conditions until the anxiety is extinguished.
Aversion	A behaviour-modification technique that uses unpleasant stimuli in a controlled fashion to change behaviour. For example, a pedophile might be given electric shocks or nausea drugs while looking at pictures of children.
Shame aversion	A behaviour-modification technique that uses shame as an unpleasant stimulus to change behaviour. For example, an exhibitionist might be asked to expose himself in front of an audience.
Orgasmic reconditioning	A behaviour-modification technique that attempts to reprogram a person's fantasies. An example would be to have a person masturbate and, when orgasm is imminent, he would switch his fantasy to a more socially desirable one in an effort to associate orgasm and erection with a preferable stimulus.
Satiation	A behavioural-modification technique in which a person masturbates to a conventional fantasy and then masturbates again to an undesirable fantasy. The decreased sex drive and low responsiveness of the second episode makes the experience less exciting. Eventually the behaviour may lose its desirability.
Pharmacotherapy	Medications are used to improve symptoms, delay progression, or reduce the urge to act on unwanted behaviours. A variety of medications have been used, including antidepressants and testosterone suppressants.
Chemotherapy	Using medication to decrease sexual drive.

effectiveness decreases over time (Laws & O'Donahue, 2008). It is interesting to note that such methods of therapy, along with others, were used primarily upon gay men and lesbians up until the 1960s and even beyond, when their behaviours were considered sex offences. These methods had little success (Duberman, 1991).

Although removing unwanted behaviours may prevent future victimization, a person who still fantasizes about that behaviour or has the same underlying attitude toward it may not be better off. The psychological underpinnings that lead to sex offences also must be changed. In systematic desensitization (Wolpe, 1958), a sex offender is taught to relax and is then taken through more and more anxiety-provoking or arousing situations until he or she learns to relax even during the most extreme situations (Hawton, 1983).

Some therapies involve masturbation in attempts to reprogram sexual fantasies. In orgasmic reconditioning therapy, people masturbate and, once orgasm is imminent, they switch to a more acceptable fantasy, hoping to increasingly associate orgasm with a preferred stimulus. Similarly, in satiation therapy, person masturbates to a conventional fantasy and then does so again as soon as possible to an undesirable fantasy (Marshall, 1979). The decreased sex drive and low responsiveness of the second episode makes the experience less exciting and eventually the behaviour may lose its desirability. In addition to behavioural therapies, pharmacotherapy or drug therapy has become more common (Chopin-Marcé, 2001). Ultimately, there is no fully effective way to change a person's sexual desires. Recidivism rates for sex offences in Canada are generally low, and treatment as well as constant surveillance, as in the case of pedophiles, has been effective.

1 What are some of the ways sex offenders are assessed? Are self-reports reliable? Why or why not?

2 Identify some of the treatment options for sex offences.

3 Explain what aversion therapy is and how it is used for the treatment of sex offenders.

4 What is the main goal of therapy for sex offenders?

Sex Scandals

If there is one phenomenon that incites what has become known as a "media feeding frenzy," it is a sex scandal where someone is caught in a compromising situation. When sex scandals reach national attention, they usually involve politicians, film stars, sports figures, or religious officials. As Gamson (2001) noted, most follow a common sequence of events. Accusations of indiscretions are put forth and followed by wide public broadcasts. Immediate denials come next, which quickly fade in the face of slowly surfacing evidence. Finally, there is a confession and a rapid fall from grace. Such was the sequence of events with anti-gay pastor Ted Haggard, who was leader of the National Association of Evangelicals in the United States. In 2006, a male prostitute claimed that Haggard had been paying him for sex for three years and had also purchased and used crystal methamphetamine ("crystal meth"). Haggard vehemently denied all accusations at first, but soon admitted to them and stepped down from his position.

Often, there is an attempt at a comeback as in the case of American televangelist and moral crusader Jimmy Swaggart, who was caught several times with prostitutes in the 1980s and 1990s. He is still involved in various ministries, although he has a smaller following. In this section, we first look at various types of sex scandals, then those involving the Catholic Church, then the residential school scandals in Canada, and finally we highlight some well-known Canadian sex scandals involving politicians.

Types of Sex Scandals

While much has been published in the media on the intricate details of major sex scandals, little has been written on them as a topic of inquiry among academics. There appear, however, to be six principal themes that underlie most sex scandals: *hypocrisy, infidelity, harassment/coercion, illicit sex, breach of trust*, and *blackmail*. Any sex scandal could have one or several themes inherent within its sequence of events and circumstances. Sometimes the central figures are guilty as charged; sometimes they are not. Often in the case of people in positions of responsibility and authority, however, the appearance of impropriety is just as important as any impropriety itself.

Hypocrisy occurs when someone has been caught engaging in the very same behaviour he or she condemns. Many American sex scandals have involved the same-sex sexual behaviour of people who themselves have publicly condemned gays and lesbians or fought against their rights. They have also involved people espousing standards of morality who have been caught with prostitutes. Aside from the downfalls of religious figures Haggard and Swaggart, American Senator Larry Craig, who openly opposed same-sex marriage, was arrested in June 2007 for soliciting sex in a men's restroom at an airport. Similarly, psychologist, Baptist minister and vehement anti-gay campaigner George Alan Rekers was caught in 2010 taking a 20-year-old male prostitute he found on a "rentboy" website on a two-week European vacation for daily nude massages. Both Craig and Rekers insisted that their actions had been misinterpreted and that they are not gay or even bisexual themselves.

Hypocrisy may also be combined with infidelity, as in the case of American politician Mark Edward Souder, who, along with a female member of his staff, publicly championed abstinence and family values and was then caught in 2010 having an extramarital affair with her. Often in such cases, one image restoration strategy has been to have the offender's wife present at press conferences

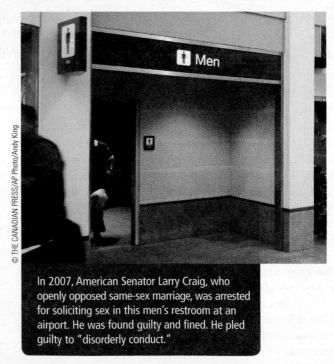

In 2007, American Senator Larry Craig, who openly opposed same-sex marriage, was arrested for soliciting sex in this men's restroom at an airport. He was found guilty and fined. He pled guilty to "disorderly conduct."

© THE CANADIAN PRESS/AP Photo/Andy King

forgiving and in support of him as he confesses (or denies) his wrongdoings (Husted, 2009). This stand-by-your-man strategy was used in 1998 when American president Bill Clinton was caught having an affair with intern Monica Lewinsky.

Harassment/coercion is a third type of sex scandal, which involves inappropriate behaviours ranging from simple unwanted touching to actual rape. In the early 1990s, American senator Brock Adams was accused of either harassing or drugging women before he raped them and at least eight of his victims came forward (Gilmore, 1992). More recently, dozens of women have come forward to accuse American comedian Bill Cosby of drugging and sexually assaulting them.

Scandals of illicit sex are those involving people caught carrying out either atypical or illegal sexual behaviour, such as engaging prostitutes, being in possession of child pornography, or having sex with someone under the age of majority. As a result, the public is able to peer into the salacious life of a public figure. In 2008, Wade Sanders, who was a deputy assistant in the American Navy, was caught with child pornography, and Robert E. Bauman, a conservative advocate in the United States House of Representatives, was caught soliciting sex from a 16-year-old male prostitute. Combining hypocrisy, infidelity, and illicit sex together, California Assemblyman Michael Duvall, who was a staunch family values advocate, was caught bragging about his sexual exploits over a live microphone of which he was unaware. He recounted sexual episodes with two women, at least one of whom was married, and bragged about how he enjoyed spanking one of them (Thompson, 2009).

Breach-of-trust scandals may involve a number of scenarios, among them school teachers caught having sex with students. In such cases, female teachers and their male students seem to attract far more attention (Angelides, 2007), as in the 1996 case of Mary Kay Letourneau and a 12-year-old student whom she later had children with and married. Letourneau spent six years in prison for her crime but, upon her release, she married the student, who by that time was 21 years old, and the two insisted that they were deeply in love.

Canadian sociologist Sheila L. Cavanagh (2007) believes that the greater attention upon female teachers has to do partially with the idea that older female/younger male relationships breach the norms of heteronormativity—that is, having a woman as the powerful one and a male as the submissive one. Given that the traditional perception of a reproductive relationship is the other way around, female teachers not only break the law in having sex with boys but they breach the norms of heteronormativity as well.

Finally, blackmail cases seem uncommon in today's political arena, although their potential figured prominently in the Cold War era of the 1950s and 1960s, where one reason used to ferret out and fire gay and lesbian employees working in government positions in Canada, the United States, and the United Kingdom was that they could be blackmailed by foreign agents.

Once a sex scandal becomes public and once there is no doubt of guilt in the public's view, the sex act that led to exposure becomes a **master status**, that is, a status that defines an individual above all else. Bill Cosby has been a successful comedian

for 50 years and yet now he is known as a rapist. Larry Craig was a successful American senator and yet now he is remembered only for soliciting sex in a public restroom.

Next we look at what is probably the largest international sex scandal of all time—child abuse and the Catholic Church.

The Catholic Church and Child Abuse Scandals

Although the Catholic Church is not the only Christian denomination involved in sexual abuse scandals, it has figured most prominently in the news over the past several decades. The numerous scandals have unfolded on two levels—first, the actual abuse of children and, second, the failure of church officials to report crimes to police. Some church officials even moved the pedophile priests around so that they could elude the police entirely. Although such scandals have occurred mainly in Ireland, the United States, and Canada, few countries in the world have not been touched by such abuse. Child sexual abuse by Catholic officials has occurred everywhere and the ensuing cover-ups have been on an international level (Pilgrim, 2011). Often, pedophile priests were deliberately moved to countries where they could not be extradited for their crimes (*USA Today*, 2004).

To name some Canadian cases, members of the Christian Brothers of Ireland in Canada were accused in the 1980s of physically and sexually abusing nearly 300 boys at the Mount Cashel Orphanage in Newfoundland. It was also found that the Department of Justice attempted to cover up the investigation of the abuse in 1975. In 2014, Catholic priest Eric Dejaeger was convicted of 24 counts of sexual abuse, mostly on boys and girls in Nunavut. There were originally many more charges, but they could not be validated since they occurred decades ago (Weber, 2014). Monseigneur Bernard A. Prince was sentenced to four years in prison in 2008 for the sexual abuse of 13 boys. His crimes were long known about by the Canadian Catholic Church and the Vatican, both of whom did little to stop them (Ha, 2010).

As for the United States, according to *bishopaccountability.org*, thousands of priests and other Catholic officials have been either accused or convicted of sexual molestation—over 500 in New York City, Chicago, and Los Angeles alone. According to the John Jay Report (United States Conference of Catholic Bishops, 2004), which looked at 10 667 abuse allegations by 4392 priests between 1950 and 2002, 23 percent of the victims were age ten or younger and 81 percent were male. Of all priests accused, most had only one allegation against them and 149 were responsible for about 3000 cases. The 4392 accused priests make up about 5 percent of all active Catholic priests in the United States. For a number of reasons, however, this figure should not be considered the actual rate of abusing priests because it is likely that many more incidents have not been reported. Victims

---

master status
A status that tends to define an individual above all other qualities and achievements.

decide not to bring charges because of shame, guilt, perceived lack of evidence, or the desire to put the abuse behind them. Furthermore, in other countries the rates of abuse may be higher or lower than 5 percent.

Several factors have been put forth as explanations for the breadth of the scandal, among them the imposition of celibacy on Catholic priests (Adams, 2003; Sipe, 2004). It is argued that pent-up sexual desire in young men that has no legitimate outlet enables many priests to look toward the children in their charge or other vulnerable individuals for relief. Some studies (e.g., Joseph, 2010) have found that many priests simply "burn out" and have affairs with women as well.

Others have argued that because 80–90 percent of victims of abuse by priests are boys, the problem is a matter of homosexuality in the priesthood and not pedophilia (Catalyst, 2010). This conflation, however, amounts to misunderstandings of the nature of homosexuality as well as pedophilia, where the former is an orientation toward adults and the latter is one toward children up to the age of puberty. One study of 352 abused children, for example, reports that abuse by gay men ranges from 0 percent to 3.1 percent, and is thus almost negligible.

Other reasons cited are the failure of seminaries to screen applicants or inform them of the challenges of celibacy; the shortage of priests, leading to the tolerance of existing ones' behaviour; and the lack of knowledge of the seriousness of child molestation in past decades.

The Canadian Residential School System

In the late 19th and most of the 20th century, the Canadian government in coalition with the Catholic, Anglican, and other churches established a system that took First Nations, Métis, and Inuit children from their homes and placed them in residential schools throughout Canada. They were sometimes placed in schools thousands of kilometres from where they grew up and never saw their parents again. By 1931, there were 80 schools in existence and in nearly a century of operation, 150 000 Native children attended. Thousands of children were physically, mentally, and sexually abused, and thousands died either of the abuse, neglect, or exposure (which at times was deliberate) to tuberculosis.

The purpose of the schools was to assimilate the children into mainstream Canadian society and, in so doing, obliterate their cultures entirely (Haig-Brown, 1991). They were forbidden to use their own languages, were schooled in Christian doctrine, and were trained either as housemaids or labourers. Only recently as testimonials emerge from the survivors of the schools have the abuses surfaced. According to the Truth Commission into Genocide in Canada (2001), many children were raped or otherwise sexually abused by teachers, clergymen, and nuns, some almost daily. Others were forcibly sterilized. On June 11, 2008, Prime Minister Stephen Harper issued a formal apology for the abuses in the residential schools.

Canadian Sex Scandals

While Canada has had its share of major sex scandals involving the Catholic Church, it has not had the same proportion of ones involving individuals compared to the United States. One of the reasons could be that in the United States, the religious convictions of politicians and other public figures are thought to be important factors in elections. As a result, when a politician is involved in a sex scandal, he or she is likely judged on religious grounds. The very few scandals that have occurred in Canada seem mainly to surround the indiscretions of politicians, but direct religious judgments seem to be absent. The following are three Canadian scandals—two provincial and one national.

John Edward Brownlee, 1930s

John Edward Brownlee, a Calgary lawyer, first became the attorney-general of Alberta and then the province's fifth premier, from 1925 to 1934. In 1930, while campaigning for re-election, Brownlee met Vivian MacMillan in Edson, Alberta. She was the daughter of the mayor and Brownlee encouraged her to study business in Edmonton. She did so and at age 18 became a stenographer in the attorney-general's office. She became friends with Brownlee's family and allegedly began an affair with the premier, which lasted three years—a claim that Brownlee vehemently denied.

In 1934, MacMillan sued Brownlee for "seduction" and a trial by jury ensued. At the time, seduction was a legally recognized civil wrong if a woman's consent to sexual intercourse was based on misrepresentation. The jury ruled in favour of MacMillan, but the judge disregarded this verdict and dismissed the case. Eventually, after an appeal, the Supreme Court of Canada upheld the jury's decision and awarded her $10 000 in damages. Brownlee's

In the early 1960s, Associate Minister of Defence Pierre Sévigny had an affair with Gerda Munsinger, an East German woman thought to be a spy.

© Frank Grant/Getty

political career came to an end. He stepped down from his position as Alberta's premier and eventually returned to his profession as a lawyer.

Gerda Munsinger, 1960s

In the middle of the Cold War, Pierre Sévigny, who was an associate minister of defence under Prime Minister John Diefenbaker, had an affair from 1958 to 1961 with an East German woman who immigrated to Canada and who had allegedly worked as a prostitute. Her name was Gerda Munsinger and, as it happened, she was suspected of being a Soviet spy and had slept with several other cabinet ministers as well. The controversy came out in 1966 after her name was mentioned in the House of Commons in reference to security leaks, which led to an RCMP inquiry. No evidence of espionage on Munsinger's part was found.

While no charges were laid, the Canadian media reported on Munsinger's affairs for weeks and the allegations of espionage and secret sexual liaisons captured the Canadian imagination at a time when James Bond films had become popular. Munsinger was deported in 1961 and was thought to be dead until a Canadian reporter found her living in East Germany. In 1974, she returned to Canada and was interviewed by journalist Barbara Frum. She told Frum that the entire affair had been greatly exaggerated. The Munsinger affair was lauded as Canada's first national sex scandal.

Graham Harle, 1980s

In 1983, Alberta Solicitor General Graham Harle was discovered by police parked outside a motel in Edmonton with a prostitute. When questioned, he said that he was merely conducting research on prostitution in the city and concluded that it "doesn't appear to be a problem right at the moment" (*Montreal Gazette*, 1983). His story that he was working undercover was not accepted and he eventually resigned from his position.

Review Questions

1 Why do you think there are so many more sex scandals in the United States than Canada?

2 Why is it that an illicit affair can ruin the entire career of a politician and not other professionals such as business executives.

3 What factors to you believe most contribute to the emergence of sex abuse in the Catholic Church?

4 Of the six types of sex scandals, which one or ones best fit the case of John Edward Brownlee?

Chapter Review

Summary Points

1 Non-conformist sexual behaviour has been called inversion, perversion, and other names over the past two centuries. By the 1950s, a "pervert" was a generic name for someone considered sick and twisted and who preyed upon women and children. Such terms did much to demonize alternative forms of sexual expression that harmed no one.

2 Societies celebrate and encourage diversity in many areas of everyday life but have long been less accepting of sexual diversity. Social value judgments rather than science typically have historically determined which sexual behaviours are acceptable in society and which are not. Such judgments vary over time and across culture.

3 In the 19th century, John Stewart Mill, in his book *On Liberty* posited that laws are justified only when they are based on preventing harm to people. Keeping this in mind, sexual behaviours can be judged not by morality but objectively with Mills's harm principle. Those that do no physical or psychological harm and involve only fully consenting adults would be left alone, while those that do cause harm, invade privacy, or involve coercion or minors would not.

4 The first edition of the *Diagnostic and Statistical Manual* (DSM) was published in 1952, and the term "sexual deviation" was used for any sexual behaviour that deviated from heterosexual intercourse. Because it had no accompanying definition, it was subject to much biased interpretation by psychiatrists. The word "paraphilia" was introduced in the third edition of the DSM in 1980 and included fetishism, transvestism, sadism, masochism, frotteurism, exhibitionism, voyeurism, and pedophilia, among other activities.

5 The fifth edition of the DSM in 2013 distinguished between a paraphilia and a paraphilic

Harmful and Antisocial Sexual Expression **439**

disorder. Merely having paraphilic interests, as do participants in BDSM, while suffering no physical or psychological ill effects, was no longer enough for treatment or definitions of mental illness. Once there is distress, discomfort, or anxiety, a sexual interest has reached the level of a disorder.

6 People with paraphilic disorders come from every socioeconomic level, every ethnic and racial group, and any sexual orientation. Factors found to be related to the development of a paraphilic disorder include growing up in a dysfunctional family and past sexual abuse. Most people with paraphilic interests in general are male.

7 A number of theories attempt to explain the development of paraphilic disorders. Biological theories look at disturbances in brain physiology or chemistry, while sociobiological theories look how the principles of evolution influence sexual behaviour. Psychoanalytic theorists suggest that the causes can be traced back to problems during the Oedipal crisis and with castration anxiety. This, however, is a circular theory and thus not falsifiable.

8 Developmental theories claim that individuals form a template in their brain that defines their ideal lover and sexual situation, and this can be disrupted in a number of ways. Paraphilic disorders may also be caused by courtship disorders in which the behaviour becomes fixed at a preliminary stage of mating that would normally lead to sexual intercourse. Behaviourists suggest that paraphilic disorders develop because a particular behaviour becomes associated with sexual pleasure through conditioning.

9 Sociologists look at ways in which a particular sexual behaviour becomes labelled as deviant, how gender interacts with sexuality in the creation of fetishes, and how culture and change contribute to the emergence of new fetishes and other sexual behaviours.

10 The DSM-5 for the first time distinguished between paraphilias and paraphilic

disorders. It lists three types: courtship disorders pertaining to disturbances in courtship sequences, algolagnic disorders pertaining to pain and humiliation, and anomalous target preferences pertaining to targets of erotic desire.

11 Courtship paraphilic disorders (voyeuristic, exhibitionistic, and frotteuristic) pertain to exposing one's genitals inappropriately ("flashers"), spying on people undressing or having sex ("peeping Toms"), and rubbing up against people in crowded places such as subways. Troilism is a situation where two people have sex while a third person watches.

12 Algolagnic disorders pertain to either sadism or masochism but go beyond simple BDSM play where the desire to hurt and humiliate or to be hurt or humiliated reaches dangerous levels. There was a controversy over whether "paraphilic coercive disorder" (e.g., rape) should have been included in the DSM. At present, it is not and is considered more of a criminal offence than a mental disorder.

13 Pedophilia is a sexual attraction toward children up until the age of puberty. Once puberty occurs, pedophilic interest wanes. Girls are twice as likely as boys to be victims of pedophilic behaviour. In 2011, there were 3822 cases of sex crimes against children in Canada ranging from "invitation to sexual touching" to luring a child via a computer.

14 The DSM-5 includes a category called "Other Specified Paraphilic Disorders" and lists telephone scatolophilia (making obscene telephone calls), zoophilia (erotic attraction to animals), and necrophilia (sex with dead bodies).

15 Sexual addiction is a much-contested concept in that many counsellors believe it to be a real mental disorder, while others believe it to be no more than a value judgment in a sex-negative society. At present, sexual addiction is not included in the DSM because of a lack of information upon which to form

legitimate diagnoses. There exist numerous organizations to help "sex addicts," some of which are counselling based while others are religion based.

16 Treatment for paraphilic disorders first involves an assessment. This can be done through self-report, behavioural observation, physiological tests, personality inventories, and phallometric tests. The most important goal of therapy is to change a person's behaviour in the case of antisocial disorders such as pedophilia and to help a person cope with their behaviour in other types of disorders. Treatments for paraphilic disorders include group, individual, and family therapy; medication; education; and self-help groups. Behavioural methods are most common. Techniques include aversion therapy, shame aversion, systematic desensitization, orgasmic reconditioning, and satiation therapy. Testosterone-suppressing drugs, antidepressants, and chemotherapy may also be used.

17 There is little academic research on sex scandals. There appear, however, to be six principal themes that underlie most sex scandals: hypocrisy, infidelity, harassment/coercion, illicit sex, breach of trust, and blackmail. Any sex scandal could have one or several themes inherent within its sequence of events and circumstances.

18 Since the 1950s, thousands of cases of sexual abuse of children by Catholic clergy have arisen. Most involve young boys. The most prominent case in Canada has been the abuse of nearly 300 boys in the Mount Cashel Orphanage in Newfoundland. Among the factors thought to be causative is the tradition of celibacy. The residential school system where Aboriginal children were taken from their families and placed in church-run schools also led to tremendous physical and sexual abuse.

19 Canada has had relatively few sex scandals compared to the United States. Those that were most prominent were the Brownlee affair in the 1930s, the Munsinger affair in the 1960s, and the Harle affair in the 1980s.

Critical Thinking Questions

1 Sexual behaviour is as varied as any other human activity. Why is it necessary to have a line drawn between what is acceptable and not acceptable? What are some of the ways of judging sexual behaviour and what is the best way to do so?

2 Why does atypical sexual behaviour evoke such strong negative reactions as opposed to atypical diets or other activities? What is it about sex in particular that evokes such negativity?

3 From the first edition of the DSM in 1952 to the latest edition in 2013, many changes have occurred in terms of what defines a mental illness. What does this say about the "objectivity" of such diagnoses?

4 Of the theories presented as to the causes of paraphilias, which one or two do you find most logical and why? Which one is the least logical?

5 Is "sexual addiction" a genuine mental disorder or is it a value judgment? Explain why.

6 Find a news story of a particular sex scandal and determine which of the six types most applies.

7 Why do you think Canada has had so few sex scandals while the United States has had so many?

Websites

Survivors Network of Those Abused by Priests (SNAP)
A resource website for people who were abused by Catholic priests containing resources, news articles, and testimonials. (http://www.snapnetwork.org/)

American Psychiatric Association—DSM-5 Development
Although parts of this website are restricted to subscribers, it contains much information about the development of the DSM, including news releases, books, etc. (http://www.dsm5.org/Pages/Default.aspx)

17 Power and Sexual Coercion

I worked as a rape crisis counsellor for many years, and while I found it enormously rewarding, it was also one of the hardest jobs I've ever had. The self-blame that many women experienced after a rape was one of the most difficult aspects of this work. We live in a blame-the-victim society that seems to take rape seriously only when a person is overcome by a stranger in a dark alley. But we all know that rapists can also be our friend, date, or classmate. Each of us makes hundreds of decisions every day, and while many of these are good decisions (such as driving the speed limit or wearing a seat belt), some may be neutral. Going to a particular party, having one too many drinks, walking home alone may not be good decisions, but a person doesn't deserve to be punished for such decisions. When something bad happens to us as a result of that decision, we often second-guess ourselves, wondering, *Why did I go to that party?* or *Why did I get drunk?* Although second-guessing

is normal, many people fail to realize that rape often involves one person disrespecting another person. All of these thoughts were running through my head when I met Meg last fall. Although she had agreed to talk to me about her recent experience being raped by an acquaintance, I knew it was going to be difficult for her to share her story with me. As she started to talk to me I could see the pain in her eyes, but I also heard hope in her voice.

Last summer, a group of friends and I decided we were going to cut loose and have fun. All the kids we invited were friends, and many of us had little time to hang out together. We organized a party at a campsite out in the woods so that our loud music and noise wouldn't bother anyone. On the drive there we drank Jäger and Red Bull. Usually I'm the one who is the designated driver because everyone thinks I'm the most responsible of our friends.

*But this night I decided I was going to have a good time.
I wasn't worried at all because I was with friends. When
we got to the campsite we brought out our coolers of beer
and some food and made a fire. Everyone was talking,
drinking, laughing, and dancing. But at one point I just
knew I had too much to drink. I felt really sick and I wanted
to lie down. One couple had brought a tent and my friends
took me there to lay down for a bit. I don't remember
getting into the tent. What I do remember is waking up
with a man on top of me and feeling absolutely terrified.*

Although Meg's story is difficult to hear, it also helps
motivate us to continue to work toward overcoming our
blame-the-victim mentality. ▮▮

Power is an aspect of all sexual relationships. Sexual relationships are healthy when power is shared and when the relationship empowers the partners. In sexuality, however, as everywhere in human life, power can also be used to degrade and oppress. For example, the act of seduction is usually an interaction between each partner's power, which is partly what makes dating and sexual anticipation so exciting. However, coercive sexuality involves the clash of personal power, with one partner overpowering the other.

Physically or psychologically forcing sexual relations on another person is usually referred to as rape in many countries. In Canada the legal system refers to rape as *sexual assault* or a *sexual offence* (Criminal Code of Canada, Part V and Section 172). Sexual contact with a minor by an adult is also a sexual assault/offence. Instances in which a person with more power entices, pressures, or encourages another person with less power into sexual activities, ranging from an unwanted glance or word to actual sexual contact, can also be called a sexual offence and is often referred to as *sexual harassment*. This chapter begins with discussions of sexual offences and sexual assault, and then goes on to explore other ways that power can be misused in relationships.

Defining Sexual Offences and Sexual Assault

The line that separates sexual offences and assault from other categories of sexual activity can be blurry because of the fine distinctions between forced and consensual sex, as well as

On Your Mind

Why does sexual assault exist?

There are several theories as to why sexual assault exists in our society. Feminists argue that the nature of the relationships between the sexes fosters sexual assault. Others argue that it exists because of the perpetrator's psychopathology. Still others claim it is because of how women dress, act, or behave. Today, most theorists agree that sexual assault is a crime of power in which sex is used as a weapon.

societal patterns of female passivity and male aggression (LaFree, 1982). For instance, societal and cultural rules often dictate that men, not women, should initiate sexual activity. These beliefs about how sex is supposed to be can make defining sexual offences or sexual assault a difficult task.

sexual assault
Coercion of a non-consenting victim to have sexual contact.

perpetrator
An individual charged with a sexual assault but not yet convicted.

offender
An individual charged with, and convicted of, a sexual assault.

Defining **sexual assault** is also complicated by the fact that sometimes unwanted sex is consensual. Studies have found that a significant percentage of college students engage in unwanted sexual activity in dating relationships (Brousseau et al., 2011; O'Sullivan & Allgeier, 1998).

Sexual assault replaced the word rape (this term is still used in the United States) in the Canadian Criminal Code in 1983. The age of consent for sexual behaviour in Canada is 16 years of age for most sexual behaviours, with the exception of anal sex, where the age of consent is 18. There are variations on the age of consent depending on the age gap between the individuals involved (see Chapter 10). In Canada when sex is not consensual it is called a sexual assault. There are three levels of sexual assault. These are:

- *Level 1 (Criminal Code Section 271):* Any form of non-consensual contact for a sexual purpose. This can range from non-consensual kissing and touching to various sex acts involving genitals.

- *Level 2 (Criminal Code Section 272):* For a sexual assault to be deemed a level two offence a weapon or the threat of a weapon must be involved. Threats of harm to others, or multiple perpetrators can also lead to a level two sexual assault charge.

- *Level 3 (Criminal Code Section 273):* Any sexual assault that involves aggravated assault or serious bodily injury that threatens a person's life is considered a level three sexual assault.

Table 17.1 outlines the terms of incarceration for each level of sexual assault, according to the Criminal Code of Canada.

Finally, any murder that includes a sexual component is automatically first-degree murder in Canada; manslaughter or second-degree murder is not an option. In Canada there is no statute of limitations on the prosecution of sexual assault. We refer to those individuals who have been charged but not convicted of sexual assault as **perpetrators** (the term that we will be using primarily in this chapter) and those that have been convicted of a sexual assault as **offenders**. These definitions apply to both males and females, and include heterosexual and homosexual sexual assault.

Animal Variations | Does Sexual Assault Happen in Other Species?

For most mammals, penile penetration of a female by a male is done only when the female is in estrus, or "heat," as it is commonly called. However, forced penetration is common in a wide variety of animal species (Lalumière et al., 2005b); for instance, male orangutans often engage in forced mating and vicious biting of the female. Sexual coercion in other non-human primates and mammals has also been documented (Smuts & Smuts, 1993).

Table 17.1	Sentencing Terms for the Three Levels of Sexual Assault in Canada	
Offence	**Sentence Terms**	**Maximum Term**
Sexual Assault (s. 271)	**By way of indictment:** ● No minimum term of incarceration ● If the victim is under the age of 16 years = minimum 1-year term of incarceration	10 years
	By way of summary: ● No minimum term of incarceration ● If the victim is under the age of 16 years = minimum 90-day term of incarceration	18 months
Sexual Assault (s. 272) With a weapon or threat of a weapon or cause bodily harm	● If a firearm is used and involves a criminal organisation = minimum 5-year term of incarceration (on first offence); 7 years on second and subsequent offences ● If a firearm is used = minimum 4-year term of incarceration ● If the victim is under the age of 16 years = minimum 5-year term of incarceration ● If none of the above criteria apply = no minimum term of incarceration	14 years
Aggravated Sexual Assault (s. 273)	● If a firearm is used and involves a criminal organization = 5 years minimum term of incarceration (on first offence); 7 years on second and subsequent offences ● If a firearm is used = minimum 4-year term of incarceration ● If the victim is under the age of 16 years = minimum 5-year term of incarceration ● If none of the above criteria apply = no minimum term of incarceration	Life

SOURCE: Personal communication Dr. Scharie Tavcer – Department of Justice Studies, Mount Royal University.

Regardless as to how sexual assault is defined, some women do not consider an assault to be sexual if a penis was not involved (Bart & O'Brien, 1985). This is because many women view sexual assault as something that is done by a penis (intercourse, fellatio, anal sex) rather than something done to a vagina (digital penetration, cunnilingus, touching).

Debate is ongoing about the appropriate term for a person who has experienced a sexual offence or sexual assault. Although the word *victim* emphasizes the person's lack of responsibility for the incident, it may also imply that the person was a passive recipient of the attack. The term *victim* can also become a permanent label. Some prefer the term *survivor,* which implies that the person had within herself or himself the strength to overcome and to survive the sexual assault. However, for clarity, in this chapter we use the term *victim* to refer to a person who has survived a sexual assault.

Sexual Assault Statistics

In 2004, according to the General Social Survey on Victimization in Canada there were about 512 000 incidents of sexual assault in individuals aged 15 or older. This works out to be about 1977 for every 100 000 people in Canada. Interestingly in 2007 only 24 200 and in 2011 only 21 800 sexual assault incidents were reported to the police, confirming a commonly held belief that the incidence of sexual assault is vastly underreported. Although both women and men can be sexually assaulted, by far the majority of victims are female (Figure 17.1). In the majority of cases, the victims know their assailants (Lawyer et al., 2010). In one study, 63 percent of sexual assaults against women and 100 percent of sexual assaults against men were committed by someone they knew (Rand, 2009). We will primarily discuss the sexual assault of women by men here and later in the chapter will explore the sexual assault of men.

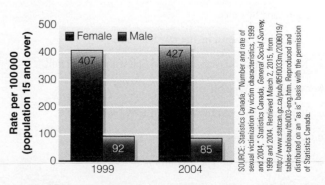

FIGURE **17.1** Reported sexual assault by sex of victim in Canada in 1999 and 2004.

Sexual offences and sexual assault are some of the most under-reported crimes in Canada, so it is difficult to assess the actual number of victims (Gonzales et al., 2005). Why are close to half of victims unlikely to report sexual assault? Like Meg, some do not report it because they feel shameful, guilty, embarrassed, or humiliated and don't want people to know (Sable et al., 2006; Shechory & Idisis, 2006). Because victims often know their assailants and may blame themselves for being with them, these factors can make them less comfortable reporting their attacks. Victims who were using drugs or alcohol before the sexual assault are much less likely to report the assault (Wolitzky-Taylor et al., 2011). Many also worry that their reports will not be taken seriously, their confidentiality will not be maintained, or the attacker will retaliate (Sable et al., 2006).

Characteristics of Sexual Assault Perpetrators

What is your image of a "rapist"? Who is it that sexually assaults others? A stranger who jumps out of a bush? A drunk at a fraternity party? What drives someone to commit a sexual assault? Anger? Frustration? Even today, the question of why someone would sexually assault another person remains largely unanswered.

Sex offenders are primarily male, single, and between the ages of 15 and 30 (Amir, 1971; D.E.H. Russell, 1984). They have been found to have high levels of impulsivity and aggression, sexist views about women, and high levels of rape/sexual assault myth acceptance (see Table 17.2; Beech et al., 2006; Giotakos et al., 2005;

Table 17.2 Sexual Assault Myths
Martha Burt (1980) defined sexual assault (rape) myths as prejudicial and stereotyped beliefs about sexual assault, victims, and perpetrators. They often lead people to justify rape by rationalizing what happened and who might be at fault. Frequently they shift the blame for sexual assault to the victims.
Although there are many sexual assault (rape) myths, below are some common most common myths.

- Only "bad" women get raped.
- Women make false reports of rape.
- Women fantasize about rape.
- Men can't be raped.
- You can tell a rapist by the way he looks.
- No woman or man can be raped against his or her will.
- A man can't rape his wife.
- Rape only happens to young, attractive women.
- Most rapists rape only once.
- False reporting of rape is common.

Copyright © Cengage Learning 2013

Lalumière et al., 2005d; Langevin et al., 2007; Masser et al., 2006). Men who commit sexual assault a often have histories of personal violence, such as child physical abuse, child sexual abuse, dating violence, or intimate partner violence (IPV; we will discuss IPV further later in this chapter; Cavanaugh et al., 2011; Lisak & Miller, 2002). Even so, despite the assumption that sex offenders are psychologically disturbed individuals, research does not support the assumption that they are very different from non-offenders (Oliver et al., 2007; Voller & Long, 2010).

Sex offenders often have multiple victims. In fact, research has found that the majority of sexual assaults are perpetrated by serial offenders who have an average of six victims (Lisak & Miller, 2002). Thus, a relatively small number of men are responsible for a large number of sexual assaults, which explains the disparities between the number of men who say they have committed sexual assault and the number of women who say they have been sexually assaulted (Lisak & Miller, 2002). Within this group of men, there are a variety of offender "types," including the power, anger, and sadistic offenders, which differentiate motivations for sexual assault (J. Douglas & Olshaker, 1998; Hazelwood & Burgess, 1987; McCabe & Wauchope, 2005; Pardue & Arrigo, 2008). Power offenders are motivated by domination and control; anger offenders are motivated by anger and use it in overt ways (i.e., force or weapons); and sadistic offenders are motivated by sexual and aggressive fantasies.

The idea of forcing or coercing a woman to engage in sex is not unusual. In a classic study about the potential to offend, 356 college-age heterosexual men were asked, "If you could be assured that no one would know and that you could in no way be punished for forcing a woman to do something she really didn't want to do (rape), how likely, if at all, would you be to commit such acts?" Sixty percent indicated that under the right circumstances, there was some likelihood that they would use force, non-consensual sexual behaviours, or both (Briere & Malamuth, 1983, p. 318). However, this study is from over 30 years ago, so it is difficult to know whether the results would be significantly different today. One study on forcing sex found that 30 percent of men admitted they might force sex under certain circumstances (Lev-Wiesel, 2004), whereas another study found that 58 percent of men reported having forced sex on a woman who was unable to consent or who had made her lack of consent clear (Parkhill & Abbey, 2008).

REAL Research One study found that 45 percent of females and 30 percent of males who were in a relationship reported being forced into sexual activity by their partner when they didn't want it (Brousseau et al., 2011). Such sexual coercion can lead to depression, anxiety, low self-esteem, and a negative view of one's sexual self.

You can protect yourself from drug-facilitated sexual assault by never accepting drinks from other people, by opening your drinks yourself, and by never leaving your drink unattended.

SEX in Real Life | *Date-Rape Drugs*

The term *date-rape drug* is slang for any drug that may be used during a sexual assault. This would include Rohypnol (also called *roofies, Forget Pill,* or *Mind Eraser*), gamma-hydroxybutyric acid (GHB; also called *Liquid Ecstasy, Georgia Home Boy,* or *Easy Lay*), and ketamine (also called *Special K, Kit Kat,* or *Cat Valium*). Today, experts refer to rapes using these drugs as "drug-facilitated sexual assault." The behavioural effects of these drugs are similar to those of Valium, but they are much more powerful. The drugs go to work quickly, and the time they last varies. If a person has been drinking alcohol when the drugs were ingested, the drug effects will last longer. Adverse effects of these drugs may include drowsiness, memory problems, lower blood pressure, sleepiness, problems talking, dizziness, and impaired motor functions. With higher doses, convulsions, vomiting, loss of consciousness, and coma or death can occur.

Rohypnol is illegal in Canada but is legal in several countries and has been smuggled into the Canada. Rohypnol comes in tablet form and is typically placed in a drink, where it quickly dissolves. Once dissolved, the tablets are

Coasters like these include test patches that can show the presence of date-rape drugs in a drink.

undetectable—there is no taste or colour change to the liquid. Ketamine is a white powder that easily dissolves in a drink, whereas GHB can come in tablet, liquid, or powder form. Ketamine and GHB are both legal and used for different medical purposes. The effects of these drugs usually begin within 30 minutes, peak within two hours, and can last a total of eight hours. An individual may feel nauseous, hot or cold, and dizzy within ten minutes after ingesting these drugs. A 2002 study in British Columbia found that 27 percent of sexual assaults involved some form of date-rape drug (Du Mont et al., 2010; McGregor et al., 2004).

Although it is important to be aware of these drugs, many experts argue that focusing on these drugs in sexual crimes often turns our attention away from other drugs, such as alcohol and/or street drugs, that are often associated with sexual assault (Németh et al., 2010). In fact, alcohol is the most common "rape drug" (Littleton et al., 2009a).

In several areas of Canada you can also purchase coasters (see the Sex In Real Life feature) called Drink Detectives that can detect several sedative-like drugs (Chung, 2010). If you think you have been drugged, it is important to go to a police station or hospital as soon as possible because a urine test can check for the presence of the drugs. These drugs can leave your body within 12 to 72 hours, so it is important to get a urine test as soon as possible. For more information about date-rape drugs, check the Websites list at the end of this chapter.

Theories about Sexual Assault

What drives someone to sexually assault another person? We discuss the most prominent theories of why sexual assault occurs, including offender psychopathology, victim precipitation, and feminist, sociological, and evolutionary theories.

Sex Offender Psychopathology: A Disease Model

Modern ideas about why sexual assault occurs evolved first from psychiatric theories, which suggested that men offend because of mental illness, uncontrollable sexual urges, or alcohol intoxication. This theory of **rapist psychopathology** suggests that it is either disease or intoxication that forces men to sexually assault their victims, and that if they did not have these problems, they would not offend.

According to this theory, the sexual assault rate can be reduced by finding these sick individuals and rehabilitating them. The theory makes people feel safer because it suggests that only sick individuals sexually assault, not "normal" people. However, research consistently fails to identify any significant distinguishing characteristics of rapists (Fernandez & Marshall, 2003). Having psychological or alcohol problems does not predispose a person to be a sex offender. In fact, men who offend are often found to be nearly "normal" in every other way. Perhaps it is easier to see offenders as somehow sick than realize that the potential to sexually assault someone exists in many of us.

rapist psychopathology
A theory of sexual assault that identifies psychological issues in a offender that contribute to sexual assault behaviour.

Theories of rapist psychopathology were very common until the 1950s, when feminist researchers began to refocus attention on sexual assault's effect on the victim rather than on the offender. However, there are still those who accept psychopathological theories today. In fact, college students often report that this theory helps to explain stranger sexual assault but does not help us to understand date or acquaintance sexual assault (Cowan, 2000).

On Your Mind

My ex-boyfriend forced me to have sex with him. Since I dated him in the past, does that mean this is not sexual assault?

It does not matter if you have had a sexual relationship with someone in the past—if it is non-consensual, it is sexual assault. Sexual assault can, and does, occur between an offender and victim who have a pre-existing relationship (often referred to as "date rape" or "acquaintance rape"), and even between spouses and partners, which we will talk about later in this chapter.

Victim Precipitation Theory: Blaming the Victim

In the chapter opening story, I discussed how many people might believe that a woman does something to put herself at risk for sexual assault. The **victim precipitation theory** explores the ways victims make themselves vulnerable to sexual assault, such as how they dress or act or where they walk (Wakelin, 2003). By focusing on the victim and ignoring the motivations of the attacker, many have labelled this a blame-the-victim theory.

The victim precipitation theory of sexual assault shifts the responsibility from the person who knowingly attacked to the innocent victim (Sawyer et al., 2002): "*She was walking home too late at night,*" "*She was drunk*" "*She was wearing a really short skirt,*" or "*She was flirting*" Women who wear suggestive clothing and drink alcohol are perceived as having greater sexual intent than women who wear neutral attire and do not drink alcohol (Maurer & Robinson, 2008). The women who wear suggestive clothing and drink alcohol are also viewed as being more responsible for a sexual assault (Maurer & Robinson, 2008).

The victim precipitation theory also serves to distance people from the reality of sexual assault and lulls them into the false assumption that it could not happen to them or someone close to them because they would not act like "those other women." If we believe bad things happen to people who take risks, then we are safe if we do not take those risks.

victim precipitation theory
A theory of sexual assault that identifies victim characteristics or behaviours that contribute to sexual assault.

feminist theory
A theory of sexual assault that contends that rape is a tool used in society to keep a woman in her place.

sociological theory
A theory of sexual assault that identifies power differentials in society as causing rape.

In Susan Brownmiller's (1975) classic work on gender and rape, she argues that rape forces a woman to stay in at night, to monitor her behaviour, and to look to men for protection. This attitude also contributes to a sexual assault victim's guilt because she then wonders, *If I hadn't worn what I did, walked where I walked, or acted as I did, maybe I wouldn't have been raped.* Overall, men are more likely than women to believe in the victim precipitation theory and to view sexual coercion as acceptable (Auster & Leone, 2001; Proto-Campise et al., 1998).

Feminist Theory: Keeping Women in Their Place

Feminist theorists contend that sexual assault and the threat of sexual assault are tools used in our society to keep women in their place. This fear keeps women in traditional sex roles, which are subordinate to men's. Feminist theorists believe that the social, economic, and political separation of the genders has encouraged sexual assault, which is viewed as an act of domination of men over women (Hines, 2007; Murnen et al., 2002). Sex-role stereotyping—which reinforces the idea that men are supposed to be strong, aggressive, and assertive, whereas women are expected to be slim, weak, and passive—encourages sexual assault in our culture (Murnen et al., 2002).

Sociological Theory: Balance of Power

Sociological theory and feminist theory have much in common; in fact, many feminist theorists are sociologists. Sociologists believe that sexual assault is an expression of power differentials in society (T.A. Martin, 2003). When men feel disempowered by society, by changing sex roles, or by their jobs, overpowering women with the symbol of their masculinity (a penis) reinforces, for a moment, men's control over the world.

Sociologists explore the ways people guard their interests in society. For example, the wealthy class in a society may fear the poorer classes, who are larger in number and envy the possessions of the upper class. Because women have been viewed as "possessions" of men throughout most of Western history, fear of the lower classes often manifested itself in a belief that lower-class males were "after our wives and daughters." During the slavery period in the United States, for example, it was widely believed that, if given the chance, Black males would rape White women, whereas White males did not find Black women attractive. Yet the truth was just the opposite: Rape of White women by Black males was relatively rare, whereas many White slave masters routinely raped their Black slaves. Once again, this supports the idea that sexual assault is a reflection of power issues rather than just sexual issues.

Evolutionary Theory: Product of Evolution

Finally, a controversial theory on the origins of sexual assault came out of evolutionary theory. Randy Thornhill and Craig Palmer, authors of *Natural History of Rape: Biological Bases of*

Sexual Coercion, propose that sexual assault or rape is rooted in human evolution (Thornhill & Palmer, 2000). According to evolutionary theory, men and women have developed differing reproductive strategies, wherein men desire frequent mating to spread their seed, which is easily made, and women are designed to protect their eggs, which are a rare biological commodity in comparison to sperm, and be more selective in choosing mates (see Chapter 2). Sexual assault has developed as a consequence of these differences in reproductive strategies.

The majority of sexual offenders are male, Thornhill and Palmer assert, because men are designed to impregnate and spread their seed.

As we pointed out, this theory is controversial, and many feminists and sociologists alike are upset about ideas proposed in this theory (Brownmiller, 2000; Roughgarden, 2004). However, controversial or not, it is an interesting argument for us to consider when discussing theories on the development of sexual assault.

Review Questions

1 Explain why there is no single definition of sexual assault.

2 Describe the various levels of sexual assault in Canada according to the Criminal Code. What are the possible sentencing options for those convicted of sexual assault in Canada?

3 Describe the problems that have been encountered in attempting to identify the actual number of sexual assaults in Canada.

4 Identify what researchers have found about the characteristics of offenders.

5 Explain the disparities between the number of women who say they were sexually assaulted and the number of men who say they have committed a sexual assault.

6 Identify and differentiate between the five theories of sexual assault.

Sexual Assault Attitudes and Cultural Variations

Researchers have found gender and ethnic variations in attitudes about sexual assault. In addition, cultural issues can affect how a society defines sexual assault and the attitudes toward it. We discuss these issues in the following sections.

Gender Differences in Attitudes about Sexual Assault

Researchers have used many techniques to measure attitudes about sexual assault and sexual assault victims, such as questionnaires, written vignettes, mock trials, videotaped scenarios, still photography, and newspaper reports. Overall, men are less empathetic and sensitive than women toward sexual assault (Black & Gold, 2008; Davies et al., 2009; Earnshaw et al., 2011; Schneider et al., 2009). Men believe more rape myths and tend to blame victims more than women (see Table 17.2; Earnshaw et al., 2011; Franiuk et al., 2008). Studies have found that heterosexual men are more likely than heterosexual women to believe that a man should expect sexual intercourse if the man pays for an expensive date (Basow & Minieri, 2011; Emmers-Sommer et al., 2010); however, there were no expectations for sex when the expenses were split. Recent research suggests that women approach the issue of sexual consent more cautiously than men and would like consent to be explicitly obtained by males from their partners before engaging in sexual behaviours (Humphreys & Herold, 2007).

However, some hope exists about changing these attitudes about sexual assault. Men who take sexual assault education workshops or college courses on violence against women have less rape myth acceptance than men who do not take such workshops or courses (Currier & Carlson, 2009; Foubert & Cremedy, 2007). Sexual assault prevention programs for male college students have also been related to both attitudinal and behavioural changes (Foubert et al., 2010a, 2010b). The Sexual Health Centre in Calgary, Alberta, has a program called "WiseGuyz" that provides education for men around the issue of explicit consent. Men who took these and other educational classes reported less likelihood to commit sexual assault when they or a potential partner was under the influence of alcohol.

Ethnic Differences in Attitudes about Sexual Assault

Although the majority of the research has examined gender differences in attitudes about sexual assault, there is also research on ethnicity differences in sexual assault attitudes. Overall, ethnic minorities have been found to have more traditional attitudes toward women, which have been found to affect sexual assault attitudes. For example, among college students, non-Hispanic Whites are more sympathetic than Blacks to women who have been sexually assaulted (Nagel et al., 2005). However, Blacks are more sympathetic than either Hispanic or Japanese college students (Fischer, 1987; Littleton et al., 2007; Yamawaki & Tschanz, 2005). Asian students have the least sympathy for women who have been sexually assaulted and are more likely to hold a sexual assault victim responsible for the assault and excuse

Sexual Entitlement and the Rape of Women and Children in South Africa

South Africa has one of the highest reported rape rates in the world. In fact, a female born in South Africa has a greater chance of being raped in her lifetime than of learning to read (Dempster, 2002). High rape rates are primarily due to a wide variety of social and cultural issues, including economic issues, gender inequality, the sexual entitlement of men, and an acceptance of violence against women (Jewkes et al., 2009a, 2009b). Poverty and economic issues often force large families to sleep in the same bedroom, which exposes young children to sex at an early age (Phillips, 2001). South African men are raised with a strong sense of male sexual entitlement. This shouldn't be surprising, especially when you consider that South Africa's president, Jacob Zuma, was tried for rape in 2006, but later acknowledged engaging in unprotected sex with the HIV-positive daughter of a family friend (McDougall, 2010). Throughout the trial, Zuma's supporters burned photographs of the woman who accused him (McDougall, 2010).

Overall, a female born in South Africa has a 50 percent chance of being raped in her lifetime (Shields, 2010). Many of these rapes involve gang rapes or involve multiple acts of penetration (Vetten et al., 2008).

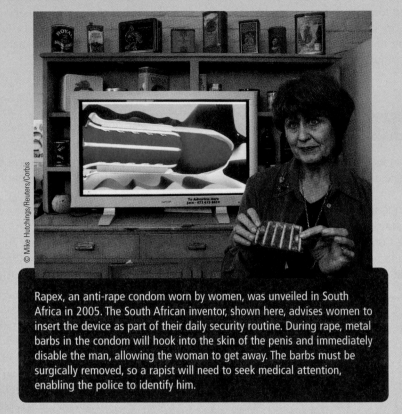

© Mike Hutchings/Reuters/Corbis

Rapex, an anti-rape condom worn by women, was unveiled in South Africa in 2005. The South African inventor, shown here, advises women to insert the device as part of their daily security routine. During rape, metal barbs in the condom will hook into the skin of the penis and immediately disable the man, allowing the woman to get away. The barbs must be surgically removed, so a rapist will need to seek medical attention, enabling the police to identify him.

Gang rapes are often viewed as a part of the culture and may be considered a form of male bonding (Jewkes et al., 2009b). In addition to high rape rates, South Africa also has the largest number of people living with HIV. In fact, a woman who is raped by a man older than 25 years has a 25 percent chance of her rapist

the offender (Devdas & Rubin, 2007; J. Lee et al., 2005; Yamawaki & Tschanz, 2005).

Researchers suggest that these differences are due to variations in cultural gender roles and conservative attitudes about sexuality. It is important to keep in mind that within these ethnic groups, there are also gender differences in attitudes about sexual assault, with women more supportive of sexual assault victims than men.

Sexual Assault in Different Cultures

Sexual assault or rape is defined differently around the world, so the incidence of sexual assault varies depending on a culture's definition (see Figure 17.2 for more information). One culture might accept sexual behaviour that is considered sexual

assault in another culture. For example, rape has been accepted as a punishment in some cultures throughout history. Among the Cheyenne, a husband who suspected his wife of infidelity could put her "out to field," where other men were encouraged to rape her (Hoebel, 1954). In the Marshall Islands of the Pacific Ocean, women were seen as the property of the males, and any male could force sexual intercourse on them (Sanday, 1981). In Kenya, the Gusii people view intercourse as an act in which males overpower their female partners and cause them considerable pain. In fact, if the female has difficulty walking the next morning, the man is seen as a "real man" and will boast of his ability to make his partner cry (Bart & O'Brien, 1985). In 2002, an 11-year-old Pakistani boy was found guilty of walking unchaperoned with a girl from a different tribe. His punishment involved the gang-raping of his 18-year-old sister, which was done to shame his family. The gang rape took place in a being HIV-positive (Jewkes et al., 2009b). Women who are raped in South Africa often do not report the rape and instead live in social isolation and fear. Those who do report the rape often face retribution and threats of murder.

A study by the Medical Research Council of South Africa found that one in four men had raped a woman or a girl in their lifetime, and nearly half of these men said they raped more than once (Jewkes et al., 2009a). Several factors were associated with the likelihood of having committed rape, including age, levels of education, and early childhood experiences. Men who raped were more likely to be between the ages of 20 and 40 years and have higher levels of education than those who did not rape (Jewkes et al., 2009a). They were also more likely to have experienced teasing, harassment, or bullying in childhood, and engage in various risky sexual behaviours, including multiple sex partners, sex with a prostitute, and a lack of condom use.

South Africa also has the highest rates of child rape in the world. It is estimated that a child is raped every 26 seconds (Jewkes et al., 2009a; McDougall, 2010). Studies have found that approximately 40 percent of girls and boys report being sexually abused at some point in their childhood. Children are often raped first by relatives in South Africa. One father, who had been raping his 11-year-old daughter for a year, said, "My child

cannot sleep with other men until I have slept with her first" (Shields, 2010). Even Oprah Winfrey was forced to take notice of these events when several girls at her exclusive school for underprivileged girls outside of Johannesburg were victims of sexual violence (Lichtenberg, 2011). For many years, a persistent myth existed that having sex with a virgin can cure AIDS (Phillips, 2001). As a result, babies, some as young as eight months old, were being gang-raped by HIV-positive men. The rape of infants poses many challenges, including the inability of the child to identify the rapist and a lack of DNA evidence because highly absorbent, disposable diapers often make it impossible to retrieve evidence (McDougall, 2010). Overall, conviction rate of child and baby rapists in South Africa is extremely low—only about 7 percent of rapists are ever found guilty (Ghanotakis, 2008).

Finally, another troubling practice in South Africa is that of *corrective rape,* in which a lesbian woman is raped to "cure" her of her sexual orientation (Kelly, 2009). Homophobia is rampant in South Africa, and this became painfully clear when Eudy Simelane, a star of South Africa's national female soccer team who was living openly as a lesbian, was gang-raped and brutally beaten and stabbed in 2008 (Bearak, 2009). A South African gay rights organization found that 86 percent of

Black lesbians say they live in fear of sexual assaults (Kelly, 2009).

Efforts to reduce the rape rates include educational campaigns, improved legislation, and increasing the prosecution of rapists and the penalties for rape. Educational interventions are now available to empower children and other adults and help them to understand sexual violence. It is hoped that all of these efforts will eventually decrease the skyrocketing rape rates in South Africa.

mud hut while hundreds of people stood by and laughed and cheered (Tanveer, 2002).

Sexual assault has also been used for initiation purposes. In East Africa, the Kikuyu previously had an initiation ritual in which a young boy was expected to rape to prove his manhood (Broude & Greene, 1976). Until he did this, he could not engage in sexual intercourse or marry a woman. In Australia, among the Arunta, rape serves as an initiation rite for girls. After the ceremonial rape, she is given to her husband, and no one else has access to her (Broude & Greene, 1976).

Many cultural beliefs and societal issues are responsible for the high rape rates in South Africa. These include the fact that South African women have a difficult time saying no to sex and that many men believe they are entitled to sex and believe that women enjoy being raped (Meier, 2002). In 2005, an anti-rape female condom was unveiled in South

Africa (Dixon, 2005). This device was controversial, with some believing that it put the responsibility for the problem on the shoulders of South African women, and others believing that the device was a valuable tool in decreasing the climbing rape rates in South Africa. (See the accompanying Sexual Diversity in Our World feature for more information about rape in South Africa.)

Asian cultures often have more conservative attitudes about sex; because of this, there is often more tolerance for rape myths (M.A. Kennedy & Gorzalka, 2002; Uji et al., 2007; Yamawaki, 2007). Research by Sanday (1981) indicates that the primary cultural factors that affect the incidence of rape in a society include relations between the sexes, the status of women, and male attitudes in the society. Societies that promote male violence have higher incidences of rape because men are socialized to be aggressive, dominating, and to use force to get what they want.

Power and Sexual Coercion **451**

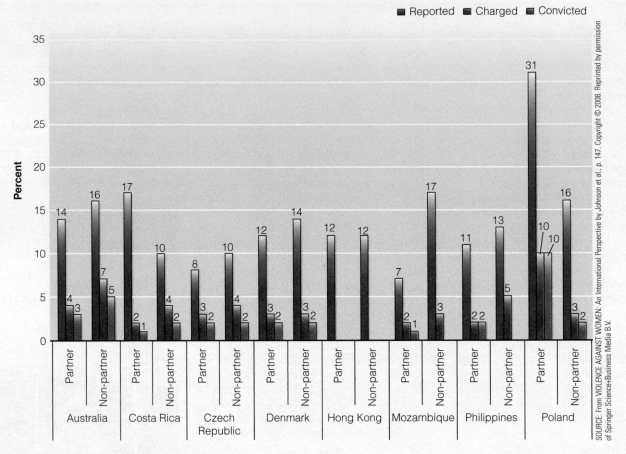

Legend: ■ Reported ■ Charged ■ Convicted

FIGURE **17.2** Reported rapes and convictions in select countries.

SOURCE: From VIOLENCE AGAINST WOMEN: An International Perspective by Johnson et al., p. 147. Copyright © 2008. Reprinted by permission of Springer Science-Business Media B.V.

Review Questions

1 Discuss the research on gender differences in attitudes about sexual assault.

2 Explain the impact of educational programs on attitudes and behaviours about sexual assault.

3 Discuss the research on ethnicity differences in attitudes about rape.

4 Explain how rape is defined differently around the world and how rape rates vary depending on a culture's definition.

Rape and Sexual Assault on Campus

Female college students are at greater risk for rape than their non-college peers (Gonzales et al., 2005). It is estimated that one of every five college women in the United States will experience a sexual assault during college. In several Canadian studies, it has been found that up to 25 percent of the undergraduate women surveyed reported that they had unwanted sexual interactions or intercourse during the last year (DeKeseredy,

Shwartz & Tait, 1993; Newton-Taylor, DeWit, & Tait, 1998). The majority of these sexual assaults will be perpetrated by someone the women know, which is why most cases are never reported (B.S. Fisher et al., 2000).

In Chapter 12, we discussed stalking in intimate relationships. Some women report being stalked on campus, either physically or through notes and e-mails. Overall, a total of 8–16 percent of women and 2–7 percent of men report being stalked at some point in their lives (Dennison & Thomson, 2005). Stalking is a serious problem, especially given that 81 percent of women who have been stalked by a heterosexual partner were also physically assaulted by that partner and 31 percent were sexually assaulted by him (Tjaden & Thoennes, 1998).

Sexual Assault Education on Campus

Many colleges and universities today sponsor rape and sexual assault prevention programs, and invite guest speakers from **sexual assault crisis centres** to discuss the problem of sexual assault between individuals that are known to one another, often through school. As we discussed earlier, researchers have found that these programs contribute to positive attitudinal and behavioural changes (Foubert et al., 2010a, 2010b). Men who attend such programs are less likely to commit sexual assaults (Currier & Carlson, 2009; Foubert & Cremedy, 2007).

Alcohol and Sexual Assault

On college and university campuses, alcohol use is one of the strongest predictors of sexual assault—up to two-thirds of sexual assault victims have voluntarily consumed alcohol before an assault (Lawyer et al., 2010; Littleton et al., 2009a). Women who are drunk are more likely to be viewed as "loose" or sexually "easy" (Parks & Scheidt, 2000). For men, alcohol seems to "sexualize" the environment around them. Cues that might be taken as neutral if the men were not drunk (such as a certain woman talking to them or dancing with them) may be seen as an indication of sexual interest (Abbey et al., 2005; Montemurro & McClure, 2005; Peralta, 2008). Alcohol also reduces inhibitions, which increases the chances of engaging in risky sexual behaviours for both men and women (Klein et al., 2007; Maisto et al., 2004; O'Hare, 2005).

Alcohol can sexualize the environment for men. A man who has been drinking may believe that a woman is signalling she is available when she is acting friendly.

© Peter M. Fisher/Corbis

On Your Mind

What if you are drunk and she is, too, and when you wake up in the morning, she says you raped her?

Claims of sexual assault must be taken seriously. This is why men and women should be very careful in using alcohol and engaging in sexual activity. The best approach would be to delay engaging in sexual activity if you have been drinking. This way, you will not find yourself in this situation.

Alcohol use on college campuses, as it relates to sexual assault, is viewed very differently for men and women. A man who is drunk and is accused of sexual assault is seen as less responsible because he was drinking ("Lighten up; he didn't even know what he was doing."), whereas a woman who has been drinking is seen as more responsible for her behaviour ("Can you believe her? She's had so much to drink that she's flirting with everyone—what a slut!"; Peralta, 2008; D. Richardson & Campbell, 1982; Scully & Marolla, 1983).

Being impaired or incapacitated during a sexual assault has been associated with self-blame, stigma, and problematic alcohol use in victims post-assault (Littleton et al., 2009a). In addition, many women might not even label the event as a sexual assault even when it clearly was (L.G. Hensley, 2002).

Athletes and Sexual Assault

Over the last few years it has become increasingly more common to hear stories in the news about college and professional athletes who are accused of rape or sexual assault (Farr & Kern, 2010; Lundstrom & Walsh, 2010; Namuo, 2010; Tramel, 2011). Participation in athletics has been found to be associated with rape-supportive attitudes and, to a lesser degree, sexually aggressive behaviour (Murnen & Kohlman, 2007). In addition, athletes who participate on teams that produce revenue have higher rates of sexually abusive behaviour than athletes on teams that do not produce revenue (McMahon, 2004). Researchers suggest that perhaps it is the sense of privilege that contributes to a view of the world in which sexual assault is legitimized. Playing sports may also help connect aggression and sexuality.

Some researchers suggest that all male groups may foster "hypermasculinity," which promotes the idea that violence and aggression are "manly" (Muehlenhard & Cook, 1988). The need to be aggressive and tough while playing sports may also help create problems off the field (Boeringer, 1999; T.J. Brown et al., 2002). Many male athletes may also have a distorted view of women, which often revolves around views expressed in the locker room. Locker room talk often includes derogatory language about women (including the use of words such as "sluts" or "bitches" to describe them), whereas those athletes who are not

sexual assault crisis centres
Organizations that offer support services to victims of sexual assault, their families, and friends. Many offer

information, referrals, support groups, counselling, educational programs, and workshops.

playing well are referred to as "girls" (McMahon, 2004; Murnen & Kohlman, 2007).

Research on female athletes has found that these athletes often believe they are less at risk than female non-athletes (McMahon, 2004). When asked about the potential for a female athlete to be sexually assaulted, one woman said:

> I think it would be a shock to a female athlete—because, we feel that we're so tough.... I always am kidding around that like, I could sit on a guy and knock the wind out of him and the idea of a guy taking advantage of me seems... well, that could never happen.... I work out all the time, I'm so strong.... I'm not some little girl. I'm tough. (McMahon, 2004, p. 16)

Female athletes are also more likely to blame the victim for a sexual assault than female non-athletes, and believe that some women who are sexually assaulted have put themselves in a bad situation (McMahon, 2004).

REAL Research When college students were asked described a bad hookup scenario, the majority focused on negative psychological consequences, such as shame, and did not identify the possibility of sexual assault (Littleton et al., 2009b).

Review Questions

1 Explain what we know about sexual assault on campus.

2 Explain the role that alcohol plays in sexual assault.

3 Explain the research on athletes, athletics, and sexual assault on college campuses.

Effects of Sexual Assault

Sexual assault is an emotionally, physically, and psychologically shattering experience for the victim. Some deny that a sexual assault has occurred at all, to avoid the pain of dealing with it. Others express self-blame, disbelief, anger, vulnerability, and increased feelings of dependency. As time goes by, the healing process begins, and feelings may shift to self-pity, sadness, and guilt. Anxiety attacks, nightmares, and fear slowly begin to decrease, although the incident is never forgotten. Some women never return to prior functioning levels and must create an entirely new view of themselves.

Rape Trauma Syndrome

Researchers Burgess and Holmstrom (1979) coined the term **rape trauma syndrome (RTS)**, which describes the effects of sexual assault. RTS is a two-stage stress response pattern characterized by physical, psychological, behavioural, sexual problems, or a combination of these, and it occurs after forced, non-consenting sexual activity. Although the *Diagnostic and Statistical Manual of Mental Disorders* does not recognize RTS, symptoms are similar to post-traumatic stress disorder (PTSD), which occurs after a traumatic event. Researchers have found that a significant number of sexual assault survivors develop PTSD within two weeks after the sexual assault (Littleton & Henderson, 2009; Taft et al., 2009).

Although not all victims respond to sexual assault or rape in the same manner, what follows is a description of what typically occurs. During the first stage of RTS, the **acute phase**, most victims fear being alone, strangers, or even their bedroom or their car if that is where the sexual assault took place. Other emotional reactions to rape include anger (at the assailant, the rape or assault itself, health care workers, family, oneself, court), anxiety, depression, confusion, shock, disbelief, incoherence, guilt, humiliation, shame, and self-blame (Frazier, 2000). A victim may also experience wide mood fluctuations. Difficulties with sleeping, including recurrent nightmares, are common. This phase begins immediately after the assault, may last from days to weeks, and involves several stress-related symptoms.

The majority of victims eventually talk to someone about the sexual assault (B.S. Fisher et al., 2003). Most of the time a victim will talk to friends or family members rather than to the police. Younger victims are more likely to tell someone than are older victims, perhaps because older victims blame themselves more for the sexual assault and may fear that others also will blame them. One study found that half of the women who were assaulted waited years before telling anyone (Monroe et al., 2005). Overall, women who speak out about their sexual assault experiences and experience negative reactions often stop talking about it (Ahrens, 2006). Negative reactions lead to increased self-blame and uncertainty about whether the experience qualified

rape trauma syndrome (RTS)	**acute phase**
A two-stage stress response pattern that occurs after a rape.	First stage of the rape trauma syndrome, in which a victim often feels shock, fear, anger, or other related feelings.

During the first stage of rape trauma syndrome, victims may feel depressed, confused, angry, guilty, or humiliated. Talking to a counsellor can be very helpful in working through these feelings.

it coming. Many also feel a sense of betrayal. Women who feel guilty or responsible for a sexual assault have lower levels of psychological well-being than women who do not feel responsible or guilty (Glenn & Byers, 2009).

Physical symptoms after a sexual assault include general body soreness, bruises, nausea, throat soreness and difficulties swallowing (if there was oral sex), genital itching or burning, and rectal bleeding or pain (if there was anal sex). In women, the emotional stress of the sexual assault may also cause menstrual irregularities. However, some of these symptoms (nausea and menstrual irregularities) are also signs of pregnancy, which is "why a pregnancy test is of utmost importance after a victim has been assaulted. Research has found there is a greater incidence of pregnancy in women who have been sexually assaulted than in women who engage in consensual unprotected vaginal intercourse (Gottschall & Gottschall, 2003). However, it is also true that women in prime fertile ages are overrepresented in sexual assault victim statistics.

Long-term reorganization, stage two of RTS, involves restoring order in the victim's lifestyle and re-establishing control. Many victims report that changing some aspect of their lives, such as changing addresses, roommates, universities, or even phone numbers, helped them to gain control. Symptoms from both stages can persist for one to two years after the sexual assault (Nadelson et al., 1982), although Burgess and Holmstrom (1979) found that 74 percent of sexual assault victims recovered within five years. Recovery is affected by the amount and quality of care that the victim received after the sexual assault. Positive crisis intervention and the support of others decrease the symptoms of the trauma.

In the past, many researchers have argued that sexual assault is a violent crime, not a sexual one. "Desexualizing" rape, or taking the sexual aspect out of it, has de-emphasized post-assault sexual concerns (Wakelin, 2003). Sexual assault is indeed a violent crime, and the majority of victims report experiencing sexual problems post-assault, even though these problems may not be lifelong (J.V. Becker et al., 1986; Burgess & Holmstrom, 1979; Van Berlo & Ensink, 2000).

Changes in sexual behaviours and sexual difficulties can persist for a considerable period after the sexual assault (Campbell et al., 2004). It can take weeks, months, or even years to work through sexual difficulties such as fear of

as sexual assault, and they increase the likelihood of PTSD (Ullman et al., 2007).

Depression often follows a sexual assault, and some victims report still feeling depressed 8 to 12 months after the sexual assault. Women who have a history of prior psychological problems, prior victimization, and/or a tendency to self-blame have a greater risk for depression (Cheasty et al., 2002; Frazier, 2000). Sometimes depression is so severe that victims' thoughts turn to suicide (Bridgeland et al., 2001).

Emotional reactions also vary depending on whether the victims knew their assailants. Women who report being sexually assaulted by strangers experience more anxiety, fear, and startle responses, whereas those sexually assaulted by acquaintances usually report more depression and guilt and decreased self-confidence (Sorenson &Brown, 1990). The majority of women who are sexually assaulted know their assailant and may have initially trusted him and agreed to be with him. After the sexual assault, they may second-guess themselves, wondering how they could have had such bad judgment or why they didn't see

On Your Mind

Do women who are raped eventually have a normal sex life?

Although it may take anywhere from a few days to months, most sexual assault victims report that their sex lives get back to what is normal for them (van Berlo & Ensink, 2000). However, research indicates that lesbian women may have more difficulties with sexual problems post-sexual assault (Long et al., 2007). Counselling, a supportive partner, and emotional support are extremely helpful.

long-term reorganization
The second stage of the rape trauma syndrome, which involves a restoration

of order in the victim's lifestyle and reestablishment of control.

sex, desire and arousal disorders, and specific problems with sexual behaviours such as sexual intercourse, genital fondling, and oral sex. Counselling can be helpful for women suffering from post-rape sexual difficulties. It is not uncommon for a woman to seek help for a sexual problem, such as anorgasmia (lack of orgasm), and during the course of therapy reveal an experience with sexual assault that she had never discussed. Some women may become more sexual after a sexual assault. In fact, one study found an increase in alcohol consumption post-assault, which increased the likelihood of engaging in risky sexual behaviours with multiple partners (Deliramich & Gray, 2008).

Silent Sexual Assault (Rape) Reaction

Some victims never discuss their sexual assault with anyone and carry the burden of the assault alone. Burgess and Holmstrom (1974) call this the **silent rape reaction**, and in many ways, it is similar to RTS. Feelings of fear, anger, and depression and physiological symptoms still exist; however, they remain locked inside. In fact, those who take longer to confide in someone usually suffer a longer recovery period (L. Cohen & Roth, 1987).

The silent rape reaction occurs because some victims deny and repress the incident until a time when they feel stronger emotionally. This may be months or even years later.

Sexual Assault of Partners and Other Special Populations

Although we have learned from the research that certain groups are at greater risk for sexual assault, we also know that some special populations are also at risk, including spouses, lesbians, older women, women with disabilities, and prostitutes.

Marital Sexual Assault

A woman's consent is often assumed when there is a marital contract (Bergen, 2006). It has been estimated that 10–14 percent of all married women are sexually assaulted by their husbands, although this number is much higher in battered women (D.E.H. Russell & Howell, 1983; Yllo & Finkelhor, 1985).

Although their symptoms are similar to those who are victims of non-marital sexual assault, many of these women report feeling extremely betrayed and may lose the ability to trust others, especially men. In addition, there is often little social support for wives who are sexually assaulted, and those who stay with their husbands often endure repeated attacks (Bergen & Bukovec, 2006). Unfortunately, marital sexual assault may be one of the least discussed types of assault.

Lesbians and Bisexuals

Sexual assault is a common experience in both lesbian and bisexual women. In fact, adult sexual assault by men is slightly higher in lesbian and bisexual women compared with heterosexual women (Balsam et al., 2005). Like heterosexual women, lesbian and bisexual women experience RTS after a rape. However, there may be more intense emotional repercussions compared with heterosexual women (Campbell, 2008; Long et al., 2007). Lesbians may also experience difficulties in assimilating the experience of sexual assault into their own self-image (Long et al., 2007). They may be "feminist-identified" in most areas of their lives, and the sexual assault may force them to re-examine the patriarchal society and their feelings about men. Some lesbians may have never experienced vaginal intercourse with a man and may be unaccustomed to dealing with the fear of pregnancy, let alone the extreme feelings of being violated and abused. Although very little research on this topic is available, lesbians can also be sexually assaulted by other women (Campbell, 2008).

Older Women

Many people believe that sexual assault happens only to younger women. It is difficult to think about our mothers or grandmothers being sexually assaulted. The stereotype that only young, attractive women are sexually assaulted prevents our thinking about the risk for older women. Although it is true that younger women are more at risk for sexual assault, older women are also assaulted (Ball, 2005; Burgess & Morgenbesser, 2005; Jeary, 2005). Older women are likely to be even more traumatized by sexual assault than younger women because many have very conservative attitudes about sexuality, have undergone physical changes in the genitals (lack of lubrication and/or thinning of the walls of the vagina) that can increase the severity of physical injury, and have less social support after a sexual assault, which reinforces and intensifies their sense of vulnerability (Burgess & Morgenbesser, 2005).

Women with Disabilities

Women with disabilities, regardless of their age, race, ethnicity, sexual orientation, or socioeconomic class, are sexually assaulted,

© Mel Curtis/Getty Images

Older women are also victims of sexual assault and may experience increased trauma because of declining physical health and more conservative attitudes about sexuality.

---

silent rape reaction
A type of rape trauma syndrome in which a victim does not talk to anyone after the rape.

and abused at a rate two times greater than women without disabilities (Cusitar, 1994; Sobsey, 1994; Wacker et al., 2008). They may be more vulnerable because of their diminished ability to fight back. In addition, persons with intellectual disabilities may have a more difficult time reading the preliminary cues that would alert them to danger. The impact of a sexual assault may be intense for these people because of a lack of knowledge about sexuality, loss of a sense of trust in others, and the lack of knowledgeable staff who can effectively work with them. In many cases, women with severe intellectual disabilities who have been sexually assaulted may not realize that their rights have been violated and, therefore, may not report the crime. Because of these factors, the intensity and length of time of RTS is usually prolonged. Educational interventions, together with solid support networks, have been found to help women with disabilities cope with sexual assaults (Foster & Sandel, 2010).

Prostitutes

Studies have found that between 68 percent and 70 percent of female prostitutes have been victims of a sexual assault (Farley & Barkan, 1998; Silbert, 1998). Because a prostitute's job is to provide sex in exchange for payment, the question of consent is often difficult to judge. Sexual assaults are also common from a prostitute's pimp. In fact, one study found that prostitutes reported being sexually assaulted an average of 16 times and beaten 58 times each year by their pimps (Chesler, 1993). Also, because of the general disapproval of prostitution, a prostitute who reports a sexual assault is often treated with disdain. People tend not to believe that she was sexually assaulted or may think that she is angry because she was not paid. Many prostitutes who

are sexually assaulted begin to question their involvement in prostitution. Believing and trusting all women's reports of sexual assault and performing a comprehensive medical checkup are imperative.

How Partners React to Sexual Assault

When a man or woman's sexual partner is sexually assaulted, the partner often feels anger, frustration, and intense feelings of revenge (M.E. Smith, 2005). Many partners express a strong desire to make the perpetrator "pay" for his or her crime. In addition, some partners experience a sense of loss, guilt, self-blame, and jealousy. Emotional reactions to the sexual assault may affect their feelings about their partner (M.E. Smith, 2005). In cases of acquaintance sexual assault, people may lose trust in their partners and worry that they might have expressed sexual interest in the perpetrator. Overall, after a date rape experience, negative judgments and reactions by a sexual assault victim's partner are common (A. Brown & Testa, 2008). These reactions further isolate the victim and reinforce feelings of guilt.

All in all, sexual assault places a great deal of stress on a relationship. Couples often avoid dealing with the incident entirely, believing that talking about it would be too stressful. Many men feel uncomfortable sharing their feelings about a sexual assault because they worry about burdening their partners. However, open communication is extremely beneficial and should be encouraged. Even though dealing with a sexual assault in a relationship can be traumatic, it has been found that women who have a stable and supportive partner recover from a sexual assault more quickly than those who do not.

Review Questions

1 Define and describe the rape trauma syndrome (RTS).

2 Identify the stages of the RTS and explain what typically happens during these stages.

3 Define and describe the silent rape reaction and discuss the long-term effects of the silent rape reaction.

4 Describe the effects of sexual assault in special populations, including married

partners, lesbians, older women, women with disabilities, and prostitutes.

5 Describe the typical reactions of men and women whose partners have been sexually assaulted.

When Men Are Sexual Assault Victims

Can a man be sexually assaulted? Although males as victims of sexual assault is more underreported than female sexual assault, it is estimated that one of every 33 men has been a victim of a completed or attempted sexual assault in North America (Tewksbury, 2007; U.S. Department of Justice, 2006). One study found a lifetime prevalence rate of sexual assault in men of 13 percent (Masho

& Anderson, 2009). The majority of men who are sexually assaulted are assaulted for the first time before the age of 18 (Masho & Anderson, 2009). Although the long-term effects of sexual assault are common in men and can include depression, anger, anxiety, self-blame, and increased vulnerability, few men ever seek out medical care or counselling (Masho & Anderson, 2009; J. Walker et al., 2005). Like for women, sexual dysfunction is common in male sexual assault victims and can continue for years after the assault (Walker et al., 2005). Also, unlike for women, some male sexual assault victims may increase their subsequent sexual activity to reaffirm their manhood.

Sexual Assault of Men by Women

Students often dismiss the idea that a man could be sexually assaulted or raped by a woman because they believe that because men are always willing to have sex, a woman would never need to sexually assault a man. However, this belief actually serves to make male sexual assault more humiliating and painful for many men.

Female offenders have been found to engage in a wide range of sexually aggressive behaviours, including forced sex and the use of verbal coercion (P.B. Anderson & Savage, 2005). In a study of male college students, 34 percent reported coercive sexual contact: 24 percent from women, 4 percent from men, and 6 percent from both sexes (Struckman-Johnson & Struckman-Johnson, 1994). The majority of male sexual assaults by women use psychological or pressured contact, such as verbal persuasion or emotional manipulation, rather than physical force. Although the majority of college men had no reaction, or a very mild negative reaction, to the unwanted female contact, 20 percent of the men experienced strong negative reactions. Because men who are sexually assaulted by women are often unwilling to define

On Your Mind

Technically, can a man really be sexually assaulted?

Some people think that it is impossible for a woman to sexually assault a man because he just would not get an erection. Even though men are anxious, embarrassed, or terrorized during a sexual assault, they are able to have erections. Having an erection while being sexually assaulted may be confusing and humiliating, just as an orgasm is for females. In fact, for some, it may be the most distressing aspect of the assault (Sarrel & Masters, 1982). Women who sexually assault men can also use dildos, hands, or other objects to penetrate the anus. In addition, men can be orally or anally sexually assaulted by men and forced to perform various sexual behaviours.

themselves as victims, many do not report these sexual assaults even though physical and psychological symptoms are common (P.B. Anderson & Savage, 2005).

Sexual Assault of Men by Men

Gay men have been found to be sexually assaulted at a higher rate than heterosexual men (Scarce, 1997). Hickson and colleagues (1994) found that in a sample of 930 gay men, close to 30 percent claimed they had been sexually assaulted at some point in their lives. Close to one-third of the victims had been sexual with the perpetrator before the sexual assault. The victims reported forced anal and oral sex and masturbation to ejaculation. The most common type of activity in the sexual assault of men by men is anal penetration followed by oral penetration (N. Groth & Burgess, 1980; Scarce, 1997).

As in the case of female sexual assault, male sexual assault is an expression of power, a show of strength and masculinity that uses sex as a weapon. The most common emotional reactions to the sexual assault of men by men include shame, embarrassment, self-blame, hostility, and depression (Scarce, 1997; Tewksbury, 2007). Like women, men who have been sexually assaulted may go through RTS (Tewksbury, 2007). Many victims question their sexual orientation and feel that the sexual assault makes them less of a "real man." Fearing others will think they are gay is a barrier to reporting for some men (Sable et al., 2006).

Men sexually assaulting men also occurs in the prison population. While the rates of male–male sexual assault in Canadian prisons is lower than that in the United States, it does still occur (Ellenbogen, 2009). Like sexual assault in other populations, inmates who have been raped also experience RTS. Because these men must continue to interact with their assailants, long-term reorganization may take longer to work through. In addition, oftentimes there are no sexual assault crisis services for those who have been sexually assaulted in prison, and there is little sympathy from prison employees.

Review Questions

1 How has the myth that a man could never be sexually assaulted by a woman made male sexual assault more humiliating for the victims?

2 Explain how female perpetrators/offenders of sexual assault use verbal persuasion or emotional manipulation more often than physical force.

3 Explain how the male sexual assault of men has been viewed as an expression of power.

4 What does the research tell us about rape in prison?

Coping with Sexual Assault, Reporting Sexual Assault, and Treating Offenders

As discussed earlier in the chapter, the majority of sexual assault victims do not report the sexual assault to the police. We now explore coping with sexual assault, reporting statistics and reasons for non-reporting, and the process of telling the police, pressing charges, and going to court. We also examine the treatment of offenders.

Coping with Sexual Assault

Sexual assault is the only violent crime in which the victim is expected to fight back. If a woman does not struggle, people question whether she wanted to have sex. Only with visible proof of a struggle (bruises and cuts) does society seem to have sympathy. Some victims of sexual assault have said that at the time of the sexual assault, they felt frozen with fear, that it was impossible to move because they just could not believe what was happening to them. One victim explains:

> Did you ever see a rabbit stuck in the glare of your headlights when you were going down a road at night? Transfixed—like it knew it was going to get it—that's what happened. (Brownmiller, 1975, p. 358)

How do people know when to fight back? What should their strategies be? If you are confronted with a potential or attempted sexual assault, the first and best strategy is to try to escape. However, this may not be possible if you are in a deserted area, if there are multiple attackers, or if your attacker has a weapon. If you cannot escape, effective strategies include verbal strategies such as screaming, dissuasive techniques ("I have my period," or "I have herpes."), empathy (listening or trying to understand), negotiation ("Let's discuss this."), and stalling for time. However, if the sex offender does not believe the victim, these techniques may cause more harm than good.

Prentky and Knight (1986) assert that the safest strategy is to attempt to talk to the attacker and try to make yourself a real person to the attacker ("I'm a stranger; why do you want to hurt me?"). Self-defence classes can help people feel more confident in their ability to fight back.

Reporting a Sexual Assault

It is estimated that about one in seven rapes is reported (Resnick et al., 2005); the likelihood of reporting is increased if the assailant was a stranger, if there was violence, or if a weapon was involved. This probably has to do with the fact that victims are clearer about intent under these conditions.

Gender differences in reporting are also common. Women are less likely to report a sexual assault if they know the attacker, whereas men are less likely to report if it jeopardizes their masculine self-identity (Pino & Meier, 1999). Women who report their sexual assault to the police have been subsequently found to have a better adjustment and fewer emotional symptoms than those who do not report it (see Table 17.3 for more information; Sable et al., 2006).

It is also important for a victim to write out exactly what happened in as much detail as possible. When did the sexual assault occur? Where was the victim? What time was it? Who was with the victim? What did the perpetrator look like? What was the perpetrator wearing? Exactly what happened? Was alcohol involved? Was anyone else present? Victims should keep this for their own records, for if they decide to press charges, it will come in handy. Over time memories fade, and victims can lose the important small details.

Telling the Police

On college campuses, campus police are often notified before the local police. Campus police may be able to take disciplinary action, often via an internal board of student conduct if the perpetrator was another student, but they are not able to press formal charges. Pressing charges with the local police may be important for two reasons. First, it alerts the police to a crime, and thus may prevent other women from being victimized. Second, if the victim decides to take legal action, he or she will need to have a formal report from the local police (not the campus police).

Although police officers have become more sensitive to the plight of sexual assault victims in the past few years, some victims still report negative experiences (Monroe et al., 2005). Society's victim-precipitated view of sexual assault also affects the attitudes of the police. To make sure that a crime did indeed occur, police must interrogate each case completely, which can be very difficult for a victim who has just been through a traumatic experience. Still, many report that taking such legal action makes them feel back in control, that they are doing something about their situation.

Pressing Charges

The decision to press official charges is a difficult one that takes much consideration. It has often been said that sexual assault

Re-living a sexual assault during a legal trial is emotionally draining. Many victims feel isolated and alone with increased feelings of guilt and self-blame.

© RubberBall/Alamy

Table 17.3 What to Do If You Are Sexually Assaulted

1. Know that it was not your fault. When a woman is sexually assaulted, she often spends a long time trying to figure out exactly what she did to put herself at risk for a sexual assault. This is probably because women have always been told to "be careful," "watch how you dress," or "don't drink too much." In reality, a sexual assault might happen anywhere and at any time. No one asks to be sexually assaulted.

2. Talk to a sexual assault crisis counsellor. Some women like to talk to a sexual assault crisis counselor before going to the hospital or police. This is very helpful because counselors can often give you advice. Besides this, they are knowledgeable about sexual assault and the aftermath of symptoms. Many hospitals have on-site counsellors. Talking to a counsellor also helps give the victim back her sense of control (see the Websites at the end of this chapter).

3. Go to a hospital for a medical examination. An immediate medical evaluation is imperative. If there is a nurse or health care provider on campus, you can see either of them, but it is better to go to a local emergency department to have a thorough physical examination. Medical evaluations are important for two reasons: to check for sexually transmitted infections that may have been transmitted during the sexual assault and to check for the presence of date-rape drugs. Because some of the sexually transmitted infections take time to show up positive on a culture, it is important to be retested in the following weeks. Recently, some women have requested AIDS tests post-sexual assault, although infection with HIV also takes time to show up. If a woman was not using birth control or has reason to suspect that she may have become pregnant, the hospital can administer emergency contraception (see Chapter 6 for more information about emergency contraception). Also, if you think you might have been drugged, you can also have a urine test to check for the drug's presence. Try not to urinate before having this test.

4. Do not throw away any evidence of the sexual assault. Do not shower before you go to the hospital. If you decide to change your clothes, do not wash or destroy what you were wearing. If anything was damaged in the assault, such as glasses, jewellery, or book bags, keep these, too. Put everything in a plastic bag and store it in a safe place. It is necessary to preserve the evidence of the sexual assault, which will be very important if you decide to press charges.

5. Decide whether you want to file a police report. You have a choice of filing either a formal or informal report. This is something that you will need to sort through and decide. A sexual assault crisis counsellor can be very helpful in this decision process.

6. Decide whether you want to press charges. Although you do not need to decide this right away, you will need to think about it as soon as possible. It is important to review this decision with a lawyer experienced in sexual assault cases.

victims go through a second assault because they can be put on trial more than the accused perpetrator. Court proceedings take up a great deal of time and energy, and they create considerable anxiety.

Victims of sexual assault report that they pressed charges because they were angry, to protect others, or they wanted justice to be served. Reasons for refusing to press charges include being afraid of revenge, wanting to just forget, feeling sorry for the perpetrator, or feeling as though it would not matter anyway because nothing would be done. In addition, often if the perpetrator is found guilty of a sexual assault, the sentence for the assault may be deemed not worth the amount of time and emotional and psychological stress that a victim goes through as part of the prosecution and court proceeds. See Table 17.4 for information on sentencing in Canada.

Going to Court

If a victim is undecided about whether to press charges, it may be helpful to sit in on a sexual assault trial if possible. Sexual assault trials can be extremely difficult for all involved. However, the purpose of sitting in is not to scare a person but to prepare oneself. It is not easy to proceed with legal action, so it can be really helpful to gather support from friends and family.

Table 17.4 Mean Sentence Length for Sexual Assault Convictions

In this table the mean sentence length (days) for all three levels of sexual assault in Canada is shown.

	2005	2006	2007	2008	2009	2010	2011	Mean Length of Sentence
Number of Convictions/Year	965	898	872	963	938	886	820	
Sentence length (days)	532	503	500	511	513	510	523	513.14 days (~1.4 years)

SOURCE: Dr. Scharie Tavcer, Department of Justice, Mount Royal University. Based on Statistics Canada, Table 252-0059, "Adult criminal courts, guilty cases by mean and median sentence length of custody annual," CANSIM (database). Retrieved September 22, 2014, from http://www5.statcan.gc.ca/cansim/a26. Reproduced and distributed on an "as is" basis with the permission of Statistics Canada.

Treating Those Who Commit Sexual Assault

Can people who sexually assault be treated so they lose their desire for this behaviour? Because the majority of offenders are male, this section concentrates on treating male offenders. Many therapies have been tried, including psychotherapy, behavioural treatment, support groups, shock treatment, and the use of Depo-Provera, a drug that can diminish a man's sex drive. The idea behind Depo-Provera is that if the sex drive is reduced, so, too, is the likelihood of sexual assault. So far these treatments have yielded inconclusive results. Many feminists argue that because violence, not sexual desire, causes sexual assault, taking away sexual desire will not decrease the incidence of sexual assault. For many men in treatment, the most important first step is to accept responsibility for their actions.

Many programs have been developed to decrease myths about rape and increase knowledge levels. All-male programs have been found to reduce significantly the belief in rape myths (Foubert & Cremedy, 2007). In another study evaluating post-education outcomes, among the 20 percent of men who indicated a possible likelihood of committing a sexual assault before participating in an educational program, 75 percent reported less likelihood of committing a sexual assault after the program (Foubert & McEwen, 1998). However, although attitudes about rape myths appear to change after these programs, researchers have yet to show that these attitude changes result in changes in sexually coercive behaviour (Foubert, 2000; Foubert & Cremedy, 2007). Treatments for high-risk sexual offenders (that is, those who are repeat offenders) have not been found to be overwhelmingly successful (Lalumière et al., 2005a).

Review Questions

1 What gender differences have been found in the reporting of sexual assault?

2 Explain how a victim-precipitated view of sexual assault might affect police attitudes.

3 Identify some of the reasons a victim might press (and not press) charges after a sexual assault.

4 Explain the process of telling the police, pressing charges, and going to court. What are some of the problems a sexual assault victim might experience along the way?

5 Explain some of the strategies given for avoiding a sexual assault. When might these strategies cause more harm than good?

6 Identify some of the therapies that have been used in the treatment of sex offenders.

Sexual Abuse of Children

So far we have been talking about forced sexual relations between adults. But what happens when the coercive behaviour involves children? **Child sexual abuse** is defined as sexual behaviour that occurs between an adult and a minor (see Chapter 10 for age of consent laws in Canada). One important characteristic of child sexual abuse is the dominant, powerful position of the adult or older teen that allows him or her to force a child into sexual activity. The sexual activity can include inappropriate touching, removing a child's clothing, genital fondling, masturbation, digital penetration with fingers or sex toys, oral sex, vaginal intercourse, or anal intercourse (Valente, 2005).

As straightforward as this seems, the definition of child sexual abuse can become fuzzy. For instance, do you consider sexual play between a 13-year-old brother and his seven-year-old sister sexual abuse? How about an adult male who persuades a 14-year-old girl to touch his genitals? A mother who caresses her two-year-old son's genitals? How about a 14-year-old-boy who willingly has sex with a 25-year-old woman? How would you define the sexual abuse of children? Personal definitions of sexual abuse affect how we perceive those who participate in this behaviour (Finkelhor, 1984).

Many researchers differentiate between child sexual abuse or molestation, which usually involves non-relatives; pedophilia, which involves a compulsive desire to engage in sex with a particular age of child; and **incest**, which is sexual contact between a child or adolescent who is related to the abuser. There are several types of incest, including father–daughter, father–son, brother–sister, grandfather–grandchild, mother–daughter, and mother–son. Incest can also occur between stepparents and stepchildren or aunts and uncles and their nieces and nephews. Sexual activity between a child and someone who is responsible for the child's care (such as a babysitter) may also be considered incest, although definitions for incest vary.

Because most children look to their parents for nurturing and protection, incest involving a parent, guardian, or someone else the child trusts can be extremely traumatic. The incestuous parent exploits this trust to fulfill sexual or power needs of his or her own. The particularly vulnerable position of children in relation to their parents has been recognized in every culture.

child sexual abuse	**incest**
Sexual contact with a minor by an adult.	Sexual contact between persons who are related or have a caregiving relationship.

The **incest taboo**—the absolute prohibition of sex between family members—is universal (J.L. Herman, 1981).

Sociologists suggest that social restrictions against incest may have originally formed to reduce role conflicts (Henslin, 2005). Parents who have sexual relationships with their child will have one role (i.e., parent) that conflicts with another (i.e., lover), which can interfere with responsibilities. We must also understand, however, that definitions of incest vary cross-culturally. The Burundi, a tribal group in tropical Africa, believe that a mother causes her son's erectile dysfunction by allowing the umbilical cord to touch his penis during birth (Henslin, 2005). To rectify this situation, the mother must engage in sexual intercourse with her son. Although this practice may sound bizarre to us, the culture of the Burundi supports this practice and does not view it as incestuous.

Although there are various types of incest, father–daughter and sibling incest are two of the most common types of incest in North America (Caffaro & Conn-Caffaro, 2005; Thompson, 2009). Many siblings play sex games with each other while growing up, and the line between harmless sex play and incest can be difficult to ascertain. Sex play often involves siblings who are no more than five years apart, is non-abusive, is mutually desired, and often involves experimentation (Kluft, 2010). Sibling incest, in contrast, often involves siblings with a large age difference, repeated sexual contact, and motivations other than curiosity (Kluft, 2010; Rudd & Herzberger, 1999; Thompson, 2009).

Although the majority of incest offenders are male, some women do engage in such behaviours. Mother–son incest is more likely to be subtle, including behaviours that may be difficult to distinguish from normal mothering behaviours (including genital touching; R.J. Kelly et al., 2002). Men who have been sexually abused by their mothers often experience more trauma symptoms than do other sexually abused men.

Incidence of Child Sexual Abuse

Accurate statistics on the prevalence of child sexual abuse are difficult to come by for many reasons: Some victims are uncertain about the precise definition of sexual abuse, might be unwilling to report, or are uncomfortable about sex and sexuality in general (Ephross, 2005; Finkelhor, 1984). The overall reported incidence has been increasing. In Kinsey and colleagues' (1953) study of 441 females, 9 percent reported sexual contact with an adult before the age of 14. By the late 1970s and early 1980s, reports of child sexual abuse in the United States were increasing dramatically; 1975 cases were reported in 1976, 22 918 in 1982 (Finkelhor, 1984), and 130 000 by 1986 (Jetter, 1991). It is estimated that one of every four girls and one of every ten boys experiences sexual abuse as a child (Fieldman & Crespi, 2002; Valente, 2005). In Canada 2012 data from police reports of sexual offences against children (Statistics Canada, 2014) revealed the following:

- Across Canada approximately 14 000 children and youth were victims of sexual assault that was reported to the police.

incest taboo
The absolute prohibition of sex between family members.

- Sexual assault Level 1 charges made up 72 percent of the total, with Level 2 and 3 making up approximately 1 percent. The remaining 27 percent were made up of charges specific to Canadian children and youth in the category of sexual interference (Canadian Criminal Code 151). In this case, "every person who, for sexual purpose, touches directly or indirectly, with a part of the body or an object, any part of the body of a person under the age of 16 years" (Justice Laws, 2015).

- The accused in these cases were primarily an acquaintance (44 percent) or family member (38 percent). Only 12 percent of perpetrators were strangers to the victim. Over 97 percent of the perpetrators were male.

Perhaps the incidence of reported child sexual abuse is a reflection of the changing sexual climate (in which there is less tolerance for such behaviour), rather than an actual increase in the number of sexual assaults on children. The women's movement and the child protection movement both have focused attention on child sexual abuse issues (Finkelhor, 1984). Women's groups often teach that child sexual abuse is due to the patriarchal social structure and must be treated through victim protection. The child protection movement views the problem as one that develops out of a dysfunctional family and is treated through family therapy.

Recently, there has been some doubt about the credibility of child sex abuse reporting. Would a child ever "make up" a story of sexual abuse? Research has shown that false reports occur in less than 10 percent of reported cases (Besharov, 1988). This is important because a child's report of sexual abuse remains the single most important factor in diagnosing abuse (Heger et al., 2002).

Victims of Child Sexual Abuse

Although research is limited because of sampling and responding rates, we do know that the median age for sexual abuse of both girls and boys is around eight or nine years old (Feinauer, 1988; Finkelhor et al., 1990). Boys are more likely to be sexually abused by strangers (40 percent of boys, 21 percent of girls), whereas girls are more likely to be sexually abused by family members (29 percent of girls, 11 percent of boys; Finkelhor et al., 1990).

Finkelhor (1984) proposes three reasons why the reported rates of male sexual abuse may be lower than those for females: Boys often feel they should be more self-reliant and should be able to handle the abuse; the stigma of homosexuality; and the fear of a loss of freedoms.

Reactions to abuse vary. Many victims are scared to reveal the abuse, because of shame, fear of retaliation, belief that they themselves are to blame, or fear that they will not be believed. Some incest victims try to get help only if they fear that a younger sibling is threatened. When they do get help, younger victims are more likely to go to a relative for help, whereas older victims may run away or enter into early marriages to escape the abuse (J.L. Herman, 1981). Victims of incest with a biological father delay reporting the longest, whereas those who have been victims of stepfathers or live-in partners have been found to be more likely to tell someone more readily (Faller, 1989).

SEX in Real Life | *Mount Cashel Orphanage*

One of the most notorious cases of sexual abuse of children in Canada occurred at Mount Cashel Orphanage in Newfoundland. The orphanage was run by the Christian Brothers of Ireland, a segment of the Roman Catholic Church. The Christian Brothers sexually abused hundreds of boys in the mid-1900s. After lengthy court proceedings, 11 staff members were convicted and over $11 million was paid to the men who had been abused as children at the orphanage (CBC News, 2013).

Another infamous case of child abuse in Canada concerns the Aboriginal residential schools. These schools, which were government mandated and church run, were part of an aggressive assimilation plan by the Canadian government to integrate Canada's Aboriginal peoples into the ways of Christianity, Canadian customs, and the English language. A great deal of physical and sexual abuse occurred at these schools, which has had a long-reaching impact on the psychological and cognitive well-being of the children placed in them (Barnes, Josefowitz, & Cole, 2006).

Bud Glunz/National Film Board of Canada, PA-134110

Aboriginal children were placed into residential schools in the late 1800s until the 1960s as part of a strategy to assimilate then into a new way of life. Children in these schools were often malnourished, physically abused, and at times sexually abused.

How Children Are Affected

There have been conflicting findings regarding the traumatic effects of sexual abuse. Some studies indicate that children are not severely traumatized by sexual abuse (Fritz et al., 1981), whereas more recent studies indicate that it may have long-lasting effects that may lead to other psychological problems. Keep in mind that what follows is a discussion of what is typically experienced by a victim of childhood sexual abuse or incest. As we have discussed before, it is impossible to predict what a child's experience will be; the reaction of each child is different. A few factors make the abuse more traumatic, including the intensity of the sexual contact and how the sexual abuse is handled in the family. If a family handles the sexual abuse in a caring and sensitive manner, the effects on the child are often reduced.

Psychological and Emotional Reactions

Sexual abuse can be devastating for a child and often causes feelings of betrayal, powerlessness, fear, anger, self-blame, low self-esteem, and problems with intimacy and relationships later in life (Martens, 2007; Thompson, 2009; Valente, 2005). Many children who were sexually abused experience antisocial behaviour, drug abuse, and prostitution later in life (Hardt et al., 2008; Jonas et al., 2011; Lu et al., 2008; Thompson, 2009). Overall, incest behaviours are the most traumatic when they occur over a long period, the offender is a person who is trusted, penetration occurs, and there is aggression (A.N. Groth, 1978). Children who hide their sexual abuse often experience shame and guilt, and fear the loss of affection from family and friends (Seymour et al., 2000). They also feel frustrated about not being able to stop the abuse.

Regardless of whether they tell someone about their sexual abuse, many victims experience psychological symptoms such as depression, increased anxiety, nervousness, emotional problems, and personality and intimacy disorders. Similar to reactions of rape victims, PTSD and depression are common symptoms, and may occur more often in victims who are abused repeatedly (Jonas et al., 2011; Thompson, 2009). Guilt is usually severe, and many children blame themselves for the sexual abuse (Thompson, 2009; Valente, 2005). Victims of sexual abuse are also more likely than non-abused children to abuse alcohol and drugs, experience eating disorders, and contemplate suicide (Jonas et al., 2011).

Victims may also try to cut themselves off from a painful or unbearable memory, which can lead to what psychiatrists refer to as a **dissociative disorder**. In its extreme form, dissociative disorder may result in a **dissociative identity disorder**, in which a person maintains two or more distinct personalities. Although it has long been a controversial issue in psychology, there is research to support the claim that some abuse victims are unable to remember past abuse (Malmo & Laidlaw, 2010). In one study of incest victims, 64 percent were found to partially repress their abuse, whereas 28 percent severely repressed it (J. Herman & Schatzow, 1987). Some experts claim that although the memories are classified as bad, disgusting, and confusing, many times they are not "traumatic." Because of this, the memories are simply forgotten and not repressed (McNally et al., 2004, 2005). This issue continues to be controversial, even though many victims of sexual abuse often report an inability to remember details or the entirety of the abuse.

Women who were sexually abused as children have higher rates of personality disorders and PTSD than those who experienced sexual abuse later in life (Jonas et al., 2011; McLean & Gallop, 2003). Earlier in this chapter, we discussed the increased risk for engaging in risky sexual behaviours post-sexual assault. Both antisocial and promiscuous sexual behaviours are also related to a history of childhood sexual behaviour (Deliramich &

Gray, 2008; Valente, 2005). The most devastating emotional effects occur when the sexual abuse is done by someone the victim trusts. In a study of the effects of sexual abuse by relatives, friends, or strangers, it was found that the stronger the emotional bond and trust between the victim and the assailant, the more distress the victim experienced (Feinauer, 1989).

Long-Term Effects

It is not uncommon for children who are sexually abused to display what Finkelhor and Browne (1985) refer to as **traumatic sexualization**. Children may begin to exhibit compulsive sex play or masturbation and show an inappropriate amount of sexual knowledge. When they enter adolescence, they may begin to show promiscuous and compulsive sexual behaviour, which may lead to sexually abusing others in adulthood (Rudd & Herzberger, 1999; Valente, 2005). These children have learned that it is through their sexuality that they get attention from adults.

Children who are sexually abused have been found to experience sexual problems in adulthood. The developmentally inappropriate sexual behaviours that they learned as children can contribute to a variety of sexual dysfunctions later in life (Najman et al., 2005). Researchers have found that a large proportion of patients who seek sex therapy have histories of incest, rape, and other forms of sexual abuse (Maltz, 2002).

Researchers have also demonstrated a connection between eating disorders and past sexual abuse (Kong & Berstein, 2009; Ross, 2009; Steiger et al., 2010; Vrabel et al., 2010). Gay and bisexual men who experience childhood sexual abuse are significantly more likely to have an eating disorder than men without a history of sexual abuse (Feldman & Meyer, 2007). Women and men who can discuss the sexual abuse are often able to make significant changes in their eating patterns.

Problems with drug and alcohol addiction are also more common in adults with a history of child sexual abuse. In fact, high rates of alcohol and drug use have been found even as early as age ten (Valente, 2005). Finkelhor and Browne (1985) hypothesize that because of the stigma that surrounds the early sexual abuse, the children believe they are "bad," and the thought of "badness" is incorporated into their self-concept (Kluft, 2010). As a result, they often gravitate toward behaviours that society sees as deviant.

It is not unusual for adults who had been abused as children to confront their offenders later in life, especially among those who have undergone some form of counseling or psychotherapy to work through their own feelings about the experience. They may feel a strong need to deal with the experience and often get help to work through it. The accompanying Sex in Real Life feature is a letter written by an 18-year-old woman who had been sexually abused by her father throughout her childhood. This letter was the first time that she had confronted him.

Characteristics of Child Sexual Abusers

Research on child sexual abusers has found several factors that distinguish abusers from those who do not abuse children. Sexual abusers are more likely to have poor social skills, low IQs,

---

dissociative disorder
Psychological disorder involving a disturbance of memory, identity, and consciousness, usually resulting from a traumatic experience.

dissociative identity disorder
A disruption of identity characterized by two or more distinct personality states.

traumatic sexualization
A common result of sexual abuse in which a child displays compulsive sex play or masturbation and shows an inappropriate amount of sexual knowledge.

SEX in Real Life Confronting the Incest Offender

The following letter was written by an 18-year-old college student to her father. She had just begun to recall past sexual abuse by her father and was in counselling working on her memories. She decided to confront her father with this letter.

Dad: I can't hide it any longer! I remember everything about when I was a little girl. For years I acted as if nothing ever happened; it was always there deep inside but I was somehow able to lock it away for many years. But Daddy, something has pried that lock open, and it will never be able to be locked away again. I remember being scared or sick and crawling into bed with my parents only to have my father's hands touch my chest and rear. I remember going on a Sunday afternoon to my father's office, innocently wanting to spend time with him, only to play with some machine that vibrated.

I remember sitting on my father's lap while he was on the phone. I had a halter top on at the time. I remember wondering what he was doing when he untied it then turned me around to face

him so he could touch my stomach and chest. I remember many hugs, even as a teenager, in which my father's hand was on my rear. I remember those words, "I like what is underneath better," when I asked my father if he liked my new outfit. But Daddy, more than anything, I remember one night when mom wasn't home. I was scared so I crawled into bed with my father who I thought was there to protect me. I remember his hands caressing my still undeveloped breast. I remember his hand first rubbing the top of my underwear then the same hand working its way down my underwear. I remember thinking that it tickled, but yet it scared me.

Others had never tickled me like this. I felt frozen until I felt something inside me. It hurt, and I was scared. I said stop and started shaking. I remember jumping out of bed and running to my room where I cried myself to sleep. I also remember those words I heard a few days later, "I was just trying to love you. I didn't mean to hurt you. No one needs to know about this. People would misunderstand what happened."

You don't have to deal with the memories of what this has done to my life, my relationships with men, my many sleepless nights, my days of depression, my feelings of filth being relieved through making myself throw up and the times of using—abusing—alcohol in order to escape. You haven't even had to see the pain and confusion in my life because of this. I have two feelings, pain and numbness. You took my childhood away from me by making me lock my childhood away in the dark corners of my mind. Now that child is trying to escape, and I don't know how to deal with her.

I felt it was only fair that you know that it is no longer a secret. I have protected you long enough. Now it is time to protect myself from all of the memories. Daddy, I must tell you, even after all that has happened, for some reason I'm not sure of, I still feel love for you—that is, if I even know what love is.

SOURCE: Author's files.

---

unhappy family histories, low self-esteem, and less happiness in their lives than non-abusers (Finkelhor et al., 1990; Hunter et al., 2003; Langevin et al., 1988; Milner & Robertson, 1990). The majority of abusers are heterosexual males (Valente, 2005). Sexual abusers, when asked how they gained access to their victims, explained how they "groomed" their victims through bribes, gifts and games. The use of persuasion and a systematic desensitization of children through conversations about sex and via the use of touch that escalates from non-sexual to sexual is also common. The grooming of the victim may occur in a larger context of grooming the family and local community who provide access to children and youth. When asked, just over half of the offenders expressed bad feelings over their behaviours (Elliot, Browne & Kilcoyne, 1995; McaLinden, 2006).

Several motivations have been identified for engaging in incestuous child sexual abuse (Kluft, 2010). An abuser with an affection motivation views the behaviours as a part of family closeness with an emphasis on the "special" relationship between the victim and abuser. An erotic-based motivation usually involves sexual contact between several family members and is motivated by an eroticization of family roles. Aggression-based and rage-based motivations revolve around the abuser's sexualized anger and frustration, which is often taken out on a victim. Rage-based motivations also involve an overly hostile and sadistic abuser.

Denying responsibility for the offence and claiming they were in a trancelike state is also common. The majority of offenders are also good at manipulation, which they develop to prevent

discovery by others. One man told his 13-year-old victim, "I'm sorry this had to happen to you, but you're just too beautiful," demonstrating the typical abuser's trait of blaming the victim for the abuse (Vanderbilt, 1992, p. 66).

The Development of a Sexual Abuser

Three prominent theoretical perspectives—learning, gender, and biological—propose factors that make abuse more likely. Proponents of learning theories believe that what children learn from their environment or those around them contributes to their behaviour later in life. Many child sex abusers were themselves sexually abused as children (Seto, 2008). Many reported an early initiation into sexual behaviour that taught them about sex at a young age. Many learned that such behaviour was how adults show love and affection to children.

Proponents of gender theories identify gender as an important aspect in the development of an abuser—sexual abusers are overwhelmingly male (Finkelhor et al., 1990; Seto, 2008). Males often are not taught how to express affection without sexuality, which leads to needing sex to confirm their masculinity, being more focused on the sexual aspect of relationships, and being socialized to be attracted to mates who are smaller (Finkelhor, 1984; Seto, 2008). Keep in mind that the incidence of female offenders may be lower because of lower reporting rates for boys or because society accepts intimate female interaction with children as normal (A.N. Groth, 1978). Although it was previously thought that about 4 percent of offenders were female (D.E.H. Russell, 1984), newer studies have found that these numbers may be significantly higher. In one study, a review of 120 000 cases of child sexual abuse, 25 percent of cases were found to involve a female offender (Boroughs, 2004).

Proponents of biological theories suggest that physiology contributes to the development of sexual abusers. One study found that male offenders had normal levels of the male sex hormone testosterone but increased levels of other hormones (Lang et al., 1990). There have also been reports of neurological differences between incest offenders and non–sex criminal offenders that are thought to contribute to violence (Langevin et al., 1988).

Treating Child Sexual Abuse

We know that sexual abuse can have many short- and long-term consequences—for victims and abusers. As a result, it is important to help victims of child sexual abuse to heal and help abusers learn ways to eliminate their abusive behaviours.

Helping the Victims Heal

Currently, the most effective treatments for victims of child sexual abuse include a combination of cognitive and behavioural psychotherapies, which teach victims how to understand and handle the trauma of their assaults more effectively. Many victims of sexual abuse also have difficulties developing and maintaining intimate relationships. Being involved in a relationship that is high in emotional intimacy and low in expectations for sex is beneficial (W. Maltz, 1990). Learning that they have the ability to say no to sex is very important and usually develops when they establish relationships based first on friendship, rather than sex.

Many times the partners of victims of sexual abuse are confused; they do not fully understand the effects of abuse in the lives of their mates, and so they may also benefit from counselling (L. Cohen, 1988).

Treating the Abusers

In the treatment of child sexual abusers the primary goal is to decrease the level of sexual arousal to inappropriate sexual objects—in this case, children. This is done through behavioural treatment, psychotherapy, or drugs. Other goals of therapy include teaching sexual abusers to interact and relate better with adults, assertiveness skills training, empathy and respect for others, increasing sexual education, and evaluating and reducing any sexual difficulties that they might be experiencing with their sexual partners (Abel et al., 1980). Because recidivism is high in these abusers, it is also important to find ways to reduce the incidence of engaging in these behaviours (Firestone et al., 2005).

Preventing Child Sexual Abuse

How can we prevent child sexual abuse? One program that has been explored is the "just say no" campaign, which teaches young children how to say no to inappropriate sexual advances by adults. This program has received much attention. How effective is such a strategy? Even if we can teach children to say no to strangers, can we also teach them to say no to their fathers or sexually abusive relatives? Could there be any negative effects of educating children about sexual abuse? These are a few questions that future research will need to address.

Increasing the availability of sex education has also been cited as a way to decrease the incidence of child sexual abuse. Children from traditional, authoritarian families who have no sex education are at greater risk for sexual abuse. Education about sexual abuse—teaching that it does not happen to all children—may help children to understand that it is wrong. Telling children where to go and whom to talk to is also important.

Another important factor in prevention is adequate funding and staffing of child welfare agencies. Social workers may be among the first to become aware of potentially dangerous situations. Physicians and educators must also be adequately trained to identify the signs of abuse.

Review Questions

1 Define child sexual abuse and discuss its incidence.

2 Discuss victims' psychological and emotional reactions to child sexual abuse.

3 Explain what the research tells us about sexual abusers and the development of such behaviour.

4 Describe the most effective treatments for victims and perpetrators of childhood sexual abuse.

5 Identify some ways in which society can help prevent childhood sexual abuse.

Intimate Partner Violence

Intimate partner violence (IPV, which may also be referred to as domestic violence) is found among all racial, ethnic, and socioeconomic classes. In 2013 in Canada, 336 000 people between the ages of 15-89 were assaulted and the crime was reported to the police. Of these reports, approximately 27 percent of these assaults were by an intimate partner. Of this 27 percent, the majority of the victims of these assaults were in dating situations (53 percent), and the remaining 47 percent of the victims were in long-term spousal relationships. Of these assaults, the majority occur in women between the ages of 20 and 29, although males are also assaulted (see Figure 17.3; Statistics Canada, 2015). The numbers of unreported IPV incidents, however, are often much higher than the numbers recorded by the police. A multi-country study by the World Health Organization reported rates of intimate partner violence against women between 15 and 71 percent, depending on the country surveyed (Garcia-Moreno, Jansen, Ellsberg, Heise, & Watts, 2006).

Although IPV is common in adolescent and college-age populations, it can happen to men and women at any age (Bonomi et al., 2007; Forke et al., 2008). It is often related to stress (Harville et al., 2011). Researchers have found that women with disabilities are significantly more likely to report experiencing IPV in their lifetime, compared with women without disabilities (Armour et al., 2008; Friedman et al., 2011).

Many women and men are killed by their violent partners (known as intimate partner homicide [IPH])—76 percent of IPH victims were women, whereas 24 percent were men (Fox & Zawitz, 2004). Studies on men who commit IPH have found that 42 percent have past criminal charges, 15 percent have a psychiatric history, and 18 percent have both (Eke et al., 2011).

REAL Research Two thirds of women with serious mental illness have histories of sexual violence (Friedman et al., 2011).

Defining Intimate Partner Violence

IPV is coercive behaviour that uses threats, harassment, or intimidation. It can involve physical (shoving, hitting, hair pulling), emotional (extreme jealousy, intimidation, humiliation), or sexual (forced sex, physically painful sexual behaviours) abuse. Some offenders even are violent toward pets, especially pets that are close to the victim. Generally there is a pattern of abuse rather than a single isolated incident.

Many women in abusive relationships claim their relationship started off well and that they believed the first incidence of

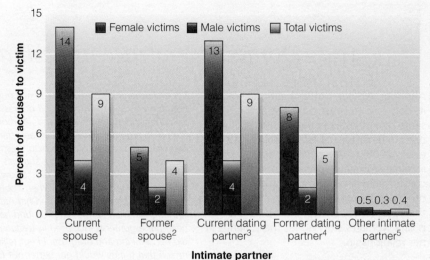

1. Refers to violence committed by currently married persons and current common-law partners. Includes victims aged 15 to 89.
2. Refers to violence committed by separated or divorced persons and former common-law partners. Includes victims aged 15 to 89.
3. Refers to violence committed by current boyfriend or girlfriend. Includes victims aged 15 to 89.
4. Refers to violence committed by former boyfriends or girlfriends. Includes victims aged 15 to 89.
5. Refers to violence committed by a person with whom the victim had a sexual relationship or a mutual sexual attraction. Includes victims ages 15 to 89.

FIGURE **17.3** The number of IPV cases in Canada in females and males, 2013.

SOURCE: Statistics Canada, *Family Violence in Canada: A statistical profile, 2013*, published January 2015, Catalogue no. 85-002-X. Retrieved March 11, 2015, from http://www.statcan.gc.ca/pub/85-002-x/2014001/article/14114/section02-eng.htm. Reproduced and distributed on an "as is" basis with the permission of Statistics Canada.

violence was a one-time occurrence that would not happen again. They often excuse their partner's behaviour and accept their partner's apologies. In time, the abuser convinces his partner that it is really her fault that he became violent and that if she changes, it won't happen again. Most women in this situation begin to believe that the problems are indeed their fault, so they stay in the abusive relationship. Many actually believe that it is safer in the relationship than outside of it. Things that may make it more difficult for some heterosexual women to leave include issues such as finances, low self-esteem, fear, or isolation.

This type of violence and abuse also occurs among college students. One 21-year-old college student told me:

No one could understand why I wanted my relationship with Billy to work. After all, no relationship is perfect. He didn't mean to slam me that hard. Why would he want to leave bruises on me? Look at him. He's a big guy. Anyone can tell he might have trouble seeing his own strength. He means well. He gives the best hugs, like a big sweet bear. He always says he's sorry. He loves me and tells me this in letters all the time. He thinks I'm sweet, pretty, and kind. Maybe my friends are just jealous. After all, he is a really good-looking guy. I know a lot of girls who want him. He tells me girls throw themselves at him every day. Why would he lie? (Author's files)

intimate partner violence (IPV) A pattern of coercive behaviour designed to exert power and control over a person in an intimate relationship through the use of intimidation, threats, or harmful or harassing behaviour.

SEX in Real Life — *Domestic Violence in Lesbian Relationships*

Although we don't often hear much about it, domestic violence occurs at about the same rate in lesbian relationships as it does in heterosexual relationships (Eaton et al., 2008; Hewlett, 2008). Many women in same-sex relationships do not feel comfortable discussing the violence with others and worry about being outed by their partner (C. Brown, 2008). Following is one woman's story about the violence in her relationship.

I met my girlfriend at a party that a friend hosted. She was intelligent, beautiful, and had a wonderful sense of humor. Our relationship developed rapidly and the closeness we shared was something I had never experienced before. It is difficult to remember exactly when the abuse began because it was subtle. She criticized me because she didn't like my cooking, and she occasionally called me names when we argued. I didn't think much about it because she had recently lost custody of her daughter to

her ex-husband because of her sexual orientation and was angry, irritable, and depressed. She often threatened suicide and attempted it during an argument that we had and then blamed me for calling 911 for help. Despite the stress she was experiencing, she was very supportive of me when my family "disowned" me after I came out to them. When I bought my first car, she insisted I put it in her name. Although we had periods of profound happiness, our arguments increased in frequency as did her drinking and drug use. I kept telling myself that things would get better but they never did. She continually accused me of being unfaithful (I wasn't) and even once raped me after claiming I had flirted with a supermarket cashier. The first time she hit me I grabbed her wrist and twisted her arm to keep from being hit again. My response frightened me so much I suggested we see a couple's counselor, and she agreed.

Couple counseling was not helpful, and although things felt worse, our therapist said

that was normal so we persevered. I began scrutinizing my own behavior believing that if I could only do things better or differently, our life together would improve. It wasn't until she pulled a knife on me that I realized that it wasn't going to change for the better...it was only going to get worse. I called a crisis line and the counselor suggested that what I was experiencing was domestic violence. That had actually never occurred to me because we were both women. Leaving her was the hardest thing I have ever done.

It's still difficult to think of my situation as domestic violence but with the help of my counselor and support group, I am learning that women can be violent to other women, that anger, stress, depression, alcohol and drugs do not cause violence, that violence is a choice the abuser makes, and finally, that I am not to blame.

SOURCE: National Coalition of Anti-Violence Programs (1998).

IPV in same-sex relationships looks similar to IPV in heterosexual relationships (Eaton et al., 2008; St Pierre & Senn, 2010). However, in same-sex relationships, additional issues may arise, including fewer social supports, less availability of medical and psychological services, and the fear of being "outed" when seeking help (C. Brown, 2008; St Pierre & Senn, 2010). Although we know less about IPV in gay relationships, studies have found that one in three men in same-sex relationships have been abused (Houston & McKirnan, 2008). Unfortunately, many gay and bisexual men are reluctant to seek help for violence in intimate relationships because there is often little social support to do so (Cruz, 2003).

Although less is known about the prevalence and experience of intimate partner violence in lesbian relationships, it is known that IPV in lesbian relationships looks similar to IPV in heterosexual relationships.

© Joel Gordon Photography

Reactions to Intimate Partner Violence

Victims of IPV experience both physical and psychological symptoms, and the symptoms depend on both the frequency and severity of the violence (Beeble et al., 2011; J.C. Campbell et al., 2002). Common psychological symptoms, similar to those experienced by victims of other coercive sexual behaviours, include depression, antisocial behaviour, increased anxiety, low self-esteem, and a fear of intimacy (Cavanaugh et al., 2011; Tjaden & Thoennes, 2000). PTSD is also common (Cavanaugh et al., 2011). Physical symptoms may include headaches, back pain, broken bones, gynecological disorders, and stomach problems.

Preventing Intimate Partner Violence

Violence tends to repeat itself in people's lives—victims of violence often experience it more than once, known as *polyvictimization* (Cavanaugh et al., 2011). IPV victims often have a history of violence in their families, child sexual abuse, and/or teen dating violence (Gómez, 2011; Leonard, 2005; Lipsky et al., 2005). In fact, men and women who are victims of child sexual abuse or teen dating violence are significantly more likely to perpetrate or become victims of IPV as adults than those who were not victims of child sexual abuse (Gómez, 2011).

Educational programs can help educate the public about IPV, and prevention programs can be designed to reach out to those who have been victimized to help them learn ways to reduce violent tendencies. Safe housing for victims of IPV can also reduce the likelihood of future abuse. Today, there are hundreds of battered women's shelters across Canada. These shelters provide women with several important things, including information and a safe haven. Increasing the availability of safe houses and counselling and education is imperative. In addition, increasing the availability of services for gay, lesbian, bisexual, transgendered, elderly, and disabled women and men will help ensure that help is available for all who may need it.

Finally, because we know that IPV increases during times of stress, it is important to have educational and prevention programs available during times of heightened stress. In addition, it is important to become aware of how various events, such as natural disasters, can increase stress. For example, the incidence of IPV increased significantly during Hurricane Katrina and its aftermath (Harville et al., 2011).

> **REAL Research** A longitudinal study found that aggression and suicide attempts during male adolescence were related to poor intimate partner relationships and an increased likelihood of partner violence in young adulthood (Kerr & Capaldi, 2011).

Review Questions

1 Define intimate partner violence (IPV) and give one example.

2 Identify some common psychological and physiological symptoms of IPV.

3 How is IPV in same-sex relationships similar to and different from heterosexual relationships?

4 Explain how IPV relates to sexual and physical abuse.

Sexual Harassment

Sexual harassment is a broad term that includes anything from jokes, unwanted sexual advances, a "friendly" pat, an "accidental" brush on a person's body, or an arm around a person (Cammaert, 1985; see Table 17.5). It can also include unwanted sexual attention online (Barak, 2005). Because of the wide variety of actions that fall under this definition, many people are confused about what exactly constitutes sexual harassment.

Under the Ontario Human Rights Code (in addition to the Canadian Human Rights Act [1977] and the Canadian Charter of Rights and Freedoms [1982]; each province or territory can define its own human rights code), sexual harassment is defined as "engaging in a course of vexatious comment or conduct that is known or ought to be known to be unwelcome" (Ontario Human Rights Commission, 2011).

It may seem that sexual harassment is not as troubling as other forms of sexual coercion, but the effects of harassment on the victim can be traumatic and often cause long-term difficulties. Fitzgerald and Ormerod (1991) claim, "There are many similarities between sexual harassment and other forms of sexual victimization, not only in the secrecy that surrounds them but also in the [myth] that supports them" (p. 2). Severe or chronic sexual harassment can cause psychological side effects similar to sexual assault, and in extreme cases, it has been known to contribute to suicide.

> **REAL Research** Cross-cultural studies on attitudes about sexual harassment have found that students from individualist countries (such as the United States, Canada, Germany, and the Netherlands) are less accepting of sexual harassment, whereas students from collectivist countries (such as Ecuador, Pakistan, the Philippines, Taiwan, and Turkey) are more accepting (Sigal et al., 2005).

Incidence and Reporting of Sexual Harassment

It is estimated that 25 to 30 percent of college students report experiences of sexual harassment (Mènard et al., 2003). Sexual harassment on campus usually involves sexist comments, jokes, or touching, and the majority of students do not report it (Mènard et al., 2003).

In Canada, sexual harassment has increased in recent years, probably in relation to the increase in women in the workforce. Several Canadian studies have found that men and women

sexual harassment
Unwanted sexual attention from someone in school or the workplace; also includes unwelcome sexual jokes, glances, or comments, or the use of status or power to coerce or attempt to coerce a person into having sex.

Table 17.5	Examples of Sexual Harassment

- Asking for sex in exchange for something, like offering to improve a test score, offering a raise or promotion at work, or withholding something like needed repairs to your apartment

- Asking for dates and not taking "no" for an answer

- Demanding hugs

- Making unnecessary physical contact, including unwanted touching

- Using rude or insulting language or making comments that stereotype girls, women, boys, or men

- Calling people unkind names that relate to their sex or gender

- Making comments about a person's physical appearance (for example, whether or not they are attractive)

- Saying or doing something because you think a person does not fit sex-role stereotypes

- Posting or sharing pornography, sexual pictures, cartoons, graffiti or other sexual images (including online)

- Making sexual jokes

- Bragging about sexual ability

- Bullying based on sex or gender

- Spreading sexual rumours or gossip (including online)

SOURCE: "Sexual and gender-based harassment: know your rights," by the Ontario Human Rights Commission. © Queen's Printer for Ontario, 2011. Reproduced with permission. Retrieved March 11, 2015, from http://www.ohrc.on.ca/en/sexual-and-gender-based-harassment-know-your-rights-brochure.

perceive harassment differently. Women are more likely than men to rate sexual content in an e-mail as offensive and to find sexual propositions from strangers offensive. Women are also less likely to be tolerant of sexual harassment than men (Kennedy & Gorzalka, 2002; Pek & Senn 2004). Because of sexual harassment, women are nine times more likely than men to quit a job, five times more likely to transfer, and three times more likely to lose their jobs (Parker & Griffin, 2002). Although the majority of people who are sexually harassed are female, it can also happen to men. Same-sex harassment also occurs (Foote & Goodman-Delahunty, 2005).

As we have discussed, many victims of sexual harassment never say anything to authorities, although they may tell a friend; this may be partly because women are socialized to keep harmony in relationships. Others verbally confront the offender or leave their jobs to get away from it. Assertiveness is the most effective strategy, either by telling someone about it or confronting the offender. Many fear, however, that confronting a boss or teacher who is harassing them could jeopardize their jobs or their grades. Also, although these strategies increase the chances that the behaviour will stop, they do not guarantee it. If you are being sexually harassed by someone in a university setting, the best advice is to talk to a counsellor or your advisor about it. Remember that you are protected by provincial and/or federal law. Colleges and universities today will not tolerate the sexual harassment of any student, regardless of sex, ethnicity, religion, or sexual orientation.

Women and men think differently about sexual harassment. In one study, females were more likely than males to experience sexual harassment and to perceive it as harmful (Hand & Sanchez, 2000). Researchers have found that a behaviour might be interpreted as sexual harassment by a woman, whereas it is interpreted as flattering to a man (Lastella, 2005).

Preventing Sexual Harassment

The first step in reducing the incidence of sexual harassment is to acknowledge the problem. Too many people deny its existence. Because sexual harassers usually have more power, it is difficult for victims to come forward to disclose their victimization. University officials and administrators need to work together to provide educational opportunities and assistance for all students, staff, and employees. Establishing policies for dealing with these problems is necessary. Workplaces also need to design and implement strong policies against sexual harassment.

Education, especially about the role of women, is imperative. Studies have shown that sexual harassment education and training can reduce these behaviours (Lonsway et al., 2008). As our society continues to change and as more and more women enter the workforce, we need to prepare men for this adjustment. Throughout history, when women have broken out of their traditional roles, there have always been difficulties. Today, we need research to explore the impact of women on the workforce.

Throughout this chapter we have explored how power can be used in sexual relationships to degrade and oppress. Rape, the sexual abuse of children, incest, IPV, and sexual harassment are problems in our society today. The first step in reducing these crimes is to acknowledge the problems and not hide them. Education, especially about the role of women, is necessary; without it, these crimes will undoubtedly continue to escalate.

Review Questions

1 Define sexual harassment and differentiate between the various types of sexual harassment.

2 Explain how sexual harassment can affect a woman's employment.

3 Identify gender differences in thoughts about sexual harassment.

4 Identify some strategies for dealing with, and preventing, sexual harassment.

Chapter Review

Summary Points

1 Physically or psychologically forcing sexual relations on another person is usually referred to as sexual assault. Sexual assault refers to sexual penetration (vaginal, oral, or anal), as well as unwanted sexual touching. Exact definitions of sexual assault are determined by the Criminal Code of Canada.

2 In the majority of cases, the victims of sexual assault know their assailants. Actual incidence rates for sexual assault are difficult to determine because forcible sexual assault is one of the most underreported crimes in Canada.

3 Women do not report sexual assault for several reasons, including that they do not think that they were really assaulted, they blame themselves, they fear no one will believe them, they worry that no legal action will be taken, or they feel shame or humiliation. Women who were using drugs or alcohol before the sexually assault are much less likely to report the assault.

4 Five theoretical perspectives are often used to explain why sexual assault occurs. These are the offender psychopathology, victim precipitation, feminist, sociological, and evolutionary theories. The offender psychopathology theory suggests that either disease or intoxication forces men to sexually assault. Victim precipitation theory shifts the responsibility from the person who knowingly attacked to the innocent victim. Feminists believe that sexual assault and the threat of it are tools used in our society to keep women in their place. Sociologists believe that sexual assault is an expression of power differentials in society. Finally some evolutionary theorists claim that sexual assault occurs due to differing reproductive roles in men and women.

5 There are also strong gender differences in attitudes toward sexual assault. Men have been found to be less empathetic and sensitive toward rape than women and to attribute more responsibility to the victim than women do. Men are more likely than women to believe that a man should expect sexual intercourse if he pays for an expensive date. Sexual assault prevention programs for male college students have also been related to both attitudinal and behavioural changes.

6 Ethnic minorities have been found to have more traditional attitudes toward women, which have been found to affect sexual assault attitudes. Non-Hispanic Whites are more sympathetic than Blacks to women who have been sexually assaulted, whereas Blacks are more sympathetic than either Hispanic or Japanese college students. Asian students have the least sympathy for women who have been sexually assaulted and are more likely to hold a sexual assault victim responsible and excuse the offender.

7 Sexual assault (rape) is defined differently around the world, so the incidence of sexual assault varies depending on a culture's definition. In some cultures, rape is accepted as a punishment for women or is used for initiation purposes. Rape has also been used during times of war as a weapon.

8 Female college students are at greater risk for sexual assault than their non-college peers. The majority of women know the person who sexually victimized them. Because many of these women know their attackers, few feel comfortable reporting or pressing charges.

9 Alcohol use is one of the strongest predictors of acquaintance sexual assault on college campuses. Up to two-thirds of sexual assault victims have voluntarily consumed alcohol before an assault. Alcohol use on college campuses, as it relates to sexual assault, is viewed very differently for men and women. Being impaired or incapacitated during a sexual assault has been associated with self-blame, stigma, and problematic alcohol use in victims post-assault.

10 Male athletes have been found to be disproportionately overrepresented as assailants of sexual assault by women surveyed. Many athletes have been found to view the world in a way that helps to legitimize sexual assault, and many feel a sense of privilege. Female athletes have been found to be more likely than non-athletes to believe in the blame-the-victim theory of rape and believe that some women put themselves in a bad situation.

11 Rape trauma syndrome (RTS) is a two-stage stress response pattern characterized by physical, psychological, behavioural, or sexual problems (or a combination of these). Two stages, the acute and long-term reorganization, detail the symptoms that many women feel after a sexual assault. Sexual assault may cause sexual difficulties that can persist for a considerable period after the sexual assault. Some victims have a silent rape reaction because they never report or talk about their sexual assault.

12 The effects of sexual assault are similar in special populations, including sexual assault between marital partners and sexual assault of lesbians, older women, women with disabilities, and prostitutes. Partners of women who have been sexually assaulted also experience emotional symptoms. Overall, sexual assault places a great deal of stress on a relationship.

13 Men can be sexually assaulted by women and also by other men. The majority of male sexual assaults by women use psychological or pressured contact, such as verbal persuasion or emotional manipulation, rather than physical force. The true incidence is unknown because the sexual assault of men by men is infrequently reported to the police. Male sexual assault is an expression of power—a show of strength and masculinity that uses sex as a weapon. Sexual assault also occurs in prison.

14 Sexual assault perpetrators and offenders are primarily from younger age groups and tend to reduce their sexual assault behaviour as they get older. They have also been found to have experienced overwhelmingly negative early interpersonal experiences; to have sexist views about women; to accept myths about rape; to have low self-esteem; and to be politically conservative.

15 Different therapies for sex offenders include shock treatment, psychotherapy, behavioural treatment, support groups, and the use of medications. Many programs have been developed to decrease myths about sexual assault and increase knowledge levels. All-male programs have been found to significantly reduce the belief in rape myths.

16 The likelihood that a sexual assault will be reported increases if the assailant was a stranger, if there was violence, or if a weapon was involved. Women who report their sexual assaults to the police have been found to have a better adjustment and fewer emotional symptoms than those who do not report. Some victims refuse to press charges because they are afraid of revenge, want to forget the event, feel sorry for the perpetrator of the sexual assault, or feel as though it would not matter anyway because nothing, or very little, will be done.

17 Incest refers to sexual contact between a child or adolescent who is related to the abuser. There are several types of incest, including father–daughter, father–son, brother–sister, grandfather–grandchild, mother–daughter, and mother–son. Sexual abuse can include undressing, inappropriate touching, oral and genital stimulation, and vaginal or anal penetration.

18 Accurate statistics on the prevalence of child sexual abuse are difficult to come by because some victims are uncertain about the definition of sexual abuse, unwilling to report, or uncomfortable about sex and sexuality in general.

19 The median age for sexual abuse of both girls and boys is around eight or nine years old, and many victims are scared to reveal the abuse. Victims of incest with a biological father delay reporting the longest, whereas those who have been victims of stepfathers or live-in partners tell more readily.

20 Children who hide their sexual abuse often experience shame and guilt and fear the loss of affection from family and friends. They also have low self-esteem and feel frustrated about not being able to stop the abuse.

21 Regardless of whether they tell someone about their sexual abuse, many victims experience psychological symptoms such as depression, increased anxiety, nervousness, emotional problems, low self-esteem, and personality and intimacy disorders. Guilt is usually severe, and many females develop a tendency to blame themselves for the sexual abuse. Men and women who have been sexually abused may not be able to recall the abuse. The most devastating emotional effects occur when the sexual abuser is someone the victim trusts.

22 Research comparing child sexual abusers with non-abusers has shown that abusers tend to have poorer social skills, lower IQs, unhappy family histories, lower self-esteem, and less happiness in their lives. Three prominent theories that propose factors that make abuse more likely are learning, gender, and biological theories.

23 Currently, the most effective treatments for victims of sexual abuse include a combination of cognitive and behavioural psychotherapies. Many victims of sexual abuse also have difficulties developing and maintaining intimate relationships. Goals for therapy of child sex abusers include decreasing sexual arousal to inappropriate sexual objects, teaching them to interact and relate better with adults, assertiveness skills training, empathy and respect for others, increasing sexual education, and evaluating and reducing any sexual difficulties that they might be experiencing with their sexual partners.

24 Increasing the availability of sex education can also help decrease child sexual abuse. Adequate funding and staffing of child welfare agencies may also be helpful.

25 Although IPV is common in adolescent and college-age populations, it can happen to men and women at any age. It is often related to stress. Researchers have reported that women with disabilities are significantly more likely to report experiencing IPV in their lifetime, compared with women without disabilities.

26 Many women and men are killed by their violent partners (known as *intimate partner homicide* [IPH]). Studies on men who commit IPH often have past criminal charges, a psychiatric history, or both.

27 Sexual harassment includes anything from jokes, unwanted sexual advances, a friendly pat, an "accidental" brush on a person's body, or an arm around a person. Severe or chronic sexual harassment can cause psychological side effects similar to those experienced by sexual assault victims, and in extreme cases, it has been known to contribute to suicide. It is estimated that 25 percent to 30 percent of college students report experiences with sexual harassment.

28 The first step in reducing the incidence of sexual harassment is to acknowledge the problem. Too many people deny its existence. Because sexual harassers usually have more power, it is difficult for victims to come forward to disclose their victimization.

Critical Thinking Questions

1 If a woman who was alone and drunk at a bar dancing very seductively with several men is sexually assaulted, do you think she is more to blame than a woman who was sexually assaulted in the street by an unknown assailant? Explain.

2 In 2003, a woman accused basketball star Kobe Bryant of rape. Do you think professional athletes make poor decisions with women who flock to them? Do you think a woman would cry sexual assault or rape without just cause? Why or why not?

3 Do you consider a 17-year-old male who has sexual intercourse with his 14-year-old girlfriend sexual abuse? How would you define the sexual abuse of children?

4 In a handful of divorce cases, one spouse accuses the other of child sexual abuse. Do you think that these accusations originate from a vengeful ex-spouse wanting custody, or do you think it might be easier to discuss the sexual abuse once the "bonds of secrecy" have been broken, as they typically are during divorce?

Adult Survivors of Child Abuse (ASCA) Designed specifically for adult survivors of physical, sexual, and emotional child abuse or neglect, ASCA offers an effective support program. This website's mission is to reach out to as many survivors of child abuse as possible, and it offers information on individual and group support groups. (http://www.ascasupport.org/)

American Women's Self-Defense Association (AWSDA) The AWSDA began with the realization that women's self-defense needs were not being met. Founded in 1990, AWSDA is an educational organization dedicated to furthering women's awareness of self-defense and rape prevention. (http://www.awsda.org/)

National Violence Against Women Prevention Research Center (United States) National Violence Against Women Prevention Research Center provides information on current topics related to violence against women and its prevention. The website contains statistics and information on many topics, including evaluations of college sexual assault programs across the United States. (https://mainweb-v.musc.edu/vawprevention/)

Men Can Stop Rape (MCSR) MCSR is a non-profit organization that works to increase men's involvement and efforts to reduce male violence. MCSR empowers male youths and the institutions that serve them to work as allies with women in preventing rape and other forms of men's violence. MCSR uses education and community groups to build men's capacity to be strong without being violent. (http://www.mencanstoprape.org/)

Male Survivor Male Survivor works to help people better understand and treat adult male survivors of childhood sexual abuse. Information about male sexual abuse and a variety of helpful links are available. (http://www.malesurvivor.org/)

Northwest Network of Bi, Trans, Lesbian and Gay Survivors of Abuse The Northwest Network provides support and advocacy for bisexual, transsexual, lesbian, and gay survivors of abuse. Information about sexual abuse and a variety of helpful links are available. (http://nwnetwork.org/)

Calgary Sexual Health Centre This website provides educational videos and resources about sexual health, sexual relationships, and boundaries. The WiseGuyz program is dedicated to the education of males and issues of consent. (http://www.calgarysexualhealth.ca/programs-workshops/wiseguyz/)

Ontario Human Rights Commission This website provides a variety of resources to help you understand what sexual harassment is and what you can do to stop it. (http://www.ohrc.on.ca/en/sexual-and-gender-based-harassment-know-your-rights-brochure)

Canadian Resource Centre for Victims of Crime This is a federal non-profit organization with a links to resources and help for those that are victims of any crime in Canada. (http://crcvc.ca/about-us/)

18 Sexual Imagery and Selling Sex

> *No community is ever unanimous as to what is required by way of legal controls on sexual materials. There are very few fixed principles; value judgments are always at the core of the matter. And in a complex society, divergent values are forced to compete for legal recognition. Advocates of either side of the controversy will employ rhetoric and invoke authority to assert contradictory value systems. The debate will take the form of rival vested interests (churches, police, helping professions, publishers and sellers) stating their case on the effect or lack of effect of certain forms of media on a "vital" but ill-defined and selectively perceived , communal value. The Commission will be pressed to acknowledge, in its legislative recommendations on obscenity, the moral supremacy of the values of one sector of the public over those of another. That the final recommendations will be read in this fashion is unquestionable. But that the criminal law on obscenity should be framed with this as an objective is unacceptable. In a pluralistic community such as Canada, the criminal law should not be modified simply in order to five effects to, or reinforce the moral standards of a powerful or vocal minority, or even a majority. Independent criteria of harmfulness such as those suggested by the Canadian Committee of Corrections must provide the measure of justification viz:*
>
> *1. No act should be criminally prescribed unless its incidence, actual or potential, is substantially damaging to society.*
> *2. No act should be criminally prohibited where its incidence may adequately be controlled by social forces other than the criminal process. . . .*

© Frédéric Neema/Sygma/Corbis

3. No law should give rise to social or personal damage greater than that is was designed to prevent.

To be a successful prostitute, you've got to have at least one of three things: good looks and a figure—and many of us are really beautiful; or the personality and individuality to make a man look at you twice, and then come back again and again; or the ability to talk or scare your clients, once you've got them back in your flat, into paying more than the original sum stipulated for extra attention, or less ordinary functions—you must persuade them into something new, or roll them, steal from them. (From the 1959 autobiographical novel Streetwalker, *anonymously written)* ||

SOURCE: Richard G. Fox, Associate Professor of Criminology and Law, University of Toronto, commenting on Canada's obscenity laws in 1972.

In a profit-driven society where people try to make as much money as they can—often more than they need—through the development and marketing of products and services, it is inevitable that sex will enter the marketplace, whether in the form of images to gaze upon, acts to be performed, or bodies to be enjoyed. Because sex is defined as a human need, and because need is the *quid pro quo* of capitalism, it is likely that there will always be exploitation and profiteering under such an economic system. The only force that prevents sex from becoming a commodity is people's values—and as the chapter-opening excerpt by Fox (1972) suggests, those values vary considerably.

We divide this chapter into two large sections—sexual imagery and prostitution. For the first, we begin with a brief history of erotic representation from the ancient world to the commercialization of pornography and the adult entertainment industry. Next we examine sexual imagery in popular film and on television, and then we look at definitions and policies on censorship in Canada over the years. In the next section, we look at prostitution and sex work, including strippers, street prostitution, and escort agencies. In so doing, we examine the policies in place in Canada on selling and soliciting sex.

Erotic Imagery in History

Representations of the human body, its genitalia, and sexual activity are one of the primary means by which we understand sexual life in ancient times. The term **pornography** (meaning "whore writing") was coined in 1850 by German archaeologist C.O. Muller to classify erotic depictions found in Pompeii (Voss, 2008). Since then, it has been used to refer to images meant to arouse and titillate viewers. One must be careful, however, of using such a label to describe depictions of nudity or sex acts in past eras. While sexuality has been commonly depicted virtually everywhere over thousands of years, it may simply have been to celebrate reproduction and sexual life rather than to arouse anyone. In other words, the term "pornography" was a 19th-century invention by an archaeologist to describe particular ancient artifacts and not a representation of the intentions of the ancient civilizations in producing them.

In this section we look at such depictions. Questions to keep in mind are what was the purpose of such imagery? Was it for sexual titillation, for celebrating sexual life, or otherwise?

Prehistoric Times

The Paleolithic era lasted about 2 million years and gave way to the Neolithic era, beginning about 10 000 B.C.E., when some hunters and gatherers began to graze cattle and till the soil. The only surviving sexual imagery comes in the form of cave drawings and paintings and figurines depicting naked or near-naked people over the years. Mere nudity, however, cannot be classified as

pornography
Any sexually oriented material that is created for the purpose of arousing the viewer.

sexual imagery since prehistoric hunters and gatherers lived their lives either naked or with animal skin covers to protect them from the cold and other harsh elements. However, given that the main purpose of cave drawings was to represent things most important to daily life (Lucie-Smith, 1991), reproduction was included.

The Venus figurines found in Europe and Asia, some of which date back at least 35 000 years, are statuettes of women with exaggerated breasts and genitalia (Conrad, 2009; Rudgley, 1999). Phallic depictions, whether drawn or carved, are also found everywhere from Melanesia to Mesopotamia as celebrations of the perceived power of the penis (Vanggaard, 1969). One recent discovery has been a series of erotic depictions on the roofs of caves in remote northern Australia dating back about 28 000 years (Conway, 2012). These charcoal drawings show oral sex, vaginal intercourse, and even anal intercourse, testifying that non-reproductive sexual activity has been around for millennia. As a more recent example, erotic paintings were found in 31 caves nestled within the Western Ghats mountain range of India, which date back to the second century B.C.E. These *Ajanta* murals told stories that included large-breasted naked dancing girls, which was ironic since the caves were the dwelling places of celibate Buddhist monks. According to historian William Dalrymple (2014), Buddhism stands in sharp contrast to Christianity, where the naked body is associated not with sin but with fertility and beauty. Sensuality was not a channel to evil but instead to the divine and, as a result, nakedness was celebrated rather than condemned.

As an example of pre-Columbian sexual imagery, the *Moche*, or the Aboriginal people of what is now Peru from 100 C.E. to 800 C.E., produced hundreds of ceramic figurines depicting masturbation, fellatio, and anal intercourse. These artifacts were funeral offerings of non-reproductive sex sent to ancestors, hoping that they would reverse them to reproductive sex and send them back to enhance fertility in the living world (Weismantal, 2004). Sexual imagery that would thus be labelled pornographic was meant not to titillate but to bolster fertility.

Ancient Egypt, Greece, and Rome

At the dawn of the Egyptian Empire, erotic images appeared on walls or papyrus as celebrations of the sexual activity in daily life (Manniche, 1987). On one papyrus, the Egyptian creation story is depicted where the sun god Ra is shown performing oral sex upon himself ("autofellatio") to give birth to two other gods, Shu and Tefenet (Hussein, 1993). The Turin Erotic Shroud, dating back to around 1150, B.C.E, depicts 12 positions of vaginal intercourse.

Ancient Greeks not only celebrated sexuality but the beauty of the human body as well. Sexual scenes, typically on terra cotta vases, depicted scenes of pederasty or satyrs and nymphs engaged in vaginal or anal intercourse with one another. Statues depicted the idealized beauty of young males as well as women (Dover, 1978). The Greeks had no concept of pornography and merely depicted scenes either of daily life or the cosmic life of their pantheon of gods. Curiously, and unlike many other cultures, Greek male figures had small penises, which were considered ideal.

Perhaps the most celebrated collection of ancient erotic art comes from the Roman city of Pompeii, which was buried by a volcanic eruption on 79 C.E. When archaeologists in the 18th and 19th centuries uncovered the city they were startled and troubled to find that there were many brothels with graphic paintings and other depictions of sex, carved phalluses protruding at every street corner, and private homes filled with erotic frescoes (Kendrick, 1987). There were frescos of Priapus with a large protruding penis, phallic wind chimes made of bronze, a sculpture of Pan copulating with a goat, frescos of men and women in idealized sexual positions, and even penises and testicles engraved in sidewalks to guide people to the entertainment district.

The fact that these images were so public was incomprehensible to the 19th-century mind that had relegated sex to privacy and secretiveness. Because of the conservative attitudes that persisted even through the 20th century, most erotic art from Pompeii was hidden away in the *Gabinetto Segreto* (Secret Museum) of Naples and in a secret room (the secretum) in the British Museum.

The sexual legacy of Pompeii had a profound effect upon scholars of the 19th century. Classical antiquity had long been held up in literature, art, architecture, and science as the best of civilization, and familiarity with it was the mark of true education. The Greek and Latin languages were compulsory subjects for boys in the upper-class preparatory school of England and knowledge of them was essential to being labelled a gentleman. The discovery of blatant sexual celebration was thus distressing and, just like the true nature (i.e., pederasty) of Plato's *Republic*, all evidence of it was suppressed. In so doing, sexuality, which was an integral part of life in classical antiquity, was removed from their lives.

India, China, and Japan

Nestled within the monuments of the 11th century Hindu and Jain Khajuraho Temples in India are some of the most sexually explicit reliefs and sculptures ever produced historically (Chandra, 1981). Not only do they depict vaginal intercourse in a variety of positions, but oral sex, group sex, and sex with animals. Similarly, the

Early erotic art was often public art. The city of Pompeii included large, erect phalluses on street corners and erotic frescoes adorned many homes.

Konark Sun Temple, built in the 13th century, also has sculptures of couples in various types of sexual embrace. Sexuality at the time was not a matter of shame but a part of life to be celebrated, as has been well documented in the *Kama Sutra*.

Chinese erotic art was not without graphic depictions of sex, even showing lesbian lovemaking. For the most part, however, it was more suggestive and subtle. Classical painters such as Zhou Fang and Qiu Ying painted numerous bed chamber and garden scenes that did not depict explicit sexuality but instead the erotic playfulness between men and women. According to Bertholet (2004), Chinese erotic art exemplified a perfect union between *yin* and *yang*, where man and woman brought in different strengths and were equal in sexual activity. There were also numerous paintings and drawings of male homosexuality, which was either celebrated or condemned depending upon the era (Hinsch, 1990).

Japanese erotic art is known as *shunga*, which means "picture of spring" (Monta, 2013). Artists such as Hishikawa Moronobu and Miyagawa Isshō of the Edo Period in the 17th and 18th centuries painted beautiful courtesans, brothel scenes, group sex, and many couples locked in naked embrace. Compared to China, Japanese culture was far more patriarchal and women were regarded as objects of pleasure rather than subjects of their own.

The Middle Ages and the Renaissance

Nudity in art was common in Europe up until the spread of Christianity, when bodies—especially those of women—were defined as evil. As a result, typical images became dominated by Biblical events such as the resurrection or the suffering of the saints. Nudity became rare and much Pagan art was thought blasphemous and destroyed. Throughout most of the Middle Ages, explicit sexual depictions were rarely seen in that they appeared only in expensive books that most could not afford or access. In the meantime, phallic art celebrating the power and glory of the penis abounded in Norse culture among the Vikings and neighbouring cultures (Vanggaard, 1969).

In contrast to this dark and lifeless period, the Renaissance saw a resurgence of celebration of the human body as is evident in the sculptures of Leonardo da Vinci and Michelangelo and in the florid nude paintings of the time. Suddenly, the bodies of naked men and women began to appear in Florence, Rome, and all over Europe. While religious themes persisted, there was a revival of classical Greek motifs of gods such as Aphrodite, Eros, and Hermes—often unabashedly naked.

Caravaggio (1571–1610), who was said never to have painted a female nude, almost certainly had an interest in boys, which influenced his art (Crompton, 2003). He produced several paintings of naked or near-naked adolescents, among them *Omnia vincit Amor* in 1602, which depicted a naked boy leering and grinning with legs spread apart. In another homoerotic painting, *St. John the Baptist*, an adolescent is seen languishing on a red cloth with a flimsy loin cloth barely covering his penis. Both works were highly sexualized. Other painters became well-known for their female nudes with rounded fleshy bodies, such as *Venus of Urbino* by Titian showing a naked woman languishing in bed with her hand coyly over her vagina, Botticelli's *The Birth of Venus* showing a naked woman standing on a sea shell, and Rubens's *The Three*

The Castrated Lion of Parliament Hill, Ottawa

In 1901, commemorating Queen Victoria's Diamond Jubilee, which marked 60 years of her reign, a marble statue of her was erected on Parliament Hill in Ottawa. At the bottom of the statue sat an "anatomically correct" lion with appendages identifying him as the king of beasts. The lion's visible testicles did not sit well with the powerful wives of Ottawa's politicians, who thought that children would be corrupted or would snicker when they should be reverent of the Queen's imposing marble presence. Soon after, in the middle of the night, a Public Works crew came with a blow torch and removed the lion's testicles, thus castrating him. The lion has never been the same.

SOURCE: Wills (1986).

Graces of three naked women embracing in the woods. Even today, to say that a woman's figure is "Rubenesque" is to say that it is rounded, fleshy, and alluringly plump.

Colonialism and Orientalism

From the 14th to the 19th century, ships sailing mostly from England, France, and Spain ventured out to new lands not only to forcibly Christianize people of the colonies but to exploit them for their gold, ivory, spices, sugar, and other commodities. This was the era of colonialism where North and South America, Australia, India, and most of Africa became the ruled colonies of European empires. By 1886, the British Empire ruled over 400 million people on every continent except Antarctica. Europeans believed that they were not there to fraternize but to rule, typically with the attitude that the native peoples of such undeveloped lands functioned best when they served. They must submit to this rule of empire for their own good and they must accept the definition of themselves as inferior and subordinate. This political position is known as **imperialism** and, when referring to Asia and the Middle East, it becomes **orientalism** (Said, 1978), where the West is defined as strong, masculine, and rational and the East as weak, feminine, and mysterious.

Imperialism and orientalism were readily apparent in the erotically charged artwork of Europeans depicting life in the colonies, where sexualization amounted to subjugation. By the late 19th century, there was an explosion of paintings by European artists depicting colonized peoples in the "exotic" settings of their own countries. Women were often naked, lying about lazily, and subjects to their men. This is seen in the works of late-19th-century post-Impressionist Paul Gauguin, who lived for a time in French-occupied Tahiti and painted many bare-breasted women. It is also seen in the "orientalist" paintings of the 19th century. One notable orientalist artist was Jean-Leon Gerome, who visited Egypt in 1856 and is famous for his *The Snake Charmer* depicting a naked boy charming a snake before an audience of older men. His other works frequently depict naked women. Sexualization of the people of the colonies served to portray them as morally opposite to the conservatism of Europe and, thus, make them into the "other."

The Victorian Era

The Victorian era was a paradox between two extremes—the staunch prudery of the upper classes, where sex was never discussed let alone depicted in any way, and the *demi-mode* of the masses, where non-marital sex in all of its forms teemed in the dilapidated houses and brothels of London and other cities.

imperialism
An attitude of colonizers maintaining that colonized peoples should live according to the colonizers' rules.

orientalism
A form of colonialism where the West (Europe, North America) is defined as strong, masculine and rational, while the East (China, Japan, the Middle East, North Africa) is defined as weak, feminine, and mysterious.

© Alinari Archives/CORBIS

Wilhelm von Gloeden photographed thousands of boys and young men in Taomina, Sicily, in the early 1900s, often using classical Greek backdrops.

During the early 20th century, John Ernest Joseph Bellocq photographed many prostitutes in Storyville, the red-light district of New Orleans.

Upper-class married men led two lives as they visited these brothels frequently and also became great consumers of sexual material. Whereas before, upper-class men would commission artists to paint graphic scenes for their private enjoyment, this was now the age of the photograph, where "French postcards," which were pictures of prostitutes and other women, often nude, were produced and passed around.

The emergence of photography, first in the form of *Daguerrotype* cameras invented in 1839, had transformed erotic images from imaginary people drawn or etched to real ones captured in light. In these earliest photographs, there was little effort in posing since women had not yet learned the choreography of modelling. They simply sat there naked. The birth of photography ultimately would lead to the proliferation of erotica in that it allowed images of nudity and sex to be mass produced. A great deal of these images came from France and French-occupied North Africa, where Arab and Berber women and girls were photographed naked or bare breasted, thus giving the erotic photograph the thinly veiled guise of anthropology rather than prurience.

Today, viewers of erotica are able to choose the types of people they would like to look at in photographs—male, female, older, younger, fatter, thinner, blonde, or otherwise. In the earliest days, it was enough that a photograph was of a naked person or a couple actually engaged in sex. With the invention of photography, a man could be viewing a woman's vagina and he was able linger on it un-self-consciously with his eyes as long as he pleased. Or he might view a penis without worrying that others will see him looking and he could compare it to his own.

Not all nude photography, however, was meant directly to be erotica. German artist Wilhelm von Gloeden (1856–1931) lived for years in Sicily and photographed thousands of boys, young men, and sometimes young girls using props such as Greek columns, vases, wreaths, and togas to suggest classical antiquity. His works were considered beautiful rather than prurient and were exhibited by the Royal Photographic Society of England and elsewhere. In the 1930s, however, when Italy was taken over by Benito Mussolini's fascist regime, several thousand negatives and prints were seized and destroyed as pornography.

Meanwhile, in New Orleans in the United States, John Ernest Joseph Bellocq (1873–1949) ventured into the red-light district of Storyville and photographed many prostitutes—some nude, some dressed. His photographs seem to tell a story of the lives of prostitutes at the time. Bellocq's life eventually became the topic of the major Hollywood film *Pretty Baby* (1978), directed by Louis Malle.

European fine artists of the time produced many paintings of nudes, which they exhibited in the salons of Paris and elsewhere. In France, William-Adolphe Bouguereau painted women and girls in angelic scenes, and François Boucher produced numerous erotic works of the same. It was not until Edouard Manet's *Olympia* (1983) that accusations of obscenity arose. According to Bernheimer (1989), this was not for its nudity or that the subject was a prostitute, it was because it differed from other nudes in that the body of the woman was not there for the male gaze and fantasy but the opposite. Because of Olympia's stare, she showed an independence that

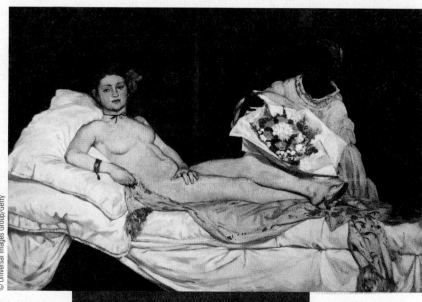

When French painter Edouard Manet exhibited *Olympia*, a portrait of a prostitute in 1863, critiques called it obscene.

strongly suggested that she was in possession of her own sexuality, thus becoming the object of the painting and not the passive subject. In most other nude paintings, women are shown as innocent and demure and their nakedness was to be enjoyed by the viewer. Olympia seemed too independent and, thus, broke the gender norms of the time. Bernheimer also points out the typical Victorian-era nudes did not have pubic hair. Instead, it was deliberately left out to feminize the subjects for the male gaze.

Review Questions

1 Why would it be inaccurate to label erotic cave paintings from 2000 years ago or the carved images of Indian temples "pornographic"?

2 Give some examples of Renaissance art that celebrated the human body or sexuality rather than condemned it. Find an example of your own.

3 Art was a way that European colonialists subjugated the colonized. Explain what this means and how it was done.

4 Define orientalism, colonialism, and imperialism.

5 If erotic images were not meant to arouse the viewer sexually, what was their purpose?

6 Explain why Eduard Manet's *Olympia* was thought to be obscene while other nude paintings of the time were not.

Sexuality in the Media

Visual or literary representations of sexuality have taken many forms over the centuries. They have existed in most cultures and have been produced for a number of reasons. As we discussed in the previous section, paintings, sculptures, and other representations of nudity and sexual activity were not typically meant to arouse viewers but instead to pay homage to fertility, sexual pleasure, the beauty of the naked body—and life itself. From the *Ajanta* murals of bare-breasted dancers in India 2000 years ago to von Gloeden's photographs of naked adolescents a century ago, erotic art was a celebration of humanity rather than an exploitation of it. Indeed, we see much nudity in the museums of Europe, Canada, and elsewhere, but accusations of pornography or harm to children are rare when images are placed under the umbrella of "fine art." The nudity in the works of Michelangelo, Titian, and Rubens is neutralized by such a definition and thus removed from any discussion of prurience or debauchery. A notable exception occurred in 1990 at the Contemporary Arts Center in Cincinnati, Ohio. At the time, artist-photographer Robert Mapplethorpe had a travelling exhibition of photographs that purposely pushed the boundaries of comfort for the viewer. Among the photographs was a self-portrait of Mapplethorpe with a bullwhip inserted into his rectum. This led to a trial where the director of the museum was acquitted and, thus, a test case for definitions of "obscenity" in the United States (Litt, 2010).

We discuss definitions of obscenity and pornography in the next section. For this section we look at written and visual erotica and pornography in contemporary society. We begin with literature, then film, television, and finally advertising. In the meantime, a question to keep in mind throughout: At what point does erotic representation become pornography?

Classic Erotic Literature

With the invention of the printing press centuries earlier, there was a proliferation of erotic literature in 17th-century Europe collectively known as the "whore dialogues," with titles such as *La Retorica delle Puttane* (The Whore's Rhetoric, 1642) and *L'École des Filles* (The School for Girls, 1655). By the 18th century, the paternalistic tendency of the clergy, the educated, and the upper classes to "protect" the masses from harm and corruption led to new efforts to control erotica whether in literature or science. Richard von Krafft-Ebing had deliberately used Latin terms such as "paraesthesia," meaning "perversion of the sexual instinct," for his *Psychopathia Sexualis* (1886) so that only the educated could understand what was written. With protectionist assumptions, it was believed that only upper-class and middle-class men would have the intellectual capacity to keep themselves from harm, while women and the poor could not. By the time of the French Revolution in 1989, however, it seemed that paternalistic forces were fighting a losing battle in that hundreds of pornographic pamphlets were sold in Le Palais Royal in Paris. Many of them were political in nature and attacked King Louis XVI and Marie Antoinette, accusing both of homosexuality.

In England, the Obscene Publications Act of 1857 forbade materials that "corrupted the morals of youth" and shocked the common decency. This led orientalist explorer and collector of materials on sexuality Richard Francis Burton to form the Kama Shastra Society, where books with sexual content were circulated privately among members. Among the works he circulated were translations of the *Kama Sutra* and a 15th-century Arabic sex manual called *The Perfumed Garden* (Wallace et al., 1981).

There were also a number of gay pornographic books by anonymous authors, among them *Teleny, or the Reverse of the Medal* (1893, attributed to Oscar Wilde) and *The Sins of the Cities of the Plain; or, The Recollections of a Mary-Ann, with Short Essays on Sodomy and Tribadism* (1881, by Jack Saul: pseudonym). Such books were distributed privately and kept well underground for their content.

In the past three centuries, there have been a number of obscenity trials involving books, poems, and other written materials that are now considered great literature. In 1748, one of the most erotic novels in history, *Memoirs of a Woman of Pleasure* (otherwise known as *Fanny Hill*) by John Cleland, was published in England. It was about a teenage girl named Frances Hill, who moved to London and became a prostitute. She had sex with numerous men, was a regular mistress to some of them, and had lesbian encounters as well. She was also preoccupied with the size of penises. The author John Cleland was arrested a year after publication and charged with "corrupting the King's subjects."

One major challenge to the Obscene Publications Act came in 1928, when the publishers of Radclyffe Hall's *The Well of Loneliness* were charged with obscenity. The novel was about an upper-class woman named "Stephen," who grows up differently, wears men's clothes, and falls in love with several women. It was one of the first lesbian novels and it popularized the ideas of Krafft-Ebing and Havelock Ellis, who were sympathetic toward homosexuality at the time (Faderman, 1977). When the judgment came down, it was decided that any book that advocated the acceptance of "inverts" was obscene by definition. Today, *The Well of Loneliness* would be considered tame. There was little erotic content—only the portrayal of lesbianism, which was sufficient at the time to label it obscene. The word "obscene" literally means "off the scene" or "off stage," thus referring to material that should not be seen.

Also in 1928, *Lady Chatterley's Lover* by D.H. Lawrence was published in England. The book was about an upper-class woman who was neglected by her husband and eventually had an affair with a servant, her estate's gamekeeper. A full version republished by Penguin Books in 1960 led to yet another obscenity trial. Not only were the class differences of the two lovers at issue, but also the frequent use of the words "fuck" and "cunt." This time the publisher was acquitted since it was decided that the novel had strong literary merit.

Beat-generation poet Allen Ginsberg was involved in an American obscenity trial after the publication of his epic poem *Howl* in 1956. *Howl* made frequent references to homosexuality, including the phrase "fucked in the ass." Publisher Lawrence Ferlinghetti and bookstore distributer Shig Murao were arrested in 1957 for distributing obscene materials. Like *Lady Chatterley's Lover*, however, it was decided that Ginsberg's work was of sufficient literary merit and the trial ended in an acquittal.

Ironically, there have been many examples of erotic literature over the centuries that have somehow escaped government scrutiny. *Justine or the Misfortune of Virtue* by the Marquis de Sade in 1791 is about a French girl subjected to rape and orgies, *The Story of O* by Pauline Réage in 1954 is about a young woman who becomes a sex slave, and *Candy* by Terry Southern in 1958 is about a naïve 18-year-old girl who has a variety of sexual encounters. Others that have not escaped scrutiny served to set precedents and help to define pornography over the years.

The Obscene Publications Act and its legal successors in Western nations were attempts to regulate act of looking at sex or reading about it. Because it was thought that sexuality was so charged with corrupting influences upon the uneducated general public, it was thought necessary to set up legal filters that would catch and then quash any material that magistrates and the clergy thought would do so. What is ironic is that the very act of labelling something obscene and quashing it serves to create obscenity by setting it apart from the rest of social life. Nothing is obscene until it is labelled as such, and the very act of labelling something as obscene creates pornography where none existed beforehand.

The Golden Age of Pulp Fiction

In the 1950s and 1960s, an entire genre of literature that appealed to popular audiences rather than "highbrow" individuals came of age (Smith, 2000). Before World War II, books were only available in bookstores, and there were usually just a few in any city. After the war, books made of wood-pulp paper could be mass-produced cheaply in paperback and were sold plentifully at drugstores, bus stations, magazine stands, and other venues where people in Canada and the United States shopped. One distinguishing feature was that they almost always had vivid art on their covers—often sexually suggestive—which hinted at the type of plot between the covers. Many of these "pocket books" were dashed off on manual typewriters within a few days by hack writers for quick profit, and many of them were thinly disguised erotic stories with titles such as *Swap Now Pay Later*, *Teach Me to Love*, and *Sally's Sinners*. There were also hundreds of lesbian-themed novels such as *Bed of Shame* and *Odd Girl Out* and gay-themed novels such as *The Beefcake Boys*, *Midtown Queen*, and *Hollywood Homo*. Although there were also pulp detective novels, western-themed stories, and romance fiction, cheap erotica seemed to consume the market. Most were tame in their treatment of sex, with euphemisms and terms such as "touched his sex" instead of "felt his penis," but others featuring bare-breasted or barely clothed women on their covers pushed the boundaries.

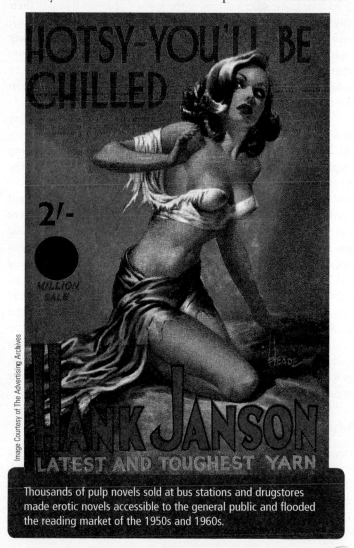

Thousands of pulp novels sold at bus stations and drugstores made erotic novels accessible to the general public and flooded the reading market of the 1950s and 1960s.

Sexual Diversity in Our World

A Canadian Enterprise—Harlequin Romances!

An entire genre of romance novels actually began in 1949 in Winnipeg, Manitoba, as a small paperback reprint company. Harlequin began to publish "medical romances"—a subgenre of romance novels involving doctors and nurses. The company enjoyed great success. It eventually moved to Toronto and was taken over by the Torstar Corporation, which is the largest newspaper publisher in Canada. Today, Harlequin romances are sold all over the world, with titles such as *A Millionaire for Cinderella* and *Meet Me under the Mistletoe*. They have remained popular as light escapes from the realities of life for many women. Unlike many other pulp novel companies, Harlequin has strict rules for its writers. The stories must centre on the heroine, the hero must be strong and trustworthy, and the sensuality must be low while the emotional feelings of romance must be high. The result is typically a tempestuous romance where both heroine and hero live happily ever after!

Lesbian-themed novels were often written by men with female pseudonyms and most either exploited lesbian sexuality for its appeal to heterosexual men or portrayed sad misguided characters who often met with tragedy or death at the end. Keller (2005) distinguished between two types: "virile adventures" and "pro-lesbian" pulps. The former often featured male characters and had graphic depictions of sexual encounters. The latter—about 50 in number (Wood, 2006)—were usually written by women and featured love stories. To lesbians of the 1950s and 1960s this was their only outlet to read about people like themselves. Purchasing such novels in a drugstore at the time was often a nerve-wracking venture since it would declare someone as a lesbian in a time when a uniform definition of deviance applied. Nevertheless, to isolated lesbians, it was worth the risk just to read about women like themselves and feel that they were not alone.

Gay pulp fiction books seemed to directly make fun of gay men by portraying them as effeminate jokes (*Color Him Gay, Mr. Fancy Panties*), sex-crazed (*Bath Boy, Bottoms Up*), or leading tragic lives (*Finistere, The Why Not, Gay but Not Happy*). In *The Why Not* (1966), the characters are either butch of fem, they blackmail each other, and there is much sadness. Along with them and often conflating sexual orientation and gender identity, there were several novels about transgender people (*Three on a Broomstick, Boy Becomes Girl*), which were equally negative. There were also "sociological studies," such as *America's Homosexual Underground* and *The Making of a Homosexual*, where M.D. or Ph.D. was placed beside the author's name to give the books an air of scientific realism. In reality, these were collections of erotic stories under the heading "case histories," which legitimized them for audiences.

In general, the pulp era produced thousands of pseudo-erotica books that provided fodder for the fantasies of millions of people, including an entire generation of curious pre-Internet Baby Boomer teenagers. For many, this was their only means of sex education.

Men's Magazines

Magazines to feature naked women appeared in the 1890s—*Le Frisson* of France being one of the first. By the 1920s, many were disguised as art magazines, with titles such as *Art Classics Magazines* and *Artists and Models*. By World War II, Canadian and American soldiers overseas typically adorned their private quarters with colourful pictures of leggy pin-up girls torn from the pages of magazines. These pictures were not typically pornographic but instead showed a wholesomeness that was said to portray the type of woman a man would like to marry when he returned home. They exhibited a type of inviting sexuality combined with an innocence that was thought to make the ideal wife for a patriotic soldier. They also emphasized legs. Betty Grable, who reportedly had her legs insured for a million dollars, was the most famous pin-up girl of the time (Williams & Wright, 2011).

After the war, along with the pulp novels, men's adventure magazines began to flood the newsstands. With titles such as *Men, Manhood, Man's Book, Man's Story,* and *Man's Action,* they typically featured illustrations of voluptuous, scantily clad women who were usually in distress and in need of a man to save them. Nazi soldiers, wild animals, or crazed "natives" (thus rekindling the old racism of colonialism) were the typical villains (Osgerby, 2000). These magazines in many ways indicated a post-war crisis in masculinity where fighting the Germans and the Japanese was

Pin-up girls were popular during World War II and adorned soldiers' barracks.

© Bettmann/CORBIS

over and there was little to replace such tests of manhood thought necessary as a rite of passage at the time. In purchasing men's adventure magazines, they could live vicariously through such stories and images. The magazines further represented an effort to put women in their "place." Because women had great independence during World War II where they filled in at jobs traditionally done by men, adventure magazines seemed to have collectedly said that a woman's place is at home and not in the battlefield or the workplace, where they were incapable of functioning (Osgerby, 2000).

Meanwhile in 1953, with rights to a naked photograph of movie star Marilyn Monroe, Hugh Hefner launched a magazine called *Playboy*, which within decades led to a billion-dollar empire. *Playboy*'s philosophy had always been to legitimize pornography. By publishing stories by authors such as Ian Fleming and even Canadian author Margaret Atwood, interviews of prominent figures, and advertisements of fine clothing and other merchandise, *Playboy* marketed itself toward the middle class, the intelligent, and the educated. Its models were not sleazy but instead as wholesome as their pin-up girl precursors. The only difference was that they were nude. By 1960, Playboy Enterprises opened up a chain of nightclubs called The Playboy Club in which men were served drinks by women dressed as bunnies with long ears and cottontails. Feminist Gloria Steinem went undercover and worked for a Playboy Club doing much to highlight the blatant sexism of the time (Steinem, 1983).

REAL Research Using a sample of college students ages 18 to 26, Reichert and Zhou (2007) tested the hypotheses that sexy models on magazine covers would positively affect interest in a magazine as well as purchase attention. Both hypotheses were supported.

By 1965, entrepreneur Bob Guccione began *Penthouse* magazine and Larry Flint began *Hustler* in 1974. In contrast to the middle-class appeal of Playboy, *Hustler* made little pretense about its purpose—it was for men to enjoy looking at naked women and nothing more. Since that time, there have been numerous magazines that straddled the path between the middle-class lifestyle philosophy of *Playboy* and the voyeuristic stance of *Hustler*, with names such as *Swank, High Society, Cocktail,* and *Velvet*. Canada seems to have far fewer home-spun magazines, *UMM: Urban Male Magazine* being one of the very few. Other magazines such as *Penthouse Forum* combined pictures of nudity with prose and featured letters about sexual experiences by readers, editorials, and stories.

A small subgenre of magazines with naked images has been nudist magazines with titles such as *Sunbathing Health Magazine* and *Urban Nudist*. Some of these magazines were thinly disguised voyeuristic efforts showing only slim young women, but others were legitimate efforts to portray a lifestyle that was healthy and showed naked families more than anything else partaking in such activities as volleyball or picnicking. According to Weinberg (1967), nudist organizations were more likely to distance themselves from sexuality so as to legitimize the lifestyle of nudism as healthy and moral and not merely an opportunity for voyeurism.

In the 1970s, and as a feminist answer to men's magazines more than anything else, at least two magazines featuring naked men and marketed toward women appeared—*Playgirl* and *Foxy Lady*. These magazines never reached the popularity level of the men's magazines and had far smaller circulations. Models eventually displayed full frontal nudity and erections. Interestingly, when *Playgirl* began marketing in Europe and elsewhere, it began to show uncircumcised men. Most men at the time were circumcised in the United States and so were *Playgirl*'s models. In Europe where circumcised males are in the minority, many subscribers could not relate to American circumcised men.

Gay erotic magazines did not appear until the 1970s. In previous decades, however, a host of magazines collectively known as "beefcake," with titles such as *Physique Pictorial*, *The Young Physique*, and *Adonis*, featured young men in athletic pouches presenting their physiques on beaches or other settings. On the surface, these magazines were for the promotion of fitness and health to other men. This is what the models were told and most of them thought no differently (Hooven, 1995). In reality, they catered to gay men.

Unlike *Playgirl* and *Foxy Lady*, gay men's magazines with titles such as *Blueboy, Mandate, Inches, In Touch,* and *Honcho* seemed to rival mainstream men's magazines, if not in circulation then at least in number. These magazines began to appear in the 1970s after the advent of what was called "gay liberation" at the time.

Today, adult magazines of any kind have taken a backseat to the Internet. Playboy, for example, is smaller, no longer features interviews with key figures, and has a far smaller circulation. While such magazines used to dominate the stands of drugstores and newsstands, they are fewer in number. With a law in Canada mandating that only their titles be visible on the top shelves to keep them away from children's reaches of views, they are far less visible as well.

Sex in Films

Hollywood movies have been around since the days of silent films at the turn of the 20th century and have come full circle in their freedom to portray sexuality, then restrictions in doing so, and then freedom once again. In an effort to clean up Hollywood in the 1920s after a series of scandals, the *Motion Picture Production Code* (the Hays Code) set down strict moral guidelines for producers to follow. Among the prohibited depictions were nudity, the inside of a woman's thigh, "sexual perversion" (undefined), white slavery (non-white slavery was acceptable), miscegenation (relationships between races), childbirth, the glorification of crime, and ridicule of the clergy, revealing the Catholic influence behind the code. Eventually, these restrictions were applied to television as well. In the heyday of the Hays Code in the 1950s, when Lucy Ricardo was to tell her husband Ricky that she was pregnant on *I Love Lucy* (1951–1957), she could not say the word "pregnant." She was "expecting" instead. On the *Dick van Dyke Show* (1961–1966) which was about a young postwar married couple (played by Dick van Dyke and Mary Tyler Moore), their bedroom had two single beds instead of one double bed. There was also the one-foot-on-the-floor rule where if a man was lying on a bed with a woman, he had to keep one foot on the floor so

Sexual Imagery and Selling Sex **483**

that he was not actually "in bed" with her. The dresses of the cartoon character *Betty Boop* went from short with low necklines and a visible garter to below the knees, no plunge in the neckline, and no garter at all, transforming her image from sexy and kittenish to matronly and dowdy.

The Hays Code was not strictly enforced until 1933. Before this time, Hollywood had made many movies that were sexually suggestive at least and showed nudity at most. D.W. Griffith's *Intolerance* (1916) showed bare-breasted women and several movies—among them, *Purity* (1916) showed fully nude women. In *Blonde Venus* (1932) and *Safe in Hell* (1931), the lead characters were prostitutes, and in *Our Betters* (1933) and *Sailor's Luck* (1933) there were openly gay characters. Clara Bow, who was dubbed the "it girl" (meaning that she is "it") in the 1920s, was shown nude in *Hula* (1927). *Wings* (1927), which won the first Oscar award, featured a long lingering kiss between men. Sexuality continued as a focus during the full enforcement of the Hays Code but it was subdued, masked in double entendre, or otherwise. Lesbian and gay characters sometimes appeared subtly on the screen but they were tolerated by the censors as long as they were comical fops or tragic figures and their sexual orientation remained unmentioned (Capsuto, 2000). In Alfred Hitchcock's *Rebecca* (1940), for example, one character, a maid, was a thinly veiled lesbian pining over her lost mistress and cherishing the smell of her clothing (Filmsite.org). It was not until the 1960s, with the emergence of the sexual revolution, that films relaxed their standards once again and sexuality was restored to film.

Meanwhile a half a world away, the Hindi film industry (popularly known as "Bollywood") has thrived as long as Hollywood. While romance and sexuality are themes in Hindi films, graphic sexuality is forbidden by Indian law. As a result, it is conveyed symbolically, through suggestion, and through innuendo. Typically, sexuality is conveyed through song and dance (Dudrah, 2006). Modern India has both the traditional culture of caste and arranged marriages and the progressive globalized philosophy of modernism and gender equality. The Hindi film industry, with its spectacular dances and often powerful women, tends to straddle both worlds and both reinforce and challenge gender inequity. Bhat (2009) believes that films can be used as a strong medium promoting the equality of women and, thus, combating domestic violence. Additionally, and as a further by-product of globalization, Bollywood has begun to explore GLBT issues with occasional gay or lesbian characters (Wilson, 2012). *Fire* (1996) about two women who marry two brothers who neglect them and they fall in love with each other and *Girlfriend* (2004) about a man coming between two lesbian lovers are prime examples.

> **REAL Research** Sabharwal and Sen (2012) compared two films from mainstream Hindi cinema to two films from alternative Hindi cinema for their treatment of sexual minorities (LGBTQ people). The mainstream films tended to treat the minorities in negative ways, with themes of sarcasm, comedy, or criminality. The alternative films tended to have more realistic and serious portrayals.

Pornographic films have been around since the early 20th century. In the 1960s, many were in the form of "loops," which were cheaply made short productions called "stag films" or "blue movies" featuring amateurs wanting to make money quickly. Many were made in Latin American countries or the United States. People would go to watch them in video arcades or what were called "adult theatres" such as the *Pussycat Theater* chain, which operated from the 1960s to 1980s, with several in Canada. In previous decades when they were illegal, they would be shown to groups of men in private homes. For many young men, they were educational in that they became their first view of actual sex and showed how it is performed. By the 1970s, such films were shown in peep-show booths in video arcades.

In mainstream theatres, films began to push the boundaries of sexual content by the late 1960s, with *I Am Curious Yellow* (1967, Sweden), *Candy* (1968, U.S.), and *Last Tango in Paris* (1972, France), the last two starring actor Marlon Brando. As a large industry, however, three films were responsible for pornography transforming to the mainstream: *Deep Throat* (1972), *Behind the Green Door* (1972), and *The Devil in Miss Jones* (1973). All showed full frontal nudity and graphic depictions of vaginal and oral sex. *Deep Throat* was a satire of oral sex about a woman born with her clitoris in her throat. Rather than being strict depictions of sex like the stag film predecessors, they had character development and stories with beginnings and endings. Together these films brought commercial pornography out of hiding and launched a trend known as "porn chic." Celebrities such as Johnny Carson admitted seeing *Deep Throat* and it became legitimate for a time for middle-class people to watch them. Much of this curiosity was fuelled by the sexual revolution, and it became acceptable to throw off one's "hang-ups" about sex and fully embrace it as a human endeavour (Pennington, 2007). In the meantime, the gay pornographic film industry was kicked off by the film *Boys in the Sand* (1971), which also featured graphic sex.

Ironically, in 1980, Linda Boreman, the main character in *Deep Throat*, whose stage name at the time was Linda Lovelace, told reporters at a press conference that she had been violently coerced into making the film with beatings and having a rifle pointed toward her head. She published her experiences in her autobiographical book *Ordeal* in the same year and became involved in the anti-pornography movement. She died of injuries sustained from a car accident in 2002 at age 53. In contrast, Marilyn Chambers of *Behind the Green Door* and Georgina Spelvin of *The Devil in Miss Jones* have not viewed their pornography careers negatively.

By the 1980s, the invention of the video cassette recorder (VCR) led to the mass closings of adult movie theatres and led to the film rental business where for $2.00 people could pick a movie and take it home to view privately on their televisions. Adult movies then began to be made available in hotels and, eventually, the Internet led to the mass closings of video stores.

Today, with the film *Fifty Shades of Grey* (2015) and its planned sequels, mainstream films that aspire to the pornographic might have a revival. The film is about a rich and successful man describing himself as a "dominant" who enters a BDSM relationship with a young woman. There is ample nudity, a red-and-black room with whips and restraints described as the "play room," and controlled whipping and spanking. While some consider it highly erotic and an effort to bring BDSM out of the closet, others (e.g., The National Center on Sexual Exploitation in the United States) consider it glorifying of violence toward women. We discuss the positive and negative viewpoints on pornography later in this chapter.

Transgender and Film

The pornographic movie industry has long included the "tranny movie" featuring a variety of gender-bending films with titles such as *Genderella*, *T-Girls*, and *Surprise I Have a Dick*, where the appeal is the blending of genders in "shemales," who have both breasts and a penis. Within the mainstream of Hollywood, there have been many films where men have cross-dressed for a variety of reasons in the early days—often to avoid detection from authorities. Actor Cary Grant dressed as a woman to enter the United States in *I Was a Male War Bride* (1949), Tony Curtis and Jack Lemmon did so to avoid mobsters in *Some Like It Hot* (1959), and Julie Andrews played a woman playing a man dressed as a woman for show business success in *Victor Victoria* (1982). In the first two, the themes were in keeping with the times and centred on the ridiculous notion of "normal" men in "unnatural" situations and invited the audience to share in the joke. There have also been films about drag queens such as *To Wong Foo, Thanks for Everything Julie Newmar* (1994) and the Australian film *The Adventures of Priscilla, Queen of the Desert* (1996). One early film by cross-dressing director Ed Wood was *Glen or Glenda* (1953), which was a sympathetic look at what is now known as transvestic paraphilic disorder.

Films about transsexuals had a rocky beginning in 1970 with the satirical *Myra Breckenridge*, based on a novel by Gore Vidal, where Myra becomes Myron. By the 1990s, however, the topic was taken more seriously. *Boys Don't Cry* (1999) depicted the true story of teenager Teena Brandon, who lived as his male identity Brandon Teena, after which he was found out and murdered. Additionally, *Transamerica* (2005) depicted a transwoman and her relationship with her teenage son, and *Normal* (2003) centred around a husband and father in the rural United States who transitions to a woman after 25 years of marriage. There have also been films depicting the points of view of men in relationships with transgender people. *Soldier's Girl* (2003) portrays an American soldier who falls in love with a transwoman, and *The Crying Game* (1992) is about an Irish man who discovers his girlfriend is a preoperative transsexual. Additionally, at least two films have dealt with passing women in history—or women who impersonated men to be free of the gendered restrictions for women of their time. *The Ballad of Little Jo* (1993) is about an upper-class woman who becomes a man and then a gold miner and sheep rancher, and *Albert Nobbs* (2011) is about a woman who lives as a man and works in a hotel as a waiter in 19th century Ireland. The treatment of transgender issues has thus gone from farcical comedy to serious exploration.

Sexuality and Television

Before television, rural families would gather around a huge radio that often amounted to a piece of furniture itself and listen to the comedy shows of *Jack Benny* and *Amos and Andy* or tune in to the latest episode of such serial dramas as *The Shadow* and *Our Miss Brooks*. Although such programs were often racist and certainly sexist, sex as a topic was almost entirely absent except for the odd vague innuendo with trite phrases such as "making whoopee." By the 1950s and after the birth of a huge generation of Baby Boomers, television dominated the living rooms of North America and the now smaller radio was relegated to the kitchen counter. With the Hays Code still in full swing, sexuality was as absent as a toilet (which also never appeared on television until an episode of *All in the Family* in the 1970s). Family shows such as *Leave It to Beaver, Father Knows Best*, and *Ozzie and Harriet* provided lessons for growing up; Western shows such as *Bonanza, Gunsmoke*, and *Cheyenne* provided heroes for boys to admire; and police shows such as *77 Sunset Strip* and *Dragnet* taught them that crime does not pay. Meanwhile, Canadian Baby Boomers grew up with *The Friendly Giant* (1958–1985), *Chez Helene* (1959–1973), and *The Forest Rangers* (1963–1965).

It was not until the 1970s that television shows became socially conscious and touched on issues such as racism, poverty, the Vietnam War, and civil unrest. As a result, it was inevitable that the newly found freedom toward sexuality that went along with the changes would permeate the once-idyllic and sexless lives of television characters. As Levine (2007) points out, most people did not participate directly in the changing culture. That is, they did not see movies such as *Deep Throat*, they did not immerse themselves in the disco culture, and they typically did not have gay or lesbian friends (that they knew of). The socio-sexual changes that took place at the time were instead experienced vicariously through television—something that most people watched regularly. In this respect, sexuality entered the airwaves in many forms—*All in the Family* dealt with homosexuality in February 1971, *Maude* dealt with abortion in November 1972, and sexually transmitted infections, premarital sex, sex for its own sake, and masturbation came soon afterward. Today, with such shows as *Two and a Half Men*, almost every major sexual issue has been a topic of one episode or another. Television programming has come to be a strong influence on life, yet the world it portrays is often biased. There is rarely the visible use of contraception, sexually transmitted infections, or worry about AIDS. The irony is that if contraception such as an IUD were used or if someone did contract syphilis, this would likely be censored as too sexually explicit. Sexuality has become acceptable but any specifics that pertain to sexual health were in question.

One consequence of portraying particular sexual situations on television is that people come to see them as a reflection of reality when in fact they may not be. For example, in 2003, the media reported on a sex game among adolescents where girls wore coloured bracelets signifying the sex acts they had or were willing to perform. Other news sources picked this up and reports of it occurred for years even though it was found to be an urban myth (Bogle & Best, 2011). An equally dubious media claim in the early 2000s was the emergence of rainbow parties. Teenage girls would wear different coloured lipstick and perform oral sex on teenage boys. The boys later compare their penises for their number of colours and proclaim a winner. Even though this too was found to be an urban myth (Lewin, 2005), it was referenced on the television show *NCIS* and was the main storyline in an episode of

Law and Order: Special Victims Unit. Early sociologist William Isaac Thomas's concept of the "definition of the situation" becomes relevant here in that "If things are defined as real, they are real in their consequences" (Hewitt, 1994).

What effect does sex on television have upon viewers? According to Eyal and Finnerty (2009), *Social cognitive theory* suggests that positive or negative consequences attached to particular modelled behaviours may either encourage or discourage viewers from participating in them. For example, if a television program depicts a young woman engaging in recreational sex and then contracting chlamydia, this may discourage young women from doing the same. This effect would be more likely when the viewer identifies with the model in terms of age, gender, or otherwise. Eyal and Finnerty thus had an interest in exploring such portrayed consequences. They looked at portrayals of sexual intercourse on 152 television programs and found that 16 percent involved teenagers or young adults. Consequences attached to episodes of sexual intercourse tended to be emotional in substance and were far more positive (e.g., being in love) than negative. Consequently, portrayals of sex on television may have a significant effect on sexual behaviour in real life.

Not all sex on television is devoid of informed sexual decision-making. One recent program that achieved tremendous popularity is *Sex and the City* (1998-2004) about four single women who talk frequently about sex and have various relationships with men. According to Jensen and Jensen (2007), who conducted a content analysis on the series, it is more likely to depict sex between established partners rather than relative strangers and there is much talk about precautions and potential consequences of sex. In other words, while its sexual content is strong, it is more likely than other shows to promote healthy sex. Similarly, the HBO serial drama *Queer as Folk* (2000-2005) depicted many episodes of sex without commitment, but all the main characters were sure to use condoms.

Even though gay and lesbian characters have become common on television, the majority of encounters or relationships are heterosexual. While this in and of itself is not a surprise, heterosexuality is depicted through heteronormative scripts that reinforce gender inequality (Kim et al., 2007). Young men are typically seen as either preoccupied with or actively pursuing sex and young women are seen as objectifying themselves through appearance while simultaneously being judged for any sexual behaviour in which they engage. In short, there is still the hunter and hunted dichotomy and the hunted are still judged for having been caught. What is also missing, according to Kelly (2007), is any significant mention of female sexual desire in storylines, especially in teenage dramas. While boys express sexual desire for girls, the reverse seems to be absent. Instead, girls are more likely to express romantic desire. As a result, heteronormative gender inequality is reinforced. At the same time, in some programs, television has shown an equality between the sexes that would never have been portrayed in previous decades.

Gay and Lesbian Characters on Television

One of the first regular gay characters on television was Jodie Dallas, played by actor Billy Crystal, on a comedy show called *Soap* (1977–1981). His debut sparked protests from the National Federation for Decency (now called the American Family Association, an organization recently designated a hate group by the Southern Poverty Law Center in the United States) and other right-wing groups, but also protests from gay activist groups. Jodie was sometimes gay, sometimes a transvestite, and sometimes a transsexual, thus conflating sexual orientation with paraphilic disorder and gender identity, and he was constantly at the centre of anti-gay jokes. His appearance on television pleased no one. Since then, gay and lesbian characters began to trickle onto the airwaves slowly: C.J. Lamb on *L.A. Law* (1986–1994), Nancy Bartlett and Leon Carp on *Rosanne* (1988–1997), Dr. Carrie Weaver on *E.R.* (1994–2009), Ellen Morgan on *Ellen* (1994–1998), Will Truman and Jack McFarland on and *Will & Grace* (1998–2006), and Dr. George Huang on *Law and Order: Special Victims Unit* (1999–present), who was also one of the first Asian gay characters on television. Today, with regular characters on *Orange Is the New Black, Skins, The Walking Dead*, and *Pretty Little Liars*, gay and lesbian characters are no longer uncommon. Interestingly enough, bisexual characters such as Kalinda Sharma on *The Good* Wife and Number Six on *Battlestar Galactica* have begun to appear, when they were rare before. Ellen DeGeneres now has her own talk show and there have also been at least two gay or lesbian serials—*Queer as Folk* (2000–2005) and *The L-Word* (2004–2009), both of which centred on the lives of a group of gay or lesbian friends and both of which were filmed in Canada.

Gay and lesbian characters have also gone from "gay" to "just happen to be gay." In other words, with early characters, their sexual orientation was central to their presence on their shows whether for shock values, as the centre of a running joke, or otherwise. Today, as exemplified by Dr. George Huang and Dr. Carrie Weaver, their sexual orientation is quite incidental to their presence on their shows and only part of their characters.

Transgender Characters on Television

Like in early films, cross-dressing on television in past decades has long been a running joke. In 1959, comedian Milton Berle dressed as "Auntie Mildred" on *I Love Lucy* and was so well received by audiences that he continued to do so occasionally well into the 1980s. Since then, television shows have used cross-dressing either as a comedic device or a sign of mental illness, as was the case with the character Max Klinger on *MASH* (1972–1983). Over time, transgender characters slowly transformed from running jokes and bizarre moments to persons in their own right. As for male-to-female transsexuals (transwomen), there is Blessing Chambers on *Hollyoaks* and Hayley Cropper on *Coronation Street*. As for female-to-male transsexuals (transmen), there is Jason Costello on *Hollyoaks*, Shannon (later Sheldon Beiste) on *Glee*, and Adam Torres on the Canadian show *Degrassi: The Next Generation*. There is even a transgender superhero cartoon character in the Australian-Canadian animated series *Shezow*. Shezow is a boy in regular life but becomes a girl when transforming to his secret identity. To do this, he spins around and says, "You go girl"! It is interesting to note that transgender characters have followed the same path as gay and lesbian ones. They began as running jokes or shock-value devices and have now become legitimate persons adding to the tapestry of the storylines.

Degrassi—Thirty Years of Teenage Canadian Melodrama

Based on a number of after-school specials, the Canadian Broadcasting Corporation (CBC) introduced Canada to *The Kids of Degrassi Street* in 1979, which centred on the lives of a group of children in Toronto. As the children grew, so did the series. *Degrassi Junior High* and *Degrassi High* followed them through their high school years, and *Degrassi: The Next Generation* (2001 to present; renamed *Degrassi* in the 10th season) saw many of them as parents and guardians of another generation. It has since become the most watched

drama on Canadian television. What was appealing from the onset about *The Kids of Degrassi Street* is that the characters looked real. They did not look like air-brushed child models but instead regular kids who sometimes dressed in ridiculous ways and often got into trouble. The series resembled a soap opera with 12-year-olds, but the homespun Toronto edge gave it a life of its own.

As they grew, the subsequent series took on critical issues such as racism and child abuse and explored sexuality issues

such as teenage pregnancy, abortion, contraception, date rape, gender identity, oral sex, homosexuality, homophobia, gay bashing, transgender, and transphobia. There have been at least five gay characters—among them, Marco del Rossi (who is gay bashed) and at least three lesbian characters. Most striking at all, the character Adam Torres has become the first teenage female-to-male transsexual (transboy) on television.

Review Questions

1 There have been a number of obscenity trials for erotic books over the years. What are the similarities between the trials involving *The Well of Loneliness* and *Howl*?

2 What made pulp books so marketable and popular in the postwar era? Why did

lesbian books sell as well as books with heterosexual themes?

3 What was the *Playboy* philosophy and how did *Playboy* magazine differ from *Hustler?*

4 What was the appeal of men's adventure magazines?

5 What was the Hays Code and how did it change the nature of television shows and film?

6 How have films and television shows involving transgender individuals changed?

Pornography and Censorship

In 1964, American Supreme Court judge Potter Stewart, when asked to give his definition of pornography, admitted that he could not do so but added, "I know it when I see it." Can pornography be defined? How does it differ from "erotica"? The history of legislation over sexually explicit materials in Canada has been the history of disagreement over definition. Some people would regard any depictions of sex or nakedness as pornographic. For example, *A & F Quarterly*, a magazine put out by the clothing company *Abercrombie and Fitch* has drawn strong criticism for its nudity and homoeroticism by conservative American groups. Other people have a far higher threshold for what constitutes pornography. At other times, sexually explicit material or depictions of nakedness has artistic merit and any definitions of obscenity become neutralized under the rubric of "art." This ultimately became the case with Cleland's *Memoires of a Woman of Pleasure*, Hall's *The Well of Loneliness*, Mapplethorpe's self-portrait, and Manet's *Olympia*. The most

accepted definition of pornography pertains to its intention—erotic material intended solely to sexually arouse the viewer (or the reader). This, however, leads to several interesting paradoxes. First, some sexually explicit material may attempt to arouse the viewer but not actually do so, instead evoking feelings of disgust, disdain, or indifference. Should pornography thus be defined by its success in achieving what it intends? Second, sexually explicit material may be arousing but not intentionally so. Bedroom scenes in major Hollywood films are typically meant to be part of a story rather than to cause men to get erections. Any sexual arousal is thus incidental. Third, there is a host of material not meant to arouse the viewer but does so nonetheless. Men, for example, have turned to the lingerie pages of the *Sears Catalogue* for more than a century anticipating models in brassieres, girdles, and sleek hosiery. Even though the intention is to sell lingerie, the *Sears Catalogue* has likely been the masturbatory material of several generations of boys and men. Because sexual desire may be channelled almost anywhere, any type of pictures of people (or objects such as high-heeled shoes) will likely be arousing to some people. The definition of pornography thus returns to intent once again—the deliberate attempt to sexually arouse people.

The Good for Her Feminist Porn Awards, Toronto, Ontario

Like the Oscars of Hollywood and the Bollywood Movie Awards, pornography has its awards for excellence. The Good for Her adult bookstore in Toronto has organized the Feminist Porn Awards annually since 2007, and the latest ceremonies were in April 2015. There are three criteria for nomination. First, women or traditionally marginalized people must be involved in the film. Second, the film must depict genuine pleasure, agency, and desire for all performers. Third, it expands the boundaries of sexual representation on film, challenges stereotypes, and presents a vision that sets it apart from mainstream pornography. Among the winners for 2015 are *Wall of Fire* as the Sexiest Short Film, *BIODILDO 2.0* as the Most Tantalizing Trans Film, and *Queen Bee Empire* for the Golden Beaver Award for Canadian Content. Winners are awarded trophies in the shape of butt plugs (anal insertion devices).

SOURCE: Feminist Porn Awards, 2015.

In this section we look at some major issues of pornography and censorship in Canada and elsewhere. We begin with a discussion of pornography in Canada and the United States, then we discuss child pornography, and then we look at the politics of pornography.

Pornography and Censorship in Canada

In 1968, the Criminal Law Amendment Act, which legalized homosexual behaviour among adults, had a ripple effect related to the sexual norms of Canada. The definition of obscenity became wider and pornography became more tolerated. Canada, like many other Western nations, has had a long history of banning books thought to have prurient content. Among those once banned are *Droll Stories* (1832–1837) by Honoré de Balzac, *Lolita* (1955) by Vladimir Nabokov, and even *The Diviners* (1974) by Canadian author Margaret Laurence. The first official campaign of censorship came during World War I (1914–1918) when the War Measures Act justified doing so for purposes of national security.

The banning of books in Canada had come to a head when two gay and lesbian bookstores were targeted in the 1980s. In Vancouver, Little Sister's Book & Art Emporium had shipments of books seized by the Canadian Border Services Agency—among them, instructions on safer sex, which were essential in informing gay communities about health risks concerning HIV/AIDS. The policy at the time was that if one book in a shipment box is deemed suspicious, then all of the books in that box would be held as well. Ironically, many of the same books shipped to other Canadian bookstores were cleared with few problems, indicating that Little Sister's had been specifically targeted (Fuller & Blackley, 1996) and proving no justification based on the material itself. Meanwhile in Toronto, Glad Day Bookshop, Canada's first gay and lesbian bookstore, which opened in 1970, was similarly targeted at one point for importing *Bad Attitude*, a feminist magazine that contained mild BDSM stories involving lesbians. At another time, readers of gay adult magazines such as *In Touch* or *Mandate* could purchase them without problems but found that pages thought to be obscene were left blank by American publishers shipping to

Canada. Both bookstores eventually sued—Little Sister's at the level of the Supreme Court of Canada and Glad Gay at the provincial level—and both won.

Another case, *Regina v. Butler*, which was heard by the Supreme Court of Canada in 1992, set a precedent for the definition of obscenity. Donald Butler, who owned a video store in Winnipeg, was arrested in 1987 and charged with 73 counts of possessing obscene material. He reopened his store several months later and was arrested again. As a framework for analysis, the court saw three types of pornography: (1) explicit sex with violence, (2) explicit sex without violence but where subjects are treated in a degrading or dehumanizing manner, and (3) explicit sex that is neither degrading nor dehumanizing. The first kind would amount to undue exploitation, the second kind would only be considered undue if there is a substantial risk of harm, and the third kind should be tolerated as long as it does not involve children. The court also provided an exception if materials have artistic value. *Regina v. Butler* thus set forth a rubric for judgment based on risks of harm rather than moral judgment (Robertson, 1992).

In Canada at present, the only time pornography is mentioned in the Criminal Code of Canada is in section 163, which makes it an offence to produce "obscene materials" or to do so for the purposes of distribution. It is also an offence to give an obscene theatre performance (Martin's Annual Criminal Code, 2006). Obscenity is defined as any *undue* exploitation of sex or sex combined with crime, horror, cruelty, or violence. While this would seem fixed and stagnate, it is actually quite flexible in that the definition of "undue" is defined by "community standards." That is to say, if a community finds the material obscene, then it becomes obscene by definition. This definition has positive and negative sides. On the positive side, where the community is tolerant and flexible, pornographic material would be allowed. On the negative side, community standards are difficult to define and it is often a matter of those who protest the loudest. Still further, as the Supreme Court of Canada pointed out in *Regina v. Butler*, community stands are less about what Canadians would not tolerate being exposed to themselves as they are about what they would not tolerate for other Canadians to be exposed to (Casavant & Robertson, 2007).

Pornography and Censorship in the United States

The United States, because of its strongly religious nature, has had a far greater opposition to pornography, with conservative special interest groups such as the American Family Association and Focus on the Family. Court cases in the country have established a three-part definition of obscenity that has determined how material is established as pornographic. For something to be obscene, it must (a) appeal to prurient interest, (b) offend community standards, and (c) lack serious literary, artistic, political, or scientific value. Important questions remain however about the definitions of "community standards" and "prurient interest." Many people have argued that such criteria are no more than subjective moral judgments and have no basis in objective law (Hunter et al., 1993).

There have been at least two presidential commissions to study pornography in the United States, one in 1970 and one in 1986. The 1970 Commission on Obscenity and Pornography used the terms "erotica" or "explicit sexual material" rather than "pornography" and looked at four areas: effects of pornography, traffic and distribution, legal issues, and positive approaches to cope with pornography (Berger et al., 1991). It concluded that no reliable evidence was found to support the idea that exposure to explicit sexual materials is related to the development of delinquent or criminal sexual behaviour and recommended that adults decide for themselves what they will view (Einsiedel, 1989). The United States Senate was disappointed with the commission's conclusions and condemned its members.

In 1986, Attorney General's Commission on Pornography (the Meese Commission) was formed. Rather than remaining objective, its mandate was to find "more effective ways in which the spread of pornography could be contained" (Berger et al., 1991, p. 25). While the 1970 Commission focused on social science, the Meese Commission listened to laypeople through public hearings, most of whom supported restricting or eliminating sexually graphic materials. Virtually every claim made by anti-pornography activists was cited in the report as fact, with little or no supporting evidence, and those who did not support the commission's positions were treated with hostility (Berger et al., 1991).

The Meese Commission divided pornography into four categories: violent pornography, degrading pornography (where they included anal intercourse, group sex, and same-sex depictions), non-violent/non-degrading pornography, and nudity. The commission claimed that the first two categories may be considered a type of social violence and that they hurt women most of all. Overall, the Meese Commission came to the opposite conclusions of the 1970 Commission and made a number of recommendations: law enforcement efforts should be increased, convicted pornographers should forfeit their profits and be liable to have property used in production or distribution of pornography confiscated, repeat offences against the obscenity laws should be considered felonies, religious and civic groups should picket and protest institutions that peddle offensive materials, and Congress should ban obscene cable television and telephone sex lines.

Note that the first commission was formed during a time of sexual revolution, while the second was formed after the election of conservative president Ronald Reagan and the rise of the Christian Right. From a social-scientific point of view, it is of little value because of its inherent biases, its method of "fact" finding, and that it admittedly placed its conclusion before its "research."

Child Pornography

In August 1984, the Committee on Sexual Offences against Children and Youth (the Badgley Committee) reported that child pornography only amounted to a small portion of all pornography in Canada and that very little is actually imported. This, however, was during the last years before the Internet and now it can be easily accessed by anyone with a computer. People under the age of majority make up a special category within pornography in that while adults are capable of informed consent in participation, children are not. Furthermore, the state (i.e., the government of Canada) assumes a protective role in shielding children from harm. Child pornography involves sexual depictions either of children or adolescents under the age of 18. These depictions may involve actual sex acts or the display of genitals, breasts, or buttocks in a manner intended for sexual gratification. To produce it, possess it, or distribute it is an indictable offence under section 163.1 of the Canadian Criminal Code and doing so can result in a prison sentence of up to ten years.

The Politics of Porn

Debates over the legitimate place of pornography in a civilized society take place on several levels. First is the moral-religious component—the idea that sex is for procreation or reserved for marriage in private. Arguments toward this end tend to vilify pornography with visceral terms such as "smut" and "filth" and condemn not only the producers but the viewers as well. Second, beginning in the 1970s, are the feminist debates—the juxtaposition of feminists who condemn pornography as violence or at least debasement of women and those who oppose censorship and see the positive agency of women in pornography. Third, by the 1980s, is the medicalization of pornographic viewing as a part of sexual addiction. Fourth is the harm component—whether the existence of pornography causes real and tangible harm to the citizens of a nation. Because we have dealt with sexual addiction previously, we will omit it from the discussion here and deal only with the remaining three issues.

Pornography and Morality

Hinduism, Sikhism, and Buddhism also do not have any specific tenets against pornography but they do emphasize simple living and moderation. Within the tenets of the three Abrahamic religions—Islam, Judaism, and Christianity—pornography is not mentioned. It is thought wrong, however, because it involves sex that is not between husband and wife in private and sex without procreation. Additionally, Islam forbids the viewing of another person's genitalia and Orthodox Judaism advises women to dress modestly. In strict Islamic nations, pornography is against Sharia law.

In the United States, conservative Christian groups have been the most outspoken against pornography. One pamphlet put out by the American conservative organization Focus on the Family, for example, says that pornography is anti-Christian in that it is idolatry, which has led to decadence in past civilizations (Kirk, 1995). Another pamphlet by the same organization warns that pornography is "destroying" American children (Kirk, 1992). What is often cited in the Bible as an anti-pornography argument is Matthew 5:28, which states, "But I tell you that everyone who gazes at a woman to lust after her has committed adultery with her already in his heart." Viewing pornography is thus considered a form of adultery.

Aside from religious organizations, Canada and the United States have had a number of citizen action groups that have rigidly campaigned against pornography. In 1965, the Citizens for Decent Literature put out a film entitled *Perversion for Profit*, where the narrator, news anchor George Putnam, began his monologue by saying that "a floodtide of filth is engulfing our country in the form of newsstand obscenity and is threatening to pervert an entire generation of our American children." Such reactions, whether based in religious tenets or otherwise, are not so much ideological as they are visceral. Pornography is condemned as perversion because sex without shame amounts to *dirt, filth, pollution*, and *disease*. These metaphors of perversion and filth may be best understood through the theoretical work of anthropologist Mary Douglas in her classic book *Purity and Danger* (1978). Douglas examined the cultural metaphors of dirt and pollution (e.g., a "dirty mind," "good clean fun") and suggested that they refer not to what something is but where it is. As she said,

> … *we are left with the old definition of dirt as matter out of place. This is a very suggestive approach. It implies two conditions: a set of ordered relationships and a contravention of that order. Dirt them is never a unique, isolated event. Where there is dirt there is a system. Dirt is the by-product of a systematic ordering and classification of matter, insofar as ordering involves rejecting inappropriate elements.* (Douglas, 1978, p. 36)

Following this logic, to say that pornography is dirty and filthy, therefore, suggests that it is "matter out of place" in an ordered system. It is thought unclean and dirty not for what it is but because it is out of place in an assumed social order. Sex, it is thought, should be in private. The fact that pornography is not private renders it out of place and, thus, "dirty."

Pornography and Feminism

Since the 1970s (and to a lesser extent before as well), feminist scholars have taken positions against pornography, against its censorship, and for its rightful place in the sexual tapestry of society. Those against see it as an assault on women and a vehicle to silence them, rendering them powerless, reinforcing male dominance, and encouraging sexual and physical abuse. Feminists against censorship believe that the suppression of sexual materials will ultimately be used to censor feminist writing and gay erotica, and would therefore endanger women's rights and freedoms of expression (Cowan, 1992). Pro-pornography feminists see it also as a matter of freedom of expression but further believe that the framing of women as victims equally silences their voices and detracts from their sexual freedom.

Catherine MacKinnon (1985, 1987, 1993) argues that pornography cannot be separated from the history of male domination. She sees pornography as less about sex than power and argues that it is a discriminatory social practice that institutionalizes the subordination of one group by another in the way segregation institutionalized the subordination of Blacks by Whites. Pornography is thus a suppressive agent toward women and is no different than hate propaganda. Andrea Dworkin (1981, 1987) agrees, in seeing pornography as a central aspect of male power, which in turn serves to elevate men to a superior position. If women are no depicted as enjoying rape and wanting it, they are depicted in positions of submission and servitude. In short, the main arguments among feminists against pornography are that it uses women, robs them of their humanity, and reinforces a system of inequality. Some of the most powerful arguments against pornography come from the producers and writers of the Canadian film *Not a Love Story: A Film about Pornography* (1982), where director Bonnie Sherr Klein shows the more violent side of films available at the time.

A number of critics have responded to the arguments put forth by MacKinnon and Dworkin (Kaminer, 1992; Posner, 1993; Wolf, 1991), claiming censorship of pornography will lead to the banning of other materials such as gay or lesbian literature. MacKinnon also makes little distinction between relatively tame erotica such as *Playboy* magazine and films showing violent rape. As a result, her argument is confusing. Many portrayals of sexuality, such as feminist pornography, are geared toward resisting society's established sexual hierarchies (Henderson, 1991). Once sexually explicit portrayals are suppressed, so are the portrayals that try to challenge sexual stereotypes.

It has been argued that "all pornography is degrading to women" and any counter response to this claim has been that there are plenty of erotic depictions of male–female sex that are not degrading. Feminist pornography, for example, which is produced by women and for women, avoids any degradation whatsoever. What is conspicuously absent in the discussion, however, is pornography that does not only degrade women but does not depict any women at all. Even though male–male pornography has been around as long as its male–female counterpart, and even though it is a large part of the adult entertainment industry, it seems ignored in any socio-political discussion, minimized as inconsequential, or dismissed as insignificant. Not only does this amount to a strong heterosexist bias but it becomes curious when considering that gay and lesbian book stores have been the frequent targets of obscenity charges in Canada and elsewhere over the years. If anything, the existence of gay pornography, by definition, negates the contention that all pornography is degrading to women.

Pornography and the Harm Principle

The federal and provincial governments have a compelling interest in any activity to the extent that it would cause harm to individuals or society in general. Murder, for example, is illegal for this very reason. The same applies to pornography involving people under the age of majority (i.e., children). It is illegal because it causes harm. By the 1970s, feminist ideology shifted the critique of pornography from the moralistic to the socio-political. In other words, feminists gave up on accusations of obscenity and "filth" and moved toward analyses of gender power relations. Men's pleasure is depicted at the expense of women. In this respect, much discussion has centred on pornography that is degrading toward women. It is speculated that with sufficient exposure to such materials, men are given the message that it is acceptable to treat women as objects and will likely do so. An analogy can be drawn between this type of pornography and hate materials that degrade racial or ethnic minorities. For example, if women were replaced in pornographic movies by Jews, Asians, or Black people and treated in the same manner, they would certainly not be acceptable in any way.

It is further speculated that pornographic materials can lead men to sexually assault women. According to a Canadian parliamentary report on pornography by Casavant and Robertson (2007), any evidence for this connection would come from two sources—statistical evidence and experimental trials where men are asked to view pornography and then respond to questionnaires. For the first, there is great difficulty in drawing any causal link. While many rapists have been exposed to pornography, so have other men who have never committed rape. According to Ferguson and Hartley (2009), who examined evidence from several countries, there has been a general failure of researchers to find any causal link between the two. In another study by Davies (1997), 194 men who rented pornographic videos were examined for their attitudes about equal rights for women, marital rape, and

date rape. No correlations were found between any of their attitudes and the number of videos rented. Davies suggests that causes of negative attitudes toward women are more deep-seated that simply viewing pornography. Kimmel and Linders (1996) examined the rape rates and circulation rates of pornographic magazines in six American cities and found that as the magazine circulation went down, the rape rates went up.

Some experimental studies have found evidence that men tend to score higher on violence on questionnaires after viewing pornography (e.g., Shim, 2007). As Casavant and Robertson (2007) point out, however, these results are not easily transferable to the real world, where a host of other variables are at play. They also point out the "catharsis theory," which suggests that pornography may even provide an outlet for aggressive tendencies and, as a result, prevent sexual assault. On the other hand, lack of compelling evidence of any direct causal links to violence should not quell the conversation entirely. Many people believe that degrading depictions of women are contrary to Canadian values and thus should not be allowed regardless. Just as racist literature maintains the walls of inequality among people, so does pornography.

Review Questions

1 Why did the Victorian upper class believe that was so important to keep images and written material on sexuality away from the poor and uneducated?

2 What major events in Canada and the United States formed present policy on definitions of obscenity?

3 Explain the significance of *Regina v. Butler.*

4 Explain the different positions on the rightful place of pornography in society.

5 How might gay-male pornography be incorporated into these arguments?

Prostitution and Other Sex Work

Like many other large industries, production is both in the form of products and services. In the last section we dealt with some of the sex industry's products—pornographic pictures, films, and literature. We now turn to the service end—namely, people who work as prostitutes, telephone sex operators, strippers, and pornographic film actors ("porn stars").

As Canadian sociologist Fran Shaver (2005) points out, there are a number of obstacles in studying sex workers. Because any sex work is stigmatized in Canada and much of it is illegal, the number of people working in the industry is unknown. This is certainly true for prostitutes and even the numbers of strippers and telephone sex operators remain unknown because many work for cash only and are not legally employed. Obtaining a random sample of any segment of the industry is thus difficult to impossible. What is known, however, is that there are more female sex workers (FSWs) with male clients than male sex workers (MSWs) with either male or female clients (Goode, 1994).

A second problem is definition. What is a prostitute? Is it someone who sells sex regularly on the street? Is it someone who occasionally does so when he or she is short on rent—perhaps three times a year? Is it someone who accepts gifts such as clothing or food in exchange for sex? What about dinner and drinks at a fine restaurant? Some people might say that anyone who sells sex once is a prostitute, while others might say that prostitution has to be more or less a career to qualify. Certainly, feminists of the 1970s claimed that marriage itself—or at least the traditional form where only the husband is employed—is a form of respectable prostitution in that sex is exchanged for financial security and protection. As a result, most research on prostitution uses only convenience samples in specific locations and, while their results may give larger views of the world of sex work, they are not generalizable to national populations.

Prostitution in Canadian History

Prostitutes have long been targeted by authorities in Canada for different reasons. They have been tolerated as a necessary evil, seen as victims of a system of male abuse and power, and condemned as fallen women (Ball, 2012). As a result, efforts were made to regulate them with the Contagious Diseases Act of 1865, rehabilitate them during the social purity movement, and eradicate them for reasons of morality.

In the early days of New France, prostitution took place through circumstance. Men would die in battle or disappear for years on hunting trips up the St. Lawrence River, leaving wives and daughters to fend for themselves. To survive, some women and girls became prostitutes, as did one of the Daughters of the King, Catherine Guichelin, when her husband deserted her. Because of her deeds, she was banished from Quebec City in 1675, becoming Canada's first officially declared prostitute. Early laws were harsh: Women could be punished for merely being prostitutes rather than actually doing prostitution.

Prostitution in 19th-century Canada and Europe was typically and practically concentrated in areas where single men congregate—military bases, naval ports, migrant worker camps, and gold rushes. In 1865, Upper and Lower Canada passed the Contagious Diseases Act modelled after the British law of the previous year, where any suspicious woman loitering near a military base or port could be arrested, detained, and forcibly given a pelvic examination. This was not an attempt to eradicate prostitute but to ensure that prostitutes did not spread disease. Prostitutes served the purpose it was thought of providing an outlet for men and preventing them from attacking "respectable" women (Backhouse, 1985). At the time of Confederation in 1867, there were laws in place to arrest vagrants who loitered at night on city streets. This was aimed at prostitutes more than anything else. By 1892, the Canadian Criminal Code not only outlawed brothels but made it illegal to both work in them and frequent them as customers.

There were other efforts to reform prostitutes as well as provide shelters for them and keep them off the streets. In the mid to late 19th century, Canada witnessed a call for "social purity" by such groups as the Woman's Christian Temperance Union. Many women with no alternatives entered prostitution and were victimized by men. Others were tricked into working in brothels by false promises of employment or marriage. It is at this time that the term "white slavery" was coined to describe such events and distinguish them from the African slave trade (Backhouse, 1985). Chinese women in Vancouver were also tricked into prostitution in that they were brought over from China as wives and then forced to take in customers procured by their husbands (Yee, 1988).

During the Fraser Valley gold rush of the 1850s in British Columbia and Klondike gold rush of the 1890s, many thousands of prospectors flooded the areas, and many women followed them and became prostitutes (Neering, 2000). At any given time, Dawson City had between 250 and 300 prostitutes (Morgan, 1998). From a purely business point of view, this was an ideal situation in that the population consisted mostly of single males and there were few available women for marriage. Brothels were opened up, as were saloons, which facilitated prostitution as well as motivated customers with alcohol.

These laws did not stop brothels from becoming common by the early 20th century. With the railroad at completion, there was a great expansion to the Prairie provinces, with more than a million settling between 1900 and 1915, many of them from the Ukraine and Scandinavian countries. Others came up from the United States. There were many young single men working as miners and cowboys and for a time the only police presence was the Northwest Mounted Police (now the Royal Canadian Mounted Police). According to Canadian historian James H. Gray in his aptly titled book *Red Lights on the Prairies* (1971), sometimes men would line up outside the brothels on pay day and be in and out in minutes. At other times brothels served as cultural centres with pianos and other entertainment where men could linger all night. They even served as conference centres where chambers of commerce would hold their meetings.

Meanwhile Vancouver was at its birth in the 1880s and rapidly growing as the terminal of the Canadian railway. There were numerous brothels by the turn of the century, and many of them in or near what is now Chinatown (Francis, 2006). Because there were so few Chinese women in Canada at the time, many Chinese men remained bachelors and sought relief at the local teahouses or restaurants where they might chat up a waitress and then make an offer of money. They would also have to pay the restaurant owners a fee. Because of anti-Chinese sentiments, the brothels of Chinatown began to close by the 1940s (Yee, 1988).

Efforts to control prostitution were renewed for a time during World War I and then again during World War II, both times with the belief that sexually transmitted diseases would dilute the Canadian fighting force. Since then, prostitutes have been targeted by the police in all Canadian cities not so much to control disease but to regulate morality.

Social Theory and Sex Work

Three traditional theoretical frameworks within sociology are functionalist theory, conflict theory, and symbolic interaction. The first maintains that everything in society, good or bad, serves a function. The very existence of something suggests that it serves a function. Because prostitution has existed since the days of ancient Babylon and has persisted despite consistent efforts to eradicate it, it can be concluded that it serves some kind of

© Petra Lambert

Xaviera Hollander, who wrote the best-selling book *The Happy Hooker* (Hollander, 1972), was one of the leading madams in the United States for many years. Today, at age 72, she operates *Xaveria's Happy House*, a bed and breakfast business out of her home in Amsterdam.

function. Kingsley Davis (1937) was one of the first sociologists to look at prostitution in the 1930s and suggested that prostitution serves the function of offering sex that is accessible and convenient without intimacy. He further says that where physical attractiveness and youth are valued in the marriage market, there will always be men who do not measure up. Consequently, prostitution serves as an outlet for such men. Prostitutes would also be likely to perform particular sex acts that men cannot enjoy elsewhere (i.e., with their wives). It is also likely that in a society where sex is condemned before marriage, particularly for women, prostitution will flourish. Kinsey et al. (1948) found that in his American sample drawn in the 1940s, two-thirds of men reported having visited a prostitute, although the vast majority did so only once. In contrast, when the double standard of sex before marriage (it's okay for men but not for women) lessens, the need for prostitution likely lessens along with it.

Davis's analysis came out in the 1930s and there were a number of critiques. First, while it is true that youth and physical attractiveness are prized in a marriage market, they are not the only elements that would attract mates. Women may also be attracted to good personalities, honesty, and stability. Second, customers of prostitutes are typically not older and unattractive, nor are most of them socially unskilled. Quite often, men in the 20s and 30s visit prostitutes for convenience in that they offer a sure thing. We will discuss customers of prostitutes shortly.

Conflict theory, which looks at conflicts between groups, has its roots in the writings of Karl Marx, who critiqued the economic system of capitalism as unjust in that it amounts to one group with greater power exploiting another. In a capitalist society, members of the elite group (the rich) control the "means of production" and the remainder must work for them to survive. In this respect, there will always be poverty and women are more likely to be poor (Stone, 1989). As a result, many will resort to prostitution to survive. As Harcourt and Donovan (2005) and Oselin (2010) say, poverty is a prime reason for prostitution. However, as early sociology Edwin H. Sutherland pointed out, economic need does not sufficiently explain crime of any sort (Sutherland, 1924). While many women (and men) do enter prostitution because they need the money, far more who are equally poor do not.

Symbolic interactionism (Blumer, 1969) takes a different approach in that it explores the meanings people hold about particular things, how these meanings arise, and how they affect people's behaviours toward the things. What becomes relevant here is how political changes in society lead to the changing of meanings toward particular things within it. Pornography and prostitution have been defined differently in different times and in different cultures. For example, because of the sexual revolution of the 1960s, pornographic films of the early 1970s (e.g., *Behind the Green Door*) were viewed positively and as a result gave rise to porn chic. Prostitution in the 1980s became even more stigmatized than it already was in that it was newly viewed as a prime means of transmission of HIV/AIDS. The swing toward conservatism in the 1980s led to the vilification or pornography, prostitution, gay and lesbian lives, and other phenomena associated with non-marital sexuality. Symbolic interactionism thus becomes useful in focusing on how meanings change and how these changes affect people's behaviour.

Sex Workers and Their Clients

Because the majority of people are heterosexual, the majority of sex work involves women as prostitutes or strippers and men as customers. There are smaller segments of the sex work industry of men available to men, men available to women, and transgender people available to men. Female customers of female prostitutes do exist, but their incidence is far less prevalent (Oselin, 2010). In this section, we discuss female, male, and transgender sex workers as well as strippers of both sexes and their clients.

Female Prostitutes (FSWs)

Canadian research on prostitution has undergone several shifts over the past years—from deviance and how to control it in the 1960s and 1970s to HIV/AIDS transmission in the 1980s and 1990s to the victimization of prostitutes and how social policy and law enforcement affects prostitutes' lives in the 2000s. In Edmonton, the bodies of 20 women have been found since 1983; Winnipeg has had 16 homicides of female sex workers, and Vancouver has had many more women go missing, some of whom were the victims of serial killer Robert Pickton, who was convicted of numerous murders in 2007 (Fong, 2008).

When attention to prostitution originally shifted from religion and the law to social work and social science, efforts to determine the "cause" were among the first to appear (e.g., Benjamin & Masters, 1964). More recently, researchers have realized that there is no cause in the sense of absolute determinism but only exacerbating factors that make prostitution in young women's lives more likely. Many prostitutes are disenfranchised women who are either poor or addicted to drugs or alcohol and, with little employment skills, the sex trade becomes a way to survive. According to Schissel and Fedec (1999), several factors are associated with entry into prostitution for teenage and young adult women. First, family traumas involving physical or sexual abuse may lead to them leaving home well before they are prepared for independence. Once they are on the street without an income, prostitution becomes a way to survive. Second, past sexual abuse, especially when it came with rewards, would likely lead young girls to learn that their bodies are marketable and, thus, prostitution becomes facilitated later on. Third, truancy, achieving poor grades, or dropping out of school leaves young girls with few marketable skills, and prostitution becomes the only activity that promises a high income. Often, women try to leave prostitution but find they cannot get the same income in low-wage shift work and return to the streets once again. With street life, time becomes less meaningful and the transition to the by-the-clock world of business is difficult. Still further, when women are constantly abused by strangers, they often become highly defensive, distrustful, and short-tempered, which may lead to them losing their jobs. This is something Canadian writer Elizabeth Hudson, who wrote of her life on the streets (Hudson, 2004), calls "feral women."

Drug and alcohol use is generally high among women in the sex trade, but why? Some researchers (e.g., Potterat, et al., 1998) have said that prostitution is a way of financing a previous drug or alcohol habit, which is likely, in that past traumas within the family, physical and sexual abuse, and other hardships lead to

Danny Cockerline

Danny Cockerline was born in North Bay, Ontario, in 1960 and went to Toronto in the early 1980s. He had long heard of Canada's main gay newspaper *The Body Politic*, went to their offices, and attached himself to the journalists there at the time. He soon became one of the newspaper's writers. His friends describe him as well-known in the gay community of Toronto, having an over-the-top personality and even getting himself thrown out of bars on Church Street for dancing naked. With a highly confrontational style, he was not afraid to speak up for what he believed was right, and quick to speak for those who could not do so for themselves.

Eventually, Danny embraced the sex trade. He starred in two pornographic films (*Midnight Sun* and *In the Grip of Passion*), was a nude model for the magazines *Honcho* and *Mandate*, and was a prostitute. During this time, he connected with male and female sex workers and showed them ways in which they could organize. He was one of the founding members of Maggie's—the Toronto Prostitutes' Community Service Project, the Sex Workers' Alliance of Toronto (SWAT), the Prostitutes Safe Sex Project, and the Coalition Advocating Safer Hustling (CASH). At the 5th International Conference on AIDS in Montreal in 1985, he was instrumental in disrupting proceedings by interrupting and yelling at speakers every chance he got. At one point, Danny took a leave of absence from the Toronto scene and embraced the prostitute communities of New York City, London, Melbourne, Sydney, and Bangkok.

Danny died in 1995 at the age of 35. His contribution to prostitute rights in Toronto laid a solid foundation for their struggle for recognition. Even 20 years after his death, he is remembered fondly by his friends at http://www.walnet .org/97_walnut/danny_cockerline/dc _memories.html.

drug abuse. Other researchers (e.g., Shaver, 1993) point out that the harshness of the sex trade leads women to drink or use drugs in order to cope. It is likely that both channels to abuse are common. Furthermore, being a street prostitute gives women access to drugs, which are also sold on the street, while they might be less likely to have access to them if they were elsewhere.

In some cities, race is an important variable, given that in Saskatoon, Regina, and Winnipeg the majority of young prostitutes are from First Nations groups (Schissel & Fedec, 1999). Because of a great deal of prejudice and discrimination, as well as holocaustic historical factors such as the devastation of generations of Aboriginal children by the residential school system (de Leeuw, 2009), a great deal of alcohol and drug abuse and family trauma has been reported by Aboriginal Canadians. Schissel and Fedec reviewed arrest and social service records of young people involved in prostitution in Canada and found that severe physical, psychological, and sexual abuse was far higher among Aboriginal than non-Aboriginal youth as was childhood neglect and running away from home.

While any one factor or any combination of factors does not necessarily lead to prostitution, they do tend to facilitate entry. An abused woman with few marketable employment skills who has no means of support becomes far more likely to enter prostitution as a means of survival.

Much literature on prostitution suggests an economic hierarchy from street prostitutes with low prices to escorts with high prices. The term "escort" is a euphemism, suggesting that men hire women so that they will have a conversational companion to accompany them to social events and important functions. High-class escorts have even been given a romantic appeal in movies such as *Pretty Woman* (1990), and escort agencies have occasionally been prominent in American scandals such as that run by high-class Madam Sydney Biddle Barrows until she was arrested in 1984, and that frequented by New York Governor Eliot Spitzer, where women were hired for between US$1000 and US$5500 an hour (Feuer, 2008).

There are many escort agencies in Canada and they are particularly common in Windsor, Ontario, which is divided by a bridge from the much larger American city of Detroit. Americans have come to Windsor for several reasons, such as the lower drinking age of 19 instead of 21. It has recently become a centre of sex tourism, with a number of escort agencies catering to same-day and overnight American tourists (Maticka-Tyndale et al., 2005).

Male Prostitutes (MSWs)

Male sex workers (MSWs) may have exclusively male or exclusively female clients or both depending upon inclination and opportunity. There are many terms to MSWs, among them "gigolo," "rent boy," hustler," and "escort." For those with male clients, they do not necessarily define themselves as gay and, like many male pornography actors, may simply be "gay for pay." Many, however, are gay or bisexual. MSWs with exclusively female clients may work for escort agencies, or they may frequent the hotels of resort areas where rich women sometimes look for company. A major difference from FSWs is that while women may serve as many customers a day as might be available, men can only have a limited number of orgasms depending upon age and health. As a result, FSWs are likely to make more money.

Male prostitution has been around for hundreds of years, as is indicated by the trials of Irish playwright Oscar Wilde in England in the 1890s when he was convicted of "gross indecency" with young men whom he paid for sex. It was not until World War II that social scientists turned their attention to the phenomenon. One of the first ethnographic studies on male prostitution was conducted by William Marlin Butts (1946) toward the end of the war, which had created an atmosphere where there were many single men in North American and European cities. Over nine months, Butts observed 121 young men and boys soliciting in a large city square. He was able to interview 38 of them and get demographic information from another 26. They ranged from 15 to 24 years old and many had left home due to abusive situations. Danish police inspector Jen Jersild (1956) conducted a study of male prostitutes in Copenhagen in the 1950s looking at where they solicited and the techniques they used to solicit customers. In both studies, it seems that there was a conflation between prostitution and simple sexual liaisons between men where there was no money exchanged.

One of the first sociologists to look at male prostitution was Albert J. Reiss Jr. (1962), who, in his study entitled *The Social Integration of Peers and Queers*, looked at the symbiotic relationship between customer and MSW. Typically, young men who did not define themselves as gay would allow themselves to be fellated by older men while they sat or stood. Their motivation for doing so was both money and sexual release. Because they were only fellated and there was no other activity, they were able to maintain their images of themselves as both heterosexual and masculine, which to the customer was appealing. Male–male activity was thus defined in terms of gender, where the fellator was seen as feminine and the fellated was seen as masculine. Had either party not stuck to their roles, the customer would have been disappointed and the MSW might have become violent in having his masculinity challenged. Today, gay male relationships of any kind have gotten away from defining insertive and receptive roles in terms of gender, but in the 1950s and 1960s this was normative.

In any city, the arrests rates of FSWs far outweigh those for MSWs. This may in part be a product of the ways that male and female prostitutes solicit their customers. In prostitute areas (known as "strolls"), FSWs are often quite assertive with potential customers—flirting with them as they pass by, smiling, and asking them if they are looking for "a date." Uninterested men will typically ignore them, or smile and say "no, thank you" before moving on. Undercover police officers posing as customers may feign interest and, as soon as the FSW refers to payment for sexual services, she is under arrest. On male prostitution strolls, the dynamics are different. An MSW cannot flirt with male pedestrians as they pass by in the same way since it assumes a gay identity, which may meet with hostility. Instead, a male prostitute will simply wait until he is approached by a customer and wait for him to make a proposition. Police officers ideally cannot do this because it would amount to entrapment. Similar obstacles exist for the arrest of customers. A female police officer can pose as an FSW, but there is often difficulty in finding male police officers who would be willing or even believable in the role of an MSW. Thus, while it is simple to make arrests on the male–female side, it is more difficult on the male–male side.

Transgender Prostitutes (TSWs)

Compared to their male and female counterparts, there is far less research on transgender sex workers (TSWs) (Ross, 2012). They have, however, long been a part of the sex work industry (Duberman, 1994; Heap, 2010). In much early research as well as historical descriptions, however, it is difficult to distinguish TSWs from MSWs, since at the time sexual orientation was often conflated with gender orientation as one and the same. Some Canadian cities such as Montreal, however, do have "tranny strolls" for men interested in TSWs.

According to Canadian historical sociologist Becki Ross (2012), who interviewed transsexual prostitutes who were active in the 1970s, dressing up in over-the-top feminine finery with thick make-up and huge hair served to identify TSWs to potential customers looking for them. They, therefore, spent much time doing so. They also decided to retain their penises rather than go through complete transsexual surgery, thus defying the societal pressure to be physically one sex or the other. While some clients may not know that they are transgender, most clients claimed liked this combination of breasts and a penis. Also, because TSWs are less common than FSWs or MSWs, they become a commodity within the sex industry and are often able to command higher prices for their services.

On Your Mind

Do sex workers enjoy having sex with clients?

Many sex workers have partners outside of their professional lives and they are no less likely to be in love. Some sex workers report that they enjoy sex with their clients but most do not. They either tolerate it or are indifferent. Some female prostitutes might experience orgasms with clients but most do not and, as a mere physical response to the activity, this is no indication of enjoying the sex they are having. Male prostitutes often have orgasms with clients since this is generally a requirement. Similarly, while this might be physically pleasurable at the time, it is likely that they may also be relieved that the job is over. In general, prostitutes tend to compartmentalize the sex they have with clients in their minds. In other words, they consider it work and nothing more, while they experience sex with their partners as intimacy.

Strippers

Strippers or "exotic dancers" are another part of the sex industry and they work either on call for parties or in nightclubs and bars where they often perform elaborate dance moves as they take off their clothes to entertain their customers. Some strippers, such as Blaze Starr and Gypsy Rose Lee, became famous in the past for their burlesque routines. Since the 1970s, clubs where men have stripped for women have opened and gay bars often have dancers or strippers nightly or on given nights.

Women may either become strippers as a career or they may do so temporarily to earn money for such things as school fees or mortgages. According to Ronai and Cross (1998), strippers of either sex often have difficulties manoeuvring their identities in everyday life because of the stigma associated with their work. For example, they may be denied housing or be socially shunned. As a result, they often are vague about what they do (e.g., "I'm an entertainer") or they selectively disclose to certain people only. They may also have difficulty in their own personal relationships, balancing the expectation of sexual exclusivity with the pressures of their work in doing such things as private lap dances (Bradley, 2007).

According to Schweitzer (2000), the striptease act offers its audience both a voyeuristic look at reality and a fantasy of forbidden sexuality. For the former, the viewer is allowed to see what

SEX
in Real Life

The Bad Trick List, Montreal, Quebec, Summer 1991

For many years, prostitutes in the larger cities of Canada have protected each other by gathering lists of "bad tricks"—men who refuse to pay after sex, become violent, or otherwise. Lists from 2003 to 2014 can be seen on the Sex Professionals of Canada (SPOC) website, but before the Internet these lists were simply photocopied and circulated. The following five out of 96 entries are from a bad trick list circulated in Montreal in the summer of 1991 (the bold type is left in):

- *White young man with curly hair. Drives a small, dark-red car with tinted*

windows. Says he is a police office. Speaks English. **PULLS OUT KNIFE**.

- *A guy who approaches a girl saying "I'll give you $125 to $200. We'll go to a classy hotel depending on your body and age."* **WANTS TO DOMINATE. PULLS OUT KNIFE**.

- *White, mustache, clean cut, good looking, chubby. SAYS "I WANT TO FUCK YOU UP THE ASS WITHOUT A CONDOM." HAS AIDS*.

- *Small red pickup with white cab.... 45–50 yrs with brown hair, clean shaven. USES AN ICE PICK*.

- *Spanish guy, scar on his right cheek, doesn't speak English. Dark hair, brown eyes, and scars on his abdomen.... Got a B.J. for $50. When he wanted a fuck too the girl told him he got what he paid for.* **HE STRANGLED HER (SHE GOT AWAY)**.

SOURCE: Used with permission of Dans la Rue.

---

is real about the stripper that would not be seen elsewhere—thus, a look into the private. For the latter, fantasy is created by sexually meaningful clothing, which is about to be taken off, as well as the context of the forbidden in that strip clubs are associated with crime and highly charged sexuality that is deemed to be unattainable in everyday life. Strippers thus create the allusion of availability of women who are both beautiful and positive about sex. In reality, however, strip clubs are typically highly controlled with bouncers and barriers between the fantasy of what is being shown and the reality of what cannot be attained.

Clients

As mentioned before, any industry is composed of producers of goods and services and consumers of those goods and services. Pornography would not exist without interested viewers and prostitution would not exist without customers. We now turn to the consumers within the sex industry, focusing on men who solicit prostitutes. They do so for a number of reasons: so that sex is guaranteed rather than just a probability, to eliminate the risk for rejection, for greater control in sexual encounters, for companionship, to have undivided attention, because of a lack of other sexual outlets, for adventure or curiosity, or even because of loneliness (Jordan, 1997; McKeganey & Bernard, 1996; Monto, 2000, 2001).

The Centre to End All Sexual Exploitation (CEASE, 2015) in Edmonton, Alberta, has recently provided information on clients of prostitutes and other illegal sexual services (e.g., massage parlours), as well as efforts by the Edmonton Police Commission to rehabilitate them. Since 1996, CEASE has conducted a prostitute offender program, otherwise known as "John School," to make convicted clients aware of the issues of sexual exploitation. It usually convenes four to seven times a year and is mainly for first-time offenders with no history of violence. Of 148 men enrolled in the program in 2012 and 2013, 26 percent were between 26 and 35 years

of age and 30 percent were 36 to 45, thus not supporting Davis's (1937) assertion that clients of prostitutes are usually much older men. Only 34 percent were single men, while 46 percent were married. The remainder were either in common-law relationships or otherwise. There also seems to be a trend in socio-economic level, where only 19 percent were professionally employed while 74 percent were either unemployed, in trade work, or did general labour. As for place of birth, 61 percent were Canadian born, 13 percent were from an Asian country, and 26 percent were from elsewhere. In another informal survey of a group of 20 in John School, two identified as sexually addicted and another 14 said that they may possibly be sexually addicted (Roth, 2014). As reported, however, John School as a means of secondary socialization has met with success, where men are made aware of the repercussions of their behaviour as opposed to excusing it as a mere dalliance.

An earlier snapshot of clients comes from research from the 1980s (Robinson & Krussman, 1982–1983), which looked at 530 men arrested while trying to solicit sex from an undercover police officer. They ranged in age from 16 to 77, with a mean age of 31 years. All had approached the officer and asked for sex acts in return for payment. The most commonly requested sex act was a combination of oral and vaginal sex known as "half and half" in the streets, where a prostitute would begin with oral sex and finish with intercourse. The men came from a variety of occupations: 17 percent were professionals, 26 percent were labourers, 9 percent were retired, and 5 percent were students.

Quite often, clients of prostitutes, both male and female, do not consider or are unwilling to use condoms for protection (Freund et al., 1991; Leonard, 1990; Morse et al., 1992). With severely drug-addicted prostitutes, this may be met with low resistance, especially if more money is offered for intercourse without a condom. Most prostitutes, however, are well aware of the importance of condom use and insist upon it with their customers. At times, however, this goes both ways, where customers will insist on condom use with prostitutes (Vanwesenbeeck, 1993).

While many clients are highly impersonal, aggressive, or threaten or carry out violence (see accompanying Sex in Real Life feature), others, as many prostitutes report, are polite and respectful, which goes against the stereotype. In general, the transaction from initial contact to termination is unproblematic (Holzman & Pines, 1982).

Community, National, and International Organizing by Prostitutes

When viewed from the perspective of work and occupation, prostitution is a difficult job with irregular hours and an unpredictable clientele. There is an ever-present threat of danger, which may be in the form of violence, HIV transmission, or otherwise. There is also a great deal of stigma attached to prostitution, where sex workers are regularly harassed in the street or elsewhere. Organizing at any level is this beneficial to sex workers regardless. Strippers have also tried to organize into unions in Canada but have been unsuccessful in doing so (Ross, 2006).

At the individual level, prostitutes often protect each other by writing down the licence plates of cars that pick up their colleagues. If the car is not back within a certain amount of time, they will put word out on the streets to look for it. At the community level, organizations such as Maggie's (the Toronto Prostitutes' Community Service Project) and Sex Workers' Alliance of Toronto (SWAT) will do such things as hand out condoms and provide safer-sex education or simply a place for sex workers to congregate on their off hours and feel safe. At the national level, organizations such as Sex Professionals of Canada (SPOC) and Sex Trade Workers of Canada (see the Websites at the end of the chapter) have provided information online for sex workers of all kinds and offer a central location of organization. A similar organization, Cast Off Your Old Tired Ethics (COYOTE), operates in the United States (Jenness, 1990).

Since the 1980s, there have also been efforts to organize at the international level. The International Committee for Prostitutes' Rights (ICPR) adopted a charter in 1985 demanding that prostitution be redefined as legitimate work and not deviance or crime. Among the demands in their charter are the decriminalization of prostitution, protection from financial exploitation by middlemen, and protection from violence from the police. In 1986, the ICPR held an international conference in Belgium to reiterate these rights, with sex worker delegates from Canada, Australia, Holland, Vietnam, and other nations (Second World Whore's Conference, 1986).

Prostitution and Social Policy in Canada—Bill C-36

The first laws dealing with prostitution emerged in Nova Scotia in 1759 (Blackhouse, 1985). By Confederation a century later, Canada modelled its Criminal Code after England and laws against pimping, procuring, and operating a brothel were firmly set in place. In most cases, prostitutes were picked up under vagrancy laws. In 1972 the "soliciting" laws came into effect and they were replaced by the "communicating" laws in 1985. At this time, prostitution became legal, but communicating for the purposes of doing so was not. This created an odd paradox where it became illegal to attempt to buy or sell a legal service. It further created dangerous situations for prostitutes who had to solicit in secret—often in areas of a city where there was no protection from violence. Also, because of the communication laws, prostitutes were unable to screen their clients and discuss conditions before getting into their cars.

Three long-time sex workers—Terry-Jean Bedford, Amy Lebovitch, and Valerie Scott—challenged the laws in the Supreme Court of Canada, arguing that the laws created dangerous atmospheres for women in sex work. After testimonies from many witnesses and experts, the communication laws were struck down on December 20, 2013, through a unanimous decision. The ruling also gave Parliament one year to rewrite the prostitution laws, and it did. The Protection of Communities and Exploited Persons Act (Bill C-36) came into effect on December 6, 2014. It places emphasis on the purchasing of sex rather than the selling of it, thus attempting to greatly reduce the demand instead of the supply. To sum up the main points of the Act, it is now illegal to sell sexual services near any area such as a school where someone under age 18 might reasonably be present. This, however, still forces prostitutes into dangerous areas. It is now illegal to communicate for purposes of buying sex but not selling it. It is illegal to advertise the sexual services of other people, thus cracking down on magazine ads and Internet ads, and it is illegal to profit from the sale of other people's sexual services, thus prohibiting escort agencies and pimping activities. As it appears, the new laws offer little improvement to the conditions of sex workers, who are still vulnerable to violence.

Review Questions

1 What are some of the laws and policies toward prostitution in Canadian history?

2 Explain the two social theories dealing with prostitution.

3 What are some of the differences among male, female, and transgender prostitutes?

4 What are the reasons for the differential arrest rates of male and female prostitutes?

5 How do strippers manage stigma in their lives?

6 How have prostitutes organized at the individual, community, national, and international levels?

7 Explain the current prostitution laws in Canada.

Chapter Review

Summary Points

1 Erotic imagery has been known since prehistoric times in the form of cave paintings, Venus figurines, phallic stone carvings, ceramic figurines, and other forms. It has also been found on papyrus and walls in ancient Egypt and in the Ghats mountain rage of India. The intention of this art was never to arouse the viewer sexually but instead to celebrate fertility and life.

2 The Ancient Greeks and Romans carved and painted many erotic images and naked statues. Most prominent is the erotic art of Pompeii, a Roman city that was subsumed by a volcanic eruption in 79 C.E. The houses and streets of Pompeii had numerous erotic depictions and objects, including murals of sex acts and even wind chimes of phalluses. Because Victorian archaeologists found them immoral and disgusting, they stored them away in secret rooms in Naples and in the British Museum.

3 Among the sexual imagery depicted by the ancients were vaginal and anal intercourse, oral sex, autofellatio, masturbation, and sex with animals. Male–male sex was also a frequent topic, especially in ancient Greece. Much of it depicted pederasty.

4 Because of sex-negativity and the power of the Church, and because books were very expensive and time-consuming to produce, there was little erotic imagery in the Middle Ages in Europe. What did exist was restricted in large part to the margins of book pages. Nudity was acceptable in paintings as long as it was of Biblical scenes and particularly when it showed the suffering of martyrs and saints.

5 During the Renaissance, the Church's influence began to weaken and there was a resurgence of appreciation of the beauty of the human body as is now evident in the paintings of Titian, da Vinci, Michelangelo, Caravaggio, Rubens, and others.

6 During the height of colonialism in the 18th and 19th centuries, paintings of the colonized people of Africa, Asia, and elsewhere began to appear and they were often depicted nude and sexualized. This sexualization was a way of subjugating them in juxtaposing them as the object for the European male gaze. Particularly prominent in the 19th century were depictions of orientalism, which juxtaposed the East as weak and feminine and the West as strong and masculine.

7 The Victorian era was characterized by the extreme prudery of the upper classes, where sex was never discussed, and the many brothels of the masses, where prostitution and premarital sex abounded. Photography had its birth with the Daguerrotype cameras in France in 1839 and, since then, many thousands of pictures of nudity and sexuality were produced, many in the form of "French postcards." Often, these pictures were of non-European women, lending an air of scientific legitimacy to erotica.

8 Photographers Wilhelm von Gloeden and John Ernest Joseph Bellocq were notable for their erotic photographs at the time. Von Gloeden photographed men and boys Sicily, and Bellocq photographed women who were prostitutes in New Orleans.

9 The mindset of the Victorians in terms of erotic literature and art was that the poor and uneducated and women must be protected from any sexual representations because they would indelibly corrupt or damage them. Erotica in any form was reserved for educated men. The Obscene Publications Act of 1857 in England forbade materials that "corrupted" the masses.

10 Erotic literature became possible for the larger population with the invention of the printing press, and erotic novels such as *The Whore's Rhetoric* and *L'École des Filles* began to appear in the 15th century.

11 Over the past three centuries, there have been many notable obscenity trials of novels and other written material now considered great literature. Among them are *The Well of Loneliness* by Radclyffe Hall, *Fanny Hill* by John Cleland, and *Howl* by Beat poet Allen Ginsberg.

12 Pulp magazines and novels appeared in North America and Europe after World War II. The men's adventure magazines with titles such as *Manhood* and *Man's Story* gave men an opportunity to revel in stereotypically masculine pursuits celebrated at the time in the absence of opportunities to fight in reality. Typically, these magazines showed women in distress and had numerous erotic images of women. The pulp novels were mass-produced erotic stories made available in bus stations, drugstores, and anywhere where people shopped.

13 There were many gay and lesbian pulp novels, although at the time they were highly negative and often portrayed comical or tragic figures who would lead miserable lives and die at the end.

14 Men's erotic magazines began to appear in the 1890s in Europe. In North America, *Playboy*, *Penthouse*, and *Hustler* built large media empires. *Playboy* and *Penthouse* attempted to make looking at erotic imagery respectable for the middle class. There was a short-lived attempt to have comparable magazines for women, but they never reached the same levels.

15 Magazines for gay men appeared long before the gay rights movement, and with titles such as *Physique Pictorial and The Young Physique* they featured men posing in g-strings and were published under the guise of promoting physical culture to young men and boys. By the 1970s, magazines that were openly gay featuring naked men began to appear and flourished.

16 Hollywood films depicted nudity and sexual imagery until the early 1930s, when the Hays Code imposed restrictions. It was not until the 1950s that sexual imagery and topics re-emerged.

17 The pornographic film industry began with four films—among them *Deep Throat* about a woman with a clitoris in her throat and *Boys in the Sand* for gay men. These films began a trend of "porn chic" in the 1970s, where for a time it became respectable for the middle class to see them.

18 Television did not begin to explore sexual issues until the 1970s. Gay, lesbian, and transgender characters have gradually emerged as legitimate characters instead of negative stereotypes.

19 Whether something is obscene in Canada is a matter of "community standards," which allows for more flexible definitions than in previous times. The Criminal Law Amendment Act of 1968 marked the beginning of a more relaxed attitude toward erotic imagery, although there were several trials involving charges of obscenity. Gay and lesbian bookstores in Canada were particularly targeted. Similar events occurred in the United States.

20 Feminists have been strongly divided on the issue of pornography. One point of view has been that it amounts only to violence and the degradation of women, another view battles censorship, and a third view sees some pornography as empowering and liberating. There is little or no evidence that viewing pornography leads men to commit rape. The harm principle maintains that if something is to be made illegal, there must be legitimate evidence that it causes harm to individuals or society. For these reasons, child pornography is illegal in Canada and virtually every other country.

21 Prostitution has long existed in Canada from the days of New France in the 15th century. There have been several laws passed and several efforts to either control it or eradicate it from society.

22 Two social theories that may apply to prostitution are functionalism and conflict theory. The first maintains that prostitution serves a purpose in society, and that purpose is to provide a sexual outlet for those who are unsuccessful in the marriage market. The second looks at conflicts between women and men, and rich and poor, that enable prostitution.

23 When doing research on prostitutes, there are at least two obstacles. First, it is impossible to get a random sample because prostitution is often hidden and one cannot know how many people are engaged in it. Second, it is difficult to define prostitution since it may involve money for sex, favours, or gifts.

24 Prostitution has arisen in Canada wherever there are large groups of single men in one area, such as migrant workers, military bases, and gold rushes. There have been different policies toward prostitution in history leading to efforts to reform prostitutes, to eradicate prostitution entirely, and merely to control it.

25 Research on female prostitution has changed over the years and today one of the priorities is safety. A large number of prostitutes, many of them Aboriginal women, have disappeared in Winnipeg, Saskatoon, Edmonton, and Vancouver. Factors that facilitate women's entry into prostitution are physical and sexual abuse, lack of education, and drug and alcohol problems.

26 In the late 1950s, Albert J. Reiss Jr. was one of the first sociologists to look at male prostitution. During this era, there was a rigid division between client and prostitute, when the prostitute would allow himself to be fellated. Because masculinity was defined by who inserts and who is penetrated, this allowed the prostitute to keep his sense of masculinity and heterosexuality.

27 Transgender prostitutes also exist and they often have their own stroll areas in the city.

They often dress up in over-the-top outfits so as to identify themselves to potential customers. Their customers prefer them because they have both breasts and a penis.

28 Women who become strippers do so either temporarily to make money quickly or they do so as a career. As an occupation, stripping is stigmatized in the general population and, thus, strippers are cautious in revealing their occupations.

29 Men solicit prostitutes for a number of reasons—among them, the guarantee of a sexual encounter, to have more control, or because they are lonely. Since 1996, the Edmonton Police Commission has operated a "John School," where offenders attend mandatory classes and are educated on matters of sexual exploitation. Typically, clients are not violent and tend to treat prostitutes with respect.

30 Sex workers have organized at the individual, community, and national level, and there have been conferences at the international level in order to promote the rights of sex workers worldwide.

Critical Thinking Questions

1 People see pictures of naked bodies in pornographic films, magazines, and elsewhere. They also see them in art museums in the paintings of Bouguereau, Titian, Rubens, and Caravaggio. Why should one depiction be considered art while the other is considered obscene? What is the difference?

2 The Hays Code of the 1930s acted to "sanitize" popular films and later on television shows. Looking back on their regulations, we see much prejudice. For example, it was forbidden to show "sexual perversion" and "miscegenation." How else was the code prejudiced, racist, or sexist?

3 Today in Canada, obscenity is defined by "community standards." That is, something is obscene only if the community in which it appears considers it so. Is this a good definition? Why or why not?

4 There is an ongoing debate among feminist scholars as to the rightful place of pornography in society. Which side would you take and why?

5 Which theory do you believe best explains prostitution—functionalism or conflict theory? What are your reasons?

6 Should prostitution be legal or illegal? What are your reasons? Are your reasons purely about personal morals or do they pertain to societal harm? Explain.

7 What do you think of the latest laws on prostitution in Canada? Are they beneficial or harmful to women and society? Why or why not?

Websites

Sex Professionals of Canada (SPOC)   SPOC is the Canadian website offering information and support to sex professionals in Canada such as prostitutes and strippers. It gives up-to-date information on court cases and laws in Canada and events related to sex work. (http://www.spoc.ca)

Sex Trade Workers of Canada   This site posts news stories and comments on relevant issues of safety for sex workers. It also raises awareness of battered women. (http://www.sextradeworkersof canada.com)

Internet Movie Data Base (IMDB)   This website offers an immense database on almost every film and television show that

has ever been made, nationally and internationally. Each entry contains a synopsis, production details, "goofs," which list mistakes in the movie, and amateur reviews. (http://www.imdb.com)

Feminist Porn Awards   The official site of the Feminist Pornography Awards held annually in Toronto, Ontario. (http://www .feministpornawards.com)

Parliament of Canada (Bill C-36)   The Protection of Communities and Exploited Persons Act—Canada's new prostitution laws. (http:// www.parl.gc.ca/HousePublications/Publication.aspx?Language =E&Mode=1&DocId=6646338&File=33&Col=1)

APPENDIX
Human Sexuality Timelines

Human Sexuality: Past and Present

200,000 years ago First *Homo sapiens* appear.

2150 B.C.E. *The Epic of Gilgamesh*.

1000 B.C.E. Early **Hebrews** develop the **Hebrew Bible**—conservative view of sexuality focuses on **marital sexuality and procreation**.

1000 B.C.E. Early **Greek** culture encourages sexual permissiveness—men and **male form is idealized**.

500 B.C.E. Early **Roman** influence leads to lessening restrictions on sexuality—**focus on "active" male and "passive" female roles** in sexual behaviour.

400 B.C.E. The *Kama Sutra*, an Indian Hindu text, encourages **sexual liberalism**.

200 B.C.E. **Chinese philosophy** focuses on the Tao, views sexual behaviour as a **natural joining of yin and yang**.

50 C.E. Christianity begins, leading to a **condemnation of sexuality,** which is **associated with sin**—attitudes about sexuality become more conservative.

500 Early Middle Ages—Church's influence further strengthens conservative attitudes about sexuality.

570 Muhammad is born. Islam emerges after his death and sexuality is viewed as **acceptable only in marriage**—attitudes become more conservative. Modesty is encouraged.

1050 High Middle Ages brings a **less conservative view** of sexuality.

1300s The **Renaissance brings increasingly liberal attitudes about sexuality** and **more gender equality**.

1400s A **backlash to growing liberalism** leads to concerns over the practice of witchcraft—**witch hunts re-establish male dominance** and acceptable roles of women.

1500s The **Protestant Reformation continues conservative views of sexuality**.

1675 Catherine Guichelin, one of the daughters of the King, is declared to be a prostitute and banished from Quebec City.

1700s The **Enlightenment brings a questioning of morals,** and with this a **more liberal attitude about sexuality**—sexual pleasure is viewed as natural and desirable.

1792 Mary Wollstonecraft pens *Vindication of the Rights of Women,* emphasizing education of women and equality of the sexes.

1837 The **Victorian Era** begins—sexual attitudes become more conservative and **women are considered delicate and fragile**.

1873 Passage of the Comstock Act in the United States prohibiting the mailing of contraceptive information (not struck down until 1965) is indicative of **attitudes about sexuality becoming more conservative**.

Late 1800s–early 1900s Medical model of sexuality and **social hygiene movement** lead to **increasingly conservative attitudes**.

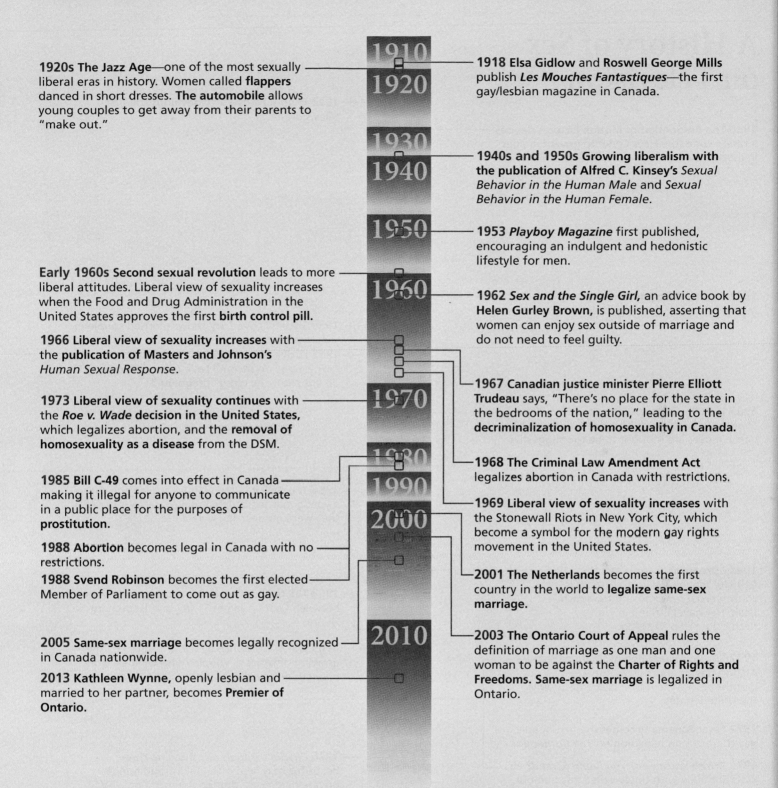

1920s The Jazz Age—one of the most sexually liberal eras in history. Women called **flappers** danced in short dresses. **The automobile** allows young couples to get away from their parents to "make out."

1918 Elsa Gidlow and **Roswell George Mills** publish *Les Mouches Fantastiques*—the first gay/lesbian magazine in Canada.

1940s and 1950s Growing liberalism with the publication of Alfred C. Kinsey's *Sexual Behavior in the Human Male* and *Sexual Behavior in the Human Female*.

1953 *Playboy Magazine* first published, encouraging an indulgent and hedonistic lifestyle for men.

Early 1960s Second sexual revolution leads to more liberal attitudes. Liberal view of sexuality increases when the Food and Drug Administration in the United States approves the first **birth control pill.**

1962 *Sex and the Single Girl,* an advice book by **Helen Gurley Brown,** is published, asserting that women can enjoy sex outside of marriage and do not need to feel guilty.

1966 Liberal view of sexuality increases with the **publication of Masters and Johnson's** *Human Sexual Response.*

1967 Canadian justice minister Pierre Elliott Trudeau says, "There's no place for the state in the bedrooms of the nation," leading to the **decriminalization of homosexuality in Canada.**

1973 Liberal view of sexuality continues with the *Roe v. Wade* decision in the United States, which legalizes abortion, and the **removal of homosexuality as a disease** from the DSM.

1968 The Criminal Law Amendment Act legalizes abortion in Canada with restrictions.

1985 Bill C-49 comes into effect in Canada making it illegal for anyone to communicate in a public place for the purposes of **prostitution.**

1969 Liberal view of sexuality increases with the Stonewall Riots in New York City, which become a symbol for the modern gay rights movement in the United States.

1988 Abortion becomes legal in Canada with no restrictions.

1988 Svend Robinson becomes the first elected Member of Parliament to come out as gay.

2001 The Netherlands becomes the first country in the world to **legalize same-sex marriage.**

2005 Same-sex marriage becomes legally recognized in Canada nationwide.

2013 Kathleen Wynne, openly lesbian and married to her partner, becomes **Premier of Ontario.**

2003 The Ontario Court of Appeal rules the definition of marriage as one man and one woman to be against the **Charter of Rights and Freedoms. Same-sex marriage** is legalized in Ontario.

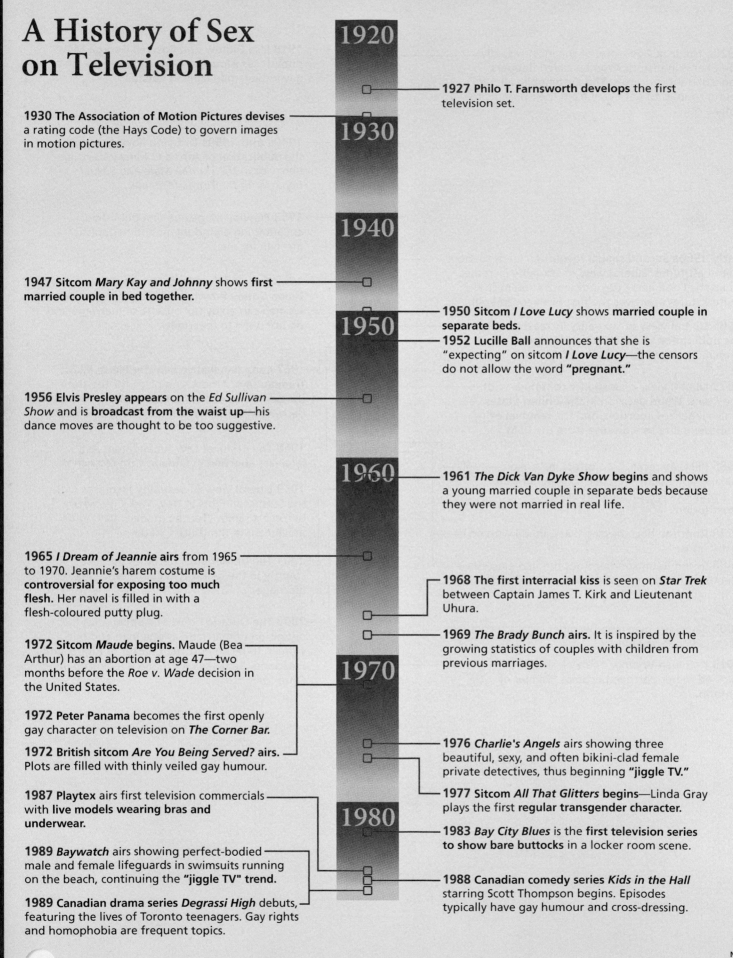

A History of Sex on Television

1920

1927 Philo T. Farnsworth develops the first television set.

1930 The Association of Motion Pictures devises a rating code (the Hays Code) to govern images in motion pictures.

1930

1940

1947 Sitcom *Mary Kay and Johnny* shows first married couple in bed together.

1950 Sitcom *I Love Lucy* shows married couple in separate beds.

1952 Lucille Ball announces that she is "expecting" on sitcom *I Love Lucy*—the censors do not allow the word **"pregnant."**

1950

1956 Elvis Presley appears on the *Ed Sullivan Show* and is **broadcast from the waist up**—his dance moves are thought to be too suggestive.

1960

1961 *The Dick Van Dyke Show* begins and shows a young married couple in separate beds because they were not married in real life.

1965 *I Dream of Jeannie* airs from 1965 to 1970. Jeannie's harem costume is **controversial for exposing too much flesh.** Her navel is filled in with a flesh-coloured putty plug.

1968 The first interracial kiss is seen on *Star Trek* between Captain James T. Kirk and Lieutenant Uhura.

1969 *The Brady Bunch* airs. It is inspired by the growing statistics of couples with children from previous marriages.

1972 Sitcom *Maude* begins. Maude (Bea Arthur) has an abortion at age 47—two months before the *Roe v. Wade* decision in the United States.

1970

1972 Peter Panama becomes the first openly gay character on television on ***The Corner Bar.***

1972 British sitcom *Are You Being Served?* airs. Plots are filled with thinly veiled gay humour.

1976 *Charlie's Angels* airs showing three beautiful, sexy, and often bikini-clad female private detectives, thus beginning **"jiggle TV."**

1987 Playtex airs first television commercials with **live models wearing bras and underwear.**

1977 Sitcom *All That Glitters* begins—Linda Gray plays the first **regular transgender character.**

1980

1983 *Bay City Blues* is the first television series to show bare buttocks in a locker room scene.

1989 *Baywatch* airs showing perfect-bodied male and female lifeguards in swimsuits running on the beach, continuing the **"jiggle TV"** trend.

1988 Canadian comedy series *Kids in the Hall* starring Scott Thompson begins. Episodes typically have gay humour and cross-dressing.

1989 Canadian drama series *Degrassi High* debuts, featuring the lives of Toronto teenagers. Gay rights and homophobia are frequent topics.

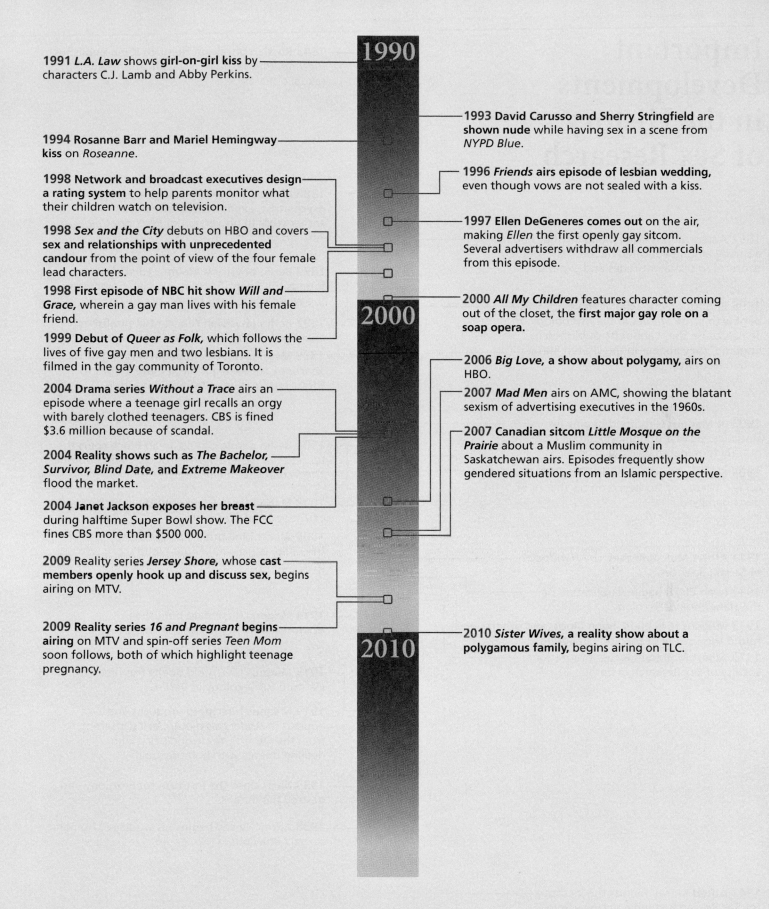

1991 *L.A. Law* shows **girl-on-girl kiss** by characters C.J. Lamb and Abby Perkins.

1994 Rosanne Barr and Mariel Hemingway **kiss** on *Roseanne*.

1998 Network and broadcast executives design **a rating system** to help parents monitor what their children watch on television.

1998 *Sex and the City* debuts on HBO and covers **sex and relationships with unprecedented candour** from the point of view of the four female lead characters.

1998 First episode of NBC hit show *Will and Grace,* wherein a gay man lives with his female friend.

1999 Debut of *Queer as Folk,* which follows the lives of five gay men and two lesbians. It is filmed in the gay community of Toronto.

2004 Drama series *Without a Trace* airs an episode where a teenage girl recalls an orgy with barely clothed teenagers. CBS is fined $3.6 million because of scandal.

2004 Reality shows such as *The Bachelor, Survivor, Blind Date,* and *Extreme Makeover* flood the market.

2004 **Janet Jackson exposes her breast** during halftime Super Bowl show. The FCC fines CBS more than $500 000.

2009 Reality series *Jersey Shore,* whose **cast members openly hook up and discuss sex,** begins airing on MTV.

2009 Reality series *16 and Pregnant* begins **airing** on MTV and spin-off series *Teen Mom* soon follows, both of which highlight teenage pregnancy.

1990

2000

2010

1993 David Carusso and Sherry Stringfield are **shown nude** while having sex in a scene from *NYPD Blue*.

1996 *Friends* airs episode of lesbian wedding, even though vows are not sealed with a kiss.

1997 Ellen DeGeneres **comes out** on the air, making *Ellen* the first openly gay sitcom. Several advertisers withdraw all commercials from this episode.

2000 *All My Children* features character coming out of the closet, the **first major gay role on a soap opera.**

2006 *Big Love,* **a show about polygamy,** airs on HBO.

2007 *Mad Men* airs on AMC, showing the blatant sexism of advertising executives in the 1960s.

2007 Canadian sitcom *Little Mosque on the Prairie* about a Muslim community in Saskatchewan airs. Episodes frequently show gendered situations from an Islamic perspective.

2010 *Sister Wives,* **a reality show about a polygamous family,** begins airing on TLC.

Important Developments in the History of Sex Research

1840

1843 Russian physician Heinrich Kaan publishes *Psychopathia Sexualis*, a classification system of sexual diseases.

1850

1860

1870

1880

1886 Richard von Krafft-Ebing, a German psychiatrist, expands and refines Kaan's earlier work in his version of *Psychopathia Sexualis*.

1890

1892 American physician Clelia Mosher begins a survey among educated middle-class women concerning sexual attitudes and experiences.

1896 English private scholar Havelock Ellis begins to write *Studies in the Psychology of Sex*. Because they cannot be published in England, they appear in the United States and in Germany.

1897 Berlin physician Magnus Hirschfeld founds the Scientific Humanitarian Committee, the world's first "gay rights" organization.

1897 Berlin physician Albert Moll publishes *Investigations into Sexuality*.

1899 Magnus Hirschfeld begins editing of the *Yearbook for Sexual Intermediate Stages* for the Scientific Humanitarian Committee.

1900

1903–4 Magnus Hirschfeld begins his statistical surveys of homosexuality. They are quickly terminated by legal action.

1905 Sigmund Freud publishes *Three Essays on the Theory of Sex* based on his theory of psychoanalysis.

1907 Berlin dermatologist Iwan Bloch coins the term *Sexualwissenschaft* (sexology) and publishes *The Sexual Life of Our Time*.

1908 Magnus Hirschfeld publishes the first issue of *The Journal for Sexology*.

1909 Albert Moll publishes *The Sexual Life of the Child*, which challenges Freud's psychoanalytic theory.

1911 Albert Moll publishes *The Handbook of Sexual Sciences*.

1912 Iwan Bloch begins publication of the *Handbook of Sexology*.

1913 Magnus Hirschfeld, Iwan Bloch, and others found the Society of Sexology in Berlin.

1913 Albert Moll founds the International Society of Sex Research in Berlin.

1910

1914 Magnus Hirschfeld publishes *Homosexuality in Men and Women*.

1919 Magnus Hirschfeld opens the first Institute for Sexology in Berlin.

1919 Magnus Hirschfeld produces and appears in *Anders als die Andern* (Different from the Others), the world's first film dealing openly with homosexuality.

1920

1930

1933 Nazis close the Institute for Sexology and destroy the data.

1938 Alfred Kinsey begins his studies of human sexual behaviour.

1940

1947 Alfred Kinsey founds the Institute for Sex Research at Indiana University.

1948 Alfred Kinsey and colleagues publish *Sexual Behavior in the Human Male*.

1949 Simone de Beauvoir publishes *The Second Sex*, which helps awaken the feminist movement.

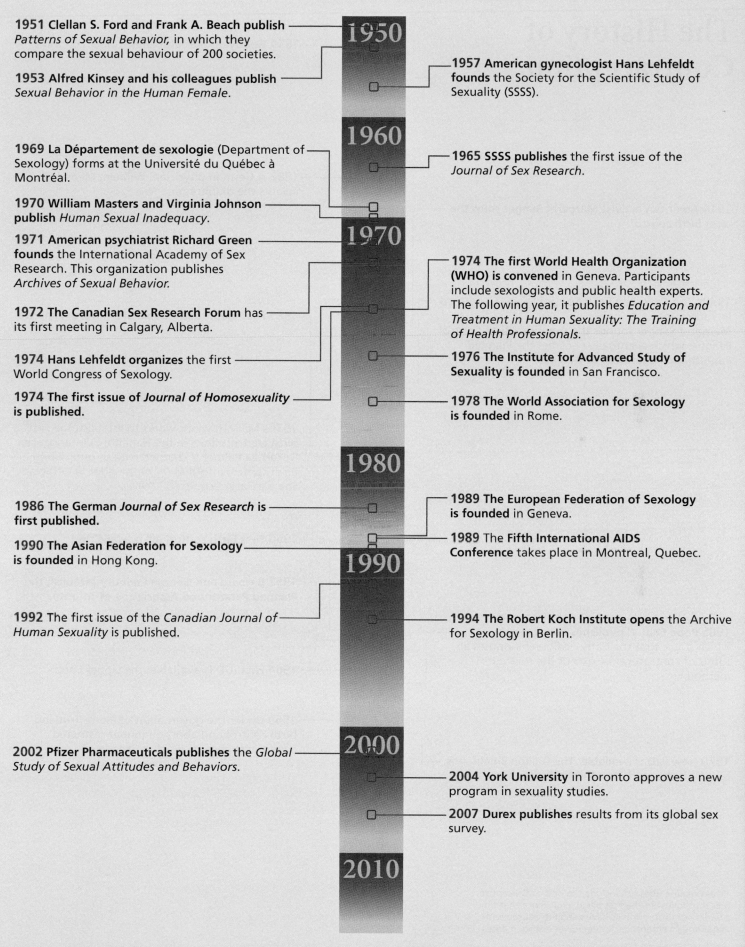

1951 Clellan S. Ford and Frank A. Beach publish *Patterns of Sexual Behavior,* in which they compare the sexual behaviour of 200 societies.

1953 Alfred Kinsey and his colleagues publish *Sexual Behavior in the Human Female.*

1957 American gynecologist Hans Lehfeldt **founds** the Society for the Scientific Study of Sexuality (SSSS).

1950

1960

1969 La Département de sexologie (Department of Sexology) forms at the Université du Québec à Montréal.

1965 SSSS publishes the first issue of the *Journal of Sex Research.*

1970 William Masters and Virginia Johnson **publish** *Human Sexual Inadequacy.*

1970

1971 American psychiatrist Richard Green **founds** the International Academy of Sex Research. This organization publishes *Archives of Sexual Behavior.*

1974 The first World Health Organization (WHO) is convened in Geneva. Participants include sexologists and public health experts. The following year, it publishes *Education and Treatment in Human Sexuality: The Training of Health Professionals.*

1972 The Canadian Sex Research Forum has its first meeting in Calgary, Alberta.

1974 Hans Lehfeldt **organizes** the first World Congress of Sexology.

1976 The Institute for Advanced Study of Sexuality is founded in San Francisco.

1974 The first issue of *Journal of Homosexuality* **is published.**

1978 The World Association for Sexology is founded in Rome.

1980

1986 The German *Journal of Sex Research* is first published.

1989 The European Federation of Sexology is founded in Geneva.

1990 The Asian Federation for Sexology is founded in Hong Kong.

1989 The **Fifth International AIDS Conference** takes place in Montreal, Quebec.

1990

1992 The first issue of the *Canadian Journal of Human Sexuality* is published.

1994 The Robert Koch Institute opens the Archive for Sexology in Berlin.

2002 Pfizer Pharmaceuticals publishes the *Global Study of Sexual Attitudes and Behaviors.*

2000

2004 York University in Toronto approves a new program in sexuality studies.

2007 Durex publishes results from its global sex survey.

2010

The History of Contraception

1830

1839 Goodyear manufactures rubber condoms.

1840

1850

1860

1870

1880

1882 A German physician, Wilhelm Mensinga, invents the diaphragm.

1914 American activist Margaret Sanger coins the term *birth control.*

1890

1900

1920s The Canadian Birth Control League is formed in Vancouver.
Margaret Sanger founds the American Birth Control League, which eventually becomes the **Planned Parenthood Federation of America.**

1910

1925 First diaphragms available in North America.

1920

1930s Mary Hawkins works to establish the first birth control clinics in the Hamilton, Ontario, area. Dorothea Palmer is charged with disseminating birth control information to the poor in Ottawa. She was later acquitted.

1930

1960 First birth control pill is available.*

1940

1961 Barbara and George Cadbury establish the Planned Parenthood Association of Toronto.

1965 Pope Paul VI publishes *Humanae Vitae,* which states that the Catholic Church opposes all forms of contraception, except the rhythm method.

1950

1960

1964 First IUD is available: the Lippes Loop.

1969 Under the government of **Pierre Trudeau,** birth control and abortion (under restricted conditions) became legal in Canada.

1970 New IUD is available: The Dalkon Shield. It is taken off the market in the 1970s.

1970

*This timeline does not include the oral contraceptive pills that followed the first pill in 1960. Since that time, a variety of different pills have been introduced with major improvements, including lower estrogen doses.

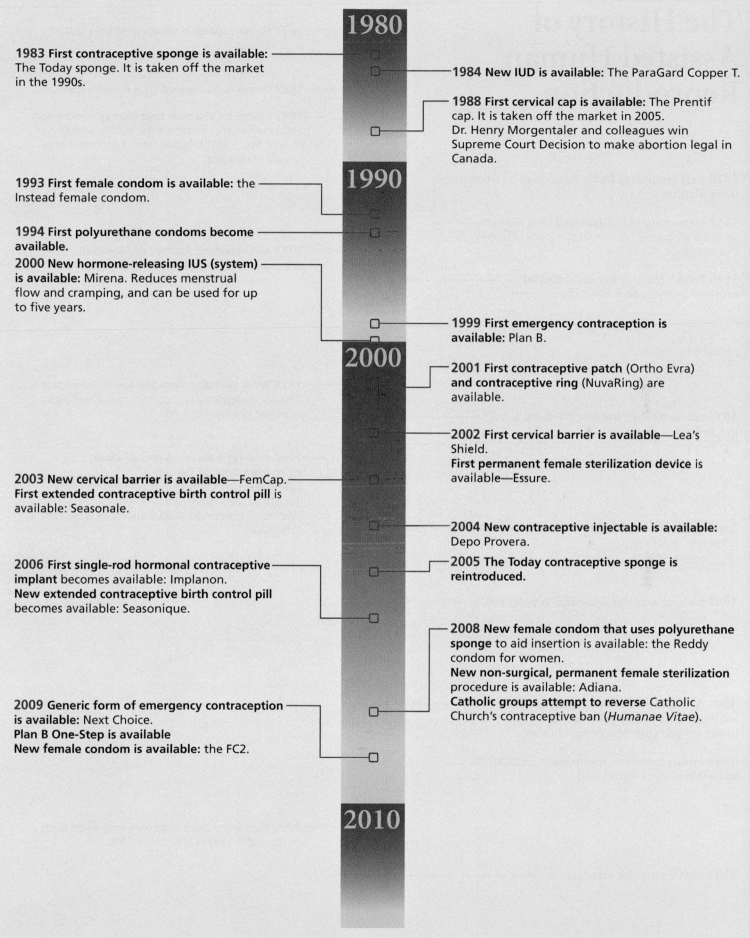

1980

1983 First contraceptive sponge is available: The Today sponge. It is taken off the market in the 1990s.

1984 New IUD is available: The ParaGard Copper T.

1988 First cervical cap is available: The Prentif cap. It is taken off the market in 2005. Dr. Henry Morgentaler and colleagues win Supreme Court Decision to make abortion legal in Canada.

1990

1993 First female condom is available: the Instead female condom.

1994 First polyurethane condoms become available.

2000 New hormone-releasing IUS (system) is available: Mirena. Reduces menstrual flow and cramping, and can be used for up to five years.

1999 First emergency contraception is available: Plan B.

2000

2001 First contraceptive patch (Ortho Evra) **and contraceptive ring** (NuvaRing) are available.

2002 First cervical barrier is available—Lea's Shield.
First permanent female sterilization device is available—Essure.

2003 New cervical barrier is available—FemCap. **First extended contraceptive birth control pill** is available: Seasonale.

2004 New contraceptive injectable is available: Depo Provera.

2006 First single-rod hormonal contraceptive implant becomes available: Implanon. **New extended contraceptive birth control pill** becomes available: Seasonique.

2005 The Today contraceptive sponge is reintroduced.

2008 New female condom that uses polyurethane sponge to aid insertion is available: the Reddy condom for women.
New non-surgical, permanent female sterilization procedure is available: Adiana.
Catholic groups attempt to reverse Catholic Church's contraceptive ban (*Humanae Vitae*).

2009 Generic form of emergency contraception is available: Next Choice.
Plan B One-Step is available
New female condom is available: the FC2.

2010

The History of Assisted Human Reproduction

1677 Human sperm is discovered by a Dutch scientist.

1827 Ovum is discovered by a Russian scientist.

1843 Scientists discover that human conception occurs when sperm enters the ovum, which reveals that contributions from both male and female create life.

1928 First pregnancy test is developed by German gynecologists.

1934 Progesterone is discovered by a German scientist who goes on to win the Nobel Prize in chemistry.

1937 *New England Journal of Medicine* **discusses** the concept of **IVF techniques.**

1945 *British Medical Journal* **discusses artificial insemination** using donor sperm.

1973 IVF is first attempted in the United States. First IVF pregnancy is reported in Australia but does not produce a child.

1978 Louise Brown, the first IVF baby, is born in Cambridge, England.

1982 First IVF babies—a pair of male twins—are born in Canada. Sperm Bank of California is opened to allow donations for unmarried women. **First baby conceived with donor ova** is born in Australia.

1984 First baby developed from a frozen embryo is born in Australia.

1987 Embryo transfer procedure is patented.

1991 A 42-year-old woman becomes a surrogate mother for her daughter after becoming pregnant with the daughter's embryo.

1992 Intracytoplasmic sperm injection (ICSI) for male infertility is introduced.

1996 First baby born that was conceived with intracellular sperm injection (ICSI).

1998 First embryonic stem cells isolated.

1600
1700
1800
1900
1910
1920
1930
1940
1950
1960
1970
1980
1990

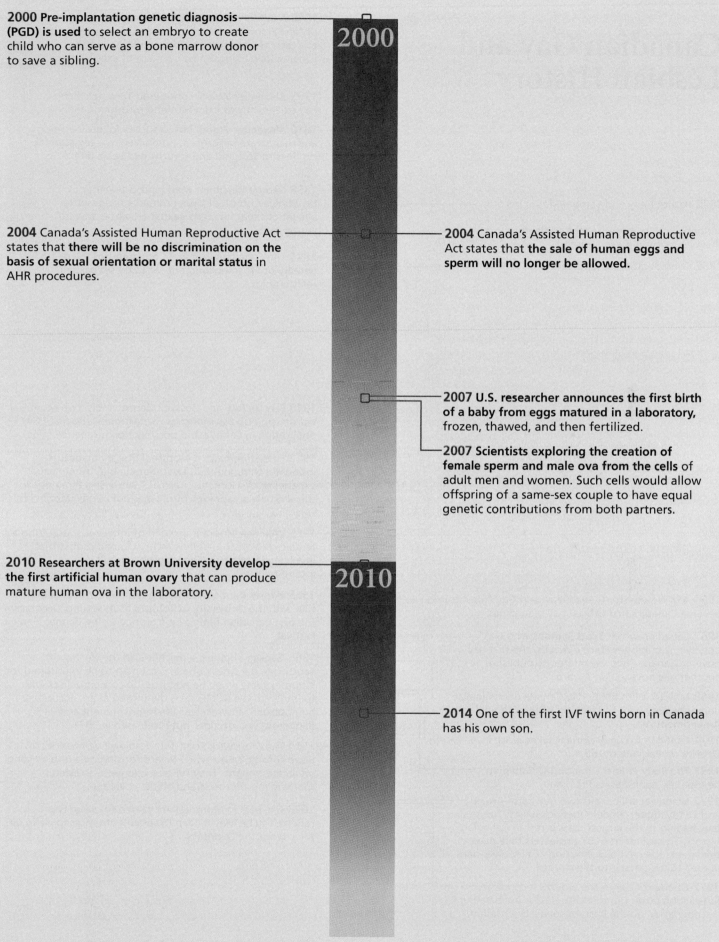

2000 Pre-implantation genetic diagnosis **(PGD) is used** to select an embryo to create child who can serve as a bone marrow donor to save a sibling.

2000

2004 Canada's Assisted Human Reproductive Act states that **there will be no discrimination on the basis of sexual orientation or marital status** in AHR procedures.

2004 Canada's Assisted Human Reproductive Act states that **the sale of human eggs and sperm will no longer be allowed.**

2007 U.S. researcher announces the first birth of a baby from eggs matured in a laboratory, frozen, thawed, and then fertilized.

2007 Scientists exploring the creation of female sperm and male ova from the cells of adult men and women. Such cells would allow offspring of a same-sex couple to have equal genetic contributions from both partners.

2010 Researchers at Brown University develop the first artificial human ovary that can produce mature human ova in the laboratory.

2010

2014 One of the first IVF twins born in Canada has his own son.

Canadian Gay and Lesbian History

1600

1648 A military drummer in Ville Marie (Montreal) of **New France** was tried for sodomy and sentenced to death. He was **freed** on the condition that he become New France's first permanent executioner.

1700

1793 Alexander Wood, considered Toronto's first gay citizen, moves from Scotland to Upper Canada.

1800

1810 Alexander Wood, now a successful businessman and magistrate in Toronto, is involved in a **sex scandal.** He flees to Scotland and returns two years later.

1842 Patrick Kelly and Samuel Moore become the first two men in Canada to be convicted of **sodomy.** Both were **sentenced to death** but their sentences were commuted.

1838 George Herchmer Markland, a member of the Legislative Council of Upper Canada, resigns after allegations that he made **sexual advances** toward young men.

1867 Confederation: Canada becomes a nation.

1841 The Canadian Criminal Code imposes the **death penalty or life imprisonment** for same-sex sexual relationships.

1900

1910

1918 Elsa Gidlow and **Roswell George Mills,** two Montreal writers, **publish** *Les Mouches Fantastiques,* the first LGBT publication in Canada and possibly North America.

1920

1930

1943 *First Statement,* a Montreal literary magazine, insinuates that poet **Patrick Anderson** has "some sexual experience of a kind not normal." Anderson threatens to sue and gets an apology but comes out as gay later in life.

1940

1950

1955 Willimae Moore is accused of indecently assaulting a female co-worker in Yellowknife in **Canada's first trial involving lesbianism.** The indecent assault was an attempted kiss.

1960

1964 *ASK Newsletter* (Vancouver) and *Gay* (Toronto) become Canada's first official gay magazines.

1965 *Winter Kept Us Warm,* a gay-themed independent film with the **University of Toronto** as its setting, becomes the **first Canadian film** to be screened at the Cannes Film Festival.

1967 Canadian writer **Scott Symons** who was openly gay publishes *Place d'Armes,* the first gay novel in Canada. Two years later he publishes another gay novel, *Civic Square.*

1965 George Klippart, a mechanic in the Northwest Territories, becomes Canada's last man to be imprisoned for homosexuality when he admitted to consensual sex with four men to the **RCMP.** He is diagnosed as an "incurable homosexual" and **receives life imprisonment** as a dangerous sex offender but is released in 1971.

1969 May 14: With **Bill C-150,** Canada decriminalizes homosexuality with the passing of the **Criminal Law Amendment Act.**

1970

1971 Canada's first gay protest takes place in Ottawa on Parliament Hill.

1974 The Brunswick Four (four lesbians) were asked to leave Toronto's Brunswick Tavern for singing a lesbian song on amateur night. They refused and were arrested, sparking much protest and media coverage.

1971 *The Body Politic,* a major gay Canadian newspaper, publishes its first issue.

1977 Montreal police raid two gay bars—**Truxx** and Le Mystique—under Quebec's bawdy house law leading to the largest mass arrest in Canadian history. Thousands of GLBT protesters take over the streets the next day shouting "Gaie, Gaie, dans la rue" (Gays, gays, into the streets).

1976 Gay bars in Montreal are raided for what was reported to be **Mayor Jean Drapeau's** attempts to clean up the city for the **Olympics.**

1977 Quebec becomes the world's second jurisdiction (after Denmark) to pass a law banning discrimination on the basis of sexual orientation.

1980

1981 Four bathhouses are raided in Toronto under **"Operation Soap."** Thousands protest in the streets once again.

1984 Pink Triangle Press launches the gay newspaper *Xtra!,* still published today.

1988 Svend Robinson becomes Canada's first elected Member of Parliament to come out as gay.

1989 Joe Rose, a gay teenager, is targeted by a gang on a Montreal bus, taunted for having pink hair, and **stabbed to death.** The gay community mobilizes and protests.

1990 Chris Lea wins leadership of the Green Party, becoming the first openly gay leader of a political party in Canada.

1990

1994 Legislation that would extend **spousal benefits** to same-sex partners is introduced in Ontario.

1996 Sexual orientation is added to the **Canadian Human Rights Act.**

1998 Glenn Murray is elected in Winnipeg, becoming Canada's first openly gay mayor of a major city.

2000

2001 PrideVision, the world's first LGBT-specific television channel, is launched.

2002 In *Marc Hall v. Durham Catholic School Board,* the Supreme Court of Canada orders the School Board to allow Marc Hall to bring a same-sex date to his high school prom.

2001 Joe Clark marches as the grand marshal of **Calgary Pride,** becoming the first former prime minister to do so in that capacity.

2005 Same-sex marriage becomes legally recognized in Canada.

2003 The Court of Appeal for Ontario rules in *Halpern v. Canada* that the definition of marriage as between one man and one woman violates the **Canadian Charter of Rights and Freedoms.** The decision immediately **legalizes same-sex marriage in Ontario.**

2005 In Toronto, **Bill Blair** becomes the first chief of police to participate in the gay pride parade.

2005 A statue honouring **Alexander Wood** as Canada's first gay citizen is erected in Toronto's gay neighbourhood at a cost of **$200 000.**

2010

2013 Kathleen Wynne wins the leadership of the **Ontario Liberal Party,** becoming both Ontario's first female premier and Canada's first openly lesbian first minister.

Same-Sex Unions around the Globe

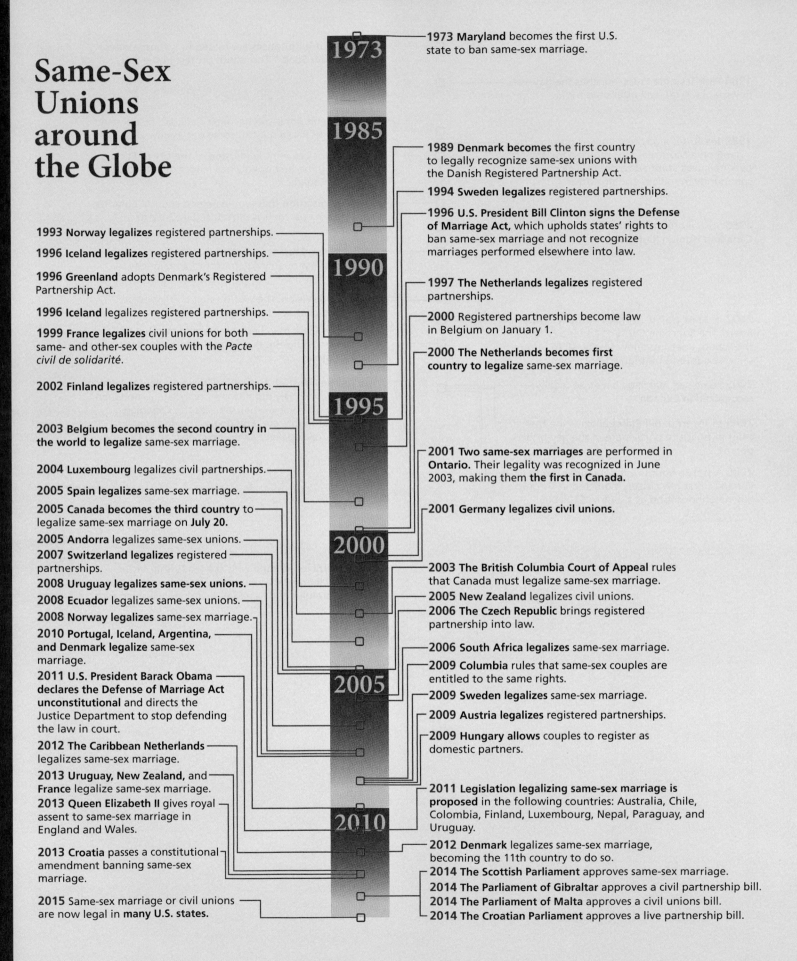

1973 **Maryland** becomes the first U.S. state to ban same-sex marriage.

1989 **Denmark becomes** the first country to legally recognize same-sex unions with the Danish Registered Partnership Act.

1994 **Sweden legalizes** registered partnerships.

1996 **U.S. President Bill Clinton signs the Defense of Marriage Act,** which upholds states' rights to ban same-sex marriage and not recognize marriages performed elsewhere into law.

1993 **Norway legalizes** registered partnerships.

1996 **Iceland legalizes** registered partnerships.

1996 **Greenland** adopts Denmark's Registered Partnership Act.

1996 **Iceland** legalizes registered partnerships.

1999 **France legalizes** civil unions for both same- and other-sex couples with the *Pacte civil de solidarité.*

1997 **The Netherlands legalizes** registered partnerships.

2000 Registered partnerships become law in Belgium on January 1.

2000 **The Netherlands becomes first country to legalize** same-sex marriage.

2002 **Finland legalizes** registered partnerships.

2003 **Belgium becomes the second country in the world to legalize** same-sex marriage.

2004 **Luxembourg** legalizes civil partnerships.

2005 **Spain legalizes** same-sex marriage.

2005 **Canada becomes the third country** to legalize same-sex marriage on **July 20.**

2005 **Andorra** legalizes same-sex unions.

2007 **Switzerland legalizes** registered partnerships.

2008 **Uruguay legalizes same-sex unions.**

2008 **Ecuador** legalizes same-sex unions.

2008 **Norway legalizes** same-sex marriage.

2010 **Portugal, Iceland, Argentina, and Denmark legalize** same-sex marriage.

2011 **U.S. President Barack Obama declares the Defense of Marriage Act unconstitutional** and directs the Justice Department to stop defending the law in court.

2012 **The Caribbean Netherlands** legalizes same-sex marriage.

2013 **Uruguay, New Zealand,** and **France** legalize same-sex marriage.

2013 **Queen Elizabeth II** gives royal assent to same-sex marriage in England and Wales.

2013 **Croatia** passes a constitutional amendment banning same-sex marriage.

2015 Same-sex marriage or civil unions are now legal in **many U.S. states.**

2001 **Two same-sex marriages** are performed in **Ontario.** Their legality was recognized in June 2003, making them **the first in Canada.**

2001 **Germany legalizes** civil unions.

2003 **The British Columbia Court of Appeal** rules that Canada must legalize same-sex marriage.

2005 **New Zealand** legalizes civil unions.

2006 **The Czech Republic** brings registered partnership into law.

2006 **South Africa legalizes** same-sex marriage.

2009 **Columbia** rules that same-sex couples are entitled to the same rights.

2009 **Sweden legalizes** same-sex marriage.

2009 **Austria legalizes** registered partnerships.

2009 **Hungary allows** couples to register as domestic partners.

2011 **Legislation legalizing same-sex marriage is proposed** in the following countries: Australia, Chile, Colombia, Finland, Luxembourg, Nepal, Paraguay, and Uruguay.

2012 **Denmark** legalizes same-sex marriage, becoming the 11th country to do so.

2014 **The Scottish Parliament** approves same-sex marriage.

2014 **The Parliament of Gibraltar** approves a civil partnership bill.

2014 **The Parliament of Malta** approves a civil unions bill.

2014 **The Croatian Parliament** approves a live partnership bill.

References

Aaronson, I., & Aaronson, A. (2010). How should we classify intersex disorders? *Journal of Pediatric Urology, 6*(5), 443–446.

Abbey, A., Zawacki, T., & Buck, P.O. (2005). The effects of past sexual assault perpetration and alcohol consumption on men's reactions to women's mixed signals. *Journal of Social & Clinical Psychology, 24*(2), 129–155.

Abboud, L.N., & Liamputtong, P. (2003). Pregnancy loss: What it means to women who miscarry and their partners. *Social Work in Health Care, 36*(3), 37–62.

Abdel-Hamid, I.A., & Saleh, E.S. (2011). Primary lifelong delayed ejaculation: Characteristics and response to bupropion. *Journal of Sexual Medicine, 8*(6), 1772–1779.

Abel, G., Becker, J., & Skinner, L. (1980). Aggressive behavior and sex. *Psychiatric Clinics of North America, 3*, 133–135.

Abma, J.C., Martinez, G.M., & Copen, C.E. (2010). Teenagers in the United States: Sexual activity, contraceptive use, and childbearing, National Survey of Family Growth 2006–2008. National Center for Health Statistics. *Vital Health Statistics, 23*(30), 1–47.

Aboriginal Affairs and Northern Development Canada. (2013). Aboriginal Demographics From the 2011 National Household Survey, May. Retrieved from https://www.aadnc-aandc.gc.ca/DAM/DAM-INTER-HQ-AI/STAGING/texte-text/abo_demo2013_1370443844970_eng.pdf.

AbouZeid, A.A., Mousa, M.H., Soliman, H.A., Hamza, A.F., & Hay, S.A. (2011). Intra-abdominal testis: Histological alterations and significance of biopsy. *Journal of Urology, 185*(1), 269–274.

Ackerman, S. (2005). *When heroes love.* New York, NY: Columbia University Press.

Adair, L.S., & Gordon-Larsen, P. (2001). Maturational timing and overweight prevalence in U.S. adolescent girls. *American Journal of Public Health, 91*(4), 642–645.

Adam, B.D. (1987). *The rise of a gay and lesbian movement.* Boston, MA: Twayne.

Adams, H.E., Wright, L.W., Jr., & Lohr, B.A. (1996). Is homophobia associated with homosexual arousal? *Journal of Abnormal Psychology, 105*, 440–445.

Adams, K.M. (2003). Clergy sex abuse: A commentary on celibacy. *Sexual Addiction & Compulsivity, 10*(2–3), 91–92.

Adapted from HIV transmission: Guidelines for assessing risk (5th ed.). (2004). Toronto: Canadian AIDS Society.

Addo, W. (2010). Body mass index, weight gain during pregnancy and obstetric outcomes. *Ghana Medicine Journal, 44*(2), 64–69.

Adler, R.B., Rosenfeld, L.B., & Proctor, R.F. (2007). *Interplay: The process of interpersonal communication* (10th ed.). New York, NY: Oxford University Press.

Afifi, T., McManus, T., Steuber, K., & Coho, A. (2009). Verbal avoidance and dissatisfaction in intimate conflict situations. *Human Communication Research, 35*(3), 357.

African and Caribbean Council on HIV/AIDS in Ontario, The (ACCHO). (2006). HIV/AIDS Stigma, Denial, Fear and Discrimination. Retrieved from http://www.accho.ca/pdf/hiv_stigma_report.pdf.

African and Caribbean Council on HIV/AIDS in Ontario, The (ACCHO). (2013). Ontario HIV/AIDS Strategy for African, Caribbean and Black Communities 2013–2018. Retrieved from http://www.accho.ca/portals/3/documents/resources/acb_strategy_web_oct2013_en.pdf.

Agaleryan, A., & Rouleau, J-L. (2014). Paraphilic coercive disorder: An unresolved issue. *Archives of Sexual Behavior, 43*(7), 1253–1256.

Ahmetoglu, G., Swami, V., & Chamorro-Premuzic, T. (2010). The relationship between dimensions of love, personality, and relationship length. *Archives of Sexual Behavior, 39*(5), 1181–1190.

Ahrens, C.E. (2006). Being silenced: The impact of negative social reactions on the disclosure of rape. *American Journal of Community Psychology, 38*, 263–274.

AIDS: Understanding AIDS. (1989). Gouvernement du Quebec, Ministere de la Sante et des Services sociaux, Quebec, Que.

Ainsworth, M.D.S., Blehar, M.C., Waters, E., & Wall, S. (1978). *Patterns of attachment: A psychological study of the strange situation.* Hillsdale, NJ: Erlbaum.

Akand, M., Ozayar, A., Yaman, O., & Demirel C. (2007). Mechanical failure with malleable penile prosthesis. *Urology, 70*(5), 1007.

Akbag, M., & Imamoglu, S. (2010). The prediction of gender and attachment styles on shame, guilt, and loneliness. *Educational Sciences: Theory and Practice, 10*(2), 669–682.

Akers, A.Y., Gold, M.A., Bost, J.E., Adimora, A.A., Orr, D.P., & Fortenberry, J.D. (2011). Variation in sexual behaviors in a cohort of adolescent females: The role of personal, perceived peer, and perceived family attitudes. *Journal of Adolescent Health, 48*(1), 87–93.

Alan Guttmacher Institute. (2002). Facts in brief: Contraceptive use. Retrieved January 14, 2003, from http://www.agi-usa.org/pubs/fb_contr_use.html.

Alan Guttmacher Institute. (2008a, January). Facts in brief: Facts on contraceptive use. Retrieved July 20, 2008, from http://www.guttmacher.org/pubs/fb_contr_use.html.

Alanis, M.C., & Lucidi, R.S. (2004, May). Neonatal circumcision: A review of the world's oldest and most controversial operation. *Obstetrical & Gynecological Survey, 59*(5), 379–395.

Alanko, K., Santtila, P., Harlaar, N., Witting, K., Varjonen, M., Jern, P., Johansson, A., von der Pahlen, B., & Sandnabba, N.K. (2010). Common genetic effects of gender atypical behavior in childhood and sexual orientation in adulthood: A study of Finnish twins. *Archives of Sexual Behavior, 39*(1), 81–92.

Albada, K.F., Knapp, M.L., & Theune, K.E. (2002). Interaction appearance theory: Changing perceptions of physical attractiveness through social interaction. *Communication Theory, 12*, 8–40.

Albers, K. (2007). Comprehensive care in the prevention of ectopic pregnancy and associated negative outcomes. *Midwifery Today with International Midwife.* (84), 26–27, 67.

Albert, A., & Porter, J.R. (1988). Children's gender-role stereotypes: A sociological investigation of psychological models. *Sociological Forum, 3*, 184–210.

Albert, B. (2009). With one voice: A 2009 survey of adults and teens on parental influence, abstinence, contraception, and the increase in the teen birth rate. National Campaign to Prevent Teen Pregnancy. Retrieved January 24, 2011, from http://www.thenationalcampaign.org/resources/pdf/pubs/WOV_Lite_2009.pdf.

Albert, R.T., Elwell, S.L., & Idelson, S. (2001). *Lesbian rabbis: The first generation.* Piscataway, NJ: Rutgers University Press.

Alberta grants new birth certificate to transgender boy. (2014). Retrieved Novmber 1, 2014, from http://www.thestar.com/news/canada/2014/06/16/alberta_grants_new_birth_certificate_to_transgender_boy.html.

Alexander, C.J., Sipski, M.L., & Findley, T.W. (1993). Sexual activities, desire, and satisfaction in males pre- and post-SCI. *Archives of Sexual Behavior, 22,* 217–228.

Alexander, M., & Rosen, R. (2008). Spinal cord injuries and orgasm: A review. *Journal of Sex and Marital Therapy, 24,* 308–324.

Alexander, M.S., Brackett, N.L., Bodner, D., Elliott, S., Jackson, A., Sonksen, J.; National Institute on Disability and Rehabilitation Research. (2009). Measurement of sexual functioning after spinal cord injury: Preferred instruments. *Journal of Spinal Cord Medicine, 32*(3), 226–236.

Alexander, M.S., Rosen, R.C., Steinberg, S., Symonds, T., Haughie, S., & Hultling, C. (2011). Sildenafil in women with sexual arousal disorder following spinal cord injury. *Spinal Cord, 49*(2), 273–279.

Alexandre, B., Lemaire, A., Desvaux, P., & Amar, E. (2007). Intracavernous injections of prostaglandin E1 for erectile dysfunction: Patient satisfaction and quality of sex life on long-term treatment. *Journal of Sexual Medicine, 4,* 426–431.

Alkhuja, S., Mnekel, R., Patel, B., & Ibrahimbacha, A. (2001). Stidor and difficult airway in an AIDS patient. *AIDS Patient Care and Sexually Transmitted Diseases, 15*(6), 293–295.

Allan, C., Forbes, E., Strauss, B., & McLachlan, R. (2008). Testosterone therapy increases sexual desire in ageing men with low-normal testosterone levels and symptoms of androgen deficiency. *International Journal of Impotence Research, 20,* 396–401.

Allen, C., Bowdin, S., Harrison, R., Sutcliffe, A., Brueton, L., Kirby, G., et al. (2008, June 3). Pregnancy and perinatal outcomes after assisted reproduction: A comparative study. *Irish Journal of Medical Science, 177*(3), 233–241.

Allen, D.J., & Oleson, T. (1999). Shame and internalized homophobia in gay men. *Journal of Homosexuality, 37*(3), 33–34.

Allen, P.L. (2000). *The wages of sin: Sex and disease, past and present.* Chicago: University of Chicago Press.

Allyn, D. (1996). Private acts—public policy: Alfred Kinsey, the American Law Institute and the privatization of American sexual morality. *Journal of American Studies, 30,* 405–428.

Allyn, D. (2000). *Make love not war: The sexual revolution: An unfettered history.* Boston, MA: Little, Brown.

Almeida, O.P., Alfonso, H., Flicker, L., Hankey, G.J., & Norman, P.E. (2012). Cardiovascular disease, depression and mortality: The Health in Men Study. *American Journal of Geriatric Psychiatry, 20*(5), 433–440.

Almosawa, S. (2013). No place for gays in Yemen. Inter Press Service News Agency. Retrieved from http://www.ipsnews.net/2013/08/no-place-for-gays-in-yemen/.

Aloni, M., & Bernieri, F.J. (2004). Is love blind? The effects of experience and infatuation on the perception of love. *Journal of Nonverbal Behavior, 28*(4), 287–295.

Al-Saleh, N. (2011). Bilateral ductal carcinoma in situ in a male breast: A case report. *Gulf Journal of Oncology, 1*(9), 68–72.

Al-Shawaf, T., Zosmer, A., Dirnfeld, M., & Grudzinskas, G. (2005). Safety of drugs used in assisted reproduction techniques. *Drug Safety, 28*(6), 513–528.

Althuis, M.D., Brogan, D.D., Coates, R.J., Daling J.R., Gammon M.D., Malone K.E., et al. (2003). Breast cancers among very young premenopausal women (United States). *Cancer Causes and Control, 14,* 151–160.

Altman, C. (2000). Gay and lesbian seniors: Unique challenges of coming out in later life. *SIECUS Report, 4,* 14.

Altman, D. (1986). *AIDS in the mind of America.* New York, NY: Anchor Press, Doubleday.

Altman, D. (1987). *AIDS in the minds of America.* Garden City, NY: Anchor Press, Doubleday.

Altman, D. (1997). Global gaze/global gays. *GLQ: A Journal of Lesbian and Gay Studies, 3*(4), 417–436.

Altman, L. (1981). Rare cancer seen in 41 homosexuals. *New York Times,* July 3, p. A-20.

Amador, J., Charles, T., Tait, J., & Helm, H. (2005). Sex and generational differences in desired characteristics in mate selection. *Psychological Reports, 96*(1), 19–25.

Amanpour, C. (2006). World fails to save Africa's AIDS orphans: Africa's HIV-infected children also ignored. *CNN Online.* Retrieved November 3, 2008 from http://www.cnn.com/2006/WORLD/africa/07/17/amanpour.africa.btsc/index.html.

Amato, P., & DeBoer, D. (2001). The transmission of marital instability across generations: Relationship skills or commitment to marriage? *Journal of Marriage and the Family, 63,* 1038–1051.

Amato, P.R., & Hohmann-Marriott, B. (2007). A comparison of high- and low-distress marriages that end in divorce. *Journal of Marriage and Family, 69,* 621–639.

Ambady, N., Koo, J., Lee, F., & Rosenthal, R. (1996). More than words: Linguistic and non-linguistic politeness in two cultures. *Journal of Personality and Social Psychology, 70,* 996–1011.

American Academy of Pediatrics Task Force on Circumcision. (2012). Male circumcision. *Pediatrics, 130*(3), 756–785.

American Cancer Society. (2007a). *How to perform a breast self exam.* Retrieved March 22, 2008, from http://www.cancer.org/docroot/CRI/content/CRI_2_6x_How_to_perform_a_breast_self_exam_5.asp.

American Cancer Society. (2007b). Overview: Prostate Cancer. Retrieved October 15, 2008, from http://www.cancer.org/docroot/CRI/CRI_2_1x.asp?dt=36.

American Cancer Society. (2010). *Cancer: Facts and figures, 2010.* Atlanta, GA: American Cancer Society. Retrieved January 5, 2011, from http://www.cancer.org/acs/groups/content/@epidemiologysurveilance/documents/document/acspc-026238.pdf.

American Cancer Society. (2011). *Breast cancer in men.* Retrieved April 19, 2011, from http://www.cancer.org/acs/groups/cid/documents/webcontent/003091-pdf.pdf.

American Psychiatric Association. (1994). *Diagnostic and statistical manual of mental disorders* (4th ed.). Washington, DC: Author.

American Psychiatric Association. (1998). *Media information: Position statement on hate crimes.* Retrieved October 4, 2008, from http://www.apa.org/releases/hate.html.

American Psychiatric Association. (2000). *Diagnostic and statistical manual of mental disorders* (4th ed., Text. Rev.). Washington, DC: Author.

American Psychiatric Association. (2013). *Diagnostic and statistical manual of mental disorders* (5th ed). Washington, DC: American Psychiatric Association.

American Psychiatric Association. (2013b). Paraphilic Disorders. Retrieved from http://www.dsm5.org/Documents/Paraphilic%20Disorders%20Fact%20Sheet.pdf.

American Psychological Association. (2005). Lesbian and gay parenting. Committee on Lesbian, Gay, and Bisexual Concerns. Retrieved September 1, 2008, from http://apa.org/pi/lgbc/publications/lgpar-enting.pdf.

Amir, M. (1971). *Patterns in forcible rape.* Chicago: University of Chicago Press.

Amis, D. (2007). Care practice #1: Labor begins on its own. *Journal of Perinatal Education, 16,* 16–20.

An, G., Huang, T.H., Wang, D.G., Xie, Q.D., Ma, L., & Chen, D.Y. (2009). In vitro and in vivo studies evaluating recombinant plasmid pCXN2-mIzumo as a potential immunocontraceptive antigen. *American Journal of Reproductive Immunology, 61*(3), 227–235.

Anderson, F.D., Gibbons, W., & Portman, D. (2006). Long-term safety of an extended-cycle oral contraceptive (Seasonale): A 2-year multimember open-label extension trial. *American Journal of Obstetrics and Gynecology, 195,* 92–96.

Anderson, P.B., & Savage, J.S. (2005). Social, legal, and institutional context of heterosexual aggression by college women. *Trauma, Violence, & Abuse, 6*(2), 130–140.

Andrews, G., Skinner, D., & Zuma, K. (2006). Epidemiology of health and vulnerability among children orphaned and made vulnerable by HIV/AIDS in sub-Saharan Africa. *AIDS Care, 18*(3), 269–276.

Angelides, S. (2007). Subjectivity under erasure: Adolescent sexuality, gender, and teacher-student sex. *Journal of Men's Studies, 15*(3), 347–360.

Angier, N. (1999). *Woman: An intimate geography.* New York, NY: Anchor Books.

Ankum, W.M., Hajenius, P.J., Schrevel, L.S., & Van der Veen, F. (1996). Management of suspected ectopic pregnancy. Impact of new diagnostic tools in 686 consecutive cases. *Journal of Reproductive Medicine, 41*(10), 724–728.

Anonymous. (1959). *Streetwalker.* New York, NY: Gramercy Publishing Company.

Antheunis, M., Valkenburg, P.M., & Peter, J. (2007). Computer-mediated communication and interpersonal attraction: An experimental test of two explanatory hypotheses. *CyberPsychology & Behavior, 10*, 831–836.

Apfel, R.J., & Handel, M.H. (1993). *Madness and loss of motherhood.* Washington, DC: American Psychiatric Press.

Arcuri, A. (2014). Dyadic perfectionism, communication patterns and relationship quality in couples. *Dissertation Abstracts International: Section B: The Sciences and Engineering*, Vol 75(2-B)(E).

Aries, E. (1996). *Men and women in interaction: Reconsidering the differences.* New York, NY: Oxford University Press.

Aries, P. (1962). *Centuries of childhood: A social history of family life.* New York, NY: Vintage Books.

Armour, B.S., Wolf, L., Mitra, M., Brieding, M. (2008). Differences in intimate partner violence among women with and without a disability. American Public Health Association's 136th Annual Meeting, San Diego, CA. October 27. Retrieved November 14, 2008, from http://apha.confex.com/apha/136am/webprogram/Paper182004.html.

Armstrong GL, Schillinger J, Markowitz L, et al. (2001). Incidence of herpes simplex virus type 2 infection in the United States. *American Journal of Epidemiology, 153*, 912–920.

Armstrong, J. (2005). Making a break from Bountiful. *Globe & Mail.* April 9, A-7.

Aron, A., Fisher, H., Mashek, D, Strong, G., Li, H., & Brown, L. (2005). Reward, motivation and emotion systems associated with early-stage intense romantic love. *Journal of Neurophysiology, 94*(1), 327–337.

Arpino, C., Compagnone, E., Montanaro, M., Cacciatore, D., DeLuca, A., Cerulli, A., Di-Girolamo, S., & Curatoio, P. (2010). Pre-term birth and neurodevelopmental outcome: A review. *Child's Nervous System, 26*(9), 1139–1149.

Arrington-Sanders, R., Dyson, J., & Ellen, J. (2007). STDs in adolescents. In J. Klausner & E. Hook (Eds.), *Current diagnosis and treatment of STDs* (pp. 160–166). New York, NY: McGraw-Hill.

Arroba, A. (2004). Costa Rica. In R.T. Francoeur & R.J. Noonan (Eds.), *The Continuum international encyclopedia of sexuality* (pp. 227–240). New York/London: Continuum International.

Atanackovic, G., Wolpin, J., & Koren, G. (2001). Determinants of the need for hospital care among women with nausea and vomiting of pregnancy. *Clinical and Investigative Medicine, 24*(2), 90–94.

Aterburn, S. (1991). *When sex becomes an addiction.* Colorado Springs, CO: Focus on the Family.

Athenstaedt, U., Haas, E., & Schwab, S. (2004). Gender role self-concept and gender-typed communication behavior in mixed-sex and same-sex dyads. *Sex Roles, 50*(1–2), 37–52.

Atta, I., Ibrahim, M., Parkash, A., Lone, S.W., Khan, Y.N., & Raza, J. (2014). Etiological diagnosis of undervirilized male/XY disorder of sex development. *Journal of the College of Physicians and Surgeons Pakistan, 24*(10), 714–718.

Aust, T.R., & Lewis-Jones, D.I. (2004). Retrograde ejaculation and male infertility. *Hospital Medicine, 65*(6), 361–364.

Auster, C.J., & Leone, J.M. (2001). Late adolescents' perspectives on marital rape. *Adolescence, 36*, 141–152.

Auster, C.J., & Ohm, S.C. (2000). Masculinity and femininity in contemporary American Society. *Sex Roles, 43*(7–8), 499–528.

Austoni, E., Colombo, F., Romano, A.L., Guarneri, A., Goumas, I.K., & Cazzaniga, A. (2005). Soft prosthesis implant and relaxing albugineal incision with saphenous grafting for surgical therapy of Peyronie's disease. *European Urology, 47*(2), 223–230.

Aveline, D. (2000). "My Son, My Son!" How parents adapt to having a gay son. *Dissertation Abstracts International. Section A: Humanities & Social Sciences, 60*(11), 4195.

Aveline, D. (2006). "Did I Have Blinders on or What?": Retrospective sense making by parents of gay sons recalling their sons' earlier years. *Journal of Family Issues, 27*(6), 777–802.

Aveline, D. (2010). Heteroracial Preferences of Gay Asian and White Men and their Reported Rationales. Presented to the 32nd Annual Guelph Sexuality Conference, June, 2010.

Aveline, D.T. (1995). A typology of perceived HIV/AIDS risk-reduction strategies used by men who "cruise" other men for anonymous sex. *The Journal of Sex Research, 32*(3), 201.

Avendano, C., Mata, A., Sanchez Sarmiento, C.A., & Doncel, G.F. (2012). Use of laptop computers connected to internet through Wi-Fi decreases human sperm motility and increases sperm DNA fragmentation. *Fertility and Sterility, 97*, 39–45.

Azadzoi, K.M., & Goldstein, I. (1992). Erectile dysfunction due to atherosclerotic vascular disease: the development of an animal model. *Journal of Urology, 147*(6), 1675–1681.

Azam, S. (2000). What's behind retro virginity? The Toronto Star Life Story. Retrieved December 29, 2002, from http://www.psurg.com/star2000.html.

Azfar, F. (2012). Genealogy of an execution: The Sodomite, the Bishop, and the Anomaly of 1726. *Journal of British Studies, 51*(3), 568–593.

Azoulay, D. (2000). *Only the lonely: Finding romance in the personal columns of Canada's Western Home Monthly 1905–1924.* Calgary, AB: Fifth House Ltd.

BabyCenter. (2015). Screening for Down Syndrome. Retrieved February 3, 2015 from, http://www.babycenter.ca/a1487/screening-for-down-syndrome.

Back, M., Stopfer, J., Vazire, S., Gaddis, S., Schmukle, B., & Gosling, S. (2010). Facebook profiles reflect actual personality, not self-idealization. *Psychological Science, 21*(3), 372–374.

Backhouse, C. (1985). Nineteenth-century Canadian prostitution law: Reflection of a discriminatory society. *Social History, 18*(35), 387–423.

Bacon, C.G., Mittleman, M.A., Kawachi, I., et al. (2003). Sexual function in men older than 50 years of age: Results from the health professionals follow-up study. *Annals of Internal Medicine, 139*, 161–168.

Badawy Z.S., Chohan K.R., Whyte D.A., Penefsky H.S., Brown O.M., & Souid A.K. (2008). Cannabinoids inhibit the respiration of human sperm. *Fertility and Sterility.* Retrieved October 13, 2008, from http://www.fertstert.org/article/S0015-0282(08)00750-4/abstract.

Bagemihl, B. (1999). *Biological exuberance: Animal homosexuality and natural diversity.* New York, NY: St. Martin's Press.

Bagley, D. (2005). Personal communication.

Bailey, A., & Hurd, P. (2005). Finger length ratio correlates with physical aggression in men but not in women. *Biological Psychology, 68*(3), 215–222.

Bailey, B.P., Gurak, L.J., & Konstan, J.A. (2003). Trust in cyberspace. In J. Ratner (Ed.),

Human factors and Web development (2nd ed., pp. 311–321). Mahwah, NJ: Erlbaum.

Bailey, J.M., & Pillard, R.C. (1993). A genetic study of male sexual orientation. *Archives of General Psychiatry 50*(3), 240–241.

Bailey, J.M., & Pillard, R.C. (1995). Genetics of human sexual orientation. *Annual Review of Sex Research, 6,* 126–150.

Bailey, R., Egesah, O., & Rosenberg, S. (2008). Male circumcision for HIV prevention: A prospective study of complications in clinical and traditional settings in Bungoma, Kenya. *Bulletin of the World Health Organization, 86,* 669–677.

Baily, D. (1968). Sexual foreplay: Do unto others. *Rational Living, 3*(1), 24–28.

Bain, J. (2001). Testosterone replacement therapy for aging men. *Canadian Family Physician, 47,* 91–97.

Baker, S.C., & MacIntyre, P.D. (2003). The role of gender and immersion in communication and second language orientations. *Language Learning,* 53(Suppl. 1), 65–96.

Bala, N. (2009). Why Canada's prohibition of polygamy is constitutionally valid and sound social policy. *Canadian Journal of Family Law, 25*(2), 165–221.

Balaban, B., Yakin, K., Alatas, C., Oktem, O., Isiklar, A., & Urman, B. (2011). Clinical outcome of intracytoplasmic injection of spermatozoa morphologically selected under high magnification: A prospective randomized study. *Reproductive Biomedicine Online, 22*(5), 472–476. Retrieved February 25, 2011, from http://www.ncbi.nlm.nih.gov/pubmed/21324747.

Baladerian, N.J. (1991). Sexual abuse of people with developmental disabilities. *Sexuality and Disability, 9,* 323–335.

Balikci, A. (1963). *The Netsilik Eskimo.* New York, NY: Natural History Press.

Ball, H. (2005). Sexual offending on elderly women: A review. *Journal of Forensic Psychiatry & Psychology, 16*(1), 127–138.

Ball, R.A. (2012). Changing images of deviance: Nineteenth-century Canadian anti-prostitution movements. *Deviant Behavior, 33,* 26–39.

Balone, R. (2012). The debate about paraphilic coercive disorder is mostly ideological and going nowhere. *Archives of Sexual Behavior, 41*(3), 535–536.

Balsam, K., Rothblum, E., & Beauchaine, T. (2005). Victimization over the life span: A comparison of lesbian, gay, bisexual and heterosexual siblings. *Journal of Counseling and Clinical Psychology, 73,* 477–487.

Balsam, K.F., Beauchaine, T., Rothblum, E., & Solomon, S. (2008). Three-year followup of same-sex couples who had civil unions in Vermont, same-sex couples not in civil unions, and heterosexual married couples. *Developmental Psychology, 44,* 101–116.

Bancroft, J. (2004). Alfred C. Kinsey and the politics of sex research. *Annual Review of Sex Research, 15,* 1–39.

Bancroft, J., Herbenick, D., Barnes, T., Hallam-Jones, R., Wylie, K., & Janssen, E. (2005). The relevance of the dual control model to male sexual dysfunction: The Kinsey Institute/BASRT collaborative project. *Sexual & Relationship Therapy, 20*(1), 13–30.

Bancroft, J., & Vukadinovic, Z. (2004). Sexual addiction, sexual compulsivity, or what? Toward a theoretical model. *Journal of Sex Research, 41*(3), 225–234.

Bandura, A. (1969). *Principles of behavior modification.* Austin, TX: Holt, Rinehart & Winston.

Banerjee, N. (2007, March 13). A place to turn when a newborn is fated to die. *New York Times.* Retrieved from http://www.nytimes.com/2007/03/13/health/13hospice.html.

Bang-Ping, J. (2009). Sexual dysfunction in men who abuse illicit drugs: A preliminary report. *The Journal of Sexual Medicine, 6*(4), 1072–1080.

Baptista, M., & Ramalho-Santos, J. (2009). Spermicides, microbicides and antiviral agents: Recent advances in the development of novel multi-functional compounds. *Mini Reviews in Medicinal Chemistry, 9*(13), 1556–1567.

Barak, A. (2005). Sexual harassment on the Internet. *Social Science Computer Review, 23*(1), 77–92.

Barbach, L. (1982). *For each other: Sharing sexual intimacy.* New York, NY: Penguin Group.

Bardeguez, A., Lindsey, J., Shannon, M., Tuomala, R., Cohn, S., Smith, E., et al. (2008). Adherence to antiretrovirals among US women during and after pregnancy. *Journal of Acquired Immune Deficiency Syndrome, 48,* 408–417.

Bardzell, J., & Bardzell, S. (2011). "Pleasure is your birthright: Digitally enabled designer sex toys as a case of third-wave HCI. Proceedings of the SIGCHI Conference on Human Factors in Computing Systems (pp. 257–266).

Barford, V. (2008, February, 25). Iran's "diagnosed transsexuals." BBC News. Retrieved December 20, 2010, from http://news.bbc.co.uk/2/hi/7259057.stm.

Barker, D.J. (1997). Maternal nutrition, fetal nutrition, and disease in later life. *Nutrition, 13*(9), 807–813.

Barner, J.M. (2003). Sexual fantasies, attitudes, and beliefs: The role of self-report sexual aggression for males and females. *Dissertation Abstracts International, 64*(4-B), 1887 (#0419–4217).

Barnes, R., Josefowitz, N., & Cole, E. (2006). Residential schools: Impact on Aboriginal students' academic and cognitive development. *Canadian Journal of Psychology, 21*(1–2), 18–32.

Baron, N.S. (2004). See you online: Gender issues in college student use of instant messaging. *Journal of Language & Social Psychology, 23*(4), 397–423.

Barratt, C., Mansell, S., Beaton, C., Tardif, S., & Oxenham, S. (2011). Diagnostic tools in male infertily—the question of sperm dysfunction. *Asian Journal of Andrology, 13*(1), 53–58.

Barrow, R., Newman, L., & Douglas, J. (2008). Taking positive steps to address STD disparities for African-American communities. *Sexually Transmitted Diseases, 35*(12), S1–S3.

Barsotti, N., & Perelle, R. (2013). Vladimir Putin & homophobia in Russia. *Capital Xtra* (Ottawa), *262,* 14.

Barth, K.R., Cook, R.L., Downs, J.S., Switzer, G.E., & Fischoff, B. (2002). Social stigma and negative consequences: Factors that influence college students' decision to seek testing for STIs. *Journal of American College Health, 50*(4), 153–160.

Bartholomew, K., & Horowitz, L. (1991). Attachment styles among young adults: A test of a four-category model. *Journal of Personality and Social Psychology, 61,* 226–244.

Bar-Yosef, Y., Greenstein, A., Beri, A., Lidawi, G., Matzkin, H., & Chen, J. (2007). Doral vein injuries observed during penile exploration for suspected penile fracture. *Journal of Sexual Medicine, 4,* 1142–1146.

Basaria, S., Coviello, A., Travison, T., Storer, T., Farwell, W., Jette, A.M., et al. (2010). Adverse events associated with testosterone administration. *New England Journal of Medicine, 363,* 109–122.

Basow, S., & Minieri, A. (2011). "You owe me": Effects of date cost, who pays, participant gender, and rape myth beliefs on perceptions of rape. *Journal of Interpersonal Violence, 26*(3), 479–497.

Bass, J. (2013). Plugged In: Sexual Fetish Communities 1970s to the Present. Retrieved August 12, 2014, from http://kinseyconfidential.org/sexual-fetish-communities-internet/.

Bassett, B., Bourbonnais, V., & McDowell, I. (2007). Living long and keeping well: Elderly Canadians account for success in aging. *Canadian Journal on Aging, 26,* 2, 113–126.

Bassil, N., & Morley, J.E. (2010). Late-life onset hypogonadism: A review. *Clinical Geriatric Medicine, 26*(2), 197–222.

Basson R. (2010). Testosterone therapy for reduced libido in women. (2010). *Therapeutic Advances in Endocrinology and Metabolism, 1*(4), 155–164.

Basson, R. (2000a). The female sexual response: A different model. *Journal of Sex and Marital Therapy, 26,* 51–65.

Basson, R. (2000b). The female sexual response revisited. *Journal of Obstetrics and Gynaecology of Canada, 22,* 383–387.

Basson, R., McInnes, R., Smith, M., Hodgson, G., & Koppiker, N. (2002). Efficacy and safety of sildenafil citrate in women with sexual dysfunction associated with female sexual arousal disorder. *Journal of Women's Health and Gender-Based Medicine, 11*(4), 367–377.

Batabyal, A.A. (2001). On the likelihood of finding the right partner in an arranged marriage. *Journal of Socio-Economics, 30*(3), 273–281.

Bates, K.G. (2010). MTV's 'teen mom' makes for teaching moments. National Public Radio. Retrieved August 10, 2010, from http://www.npr.org/templates/story/story.php?storyId5128626258.

Bauer, G.R., & Welles, S.L. (2001). Beyond assumptions of negligible risk: STDs and women who have sex with women. *American Journal of Public Health, 91*(8), 1282–1287.

Bauermeister, J.A., Johns, M.M., Sandfort, T.G., Eisenberg, A., Grossman, A.H., & D'Augelli, A.R. (2010). Relationship trajectories and psychological well-being among sexual minority youth. *Journal of Youth and Adolescence, 39*(10), 1148–1163.

Baumann, E.E. (1991). Negotiating respectability in ambiguous commerce: selling sex paraphernalia at home parties. *Canadian Review of Sociology & Anthropology, 28*(3), 376–392.

Baumeister, L.M., Flores, E., & Marin, B.V. (1995). Sex information given to Latina adolescents by parents. *Health Education Research, 10*(2), 233–239.

Baxter, J., & Hewitt, B. (2010). Pathways into marriage: Cohabitation and the domestic division of labor. *Journal of Family Issues, 31*(11), 1507–1529.

Bayer, R. (1981). *Homosexuality and American psychiatry: The politics of diagnosis.* New York, NY: Basic Books.

Bayer, R. (1987). *Homosexuality and American Psychiatry.* Princeton, NJ: Princeton University Press.

Baylin, A., Hernandez-Diaz, S., Siles, X., Kabagambe, E., & Campos, H. (2007). Triggers of nonfatal myocardial infarction in Costa Rica: Heavy physical exertion, sexual activity, and infection. *Annals of Epidemiology, 17,* 112–118.

BBC News. (2000). Cheeky anarchists in palace protest. June 3. Retrieved from http://news.bbc.co.uk/2/hi/uk_news/775725.stm.

BBC News. (2006). Dutch will allow paedophile group. Retrieved from http://news.bbc.co.uk/2/hi/europe/5187010.stm.

Beals, K.P., & Peplau, L.A. (2005). Identity support, identity devaluation, and well-being among lesbians. *Psychology of Women Quarterly, 29*(2), 140–148.

Bearak, B. (2009, September 22). Mixed verdict in S. African lesbian's murder trial. *New York Times.* Retrieved April 20, 2011, from http://www.nytimes.com/2009/09/23/world/africa/23safrica.html.

Bearman, P., & Bruckner, H. (2001). Promising the future: Virginity pledges and first intercourse. *American Journal of Sociology, 106*(4), 859–912.

Bearman, P., & Bruckner, H. (2005). After the promise: The STD consequences of adolescent virginity pledges, *Journal of Adolescent Health, 36*(4), 271–278.

Beaton, A.A., & Mellor, G. (2007). Direction of hair whorl and handedness. *Laterality, 12,* 295–301.

Beaudreau, S.A., Rideaux, T., & Zeiss, R.A. (2011). Clinical characteristics of older male military veterans seeking treatment for erectile dysfunction. *International Psychogeriatrics, 23*(1), 155–160.

Becker, J.V., et al. (1986). Level of postassault sexual functioning in rape and incest victims. *Archives of Sexual Behavior, 15,* 37–50.

Beckett, M.K., Elliott, M.N., Martino, S., Kanouse, D.E., Corona, R., Klein, D.J., & Schuster, M.A. (2010). Timing of parent and child communication about sexuality relative to children's sexual behaviors. *Pediatrics, 125*(1), 34–42.

Beeble, M., Sullivan, C., & Bybee, D. (2011). The impact of neighborhood factors on the well-being of survivors of intimate partner violence over time. *American Journal of Community Psychology, 47*(3–4), 287–306.

Beeby, S. (1992). Hundreds of civil servants fired in '60s gay witchhunt. *The Montreal Gazette.* April 24, pp. A1–A2.

Beech, A., Ward, T., & Fisher, D. (2006). The identification of sexual and violent motivations in men who assault women: Implication for treatment. *Journal of Interpersonal Violence, 21,* 1635.

Begley, S. (2010, July 2). The anti-lesbian drug. *Newsweek.* Retrieved November 16, 2010, from http://www.newsweek.com/2010/07/02/the-anti-lesbian-drug.html.

Begley, S. (2012). Insight: New doubts about prostate cancer vaccine Provenge. *Reuters U.S. Edition,* March 30.

Bell, A.P., Weinberg, M.S., & Hammersmith, S.K. (1981). *Sexual preference: Its development in men and women.* Bloomington: Indiana University Press.

Bella, A.J., & Shamloul, R. (2014). Psychotropics and sexual dysfunction. *Central European Journal of Urology, 66*(4), 466–471.

Bellino, S., Renocchio, M., Zizzo, M., Rocca, G., Bogetti, P., & Bogetto, F. (2010). Quality of life of patients who undergo breast reconstruction after mastectomy: Effects of personality characteristics. *Plastic Reconstructive Surgery, 127*(1), 10–17.

Belsky, J., Houts, R., & Fearon, R. (2010). Infant attachment security and the timing of puberty: Testing an avolutionary hypothesis. *Psychological Science, 21*(9), 1195–1201.

Bem, S.L. (1974). The measurement of psychological androgyny. *Journal of Consulting and Clinical Psychology, 42,* 155–162.

Bem, S.L. (1977). On the utility of alternative procedures for assessing psychological androgyny. *Journal of Consulting and Clinical Psychology, 45,* 196–205.

Bem, S.L. (1981). Gender schema theory: A cognitive account of sex-typing. *Psychological Review, 88,* 354–364.

Bendriss, N. (2008). Report on the Practice of Forced Marriage in Canada: Interviews with Frontline Workers: Exploratory Research Conducted in Montreal and Toronto in 2008. Presented to: Family, Children and Youth Section Department of Justice Canada. November.

Benevento, B.T., & Sipski, M.L. (2002). Neurogenic bladder, neurogenic bowel, and sexual dysfunction in people with spinal cord injury. *Physical Therapy, 82*(6), 601–612.

Benjamin, H., & Masters, R.E.L. (1964). *Prostitution and morality.* New York, NY: The Julian Press.

Bennett, J. (2009). Only you. And you. And you. *Newsweek.* Retrieved July 3, 2011, from http://www.newsweek.com/2009/07/28/only-you-and-you-and-you.html.

Benokraitis, N.V. (1993). *Marriages and families.* Englewood Cliffs, NJ: Prentice Hall.

Benson, A., Ost, L., Noble, M., & Laakin, M. (2009). Premature ejaculation. *Emedicine.* Retrieved March 25, 2010, from http://emedicine.medscape.com/article/435884-overview.

Ben-Zion, I., & Shiber, A. (2006). Heart to heart: Rehabilitation of sexuality in cardiac patients. *Harefuah, 145,* 350–351.

Berenbaum, S.A., & Snyder, E. (1995). Early hormonal influences on childhood sex-typed activity and playmate preferences. *Developmental Psychology, 31*(1), 31–43.

Bergen, R. (2006). Marital rape: New research and directions. National Sexual Violence Resource Center. Retrieved June 26, 2011, from http://new.vawnet.org/Assoc_Files_VAWnet/AR_MaritalRapeRevised.pdf.

Bergen, R., & Bukovec, P. (2006). Men and intimate partner rape: Characteristics of men who sexually abuse their partner. *Journal of Interpersonal Violence, 21,* 1375.

Berger, R.J., Searles, P., & Cottle, C.E. (1991). *Feminism and pornography*. New York, NY: Praeger.

Bergmark, K., Avall-Lundqvist, E., Dickman, P., Henningsohn, L., & Steineck, G. (1999). Vaginal changes and sexuality in women with a history of cervical cancer. *New England Journal of Medicine, 340,* 1383–1389.

Bergstrand, C., & Williams, B. (2000, October 10). Today's alternative marriage styles: The case of swingers. *Electronic Journal of Human Sexuality, 3*. Retrieved September 14, 2008, from http://www.ejhs.org/volume3/swing/body.htm.

Berkey, B.R., Perelman-Hall, T., & Kurdek, L.A. (1990). The multidimensional scale of sexuality. *Journal of Homosexuality, 19,* 67–87.

Berkow, R., Beers, M.H., Fletcher, A.J., & Bogin, R.M. (Eds). (2000). *Merck manual of medical information* (Home ed.). White-house Station, NJ: Merck & Co.

Berkowitz, D., & Marsiglio, W. (2007). Gay men: Negotiating procreative, father, and family identities. *Journal of Marriage and Family, 69,* 366–382.

Berkowitz, E. (2012). *Sex and punishment*. Berkeley, CA: Counterpoint.

Berman, J., Berman, L., Toler, S., Gill, J., Haughie, S., & the Sildenafil Study Group. (2003). Safety and efficacy of sildenafil citrate for the treatment of female sexual arousal disorder: A double-blind, placebo controlled study. *Journal of Urology, 170*(6 Pt. 1), 2333–2338.

Berner, W., & Briken, P. (2012). Pleasure seeking and the aspect of longing for an object in perversion: A neuropsychoanalytical perspective. *American Journal of Psychotherapy, 66*(2), 129–150.

Bernheimer, C. (1989). Manet's Olympia: The figuration of scandal. *Poetics Today, 10*(2), 255–277.

Bernstein, D.I., Earwood, J.D., Bravo, F.J., Cohen, G.H., Eisenberg, R.J., Clark, J.R., Fairman, J., & Cardin, R.D. (2011). Effects of herpes simplex virus type 2 glycoprotein vaccines and CLDC adjuvant on genital herpes infection in the guinea pig. *Vaccine, 29*(11), 2071–2078.

Bersamin, M.M., Fisher, D.A., Walker, S., Hill, D.L., & Grube, J.W. (1995). Defining virginity and abstinence: Adolescents' interpretations of sexual behaviors. *Journal of Adolescent Health, 41*(2), 182–188.

Bertholet, F.M. (2004). *Gardens of pleasure: Eroticism and art in China*. New York, NY: Prestel Publishing.

Besharov, D. (1988). *Protecting children from abuse and neglect: Policy and practices*. Springfield, IL: Charles C. Thomas.

Bessede, T., Massard, C., Albouy, B., Leborgne, S., Gross-Goupil, M., Droupy, S., Patard, J.J., Fizazi, K., & Escudier, B. (2011). Sexual life of male patients with advanced renal cancer treated with angiogenesis inhibitors. *Annals of Oncology, 22*(10), 2320-2324.

Bestard, A.D. (2008). Feederism: an exploratory study into the stigma of erotic weight gain. Masters Thesis, University of Waterloo, Departmento of Sociology.

Bestic, L. (2005). When a patch works. Retrieved August 30, 2005, from http://www.timesonline.co.uk/article/0,,8124-1716899,00.html.

Bettocchi, C., Palumbo, F., Spilotros, M., Lucarelli, G., Palazzo, S., Battaglia, M., Selvaggi, F., & Ditonno, P. (2010). Patient and partner satisfaction after AMS inflatable penile prosthesis implant. *Journal of Sexual Medicine, 7*(1 Pt 1), 304–309.

Bettocchi, C., Verze, P., Palumbo, F., Arcaniolo, D., & Mirone, V. (2008). Ejaculatory disorders: Pathophysiology and management. *Nature Clinical Practice Urology, 5*(2), 93–103.

Bhat, M. (2009). A feminist critique of the representation of women in films: Bollywood under the microscope. Conference Papers—American Society of Criminology. Annual Meeting, p1.

Bhide, A., Nama, V., Patel, S., & Kalu, E. (2010). Microbiology of cysts/abscesses of Bartholin's gland: Review of empirical antibiotic therapy against microbial culture. *Journal of Obstetrics and Gynecology, 30*(7), 701–703.

Bialik, C. (2007). Sorry you have gone over your limit of network friends. *Wall Street Journal*. Retrieved February 10, 2008, from http://online.wsj.com/article/SB119518271549595364.html?mod=googlenews_wsj.

Bialik, C. (2010a, October 8). Sex, and studying it, are complicated. *Wall Street Journal*. Retrieved October 10, 2010, from http://blogs.wsj.com/numbersguy/sex-and-studying-it-is-complicated-998/.

Bialik, C. (2010b). Research into human sexuality leaves a lot to be desired. *Wall Street Journal*, October 9, p. A2.

Bick, R.L., Maden, J., Heller, K.B., & Toofanian, A. (1998). Recurrent miscarriage: Causes, evaluation, and treatment. *Medscape Women's Health, 3*(3), 2.

Bieber, I., et al. (1962). *Homosexuality: A psychoanalytic study*. New York, NY: Basic Books.

Bigelow, B.J. (1977). Children's friendship expectations: A cognitive developmental study. *Child Development, 48,* 246–253.

Biglia, N., Moggio, G., Peano, E., Sgandurra, P., Ponzone, R., Nappi, R.E., & Sismondi, P. (2010). Effects of surgical and adjuvant therapies for breast cancer on sexuality, cognitive functions, and body weight. *Journal of Sexual Medicine, 7*(5), 1891–1900.

Bird, M.H. (2006). Sexual addiction and marriage and family therapy: Facilitating individual and relationship healing through couple therapy. *Journal of Marital and Family Therapy, 32*(3), 297–310.

Birdthistle, I., Floyd, S., Machingura, A., Mudziwapasi, N., Gregson, S., Glynn, J.R. (2008). From affected to infected? Orphanhood and HIV risk among female adolescents in urban Zimbabwe. *Epidemiology and Social AIDS, 22*(6), 759–766.

Birnbaum, G., Glaubman, H., & Mikulincer, M. (2001). Women's experience of heterosexual intercourse. *Journal of Sex Research, 38*(3), 191–194.

Biro, F., Galvez, M., Greenspan, L., Succop, P., Vangeepuram, N., Pinney, S., Teitelbaum, S., Windham, G., Kushi, L., & Wolff, M. (2010). Pubertal assessment method and baseline characteristics in a mixed longitudinal study of girls. *Pediatrics, 6*(11), 595.

Bish, C.L., Chu, S.Y., Shapiro-Mendoza, C., Sharma, A., & Blanck, H. (May 1, 2008). Trying to lose or maintain weight during pregnancy—United States, 2003. *Maternal and Child Health Journal*. Retrieved October 14, 2008, from http://www.springer-link.com/content/n76tk678r07j87v1/?p=13a04154744143e6be60537c74733c0d&pi=1.

Bittles, A.H., & Black, M.L. (2010a). Consanguineous marriage and human evolution. *Annual Review of Anthropology, 39*(1), 193–207.

Bittles, A.H., & Black, M.L. (2010b). Evolution in health and medicine Sackler colloquium: Consanguinity, human evolution, and complex diseases. *Proceedings of the National Academy of Science, 107*(Suppl 1), 1779–1786.

Bivona, J.M., & Critelli, J.W. (2009). The nature of women's rape fantasies: An analysis of prevalence, frequency, and contents. *Journal of Sex Research, 46,* 33–45.

Bivona, J.M., Critelli, J.W., & Clark, M.J. (2012). Women's rape fantasies: An empirical evaluation of the major explanations. *Archives of Sexual Behavior, 21,* 1107–1119.

Black, A., Yang, Q., Wu., Wen, S., Lalonde, A.B., Guilbert, E., & Fisher, W. (2009). Contraceptive use among Canadian women of reproductive age: Results of a national survey. *Journal of Obstetrics and Gynaecology Canada, 31*(7), 627-640.

Black, K., & Gold, D. (2008). Gender differences and socioeconomic status biases in judgments about blame in date rape scenarios. *Violence and Victims, 23*(1), 115–128.

Black, M., Shetty, A., & Bhattacharya, S. (2008). Obstetric outcomes subsequent to intrauterine death in the first pregnancy. *British Journal of Gynecology, 115,* 269–274.

Black, S.L., & Biron, C. (1982). Androstenol as a human pheromone: No effect on perceived physical attractiveness. *Behavioral & Neural Biology, 34*(3), 326–330.

Blackhouse, C. (2008). Canada's first capital "L" lesbian sexual assault trial: Yellowknife 1955." Conference Papers—Law & Society. 2008 Annual Meeting.

Blackhouse, C. (1985). Nineteenth-century Canadian prostitution law reflection of a discriminatory society. *Social History, 18*(36), 387–423.

Blackwood, E. (1983). "Sexuality and gender in certain Native American tribes: The case of cross-gender females." *Signs: Journal of Women in Culture & Society, 10*(1), 4–23.

Blackwood, E. (1994). Sexuality and gender in Native American tribes: The case of cross-gender females. In A.C. Herrmann & A.J. Stewart (Eds.), *Theorizing feminism: Parallel trends in the humanities and social sciences* (pp. 301–315). Boulder, CO: Westview Press.

Blair, A. (2000) Individuation, love styles and health-related quality of life among college students. *Dissertation Abstracts International,* University of Florida, #0–599–91381–9.

Blair, K.L., & Pukall, C.F. (2014). Can less be more? Comparing duration vs. frequency of sexual encounters in same-sex and mixed-sex relationships. *Canadian Journal of Human Sexuality, 23*(2), 123–136.

Blake, S.M., Ledsky, R., Lehman, T., Goodenow, C., Sawyer, R., & Hack, T. (2001). Preventing sexual risk behaviors among gay, lesbian, and bisexual adolescents: The benefits of gay-sensitive HIV instruction in schools. *American Journal of Public Health, 91,* 940–946.

Blakemore, J.E. (2003). Children's beliefs about violating gender norms: Boys shouldn't look like girls, and girls shouldn't act like boys. *Sex Roles, 48*(9–10), 411–419.

Blanchard, M.A., & Semoncho, J.E. (2006). Anthony Comstock and his adversaries: The mixed legacy of the battle for free speech. *Communication and Public Policy, 11,* 317–366.

Blanchard, R., & Klassen, P. (1997). H-Y antigen and homosexuality in men. *Journal of Theoretical Biology, 185*(3), 373–378.

Blanchard, R. (1997). Birth order and sibling sex ratio in homosexual versus heterosexual males and females. *Annual Review of Sex Research, 8,* 27–67.

Blanchard, R. (2004). Quantitative and theoretical analyses of the relation between older brothers and homosexuality in men. *Journal of Theoretical Biology, 230*(2), 173–187.

Blanchard, R. (2008). Review and theory off-handedness, birth order, and homosexuality in men. *Laterality, 13,* 51–70.

Blanchard, R., Cantor, J.M., Bogaert, A., Breedlove, S., & Ellis, L. (2006). Interaction of fraternal birth order and handedness in the development of male homosexuality. *Hormones & Behavior, 49,* 405–414.

Bleakley, A., Hennessey, M., & Fishbein, M. (2006). Public opinion on sex education in U.S. schools. *Archives of Pediatrics and Adolescent Medicine, 160,* 1151–1156.

Blell, M., Pollard, T., & Pearce, M. (2008). Predictors of age at menarche in the Newcastle Thousand Families Study. *Journal of Biosocial Science, 40,* 563–575.

Blow, A.J., & Hartnett, K. (2005). Infidelity in committed relationships: A methodological review. *Journal of Marital and Family Therapy, 31*(2), 183–216.

Blumer, H. (1969). *Symbolic interaction: Perspective and method.* Englewood Cliffs, NJ: Prentice Hall.

Blumstein, H. (2001). Bartholin gland disease. Retrieved September 9, 2002, from http://www.emedicine.com/emeg/topic54.htm.

Blumstein, P., & Schwartz, P. (1983). *American couples.* New York, NY: William Morrow.

Boardman, L.A., & Stockdale, C.K. (2009). Sexual pain. *Clinical Obstetrics and Gynecology, 52*(4), 682–690.

Bocklandt, S., & Vilain, E. (2007). Sex differences in brain and behavior: Hormones versus genes. *Advances in Genetics, 59,* 245–266.

Bodenmann, G., Meuwly, N., Bradbury, T., Gmelch, S., & Ledermann, T. (2010). Stress, anger, and verbal aggression in intimate relationships: Moderating effects of individual and dyadic coping. *Journal of Social and Personal Relationships, 27*(3), 408–424.

Boehmer, U. (2002). Twenty years of public health research: Inclusion of lesbian, gay, bisexual and transgender populations. *American Journal of Public Health, 92*(7), 1125–1131.

Boeke, A.J., van Bergen, J.E., Morre, S.A., & van Everdingen, J.J. (2005). The risk of pelvic inflammatory disease associated with urogenital infection with chlamydia trachomatis: Literature review. *Ned Tijdschr Geneeskd, 149*(16), 878–884.

Boeringer, S. (1999). Associations of rape-supportive attitudes with fraternal and athletic participation. *Violence Against Women, 5*(1), 81–90.

Bogaert, A. (1996). Volunteer bias in human sexuality research: Evidence for both sexuality and personality differences in males. *Archives of Sexual Behavior, 25*(2), 125–140.

Bogaert, A.F. (2004). Asexuality: Prevalence and associated factors in a national probability sample. *The Journal of Sex Research, 4*(3), 279–287.

Bogaert, A.F. (2005). Gender role/identity and sibling sex ratio in homosexual men. *Journal of Sex and Marital Therapy, 31,* 217–227.

Bogaert, A.F., & Skorska, M. (2011). Sexual orientation, fraternal birth order, and the maternal immune hypothesis: A review. *Frontiers in Neuroendocrinology, 32*(2), 247–254.

Bogaerts, S., Vanheule, S., Leeuw, F., & Desmet, M. (2006). Recalled parental bonding and personality disorders in a sample of exhibitionists: A comparative study. *Journal of Forensic Psychiatry & Psychology, 17*(4), 636–646.

Bogle, K., & Best, J. (2011). The role of television in spreading the "sex bracelet" urban legend. Conference Papers, American Sociological Association, Annual Meeting, p. 1771.

Bohm-Starke, N. (2010). Medical and physical predictors of localized provoked vulvodynia. *Acta Obstetrics and Gynecology Scandinavia, 89*(12), 1504–1510.

Bohring, C., & Krause, W. (2005). The role of antisperm antibodies during fertilization and for immunological infertility. *Chemical Immunology and Allergy, 88,* 15–26.

Boin, A.C., Nozoe, K.T., Polesel D.N., Andersen M.L., & Tufik S. (2014). The potential role of sleep in sexual dysfunction in patients with schizophrenia. *Schizophrenia Research, 154*(1–3), 126–127.

Bolton, M., van der Straten, A., & Cohen, C. (2008). Probiotics: Potential to prevent HIV and sexually transmitted infections in women. *Sexually Transmitted Diseases, 35*(3), 214–225.

Bonetti, A., Tirelli, F., Catapano, A., Dazzi, D., Dei Cas, A., Solito, F., et al. (2007). Side effects of anabolic androgenic steroids abuse. *International Journal of Sports Medicine, 29*(8), 679–687.

Bonomi, A., Anderson, M., Reid, R., Carrell, D., Fishman, P., Rivara, F., & Thompson, R. (2007). Intimate partner violence in older women. *The Gerontologist, 47,* 34–41.

Boomer, D.S. (1963). Speech disturbances and body movement in interviews. *Journal of Nervous and Mental Disease, 136,* 263–266.

Boon, S., & Alderson, K. (2009). A phenomenological study of women in same-sex relationships who were previously married to men. *Canadian Journal of Human Sexuality, 18*(4), 149–169.

Boonstra, H. (2005, May). Condoms, contraceptives and nonoxynol-9: Complex issues obscured by ideology. *The Guttmacher Report on Public Policy, 8*(2), pp. 4–7.

Boonstra, H., Gold, R., Richard, C., & Finer, L. (2006). *Abortion in women's lives.* New York, NY: Guttmacher Institute. Retrieved June 4, 2011, from http://www.guttmacher.org/pubs/2006/05/04/AiWL.pdf.

Borg, C., de Jong, P.J., & Schultz, W.W. (2010). Vaginismus and dyspareunia: Automatic vs. deliberate disgust responsivity. *Journal of Sexual Medicine, 7*(6), 2149–2157.

Borg, C., de Jong, P.J., & Weijmar Schultz, W. (2011). Vaginismus and dyspareunia: Relationship with general and sex-related moral standards. *Journal of Sexual Medicine, 8*(1), 223–231.

Borini, A., Cattoli, M., Bulletti, C., & Coticchio, G. (2008). Clinical efficiency of oocyte and embryo cryopreservation. *Annals of the New York Academy of Sciences, 1127,* 49–58.

Borisoff, J., Elliott, S., Hocaloski, S., & Birch, G. (2010). The development of a sensory substitution system for the sexual rehabilitation of men with chronic spinal cord injury. *Journal of Sexual Medicine, 7*(11), 3647–3658.

Born, K., Konklin, J., Tepper, J., & Okun, N. (2014). Pulling back the curtain on Canada's rising c-section rate. Retrieved February 5, 2015, from, http://healthydebate.ca/2014/05/topic/quality/c-section-variation.

Bornstein, D. (Ed.). (1979). *The feminist controversy of the Renaissance.* Delmar, NY: Scholars' Facsimiles & Reprints.

Boroughs, D.S. (2004). Female sexual abusers of children. *Children & Youth Services Review, 26*(5), 481–487.

Bos, H., & Gartrell, N. (2010). Adolescents of the USA National Longitudinal Lesbian Family Study: Can family characteristics counteract the negative effects of stigmatization? *Family Process, 49*(4), 559–572.

Bosello, R., Favaro, A., Zanetti, T., Soave, M., Vidotto, G., Huon, G., & Santanastaso, P. (2010). Tattoos and piercings in adolescents: Family conflicts and temperament. *Rivesta di Psichiatria, 45*(2), 102–106.

Boswell, J. (1980). *Christianity, social tolerance, and homosexuality: Gay people in western Europe from the beginning of the Christian era to the fourteenth century.* Chicago: The University of Chicago Press.

Bouchlariotou, S., Tsikouras, P., Dimitraki, M., Athanasiadis, A., Papoulidis, I., Maroulis, G., Liberis, A., & Liberis, V. (2011). Turner's syndrome and pregnancy: Has the 45, X/47, XXX mosaicism a different prognosis? *Journal of Maternal and Fetal Neonatal Medicine, 24*(5), 668–672.

Bounhoure, J., Galinier, M., Roncalli, J., Assoun, B., & Puel, J. (2008). Myocardial infarction and oral contraceptives. *Bulletin of the Academy of National Medicine, 192,* 569–579.

Bowlby, J. (1969). *Attachment and loss: Attachment.* New York, NY: Basic Books.

Bowler, A., Leon, C., & Lilley, T. (2013). "What shall we do with the young prostitute? reform her or neglect her?": Domestication as reform at the New York State Reformatory for Women at Bedford, 1901–1913. *Journal of Social History, 47*(2), 458–481.

Boyd, L. (2000). Morning sickness shields fetus from bugs and chemicals. *RN, 63*(8), 18–20.

Boyd, M., & Li, A. (2003). May-December: Canadians in age-discrepant relationships. Statistics Canada, Canadian Social Trends, Catalogue # 11–008.

Boyle, C., Berkowitz, G., & Kelsey, J. (1987). Epidemiology of premenstrual symptoms. *American Journal of Public Health, 77*(3), 349–350.

Bozkurt, I.H., Yonguc, T., Arslan, B., Kozacioglu, Z., Degirmenci, T., Polat, S., & Minareci, S. (2014). Spontaneous bilateral rod fracture of malleable penile prosthesis. *Canadian Urology Association Journal, 8,* 9–10.

Bradley, M.S. (2007). Girlfriends, wives, and strippers: Managing stigma in exotic dancer romantic relationships. *Deviant Behavior, 28*(4), 379–406.

Bradshaw, C., Kahn, A., & Saville, B. (2010). To hook up or date: Which gender benefits? *Sex Roles, 62*(9–10), 661–669.

Brandberg, Y., Sandelin, K., Erikson, S., Jurell, G., Liljegren, A., Lindblom, A., et al. (2008). Psychological reactions, quality of life, and body image after bilateral prophylactic mastectomy in women at high risk for breast cancer: A prospective 1-year follow-up study. *Journal of Clinical Oncology, 26,* 3943–3949.

Brandes, M., Hamilton, C.J., Bergevoet, K.A., de Bruin, J.P., Nelen, W.L., & Kremer, J.A. (2010). Origin of multiple pregnancies in a subfertile population. *Acta Obstetricia et Gynecologica Scandinavica, 89*(9), 1149–1154.

Brans, R., & Yao, F. (2010). Immunization with a dominant-negative recombinant Herpes Simplex Virus (HSV) type 1 protects against HSV-2 genital disease in guinea pigs. *BMC Microbiology, 10,* 163.

Branson, K. (2011, March 4). Gender-neutral housing. *Rutgers Today.* Retrieved April 17, 2011, from http://news.rutgers.edu/medrel/special-content/hot-topic-gender-neu-20110304.

Braume, G.G. (2011). *The truth about sex.* Vancouver, BC: CCB Publishing.

Braun, J. (2008). From policy to personal: One queer Mennonite's journey. *Journal of Mennonite Studies, 26,* 69–80.

Brecher, E.M., & Brecher, J. (1986). Extracting valuable sexological findings from severely flawed and biased population samples. *Journal of Sex Research, 22,* 6–20.

Breech, L., & Braverman, P. (2010). Safety, efficacy, actions, and patient acceptability of drospirenone/ethinyl estradiol contraceptive pills in the treatment of premenstrual dysphoric disorder. *International Journal of Women's Health, 1,* 85–95.

Brennan, A., Ayers, S., Ahmed, H., & Marshall-Lucette, S. (2007). A critical review of the Couvade syndrome: The pregnant male. *Journal of Reproductive and Infant Psychology, 25*(3), 173–189.

Brennan, B.P., Kanayama, G., Hudson, J.I., & Pope, H.G., Jr. (2011). Human growth hormone abuse in male weightlifters. *American Journal of Addiction, 20*(1), 9–13.

Brennan, D.J., Ross, L.E., Dobinson, C., Veldhuizen, S., & Steele, L.S. (2010). Men's sexual orientation and health is Canada. *Canadian Journal of Public Health, 101*(3), 233–258.

Breuss, C.E., & Greenberg, S. (1981). *Sex education: Theory and practice.* Belmont, CA: Wadsworth.

Brewis, A., & Meyer, M. (2005). Marital coitus across the life course. *Journal of Biosocial Sciences, 37,* 499–518.

Brewster, K.L., & Tillman, K.H. (2008). Who's doing it? Patterns and predictors of youths' oral sexual experiences. *Journal of Adolescent Health, 42,* 73–80.

Brewster, P., Mullin, C., Dobrin, R., & Steeves, J. (2010). Sex differences in face processing are mediated by handedness and sexual orientation. *Laterality, 9,* 1–13.

Bridgeland, W.M., Duane, E.A., & Stewart, C.S. (2001). Victimization and attempted suicide among college students. *College Student Journal, 35*(1), 63–76.

Briere, J., & Malamuth, N. (1983). Self-reported likelihood of sexually aggressive behavior: Attitudinal versus sexual explanations. *Journal of Research in Personality, 17,* 315–323.

Brinig, M.F., & Allen, D.A. (2000). "These boots are made for walking": Why most divorce filers are women. *American Law and Economics Review, 2,* 126–169.

Brinton, L. (2007). Long-term effects of ovulation-stimulating drugs on cancer risk. *Reproductive Biomedicine Online, 15,* 38–44.

Brinton, L., Richesson, D., Gierach, G., & Lacey, J. (2008). Prospective evaluation of risk factors for male breast cancer. *Journal of the National Cancer Institute, 100*(20), 1477–1482.

Brinton, L.A., & Schairer, C. (1997). Postmenopausal hormone-replacement therapy: Time for a reappraisal? *New England Journal of Medicine, 336*(25), 1821–1822.

Brizendine, L., & Allen, B.J. (2010). Are gender differences in communication biologically determined? In B. Slife (Ed.), *Clashing views on psychological issues* (16th ed., pp. 72–88). New York, NY: McGraw-Hill.

Brizendine, L. (2006). *The female brain.* New York, NY: Broadway Publishing.

Brockman, N. (2004). Kenya. In R.T. Francoeur & R.J. Noonan (Eds.), *The Continuum international encyclopedia of sexuality* (pp. 679–691). New York/London: Continuum International.

Brongersma, E. (1990). Boy-lovers and their influence on boys: Distorted research and anecdotal observations. *Journal of Homosexuality, 20,* 145–173.

Brooks-Gunn, J., & Furstenberg, F.F. (1989). Adolescent sexual behavior. *American Psychologist, 44,* 249–257.

Brooks-Gunn, J., & Furstenberg, F.F. (1990). Coming of age in the era of AIDS: Puberty, sexuality, and contraception. *Mil-bank Quarterly, 68,* 59–84.

Brotman, S., Ryan, B., Collins, S., Chamberland, L., Julien, D., Meyer, E., Peterkin, A., & Richard, B. (2007). Coming out to care: Caregivers of gay and lesbian seniors in Canada. *Gereontologist, 47*(4), 490–503.

Brotto, L.A., & Basson, R. (2014). Group mindfulness-based therapy significantly improves sexual desire in women. *Behaviour Research and Therapy, 57,* 43–54.

Brotto, L.A., Basson, R., Carlson, M., & Zhu, C. (2013). Impact of an integrated mindfulness and cognitive behavioural treatment for Provoked Vestibulodynia (IMPROVED): A qualitative study. *Sexual and Relationship Therapy, 28*(1–2), 3–19.

Broude, G.J., & Greene, S.J. (1976). Cross-cultural codes on twenty sexual attitudes and practices. *Ethnology, 15,* 409–428.

Brousseau, M., Bergeron, S., & Hebert, M. (2011). Sexual coercion victimization and perpetration in heterosexual couples: A dyadic investigation. *Archives of Sexual Behavior, 40*(2), 363–372.

Brown, A., & Testa, M. (2008). Social influences on judgments of rape victims: The role of the negative and positive social reactions of others. *Sex Roles, 58,* 490–501.

Brown, B.B., Dolcini, M.M., & Leventhal, A. (1997). Transformations in peer relationships at adolescence: Implications for healthrelated behavior. In J. Schulenberg, J.L. Maggs, & K. Hurrelmann (Eds.), *Health risks and developmental transitions during adolescence* (pp. 161–189). Cambridge, UK: Cambridge University Press.

Brown, C. (2008). Gender-role implications on same-sex intimate partner abuse. *Journal of Family Violence, 23,* 457–463.

Brown, D.L., & Frank, J.E. (2003). Diagnosis and management of syphilis. *American Family Physician, 68*(2), 283–290.

Brown, D.J., Hill, S.T., & Baker, H.W. (2005). Male fertility and sexual function after spinal cord injury. *Progress in Brain Research, 152,* 427–439.

Brown, H.G. (1962). *Sex and the single girl.* New York, NY: Giant Cardinal.

Brown, J., & Trevethan, R. (2010). Shame, internalized homophobia, identity formation, attachment style, and the connection to relationship status in gay men. *American Journal of Men's Health, 4*(3), 267–276.

Brown, J., Pan, A., & Hart, R.J. (2010). Gonadotrophin-releasing hormone analogues for pain associated with endometriosis.

Cochrane Database of Systematic Reviews, 12, CD008475.

Brown, J., Ramirez, O.M., & Schniering, C. (2013). Finding love: Passion, intimacy, and commitment in the relationships of gay men. *Australian and New Zealand Journal of Family Therapy, 34*(1), 32–53.

Brown, J.C. (1983). Paraphilias: Sadomasochism, fetishism, transvestism and transsexuality. *British Journal of Psychiatry, 143,* 227–231.

Brown, M.S., & Brown, C.A. (1987). Circumcision decision: Prominence of social concerns. *Pediatrics, 80,* 215–219.

Brown, T.J., Sumner, K.E., & Nocera, R. (2002). Understanding sexual aggression against women: An examination of the role of men's athletic participation and related variables. *Journal of Interpersonal Violence, 17*(9), 937–952.

Brown, V.W., Lamb, S.M., Perkins, A.M., Naim, D.W., & Starling, S.P. (2014). Knowledge regarding hymens and the sex education of parents. *Journal of Child Sexual Abuse* [Epub ahead of print].

Brownmiller, S. (1975). *Against our will: Men, women, and rape.* New York, NY: Simon & Schuster.

Brownmiller, S. (2000). Rape on the brain: A review of Randy Thornhill and Craig Palmer. Retrieved December 5, 2005, from http://www.susanbrownmiller.com/html/review-thornhill.html.

Brubaker, L., Handa, V., Bradley, C., Connolly, A., Moalli, P., Brown, M., & Weber, A. (2008). Sexual function 6 months after first delivery. *Obstetrics and Gynecology, 111,* 1040–1044.

Bruce, K., & Walker, L. (2001). College students' attitudes about AIDS: 1986 to 2000. *AIDS Education and Prevention, 13*(5), 428–437.

Brucker, C., Karck, U., & Merkle, E. (2008). Cycle control, tolerability, efficacy and acceptability of the vaginal contraceptive ring, NuvaRing: Results of clinical experience in Germany. *European Journal of Contraceptive Reproductive Health Care, 13,* 31–38.

Brugman, M., Caron, S., & Rademakers, J. (2010). Emerging adolescent sexuality: A comparison of American and Dutch college women's experiences. *International Journal of Sexual Health, 22*(1), 32–46.

Brumbaugh, C., & Fraley, C. (2010). Adult attachment and dating strategies: How do insecure people attract dates? *Personal Relationships, 17*(4), 599–614.

Brumberg, J.J. (1997). *The body project: An intimate history of American girls.* New York, NY: Vintage Books.

Bruni, V., Pontello, V., Luisi, S., & Petraglia, F. (2008). An open-label multicentre trial to evaluate the vaginal bleeding pattern of the combined contraceptive vaginal ring

NuvaRing. *European Journal of Obstetrics and Gynecological Reproductive Biology, 139,* 65–71.

Brunner Huber, L.R., & Ersek, J.L. (2011). Perceptions of contraceptive responsibility among female college students: An exploratory study. *Annals of Epidemiology, 21*(3), 197–203.

Brunner-Huber, L., & Toth, J. (2007). Obesity and oral contraceptive failure: Findings from the 2002 National Survey of Family Growth. *American Journal of Epidemiology, 166,* 1306–1311.

Buckett, W., Chian, R., Holzer, H., Dean, N., Usher, R., & Tan, S. (2007). Obstetric outcomes and congenital abnormalities after in vitro maturation, IVF, and ICSI. *Obstetrics and Gynecology, 110,* 885–891.

Buffardi, A.L., Thomas, K.K., Holmes, K.K., & Manhart, L.E. (2008). Moving upstream: Ecosocial and psychosocial correlates of sexually transmitted infections among young adults in the United States. *American Journal of Public Health, 98,* 1128–1137.

Buisson, O., Foldes, P., Jannini, E., & Mimoun, S. (2010). Coitus as revealed by ultrasound in one volunteer couple. *Journal of Sexual Medicine, 7*(8), 2750–2754.

Bull, S.S., & Melian, L.M. (1998). Contraception and culture: The use of Yuyos in Paraguay. *Health Care for Women International, 19*(1), 49–66.

Bulletin of the World Health Organization (2010). Thailand's new condom crusade, 88(6), 404–405.

Bullivant, S., Sellergren, S., Stern, K., Spencer, N., Jacob, S., Mennella, J., & McClintock, M. (2004). Women's sexual experience during the menstrual cycle: Identification of the sexual phase by noninvasive measurement of luteinizing hormone. *Journal of Sex Research, 41*(1), 82–93.

Bullough, V. (1994). *Science in the bedroom: The history of sex research.* New York, NY: Basic Books.

Bullough, V.L. (1973). *The subordinate sex: A history of attitudes toward women.* Urbana: University of Illinois Press.

Bullough, V.L. (1979). *Homosexuality: A history.* New York, NY: New American Library.

Bullough, V.L. (1998). Alfred Kinsey and the Kinsey Report: Historical overview and lasting contributions. *Journal of Sex Research, 35*(2), 127–131.

Bumpass, L., & Lu, H-H. (2000). Trends in cohabitation and implications for children's family contexts in the United States. *Population Studies, 54*(1), 29–41.

Burdette, A.M., Ellison, C.G., Sherkat, D.E., & Gore, K.A. (2007). Are there religious variations in marital infidelity? *Journal of Family Issues, 28,* 1553.

Burgess, A., & Holmstrom, L. (1979). Rape: Sexual disruption and recovery. *American Journal of Orthopsychiatry, 131,* 981–986.

Burgess, A.W., & Holmstrom, L.L. (1979). *Rape: Crisis and recovery.* Bowie, MD: Robert J. Brady.

Burgess, A.W., & Morgenbesser, L.I. (2005). Sexual violence and seniors. *Brief Treatment & Crisis Intervention, 5*(2), 193–202.

Burgess, A.W., & Holmstrom, L.L. (1974). Rape trauma syndrome. *American Journal of Psychiatry, 131*(9), 981–986.

Burgoyne, R.W. (2001). The relationship assessment measure for same-sex couples (RAM-SSC): A standardized instrument for evaluating gay couple functioning. *Journal of Sex & Marital Therapy, 27*(3), 279–287.

Burke, A.E., Barnhart, K., Jensen, J.T., Creinin, M.D., Walsh, T.L., Wan, L.S., Westhoff, C., Thomas, M., Archer, D., Wu, H., Liu, J., Schlaff, W., Carr, B.R., & Blithe, D. (2010). Contraceptive efficacy, acceptability, and safety of C31G and nonoxynol-9 spermicidal gels: A randomized controlled trial. *Obstetrics and Gynecology, 116*(6), 1265–1273.

Burke, D. (2008, July 26). Birth control ban marks 40 years. *The Ledger.* Retrieved October 28, 2008, from http://www.theledger.com/article/20080726/NEWS/807260367/1326&title=Birth_Control_Ban_Marks_40_Years.

Burkeman, O., & Younge, G. (2005). Being Brenda. Retrieved February 24, 2005, from http://www.godspy.com/life/Being-Brenda.cfm.

Burkman, R., Schlesselman, J.J., & Zieman, M. (2004). Safety concerns and health benefits associated with oral contraception. *American Journal of Obstetrics and Gynecology, 190*(Suppl. 4), S5–22.

Burkman, R.T. (2002). The transdermal contraceptive patch: A new approach to hormonal contraception. *International Journal of Fertility and Women's Medicine, 47*(2), 69–76.

Burleson, B.R. (2003). The experience and effects of emotional support: What the study of cultural and gender differences can tell us about close relationships, emotion and interpersonal communication. *Personal Relationships, 10*(1), 1–23.

Burleson, B.R., Kunkel, A.W., Samter, W., & Werking, K. (1996). Men's and women's evaluations of communication skills in personal relationships: When sex differences make a difference—and when they don't. *Journal of Social and Personal Relationships, 13,* 201–224.

Burns, M., Costello, J., Ryan-Woolley, B., & Davidson, S. (2007). Assessing the impact of late treatment effects in cervical cancer: An exploratory study of women's sexuality. *European Journal of Cancer Care, 16,* 364–372.

Burt, M. (1980). Cultural myths and support for rape. *Journal of Personality and Social Psychology, 38,* 217–230.

Burton, K. (2005). Attachment style and perceived quality of romantic partner's opposite-sex best friendship: The impact on romantic relationship satisfaction. *Dissertation Abstracts International, 65*(8-B), 4329, # 0419–4217.

Busby, D., Carroll, J., & Willoughby, B. (2010). Compatibility or restraint? The effects of sexual timing on marriage relationships. *Journal of Family Psychology, 24*(6), 766–774.

Buss, D. (1989). Sex differences in human mate preferences: Evolutionary hypotheses tested in 37 cultures. *Behavioral and Brain Sciences, 12,* 1–49.

Buss, D.M. (1994). *The evolution of desire: Strategies of human mating.* New York, NY: Basic Books.

Buss, D.M. (2003). The dangerous passion: Why jealousy is as necessary as love and sex. *Archives of Sexual Behavior, 32*(1), 79–80.

Buss, D.M., Shackelford, T.K., Kirkpatrick, L., & Larsen, R.J. (2001). A half century of mate preferences: The cultural evolution of values. *Journal of Marriage & the Family, 63*(2), 491–503.

Busse, P., Fishbein, M., Bleakley, A., & Hennessy, M. (2010). The role of communication with friends in sexual initiation. *Communication Research, 37*(2), 239–255.

Butrick, C.W. (2009). Pelvic floor hypertonic disorders: Identification and management. *Obstetrics and Gynecology Clinics of North America, 36*(3), 707–722.

Butts, W.M. (1946). Boy prostitutes of the metropolis. *Journal of Clinical Psychopathology, 8,* 673–681.

Buvat, J., Tesfayae, F., Rothman, M., Rivas, D.A., & Giuliano, F. (2009). Dapoxetine for the treatment of premature ejaculation: Results from a randomized, double blind, placebo-controlled phase 3 trial in 22 countries. *European Urology, 55,* 957–968.

Byers, E., Henderson, J., & Hobson, K. (2009). University students' definitions of sexual abstinence and having sex. *Archives of Sexual Behavior, 38*(5), 665–674.

Byers, S.E., Sears, H.A., Voyer, S.D., et al. (2003a). An adolescent perspective on sexual health education at school and at home: I. High school students. *The Canadian Journal of Human Sexuality, 12,* 1–17.

Byers, S.E.., Sears, H.A., Voyer, S.D., et al. (2003b). An adolescent perspective on sexual health education at school and at home: II. Middle school students. *The Canadian Journal of Human Sexuality, 12,* 19–33.

Byrne, D., & Murnen, S.K. (1988). Maintaining loving relationships. In R. Sternberg & M.L. Barnes (Eds.), *Psychology of love* (pp. 293–310). New Haven, CT: Yale University Press.

Cabaret, A.S., Leveque, J., Dugast, C., Blanchot, J., & Grall, J.Y. (2003). Problems raised by the gynaecologic management of women with BRCA 1 and 2 mutations. *Gynecology, Obstetrics and Fertility, 31*(4), 370–377.

Cado, S., & Leitenberg, H. (1990). Guilt reactions to sexual fantasies during intercourse. *Archives of Sexual Behavior 19*(1), 49–63.

Caffaro, J., & Conn-Caffaro, A. (2005). Treating sibling abuse families. *Aggression and Violent Behavior, 10*(5), 604–623.

Cahill, S., South, K., & Spade, J. (2000). *Outing age: Public policy issues affecting gay, lesbian, bisexual and transgender elders.* Washington, DC: National Gay and Lesbian Task Force.

Cai, D., Wilson, S.R., & Drake, L.E. (2000). Culture in the context of intercultural negotiation: Individualism-collectivism and paths to integrative agreements. *Human Communication Research, 26*(4), 591–617.

Cai, L.Q.,, Zhu, Y.S., Katz, M.D., Herrera, C., Baéz J, DeFillo-Ricart, M., Shackleton, C.H., & Imperato-McGinley, J.J. (1996). Alpha-reductase-2 gene mutations in the Dominican Republic. *Journal of Clinical Endocrinology and Metabolism, 81*(5), 1730–1735.

Cain, R., Jackson, R., Prentice, T., Mill, J., Collins, E., & Barlow, K. (2013). Depression Among Aboriginal People Living With HIV in Canada. Canadian Journal of Community Mental Health. Vol. 30 Issue 1, p105–120.

Cakin-Memik, N., Yildiz, O., Sişmanlar, S.G., Karakaya, I., & Agaoglu, B. (2010). Priapism associated with methylphenidate: A case report. *Turkish Journal of Pediatrics, 52*(4), 430–434.

Calderone, M. (1983). On the possible prevention of sexual problems in adolescence. *Hospital and Community Psychiatry, 34,* 528–530.

Calgary Herald. (2007). Health Canada approves Seasonale. Retrieved March 12, 2015, from http://www.canada.com/story.html?id=af6f4a7b-fc74-4433-816d-7fc5862745da.

Califia, P. (1979). Lesbian sexuality. *Journal of Homosexuality, 4*(3), 255–266.

Callens, N., De Cuypere, G., Van Hoecke, E., T'sjoen, G., Monstrey, S., Cools, M., & Hoebeke, P. (2013). Sexual quality of life after hormonal and surgical treatment, including phalloplasty, in men with micropenis: A review. *Journal of Sexual Medicine, 10*(12), 2890–2903.

Calzavara, L.M., Bullock, S.L., Myers, T., Marshall, V.W., & Cockhill, R. (1999). Sexual partnering and risk of HIV/STD among aboriginals. *Canadian Journal of Public Health, 90,* 186–191.

Calzavara, L.M., Burchell, A.N., Lebovic, G., Myers, T., Remis, R.S., Raboud, J., Corey, P., Swantee, C., & Hart, T.A. (2011). The impact of stressful life events on unprotected anal intercourse among gay and bisexual men. *AIDS Behavior.* Retrieved February 20, 2011, from http://www.ncbi.nlm.nih.gov/pubmed/21274612.

Camacho, M., & Reyes-Ortiz, C. (2005). Sexual dysfunction in the elderly: Age or disease? *International Journal of Impotence Research, 17,* S52–S56.

Cameron, S., Glasier, A., Dewart, H., & Johnstone, A. (2010). Women's experiences of the final stage of early medical abortion at home: Results of a pilot survey. *Journal of Family Planning and Reproductive Health Care, 36*(4), 213–216.

Cammaert, L. (1985). How widespread is sexual harassment on campus? Special issue: Women in groups and aggression against women. *International Journal of Women's Studies, 8,* 388–397.

Campbell, J.C., Webster, D., Koziol-McLain, J., Block, C., Campbell, D., Curry, M.A., et al. (2002). Intimate partner violence and physical health consequences. *Archives of Internal Medicine, 162*(10), 1157–1163.

Campbell, L., Simpson, J., Boldry, J., & Rubin, H., (2010). Trust, variability in relationship evaluations, and relationship processes. *Journal of Personality and Social Psychology, 99*(1), 14–21.

Campbell, P.P. (2008). Sexual violence in the lives of lesbian rape survivors. St. Louis: Saint Louis University, AAT #3324148.

Campbell, R., Lichty, L., Sturza, M., & Raja, S. (2006). Gynecological health impact of sexual assault. *Research in Nursing and Health, 29,* 399–413.

Campbell, R., Sefl, T., & Ahrens, C.E. (2004). The impact of rape on women's sexual health risk behaviors. *Health Psychology, 23*(1), 67–74.

Campbell, R. (2008). The psychological impact of rape victims. *American Psychologist, 63*(8), 702–717.

Camperio-Ciani, A., Corna, F., & Capiluppi, C. (2004). Evidence for maternally inherited factors favouring male homosexuality and promoting female fecundity. *Proceedings: Biological Sciences, 271*(1554), 2217–2221.

Campos, B., Graesch, A., Repetti, R., Bradbury, T., & Ochs, E. (2009). Opportunity for interaction? A naturalistic observation study of dual-earner families after work and school. *Journal of Family Psychology, 23*(6), 798–807.

Canadian Cancer Society. (2015a). Breast cancer. Retrieved February 17, 2015, from http://www.cancer.ca/en/cancer-information/cancer-type/breast/statistics/?region=bc.

Canadian Cancer Society. (2015b). Cervical cancer. Retrieved February 18, 2015, from http://www.cancer.ca/en/cancer-information/cancer-type/cervical/screening/?region=bc.

Canadian Cancer Society. (2015c). Cervical cancer prevention and screening. Retrieved February 18, 2015, from http://www.cancer.ca/en/prevention-and-screening/be-aware/viruses-and-bacteria/human-papillomavirus-hpv/?region=bc.

Canadian Cancer Society. (2015d). Uterine Cancer. Retrieved February 20, 2015, from http://www.cancer.ca/en/cancer-information/cancer-type/uterine/statistics/?region=bc.

Canadian Cancer Society. (2015e). Ovarian cancer. Retrieved February 21, 2015, from http://www.cancer.ca/en/cancer-information/cancer-type/ovarian/signs-and-symptoms/?region=bc.

Canadian Cancer Society. (2015f). Breast Cancer. Retrieved September 2, 2014, from, http://www.cancer.ca/en/cancer-information/cancer-type/breast/breast-cancer/breast-cancer-in-men/?region=ab.

Canadian Cancer Society. (2015g). Testicular cancer. Retrieved September 4, 2014 from, http://www.cancer.ca/en/cancer-information/cancer-type/testicular/statistics/?region=bc.

Canadian Cancer Society. (2015h). Prostate cancer. Retrieved September 6, 2014 from, http://www.cancer.ca/en/cancer-information/cancer-type/prostate/statistics/?region=ab.

Canadian Divorce News. (2013). Retrieved from http://canadiandivorcelaws.com/annulment.

Canadian Institute for Health Information. (2015). Retrieved Dec 17, 2015, from https://www.cihi.ca/sites/default/files/document/ta_10_alldatatables20120417_en.pdf.

Canadian Maternity Experiences Survey. (2009). Retrieved April 22, 2015 from http://www.phac-aspc.gc.ca/rhs-ssg/survey-enquete/mes-eem-eng.php.

Canadian Sex Research Forum. (n.d.). Retrieved from http://www.canadiansexresearchforum.com.

Canadian Youth, Sexual Health and HIV/AIDS Study (CYSHHAS). (2003). Council of Ministers of Education, Canada.

Candolin, U. (2000). Male-male competition ensures honest signaling of male parental ability in the three-spines stickleback (*Gaterosteus aculeatus*). *Behavioral Ecology and Sociobiology, 49,* 57–61.

Cantor, J.M., Blanchard, R., Paterson, A.D., & Bogaert, A.F. (2002). How many gay men owe their sexual orientation to fraternal birth order? *Archives of Sexual Behavior, 31*(1), 63–71.

Capsuto, S. (2000). *Alterate channels: The uncensored story of gay and lesbian images on radio and television.* New York, NY: Ballantine Books.

Carcopino, X., Shojai, R., & Boubli, L. (2004). Female genital mutilation: Generalities, complications and management during obstetrical period. *Journal of Gynecology, Obstetrics, & Biological Reproduction, 33*(5), 378–383.

Cardoso, F.L., Savall, A.C., & Mendes, A.K. (2009). Self-awareness of the male sexual response after spinal cord injury. *International Journal of Rehabilitation Research, 32*(4), 294–300.

Carey, B. (2005). Straight, gay or lying? Bisexuality revisited. Retrieved July 5, 2005, from http://www.thetaskforce.org/downloads/07052005NYTBisexuality.pdf.

Cargill, W.M., & MacKinnon, C.J. (2004). Guidelines for operative vaginal birth. *Journal of Obstetreics and Gynaecolology Canada, 26*(8), 747–753.

Carlson, H. (2011). Approach to the patient with gynecomastia. *Journal of Clinical Endocrinological Metabolism, 96*(1), 15–21.

Carlton, C.L., Nelson, E.S., & Coleman, P.K. (2000). College students' attitudes toward abortion and commitment to the issue. *Social Science Journal, 37*(4), 619–625.

Carnes, P. (2001). *Out of the shadows: Understanding sexual addiction.* Center City, MN: Hazelden Information Education.

Carpentier, M.Y., & Fortenberry, J.D. (2010). Romantic and sexual relationships, body image, and fertility in adolescent and young adult testicular cancer survivors: A review of the literature. *Journal of Adolescent Health, 47*(2), 115–125.

Carr, R.R., & Ensom, M.H. (2002). Fluoxetine in the treatment of premenstrual dysphoric disorder. *Annuals of Pharmacotherapy, 36*(4), 713–717.

Carrell, D.T., Wilcox, A.L., Lowry, L., Peterson, C.M., Jones, K.P., Erickson, L., et al. (2003). Elevated sperm chromosome aneuploidy and apoptosis in patients with unexplained recurrent pregnancy loss. *Obstetrics and Gynecology, 101*(6), 1229–1235.

Carrigan, M. (2011). There's more to life than sex? Differences and commonality within the asexual community. *Sexualities, 14*(4), 462–478.

Carrington, B., & McDonald, I. (2007). The ontological impossibility of the black streaker: Towards a sociology of streaking. Conference Papers—American Sociological Association. 2007 Annual Meeting, pp.1–20.

Carroll, J. (2009). *The day Aunt Flo comes to visit.* Avon, CT: Best Day Media.

Carter, F., Carter, J., Luty, S., Jordan, J., McIntosh, V., Bartram, A., et al. (2007). What is worse for your sex life: Starving, being depressed, or a new baby? *International Journal of Eating Disorders, 40,* 664–667.

Carter, J., Goldfrank, D., & Schover, L. (2011). Simple strategies for vaginal health promotion in cancer survivors. *Journal of Sexual Medicine, 8*(2), 549–559.

Carter, J.S., Corra, M., & Carter, S.K. (2009). The interaction of race and gender: Changing gender-role attitudes, 1974–2006. *Social Science Quarterly, 90*(1), 196–212.

Caruso, S., Iraci Sareri, M., Agnello, C., Romano, M., Lo Presti, L., Malandrino, C., & Cianci, A. (2011). Conventional vs. extended-cycle oral contraceptives on the quality of sexual life: Comparison between two regimens containing 3 mg drospire-none and 20 mg ethinyl estradiol. *Journal of Sexual Medicine, 8*(5), 1478–1485.

Caruso, S., Rugolo, S., Agnello, C., Intelisano, G., DiMari, L., & Cianci, A. (2006). Sildenafil improves sexual functioning in pre-menopausal women with type 1 diabetes who are affected by sexual arousal disorder: A double-blind, crossover, placebo-controlled pilot study. *Fertility and Sterility, 85,* 1496–1501.

Casavent, L., & Robertson, J.R. (2007). the evolution of pornography law in Canada. Parliament of Canada. Retrieved from http://www.parl.gc.ca/Content/LOP/researchpublications/843–e.htm.

Case, P., Austin, S.B., Hunter, D., Manson, J., Malpeis, S., Willett, W., & Spiegelman, D. (2004). Sexual orientation, health risk factors, and physical functioning in the nurses' health study II. *Journal of Women's Health, 13*(9), 1033–1047.

Caspi, A., Williams, B., Kim-Cohen, J., Craig, I., Milne, B., Poulton, R., et al. (2007). Moderation of breastfeeding effects on the IQ by genetic variation in fatty acid metabolism. *Proceedings of the National Academy of Sciences of the United States of America, 104,* 18860–18865.

Cass, V.C. (1979). Homosexual identity formation: A theoretical model. *Journal of Homosexuality, 4,* 219–235.

Cass, V.C. (1984). Homosexual identity formation: Testing a theoretical model. *The Journal of Sex Research, 20,* 143–167.

Casteels, K., Wouters, C., VanGeet, C., & Devlieger, H. (2004). Video reveals self-stimulation in infancy. *Acta Paediatrics, 93*(6), 844–846.

Catalyst. (2010). Homosexuality and sexual abuse. Catholic League for Religious and Civil Rights. September, http://www.catholicleague.org/homosexuality-and-sexual-abuse/.

Catania, J.A., Binson, D., Van Der Straten, A., & Stone, V. (1995). Methodological research on sexual behavior in the AIDS era. *Annual Review of Sex Research, 6,* 77–125.

Catania, J.A., McDermott, L.J., & Pollack, L.M. (1986). Questionnaire response bias and face-to-face interview sample bias in sexuality research. *Journal of Sex Research, 22,* 52–72.

Caughey, A., Hopkins, L., & Norton, M. (2006). Chorionic villus sampling compared with amniocentesis and the difference in the rate of pregnancy loss. *Obstetrics and Gynecology, 108,* 612–616.

Cavanagh, S.L. (2007). *Sexing the teacher: School sex scandals and queer pedagogies.* Vancouver: UBC Press.

Cavanaugh, C., Messing, J., Petras, H., Fowler, B., LaFlair, L., Kub, J., Agnew, J., Fitzgerald, S., Bolyard, R., & Campbell, J. (2011). Patterns of violence against women: A latent class analysis. *Psychological Trauma: Theory, Research, Practice, and Policy.* Retrieved August 26, 2011, from http://psycnet.apa.org/index.cfm?fa=buy.optionToBuy&id=2011-07605-001.

CBC. (2014). Retrieved from http://www.cbc.ca/radio/unreserved/remembering-mmiw-iceis-rain-on-two-spirited-success-and-cellist-cris-derksen-s-unique-musical-genre-1.3254088/businessman-massey-whiteknife-transforms-into-diva-iceis-rain-1.3254252.

CBC News. (2013). Mount Cashel abuse settlement sets the stage for more suits. Retrieved April 15, 2015, from http://www.cbc.ca/news/canada/newfoundland-labrador/mount-cashel-abuse-settlement-sets-stage-for-more-suits-1.1311548.

Cecchetti, J.A. (2007). Women's attachment representations of their fathers and the experience of passionate love in adulthood. *Dissertation Abstracts International: Section B: The Sciences and Engineering, 68,* 3389.

Cederroth, C.R., Auger, J., Zimmermann, C., Eustache, F., & Nef, S. (2010). Soy, phytooestrogens and male reproductive function: A review. *International Journal of Andrology, 33*(2), 304–316.

Centers for Disease Control and Prevention. (2007a). *2005 assisted reproductive technology success rates: National summary and fertility clinic reports.* Atlanta, GA: Author.

Centers for Disease Control and Prevention. (2008h, February). Male circumcision and risk for HIV transmission and other health conditions: Implications for the United States. Department of Health and Human Services. Retrieved December 18, 2008, from http://www.cdc.gov/hiv/resources/factsheets/circumcision.htm.

Centers for Disease Control and Prevention. (2009c). *Oral sex and HIV risk. CDC HIV/AIDS facts.* Retrieved April 1, 2011, from http://www.cdc.gov/hiv/resources/factsheets/PDF/oralsex.pdf.

Centers for Disease Control and Prevention. (2010a). 2008 assisted reproductive technology success rates: National summary and fertility clinic reports. Atlanta, GA: U.S. Department of Health and Human Services. Retrieved March 1, 2011, from http://www.cdc.gov/art/ART2008/PDF/ART_2008_Full.pdf.

Centers for Disease Control and Prevention. (2010c). Hepatitis A information for health professionals. Retrieved April 1, 2011, from http://www.cdc.gov/hepatitis/Statistics/2008Surveillance/Commentary. htm.

Centers for Disease Control and Prevention. (2010g). Youth Risk Behavior Surveillance—United States, 2009. *Morbidity and Mortality Weekly Report Surveillance Summaries, 59*(5), 1–142.

Centers for Disease Control and Prevention. (2014). HIV Surveillance Report, 2012; vol. 24. Published November 2014. Retrieved from http://www.cdc.gov/hiv/statistics/basics/ataglance.html#ref3.

Centre to End All Sexual Exploitation. (2015). A Snapshot—Sexual Exploitation in Edmonton. Edmonton Police Commission, February 19, 2015. Retrieved from http://www.edmontonpolicecommission.com/wp-content/uploads/2015/02/EPC-Feb-19-2015-Snapshot-on-Sexual-Exploitation.pdf.

Cetinkaya, H., & Domjan, M. (2006). Sexual fetishism in a quail (Coturnix japonica) model system: Test of reproductive success. *Journal of Comparative Psychology, 120*(4), 427–432.

Chakraborty, A., McManus, S., Brugha, T.S., Bebbington, P., & King, M. (2011). Mental health of the non-heterosexual population of England. *British Journal of Psychiatry, 198,* 143–148.

Chalett, J.M., & Nerenberg, L.T. (2000). "Blue balls": A diagnostic consideration in testiculoscrotal pain in young adults: A case report and discussion. *Pediatrics, 106,* 843.

Chalkley, A.J., & Powell, G.E. (1983). The clinical description of forty-eight cases of sexual fetishism. *British Journal of Psychiatry, 142,* 292–295.

Chan, J., Olivier, B., deJong, R., Snoeren, E., Kooijman, E., vanHasselt, F., et al. (2008). Translational research into sexual disorders: Pharmacology and genomics. *European Journal of Pharmacology, 585,* 426–435.

Chandra, P. (1981). The sculpture and architecture of Northern India. In B. Gray (Ed.), *The Arts of India.* New Delhi, India: Vikas Publishing House.

Chang, Q., Qian, X., Xu, Z., & Zhang, C. (2010). Effects of combined administration of low-dose gossypol with steroid hormones on the mitotic phase of spermatogenesis of rat. *Journal of Experimental Zoology, 313*(10), 671–679.

Chang, S., Chen, K., Lin, H., Chao, Y., & Lai, Y. (2011). Comparison of the effects of episiotomy and no episiotomy on pain, urinary incontinence, and sexual function 3 months postpartum: A prospective follow-up study. *International Journal of Nursing Studies, 48*(4), 409–418.

Chaplin, S. (2007). *Japanese love hotels: A cultural history.* London: Routledge.

Chasin, C.J.D. (2013). Reconsidering asexuality and its radical potential. *Feminist Studies, 39*(2), 405–426.

Chatterjee, E. (2010). Movements towards equality: A study of lesbian and gay rights movements in India. Conference Papers—American Sociological Association. 2010 Annual Meeting, pp. 892–892.

Chaudhury, R.R. (1985). Plant contraceptives translating folklore into scientific application. In D.B. Jelliffe & E.F. Jelliffe (Eds.), *Advances in international maternal and child health* (pp. 107–114). Oxford, UK: Claredon Press.

Chauncey, G. (1994). *Gay New York, NY: Gender, urban culture, and the making of the gay male world, 1890–1940.* New York, NY: Harper Collins.

Chavarro, J.E., Willett, W.C., & Skerrett, P.J. (2007b). *The fertility diet.* New York, NY: McGraw Hill.

Cheasty, M., Clare, A.W., & Collins, C. (2002). Child sexual abuse: A predictor of persistent depression in adult rape and sexual assault victims. *Journal of Mental Health, 11*(1), 79–84.

Check, J.H. (2010). The future trends of induction of ovulation. *Minerva Endocrinology, 35*(4), 227–246.

Chemes, H., & Rawe, V. (2010). The making of abnormal spermatozoa: Cellular and molecular mechanisms. *Cell Tissue Research, 341*(3), 349–357.

Chen, Z., & Shi, Y. (2010). Polycystic ovary syndrome. *Front Medicine China, 4*(3), 280–284.

Cheng, D., Kettinger, L., Uduhiri, K., & Hurt, L. (2011). Alcohol consumption during pregnancy: Prevalence and provider assessment. *Obstetrics and Gynecology, 117*(2 Pt 1), 212–217.

Chenier, I. (2012). The natural order of disorder: Pedophilia, stranger danger and the normalising family. *Sexuality & Culture: An Interdisciplinary Quarterly, 16*(2), 172–186.

Cherkowski, S., & Bosetti, L. (2014). Behind the veil: Academic women negotiating demands of femininity. *Women's Studies International Forum, 45*, 19–26.

Chesler, P. (1993, October). Sexual violence against women and a woman's right to self-defense: The case of Aileen Carol Wuornos. *Criminal Practice Law Report, 1*(9). Retrieved May 1, 2011, from http://www.phyllis-chesler.com/114/sexual-violence-against-women-self-defense-wuornos.

Chesney, K. (1970). *The Victorian underworld.* London: Penguin Books.

Chia, M., & Abrams, D. (1997). *The multiorgasmic man: Sexual secrets every man should know.* San Francisco: HarperCollins.

Chinas, B. (1995). Isthmus Zapotec attitudes toward sex and gender anomalies. In S.O. Murray (Ed.), *Latin American male homosexualities* (pp. 293–302). Albuquerque: University of New Mexico Press.

Chin-Hong, P., Berry, J., Cheng, S., Catania, J., DaCosta, M., Darragh, T., et al. (2008). Comparison of patient- and clinician-collected anal cytology samples to screen for human papillomavirus-associated anal intraepithelial neoplasia in men who have sex with men. *Annals of Internal Medicine, 149*, 300–306.

Choi, N. (2004). Sex role group differences in specific, academic, and general self-efficacy. *Journal of Psychology: Interdisciplinary & Applied, 138*(2), 149–159.

Chopin-Marcé, M.J. (2001). Exhibitionism and psychotherapy: A case study. *International Journal of Offender Therapy & Comparative Criminology, 45*(5), 626–633.

Chow, E.W., & Choy, A.L. (2002). Clinical characteristics and treatment response to SSRI in a female pedophile. *Archives of Sexual Behavior, 31*(2), 211–215.

Christal, J., & Whitehead, H. (2001). Social affiliations within sperm whale (Physeter macrocephalus) groups. *Ethology, 107*(4), 323–340.

Christiansen, O.B. (1996). A fresh look at the causes and treatments of recurrent miscarriage, especially its immunological aspects. *Human Reproduction Update, 2*(4), 271–293.

Christofides, E., Muise, A., & Desmarais, S. (2009). Information disclosure and control on Facebook: Are they two sides of the same coin or two different processes? *CyberPsychology & Behavior, 12*(3), 341–345.

Chuang, S.S., & Yanjie, S. (2009). Do We See Eye to Eye? Chinese Mothers' and Fathers' Parenting Beliefs and Values for Toddlers in Canada and China. *Journal of Family Psychology, 23*(3), 331–341.

Chudakov, B., Cohen, H., Matar, M., & Kaplan, Z. (2008). A naturalistic prospective open study of the effects of adjunctive therapy of sexual dysfunction in chronic PTSD patients. *Israel Journal of Psychiatry Related Sciences, 45*, 26–32.

Chughtai, B., Sawas, A., O'Malley, R.L., Naik, R.N., Khan, S.A., & Pentyala, S. (2005). A neglected gland: A review of Cowper's gland. *International Journal of Andrology, 28*(2), 74–77.

Chumlea, W.C., Schubert, C.M., Roche, A.F., Kulin, H.E., Lee, P.A., Himes, J.H., & Sun, S.S. (2003). Age at menarche and racial comparisons in U.S. girls. *Pediatrics, 111*, 110–113.

Chung, A. (2010). Simple card detects date-rape drugs. *Toronto Star*, July 6, A6.

Chung, E., Solomon, M., DeYoung, L., & Brock, G.B. (2014). Clinical outcomes and patient satisfaction rates among elderly male aged ≥75 years with inflatable penile prosthesis implant for medically refractory erectile dysfunction. *World Journal of Urology, 32*(1),173–177.

Cianciotto, J., & Cahill, S. (2006). *Youth in the crosshairs: The third wave of the ex-gay movement.* National Gay and Lesbian Task Force Policy Institute. Retrieved October 2, 2008, from http://www.thetaskforce.org/downloads/reports/reports/YouthIn-TheCrosshairs.pdf.

Cibula, D., Gompel, A., Mueck, A.O., La Vecchia, C., Hannaford, P.C., Skouby, S.O., Zikan, M., & Dusek, L. (2010). Hormonal contraception and risk of cancer. *Human Reproduction Update, 16*(6), 631–650.

Cigna, E., Tarallo, M., Fino, P., DeSanto, L., & Scuderi, N. (2011). Surgical correction of gynecomastia in thin patients. *Aesthetic Plastic Surgery, 35*(4), 439–445.

Cila, J., & Lalonde, R.N. (2014). Personal openness toward interfaith dating and marriage among Muslim young adults: The role of religiosity, cultural identity, and family connectedness. *Group Processes & Intergroup Relations, 17*(3), 357–370.

Clapp, I., & Lopez, B. (2007). Size at birth, obesity and blood pressure at age five. *Metabolic Syndrome and Related Disorders, 5,* 116–126.

Clapp, J.F. (1996). Morphometric and neurodevelopmental outcome at age five years of the offspring of women who continued to exercise regularly throughout pregnancy. *Journal of Pediatrics, 129*(6), 856–863.

Clark, A.M., Ledger, W., Galletly, C., Tomlinson, L., Blaney, F., Wang, X., & Norman R.J. (1995). Weight loss results in significant improvement in pregnancy and ovulation rates in anovulatory obese women. *Human Reproduction, 10,* 2705–2712.

Clark, M.S., & Reis, H.T. (1988). Interpersonal processes in close relationships. *Annual Review of Psychology, 39,* 609–672.

Clark, P.M., Atton, C., Law, C.M., Shiell, A., Godfrey, K., & Barker, D.J. (1998). Weight gain in pregnancy, triceps skinfold thickness, and blood pressure in offspring. *Obstetrics and Gynecology, 91*(1), 103–107.

Clarke, A.K., & Miller, S.J. (2001). The debate regarding continuous use of oral contraceptives. *Annals of Pharmacotherapy, 35,* 1480–1484.

Clarke, L., & Korotchenko, A. (2010). Shades of grey: To dye or not to dye one's hair in later life. *Ageing and Society, 30*(6), 1011–1026.

Claxton, A., & Perry-Jenkins, M. (2008). No fun anymore: Leisure and marital quality across the transition to parenthood. *Journal of Marriage and Family, 70,* 28–44.

Clayton, A.H. (2008). Symptoms related to the menstrual cycle: Diagnosis, prevalence, and treatment. *Journal of Psychiatric Practices, 14,* 13–21.

Clinton, C., & Gillespie, M. (1997). *Sex and race in the early South.* Oxford, England: Oxford University Press.

Cluver, L., & Gardner, F. (2007). Risk and protective factors for psychological well-being of children orphaned by AIDS in Cape Town: A qualitative study of children and caregivers' perspectives. *19*(3), 318–325.

Coast, E. (2007). Wasting semen: Context and condom use among the Maasai. *Culture, Health and Sexuality, 9,* 387–401.

Coccia, M., & Rizzello, F. (2008). Ovarian reserve. Assessment of human reproductive function. *Annals of the New York Academy of Science, 1127,* 27–30.

Coccia, M., Rizzello, F., Cammilli, F., Bracco, G., & Scarselli, G. (2008). Endometriosis and infertility surgery and ART: An integrated approach for successful management. *European Journal of Obstetrics, Gynecology, and Reproductive Biology, 138,* 54–59.

Cochran, B.M., Ginzler, J., & Cauce, A. (2002). Challenges faced by homeless sexual minorities: Comparison of gay, lesbian, bisexual, and transgendered homeless sexual minorities with their heterosexual counterparts. *Journal of Public Health, 92,* 773–777.

Cochran, S.D., & Mays, V.M. (1990). Sex, lies, and HIV [letter]. *New England Journal of Medicine, 322*(11), 774–775.

Cochran, S.D., Mays, V.M., Alegria, M., Ortega, A.N., & Takeuchi, D. (2007). Mental health and substance use disorders among Latino and Asian American lesbian, gay, and bisexual adults. *Journal of Consulting and Clinical Psychology, 75*(5), 785–794.

Cohan, C., & Kleinbaum, S. (2002). Toward a greater understanding of the cohabitation effect. *Journal of Marriage and Family, 64*(1), 180–193.

Cohen, C., Brandhorst, B., Nagy, A., Leader, A., Dickens, B., Isasi, R., Evans, D., & Knoppers, B. (2008). The use of fresh embryos in stem cell research: Ethical and policy issues. *Cell Stem Cell, 2,* 416–421.

Cohen, F., Kemeny, M., Kearney, K., Zegans, L., Neuhaus, J., & Conant, M. (1999). Persistent stress as a predictor of genital herpes recurrence. *Archives of Internal Medicine, 159,* 2430–2436.

Cohen, J., Byers, E., & Walsh, L. (2008). Factors influencing the sexual relationships of lesbians and gay men. *International Journal of Sexual Health, 20*(3), 162–176.

Cohen, J.K., Miller, R.J., Ahmed, S., Lotz, M.J., & Baust, J. (2008c). Ten-year biochemical disease control for patients with prostate cancer treated with cryosurgery as primary therapy. *Urology, 71,* 515–518.

Cohen, J.N., Byers, E.S., Sears, H.A., & Weaver, A.D. (2004). Sexual health education: Attitudes, knowledge and comfort of teachers in New Brunswick schools. *Canadian Journal of Human Sexuality, 13*(1), 1–15.

Cohen, K.M., & Savin-Williams, R.C. (1996). Developmental perspectives on coming out to self and others. In R.C. Savin-Williams & K.M. Cohen (Eds.), *The lives of lesbians, gays, and bisexuals: Children to adults* (pp. 113–151). Fort Worth, TX: Harcourt Brace.

Cohen, L. (1988). Providing treatment and support for partners of sexual-assault survivors. *Psychotherapy, 25,* 94–98.

Cohen, L., & Roth, S. (1987). The psychological aftermath of rape: Long-term effects and individual differences in recovery. *Journal of Social and Clinical Psychology, 5,* 525–534.

Cohen, L.S., Soares, C., Otto, M., Sweeney, B., Liberman, R., & Harlow, B. (2002). Prevalence and predictors of premenstrual dysphoric disorder (PMDD) in older premenopausal women. The Harvard Study of Moods and Cycles. *Journal of Affective Disorders, 70*(2), 125–132.

Cohen, M.S., Hellmann, N., Levy, J.A., Decock, K., & Lange, J. (2008d). The spread, treatment, and prevention of HIV-1: Evolution of a global pandemic. *Journal of Clinical Investigation, 118,* 1244–1254.

Cohen, S.A. (2009). Facts and consequences: Legality, incidence and safety of abortion worldwide. *Guttmacher Policy Review, 12*(4). Retrieved June 4, 2010, from http://www.guttmacher.org/pubs/gpr/12/4/gpr120402.html.

Cohen-Bendahan, C., van de Beek, C., & Berenbaum, S. (2005). Prenatal sex hormone effects on child and adult sex-typed behavior: Methods and findings. *Neuroscience & Biobehavioral Reviews, 29*(2), 353–384.

Cohn, D. (2009). The states of marriage and divorce. Pew Research Council, October 15, Retrieved July 4, 2011, from http://pewresearch.org/pubs/1380/marriage-and-divorce-by-state.

Coker, A.L. (2007). Does physical intimate partner violence affect sexual health? A systematic review. *Trauma Violence Abuse, 8,* 149–177.

Cokkinos, D.D., Antypa, E., Tserotas, P., Kratimenou, E., Kyratzi, E., Deligiannis, I., Kachrimanis, G., & Piperopoulos, P.N. (2011). Emergency ultrasound of the scrotum: A review of the commonest pathologic conditions. *Current Problems in Diagnostic Radiology, 40*(1), 1–14.

Colapinto, J. (2001). *As nature made him: The boy who was raised as a girl.* New York, NY: HarperCollins.

Coleman, E. (1982). Developmental stages of the coming-out process. *American Behavioral Scientist, 25,* 469–482.

Coleman, M., & Ganong, L.H. (1985). Love and sex role stereotypes: Do macho men and feminine women make better lovers? *Journal of Personality & Social Psychology, 49*(1), 170–176.

Coleman, M., Ganong, L., & Fine, M. (2000). Reinvestigating remarriage: Another decade of progress. *Journal of Marriage and Family, 62*(4), 1288–1308.

Coleman, P. (2002). *How to say it for couples.* New York, NY: Prentice Hall Press.

Coleman, P.K. (2006). Resolution of unwanted pregnancy during adolescence through abortion versus childbirth: Individual and family predictors and psychological consequences. *Journal of Youth and Adolescence, 35,* 903–911.

Coles, R., & Stokes, G. (1985). *Sex and the American teenager.* New York, NY: Harper & Row.

Collaborative Group on Hormonal Factors in Breast Cancer. (2001). Familial breast cancer. *The Lancet, 358*(9291), 1389–1399.

Colley, A., Todd, Z., White, A., & Turner-Moore, T. (2010). Communication using camera phones among young men and women: Who sends what to whom? *Sex Roles, 63*(5/6), 348–360.

Collier, J.F., & Rosaldo, M.Z. (1981). Politics and gender in simple societies. In S. Ortner & H. Whitehead (Eds.), *Sexual meanings* (pp. 275–329). Cambridge, UK: Cambridge University Press.

Collins, K.A., Davis, G.J., & Lantz, P.E. (1994). An unusual case of maternal-fetal death due to vaginal insufflation of cocaine. *American Journal of Forensic Medical Pathology, 15*(4), 335–339.

Collins, P.H. (1998). The tie that binds: Race, gender and U.S. violence. *Ethnic and Racial Studies, 21*(5), 917–939.

Collins, P.H. (2000). It's all in the family. *Women and Language, 23*(2), 65–69.

Collins, R. (2005). Sex on television and its impact on American youth: Background and results from the RAND television and adolescent sexuality study. *Child & Adolescent Psychiatric Clinics of North America, 14*(3), 371–385.

Collins, R.L., Ellickson, P.L., & Klein, D.J. (2007). Research report: The role of substance use in young adult divorce. *Addiction, 102,* 786.

Comfort, A., & Rubenstein, J. (1992). The new joy of sex: A gourmet guide to lovemaking in the nineties. New York, NY: Simon & Schuster.

Condon, P. (2010, July 8). Presbyterian church's general assembly oks gay clergy. *Huffington Post*. Retrieved February 20, 2011, from http://www.huffingtonpost.com/2010/07/08/presbyterian-gay-clergy_n_640189.html.

Connolly, P.H. (2006). Psychological functioning of bondage/domination/sado-masochism (BDSM) practitioners. *Journal of Psychology & Human Sexuality, 18*(1), 79–120.

Conrad, N.J. (2009). A female figurine from the basal Aurignacian of Hohle Fels Cave in southwestern Germany. Letter. *Nature, 459*, 248–252.

Conron, K.J., Mimiaga, M.J., & Landers, S.J. (2010). A population-based study of sexual orientation identity and gender differences in adult health. *American Journal of Public Health, 100*(10), 1953–1960.

Conway, A.M. (2005). Girls, aggression, and emotional regulation. *American Journal of Orthopsychiatry, 75*(2), 334–339.

Conway, G., Band, M., Doyle, J., & Davies, M. (2010). How do you monitor the patient with Turner's syndrome in adulthood? *Clinical Endocrinology, 73*(6), 696–699.

Conway, L. (2012). Aboriginal erotic rock art proves that—even 28,000 years ago—men had ONE thing on their minds. Retrieved from http://www.dailymail.co.uk/news/article-2161118/Aboriginal-erotic-rock-art-proves—28-000-years-ago—men-ONE-thing-minds.html.

Cook, R., & Dickens, B. (2009). Hymen reconstruction: Ethical and legal issues. *International Journal of Gynecology and Obstetrics, 107*(3), 266–269.

Cooper, A.M. (1991). The unconscious core of perversion. In G.I. Fogel & W.A. Myers (Eds.), *Perversions and near-perversions in clinical practice: New psychoanalytic perspectives* (pp. 17–35). New Haven: Yale University Press.

Coordt, A.K. (2005). Young adults of childhood divorce: Intimate relationships prior to marriage. *Dissertation Abstracts International, Section A: Humanities and Social Sciences, 66*, 500.

Copen, C., Chandra, A., & Martinez, G. (2012). Prevalence and timing of oral sex with opposite-sex partners among females and males aged 15–24 years: U.S., 2007–2010. *National Health Statistics Reports, 56*. Retrieved March 27, 2014, from http://www.cdc.gov/nchs/data/nhsr/nhsr056.pdf.

Coppola, M.A., Klotz, K.L., Kim, K.A., Cho, H.Y., Kang, J., Shetty, J., Howards, S.S., Flickinger, C.J., & Herr, J.C. (2010). Sperm-Check Fertility, an immunodiagnostic home test that detects normozoo-spermia and severe oligozoospermia. *Human Reproduction, 25*(4), 853–861.

Corey, L., & Handsfield, H. (2000). Genital herpes and public health. *Journal of the American Medical Association, 283*, 791–794.

Cormie P., Newton R.U., Taaffe D.R., Spry N., & Galvão D.A. (2013). Exercise therapy for sexual dysfunction after prostate cancer. *Nature Reviews Urology, 10*(12), 731–736.

Corneanu, L.M., Stànculescu, D., & Corneanu, C. (2011). HPV and cervical squamous intraepithelial lesions: Clinicopathological study. *Romanian Journal of Morphology and Embryology, 52*(1), 89–94.

Cornelius, T., Shorey, R., & Beebe, S. (2010). Self-reported communication variables and dating violence: Using Gottman's marital communication conceptualization. *Journal of Family Violence, 25*(4), 439.

Corona, G., Jannini, E.A., Lotti, F., Boddi, V., De Vita, G., Forti, G., Lenzi, A., Mannucci, E., & Maggi, M. (2011). Premature and delayed ejaculation: Two ends of a single continuum influenced by hormonal milieu. *International Journal of Andrology, 34*(1), 41–48.

Corso, P., Edwards, V., Fang, X., & Mercy, J. (2008). Health-related quality of life among adults who experience maltreatment during childhood. *American Journal of Public Health, 98*, 1094–1100.

Corty, E.W., & Guardiani, J.M. (2008). Canadian and American sex therapists' perceptions of normal and abnormal ejaculatory latencies: How long should intercourse last? *Journal of Sexual Medicine, 5*, 1251–1256.

Costabile, R., Mammen, T., & Hwang, K. (2008). An overview and expert opinion on the use of alprostadil in the treatment of sexual dysfunction. *Expert Opinions in Pharmacotherapy, 9*, 1421–1429.

Costello, C., Hillis, S.D., Marchbanks, P.A., Jamieson, D.J., & Peterson, H.B. (2002). The effect of interval tubal sterilization on sexual interest and pleasure. *Obstetrics and Gynecology, 100*(3), 511–518.

Cottrell, B.H. (2010). An updated review of of evidence to discourage douching. *MCN: The American Journal of Maternal/Child Nursing, 35*(2),102–107.

Coulson, N.J. (1979). Regulation of sexual behavior under traditional Islamic law. In Al- Sayyid-Marsot & A. Lutfi (Eds.), *Society and the sexes in medieval Islam* (pp. 63–68). Malibu, CA: Undena Publications.

Courtenay, W.H. (2000). Behavioral factors associated with disease, injury, and death among men: Evidence and implications for prevention. *The Journal of Men's Studies, 9*(1), 81–142.

Cowan, G. (1992). Feminist attitudes toward pornography control. *Psychology of Women Quarterly,* 165–177.

Cowan, G. (2000). Beliefs about the causes of four types of rape. *Sex Roles, 42*(9–10), 807–823.

Cox, N., Vanden Berghe, W., Dewaele, A., & Vincke, J. (2010). Acculturation strategies and mental health in gay, lesbian, and bisexual youth. *Journal of Youth and Adolescence, 39*(10), 1199–1210.

Coyne Kelly, K., & Leslie, M. (Eds.). (1999). *Menacing virgins: Representing virginity in the Middle Ages and Renaissance*. Cranbury, NJ: Associated University Presses.

Cramer, R., Golom, F., LoPresto, C., & Kirkley, S. (2008). Weighing the evidence: Empirical assessment and ethical implications of conversion therapy. *Ethics & Behavior, 18*, 93–114.

Crawford, A. (2008, July 13). Male fertility options growing. *Chicago Tribune*. Retrieved July 29, 2008, from http://www.chicagotribune.com/features/lifestyle/chi-0713-guy-birth-control-for-mjul13,0,1337399.story.

Crawford, J., Boulet, M., & Drea, C. (2011). Smelling wrong: Hormonal contraception in lemurs alters critical female odour cues. *Proceedings of the Royal Society B, 278*, 122–130.

Crawford, J.T., Leynes, P.A., Mayhorn, C.B., & Bink, M.L. (2004). Champagne, beer, or coffee? A corpus of gender-related and neutral words. *Behavior Research Methods, Instruments & Computers, 36*(3), 444–459.

Crawford, M. (2006). *Transformations: Women, gender & psychology*. New York, NY: McGraw-Hill.

Creek, S.J. (2013). "Not getting any because of Jesus": The centrality of desire management to the identity work of gay, celibate Christians. *Symbolic Interaction, 36*(2), 119–136.

Cremer, M., Phan-Weston, S., & Jacobs, A. (2010). Recent innovations in oral contraception. *Seminars in Reproductive Medicine, 28*(2), 140–146.

Critelli, J.W., Myers, E.J., & Loos, V.E. (1986). The components of love: Romantic attraction and sex role orientation. *Journal of Personality, 54*(2), 354–370.

Crittenden, A. (2001). *The price of motherhood*. New York, NY: Metropolitan Books.

Croft, M.L., Morgan, V., Read, A.W., & Jablensky, A.S. (2010). Recorded pregnancy histories of the mothers of singletons and the mothers of twins. *Twin Research and Human Genetics, 13*(6), 595–603.

Crompton, L. (2003). *Homosexuality & civilization*. Cambridge, MA: Harvard University Press.

Crompton, S., & Geran, L. (1995). Women as main wag-earners. *Perspectives* (Statistics Canada), Winter, 26–29.

Crosby, R., & Diclemente, R. (2004). Use of recreational Viagra among men having sex with men. *Sexually Transmitted Infections, 80*, 466–468.

Crosby, R., Milhausen, R., Yarber, W., Sanders, S., & Graham, C. (2008b). Condom "turn offs" among adults: An exploratory study. *International Journal of STDs and AIDS, 19,* 590–594.

Crow, S., Agras, W., Crosby, R., Halmi, K., & Mitchell, J. (2008). Eating disorder symptoms in pregnancy: A prospective study. *International Journal of Eating Disorders, 41,* 277–279.

Crowley, I.P., & Kesner, K.M. (1990). Ritual circumcision (umkhwetha) amongst the Xhosa of the Ciskei. *British Journal of Urology, 66*(3), 318–321.

Crum, N., Riffenburgh, R., Wegner, S., Agan, B., Tasker, S., Spooner, K., et al.; Triservice AIDS Clinical Consortium. (2006). Comparisons of causes of death and mortality rates among HIV-infected patients. Analysis of the pre-, early, and late HAART (highly active antiretroviral therapy) eras. *Journal of Acquired Immune Deficiency Syndromes, 41,* 194–200.

Cruz, J.M. (2003). "Why doesn't he just leave?": Gay male domestic violence and the reasons victims stay. *Journal of Men's Studies, 11,* 309.

Cunningham, G.R., & Toma, S.M. (2011). Why is androgen replacement in males controversial? *Journal of Clinical Endocrinological Metabolism, 96*(1), 38–52.

Currier, D., & Carlson, J. (2009). Creating attitudinal change through teaching: How a course on "women and violence" changes students' attitudes about violence against women. *Journal of Interpersonal Violence, 24*(10), 1735–1754.

Cusitar, L. (1994). *Strengthening the link: Stopping the violence.* Toronto: Disabled Women's Network.

Czuchry, M., Timpson, S., Williams, M.L., Bowen, A.M., & Ratliff, E.A. (2009). Improving condom self-efficacy and use among individuals living with HIV: The positive choices mapping intervention. *Journal of Substance Use, 14*(3/4), 230–239.

Dade, L.R., & Sloan, L.R. (2000). An investigation of sex-role stereotypes in African Americans. *Journal of Black Studies, 30*(5), 676.

Dahl, A., Bremnes, R., Dahl, O., Klepp, O., Wist, E., & Fossa, S. (2007). Is the sexual function compromised in long-term testicular cancer survivors? *European Urology, 52,* 1438–1447.

Dahlen, H., Homer, C., Leap, N., & Tracy, S. (in press). From social to survival: Historical perspectives on perineal care during labour and birth. *Women and Birth.*

Dake, J.A., Price, J.H., Ward, B.L., & Welch, P.J. (2011). Midwestern rural adolescents' oral sex experience. *Journal of School Health, 81*(3), 159–165.

D'Aloisio, A., Baird, D., DeRoo, L., & Sandler, D. (2010). Association of intrauterine and early-life exposures with diagnosis of uterine leiomyomata by 35 years of age in the sister study. *Environmental Health Perspectives, 118*(3), 375–381.

Dalrymple, W. (2014). A Point of View: The sacred and sensuous in Indian art. Retrieved from http://www.bbc.com/news/magazine-26873149.

Dalton, A. (2000). Retrieved from https://www.psychologytoday.com/articles/200001/the-ties-unbind.

Daltveit, A., Tollances, M., Pihlstrom, H., & Irgens, L. (2008). Cesarean delivery and subsequent pregnancies. *Obstetrics and Gynecology, 111,* 1327–1334.

d'Amora, D., & Hobson, B. (2003). Sexual offender treatment. Retrieved March 31, 2003, from http://www.smith-lawfirm.com/Connsacs_offender_treatment.htm.

Danby, C., & Margesson, L. (2010). Approach to the diagnosis and treatment of vulvar pain. *Dermatology Therapy, 23*(5), 485–504.

Dancey, C.P. (1990). Sexual orientation in women: An investigation of hormonal and personality variables. *Biological Psychology, 30,* 251–264.

Danielou, A. (Translator). (1994). *The complete Kama Sutra.* Rochester, VT: Park Street Press.

Daniels M.C., & Adair, L.S. (2005). Breast-feeding influences cognitive development in Filipino children. *Journal of Nutrition, 135*(11), 2589–2595.

Dansky, S. (2013). On the persistence of camp. *Gay & Lesbian Review Worldwide, 20*(2), 15–18.

Darcangelo, S. (2008). Fetishism: Psychopathology and theory. In D. Laws & W. O'Donohue (Eds.), *Sexual deviance: Theory, assessment and treatment* (2nd ed., pp. 108–118). New York, NY: Guilford Press.

Dare, R.O., Oboro, V.O., Fadiora, S.O., Orji, E.O., Sule-Edu, A.O., & Olabode, T.O. (2004). Female genital mutilation: An analysis of 522 cases in South-Western Nigeria. *Journal of Obstetrics & Gynaecology, 24*(3), 281–283.

Das, A. (2007). Masturbation in the U.S. *Journal of Sex and Marital Therapy, 33*(4), 301–317.

Das, M. (2010) Gender role portrayals in Indian television ads. *Sex Roles, 64,* 208–222.

Dattijo, L.M., Nyango, D.D., & Osagie, O.E. (2010). Awareness, perception and practice of female genital mutilation among expectant mothers in Jos University Teaching Hospital Jos, north-central Nigeria. *Nigerian Journal of Medicine, 19*(3), 311–315.

D'Augelli, A.R. (2005). Stress and adaptation among families of lesbian, gay, and bisexual youth: Research challenges. *Journal of GLBT Family Studies, 1,* 115–135.

D'Augelli, A.R., Grossman, A., Salter, N., Vasey, J., Starks, M., & Sinclair, K. (2005b). Predicting the suicide attempts of lesbian, gay, and bisexual youth. *Suicide and Life-Threatening Behavior, 35,* 646–660.

D'Augelli, A.R., Grossman, A.H., & Starks, M. (2006). Childhood gender atypicality, victimization, and PTSD among lesbian, gay, and bisexual youth. *Journal of Interpersonal Violence, 21,* 1462–1482.

D'Augelli, A.R., Grossman, A.H., Hershberger, S., & O'Connell, T. (2001). Aspects of mental health among older lesbian, gay, and bisexual adults. *Aging and Mental Health, 5,* 149–158.

Davé, S., Petersen, I., Sherr, L., & Nazareth, I. (2010). Incidence of maternal and paternal depression in primary care. *Archives of Pediatriac Adolescent Medicine, 164*(11), 1038–1044.

Davidsen, L., Vistulien, B., & Kastrup, A. (2007). Impact of the menstrual cycle on determinants of energy balance: A putative role in weight loss attempts. *International Journal of Obesity, 31,* 1777–1785.

Davidson, J. (2002). Working with polyamorous clients in the clinical setting. *Electronic Journal of Human Sexuality, 5.* Retrieved September 13, 2008, from http://www.ejhs.org/volume5/polyoutline.html.

Davidson, J., Moore, N., Earle, J., & Davis, R. (2008). Sexual attitudes and behavior at four universities: Do region, race, and/or religion matter? *Adolescence, 433*(170), 189–220.

Davies, B., Ward, H., Leung, S., Turner, K.M.E., Garnett, G.P., Blanchard, J.F., & Yu, B.N. (2014). Heterogeneity in risk of pelvic inflammatory diseases after Chlamydia infection: a population-based study in Manitoba, Canada. *Journal of Infectious Diseases, 210*(Suppl. 2), S549–S555.

Davies, K.A. (1997). Voluntary exposure to pornography and men's attitudes toward feminism and rape. *Journal of Sex Research, 34*(2), 131–138.

Davies, M., Boulle, A., Fakir, T., Nuttall, J., & Eley B. (2008). Adherence to antiretroviral therapy in young children in Cape Town, South Africa, measured by medication return and caregiver self-report: A prospective cohort study. *BMC Pediatrics, 4*(8), 34.

Davies, M., Rogers, P., & Whitelegg, L. (2009). Effects of victim gender, victim sexual orientation, victim response and respondent gender on judgments of blame in a hypothetical adolescent rape. *Legal and Criminological Psychology, 14*(2), 331–338.

Davies, P. (1997). The role of disclosure in coming out among gay men." In K. Plummer. (Ed.), *Modern homosexualities* (pp. 75–83). New York, NY: Routledge.

Davis, K. (1937). The sociology of prostitution. *American Sociological Review, 2*(5), 744–755.

Davis, K.E., & Latty-Mann, H. (1987). Love styles and relationship quality: A contribution to validation. *Journal of Social & Personal Relationships, 4*(4), 409–428.

Davis, M.G., Reape, K.Z., & Hait, H. (2010a). A look at the long-term safety of an extended-regimen OC. *Journal of Family Practitioner, 59*(5), E3.

Davis, S.C., Meneses, K., & Hilfinger Messias, D.K. (2010b). Exploring sexuality & quality of life in women after breast cancer surgery. *Nurse Practioner, 35*(9), 25–31.

Daw, J. (2002). Hormone therapy for men? *Monitor on Psychology, 33*(9), 53.

Dawar, A. (2006, November 28). British scientists invent male pill. *Telegraph*. Retrieved October 28, 2008, from http://www. telegraph .co.uk/news/migrationtemp/1535304/British -scientists-invent-male-pill.html.

Day, R.D., & Padilla-Walker, L.M. (2009). Mother and father connectedness and involvement during early adolescence. *Journal of Family Psychology, 23*(6), 900–904.

D'Cruz, H., & Stagnitti, K. (2010). When parents love and don't love their children: Some children's stories. *Child & Family Social Work, 15*(2), 216.

DeBellis, M.D., Keshavan, M.S., Beers, S.R., Hall, J., Frustaci, K., Masalehdan, A., et al. (2001) Sex differences in brain maturation during childhood and adolescence. *Cerebral Cortex, 11*(6), 552–557.

DeCuypere, G., T'Sjoen, G., Beerten, R., Selvaggi, G., Sutter, P., Hoebeke, P., et al. (2005). Sexual and physical health after sex reassignment surgery. *Archives of Sexual Behavior, 34,* 679–690.

Deepinder, R., Makker, K., & Agarwal, A. (2007). Cell phones and male infertility: Dissecting the relationship. *Reproductive BioMedicine Online, 15*(3), 266–270.

de Freitas, S. (2004). Brazil. In R.T. Francoeur & R.J. Noonan (Eds.), *The Continuum complete international encyclopedia of sexuality* (pp. 98–113). New York/London: Continuum International.

Degges-White, S., & Marszalek, J. (2008). An exploration of long-term, same-sex relationships: Benchmarks, perceptions, and challenges. *Journal of Lesbian, Gay, Bisexual, and Transgendered Issues in Counseling, 1,* 99–119.

de Graaf, H., & Rademakers, J. (2011). The psychological measurement of childhood sexual development in Western societies: methodological challenges. *The Journal of Sex Research, 48*(2–3), 118–129.

De Hert, M., Detraux, J., & Peuskens J. (2014). Second-generation and newly approved antipsychotics, serum prolactin levels and sexual dysfunctions: A critical literature review. *Expert Opinions on Drug Safety, 13*(5), 604–624.

DeJonge, A., Teunissen, D., van Diem, M., Scheepers, P., & Lagro-Janssen, A. (2008). Woman's positions during the second stage of labour: Views of primary care midwives. *Journal of Advanced Nursing, 63,* 347–356.

DeKeseredy, W.S., Schwartz, M.D., & Tait, K. (1993). Sexual assault and stranger aggression on a canadian university campus. *Sex Roles, 28*(5–6), 263–277.

de Klerk, V. (2001). Language usage and attitudes in a South African prison: Who calls the shots? *International Journal of the Sociology of Language, 2001*(153), 97–115.

DeLamater, J. (1987). A sociological approach. In J.H. Geer & W.T. O'Donohue (Eds.), *Theories of human sexuality* (pp. 237–253). New York, NY: Plenum Press.

DeLange, J. (1995). Gender and communication in social work education: A cross-cultural perspective. *Journal of Social Work Education, 31*(1), 75–82.

de Leeuw, S. (2009). "If anything is to be done with the Indian, we must catch him very young": Colonial constructions of aboriginal children and the geographies of Indian residential schooling in British Columbia, Canada. *Children's Geographies, 7*(2), 123–140.

Deligeoroglou, E., Michailidis, E., & Creatsas, G. (2003). Oral contraceptives and reproductive system cancer. *Annals of New York Academy of Science, 997,* 199–208.

Deliramich, A., & Gray, M. (2008). Changes in women's sexual behavior following sexual assault. *Behavior Modification, 32*(5), 611–621.

D'Emilio, J. (1998). *Sexual politics, sexual communities*. Chicago: University of Chicago Press.

D'Emilio, J., & Freedman, E. (1988). *Intimate matters: A history of sexuality in America*. New York, NY: Harper & Row.

D'Emilio, J., & Freedman, S. (1988). *A history of sexuality in America*. Chicago: The University of Chicago Press.

Dempster, C. (2002). Silent war on South African women. Retrieved April 10, 2003, from www.new.bbc.co.uk/hi/english/world/ africa/newsid_1909000011909220.stm.

Denizet-Lewis, B. (2009, September 23). Coming out in middle school. *New York Times*. Retrieved February 20, 2011, from http://www.nytimes.com/2009/09/27/ magazine/27out-t.html?pagewanted54&_r51.

Dennerstein, L., Dudley, E., Guthrie, J., & Barrett-Connor, E. (2000). Life satisfaction, symptoms, and the menopausal transition. *Medscape Women's Health, 5*(4), E4.

Dennison, S.M., & Tomson, D.M. (2005). Criticisms of plaudits for stalking laws? What psycholegal research tells us about proscribing stalking. *Psychology, Public Policy, & Law, 11*(3), 384–406.

Denton, T. (1975). Canadian Indian migrants and impression management of ethnic stigma. *Canadian Review of Sociology & Anthropology, 12*(1), 65–71.

DeSteno, D., Barlett, M.T., Braverman, J., & Salovey, P. (2002). Sex differences in jealousy: Evolutionary mechanism or artifact of measurement? *Journal of Personality and Social Psychology, 83*(5), 1103–116.

Devdas, N., & Rubin, L. (2007). Rape myth acceptance among first-and second -generation south Asian American women. *Sex Roles, 56,* 701–705.

Deveau, V. (2006). Getting even: An investigation of revenge in romantic relationships. *Dissertation Abstracts International Section A: Humanities and Social Sciences, 67*(4–A), 1221.

deVisser, R., & McDonald, D. (2007). Swings and roundabouts: Management of jealousy in heterosexual "swinging" couples. *British Journal of Social Psychology, 46,* 459–476.

Dhir, R.R., Lin, H.C., Canfield, S.E., & Wang, R. (2011). Combination therapy for erectile dysfunction: An update review. *Asian Journal of Andrology, 13*(3), 382–390.

Diamanduros, T., Jenkins, S.J., & Downs, E. (2007). Analysis of technology ownership and selective use among undergraduates. *College Student Journal, 41,* 970–976.

Diamant, A.L., Lever, J., & Schuster, M. (2000). Lesbians' sexual activities and efforts to reduce risks for sexually transmitted diseases. *Journal of the Gay and Lesbian Medical Association, 4*(2), 41–48.

Diamanti-Kandarakis, E. (2007). Role of obesity and adiposity in polycystic ovary syndrome. *International Journal of Obesity, 31,* s8-s13.

Diamond, L., & Fagundes, C. (2010). Psychobiological research on attachment. *Personal Relationships, 27*(2), 218.

Diamond, L., Earle, D., Heiman, J., Rosen, R., Perelman, M., & Harning, R. (2006). An effect on the subjective sexual response in premenopausal women with sexual arousal disorder by bremelanotide (PT-141), a melanocortin receptor agonist. *Journal of Sexual Medicine, 3,* 628–638.

Diamond, L.M. (2000). Sexual identity, attractions, and behavior among young sexual minority women over a 2-year period. *Developmental Psychology, 36*(2), 241–250.

Diamond, L.M. (2005). A new view of lesbian subtypes: Stable versus fluid identity trajectories over an 8-year period. *Psychology of Women Quarterly, 29*(2), 119–128.

Diamond, M. (1993). Homosexuality and bisexuality in different populations. *Archives of Sexual Behavior, 22,* 291–310.

Diamond, M., & Diamond, G.H. (1986). Adolescent sexuality: Biosocial aspects and intervention. In P. Allen-Meares & D.A.

Shore (Eds.), *Adolescent sexualities: Overviews and principles of intervention* (pp. 3–13). NewYork: Haworth Press.

Diamond, M., & Sigmundson, H.K. (1997). Sex reassignment at birth: Long-term review and clinical implications. *Archives of Pediatric Medicine, 151*, 290–297.

Diaz, R.M., Ayala, G., Bein, E., Henne, J., & Marin, B.V. (2001). The impact on homophobia, poverty, and racism on the mental health of gay and bisexual Latino men. *American Journal of Public Health, 41*(6), 927–933.

Dibble, S.L., & Swanson, J.M. (2000). Gender differences for the predictors of depression in young adults with genital herpes. *Public Health Nursing, 17*(3), 187–194.

Dietz, A., & Nyberg, C. (2011). Genital, oral, and anal human papillomavirus infection in men who have sex with men. *Journal of the American Osteopathic Association, 111*(3 Suppl. 2), S19–S25.

Dietz, H.P. (2006). Pelvic floor trauma following vaginal delivery. *Current Opinions in Obstetrics and Gynecology, 18*, 528–537.

Dillow, M., Dunleavy, K., & Weber, K. (2009). The impact of relational characteristics and reasons for topic avoidance on relational closeness. *Communication Quarterly, 57*(2), 205.

Dimah, K., & Dimah, A. (2004). Intimate relationships and sexual attitudes of older African American men and women. *The Geronotologist, 44*, 612–613.

diMauro, D. (1995). *Sexuality research in the United States: An assessment of the social and behavioral sciences.* New York, NY: Social Science Research Council.

DiNapoli, L., & Capel, B. (2008). SRY and the standoff in sex determination. *Molecular Endocrinology, 22*, 1–9.

Dindia, K., & Canary, D.J. (2006). (Eds.), *Sex differences and similarities in communication* (2nd. ed.). Mahwah, NJ: Erlbaum.

Dindyal, S. (2004). The sperm count has been decreasing steadily for many years in Western industrialised countries: Is there an endocrine basis for this decrease? *The Internet Journal of Urology 2*(1). Retrieved December 18, 2008, from http://www.ispub.com/ostia/index.php?xmlFilePath=journals/iju/vol2n1/sperm.xml.

Dinger, J., Minh, T.D., Buttmann, N., & Bardenheuer, K. (2011). Effectiveness of oral contraceptive pills in a large U.S. cohort comparing progestogen and regimen. *Obstetrics and Gynecology, 117*(1), 33–40.

Dinh, M., Fahrbach, K., & Hope, T. (2011). The role of the foreskin in male circumcision: An evidence-based review. *American Journal of Reproductive Immunlogy, 65*(3), 279–283.

Dion, K., & Dion, K. (1996). Cultural perspectives on romantic love. *Personal Relationships, 3*(1), 5–17.

Dittmar, M. (2000). Age at menarche in a rural Aymara-speaking community located at high altitude in northern Chile. *Mankind Quarterly, 40*(4), 38–52.

Dixon, R. (2005). Controversy in South Africa over device to snare rapists. Retrieved October 19, 2005, from http://www.smh.com.au/news/world/controversy-in-south-africa-over-device-to-snare-rapists/2005/09/01/1125302683893.html.

Dodd, S.M. (2010). Ambivalent social support and psychneuroimmunologic relationships among women undergoing surgery for suspected endometrial cancer. University of Florida, AAT #34366330.

Dodge, B., Reece, M., Herbenick, D., Schick, V., Sanders, S.A., & Fortenberry, J.D. (2010). Sexual health among U.S. black and Hispanic men and women: A nationally representative study. *Journal of Sexual Medicine, 7*(Suppl. 5): 330–345.

Dodson, B. (1993). *Sex for one: The joy of self-loving.* New York, NY: Crown.

Doell, F.K. (2011). Enhancing couples' communication through systemic-constructivist couple therapy: The relationship between marital listening and relationship quality. *Dissertation Abstracts International: Section B: The Sciences and Engineering, 71*(9–B), 5786.

Doll, L.S., Petersen, L.R., White, C.R. Johnson, C.S., Ward, J.W., & The Blood Donor Study Group. (1992). Homosexually and nonhomosexually identified men who have sex with men: A behavioural comparison. *The Journal of Sex Research, 29*(1), 1–14.

Dolnick, S. (2007). India leads way in making commercial surrogacy a viable industry. *Hartford Courant,* December 31, p. A3.

Dong, Q., Deng, S., Wang, R., & Yuan, J. (2011). In vitro and in vivo animal models in priapism research. *Journal of Sexual Medicine, 8*(2), 347–359.

Donnelly, D.A., & Burgess, E.O. (2008). The decision to remain in an involuntarily celibate relationship. *Journal of Marriage and Family, 70*(2), 519–536.

Donovan, K., Taliaferro, L., Alvarez, E., Jacobsen, P., Roetzheim, R., & Wenham, R. (2007). Sexual health in women treated for cervical cancer: Characteristics and correlates. *Gynecological Oncology, 104,* 428–434.

Dorf, J. (2013). Fighting homophobia in Russia is an LGBT tradition. *Bay Area Reporter, 43*(34), 6–6.

Dorner, G., Schenk, B., Schmiedel, B., & Ahrens, L. (1983). Stressful events in perinatal life of bi- and homosexual men. *Experimental and Clinical Endocrinology, 81*(1), 83–87.

Dorr, C. (2001). Listening to men's stories: Overcoming obstacles to intimacy from childhood. *Families in Society, 82,* 509–515.

Dort, M. (2010). Undeard vioces: Adoption narratives of same-sex couples. *Canadian Journal of Family Law, 26*(2), 289–338.

Doty, N.D., Willoughby, B.L., Lindahl, K.M., & Malik, N.M. (2010). Sexuality related social support among lesbian, gay, and bisexual youth. *Journal of Youth and Adolescence, 39*(10), 1134–1147.

Dougherty, C. (2010, September 29). New vow: I don't take thee. *Wall Street Journal.* Retrieved October 5, 2010, from http://on-line.wsj.com/article/SB100014240527487038824045755198714447705214.html.

Douglas, J., & Olshaker, M. (1998). *Obsession.* Sydney: Pocket Books.

Douglas, M. (1978). *Purity and danger: An analysis of concepts of pollution and taboo.* London: Routledge & Kegan Paul.

Dover, K.J. (1978). *Greek homosexuality.* New York, NY: Random House.

Doyle, D. (2005). Ritual male circumcision: A brief history. *Journal of the Royal College of Physicians, 35,* 279–285. Retrieved April 8, 2008, from http://www.rcpe.ac.uk/publications/articles/journal_35_3/doyle_circumcision.pdf.

Draganowski, L. (2004). Unlocking the closet door: The coming out process of gay male adolescents. *Dissertation Abstracts International, 64*(11-B). (#0419–4217).

Drain, P.K., Halperin, D.T., Hughes, J.P., Klausner, J.D., & Bailey, R.C. (2006). Male circumcision, religion, and infections diseases: An ecologic analysis of 118 developing countries. *BMC Infectious Diseases, 6,* 172.

Dreger, A., Feder, E., & Tamar-Mattis, A. (2010, June 29). Preventing homosexuality (and uppity women) in the womb? The Hastings Center. Retrieved November 13, 2010, from http://www.thehastingscenter.org/Bioethicsforum/Post.aspx?id54754.

Dresner, E., & Herring, S. (2010). Functions of the nonverbal in CMC: Emoticons and illocutionary force. *Communication Theory, 20*(3), 249.

Droupy, S. (2010). [Sexual dysfunctions after prostate cancer radiation therapy]. *Cancer Radiotherapy, 14*(6–7), 504–509.

Duarte Freitas, P., Haida, A., Bousquet, M., Richard, L., Mauriège, P., & Guiraud T. (2011). Short-term impact of a 4-week intensive cardiac rehabilitation program on quality of life and anxiety-depression. *Annals of Physical and Rehabilitation Medicine, 54*(3), 132–143.

Duberman, G. (1994). *Gay New York, NY: Gender, urban culture, and the making of the gay male world, 1890–1940.* New York, NY: Harper Collins.

Duberman, M. (1991). *Cures: A gay man's odyssey*. New York, NY: Dutton.

Dubuc, S., & Coleman, D. (2007). An increase in the sex ratio of births to India-born mothers in England and Wales: Evidence for sex-selective abortion. *Population and Development Review, 33*, 383–400.

Dudrah, R.K. (2006). *Bollywood: Sociology goes to the movies*. New Dehli: Sage Publications India.

Duffy, J., Warren, K., & Walsh, M. (2001). Classroom interactions: Gender of teacher, gender of student and classroom subject. *Sex Roles, 45*(9–10), 579–593.

Duijts, L., Jaddoe, V., Hofman, A., & Moll, H. (2010). Prolonged and exclusive breastfeeding reduces the risk of infectious diseases in infancy. *Pediatrics, 126*, e18–e25.

Du Mont, J., et al., (2010). Drug facilitated sexual assault in Ontario Canada: Toxicological and DNA findings. *Journal of Forensic and Legal Medicine, 17*, 333–338.

Dunbar, R. (1998). *Grooming, gossip, and the evolution of language*. Boston, MA: Harvard University Press.

Dunham, C., Myers, F., McDougall, A., & Barnden, N. (1992). *Mamatoto: A celebration of birth*. New York, NY: Penguin Group.

Dunn, M.E., & Trost, J.E. (1989). Male multiple orgasms: A descriptive study. *Archives of Sexual Behavior, 18*, 377–387.

Dunne, E. (2007). *Genital warts*. U.S. Centers for Disease Control, Division of STD Prevention. Retrieved September 17, 2008, from http://www.cdc.gov/vaccines/recs/acip/downloads/mtg-slides-oct07/23HPV.pdf.

Dupre, M.E., & Meadows, S.O. (2007). Disaggregating the effects of marital trajectories on health. *Journal of Family Issues, 28*, 623–652.

Durex.com. (2007). *Sexual wellbeing global study 2007–2008*. Retrieved on January 20, 2008, from http://durex.com/cm/sexual_wellbeing_globeflash.asp.

Durham, L., Veltman, L., Davis, P., Ferguson, L., Hacker, M., Hooker, D., et al. (2008). Standardizing criteria for scheduling elective labor inductions. *American Journal of Maternal Child Nursing, 33*, 159–165.

Durmaz, E., Oxzmert, E., Erkekoglu, P., Giray, B., Derman, O., Hincal, F., & Yurdakôk, K. (2010). Plasma phthalate levels in pubertal gynecomastia. *Pediatrics, 125*(1), 122.

Dush, C., & Amato, P.R. (2005). Consequences of relationship status and quality for subjective well-being. *Journal of Social and Personal Relationships, 22*, 607.

Dworkin, A. (1981). *Pornography: Men possessing women*. New York, NY: Putnam.

Dworkin, A. (1987). *Intercourse*. New York, NY: The Free Press.

Dye, C., & Upchurch, D.M. (2006). Moderating effects of gender on alcohol use: Implications for condom use at first intercourse. *Journal of School Health, 76*(3), 111–116.

Dzelme, K., & Jones, R.A. (2001). Male cross-dressers in therapy: A solution-focused perspective for marriage and family therapists. *American Journal of Family Therapy, 29*, 293–305.

Eaker, E.D., Sullivan, L.M., Kelly-Hayes, M., D'Agostino, R.B., Sr., & Benjamin, E.J. (2007). Marital status, marital strain and the risk of coronary heart disease or total mortality: The Framingham Offspring Study. *Psychosomatic Medicine, 69*, 509–513.

Eardley, I. (2010). Oral therapy for erectile dysfunction. *Archives of Españoles Urology, 63*(8), 703–714.

Earl, W.L. (1990). Married men and same sex activity: A field study on HIV risk among men who do not identify as gay or bisexual. *Journal of Sex & Marital Therapy, 16*(4), 251–257.

Earnshaw, V., Pitipitan, E., & Chaudoir, S. (2011). Intended responses to rape as functions of attitudes, attributions of fault, and emotions. *Sex Roles, 64*(5–6), 382–393.

Easton, J.A., Confer, J.C., Goetz, C.D., & Buss, D.M. (2010). Reproduction expediting: Sexual motivations, fantasies, and the ticking biological clock. *Personality and Individual Differences, 49*, 516–520.

Eaton, D.K., Kann, L., Kinchen, S., Ross, J., Hawkins, J., Harris, W., et al. (2006, June 9). Youth risk behavior surveillance—United States, 2005. Surveillance Summaries. *Morbidity and Mortality Weekly Report, 55*(no. SS-5). Hyattsville, MD: U.S.

Eaton, L., Kaufman, M., Fuhrel, A., Cain, D., Cherry, C., Pope, H., & Kalichman, S. (2008). Examining factors co-existing with interpersonal violence in lesbian relationships. *Journal of Family Violence, 23*, 697–706.

Ebsworth, M., & Lalumiere, M.L. (2012). Viewing time as a measure of bisexual sexual interest. *Archives of Sexual Behavior, 41*(1), 161–172.

Eckstein, D., & Goldman, A. (2001). The couples' gender-based communication questionnaire. *Family Journal of Counseling and Therapy for Couples and Families, 9*(1), 62–74.

Edwards, J. (2010, March 12). Sequenom's disappearing Down syndrome test mystery—solved! CBS Business Network. Retrieved March 1, 2011, from http://www.bnet.com/blog/drug-business/sequenom-8217s-disappearing-down-syndrome-test-mystery-8212-solved/4388.

Edwards, R. (1998). The effects of gender, gender role, and values. *Journal of Language and Social Psychology, 17*(1), 52–72.

Edwards, R., & Hamilton, M.A. (2004). You need to understand my gender role: An empirical test of Tannen's model of gender and communication. *Sex Roles, 50*(7–8), 491–504.

Egan, C.E. (2001). Sexual behaviours, condom use and factors influencing casual sex among backpackers and other young international travellers. *Canadian Journal of Human Sexuality, 10*, 1–2, Spring/Summer, 41–58.

Ehrich, K., Williams, C., Farsides, B., Sandall, J., & Scott, R. (2007). Choosing embryos: Ethical complexity and relational autonomy in staff accounts of PGD. *Sociology of Health and Illness, 29*, 1091–1106.

Einsiedel, E. (1989). Social science and public policy: Looking at the 1986 commission on pornography. In S. Gubar & J. Hoff (Eds.), *For adult users only* (pp. 87–107). Bloomington: Indiana University Press.

Eisinger, F., & Burke, W. (2002). Breast cancer and breastfeeding. *Lancet, 360*(9328), 187–195.

Eke, A., Hilton, N., Harris, G., Rice, M., & Houghton, R. (2011). Intimate partner homicide: Risk assessment and prospects for prediction. *Journal of Family Violence, 26*(3), 211–216.

Ekman, P., & Friesen, W. (1969). The repertoire of nonverbal behavior: Categories, origins, usage and coding. *Semiotica, 1*, 49–98.

Eldar-Avidan, D., Haj-Yahia, M., & Green-baum, C. (2009). Divorce is a part of my life. Resilience, survival, and vulnerability. Young adults' perception of the implications of parental divorce. *Journal of Marital and Family Therapy, 35*(1), 30–47.

Eley, A., & Pacey, A.A. (in press). The value of testing semen for Chlamydia trachomatis in men of infertile couples. *International Journal of Andrology*, Retrieved May 29, 2011, from http://onlinelibrary.wiley.com/doi/10.1111/j.1365-2605.2010.01099.x/abstract.

Elgar, F.J., Craig, W., & Trites, S.J. (2013). Family dinners, communication, and mental health in Canadian adolescents. *Journal of Adolescent Health, 52*(4), 433–438.

Elhanbly, S., Elkholy, A., Elbayomy, Y., Elsaid, M., & Abdel-gaber, S. (2009). Nocturnal penile erections: The diagnostic value of tumescence and rigidity activity units. *International Journal of Impotence Research, 21*(6), 376–381.

El-Helaly, M., Awadalla, N., Mansour, M., & El-Biomy, Y. (2010). Workplace exposures and male infertility: A case-control study. *International Journal of Occupational Medicine and Environmental Medicine, 23*(4), 331–338.

Elias, M. (2007, February 11). Gay teens coming out earlier to peers and family. *USA Today*. Retrieved October 2, 2008, from http://www.usatoday.com/news/nation/2007-02-07-gay-teens-cover_x.htm.

Eliason, M.J. (1997). The prevalence and nature of biphobia in heterosexual undergraduate students. *Archives of Sexual Behavior, 26,*(3), 317–326.

Eliot, L. (2009). *Pink brains, blue brains: How small differences grow into troublesome gaps—and what we can do about it.* Orlando, FL: Houghton Mifflin Harcourt.

Ellenbogen, P. (2009). Beyond the border: A comparative look at prison rape in the United States and Canada. *Columbia Journal of Law and Social Problems, 42,* 335–372.

Elliot, D. (1999). Fallen bodies: Pollution, sexuality, & demonology in the Middle Ages. Philadelphia, PA: University of Pennsylvania Press.

Elliot, M., Browne, K., & Kilcoyne, J. (1995). Child sexual abuse prevention: What offenders tell us. *Child Abuse & Neglect, 19*(5), 579–594.

Elliott, S. (2010). Parents' constructions of teen sexuality: Sex panics, contradictory discourses, and social inequality. *Symbolic Interaction, 33*(2), 191–212.

Elliott, S., Latini, D., Walker, L., Wassersug, R., & Robinson, J. (2010). Androgen deprivation therapy for prostate cancer: Recommendations to improve patient and partner quality of life. *Journal of Sexual Medicine, 7*(9), 2996–3010.

Elliott, S., & Umberson, D. (2008). The performance of desire: Gender and sexual negotiation in long-term marriages. *Journal of Marriage and Family, 70,* 392–407.

Ellis, B.J., & Essex, M.J. (2007). Family environments, adrenarche, and sexual maturation: A longitudinal test of a life history model. *Child Development, 78,* 1799–1817.

Ellis, H. (1910). *Studies in the psychology of sex* (Vols. I-VI). Philadelphia, PA: F.A. Davis.

Ellis, L. (1988). Sexual orientation of human offspring may be altered by severe maternal stress during pregnancy. *Journal of Sex Research, 25*(1), 152–157.

Ellis, L., Burke, D., & Ames, M. (1987). Sexual orientation as a continuous variable: A comparison between the sexes. *Archives of Sexual Behavior, 16,* 523–529.

Ellison, C.R. (2000). *Women's sexualities.* Oakland, CA: New Harbinger.

Ellison, C.R. (2006). *Women's sexualities: Generations of women share intimate secrets of sexual self-acceptance.* Oakland, CA: New Harbinger Publications.

Elmslie, B., & Tebaldi, E. (2007). Sexual orientation and labor market discrimination. *Journal of Labor Research, 28*(3), 436–453.

Eloi-Stiven, M., Channaveeraiah, N., Christos, P., Finkel, M., & Reddy, R. (2007). Does marijuana use play a role in the recreational use of sildenafil? *Journal of Family Practitioner, 56,* E1–E4.

Ely, G., Flaherty, C., & Cuddeback, G. (2010). The relationship between depression and other psychosocial problems in a sample of adolescent pregnancy termination patients. *Child and Adolescent Social Work Journal, 27*(4), 269–282.

Emilee, G., Ussher, J.M., & Perz, J. (2010). Sexuality after breast cancer: A review. *Maturitas, 66*(4), 397–407.

Emmers-Sommer, T., Farrell, J., Gentry, A., Stevens, S., Eckstein, J., Battocletti, J., & Gardener, C. (2010). First date sexual expectations: The effects of who asked, who paid, date location, and gender. *Communication Studies, 61*(3), 339–355.

Emons, G., Fleckenstein, G., Hinney, B., Huschmand, A., & Heyl, W. (2000). Hormonal interactions in endometrial cancer. *Endocrine-Related Cancer, 7,* 227–242.

Employment and Social Development Canada. (2015). Retrieved from http://www4.hrsdc.gc.ca/h.4m.2@-eng.jsp.

Engman, M., Wijma, K., & Wijma, B. (2010). Long-term coital behaviour in women treated with cognitive behaviour therapy for superficial coital pain and vaginismus. *Cognitive and Behavioral Therapy, 39*(3), 193–202.

Ensign, J., Scherman, A., & Clark, J. (1998). The relationship of family structure and conflict to levels of intimacy and parental attachment in college students. *Adolescence, 33*(131), 575–582.

Ephross, P.H. (2005). Group work with sexual offenders. In G.L. Greif (Ed.), *Group work with populations at risk* (pp. 253–266). New York, NY: Oxford University Press.

Epp, A., Larochelle, A., Lovatsis, D., Walter, J., Easton, W., Farrell, S., Girouard, L., Gupta, C., Harvey, M., Robert, M., et al. (2010). Recent urinary tract infections. *Journal of Obstetrics and Gynecology, 32*(11), 1082–1090.

Epp, M. (1958). *Mennonite women in Canada: A history.* Winnipeg, MA: University of Manitoba Press.

Epps, J., & Kendall, P.C. (1995). Hostile attributional bias in adults. *Cognitive Therapy and Research, 19,* 159–178.

Epstein, C.F. (1986). Symbolic segregation: Similarities and differences in the language and non-verbal communication of women and men. *Sociological Forum, 1,* 27–49.

Epstein, C.F. (1988). *Deceptive distinctions: Sex, gender, and the social order.* New Haven, CT: Yale University Press.

Epstein, M., & Ward, L.M. (2008). "Always use protection": Communication boys receive about sex from parents, peers, and the media. *Journal of Youth and Adolescence, 37,* 113–127.

Eraslan D., Ertekin E., Ertekin B.A., & Oztürk O. (2014). Treatment of insomnia with hypnotics resulting in improved sexual functioning in post-menopausal women. *Psychiatric Danubina, 26*(4), 353–357.

Ericksen, J.A. (1999). *Kiss and tell: Surveying sex in the twentieth century.* Cambridge, MA: Harvard University Press.

Erogul, O., Oztas, E., Yildirim, I., Kir, T., Aydur, E., Komesli, G., et al. (2006). Effects of electromagnetic radiation from a cellular phone on human sperm motility: An in vitro study. *Archives of Medical Research, 37,* 840–843.

Errington, J. (1988). Pioneers and suffragists. In S. Burt, L. Code, and L. Dorney (Eds.), *Changing patterns: Women in Canada.* Toronto: McClelland & Stewart.

Ersoy, B., Balkan, C., Gunay, T., & Egemen, A. (2005). The factors affecting the relation between the menarcheal age of mother and daughter. *Child: Care, Health & Development, 31*(3), 303–308.

Escoffier, J. (2003). *Sexual revolution.* New York, NY: Thunder's Mouth Press.

Eskenazi, B., Wyrobek, A.J., Sloter, E., Kidd, S.A., Moore, L., Young, S., & Moore, D. (2003). The association of age and semen quality in healthy men. *Human Reproduction, 18,* 447–454.

Espelage, D.L., Aragon, S.R., Birkett, M., & Koenig, B.W. (2008). Homophobic teasing, psychological outcomes, and sexual orientation among high school students: What influence do parents and schools have? *School Psychology Review, 37,* 202–216.

Esposito, J.L. (2002). *Women in Muslim family law.* New York, NY: Syracuse University Press.

Esposito, K., Giugliano, F., Ciotola, M., De Sio, M., D'Armiento M., & Giugliano, D. (2008). Obesity and sexual dysfunction, male and female. *International Journal of Impotence Research, 20*(4), 358–365.

Esposito, K., Maiorino, M.I., Bellastella, G., Giugliano, F., Romano, M., & Giugliano, D. (2010). Determinants of female sexual dysfunction in type 2 diabetes. *International Journal of Impotence Research, 22*(3), 179–184.

Essén, B., Blomkvist, A., Helström, L., & Johns-dotter, S. (2010). The experience and responses of Swedish health professionals to patients requesting virginity restoration. *Reproductive Health Matters, 18*(35), 38–46.

Estacion, A., & Cherlin, A. (2010). Gender distrust and intimate unions among low-income Hispanic and African American women. *Journal of Family Issues, 31*(4), 475.

Estephan, A., & Sinert, R. (2010, February 1). *Dysfunctional uterine bleeding.* Retrieved December 26, 2010, from http://emedicine.medscape.com/article/795587-over-view.

Ettala O.O., Syvänen K.T., Korhonen P.E., Kaipia A.J., Vahlberg T.J., Boström P.J., & Aarnio P.T. (2014). High-intensity physical activity, stable relationship, and high education level associate with decreasing risk of erectile dysfunction in 1,000 apparently healthy cardiovascular risk subjects. *Journal of Sexual Medicine*, 11(9), 2277–2284.

Evans, A., Scally, A., Wellard, S., & Wilson, J. (2007). Prevalence of bacterial vaginosis in lesbians and heterosexual women in a community setting. *Sexually Transmitted Infections*, 83, 424–425.

Evans-Pritchard, E.E. (1970). Sexual inversion among the Azande. *American Anthropologist*, 72, 1428–1434.

Eyada, M., & Atwa, M. (2007). Sexual function in female patients with unstable angina or non-ST-elevation myocardial infarction. *Journal of Sexual Medicine*, 4(5), 1373–1380.

Eyal, K., & Finnerty, K. (2009). The portrayal of sexual intercourse on television: How, who, and with what consequence? *Mass Communication & Society*, 12(2), 143–169.

Eysenck, H. (1993). *Decline and fall of the Freudian empire*. New York, NY: Viking-Penguin.

Fabes, R., Martin, C., & Hanish, L. (2003). Young children's play qualities in same-, other-, and mixed-sex peer groups. *Child Development*, 74(3), 921–932.

Fabre, L.F., Brown, C.S., Smith, L.C., & Derogatis, L.R. (2011). Gepirone-ER treatment of hypoactive sexual desire disorder (HSDD) associated with depression in women. *Journal of Sexual Medicine*, 8(5), 1411–1419.

Faderman, L. (1978). The morbidification of love between women by 19th-century sexologists. *Journal of Homosexuality*, 4(1), 73–91.

Faderman, L. (1981). *Surpassing the love of men: Romantic friendship and love between women from the Renaissance to the present*. New York, NY: William Morrow.

Falagas, M., Betsi, G., & Athanasiou, S. (2006). Probiotics for prevention of recurrent vulvovaginal candidiasis: A review. *Journal of Antimicrobial Chemotherapy*, 58(2), 266–272.

Faller, K.C. (1989). The role relationship between victim and perpetrator as a predictor of characteristics of intrafamilial sexual abuse. *Child and Adolescent Social Work Journal*, 6, 217–229.

Faludi, S. (1991). *Backlash: The undeclared war against American women*. New York, NY: Crown.

Farage, M.A., Lennon, L., Ajayi, F. (2011). Products used on female genital mucosa. *Current Problems in Dermatology*, 40, 90–100.

Farley, M., & Barkan, H. (1998). Prostitution, violence, and post-traumatic stress disorder. *Women and Health*, 27(3), 37–49.

Farr, C., Brown, J., & Beckett, R. (2004). Ability to empathise and masculinity levels: Comparing male adolescent sex offenders with a normative sample of non-offending adolescents. *Psychology, Crime & Law*, 10(2), 155–168.

Farr, R., Forssell, S., & Patterson, C. (2010). Parenting and child development in adoptive families: Does parental sexual orientation matter? *Applied Developmental Science*, 14(3), 164–178.

Farr, S., & Kern, M. (2010, November 24). Temple football players eyed in rape of student. *McClatchy-Tribune Business News*. Retrieved April 13, 2011, from http://articles.philly.com/2010-11-24/news/24955668_1_temple-students-temple-officials-al-golden.

Faulkner, A.H., & Cranston, K. (1998). Correlates of same-sex sexual behavior in a random sample of Massachusetts high school students. *American Journal of Public Health*, 88(2), 262–266.

Faulkner, S., & Lannutti, P. (2010). Examining the content and outcomes of young adults' satisfying and unsatisfying conversations about sex. *Qualitative Health Research*, 20(3), 375.

Fava, M., Dording, C., Baker, R., Mankoski, R., Tran, Q., Forbes, R., et al. (2011). Effects of adjunctive aripiprazole on sexual functioning in patients with major depressive disorder and an inadequate response to standard antidepressant monotherapy. *Primary Care Companion for CHS Disorders*, 13(1). Retrieved August 2, 2011, from http://www.ncbi.nlm.nih.gov/pmc/articles/PMC3121211/?tool5gateway.

Fechner, A.J., & McGovern, P.G. (2011). The state of the art of in vitro fertilization. *Frontiers in Bioscience*, 3, 264–278.

Federation of Feminist Women's Health Centers. (1991). *A new view of a woman's body: An illustrated guide*. Los Angeles: The Feminist Press.

Feeney, J.A., & Noller, P. (1990). Attachment style as a predictor of adult romantic relationships. *Journal of Personality & Social Psychology*, 58(2), 281–291.

Feinauer, L. (1988). Relationship of long term effects of childhood sexual abuse to identity of the offender: Family, friend, or stranger. *Women and Therapy*, 7, 89–107.

Feinauer, L. (1989). Comparison of long-term effects of child abuse by type of abuse and by relationship of the offender to the victim. *American Journal of Family Therapy*, 17, 46–48.

Feldhaus-Dahir, M. (2010). Treatment options for female sexual arousal disorder: Part II. *Urologic Nursing*, 30(4), 247–251.

Feldman M.P. (1966). Aversion therapy for sexual deviations: A critical review. Psychological Bulletin, 65(2), February, 65–79.

Feldman, M., & Meyer. I. (2007). Childhood abuse and eating disorders in gay and bisexual men. *International Journal of Eating Disorders*, 40(5), 418–423.

Female Condoms: Questions and Answers. (2010). Retrieved from http://www.bccdc.ca/NR/rdonlyres/6553335D-039E-4B61-B95D-92E9671464E2/0/FemaleCondomsQAAug10.pdf.

Feminist Porn Awards. (2015). Retrieved from http://www.feministpornawards.com/.

Fenwick, W. (2014). Why Russia's anti-gay backlash will backfire. Gay & Lesbian Review Worldwide, 21, 4, p.5.

Ferdenzi, C., Schaal, B., & Roberts, S.C. (2009). Human axillary odor: Are there side-related perceptual differences? *Chemical Senses*, 34(7), 565–571.

Ferguson, C.J., & Hartley, R.D. (2009). The pleasure is momentary … the expense damnable? The influence of pornography on rape and sexual assault. *Aggression and Violent Behavior*, 14(5), 323–329.

Fergusson, D.M., Horwood, L.J., & Boden, J.M. (2009). Reactions to abortion and subsequent mental health. *British Journal of Psychiatry*, 195(5), 420–426.

Fernandez, Y.M., & Marshall, W.L. (2003). Victim empathy, social self-esteem, and psychopathology in rapists. *Sexual Abuse: Journal of Research and Treatment*, 15(1), 11–26.

Ferree, M.M., & Hess, B.B. (1985). *Controversy and coalition: The new feminist movement*. Boston, MA: Twayne.

Ferreira-Poblete, A. (1997). The probability of conception on different days of the cycle with respect to ovulation: An overview. *Advances in Contraception*, 13(2–3), 83–95.

Ferreiro-Velasco, M.E., Barca-Buyo, A., de la Barrera, S.S., Montoto-Marques, A., Vazquez, X.M., & Rodriguez-Sotillo, A. (2005). Sexual issues in a sample of women with spinal cord injury. *Spinal Cord*, 43(1), 51–55.

Feuer, A. (2008). Four charged with running online prostitution ring. *New York Times*, March 7. Retrieved from http://www.nytimes.com/2008/03/07/nyregion/07prostitution.html?_r=0.

Fieldman, J.P., & Crespi, T.D. (2002). Child sexual abuse: Offenders, disclosure and school-based initiatives. *Adolescence*, 37(145), 151–160.

Fincham, F., & Beach, S. (2010). Marriage in the new millennium: A decade of review. *Journal of Marriage and Family*, 72(3), 630–650.

Finer, L., & Philbin, J. (2013). Sexual initiation, contraceptive use, and pregnancy among young adolescents. *Pediatrics*, 131(5), 886–891.

Finer, L., Frohwirth, L., Dauphinee, L., Singh, S., & Moore, A. (2006). Timing of steps and reasons for delays in obtaining abortions in the United States. *Contraception*, 74(4), 334–344.

Finer, L.B., & Henshaw, S.K. (2006). Disparities in rates of unintended pregnancy in the United States, 1994 and 2001. *Perspectives on Sexual and Reproductive Health, 38,* 90–96.

Fink, H.A., MacDonald, R., Rutks, I.R., & Nelson, D.B. (2002). Sildenafil for male erectile dysfunction: A systematic review and meta-analysis. *Archives of Internal Medicine, 162*(12), 1349–1360.

Finkelhor, D. (1980). Sex among siblings: A survey on prevalence, variety, and effects. *Archives of Sexual Behavior, 9,* 171–194.

Finkelhor, D. (1984). *Child sexual abuse: New theory and research.* New York, NY: The Free Press.

Finkelhor, D., & Browne, A. (1985). The traumatic impact of child sexual abuse. *American Journal of Ortho-Psychiatry, 55,* 530–541.

Finkelhor, D., Hotaling, G., Lewis, I.A., & Smith, C. (1990). Sexual abuse in a national survey of adult men and women: Prevalence, characteristics, and risk factors. *Child Abuse and Neglect, 14,* 19–28.

Finster, M., & Wood, M. (2005). The Apgar score has survived the test of time. *Anesthesiology, 102*(4), 855–857.

Firestone, P., Nunes, K.L., Moulden, H., Broom, I., & Bradford, J.M. (2005). Hostility and recidivism in sexual offenders. *Archives of Sexual Behavior, 34*(3), 277–283.

Fischer, G.J. (1987). Hispanic and majority student attitudes toward forcible date rape as a function of differences in attitudes toward women. *Sex Roles, 17*(1–2), 93–101.

Fisher, B.S., Cullen, F.T., & Turner, M.G. (2000). *Sexual victimization of college women.* Washington, DC: U.S. Department of Justice, National Institute of Justice.

Fisher, B.S., Daigle, L.E., Cullen, F.T., & Turner, M.G. (2003). Reporting sexual victimization to the police and others: Results from a national-level study of college women. *Criminal Justice & Behavior, 30*(1), 6–38.

Fisher, D., Malow, R., Rosenberg, R., Reynolds, G., Farrell, N., & Jaffe, A. (2006). Recreational Viagra use and sexual risk among drug abusing men. *American Journal of Infectious Disease, 2,* 107–114.

Fisher, H. (2004). *Why we love: The nature and chemistry of romantic love.* New York, NY: Henry Holt.

Fisher, H., Brown, L., Aron, A., Strong, G., & Mashek, D. (2010). Reward, addiction, and emotion regulation systems associated with rejection in love. *Journal of Neuro-physiology, 104*(1), 51–60.

Fisher, T. (1997). *Prostitution and the Victorians.* New York, NY: St. Martin's Press.

Fitzgerald, L.F., & Ormerod, A.J. (1991). Perceptions of sexual harassment: The influence of gender and academic context. *Psychology of Women Quarterly, 15,* 281–294.

Flanigan, C., Suellentrop, K., Albert, B., Smith, J., & Whitehead, M. (2005, September 15). Science says #17: Teens and oral sex. Retrieved September 17, 2005, from http://www.teenpregnancy.org/works/pdf/ScienceSays_17_OralSex.pdf.

Fleischmann, A.A., Spitzberg, B.H., Andersen, P.A., Roesch, S.C., & Metts, S. (2005). Tickling the monster: Jealousy induction in relationships. *Journal of Social and Personal Relationships, 22*(1), 49–73.

Flowers, A. (1998). *The fantasy factory: An insider's view of the phone sex industry.* Philadelphia, PA: University of Pennsylvania Press.

Focus on the Family. (2005). *Kinsey: Myths, facts and reform.* Boulder, CO: Focus on the Family.

Foldes, P., & Buisson, O. (2009). The clitoral complex: A dynamic sonographic study. *Journal of Sexual Medicine, 6*(5), 1223–1231.

Fong, P. (2008). Edmonton killer preying on prostitutes. Retrieved from http://www.missingpeople.net/edmonton_killer_preying.htm.

Foote, W.E., & Goodman-Delahunty, J. (2005). Harassers, harassment contexts, same-sex harassment, workplace romance, and harassment theories. In W.E. Foote & J. Goodman-Delahunty (Eds.), *Evaluating sexual harassment: Psychological, social, and legal considerations in forensic examinations* (pp. 27–45). Washington, DC: American Psychological Association.

Ford, F. (2012). Focus on the Family pushing 'license to discriminate initiative in Colorado. Retrieved from http://thinkprogress.org/lgbt/2012/03/15/445629/focus-on-the-family-pushing-license-to-discriminate-initiative-in-colorado/.

Forhan, S. (2008, March). *Prevalence of STIs and bacterial vaginosis among female adolescents in the U.S.: Data from the National Health and Nutritional Examination Survey 2003–2004.* Presented at the 2008 National STD Prevention Conference, Chicago, IL. Retrieved May 29, 2008, from http://www.cdc.gov/STDConference/2008/media/summaries-11march2008.htm#tues1.

Forke, C., Myers, R., Catallozzi, M., & Schwarz, D. (2008). Relationship violence among female and male college undergraduate students. *Archives of Pediatric Adolescent Medicine, 162,* 634–641.

Forry, N.D., Leslie, L.A., & Letiecq, B.L. (2007). Marital quality in interracial relationships. *Journal of Family Issues, 28,* 1538.

Forstein, M. (1988). Homophobia: An overview. *Psychiatric Annals, 18,* 33–36.

Fortenberry, J., Schick, V., Herbenick, D., Sanders, S., Dodge, B., & Reece, M. (2010). Sexual behaviors and condom use at least vaginal intercourse: A national sample of adolescents age 14 to 17 years. *Journal of Sexual Medicine, 7*(Suppl. 5), 305–314.

Fortenberry, J.D. (2013). Puberty and adolescent sexuality. *Hormones and Behavior, 64*(2), 280–287.

Forti, G., Corona, G., Vignozzi, L., Krausz, C., & Maggi, M. (2010). Klinefelter's syndrome: A clinical and therapeutical update. *Sex Development, 4*(4–5), 249–258.

Forti, G., & Krausz, C. (1998). Clinical review 100: Evaluation and treatment of the infertile couple. *Journal of Clinical Endocrinology Medicine, 83*(12), 4177–4188.

Forum Research. (2012). One twentieth of Canadians claim to be LGBT. Retrieved from http://www.forumresearch.com/forms/News%20Archives/News%20Releases/67741_Canada-wide_-_Federal_LGBT_%28Forum_Research%29_%2820120628%29.pdf.

Foster, G. (2002). Supporting community efforts to assist orphans in Africa. *New England Journal of Medicine, 346,* 1907–1911.

Foster, G. (2006). Children who live in communities affected by AIDS. *The Lancet, 367*(9511), 700–701.

Foster, K., & Sandel, M. (2010). Abuse of women with disabilities: Toward an empowerment perspective. *Sexuality and Disability, 28*(3), 177–187.

Foubert, J., & Cremedy, B. (2007). Reactions of men of color to a commonly used rape prevention program. *Sex Roles, 57,* 137–144.

Foubert, J., Godin, E., & Tatum, J. (2010a). In their own words: Sophomore college men describe attitude and behavior changes resulting from a rape prevention program 2 years after their participation. *Journal of Interpersonal Violence, 25*(12), 2237–2257.

Foubert, J., Tatum, J., & Godin, E. (2010b). First-year male students' perceptions of a rape prevention program 7 months after their participation: Attitude and behavior changes. *Journal of College Student Development, 51*(6), 707–715.

Foubert, J.D. (2000). The longitudinal effects of a rape: Prevention program on fraternity men's attitudes. *Journal of American College Health, 48*(4), 158–163.

Foubert, J.D., & McEwen, M.K. (1998). An all-male rape prevention peer education program: Decreasing fraternity men's behavioral intent to rape. *Journal of College Student Development, 39,* 548–556.

Fowers, B.J. (1998). Psychology and the good marriage. *American Behavioral Scientist, 41*(4), 516.

Fowler, G.A. (2012). Retrieved from https://www.google.ca/?gfe_rd=cr&ei=HBB2VtjDNKmi8weRqamgCg&gws_rd=ssl#q=nathalie+blanchard+facebook.

Fox, J.A., & Zawitz, M.W. (2004). Homicide trends in the United States. Retrieved

October 23, 2005, from www.ojp.usdoj.gov/bjs/homicide/homtrnd.htm.

Fox, M., & Thomson, M. (2010). HIV/AIDS and circumcision: Lost in translation. *Journal of Medical Ethics, 36*(12), 798–801.

Fox, R.G. (1972). Study Paper on Obscenity. Prepared for the Law Reform Commission of Canada. June. KE 9070 A72 F68 1972.

Fraccaro, P.J., O'Connor, J.J. M., Re, D.E., DeBruine, L.M., & Feinberg, D.R. (2013). Faking it: Deliberately altering voice pitch and vocal attractiveness. *Animal Behavior, 85*(1), 127–136.

Frackiewicz, E.J. (2000). Endometriosis: An overview of the disease and its treatment. *Journal of the American Pharmaceutical Association, 40*(5), 645–657.

France-Presse, A. (2010, September 28). Bishops to support protests against birth control. ABS/CBN News. Retrieved March 2, 2011, from http://www.abs-cbnnews.com/nation/09/28/10/bishops-support-protests-against-birth-control.

Franceschi, S. (2005). The IARC commitment to cancer prevention: The example of papillomavirus and cervical cancer. *Recent Results in Cancer Research, 166,* 277–297.

Francis, A. (2008). Family and sexual orientation: The family-demographic correlates of homosexuality in men and women. *Journal of Sex Research, 45*(4), 371–377.

Francis, D. (2006). *Red light neon: A history of Vancouver sex trade.* Vancouver: Subway Books.

Francoeur, R.T., & Noonan, R.J. (Eds.). (2004). *The Continuum International encyclopedia of sexuality.* New York/London: Continuum International.

Francucci, C.M., Ceccoli, L., Caudarella, R., Rilli, S., & Boscaro, M. (2010). Skeletal effect of natural early menopause. *Journal of Endocrinological Investigations, 33*(7 Suppl.), 39–44.

Franiuk, R., Seefelt, J., & Vandello, J. (2008). Prevalence of rape myths in headlines and their effects on attitudes toward rape. *Sex Roles, 58,* 790–802.

Frank, E., Anderson, C., & Rubinstein, D.N. (1978). Frequency of sexual dysfunction in normal couples. *New England Journal of Medicine, 299,* 111–115.

Frank, L.G. (1997). Evolution of genital masculinization: Why do female hyaenas have such a large 'penis'? *Trends in Ecology and Evolution, 12*(2), 58–62.

Frankel, L. (2002). "I've never thought about it": Contradictions and taboos surrounding American males' experiences of first ejaculation (semenarche). *Journal of Men's Studies, 11*(1), 37–54.

Frappier, J.-Y. et al. (2008). Sex and sexual health: A survey of Canadian youth and mothers. *Pediatric and Child Health, 13*(1), 25–30.

Fraser, C.M. (1997). The impact of an undergraduate HIV/AIDS education course on students' AIDS knowledge, attitudes, and sexual risk behaviour. *Dissertation Abstracts International: Section B: The Sciences and Engineering, 58*(4–B), 1830.

Fraser, I.S. (2000). Forty years of combined oral contraception: the evolution of a revolution. *Medical Journal of Australia, 173*(10), 541–544.

Frazier, P.A. (2000). The role of attributions and perceived control in recovery from rape. *Journal of Personal and Interpersonal Loss, 5*(2/3), 203–225.

Fredriksson, J., Kanabus, A., Pennington, J., & Pembrey, G. (2008). AIDS orphans. Avert International AIDS Charity. Retrieved November 3, 2008, from http://www.avert.org/aidsorphans.htm.

Freedman, D., Khan, L., Serdula, M., Dietz, W., Srinivasan, S.R., & Berenson, G.S. (2002). Relation of age at menarche to race, time period, and anthropometric dimensions: The Bogalusa Heart Study. *Pediatrics, 110*(4), E43.

Freeman et al. (2011). *The health of Canada's Young People: A mental health focus.* Ottawa, ON: Public Health Agency of Canada.

Freeman, R. (2010). Gay rights and northern wrongs. *Up Here, 26*(3), 72, 75–75.

Freeman, S.B. (2008). Continuous oral contraception. Strategies for managing breakthrough bleeding. *Advance for Nurse Practitioners 16*(8), 36–38.

Freire, G.C. (2013). Cranberries for preventing urinary tract infections. *Sao Paulo Medical Journal, 131*(5).

French, S.E., & Holland, K.J. (2013). Condom negotiation strategies as a mediator of the relationship between self-efficacy and condom use. *The Journal of Sex Research, 50*(1), 48.

Fretts, R.C., Boyd, M.E., Usher, R.H., & Usher, H.A. (1992). The changing pattern of fetal death, 1961–1988. *Obstetrics and Gynecology, 79*(1), 35–39.

Freud, S. (1953). Three essays on the theory of sexuality. In J. Strachey (Ed. & Trans.), *The standard edition of the complete psychological works of Sigmund Freud* (Vol. 7, pp. 130–243). London: Hogarth Press. (Original work published 1905.)

Freund, K., & Blanchard, R. (1986). The concept of courtship disorder. *Journal of Sex and Marital Therapy, 12,* 79–92.

Freund, K., Scher, H., & Hucker, S. (1983). The courtship disorders. *Archives of Sexual Behavior, 12,* 369–379.

Freund, K., Scher, H., & Hucker, S. (1984). The courtship disorders: A further investigation. *Archives of Sexual Behavior, 13,* 133–139.

Freund, M., Lee, N., & Leonard, T. (1991). Sexual behavior of clients with street prostitutes in Camden, New Jersey. *Journal of Sex Research, 28,* 579–591.

Freymiller, L. (2005, May). Separate or equal?: Gay viewers respond to same-sex and gay/straight relationships on TV. Presented at the 2005 Annual Meeting of the International Communication Association, New York, NY.

Frick, K.D., Clark, M.A., Steinwachs, D.M., Langenberg, P., Stovall, D., Munro, M.G., & Dickersin, K.; STOP-DUB Research Group. (2009). Financial and quality-of-life burden of dysfunctional uterine bleeding among women agreeing to obtain surgical treatment. *Womens Health Issues, 19*(1), 70–78.

Friebe, A., & Arck, P. (2008). Causes for spontaneous abortion: What the bugs 'gut' to do with it? *International Journal of Biochemistry and Cell Biology, 40*(11), 2348–2352.

Friedler, S., Glasser, S., Azani, L., Freedman, L., Raziel, A., Strassburger, D., Ron-El, R., & Lerner-Geva, L. (2011). The effect of medical clowning on pregnancy rates after in vitro fertilization and embryo transfer. *Fertility and Sterility, 95*(6), 2127–2130.

Friedman, C. (2007). First comes love, then comes marriage, then comes baby carriage: Perspectives on gay parenting and reproductive technology. *Journal of Infant, Child, and Adolescent Psychotherapy, 6,* 111–123.

Friedman-Kien, A.E., & Farthing, C. (1990). Human immunodeficiency virus infection: A survey with special emphasis on mucocutaneous manifestations. *Seminars in Dermatology, 9,* 167–177.

Friedrich, W.N. (1998). Behavioral manifestations of child sexual abuse. *Child Abuse and Neglect, 22*(6), 523–531.

Friedrich, W.N., Fisher, J., Broughton, D., Houston, M., & Shafran, C.R. (1998). Normative sexual behaviour in children: A contemporary sample. *Pediatrics, 101*(4), e9.

Friedrich, W.N., Grambsch, P., Broughton, D., Kuiper, J., & Beilke, R.L. (1991). Normative sexual behavior in children. *Pediatrics, 88,* 456–464.

Fritz, G.S., Stoll, K., & Wagner, N.N. (1981). A comparison of males and females who were sexually molested as children. *Journal of Sex & Marital Therapy, 7*(1), 54–59.

Frohlich, P.F., & Meston, C.M. (2000). Evidence that serotonin affects female sexual functioning via peripheral mechanisms. *Physiology and Behavior, 71*(3–4), 383–393.

Frost, J.J., & Driscoll, A.K. (2006). *Sexual and reproductive health of U.S. Latinas: A literature review.* New York, NY: Alan Guttmacher Institute. Retrieved May 27, 2008, from http://www.guttmacher.org/pubs/2006/02/07/or19.pdf.

Frost, J.J., Darroch, J.E., & Remez, L. (2008). Improving contraception use in the United States. *In Brief, 1.* New York, NY: Alan Guttmacher Institute.

Frostino, A. (2007). Guilt and jealousy associated with sexual fantasies among heterosexual married individuals. Widener University. *Dissertation Abstracts International: Section B: The Sciences and Engineering, 68*(3-B), 1924.

Fruth, A. (2007). Dating and adolescents' psychological well-being. *Dissertation Abstracts International Section A: Humanities and Social Sciences, 68*(1-A), 360.

Fu, Y. (2010). Interracial marriage formation: Entry into first union and transition from cohabitation to marriage. University of North Carolina at Chapel Hill, AAT #1483777.

Fuller, J., & Blackley, S. (1996). *Restricted entry: Censorship on trial.* Vancouver, BC: Press Gang Publishers.

Fuller-Fricke., R.L. (2007). Interaction of relationship satisfaction, depressive symptoms, and self-esteem in college-aged women. *Fuller Theological Seminary, Dissertation Abstracts,* UMI #3267404.

Gaetz, S. (2004). Safe streets for whom? Homeless youth, social exclusion, and criminal victimization. *Canadian Journal of Criminology and Criminal Justice, 46,* 423–456.

Gaffield, M.E., Culwell, K.R., & Ravi, A. (2009). Oral contraceptives and family history of breast cancer. *Contraception, 80*(4), 372–380.

Gahler, M., Hong, Y., & Bernhardt, E. (2009). Parental divorce and union disruption among young adults in Sweden. *Journal of Family Issues, 30*(5), 688–713.

Gaither, G.A. (2000). The reliability and validity of three new measures of male sexual preferences (Doctoral dissertation, University of North Dakota). *Dissertation Abstracts International, 61,* 4981.

Gaither, G.A., Sellbom, M., & Meier, B.P. (2003). The effect of stimulus content on volunteering for sexual interest research among college students. *Journal of Sex Research, 40*(3), 240–249.

Galis, F., Broek, C., Van Dongen, S., & Wijnaendts, L. (2010). Sexual dimorphism in the prenatal digit ratio (2D:4D). *Archives of Sexual Behavior, 39,* 57–62.

Gallagher, J. (2001). Normal, China—The Chinese Psychiatric Association decides that being gay is no longer a disease. *The Advocate.* p. 22.

Gallo, R.V. (2000). Is there a homosexual brain? *Gay and Lesbian Review, 7*(1), 12–16.

Galloway, T., Cipelli, R., Guralnick, J., Ferrucci, L., Bandinelli, S., Corsi, A.M., Money, C., McCormack, P., & Melzer, D. (2010). Daily bisphenol A excretion and associations with sex hormone concentrations: Results from the InCHIANTI Adult Population Study. *Environmental Health Perspectives, 118*(11), 1603–1608.

Gallup, G.G. Jr., Rebecca, L. Burch, M., Zappieri, L., Rizwan, A. Parvez, M., Stockwell, L., & Davis, J.A. (2003). The human penis as a semen displacement device. *Evolution & Human Behavior,* 24(4), 277–289,

Galupo, M.P. (2006). Sexism, heterosexism, and biphobia: The framing of bisexual women's friendships. *Journal of Bisexuality, 6,* 35–45.

Gamel, C., Hengeveld, M., Davis, B. (2000). Informational needs about the effects of gynaecological cancer on sexuality: A review of the literature. *Journal of Clinical Nursing, 9*(5), 678–688.

Gamson, J. (1990). Rubber Wars: Struggles over the Condom in the United States. *Journal of the History of Sexuality, 1*(2), 262-282.

Gan, C., Zou, Y., Wu, S., Li, Y., & Liu, Q. (2008). The influence of medical abortion compared with surgical abortion on subsequent pregnancy outcome. *International Journal of Gynecology and Obstetrics, 101,* 231–238.

Gannon, S. (2011). Exclusion as language and the language of exclusion: Tracing regimes of gender through linguistic representations of the "eunuch." *Journal of the History of Sexuality, 20*(1), 1–27.

Garbin, C., Deacon, J., Rowan, M., Hartmann, P., & Geddes, D. (2009). Association of nipple piercing with abnormal milk production and breastfeeding. *Journal of the American Medical Association, 301*(24), 2550–2551.

Garcia-Falgueras, A., & Swaab, D.F. (2010). Sexual hormones and the brain: An essential alliance for sexual identity and sexual orientation. *Endocrine Development, 17,* 22–35.

Garcia-Moreno, C., Jansen, H.A.F.M., Ellsberg, M., Heise, L., & Watts, C.H. (2006). Prevalence of intimate partner violence: findings from the WHO multi-country study on women's health and domestic violence. *The Lancet, 368*(9543), 1260–1269.

Gardiner, P., Stargrove, M., & Low, D. (2011). Concomitant use of prescription medications and dietary supplements in menopausal women: An approach to provider preparedness. *Maturitas, 68*(3), 251–255.

Gardner, A. (2004). *Excess weight can compromise birth control pills.* Sexual Health Network. Retrieved October 1, 2008, from http://sexualhealth.ehealthsource.com/?p=news1&id=523135.

Gardner, C. (2011). *Making chastity sexy: The rhetoric of evangelical abstinence campaigns.* Berkeley, CA: University of California Press.

Gardner, R.A. (1993). A theory about the variety of human sexual behavior. http://www.ipt-forensics.com/journal/volume5/j5_2_8.htm.

Garner, M., Turner, M.C., Ghadirian, P., Krewski, D., & Wade, M. (2008). Testicular cancer and hormonally active agents. *Journal of Toxicology and Environmental Health, 11,* 260–275.

Garnock-Jones, K.P., & Giuliano, A.R. (2011) Quadrivalent human papillomavirus (HPV) types 6, 11, 16, 18 vaccine: For the prevention of genital warts in males. *Drugs, 71*(5), 591–602.

Gartrell, N., & Bos, H. (2010). The US national longitudinal lesbian family study: Psychological adjustment of the 17-year-old adolescents. Retrieved June 7, 2010, from http://pediatrics.aappublications.org/cgi/content/abstract/peds.2009–3153v1.

Garver-Apgar, C.E., Gangestad, S.W., Thorn-hill, R., Miller, R.D., & Olp, J.J. (2006). Major histocompatibility complex alleles, sexual responsivity, and unfaithfulness in romantic couples. *Psychological Science, 17,* 830–835.

Gavard, J., & Artal, R. (2008). Effect of exercise on pregnancy outcome. *Clinical Obstetrics and Gynecology, 51,* 467–480.

Gebhard, P., & Johnson, A. (1979). *The Kinsey data: Marginal tabulations of the 1938–1963 interviews conducted by the Institute for Sex Research.* Philadelphia: W.B. Saunders.

Geer, J.H., & O'Donohue, W.T. (1987). A sociological approach. In J.H. Geer & W.T. O'Donohue (Eds.), *Theories of human sexuality* (pp. 237–253). New York, NY: Plenum Press.

Gelbard, M. (1988). Dystrophic penile classification in Peyronie's disease. *Journal of Urology, 139,* 738–740.

Gemelli, R.J. (1996). *Normal child and adolescent development.* Arlington, VA: American Psychiatric Press.

Gentzler, A., Kerns, K., & Keener, E. (2010). Emotional reactions and regulatory responses to negative and positive events: Associations with attachment and gender. *Motivation and Emotion, 34*(1), 78.

George, C., Adam, B.A., Read, S.E. Husbands, W.C., Remis, R.S., Makoroka, L., & Rourke, S.B. (2012). The MaBwana Black men's study: Community and belonging in the lives of African, Caribbean and other Black gay men in Toronto. *Culture, Health & Sexuality,* Vol 14(5), 549–562.

Geraghty, P. (2010). Beyond birth control. The health benefits of hormonal contraception. *Advanced Nurse Practitioner, 17*(2), 47–48, 50, 52.

Getahun, D. Ananth, C.V., Selvam, N., & Demissie, K. (2005). Adverse perinatal outcomes among interracial couples in the

United States. *Obstetrics and Gynecology, 106*(1), 81–88.

Ghanotakis, E. (2008, January 10). South Africa: An everyday crime. *Frontline Rough Cut.* Retrieved April 30, 2011, from http://www.pbs.org/frontlineworld/rough/2008/01/south_africa_ev.html.

Ghaziani, A. (2005). Breakthrough: The 1979 national march. *Gay & Lesbian Review Worldwide, 12*(2), 31–33.

Ghidini, A., & Bocchi, C. (2007). Direct fetal blood sampling: Cordocentesis. In J.T. Queenan, C.Y. Spong, & C.J. Lockwood (Eds.), *Management of high-risk pregnancy: An evidence-based approach.* Hoboken, NJ: Wiley Blackwell.

Ghosh, M.K. (2005). Breech presentation: Evolution of management. *Journal of Reproductive Medicine, 50*(2), 108–116.

Gibbs, J.L., Ellison, N.B., & Heino, R.D. (2006). Self-presentation in online personals: The role of anticipated future interaction, self-disclosure, and perceived success in Internet dating. *Communication Research, 33*, 152–177.

Gibbs, N. (2010, April 22). The pill at 50: Sex, freedom and paradox. *Time Magazine.* Retrieved September 6, 2010, from http://www.time.com/time/health/article/0,8599,1983712,00.html.

Gibson, B. (2010). Care of the child with the desire to change genders—female to male transition. *Pediatric Nursing, 36*(2), 112–119.

Gibson, M. (1997). Clitoral corruption: Body metaphors and American doctors' constructions of female homosexuality, 1870–1900. In V.A. Rosario (Ed.), *Science and homosexualities.* London: Routledge.

Gill, S. (2009). Honour killings and the quest for justice in black and minority ethnic communities and in the UK. United Nations Division for the Advancement of Women, Expert Group Meeting on good practices in legislation to address harmful practices against women. Retrieved March 30, 2011, from http://www.un.org/womenwatch/daw/egm/vaw_legislation_2009/Expert%20Paper%20EGMGPLHP %20_Aisha%20Gill%20revised_pdf.

Gilleard, C., & Higgs, P. (2000). *Cultures of ageing: Self, citizen and the body.* Upper Saddle River, NJ: Prentice Hall Publishers.

Gilmore, A.K., Schacht, R.L., George, W.H., Otto, J.M., Davis, K.C., Heiman, J.R., Norris, J., & Kajumulo, K.F. (2010). Assessing women's sexual arousal in the context of sexual assault history and acute alcohol intoxication. *Journal of Sexual Medicine, 7*(6), 2112–2119.

Gilmore, D.D. (1990). *Manhood in the making: Cultural concepts of masculinity.* New Haven, CT: Yale University Press.

Gilmore, S. (1992). 8 more women accuse Adams—allegations of two decades of sexual harassment, abuse—and a rape. *The Seattle Times*, March 1, http://community.seattletimes.nwsource.com/archive/?date=19920301&slug=1478550.

Gilson, R.J., & Mindel, A. (2001). Sexually transmitted infections. *British Medical Journal, 322*(729S), 1135–1137.

Giltay, J.C., & Maiburg, M.C. (2010). Klinefelter syndrome: Clinical and molecular aspects. *Expert Review of Molecular Diagnostics, 10*(6), 765–776.

Ginty, M.M. (2005). New pills launch debate over menstruation. Retrieved March 19, 2005, from http://www.womensenews.org/article.cfm/dyn/aid/1879/context/archive.

Giotakos, O., Markianos, M., & Vaidakis, N. (2005). Aggression, impulsivity, and plasma sex hormone levels in a group of rapists, in relation to their history of childhood attention-deficit/hyperactivity disorder symptoms. *Journal of Forensic Psychiatry & Psychology, 16*(2), 423–433.

Giraldi, A., & Kristensen, E. (2010). Sexual dysfunction in women with diabetes mellitus. *Journal of Sex Research, 47*(2), 199–211.

Girsh, E., Katz, N., Genkin, L., Girtler, O., Bocker, J., Bezdin, S., & Barr, I. (2008). Male age influences oocyte-donor program results. *Journal of Assisted Reproductive Genetics, 25*(4), 137–143.

Glasser, M., Kolvin, I., Campbell, D., Glasser, A., Leitch, I., & Farrelly, S. (2001). Cycle of child sexual abuse: Links between being a victim and becoming a perpetrator. *British Journal of Psychiatry, 179*, 482–494.

Gleicher, N., Weghofer, A., & Barad, D. (2008). Preimplantation genetic screening: "Established" and ready for prime time? *Fertility and Sterility, 89*, 780–788.

Glenn, N., & Marquardt, E. (2001). Hooking up, hanging out and hoping for Mr. Right: College women on mating and dating today. Retrieved October 19, 2005, from http://www.americanvalues.org/Hooking_Up.pdf.

Glenn, S., & Byers, E. (2009). The roles of situational factors, attributions, and guilt in the well-being of women who have experienced sexual coercion. *Canadian Journal of Human Sexuality, 18*(4), 201–220.

Glenwright, M., & Pexman, P.M. (2010). Development of children's ability to distinguish sarcasm and verbal irony. *Journal of Child Language, 37*(2), 429–451.

Glina, S., Sharlip, I.D., & Hellstrom, W.J. (2013). Modifying risk factors to prevent and treat erectile dysfunction. *Sexual Medicine, 10*(1), 111–119.

Godeau, E., Gabhainn, S., Vignes, C., Ross, J., Boyce, W., & Todd, J. (2008). Contraceptive use by 15-year old students at their last sexual intercourse. *Archives of Pediatric and Adolescent Medicine, 162*(1), 66–73.

Godfrey, K., Robinson, S., Barker, D.J., Osmond, C., & Cox, V. (1996). Maternal nutrition in early and late pregnancy in relation to placental and fetal growth. *British Medical Journal, 312*(7028), 410–414.

Goffman, E. (1967). *Interaction ritual.* New York, NY: Doubleday.

Gokyildiz, S., & Beji, N.K. (2005). The effects of pregnancy on sexual life. *Journal of Sex and Marital Therapy, 31*(3), 201–215.

Gold, J.C. (2004). Kiss of the yogini: "Tantric sex" in its South Asian contexts. *Journal of Religion, 84*(2), 334–336.

Goldberg, A., Smith, J., & Kashy, D. (2010). Preadoptive factors predicting lesbian, gay, and heterosexual couples' relationship quality across the transition to adoptive parenthood. *Journal of Family Psychology, 24*(3), 221–232.

Golden, G.H. (2001). Dyadic-dystonic compelling eroticism: Can these relationships be saved? *Journal of Sex Education & Therapy, 26*(1), 50.

Goldman, R. (1999). The psychological impact of circumcision. *British Journal of Urology International, 83*, 93–102.

Goldman-Mellor, S., Brydon, L., & Steptoe, A. (2010). Psychological distress and circulating inflammatory markers in healthy young adults. *Psychological Medicine, 40*, 2079–2087.

Goldstein, A.T., & Burrows, L. (2008). Vulvodynia. *Journal of Sexual Medicine, 5*, 5–15.

Goleman, D. (1992, April 14). Therapies offer hope for sexual offenders. *The New York Times*, pp. C1, C11.

Golen, S. (1990). A factor analysis of barriers to effective listening. *Journal of Business Communication, 27*, 25–36.

Gollapalli, V., Liao, J., Dudakovic, A., Sugg, S., Scott-Conner, C., & Weigel, R. (2010). Risk factors for development and recurrence of primary breast abscesses. *Journal of the American College of Surgeons, 211*(1), 41–48.

Gómez, A. (2011). Testing the cycle of violence hypothesis: Child abuse and adolescent dating violence as predictors of intimate partner violence in young adulthood. *Youth and Society, 43*(1), 171–192.

Gonçalves, M.A., Guilleminault, C., Ramos, E., Palha, A., & Paiva, T. (2005). Erectile dysfunction, obstructive sleep apnea syndrome and nasal CPAP treatment. *Sleep Medicine, 6*(4), 333–339.

Gonzaga, G., Haselton, M., Smurda, J., Davies, M., & Poore, J. (2008). Love, desire, and the suppression of thoughts of romantic alternatives. *Evolution and Human Behavior, 29*, 119–126.

Gonzales, A., Schofield, R., & Schmitt, G. (2005). Sexual assault on campus: What colleges and universities are doing about it. U.S. Department of Justice. Retrieved April 25, 2011, from http://www.publicintegrity.org/investigations/campus_assault/assets/pdf/Fisher_report_3.pdf.

González, M., Viáfara, G., Caba, F., Molina, T., & Ortiz, C. (2006). Libido and orgasm in middle-aged women. *Maturitas, 53,* 1–10.

Goode, E. (1994). *Deviant behavior.* Englewood Cliffs, NJ: Prentice Hall.

Goodell, T.T. (2007). Sexuality in chronic lung disease. *The Nursing Clinics of North America, 42*(4), 631–638.

Goodman, A. (1993). Diagnosis and treatment of sexual addiction. *Journal of Sex and Marital Therapy, 19*(3), 225–251.

Goodman, E., & Vertesi, J. (2012). :Design for X? Distribution choices and ethical design." CHI EA '12: Proceedings of the 2012 Annual Conference. Extended Abstracts. Pages 81–90.

Goodman, M., Shvetsov, Y., McDuffie, K., Wilkens, L., Zhu, X., Ning, L., et al. (2008). Acquisition of anal human papillomavirus infection in women: The Hawaii HPV cohort study. *Journal of Infectious Diseases, 197,* 957–966.

Goodman, M.P. (2009). Female cosmetic genital surgery. *Obstetrics and Gynecology, 113*(1), 154–159.

Goodman, M.P., Placik, O., Benson, R., Miklos, J., Moore, R., Jason, R., Matlock, D., Simopoulos, A., Stern, B., Stanton, R., et al. (2010). A large multicenter outcome study of female genital plastic surgery. *Journal of Sexual Medicine, 7*(4 Pt 1), 1565–1577.

Gooren, L. (2006). The biology of human psychosexual differentiation. *Hormones & Behavior, 50,* 589–601.

Gordon, B.N., & Schroeder, C.S. (1995). *Sexuality: A developmental approach to problems.* Chapel Hill, NC: Clinical Child Psychology Library.

Gordon, L. (2010, March 15). Mixed-gender dorm rooms are gaining acceptance. *Los Angeles Times.* Retrieved November 6, 2010, from http://articles.latimes.com/2010/mar/15/local/la-me-dorm-gender15-2010mar15.

Gordon, S. (1986). What kids need to know. *Psychology Today, 20,* 22–26.

Gottman, J., & Silver, N. (2000). *The seven principles for making marriage work.* New York, NY: Crown.

Gottman, J., Levenson, R., Swanson, C., Swanson, K., Tyson, R., & Yoshimoto, D. (2003). Observing gay, lesbian and heterosexual couples' relationships: Mathematical modeling of conflict interaction. *Journal of Homosexuality, 45,* 65–91.

Gottman, J.M. (1994). *Why marriages succeed or fail.* New York, NY: Simon & Schuster.

Gottschall, J.A., & Gottschall, T.A. (2003). Are perincident rape-pregnancy rates higher than per-incident consensual pregnancy rates? *Human Nature, 14*(1), 1–20.

Gould, S.J. (1981). *The mismeasure of man.* New York, NY: Norton.

Gourley, C. (2007). *Flappers and the new American woman: Perceptions of women from 1918 through the 1920s.* Breckenridge, CO: Twenty-First Century Books.

Government of Canada. (2013). Infertility. Retrieved November 28, 2014, from http://healthycanadians.gc.ca/healthy-living-vie-saine/pregnancy-grossesse/fertility-fertilite/fert-eng.php.

Government of Canada, Department of Justice. (2015). Age of consent to sexual activity. Retrieved February 28, 2015, from http://www.justice.gc.ca/eng/rp-pr/other-autre/clp/faq.html.

Government of Canada, Justice Laws. (2015). Criminal Code. Retrieved April 17, 2015, from http://laws-lois.justice.gc.ca/eng/acts/C-46/.

Gowing, L. (2012). Women's bodies and the making of sex in seventeenth-century England. *Signs, 37*(4), 813–822.

Goy, R.W., & Wallen, K. (1979). Experiential variables influencing play, foot-clasp mounting and adult sexual competence in male rhesus monkeys. *Psychoneuroendocrinology, 4*(1), 1–12.

Grace, A.P. (2005). Reparative Therapies: A Contemporary Clear and Present Danger Across Minority Sex, Sexual, and Gender Differences. *Canadian Woman Studies; Winter/Spring2005, Vol. 24* Issue 2/3, 145–151.

Grace, A.P. (2008).The Charisma and Deception of Reparative Therapies: When Medical Science Beds Religion. *Journal of Homosexuality; 2008, Vol. 55* Issue 4, 545.

Graham, C., Bancroft, J., Doll, H., Greco, T., & Tanner, A. (2007). Does oral contraceptive-induced reduction in free testosterone adversely affect the sexuality or mood of women? *Psychneuroendocrinology, 32,* 246–255.

Grant, V.J. (2006). Entrenched misinformation about X and Y sperm. *British Medical Journal, 332*(7546), 916.

Gray, J.H. (1971). *Red lights on the Prairies.* Calgary, AB: Fifth House Publishers.

Graziottin, A. (2007). Prevalence and evaluation of sexual health problems—HSDD in Europe. *Journal of Sexual Medicine, 4*(Suppl 3), 211–219.

Grce, M., & Davies, P. (2008). Human papillomavirus testing for primary cervical cancer screening. *Expert Review of Molecular Diagnostics, 8,* 599–605.

Green, A.I. (2007). On the horns of a dilemma: Institutional dimensions of the sexual career in a sample of middle-class, urban, Black, gay men. *Journal of Black Studies, 37*(5), 753–774.

Green, D., Tarasaoff, L.A., & Epstien, R. (2012). Meeting the Assisted Human Reproduction (AHR) needs of lesbian, gay, bisexual, trans and queer (LGBTQ) People in Canada. Retrieved February 21, 2015, from http://www.cfas.ca/images/stories/pdf/factsheet_lgbtq_english.pdf.

Green, R. (1987). *The "sissy boy syndrome" and the development of homosexuality.* New Haven, CT: Yale University Press.

Green, R. (1988). The immutability of (homo)-sexual orientation: Behavioral science implications for a constitutional (legal) analysis. *The Journal of Psychiatry and the Law, 16,* 537–575.

Green, R.J. (2008a). Gay and lesbian couples: Developing resilience in response to social injustice. In M. McGoldrick & K. Hardy (Eds.), *Revisioning family therapy: Race, culture, and gender in clinical practice* (2nd ed.). New York, NY: Guilford Press.

Green, R.J. (2008b, January 11). *What straights can learn from gays about relationships and parenting.* San Francisco: Rockway Institute. Retrieved December 19, 2008, from http://www.newswise.com/articles/view/536799/.

Green, R.J., Bettinger, M., & Zacks, E. (1996). Are lesbian couples fused and gay male couples disengaged? Questioning gender straightjackets. In J. Laird & R.J. Green (Eds.), *Lesbians and gays in couples and families: A handbook for therapists* (pp. 185–230). New York, NY: Jossey-Bass.

Green, R.J., & Mitchell, V. (2002). Gay and lesbian couples in therapy: Homophobia, relational ambiguity, and social support. In A.S. Gurman & N.S. Jacobson (Eds.), *Clinical handbook of couple therapy* (3rd ed., pp. 546–568). New York, NY: Guilford Press.

Greenberg, M., Cheng, Y., Hopkins, L., Stotland, N., Bryant, A., & Caughey, A. (2006). Are there ethnic differences in the length of labor? *American Journal of Obstetrics and Gynecology, 195,* 743–748.

Greenberg, M., Cheng, Y., Sullivan, M., Norton, L., & Caughey, A. (2007). Does length of labor vary by maternal age? *American Journal of Obstetrics and Gynecology, 197,* 428.

Greenfeld, D.A. (2005). Reproduction in same sex couples: Quality of parenting and child development. *Current Opinions in Obstetrics and Gynecology, 17,* 309–312.

Greenlinger, V., & Byrne, D. (1987). Coercize sexual fantasies of college men as predictors of self-reported likelihood to rape and overt sexual aggression. *The Journal of Sex Research, 23*(1), 1–11.

Greenwald, E., & Leitenberg, H. (1989). Long-term effects of sexual experiences with siblings and nonsiblings during childhood. *Archives of Sexual Behavior, 18,* 289–400.

Greenwald, H., & McCorkle, R. (2008). Sexuality and sexual function in long-term survivors of cervical cancer. *Journal of Women's Health, 17,* 955–963.

Greenwald, J.L., Burstein, G., Pincus, J., & Branson, G. (2006). A rapid review of rapid HIV antibody tests. *Current Infectious Disease Reports, 8,* 125–131.

Greer, J.B., Modugno, F., Allen, G.O., & Ness, R.B. (2005). Androgenic progestins in oral contraceptives and the risk of epithelial ovarian cancer. *Obstetrics and Gynecology, 105,* 731–740.

Gregson, S., Nyamukapa, C., Garnett, G., Wambe, M., Lewis, J., Mason, P., Chandiwana, S., & Anderson, R. (2005). HIV infection and reproductive health in teenage women orphaned and made vulnerable by AIDS in Zimbabwe. *AIDS Care, 17*(7), 785–794.

Grew, T. (2008). Human rights group criticises Jamaica's homophobic violence. PinkNews.co.uk, December 8, 2008.

Griffin, S.A. (2006). A qualitative inquiry into how romantic love has been portrayed by contemporary media and researchers. *Dissertation Abstracts International Section A: Humanities and Social Sciences, 67,* 2272.

Griffiths, M.D. (2000). Excessive Internet use: Implications for sexual behavior. *Cyberpsychology and Behavior, 3,* 537–552.

Griffitt, W., & Veitch, R. (1971). Hot and crowded: Influences of population density and temperature on interpersonal affective behavior. *Journal of Personality and Social Psychology, 17,* 92–98.

Grimbizis, G.F., & Tarlatzis, B.C. (2010). The use of hormonal contraception and its protective role against endometrial and ovarian cancer. *Best Practice & Research: Clinical Obstetrics & Gynaecology, 24*(1), 29–38.

Grimbos T., Dawood K., Burriss R.P., Zucker K.J., & Puts D.A. (2010). Sexual orientation and the second to fourth finger length ratio: A meta-analysis in men and women. *Behavioral Neuroscience, 124*(2), 278–287.

Grob, C.S. (1985). Single case study: Female exhibitionism. *Journal of Nervous and Mental Disease, 173,* 253–256.

Groer, M.W. (2005). Differences between exclusive breastfeeders, formula-feeders, and controls: A study of stress, mood, and endocrine variables. *Biological Research for Nursing, 7*(2), 106–117.

Gross, J. (2007, October 9). Aging and gay, and facing prejudice in twilight. *New York Times.* Retrieved September 3, 2008, from http://www.nytimes.com/2007/10/09/us/09aged.html.

Grosskurth, P. (1980). *Havelock Ellis: A biography.* New York, NY: Alfred A. Knopf.

Groth, A.N. (1978). Patterns of sexual assault against children and adolescents. In A.W. Burgess, A.N. Groth, L.L. Holmstrom, & S.M. Sgroi (Eds.), *Sexual assault of children and adolescents.* Toronto: Lexington Books.

Groth, N., & Burgess, A. (1980). Male rape: Offenders and victims. *American Journal of Psychiatry, 137,* 806–810.

Grover, S., Mattoo, S.K., Pendharkar, S., & Kandappan, V. (2014). Sexual dysfunction in patients with alcohol and opioid dependence. *Indian Journal of Psychological Medicine, 36*(4), 355–365.

Groysman, V. (2010). Vulvodynia: New concepts and review of the literature. *Dermatology Clinics, 28*(4), 681–696.

Gruber, A.J., & Pope, H.G. (2000). Psychiatric and medical effects of anabolic-androgenic steroid use in women. *Psychotherapy and Psychosomatics, 69*(1), 19–26.

Gruenbaum, E. (2006). Sexuality issues in the movement to abolish female genital cutting in Sudan. *Medical Anthropology Quarterly, 20,* 121.

Grunbaum, J.A., Kann, L., Kinchen, S.A., Williams, B., Ross, J.G., Lowry, R., & Kolbe, L. (2002). Youth risk behavior surveillance: United States, 2001. *Morbidity and Mortality Weekly Report, 51*(no. SS-4).

Guadagno, R., & Sagarin, B. (2010). Sex differences in jealousy: An evolutionary perspective on online infidelity. *Journal of Applied Social Psychology, 40*(10), 2636–2655.

Gudjonsson, G.H. (1986). Sexual variations: Assessment and treatment in clinical practice. *Sexual and Marital Therapy, 1,* 191–214.

Gudykunst, W., Ting-Toomey, S., & Nishida, T. (1996). *Communication in personal relationships across cultures.* Thousand Oaks, CA: Sage Publications.

Guerrero, L., & Bachman, G. (2010). Forgiveness and forgiving communication in dating relationships: An expectancy-investment explanation. *Journal of Social and Personal Relationships, 27*(6), 801.

Guerrero, L.K., & Afifi, W. (1999). Toward a goal-oriented approach for understanding communicative responses to jealousy. *Western Journal of Communication, 63*(2), 216–248.

Guerrero, L.K., Spitzberg, B.H., & Yoshimura, S.M. (2004). Sexual and emotional jealousy. In J.H. Harvey, A. Wenzel, & S. Sprecher (Eds.), *The handbook of sexuality in close relationships* (pp. 311–345). Mahwah, NJ: Erlbaum.

Guffey, M.E. (1999). *Business communication: Process & product* (3rd ed.). Belmont, CA: Wadsworth.

Guha, C., Shah, S.J., Ghosh, S.S., Lee, S.W., Roy-Chowdhury, N., & Roy-Chowdhury, J. (2003). Molecular therapies for viral hepatitis. *BioDrugs, 17*(2), 81–91.

Gundersen, B.H., Melas, P.S., & Skar, J.E. (1981). Sexual behavior of preschool children: Teachers' observations. In L.L. Constantine & F.M. Martinson (Eds.), *Children and sex: New findings, new perspectives* (pp. 45–61). Boston, MA: Little, Brown.

Gunter, J. (2007). Vulvodynia: New thoughts on a devastating condition. *Obstetrics and Gynecological Survey, 62,* 812–819.

Gupta, J.K., & Nikodem, V.C. (2000). Woman's position during second stage of labour. *Cochrane Database of Systematic Reviews, 2,* CD002006.

Gusarova, I., Fraser, V., & Alderson, K.G. (2012). A quantitative study of "friends with benefits" relationships. *Canadian Journal of Human Sexuality, 21*(1), 41–59.

Gutkin, M. (2010). Internet versus face-to-face dating: A study of relationship satisfaction, commitment, and sustainability. *Dissertation Abstracts International, 71*(08). University of Delaware, AAT #3417180.

Guzzo, K. (2009). Marital intentions and the stability of first cohabitations. *Journal of Family Issues, 30*(2), 179–205.

Ha, T.T. (2010). Vatican, Canadian church officials tried to keep sex scandal secret. *The Globe and Mail,* April 9. http://www.theglobeandmail.com/news/national/vatican-canadian-church-officials-tried-to-keep-sex-scandal-secret/article4315371/.

Hack, W.W., Meijer, R.W., Bos, S.D., & Haas-noot, K. (2003). A new clinical classification for undescended testis. *Scandinavian Journal of Nephrology, 37*(1), 43–47.

Hackett, G. (2009). The burden and extent of comorbid conditions in patients with erectile dysfunction. *International Journal of Clinical Practice, 63*(8), 1205–1213.

Hader, S.L., Smith, D.K., Moore, J.S., & Holmberg, S.D. (2001). HIV infection in women in the U.S.: Status at the millennium. *Journal of the American Medical Association, 285*(9), 1186–1192.

Haeberle, E.J. (1982). The Jewish contribution to the development of sexology. *Journal of Sex Research, 18,* 305–323.

Haegert, S.A. (1999). How does love grow? attachment processes in older adoptees and foster children as illustrated by fictional stories. *Dissertation Abstracts International Section A: Humanities and Social Sciences, 60*(6–A), 1903.

Haggerty, C.L., Gottlieb, S.L., Taylor, B.D., Low, N., Xu, F., & Ness, R.B. (2010). Risk of sequelae after Chlamydia trachomatis genital infection in women. *Journal of Infectious Disease, 201*(Suppl. 2), S134-S155.

Haglund, K. (2003). Sexually abstinent African American Adolescent females' descriptions of abstinence. *Journal of Nursing Scholarship, 35*(3), 231–236.

Hahlweg, K., Kaiser, A., Christensen, A., Fehm-Wolfsdorf, G., & Grother, T. (2000). Self-report and observational assessment of couples' conflict. *Journal of Marriage and Family, 62*(1), 61.

Hahm, H., Lee, J., Zerden, L., & Ozonoff, A. (2008). Longitudinal effects of perceived maternal approval on sexual behaviors of Asian and Pacific Islander (API) young adults. *Journal of Youth and Adolescence, 37*, 74–85.

Haig-Brown, C. (1988). *Resistance and renewal: Surviving the Indian residential school.* Vancouver, BC: Tillacum Library.

Haji, R., Lalonde, R.N., Durbin, A., & Naveh-Benjamin, I. (2011). A multidimensional approach to identity: Religious and cultural identity in young Jewish Canadians. *Group Processes & Intergroup Relations, 14*(1), 3–18.

Hall, E.T. (1976). *Beyond culture.* New York, NY: Doubleday.

Hall, E.T. (1990). *Understanding cultural differences, Germans, French and Americans.* Yarmouth, ME: Intercultural Press.

Hall, J. (2005). Neuroscience and education (SCRE Research Report No. 121). Glasgow, Scotland: University of Glasgow, the Scottish Council for Research in Education Centre.

Hall, K. (2012). Christian groups take issue with anti-bullying laws. *Huffington Post.* May 5th. http://www.huffingtonpost.com/2012/04/05/anti-bullying-laws-christian-religious-freedom_n_1406757.html.

Hall, P., & Schaeff, C. (2008). Sexual orientation and fluctuating symmetry in men and women. *Archives of Sexual Behavior, 37*(1), 158–165.

Halldorsson, T.I., Strom, M., Petersen, S.B., & Olsen, S.F. (2010). Intake of artificially sweetened soft drinks and risk of preterm delivery: A prospective cohort study in 59,334 Danish pregnant women. *American Journal of Clinical Nutrition, 92*(3), 626–633.

Hallinan, R., Byrne, A., Agho, K., McMahon, C., Tynan, P., & Attia J. (2008). Erectile dysfunction in men receiving methadone and buprenorphine maintenance treatment. *Journal of Sexual Medicine, 5*(3), 684–692.

Hallinan, R., Byrne, A., Agho, K., McMahon, C.G., Tynan, P., & Attia J. (2009). Hypogonadism in men receiving methadone and buprenorphine maintenance treatment. *International Journal of Andrology, 32*(2), 131–139.

Halpern, C., Joyner, K., Udry, R., & Suchindran, C. (2000). Smart teens don't have sex (or kiss much either). *Journal of Adolescent Health, 26*(3), 213–222.

Halpern-Felsher, B., Kropp, R., Boyer, C., Tschann, J., & Ellen, J. (2004). Adolescents' self-efficacy to communicate about sex: Its role in condom attitudes, commitment, and use. *Adolescence, 39*(155), 443–457.

Halsall, P. (1996). *Thomas Aquinas: Summa theologiae.* Retrieved April 10, 2008, from http://www.fordham.edu/halsall/source/aquinas1.html.

Hamachek, D.E. (1982). *Encounters with others: Interpersonal relationships and you.* New York, NY: Holt, Rinehart & Winston.

Hamamy, H. (2011). Consanguineous marriages: Preconception consultation in primary health care settings. *Journal of Community Genetics, 3*(3), 185–192.

Hamberg, K. (2000). Gender in the brain: A critical scrutiny of the biological gender differences. *Lakartidningen, 97*, 5130–5132.

Hamburg, B.A. (1986). Subsets of adolescent mothers: Developmental, biomedical, and psychosocial issues. In J.B. Lancaster & B.A. Hamburg (Eds.), *School-age pregnancy and parenthood: Biosocial dimensions* (pp. 115–145). New York, NY: Aldine DeGruyter.

Hamer, D.H., et al. (1993). A linkage between DNA markers on the X chromosome and male sexual orientation. *Science, 261*, 321–327.

Hamilton, A. (1981). Sexual problems in arthritis and allied conditions. *International Rehabilitation Medicine, 3*(1), 38–42.

Hand, J.Z., & Sanchez, L. (2005). Badgering or bantering? Gender differences in experience of, and reactions to, sexual harassment among U.S. high school students. *Gender & Society, 14*(6), 718–746.

Handler, A., Davis, F., Ferre, C., & Yeko, T. (1989). The relationship of smoking and ectopic pregnancy. *American Journal of Public Health, 79*, 1239–1242.

Handwerk, B. (2005, February 25). 4-D ultrasound gives video view of fetuses in the womb. *National Geographic News.* Retrieved October 14, 2008, from http://news.national-geographic.com/news/pf/80752382.html.

Hankins, G. (1995). *Operative obstetrics.* Appleton and Lange, Stamford, CT.

Hannaford, P.C., Iversen, L., Macfarlane, T.V., Elliott, A.M., Angus, V., & Lee, A.J. (2010). Mortality among contraceptive pill users: Cohort evidence from Royal College of General Practitioners' Oral Contraception Study. *British Medical Journal, 340*, c927.

Hans, J.D., & Kimberly, C. (2011). Abstinence, sex, and virginity: Do they mean what we think they mean? *American Journal of Sexuality Education, 6*(4), 329–342.

Harcourt, C., & Donovan, B. (2005). The many faces of sex work. *Sexually Transmitted Diseases, 81*, 201–206.

Hardt, J., Sidor, A., Nickel, R., Kappis, B., Petrak, P., & Egle, U.T. (2008). Childhood adversities and suicide attempts: A retrospective study. *Journal of Family Violence, 23*, 713–719.

Hardy, S., & Raffaelli, M. (2003). Adolescent religiosity and sexuality: An investigation of reciprocal influences. *Journal of Adolescence, 26*(6), 731–739.

Harlan, L.C., Potosky, A., Cilliland, F.D., Hoffman, R., Albertsen, P.C., Hamilton, A.S., Eley, J.W., Stanford, J.L., & Stephenson, R.A. (2001). Factors associated with initial therapy for clinically localized prostate cancer: Prostate cancer outcomes study. *Journal of the National Cancer Institute, 93*(24), 1864–1871.

Harlow, H.F. (1959). Love in infant monkeys. *Scientific American, 200*, 68–70.

Harmon, A. (2007, September 16). Cancer free at 33, but weighing a mastectomy. *New York Times.* Retrieved March 20, 2008, from http://www.nytimes.com/2007/09/16/health/16gene.html.

Harris, C.R. (2002). Sexual and romantic jealousy in heterosexual and homosexual adults. *Psychological Science, 13*(1), 7–12.

Harris, C.R. (2003). A review of sex differences in sexual jealousy, including self-report data, psychophysiological responses, interpersonal violence, and morbid jealousy. *Personality and Social Psychology Review, 7*(2), 102–128.

Harry, J. (1974). Urbanization and the gay life. *Journal of Sex Research, 10*(3), 238–247.

Harte, C.B. (2014). Concurrent relations among cigarette smoking status, resting heart rate variability, and erectile response. *Journal of Sexual Medicine, 11*(5), 1230–1239.

Hartmann, K., Viswanathan, M., Palmieri, R., Gartlehner, G., Thorp, J., & Lohr, K. (2005). Outcomes of routine episiotomy: A systematic review. *Journal of the American Medical Association, 293*(17), 2141–2148.

Harvey, J.F. (2007). *Homosexuality and the Catholic Church.* West Chester, PA: Ascension Press.

Harvey, K. (2002). Camp talk and citationality: a queer take on 'authentic' and 'represented' utterance. *Journal of Pragmatics, 34*(9), 1145-1166.

Harville, E., Taylor, C., Tesfai, H., Xiong, X., & Buekens, P. (2011). Experience of hurricane Katrina and reported intimate partner violence. *Journal of Interpersonal Violence, 26*(4), 833–845.

Haselton, M.G., Mortezaie, M., Pillsworth, E.G., Bleske-Recheck, A.E., & Frederick, D.A. (2007). Ovulation and human female ornamentation: Near ovulation, women dress to impress. *Hormones and Behavior, 51*, 40–45.

Hatano, Y., & Shimazaki, T. (2004). Japan. In R.T. Francoeur & R.J. Noonan (Eds.), *The Continuum International encyclopedia of sexuality* (pp. 636–678). New York/London: Continuum International.

Hatcher, R.A., Trussell, J., Nelson, A., Cates, W., Kowal, D., & Policar M. (2011). *Contraceptive technology* (20th ed.). New York, NY: Ardent Media.

Hatcher, R.A., Trussell, J., Nelson, A., Cates, W., Steward, F., & Kowal, D. (2007). *Contraceptive technology* (19th ed.). New York, NY: Ardent Media.

Hatcher, R.A., Trussell, J., Stewart, F.H., Nelson, A.L., Cates, W., Guest, F., & Kowal, D. (2004). *Contraceptive technology* (18th Rev. ed.). New York, NY: Ardent Media.

Hatfield, E. (1988). Passionate and companionate love. In R.J. Sternberg & R.J. Barnes (Eds.), *Psychology of love* (pp. 191–217). New Haven, CT: Yale University Press.

Hatfield, E., & Sprecher, S. (1986). Measuring passionate love in intimate relationships. *Journal of Adolescence, 9*(4), 383–410.

Hathaway, J.E., Willis, G., Zimmer, B., & Silverman, J.G. (2005). Impact of partner abuse on women's reproductive lives. *Journal of the American Medical Women's Association, 60*(1), 42–45.

Hawton, K. (1983). Behavioural approaches to the management of sexual deviations. *British Journal of Psychiatry, 143,* 248–255.

Hayashi, A. (2004, August 20). Japanese women shun the use of the pill. *CBS News.* Retrieved October 28, 2008, from http://www.cbsnews.com/stories/2004/08/20/health/main637523.shtml.

Hazelwood, R., & Burgess, A. (1987). *Practical aspects of rape investigation: A multidisciplinary approach.* New York, NY: Elsevier.

Health Canada. (2014). Information Update: Possible cardiovascular problems associated with testosterone products. Retrieved August 30, 2014, from http://healthycanadians.gc.ca/recall-alert-rappel-avis/hc-sc/2014/40587a-eng.php.

Health Canada. (2014). Retrieved August 10, 2014, http://www.hc-sc.gc.ca/dhp-mps/medeff/reviews-examens/testosterone-eng.php.

Health Canada. (2015a). Infant feeding. Retrieved April 23, 2015, from http://www.hc-sc.gc.ca/fn-an/nutrition/infant-nourisson/index-eng.php.

Health Canada. (2015b). Drug and health products. Retrieved March 3, 2015, from http://www.hc-sc.gc.ca/dhp-mps/prodpharma/activit/fs-fi/reviewfs_examenfd-eng.php.

Heap, C. (2010). Slumming: Sexual and Racial Encounters in American Nightlife, 1885–1940. Chicago, Ill: University of Chicago Press.

Hébert, A., & Weaver, A. (2014). An examination of personality characteristics associated with BDSM orientations. *Canadian Journal of Human Sexuality. 2014, Vol. 23 Issue 2,* 106–115.

Hebert, K., Lopez, B., Castellanos, J., Palacio, A., Tamariz, L., & Arcement, L. (2008). The prevalence of erectile dysfunction in heart failure patients by race and ethnicity.

International Journal of Impotence Research, 20(5), 507–511.

Heger, A., Ticson, L., Velasquez, O., & Bernier, R. (2002). Children referred for possible sexual abuse: Medical findings in 2384 children. *Child Abuse & Neglect, 26*(6–7), 645–659.

Heger, H. (1980). *The men with the pink triangle.* New York, NY: Alyson Books.

Hegna, K., & Rossow, I. (2007). What's love got to do with it? Substance use and social integration for young people categorized by same-sex experience and attractions. *Journal of Drug Issues, 37,* 229–256.

Heidari, M., Nejadi, J., Ghate, A., Delfan, B., & Iran-Pour, E. (2010). Evaluation of intralesional inject of verapamil in treatment of Peyronie's disease. *Journal of the Pakistan Urological Association, 60*(4), 291–293.

Heiman, J. (2002). Sexual dysfunction: Overview of prevalence, etiological factors, and treatments. *Journal of Sex Research, 39*(1), 73–79.

Heiman, J., & LoPiccolo, J. (1992). *Becoming orgasmic: A sexual and personal growth program for women.* New York, NY: Simon & Schuster.

Heiman, J., & Meston, M. (1997). Empirically validated treatment for sexual dysfunction. *Annual Review of Sex Research, 8,* 148–194.

Hellerstein, E., Olafson, L., Parker, H., & Offen, K.M. (1981). *Victorian women: A documentary account of women's lives in nineteenth-century England, France, and the United States.* Stanford, CA: Stanford University Press.

Hellstrom, W.J. (2006). Current and future pharmacotherapies of premature ejaculation. *Journal of Sexual Medicine, 3*(Suppl 4), 332–341.

Helmore, K. (2010, July 1). Empowering women to protect themselves: Promoting the female condom in Zimbabwe. United Nations Population Fund. Retrieved March 15, 2011, from http://www.unfpa.org/public/News/pid/3913.

Hemmings, C. (2007). Rescuing lesbian camp. *Journal of Lesbian Studies, 11*(1/2), 159–166.

Hemphill, E. (1991). *Brother to brother: New writings by black gay men.* Boston, MA: Alyson.

Hemstrom, O. (1996). Is marriage dissolution linked to differences in mortality risks for men and women? *Journal of Marriage and the Family, 58,* 366–378.

Hencken, J.D. (1984). Conceptualizations of homosexual behaviour which preclude homosexual self-labeling. *Journal of Homosexuality, 9,* 53–63.

Henderson, A., Lehavot, K., & Simoni, J. (2009). Ecological models of sexual satisfaction among lesbian/bisexual and heterosexual women. *Archives of Sexual Behavior, 38*(1), 50–66.

Henderson, L. (1991). Lesbian pornography: Cultural transgression and sexual demystification. *Women and Language, 14,* 3–12.

Hendrick, C., & Hendrick, S.S. (1989). Research on love: Does it measure up? *Journal of Personality & Social Psychology, 56*(5), 784–794.

Hendrick, C., & Hendrick, S.S. (2000). *Close relationships: A sourcebook.* Thousand Oaks, CA: Sage.

Henline, B., Lamke, L., & Howard, M. (2007). Exploring perceptions of online infidelity. *Personal Relationships, 14,* 113–238.

Hennessy, M., Bleakley, A., Fishbein, M., & Jordan, A. (2009). Estimating the longitudinal association between adolescent sexual behavior and exposure to sexual media content. *Journal of Sex Research, 46,* 586–596.

Hensel, D.J., Fortenberry, J.D., Harezlak, J., Anderson, J.G., & Orr, D.P. (2004). A daily diary analysis of vaginal bleeding and coitus among adolescent women. *Journal of Adolescent Health, 34*(5), 392–394.

Hensley, L.G. (2002). Treatment of survivors of rape: Issues and interventions. *Journal of Mental Health Counseling, 24*(4), 331–348.

Henslin, J.M. (2005). The sociology of human sexuality. In J.M. Henslin, *Sociology: A down-to-earth approach.* Online chapter retrieved November 30, 2005, from http://www.ablongman.com/html/henslintour/henslinchapter/ahead3.html.

Herbenick, D., Reece, M., Schick, V., Sanders, S., Dodge, B., & Fortenberry, D. (2010a). Sexual behavior in the United States: Results from a National Probability Sample of men and women ages 14–94. *Journal of Sexual Medicine, 7*(Suppl. 5), 255–265.

Herbenick, D., Reece, M., Schick, V., Sanders, S., Dodge, B., & Fortenberry, J.D. (2010b). Sexual behaviors, relationships, and perceived health status among adult women in the U.S.: Results from a national probability sample. *Journal of Sexual Medicine, 7*(Suppl. 5), 277–290.

Herbruck, L.F. (2008). The impact of childbirth on the pelvic floor. *Urlogical Nursing, 28,* 173–184.

Herdt, G. (1989). Introduction: Gay and lesbian youth, emergent identities, and cultural scenes at home and abroad. In G. Herdt (Ed.), *Gay and lesbian youth* (pp. 1–42). New York, NY: Harrington Park Press.

Herdt, G., & Stoller, R. (1990). *Intimate communications: Erotics and the study of culture.* New York, NY: Columbia University Press.

Herek, G. (2002). Heterosexuals' attitudes toward bisexual men and women in the United States. *Journal of Sex Research, 39*(4), 264–274.

Herek, G. (2006). Legal recognition of same-sex relationship in the United States: A social science perspective. *American Psychologist, 61,* 606–621.

Herek, G., Cogan, J.C., & Gillis, J. (2002). Victim experiences in hate crimes based on sexual orientation. *Journal of Social Issues, 58*(2), 319–339.

Herek, G.M. (1984). Beyond "homophobia": A social psychological perspective on attitudes toward lesbians and gay men. In J.P. DeCecco (Ed.), *Homophobia: An overview* (pp. 1–21). New York, NY: The Haworth Press.

Hergemoller, B-U. (2006). *The Middle Ages.* In R. Aldrich (Ed.), *Gay life and culture: A world history* (pp. 57–77). London: Thames & Hudson Ltd.

Herman, J., & Schatzow, E. (1987). Recovery and verification of memories of childhood sexual trauma. *Psychoanalytic Psychology, 4,* 1–14.

Herman, J.L. (1981). *Father-daughter incest.* Cambridge, MA: Harvard University Press.

Heron, J., McGuinness, M., Blackmore, E., Craddock, N., & Jones, I. (2008). Early post-partum symptoms in puerperal psychosis. *British Journal of Obstetrics and Gynecology, 115,* 348–353.

Herrick, A.L., Matthews, A.K., & Garofalo, R. (2010). Health risk behaviors in an urban sample of young women who have sex with women. *Journal of Lesbian Studies, 14*(1), 80–92.

Herz, R. (2007). *The scent of desire: Discovering our enigmatic sense of smell.* New York, NY: William Morrow Publishers.

Heston, L.L., & Shields, J. (1968). Homosexuality in twins—A family study and a registry study. *Archives of General Psychiatry,18,*149–160.

Hetherington, E. (2003). Intimate pathways: Changing patterns in close personal relationships across time. *Family Relations, 52,* 318–331.

Hewitt, E.C., & Moore, L.D. (2002). The role of lay theories of the etiologies of homosexuality in attitudes towards lesbians and gay men. *Journal of Lesbian Studies, 6*(3–4), 59–72.

Hewitt, J.P. (1994). *Self and society: A symbolic interactionist social psychology.* Boston, MA: Allyn & Bacon.

Hewlett, M. (2008, September 17). Getting help is hard for gay domestic violence victims. *McClatchy—Tribune Business News.* Retrieved October 5, 2008, from http://libill.hartford.edu:2083/pqdweb?index=2&did=1556431461&SrchMode=1&sid=1&Fmt=3 &VInst=PROD&VType=PQD&RQT=309&VName=PQD&TS=1223252228&clientId=3309.

Heymann, J., Earle, A., Rajaraman, D., Miller, C., & Bogen, K. (2007). Extended family caring for children orphaned by AIDS: Balancing essential work and caregiving in a high HIV prevalence nation. *AIDS Care, 19*(3), 337–345.

Hickman, S.E., & Muehlenhard, C.L. (1999). By the semi-mystical appearance of a condom: How young women and men communicate sexual consent in heterosexual situations. *Journal of Sex Research, 36*(3), 258–272.

Hicks, C.W., & Rome, E.S. (2010). Menstrual manipulation: Options for suppressing the cycle. *Cleveland Clinic Journal of Medicine, 77*(7), 445–453.

Hicks, S. (2005). Is gay parenting bad for kids? Responding to the "very idea of difference" in research on lesbian and gay parents. *Sexualities, 8*(2), 153–168.

Hicks, T., & Leitenberg, H. (2001). Sexual fantasies about one's partner versus someone else: Gender differences in incidence and frequency. *Journal of Sex Research, 38,* 43–50.

Hickson, F.C.I., Davies, P.M., & Hunt, A.J. (1994). Gay men as victims of nonconsensual sex. *Archives of Sexual Behavior, 23*(3), 281–294.

Hildebrand, R. (2008). The Oneida community. Retrieved April 10, 2008, from http://www.nyhistory.com/central/oneida.htm.

Hill, B.F., & Jones, J.S. (1993). Venous air embolism following orogenital sex during pregnancy. *American Journal of Emergency Medicine, 11,* 155–157.

Hill, S. (2007). Overestimation bias in mate competition. *Evolution and Human Behavior, 28*(2), 118–123.

Hill, S.A. (2002). Teaching and doing gender in African American families. *Sex Roles, 47,* 493–506.

Hinchley, G. (2007). Is infant male circumcision an abuse of the rights of the child? Yes. *British Medical Journal, 8,* 335(7631), 1180.

Hines, D.A. (2007). Predictors of sexual coercion against women and men: A multilevel, multinational study of university students. *Archives of Sexual Behavior, 36,* 403–422.

Hinsch, B. (1990). *Passions of the cut sleeve: The male homosexual tradition in China.* Berkeley, CA: University of California Press.

Hirshkowitz, M., & Schmidt, M.H. (2005). Sleep-related erections: Clinical perspectives and neural mechanisms. *Sleep Medicine Reviews, 9*(4), 311–329.

Hisasue, S., Furuya, R., Itoh, N., Kobayashi, K., Furuya, S., & Tsukamoto, T. (2006). Ejaculatory disorder caused by alpha-1 adrenoceptor antagonists is not retrograde ejaculation but a loss of seminal emission. *International Journal of Urology, 13*(10), 1311–1316.

Hitsch, G., Hortacsu, A., & Ariely, D. (2010). What makes you click? Mate preferences in online dating. *Quantitative Marketing and Economics, 8*(4), 393.

Hitti, M. (2008, January 18). *FDA strengthens warning on blood clot risk for users of Ortho Evra birth control skin patch.* WebMD.

Retrieved October 28, 2008, from http://www.webmd.com/sex/birth-control/news/20080118/birth-control-patch-stronger-warning.

Hjelmstedt, A., Andersson, L., Skoog-Syanberg, A., Bergh, T., Boivin, J., & Collins, A. (1999). Gender differences in psychological reactions to infertility among couples seeking IVF and ICSI treatment. *Acta Obstetricia et Gynecologica Scandinavica, 78*(1), 42–48.

Ho, V.P., Lee, Y., Stein, S.L., & Temple, L.K. (2011). Sexual function after treatment for rectal cancer: A review. *Diseases of the Colon and Rectum, 54*(1), 113–125.

Hobbs, K., Symonds, T., Abraham, L., May, K., & Morris, M. (2008). Sexual dysfunction in partners of men with premature ejaculation. *International Journal of Impotence Research, 20*(5):512–517.

Hoburg, R., Konik, J., Williams, M., & Crawford, M. (2004). Bisexuality among self-identified heterosexual college students. *Journal of Bisexuality, 4,* 25–36.

Hoebel, E.A. (1954). *The law of primitive man.* Cambridge, MA: Harvard University Press.

Hofer, S. (1962). *The Hutterites: Lives and images of a communal people.* Saskatoon, SK: Hofer Publishers.

Hoffman, M.C. (2008, July 23). Philippines in struggle against abortionist population control initiative. *LifeSite News.com.* Retrieved October 28, 2008, from http://www.lifesitenews.com/ldn/2008/jul/08072201.html.

Hoffstetter, S., Barr, S., LeFevre, C., Leong, F., & Leet, T. (2008). Self-reported yeast symptoms compared with clinical wet mount analysis and vaginal yeast culture in a specialty clinic setting. *Journal of Reproductive Medicine, 53,* 402–406.

Hofman, B. (2005). "What is next?": Gay male students' significant experiences after coming-out while in college. *Dissertation Abstracts International Section A: Humanities & Social Sciences, 65*(8-A), #04194209.

Hollander, D. (1997). Who's at risk for condom failure? *Family Planning Perspectives, 29*(4), 151–151.

Hollander, D. (2000, March/April). Fertility drugs do not raise breast, ovarian or uterine cancer risk. *Family Planning Perspectives, 32*(2), 100–103.

Hollander, D. (2001). Users give new synthetic and latex condoms similar ratings on most features. *Family Planning Perspectives, 33*(1), 45–48.

Hollander, X. (1972). *The happy hooker.* New York, NY: Dell Publishing.

Holmes, J.G., & Rempel, J.K. (1989). Trust in close relationships. In C. Hendrick (Ed.), *Close relationships* (Vol. 10, pp. 187–219). Newbury Park, CA: Sage.

Holmes, M.C. (2004). Reconsidering a "woman's issue:" Psychotherapy and one man's posta-bortion experiences. *American Journal of Psychotherapy, 58*(1), 103–115.

Holmes, R. (1991). *Sex crimes*. Newbury Park, CA: Sage.

Holzman, H.R., & Pines, S. (1982). Buying sex: The phenomenology of being a john. *Deviant Behavior, 4*, 89–116.

Hooghe, M., Claes, E., Harell, A., Quintelier, E., & Dejaeghere, Y. (2010). Anti-gay sentiment among adolescents in Belgium and Canada: A comparative investigation into the role of gender and religion. *Journal of Homosexuality, 57*(3), 384–400.

Hooker, E. (1957). The adjustment of the male overt homosexual. *Journal of Projective Techniques, 21*, 18–31.

Hooton, T.M. (2003). The current management strategies for community-acquired urinary tract infection. *Infectious Disease Clinics of North America, 17*(2), 303–332.

Hooven, F.V. (1995). *Beefcake: The muscle magazines of America* 1950–1970. Taschen.

Hope, M.E., Farmer, L., McAllister, K.F., & Cumming, G.P. (2010). Vaginismus in peri- and postmenopausal women: A pragmatic approach for general practitioners and gynaecologists. *Menopause International, 16*(2), 68–73.

Horner, T. (1978). *Jonathan loved David: Homosexuality in Biblical times*. Philadelpia, PA: The Westminster Press.

Horowitz, S.M., Weis, D.L., & Laflin, M.T. (2001). Differences between sexual orientation behavior groups and social background, quality of life, and health behaviors. *Journal of Sex Research, 38*(3), 205–219.

Horrigan, J.B., Rainie, L., & Fox, S. (2001). Online communities: Networks that nurture long-distance relationships and local ties. Pew Internet and American Life Project. Retrieved April 26, 2008, from http://www.pewinternet.org/pdfs/pip_communities_report.pdf.

Hou, F., & Myles, J. (2007). The changing role of education in the marriage market: Assortative marriage in Canada and the United States Since the 1970s. Research paper, Statistics Canada, Catalogue No. 11F0019MIE—No. 299

Houston, E., & McKirnan, D. (2008). Intimate partner abuse among gay and bisexual men: Risk correlates and health outcomes. *Journal of Urban Health, 84*, 681–690.

How to Use Condoms Correctly. (n.d.). Retrieved from http://trojanprofessional.ca/pdfs/HowtoUseCondomsCorrectly.pdf.

Howard, L.M., Hoffbrand, S., Henshaw, C., Boath, L., & Bradley, E. (2005). Antidepressant prevention of postnatal depression. *The Cochrane Database of Systematic Reviews, 2*, art. no. CD004363.

Howden, K.J. (2004). Androgen insensitivity syndrome in a thoroughbred mare (64, XY—testicular feminization). *Canadian Vetrinary Journal, 45*(6), 501–503.

Howe, N., Rinaldi, C., & Recchia, H. (2010). Patterns in mother-child internal state discourse across four contexts. *Merrill-Palmer Quarterly, 56*(1), 1–20.

Howlett, K., Koetters, T., Edrington, J., West, C., Paul, S., Lee, K., Aouizerat, B.E., Wara, W., Swift, P., & Miaskowski, C. (2010). Changes in sexual function on mood and quality of life in patients undergoing radiation therapy for prostate cancer. *Oncology Nursing Forum* 37(1):E58–E66.

Hu, K., He, X., Yu, F., Yuan, X., Hu, W., Liu, C., Zhao, F., & Dou, J. (2011). Immunization with DNA vaccine expressing herpes simplex virus type 1 gD and IL-21 protects against mouse herpes keratitis. *Immunology Invest, 40*(3), 265–278.

Hu, X., Cheng, L., Hua, X., & Glasier, A. (2005). Advanced provision of emergency contraception to postnatal women in China makes no difference in abortion rates: A randomized controlled trial. *Contraception, 72*, 111–116.

Huang, C.Y., Yao, C.J., Wang, C., Jiang, J.K., & Chen, G. (2010). Changes of semen quality in Chinese fertile men from 1985 to 2008. *National Journal of Andrology, 16*(8), 684–688.

Huang, J. (2007). Hormones and female sexuality. In M. Tepper & A.F. Owens (Eds.), *Sexual Health, Vol 2: Physical Foundations* (pp. 43–78). Westport, CT: Praeger.

Hubacher, D., Finerb, L., & Espeyc, E. (2010). Renewed interest in intrauterine contraception in the United States: Evidence and explanation. *Contraception, 83*(4), 291–294.

Hubayter, Z., & Simon, J. (2008). Testosterone therapy for sexual dysfunction in postmenopausal women. *Climacteric, 11*, 181–191.

Hudson, D.J. (2010). Standing OUT/fitting IN: Identity, appearance, and authenticity in gay and lesbian communities. *Symbolic Interaction, 33*(2), 213–233.

Hudson, E. (2004). *Snow bodies*. Edmonton, AB: NeWest Press.

Hudson-Sonnen, N. (2012). Canada hides from its embarrassing abortion statistics. Retrieved March 3, 2015, from, http://news.nationalpost.com/full-comment/natalie-hudson-sonnen-canada-hides-from-its-embarrassing-abortion-statistics.

Huff-Hannon, J. (2011). A campaign goes viral to stop 'corrective rape,' used to 'cure' south African women of homosexuality. Retrieved February 20, 2011, from http://www.alternet.org/rights/149491/a_campaign_goes_viral_to_stop_%2527corrective_rape%252C%2527_used_to_%2527cure%2527_south_african_women_of_homosexuality/.

Huffstutter, P.J. (2004). Smallest surviving preemie will go home soon. Retrieved December 23, 2004, from http://www.latimes. come/news/nationworld/nation/la-na-baby22dec,0,3320847,print.story.

Hughes, J.R. (2006). A general review of recent reports on homosexuality and lesbianism. *Sexuality and Disability, 24*, 195–205.

Hughes, L.M., Griffith, R., Aitken, R. (2007). The search for a topical dual action spermicide/microbicide. *Current Medicinal Chemistry, 14*, 775–786.

Hulbert, F. (1989). Barriers to effective listening. *Bulletin for the Association for Business Communication, 52*, 3–5.

Hull, S., Hennessy, M., Bleakley, A., Fishbein, M., & Jordan, A. (2010). Identifying the causal pathways from religiosity to delayed adolescent sexual behavior. *Journal of Sex Research, 19*, 1–11.

Humble, A. (2013). Moving from ambivalence to certainly: Older same-sex couples marry in Canada. *Canadian Journal of Aging, 32*(2), 131–144.

Hummer, M., Kemmler, G., Kurz, M., Kurzthaler, I., Oberbauer, H., & Fleischhacker W.W. (1999). Sexual disturbances during clozapine and haloperidol treatment for schizophrenia. *American Journal of Psychiatry, 156*(4), 631–633.

Humphreys, T., & Herold, E. (2007). Sexual consent in heterosexual relationships: Development of a new measure. *Sex Roles, 57*(3–4), 305–315.

Hung, C.T. (2006). Arranging "Traditional" marriages across the Vietnamese diaspora. Conference papers—American Sociological Association, Annual Meeting, Montreal, pp. 1–23.

Hunt, A., & Curtis, B. (2006). A genealogy of the genital kiss: Oral sex in the twentieth century. *Canadian Journal of Human Sexuality, 15*(2), 69–84.

Hunt, M. (1974). *Sexual behavior in the 1970's*. New York, NY: Dell.

Hunter, I., Saunders, D., & Williamson, D. (1993). *On pornography: Literature, sexuality and obscenity law*. New York, NY: St. Martin's Press.

Hunter, J.A., Figueredo, A.J., Malamuth, N.M., & Becker, J.V. (2003). Juvenile sex offenders: Toward the development of a typology. *Sexual Abuse: Journal of Research & Treatment, 15*(1), 27–48.

Huober-Zeeb, C., Lawrenz, B., Popovici, R.M., Strowitzki, T., Germeyer, A., Stute, P., & von Wolff, M. (2011). Improving fertility preservation in cancer: Ovarian tissue cryobanking followed by ovarian stimulation can be efficiently combined. *Fertility and Sterility, 95*(1), 342–344.

Huppertz, B. (2011). Placental pathology in pregnancy complications. *Thombosis Research, 127*(Suppl. 3), S96–S99.

Husbands, W., Makoroka, L., Walcott, R. Adam, B.D., George, C., Remis, R.S., & Rourke, S.B.2013). Black gay men as sexual subjects: Race, racialisation and the social relations of sex among Black gay men in Toronto. *Culture, Health & Sexuality, 15*(4), 434–449.

Hussain, A., Nicholls, J., & El-Hasani, S. (2010). Technical tips following more than 2000 transabdominal preperitoneal (TAPP) repair of the groin hernia. *Surgical Laparoscopy, Endoscopy, and Percutaneous Techniques, 20*(6), 384–388.

Hussein M.I. (1993). Mental Health and Psychological Medicine at the Time of the Pharaohs, MS Thesis, Department of Psychiatry, Faculty of Medicine, Cairo University.

Husted, R. (2009). Some Little Tammy Wynette: The 'Stand by Your Man' Strategy of Image Restoration in Political Sex Scandals. Conference Papers—National Communication Association, p. 1.

Hutcheon, J.A., Lisonkova, S., & Joseph, K.S. (2011). Epidemiology of pre-eclampsia and the other hypertensive disorders of pregnancy. *Best Practice and Research in Clinical Obstetrics and Gynecology, 25*(4), 391–403.

Hutson, J.M., Baker, M., Terada, M., Zhou, B., & Paxton, G. (1994). Hormonal control of testicular descent and the cause of cryptorchidism. *Reproduction, Fertility and Development, 6*(2), 151–156.

Hutson, J.M., & Hasthorpe S.J. (2005). Testicular descent and cryptorchidism: The state of the art in 2004. *Pediatric Surgery, 40*(2), 297–302.

Hutton, I.E. (1936). *The sex technique in marriage.* New York, NY: Emerson Books, Inc.

Huyghe, E., Delannes, M., Wagner, F., Delaunay, B., Nohra, J., Thoulouzan, M., Shut-Yee, J.Y., Plante, P., Soulie, M., Thonneau, P., & Bachaud, J.M. (2009). Ejaculatory function after permanent 125I prostate brachytherapy for localized prostate cancer. *International Journal of Radiation Oncology, 74*(1), 126–132.

Hwu, J.R., Lin, S.Y., Tsay, S.C., De Clercq, E., Leyssen, P., & Neyts, J. (2011). Coumarin-purine ribofuranoside conjugates as new agents against hepatitis C virus. *Journal of Medical Chemistry, 54,* 2114–2126.

Hyde, J., & Mertz, J. (2008). Gender, culture, and mathematics. *Proceedings of the National Academy of Science, 106*(22), 8801–8807.

Ignatius, E., & Kokkonen, M. (2007). Factors contributing to verbal self-disclosure. *Nordic Psychology, 59*(4), 362–391.

Imperato-McGinley, J., Guerrero, L., Gautier, T., Peterson, R.E. (1974). Steroid 5alpha-reductase deficiency in man: an inherited form of male

pseudohermaphroditism. *Science, 186*(4170), 1213–1215.

Impett, E.A., Beals, K.P., & Peplau, L.A. (2001). Testing the investment model of relationship commitment and stability in a longitudinal study of married couples. *Current Psychology, 20*(4), 312–327.

Incerpi, M.H., Miller, D.A., Samadi, R., Settlage, R.H., & Goodwin, T.M. (1999). Stillbirth evaluation: What tests are needed? *American Journal of Obstetrics and Gynecology, 180*(6 Pt 1), 1595–1596.

International Gay and Lesbian Human Rights Commission (IGLHRC). (2011). Human Rights Violations on the Basis of Sexual Orientation, Gender Identity, and Homosexuality in the Islamic Republic of Iran. Submission to the 103rd Session of the Human Rights Committee (17 October–4 November 2011).

International Gay and Lesbian Human Rights Commission. (2010). Middle East and North America. Retrieved August 26, 2011, from http://www.iglhrc.org/cgibin/iowa/region/10.html.

Irvine, J. (1990). *Disorders of desire, sex, and gender in modern American sexology.* Philadelphia: Temple University Press.

Irving, C., Basu, A., Richmond, S., Burn, J., & Wren, C. (2008, July 2). Twenty-year trends in prevalence of survival of Down syndrome. *European Journal of Human Genetics.* Retrieved October 14, 2008, from http://www.nature.com/ejhg/journal/vaop/ncurrent/abs/ejhg2008122a.html.

Irwig, M.S., & Kolukula, S. (2011). Persistent sexual side effects of finasteride for male pattern hair loss. *Journal of Sexual Medicine, 8*(6), 1747–1753.

Isaiah Green, A. (2007). Queer theory and sociology: Locating the subject and the self in sexuality studies. *Sociological Theory, 25,* 26–45.

Ishak, W., Bokarius, A., Jeffrey, J., Davis, M., & Bakhta, Y. (2010). Disorders of orgasm in women: A literature review of etiology and current treatments. *Journal of Sexual Medicine, 7*(10), 3254–3268.

Ishak, W.W., Berman, D.S., & Peters, A. (2008). Male anorgasmia treated with oxytocin. *Journal of Sexual Medicine, 5,* 1022–1024.

Ishibashi, K.L., Koopmans, J., Curlin, F.A., Alexander, K., & Ross, L. (2008). Paediatricians' attitudes and practices towards HPV vaccination. *Acta Paediatrician, 97*(11), 1550–1556.

Isidori, A., Giannetta, E., Gianfrilli, D., Greco, E., Bonifacio, V., Aversa, A., et al. (2005). Effects of testosterone on sexual function in men: Results of a meta-analysis. *Clinical Endocrinology, 63,* 381–394.

Israelstam, S., & Lambert, S. (1984). Gay bars. *Journal of Drug Issues, 14,* 637–653.

Israilov, S., Niv, E., Livne, P.M., Shmeuli, J., Engelstein, D., Segenreich, E., & Baniel, J. (2002). Intracavernous injections for erectile dysfunction in patients with cardiovascular diseases and failure or contraindications for sildenafil citrate. *International Journal of Impotence Research, 14*(1), 38–43.

Ivarsson, B., Fridlund, B., & Sjöberg, T. (2010). Health professionals' views on sexual information following MI. *British Journal of Nursing, 19*(16), 1052–1054.

Jackman, L.P., Williamson, D.A., Netemeyer, R.G., & Anderson, D.A. (1995). Do weight-preoccupied women misinterpret ambiguous stimuli related to body size? *Cognitive Therapy and Research, 19,* 341–355.

Jackson, B. (1998). *Splendid slippers: A thousand years of an erotic tradition.* Berkeley, CA: Ten Speed Press.

Jackson, M. (1984). Sex research and the construction of sexuality: A tool of male supremacy? *Women's Studies International Forum, 7,* 43–51.

Jacobs, S.E., Thomas, W., & Lang, S. (1997). *Two-spirit people: Native American gender identity, sexuality, and spirituality.* Chicago: University of Illinois Press.

Jacquet, S.E., & Surra, C.A. (2001). Parental divorce and premarital couples: Commitment and other relationship characteristics. *Journal of Marriage and Family, 63*(3), 627–639.

Jain, J.K., Minoo, P., Nucatola, D.L., & Felix, J.C. (2005). The effect of nonoxynol-9 on human endometrium. *Contraception, 71*(2), 137–142.

Jakimiuk, A., Fritz, A., Grzybowski, W., Walecka, I., & Lewandowski, P. (2007). Diagnosing and management of iatrogenic moderate and severe ovarian hyperstymulation syndrome in clinical material. *Polish Academy of Sciences, 45*(Suppl. 1), S105–108.

Jamanadas, K. (2008). Sati was started for preserving caste. Retrieved April 8, 2008, from http://www.ambedkar.org/research/Sati_Was_Started_For_Preserving_Caste.htm.

James, D., & Drakich, J. (1993). Understnading gender differences in amount of talk: A critical review of research. In D. Tannen (Ed.), *Gender and conversational interaction* (pp. 281–312). New York, NY: Oxford University Press.

Jamieson, D., Kaufman, S., Costello, C., Hillis, S., Marchbanks, P., & Peterson, H. (2002). A comparison of women's regret after vasectomy versus tubal sterilization. *Obstetrics and Gynecology, 99,* 1073–1079.

Jannini, E., Whipple, B., Kingsberg, S., Buisson O., Foldès, & Vardi, Y. (2010).Who's afraid of the g-spot? *Journal of Sexual Medicine, 7*(1 Pt 1), 25–34.

Japsen, B. (2003). Viagra faces 1st rivals by year's end. Retrieved July 18, 2003, from http://www.webprowire.com/summaries/5357111.html.

Jaspal, R. (2014). Arranged marriage, identity, and well-being among British Asian gay men. *Journal of GLBT Family Studies, 10*(5), 425–448.

Jaworowicz, D. (2007). Novel risk factors for breast cancer. Presented at the 40th Annual Meeting of the Society for Epidemio-logic Research, Boston, MA.

Jayne, C. (1981). A two-dimensional model of female sexual response. *Journal of Sex and Marital Therapy, 7,* 3–30.

Jeary, K. (2005). Sexual abuse and sexual offending against elderly people: A focus on perpetrators and victims. *Journal of Forensic Psychiatry & Psychology, 16*(2), 328–343.

Jelovsek, J.E., Walters, M.D., & Barber, M.D. (2008). Psychosocial impact of chronic vul-vovaginal conditions. *Journal of Reproductive Medicine, 53,* 75–82.

Jemal, A., Murray, T. Ward, E., Samuels, A., Tiwari, R.C., Ghafoor, A., Feuer, E.J., & Thun, M.J. (2005). Cancer statistics, 2005. *CA: A Cancer Journal for Clinicians, 55,* 10–30.

Jenkins, D., & Johnston, L. (2004). Unethical treatment of gay and lesbian people with conversion therapy. *Families in Society, 85*(4), 557–561.

Jenkins, S. (2009). Marital splits and income changes over the longer term. In M. Brynin & J. Ermisch (Eds.), *Changing relationships.* London: Routledge.

Jenkins, W. (2010). Can anyone tell me why I'm gay? What research suggests regarding the origins of sexual orientation. *North American Journal of Psychology, 12*(2), 279–296.

Jenness, V. (1990). From sex as sin to sex as work: COYOTE and the reorganization of prostitution as a social problem. *Social Problems, 37,* 403–420.

Jensen, J.T. (2008). A continuous regimen of levonorgestrel/ethinyl estradiol for contra-ception and elimination of menstruation. *Drugs Today, 44,* 183–195.

Jensen, R., & Jenson, K. (2007). Entertain-ment media and sexual health: A content analysis of sexual talk, behavior, and risks in a popular television series. *Sex Roles, 56*(5/6), 275–284.

Jern, P., Santtila, P., Johansson, A., Varjonen, M., Witting, K., von der Pahlen, B., & Sandnabba, N.K. (2009). Evidence for a genetic etiology to ejaculatory dysfunction. *International Journal of Impotence Research, 21*(1), 62–67.

Jersild, J. (1956). *Boy prostitutes.* Copenhagen: G.E.C. Gad.

Jetter, A. (1991). Faye's crusade. *Vogue, 147*–151, 202–204.

Jewkes, R., Abrahams, N., Mathews, S., Seedat, M., Niekerk, A., Suffla, S., & Ratele, K. (2009a). Preventing rape and violence in South Africa: Call for leadership in a new agenda for action. MRC Policy Brief. Retrieved April 30, 2011, from http://www.mrc.ac.za/gender/prev_rapedd041209.pdf.

Jewkes, R., Sikweyiya, Y., Morrell, R., & Dunkle, K. (2009b). Understanding men's health and use of violence: Interface of rape and HIV in South Africa. Medical Research Council of South Africa. Retrieved April 30, 2011, from http://gender. care2share.wikispaces.net/file/view/MRC-ISA1men1and1rape1ex1summary-1june2009.pdf.

Jha, A. (2010, October 4). British IVF pioneer Robert Edwards wins Nobel prize for medi-cine. Retrieved March 1, 2011, from http://www.guardian.co.uk/science/2010/oct/04/ivf-pioneer-robert-edwards-nobel-prize-medicine.

Jha, P., Kumar, R., Vasa, P., Dhingra, N., Thiruchelvam, D., & Moineddin, R. (2006). Low male-to-female sex ratio of children born in India: National survey of 1.1 million households. *The Lancet, 367,* 211–218.

Jha, R.K., Jha, P.K., & Guha, S.K. (2009). Smart RISUG: A potential new contraceptive and its magnetic field-mediated sperm interac-tion. *International Journal of Nanomedicine, 4,* 55–64.

Jick, S., & Hernandez, R. (2011). Risk of non-fatal venous thromboembolism in women using oral contraceptives containing dro-spirenone compared with contraceptives containing levonorgestrel. *British Medical Journal.* Retrieved June 5, 2011, from http://www.bmj.com/content/342/bmj. d2151.full.

Johannsen, T., Ripa, C., Carlsen, E., Starup, J., Nielsen, O., Schwartrz, M., Drzewiecki, K., Mortensen, E., & Main, K. (2010). Long-term gynecological outcomes in women with congenital adrenal hyperplasia due to 21-hydroxylase deficiency. *International Journal of Pediatric Endocrinology.* Retrieved November 13, 2010, from http://www.ncbi.nlm.nih.gov/pmc/articles/PMC2963122/.

Johansen, R.E.B. (2007). Experiencing sex in exile—Can genitals change their gender? In Y. Hernlund & B. Shell-Duncan (Eds.), *Transcultural bodies: Female cutting in global context* (pp. 248–277). New Brunswick, NJ: Rutgers University Press.

Johansson, A., Sundbom, E., Hojerback, T., & Bodlund, O. (2010). A five-year follow-up study of Swedish adults with gender identity disorder. *Archives of Sexual Behavior, 39*(6), 1429–1437.

Johnson, A.M. (2001). Popular belief in gender-based communication differences and relationship success. *Dissertation Abstracts.* Amherst, MA: University of Massachusetts.

Johnson, D.K. (2004). *The lavender scare: The Cold War persecution of gays and lesbians in the federal government.* Chicago, IL: University of Chicago Press.

Johnson, J. (2001). *Male multiple orgasm: Step by step* (4th ed). Jack Johnson Seminars.

Johnson, J., & Alford, R. (1987). The adolescent quest for intimacy: Implications for the therapeutic alliance. *Journal of Social Work and Human Sexuality* (Special issue: Intimate Relationships), *5,* 55–66.

Johnson, K., Gill, S., Reichman, V., Tassinary, L. (2007). Swagger, sway, and sexuality: Judging sexual orientation from body motion and morphology. *Journal of Personality and Social Psychology, 93*(3), 321–334.

Johnson, K.C., & Daviss, B.A. (2005). Outcomes of planned home births with certified profes-sional midwives: Large prospective study in North America. *British Medical Journal, 330*(7505), 1416–1420.

Johnson, L.A. (2005). Experts urge routine HIV tests for all. Retrieved February 11, 2005, from http://abcnews.go.com/Health/wireStory?id=485527.

Johnson, R., & Murad, H. (2009). Gynecomastia: Pathophysiology, evaluation, and management. *Mayo Clinic Proceedings, 84*(11), 1010–1015.

Johnson, S.L., Dunleavy, J., Gemmell, N.J., & Nakagawa, S. (2015). Consistent age-dependent declines in human semen quality: A systematic review and meta-analysis. *Ageing Research Review, 19,* 22–33.

Joint United Nations Programme on HIV/AIDS (UNAIDS). (2000). *Condom social mar-keting: Selected case studies.* UNAIDS 2000.

Jonas, S., Bebbington, P., McManus, S., Meltzer, H., Jenkins, R., Kuipers, E., Cooper, C., King, M., & Brugha, T. (2011). Sexual abuse and psychiatric disorder in England: Results from the 2007 adult psychiatric morbidity survey. *Psychological Medicine, 41*(4), 709–720.

Jones, J.H. (1997). *Alfred C. Kinsey: A public/pri-vate life.* New York, NY: W.W. Norton.

Jones, R. (1984). *Human reproduction and sexual behavior.* Englewood Cliffs, NJ: Prentice Hall.

Jones, R., Darroch, J., & Singh, S. (2005). Religious differentials in the sexual and reproductive behaviors of young women in the United States. *Journal of Adolescent Health, 36*(4), 279–288.

Jones, R., Finer, L., & Singh, S. (2010, May). Characteristics of U.S. abortion patients, 2008. New York, NY: Alan Guttmacher Insti-tute. Retrieved June 5, 2011, from http://www.guttmacher.org/pubs/US-Abortion-Patients.pdf.

Jones, R., & Kooistra, K. (2011). Abortion inci-dence and access to services in the U.S., 2008. *Perspectives in Sex and Reproductive Health, 43*(1), 41–50.

Jones, R.K., Moore, A.M., & Frohwirth, L.F. (2011). Perceptions of male knowledge and support among U.S. women obtaining abortions. *Women's Health Issues, 21*(2), 117–123.

Jongpipan, J., & Charoenkwan, K. (2007). Sexual function after radical hysterectomy for early-stage cervical cancer. *Journal of Sexual Medicine, 4,* 1659–1665.

Jordan, J. (1997). User buys: Why men buy sex. *Australian and New Zealand Journal of Criminology, 30,* 55–71.

Jorgensen, C. (1967). *Christine Jorgenson: Personal biography.* New York, NY: Erickson.

Joseph, E. (2010). Does commitment to celibacy lead to burnout or enhance engagement? *European Journal of Mental Health, 5*(2), 187–204.

Joung, I.M., Stronks, K., & van de Mheen, H. (1995). Health behaviours explain part of the differences in self-reported health associated with partner/marital status in the Netherlands. *Journal of Epidemiology and Community Health, 49*(5), 482–488.

Jozkowski, K.N., Schick, V., Herbenick, D., & Reece, M. (2012). sexuality information seeking and sexual function among women attending in-home sex toy parties. *International Journal of Sexual Health, 24*(2), 112–123.

Juenemann, K.P., Lue, T.F., Luo, J.A., Benowitz, N.L., Abozeid M., & Tanagho, E.A. (1987). The effect of cigarette smoking on penile erection. *The Journal of Urology, 138*(2), 438–441.

Juntti, S.A., Tollkuhn, J., Wu, M.V., Fraser, E., Soderborg, T., Tan, S., Honda, S., Harada, N., & Shah, N.M. (2010). The androgen receptor governs the execution, but not the programming, of male sexual and territorial behavior. *Neuron, 66*(2), 167–169.

Juraskova I., Jarvis S., Mok K., Peate M., Meiser B., Cheah B.C., Mireskandari S., & Friedlander M. (2013). The acceptability, feasibility, and efficacy (phase I/II study) of the OVERcome (Olive Oil, VaginalExercise, and MoisturizeR) intervention to improve dyspareunia and alleviate sexual problems in women with breast cancer. *Journal of Sexual Medicine, 10*(10), 2549–2558.

Kaats, G.R., & Davis, K.E. (1971). Effects of volunteer biases in studies of sexual behavior and attitudes. *Journal of Sex Research, 7,* 26–34.

Kaczorowski, J. (1998). *Physical attractiveness and economic success.* Dissertation, Department of Sociology, McGill University, Montreal, PQ.

Kaestle, C., & Allen, K. (2011). The role of masturbation in healthy sexual development: Perceptions of young adults. *Archives of Sexual Behavior,* Retrieved February 4, 2011, from http://www.springerlink.com/content/a61r62w728335l00/.

Kafka, M.P. (2010). Hypersexual disorder: A proposed diagnosis for DSM-V. *Archives of Sexual Behavior, 39*(2), 377–400.

Kahr, B. (2008). *Who's been sleeping in your head: The secret world of sexual fantasies.* New York, NY: Basic Books.

Kain, E.L. (1987). A note on the integration of AIDS into the Sociology of Human Sexuality. *Teaching Sociology, 15,* 320–323.

Kalfa, N., Philibert, P., & Sultan, C. (2009). Is hypospadias a genetic, endocrine or environmental disease, or still an unexplained malformation? *International Journal Andrology, 32*(3), 187–197.

Kallmann, F.J. (1953). *Heredity in health and mental disorder: Principles of psychiatric genetics in the light of comparative twin studies.* New York, NY: Norton.

Kalsi, J., Thum, M.Y., Muneer, A., Pryor, J., Abdullah, H., & Minhas, S. (2011). Analysis of the outcome of intracytoplasmic sperm injection. *British Journal of Urology, 107*(7), 1124–1128.

Kalu, E., Thum, M., & Abdalla, H. (2011). Prognostic value of first IVF cycle on success of a subsequent cycle. *Journal of Assisted Reproductive Genetics, 28*(4), 379–382.

Kalyani, R., Basavaraj, P.B., & Kumar, M.L. (2007). Factors influencing quality of semen: A two year prospective study. *Indian Journal of Pathology and Microbiology, 50,* 890–895.

Kamali, H. (2010, December 20). Personal communication.

Kaminer, W. (1992, November). Feminists against the first amendment. *Atlantic Monthly,* pp. 111–117.

Kanayama, G., Hudson, J.I., & Pope, H.G., Jr. (2010). Illicit anabolic-androgenic steroid use. *Hormones and Behavior, 58*(1), 111–121.

Kantor, L. (1992). Scared chaste? Fear based educational curricula. *SIECUS Reports, 21,* 1–15.

Kaplan, G. (1977). Circumcision: An overview. *Current Problems in Pediatrics, 1,* 1–33.

Kaplan, H., Sadock, B., & Grebb, J. (1994). *Synopsis of psychiatry* (7th ed.). Baltimore, MD: Williams and Wilkins.

Kaplan, H.S. (1974). *The new sex therapy.* New York, NY: Bruner/Mazel.

Kaplan, L.J. (1991). Women masquerading as women. In G.I. Fogel & W.A. Meyers (Eds.), *Perversions and near-perversions in clinical practice: New psychoanalytic perspectives* (pp. 127–152). New Haven, CT: Yale University Press.

Kaplan, S.A. (2009). Side effects of alpha-blocker use: Retrograde ejaculation. *Reviews in Urology, 11*(Suppl. 1), S14–S18.

Kaplowitz, P.B. (2008). Link between body fat and the timing of puberty. *Pediatrics, 121*(Suppl 3), S208–217.

Kaplowitz, P.B., Slora, E.J., Wasserman, R.C., Pedlow, S.E., & Herman-Giddens, M.E. (2001). Earlier onset of puberty in girls: Relation to increased body mass index and race. *Pediatrics, 2108*(2), 347–354.

Kapoor, S. (2008). Testicular torsion: A race against time. *International Journal of Clinical Practices, 62,* 821–827.

Kapsimalakou, S., Grande-Nagel, I., Simon, M., Fischer, D., Thill, M., & Stôkelhuber, B. (2010). Breast abscess following nipple piercing: A case report and review of the literature. *Archives of Gynecology and Obstetrics, 282*(6), 623–626.

Karatas, O., Baltaci, G., Ilerisoy, Z., Bayrak, O., Cimentepe, E., Irmak, R., & Unal, D. (2010). The evaluation of clitoral blood flow and sexual function in elite female athletes. *Journal of Sexual Medicine, 7*(3), 1185–1189.

Karlsson, A., Sterlund, A., & Forss, N. (2011). Pharyngeal chlamydia trachomatis is not uncommon any more. *Scandinavian Journal of Infectious Disease, 43,* 344–348.

Karniol, R. (2001). Adolescent females' idolization of male media stars as a transition into sexuality. *Sex Roles, 44*(1–2), 61–77.

Kaschak, E., & Tiefer, L. (2001). *A new view of women's sexual problems.* Binghamton, NY: Haworth Press.

Kask, A.S., Chen, X., Marshak, J.O., Dong, L., Saracino, M., Chen, D., Jarrahian, C., Kendall, M.A., & Koelle, D.M. (2010). DNA vaccine delivery by densely-packed and short microprojection arrays to skin protects against vaginal HSV-2 challenge. *Vaccine, 28*(47), 7483–7491.

Kassler, W.J., & Cates, W. (1992). The epidemiology and prevention of sexually transmitted diseases. *Urologic Clinics of North America, 19,* 1–12.

Katz, J. (1976). *Gay American history: Lesbians and gay men in the U.S.A.* New York, NY: Thomas Y. Crowell Company.

Katz, M.H., Schwarcz, S.K., Kellogg, T.A., Klausner, J.D., Dilley, J.W., Gibson, S., et al. (2002). Impact of highly active antiretroviral treatment on HIV seroincidence among men who have sex with men. *American Journal of Public Health, 92*(3), 388–395.

Kaufman, B.S., Kaminsky, S.J., Rackow, E.C., & Weil, M.H. (1987). Adult respiratory distress syndrome following orogenital sex during pregnancy. *Critical Care Medicine, 15,* 703–704.

Kaunitz, A. (2002). Current concepts regarding use of DMPA. *Journal of Reproductive Medicine, 47*(9 Suppl.), 785–789.

Kaunitz, A.M., Arias, R., & McClung, M. (2008). Bone density recovery after depot medroxyprogesterone acetate injectable contraception use. *Contraception, 77,* 67–76.

Kazemi-Saleh, D., Pishgou, B., Assari, S., & Tavallaii, S. (2007). Fear of sexual intercourse in patients with coronary artery disease:

A pilot study of associated morbidity. *Journal of Sexual Medicine, 4,* 1619–1625.

Keasler, M. (2006). *Love hotels.* San Francisco: Chronicle Books.

Keegan, J. (2001). The neurobiology, neuropharmacology and pharmacological treatment of the paraphilias and compulsive sexual behavior. *Canadian Journal of Psychiatry, 46*(1), 26–33.

Keller, J.C. (2005). Straight talk about the gay gene. *Science & Spirit, 16,* 21.

Keller, Y. (2005). "Was it right to love her brother's wife so passionately?: Lesbian pulp novels and US lesbian identity, 1950–1965." *American Quarterly, 57*(2), 385–410.

Kelley, M.L., & Fals-Stewart, W. (2002). Couples- versus individual-based therapy for alcohol and drug abuse: effects on children's psychosocial functioning. *Journal of Consulting and Clinical Psychology, 70*(2), 417–427.

Kelly, A. (2009, March 12). Raped and killed for being a lesbian: South Africa ignores 'corrective' attacks. *The Guardian.* Retrieved April 30, 2011, from http://www.guardian .co.uk/world/2009/mar/12/eudy-simelane -corrective-rape-south-africa.

Kelly, B., Leader, A., Mittermaier, D., Hornik, R., & Cappella, J. (2009). The HPV vaccine and the media: How has the topic been covered and what are the effects on knowledge about the virus and cervical cancer? *Patient Education and Counseling, 77,* 308–313.

Kelly, C.K. (2000). Performing virginity and testing chastity in the Middle Ages. London: Routledge.

Kelly, D.L., & Conley, R.R. (2004). Sexuality and schizophrenia: A review. *Schizophrenia Bulletin, 30*(4), 767–779.

Kelly, D.L., & Conley, R.R. (2006). A randomized double-blind 12–week study of quetiapine, risperidone or fluphenazine on sexual functioning in people with schizophrenia. *Psychoneuroendocrinology, 31*(3), 340–346.

Kelly, J.M. (2005). *Zest for life: Lesbians' experiences of menopause.* North Melbourne, Australia: Spinifex Press.

Kelly, M. (2007). Discursive Framing of Teenage Sexuality: Virginity Loss on "Teen Drama" Television Programs. Conference Papers—American Sociological Association. Annual Meeting, pp. 1–40.

Kelly, M.P., Strassberg, D.S., & Kircher, J.R. (1990). Attitudinal and experiential correlates of anorgasmia. *Archives of Sexual Behavior, 19,* 165–177.

Kelly, R.J., Wood, J., Gonzalez, L., MacDonald, V., & Waterman, J. (2002). Effects of mother-son incest and positive perceptions of sexual abuse experiences on the psychosocial adjustment of clinic-referred men. *Child Abuse and Neglect, 26*(4), 425–441.

Kelly-Vance, L., Anthis, K.S., & Needelman, H. (2004). Assisted reproduction versus spontaneous conception: A comparison of the developmental outcomes in twins. *Journal of Genetic Psychology, 165*(2), 157–168.

Kempeneers, P., Andrianne, R., & Mormont, C. (2004). Penile prosthesis, sexual satisfaction and representation of male erotic value. *Sexual & Relationship Therapy, 19*(4), 379–392.

Kendrick, W.M. (1987). *The secret museum: Pornography in modern culture.* New York, NY: Viking.

Kennedy, M.A., & Gorzalka, B.B. (2002). Asian and non-Asian attitudes toward rape, sexual harassment and sexuality. *Sex Roles, 46*(7–8), 227–238.

Kerckhoff, A. (1964). Patterns of homogamy and the field of eligibles. *Social Forces, 42*(3), 289–297.

Kerr, D., & Capaldi, D. (2011). Young men's intimate partner violence and relationship functioning: Long-term outcomes associated with suicide attempt and aggression in adolescence. *Psychological Medicine, 41*(4), 759–769.

Kerrigan, D., Mobley, S., Rutenberg, N., Fisher, A., & Weiss, E. (2000). The female condom: Dynamics of use in urban Zimbabwe. New York, NY: The Population Council. Retrieved July 24, 2008, from http://www.popcouncil .org/pdfs/horizons/fcz.pdf.

Kertzner, R.M., Meyer, I.H., Frost, D.M., & Stirratt, M.J. (2009). Social and psychological well-being in lesbians, gay men, and bisexuals: The effects of race, gender, age, and sexual identity. *American Journal of Orthopsychiatry, 79*(4), 500–510.

Khadivzadeh, T., & Parsai, S. (2005). Effect of exclusive breastfeeding and complementary feeding on infant growth and morbidity. *Eastern Mediterranean Health Journal, 10*(3), 289–294.

Khoo, J., Ling, P.S., Tan, J., Teo, A., Ng, H.L., Chen, R.Y., Tay, T.L., Tan, E., & Cheong, M. (2014). Comparing the effects of meal replacements with reduced-fat diet on weight, sexual and endothelial function, testosterone and quality of life in obese Asian men. *International Journal of Impotence Research, 26*(2), 61–66.

Kidman, R., Petrow, S., & Heymann, S. (2007). Africa's orphan crisis: Two community-based models of care. *AIDS Care, 19*(3), 326–329.

Killick, S., Leary, C., Trussell, J., & Guthrie, K. (2010). Sperm content of pre-ejaculatory fluid. *Human Fertility, 14*(1), 48–52.

Kim, H.M., Ryu, J., Kim, K.S., & Song, S.W. (2013). Effects of yoga on sexual function in women with metabolic syndrome: a randomized controlled trial. *Journal of Sexual Medicine, 10*(11), 2741–2751.

Kim, I.W., Khadilkar, A.C., Ko, E.Y., Sabanegh, E.S. Jr. (2013). 47,XYY syndrome and male infertility. *Reviews in Urololgy, 15*(4), 188–196.

Kim, J., & Hatfield, E. (2004). Love types and subjective well-being: A cross-cultural study. *Social Behavior and Personality, 32,* 173–182.

Kim, J.L., Sorsoli, C.L., Collins, K., Zylbergold, B.A., Schooler, D., & Tolman, D.L. (2007). From sex to sexuality: Exposing the heterosexual script on primetime network television. *Journal of Sex Research, 44*(2), 145–157.

Kim, K., & Smith, P.K. (1999). Family relations in early childhood and reproductive development. *Journal of Reproductive and Infant Psychology, 17*(2), 133–149.

Kim, Y., Yang, S., Lee, J., Jung, T., & Shim, H. (2008). Usefulness of a malleable penile prosthesis in patients with a spinal cord injury. *International Journal of Urology, 15*(10), 919–923.

Kimberlin, D.W. (2007). Herpes simplex virus infections of the newborn. *Seminars in Perinatology, 31*(1), 19–25.

Kimmel, M.S., & Linders, A. (1996). Does censorship make a difference? An aggregate empirical analysis of pornography and rape. Journal *of Psychology & Human Sexuality, 8*(3), 1–20.

Kimmel, M.S., & Plante, R.F. (2007). Sexualities. *Contexts, 6,* 63–65.

King, M., Semlyen, J., Tai, S., Killaspy, H., Osborn, D., Popelyuk, D., & Nazareth, I. (2008). A systematic review of mental disorder, suicide, and deliberate self harm in lesbian, gay and bisexual people. *BMC Psychiatry, 8,* 70. Retrieved January 24, 2011, fromhttp://www.biomedcentral .com/1471–244X/8/70.

King, P., & Boyatzis, C. (2004). Exploring adolescent spiritual and religious development: Current and future theoretical and empirical perspectives. *Applied Developmental Science, 8,* 2–6.

Kingsberg, S.A., & Knudson, G. (2011). Female sexual disorders: Assessment, diagnosis, and treatment. *Urological Clinics of North America, 34*(4), 497–506.

Kinkade, S., & Meadows, S. (2005). Does neonatal circumcision decrease morbidity? *The Journal of Family Practice, 54*(1), 81–82.

Kinnunen, L.H., Moltz, H., Metz, J., & Cooper, M. (2004). Differential brain activation in exclusively homosexual and heterosexual men produced by the selective serotonin reuptake inhibitor, fluoxetine. *Brain Research, 1024*(1–2), 251–254.

Kinsey, A., Pomeroy, W.B., & Martin, C.E. (1948). *Sexual behavior in the human male.* Philadelphia: Saunders.

Kinsey, A.C., Pomeroy, W., Martin, C.E., & Gebhard, P. (1953). *Sexual behavior in the human female.* Philadelphia: Saunders.

Kinsman, G. (1987). *The regulation of desire: Sexuality in Canada*. Montreal: Black Rose Books.

Kirby, D. (1992). Sexuality education: It can reduce unprotected intercourse. *SIECUS Report, 21,* 19–25.

Kirby, D. (2001, May). Emerging answers: Research findings on programs to reduce teen pregnancy. National Campaign to Prevent Teen Pregnancy.

Kirby, D. (2007). Emerging answers: 2007. Research findings on programs to reduce teen pregnancy and sexually transmitted diseases. Washington, DC: National Campaign to Prevent Teen and Unplanned Pregnancy. Retrieved May 29, 2008, fromhttp://www .thenationalcampaign.org/EA2007/EA2007 _full.pdf.

Kirk, J.R. (1992). *The power of the picture* (pamphlet). Boulder, CO: Focus on the Family.

Kirk, J.R. (1995). *What the Bible says about pornography* (pamphlet). Boulder, CO: Focus on the Family.

Kirkey, S. (2013). Canada's pediatricians set to reveal new policy on circumcision. Retrieved August 30, 2014, from http://o.canada.com/ news/canadas-pediatricians-set-to-reveal -new-policy-on-circumcision.

Kirkpatrick, B. (2010). 'It beats rocks and tear gas': Streaking and cultural politics in the post-Vietnam era. *Journal of Popular Culture, 43*(5), 1023–1047.

Kitazawa, K. (1994). Sexuality issues in Japan. *SIECUS Report,* 7–11.

Kito, M. (2005). Self-disclosure in romantic relationships and friendships among American and Japanese college students. *Journal of Social Psychology, 145,* 127–140.

Klausen, P. (2007). *Trends in birth defect research.* Hauppauge, NY: Nova Science Publishers.

Klein, C., & Gorzalka, B. (2009). Sexual functioning in transsexuals following hormone therapy and genital surgery: A review. *Journal of Sexual Medicine, 6*(11), 2922–2932.

Klein, F. (1990). The need to view sexual orientation as a multivariable dynamic process: A theoretical perspective. In D.P. McWhirter, S.A. Sanders, & J.M. Reinisch (Eds.), *Homosexuality/heterosexuality: Concepts of sexual orientation* (pp. 277–282). New York, NY: Oxford University Press.

Klein, F. (1993). *The bisexual option* (2nd ed.). Philadelphia: Haworth Press.

Klein, F., Sepekoff, B., & Wolf, T.J. (1985). Sexual orientation. *Journal of Homosexuality, 11*(1/2), 35–49.

Klein, W., Geaghan, T., & MacDonald, T. (2007). Unplanned sexual activity as a consequence of alcohol use: A prospective study of risk perceptions and alcohol use among college freshman. *Journal of American College Health, 56,* 317–323.

Kleinplatz, P., & Moser, C. (2004). Toward clinical guidelines for working with BDSM clients. *Contemporary Sexuality, 38*(6), 1–4.

Kleinplatz, P.J., Ménard A.D., & Wannamaker C. (2014), "Personal contributors to optimal sexual experiences." In A.C. Michalos (Ed.), *Encyclopedia of quality of life and well-being research* (pp. 4724–4727). Dordrecht, Netherlands, Springer.

Klephart, W.M. (1976). *Extraordinary groups: The sociology of unconventional life-styles.* New York, NY: St. Martin's Press.

Kline, P. (1987). Sexual deviation: Psychoanalytic research and theory. In G.D. Wilson (Ed.), *Variant sexuality: Research and theory* (pp. 150–175). Baltimore: Johns Hopkins University Press.

Klonoff-Cohen, H., Natarajan, L., & Chen, R. (2006). A prospective study of the effects of female and male marijuana use on in vitro fertilization (IVF) and gamete intra-fallopian transfer (GIFT) outcomes. *American Journal of Obstetrics and Gynecology, 194*(2), 369–376.

Kluft, R. (2010). Ramifications of incest. *Psychiatric Times, 27*(12), 48–56.

Kluger, J. (2008, January 17). The science of romance: Why we love. *Time Magazine.* Retrieved August 17, 2008, from http:// www.time.com/time/magazine/article/ 0,9171,1704672–2,00.html.

Kluger, N. (2010). Body art and pregnancy. *European Journal of Obstetrics and Gynecological Reproductive Biology, 153*(1), 3–7.

Knaapen, L., & Weisz, G. (2008). The biomedical standardization of premenstrual syndrome. *Studies in History and the Philosophy of Biology and Biomedical Science, 39,* 120–134.

Knapp, M.L., & Hall, J.A. (2005). *Nonverbal communication in human interaction* (6th ed.). Belmont, CA: Wadsworth.

Knight, R.A., Sime-Knight, J., & Guay, J.-P. (2013). Is a separate diagnostic category defensible for paraphilic coercion? *Journal of Criminal Justice, 41*(2), 90–99.

Knight, S.J., & Latini, D.M. (2009). Sexual side effects and prostate cancer treatment decisions: Patient information needs and preferences. *Cancer Journal, 15*(1), 41–44.

Knoester, M., Helmerhorst, F., Vandenbroucke, J., van der Westerlaken, L., Walther, F., Veen, S., et al. (2008). Perinatal outcome, health growth, and medical care utilization of 5- to 8- year old intracytoplasmic sperm injection singletons. *Fertility and Sterility, 89,* 1133–1146.

Knöfler, T., & Imhof, M. (2007). Does sexual orientation have an impact on nonverbal behavior in interpersonal communication? *Journal of Nonverbal Behavior, 31,* 189–204.

Knox, D., Breed, R., & Zusman, M. (2007). College men and jealousy. *College Student Journal, 41,* 435–444.

Knox, D., Zusman, M., & McNeely, A. (2008). University student beliefs about sex: Men vs. women. *College Student Journal, 42,* 181–186.

Knox, D., Zusman, M.E., & Mabon, L. (1999). Jealousy in college student relationships. *College Student Journal, 33*(3), 328–329.

Knox, D., Zusman, M.E., Buffington, C., & Hemphill, G. (2000). Interracial dating attitudes among college students. *College Student Journal, 434*(1), 69–72.

Ko, D. (2001). *In every step a lotus: Shoes for bound feet.* Berkeley: University of California Press.

Koci, A.F. (2004). Marginality, abuse and adverse health outcomes in women. *Dissertations Abstracts International,* 0419–4217.

Koda, T., Ishida, T., Rehm, M., & Andre, E. (2009). Avatar culture: Cross-cultural evaluations of avatar facial expressions. *Artificial Intelligence & Society, 24,* 237–250.

Koerner, A., & Fitzpatrick, M. (1997). Family type and conflict: The impact of conversation orientation and conformity orientation on conflict in the family. *Communication Studies, 48,* 59–75.

Koh, A.S., Gomez, C.A., Shade, S., & Rowley, E. (2005). Sexual risk factors among self-identified lesbians, bisexual women, and heterosexual women accessing primary care settings. *Sexually Transmitted Diseases, 32*(9), 563–569.

Kohl, J.V., & Francoeur, R. (2002). *The scent of eros: Mysteries of odor in human sexuality.* Lincoln, NE: iUniverse, Author's Choice Press.

Kohler, P.K., Manhart, L.E., & Lafferty, W.E. (2008). Abstinence-only and comprehensive sex education and the initiation of sexual activity and teen pregnancy. *Journal of Adolescent Health, 42,* 344–351.

Kohn, C., Hasty, S., & Henderson, C.W. (2002, September 3). Study confirms infection from receptive oral sex occurs rarely. *AIDS Weekly,* 20–22.

Kon, I.S. (2004). Russia. In R.T. Francoeur & R.J. Noonan (Eds.), *The Continuum International encyclopedia of sexuality* (pp. 888–908). New York/London: Continuum International.

Kong, S., & Bernstein, K. (2009). Childhood trauma as a predictor of eating psychopathology and its mediating variables in patients with eating disorders. *Journal of Clinical Nursing, 18*(13), 1897–1907.

Kontula, O., & Haavio-Mannila, E. (2004). Finland. In R.T. Francoeur & R.J. Noonan (Eds.), *The Continuum International encyclopedia of sexuality* (pp. 381–411). New York/ London: Continuum International.

Kopelman, L. (1988). The punishment concept of disease. In C. Pierce & D. Vandeveer (Eds.), *AIDS, ethics, and public policy.* Belmont, CA: Wadsworth.

Korinek, B. (2012). "We're the girls of the pansy parade": Historicizing Winnipeg's queer subcultures, 1930s–1970. *Histoire sociale/Social History, 45,* 117–55

Kosfeld, M., Heinrichs, M., Zak, P.J., Fisch-bacher, U., & Fehr, E. (2005). Oxytocin increases trust in humans. *Nature, 435,* 673–676.

Koskimàki, J., Shiri, R., Tammela, T., Hàkkinen, J., Hakama, M., & Auvinen, A. (2008). Regular intercourse protects against erectile dysfunction: Tampere aging male urologic study. *American Journal of Medicine, 121,* 592–596.

Kotchick, B.A., Dorsey, S., & Miller, K.S. (1999). Adolescent sexual risk-taking behavior in single-parent ethnic minority families. *Journal of Family Psychology, 13*(1), 93–102.

Kotlyar, I., & Ariely, D. (2013). The effect of nonverbal cues on relationship formation. *Computers in Human Behavior, 29*(3), 544–551.

Kral, M.J., Idlout, L., Minore, J.B., Dyck, R.J., & Kirmayer, L.J. (2011). Unikkaartuit: Meanings of well-being, unhappiness, health, and community change among Inuit in Nunavut, Canada. *American Journal of Community Psychology, 48*(3–4), 426–438.

Kreider, R.M. (2005). Number, timing and duration of marriages and divorces: 2001. *Current Population Reports* (P70–97). Washington, DC: U.S. Census Bureau.

Kreuter, M., Siosteen, A., & Biering-Sorensen, F. (2008). Sexuality and sexual life in women with spinal cord injury: A controlled study. *Journal of Rehabilitative Medicine, 40,* 61–69.

Kreuter, M., Taft, C., Siôsteen, A., & Biering-Sorensen, F. (2011). Women's sexual functioning and sex life after spinal cord injury. *Spinal Cord, 49*(1), 154–160.

Kriebs, J. (2008). Understanding herpes simplex virus: Transmission, diagnosis, and considerations in pregnancy management. *Journal of Midwifery Women's Health, 53,* 202–208.

Krikorian, T. (2004, February 25). Hymeno-plasty surgery result of a sexist society. *Spartan Daily.* Retrieved January 13, 2011, from http://www.urogyn.org/documents/Hymenoplasty_surgery_result_of_sexist_society.pdf.

Krone, N., Hanley, N., & Arlt, W. (2007). Age-specific changes in sex steroid biosynthesis and sex development. *Clinical Endocrinology and Metabolism, 21*(3), 393–401.

Krstic, Z.D., Smoljanic, Z., Vukanic, D., Varinac, D., & Janiic, G. (2000). True hermaphroditism: 10 years' experience. *Pediatric Surgery International, 16*(8), 580–583.

Krueger, R.B. (2009). The DSM diagnostic criteria for sexual sadism. *Archives of Sexual Behavior, 39*(2), 325–345.

Krüger, T., Schiffer, B., Eikermann, M., Haake, P., Gizewski, E., & Schedlowsk, M. (2006). Serial neurochemical measurement of cerebrospinal fluid during the human sexual response cycle. *European Journal of Neuroscience, 24,* 3445–3452.

Kuczkowski, K.M. (2006). Labor analgesia for the parturient with lumbar tattoos: What does an obstetrician need to know? *Archives of Gynecology and Obstetrics, 274,* 310–312.

Kuefler, M. (2006). *The Boswell thesis: Essays on Christianity, social tolerance, and homosexuality.* Chicago: University of Chicago Press.

Kuliev, A., & Verlinsky, Y. (2008). Impact of preimplantation genetic diagnosis for chromosomal disorders on reproductive outcome. *Reproductive Biomedical Online, 16,* 9–10.

Kulig, J., Pfeuti, L., Thorpe, K., & Hall, B. (1999). Multicultural issues within universities: Identifying trends and challenges. *Indian Journal of Social Work, 60*(2), 209–232.

Kumar, S., Roy, S., Chaudhury, K., Sen, P., & Guha, S.K. (2008). Study of the microstructural properties of RISUG—a newly developed male contraceptive. *Journal of Biomedical Materials Research, 86*(1), 154–161.

Kunin, C.M. (1997). *Urinary tract infections: Detection, prevention and management.* (5th ed.) Baltimore: Williams & Wilkins.

Kunkel, A.W., & Burleson, B.R. (1998). Social support and the emotional lives of men and women: An assessment of the different cultures perspective. In D. Canary & K. Dindia (Eds.), *Sex differences and similarities in communication: Critical essays and empirical investigations of sex and gender in interaction* (pp. 101–125). Mahwah, NJ: Lawrence Erlbaum Associates.

Kurdek, L.A. (2006). Differences between partners from heterosexual, gay, and lesbian cohabiting couples. *Journal of Marriage and Family, 68,* 509–528.

Kürzinger, M., Pagnier, J., Kahn, J., Hampshire, R., Wakabi, T., & Dye, T. (2008). Education status among orphans and non-orphans in communities affected by AIDS in Tanzania and Burkina Faso. *AIDS Care, 20*(6), 726–732.

Kwan, I., Bhattacharya, S., McNeil, A., & van Rumste, M. (2008). Monitoring of stimulated cycles in assisted reproduction. *Co-chrane Database of Systematic Reviews, 16,* CD005289.

Kyongseok, K., Hye-Jin, P., & Jordan, L. (2010). A content analysis of smoking fetish videos on youtube: Regulatory implications for tobacco control. *Health Communication, 25,* 97–106.

Labbate, L. (2008). Psychotropics and sexual dysfunction: The evidence and treatments. *Advances in Psychosomatic Medicine, 29,* 107–130.

Labruce, B. (2014). Notes on camp—and anti-camp. *Gay & Lesbian Review Worldwide, 21*(2), 10–13.

Lacerda, H.M., Richiardi, L., Pettersson, A., Corbin, M., Merletti, F., & Akre, O. (2010). Cancer risk in mothers of men operated for undescended testis. *PLoS One, 5*(12), e14285.

LaFree, G. (1982). Male power and female victimization. *American Journal of Sociology, 88,* 311–328.

Lahaie, M.A., Boyer, S.C., Amsel, R., Khalifé, S., & Binik, Y.M. (2010). Vaginismus: A review of the literature on the classification/diagnosis, etiology and treatment. *Womens Health, 6*(5), 705–719.

Lahaie, M.A., Amsel, R., Khalifé, S., Boyer, S., Faaborg-Andersen, M., & Binik, Y.M. (2014). Can fear, pain, and muscle tension discriminate vaginismus from dyspareunia/provoked vestibulodynia? Implications for the new DSM-5 diagnosis of genito-pelvic pain/penetration disorder. *Archives of Sexual Behavior,* [Epub ahead of print].

Lahey, K.A., & Alderson, K. (2004). *Same-sex marriage: The personal and the political.* Toronto: Insomniac Press.

Lai, C.H. (2011). Major depressive disorder: Gender differences in symptoms, life quality, and sexual function. *Journal of Clinical Psychopharmacology, 31*(1), 39–44.

Lakhey, M., Ghimire, R., Shrestha, R., & Bhatta, A.D. (2010). Correlation of serum free prostate-specific antigen level with histological findings in patients with prostatic disease. *Kathmandu University Medical Journal, 8*(30), 158–163.

Lakoff, R. (1975). *Language and woman's place.* New York, NY: Harper.

Lalor, K., & McElvaney, R. (2010). Child sexual abuse, links to later sexual exploitation/high-risk sexual behavior, and prevention/treatment programs. *Trauma Violence Abuse, 11*(4), 159–177.

Lalumière, M.L., Harris, G.T., Quinsey, V., & Rice, M.E. (2005a). Clinical assessment and treatment of rapists. In M.L. Lalumière & G. Harris (Eds.), *Causes of rape: Understanding individual differences in male propensity for sexual aggression* (pp. 161–181). Washington, DC: American Psychological Association.

Lalumière, M.L., Harris, G.T., Quinsey, V., & Rice, M.E. (2005b). Forced copulation in the animal kingdom. In M.L. Lalumière & G. Harris (Eds.), *Causes of rape: Understanding individual differences in male propensity for sexual aggression* (pp. 31–58). Washington, DC: American Psychological Association.

Lalumière, M.L., Harris, G.T., Quinsey, V., & Rice, M.E. (2005c). Rape across cultures and time. In M.L. Lalumière & G. Harris (Eds.), *Causes of rape: Understanding individual differences in male propensity for sexual aggression* (pp. 9–30). Washington, DC: American Psychological Association.

Lalumière, M.L., Harris, G.T., Quinsey, V., & Rice, M.E. (2005d). Sexual interest in rape. In M.L. Lalumière & G. Harris (Eds.), *Causes of rape: Understanding individual differences in male propensity for sexual aggression* (pp. 105–128). Washington, DC: American Psychological Association.

Lam, A.G., Russell, S.T., Tan, T.C., & Leong, S.J. (2008). Maternal predictors of noncoital sexual behavior: Examining a nationally representative sample of Asian and White American adolescents who have never had sex. *Journal of Youth and Adolescence, 37*, 62–74.

Lamont, J.A. (1977). Sex research and therapy groups. *Canadian Medical Association Journal, 116*(1), 15, 18.

Lampiao, F. (2009). Variation of semen parameters in healthy medical students due to exam stress. *Malawi Medical Journal, 21*(4), 166–170.

Lancet, The. (2009). "Redemption for the pope?" 373, 9669, p. 1054.

Lang, R., Flor-Henry, P., & Frenzel, R. (1990). Sex hormone profiles in pedophilic and incestuous men. *Annals of Sex Research, 3*, 59–74.

Lange R.A., & Levine G.N. (2014). Sexual activity and ischemic heart disease. *Current Cardiology Reports, 16*(2), 445.

Langevin, R., & Lang, R.A. (1987). The courtship disorders. In G.D. Wilson (Ed.), *Variant sexuality: Research and theory* (pp. 202–228). Baltimore: Johns Hopkins University Press.

Langevin, R., Langevin, M., & Curnoe, S. (2007). Family size, birth order, and parental age among male paraphilics and sex offenders. *Archives of Sexual Behavior, 36*, 599–609.

Langevin, R., Wortzman, G., Dickey, R., Wright, P., et al. (1988). Neuropsychological impairment in incest offenders. *Annals of Sex Research, 1*, 401–415.

Långström N., & Seto, M.C. (2006). Exhibitionistic and voyeuristic behavior in a Swedish national population survey. *Archives of Sexual Behavior, 35*(4), 427–435.

Långström, N. (2010). The DSM diagnostic criteria for exhibitionism, voyeurism, and frotteurism. *Archives of Sexual Behavior, 29*(2), 317–324.

Långström, N., Grann, M., & Lindblad, F. (2000). A preliminary typology of young sex offenders. *Journal of Adolescence, 23*, 319–329.

Laqueur, T.W. (2003). *Solitary sex: A cultural history of masturbation.* Cambridge, MA: Zone Books.

Larivière, S., & Ferguson, S.H. (2002). On the evolution of the mammalian baculum: vaginal friction, prolonged intromission or induced ovulation? *Mammal Review, 32*(4), 283–294.

Larkin, M. (1992). Reacting to patients with sexual problems. *Headlines, 3*(2), 3, 6, 8.

Larsson, P.G., Bergström, M., Forsum, U., Jacobsson, B., Strand, A., & Wölner-Hanssen, P. Bacterial vaginosis. Transmission, role in genital tract infection and pregnancy outcome: an enigma. *APMIS, 113*(4), 233–245.

LaSala, M.C. (2000). Lesbians, gay men and their parents: Family therapy for the coming out crisis. *Family Process, 39*(2), 257–266.

LaSala, M.C. (2001). The importance of partners to lesbians' intergenerational relationships. *Social Work Research, 25*(1), 27–36.

Lastella, D.D. (2005). Sexual harassment as an interpersonal dynamic: The effect of race, attractiveness, position power and gender on perceptions of sexual harassment. *Dissertation Abstracts International: Section B.,* #0419–4217.

Lau, J., Kim, J.H., & Tsui, H.Y. (2005). Prevalence of male and female sexual problems, perceptions related to sex and association with quality of life in a Chinese population. *International Journal of Impotence Research, 17*(6), 494–505.

Laughlin, S., Schroeder, J., & Baird, D. (2010). New directions in the epidemiology of uterine fibroids. *Seminars in Reproductive Medicine, 28*(3), 204–217.

Laumann, E., Nicolosi, A., Glasser, D., Paik, A., Gingell, C., Moreira, E., Wang, T., for the GSSAB Investigators' Group. (2005). Sexual problems among women and men aged 40–80-y: Prevalence and correlates identified in the Global Study of Sexual Attitudes and Behaviors. *International Journal of Impotence Research, 17*, 39–57.

Laumann, E.O., Gagnon, J., Michael, R., & Michaels, S. (1994). *The social organization of sexuality: Sexual practices in the United States.* Chicago: University of Chicago Press.

Laumann, E.O., Paik, A., & Rosen, R. (1999). Sexual dysfunction in the United States. *Journal of the American Medical Association, 281*, 537–544.

Laumann, E.O., Paik, A., Glasser, D.B., Kang, J., Wang, T., Levinson, B., et al. (2006). A cross-national study of subjective sexual well-being among older women and men: Findings from the Global Study of Sexual Attitudes and Behaviors. *Archives of Sexual Behavior, 35*, 145–161.

Laurence, J. (2006). Treating HIV infection with one pill per day. *AIDS Patient Care and STDs, 20*, 601–603.

Lavee, Y. (1991). Western and non-Western human sexuality: Implications for clinical practice. *Journal of Sex and Marital Therapy, 17*, 203–213.

La Vignera, S., Rosita, A., Condorelli, E.V., D'Agata, R., & Calogero, A.E. (2012). Effects of the exposure to mobile phones on male reproduction: a review of the literature. *Journal of Andrology, 33*(3), 350–356.

Lavin, M. (2008). Voyeurism: Psychopathology and theory. In D. Laws & W. O'Donohue (Eds.), *Sexual deviance: Theory, assessment and treatment* (2nd ed., pp. 305–319). New York, NY: Guilford Press.

Lawrence, A.A. (2006). Patient-reported complications and functional outcomes of male and female sex reassignment surgery. *Archives of Sexual Behavior, 35*, 717–727.

Laws, D., & O'Donohue, W. (2008). *Sexual deviance: Theory, assessment, and treatment.* New York, NY: Guilford Press.

Lawyer, S., Resnick, H., Bakanic, V., Burkett, T., & Kilpatrick, D. (2010). Forcible, drug-facilitated, and incapacitated rape and sexual assault among undergraduate women. *Journal of American College Health, 58*(5), 453–461.

Layton-Tholl, D. (1998). Extramarital affairs: The link between thought suppression and level of arousal. *Dissertation Abstracts,* Miami Institute of Psychology of the Caribbean Center for Advanced Studies, #AAT9930425.

Lazarou, S., & Morgentaler, A. (2008). The effect of aging on spermatogenesis and pregnancy outcomes. *Urologic Clinics of North America, 35*(2), 331–339.

Leaper, C. (2000). The social construction and socialization of gender during development. In P.H. Miller & E.K. Scholnick (Eds.), *Toward a feminist developmental psychology* (pp. 127–152). New York, NY: Routledge.

Ledbetter, A. (2010). Communication patterns and communication competence as predictors of online communication attitude: Evaluating a dual pathway model. *Journal of Family Communication, 10*(2), 99–115.

Ledermann, T., Bodenmann, G., Rudaz, M., & Bradbury, T. (2010). Stress, communication, and martial quality in couples. *Family Relations, 59*(2), 195–207.

Ledger, W. (2004). Implications of an irreversible procedure. *Fertility and Sterility, 82*, 1473.

Leduc D., Biringer A., Lee, L., & Dy, J. (2013). Induction of labour. *Journal of Obstetrics and Gynaecology Canada, 35*(9), 840–860.

Lee, J., Pomeroy, E.C., Yoo, S., & Rheinboldt, K. (2005). Attitudes toward rape: A comparison between Asian and Caucasian college students. *Violence Against Women, 11*(2), 177–196.

Lee, J.A. (1974). The styles of loving. *Psychology Today, 8,* 43–51.

Lee, J.A. (1988). Love-styles. In R. Sternberg & M. Barnes (Eds.), *The psychology of love.* New Haven, CT: Yale University Press.

Lee, J.A. (1998). Ideologies of lovestyle and sexstyle. In V.de Munck (Ed.), *Romantic love and sexual behavior* (pp. 33–76). Westport, CT: Praeger.

Lee, P., Houk, C., Ahmed, S., Hughes, I., & the International Consensus Conference on Intersex Organized by the Lawson Wilkins Pediatric Endocrine Society and the European Society of Paediatric Endocrinology. (2006). Consensus statement on management of intersex disorders. *Pediatrics, 118,* 488–500.

Lee, S., Liong, M., Yuen, K., Leong, W., Cheah, P., Khan, N., & Krieger, J. (2008). Adverse impact of sexual dysfunction in chronic prostatitis/chronic pelvic pain syndrome. *Urology, 71,* 79–84.

Leiblum, S., Koochaki, P., Rodenberg, X., Barton, I., & Rosen, R. (2006). Hypoactive sexual desire disorder in postmenopausal women: US results from the women's international study of health and sexuality. *Menopause, 13,* 46–56.

Leiblum, S.R., & Goldmeier, D. (2008). Persistent genital arousal disorder in women: Case reports of association with anti-depressant usage and withdrawal. *Journal of Sex and Marital Therapy, 34*(2), 150–159.

Leiblum, S.R., & Seehuus, M. (2009). FSFI scores of women with persistent genital arousal disorder compared with published scores of women with female sexual arousal disorder and healthy controls. *Journal of Sexual Medicine, 6,* 469–473.

Leibo, S.P. (2008). Cryopreservation of oocytes and embryos: Optimization by theoretical versus empirical analysis. *Theriogenology, 69,* 37–47.

Leite, R., Prestes, J., Pereira, G., Shiguemoto, G., & Perez, S. (2010). Menopause: Highlighting the effects of resistance training. *International Journal of Sports Medicine, 31*(11), 761–767.

Leitenberg, H., & Henning, K. (1995). Sexual fantasy. *Psychological Bulletin, 117*(3), 469–496.

Lenius, S. (2001). Bisexuals and BDSM: Bisexual people in a pansexual community. *Journal of Bisexuality, 1*(4), 70–78.

Leo, S., & Sia, A. (2008). Maintaining labour epidural analgesia: What is the best option? *Current Opinions in Anesthesiology, 21,* 263–269.

Leonard, A.S. (2006, September 25). Hong Kong appeals court strikes down differential age of consent law on "buggery." Leonard Link, New York Law School. Retrieved October 2, 2008, from http://newyorklawschool.typepad.com/leonardlink/2006/09/hong_kong_appea.html.

Leonard, K.E. (2005). Editorial: Alcohol and intimate partner violence: When can we say that heavy drinking is a contributing cause of violence? *Addiction, 100*(4), 422–425.

Leonard, T.L. (1990). Male clients of female prostitutes: Unseen partners in sexual disease transmission. *Medical Anthropology Quarterly, 4*(1), 41–55.

Leonard, T.M. (2006). *Encyclopedia of the developing world* (Vol. 2). Philadelphia: Taylor & Francis.

Leone, T., & Padmadas, S. (2007). The proliferation of a sterilization culture in women's lives: A comparison of Brazil and India. London School of Economics. *Genus, 63*(3/4), 77–97.

Lerner, H. (1998). *The mother dance: How children change your life.* New York, NY: HarperCollins.

Lerner-Geva, L., Keinan-Boker, L., Blumstein, T., Boyko, V., Olmar, L., Mashiach, S., et al. (2006). Infertility, ovulation induction treatments and the incidence of breast cancer—a historical prospective cohort of Israeli women. *Breast Cancer Research and Treatment, 100,* 201–212.

LeVay, S. (1991). A difference in hypothalamic structure between heterosexual and homosexual men. *Science, 253,* 1034–1037.

Lever, J., Grov, C., Royce, T., & Gillespie, B. (2008). Searching for love in all the "write" and "wrong" places: Exploring Internet personals use by sexual orientation, gender, and age. *International Journal of Sexual Health, 20*(4), 233.

Levin, R., & Wylie, K. (2010). Persistent genital arousal disorder: A review of the literature and recommendations for management. *International Journal of STDs and AIDS, 21*(5), 379–380.

Levin, R.J. (2007). Sexual activity, health and well-being—the beneficial roles of coitus and masturbation. *Sexual and Relationship Therapy, 22,* 135–148.

Levine, D. (2007). Ectopic pregnancy. *Radiology, 245,* 385–397.

Levine, D.A., & Gemignani, M.L. (2003). Prophylactic surgery in hereditary breast/ovarian cancer syndrome. *Oncology, 17*(7), 932–941.

Levine, E. (2007). *Wallowing in sex: The new sexual culture of 1970s American television.* Durham, NC: Duke University Press.

Levine, M.P., & Troiden, R.R. (1988). The myth of sexual compulsivity. *The Journal of Sex Research, 25*(3), 347–363.

Levine, R., Sato, S., & Hashimoto, T. (1995). Love and marriage in eleven cultures. *Journal of Cross-Cultural Psychology, 26*(5), 554–571.

Levine, S.B., Risen, C.B., & Althof, S.E. (1990). Essay on the diagnosis and nature of paraphilia. *Journal of Sex and Marital Therapy, 16*(2), 89–102.

Lev-Wiesel, R. (2004). Male university students' attitudes toward rape and rapists. *Child & Adolescent Social Work Journal, 21,* 199.

Levy, D. (2007). Love and sex with robots: The evolution of human-robot relations. New York, NY: HarperCollins.

Lewin, R. (1988). New views emerge on hunters and gatherers. *Science, 240*(4856), 1146–1148.

Lewin, T. (2005). Are these parties for real? *New York Times.* June 30. Retrieved from http://www.nytimes.com/2005/06/30/fashion/thursdaystyles/30rainbow.html?_r=0.

Lewis, M. (1987). Early sex role behavior and school age adjustment. In J.M. Reinish, L.A. Rosenblum, & S.A. Sanders (Eds.), *Masculinity/femininity: Basic perspectives* (pp. 202–226). New York, NY: Oxford University Press.

Lewis, R., & Ford-Robertson, J. (2010). Understanding the occurrence of interracial marriage in the United States through differential assimilation. *Journal of Black Studies, 41*(2), 405–420.

Lewis, R.J., & Janda, L.H. (1988). The relationship between adult sexual adjustment and childhood experiences regarding exposure to nudity, sleeping in the parental bed, and parental attitudes toward sexuality. *Archives of Sexual Behavior, 17,* 349–362.

Lewis, S.E., Agbaje, I., & Alvarez, J. (2008). Sperm DNA tests as useful adjuncts to semen analysis. *Systems Biology in Reproductive Medicine, 54,* 111–125.

Ley, D.J. (2012). *The myth of sexual addiction.* London: Rowman & Littlefield Publishers.

Leyendecker, G., Kunz, G., Herbertz, M., Beil, D., Huppert, P., Mall, G., Kissler, S., Noe, M., & Wildt, L. (2004, December). Uterine peristaltic activity and the development of endometriosis. *Annals of the New York Academy of Sciences, 1034,* 338–355.

Leyson, J.F. (2004). Philippines. In R.T. Francoeur & R.J. Noonan (Eds.), *The Continuum International encyclopedia of sexuality* (pp. 825–845). New York/London: Continuum International.

Leznoff. M. (1954). The Homosexual in Urban Society. Masters Thesis. McGill University, Montreal, Quebec.

LGBT in the Workplace. (2016). Angus Reid Public Opinion Poll. Retrieved from http://www.angusreidglobal.com/wp-content/uploads/2011/11/2011.11.15_LGBT.pdf.

Li, C.C., & Rew, L. (2010). A feminist perspective on sexuality and body image in females with colorectal cancer: An integrative review. *Journal of Wound Ostomy and Continence Nursing, 37*(5), 519–525.

Li, C.I., Chlebowski, R.T., Freiberg, M., Johnson, K.C., Kuller, L., Lane, D., Lessin, L., O'Sullivan, M.J., Wactawski-Wende, J., Yasmeen, S., & Prentice, R. (2010a). Alcohol consumption and risk of postmenopausal breast cancer by subtype: The Women's Health Initiative Observational Study. *Journal of the National Cancer Institute, 102*(18), 1422.

Li, C.I., Malone, K.E., Daling, J.R., Potter, J.D., Bernstein, L., Marchbanks, P.A., et al. (2008). Timing of menarche and first full-term birth in relation to breast cancer risk. *Journal of Epidemiology, 167,* 230–239.

Li, D.K., Zhou, Z., Miao, M., He, Y., Wang, J., Ferber, J., Herrinton, L.J., Gao, E., & Yuan, W. (2011). Urine bisphenol-A (BPA) level in relation to semen quality. *Fertility and Sterility, 95*(2), 625–630.e1–e4.

Li, G., Li, G.Y., Ji, H.J., Zhao, W.J., Chu, S.F., & Chen, N.H. (2010b). [Effect of testosterone on the expression of CMTM family of the male spermatogenesis suppression rats]. *Yao XueXue Bao, 45*(8), 995–1000.

Liao, C., Wei, J., Li, Q., Li, L., Li, J., & Li, D. (2006). Efficacy and safety of cordocentesis for prenatal diagnosis. *International Journal of Gynecology and Obstetrics, 93,* 13–17.

Liao, L., Michala, L., & Creighton, S. (2010). Labial surgery for well women: A review of the literature. *British Journal of Obstetrics and Gynecology, 117*(1), 20–25.

Liao, L.M., & Creighton, S.M. (2007). Requests for cosmetic genitoplasty: How should healthcare providers respond? *British Medical Journal, 334*(7603), 1090–1092.

Liben, L.S., & Bigler, R.S. (2002). The developmental course of gender differentiation. *Monographs of the Society of Research in Child Development, 67*(2), vii–147.

Lichtenberg, I. (2011, February 27). Child rape in South Africa persists unabated. *Monsters and Critics News.* Retrieved April 30, 2011, from http://www.monstersandcritics.com/news/africa/features/article_1622267.php/Child-rape-in-South-Africa-persists-unabated-Feature.

Lie, D. (2000). Contraception update for the primary care physician. Retrieved May 17, 2001, from http://www.medscape.com/medscape/CNO/200/AAFP/AAFP-06.html.

Lie, M.L., Robson, S.C., & May, C.R. (2008). Experiences of abortion: A narrative review of qualitative studies. *BMC Health Services Research, 8,* 150.

Lilley, L.L., & Schaffer, S. (1990). Human papillomavirus: A sexually transmitted disease with carcinogenic potential. *Cancer Nursing, 13,* 366–372.

Lim, M.M., & Young, L.J. (2006). Neuropeptidergic regulation of affiliative behavior and social bonding in animals. *Hormones and Behavior, 50,* 506–517.

Limin, M., Johnsen, N., & Hellstrom, W.J. (2010). Avanafil, a new rapidonset phosphodiesterase 5 inhibitor for the treatment of erectile dysfunction. *Expert Opinion on Investigational Drugs, 19*(11), 1427–1437.

Lindau, S., & Gavrilova, N. (2010). Sex, health, and years of sexually active life gained due to good health: Evidence from two US population based cross sectional surveys of ageing. *British Medical Journal, 340,* c810. Retrieved from http://www.bmj.com/content/340/bmj.c810.full.pdf.

Lindau, S., Gavrilova, N., & Anderson, D. (2007). Sexual morbidity in very long term survivors of vaginal and cervical cancer: A comparison to national norms. *Gynecologic Oncology, 106*(2), 413–418.

Lindberg, L.D., Jones, R., & Santelli, J.S. (2008, July). Non-coital sexual activities among adolescents. *Journal of Adolescent Health.* Retrieved May 26, 2008, from http://www.guttmacher.org/pubs/JAH_Lindberg.pdf.

Linton, K.D., & Wylie, K.R. (2010). Recent advances in the treatment of premature ejaculation. *Journal of Drug Design, Development and Therapy, 18*(4), 1–6.

Lippa, R.A., & Tan, F.P. (2001). Does culture moderate the relationship between sexual orientation and gender-related personality trait? *Journal of Comparative Social Science, 35*(1), 65–87.

Lips, H. (2008). *Sex & gender: An introduction* (6th ed.). New York, NY: McGraw-Hill.

Lipsky, S., Caetono, R., Field, C.A., & Larkin, G. (2005). Psychosocial and substanceuse risk factors for intimate partner violence. *Drug & Alcohol Dependence, 78*(1), 39–47.

Lipton, L. (2003). The erotic revolution. In J. Escoffier (Ed.), *Sexual revolution* (pp. 20–30). New York, NY: Thunder's Mouth Press.

Lisak, D., & Miller, P. (2002). Repeat rape and multiple offending among undetected rapists. *Violence and Victims, 17*(1), 73–84.

Litosseliti, L. (2006). *Gender and language: Theory and practice.* London: Arnold.

Litt, S. (2010). Dennis Barrie looks back on his Cincinnati obscenity trail 20 years after his acquittal. Retrieved from http://www.cleveland.com/arts/index.ssf/2010/10/dennis_barrie_looks_back_on_hi.html.

Little, A.C., Burt, D.M., & Perrett, D.I. (2006). What is good is beautiful: Face preference reflects desired personality. *Personality and Individual Differences, 41,* 1107–1118.

Little, B., & White, M. (2005). Treatment options for paraphimosis. International Journal of Clinical Practice, 59(5), 591–593.

Littleton, H., Breitkopf, C., & Berenson, A. (2007). Rape scripts of low-income European American and Latina women. *Sex Roles, 56,* 509–516.

Littleton, H., Grills-Taquechel, A., & Axsom, D. (2009a). Impaired and incapacitated rape victims: Assault characteristics and post-assault experiences. *Violence and Victims, 24*(4), 439–457.

Littleton, H., & Henderson, C. (2009). If she is not a victim, does that mean she was not traumatized? Evaluation of predictors of PTSD symptomatology among college rape victims. *Violence Against Women, 15*(2), 148–167.

Littleton, H., Tabernik, H., Canales, E., & Backstrom, T. (2009b). Risky situation or harmless fun? A qualitative examination of college women's bad hook-up and rape scripts. *Sex Roles, 60*(11–12), 793–805.

Liu, D.F., Jiang, H., Hong, K., Zhao, L.M., Tang, W.H., & Ma, L.L. (2010). Influence of erectile dysfunction course on its progress and efficacy of treatment with phosphodiesterase type 5 inhibitors. *Chinese Medical Journal, 123*(22), 3258–3261.

Ljepava, N., Orr, R.R., Locke, S., & Ross, C. (2013). Personality and social characteristics of Facebook non-users and frequent users. *Computers in Human Behavior, 29*(4), 1602–1607.

Lloyd, J., Crouch, N.S., Minto, C.L., Liao, L.M., & Creighton, S.M. (2005). Female genital appearance: "normality" unfolds. *BJOG: An International Journal of Obstetrics & Gynaecology, 112*(5), 643–646.

Lloyd, T., Petit, M.A., Lin, H.M., & Beck, T.J. (2004). Lifestyle factors and the development of bone mass and bone strength in young women. *Journal of Pediatrics, 144*(6), 776–782.

Lock, J., & Steiner, H. (1999). Gay lesbian and bisexual youth risks for emotional, physical, and social problems: Results from a community-based survey. *Journal of American Academy of Child and Adolescent Psychiatry 38*(3), 297–305.

Locker, L., McIntosh, W., Hackney, A., Wilson, J., & Wiegand, K. (2010). The breakup of romantic relationships: Situational predictors of perception of recovery. *North American Journal of Psychology, 12*(3), 565–578.

Lockwood, S. (2008, April 7). Homeless GLBT youths often face violent life on the streets. *Columbia Spectator.* Retrieved October 2, 2008, from http://www.columbiaspectator.com/node/30281.

Lohiya, N.K., Suthar, R., Khandelwal, A., Goyal, S., Ansari, A.S., & Manivannan, B. (2010). Sperm characteristics and teratology in rats following vas deferens occlusion with RISUG and its reversal. *International Journal of Andrology, 33*(1), e198–e206.

Loke, A., & Poon, C. (2011). The health concerns and behaviours of primigravida: Comparing advanced age pregnant women with their younger counterparts. *Journal of Clinical Nursing, 20,* 1141–1150.

Lombardi, G., Del Popolo, G., Macchiarella, A., Mencarini, M., & Celso, M. (2010). Sexual rehabilitation in women with spinal cord injury: A critical review of the literature. *Spinal Cord, 48*(12), 842–849.

Lombardi, G., Macchiarella, A., Cecconi, F., & Del Popolo, G. (2009). Ten-year follow-up of sildenafil use in spinal cord-injured patients with erectile dysfunction. *Journal of Sexual Medicine, 6*(12), 3449–3457.

Lombardo, W., Cretser, G., & Roesch, S. (2001). For crying out loud—the differences persist into the '90s. *Sex Roles, 45*(7–8), 529–547.

Long, S., Ullman, S., Long, L., Mason, G., & Starzynski, L. (2007). Women's experiences of male-perpetrated sexual assault by sexual orientation. *Violence and Victims, 22,* 684–701.

Long, V.E. (2003). Contraceptive choices: New options in the U.S. market. *SIECUS Report, 31*(2), 13–18.

Longua, P. (2010). "I love you" (but I can't look you in the eyes): Explicit and implicit self-esteem predict verbal and nonverbal response to relationship threat. Chicago: Loyola University, AAT #3434370.

Lonsway, K., Cortina, L., & Magley, V. (2008). Sexual harassment mythology: Definition, conceptualization, and measurement. *Sex Roles, 58,* 599–616.

Lopez, L., Grimes, D.A., Gallo, M., & Schulz, K. (2008). Skin patch and vaginal ring versus combined oral contraceptives for contraception. *Cochrane Database Systems Review, 23,* CD003552.

LoPiccolo, J., & Lobitz, W.C. (1972). The role of masturbation in the treatment of orgasmic dysfunction. *Archives of Sexual Behavior, 2,* 163–171.

LoPiccolo, J., & Stock, W.E. (1986). Treatment of sexual dysfunction. *Journal of Consulting and Clinical Psychology, 54,* 158–167.

Lo Presto, C.T., Sherman, M.F., & Sherman, N.C. (1985). The effects of a masturbation seminar on high school males' attitudes, false beliefs, guilt, and behavior. *Journal of Sex Research, 21*(2), 142.

Loriggio, P. (2014). Sexuality a 'non-issue' during Wynne's election campaign: Expert. *National Post,* June 14. http://news.nationalpost.com/2014/06/14/sexuality-a-non-issue-during-wynnes-election-campaign-expert/.

Lott, A.J., & Lott, B.E. (1961). Group cohesiveness, communication level, and conformity. *Journal of Abnormal & Social Psychology, 62,* 408–412.

Loucks, A.B., & Nattiv, A. (2005). The female athlete triad. *Lancet, 366,* s49–s50.

Love, E., Bhattacharya, S., Smith, N., & Bhattacharya, S. (2010). Effect of interpregnancy interval on outcomes of pregnancy after miscarriage: Retrospective analysis of hospital episode statistics in Scotland. *British Medical Journal, 341,* c3967.

Lovejoy, F.H., & Estridge, D. (Eds.). (1987). *The new child health encyclopedia.* New York, NY: Delacorte Press.

Low, W.Y., Wong, Y.L., Zulkifli, S.W., & Tan, H. (2002). Malaysian cultural differences in knowledge, attitudes and practices related to erectile dysfunction. *International Journal of Impotence Research, 14*(6), 440–445.

Lu, W., Mueser, K., Rosenberg, S., & Jankowski, M. (2008). Correlates of adverse childhood experiences among adults with severe mood disorders. *Psychiatric Services, 59,* 1018–1026.

Lucie-Smith, E. (1991). *Sexuality in western art.* London: Thames & Hudson.

Ludermir, A., Lewis, G., Valongueiro, S., de Araujo, T., & Araya, R. (2010). Violence against women by their intimate partner during pregnancy and postnatal depression: A prospective cohort study. *Lancet, 376*(9744), 903–910.

Lue, T. (2000). Erectile dysfunction. *New England Journal of Medicine, 342*(24), 1802–1813.

Lundstrom, M., & Walsh, D. (2010, November 14). Secrecy shrouds UOP sexual attack suit. *The Sacramento Bee.* Retrieved May 1, 2011, from http://www.sacbee.com/2010/11/14/v-mobile/3183395/secrecy-shrouds-sexual-assault.html.

Lutfey, K.E., Link, C., Rosen, R., Wiegel, M., & McKinlay, J. (2008, January 11). Prevalence and correlates of sexual activity and function in women: Results from the Boston Area Community Health (BACH) survey. *Archives of Sexual Behavior.* Retrieved October 30, 2008, from http://www.springerlink.com/content/f47306253471w048/?p=efd510bd7d9a43c29bd1f1b7ca8b3 3b3&pi=0.

Lynch, D. (2007). Rehearsing for real: Children's identity development in virtual spaces. *Dissertation Abstracts International Section A: Humanities and Social Sciences, 68*(3-A), 780.

Lyndon, A., Bonds-Raacke, J., & Cratty, A.D. (2011). College students/ Facebook stalking of ex-partners. *Cyberpsychology, Behavior, and Social Networking, 14*(12), 711–16.

Maas, C.P., ter Kuile, M.M., Laan, E., Tuynman, C.C., Weyenborg, P., Trimbos, J.B., & Kenter, G.G. (2004). Objective assessment of sexual arousal in women with a history of hysterectomy. *British Journal of Obstetrics and Gynaecology, 111,* 456–462.

Maas, J. (1998). *Power sleep.* New York, NY: HarperCollins.

Maccio, E.M. (2010). Influence of family, religion, and social conformity on client participation in sexual reorientation therapy. *Journal of Homosexuality, 57*(3), 441–458.

Maccoby, E.E. (2002). Gender and group process: A developmental perspective. *Current Directions in Psychological Science, 11*(2), 54–58.

Maccoby, E.E., & Jacklin, C.N. (1987). Gender segregation in childhood. In H.W. Reese (Ed.), *Advances in child development and behavior,* (Vol. 20, pp. 239–287). San Diego, CA: Academic Press.

Macdorman, M.F., Declercq, E., & Menacker, F. (2011). Trends and characteristics of home births in the United States by race and ethnicity, 1990–2006. *Birth, 38*(1), 17–23.

MacDorman, M.F., Mathews, T.J., Martin, J.A., & Malloy, M.H. (2002). Trends and characteristics of induced labour in the U.S., 1989–1998. *Paediatric & Perinatal Epidemiology, 16*(3), 263–274.

MacDougall, H. (1994). Sexually transmitted diseases in Canada, 1800–1992. *Genitourinary Medicine, 70*(1), 56–63.

Macdowall, W., Wellings, K., Stephenson, J., & Glasier, A. (2008). Summer nights: A review of the evidence of seasonal variations in sexual health indicators among young people. *Health Education, 108,* 40.

MacGaffey, W. (1994). African objects and the idea of fetish. *RES: Anthropology and Aesthetics, 25*(Spring), 123–131.

MacInnis, C.C., & Hodson, G. (2013). Is homophobia associated with an implicit same-sex attraction? *Journal of Sex Research, 50*(8), 777–785.

MacIntosh, H., Reissing, E.D., & Andruff, H. (2010). Same-sex marriage in Canada: The impact of legal marriage on the first cohort of gay and lesbian Canadians to wed. *Canadian Journal of Human Sexuality, 19*(3), 79–90.

Mackay, J. (2000). *The Penguin atlas of human sexual behavior.* New York, NY: Penguin.

Mackenzie, C. (2011, April 7). Personal communication.

MacKinnon, C.A. (1985, March 26). Pornography: Reality, not fantasy. *The Village Voice.*

MacKinnon, C.A. (1986). Pornography: Not a moral issue. (Special Issue: Women and the law.) *Women's Studies International Forum, 9,* 63–78.

MacKinnon, C.A. (1987). *Feminism unmodified: Discourses on life and law.* Cambridge, MA: Harvard University Press.

Macklon, N., & Fauser, B. (2000). Aspects of ovarian follicle development throughout life. *Hormone Research, 52,* 161–170.

Maclean's. (2012). Retrieved from http://www.macleans.ca/news/facebook-releases-stats-about-canadian-usage-14-million-daily-users/.

MacLeod, A.A.N., Laukys, K., & Rvachew, S. (2011). The impact of bilingual language learning on whole-word complexity and segmental accuracy among children aged 18 and 26 months. *International Journal of Speech-Language Pathology, 13*(6), 490–499.

Macneil, S. (2004). It takes two: Modeling the role of sexual self-disclosure in sexual satisfaction. *Dissertation Abstracts International: Section B: The Sciences & Engineering, 65*(1–B), 481. (#0419–4217).

Madan, R.A., & Gulley, J.L. (2010). The current and emerging role of immunotherapy in prostate cancer. *Clinical Genitourinary Cancer, 8*(1), 10–16.

Madan, R.A., & Gulley, J.L. (2011). Therapeutic cancer vaccine fulfills the promise of immunotherapy in prostate cancer. *Immunotherapy, 3*(1), 27–31.

Madanikia, Y., Batholomew, K., & Cytrynbaum, J.B. (2013). Depiction of masturbation in North American movies. *Canadian Journal of Human Sexuality, 22*(2),106–115.

Maestripieri, D. (2012). Games primates play: The evolution and economics of human relationships. *Psychology Today.* http://www.psychologytoday.com/blog/games-primates-play/201203/the-evolutionary-history-love.

Maffini, M.V., Rubin, B.S., Sonnenschein, C., & Soto, A.M. (2006). Endocrine disruptors and reproductive health: The case of bisphenol-A. *Molecular and Cellular Endocrinology, 254–255,* 179–186.

Mah, K., & Binik, Y. (2005). Are orgasms in the mind or the body? Psychosocial versus physiological correlates of orgasmic pleasure and satisfaction. *Journal of Sex & Marital Therapy, 31*(3), 187–200.

Mahabir, S., Spitz, M.R., Barrera, S.L., Dong, Y.Q., Eastham, C., & Forman, M.R. (2008). Dietary boron and hormone replacement therapy as risk factors for lung cancer in women. *American Journal of Epidemiology* (Epub). Retrieved March 18, 2008, from http://www.ncbi.nlm.nih.gov/sites/entrez.

MaHood, J., & Wenburg, A.R. (1980). *The Mosher survey.* New York, NY: Arno.

Maines, R. (1999). *Hysteria, the vibrator, and women's sexual satisfaction.* Baltimore: The Johns Hopkins University Press.

Maisto, S.A., Carey, M.P., Carey, K.B., Gordon, C.M., Schum, J., & Lynch, K. (2004). The relationship between alcohol and individual differences variables on attitudes and behavioral skills relevant to sexual health among heterosexual young adult men. *Archives of Sexual Behavior, 33*(6), 571–584.

Makarainen, L., van Beek, A., Tuomivaara, L., Asplund, B., & Coelingh-Bennink, B. (1998). Ovarian function during the use of a single contraceptive implant: Impla-non compared with Norplant. *Fertility and Sterility, 69,* 714–721.

Makrantonaki, E., Schônknecht, P., Hossini, A.M., Kaiser, E., Katsouli, M.M., Adjaye, J., Schrôder, J., & Zouboulis, C.C. (2010). Skin and brain age together: The role of hormones in the ageing process. *Experimental Gerontology, 45*(10), 801–813.

Malmo, C., & Laidlaw, T. (2010). Symptoms of trauma and traumatic memory retrieval in adult survivors of childhood sexual abuse. *Journal of Trauma and Dissociation, 11*(1), 22–43.

Malone, F.D., Canick, J.A., Ball, R.H., Nyberg, D.A., Comstock, C.H., Bukowski, R., Berkowitz, R.L., Gross, S.J., Wolfe, H.M., et al. (2005). First-trimester or second-trimester screening, or both, for Down's syndrome. *The New England Journal of Medicine, 353*(19), 2001–2011.

Malone, P., & Steinbrecher, H. (2007). Medical aspects of male circumcision. *British Medical Journal, 335*(7631), 1206–1290.

Maltz, D.W., & Borker, R.A. (1982). A cultural approach to male-female communication. In J.J. Gumperz (Ed.), *Language and social identity* (pp. 196–216). New York. Cambridge University Press.

Maltz, W. (1990, December). Adult survivors of incest: How to help them overcome the trauma. *Medical Aspects of Human Sexuality,* 38–43.

Maltz, W. (2002). Treating the sexual intimacy concerns of sexual abuse survivors. *Sexual and Relationship Therapy, 17*(4), 321–327.

Maltz, W., & Boss, S. (2001). *Private thoughts: Exploring the power of women's sexual fantasies.* Novato, CA: New World Library.

Mandelbaum, J. (2010). What motivates female suicide bombers? Open Salon. Retrieved April 10, 2010, from http://open.salon.com/blog/judy_mandelbaum/2010/04/05/what_motivates_female_suicide_bombers.

Maness, D.L., Reddy, A., Harraway-Smith, C.L., Mitchell, G., & Givens, V. (2010). How best to manage dysfunctional uterine bleeding. *Journal of Family Practice, 59*(8), 449–458.

Manganiello, A., Hoga, L., Reberte, L., Miranda, C., & Rocha, C. (2011). Sexuality and quality of life of breast cancer patients post mastectomy. *European Journal of Oncology Nursing, 15*(2), 167–172.

Manniche, L. (1987). *Sexual life in ancient Egypt.* London: KPI Ltd.

Manson, J.E. (2004, December). Your doctor is in. *Glamour,* p. 104.

Mansour, D. (2010). Nexplanon: What Implanon did next. *Journal of Family Planning and Reproductive Health Care, 36*(4), 187–189.

Mantica, A. (2005). Better test for a stealthy cancer. *Prevention, 57*(3), 48–51.

Maranghi, F., Mantovani, A., Macri, C., Romeo, A., Eleuteri, P., Leter, G., Rescia, M., Spanó, M., & Saso, L. (2005). Long-term effects of lonidamine on mouse testes. *Contraception, 72*(4), 268–272.

Marcellus, L. (2008). (Ad)ministering love: Providing family foster care to infants with prenatal substance exposure. *Qualitative Health Research, 18*(9), 1220–1230.

Marchbanks, P.A., McDonald, J.A., Wilson, H.G., Folger S.G., Mandel M.G., Daling J.R., et al. (2002). Oral contraceptives and the risk of breast cancer. *New England Journal of Medicine, 346,* 2025–2032.

Margolis, J. (2004). *O: The intimate history of the orgasm.* New York, NY: Grove/Atlantic Press.

Margulis, L., & Sagan, D. (1991). *Mystery dance: On the evolution of human sexuality.* New York, NY: Summit Books.

Marinakis, G., & Nikolaou, D. (2011). What is the role of assisted reproduction technology in the management of age-related infertility? *Human Fertility, 14,* 8–15.

Marino, T. (2010). Embryology and disorders of sexual development. *Perspectives of Biological Medicine, 53*(4), 482–490.

Maritz, G.S. (2008). Nicotine and lung development. *Birth Defects Research, Part C.84,* 45–53.

Mark, K., Wald, A., Mageret, A., Selke, S., Olin, L, Huang, M., & Corey, L. (2008). Rapidly cleared episodes of herpes simplex virus reactivation in immunocompetent adults. *Journal of Infectious Disease.* Epub ahead of print. Retrieved September 19, 2008, from http://www.ncbi.nlm.nih.gov/sites/entrez.

Marrazzo, J. (2004). Barriers to infectious disease care among lesbians. *Emerging Infectious Disease, 10,* 1974–1978.

Marrazzo, J., Cook, R., Wiesenfeld, H., Murray, P., Busse, B., Krohn, M., & Hillier, S. (2007). *Lactobacillus* capsule for the treatment of bacterial vaginosis. *Journal of Women's Health, 15,* 1053–1060.

Marrazzo, J., Thomas, K., Fiedler, T., Ring-wood, K., & Fredricks, D. (2008). Relationship of specific vaginal bacteria and bacterial vaginosis treatment failure in women who have sex with women. *Annals of Internal Medicine, 149,* 20–28.

Marrazzo, M., Thomas, K., Fiedler, T., Ring-wood, K., & Fredricks, D. (2010). Risks for acquisition of bacterial vaginosis among women who report sex with women: A cohort study. *PLoS One, 5*(6), e11139.

Marshal, M.P., Friedman, M.S., Stall, R., & Thompson, A.L. (2009). Individual trajectories of substance use in lesbian, gay and bisexual youth and heterosexual youth. *Addiction, 104*(6), 974–981.

Marshall, D.S. (1971). Sexual behavior on Mangaia. In D.S. Marshall & R.C. Suggs (Eds.), *Human sexual behavior.* New York, NY: Basic Books.

Marshall, W.L. (1979). Satiation therapy: A procedure for reducing deviant sexual arousal. *Journal of Applied Behavior Analysis, 12*(3), 377–389.

Martens, W. (2007). Optimism therapy: An adapted psychotherapeutic strategy for adult female survivors of childhood sexual abuse. *Annals of the American Psychotherapy Association, 10,* 30–38.

Martin, D., Martin, M., & Carvalho, K. (2008). Reading and learning-disabled children: Understanding the problem. *The Clearing House, 81,* 113–118.

Martin, H.P. (1991). The coming-out process for homosexuals. *Hospital and Community Psychiatry, 42,* 158–162.

Martin, J.A., Hamilton, B.E., Sutton, P., Ventura, S., Menacker, F., Kirmeyer, S., & Munson, M. (2007, December 5). Births: Final data for 2005. *National Vital Statistics Report, 56*(6). Retrieved May 31, 2008, from http://www .cdc.gov/nchs/data/nvsr/nvsr56/nvsr56_06 .pdf.

Martin, J.T., Puts, D.A., & Breedlove, S.M. (2008). Hand asymmetry in heterosexual and homosexual men and women: Relationship to 2D:4D digit ratios and other sexually dimorphic anatomical traits. *Archives of Sexual Behavior, 37*(1), 119–132.

Martin, K., & Luke, K. (2010). Gender differences in the ABC's of the birds and bees: What mothers teach young children about sexuality and reproduction, *Sex Roles, 62*(3–4), 278–291.

Martin, R.P., Dombrowski, S.C., Mullis, C., Wisenbaker, J., & Huttunen, M.O. (2005, July 7). Smoking during pregnancy: Association with childhood temperament, behavior, and academic performance. *Journal of Pediatric Psychology,* Epub ahead of print. Retrieved July 17, 2005, from http://www .ncbi.nlm.nih.gov/entrez/query.fcgi?cmd =Retrieve&db=pubmed&dopt=Abstrac t&list_uids=16002482&query_hl=23.

Martin, T.A. (2003). Power and consent: Relation to self-reported sexual assault and acquaintance rape. *Dissertation Abstracts International: Section B: The Sciences & Engineering, 64*(3–B), #0419–4217.

Martin's Annual Criminal Code. (2006). Aurora, ON: Canada Law Book Inc.

Martinez, G.M., Chandra, A., Abma, J.C., Jones, J., & Mosher, W.D. (2006). Fertility, contraception, and fatherhood: Data on men and women from cycle 6 (2002) of the National Survey of Family Growth. *Vital Health Statistics, 23*(26). Hyattsville, MD: National Center for Health Statistics, Centers for Disease Control.

Martínez-Burgos, M., Herrero, L., Megías, D., Salvanes, R., Montoya, M.C., Cobo, A.C., & Garcia-Velasco, J.A. (2011). Vitrification versus slow freezing of oocytes: Effects on morphologic appearance, meiotic spindle configuration, and DNA damage. *Fertility and Sterility, 95*(1), 374–377.

Martinson, F.M. (1981). Eroticism in infancy and childhood. In L.L. Constantine & F.M. Martinson (Eds.), *Children and sex: New findings, new perspectives* (pp. 23–35). Boston, MA: Little, Brown.

Maruo, T., Ohara, N., Yoshida, S., Nakabayashi, K., Sasaki, H., Xu, Q., Chen, W., & Yamada, H. (2010). Translational research with progesterone receptor modulator motivated by the use of levonorgestrel-releasing intrauterine system. *Contraception, 82*(5), 435–441.

Masho, S., & Anderson, L. (2009). Sexual assault in men: A population-based study of Virginia. *Violence and Victims, 24*(1), 98–110.

Mason, M.A., Fine, M.A., & Carcochan, S. (2001). Family law in the new millennium: For whose families? *Journal of Family Issues, 22*(7), 859–882.

Masoomi, M., Zare, J., Kahnooj, M., Mirzazadeh, A., & Sheikhvatan, M. (2010). Sex differences in potential daily triggers of the onset of acute myocardial infarction: A case-crossover analysis among an Iranian population. *Journal of Cardiovascular Medicine, 11*(10), 723–726.

Massa, G., Verlinde, F., DeSchepper, J., Thomas, M., Bourguignon, J.P, Craen, M., de Segher, F., Francois, I., Du Caju, M., Maes, M., & Heinrichs, C. (2005). Trends in age at diagnosis of Turner syndrome. *Archives of Disease in Childhood, 90*(3), 267–275.

Massart, F., & Saggese, G. (2010). Morphogenetic targets and genetics of undescended testis. *Sexual Development, 4*(6), 326–335.

Masser, B., Viki, T., & Power, C. (2006). Hostile sexism and rape proclivity amongst men. *Sex Roles, 54,* 565–574.

Masters, W.H., & Johnson, V.E. (1966). *Human sexual response.* Boston, MA: Little, Brown.

Masters, W.H., & Johnson, V.E. (1970). *Human sexual inadequacy.* Boston, MA: Little, Brown.

Masters, W.H., & Johnson, V.E. (1979). *Homosexuality in perspective.* Boston, MA: Little, Brown.

Masters, W.H., Johnson, V.E., & Kolodny, R.C. (1982). *Human sexuality.* Boston, MA: Little, Brown.

Masterton, G. (1987). *How to drive your woman wild in bed.* New York, NY: Penguin Books.

Matek, O. (1988). Obscene phone callers. (Special issue: The sexually unusual: Guide to understanding and helping.) *Journal of Social Work and Human Sexuality, 7,* 113–130.

Mather, M., & Lavery, D. (2010). In U.S., proportion married at lowest recorded levels. Population Reference Bureau. Retrieved May 11, 2011, from http://www.prb.org/Articles/2010/ usmarriagedecline.aspx.

Mathers, M., Degener, S., & Roth, S. (2011). Cryptorchidism and infertility from the perspective of interdisciplinary guidelines. *Urologe A, 50*(1), 20–25.

Mathes, E.W. (2005). Relationship between short-term sexual strategies and sexual jealousy. *Psychological Reports, 96*(1), 29–35.

Maticka-Tyndale, E., Herold, E.S., & Mewhinney, D. (1998). Casual sex on spring break: Intentions and behaviors of Canadian students. *Journal of Sex Research, 35*(3), 254–264.

Maticka-Tyndale, E., Lewis, J., & Street, M. (2005). Making a place for escort work: A case study. *The Journal of Sex Research, 42*(1), 46–53.

Maticka-Tyndale, E., Shirpak, K.R., & Chinichian, M. (2007). Providing for the sexual health needs of canadian immigrants: The experience of immigrants from Iran. *Canadian Journal of Public Health, 98*(3), 183–186.

Matsumoto, D. (1996). *Culture and psychology.* Pacific Grove, CA: Brooks/Cole.

Matthews, A., Dowswell, T., Haas, D.M., Doyle, M., & O'Mathúna, D.P. (2010). Interventions for nausea and vomiting in early pregnancy. *Cochrane Database Systems Review, 8*(9), CD007575.

Maunder, R., & Hunter, J. (2008). Attachment relationships as determinants of physical health. *Journal of the American Academy of Psychoanalysis and Dynamic Psychiatry, 36*(1), 11–33.

Maurer, T., & Robinson, D. (2008). Effects of attire, alcohol, and gender on perceptions of date rape. *Sex Roles, 58,* 423–435.

Mayer, J. (2011). Gay rights in Costa Rica: Pura vida. *The Costa Rica News.* Retrieved February 20, 2011, from http://thecostaricanews.com/ gay-rights-in-costa-rica/5650.

Maynard, E., Carballo-Dieguez, A., Ventuneac, A., Exner, T., & Mayer, K. (2009). Women's experiences with anal sex: Motivations and implications for STD prevention. *Perspectives on Sexual and Reproductive Health, 41*(3), 142–149.

Mays, V.M., Yancy, A.K., Cochran, S.D., Weber, M., & Fielding, J.E. (2002). Heterogeneity of health disparities among African-American, Hispanic and Asian American women. *American Journal of Public Health, 92*(4), 632–640.

Mbügua, K. (2006). Reasons to suggest that the endocrine research on sexual preference is a degenerating research program. *History & Philosophy of the Life Sciences, 28,* 337–358.

McAdams, M. (1996). Gender without bodies. Retrieved September 3, 2005, from http:// www.december.com/cmc/mag/1996/mar/ mcadams.html.

Mcalinden, A.-M. (2006). 'Setting 'Em Up': Personal, familial and institutional grooming in the sexual abuse of children. *Social Legal Studies, 15*(3), 339–362.

McCabe, M., & Wauchope, M. (2005). Behavioral characteristics of men accused of rape:

Evidence for different types of rapists. *Archives of Sexual Behavior, 34,* 241–253.

McCabe, M.P. (2002). Relationship functioning among people with MS. *Journal of Sex Research, 39*(4), 302–309.

McCabe, S., Bostwick, W., Hughes, T., West, B., & Boyd, C. (2010). The relationships between discrimination and substance use disorders among lesbian, gay, and bisexual adults in the U.S. *American Journal of Public Health, 100*(10), 1946–1952.

McCall-Hosenfeld, J.S., Freund, K.M., Legault, C., Jaramillo, S.A., Cochrane, B.B., Manson, J.E., Wenger, N.K., Eaton, C.B., Mc-Neeley, S.G., Rodriguez, B.L., & Bonds, D. (2008). Sexual satisfaction and cardiovascular disease: The Women's Health Initiative. *American Journal of Medicine, 121*(4), 295–301.

McCarthy, B., & Casey, T. (2008). Love, sex, and crime: Adolescent romantic relationships and offending. *American Sociological Review, 73*(6), 944–969.

McCarthy, B.W., & Fucito, L.M. (2005). Integrating medication, realistic expectations, and therapeutic interventions in the treatment of male sexual dysfunction. *Journal of Sex and Marital Therapy, 31*(4), 319–328.

McCarthy, B.W., & Ginsberg, R.L. (2007). Second marriages: Challenges and risks. *Family Journal, 15,* 119.

McClintock, M.K. (1971). Menstrual synchorony and suppression. *Nature, 229*(5282), 244–245.

McConaghy, N., Hadzi-Pavlovic, D., Stevens, C., Manicavasagar, V., Buhrich, N., & Vollmer-Conna, U. (2006). Fraternal birth order and ratio of heterosexual/homosexual feelings in women and men. *Journal of Homosexuality, 51*(4), 161–174.

McCormack, M. (2014). Innovative sampling and participant recruitment in sexuality research. *Journal of Social & Personal Relationships, 31*(4), 475–481.

McCoubrey, C. (2002, May 24). Alan P. Bell, 70, researcher of influences on homosexuality. *New York Times.* Retrieved October 12, 2010, from http://www.nytimes.com/2002/05/24/us/alan-p-bell-70-researcher-of-influences-on-homosexuality.html.

McCracken, P. (2006, August 20). Bullying women into suicide to restore honor. *San Francisco Chronicle.* Retrieved October 5, 2010, from http://www.sfgate.com/cgibin/article.cgi?file5/chronicle/archive/2006/08/20/INGD9KJ5U61.DTL.

McCreary, D.R. (1994). The male role and avoiding femininity. *Sex Roles, 31*(9–10), 517–531.

McDougall, D. (2010, May 30). Cries from the beloved country. *The Sunday Times.*

Retrieved April 30, 2011, from http://www.timesonline.co.uk/tol/news/world/africa/article7133312.ece.

McDowall, A., & Khan, S. (2004, November 25). The Ayatollan and the transsexual. *The Independent.* Retrieved December 20, 2010, from http://www.independent.co.uk/news/world/middle-east/the-ayatollah-and-the-transsexual-534482.html.

McFadden, D. (2011). Sexual orientation and the auditory system. *Front Neuroendocrinology.* Retrieved February 20, 2011, from http://www.ncbi.nlm.nih.gov/pubmed/21310172.

McFadden, D., Loehlin, J.C., Breedlove, S., Lippa, R.A., Manning, J.T., & Rahman, Q. (2005). A reanalysis of five studies on sexual orientation and the relative length of the 2nd and 4th fingers (the 2D:4D). *Archives of Sexual Behavior, 34,* 341–356.

McGlynn, K.A., & Trabert, B. (2012). Adolescent and adult risk factors for testicular cancer. *Nature Reviews Urology, 9*(6), 339–349.

McGlynn, K.A., Sakoda, L.C., Rubertone, M.V., Sesterhenn, I.A., Lyu, C., Graubard, B.I., & Erickson, R.L. (2007). Body size, dairy consumption, puberty, and risk of testicular germ cell tumors. *American Journal of Epidemiology, 165*(4), 355–363.

McGregor, M.J., Ericksen, J., Ronald, L.A., Janssen, P.A., Van Vliet, A., & Schultzer, M. (2004). Rising incidence of hospital reported drug-facilitated sexual assault in a large urban community in Canada. *Canadian Journal of Public Health, 95*(6), 441–445.

McKay, A. (1999). Sexual partnering and risk of HIV/STD among aboriginals. *Canadian Journal of Human Sexuality, 8*(2), 143–144.

McKay, A. (2012). Trends in Canadian national and provincial/territorial teen pregnancy rates. *The Canadian Journal of Human Sexuality, 21*(2–4), 161–175.

McKeganey, N., & Bernard, M. (1996). *Sex work on the streets: Prostitutes and their clients.* Philadelphia: Open University Press.

McLaren, A. (1990). *A history of contraception.* Cambridge, MA: Basil Blackwell.

McLean, L.M., & Gallop, R. (2003). Implications of childhood sexual abuse for adult borderline personality disorder and complex post traumatic stress disorder. *American Journal of Psychiatry, 160*(2), 369–371.

McMahon, C.G. (2014). Management of ejaculatory dysfunction. *Internal Medicine Journal, 44*(2), 124–131.

McMahon, S. (2004). Student-athletes, rape-supportive culture, and social change. Retrieved October 16, 2005, from http://sexualassault.rutgers.edu/pdfs/student-athletes_rape-supportive_culture_and_social_change.pdf.

McManus, A.J., Hunter, L., & Renan, H. (2006). Lesbian experiences and needs during child-

birth: Guidance for health care providers. *Journal of Obstetrics and Gynecology in Neonatal Nursing, 35,* 13–23.

McNall, M., & Gary Remafedi, G. (1999). Relationship of amphetamine and other substance use to unprotected intercourse among young men who have sex with men. *Archives of Pediatric and Adolescent Medicine, 153*(11), 1130–1135.

McNally, R.J., Clancy, S.A., Barrett, H.M., & Parker, H.A. (2004). Inhibiting retrieval of trauma cues in adults reporting histories of childhood sexual abuse. *Cognition and Emotion, 18*(4), 479–493.

McNally, R.J., Clancy, S.A., Barrett, H.M., & Parker, H.A. (2005). Reality monitoring in adults reporting repressed, recovered, or continuous memories of childhood sexual abuse. *Journal of Abnormal Psychology, 114*(1), 147–152.

Mead, M. (1935/1988/2001). *Sex and temperament in three primitive societies.* New York, NY: William Morrow.

Mehl, M.R., Vazire, S., Ramirez-Esparza, N., Slatcher, R.B., & Pennebaker, J.W. (2007). Are women really more talkative than men? *Science, 317,* 82.

Mehrabian, A. (2009). *Nonverbal communication.* Piscataway, NJ: Transaction Publishers.

Mehta, C., & Strough, J. (2010). Gender segregation and gender-typing in adolescence. *Sex Roles, 64*(3–4), 251–263.

Meier, E. (2002). Child rape in South Africa. *Pediatric Nursing, 28*(5), 532–535.

Meirik, O., Fraser, I., & d'Arcangues, C. (2003). Implantable contraceptives for women. *Human Reproduction Update, 9*(1), 49–59.

Melisko, M.E., Goldman, M., & Rugo, H.S. (2010). Amelioration of sexual adverse effects in the early breast cancer patient. *Journal of Cancer Survivorship, 4*(3), 247–255.

Melody, M.E., & Peterson, L.M. (1999). Teaching america about sex: Marriage guides and sex manuals from the late Victorians to Dr. Ruth. New York, NY: New York University Press.

Meltzer, D. (2005). Complications of body piercing. *American Family Physician, 72*(10), 2029–2034.

Ménard, K.S., Nagayama Hall, G., Phung, A., Erian Ghebrial, M., & Martin, L. (2003). Gender differences in sexual harassment and coercion in college students. *Journal of Interpersonal Violence, 18*(10), 1222–1239.

Menke, L., Sas, T., Keizer-Schrama, S., Zandwijken, G., Ridder, M., Odink, R., Jansen, M., et al. (2010). Efficacy and safety of oxandrolone in growth hormone-treated girls with Turner syndrome. *Journal of Clinical Endocrinology & Metabolism, 95*(3), 1151–1160.

Mennonites also face gay issue. (2000). *Christian Century, 117*(13), 452–453.

Menon, R. (2008). Spontaneous preterm birth, a clinical dilemma: Etiologic, pathophysiologic and genetic heterogeneities and racial disparity. *Acta Obstetrica Gynecologic Scandinavica, 87*, 590–600.

Menzler, K., Belke, M., Wehrmann, E., Kradow, K., Lengler, U., Jansen, A., Hamer, H., Oertel, W., Rosenow, F., & Knake, S. (2011). Men and women are different: Diffusion tensor imaging reveals sexual dimorphism in the microstructure of the thalamus, corpus callosum and cingulum. *Neuroimage, 54*, 2557–2562.

Merki-Feld, G.S., & Hund, M. (2007). Clinical experience with NuvaRing in daily practice in Switzerland: Cycle control and acceptability among women of all reproductive ages. *European Journal of Contraceptive and Reproductive Health Care, 12*, 240–247.

Merki-Feld, G.S., Seeger, H., & Mueck, A.O. (2008). Comparison of the proliferative effects of ethinylestradiol on human breast cancer cells in an intermittent and a continuous dosing regime. *Hormone and Metabolic Research.* Retrieved March 18, 2008, from http://www.thieme-connect.com/ejournals/abstract/hmr/doi/10.1055/s-2007–1004540.

Mertz, G. (2008). Asymptomatic shedding of herpes simplex virus 1 and 2: Implications for prevention of transmission. *Journal of Infectious Diseases, 198*(8), 1098–1100.

Meschke, L.L., Bartholomae, S., & Zentall, S.R. (2000). Adolescent sexuality and parent-adolescent processes: Promoting healthy teen choices. *Family Relations, 49*(2), 143–155.

Messenger, J.C. (1993). Sex and repression in an Irish folk community. In D.N. Suggs & A.W. Miracle (Eds.), *Culture and human diversity.* Pacific Grove, CA: Brooks/Cole.

Messina, M. (2010). Soybean isoflavone exposure does not have feminizing effects on men: A critical examination of the clinical evidence. *Fertility and Sterility, 93*(7), 2095–2104.

Meston, C.M., Hull, E., Levin, R., & Sipski, M. (2004). Disorders of orgasm in women. *Journal of Sexual Medicine, 1*, 66–68.

Meston, C.M., Trapnell, P.D., & Gorzalka, B.B. (1996). Ethnic and gender differences in sexuality: Variations in sexual behavior between Asian and non-Asian university students. *Archives of Sex Behavior, 25*(1), 33–71.

Metropolitan Community Churches. (2005). About us. Retrieved November 7, 2005, from http://www.mcchurch.org/AM/TextTemplate.cfm?Section=About_Us&Template=/CM/HTMLDisplay. cfm&ContentID=877.

Meyer-Bahlburg, H., Ehrhardt, A., Feldman, J., Rosen, L., Veridiano, N., & Zimmerman, I. (1985). Sexual activity level and sexual functioning in women prenatally exposed to diethylstilbestrol. *Psychosomatic Medicine, 47*(6), 497–511.

Meyer-Bahlburg, H.F., Dolezal, C., Baker, S.W., & New, M.I. (2008). Sexual orientation in women with classical or non-classical CAH as a function of degree of prenatal androgen excess. *Archives of Sexual Behavior, 37*, 85–99.

Meyers-Wallen, V.N. (2012). Gonadal and sex differentiation abnormalities of dogs and cats. *Sexual Development, 6*(1–3), 46–60.

Meyers-Wallen, V.N., Wilson, J.D., Griffin, J.E., Fisher, S., Moorhead, P.H., Goldschmidt, M.H., Haskins, M.E., & Patterson, D.F. (1989). Testicular feminization in a cat. *Journal of the American Verterinary Medical Association, 195*(5), 631–634.

Mi, T., Abbasi, S., Zhang, H., Uray, K., Chunn, J., Wei, L., Molina, J., Weisbrodt, N., Kellems, R., Blackburn, M., & Xia, Y. (2008). Excess adenosine in murine penile erectile tissues contributes to priapism via A2B adenosine receptor signaling. *Journal of Clinical Investigation, 118*(4), 1491–1501.

Michael, R.T., Gagnon, J.H., Laumann, E.O., & Kolata, G. (1994). *Sex in America.* Boston, MA: Little, Brown.

Mihalik, G. (1988). Sexuality and gender: An evolutionary perspective. *Psychiatric Annals, 18*, 40–42.

Mikulincer, M., & Shaver, P. (2005). Attachment theory and emotions in close relationships: Exploring the attachment-related dynamics of emotional reactions to relational events. *Personal Relationships, 12*(2), 149–168.

Milan, A. (2013). Marital Status: Overview, 2011. Statistics Canada, Catalogue no. 91-209-X.

Milan, A., & Hamm, B. (2004). Mixed Unions. Canadian Social Trends, Statistics Canada, Catalogue # 11-008.

Milhausen, R.R., McKay, A., Graham, C.A., Crosby, R.A., Yarber, W.L., & Sanders, S.A. (2013). Prevalence and predictors of condom use in a national sample of Canadian university students. *Canadian Journal of Human Sexuality, 22*(3), 142–151.

Miller, E., Decker, M.R., Reed, E., Raj, A., Hathaway, J.E., & Silverman, J.G. (2007). Male partner pregnancy-promoting behaviors and adolescent partner violence: Findings from a qualitative study with adolescent females. *Ambulatory Pediatrics, 7*(5), 360–366.

Miller, S.A., & Byers, E.S. (2004). Actual and desired duration of foreplay and intercourse: Discordance and misperceptions within heterosexual couples. *Journal of Sex Research, 41*(3), 301–309.

Milner, J., & Robertson, K. (1990). Comparison of physical child abusers, intrafamilial sexual child abusers, and child neglecters. *Journal of Interpersonal Violence, 5*, 37–48.

Milner, J., Dopke, C., & Crouch, J. (2008). Paraphilia not otherwise specified. In D. Laws & W. O'Donohue (Eds.), *Sexual deviance: Theory, assessment and treatment* (2nd ed., pp. 384–418). New York, NY: Guilford Press.

Mindel, A., & Sawleshwarkar, S. (2008). Condoms for sexually transmissible infection prevention: Politics versus science. *Sexual Health, 5*, 1–8.

Miner, M.H., Coleman, E., Center, B., Ross, M., & Simon Rosser, B. (2007). The compulsive sexual behavior inventory: Psychometric properties. *Archives of Sexual Behavior, 36*(4), 579–587.

Minervini, A., Ralph, D., & Pryor, J. (2006). Outcome of penile prosthesis implantation for treating erectile dysfunction: Experience with 504 procedures. *British Journal of Urology, 97*, 129–133.

Minna, S., & Aruundhati, C. (2014). Semen loss and sexual anxiety among young unmarried men: Being young and vulnerable in rural India. *Sexuality and Culture, 18*(1), 103–118.

Mishna, F., Newman, P., Daley, A., & Soloman, S. (2008, January 5). Bullying of lesbian and gay youth: A qualitative investigation. *British Journal of Social Work.* Retrieved October 2, 2008, from http://bjsw.oxford-journals.org/cgi/content/abstract/bcm148.

Misra, G. (2009). Decriminalising homosexuality in India. *Reproductive Health Matters, 17*(34), 20–28.

Misri, S., Kostaras, X., Fox, D., & Kostaras, D. (2000). The impact of partner support in the treatment of postpartum depression. *Canadian Journal of Psychiatry, 45*(6), 554–559.

Mitchell, J.E., & Popkin, M.K. (1982). Antipsychotic drug therapy and sexual dysfunction in men. *American Journal of Psychiatry, 139*(5), 633–637.

Mitchell, P.J. (2009). Rated PG: How parental influence impacts teen sexual activity. Ottawa, ON: Institute of Marriage and Family Canada.

Mittendorf, R., Williams, M.A., Berkey, C.S., & Cotter, P.F. (1990). The length of uncomplicated human gestation. *Obstetrics and Gynecology, 75*(6), 929–932.

Mocarelli, P., Gerthoux, P.M., Patterson, D., Milani, S., Limonta, G., Bertona, M., et al. (2008). Dioxin exposure, from infancy through puberty, produces endocrine disruption and affects human semen quality. *Environmental Health Perspectives, 116*, 70–77.

Mock, S.E., & Cornelius, S.W. (2007). Profiles of interdependence: The retirement planning of married, cohabiting, and lesbian couples. *Sex Roles, 56*(11–12), 793–800.

Modan, B., Hartge, P., Hirsh-Yechezkel, G., Chetrit A., Lubin F., Beller U., et al. (2001). Parity, oral contraceptives, and the risk of ovarian cancer among carriers and noncarriers of a BRCA1 or BRCA2 mutation. *New England Journal of Medicine, 345*, 235–240.

Moegelin, L., Nilsson, B., & Helström, L. (2010). Reproductive health in lesbian and bisexual women in Sweden. *Acta Obstet Gynecol Scand, 89*(2), 205–209.

Moen, V., & Irestedt, L. (2008). Neurological complications following central neuraxial blockades in obstetrics. *Current Opinions in Anesthesiology, 21,* 275–280.

Mofrad, S., Abdullah, R., & Uba, I. (2010). Attachment patterns and separation anxiety symptom. *Asian Social Science, 6*(11), 148–153.

Moller, L.C., Hymel, S., & Rubin, K.H. (1992). Sex typing in play and popularity in middle childhood. *Sex Roles, 26*(7–8), 331–353.

Moller, N.P., Fouladi, R.T., McCarthy, C.J., & Hatch, K.D. (2003). Relationship of attachment and social support to college students' adjustment following a relationship breakup. *Journal of Counseling & Development, 81,* 354–369.

Molnár, Z., Berta, E., Benyó, M., Póka, R., Kassai, Z., Flaskó, T., Jakab, A., & Bodor, M. (2014). Fertility of testicular cancer patients after anticancer treatment-experience of 11 years. *Pharmazie, 69*(6), 437–441.

Mommers, E., Kersemaekers, J., Kepers, M., Apter, D., Behre, H., Beynon, J., et al. (2008). Male hormonal contraception: A double-blind, placebo-controlled study. *Journal of Clinical Endocrinology and Metabolism, 93,* 2572–2580.

Monasch, R., & Boerma, J. (2004). Orphanhood and childcare patterns in sub-Saharan Africa: An analysis of national survey from 40 countries. *AIDS, 18, (suppl 2), S55–S65.*

Monat-Haller, R.K. (1992). *Understanding and experiencing sexuality.* Baltimore: Brookes.

Money, J. (1955). Hermaphroditism, gender, and precocity in hyper-adrenocorticism: Psychologic findings. *Bulletin of the Johns Hopkins Hospital, 96,* 253–254.

Money, J. (1975). Ablatio penis: Normal male infant sex-reassigned as a girl. *Archives of Sexual Behavior, 4*(1), 65–71.

Money, J. (1984). Paraphilias: Phenomenology and classification. *American Journal of Psychotherapy, 38,* 164–179.

Money, J. (1986). *Venuses penuses: Sexology, sexophy, and exigency theory.* Buffalo, NY: Prometheus Books.

Money, J. (1990). Pedophilia: A specific instance of new phylism theory as applied to paraphiliac lovemaps. In J. Feierman (Ed.), *Pedophilia: Biosocial dimensions* (pp. 445–463). New York, NY: Springer-Verlag.

Mongiat-Artus, P. (2004) Torsion of the spermatic cord and testicular annexes. *Annals of Urology, 38*(1), 25–34.

Monroe, L.M., Kinney, L., Weist, M., Dafeamekpor, D., Dantzler, J., & Reynolds, M. (2005). The experience of sexual assault: Findings from a statewide victim needs assessment.

Journal of Interpersonal Violence, 20(7), 767–776.

Monta, H. (2013). Who were the audiences of Shunga? *Japan Review, 26*(Special Issue), 17–36.

Montemurro, B., & McClure, B. (2005). Changing gender norms for alcohol consumption. *Sex Roles, 52,* 279–288.

Montirosso, R., Peverelli, M., Frigerio, E., Crespi, M., & Borgatti, R. (2010). The development of dynamic facial expression recognition at different intensities in 4- to 18-year-olds. *Social Development, 19*(1), 71.

Monto, M.A. (2000). Why men seek out prostitutes. In R. Weitzer (Ed.), *Sex for sale: Prostitution, pornography, and the sex industry* (pp. 67–83). New York, NY: Routledge.

Monto, M.A. (2001). Prostitution and fellatio. *Journal of Sex Research, 38*(2), 140–146.

Monto, M.A. (2004). Cultural Contradictions and the Customers of Prostitutes. Conference Papers—American Sociological Association. 2004 Annual Meeting, San Francisco, pp. 1–20.

Montorsi, F., &, Oettel, M. (2005). Testosterone and sleep-related erections: an overview. *Journal of Sexual Medicine, 2*(6), 771–784.

Montreal Gazette. (1983). Minister out after meeting prostitute. November 17, p. A-1.

Montsori, F. (2005). Prevalence of premature ejaculation: A global and regional perspective. *Journal of Sexual Medicine*, Supplement 2, 96–102.

Mookodi, G., Ntshebe, O., & Taylor, I. (2004). Botswana. In R.T. Francoeur & R.J. Noonan (Eds.), *The Continuum International encyclopedia of sexuality* (pp. 89–97). New York/London: Continuum International.

Moor, B., Crone, E., & der Molen, M. (2010). The heartbrake of social rejection: Heart rate deceleration in response to unexpected peer rejection. *Psychological Science, 21*(9), 1326–1333.

Moore, M. (1994, October 8). Changing India: Arranged marriages persist with 90s twist. *The Washington Post.*

Moore, M.E. (2010). Communication involving long-term dating partners' sexual conversations: The connection between religious faith and sexual intimacy. *Dissertation Abstract International,* 48/05. University of Arkansas, AAT #1484652.

Morales, A. (2004). Andropause (or symptomatic late-onset hypogonadism): Facts, fiction and controversies. *Aging Male, 7*(4), 297–304.

Morales, A.M., Casillas, M., & Turbi, C. (2011). Patients' preference in the treatment of erectile dysfunction: A critical review of the literature. *International Journal of Impotence Research, 23*(1), 1–8.

Morbidity and Mortality Weekly Report (MMWR). (1982). Current Trends Update

on Acquired Immune Deficiency Syndrome (AIDS)—United States. September 24, *31*(37), 507–508, 513–514.

Morbidity and Mortality Weekly Report (MMWR). (2008). Retrieved from http://www.cdc.gov/mmwr/PDF/wk/mm5701.pdf.

Morello, C.S., Levinson, M.S., Kraynyak, K.A., & Spector, D.H. (2011). Immunization with herpes simplex virus 2 (HSV-2) genes plus inactivated HSV-2 is highly protective against acute and recurrent HSV-2 disease. *Journal of Virology, 85*(7), 3461–3472.

Morency, J-D., & LaPlante, B. (2010). L'action publique et la première naissance au Canada. *Cahiers Quebecois de Demographie, 39*(2), 201–241.

Moreno, V., Bosch, F.X., Munoz, N., Meijer C.J., Shah K.V., Walboomers J.M., et al. (2002). Effect of oral contraceptives on risk of cervical cancer in women with human papillomavirus infection: The IARC multicentric case-control study. *Lancet, 359,* 1085–1092.

Moreno-Garcia, M., Fernandez-Martinez, F.J., & Miranda, E.B. (2005). Chromosomal anomalies in patients with short stature. *Pediatric International, 47*(5), 546–549.

Morgan, L. (1998). *Good time girls of the Alaska-Yukon Gold Rush.* Seattle, Wash: Epicenter Press.

Morgan, S.P., & Rindfuss, R. (1985). Marital disruption: Structural and temporal dimensions. *American Journal of Sociology, 90*(5), 1055–1077.

Morotti, M., Remorgida, V., Venturini, P.L., Ferrero, S. (2012). Endometriosis in menopause: A single institution experience. *Archives of Gynecology and Obstetrics, 286*(6), 1571–1575.

Morris, B.J. (2007). Why circumcision is a biomedical imperative for the 21st century. *Bioessays, 29,* 1147–1158.

Morris, R.J. (1990). Aikane: Accounts of Hawaiian same-sex relationships in the journals of Captain Cook's third voyage (1776–1780). *Journal of Homosexuality, 19,* 21–54.

Morrison-Beedy, D., Carey, M.P., Cote-Arsenault, D., Seibold-Simpson, S., & Robinson, K.A. (2008). Understanding sexual abstinence in urban adolescent girls. *Journal of Obstetric, Gynecologic, and Neonatal Nursing, 37,* 185.

Morrow, K.M., & Allsworth, J.E. (2000). Sexual risk in lesbians and bisexual women. *Journal of Gay and Lesbian Medical Association, 4*(4), 159–165.

Morse, E.V., Simon, P.M., Balson, P.M., & Osofsky, H.J. (1992). Street behavior patterns of customers of male street prostitutes. *Archives of Sexual Behavior, 21*(4), 347–357.

Mortenson, S.T. (2002). Sex, communication, values, and cultural values. *Communication Reports, 15*(1), 57–71.

Mosconi, A.M., Roila, F., Gatta, G., & Theodore, C. (2005). Cancer of the penis. *Critical Reviews in Oncology/Hematology, 53*(2), 165–178.

Mosher, W.D., & Jones, J. (2010). Use of contraception in the United States: 1982–2008. *Vital Health Statistics, 23*(29), 1–44.

Mosher, W.D., Martinez, G.M., Chandra, A., Abma, J.C., & Wilson, S.J. (2004). Use of contraception and use of family planning services in the United States: 1982–2002. *Advance Data from Vital and Health Statistics,* no. 350. Retrieved May 27, 2008, from http://www.cdc.gov/nchs/data/ad/ad350.pdf.

Moskowitz, C. (2008, May 16). Same sex couples common in the wild. *LiveScience.* Retrieved October 2, 2008, from http://www.livescience.com/animals/080516-gay-animals.html.

Mruk, D.D. (2008). New perspectives in non-hormonal male contraception. *Trends in Endocrinology and Metabolism, 19*(2), 57–64.

Mueck, A.O., & Seeger, H. (2008). The World Health Organization defines hormone replacement therapy as carcinogenic: Is this implausible? *Gynecological Endocrinology, 24,* 129–132.

Mueck, A.O., Seeger, H., & Rabe, T. (2010). Hormonal contraception and risk of endometrial cancer: A systematic review. *Endocrine Related Cancer, 17*(4), R263–R271.

Muehlenhard, C., & Shippee, S. (2010). Men's and women's reports of pretending orgasm. *Journal of Sex Research, 47*(6), 552–567.

Muehlenhard, C.L., & Cook, S.W. (1988). Men's self-reports of unwanted sexual activity. *Journal of Sex Research, 24,* 58–72.

Mufti, U., Ghani, K., Samman, R., Virdi, J., & Potluri, B. (2008). Anejaculation as an atypical presentation of prostate cancer: A case report. *Cases Journal, 1,* 81.

Mukherjee, B., & Shivakumar, T. (2007). A case of sensorineural deafness following ingestion of sildenafil. *Journal of Laryngology and Otology, 121,* 395–397.

Mukonyora, B. (2005). Churches! Whose side are you on? Retrieved from http://archive.kubatana.net/html/archive/opin/050622bm.asp?sector=HIVAID&range_start=1.

Mulders, T.M., & Dieben, T. (2001). Use of the novel combined contraceptive vaginal ring NuvaRing® for ovulation inhibition. *Fertility and Sterility, 75,* 865–870.

Mulick, P.S., & Wright, L.W. (2002). Examining the existence of biphobia in the heterosexual and homosexual populations. *Journal of Bisexuality, 2,* 45–65.

Muller, J.E., Mittleman, M.A., Maclure, M., Sherwood, J.B., & Toffer, G.H. (1996). Triggering myocardial infarction by sexual activity. *Journal of the American Medical Association, 275*(18), 1405–1409.

Mulligan, E., & Heath, M. (2007). Seeking open minded doctors. How women who identify as bisexual, queer or lesbian seek quality health care. *Australian Family Physician, 36,* 385–480.

Mulvaney, B.M. (1994). Gender differences in communication: An intercultural experience. Paper prepared by the Department of Communication, Florida Atlantic University.

Munk-Olsen, T., Laursen, T.M., Pedersen, C.B., Lidegaard, 0., & Mortensen, P.B. (2011). Induced first-trimester abortion and risk of mental disorder. *New England Journal of Medicine, 364*(4), 332–339.

Muratori, M., Marchiani, S., Tamburrino, L., Forti, G., Luconi, M., & Baldi, E. (2011). Markers of human sperm functions in the ICSI era. *Frontiers in Bioscience, 1*(16), 1344–1363.

Murdock, G.P. (1967). Ethnographic atlas: A summary. *Ethnology, 6,* 109–236.

Murina F., Bernorio R., & Palmiotto, R. (2008). The use of amielle vaginal trainers as adjuvant in the treatment of vestibulodynia: An observational multicentric study. *Medscape Journal of Medicine, 10*(1), 23.

Murina, F., Bianco, V., Radici, G., Felice, R., & Signaroldi, M. (2010). Electrodiagnostic functional sensory evaluation of patients with generalized vulvodynia: A pilot study. *Journal of Lower Genital Tract Diseases, 14*(3), 221–224.

Murnen, S., & Kohlman, M. (2007). Athletic participation, fraternity membership, and sexual aggression among college men: A meta-analysis review. *Sex Roles, 57,* 145–157.

Murnen, S.K., Wright, C., & Kaluzny, G. (2002). If boys will be boys then girls will be victims? A meta-analytic review of the research that relates masculine ideology to sexual aggression. *Sex Roles, 46*(11–12), 359–375.

Murphy, L.R. (1990). Defining the crime against nature: Sodomy in the United States appeals courts, 1810–1940. *Journal of Homosexuality, 19,* 49–66.

Murphy, W., & Page, J. (2008). Exhibitionism: Psychopathology and theory. In D. Laws & W. O'Donohue (Eds.), *Sexual deviance: Theory, assessment and treatment* (2nd ed., pp. 61–75). New York, NY: Guilford Press.

Murray, H., Baakdah, H., Bardell, T., & Tulandi, T. (2005). Diagnosis and treatment of ectopic pregnancy. *Canadian Medical Assoiation Journal, 173*(8), 905–912.

Murray, J. (2000). Psychological profile of pedophiles and child molesters. *Journal of Psychology, 134*(2), 211–224.

Murray, S., & Dynes, W. (1999). Latin American gays: Snow Whites and snake charmers. *The Economist, 353*(8150), 82.

Murray, S.O. (1997). The Solari Khanith. In S.O. Murray and W. Roscoe (Eds.), *Islamic homosexualities.* New York, NY: New York University Press.

Murray, S.O. (1999). Increasingly gay self-representations of male-male sexual experiences in Thailand. *Journal of Gay & Lesbian Social Services, 9*(2/3), 81–96.

Musacchio, N., Hartrich, M., & Garofalo, R. (2006). Erectile dysfunction and Viagra use: What's up with college males? *Journal of Adolescent Health, 39,* 452–454.

Mustanski, B. (2001). Getting wired: Exploiting the internet for the collection of valid sexuality data. *Journal of Sex Research, 38*(4), 292–302.

Musters, A.M., Taminiau-Bloem, E.F., van den Boogaard, E., van der Veen, F., & Goddijn, M. (2011). Supportive care for women with unexplained recurrent miscarriage: Patients' perspectives. *Human Reproduction, 26,* 873–877.

Muula, A.S. (2010). "I can't use a condom, I am a Christian." Salvation, death, and…naivity in Africa. *Croatian Medical Journal, 51,* 468–471.

Myslewski, R. (2009, September 29). UK, France mull photoshop fakery laws. *The Register.* Retrieved October 1, 2010, from http://www.theregister.co.uk/2009/09/29/photoshop_laws/.

Nadelson, C.C., Notman, M.T., Zackson, H., & Gornick, J. (1982). A follow-up study of rape victims. *American Journal of Psychiatry, 139,* 1266–1270.

Nader, S. (2010). Infertility and pregnancy in women with polycystic ovary syndrome. *Minerva Endocrinology, 35*(4), 211–225.

Nagai, A., Hara, R., Yokoyama, T., Jo, Y., Fujii, T., & Miyaji, Y. (2008). Ejaculatory dysfunction caused by the new alpha1-blocker silodosin: A preliminary study to analyze human ejaculation using color Doppler ultrasonography. *International Journal of Urology, 15*(10), 915–918.

Nagel, B., Matsuo, H., McIntyre, K.P., & Morrison, N. (2005). Attitudes toward victims of rape: Effects of gender, race, religion, and social class. *Journal of Interpersonal Violence, 20*(6), 725–737.

Nahshoni, K. (2010, July 28). US rabbis: Accept homosexuals. *Ynet news.* Retrieved February 19, 2011, from http://www.ynetnews.com/articles/0,7340,L-3926452,00.html.

Nair, V.R., & Baguley, S. (2010). Tracking down chlamydia infection in primary care. *Practitioner, 254*(1732), 24–26, 3.

Najman, J.M., Dunne, M.P., Purdie, D.M., Boyle, F.M., & Coxeter, P.D. (2005). Sexual abuse in childhood and sexual dysfunction in adulthood: An Australian population-based study. *Archives of Sexual Behavior, 34*(5), 517–526.

Namuo, C. (2010). UNH football player charged with rape. Manchester, NH: *The Union Leader,* October 8, p. A1.

Nanda, S. (2001). *Gender diversity: Crosscultural variations.* Prospect Heights, IL: Waveland Press.

Nappi, R., Albani, F., Santamaria, V., Tonani, S., Martini, E., Terreno, E., Brambilla, E., & Polatti, F. (2010). Menopause and sexual desire: The role of testosterone. *Menopause International, 16*(4), 162–168.

Narod, S.A., Dube, M.P., Klijn, J., Lubinski, J., Lynch, H.T., Ghadirian, P., Provencher, D., Heimdal, K., Moller, P., Robson, M., Offit, K., Isaacs, C., Weber, B., Friedman, E., et al. (2002). Oral contraceptives and the risk of breast cancer in BRCA1 and BRCA2 mutation carriers. *Journal of National Cancer Institute, 94*(23), 1773–1779.

Narod, S.A., Sun, P., Ghadirian, P., Lynch, H., Isaacs, C., Garber, J., Weber, B., Karlan, B., Fishman, D., Rosen, B., Tung, N., & Neuhausen, S.L. (2001). Tubal ligation and risk of ovarian cancer in carriers of BRCA1 or BRCA2 mutations: A case-control study. *Lancet, 357*(9267), 843–844.

Narod, S.A., Sun, P., Wall, C., Baines, C., & Miller, A.B. (2014). Impact of screening mammography on mortality from breast cancer before age 60 in women 40 to 49 years of age. *Annals of Oncology, 21*(5), 217–221.

Natali, A., & Turek, P. (2011). An assessment of new sperm tests for male infertility. *Urology, 77*(5), 1027–1034.

National Cancer Institute. (2009). Human papillomavirus (HPV) vaccines. U.S. National Institutes of Health, National Cancer Institute. Retrieved April 1, 2010, from http://www. cancer. gov/cancertopics/factsheet/prevention/HPV-vaccine.

National Coalition of Anti-Violence Programs. (1998, October 6). Annual report on lesbian, gay, bisexual, and transgender domestic violence. Retrieved May 23, 2003, from http://www.hrc.org/issues/hate_crimes/antiviolence.asp.

National Health and Social Life Survey. (1992). Retrieved from http://www.socio.com/aid1213.php.

National Student GenderBlind. (2010). 2010 Campus Equality Index: Colleges and universities with inclusive rooming policies. Retrieved November 13, 2010, from http://www.genderblind.org/wpcontent/uploads/2010/07/2010CampusEqualityIndex.pdf.

National Telecommunications and Information Administration and the U.S. Department of Commerce. (1999). Falling through the Net: Defining the digital divide: A report on the telecommunications and information technology gap in America. Retrieved June 1, 2002, from http://www.ntia.doc.gov/ntiahome/fttn99/contents.html.

Nauru, T., Suleiman, M., Kiwi, A., Anther, M., Wear, S.Q., Irk, S., & Rive, J. (2008).

Intra-cytoplasmic sperm injection outcome using ejaculated sperm and retrieved sperm in azoospermic men. *Urology, 5,* 106–110.

Navai, R. (2009, March 27). Women told: 'You have dishonoured your family, please kill yourself.' *The Independent.* Retrieved October 5, 2010, from http://www.independent.co.uk/news/world/europe/women-told-you-have-dishonoured-your-family-please-kill-yourself-1655373.html.

Nayak, G., Kamath, A., Kumar, P.N., & Rao, A. (2014). Effect of yoga therapy on physical and psychological quality of life of perimenopausal women in selected coastal areas of Karnataka. *Indian Journal of Midlife Health, 5*(4), 180–185.

Naz, R.K. (2004). Modalities for treatment of antisperm antibody mediated infertility: Novel perspectives. *American Journal of Reproductive Immunology, 51*(5), 390–397.

Naz, R.K. (2005). Contraceptive vaccines. *Drugs, 65,* 593–603.

Naz, R.K. (2009). Development of genetically engineered human sperm immunocontraceptives. *Journal of Reproductive Immunology, 83*(1–2), 145–150.

Naziri, D. (2007). Man's involvement in the experience of abortion and the dynamics of the couple's relationship: A clinical study. *European Journal of Contraceptive and Reproductive Health Care, 12,* 168–174.

Neal, J., & Frick-Horbury, D. (2001). The effects of parenting styles and childhood attachment patterns on intimate relationships. *Journal of Instructional Psychology, 28*(3), 178–183.

Nebehay, S. (2004). Cervical cancer epidemic in poor countries. Retrieved December 12, 2004, from http://www.reuters.co.uk/printerFriendlyPopup.jhtml?type=healthNews&storyID=7114888.

Needham, B.L., & Austin, E.L. (2010). Sexual orientation, parental support, and health during the transition to young adulthood. *Journal of Youth and Adolescence, 39*(10), 1189–1198.

Neergaard, L. (2005). Doctors are holding off on surgery for newborns of uncertain gender. Retrieved February 22, 2005, from http://www.cleveland.com/health/plain-dealer/index.ssf?/base/news/110889699317860.xml.

Neering, R. (2000). *Wild West women.* Vancouver BC: Whitecap Books.

Neff, C., Kurisu, T., Ndolo, T., Fox, K., & Akkina, R. (2011). A topical microbicide gel formulation of CCR5 antagonist maraviroc prevents HIV-1 vaginal transmission in humanized RAG-hu mice. *PLoS One, 6*(6). Retrieved July 27, 2011, from http://www.plosone.org/article/info%3Adoi%2F10.1371%2Fjournal.pone.0020209.

Neff, L., & Karney, B. (2005). To know you is to love you: The implications of global adoration and specific accuracy for marital relationships. *Journal of Personality & Social Psychology, 88*(3), 480–497.

Neisen, J.H. (1990). Heterosexism: Redefining homophobia for the 1990s. *Journal of Gay and Lesbian Psychotherapy, 1,* 21–35.

Nelson, A.L. (2007). Communicating with patients about extended-cycle and continuous use of oral contraceptives. *Journal of Women's Health, 16,* 463–470.

Nelson, C., Ahmed, A., Valenzuela, R., & Melhall, J. (2007). Assessment of penile vibratory stimulation as a management strategy in men with secondary retarded orgasm. *Urology, 69,* 552–555.

Nelson, H.D. (2008). Menopause. *Lancet, 372,* 760–770.

Nelson, R. (2005). Gottman's sound medical house model. Retrieved September 3, 2005, from http://www.psychpage.com/family/library/gottman.html.

Németh, Z., Kun, B., & Demetrovics, Z. (2010). The involvement of gammahydroxybutyrate in reported sexual assaults: A systematic review. *Journal of Psychopharmacology, 24*(9), 1281–1287.

Neri, Q., Takeuchi, T., & Palermo, G. (2008). An update of assisted reproductive technologies results in the U.S. *Annals of the New York Academy of Sciences, 1127,* 41–49.

Neruda, B. (2005). Development and current status of combined spinal epidural anaesthesia [article in German]. *Anasthesiol Intensivemed Nofallmed Schmerzther, 40*(8), 4590–460.

Ness, R.B., Dodge, R.C., Edwards, R.P., Baker, J.A., & Moysich, K.B. (2011). Contraception methods, beyond oral contraceptives and tubal ligation, and risk of ovarian cancer. *Annals of Epidemiology, 21*(3), 188–196.

Netting, N. (2006). Two-lives, one partner: Indo-Canadian youth between love and arranged marriages. *Journal of Comparative Family Studies, 37*(1), 129–146.

New, J.F.H. (1969). *The Renaissance and Reformation: A short history.* New York, NY: Wiley.

Newcomb, M.E., & Mustanski, B. (2010). Internalized homophobia and internalizing mental health problems: A meta-analytic review. *Clinical Psychology Review, 30*(8), 1019–1029.

Newfield, E., Hart, S., Dibble, S., & Kohler, L. (2006). Female-to-male transgender quality of life. *Quality of Life Research, 15,* 1447–1457.

Newman, A.M. (2007). Arthritis and sexuality. *The Nursing Clinics of North America, 42*(4), 621–630.

Newman, L., & Nyce, J. (Eds.). (1985). *Women's medicine: A cross-cultural study of indigenous fertility regulation.* New Brunswick, NJ: Rutgers University Press.

Newring, K., Wheeler, J., & Draper, C. (2008). Transvestic fetishism: Assessment and treatment. In D. Laws & W. O'Donohue (Eds.), *Sexual deviance: Theory, assessment and treatment* (2nd ed., pp. 285–304). New York, NY: Guilford Press.

Newton-Taylor, B., DeWit, D., & Gliksman, L. (1998). Prevalence and factors associated with physical and sexual assault of female university students in Ontario. *Health Care for Women International, 19*(2),155–164.

Ng, E., & Ma, J.L. (2004). Hong Kong. In R.T. Francoeur & R.J. Noonan (Eds.), *The Continuum International encyclopedia of sexuality* (pp. 489–502). New York/London: Continuum International.

Ngun, T.C., Ghahramani, N., Sanchez, F.J., Bocklandt, S., & Vilain, E. (2011). The genetics of sex differences in brain and behavior. *Frontiers in Neuroendocrinology, 32*(2), 227–246.

Nicholas, D.R. (2000). Men, masculinity and cancer. *Journal of American College Health, 49*(1), 27–33.

Nicolaides, K.H., Spencer, K., Avgidou, K., Faiola, S., & Falcon, O. (2005). Multicenter study of first-trimester screening for trisomy 21 in 75,821 pregnancies: Results and estimation of the potential impact of individual risk-orientated two-stage first-trimester screening. *Ultrasound Obstetrics and Gynecology, 25*(3), 221–226.

Nicoll, L.M., & Skupski, D.W. (2008). Venous air embolism after using a birth-training device. *Obstetrics and Gynecology, 111,* 489–491.

Niedzviecki, H. (2009). *The peep diaries: How we're learning to love watching ourselves and our neighbors.* San Francisco, CA: City Lights Books.

Nielsen, T.M. (2002). Streets, strangers and solidarity: A study of lesbian interaction in the public realm. Dissertation. The University of Manitoba. August 13.

Nieman, L.K., Blocker, W., Nansel, T., Mahoney, S., Reynolds, J., Blithe, D., Wesley, R., & Armstrong, A. (2011). Efficacy and tolerability of CDB-2914 treatment for symptomatic uterine fibroids: A randomized, double-blind, placebo-controlled, phase IIb study. *Fertility and Sterility, 95*(2), 767–772.e1–2.

Nilsson, L. (1990). *A child is born.* New York, NY: Delacorte Press, Bantam Books.

Noel, T.J. (1978). Gay bars and the emergence of the Denver homosexual community. *The Social Sciences Journal, 15,* 59–74.

Noland, C.M. (2010). *Sex talk: The role of communication in intimate relationships.* Portland, OR: Praeger Publishing.

Noller, P. (1993, March-June). Gender and emotional communication in marriage: Different cultures or differential social power? *Journal of Language & Social Psychology, 12*(1–2), 132–152.

Nonnemaker, J., McNeely, C., & Blum, R. (2003). Public and private domains of religiosity and adolescent health risk behaviors: Evidence from the National Longitudinal Study of Adolescent Health. *Social Science & Medicine, 57*(11), 2049–2054.

Noonan, V.K., Fingas, M., Farry, A., Baxter, D., Singh, A., Fehlings, M.G., & Dvorak, M.F. (2012). Incidence and prevalence of spinal cord injury in Canada: a national perspective. *Neuroepidemiology, 38*(4), 219–226.

Nordling, N., Sandnabba, N., Santilla, P., & Alison, L. (2006). Differences and similarities between gay and straight individuals involved in the SM subculture. *Journal of Homosexuality, 50*(2–3), 41–67.

Nordtveit, T., Melve, K., Albrechtsen, S., & Skjaerven, R. (2008). Maternal and paternal contribution to intergenerational recurrence of breech delivery: Population based cohort study. *British Medical Journal, 336,* 843–844.

Norwood, S.J., Murray, M., Nolan, A., & Bowker, A. (2011). Beautiful from the inside out: A school-based programme designed to increase self-esteem and positive body image among preadolescents. *Canadian Journal of School Psychology, 26*(4), 263–282.

Notman, M.T. (2002). Changes in sexual orientation and object choice in midlife in women. *Psychoanalytic Inquiry, 22,* 182–195.

Nour, N.M. (2004). Female genital cutting: Clinical and cultural guidelines. *Obstetrical & Gynecological Survey, 59*(4), 272–279.

Novák, A., de la Loge, C., Abetz, L., & van der Meulen, E. (2003). The combined contraceptive vaginal ring, NuvaRing: An international study of user acceptability. *Contraception, 67,* 187–194.

Nunes, L.V., Moreira, H.C., Razzouk, D., Nunes, S.O., & Mari Jde, J. (2012). Strategies for the treatment of antipsychotic-induced sexual dysfunction and/or hyperprolactinemia among patients of the schizophrenia spectrum: A review. *Journal of Sex and Marital Therapy, 38*(3), 281–301.

Nunn, G. (2011). A challenge to the Guardian: it's time to drop the word 'homosexual'. Retrieved from http://www.theguardian.com/media/mind-your-language/2011/nov/18/mind-your-language-word-homosexual.

NuvaRing now available for Australian women. (2007, April 8). *Women's Health Law Weekly.* NewsRX. Retrieved December 19, 2008, from http://www.newsrx.com/article.php?articleID=519768.

Oakes, M., Eyvazzadeh, A., Quint, E., & Smith, Y. (2008). Complete androgen insensitivity syndrome—a review. *Journal of Pediatric and Adolescent Gynecology, 21,* 305–310.

Obstetricians and Gynecologist Society of Canada. (2013). Retrieved on March, 15, 2015, from http://sogc.org/.

O'Bryne, P.W., & Watts, J.A. (2011). Exploring sexual networks: A pilot study of swingers' sexual behaviour and health-care-seeking practices. *CJNR: Canadian Journal of Nursing Research, 43*(1), 80–97.

Ochoa, S.C., & Sapalis, J. (2014). Risk perception and vulnerability to STIs and HIV/AIDS among immigrant Latin-American women in Canada. *Culture, Health & Sexuality, 16*(4), 412–425.

Ochsenkühn, R., Hermelink, K., Clayton, A.H., von Schônfeldt, V., Gallwas, J., Ditsch, N., Rogenhofer, N., & Kahlert, S. (2011). Menopausal status in breast cancer patients with past chemotherapy determines long-term hypoactive sexual desire disorder. *Journal of Sexual Medicine, 8*(5), 1486–1494.

O'Connell, H.E., & DeLancey, D.O. (2005). Clitoral anatomy in nulliparous, healthy, premenopausal volunteers using enhanced magnetic resonance imaging. *Journal of Urology, 173,* 2060–2063.

O'Connor, M. (2008). Reconstructing the hymen: Mutilation or restoration? *Journal of Law, Medicine, and Ethics, 16*(1), 161–175.

Office on Women's Health, U.S Department of Health and Human Services. (2010). *Pregnancy.* Retrieved December 4, 2014, from http://www.womenshealth.gov/pregnancy/you-are-pregnant/body-changes-discomforts.html.

Ofman, U. (2004). ",,, And how are things sexually?": Helping patients adjust to sexual changes before, during, and after cancer treatment. *Supportive Cancer Therapy, 1,* 243–247.

Ogletree, S.M., & Ginsburg, H.J. (2000). Kept under the hood: Neglect of the clitoris in common vernacular. *Sex Roles, 43*(11–12), 917–927.

O'Grady, R. (2001). Eradicating pedophilia toward the humanization of society. *Journal of International Affairs, 55*(1), 123–140.

O'Hare, T. (2005). Risky sex and drinking contexts in freshman first offenders. *Addictive Behaviors, 30*(3), 585–588.

Ohl, D.A., Quallich, S.A., Sonksen, J., Brackett, N.L., & Lynne, C.M. (2008). Anejaculation and retrograde ejaculation. *Urology Clinics of North America, 35*(2), 211–220.

Ojanen, T., Sijtsema, J., Hawley, P., & Little, T. (2010). Intrinsic and extrinsic motivation in early adolescents' friendship development: Friendship selection, influence, and prospective friendship quality. *Journal of Adolescence, 33*(6), 837.

Okabe, M. (2013). The cell biology of mammalian fertilization. *Development, 140*(22), 4471–4479.

Okami, P. (1990). Sociopolitical biases in the contemporary scientific literature on adult human sexual behavior with children and adolescents. In J. Feierman (Ed.), *Pedophilia* (pp. 91–121). New York, NY: Springer Verlag.

Okami, P., Olmstead, R., & Abramson, P.R. (1997). Sexual experiences in early childhood: 18-year longitudinal data from the UCLA Family Lifestyles Project. *Journal of Sex Research, 34*(4), 339–347.

Okami, P., Olmstead, R., & Abramson, P.R. (1998). Early childhood exposure to parental nudity and scenes of parental sexuality ("primal scenes"): An 18-year longitudinal study of outcome. *Archives of Sexual Behavior, 27*(4), 361–384.

Oliver, C., Beech, A., Fisher, D., & Beckett, R. (2007). A comparison of rapists and sexual murderers on demographic and selected psychometric measures. *International Journal of Offender Therapy and Comparative Criminology, 51,* 298.

Olivier, M., Bobbins, W., Beauregard, D., Brayton, J., & Sauvé, G. (2006). Feminist Activists On-line: A Study of the PAR-L Research Network. *Canadian Review of Sociology & Anthropology, 43*(4), 445–464.

Olsson, S.E., & Möller, A. (2006). Regret after sex reassignment surgery in a male-to-female transsexual: A long-term follow up. *Archives of Sexual Behavior, 35,* 501–506.

Once taboo, fetishes now flourishing. (2001). *Contemporary Sexuality, 35*(7), 9.

O'Neill, N., & O'Neill, G. (1972). *Open marriage: A new life style for couples.* New York, NY: Evans.

Oner, B. (2001). Factors predicting future time orientation for romantic relationships with the opposite sex. *Journal of Psychology: Interdisciplinary & Applied, 135*(4), 430–438.

Ong, K.K., Northstone, K., Wells, J.C., Rubin, C., Ness, A.R., Golding, J., & Dunger, D.B. (2007). Earlier mother's age at menarche predicts rapid infancy growth and childhood obesity. *PLoS Med, 4*(4), e132.

Ontario Funeral Home Association. (2011). Perinatal bereavement services in Ontario .Retrieved April 18, 2015, from http://www .ofsa.org/Perinatal_Bereavement_Services _Ontario_919553.html.

Ontario Human Rights Commission (Retrieved March 11, 2015). Sex and gender based harassment: Know your rights (brochure). Retrieved from http://www.ohrc.on.ca/en/ sexual-and-gender-based-harassment-know -your-rights-brochure.

Ontario Human Rights Commission. (2011). Sex and gender based harassment. Retrieved March 12, 2015, from http://www.ohrc.on.ca/ en/sexual-and-gender-based-harassment -know-your-rights-brochure.

Ontario Ministry of Children and Youth Services. (2013). Infertility and assisted reproduction in Ontario. Retrieved November 29, 2014, from http://www .children.gov.on.ca/htdocs/English/ infertility/report/caretoproceed.aspx.

Oosterhuis, H. (2012). Sexual modernity in the works of Richard von Krafft-Ebing and Albert Moll. *Medical History, 56*(2), 133–155.

O'Rell, M. (1903). *Her Royal Highness—Woman.* London: Chatto & Windus.

Oriel, J.D., & Hayward, A.H.S. (1974). Sexually transmitted diseases in animals. *British Journal of Venereal Disease, 50,* 412–420.

Oriel, K.A., & Schrager, S. (1999). Abnormal uterine bleeding. *American Family Physician, 60*(5), 1371–1380.

Orlandi, F., Rossi, C., Orlandi, E., Jakil, M.C., Hallahan, T.W., Macri, V.J., & Krantz, D.A. (2005). First-trimester screening for tisomy-21 using a simplified method to assess the presence or absence of the fetal nasal bone. *American Journal of Obstetrics & Gynecology, 192*(4), 1107–1111.

Ornish, D. (1999). *Love and survival: The scientific basis for the healing power of intimacy.* New York, NY: Harper Paperbacks.

Orr, P.H., & Brown, R. (1998). Incidence of ectopic pregnancy and sexually transmitted disease in the Canadian Central Arctic. *International Journal of Circumpolar Health, 57*(Suppl 1), 127–134.

Ortigue, S., Bianchi-Demicheli, F., Patel, N., Frum, C., & Lewis, J. (2010). Neuroimaging of love: fMRI metaanalysis evidence toward new perspectives in sexual medicine. *Journal of Sexual Medicine, 7*(11), 3541–3552.

Oselin, S. (2010). Weighing the consequences of a deviant career: Factors leading to an exit from prostitution. *Sociological Perspectives, 53*(4), 527–549.

Osgerby, B. (2000). Muscular manhood and salacious sleaze: The singular world of the 1950s macho pulps. In N. Abrams and J. Hughes (Eds.), *Containing America: cultural production and consumption in Fifties America.* New York, NY: Continuum International Publishing Group.

O'Sullivan, L., & Allgeier, E. (1998). Feigning sexual desire: Consenting to unwanted sexual activity in heterosexual dating relationships. *Journal of Sex Research, 35,* 234–243.

O'Sullivan, L.F., Udell, W., Montrose, V.A., Antoniello, P., & Hoffman, S. (2010). A cognitive analysis of college students' explanations for engaging in unprotected sexual intercourse. *Archives of Sexual Behavior, 39*(5), 1121–1131.

Oswald, R., & Clausell, E. (2005). Same-sex relationships and their dissolution. In M. Fine & J. Harvey (Eds.), *Handbook of divorce and relationship dissolution* (pp. 499–513). New York, NY: Routledge.

Oultram, S. (2009). All hail the new flesh: Some thoughts on scarification, children and adults. *Journal of Medical Ethics, 35*(10), 607–610.

Ovarian Cancer Canada. (2014). Ovarian cancer. Retrieved February 21, 2015, from http://www .ovariancanada.org/about-ovarian-cancer.

Oversey, L. (1969). Homosexuality and pseudohomosexuality. New York, NY: Science House.

Owen, R. (2009). Dapoxetine: A novel treatment for premature ejaculation. *Drugs Today, 45*(9), 669–678.

Ozdemir, O., Simsek, F., Ozkardes, S., Incesu, C., & Karakoc, B. (2008). The unconsummated marriage: Its frequency and clinical characteristics in a sexual dysfunction clinic. *Journal of Sex and Marital Therapy, 34,* 268–279.

Pacey, A. (2010). Environmental and lifestyle factors associated with sperm DNA damage. *Human Fertility, 13*(4), 189–193.

Pachankis, J.E., & Goldfried, M.R. (2004). Clinical issues in working with lesbian, gay, and bisexual clients. *Psychotherapy: Theory, Research, Practice, Training, 41,* 227–246.

Pacik, P.T. (2009). Botox treatment for vaginismus. *Plastic and Reconstructive Surgery, 124*(6), 455e–456e.

Paek, H., Nelson, M., & Vilela, A. (2010). Examination of gender-role portrayals in television advertising across seven countries. *Sex Roles, 64,* 192–207.

Palacios, S. (2011). Hypoactive sexual desire disorder and current pharmacotherapeutic options in women. *Womens Health, 7*(1), 95–107.

Paladin Labs. (2011). SEASONIQUE™ Now available in Canada, the next generation extended cycle pill designed to provide 4 menstrual periods per year. Retrieved March 12, 2015, from http://www.marketwired.com/ press-release/seasonique-now-available -canada-next-generation-extended-cycle -pill-designed-provide-tsx-plb-1503701.htm.

Palefsky, J. (2008). Human papillomavirus and anal neoplasia. *Current HIV/AIDS Report, 5,* 78–85.

Palit, V., & Eardley, I. (2010). An update on new oral PDE5 inhibitors for the treatment of erectile dysfunction. *Nature Reviews Urology, 7*(11), 603–609.

Palmer, D., & El Miedany, Y. (2011). Sexual dysfunction in rheumatoid arthritis: A hot but sensitive issue. *British Journal of Nursing, 20*(17), 1134–1137.

Palmer, L.S. (2013). Hernias and hydroceles. *Pediatrics Review, 34*(10), 457–464.

Palomares, N., & Lee, E. (2010). Virtual gender identity: The linguistic assimilation to gendered avatars in computer-mediated communication. *Journal of Language and Social Psychology, 29*(1), 5.

Pan American Health Organization (PAHO). (2012). "Therapies" to change sexual orientation lack medical justification and threaten health. Press Release. http://www.paho.org/hq/index.php?option=com_content&view=article&id=6803%3Atherapies-change-sexual-orientation-lack-medical-justification-threaten-health-&catid=740%3Anews-press-releases&Itemid=1926&lang=en.

Pandey, M.K., Rani, R., & Agrawal, S. (2005). An update in recurrent spontaneous abortion. *Archives of Gynecology & Obstetrics, 272*(2), 95–108.

Pandey, S., & Bhattacharyta, S. (2010). Impact of obesity on gynecology. *Women's Health, 6*(1), 107–117.

Panjari, M., Bell, R., & Davis, S. (2011). Sexual function after breast cancer. *Journal of Sexual Medicine, 8*(1), 294–302.

Papalia, D.E., Sterns, H.L., Feldman, R., & Camp, C. (2002). *Adult development and aging* (2nd ed.). Boston, MA: McGraw-Hill.

Papamarko, S. (2011). Childless by choice through sterilization. Retrieved March 3, 2015, from http://www.thestar.com/news/insight/2011/05/06/childless_by_choice_through_sterilization.html.

Pappo, I., Lerner-Geva, L., Halevy, A., Olmer, L., Friedler, S., Raziel, A., et al. (2008). The possible association between IVF and breast cancer incidence. *Annals of Surgical Oncology, 15,* 1048–1055.

Pardue, A., & Arrigo, B. (2008). Power, anger, and sadistic rapists: Toward a differentiated model of offender personality. *International Journal of Offender Therapy and Comparative Criminology, 52,* 378–400.

Park, A.J., & Paraiso, M.F. (2009). Successful use of botulinum toxin type A in the treatment of refractory postoperative dyspareunia. *Obstetrics and Gynecology, 114*(2 Pt 2), 484–487.

Parker, S.E., Mai, C.T., Canfield, M.A., Rickard, R., Wang, Y., Meyer, R.E., Anderson, P., Mason, C.A., Collins, J.S., Kirby, R.S., & Correa, A. (2010). Updated national birth prevalence estimates for selected birth defects in the United States, 2004–2006. National Birth Defects Prevention Network. *Birth Defects Research: Part A, Clinical and Molecular Teratology, 88*(12), 1008–1016.

Parker, S.K., & Griffin, M.A. (2002). What is so bad about a little name calling? *Journal of Occupational Health Psychology, 7*(3), 195–210.

Parker-Pope, T. (2010). *For better: The science of marriage.* Boston, MA: Dutton.

Parkhill, M., & Abbey, A. (2008). Does alcohol contribute to the confluence model of sexual

assault perpetration? *Journal of Social and Clinical Psychology, 27,* 529–554.

Parks, K.A., & Scheidt, D.M. (2000). Male bar drinkers' perspective on female bar drinkers. *Sex Roles, 43*(11/12), 927–935.

Parrott, D., & Peterson, J. (2008). What motivates hate crimes based on sexual orientation? Mediating effects of anger on antigay aggression. *Aggressive Behavior, 34,* 306–318.

Parry, B.L. (2008). Perimenopausal depression. *American Journal of Psychiatry, 165,* 23–27.

Parsonnet, J., Hansmann, M., Delaney, M., Modern, P., Dubois, A., Wieland-Alter, W., Wissemann, K., Wild, J., Jones, M., Seymour, J., & Onderdonk, A. (2005). Prevalence of toxic shock syndrome toxin 1-producing Staphylococcus aureus and the presence of antibodies to this superantigen in menstruating women. *Journal of Clinics in Microbiology, 43*(9), 4628–4634.

Passel, J., Wang, W., & Taylor, P. (2010). Marrying out: One-in-seven new U.S. marriages is interracial or interethnic. Pew Research Center. Retrieved May 11, 2011, from http://pewresearch.org/pubs/1616/american-marriage-interracial-interethnic.

Passie, T., Hartmann, U., Schneider, U., Emrich, H.M., & Tillmann, H.C.K. (2005). Ecstasy (MDMA) mimics the post-orgasmic state: Impairment of sexual drive and function during acute MDMA-effects may be due to increased prolactin secretion. *Medical Hypotheses, 64*(5), 899–903.

Pasterski, V., Hindmarsh, P., Geffnew, M., Brook, C., Brain, C., & Hines, M. (2007). Increased aggression and activity level in 3- to 11-year old girls with congenital adrenal hyperplasia (CAH). *Hormones and Behavior, 52,* 368–374.

Pasterski, V.L., Brain, C., Geffner, M.E., Hindmarsh, P., Brook, C., & Hines, M. (2005). Prenatal hormones and postnatal socialization by parents as determinants of male-typical toy play in girls with congenital adrenal hyperplasia. *Child Development, 76*(1), 264–279.

Pastor, Z. (2010). G spot—Myths and realities. *Czechoslovakian Gynecology, 75*(3), 211–217.

Pasupathy, D., & Smith, G.C. (2005). The analysis of factors predicting antepartum stillbirth. *Minerva Ginecology, 57*(4), 397–410.

Patrick, K. (2007). Is infant male circumcision an abuse of the rights of the child? No. *British Medical Journal, 335*(7631), 1181.

Pattatucci, A.M. (1998). Molecular investigations into complex behavior: Lessons from sexual orientation studies. *Human Biology, 70*(2), 367–387.

Patton, G.C., & Viner, R. (2007). Pubertal transitions in health. *Lancet, 369,* 1130–1139.

Patton, M.S. (1986). Twentieth-century attitudes toward masturbation. *Journal of Religion and Health, 25*(4), 291–302.

Pauktuutit Inuit Women of Canada. (2006). *The Inuit way: A guide to Inuit culture.* Ottawa: Heritage Canada.

Paul, J.P. (1984). The bisexual identity: An idea without social recognition. *Journal of Homosexuality, 9,* 45–63.

Pauls, R.N., Crisp, C.C., Novicki, K., Fellner, A.N., & Kleeman, S.D. (2013). Impact of physical therapy on quality of life and function after vaginal reconstructive surgery. *Female Pelvic and Medical Reconstructive Surgery, 19*(5), 271–277.

Pawelski, J.G., Perrin, E.C., Foy, J.M., Allen, C.E., Crawford, J.E., Del Monte, M., et al. (2006). The effects of marriage, civil union, and domestic partnership laws on the health and well-being of children. *Pediatrics, 118,* 349–364.

Payer, P.J. (1991). Sex and confession in the thirteenth century. In J.E. Salisbury (Ed.), *Sex in the Middle Ages.* New York, NY: Garland.

Payton, L. (2015). Abortion drug decision pushed back by Health Canada: Mifepristone under consideration at Health Canada since December 2012. Retrieved March 5, 2015, from, http://www.cbc.ca/news/politics/abortion-drug-decision-pushed-back-by-health-canada-1.2899723.

Pearce, A., Chuikova, T., Ramsey, A., & Galy-autdinova, S. (2010). A positive psychology perspective on mate preferences in the U.S. and Russia. *Journal of Cross-Cultural Psychology, 41*(5–6), 742.

Pearson, J.C., Turner, L.H., & Todd-Mancillas, W. (1991). *Gender and communication* (2nd ed.). Dubuque, IA: William C. Brown.

Peck, S. (1978). *The road less traveled: A new psychology of love, traditional values and spiritual growth.* Oxford, England: Simon & Schuster.

Pedrera-Zamorano, J.D., Lavado-Garcia, J.M., Roncero-Martin, R., Calderon-Garcia, J.F., Rodriguez-Dominguez, T., & Canal-Macias, M.L. (2009). Effect of beer drinking on ultrasound bone mass in women. *Nutrition, 25*(10), 1057–1063.

Peele, S., & Brodsky, A. (1991). *Love and addiction.* Jersey City, NJ: Parkwest.

Pek, N.K., & Senn, C.Y. (2004). Not wanted in the inbox! Evaluations of unsolicited and harassing e-mail. *Psychology of Women Quarterly, 28,* 204–214.

Pellis, S.M., Field, E.F., Smith, L.K., & Pellis, V.C. (1997). Multiple differences in the play fighting of male and female rats. Implications for the causes and functions of play. *Neuroscience and Biobehavioural Reviews, 21*(1), 105–120.

Penke, L., & Asendorpf, J.B. (2008). Evidence for conditional sex differences in emotional but not in sexual jealousy at the automatic level of cognitive processing. *European Journal of Personality, 22,* 3–30.

Pennington, J. (2007). *The history of sex in American film.* Greenwood Publishing Group.

Peplau, L.A., & Conrad, E. (1989). Beyond nonsexist research: The perils of feminist methods in psychology. *Psychology of Women Quarterly, 13,* 381–402.

Peplau, L.A., & Fingerhut, A. (2004). The paradox of the lesbian worker. *Journal of Social Issues, 60*(4), 719–736.

Peraldi, F. (1992). Heterosexual presumption. *American Imago, 49*(3), 357–370.

Peralta, R.L. (2008). "Alcohol allows you to not be yourself": Toward a structured understanding of alcohol use and gender difference among gay, lesbian, and heterosexual youth. *Journal of Drug Issues, 38,* 373–400.

Perelman, M. (2007). Clinical application of CNS-acting agents in FSD. *Journal of Sexual Medicine, 4*(Suppl. 4), 280–290.

Perelman, M., & Rowland, D. (2006). Retarded ejaculation. *World Journal of Urology, 24,* 645–652.

Perilloux, C., & Buss, D. (2008). Breaking up romantic relationships: Costs experienced and coping strategies deployed. *Evolutionary Psychology, 6*(1), 164–181.

Perovic, S.V., & Djinovic, R.P. (2010). Current surgical management of severe Peyronie's disease. *Archives of Españoles Urology, 63*(9), 755–770.

Perrigouard, C., Dreval, A., Cribier, B., & Lipsker, D. (2008). Vulvar vestibulitis syndrome: A clinicopathological study of 14 cases. *Annals of Dermatologie et de Venereologie, 135,* 367–372.

Perrin, E.C. (2002). Technical report: Coparent or second-parent adoption by same-sex parents. *Pediatrics, 109*(2), 341–345.

Perrow, C., & Guillén, M.F. (1990). *The AIDS disaster.* New Haven, CT: Yale University Press.

Peterson, H.B. (2008). Sterilization. *Obstetrics and Gynecology, 111,* 189–203.

Pew Research Center. (2010). The decline of marriage and rise of new families. Pew Research Center's Social and Demographic Trends Project. Retrieved May 12, 2011, from http://pewsocialtrends.org/files/2010/11/pew-social-trends-2010-families.pdf.

Pfaus, J., Giuliano, F., & Gelez, H. (2007). Bremelanotide: An overview of preclinical CHS effects of female sexual function. *Journal of Sexual Medicine, 4*(Suppl. 4), 269–279.

Pfaus, J.G., Erickson, K.A., & Talianakis, S. (2013). Somatosensory conditioning of sexual arousal and copulatory behavior in the male rat: A model of fetish development. *Physiology & Behavior, 122,* 1–7.

Phillips, B. (2001, December 11). Baby rapes shock South Africa. BBC News. Retrieved April 30, 2011, from http://news.bbc.co.uk/2/hi/africa/1703595.stm.

Phipps, W., Saracino, M., Magaret, A., Selke, S., Remington, M., Huang, M.L., Warren, T., Casper, C., Corey, L., & Wald, A. (2011). Persistent genital herpes simplex virus-2 shedding years following the first clinical episode. *Journal of Infectious Disease, 203*(2), 180–187.

Piaget, J. (1951). *Play, dreams, and imitation in children.* New York, NY: Norton.

Pialoux, G., Vimont, S., Moulignier, A., Buteux, M., Abraham, B., & Bonnard, P. (2008). Effect of HIV infection on the course of syphilis. *AIDS Review, 10,* 85–92.

Picard, A. (2013). Midwives: Underused and misused assets in Canada. Retrieved February 8, 2015, from http://www.theglobeandmail.com/life/health-and-fitness/health/midwives-underused-and-misused-assets/article13133123/.

Piccinino, L.J., & Mosher, W.D. (1998). Trends in contraceptive method use in the United States: 1982–1994. *Family Planning Perspectives, 30,* 4–10.

Pilgrim D. (2011). The child abuse crisis in the Catholic Church: international, national and personal policy aspects. Policy & Politics 39 (3): 309–324.

Pillard, R.C. (1991). Masculinity and femininity in homosexuality: "Inversion" revisited. In J.C. Gonsiorek & J.D. Weinrich (Eds.), *Homosexuality: Research implications for public policy* (pp. 32–43). Newbury Park, CA: Sage.

Pillard, R.C. (1998). Biologic theories of homosexuality. *Journal of Gay and Lesbian Psychotherapy, 2*(4), 75–76.

Pillard, R.C., & Bailey, J.M. (1998). Human sexual orientation has a heritable component. *Human Biology, 70*(2), 347–366.

Piller, I. (2009). "I always wanted to marry a cowboy": Bilingual couples, language, and desire. In T.A. Karis & K.D. Killian (Ed.), *Intercultural couples: Exploring diversity in intimate relationships* (pp. 53–70). New York, NY: Routledge.

Pines, A. (2011). Male menopause: Is it a real clinical syndrome? *Climacteric, 14*(1), 15–17.

Ping, W. (2002). *Aching for beauty: Footbinding in China.* New York, NY: Random House.

Pinheiro, A.P., Raney, T.J., Thornton, L.M., Fichter, M.M., Berrettini, W.H., Goldman, D., Halmi, K.A., Kaplan, A.S., Strober, M., Treasure, J., Woodside, D.B., Kaye, W.H., & Bulik, C.M. (2010). Sexual functioning in women with eating disorders. *International Journal of Eating Disorders, 43*(2), 123–129.

Pinheiro, A.P., Thorton, L., & Plotonicov, K. (2007). Patterns of menstrual disturbance in eating disorders. *International Journal of Eating Disorders, 40*(5), 424.

Pinkerton, J., & Stovall, D. (2010). Reproductive aging, menopause, and health outcomes. *Annals of the New York Academy of Science, 1204,* 169–178.

PinkNews. (2014a). Taiwanese Parliament considers same-sex marriage for the first time. December 22. http://www.pinknews.co.uk/2014/12/22/taiwanese-parliament-considers-same-sex-marriage-for-the-first-time/.

PinkNews. (2014b). Family Research Council 'doesn't know' if gays should be executed. December 16. http://www.pinknews.co.uk/2014/12/16/family-research-council-doesnt-know-if-gays-should-be-executed/.

PinkNews. (2015). Meet India's first ever out transgender mayor. January 5. http://www.pinknews.co.uk/2015/01/05/meet-indias-first-ever-out-transgender-mayor/.

Pino, N.W., & Meier, R.F. (1999). Gender differences in rape reporting. *Sex Roles, 40*(11–12), 979–990.

Pinquart, M., Stotzka, C., & Silberreisen, R., (2008). Personality and ambivalence in decisions about becoming parents. *Social Behavior and Personality, 36,* 87–96.

Piot, P. (2000). Global AIDS epidemic: Time to turn the tide. *Science, 288*(5474), 2176–2188.

Pipitone, R., & Gallup, G. (2008). Women's voice attractiveness varies across the menstrual cycle. *Evolution and Human Behavior, 29*(4), 268–274.

Pisetsky, E.M., Chao, Y., Dierker, L.C., May, A.M., & Striegel-Moore, R. (2008). Disordered eating and substance use in high-school students: Results from the Youth Risk Behavior Surveillance System. *International Journal of Eating Disorders, 41,* 464.

Pitkin, J. (2010). Cultural issues and the menopause. *Menopause International, 16*(4), 156–161.

Pitts, S., & Emans, S. (2008). Controversies in contraception. *Current Opinion in Pediatrics, 20*(4), 383–389.

Pivarnik, J.M. (1998). Potential effects of maternal physical activity on birth weight: Brief review. *Med Science Sports Exercise, 30*(3), 400–406.

Plante, A.F., & Kamm, M.A. (2008). Life events in patients with vulvodynia. *British Journal of Obstetrics and Gynecology, 115,* 509–514.

Plante, C.N., Mock, S., Reysen, S., & Gerbasi, K.C. (2011). International Anthropomorphic Research Project: Winter 2011 Online Survey Summary. https://sites.google.com/site/anthropomorphicresearch/past-results/international-online-furry-survey-2011.

Platoni, K. (2010). The sex scholar. Stanford Magzine, March/April, 2010. Retrieved from http://alumni.stanford.edu/get/page/magazine/article/?article_id=29954.

Plaud, J.J., Gaither, G.A., Hegstand, H.J., Rowan, L., & Devitt, M.K. (1999). Volunteer bias in human psychophysiological sexual arousal research: To whom do our research results apply? *The Journal of Sex Research, 36,* 171–179.

Plaut, A., & Kohn-Speyer, A.C. (1947). The carcinogenic action of smegma. *Science, 105,* 392.

Plosker, G.L. (2011). Sipuleucel-T: In metastatic castration-resistant prostate cancer. *Drugs, 71*(1), 101–108.

Pluchino, N., Bucci, F., Cela, V., Cubeddu, A., & Genazzani, A. (2011). Menopause and mental well-being: Timing of symptoms and timing of hormone treatment. *Women's Health, 7*(1), 71–80.

Plummer, K. (1991). Understanding childhood sexualities. *Journal of Homosexuality, 20,* 231–249.

Poimenova, A., Markaki, E., Rahiotis, C., & Kitraki, E. (2010). Corticosterone-regulated actions in the rat brain are affected by perinatal exposure to low dose of bisphenol A. *Neuroscience, 167*(3), 741–749.

Pollock, N.L., & Hashmall, J.M. (1991). The excuses of child molesters. *Behavioral Sciences and the Law, 9,* 53–59.

Polman, R., Kaiseler, M., & Borkoles, E. (2007). Effect of a single bout of exercise on the mood of pregnant women. *Journal of Sports Medicine and Physical Fitness, 47,* 102–111.

Pomeroy, W.B. (1982). *Dr. Kinsey and the Institute for Sex Research.* New Haven, CT: Yale University Press.

Poon, M. (2006). The discourse of oppression in contemporary gay asian diasporal literature: Liberation or limitation? *Sexuality & Culture: An Interdisciplinary Quarterly, 10*(3), 29–58.

Poon, M., & Ho, P.T. (2002). A qualitative analysis of cultural and social vulnerabilities to HIV infection among gay, lesbian, and bisexual Asian youth. *Journal of Gay & Lesbian Social Services: Issues in Practice, Policy & Research, 14*(3), 43–78.

Poon, M., & Ho, P.T. (2008). Negotiating social stigma among gay Asian men. *Sexualities, 11*(1–2), 245–268.

Poon, M., Wong, J.P., Wong, G., & Lee, R.Ho, P.T. (2005). Psychosocial experiences of East and Southeast Asian men who use gay internet chatrooms in Toronto: An implication for HIV/AIDS Prevention. *Ethnicity & Health, 10*(2), 145–167.

Popovic, M. (2005). Intimacy and its relevance in human functioning. *Sexual and Relationship Therapy, 20*(1), 31–49.

Porter, R. (1982). Mixed feelings: The Enlightenment and sexuality in eighteenth-century Britain. In P.-G. Goucé (Ed.), *Sexuality in eighteenth-century Britain* (pp. 1–27). Manchester, UK: Manchester University Press.

Posey, C., Lowry, P., Roberts, T., & Ellis, T. (2010). Proposing the online community self-disclosure model: The case of working professionals in France and the UK who use online communities. *European Journal of Information Systems, 19*(2), 181–196.

Posner, R.A. (1993). Obsession. *The New Republic, 209,* 31–36.

Potter, B., Gerofi, J., Pope, M., & Farley, T. (2003). Structural integrity of the polyurethane female condom after multiple cycles of disinfection, washing, drying and relubrication. *Contraception, 67*(1), 65–72.

Potterat, J.J., Rothenberg, R.B., Muth, S.Q., Darrow, W.W., & Phillips-Plummer, L. (1998). Pathways to prostitution: The chronology of sexual and drug abuse milestones. *Journal of Sex Research, 35*(4), 333–340.

Pouriayevali, M.H., Bamdad, T., Parsania, M., & Sari, R. (2011). Full length antigen priming enhances the CTL epitope-based DNA vaccine efficacy. *Cell Immunology, 268*(1), 4–8.

Povey, A., & Stocks, S. (2010). Epidemiology and trends in male subfertility. *Human Fertility, 13*(4), 182–188.

Pozniak, A. (2002). Pink versus blue: The things people do to choose the sex of their baby. Retrieved June 3, 2002, from http://abcnews .go.com/sections/living/DailyNews/ choosingbabysex020603.html.

Predrag, S. (2005). LGBT news and views from around the world. *Lesbian News, 30*(9), 19–21.

Prentice, A. (2001). Endometriosis. *British Medical Journal, 323*(7304), 93–96.

Prentky, R.A., & Knight, R.A. (1986). Impulsivity: In the lifestyle and criminal behavior of sexual offenders. *Criminal Justice and Behavior, 13*(2), 141.

Previti, D., & Amato, P. (2004). Is infidelity a cause or a consequence of poor marital quality? *Journal of Social and Personal Relationships, 21*(2), 217–230.

Price, J. (2008). Parent-child quality time: Does birth order matter? *Journal of Human Resources, 43,* 240–265.

Price, M., Kafka, M., Commons, M., Gutheil, T., & Simpson, W. (2002). Telephone scatologia: Comorbidity with other paraphilias and paraphilia-related disorders. *International Journal of Law & Psychiatry, 25*(1), 37–49.

Prior, V., & Glaser, D. (2006). *Understanding attachment and attachment disorders: Theory, evidence and practice.* London: Jessica Kingsley.

Prostate Cancer Canada. (2015). Prostate cancer. Retrieved August 30, 2014, from http://www.prostatecancer.ca/In-The-News/ Foundation-News-Releases/Prostate-Cancer -Canada-Releases-New-Recommendation# .U9wSco4rU7p.

Proto-Campise, L., Belknap, J., & Wooldredge, J. (1998). High school students' adherence to rape myths. *Violence Against Women, 4,* 308–328.

Pryzgoda, J., & Chrisler, J.C. (2000). Definitions of gender and sex: The subtleties of meaning. *Sex Roles, 43*(7–8), 499–528.

Przybylo, E. (2011). Crisis and safety: The asexual in sexusociety. *Sexualities, 14*(4), 444–461.

Public Health Agency of Canada. (2008). Canadian Guidelines for Sexual Health Education. Retrieved from http://www.phac -aspc.gc.ca/aids-sida/publication/epi/2010/ pdf/EN_Chapter4_Web.pdf.

Public Health Agency of Canada. (2008). Report on Sexually Transmitted Infections in Canada: 2008. Retrieved from http://www .phac-aspc.gc.ca/std-mts/report/sti-its2008/ index-eng.php.

Public Health Agency of Canada. (2010). *Gender ideneity in schools: Questions & answers.* Ottawa: Public Health Agency of Canada.

Public Health Agency of Canada. (2010). Life with arthritis in Canada: A personal and public health challenge. Retrieved February 10, 2015, from http://www.phac-aspc.gc.ca/ cd-mc/arthritis-arthrite/lwaic-vaaac-10/pdf/ arthritis-2010-eng.pdf.

Public Health Agency of Canada. (2013). HIV and AIDS in Canada: Report to December 31, 2013. http://www.phac-aspc.gc.ca/aids -sida/publication/survreport/2013/dec/index -eng.php.

Public Health Agency of Canada. (2014). Cervical cancer. Retrieved February 18, 2015, from http://www.phac-aspc.gc.ca/cd-mc/ cancer/cervical_cancer-cancer_du_col _uterus-eng.php.

Puente, S., & Cohen, D. (2003). Jealousy and the meaning (or nonmeaning) of violence. *Personality and Social Psychology Bulletin, 29*(4), 449–460.

Puhl, R.M., & Boland, F.J. (2001). Predicting female attractiveness: Waist-to-hip ratio versus thinness. *Psychology, Evolution & Gender, 3*(1), 27–46.

Pyke, S.W. (1985). Androgyny: An integration. *International Journal of Women's Studies, 8*(5), 529–539.

QMI Agency. (2012). Preterm births on the rise. Retrieved February 10, 2015, from http://www.torontosun.com/2012/05/02/ preterm-births-on-the-rise-report.

Quaglio, G., Lugoboni, F., Pattaro, C., Melara, B., Mezzelani, P., & Des Jarlais D.C. (2009). Erectile dysfunction in male heroin users, receiving methadone and buprenorphine maintenance treatment. *Drug and Alcohol Dependence, 94*(1–3), 12–18.

Quinsey, V.L., & Lalumiere, M.L. (1995). Evolutionary perspectives on sexual offending. *Sexual Abuse: A Journal of Research and Treatment, 7,* 301–315.

Rabin, R.C. (2010a, October 9). Grown-up, but still irresponsible. *New York Times.* Retrieved October 10, 2010, from http://www.nytimes.com/2010/10/10/weekinreview/10rabin.html.

Rabinovici, J., David, M., Fukunishi, H., Morita, Y., Gostout, B.S., & Stewart, E.A.; MRgFUS Study Group. (2010). Pregnancy outcome after magnetic resonance-guided focused ultrasound surgery (MRgFUS) for conservative treatment of uterine fibroids. *Fertility and Sterility, 93*(1), 199–209.

Rabinowitz Greenberg, S.R., Firestone, P., Bradford, J., & Greenberg, D.M. (2002). Prediction of recidivism in exhibitionists: Psychological, phallometric, and offense factors. *Sexual Abuse: Journal of Research & Treatment, 14*(4), 329–347.

Radestad, I., Olsson, A., Nissen, E., & Rubertsson, C. (2008). Tears in the vagina, perineum, spincter ani, and rectum and first sexual intercourse after childbirth: A nationwide follow up. *Birth, 35,* 98–106.

Radford, B. (2006). Predator panic. *The Skeptical Inquirer, 20,* 20–23.

Rado, S. (1949, rev. 1955). An adaptional view of sexual behavior. *Psychoanalysis of behavior: Collected papers.* New York, NY: Grune & Stratton.

Raffaelli, M., & Green, S. (2003). Parent-adolescent communication about sex; retrospective reports by Latino college students. *Journal of Marriage and the Family, 65,* 474–481.

Rahman, Q. (2005). Fluctuating asymmetry, second to fourth finger length ratios and human sexual orientation. *Psychoneuroendocrinology, 30*(4), 382–391.

Rahman, Q., & Koerting, J. (2008). Sexual orientation-related differences in allocentric spatial memory tasks. *Hippocampus, 18,* 55–63.

Rahman, Q., & Symeonides, D. (2008). Neurodevelopmental correlates of paraphilic sexual interests in men. *Archives of Sexual Behavior, 37,* 166–171.

Rahnama, P., Hidarnia, A., Amin Shokravi, F., Kazemnejad, A., Ghazanfari, Z., & Montazeri, A. (2010). Withdrawal users' experiences of and attitudes to contraceptive methods: A study from Eastern district of Tehran, Iran. *BMC Public Health, 10,* 779.

Ramjee, G., Kamali, A., & McCormack, S. (2010). The last decade of microbicide clinical trials in Africa: From hypothesis to facts. *AIDS, 24*(Suppl. 4), S40–S49.

Ramlau-Hansen, C., Thulstrup, A., Storgaard, L., Toft, G., Olsen, J., & Bonde, J.P. (2007). Is prenatal exposure to tobacco smoking a cause of poor semen quality? A follow-up study. *American Journal of Epidemiology, 165*(12), 1372–1379.

Rammouz, I., Tahiri, D., Aalouane, R., Kjiri, S., Belhous, A., Ktiouet, J., & Sekkat, F. (2008). Infanticide in the postpartum period: About a clinical case. *Encephale, 34,* 284–288.

Ramsey, F., Hill, M., & Kellam, C. (2010). Black lesbians matter: An examination of the unique experiences, perspectives, and priorities of the Black lesbian community. Retrieved February 20, 2011, from http://zunainstitute.org/2010/research/blm/blacklesbiansmatter.pdf.

Rancour-Laferriere, D. (1985). *Signs of the flesh.* New York, NY: Mouton de Gruyter.

Rand, M.R. (2009). Criminal victimization, 2008. National Crime Victimization Survey, Bureau of Justice Statistics. *Bureau of Justice Statistics Bulletin.* Retrieved April 13, 2011, from http://bjs.ojp.usdoj.gov/content/pub/pdf/cv08.pdf.

Randall, H.E., & Byers, E.S. (2003). What is sex?: Students' definitions of having sex, sexual partner, and unfaithful sexual behaviour. *Canadian Journal of Human Sexuality, 12,* 87–96.

Ranger, R., & Fedoroff, P. (2014). Commentary: Zoophilia and the Law. *Journal of the American Academy of Psychiatry and the Law Online, 42*(4), 421–426.

Rankin, P.T. (1952). The measurement of the ability to understand spoken language. *Dissertation Abstracts.* University of Michigan, 1953–06117–001.

Rapkin, A., Berman, S., Mandelkern, M., Silverman, D., Morgan, M., & London, E. (2011). Neuroimaging evidence of cerebellar involvement in premenstrual dysphoric disorder. *Biological Psychiatry, 69*(4), 374–380.

Rapkin, A.J., & Winer, S.A. (2008). The pharmacologic management of premenstrual dysphoric disorder. *Expert Opinions in Pharmacotherapy, 9,* 429–445.

Raskin, N.J., & Rogers, C.R. (1989). Person-centered therapy. In R.J. Corsini & D. Wedding (Eds.), *Current psychotherapies* (4th ed., pp. 155–196), Pacific Grove, CA: F.E. Peacock.

Rauer, A.J., & Volling, B.L. (2007). Differential parenting and sibling jealousy: Developmental correlates of young adults' romantic relationships. *Personal Relationships, 14,* 495–511.

Raval, A.P., Hirsch, N., Dave, K.R., Yavagal, D.R., Bramlett, H., & Saul, I. (2011). Nicotine and estrogen synergistically exacerbate cerebral ischemic injury. *Neuroscience, 181,* 216–225.

Ravelli, B., & Webber, M. (2010). *Exploring sociology: A Canadian perspective.* Toronto, ON: Pearson.

Ravert, A.A., & Martin, J. (1997). Family stress, perception of pregnancy, and age of first menarche among pregnant adolescents. *Adolescence, 32*(126), 261–269.

Rawana, J.S., & Morgan, A.S. (2014). Trajectories of depressive symptoms from adolescence to young adulthood: The role of self-esteem and body-related predictors. *Journal of Youth and Adolescence, 43*(4), 597–611.

Ray, N. (2006). Lesbian, gay, bisexual and transgendered youth: An epidemic of homelessness. National Gay and Lesbian Task Force Policy Institute. Retrieved February 17, 2011, from http://www.thetaskforce.org/downloads/reports/reports/HomelessYouth.pdf.

Ray, N. (2007). Lesbian, gay, bisexual, and transgendered youth: An epidemic of homelessness. National Gay and Lesbian Task Force Policy Institute. Retrieved October 3, 2008, from http://www.thetaskforce.org/downloads/HomelessYouth.pdf.

Raymond, E., Stewart, F., Weaver, M., Monteith, C., & Van Der Pol, B. (2006). Impact of increased access to emergency contraceptive pills: A randomized controlled trial. *Obstetrics and Gynecology, 108,* 1098–1106.

Read, C.M. (2010). New regimens with combined oral contraceptive pills—moving away from traditional 21/7 cycles. *European Journal of Contraceptive and Reproductive Health Care, 15*(Suppl. 2), S32–S41.

Reece, M., Herbenick, D., Sanders, S., Dodge, B., Ghassemi, A., & Fortenberry, J. (2010a). Prevalence and predictors of testicular self-exam among a nationally representative sample of men in the U.S. *International Journal of Sexual Health, 22*(1), 1–4.

Reece, M., Herbenick, D., Schick, V., Sanders, S., Dodge, B., & Fortenberry, J.D. (2010b). Background and considerations on the National Survey of Sexual Health and Behavior (NSSHB). *Journal of Sexual Medicine, 7*(Suppl. 5), 243–245.

Reece, M., Herbenick, D., Schick, V., Sanders, S., Dodge, B., & Fortenberry, D. (2010c). Condom use rates in a national probability sample of males and females ages 14–94 in the United States. *Journal of Sexual Medicine, 7*(Suppl. 5), 266–276.

Reed, S.C., Levin, F.R., & Evans, S.M. (2008). Changes in mood, cognitive performance and appetite in the late luteal and follicular phases of the menstrual cycle in women with and without PMDD (premenstrual dysphoric disorder). *Hormonal Behavior, 54*(1), 185–193.

Reese, J.B. (2011). Coping with sexual concerns after cancer. *Current Opinions in Oncology, 23*(4), 313–321.

Reese, J.B., Keefe, F.J., Somers, T.J., & Abernethy, A.P. (2010). Coping with sexual concerns after cancer: The use of flexible coping. *Support Care Cancer, 18*(7), 785–800.

Regan, P.C. (2006). Love. In R.D. McAnulty & M.M. Burnette (Eds.), *Sex and sexuality: Sexual functions and dysfunctions* (pp. 87–113). Westport, CT: Praeger.

Regnerus, M.D., & Luchies, L.B. (2006). The parent-child relationship and opportunities for adolescents' first sex. *Journal of Family Issues, 27,* 159–183.

Rehm, J., Shield, K.D., Joharchi, N., & Shuper, P.A. (2012). Alcohol consumption and the intention to engage in unprotected sex: systematic review and meta-analysis of experimental studies. *Addiction,* 107(1), 51–59.

Rehman, U., Janssen, E., Newhouse, S., Heiman, J., Holtzworth-Munroe, A., Fallis, E., & Rafaeli, E. (2011). Marital satisfaction and communication behaviors during sexual and nonsexual conflict discussions in newlywed couples. *Journal of Sex and Marital Therapy,* 37(2), 94–103.

Rehman, U.S., & Holtzworth-Munroe, A. (2007). A cross-cultural examination of the relation of marital communication behavior to marital satisfaction. *Journal of Family Psychology, 21,* 759–763.

Reichert, T., & Zhou, S. (2007). Consumer responses to sexual magazine covers on a men's magazine. *Journal of Promotion Management,* 13(1/2), 127–145.

Reid, R., & Society of Obstetricians and Gynaecologists of Canada. (2010). SOGC clinical practice guideline. No. 252, December 2010. Oral contraceptives and the risk of venous thromboembolism: An update. *Journal of Obstetrics and Gynecology,* 32(12), 1192–1204.

Reid, R.C., Carpenter, B.N., Hook, J.N., Garos, S., Manning, J.C, Gilliland, R., Cooper, B.C., McKittrick, H., Davtian, M., & Fong, T. (2012). Report of findings in a DSM-5 field trial for hypersexual disorder. *Journal of Sexual Medicine,* 9(11), 2868–2877.

Reips, U.D. (2000). The Web experiment method: Advantages, disadvantages, and solutions. In M.H. Birnbaum (Ed.), *Psychological experiments on the Internet* (pp. 89–114). San Diego, CA: Academic Press.

Reips, U.D., & Bachtiger, M.T. (2000). Are all flies drosophilae? Participant selection bias in psychological research. Unpublished manuscript.

Reis, L.O., Dias, F.G., Castro, M.O., & Ferreira, U. (2011). Male breast cancer. *Aging Male,* 14(2), 99–109.

Reiss, I.L. (1982). Trouble in paradise: The current status of sexual science. *Journal of Sex Research, 18,* 97–113.

Reiss, I.L. (1986). A sociological journey into sexuality. *Journal of Marriage and Family,* 48(2), 233–242.

Reiss, I.L. (1986). *Journey into sexuality: An exploratory voyage.* Englewood Cliffs, NJ: Prentice Hall.

Reiss, Jr., A.J. (1961). The social integration of queers and peers. *Social Problems,* 9(2), 102.

Rellini, A.H., & Meston, C.M. (2011). Sexual self-schemas, sexual dysfunction, and the sexual responses of women with a history of childhood sexual abuse. *Archives of Sexual Behavior,* 40(2), 351–362.

Remafedi, G. (1987). Male homosexuality: The adolescent perspective. *Pediatrics, 79*(3), 326–330.

Remez, L. (2000, November/December). Oral sex among adolescents: Is it sex or is it abstinence? *Family Planning Perspectives,* 32(6), 298–304.

Rempel, J.K., & Baumgartner, B. (2003). The relationship between attitudes towards menstruation and sexual attitudes, desires, and behavior in women. *Archives of Sexual Behavior,* 32(2), 155–163.

Remsberg, K.E., Demerath, E.W., Schubert, C.M., Chumlea, C., Sun, S.S., & Siervogel, R.M. (2005). Early menarche and the development of cardiovascular disease risk factors in adolescent girls: The Fels Longitudinal Study. *Journal of Clinical Endocrinology & Metabolism,* published online ahead of print. Retrieved March 22, 2005, from http://jcem.endojournals.org/cgi/content/abstract/jc.2004–1991v1

Renaud, C.A., & Byers, E.S. (1999). Exploring the frequency, diversity, and content of university students' positive and negative sexual cognitions. *Canadian Journal of Human Sexuality,* 8(1), 17–30.

Rendas-Baum, R., Yang, M., Gricar, J., & Wallenstein, G. (2010). Cost-effectiveness analysis of treatments for premenstrual dysphoric disorder. *Applied Health Economics and Health Policy,* 8(2), 129–140.

Rensberger, B. (1994). Contraception the natural way: Herbs have played a role from ancient Greece to modern-day Appalachie. *Washington Post,* July 25, p. A3.

Renshaw, D.C. (2005). Premature ejaculation-revisted—2005. *Family Journal: Counseling & Therapy for Couples and Families,* 13(2), 150–152.

Resnick, H., Acierno, R., Kilpatrick, D.G., & Holmes, M. (2005). Description of an early intervention to prevent substance abuse and psychopathology in recent rape victims. *Behavior Modification,* 29(1), 156–188.

Resnick, M.D., Bearman, P.S., Blum, R.W., Bauman, K.E., Harris, K.M., Jones, J., et al. (1997). Protecting adolescents from harm: Findings from the National Longitudinal Study on Adolescent Health. *Journal of the American Medical Association,* 278(10), 823–832.

Rettenmaier, N., Rettenmaier, C., Wojciechowski, T., Abaid, L., Brown, J., Micha, J., & Goldstein, B. (2010). The utility and cost of routine follow-up procedures in the surveillance of ovarian and primary peritoneal carcinoma: A 16-year institutional review. *British Journal of Cancer,* 103(11), 1657–1662.

Reynaert, C., Zdanowicz, N., Janne, P., & Jacques, D. (2010). Depression and sexuality. *Psychiatria Danubina,* 22(Suppl. 1), S111–S113.

Reynolds, T., Vranken, G., Nueten, J.V., & Aldis, J. (2008). Down's syndrome screening: Population statistic dependency of screening performance. *Clinical Chemistry and Laboratory Medicine,* 46(5), 639–647.

Rhoades, G.K., Stanley, S.M., & Markman, H.J. (2009). The pre-engagement cohabitation effect: A replication and extension of previous findings. *Journal of Family Psychology,* 23(1), 107–111.

Rhoads, J.M., & Boekelheide, P.D. (1985). Female genital exhibitionism. *The Psychiatric Forum,* Winter, 1–6.

Ricciardelli, R., & Moir, M. (2013). Stigmatized among the stigmatized: Sex offenders in Canadian penitentiaries. *Canadian Journal of Criminology and Criminal Justice,* 55(3), 353–385.

Rich, A. (1983). Compulsory heterosexuality and lesbian existence. In A. Snitow, C. Stinsell, & S. Thompson (Eds.), *Powers of desire: The politics of sexuality* (pp. 177–205). New York, NY: Monthly Review Press.

Richardson, B.A. (2002). Nonoxynol-9 as a vaginal microbicide for prevention of sexually transmitted infections. *Journal of American Medication Association, 287,* 1171–1172.

Richardson, C.T., & Nash, E. (2006). Misinformed consent: The medical accuracy of state-developed abortion counseling materials. *Guttmacher Policy Review,* 9(4). Retrieved March 18, 2011, from http://www.guttmacher.org/pubs/gpr/09/4/gpr090406.html.

Richardson, D., & Campbell, J.L. (1982). The effect of alcohol on attributions of blame for rape. *Personality and Social Psychology Bulletin, 8,* 468–476.

Richardson, D., Nalabanda, A., & Goldmeier, D. (2006). Retarded ejaculation: A review. *International Journal of STDs and AIDS, 17,* 143–150.

Richters, J., Grulich, A.E., De Visser, R.O., & Rissel, C.E. (2003). Sex in Australia: Autoerotic, esoteric and other sexual practices engaged in by a representative sample of adults. *Australian & New Zealand Journal of Public Health,* 27(2), p180–190.

Richters, J., Hendry, O., & Kippax, S. (2003). When safe sex isn't safe. *Culture, Health & Sexuality,* 5(1), 37–52.

Rideout, V.J., Foehr, U.G., & Roberts, D.F. (2010). *Generation M2: Media in the lives of 8- to 18-year-olds.* Menlo Park, CA: Kaiser Family Foundation.

Ridge, R.D., & Reber, J.S. (2002). "I think she's attracted to me": The effect of men's beliefs on women's behavior in a job interview scenario. *Basic and Applied Social Psychology, 24*(1), 1–14.

Rieger, G., Chivers, M.L., & Bailey, J.M. (2005). Sexual arousal patterns of gay men. *Psychological Science, 16*(8), 579–584.

Riggle, E., Rostosky, S., & Horne, S. (2010). Psychological distress, well-being, and legal recognition in same-sex couple relationships. *Journal of Family Psychology, 24*(1), 82–86.

Riggs, J.M. (2005). Impressions of mothers and fathers on the periphery of child care. *Psychology of Women Quarterly, 29*(1), 58.

Ringdahl, E., & Teague, L. (2006). Testicular torsion. *American Family Physician, 74*(10), 1739–1743.

Riordan, M., & Kreuz, R. (2010). Cues in computer-mediated communication: A corpus analysis. *Computers in Human Behavior, 26*(6), 1806–1817.

Rischer, C.E., & Easton, T. (1992). *Focus on Human Biology*. New York, NY: HarperCollins.

Risman, B., & Schwartz, P. (1988). Sociological research on male and female homosexuality. *Annual Review of Sociology, 14*, 125–147.

Rittenhouse, C.A. (1991). The emergence of premenstrual syndrome as a social problem. *Social Problems, 38*(3), 412–425.

Rivers, I., & Noret, N. (2008). Well-being among same-sex- and opposite-sex-attracted youth at school. *School Psychology Review, 37*, 174–187.

Rivers, J., Mason, J., Silvestre, E., Gillespie, S., Mahy, M., & Monasch, R. (2008). Impact of orphanhood on underweight prevalence in sub-Saharan Africa. *Food and Nutrition Bulletin, 29*(1), 32–42.

Rizwan, S., Manning, J., & Brabin, B.J. (2007). Maternal smoking during pregnancy and possible effects of in utero testosterone: Evidence from the 2D:4D finger length ratio. *Early Human Development, 83*, 87–90.

Roan, S. (2010, August 15). Medical treatment carries possible side effect of limiting homosexuality. *Los Angeles Times*. Retrieved October 15, 2010, from http://articles.latimes.com/2010/aug/15/science/la-sci-adrenal-20100815.

Roberts, A., Austin, S., Corliss, H., Vandermor-ris, A., & Koenen, K. (2010). Pervasive trauma exposure among US sexual orientation minority adults and risk of post-traumatic stress disorder. *American Journal of Public Health, 100*(12), 2433–2441.

Roberts, D.F., Foehr, U.G., & Rideout, V. (2005). Generation M: Media in the lives of 8–18-year-olds. Retrieved November 3, 2005, from http://www.kff.org/entmedia/upload/Generation-M-Media-in-the-Lives-of-8-18-Year-olds-Report.pdf.

Roberts, J.E., & Oktay, K. (2005). Fertility preservation: A comprehensive approach to the young woman with cancer. *Journal of the National Cancer Institute Monograph, 34*, 57–59.

Roberts, L.W., Clifton, R.A., Ferguson, B., Kampen, K., & Langlois, S. (Eds.). (2005). *Recent social trends in Canada—1960–2000*. Montreal: McGill-Queens University Press.

Roberts, S. (2010, September 15). Study finds wider view of family. *New York Times*. Retrieved September 15, 2010, from http://query.nytimes.com/gst/fullpage.html?res59504E7DE163AF936A2575AC0A9669D8B63.

Roberts, S., Gosling, L., Carter, V., & Petrie, M. (2008). MHC-correlated odour preferences in humans and the use of oral contraceptives. *Proceedings of the Royal Society B, 275*(1652), 2715–2722.

Roberts, S., & Roiser, J.P. (2010). In the nose of the beholder: Are olfactory influences on human mate choice driven by variation in immune system genes or sex hormone levels? *Experimental Biology and Medicine, 235*(11), 1277–1281.

Robertson, J.R. (1992). Obscenity: The decision of the Supreme Court of Canada in *R. v. Butler*. Ottawa, ON: Minister of Supply and Services.

Robin, G., Boitrelle, F., Marcelli, F., Colin, P., Leroy-Martin, B., Mitchell, V., Dewailly, D., & Rigot, J.M. (2010). Cryptorchidism: From physiopathology to infertility. *Gynecological Obstetrics and Fertility, 38*(10), 588–599.

Robinson, E.D., & Evans, B.G.I. (1999). Oral sex and HIV transmission. *AIDS, 16*(6), 737–738.

Robinson, P. (1993). *Freud and his critics*. Berkeley, CA: University of California Press.

Robinson, S.E., & Krussman, H.W. (1982–1983). *Sex for money: Profile of a John. Research Reports, Journal of Sex Education and Therapy*, 8–9.

Robson, J. (2013). *Sex and sexuality in classical Athens*. Edinburgh: Edinburgh University Press.

Roby, J.L., & Shaw, S.A. (2006). The African orphan crisis and international adoption. *Social Work, 51*(3), 199–210.

Rodriguez, I. (2004). Pheromone receptors in mammals. *Hormones & Behavior, 46*(3), 219–230.

Rogers, S.C. (1978). Woman's place: A critical review of anthropological theory. *Comparative Studies in Society and History, 20*, 123–162.

Roisman, G., Clausell, Holland, A., Fortuna, K., & Elieff, C. (2008). Adult romantic relationships as contexts of human development: A multimethod comparison of same-sex couples with opposite-sex dating, engaged, and married dyads. *Developmental Psychology, 44*(1), 91–101.

Rome, E. (1998). Anatomy and physiology of sexuality and reproduction. In The Boston Women's Health Collective (Eds.), *The new our bodies, ourselves* (pp. 241–258). Carmichael, CA: Touchstone Books.

Romer, D., Sznitman, S., DiClemente, R., Salazar, L., Vanable, P., Carey, M., Hennessy, M., Brown, L., Valois, R., Stanton, B., Fortune, T., & Juzang, I. (2009). Mass media as an HIV-prevention strategy: Using culturally sensitive messages to reduce HIV-associated sexual behavior of at-risk African American youth. *American Journal of Public Health, 99*, 2150–2159.

Ronai, C.R., & Cross, R. (1998). Dancing with identity: Narrative resistance of male and female stripteasers. *Deviant Behavior, 19*(2), 99–129.

Röndahl, G., Innala, S., & Carlsson, M. (2004). Nurses' attitudes towards lesbians and gay men. *Journal of Advanced Nursing, 47*, 386–392.

Rosa, M., & Masood, S. (2012). Cytomorphology of male breast lesions: Diagnostic pitfalls and clinical implications. *Diagnostic Cytopathology, 40*(2), 179–184.

Rosario, M., Schrimshaw, E., & Hunter, J. (2004). Predictors of substance use over time among gay, lesbian, and bisexual youths. An examination of three hypotheses. *Addictive Behaviors, 29*(8), 1623–1631.

Rosen, R.C., & Leiblum, S.R. (1987). Current approaches to the evaluation of sexual desire disorders. *Journal of Sex Research, 23*, 141–162.

Rosenbaum, T. (2011). Addressing anxiety in vivo in physiotherapy treatment of women with severe vaginismus: A clinical approach. *Journal of Sex and Marital Therapy, 37*(2), 89–93.

Rosenblatt, P.C., Karis, T.A., & Powell, R.D. (1995). *Multiracial couples*. Thousand Oaks, CA: Sage.

Rosenthal, R., & Rosnow, R.L. (1975). *The volunteer subject*. New York, NY: Wiley.

Rosman, J.P., & Resnick, P.J. (1989). Sexual attraction to corpses: A psychiatric review of necrophilia. *Bulletin of the American Academy of Psychiatry and the Law, 17*, 153–163.

Ross, B.L. (2006). "Troublemakers" in tassels and g-strings: Striptease dancers and the union question in Vancouver, 1965–1980. *Canadian Review of Sociology & Anthropology, 43*(3), 329–344.

Ross, B.L. (2012). "Outdoor brothel culture: the un/making of a transsexual stroll in Vancouver's West End, 1975–1984," *Journal of Historical Sociology, 25*, 126–150

Ross, C.A. (2009). Psychodynamics of eating disorder behavior in sexual abuse survivors. *American Journal of Psychotherapy, 63*(3), 211–227.

Ross, L.E. (2005). Perinatal mental health in lesbian mothers: A review of potential risk and protective factors. *Women Health, 41*(3), 113–128.

Ross, L.E., Steele, L., & Epstein, R. (2006a). Lesbian and bisexual women's recommendations for improving the provision of assisted reproductive technology services. *Fertility and Sterility, 86,* 735–738.

Ross, L.E., Steele, L., & Sapiro, B. (2005). Perceptions of predisposing and protective factors for perinatal depression in same-sex parents. *Journal of Midwifery Women's Health, 50,* 65–70.

Ross, L.E., Steele, L., Goldfinger, C., & Strike, C. (2007). Perinatal depressive symptomatology among lesbian and bisexual women. *Archives of Women's Mental Health, 10,* 1434–1816.

Ross, L.E., Steele, L.S., & Epstein, R. (2006b). Service use and gaps in services for lesbian and bisexual women during donor insemination, pregnancy, and the postpartum period. *Journal of Obstetrics and Gynecology Canada, 28,* 505–511.

Ross, P., & Blum, I. (2013). Sexuality and HIV/AIDS: An exploration of older heterosexual women's knowledge levels. *Journal of Women & Aging, 25*(2), 165–182.

Rossato M., Pagano C., & Vettor R. (2008). The cannabinoid system and male reproductive functions. *Journal of Neuroendocrinology, 20*(Suppl 1), 90–93.

Rossi, A.S. (1978). The biosocial side of parenthood. *Human Nature, 1,* 72–79.

Rossi, W.A. (1993). *The sex life of the foot and shoe.* Melbourne, FL: Krieger.

Rotermann, M. (2005). Sex, condoms and STDs among young people. *Health Reports, 16,* 38–45.

Rotermann, M. (2008). Trends in teen sexual behaviour and condom use. *Health Reports, 19*(3), 1–5.

Rotermann, M. (2012). Sexual behaviour and condom use of 15- to 24-year-olds in 2003 and 2009/2010. *Health Reports, 23*(1), 1–5.

Roth, P. (2014). Edmonton John school finding success curbing sexual exploitation. *Edmonton Sun,* January 25, http://www.edmontonsun.com/2014/01/25/edmonton-john-school-finding-success-curbing-sexual-exploitation.

Rothman, S.M. (1978). *Woman's proper place.* New York, NY: Basic Books.

Rothon, R. (1007). The forgotton hero. *Daily Xtra,* January 18. http://dailyxtra.com/vancouver/ideas/the-forgotten-hero-10321s

Rothschild, B.M. (2005). History of syphilis. *Clinical Infectious Diseases, 40*(10), 1454–1463.

Rotondi, N.K., Bauer, G., Scanlon, K., Kaay, M. Travers, R., & Travers, A. (2013). Non-prescribed hormone use and self-performed surgeries: "Do-it-yourself" transitions in transgender communities in Ontario, Canada. *American Journal of Public Health, 103*(10), 1830–1836.

Roughgarden, J. (2004). A review of evolution, gender, and rape. *Ethology, 110*(1), 76.

Rowland, D., McMahon, C.G., Abdo, C., Chen, J., Jannini, E., Waldinger, M.D., & Ahn, T.Y. (2010). Disorders of orgasm and ejaculation in men. *Journal of Sexual Medicine, 7*(4 Pt 2), 1668–1686.

Rowlands, S., Sujan, M.A., & Cooke, M. (2010). A risk management approach to the design of contraceptive implants. *Journal of Family Planning and Reproductive Health Care, 36*(4), 191–195.

Roy, J.R., Chakraborty, S., & Chakraborty, T.R. (2010). Estrogen-like endocrine disrupting chemicals affecting puberty in humans—a review. *Medical Science Monitor, 15*(6), 137–145.

Royal Canadian Mounted Police. (2012). Criminal Harassment: Stalking—It's NOT Love. Retrieved from http://www.rcmp-grc.gc.ca/cp-pc/crimhar-eng.htm.

Ruan, F., & Lau, M.P. (2004). China. In R.T. Francoeur & R.J. Noonan (Eds.), *The Continuum International encyclopedia of sexuality* (pp. 182–209). New York/London: Continuum International.

Rubin, B., & Soto, A. (2009). Bisphenol A: Perinatal exposure and body weight. *Molecular and Cellular Endocrinology, 302*(1–2), 55–62.

Rubin, G. (2011). *Devitions: A Gayle Rubin reader.* Durham, NC: Duke University Press.

Rubin, R.H. (2001). Alternative lifestyles revisited, or whatever happened to swingers, group marriages, and communes. *Journal of Family Issues, 22*(6), 711–728.

Rubin, Z. (1970). Measurement of romantic love. *Journal of Personality & Social Psychology, 16*(2), 265–273.

Rubin, Z. (1973). *Liking and loving: An invitation to social psychology.* Oxford, England: Holt, Rinehart & Winston.

Rudd, J.M., & Herzberger, S.D. (1999). Brother-sister incest, father-daughter incest: A comparison of characteristics and consequences. *Child Abuse and Neglect, 23*(9), 915–928.

Rudgley, R. (1999). *The lost Civilizations of the Stone Age.* New York, NY: Simon and Schuster.

Rudolph, K., Caldwell, M., & Conley, C. (2005). Need for approval and children's well-being. *Child Development, 76*(2), 309–323.

Rudy, K. (2000). Queer theory and feminism. *Women's Studies, 29*(2), 195–217.

Rue, V.M., Coleman, P.K., Rue, J.J., & Reardon, D.C. (2004). Induced abortion and traumatic stress: A preliminary comparison of American and Russian women. *Medical Science Monitor, 10*(10), SR5–SR16.

Ruffman, T., Halberstadt, J., & Murray, J. (2009). Recognition of facial, auditory, and bodily emotions in older adults. *Journals of Gerontology, 64B*(6), 696.

Ruhl, M., Knuschke, T., Schewior, K., Glavinic, L., Neumann-Haefelin, C., Chang, D.I., Klein, M., Heinemann, F.M., Tenckhoff, H., Wiese, M., Horn, P.A., Viazov, S., Spengler, U., Roggendorf, M., Scherbaum, N., Nattermann, J., Hoffmann, D., Timm, J.; East German HCV Study Group. (2011). The CD81 T-cell response promotes evolution of hepatitis C virus non-structural proteins. *Gastroenterology, 140*(7), 2064–2073.

Rupp, J. (2007). The photography of Joseph Rupp: Bound feet. Retrieved December 19, 2008, from http://www.josephrupp.com/.

Russell, D.E.H. (1984). *Sexual exploitation: Rape, child sexual abuse, and workplace harassment.* Beverly Hills, CA: Sage.

Russell, D.E.H., & Howell, N. (1983). The prevalence of rape in the United States revisited. *Signs: Journal of Women in Culture and Society,* 688–695.

Russell, S., Driscoll, A., & Truong, N. (2002). Adolescent same-sex romantic attractions and relationship: Implications for substance use and abuse. *American Journal of Public Health, 92*(2), 198–202.

Rust, P.C.R. (2000). *Bisexuality in the U.S.* New York, NY: Columbia University Press.

Ryan, C., & Futterman, D. (2001). Social and developmental challenges for lesbian, gay, bisexual youth. *SIECUS Report, 29*(4), 5–18.

Ryan, C., Huebner, D., Diaz, R.M., & Sanchez, J. (2009). Family rejection as a predictor of negative health outcomes in white and Latino lesbian, gay, and bisexual young adults. *Pediatrics, 123*(1), 346–352.

Ryan, C.J., & Small, E.J. (2005). Progress in detection and treatment of prostate cancer. *Current Opinion in Oncology, 17*(3), 257–260.

Rye, B.J., & Meaney, G.J. (2007). Voyeurism: It is good as long as we do not get caught. *International Journal of Sexual Health, 19*(1), 47–56.

Sabatier, R. (1988). *Blaming others: Prejudice, race and worldwide AIDS.* Philadelphia, PA: New Society Publishers.

Sabelli, H., Fink, P., Fawcett, J., & Tom, C. (1996). Sustained antidepressant effect of PEA replacement. *Journal of Neuropsychiatry and Clinical Neuroscience, 8*(2), 168–171.

Sabharwal, S.K., & Sen, R. (2012). Portrayal of sexual minorities in Hindi films. *Global Media Journal: Indian Edition, 3*(1), 1–13.

Sable, M., Danis, F., Mauzy, D., & Gallagher, S. (2006). Barriers to reporting sexual assault for women and men: Perspectives of college students. *Journal of American College Health, 55,* 157–162.

Sabo, D.S., & Runfola, R. (1980). *Jock: Sports and male identity.* New York, NY: Prentice Hall.

Saewyc, E.M., Bearinger, L.H., Heinz, P.A., Blum, R.W., & Resnick, M. (1998). Gender differences in health and risk behaviors among bisexual and homosexual adolescents. *Journal of Adolescent Health, 23*(2), 181–188.

Safarinejad, M.R. (2008). Evaluation of the safety and efficacy of bremelanotide, a melanocortin receptor agonist, in female subjects with arousal disorder: A double-blind placebo-controlled, fixed dose, randomized study. *Journal of Sexual Medicine, 5,* 887–897.

Saftlas, A., Wallis, A., Shochet, T., Harland, K., Dickey, P., & Peek-Asa, C. (2010). Prevalence of intimate partner violence among an abortion clinic population. *American Journal of Public Health, 100*(8), 1412–1415.

Saha, P., Majumdar, S., Pal, D., Pal, B.C., & Kabir, S.N. (2010). Evaluation of spermicidal activity of MI-saponin A. *Reproductive Science, 17*(5), 454–464.

Said, E. (1978). *Orientalism.* New York, NY: Pantheon Books.

Saikaku, I. (1990). *The great mirror of male love* (Translated with an introduction by Paul Gordon Schlalow). Stanford: Stanford University Press.

Sakorafas, G.H. (2005). The management of women at high risk for the development of breast cancer: Risk estimation and preventative strategies. *Cancer Treatment Reviews, 29*(2), 79–89.

Salazar-Gonzalez, J.F., Salazar, M.G., Learn, G.H., Fouda, G.G., Kang, H.H., Mahlokozera, T., Wilks, A.B., Lovingood, R.V., et al. (2011). Origin and evolution of HIV-1 in breast milk determined by single-genome amplification and sequencing. *Journal of Virology, 85*(6), 2751–2763.

Saleh, F.M., & Berlin, F. (2003). Sex hormones, neurotransmitters, and psychopharmacological treatments in men with paraphilic disorders. *Journal of Child Sexual Abuse, 12,* 233–253.

Salehi, R., & Flicker, S. (2010). Predictors of exposure to sexual health education among teens who are newcomers to Canada. *Canadian Journal of Human Sexuality, 19*(4), 157–158.

Salter, D., McMillan, D., Richards, M., Talbot, T., Hodges, J., Bentovim, A., et al. (2003). Development of sexually abusive behavior in sexually victimized males. *Lancet, 361*(9356), 471–476.

Samter, W., & Burleson, B.R. (2005). The role of communication in same-sex friendships: A comparison among African Americans, Asian Americans, and European Americans. *Communication Quarterly, 53,* 265–284.

Samuel, A.S., & Naz, R.K. (2008). Isolation of human single chain variable fragment antibodies against specific sperm antigens or immunocontraceptive development. *Human Reproduction, 23*(6), 1324–1337.

Samuel, L. (2010). Mating, dating and marriage: Intergenerational cultural retention and the construction of diasporic identities among South Asian immigrants in Canada. *Journal of Intercultural Studies, 31*(1), 95–110.

Sánchez, F., & Vilain, E. (2010). Genes and brain sex differences. *Progress in Brain Research, 186,* 65–76.

Sánchez, J.M., Milam, M.R., Tomlinson, T.M., & Beardslee, M.A. (2008). Cardiac troponin I elevation after orogenital sex during pregnancy. *Obstetrics and Gynecology, 111,* 487–489.

Sanday, P.R. (1981). The sociocultural context of rape: A cross-cultural study. *Journal of Social Issues, 37,* 5–27.

Sanders, S.A., & Reinisch, J.M. (1999). Would you say you "had sex" if... ? *Journal of the American Medical Association, 281*(3), 275–277.

Sandnabba, N.K., & Ahlberg, C. (1999). Parents' attitudes and expectations about children's cross-gender behavior. *Sex Roles, 40*(3–4), 249–263.

Sandowski, C.L. (1989). *Sexual concerns when illness or disability strikes.* Springfield, IL: Charles C. Thomas.

Santa Ana, R. (2008, June 30). Watermelon may have Viagra-effect. *Texas A&M Agricultural Communication.* Retrieved August 31, 2008, from http://vfic.tamu.edu/Documents/News/2008/0630%20agnews%20watermelon.pdf.

Santos, P., Schinemann, J., Gabarcio, J., & da Graca, G. (2005). New evidence that the MHC influences odor perception in humans: A study with 58 Southern Brazilian students. *Hormones and Behavior, 47*(4), 384–388.

Sarrel, P., & Masters, W. (1982). Sexual molestation of men by women. *Archives of Sexual Behavior, 11,* 117–131.

Sartorius, A., Ruf, M., Kief, C., & Demirakca, T. (2008). Abnormal amygdala activation profile in pedophilia. *European Archives of Psychiatry and Clinical Neuroscience, 258,* 271–279.

Saslow, B., Boetes, C., Burke, W., Harms, S., Leach, M., Lehman, C., et al. (2007). American Cancer Society guidelines for breast screening with MRI as an adjunct to mammography. *CA Cancer Journal for Clinicians, 57,* 75–89.

Sassler, S., Cunningham, A., & Lichter, D. (2009). Intergenerational patterns of union formation and relationship quality. *Journal of Family Issues, 30*(6), 757–786.

Sati, N. (1998). Equivocal lifestyles. The Living Channel. Retrieved July 7, 2003, from http://www.glas.org/ahbab/Articles/arabia1.html.

Sato, S.M., Schulz, K.M., Sisk, C.L., & Wood, R.I. (2008). Adolescents and androgens, receptors and rewards. *Hormones and Behavior 53*(5), 647–658.

Sauerteig, L.D.H. (2012). Loss of innocence: Albert Moll, Sigmund Freud and the invention of childhood sexuality around 1900. *Medical History, 56*(2), 156–183.

Saulny, S. (2010, January 30). Black? White? Asian? More young Americans choose all of the above. *New York Times.* Retrieved January 30, 2011, from http://www.nytimes.com/2011/01/30/us/30mixed.html?src5twrhp.

Savareux, L., Droupy, S.; les membres du comité d'andrologie de l'AFU. (2009). [Evaluation of sexual dysfunction in prostate cancer management]. *Progress in Urology, 19*(Suppl. 4), S189–S192.

Savic, I., Berglund, H., & Lindström, P. (2005). Brain response to putative pheromones in homosexual men. *Proceedings of the National Academy of Sciences, 102,* 7356–7361.

Savic, I., Garcia-Falgueras, A., & Swaab, D. (2010). Sexual differentiation of the human brain in relation to gender identity and sexual orientation. *Progress in Brain Research, 186,* 41–62.

Savin-Williams, R.C. (2001). *"Mom, Dad. I'm gay." How families negotiate coming out.* Washington, DC: American Psychological Association.

Savin-Williams, R.C., & Diamond, L.M. (2000). Sexual identity trajectories among sexual minority youths: Gender comparisons. *Archives of Sexual Behavior, 29,* 607–627.

Savin-Williams, R.C., & Dube, E.M. (1998). Parental reactions to their child's disclosure of a gay/lesbian identity. *Family Relations, 47,* 7–13.

Sawyer, R.G., Thompson, E.E., & Chicorelli, A.M. (2002). Rape myth acceptance among intercollegiate student athletes. *American Journal of Health Studies, 18*(1), 19–25.

Sayal, K., Heron, J., Golding, J., & Emond, A. (2007). Prenatal alcohol exposure and gender differences in childhood mental health problems: A longitudinal population-based study. *Pediatrics, 119,* 426–434.

Scaravelli, G., Vigiliano, V., Mayorga, J.M., Bolli, S., De Luca, R., & D'Aloja, P. (2010). Analysis of oocyte cryopreservation in assisted reproduction: The Italian National Register data from 2005 to 2007. *Reproductive Biomedicine Online, 21*(4), 496–500.

Scarce, M. (1997). *The hidden toll of stigma and shame.* New York, NY: De Capo Press.

Schachter, S., & Singer, J. (1962). Cognitive, social, and physiological determinants of emotional state. *Psychological Review, 69*(5), 379–399.

Schachter, S., & Singer, J. (2001). Cognitive, social, and physiological determinants of emotional state. In W. Parrott (Ed.), *Emotions in social psychology: Essential readings* (pp. 76–93). New York, NY: Psychology Press.

Schick, V., Herbenick, D., Jozkowski, K.N., Jawad-Wessel, S., & Reece, M. (2013). The sexual consumer: Characteristics, expectations, and experiences of women attending in-home sex toy parties. *Journal of Sex & Marital Therapy, 39*(2), 160–175.

Schick, V., Herbenick, D., Reece, M., Sanders, S.A., Dodge, B., Middlestadt, S.E., & Fortenberry, J.D. (2010). Sexual behaviors, condom use, and sexual health of Americans over 50: Implications for sexual health promotion for older adults. *Journal of Sexual Medicine, 7*(Suppl. 5), 315–329.

Schiffer, J.T., Abu-Raddad, L., Mark, K.E., Zhu, J., Selke, S., Koelle, D.M., Wald, A., & Corey, L. (2010). Mucosal host immune response predicts the severity and duration of herpes simplex virus-2 genital tract shedding episodes. *Proceedings of the National Academy of Sciences, 107*(44), 18973–18978.

Schiffrin, H., Edelman, A., Falkenstern, M., & Stewart, C. (2010). The associations among computer-mediated communication, relationships, and well-being. *Cyber-psychology, Behavior, and Social Networking, 13*(3), 299–306.

Schildkraut, J.M., Calingaert, B., Marchbanks, P.A., Moorman, P.G., & Rodriguez, G.C. (2002). Impact of progestin and estrogen potency in oral contraceptives on ovarian cancer risk. *Journal of the National Cancer Institute, 94*, 32–38.

Schindler, A.E. (2010). Non-contraceptive benefits of hormonal contraceptives. *Minerva Ginecol, 62*(4), 319–329.

Schissel, B., & Fedec, K. (1999). The selling of innocence: The gestalt of danger in the lives of youth prostitutes. *Canadian Journal of Criminology, 41*(1), 33–56.

Schlegel, R. (2007, January 17). HPV vaccine. *Washington Post*. Retrieved September 16, 2008, from http://www.washingtonpost.com/wp-dyn/content/discussion/2007/01/16/DI2007011600929.html.

Schlicter, A. (2004). Queer at last? *GLW: A Journal of Lesbian and Gay Studies, 10*(4), 543-565.

Schmidt, H.M., Hagen, M., Kriston, L., Soares-Weiser, K., Maayan, N., & Berner, M.M. (2012). Management of sexual dysfunction due to antipsychotic drug therapy. *The Cochrane Database of Systematic Reviews*, Nov 14, 11.

Schneider, F., Habel, U., Kessler, C., Salloum, J.B., & Posse, S. (2000). Gender differences in regional cerebral activity during sadness. *Human Brain Mapping, 9*(4), 226–238.

Schneider, L., Mori, L., Lambert, P., & Wong, A. (2009). The role of gender and ethnicity in perceptions of rape and its aftereffects. *Sex Roles, 60*(5–6), 410–422.

Schneider, M. (1989). Sappho was a right-on adolescent: Growing up lesbian. *Journal of Homosexuality, 17*, 111–130.

Schover, L., & Jensen, S.B. (1988). *Sexuality and chronic illness*. New York, NY: Guilford Press.

Schrodt, P. (2009). Family strength and satisfaction as functions of family communication environments. *Communication Quarterly, 57*(2), 171–186.

Schrodt, P., & Ledbetter, A. (2007). Communication processes that mediate family communication patterns and mental well-being: A means and covariance structures analysis of young adults from divorced and non-divorced families. *Human Communication Research, 33*, 330–356.

Schrodt, P., Ledbetter, A., Jembert, K., Larson, L., Brown, N., & Glonek, K. (2009). Family communication patterns as mediators of communication competence in the parent-child relationship. *Journal of Social and Personal Relationships, 26*(6–7), 853–874.

Schuberg, K. (2009, October 16). Despite widespread contraceptive use, 1/3 of pregnancies in France 'unplanned,' new study confirms. CBS News. Retrieved October 17, 2009, from http://www.cnsnews.com/node/55580.

Schuler, P., Vinci, D., Isosaari, R., Philipp, S., Todorovich, J., Roy, J., & Evans, R. (2008). Body-shape perceptions and body mass index of older African American and European American Women. *Journal of Cross-Cultural Gerontology, 23*(3), 255–264.

Schultheiss, D. (2008). Urogenital infections and male sexuality: Effects on ejaculation and erection. *Andrologia, 40*, 125–129.

Schumann, K., & Ross, M. (2010). Why women apologize more than men: Gender differences in threshholds for perceiving offensive behavior. *Psychological Science, 21*(11), 1649–1655.

Schützwohl, A. (2008). The intentional object of romantic jealousy. *Evolution and Human Behavior, 29*, 92–99.

Schwartz, D. (2013). We're happy with our sex lives, Canadian university students say. http://www.cbc.ca/m/news/health/we-re-happy-with-our-sex-lives-canadian-university-students-say-1.1376119.

Schwartz, G., Kim, R., Kolundzija, A., Rieger, G., & Sanders, A. (2010). Biodemographic and physical correlates of sexual orientation in men. *Archives of Sexual Behavior, 39*, 93–109.

Schwartz, J.L., & Gabelnick, H.L. (2002). Current contraceptive research. *Perspectives on Sexual and Reproductive Health, 34*(6), 310–316.

Schweitzer, D. (2000). Striptease: The art of spectacle and transgression. *Journal of Popular Culture, 34*(1), 65–75.

Scott-Sheldon, L.A., Carey, M.P., Vanable, P.A., Senn, T.E., Coury-Doniger, P., & Urban, M.A. (2009). Alcohol consumption, drug use, and condom use among STD clinic patients. *Journal of Studies on Alcohol & Drugs, 70*(5), 762–770.

Scully, D., & Marolla, J. (1983). *Incarcerated rapists: Exploring a sociological model*. Final Report for Department of Health and Human Services, NIMH.

Searcy, W.A., & Nowicki, S. (2005). *The evolution of animal communication*. Princeton, NJ: Princeton University Press.

Second World Whore's Conference, (1986). Draft statement on prostitution and human rights, Internation Committee for Prostitutes' Rights, European Parliament, Brussels, October 1–4 (Author Aveline's files).

Sedgh, G., Hussain, R., Bankole, A., & Singh, S. (2007a). Unmet need for contraception in developing countries: Levels and reasons for not using a method. Alan Guttmacher Institute, Occasional Report No. 37. Retrieved July 29, 2008, from http://www.guttmacher.org/pubs/2007/07/09/or37.pdf.

Seeber, B., & Barnhart, K. (2006). Suspected ectopic pregnancy. *Obstetrics and Gynecology, 107*(2 pt 1), 399–413.

Sehovic, N., & Smith, K.P. (2010). Risk of venous thromboembolism with drospire-none in combined oral contraceptive products. *Annals of Pharmacotherapy, 44*(5), 898–903.

Seidman, S.N. (2007). Androgens and the aging male. *Psychopharmacological Bulletin, 40*, 205–218.

Seidman, S.N., & Rieder, R.O. (1994). A review of sexual behavior in the U.S. *American Journal of Psychiatry, 151*, 330–341.

Seiffge-Krenke, I., Shulman, S., & Klesinger, N. (2001). Adolescent precursors of romantic relationships in young adulthood. *Journal of Social & Personal Relationships, 18*(3), 327–346.

Seki, K., Matsumoto, D., & Imahori, T.T. (2002). The conceptualization and expression of intimacy in Japan and the United States. *Journal of Cross Cultural Psychology, 33*, 303–319.

Seligman, L., & Hardenburg, S.A. (2000). Assessment and treatment of paraphilias. *Journal of Counseling and Development, 78*(1), 107–113.

Sell, R., Wells, J., & Wypij, D. (1995). The prevalence of homosexual behavior and attraction in the U.S., the U.K and France: Results of a national population-based sample. *Archives of Sexual Behavior, 24*, 235–249.

Seltzer, J.A. (2000). Families formed outside of marriage. *Journal of Marriage and Family, 62*(4), 1247.

Sepilian, V., & Wood, E. (2004). Ectopic pregnancy. Retrieved July 19, 2005, from http://www.emedicine.com/med/topic3212.htm.

Seppa, N. (2001). Study reveals male link to pre-eclampsia. *Science News, 159*(12), 181–182.

Serati, M., Salvatore, S., Siesto, G., Cattoni, E., Zanirato, M., Khullar, V., Cromi, A., Ghezzi, F., & Bolis, P. (2010). Female sexual function during pregnancy and after child-birth. *Journal of Sexual Medicine, 7*(8), 2782–2790.

Serbin, L.A., & Sprafkin, C. (1986). The salience of gender and the process of sex typing in three- to seven-year-old children. *Child Development, 57*(5), 1188–1199.

Serefoglu, E.C., Yaman, O., Cayan, S., Asci, R., Orhan, I., Usta, M.F., Ekmekcioglu, O., Kendirci, M., Semerci, B., & Kadioglu, A. (2011). Prevalence of the complaint of ejaculating prematurely and the four premature ejaculation syndromes: Results from the Turkish Society of Andrology Sexual Health Survey. *Journal of Sexual Medicine, 8*(2), 540–548.

Serino, L., Moriel, D., Rappuoli, R., & Pizza, M. (2010). Towards a vaccine against Esche-richia coliassociated urinary tract infections. *Future Microbiology, 5*(3), 351–354.

Sethi, A. (2007). Domestic sex trafficking of Aboriginal girls in Canada: Issues and implications. *First Peoples Child & Family Review, 3*(3), 57–71.

Seto, M. (2008). Pedophilia: Psychopathology and theory. In D. Laws & W. O'Donohue (Eds.), *Sexual deviance: Theory, assessment and treatment* (2nd ed., pp. 164–183). New York, NY: Guilford Press.

Seveso, M., Taverna, G., Giusti, G., Benetti, A., Maugeri, O., Piccinelli, A., & Graziotti, P. (2010). Corporoplasty by plication: Outpatient surgery for the correction of penile cancer. *Archives of Italian Urological Andrology, 82*(3), 164–166.

Sex Information and Education Council of Canada (SIECCAN). (2009). Sexual health education in the schools: Questions and answers (3rd ed.). *Canadian Journal of Human Sexuality, 18*(1–2), 47–60.

Sex Information and Education Council of Canada (SIECCAN). (2010). *Sexual health education in the schools: Questions & answers* (3rd ed.). Toronto: SIECCAN.

Sexual Health Toronto. (2007). Retrieved January 10, 2015, from http://www.toronto.ca/legdocs/mmis/2007/hl/bgrd/backgroundfile-7293.pdf.

Sexuality Education and Information Council of the United States (SEICUS). (2007). Fact sheet: What the research says. Retrieved from http:// http://www.siecus.org/_data/global/images/research_says.pdf.

sexualityandU.ca. (2012). Retrieved December 16, 2015, from http://www.sexualityandu.ca/sexual-health/statistics1/statistics-on-sexual-intercourse-experience-among-canadian-teenagers.

Seymour, A., Murray, M., Sigmon, J., Hook, M., Edmunds, C., Gaboury, M., et al. (Eds.).

(2000). Retrieved May 22, 2003, from http://www.ojp.usdoj.gov/ovc/assist/nvaa2000/academy/welcome.html.

Shackelford, T.K., & Goetz, A.T. (2007). Adaptation to sperm competition in humans. *Current Directions in Psychological Science, 16*, 47–50.

Shadiack, A., Sharma, S., Earle, D., Spana, C., & Hallam, T. (2007). Melanocortins in the treatment of male and female sexual dysfunction. *Current Topics in Medical Chemistry, 7,* 1137–1144.

Shafaat, A. (2004). Punishment for adultery in Islam: A detailed examination. Retrieved April 10, 2008, from http://www.islamicperspectives.com/Stoning4.htm.

Shamloul, R. (2005). Treatment of men complaining of short penis. *Urology, 65*(6), 1183–1185.

Shamloul, R. (2010). Natural aphrodisiacs. *Journal of Sexual Medicine, 7*(1 Pt 1), 39–49.

Shapiro, J., Radecki, S., Charchian, A.S., & Josephson, V. (1999). Sexual behavior and AIDS-related knowledge among community college students in Orange County, California. *Journal of Community Health, 24*(1), 29–43.

Shapiro, S., & Dinger, J. (2010). Risk of venous thromboembolism among users of oral contraceptives: A review of two recently published studies. *Journal of Family Planning and Reproductive Health Care, 36*(1), 33–38.

Sharma, O., & Haub, C. (2008). Sex ratio at birth begins to improve in India. Population Reference Bureau. Retrieved February 24, 2011, from http://www.prb.org/Articles/2008/indiasexratio.aspx.

Sharp, P.M., Bailes, E., Chaudhuri, R.R., Rodenburg, C.M., Santiago, M.O., & Hahn, B.H. (2001). The originals of acquired immuno-deficiency viruses: Where and when. *Philosophical Transactions of the Royal Society B: Biological Sciences, 236,* 867–876.

Sharpe, R.M., & Skakkebaek, N.E. (2008). Testicular dysgenesis syndrome: Mechanistic insights and potential new downstream effects. *Fertility and Sterility, 89*(Suppl. 2), e33–38.

Sharpsteen, D.J., & Kirkpatrick, L.A. (1997). Romantic jealousy and adult romantic attachment. *Journal of Personality & Social Psychology, 72*(3), 627–640.

Shaughnessy, K., Byers, S., Clowater, S.L., & Kalinowski, A. (2013). "Self-appraisals of arousal-oriented online sexual activities in university and community samples." *Archives of Sexual Behavior*, June.

Shaver, F.M. (1993). Prostitution a female crime? In E. Adelberg and C. Currie (Eds.), *In conflict with the law: Women and the Canadian justice system*. Vancouver BC: Press Gang.

Shaver, F.M. (2005). Sex work research: Methodological and ethical challenges. *Journal of Interpersonal Violence, 20*(3), 296–319.

Shaver, P., & Hazan, C. (1987). Being lonely, falling in love: Perspectives from attachment theory. *Journal of Social Behavior & Personality, 2*(2, Pt 2), 105–124.

Shaver, P.R., Wu, S., & Schwartz, J.C. (1992). Cross-cultural similarities and differences in emotion and its representation: A prototype approach. In M.S. Clark (Ed.), *Emotion* (pp. 175–212). Newbury Park, CA: Sage.

Sheaffer, A.T., Lange, E., & Bondy, C.A. (2008). Sexual function in women with Turner syndrome. *Journal of Women's Health, 17,* 27–33.

Shear, M.D. (2010, April 16). Obama extends hospital visitation rights to same-sex partners of gays. *The Washington Post*. Retrieved May 11, 2011, from http://www.washingtonpost.com/wp-dyn/content/article/2010/04/15/AR2010041505502. html.

Shechory, M., & Idisis, Y. (2006). Rape myths and social distance toward sex offenders and victims among therapists and students. *Sex Roles, 54,* 651–658.

Sheehan, P. (2007). Hyperemesis gravidarum—assessment and management. *Australian Family Physician, 36,* 698–701.

Sheets, V.L., & Wolf, M.D. (2001). Sexual jealousy in heterosexuals, lesbians, and gays. *Sex Roles, 44*(5–6), 255–276.

Sheldon, K.M. (2007). Gender differences in preferences for singles ads that proclaim extrinsic versus intrinsic values. *Sex Roles, 57,* 119–130.

Shellenbarger, S. (2008). Why some single women choose to freeze their eggs. *Wall Street Journal*, February 14, p. D1.

Shelton, J.F., Tancredi, D.J., & Hertz-Picciotto, I. (2010). Independent and dependent contributions of advanced maternal and paternal ages to autism risk. *Autism Research, 3*(1), 30–39.

Sheppard, C., & Wylie, K.R. (2001). An assessment of sexual difficulties in men after treatment for testicular cancer. *Sexual and Relationship Therapy, 16*(1), 47–58.

Sherfey, J. (1972). *The nature and evolution of female sexuality*. New York, NY: Random House.

Sherr, L., Varrall, R., Mueller, J., Richter, L., Wakhweya, A., Adato, M., Belsey, M., Chandan, U., Drimie, S., Haour-Knipe, V., Hosegood, M., Kimou, J., Madhavan, S., Mathambo, V., & Desmond, C. (2008). A systematic review on the meaning of the concept 'AIDS orphan': Confusion over definitions and implications for care. *AIDS Care, 20*(5), 527–536.

Shettles, L., & Rorvik, D. (1970). *Your baby's sex: Now you can choose*. New York, NY: Dodd, Mead.

Sheynkin, Y., Jung, M., Yoo, P., Schulsinger, D., & Komaroff, E. (2005). Increase in scrotal temperature in laptop computer users. *Human Reproduction, 20*(2), 452–455.

Shibusawa, T. (2009). A commentary on "gender perspectives in cross-cultural couples." *Clinical Social Work Journal, 37*, 230–233.

Shields, R. (2010, May 16). South Africa's shame: The rise of child rape. *The Independent UK.* Retrieved April 20, 2011, from http://www.independent.co.uk/news/world/africa/south-africas-shame-the-rise-of-child-rape-1974578.html.

Shifren, J.L., & Avis, N.E. (2007). Surgical menopause: Effects on psychological well-being and sexuality. *Menopause, 14*, 586–591.

Shifren, J.L., Monz, B.U., Russo, P., Segreti, A., & Johannes, C. (2008). Sexual problems and distress in United States women. *Obstetrics & Gynecology, 112*, 970–978.

Shih, C., Cold, C.J., & Yang, C.C. (2013). Cutaneous corpuscular receptors of the human glans clitoris: Descriptive characteristics and comparison with the glans penis. *The Journal of Sexual Medicine, 10*(7), 1783–1789.

Shih, G., Turok, D.K., & Parker, W.J. (2011). Vasectomy: The other (better) form of sterilization. *Contraception, 83*(4), 310–315.

Shilts, R. (2000). *And the band played on: Politics, people, and the AIDS epidemic.* New York, NY: St. Martin's Press.

Shim, J.W. (2007). Online pornography and rape myth acceptance: Sexually degrading content, anonymous viewing conditions, and the activation of antisocial attitudes. *Dissertation Abstracts International Section A: Humanities and Social Sciences, 67*(12–A), 4378.

Shindel, A.W., Ando, K.A., Breyer, C.J., Lue, B.N., Smith, T.F., & James, F. (2010). Medical student sexuality: How sexual experience and sexuality training impact U.S. and Canadian medical students' comfort in dealing with patients' sexuality in clinical practice. *Academic Medicine, 85*(8), 1321.

Shirpak, K.R., Maticka-Tyndale, E., & Chinichian, M. (2008). Iranian immigrants' perceptions of sexuality in Canada: A symbolic interactionist approach. *The Canadian Journal of Human Sexuality, 16*(3–4), 113–128.

Shoveller, J.A., Johnson, J.L., Langille, D.B., Mitchell, T. (2004). Socio-cultural influences on young people's sexual development. *Social Science & Medicine, 59*(3), 473–487.

Shrewsberry, A., Weiss, A., & Ritenour, C.W. (2010). Recent advances in the medical and surgical treatment of priapism. *Current Urological Reports, 11*(6), 405–413.

Shtarkshall, R.A., & Zemach, M. (2004). Israel. In R.T. Francoeur & R.J. Noonan (Eds.), *The Continuum International encyclopedia of sexuality* (pp. 581–619). New York/London: Continuum International.

Shteynshlyuger, A., & Freyle, J. (2011). Familial testicular torsion in three consecutive generations of first-degree relatives. *Journal of Pediatric Urology, 7,* 86–91.

Shufaro, Y., & Schenker, J.G. (2010). Cryo-preservation of human genetic material. *Annals of New York Academy of Science, 1205,* 220–224.

Shulman, J.L., & Home, S.G. (2003). The use of self-pleasure: Masturbation and body image among African American and European American women. *Psychology of Women Quarterly, 27*(3), 262–269.

Shulman, L.P. (2010). Gynecological management of premenstrual symptoms. *Current Pain and Headache Reports, 14*(5), 367–375.

Shulman, S., Davilla, J., & Shachar-Shapira, L. (2010). Assessing romantic competence among older adolescents. *Journal of Adolescence, 34*(3), 397–406.

Shutty, M.S., & Leadbetter, R.A. (1993). Case report: Recurrent pseduocyesis in a male patient with psychosis, intermittent hyponatremia, and polydipsia. *Psychosomatic Medicine, 55,* 146–148.

Siegel, K., & Raveis, V.H. (1993). AIDS-related reasons for gay men's adoption of celibacy. *AIDS Education and Prevention, 5*(4), 302–310.

Siegel, K., & Schrimshaw, E.W. (2003). Reasons for adopting celibacy among older men and women living with HIV/AIDS. *Journal of Sex Research, 40*(2), 189–200.

Sierra, J.C., Perla, F., & Gutiérrez-Quintanilla, R. (2010). Actitud hacia la masturbación en adolescentes: Propiedades psicométricas de la versión Española del Attitudes Toward Masturbation Inventory. *Universitas Psychologica, 9*(2), 531–542.

Sigal, J., Gibbs, M.S., Goodrich, C., Rashid, T., Anjum, A., Hsu, D., Perrino, C., Boratrav, H., Carson-Arenas, A., et al. (2005). Cross-cultural reactions to academic sexual harassment: Effects of individualist vs. collectivist culture and gender of participants. *Sex Roles, 52*(3–4), 201–215.

Sigusch, V. (2012). The sexologist Albert Moll—between Sigmund Freud and Magnus Hirschfeld. *Medical History, 56*(2), 184–200.

Siker, J.S. (1994). *Homosexuality in the Church: Both sides of the debate.* Louisville, KY: Westminster John Knox Press.

Silbert, M. (1998). Compounding factors in the rape of street prostitutes. In A.W. Burgess (Ed.), *Rape and sexual assault II.* London: Taylor & Francis.

Silverman, E.K. (2004). Anthropology and circumcision. *Annual Reviews in Anthropology, 33*(1), 419–445.

Silverman, J., Decker, M., McCauley, H., Gupta, J., Miller, E., Raj, A., & Goldberg, A. (2010). Male perpetration of intimate partner violence and involvement in abortions: An abortion-related conflict. *American Journal of Public Health, 1100*(8), 1415–1417.

Simforoosh, N., Tabibi, A., Khalili, S., Soltani, M., Afjehi, A., Aalami, F., & Bodoohi, H. (2012). Neonatal circumcision reduces the incidence of asymptomatic urinary tract infection: A large prospective study with long-term follow up using Plastiball. *Journal of Pediatric Urology, Journal of Pediatric Urology, 8*(3), 320–323.

Simmons, M., & Montague, D. (2008). Penile prosthesis implantation: Past, present and future. *International Journal of Impotence Research, 20,* 437–444.

Simon, J.A., & Maamari, R.V. (2013). Ultra-low-dose vaginal estrogen tablets for the treatment of postmenopausal vaginal atrophy. *Climacteric, 16*(Suppl. 1), 37–43.

Simon, R.W. (2002). Revisiting the relationships among gender, martial status, and mental health. *American Journal of Sociology, 107*(4), 1065–1097.

Simpson, J., Collins, W., Tran, S., & Haydon, K. (2007). Attachment and the experience and expression of emotions in romantic relationships: A developmental perspective. *Journal of Personality and Social Psychology, 92*(2), 355–367.

Simpson, J.L., & Lamb, D.J. (2001). Genetic effects of intracytoplasmic sperm injection. *Seminars in Reproductive Medicine, 19*(3), 239–249.

Singer, S.M., Willms, D.G., Adrien, A., Baxter, J., Brabazon, C., Leaune, V., Godin, G. Maticka-Tyndale, E., & Cappon, P. (1996). Many voices—sociocultural results of the ethnocultural communities facing AIDS study in Canada. *Canadian Journal of Public Health/Revue Canadienne De Santé Publique, 87*(Suppl. 1), S26–S32, S28–S35.

Singh, A., Wong, T., & De, P. (2008). Characteristics of primary and late latent syphilis cases which were initially non-reactive with the rapid plasma regain as the screening test. *International Journal of STDs and AIDS, 19,* 464–468.

Singh, J. (2007). India rattled by vibrating condom. June 20. BBC News. http://news.bbc.co.uk/2/hi/6221540.stm.

Sipe, A.W.R. (2004). The crisis of sexual abuse and the celibate/sexual agenda of the church. In T.G. Plante (Ed.), *Sin against the innocents: Sexual abuse by priests and the role of the Catholic Church.* Westport, CT: Praeger Publishers/Greenwood Publishing Group.

Sipski, M., Alexander, C., & Gomez-Marin, O. (2006). Effects of level and degree of spinal cord injury on male orgasm. *Spinal Cord, 44,* 798–804.

Skinner, B.F. (1953). *Science and human behavior.* New York, NY: Macmillan.

Slavney, P.R. (1990). *Perspectives on hysteria.* Baltimore, MD: Johns Hopkins University Press.

Slevin, K.F. (2010). "If I had lots of money...I'd have a body makeover": Managing the aging body. *Social Forces, 88*(3), 1003–1020.

Smith, A., Nes, N., Berg, K.A., Valtonen, M., Mäkinen, A., Lukola, A. (1983). Testicular feminization in the Finnish racoon dog (Nyctereutes procyonoides). *Nordisk Veterinaermedicin, 35*(12), 452–459.

Smith, C.J., McMahon, C., & Shabsigh, R. (2005). Peyronie's disease: The epidemiology, aetiology and clinical evaluation of deformity. *British Journal of Urology International, 95*(6), 729–732.

Smith, C.Y. (2007). Celibacy in marriage: Female object relations and their adult manifestations. Dissertation *Abstracts International: Section B: The Sciences and Engineering, 67*(9–B), 5472.

Smith, D. (1987). *The everyday world as problematic: A feminist sociology.* Boston, MA: Northeast University Press.

Smith, D.K., Taylor, A., Kilmarx, P.H., Sullivan, P., Warner, L., Kamb, M., Bock, N., Kohmescher, B., & Mastro, T.D. (2010). Male circumcision in the United States for the prevention of HIV infection and other adverse health outcomes: Report from a CDC consultation. *Public Health Report, 25*(Suppl. 1), 72–82.

Smith, E.A. (2000). *Hard-boiled: Working-class readers and pulp magazines.* Philadelphia, PA: Temple University Press.

Smith, G., Bartlett, A., & King, M. (2004). Treatments of homosexuality in Britain since the 1950s—an oral history: The experience of patients. *British Medical Journal, 328*, 427.

Smith, G.D., & Travis, L. (2011). Getting to know human papillomavirus (HPV) and the HPV vaccines. *Journal of the American Osteopathic Association, 111*(3 Suppl. 2), S29–S34.

Smith, L.E. (2010). Sexual function of the gynecologic cancer survivor. *Oncology, 24*(10 Suppl.), 41–44.

Smith, M.D., & Morra, N.N. (1994). Obscene and threatening telephone calls to women: Data from a Canadian National Survey. *Gender & Society, 8*(4), 584–596.

Smith, M.E. (2005). Female sexual assault: The impact on the male significant other. *Issues in the Mental Health Nursing, 26*(2), 149–167.

Smith, S.A., & Michel, Y. (2006). A pilot study on the effects of aquatic exercises on discomforts of pregnancy. *Journal of Obstetrics and Gynecological Neonatal Nursing, 35*, 315–323.

Smuts, B.B., & Smuts, R.W. (1993). Male aggression and sexual coercion of females in nonhuman primates and other mammals: Evidence and theoretical implications. *Advances in the Study of Behaviour, 22,* 1–63.

Smylie, L., Maticka-Tyndale, E., & Boyd. D. (2008). Evaluation of a school-based sex education programme delivered to grade nine students in Canada. *Sex Education, 8*(1), 25–46.

Snabes M.C., Zborowski J., & Siems S. (2012). Libigel (testosterone gel) does not differentiate from placebo therapy in the treatment of hypoactive sexual desire disorder in postmenopausal women. *Journal of Sexual Medicine, 9*(Suppl. 3), S171.

So, H.W., & Cheung, F.M. (2005). Review of Chinese sex attitudes & applicability of sex therapy for Chinese couples with sexual dysfunction. *Journal of Sex Research, 42*(2), 93–102.

Soares, C. (2010). Can depression be a menopause-associated risk? *BMC Medicine, 8,* 79.

Sobsey, D. (1994). *Violence and abuse in the lives of people with disabilities.* Baltimore, MD: Paul H. Brookes.

Society for Obstetrics and Gynecology in Canada. (2007). Retrieved from http://sogc.org/wp-content/uploads/2013/01/gui262CPG1107E.pdf .

Soloman, S.E., Rothblum, D., & Balsam, K.F. (2005). Money, housework, sex, and conflict: Same-sex couples in civil unions, those not in civil unions, and heterosexual married siblings. *Sex Roles, 52,* 561–575.

Song, A., & Halpern-Felsher, B. (2011). Predictive relationship between adolescent oral and vaginal sex: Results from a prospective, longitudinal study. *Archives of Pediatrics & Adolescent Medicine, 165*(3), 243–249.

Song, L.M., Gu, Y., Lu, W., Liang, X., & Chen, Z. (2006). A phase II randomized controlled trial of a novel male contraception, an intravas device. *International Journal of Andrology, 29,* 489–495.

Sontag, S. (1979). The double-standard of aging. In J.H. Williams (Ed.), *Psychology of women: Selected readings* (pp. 462–478). New York, NY: W.W. Norton Publishers.

Soon, J.A., Levine, M., Osmond, B.L., Ensom, M.H., & Fielding, D.W. (2005). Effects of making emergency contraception available without a physician's prescription: A population-based study. *Canadian Medical Association Journal, 172*(7), 878–883.

Soper, D.E. (2010). Pelvic inflammatory disease. *Obstetrics and Gynecology, 116*(2 Pt 1), 419–428.

Sorenson, S., & Brown, V. (1990). Interpersonal violence and crisis intervention on the college campus. *New Directions for Student Services, 49,* 57–66.

Southern Poverty Law Center. (2015). Retrieved from http://www.splcenter.org/get-informed/intelligence-files/ideology/anti-gay/active_hate_groups.

Spence, J.T. (1984). Gender identity and its implications for the concepts of masculinity and femininity. In T.B. Sonderegger (Ed.), *Psychology and gender* (pp. 59–95). Lincoln: University of Nebraska Press.

Spolan, S. (1991). Oh, by the way. *Philadelphia City Paper,* March 22, p. 7.

Sprecher, S. (2002). Sexual satisfaction in premarital relationships: Associations with satisfaction, love, commitment and stability. *Journal of Sex Research, 39*(3), 190–196.

Sprecher, S., & Hendrick, S. (2004). Self-disclosure in intimate relationships: Associations with individual and relationship characteristics over time. *Journal of Social and Clinical Psychology, 23*(6), 857–877.

Sprecher, S., & Regan, P. (1996). College virgins: How men and women perceive their sexual status. *Journal of Sex Research, 33*(1), 3–16.

Sprecher, S., & Regan, P. (2002). Liking some things (in some people) more than others: Partner preferences in romantic relationships and friendships. *Journal of Social & Personal Relationships, 19*(4), 463–481.

Sprecher, S., & Toto-Morn, M. (2002). A study of men and women from different sides of earth to determine if men are from Mars and women are from Venus in their beliefs about love and romantic relationships. *Sex Roles, 46*(5–6), 131–147.

Sprecher, S., Cate, R., & Levin, L. (1998). Parental divorce and young adults' beliefs about love. *Journal of Divorce & Remarriage, 28*(3–4), 107–120.

Srivastava, R., Thakar, R., & Sultan, A. (2008). Female sexual dysfunction in obstetrics and gynecology. *Obstetrics and Gynecology Survey, 63,* 527–537.

St. Pierre, M., & Senn, C. (2010). External barriers to help-seeking encountered by Canadian gay and lesbian victims of intimate partner abuse: An application of the barriers model. *Violence and Victims, 25*(4), 536–551.

Stacey, D. (2008). No more periods: The safety of continuous birth control. Retrieved March 18, 2008, from http://contraception.about.com/od/prescriptionoptions/p/MissingPeriods.htm.

Stahlhut, R.W., vanWijngaarden, E., Dye, T.D., Cook, S., & Swan, S.H. (2007). Concentrations of urinary phthalate metabolites are associated with increased waist circumference and insulin resistance in adult U.S. males. *Environmental Health Perspectives, 115,* 876–882.

Stanford, E.K. (2002). Premenstrual syndrome. Retrieved July 18, 2002, from http://www.medical-library.org/journals/secure/gynecol/secure/Premenstrual%20 syndromes.

Stanger, J.D., Vo, L., Yovich, J.L., & Almahbobi, G. (2010). Hypoosmotic swelling test identifies individual spermatozoa with minimal DNA fragmentation. *Reproductive Biomedicine Online, 21*(4), 474–484.

Stark, R. (1996). *The rise of Christianity.* Princeton, NJ: Princeton University Press.

Starkman, N., & Rajani, N. (2002). The case for comprehensive sex education. *AIDS Patient Care and STDs, 16*(7), 313–318.

Starkweather, K., & Hames, R. (2012). A survey of non-classical polyandry. *Human Nature, 23*(2), 149–172.

Starling, K. (1999). How to bring the romance back. *Ebony, 54*(4), 136–137.

Statistics Canada, National Household Survey. (2011). Mixed Unions in Canada. Catalogue no. 99–010–X2011003.

Statistics Canada. (2002). Changing conjugal life in Canada. Catalogue @ 89–576–XIE.

Statistics Canada. (2011). Police-reported Crime Statistics in Canada, 2011. Statistics Canada. http://www.statcan.gc.ca/pub/85-002-x/2012001/article/11692-eng.htm.

Statistics Canada. (2011). Police-reported hate crimes in Canada, 2011. Juristat Article. http://www.statcan.gc.ca/pub/85-002-x/2013001/article/11822-eng.pdf.

Statistics Canada. (2011a). Canada Year Book 2011. Catalogue # 11–402–X.

Statistics Canada. (2011b). The Canadian Population in 2011: Age and Sex. Statistics Canada, Analytical Document, Catalogue no. 98–311–X2011001.

Statistics Canada. (2013). 2011 National Household Survey: Aboriginal Peoples in Canada: First Nations People, Métis and Inuit.

Statistics Canada. (2013). 2011 National Household Survey: Immigration, place of birth, citizenship, ethnic origin, visible minorities, language and religion. http://www.statcan.gc.ca/daily-quotidien/130508/dq130508b-eng.pdf.

Statistics Canada. (2013a). Canadian Use of the Internet in 2012. Retrieved September 10, 2014, from http://www.statcan.gc.ca/daily-quotidien/131126/dq131126d-eng.htm.

Statistics Canada. (2013b). Table 102-4502 Live births by age of mother, Canada, provinces and territories. Retrieved February 2, 2015 from http://www5.statcan.gc.ca/cansim/a05?lang=eng&id=1024503&pattern=1024503&searchTypeByValue=1&p2=35.

Statistics Canada. (2013c). Breast feeding trends in Canada. Retreived April 23, 2015 from, http://www.statcan.gc.ca/pub/82-624-x/2013001/article/11879-eng.htm.

Statistics Canada. (2014). Portrait of Families and Living Arrangements in Canada. http://www12.statcan.ca/census-recensement/2011/as-sa/98-312-x/98-312-x2011001-eng.cfm.

Statistics Canada. (2014a). Causes of Death. Retrieved February 23, 2015 from, http://www.statcan.gc.ca/tables-tableaux/sum-som/l01/cst01/hlth36a-eng.htm.

Statistics Canada. (2014b). Police reported sexual offences against children and youth, 2012. Retrieved March 31,2015 from, http://www.statcan.gc.ca/pub/85-002-x/2014001/article/14008/hl-fs-eng.htm.

Statistics Canada. (2015). Aging populations. Retrieved November 26, 2014 from, http://www.statcan.gc.ca/tables-tableaux/sum-som/l01/cst01/demo10a-eng.htm.

Statistics Canada. (2015). Teen pregnancy. Retreived April 24, 2015 from, http://www.statcan.gc.ca/eng/help/bb/info/teen.

Steiger, H., Richardson, J., Schmitz, N., Israel, M., et al. (2010). Trait-defined eating disorder subtypes and history of childhood abuse. *International Journal of Eating Disorders, 43*(5), 428–432.

Stein, J.H., & Reiser, L.W. (1994). A study of white, middle-class adolescent boys' responses to 'semenarche'. *Journal of Youth and Adolescence, 23*(3), 373–384.

Stein, R. (2008, May 20). A debunking on teenagers and "technical virginity"; researchers find that oral sex isn't commonplace among young people who avoid intercourse. *The Washington Post.* Retrieved May 29, 2008, from http://www.guttmacher.org/media/nr/nr_euroteens.html.

Steinem, G. (1983). *Outrageous acts and everyday rebellions.* New York, NY: Holt, Rinehart and Winston.

Steiner, A.Z., DAloisio, A.A., DeRoo, L.A., Sandler, D.P., & Baird, D.D. (2010). Association of intrauterine and early-life exposures with age at menopause in the Sister Study. *American Journal of Epidemiology, 172*(2), 140–148.

Stengers, J., & Van Neck, A. (2001). *Masturbation: The history of a great terror.* New York, NY: Palgrave/St. Martins.

Sternberg, R.J. (1985): *Beyond IQ: A triarchic theory of human intelligence.* New York, NY: Cambridge University Press.

Sternberg, R.J. (1987). Liking versus loving: A comparative evaluation of theories. *Psychological Bulletin, 102*(3), 331–345.

Sternberg, R.J. (1998). *Cupid's arrow: The course of love through time.* New Haven, CT: Yale University Press.

Sternberg, R.J. (1999). *Love is a story.* New York, NY: Oxford University Press.

Sternberg, S. (2006). Once-a-day drug cocktail—in one pill—wins FDA approval. *USAToday.* Retrieved October 8, 2008, from http://www.usatoday.com/news/health/2006-07-12-hiv-pill_x.htm.

Sternfeld, B., Swindle, R., Chawla, A. Long, S., & Kennedy, S. (2002). Severity of premenstrual symptoms in a health maintenance organization population. *Obstetrics & Gynecology, 99*(6), 1014–1024.

Stevenson, B., & Isen, A. (2010). Who's getting married? Education and marriage today and in the past. A briefing paper prepared for the Council on Contemporary Families, January 26, 2010. Retrieved January 29, 2011, from http://www.contemporary-families.org/images/stories/homepage/orange_border/ccf012510.pdf.

Stevenson, B., & Wolfers, J. (2007). Marriage and divorce: Changes and their driving forces. *Journal of Economic Perspectives, 21*(2), 27–52.

Stevenson, B., & Wolfers, J. (2008). Marriage and the market. Cato Institute. Retrieved January 29, 2011, from http://bpp.wharton.upenn.edu/betseys/papers/Policy%20Papers/Cato%20Unbound.pdf.

Stewart, F., & Gabelnick, H.L. (2004). Contraceptive research and development. In R.A. Hatcher et al. (Eds.), *Contraceptive technology* (18th rev. ed., pp. 601–616). New York, NY: Ardent Media.

Stewart, F.H., Ellertson, C., & Cates, W. (2004). Abortion. In R.A. Hatcher et al. (Eds.), *Contraceptive technology* (18th rev. ed., pp. 673–700). New York, NY: Ardent Media.

Stewart, H. (2005). Senoritas and princesses: The quinceanera as a context for female development. *Dissertation Abstracts, 65*(7-A), 2770, #0419–4209.

Stewart, J. (1990). *The complete manual of sexual positions.* Chatsworth, CA: Media Press.

Stiles, B.L., & Clark, R.E. (2011). BDSM: A subcultural analysis of sacrifices and delights. *Deviant Behavior, 32*(2), 158–189.

Stojanovska, L., Apostolopoulos, V., Polman, R., & Borkoles, E. (2014). To exercise, or, not to exercise, during menopause and beyond. *Maturitas, 77*(4), 318–323.

Stokes, C., & Ellison, C. (2010). Religion and attitudes toward divorce laws among U.S. adults. *Journal of Family Issues, 31*(10), 1279–1304.

Stoller, R.J. (1996). The gender disorders. In I. Rosen (Ed.), *Sexual deviation* (3rd ed., pp. 111–133). London: Oxford University Press.

Stone, R.I. (1989). The feminization of poverty. *Women's Studies Quarterly, 17*(1–2), 20–34.

Storgaard, L., Bonde, J.P., Ernst, E., Spano, M., Andersen, C.Y., Frydenberg, M., & Olsen, J. (2003). Does smoking during pregnancy affect sons' sperm counts? *Epidemiology, 14*(3), 278–286.

Storm, L. (2011). Nurturing touch helps mothers with postpartum depression and their infants. Interview by Deb Discenza. *Neonatal Network, 30*(1), 71–72.

Storm, T., & Storm, C. (1984). Canadian students' beliefs about the relationships among love, sex and intimacy. *Social Behavior & Personality: An International Journal, 12*(2), 191–197.

Storms, M.D. (1980). Theories of sexual orientation. *Journal of Personality and Social Psychology, 38,* 783–792.

Storms, M.D. (1981). A theory of erotic orientation development. *Psychological Review, 88,* 340–353.

Stout, A.L., Grady, T.A., Steege, J.F., Blazer, D.G., George, L.K., & Melville, M.L. (1986). Premenstrual symptoms in Black and White community samples. *American Journal of Psychiatry, 143*(11), 1436–1469.

Strand, L.B., Barnett, A.G., & Tong, S. (2011). The influence of season and ambient temperature on birth outcomes: A review of the epidemiological literature. *Environmental Research, 111,* 451–462.

Strandberg, K., Peterson, M., Schaefers, M., Case, L., Pack, M., Chase, D., & Schlievert, P. (2009). Reduction in staphylococcus aureus growth and exotoxin production and in vaginal interleukin 8 levels due to glycerol monolaurate in tampons. *Clinics in Infectious Diseases, 49*(11), 1718–1717.

Strasburger, V.C. (2005). Adolescents, sex, and the media: Oooo, baby, baby—a Q&A. *Adolescent Medicine Clinics, 16*(2), 269–288.

Strasburger, V.C., & The Council on Communications and Media. (2010). Sexuality, contraception, and the media. *Pediatrics, 126,* 576–582.

Strassberg, D.S., & Lockerd, L.K. (1998). Force in women's sexual fantasies. *Archives of Sexual Behavior, 27*(4), 403–415.

Strassman, B.I. (1999). Menstrual synchrony pheromones: Cause for doubt. *Human Reproduction, 14,* 579–580.

Strine, T.W., Chapman, D.P., & Ahluwalia, I.B. (2005). Menstrual-related problems and psychological distress among women in the United States. *Journal of Women's Health, 14*(4), 316–323.

Strohmaier, J., Wüst, S., Uher, R., Henigsberg, N., Mors, O., Hauser, J., Souery, D., Zobel, A., Jordan, R., Hallam, T.J., Molinoff, P., & Spana, C. (2011). Developing treatments for female sexual dysfunction. *Clinical Pharmacology and Therapeutics, 89*(1), 137–141.

Stromsvik, N., Raheim, M., Oyen, N., Enge-bretsen, L., & Gjengedal, E. (2010). Stigmatization and male identity: Norwegian males' experience after identification as BRCA1/2 mutation carriers. *Journal of Genetic Counseling, 19*(4), 360.

Struble, C.B., Lindley, L.L., Montgomery, K., Hardin, J., & Burcin, M. (2010). Overweight and obesity in lesbian and bisexual college women. *Journal of American College Health, 59*(1), 51–56.

Struckman-Johnson, C., & Struckman-Johnson, D. (1994). Men pressured and forced into

sexual experience. *Archives of Sexual Behavior, 23,* 93–115.

Stuebe, A.M., Willett, W.C., Xue, F., & Michels, K.B. (2009). Lactation and incidence of premenopausal breast cancer. *Archives of Internal Medicine, 169*(15), 1364–1371.

St-Yves, A., Freeston, M.H., Jacques, C., & Robitaille, C. (1990). Love of animals and interpersonal affectionate behavior. *Psychological Reports, 67*(3, Pt 2), 1067–1075.

Su, J., Berman, S., Davis, D., Weinstock, H., & Kirkcaldy, R. (2010). Congenital syphilis, US, 2003–2008. Centers for Disease Control and Prevention. *MMWR Morbidity and Mortality Weekly Report, 59,* 413–417.

Suarez, S.S., & Pacey, A.A. (2006). Sperm transport in the female reproductive tract. *Human Reproduction Update, 12*(1), 23–37.

Sulak, P.J., Kuehl, T.J., Ortiz, M., & Shull, B.L. (2002). Acceptance of altering the standard 21-day/7-day oral contraceptive regimen to delay menses and reduce hormone withdrawal symptoms. *American Journal of Obstetrics and Gynecology, 186*(6), 1142–1149.

Sulak, P.J., Scow, R.D., Preece, C., Riggs, M., & Kuehl, T. (2000). Withdrawal Symptoms in Oral Contraceptive Users. *Obstetrics & Gynecology, 95,* 261–266.

Sullian, R., & Harrington, M. (2009). The politics and ethics of same-sex adoption. *Journal of GLBT Family Studies, 5*(3), 235–246.

Sun, L., Huang, X., Suo, J., Fan, B., Chen, Z., Yang, W., & Li, J. (2011). Biological evaluation of a novel copper-containing composite for contraception. *Fertility and Sterility, 95*(4), 1416–1420.

Sutherland, E.H. (1924). *Principles of criminology.* Chicago, IL: University of Chicago Press.

Sutphin, S.T. (2010). Social exchange theory and the division of household labor in same-sex couples. *Marriage and Family Review, 46*(3), 191–209.

Svoboda, E. (2006, December 5). All the signs of pregnancy except one: A baby. Retrieved from http://www.nytimes.com/2006/12/05/health/05pseud.html.

Svoboda, E. (2011). Breaking up in hard to do. *Psychology Today, 44*(1), 64.

Swaab, D.F. (2004). Sexual differentiation of the human brain: Relevance for gender identity, transsexualism and sexual orientation. *Gynecological Endocrinology, 19*(6), 201–312.

Swaab, D.F., & Hofman, M.A. (1990). An enlarged suprachiasmatic nucleus in homosexual men. *Brain Research, 537,* 141–148.

Swami, V., & Furnham, A. (2008). *The Psychology of Physical Attraction.* New York, NY: Routledge/Taylor & Francis Group.

Swan, S. (2006). Semen quality in fertile U.S. men in relation to geographical area and

pesticide exposure. *International Journal of Andrology, 29,* 62–68.

Swanson, J.M., Dibble, S., & Chapman, L. (1999). Effects of psychoeducational interventions on sexual health risks and psychosocial adaptation in young adults with genital herpes. *Journal of Advanced Nursing, 29*(4), 840–851.

Swearingen, S., & Klausner, J.D. (2005). Sildenafil use, sexual risk behavior, and risk for sexually transmitted diseases, including HIV infection. *American Journal of Medicine, 118,* 571–577.

Swenson, L.W., Carmel, S., & Varnhagen, C.K. (1997). A review of the knowledge, attitudes and behaviours of university students concerning HIV/AIDS. *Health Promotion International, 12*(1), 61–68.

Switonski, M., Payan-Carreira, R., Bartz, M., Nowacka-Woszuk, J., Szczerbal, I., Colaço, B., Pires, M.A., Ochota, M., & Nizanski, W. (2012). Hypospadias in a male (78,XY; SRY-positive) dog and sex reversal female (78,XX; SRY-negative) dogs: clinical, histological and genetic studies. *Sexual Development, 6*(1–3), 128–134.

Szasz, T.S. (1974). *The myth of mental illness.* New York, NY: Harper and Row.

Szymanski, D.M., Chung, Y., & Balsam, K. (2001). Psychosocial correlates of internalized homophobia in lesbians. *Measurement and Evaluation in Counseling and Development, 34*(1), 27–39.

Taft, C., Resick, P., Watkins, L., & Panuzio, J. (2009). An investigation of posttraumatic stress disorder and depressive symptomatology among female victims of interpersonal trauma. *Journal of Family Violence, 24*(6), 407–416.

Tai, Y.C., Domchek, S., Parmigiani, G., & Chen, S. (2007). Breast cancer risk among male BRCA1 and BRCA2 mutation carriers. *Journal of the National Cancer Institute, 99,* 1811–1814.

Taioli, E., Marabelli, R., Scortichini, G., Migliorati, G., Pedotti, P., Cigliano, A., & Caporale, V. (2005). Human exposure to dioxins through diet in Italy. *Chemosphere, 61,* 1672–1676.

Tait, R. (2005, July 28). A fatwa for transsexuals. *Salon.* Retrieved December 14, 2010, from http://dir.salon.com/story/news/feature/2005/07/28/iran_transsexuals.

Talakoub, L., Munarriz, R., Hoag, L., Gioia, M., Flaherty, E., & Goldstein, I. (2002). Epidemiological characteristics of 250 women with sexual dysfunction who presented for initial evaluation. *Journal of Sex and Marital Therapy, 28* (Suppl. 1), 217–224.

Talbot, J., Baker, J., & McHale, J. (2009). Sharing the love: Prebirth adult attachment status and coparenting adjustment during early infancy. *Parenting: Science & Practice, 9*(1), 56–77.

Talwar, G.P., Vyas, H.K., Purswani, S., & Gupta, J.C, (2009), Gonadotropin-releasing hormone/human chorionic gonadotropin beta based recombinant antibodies and vaccines. *Journal of Reproductive Immunology, 83*(1–2), 158–163.

Tamiello, M., Castelli, L., Vighetti, S., Perozzo, P., Geminianib, G., & Weiskrantz, http://www.pnas.org/content/early/2009/10/02/0908994106.abstract-aff-6#aff-6 L., et al. (2009). Unseen facial and bodily expressions trigger fast emotional reactions. *Proceedings of the National Academy of Sciences of the United States of America, 106*(42), 17661.

Tan, D.H., Kaul, R., Raboud, J.M., & Walmsley, S.L. (2011). No impact of oral tenofovir disoproxil fumarate on herpes simplex virus shedding in HIV-infected adults. *AIDS, 25*(2), 207–210.

Tang, S., & Gui, G. (2011). A review of the oncologic and survival management of breast cancer in the augmented breast: Diagnostic, surgical, and surveillance challenges. *Annals of Surgical Oncology.* Annals of Surgical Oncology, *18*(8), 2173–2181.

Tannahill, R. (1980). *Sex in history.* New York, NY: Stein & Day.

Tannen, D. (1990). *You just don't understand: Women and men in conversation.* New York, NY: Ballantine Books.

Tannen, D., Kendall, S., & Gordon, C. (2007). *Family talk: Discourse and identity in four American families.* New York, NY: Oxford University Press.

Tanveer, K. (2002, July 7). In Pakistan, gang rape as a tribal punishment. *The Hartford Courant,* A2.

Tao, G. (2008). Sexual orientation and related viral sexually transmitted disease rates among U.S. women aged 15–44 years. *American Journal of Public Health, 98,* 1007–1009.

Tarkovsky, A. (2006). Sperm taste: 10 simple tips for better tasting semen. Ezine articles. Retrieved August 10, 2008, from http://ezinearticles.com/?Sperm-Taste—-10-Simple-Tips-For-Better-Tasting-Semen&id=164106.

Taub, D.E. (1982). Public sociability of college-aged male homosexuals: The gay bar and the cruising block. *Sociological Spectrum, 2,* 291–303.

Tay, J.I., Moore, J., & Walker, J.J. (2000). Ectopic pregnancy. *British Medical Journal, 320*(7239), 916–920.

Taylor, C., & Peter., with McMinn, T.L., Elliott, T., Beldom, S., Ferry, A., Gross, Z., Paquin, S., & Schachter, K. (2011). Every class in every school: The first national climate survey on homophobia, biphobia, and transphobia in Canadian schools. Final Report. Toronto, ON: Egale Canada Human Rights Trust. http://egale.ca/wp-content/uploads/2011/05/EgaleFinalReport-web.pdf.

Taylor, G.W., & Ussher, J.M. (2001). Making sense of S&M: A discourse analytic account. *Sexualities,* 4(Issue 3), 293–314.

Taylor, H.E. (2000). Meeting the needs of lesbian and gay young adults. *The Clearing House, 73*(4), 221.

Taylor, M.A. (1998). "The masculine soul heaving in the female bosom": Theories of inversion and The Well of Loneliness. *Journal of Gender Studies, 7*(3), 287–296.

Teitelman, A. (2004). Adolescent girls' perspectives of family interactions related to menarche and sexual health. *Qualitative Health Research, 14*(9), 1292–1308.

Teitelman, A. (2010). Can anything prevent recurrent bacterial vaginosis? January 14, 2010. Retrieved from http://www.medscape.com/viewarticle/714690#2.

Teles, M., Bianco, S., Brito, V., Trarbach, E., Kuohung, W., Xu, S., Seminara, S., Mendonca, B., Kaiser, U., & Latronico, A. (2008). A GPR54-activiting mutation in a patient with central preconscious puberty. *New England Journal of Medicine, 358,* 709–715.

Tepavcevic, D., Kostic, J., Basuroski, I., Stojsavljevic, N., Pekmezovic, T., & Drulovic, J. (2008). The impact of sexual dysfunction on the quality of life measured by MSQoL-54 in patients with multiple sclerosis. *Multiple Sclerosis, 14*(8), 1131–1136.

Terada, Y., Schatten, G., Hasegawa, H., & Yae-gashi, N. (2010). Essential roles of the sperm centrosome in human fertilization: Developing the therapy for fertilization failure due to sperm centrosomal dysfunction. *Tohoku Journal of Experimental Medicine, 220*(4), 247–258.

Terry, J. (1990). Lesbians under the medical gaze: Scientists search for remarkable differences. *The Journal of Sex Research, 27,* 317–339.

Tesher, E. (2014). Today's advice column, October 9. Retrieved from http://ellieadvice.com/both-parties-have-to-want-it-to-make-it-work/.

Teuscher, U., & Teuscher, C. (2006). Reconsidering the double standard of aging: Effects of gender and sexual orientation on facial attractiveness ratings. *Personality and Individual Differences, 42*(4), 631–639.

Tewksbury, R. (2007). Effects of sexual assaults on men: Physical, mental and sexual consequences. *International Journal of Men's Health, 6,* 22–36.

Thalidomide Victims Association of Canada. (2015). The Canadian tragedy. Retrieved January 30, 2015, from http://www.thalidomide.ca/the-canadian-tragedy.

Thankamony, A., Ong, K.K., Dunger, D.B., Acerini, C.L., & Hughes, I.A. (2009). Anogenital distance from birth to 2 years: a population study. *Environmental Health Perspectives, 117*(11), 1786–1790.

This, P. (2008). Breast cancer and fertility: Critical review, considerations and perspectives. *Bulletin du Cancer, 95,* 17–25.

Thomas, S.L., & Ellertson, C. (2000). Nuisance or natural and healthy: Should monthly menstruation be optional for women? *Lancet, 355,* 922–924.

Thomasset, C. (1992). The nature of woman. In C. Klapisch-Zuber (Ed.), *A history of women in the West, Volume II: Silences of the Middle Ages* (pp. 43–70). Cambridge, UK: Belknap Press.

Thompson, A.P. (1984). Emotional and sexual components of extramarital relations. *Journal of Marriage and the Family, 46,* 35–42.

Thompson, J.L.P., Yager, T.J., & Martin, J.L. (1993). Condom failure and frequency of condom use among gay men. *American Journal of Public Health, 83*(10), 1409–1413.

Thompson, K.M. (2009). Sibling incest: A model for group practice with adult female victims of brother-sister incest. *Journal of Family Violence, 24,* 531–537.

Thompson, P. (2009). The spanking senator: Politician friend of Schwarzenegger caught on camera bragging about extra-marital affair. Mail Online, September 10. http://www.dailymail.co.uk/news/article-1212286/The-spanking-senator-Politician-friend-Schwarzenegger-bragging-mike-extra-marital-affair.html.

Thomson, R., & Murachver, T. (2001). Predicting gender from electronic discourse. *British Journal of Social Psychology, 40*(2), 193–208.

Thomson, R., Finau, S., Finau, E., Ahokovi, L., & Tameifuna, S. (2007). Circumcision of Pacific boys: Tradition at the cutting edge. *Pacific Health Dialogue, 13,* 115–122.

Thonneau, P., Bujan, L., Multigner, L., & Mieusset, R. (1998). Occupational heat exposure and male fertility: A review. *Human Reproduction, 13*(8), 2122-2125.

Thorne, N., & Amrein, H. (2003). Vomeronasal organ: Pheromone recognition with a twist. *Current Biology, 13*(6), R220–R222.

Thornhill, R., & Palmer, C.T. (2000). *A natural history of rape: Biological bases of sexual coercion.* Boston, MA: MIT Press.

Thorp, J.M., Hartmann, K.E., & Shadigian, E. (2003). Long-term physical and psychological health consequences of induced abortion: Review of the evidence. *Obstetrical and Gynecological Survey, 58*(1), 67–79.

Thorup, J., McLachlan, R., Cortes, D., Nation, T.R., Balie, A., Southwell, B.R., & Hutson, J. (2010). What is new in cryptorchidism and hypospadias—a critical review on the testicular dysgenesis hypothesis. *Pediatric Surgery, 45*(10), 2074–2086.

Thurston, M. (2007). *The fourth path: Gay, Mormon, celibate*. Retrieved from https://www.sunstonemagazine.com/the-fourth-path-gay-mormon-celibate/.

Tiefer, L. (1991). Historical, scientific, clinical and feminist criticisms of "the Human Sexual Response Cycle" model. *Annual Review of Sex Research, 2,* 1–23.

Tiefer, L. (2001). A new view of women's sexual problems: Why new? Why now? *Journal of Sex Research, 38*(2), 89–96.

Tiefer, L. (2004). *Sex Is Not a Natural Act and Other Essays*. Boulder, CO: Westview Press.

Tiefer, L. (2006). Female sexual dysfunction: A case study of disease mongering and activist resistance. PLoS Medicine, 3(4). Retrieved June 19, 2008, from http://medicine.plosjournals.org/perlserv/?request=get-document&doi=10.1371/journal.pmed.0030178&ct=1.

Timmreck, T.C. (1990). Overcoming the loss of a love: Presenting love addiction and promoting positive emotional health. *Psychological Reports, 66*(2), 515–528.

Timur, S., & Sahin, N. (2010). The prevalence of depression symptoms and influencing factors among perimenopausal and post-menopausal women. *Menopause, 17*(3), 545–551.

Ting-Toomey, S., Gao, G., & Trubisky, P. (1991). Culture, face maintenance, and styles of handling interpersonal conflicts: A study in five cultures. *International Journal of Conflict Management, 2*(4), 275–296.

Tirabassi, R.S., Ace, C.I., Levchenko, T., Torchilin, V.P., Selin, L.K., Nie, S., Guberski, D.L., & Yang, K. (2011). A mucosal vaccination approach for herpes simplex virus type 2. *Vaccine, 29*(5), 1090–1098.

Tjaden, P., & Thoennes, N. (1998). *Stalking in America: Findings from the National Violence Against Women Survey*. National Institute of Justice and the Centers for Disease Control and Prevention.

Tjaden, P., & Thoennes, N. (2000). *Extent, nature, and consequences of intimate partner violence: Findings from the National Violence Against Women Survey*. Washington, DC: National Institute of Justice and the Centers for Disease Control and Prevention.

Tjepkema, M. (2008). Health care use among gay, lesbian and bisexual Canadians. *Health Reports, 19,* 53–64.

Tjioe, M., & Vissers, W. (2008). Scabies outbreaks in nursing homes for the elderly: Recognition, treatment options, and control of reinfestation. *Drugs Aging, 25*(4), 299–306.

Tobian, A.A., Gray, R.H., & Quinn, T.C. (2010). Male circumcision for the prevention of acquisition and transmission of sexually transmitted infections: The case for neonatal circumcision. *Archives of Pediatric Adolescent Medicine, 164*(1), 78–84.

Tokushige, N., Markham, R., Crossett, B., Ah, S., Nelaturi, V., Khan, A., & Fraser, I. (2011). Discovery of a novel biomarker in the urine in women with endometriosis. *Fertility and Sterility, 95*(1), 46–49.

Tom, S., Kuh, D., Guralnik, J., & Mishra, G. (2010). Self-reported sleep difficulty during the menopausal transition: Results from a prospective cohort study. *Menopause, 17*(6), 1128–1135.

Tomaso, B. (2008, July 25). After 40 years, birth control decree still divides American Catholics. *Dallas News*. Retrieved October 28, 2008, from http://religionblog.dallasnews.com/archives/2008/07/after-40-years-birth-control-d.html.

Tommola, P., Unkila-Kallio, L., & Paavonen, J. (2010). Surgical treatment of vulvar vestibulitis: A review. *Acta Obstetrics and Gynecology Scandinavia, 89*(11), 1385–1395.

Toppari, J., Virtanen, H.E., Main, K.M., & Skakkebaek, N.E. (2010). Cryptorchidism and hypospadias as a sign of testicular dysgenesis syndrome (TDS): Environmental connection. *Birth Defects Research, 88*(10), 910–919.

Toussaint, I., & Pitchot, W. (2013). Hypersexual disorder will not be included in the DSM V: A contextual analysis. *Review Medical Liege, 68*(5–6), 348–353.

Tovar, J., Bazaldua, O., Vargas, L., & Reile, E. (2008). Human papillomavirus, cervical cancer, and the vaccines. *Postgraduate Medicine, 120,* 79–84.

Towne, B., Czerwinski, S.A., Demerath, E.W., Blangero, J., Roche, A.F., & Siervogel, R.M. (2005). Heritability of age at menarche in girls from the Fels Longitudinal Study. *American Journal of Physical Anthropology,* published online ahead of print. Retrieved March 22, 2005, from http://www.ncbi.nlm.nih.gov/entrez/query.fcgi?cmd=Retrieve&db=pubmed&dopt=Abstract&list_uids=15779076.

Trabert, B., Sigurdson, A.J., Sweeney, A.M., Strom, S.S., & McGlynn, K.A. (2011). Marijuana use and testicular germ cell tumors. *Cancer, 117*(4), 848–853.

Tramel, J. (2011, April 5). Cowboy to stand trial for rape charges. *McClatchy-Tribune Business News*. Retrieved April 13, 2011, from http://www.tulsaworld.com/news/article.aspx?no5subj&articleid520110405_93_B5_CUTLIN644366&.

Treas, J., & Giesen, D. (2000). Sexual infidelity among married and cohabiting Americans. *Journal of Marriage and Family, 62*(1), 48–61.

Trends in HIV/AIDS Diagnoses. (2005, November 18). Trends in HIV/AIDS Diagnoses—33 States, 2001–2004. *Morbidity and Mortality Weekly Report, 54,* 1149–1153.

Trenholm, C., Devaney, B., Fortson, K., Quay, L., Wheeler, J., & Clark, M. (2007). Impact of four Title V, Section 510 Abstinence Education Programs. Princeton, NJ: Mathematic Policy Research. Retrieved from http://www.mathematicampr.com/publications/PDFs/impactabstinence.pdf.

Trevithick, A. (1997). On a panhuman preference for monandry: Is polyandry an exception? *Journal of Comparative Family Studies, 28*(3), 154–181.

Triadafilopoulos, T. (2012). *Becoming multicultural: Immigration and the politics of membership in Canada and Germany*. Vancouver: UBC Press.

Trigger, B.G. (1969). *The Huron: Farmers of the North*. Montreal: Holt, Rinehart and Winston.

Tristano, A.G. (2009). The impact of rheumatic diseases on sexual function. *Rheumatology International, 29*(8), 853–860.

Troiden, R.R. (1989). The formation of homosexual identities. In G. Herdt (Ed.), *Gay and lesbian youth* (pp. 43–73). New York, NY: Harrington Park Press.

Trotter, E.C., & Alderson, K.G. (2007). University students' definitions of having sex, sexual partner, and virginity loss: The influence of participant gender, sexual experience, and contextual factors. *Canadian Journal of Human Sexuality, 16,* 11–20.

Trudel, G., & Desjardins, G. (1992). Staff reactions toward the sexual behaviors of people living in institutional settings. *Sexuality and Disability, 10,* 173–188.

Trumbach, R. (1989). The birth of the queen: Sodomy and the emergence of gender equality in modern culture, 1660–1750. In M. Duberman, M. Vicinus, & G. Chauncey Jr. (Eds.), *Hidden from history: Reclaiming the gay and lesbian past* (pp. 129–140). New York, NY: Penguin Books.

Trumbach, R. (1990). Is there a modern sexual culture in the West, or, did England never change between 1500 and 1900? *Journal of the History of Sexuality, 1,* 206–309.

Truth Commission into Genocide in Canada, The. (2001). *Hidden from history: The Canadian Holocaust*. Retrieved from http://canadiangenocide.nativeweb.org/genocide.pdf.

Tsai, S., Stafanick, M., & Stafford, R. (2011). Trends in menopausal hormone therapy use of US office-based physicians, 2000–2009. *Menopause, 18*(4), 385–392.

Tsang, A.K., Fuller-Thompson, E., & Lai, D. (2012). Sexuality and health among Chinese seniors in Canada. *Journal of International Migration & Integration, 13*(4), 525–540.

Tsang, S. (2010). When size matters: A clinical review of pathological micropenis. *Journal of Pediatric Health Care, 24*(4), 231–240.

Tse, J.K.H., & Waters, J.L. (2013). Transnational youth transitions: Becoming adults between Vancouver and Hong Kong. *Global Networks, 13*(4), 535–550.

Tsivian, M., Mayes, J.M., Krupski, T.L., Mouraviev, V., Donatucci, C.F., & Polascik, T.J. (2009). Altered male physiologic function after surgery for prostate cancer: Couple perspective. *International Brazilian Journal of Urology, 35*(6), 673–682.

Tsui-Sui, A., Loveland-Cherry, C., & Guthrie, B. (2010). Maternal influences on Asian American-Pacific Islander adolescents' perceived maternal sexual expectations and their sexual initiation. *Journal of Family Issues, 31*(3), 381–406.

Tsunokai, G., Kposowa, A., & Adams, M. (2009). Racial preferences in internet dating: A comparison of four birth cohorts. *Western Journal of Black Studies, 33*(1), 1–16.

Tuller, E.R. (2010, December 26). Personal communication.

Turcotte, M. (2013). Living Apart Together. Statistics Canada, Insights on Canadian Society, March, Catalogue #75-006-X.

Turner, W. (2000). *A genealogy of queer theory.* Philadelphia: Temple University Press.

Twiss, J., Wegner, J., Hunter, M., Kelsay, M., Rathe-Hart, M., & Salado, W. (2007). Perimenopause symptoms, quality of life, and health behaviors in users and nonusers of hormone therapy. *Journal of the American Academy of Nurse Practitioners, 19*, 602–613.

Tye, M.H. (2006). Social inequality and well-being: Race-related stress, gay-related stress, self-esteem, and life satisfaction among African American gay and bisexual men. *Dissertation Abstracts International: Section B, 67*(4–B), 0419–4217.

Tzeng, J.M. (2000). Ethnically heterogamous marriages: The case of Asian Canadians. *Journal of Comparative Family Studies, 31*(3), 321–337.

Tzeng, O. (1992). Cognitive/comparitive judgment paradigm of love. In O. Tzeng (Ed.), *Theories of love development, maintenance, and dissolution: Octagonal cycle and differential perspectives*, pp. 133–149.

Tzortzis, V., Skriapas, K., Hadjigeorgiou, G., Mitsogiannis, I., Aggelakis, K., Gravas, S., et al. (2008). Sexual dysfunction in newly diagnosed multiple sclerosis women. *Multiple Sclerosis, 14*, 561–563.

U.S. Census Bureau. (2007, September 19). *Most people make only one trip down the aisle, but first marriages shorter, census bureau reports.* Retrieved September 20, 2007, from http://www.census.gov/Press-Release/www/releases/archives/marital_status_living_arrangements/010624.html.

U.S. Department of Justice, Bureau of Justice Statistics. (2006). Criminal victimization in the United States, 2005 statistical tables (U.S. Department of Justice Publication NCH 2152244, Table 2, Number of victimizations and victimization rates for persons age 12 and over, by type of crime and gender of victims). Washington, DC: Author.

U.S. Food and Drug Administration, Office of Women's Health. (2006, June). *Human papillomavirus.* Retrieved September 16, 2008, from http://www.fda.gov/WOMENS/getthefacts/hpv.html.

U.S. Food and Drug Administration. (2008, January 18). *FDA approves update to label on birth control patch.* Retrieved October 28, 2008, from http://www.fda.gov/bbs/topics/NEWS/2008/NEW01781.html.

U.S. National Longitudinal Study of Adolescent Health. (2002). Retrieved December 16, 2015, from http://www.socio.com/dapq1q9.php.

Uji, M., Shono, M., Shikai, N., & Kitamura, T. (2007). Case illustrations of negative sexual experiences among university women in Japan: Victimization disclosure and reactions of the confidant. *International Journal of Offender Therapy and Comparative Criminology, 51,* 227–242.

Ullman, S., Townsend, S., Filipas, H., & Star-zynski, L. (2007). Structural models of the relations of assault severity, social support, avoidance coping, self-blame, and PTSD among sexual assault survivors. *Psychology of Women Quarterly, 31,* 23–37.

UNAIDS. (2005). AIDS Epidemic Update: December, 2005. Retrieved November 22, 2005, from http://www.unaids.org/epi2005/doc/report_pdf.html.

UNAIDS. (2008). 2008: Report on the global AIDS epidemic. UNAIDS Joint United Nations Programme on HIV/AIDS. Retrieved November 3, 2008, from http://www.unaids.org/en/KnowledgeCentre/HIVData/GlobalReport/2008/2008_Global_report.asp.

UNAIDS. (2008a). Eastern Europe and Central Asia: AIDS Epidemic Update: Regional Summary. UNAIDS, 2008.

UNAIDS. (2008b). Latin America: AIDS Epidemic Update: Regional Summary. UNAIDS, 2008.

UNAIDS. (2010). Global report on the AIDS epidemic. Joint United Nations Programme on HIV/AIDS. Retrieved April 1, 2011, from http://www.unaids.org/globalreport/documents/20101123_GlobalReport_full_en.pdf.

UNAIDS. (2013a). Global Report: UNAIDS Report on the Global AIDS Epidemic, 2013.

UNAIDS. (2013b). HIV in Asia and the Pacific. UNAIDS Report 2013.

UNAIDS. (2013c). HIV in Asia and the Pacific. Update: How Africa Turned AIDS Around, 2013.

UNAIDS. (2014a). The Cities Report. UNAIDS Report: 2014.

UNAIDS. (2014b). Fact Sheet 2014: Global Statistics.

United Nations Educational, Scientific, and Cultural Organization (UNESCO). (2008). Review of sex, relationships, and HIV education in the schools. UNESCO Global Advisory Group. Retrieved January 26, 2011, from http://unesdoc.unesco.org/images/0016/001629/162989e.pdf.

United Nations Educational, Scientific, and Cultural Organization (UNESCO). (2009). International technical guidance on sexuality education: An evidence-informed approach for schools, teachers, and health educators. Retrieved May 10, 2011, from http://unesdoc.unesco.org/images/0018/001832/183281e.pdf.

United Nations Population Fund (UNFPA). (2004). Position Statement on Condoms and HIV Prevention, July, 2004. http://www.unfpa.org/sites/default/files/faqs/condom_statement.pdf.

United States Conference of Catholic Bishops. (2004). The Nature and Scope of Sexual Abuse of Minors by Catholic Priests and Deacons in the United States, 1950 – 2002. A Research Study conducted bt the John Jay College of Criminal Justice, February. http://www.bishop-accountability.org/reports/2004_02_27_JohnJay_revised/2004_02_27_John_Jay_Main_Report_Optimized.pdf.

Upchurch, D.M., Aneshensel, C.S., Mudgal, J., & McNeely, C.S. (2001). Sociocultural contexts of time to first sex among Hispanic adolescents. *Journal of Marriage and Family, 63*(4), 1158.

Upchurch, D.M., Levy-Storms, L., et al. (1998). Gender and ethnic differences in the timing of first sexual intercourse. *Family Planning Perspectives, 30*(3), 121–128.

Urato, A.C., & Norwitz, E.R. (2011). A guide towards pre-pregnancy management of defective implantation and placentation. *Best Practices and Research in Clinical Obstetrics and Gynecology, 25*(3), 367–387.

USA Today. (2014). Report: Accused priests shuffled worldwide. June 19. http://usatoday30.usatoday.com/news/religion/2004-06-19-church-abuse_x.htm.

Usatine, R.P., & Tinitigan, R. (2010). Nongenital herpes simplex virus. *American Family Physician, 82*(9), 1075–1082.

Uskel, A.K., Lalonde, R.N., & Cheng, L. (2007). Views on interracial dating among Chinese and European Canadians: The roles of culture, gender, and mainstream cultural identity. *Journal of Social & Personal Relationships, 24*(6), 891–911.

Uskel, A.K., Lalonde, R.N., & Konanur, S. (2011). The role of culture in intergenerational value discrepancies regarding intergroup dating. *Journal of Cross-Cultural Psychology, 42*(7), 1165–1178.

Ussher, J., & Perz, J. (2008). Empathy, egalitarisnism and emotion work in the relationship negotiation of PMS: The experience of women in lesbian relationships. *Feminism and Psychology, 18*(1), 87–111.

Vaast, E. (2007). Playing with masks: Fragmentation and continuity in the presentation of self in an occupational online forum. *Information Technology & People, 20*(4), 334–351.

Valente, S.M. (2005). Sexual abuse of boys. *Journal of Child and Adolescent Psychiatric Nursing, 18*(1), 10–16.

Valenzuela, C.Y. (2008). Prenatal maternal mnemonic effects on the human neuropsychic sex: A new proposition from fetus-maternal tolerance-rejection. *La Revista Medica de Chile, 136*(12), 1552–1558.

Valenzuela, C.Y. (2010). Sexual orientation, handedness, sex ratio and fetomaternal tolerance-rejection. *Biological Research, 43*(3), 347–356.

van Aerde, J. (2001). Guidelines for health care professionals supporting families experiencing a perinatal loss. *Paediatric Child Health, 6*, 469–477.

van Basten, J.P., Van Driel, M.F., Hoekstra, H.J., Sleijfer, D.T., van de Wiel, H.B., Droste, J.H., et al. (1999). Objective and subjective effect of treatment for testicular cancer on sexual function. *British Journal of Urology, 84*(6), 671–678.

Van Berlo, W., & Ensink, B. (2000). Problems with sexuality after sexual assault. *Annual Review of Sex Research, 11*, 235–257.

Van De Geyn, L. (2013). The latest breast augmentation & lift surgery advancements. *Elevate magazine*, October 29, 2013, http://www.elevatemagazine.com/plastic-surgery/articles/1018-the-latest-breast-aguemtnation-lift-surgery-advancements.

Van den Heuvel, M., van Bragt, A., Alnabawy, A., & Kaptein, M. (2005). Comparison of ethinylestradial pharmacokinetics in three hormonal contraceptive formulation: The vaginal ring, the transdermal patch and an oral contraceptive. *Contraception, 72*, 168–174.

Vanderbilt, H. (1992). Incest: A chilling report. *Lears*, (Feb.), 49–77.

Van der Horst, C., Stuebinger, H., Seif, C., Melchior, D., Martínez-Portillo, F.J., & Juenemann, K.P. (2003). Priapism—etiology, pathophysiology and management. *International Brazillian Journal of Urology, 29*(5), 391-400.

VanderLaan, D., & Vasey, P. (2008). Mate retention behavior of men and women in heterosexual and homosexual relationships. *Archives of Sexual Behavior, 37*, 572–586.

VanderLaan, D.P., & Vasey, P.L. (2012). Relationship status and elevated avuncularity in Samoan fa'afafine. *Personal Relationships, 19*(2), 326–339.

van der Zanden, L.F., van Rooij, I.A., Feitz, W.F., Franke, B., Knoers, N.V., & Roeleveld, N. (2012). Aetiology of hypospadias: A systematic review of genes and environment. *Human Reproduction Update, 8*(3), 260–283.

Vanfossen, B. (1996). ITROWs women and expression conference. Institute for Teaching and Research on Women, Towson University, Towson, MD. Retrieved April 15, 2003, from http://www.towson.edu/itrow.

Vanggaard, T. (1969). *Phallos: A symbol and its history in the male world*. New York, NY: International Universities Press.

Vanier Institute of the Family, The. (2013). Same-sex families raising children. *Facinating Families*, March, Issue 51. http://www.vanierinstitute.ca/include/get.php?nodeid=2817.

Vanier, S.A., & Byers, E.S. (2013). A qualitative study of university students' perceptions of oral sex, intercourse, and intimacy. *Archives of Sexual Behavior, 42*(8), 1573–1581.

van Lankveld, J., Everaerd, W., & Grotjohann, Y. (2001). Cognitive-behavioral bibliotherapy for sexual dysfunctions in heterosexual couples: A randomized waiting-list controlled clinical trial in the Netherlands. *Journal of Sex Research, 38*(1), 51–67.

van Lankveld, J.J., Granot, M., Weijmar Schultz, W.C., Binik, Y.M., Wesselmann, U., Pukall, C.F., Bohm-Starke, N., & Achtrari, C. (2010). Women's sexual pain disorders. *Journal of Sexual Medicine, 7*(1 Pt 2), 615–631.

Vannier, S.A., & O'Sullivan, L.F. (2012). Why gives and who gets: Why, when and with whom young people engage in oral sex. *Journal of Youth and Adolescence, 42*(5), 572–582.

van Teijlingen, E., Reid, J., Shucksmith, J., Harris, F., Philip, K., Imamura, M., Tucker, J., & Penney, G. (2007). Embarrassment as a key emotion in young people talking about sexual health. *Sociological Research, 12*(2). Retrieved April 15, 2011, fromhttp://www.socresonline.org.uk/12/2/van_teijlingen.html.

Van Voorhis, B.J. (2006). Outcomes from assisted reproductive technology. *Obstetrics and Gynecology, 107*, 183–200.

Vanwesenbeeck, I., de Graaf, R., van Zessen, G., Straver, C.J., & Visser, J.H. (1993). Protection styles of prostitutes' clients: Intentions, behavior, and considerations in relation to AIDS. *Journal of Sex Education and Therapy, 19*(2), 79–92.

Van Wormer, H.M. (2006). The Ties That Bind: Ideology, Material Culture, and the Utopian Ideal Historical Archaeology Vol. 40, No. 1, 37–56.

Vardi, Y., McMahon, C., Waldinger, M., Rubio-Aurioles, E., & Rabinowitz, D. (2008). Are premature ejaculation symptoms curable? *Journal of Sexual Medicine, 5*, 1546–1551.

Venâncio, D.P., Tufik, S., Garbuio, S.A., da Nóbrega, A.C., & de Mello, M.T. (2008). Effects of anabolic androgenic steroids on sleep patterns of individuals practicing resistance exercise. Retrieved April 6, 2008, from http://www.ncbi.nlm.nih.gov/pubmed/18043934?ordinalpos=2&itool=EntrezSystem2.PEntrez.Pubmed.Pubmed_ResultsPanel.Pubmed_RVDocSum.

Vendittelli, F., Riviere, O., Crenn-Hebert, C., Rozan, M., Maria, B., & Jacquetin, B. (2008). Is a breech presentation at term more frequent in women with a history of cesarean delivery? *American Journal of Obstetrics and Gynecology, 198*, 521.

Venkat, P., Masch, R., Ng, E., Cremer, M., Rich-man, S., & Arslan, A. (2008, May 23). Knowledge and beliefs about contraception in urban Latina women. *Journal of Community Health, 33*(5), 357–362.

Venkatesh, K., Biswas, J., & Kumarasamy, N. (2008). Impact of highly active antiretroviral therapy on ophthalmic manifestations in human immunodeficiency virus/acquired immune deficiency syndrome. *Indian Journal of Ophthalmology, 56*(5), 391–393.

Ventura, S.J., Abma, J.C., Mosher, W.D., & Henshaw, S.K. (2007). *Recent trends in teenage pregnancy in the United States, 1990–2002*. Hyattsville, MD: National Center for Health Statistics, Centers for Disease Control. Retrieved May 27, 2008, from http://www.cdc.gov/nchs/products/pubs/pubd/hestats/teenpreg1990–2002/teenpreg1990–2002.htm.

Verberg, M.F., Gillott, D.J., Al-Fardan, N., & Grudzinskas, J.G. (2005). Hyperemesis gravidarum, a literature review. *Human Reproduction Update, 11*(5), 527–539.

Verkasalo, P.K., Thomas, H.V., Appleby, P.N., Davey, G.K., & Key, T.J. (2001). Circulating levels of sex hormones and their relation to risk factors for breast cancer: A cross-sectional study in 1092 pre- and postmenopausal women. *Cancer Causes and Control, 12*(1), 47–59.

Versfeld, N.J., & Dreschler, W.A. (2002). The relationship between the intelligibility of time-compressed speech and speech-innoise in young and elderly listeners. *Journal of the Acoustical Society of America, 111*, 401–408.

Verweij, K., Shekar, S., Zietsch, B., Eaves, L., Bailey, J., Boomsma, D., & Martin, N. (2008). Genetic and environmental influences on individual differences in attitudes toward homosexuality: An Australian twin study. *Behavior Genetics, 38*, 257–265.

Vessey, M., Yeates, D., & Flynn, S. (2010). Factors affecting mortality in a large cohort study with special reference to oral contraceptive use. *Contraception, 82*(3), 221–229.

Vetten, L., Jewkes, R., Sigsworth, R., Christofides, N., Loots, L., & Dunseith, O. (2008). "Tracking justice: The attrition of rape cases through the criminal justice system in Gauteng." Johannesburg, South Africa: Tsh-waranang Legal Advocacy Centre, the South African Medical Research Council and the Centre for the Study of Violence and Reconciliation.

Vigano, P., Parazzini, F., Somigliana, E., & Vercellini, P. (2004). Endometriosis: Epidemiology and aetiological factors. *Best Practice & Research Clinical Obstetrics & Gynaecology, 18*(2), 177–200.

Vincent, M.V., & Mackinnon, E.J. (2005). The response of clinical balanitis xerotica obliterans to the application of topical steroid-based creams. *Pediatric Surgery, 40*(4), 709–712.

Vincke, J., & van Heeringen, K. (2002). Confidant support and the mental well-being of lesbian and gay young adults: A longitudinal analysis. *Journal of Community and Applied Social Psychology, 12*, 181–193.

Voigt, H. (1991). Enriching the sexual experience of couples: The Asian traditions and sexual counseling. *Journal of Sex and Marital Therapy, 17*, 214–219.

Voiland, A. (2008). More problems with plastics: Like BPA, chemical called phthalates raise some concerns. *U.S. News and World Report, 144*, 54.

Voller, E., & Long, P. (2010). Sexual assault and rape perpetration by college men: The role of the big five personality traits. *Journal of Interpersonal Violence, 25*(3), 457–480.

Von Sydow, K. (2000). Sexuality of older women: The effect of menopause, other physical and social and partner-related factors. *Arztl Fortbild Qualitatssich, 94*(3), 223–229.

Vorsanova, S., Iurov, I., Kolotii, A., Beresheva, A., Demidova, I., Kurinnaia, O., Kravets, V., Monakhov, V., Solov'ev, I., & Iurov, I. (2010). Chromosomal mosaicism in spontaneous abortions: Analysis of 650 cases. *Genetika, 46*(10), 1356–1359.

Vrabel, K., Hoffart, A., Ro, O., Martinsen, E., & Rosenvinge, J. (2010). Co-occurrence of avoidant personality disorder and child sexual abuse predicts poor outcome in long-standing eating disorder. *Journal of Abnormal Psychology, 119*(3), 623–629.

Waal, F.B.M. (1995). Bonobo sex and society. *Scientific American*, 82–88. Retrieved July 4, 2003, from http://songweaver.com/info/bonobos.html.

Wacker, J., Parish, S., & Macy, R. (2008). Sexual assault and women with cognitive disabilities: Codifying discrimination in the United States. *Journal of Disability Policy Studies, 19*, 86–95.

Wakelin, A. (2003). Effects of victim gender and sexuality on attributions of blame to rape victims. *Sex Roles, 49*(9–10), 477–487.

Walch, K., Eder, R., Schindler, A., & Feichtinger, W. (2001). The effect of single-dose oxytocin application on time to ejaculation and seminal parameters in men. *Journal of Assisted Reproductive Genetics, 18*, 655–659.

Wald, A., Zeh, J., Selke, S., Warren, T., Ryncarz, A.J., Ashley, R., et al. (2000). Reactivation of genital herpes simplex virus type-2 infection in asymptomatic seropositive persons. *New England Journal of Medicine, 342*(12), 844–850.

Waldinger, M. (2005). Lifelong premature ejaculation: Definition, serotonergic neurotransmission and drug treatment. *World Journal of Urology, 23*, 102–108.

Waldinger, M.D. (2002). The neurobiological approach to premature ejaculation. *Journal of Urology, 168*, 2359–2367.

Waldinger, M.D., & Schweitzer, D.H. (2009). Persistent genital arousal disorder in 18 Dutch women: Part II.A syndrome clustered with restless legs and overactive bladder. *Journal of Sexual Medicine, 6*(2), 482–497.

Waldinger, R., & Schulz, M. (2010). What's love got to do with it? Social functioning, perceived health, and daily happiness in married octogenarians. *Psychology and Aging, 25*(2), 422–431.

Walen, S.R., & Roth, D. (1987). A cognitive approach. In J.H. Geer & W.T. O'Donahue (Eds.), *Theories of human sexuality* (pp. 335–360). New York, NY: Plenum Press.

Walker, J., & Milton, J. (2006). Teachers' and parents' roles in the sexuality education of primary school children: A comparison of experiences in Leeds, UK and in Sydney, Australia. *Sex Education, 6*(4), 415–428.

Walker, J., Archer, J., & Davies, M. (2005). Effects of rape on men: A descriptive analysis. *Archives of Sexual Behavior, 34*(1), 69–80.

Wallace, I., Wallace, A., Wallechinsky, D., & Wallace, S. (1981). *The intimate sex lives of famous people*. New York, NY: Delacorte Press.

Wallerstein, E. (1980). *Circumcision: An American health fallacy*. New York, NY: Springer.

Walters, G.D., Knight, R.A., & Långström, N. (2011). Is hypersexuality dimensional? Evidence for the DSM-5 from general population and clinical samples. *Archives of Sexual Behavior, 40*(6) 1309–1321.

Wampler, S.M., & Llanes, M. (2010). Common scrotal and testicular problems. *Primary Care, 37*(3), 613–626.

Wang, H., & Amato, P.R. (2000). Predictors of divorce adjustment: Stressors, resources and definitions. *Journal of Marriage and Family, 62*(3), 655–669.

Wang, M., Lv, Z., Shi, J., Hu, Y., & Xu, C. (2009a). Immunocontraceptive potential of the Ig-like domain of Izumo. *Molecular Reproduction and Development, 76*(8), 794–801.

Wang, M., Shi, J.L., Cheng, G.Y., Hu, Y.Q., & Xu, C. (2009b). The antibody against a nuclear autoantigenic sperm protein can result in reproductive failure. *Asian Journal of Andrology, 11*(2), 183–192.

Wang, S. (2007). Fertility therapies under the microscope. *Wall Street Journal*, November 15, p. D1.

Wanja, J. (2010, June 2). Young Kenyan women top contraception users. *Daily Nation*. Retrieved June 3, 2010, from http://www.nation.co.ke/News/Contraception%20high%20among%20women%20in%20mid%2020s/-/1056/930606/-/5an94h/-/.

Ward, P. (1990). *Courtship, love, and marriage in nineteenth-century English Canada*. Montreal and Kingston: McGill-Queen's University Press.

Warin, J. (2000). The attainment of self-consistency through gender in young children. *Sex Roles, 41*, 209–232.

Warne, G.L., Grover, S., & Zajac, J.D. (2005). Hormonal therapies for individuals with intersex conditions: Protocol for use. *Treatments in Endocrinology, 4*(1), 19–29.

Warner, T. (2002). *Never going back: A history of queer activism in Canada*. Toronto: University of Toronto Press.

Warren, J., Harvey, S., & Henderson, J. (2010). Do depression and low self-esteem follow abortion among adolescents? Evidence from a national study. *Perspectives on Sexual and Reproductive Health, 42*(4), 230–235.

Warren, M.P., Brooks-Gunn, J., Fox, R.P., Holderness, C.C., Hyle, E.P., & Hamilton, W.G. (2002). Osteopenia in exercise-associated amenorrhea using ballet dancers as a model: A longitudinal study. *Journal of Clinical Endocrinology Metabolism, 87*(7), 3162–3168.

Washington Blade, The. (1982, April 16). Gay cancer focus of hearing.

Wasley, A., Fiore, A., & Bell, B.P. (2006). Hepatitis A in the era of vaccination. *Epidemiologic Reviews, 28*(1), 101–111.

Watson, C., & Calabretto, H. (2007). Comprehensive review of conventional and non-conventional methods of management of recurrent vulvovaginal candidiasis. *Australian and New Zealand Journal of Obstetrics and Gynaecology, 47*(4), 262–272.

Watson, W., Miller, R., Wax, J., Hansen, W., Yamamura, Y., & Polzin, W. (2008). Sonographic findings of trisomy 18 in the second trimester of pregnancy. *Journal of Ultrasound in Medicine, 27*, 1033–1038.

Wattleworth, R. (2011). Human papillomavirus infection and the links to penile and cervical cancer. *Journal of the American Osteopathic Association, 111* (3 Suppl. 2), S3–S10.

Wdowiak, A., Wdowiak, L., & Wiktor, H. (2007). Evaluation of the effect of using mobile phones on male fertility. *Annals of Agricultural and Environmental Medicine, 14,* 169–172.

Weatherall, A. (2002). *Gender, language and discourse.* London: Hove Routledge.

Weaver, K., Campbell, R., Mermelstein, R., & Wakschlag, L. (2008). Pregnancy smoking in context: The influence of multiple levels of stress. *Nicotine and Tobacco Research, 10,* 1065–1073.

Weaver, T.L. (2009). Impact of rape on female sexuality: Review of selected literature. *Clinics in Obstetrics and Gynecology, 52*(4), 702–711.

Weber, B. (2014). Eric Dejaeger found guilty of 24 out of 68 sex-related charges. CBC News, September 12. http://www.cbc.ca/news/canada/north/eric-dejaeger-found-guilty-of-24-out-of-68-sex-related-charges-1.2763590.

Weed, S.E. (2008). Marginally successful results of abstinence-only program erased by dangerous errors in curriculum. *American Journal of Health Behavior, 32,* 60–73.

Weeks, J. (1989). Inverts, perverts, and Mary-Annes: Male prostitution and the regulation of homosexuality in England in the nineteenth and early twentieth centuries. In M. Duberman, M. Vicinus, & G. Chauncey Jr. (Eds.), *Hidden from history: Reclaiming the gay and lesbian past* (pp. 195–211). New York, NY: Penguin Books.

Wei, E.H. (2000). Teenage fatherhood and pregnancy involvement among urban, adolescent males: Risk factors and consequences. *Dissertation Abstracts International: Section B, 61*(1–B), #0419–4217.

Weigel, D.J. (2007). Parental divorce and the types of commitment-related messages people gain from their families of origin. *Journal of Divorce and Remarriage, 47,* 15.

Weinberg, G. (1972). *Society and the healthy homosexual.* New York, NY: MacMillan and Company.

Weinberg, M.S. (1967). The nudist camp: Way of life and social structure. *Human Organization, 26*(3), 91.

Weinberg, M.S., Williams, C.J., & Moser, C. (1984). The social constituents of sadomasochism. *Social Problems, 31*(4), 379–389.

Weinberg, M.S., Williams, C.J., & Pryor, D.W. (1994). *Dual attraction: Understanding bi-sexuality.* New York, NY: Oxford University Press.

Weinrich, J.D., Snyder, P.J., Pillard, R.C., Grant, I., Jacobson, D.L., Robinson, S.R., & McCutchan, J.A. (1993). A factor analysis of the Klein sexual orientation grid in two disparate samples. *Archives of Sexual Behavior, 22*(2), 157–168.

Weinstock, H., Berman, S., & Cates, W. (2004). Sexually transmitted diseases among American youth: Incidence and prevalence estimates, 2000. *Perspectives in Sex and Reproductive Health, 36*(1), 6–10.

Weisel, J.J., & King, P.E. (2007). Involvement in a conversation and attributions concerning excessive self-disclosure. *Southern Communication Journal, 72,* 345–354.

Weismantel, M. (2004). Moche sex pots: Reproduction and temporality in ancient South America. *American Anthropologist, 106*(3), 495–496.

Weiss, H., Dickson, K., Agot, K., & Hankins, C. (2010). Male circumcision for HIV prevention: Current research and programmatic issues. *AIDS* (Suppl. 4), S61–S69.

Weiss, P., & Brody, S. (2009). Women's partnered orgasm consistency is associated with greater duration of penile-vaginal intercourse but not of foreplay. *Journal of Sexual Medicine, 6*(1), 135–141.

Weiss, R.A. (2009). Apes, lice and prehistory. Journal of Biology, 8, 2, 20.

Weitzman, G.D. (1999). What psychology professionals should know about polyamory: The lifestyles and mental health concerns of polyamorous individuals. Paper presented at the 8th Annual Diversity Conference. Retrieved June 11, 2005, fromhttp://www.polyamory.org/~joe/polypaper.htm.

Weller, A., & Weller, L. (1998). Prolonged and very intensive contact may not be conducive to menstrual synchrony. *Psychoneuroendocrinology, 23,* 19–32.

Wellings, K., Collumbien, M., Slaymaker, E., Singh, S., Hodges, Z., et al. (2006). Sexual behavior in context: A global perspective. *Lancet, 368,* 1706–1728.

Wellisch, M. (2010). Communicating love or fear: The role of attachment styles in pathways to giftedness. *Roeper Review, 32,* 116–126.

Wells, K., Roberts, G., & Allan, C. (2012). Supporting transgender and transsexual students in K-12 schools: A guide for educators. Retrieved March 12, 2015, from http://gendercreativekids.ca/wp-content/uploads/2013/10/Supporting-Transgender-and-Transsexual-Students-web.pdf.

Welty, S.E. (2005). Critical issues with clinical research in children: The example of premature infants. *Toxicology and Applied Pharmacology,* Epub ahead of print. Retrieved July 19, 2005, from http://www.ncbi.nlm.nih.gov/entrez/query.fcgi?cmd= Retrieve&db=pubmed&dopt=Abstract&list_uids=16023161&query_hl=14.

Wesley, S. (2014). Twin-Spirited Woman: Sts'iyóye smestíyexw slhá:li. Transgender Archives Symposium. University of Victoria, BC.

Wespes, E., & Schulman, C.C. (2002). Male and ropause: Myth, reality and treatment. *International Journal of Impotence Research, 14*(Suppl. 1), 593–598.

West, K., & Hewstone, M. (2013). Culture and contact in the promotion and reduction of anti-gay prejudice: Evidence from Jamaica and Britain. *Journal of Homosexuality, 59*(1), 44–66.

Westheimer, R. (1992). *Dr. Ruth's guide to safer sex: Exciting, sensible directions for the 1990s.* New York, NY: Warner Books.

Whalen, R.E., Geary, D.C., & Johnson, F. (1990). Models of sexuality. In D.P. McWhirter, S.A. Sanders, & J.M. Reinisch (Eds.), *Homosexuality/heterosexuality: Concepts of sexual orientation* (pp. 61–70). New York, NY: Oxford University Press.

Whelan, C.I., & Stewart, D.E. (1990). Pseudocyesis: A review and report of six cases. *International Journal of Psychiatry in Medicine, 20,* 97–108.

Whipple, B. (2000). Beyond the G spot. *Scandinavian Journal of Sexology, 3,* 35–42.

Whitam, F.L., Daskalos, C., Sobolewski, C.G., & Padilla, P. (1999). The emergence of lesbian sexuality and identity cross-culturally. *Archives of Sexual Behavior, 27*(1), 31–57.

White, R.C., & Carr, R. (2005). Homosexuality and HIV/AIDS stigma in Jamaica. *Culture, Health & Sexuality, 7*(4), 347–359.

White, S.D., & DeBlassie, R.R. (1992). Adolescent sexual behavior. *Adolescence, 27,* 183–191.

Whitehead, C.S., & Hoff, C.A. (1928). *Ethical sex relations or the new eugenics: A safe guide for young men—young women.* Chicago, IL: The John A. Hertel Company.

Whiting, B., & Edwards, C.P. (1988). A cross-cultural analysis of sex differences in the behavior of children aged 3 through 11. In G. Handel (Ed.), *Childhood socialization* (pp. 281–297). New York, NY: Aldine De Gruyter.

Whiting, B.B., & Whiting, J.W. (1975). *Children of six cultures: A psycho-cultural analysis.* Cambridge, MA: Harvard University Press.

Whitley, R.J., & Roizman, B. (2001). Herpes simplex virus infections. *Lancet, 357*(9267), 1513–1519.

Whittaker, P.G., Merkh, R.D., Henry-Moss, D., & Hock-Long, L. (2010). Withdrawal attitudes and experiences: A qualitative perspective among young urban adults. *Perspectives in Sex and Reproductive Health, 42*(2), 102–109.

Whitty, M.T., & Quigley, L (2008). Emotional and sexual infidelity offline and in cyberspace. *Journal of Marital and Family Therapy, 34*(4), 461–468.

Wiederman, M.W. (1999). Volunteer bias in sexuality research using college student participants. *Journal of Sex Research, 36(1),* 59–66.

Wienke, C., & Hill, G. (2008). Does the "marriage benefit" extend to partners in gay and lesbian relationships? Evidence from a random sample of sexually active adults. *Journal of Family Issues, 30(2),* 259–289.

Wiesemann, C., Ude-Koeller, S., Sinnecker, G., & Thyen, U. (2010). Ethical principles and recommendations for the medical management of differences of sex development (DSD)/intersex in children and adolescents. *European Journal of Pediatrics, 169(6),* 671–679.

Wikan, U. (1977). Man becomes woman: Transsexualism in Oman as a key to gender roles. *Man, 12,* 304–391.

Wilcox, A.J., Weinberg, C.R., & Baird, D.D. (1995). Timing of sexual intercourse in relation to ovulation. Effects on the probability of conception, survival of the pregnancy, and sex of the baby. *New England Journal of Medicine, 333(23),* 1517–1521.

Wilcox, W.B., & Nock, S.L. (2006). What's love got to do with it? Equality, equity, commitment and women's marital quality. *Social Forces, 84,* 1321–1346.

Wildemeersch, D., & Andrade, A. (2010). Review of clinical experience with the frameless LNG-IUS for contraception and treatment of heavy menstrual bleeding. *Gynecological Endocrinology, 26(5),* 383–389.

Wilkinson, D., Tholandi, M., Ramjee, G., & Rutherford, G.W. (2002). Nonoxynol-9 spermicide for prevention of vaginally acquired HIV and other sexually transmitted infections: Systematic review and meta-analysis of randomised controlled trials including more than 5000 women. *Lancet Infectious Diseases, 2,* 613–617.

Williams, A. (2010, February 5). The new math on campus. *New York Times.* Retrieved January 26, 2011, from http://www.nytimes.com/2010/02/07/fashion/07campus.html.

Williams, C.A. (2010). *Roman homosexuality* (2nd ed.). Oxford: Oxford University Press.

Williams, J.E., & Best, D.L. (1994). Cross-cultural views of women and men. In W.J. Lonner & R. Malpass (Eds.), *Psychology and culture.* Boston, MA: Allyn & Bacon.

Williams, K., & Umberson, D. (2004). Marital status, marital transitions, and health: A gendered life course perspective. *Journal of Health and Social Behavior, 45,* 81–99.

Williams, M., & Wright, E. (2011). Betty Grable: An American icon in wartime Britain. *Historical Journal of Film, Radio & Television, 31(4),* 543–559.

Williams, W.L. (1986). *The spirit and the flesh: Sexual diversity in American Indian culture.* Boston, MA: Beacon Press.

Wills, T. (1986). Statue to bring Diefenbaker back to Parliament he loved so well. *The Montreal Gazette,* August 18, p. 1.

Wilmington Morning Star. (1992). Defense claims Dahmer was a "killing machine." *Star News,* February 15, p. 3A.

Wilson, C. (2005). Recurrent vulvovaginitis candidiasis: An overview of traditional and alternative therapies. *Advanced Nurse Practitioner, 13(2),* 24–29.

Wilson, C.A., & Davies, D.C. (2007). The control of sexual differentiation of the reproductive system and brain. *Reproduction, 133,* 331–359.

Wilson, E., Dalberth, B., & Koo, H. (2010). "We're the heroes!": Fathers' perspectives on their role in protecting their preteen-age children from sexual risk. *Perspectives on Sexual and Reproductive Health, 42(2),* 117–124.

Wilson, G.D. (1987). An ethological approach to sexual deviation. In G.D. Wilson (Ed.), *Variant sexuality: Research and theory* (pp. 84–115). Baltimore: Johns Hopkins University Press.

Wilson, J.C. (2012). Bollywood explores gay-related themes. *Windy City Times, 28(2),* 26.

Wilson, P. (1994). Forming a partnership between parents and sexuality educators. *SIECUS Report, 22,* 1–5.

Wilson, R.F. (2008). Keeping women in business (and the family). (Washington Lee Legal Studies Paper No. 2008–34.) Retrieved December 18, 2008, from http://ssrn.com/abstract=1113468.

Wilson, S.K., Delk, J.R., 2nd, & Billups, K.L. (2001). Treating symptoms of female sexual arousal disorder with the Eros-Clitoral Therapy Device. *Journal of Gender Specific Medicine, 4(2),* 54–58.

Wind, R. (2008). Perception that teens frequently substitute oral sex for intercourse a myth. [News release]. New York, NY: Alan Guttmacher Institute. Retrieved September 2, 2008, from http://www.guttmacher.org/media/nr/2008/05/20/index.html.

Wise, L.A., Cramer, D.W., Hornstein, M.D., Ashby, R.K., & Missmer, S.A. (2011). Physical activity and semen quality among men attending an infertility clinic. *Fertility and Sterility 95(3),* 1025–1030.

Wittchen, H.U., Becker, E., Lieb, R., & Krause, P. (2002). Prevalence, incidence and stability of premenstrual dysphoric disorder in the community. *Psychological Medicine, 32(1),* 119–132.

Wittenberg, A., & Gerber, J. (2009). Recommendations for improving sexual health curricula in medical schools: Results from a two-arm study collecting data from patients and medical students. *Journal of Sexual Medicine, 6,* 362–368.

Wittmann, D., Foley, S., & Balon, R. (2011). A biopsychosocial approach to sexual recovery after prostate cancer surgery: The role of grief and mourning. *Journal of Sex and Marital Therapy, 37(2),* 130–144.

Wojnar, D. (2007). Miscarriage experiences of lesbian couples. *Journal of Midwifery Women's Health, 52,* 479–485.

Wolf, N. (1991). *The beauty myth: How images of beauty are used against women.* New York, NY: W. Morris.

Wolfinger, N.H. (2000). Beyond the intergenerational transmission of divorce. *Journal of Family Issues, 21,* 1061–1086.

Wolitzky-Taylor, K., Resnick, H., McCauley, J., Amstadter, A., et al. (2011). Is reporting of rape on the rise? A comparison of women with reported versus unreported rape experiences in the National Women's Study-Replication. *Journal of Interpersonal Violence, 26(4),* 807–832.

Wolpe, J. (1958). *Psychotherapy by reciprocal inhibition.* Stanford, CA: Stanford University Press.

Wong, E.W., & Cheng, C.Y. (2011). Impacts of environmental toxicants on male reproductive dysfunction. *Trends Pharmacological Science, 32(5),* 290–299.

Woo, J., Fine, P., & Goetzl, L. (2005). Abortion disclosure and the association with domestic violence. *Obstetrics & Gynecology, 105(6),* 1329–1334.

Wood, C. (2006). From barracks to barstools: A sociological reading of the lesbian pulp fiction genre. Conference Papers, American Sociological Association, Annual Meeting, Montreal, p. 1–20.

Wood, J. (1999). *Gendered lives: Communication, gender, and culture.* Belmont, CA: Wadsworth.

Woods, G. (1998). *A history of gay literature.* Hong Kong: World Print Ltd.

Woods, N.F., Most, A., & Dery, G.K. (1982). Prevalence of perimenstrual symptoms. *American Journal of Public Health, 72(11),* 1257–1264.

Wooltorton, E. (2006). Visual loss with erectile dysfunction medications. *Canadian Medical Association Journal, 175,* 355.

Workowski, K., & Berman, S. (2010). Sexually transmitted disease treatment guidelines, 2010. *Morbidity and Mortality Weekly Report, 59(RR-12),* 1–110.

World Contraceptive Use 2009. (2009). New York, NY: United Nations, Department of Economic and Social Affairs, Population Division. Retrieved from http://www.un.org/esa/population/publications/contraceptive2009/contraceptive2009.htm.

World Health Organization (2009). Reference values for human semen composition. *Human Reproduction Update, 16(3),* 231–245.

World Health Organization. (2006). Fifty-Ninth World Health Assembly. Geneva, 22–27 May. WHA59/2006/REC/1.

World Health Organization. (2008). *Eliminating female genital mutilation: An interagency statement.* Retrieved March 22, 2008, from http://data.unaids.org/pub/BaseDocument/2008/20080227_interagencystatement_eliminating_fgm_en.pdf.

World Health Organization. (2008). Hepatitis B. Fact sheet no. 204. Geneva, Switzerland: World Health Organization.

World Health Organization. (2013). HIV/AIDS. Fact sheet N-360. November.

World Professional Organization for Transgender Health. (2001). "The Harry Benjamin International Gender Dysphoria Association's Standards of Care for Gender Identity Disorders, Sixth Version." Retrieved April 17, 2011, from http://wpath.org/Documents2/socv6.pdf.

Wright, K. (1994). The sniff of legend—human pheromones. Chemical sex attractants? A sixth sense organ in the nose? What are we animals? *Discover, 15*(4), 60.

Wright, L., Mulick, P., & Kincaid, S. (2006). Fear of and discrimination against bisexuals, homosexuals, and individuals with AIDS. *Journal of Bisexuality, 6,* 71–84.

Wright, S. (2010). Depathologizing consensual sexual sadism, sexual masochism, transvestic fetishism, and fetishism. *Archives of Sexual Behavior, 39*(6), 1229–1230.

Wright, V.C., Chang, J., Jeng, G., & Macaluso, M. (2008). Assisted reproductive technology surveillance—United States. *Morbidity and Mortality Weekly Report, 57,* 1–23.

Wu, F., Tajar, A., Beynon, J., Pye, S., Phil, M., Silman, A., Finn, J., O'Neill, T., & Bartfai, G. (2010). Identification of late-onset hypogonadism in middle-aged and elderly men. *New England Journal of Medicine, 363,* 123–135.

Wu, M.V., & Shah, N.M. (2011). Control of masculinization of the brain and behavior. *Current Opinions in Neurobiology, 21,* 116–123.

Wu, S.C. (2010). Family planning technical services in China. *Frontiers of Medicine in China. 4*(3), 285–289.

Wuthnow, R. (1998). Islam. In *Encyclopedia of politics and religion* (pp. 383–393). Washington, DC: Congressional Quarterly Books.

Wynne, A., & Currie, C.L. (2011). Social exclusion as an underlying determinant of sexually transmitted infections among Canadian Aboriginals. *Pimatisiwin: A Journal of Aboriginal & Indigenous Community Health, 9* (1), 113–127.

Wysoczanski, M., Rachko, M., & Bergmann, S.R. (2008, April 2). Acute myocardial-infarction in a young man using anabolic-steroids. *Angiology, 59*(3), 376–378.

Xiaohe, X., & Whyte, M. (1990). Love matches and arranged marriages: A Chinese replication. *Journal of Marriage and the Family, 53*(3), 709–722.

Xu, F., Sternberg, M., Kottiri, B., McQuillan, G., Lee, F., Nahmias, A., Berman, S., & Markowitz, L.E. (2006). Trends in herpes simplex virus type 1 and type 2 seroprevalence in the U.S. *Journal of the American Medical Association, 296,* 964–973.

Yamawaki, N. (2007). Differences between Japanese and American college students in giving advice about help seeking to rape victims. *Journal of Social Psychology, 147,* 511–530.

Yamawaki, N., & Tschanz, B.T. (2005). Rape perception differences between Japanese and American college students: On the mediating influence of gender role traditionality. *Sex Roles, 52*(5–6), 379–392.

Yanagimachi, R. (2011). Problems of sperm fertility: A reproductive biologist's view. *Systems in Biological Reproductive Medicine, 57*(1–2), 102–114.

Yancey, G. (2007). Homogamy over the net: Using Internet advertisements to discover who interracially dates. *Journal of Social and Personal Relationships, 24,* 913–930.

Yang, X., & Reckelhoff, J. (2011). Estrogen, hormonal replacement therapy and cardiovascular disease. *Current Opinions in Nephrology and Hypertension, 20*(2), 133–138.

Yao, M.Z., Mahood, C., & Linz, D. (2010). Sexual priming, gender stereotyping, and likelihood to sexually harass: Examining the cognitive effects of playing a sexually-explicit video game. *Sex Roles, 62*(1), 77–88.

Yassin, A.A., & Saad, F. (2008). Testosterone and sexual dysfunction. *Journal of Andrology, 29*(6), Epub ahead of print. Retrieved October 29, 2008, from http://www.andrologyjournal.org/cgi/content/abstract/29/6/593.

Yates, C. (2012). Sexuality and South Asian diaspora. *Xtra* (Toronto), *713,* 12.

Yee, L. (2010). Aging and sexuality. *Australian Family Physician, 39*(10), 718–721.

Yee, P. (1988). Saltwater city: An illustrated history of the Chinese in Vancouver. Vancouver: Douglas and McIntyre.

Yen, J., Chang, S., Ko, C., Yen, C., Chen, C., Yeh, Y., & Chen, C. (2010). The high-sweet-fat food craving among women with PMDD: Emotional response, implicit attitudes and rewards sensitivity. *Psychoneuroendocrinology, 35*(8), 1203–1212.

Yllo, K., & Finkelhor, D. (1985). Marital rape. In A.W. Burgess (Ed.), *Rape and sexual assault* (pp. 146–158). New York, NY: Garland.

Yost, M.R. (2010). Development and validation of the attitudes about sadomasochism scale. *Journal of Sex Research, 47*(1), 79–91.

Young, K.A., Liu, Y., & Wang, Z. (2008, March 2). The neurobiology of social attachment: A comparative approach to behavioral, neuroanatomical, and neurochemical studies. *Comparative Biochemistry and Physiology: Toxicology and Pharmacology.* Retrieved October 3, 2008, from http://www.ncbi.nlm.nih.gov/pubmed/18417423?ordinalpos=1&itool=EntrezSystem2.PEntrez.Pubmed.Pubmed_ResultsPanel.Pubmed_RVDocSum.

Young, K.S., Griffin-Shelley, E., Cooper, A., O'Mara, J., & Buchanan, J. (2000). Online infidelity. In A. Cooper (Ed.), *Cybersex: The dark side of the force* (pp. 59–74). Philadelphia, PA: Brunner Routledge.

Young, L. (2015). Sexual education compared across Canada. Retrieved from http://globalnews.ca/news/1847912/sexual-education-compared-across-canada/.

Young, L.J., & Wang, Z. (2004). The neurobiology of pair bonding. *Nature, 7,* 1048–1054.

Youssry, M., Ozmen, B., Zohni, K., Diedrich, K., & Al-Hasani, S. (2008). Current aspects of blastocyst cryopreservation. *Reproductive Biomedicine Online, 16,* 311–320.

Yule, M.A., Brotto, L.A., & Gorzalka, B.B. (2014). Sexual fantasy and masturbation among asexual individuals. *Canadian Journal of Human Sexuality, 23*(2), 89–95.

Zaazaa, A., Bella, A.J., & Shamloul, R. (2013). Drug addiction and sexual dysfunction. *Endocrinology and Metabolic Clinics of North America, 42*(3), 585–592.

Zacur, H.A., Hedon, B., Mansourt, D., Shang-old, G.A., Fisher, A.C., & Creasy, G.W. (2002). Integrated summary of Ortho Evra contraceptive patch adhesion in varied climates and conditions. *Fertility and Sterility, 77* (2 Suppl. 2), 532–535.

Zaidi, A.U., & Shuraydi, M. (2002). Perceptions of arranged marriages by young pakistani muslim women living in a western society. *Journal of Comparative Family Studies, 33*(4), 495.

Zain Al-Dien, M.M. (2010). Perceptions of sex education among Muslim adolescents in Canada. *Journal of Muslim Minority Affairs, 30*(3), 391–407.

Zak, A., Collins, C., & Harper, L. (1998). Self-reported control over decision-making and its relationship to intimate relationships. *Psychological Reports, 82*(2), 560–562.

Zanetti-Dallenbach, R.A., Krause, E.M., Lapaire, O., Gueth, U., Holzgreve, W.,

Wight, E. (2008). Impact of hormone replacement therapy on the histologic subtype of breast cancer. Epub retrieved on March 18, 2008, from http://www.ncbi.nlm.nih.gov/pubmed/18335229?ordinalpos=1&itool=EntrezSystem2.PEntrez.Pubmed.Pubmed_ResultsPanel.Pubmed_RVDocSum.

Zaslow, J. (2007, August 23). Are we teaching our kids to be fearful of men? *Wall Street Journal.* Retrieved June 10, 2008, from http://online.wsj.com/public/article/SB118782905698506010.html.

Zemishlany, Z., Aizenberg, D., & Weizman, A. (2001). Subjective effects of MDMA ('Ecstasy') on human sexual function. *European Psychiatry, 16*(2), 127–130.

Zhang, X.H., Filippi, S., Morelli, A., Vignozzi, L., Luconi, M., Donati, S., Forti, G., Maggi, M. (2006). Testosterone restores diabetes-induced erectile dysfunction and sildenafil responsiveness in two distinct animal models of chemical diabetes. *Journal of Sexual Medicine, 3*(2), 253–264.

Zhao, Y., Garcia, J., Jarow, J., & Wallach, E. (2004). Successful management of infertility due to retrograde ejaculation using assisted reproductive technologies: A report of two cases. *Archives of Andrology, 50*(6), 391–394.

Zhao, Y., Montoro, R., Igartua, K., & Thombs, B.D. (2010). Suicidal ideation and attempt among adolescents reporting "unsure" sexual identity or heterosexual identity plus same-sex attraction or behavior: Forgotten groups? *Journal of the American Academy of Child and Adolescent Psychiatry, 49*(2), 104–113.

Zieman, M., Guillebaud, J., Weisberg, E., Shangold, G., Fisher, A., & Creasy, G. (2002). Contraceptive efficacy and cycle control with the Ortho Evra transdermal system: The analysis of pooled data. *Fertility and Sterility, 77,* S13–18.

Zimmer-Gembeck, M.J., & Helfand, M. (2008). Ten years of longitudinal research on U.S. adolescent sexual behavior: Developmental correlates of sexual intercourse, and the importance of age, gender and ethnic background. *Developmental Review, 28,* 153–224.

Zinaman, M.J., Clegg, E.D., Brown, C.C., O'Connor, J., & Selevan, S.G. (1996). Estimates of human fertility and pregnancy loss. *Journal of Fertility and Sterility, 65*(3), 503–509.

Zolese, G., & Blacker, C.V.R. (1992). The psychological complications of therapeutic abortion. *British Journal of Psychiatry, 160,* 742–749.

Zucker, K.J. (1990). Psychosocial and erotic development in cross-gender identified children. *Canadian Journal of Psychiatry, 35,* 487–495.

Zukov, I., Ptacek, R., Raboch, J., Domluvilova, D., Kuzelova, H., Fischer, S., & Kozelek, P. (2010). PMDD—Review of actual findings about mental disorders related to menstrual cycle and possibilities of their therapy. *Prague Medical Reports, 111*(1), 12–24.

Zurbriggen, E.L., & Yost, M.R. (2004). Power, desire, and pleasure in sexual fantasies. *Journal of Sex Research, 41*(3), 288–300.

Name Index

Briken, P., 423
Brinig, M. F., 356
Brinton, L., 80, 108, 129
Brizendine, L., 148, 300
Brock, G. B., 398
Brockman, N., 177
Brodsky, A., 333
Brody, S., 372
Brongersma, E., 428
Brooks-Gunn, J., 278, 283
Brotman, S., 258
Brotto, L. A., 393, 408
Broude, G. J., 451
Broughton, D., 272
Brousseau, M., 444, 446
Brown, A., 457
Brown, B. B., 278–279
Brown, C., 468
Brown, D. J., 412
Brown, D. L., 200
Brown, Helen Gurley, 21
Brown, J., 255
Brown, J. C., 82, 328, 418
Brown, Louise, 130
Brown, M. S., 95
Brown, R., 137
Brown, T. J., 453
Brown, V. W., 61, 455
Browne, A., 464
Brownlee, John Edward, 438–439
Brownmiller, Susan, 448–449
Brubaker, L., 147
Brucker, Co., 170
Bruckner, H., 211
Brumbaugh, C., 324
Brumberg, J. J., 277
Bruni, V., 170
Brunner-Huber, L. R., 154, 169
Buckett, W., 129
Buffardi, A. L., 282
Buisson, O., 62
Bukovec, P., 456
Bull, S. S., 155
Bullivant, S., 121
Bullough, V. L., 12, 14–15, 20, 34, 37, 39, 249
Bumpass, L., 341
Burdette, A. M., 346
Burgess, A., 446, 455–456, 458
Burgess, E. O., 345, 363
Burgoyne, Robert, 302
Burke, A. E., 155, 160
Burke, W., 86
Burkeman, O., 221
Burkman, R., 169, 171
Burleson, R. R., 298–300
Burns, M., 409
Burrows, L., 83
Burton, K., 324
Burton, Richard Francis, 480
Busby, D., 340
Buss, D. M., 227, 326–327, 333, 340
Busse, P., 283

Butler, Donald, 487
Butrick, C. W., 405
Butts, William Marlin, 494–495
Buvat, J., 403
Byers, E., 287, 374
Byers, E. S., 365, 372, 383
Byers, S. E., 286
Byrne, D., 326, 367

C

Cabaret, A. S., 86
Cadbury, Barbara, 155
Cadbury, George, 155
Cado, S., 365
Caffaro, J., 462
Cahill, S., 247, 258
Cai, D., 102–103
Cai, L. Q., 301, 329
Cain, R., 209
Cakin-Memik, N., 107
Calabretto, H., 202
Calderone, M., 286
Califia, P., 369
Callens, N., 103
Calvin, John, 14
Calzavara, L. M., 195, 255
Camacho, M., 391
Cameron, S., 186
Cammaert, L., 469
Campbell, J. C., 468
Campbell, J. L., 453
Campbell, L., 308, 393
Campbell, P. P., 456
Campbell, R., 455
Camperio-Ciani, A., 245
Campos, B., 354
Canadian AIDS Society (CAS), 194
Canadian Cancer Society, 84, 86–87, 108–109
Canadian Criminal Code, 462
Canadian Quality of Life Survey, 326
Canary, D. J., 300
Candolin, U., 300
Cantor, J. M., 245
Capaldi, D., 469
Capel, B., 100
Capsuto, S., 484
Caravaggio, 477
Carcopino, X., 60
Card, Charles Ora, 352
Carey, B., 263, 330
Cargill, W. M., 143
Carlson, H., 100
Carlson, J., 449, 453
Carlson, M., 393, 408
Carlton, C. L., 183
Carnegie, Andrew, 35
Carnes, Patrick, 433
Carpentier, M. Y., 409
Carr, R. R., 78, 215
Carrell, D. T., 138
Carrigan, M., 365
Carrington, B., 427

Carroll, J, 278, 366, 429
Carter, F., 223
Carter, J., 393, 410
Caruso, S., 168, 393
Casavent, L., 491
Case, P., 262
Casey, T., 280
Caspi, A., 148
Cass, Vivienne, 254–255
Casteels, K., 271
Catalyst, 438
Catania, J. A., 45
Cates, W., 205
Caughey, A., 139
Cavanagh, Sheila L., 437
Cavanaugh, C., 446, 468
Cecchetti, J. A., 325
Cederroth, C. R., 97
Centers for Disease Control and Prevention, 95, 128, 129, 130, 131, 195, 208, 282
Cetinkaya, H., 381
Chakraborty, A., 255–256
Chalett, J. M., 120
Chalkley, A. J., 380
Chambers, Marilyn, 484
Chan, J., 403
Chandra, P., 477
Chang, Q., 143
Chang, S., 181
Chaplin, S., 381
Charcot, Jean-Martin, 34
Charoenkwan, K., 410
Chasin, C. J. D., 364
Chatterjee, E., 252
Chaudhury, R. R., 155
Chauncey, G., 246
Chavarro, J. E., 97, 128
Cheasty, M., 455
Check, J. H., 129
Chemes, H., 130
Chen, Z., 82
Cheng, C. Y., 128
Cheng, D., 135
Chenier, I., 418
Cherkowski, S., 228
Cherlin, A., 333
Chesney, K., 418
Cheung, F. M., 395
Chia, M., 120
Chinas, B., 232
Chin-Hong, P., 204
Chinichian, M., 282
Choi, N., 328
Chopin-Marcé, M. J., 435
Chow, E. W., 429
Choy, A. L., 429
Chrisler, J. C., 66, 220
Christal, Jenny, 329
Christian Brothers of Ireland in Canada, 437
Christiansen, O. B., 138
Christofides, E., 296
Chudakov, B., 394

Tannen, Deborah, 298–299
Tanveer, K., 451
Tao, G., 10
Tarasaoff, L. A., 128
Tarkovsky, A., 376
Taub, D. E., 257
Taylor, C., 355
Taylor, G. W., 382
Taylor, H. E., 254, 256
Taylor, M. A., 418
Teague, L., 106
Tebaldi, E., 256
Teen Pregnancy, 284
Teitelman, A., 84
Teles, M., 73
Tepavcevic, D., 412
Tepper, J., 145
Terada, Y., 130
Terry, J., 243
Tesfayae, F., 403
Tesher, Ellie, 299
Testa, M., 457
Teuscher, C., 235
Teuscher, U., 235
Tewksbury, R., 457–458
Thalidomide Victims Association of
    Canada, 135
Thankamony, A., 61
Thoennes, N., 453, 468
Thomas, S. L., 78–79, 166
Thomasset, C., 13
Thompson, A. P., 346, 437
Thompson, C., 194
Thompson, K. M., 462, 464
Thomson, M., 95
Thomson, R., 95, 305
Thorne, N., 323
Thornhill, Randy, 448–449
Thorp, J. M., 186
Thorup, J., 103
Tiefer, Leonore, 33, 36, 390
Tillmann, H. C. K, 406
Timmreck, C., 331
Ting-Toomey, S., 329
Tinitigan, R., 203
Tipton, Billy, 229
Tissot, Samuel-Auguste, 368
Tjaden, P., 453, 468
Tjepkema, M., 195
Tjoe, M., 196
Tokushige, N., 82
Toma, S. M., 105
Tomaso, B., 155
Tommola, P., 83
Tomson, D. M., 452
Toppari, J., 97, 103
Toro-Morn, M., 329
Toth, J., 169
Toussaint, I., 399
Tovar, J., 204, 206
Towne, B., 74
Trabert, B., 109

Tralatzis, B. C., 169
Tramel, J., 453
Travis, L., 204
Treas, J., 346
Trenholm, C., 290
Trevethan, R., 255
Trevithick, A., 351
Trigger, B. G., 17
Tristano, A. G., 412
Troiden, R.R., 254, 432–433
Trost, J. E., 120
Trotter, E. C., 281
Trudeau, Pierre Elliott, 239, 348
Trudel, G., 413
Trumbach, R., 15, 249
Tsai, S., 80–81
Tsang, A. K., 235
Tschanz, B. T., 449–451
Tse, J. K.-H., 350
Tsivian, M., 402
Tsui-Sui, A., 283
Tsunokai, G., 339
Tufik, S., 408
Tulandi, T., 137
Turcotte, M., 343
Turek, P., 128
Turner, W., 34, 333
Twiss, J., 79
Tye, M. H., 264
Tzeng, J. M., 322, 344
Tzortzis, V., 412

U

Uittenbogaard, Martin, 429
Uji, M., 451
Ullman, S., 455
Umberson, D., 345
UNAIDS, 208, 211–215
Upchurch, D. M., 193, 280, 282
Usatine, R. P., 203
USA Today, 437
U.S. Census Bureau, 356
U.S. Department of Justice, 457
Uskel, A. K., 339
U.S. National Survey on Sexual Health and
    Behavior, 118
U.S. Preventive Services Task Force, 87
Ussher, J. M., 262, 382

V

Valente, S. M., 461–462, 464
Valenzuela, C. Y., 244–245
van Aerde, J., 146
van Basten, J. P., 411
Van Berlo, W., 455
Van De Geyn, L., 65
van den Berg, Ad, 429
van den Heuvel, M., 170
Vanderbilt, H., 465
Van der Horst, C., 107
VanderLaan, 195, 232
Van der Zanden, L. F., 103

Vanfossen, B., 298
Vanggaard, T., 476–477
van Heeringen, K., 254
Vanier, S. A., 374
Vanier Institute of the Family, 355
van Lankveld, J., 401
Van Neck, A., 368
Vannier, Sarah, 338
van Teijlingen, E., 309
Van Voorhis, B. J., 129
Vanwesenbeeck, I., 496
Van Wormer, H. M., 352
Vasey, P., 103, 195
Veitch, R., 321
Venancio, D. P., 108
Venkat, P., 171
Ventura, S. J., 282
Venturini, P. L., 82
Verberg, M. F., 125
Verkasalo, P. K., 86
Verlinsky, Y., 127, 138
Versfeld, N. J., 310
Vertesi, J., 371
Verweij, K., 259
Vessey, M., 169
Vetten, L., 450
Vigano, P., 82
Vilain, E., 24, 70
Vincent, M. V., 107
Vincke, J., 254
Viner, R., 74
Vissers, W., 196
Voight, H., 395
Voiland, A., 97
Voller, E., 446
Volling, B. I., 324
Von Gloeden, Wilhelm, 478–479
Vorsanova, S., 138
Vrabel, K., 464
Vukadinovic, Z., 433

W

Waal, F. B. M., 246
Wacker, J., 457
Wahlberg, Mark, 379
Wakelin, A., 448, 455
Walch, K., 114
Wald, A., 203
Waldinger, M., 399, 402, 403
Waldinger, R., 345
Walen, S. R., 30–31
Walker, J., 286, 457
Wall, C., 84
Wallen, K., 275
Wallerstein, E., 95
Walsh, D., 453
Walsh, John, 223
Walters, G. D., 399
Wampler, S. M., 106
Wang, H., 357
Wang, M., 138
Wang, S., 182

Subject Index

Bold entries and page references indicate definitions.

artificial insemination, 129
asceticism, 14
asexual relationships, 345, 363–365
Asia and the Pacific countries
    HIV/AIDS in, 212–213
    homosexuality in, 252
Asian immigrants, sexual assault attitudes
        among, 449–450
*As Nature Made Him: The Boy Who Was Raised
        as a Girl* (Colapinto), 221
assisted human reproduction (AHR), 128–129, 136
asymptomatic infection, 195
atheoretical research, 39
athletes
    amenorrhea in, 76–77
    male identity and, 328
    sexual assault and, 453–454
attachment, bonding and, 271, 323–324
attraction
    gender inequity and, 327
    love and, 326–327
Austin Powers: International Man of Mystery
        (film), 399
autinoculate, 203
auto-fellatio, 369
autosomes, 67
avatars, 305
aversion therapy, 30
    sexual disorders, 434–435

B

back-alley abortions, 183
bacterial vaginosis, 83, 201
baculum, 94
Bad Trick List, 496
balanitis, 107
Bartholin's glands, 61, 83
basal body temperature (BBT), 176
BDSM (bondage & discipline, dominance &
        submission), 382–383, 418–420, 428
    film images of, 484–485
beauty, Chinese concepts of, 11
beer consumption, bone density and, 80
behavioural reinforcement theory, 321–322
behaviourists, 30
behaviour modification, 30
behavioural theory, 30
    paraphilias and, 423
    sex research and, 38, 48
    sexual orientation and, 247
Be Like Others (film), 229
Bem Sex-Role Inventory, 226–229, 328
benign mass, 84
benign prostatic hypertrophy (BPH), 109–110
bestiality, 8, 431–432
bibliotherapy, 400–401
bigamy, 351
bilingualism, communication and, 302
Bill C-36, 497
Bill C-38 (Canada), 348–349
Bill C-150 (Canada), 239
Bill C-279 (Canada), 230

biological clock phenomenon, 136
biological theory, 31, 48
    gender differences and, 224
    love and, 323
    paraphilias and, 422
    sexual orientation and, 243–245
biphasic pill, 167
biphobia, 263
birth control, 156. *See also* contraception; oral
        contraceptives
    combination birth control pill, 166
    education about, 4
    emergency contraception and, 180–181
    forgetting to use, 167
    gender roles in, 154–156
    progestin-only methods, 172–173
    sexually transmitted infections and, 195–196
    unreliable methods for, 157
Birth Control League, 22
birth defects, 138–139
birthing positions, 142
birth order
    sexuality and, 272
    sexual orientation and, 244–245
birthplace choices, 141
birth process, 140–144
birth rates, 122
bisexuality, 262–263
    hate crimes and, 260
    organizations for, 258
    prevalence measurements, 241–242
    sexual assault and, 456
    sexually transmitted infections and, 195
    on television, 486
bisphenol A, 73
blackmail, sex scandals and, 437
blastocyst, 123–124
blood tests, 126
"blue balls," 120
bluedildonics, 371
body art, female genitalia, 64
body image, 277
    sexual communication and, 307
bonding, in early childhood, 271, 323–324
bone density tests, 79–80
Borat (film), 369
The Bostonians (James), 249
"Boston marriages," 20, 249
brain
    differentiation and development, 69–70
    gender differences in, 224
    love and, 330
Braxton-Hicks contractions, 133
BRCA genes, 86–87, 108
breaking up, 340–341
breakthrough bleeding, 167
breast buds, 273–274
breast cancer
    in men, 100, 108–109
    morning sickness and, 126
    sexual dysfunction and, 410
    in women, 84–87

breastfeeding, 147–148
    birth control and, 157
breasts
    augmentation, 65
    exposure of, in Canada, 19
    female anatomy, 64–65
    male anatomy, 100
    self-examination, 85
    sexual response cycle and, 115–117
breech position, 141, 145
Brenda/Bruce, 221
*Brother to Brother: New Writings by Black Gay
        Men* (Hemphill), 264
brucella parasite, 205
bulbourethral gland, 99

C

camp, 247
Canada
    abortion in, 183–184
    arranged marriages in, 350
    assimilation policies toward Aboriginal
        people in, 17–18
    breastfeeding in, 147–148
    Catholic Church child abuse scandals in,
        437–439
    cesarean section statistics in, 145–146
    child sex abuse in, 462
    common-law unions, 342–343
    consanguineous marriages in, 353–354
    contraception in, 154–156
    criminal sexual psychopath laws in, 418
    cybersex in, 370–371
    dating in, 338–339
    divorce in, 355–356
    ectopic pregnancies in, 137–138
    fertility statistics and current trends in,
        120–123, 128–131
    French colonization in, 18
    gay rights in, 19, 256
    gay-themed films in, 261
    history of sexuality in, 17–18
    HIV/AIDS in, 207–208
    intimate partner violence in, 467
    legalization of homosexuality in, 238–239
    marriage trends and statistics in, 342
    oral sex in, 374–375
    pedophilia in, 429–430
    polygamous marriages in, 351–352
    pornography and censorship in, 487–491
    prostitution in, 491–492, 493–497
    race and homosexuality in, 263–264
    romance novels published in, 482
    same-sex marriage in, 348–349
    sex education programs in, 4, 6, 286–292
    sex research in, 43–44
    sex scandals in, 438–439
    sex and single college students in, 362–363
    sex therapy in, 395
    sexual assault statistics in, 445–446
    sexual harassment in, 469–470
    sexuality in, 32–33

femininity (*continued*)
    sexual orientation and, 243
    stereotypes of, 228
feminist standpoint theory, 33
feminist theory, 448–449
    pornography and, 490–491
    sexuality and, 33, 48, 228–229
    in United States, 21–22
fertility, 120–127
    drugs for, 129
    statistics and current trends, 120–121
fertility awareness, 176
fertility awareness-based methods, 176
fertilization, 67
fetal alcohol spectrum disorder (FASD), 135
fetal distress, 145
fetishistic disorder, 428, 430
fetishistic sexual activity, 379–381, 424
    in animals, 381
    incidence and categories, 379–381
    Internet communities, 381
Fetlife, 381
fetus, 67
field of eligibles, 326
Fifty Shades of Grey (film), 484
fighting, communication and, 311–312
films. *See also* specific films
    sexuality in, 483–485
    transgender images, 485
fimbriae, 64
First Nations cultures (Canada). *See also*
        aboriginal cultures; Métis culture in Canada.
    Canadian residential school system and
        abuse of, 438, 463
    communication and culture in, 301
    consanguineous marriages and, 353–354
    HIV/AIDS and, 209
    intermarriage with colonists and, 18
    music artists from, 318
    polyandry and, 351
    prostitution and, 494
    sexuality and, 17–18, 33
5-alpha reductase deficiency, 101–103
fixation, 29
flagellum, 98
follicle-stimulating hormone (FSH), 70
    in males, 104, 108
    menstruation, 73
    oral contraceptives, 167
follicular phase, 74
Food and Drug Administration (FDA),
        156–157
foot binding, Chinese practice of, 11
forced marriages, 350–351
For Each Other: Sharing Sexual Intimacy
        (Barbach), 309
foreplay, 372
foreskin, 92–93
The 40 Year Old Virgin (film), 369
fraternal twins, 124
free love movement, 20
frenulum, 92

friends with benefits, 339
frotteuristic disorder, 425, 427–428
Fundamentalist Church of Jesus Christ of
        Latter Day Saints (FLDS), 352
furries, 381

G

gamete, female, 66
**gamete intra-Fallopian tube transfer
        (GIFT),** 130
gang rape, 450–451
gay rights
    in Africa, 252–253
    in Asia and Pacific, 252
    assisted human reproduction and, 128–129
    in Canada, 19, 249–250
    censorship and, 487–491
    cross-cultural comparisons, 251–253
    gay-themed Canadian films and, 261
    globalization and, 253–254
    hate crimes and, 260
    homophobia and, 259–261
    in Iran, 229
    in Latin America, 251
    lifestyle issues and, 256–258
    in Middle East and North Africa,
        251–252
    organizations for, 258
    parenting and, 257
    persecution of homosexuality and,
        418–420
    race and, 263–264
    seniors and, 257–258
    in South Africa, 451
    in United States, 22–23
The Gay Mystique (Fisher), 348
gender, 66, 220. *See also* females; males
    in Canadian Aboriginal culture, 17
    communication and, 298–301
    contraceptives and, 154–156
    in early childhood, 271
    extramarital sex and, 346
    femininity, 222–223
    masculinity, 222–223
    rape and sexual assault attitudes and, 449,
        459–461
    sexual fantasies and, 367
    sexually transmitted infections and,
        194–195
    sexual revolution and role of, 21–22
    social networking and, 304–306
    stereotypes, 222–223
    varieties of, 227–233
gender bias, 41
gender binary, 229
gender constancy, 271
gender diversity, 230
gender dysphoria, 230
gender equality, 235–236
gender-identity disorder, 234
gender inequity, in attraction, 327
genderlect theory, 299

gender roles, 222
    coming out and, 254–256
    as innate, 223–224
    non-conformity with, 246–247
    theories, 225–226
    throughout life span, 234–236
gender schema, 226
gender spectrum, 229
gender traits, 222
generalizable research, 40–41
generalizable sexual problem, 391
genetics
    breast cancer, 86
    homosexuality and, 243–244
    sexuality and, 37
    sexual orientation, 243–244
genital congestion, 16
genital herpes, 202–204
genital self-examination, females, 57
genital stage, 29
genital touching, in early childhood,
        272–273
genital warts, 204
genito-pelvic pain/penetration disorders,
        404–405
germ cell, 66
gerontophilia, 428–429
gestation, 67, 220
    in animals, 140
ginseng, 394
glans clitoris, 59
glans penis, 92–93
GLBTTQQIAAP2S, 240
globalization
    homosexuality and, 253–254
    sex education and, 291
Global Study of Sexual Attitudes and
        Behaviors, 49–50
gonadotropin-releasing hormone (GnRH),
        70, 73, 104, 108
gonads, 220
    female, 66
gonococcus bacterium, 198
gonorrhea, 197–199
Gossip Girl (television program), 6
gossypol, 181
granulosa cells, 76
Grifenberg spot (G-spot), 62
gynandromorphophilia, 425
gynecologic health concerns, 81–84
gynecologist, 56
gynecomastia, 100
Gynefix, 176

H

"half-age-plus-seven rule," 339
haploid cell, 67
The Happy Hooker (Hollander), 492
harassment/coercion, 436–437. *See also* sexual
        harassment
    sexual assault and, 445–447
harems, 13

Harlequin Romances, 482
harm principle, pornography and, 490–491
Hassle Free Clinic, 199
hate crimes, 260
Health Canada, 156–157, 180–181
health status, sexual function and, 408
hebephilia, 428–429
Hebrew Bible
    love in, 317
    sexual fantasy in, 366–367
    sexuality in, 8
hedge words, 299
hemiplegia, 409
herbs
    as contraceptives, 155
    oral contraceptive interaction with, 168
hermaphroditism, in females, 71–73
herpes simplex 1 (HSV-1), 202–204
herpes simplex 2 (HSV-2), 202–204
herpes viruses, 202–203
Her Royal Highness—Woman (O'Rell), 339
heterocentrism, 260
heteronormativity, 33
    homosexuality and, 235–236, 260
heterophobia, 263
heterosexism, 259–260
heterosexuality
    BDSM and, 382–383
    gender roles and, 223–224
    HIV/AIDS and, 208–209
    intercourse in adolescence, 281–282
    jealousy and, 332–333
    sexually transmitted infection and, 195
    as sexual orientation, 240
**highly active antiretroviral therapy
    (HAART),** 210
Hijra, 233
Hinduism, sexuality in, 9
HIV/AIDS. *See also* acquired immune
    deficiency syndrome; human
    immunodeficiency virus
    African orphans from, 214
    in animals, 208
    celibacy and, 363
    circumcision as protection, 95
    diagnosis and treatment, 210
    education and popular culture and, 215
    fetishism and, 380
    gay rights in U.S. and, 22–23
    global aspects of, 211–216
    incidence and prevalence, 207–209
    oral sex and, 374
    partnered sexual activity and, 372
    prevention, 210–211
    sex research and, 35–36
    sexual behaviour and, 209, 216
    symptoms, 209–210
HIV RNA testing, 210
home births, 141
homoeroticism, 9
    in Arab poetry, 252
    Renaissance sexual imagery and, 477–478

homologous tissues, 101
homophobia, 259–260
    in Africa, 252–253
    combating, 260–262
"The Homosexual in Urban Society" (Leznoff),
    19
Homosexualities (Weinberg and Williams), 41
homosexuality
    anal intercourse and, 378
    in ancient cultures, 8–9
    in animals, 246
    BDSM and, 382–383
    biological theories of, 243–245
    birth order and, 244–245
    in Canada, 19
    celibacy and, 363
    Chinese attitudes concerning, 10
    Christianity and, 8, 12–14
    coming out process, 254–256
    communication and, 302
    cross-cultural comparisons, 251–253
    in Enlightenment and Victorian eras, 15
    in films, 484–485
    gay erotic magazines and, 483
    gay-themed Canadian films and, 261
    globalization and, 253–254
    hate crimes and, 260
    homophobia and, 259–261
    in history, 248–250
    in Japan, 10
    jealousy and, 333
    legalization in Canada of, 238–239
    life issues and, 256–258
    in literature, 480–481
    male prostitution and, 493–495
    organizations for, 258
    as perversion, 418–420
    prevalence measurements, 241–242
    psychoanalytic theory and, 245–246
    pulp fiction and, 481–482
    queer theory and, 33–34
    race and, 263–264
    religion and, 249–250, 264–265
    reparative therapy and, 247
    research in United States on, 38–41
    sexology research on, 37, 41–42
    sexual fantasies and, 367
    sexually transmitted infection and, 195
    sexual techniques in, 375–376
    sociological theory and, 32, 247–248
    stigmatization and, 256
    on television, 485–487
    transsexuality and, 229
    in United States, 20–23, 22
homosocial play, 234
honour killings, 13
hookups, 339
hormonal conditions
    females, 71–72
    males, 101–102, 108
hormonal patch, 170–171
hormonal ring, 170

hormone replacement therapy (HRT), 80–81
    transsexuals, 231–232
hormones
    contraception based on, 166–173
    development and, 69
    erectile dysfunction therapy, 397
    female cycle of, 76
    injectable, 173
    male cycle of, 104–105
    sexual orientation and, 244
    sexual response and, 114
hot flashes, 78
Howl (Ginsberg), 481
How to Drive Your Woman Wild in Bed
    (Masterton), 307
Humanae Vitae, 155
human chorionic gonadotropin (hCG),
    126, 139
human-computer interaction, 371
human immunodeficiency virus (HIV), 207
humanistic theory, 31, 48
human papillomavirus HPV, 204–206
    cervical cancer, 86
human rights, sex research and, 50–52
Human Rights Watch, 251
Human Sexual Behavior (Marshall and Suggs),
    49
Human Sexual Response (Masters and
    Johnson), 41–42
Hustler magazine, 483
Hutterites, 32, 340
H-Y antigen, 244–245
hydrocele, 106
hymen, 61
hymenoplasty, 61
hypermasculinity, 227
    sexual assault and, 453–454
hyperphilia, 423
hypersexual disorder, 399
    paraphilias and, 422
hypersexuality, 432–433
hypertension, 408–409
hypoactive sexual desire disorder, 364,
    392–393
hypocrisy, sex scandals and, 436–439
hypophilia, 423
hyposexuality, 409
hypospadias, 103
hypothalamus, sexual orientation and, 245
hysterectomy, 83, 86, 231, 410
hysteria, sexuality and, 16
hysteroscopy, 129

I

id, 28
identical twins, 124
illness, sexual functioning and, 407–413
immigration
    arranged marriages and, 350
    homosexuality and, 264
    interracial/intercultural dating and, 339
    sex research and, 50–52

living apart together, 343
L'Onanisme (Tissot), 368
London School of Hygiene, 50
long-term reorganization, 455
Looking for Mr. Goodbar (film), 432
love
    Aboriginal love songs, 318
    as addiction, 333–334
    in adolescence, 324–325
    attraction and, 326–327
    in childhood, 323–324
    colours of, 318–319
    forms and measures of, 317–321
    in history, 316–317
    life stages and, 323–325
    long-term commitment and, 331, 345
    loss of, 331
    measurement of, 320–321
    negative aspects of, 332–334
    romantic *vs.* companionate love, 317–318
    sexuality and, 332–334
    theories concerning, 321–323
    triangles, 319–320
Love and Addiction (Peele and Brodsky), 333
Love and Survival: The Scientific Basis for the Healing Power of Intimacy (Ornish), 316
lovemaps, 423
"love scale," 320–321
Luleki Sizwe group, 253
lumbar tatoos, epidural injections and, 143
lumpectomy, 84
luteal phase, 74
luteinizing hormone (LH), 70
    in males, 104, 108
    menstruation, 73
    oral contraceptives and, 167
Lybrel oral contraceptive, 78

M

machismo, 251
Mahu of Tahiti, 232
major depression, 413
major histocompatibility complex (MHC), 323
male hypoactive sexual desire disorder, 392–393
male-on-top sexual position, 377
male prostitutes, 494–495
males
    abortion reactions in, 187
    adolescence in, 278
    in antiquity, 7–11
    in Canadian Aboriginal culture, 17–18
    in Christianity, 12–14
    circumcision in, 95
    condoms for, 159–161
    contraception in, 154–156, 181
    in Enlightenment and Victorian eras, 15
    external genitalia, 91–97, 101
    fear of, 223
    gender roles and traits, 222
    homosexuality in, 40

    as infants and toddlers, 271
    infertility in, 128–131
    internal sex organs, 97–100
    intimacy in, 327–328
    maturation cycle, 104–106
    in Middle Ages, 13
    natural contraception for, 176–177
    non-verbal communication in, 303–304
    pregnancy in, 125
    prenatal development, 100–101
    puberty in, 104–105
    reproductive health in, 106–110
    sexual and reproductive system, 92–99
    sexual assault on men by, 458
    sexual communication in, 307–309
    sexual health in, 106–110
    sexual response cycle in, 118–120
    sterilization in, 178
male-to-female (MTF) transsexuals, 231–232
malignant mass, 84
mammography, 84
manual sex, 373
marijuana, 394
    fertility and, 135
marital sexual assault, 456
marriage
    in ancient Rome, 9
    arranged marriages, 350
    in Canadian Aboriginal culture, 17–18
    in Christianity, 12–14
    cohabitation and, 341–342
    consanguineous marriages, 352–354
    endogamous and exogamous, 343–344
    in Enlightenment and Victorian eras, 15
    forced marriages, 350–351
    in French colonial Canada, 18
    in India, 9
    interracial marriage, 20–23
    in Islam, 13–14
    in later life, 344
    in Métis culture (Canada), 18
    non-exclusive marriages, 346–347
    polygamous marriages, 351–352
    satisfaction in, 344–345
    sexual activity outside, 345–346
    sexual assault in, 456
    sex within, 345–346
    statistics and current trends, 342
    U.S. cultural attitudes about, 20–23
Mary, the Virgin, 12–13
masculinity, 222–223
    in adolescence, 234–235
    androgyny and, 228–229
    in early childhood, 271–272
    expectations of, 227–228
    gender role non-conformity and, 246–247
    in men's magazines, 482–483
    sexual orientation and, 243
masochism, 382. *See also* sexual masochism disorder
mastectomy, 410

master status, 437
masturbation, 368–370
    in adolescence, 279–280
    in animals, 368
    cultural attitudes toward, 369
    frequency, 369
    history of, 368, 418
    Indian attitudes concerning, 10
    in middle childhood and preadolescence, 274–275
    mutual masturbation, 373
    orgasm during, 117
    orgasmic disorder and, 400
    research in U.S. on, 21
    sex toys and, 369–370
    traumatic sexualization and, 464
"matching hypothesis," love and, 326
maternal immune hypothesis, 244
maternal-serum alpha-fetoprotein screening (MSAFP), 138–139
matrilineal societies, in Canadian Aboriginal culture, 17
Mattachine Society, 22
media
    fetishism and, 380
    homosexuality in, 262
    sex scandals in, 436–439
    sexuality and, 5–6
    sexuality in, 480–487
medicalization of sexuality, 20–21, 33–34, 38
    erectile dysfunction and, 397
    gender procedures, 230–232
meditation, 408
Meese Commission, 488
Memoirs of a Women of Pleasure (Fanny Hill) (Cleland), 480–481
menarche, 74
    adolescence and, 277–278
Mennonites, 32
menopause, 66, 79–81
    cancer and, 410
    sexual functioning and, 408–413
menorrhagia, 77
menses, 75
men's magazines, 482–483
menstrual manipulation, 78
menstrual phase, 75
menstrual suppression, 78
menstrual synchronicity, 76
menstrual toxic shock syndrome, 82
menstruation, 74–79
    sexual behaviour and, 79
    variations in, 76–77
mental illness
    abnormal sexual expression and, 418–420
    child sexual abuse and, 464
    sexual dysfunction and, 412–413
    sexual violence and, 467
message interpretation, 310
Métis culture in Canada, 18, 302
    Canadian residential school system and, 438

ovarian hyperstimulation syndrome, 129
ovaries, 64
  cancer of, 87
overgeneralizations, 311
overkill, 311
oviducts, 63–64
ovulation, 63, 121–124
ovulatory phase, 74
ovum, 62–63
oxytocin, 65, 70

P

Papanicolaou (Pap) smear, 81, 86
  human papilloma virus and, 206
ParaGard IUD, 175
Paragraph 175 law, 37
parallel cousins, marriage to, in Canadian
    Aboriginal culture, 17
paraphilias, 421
  algolagnic disorders, 428
  anomalous target preferences, 428–430
  assessment and treatment, 434–435
  classification of, 421, 425–431
  theories concerning, 421–422
"paraphilic coercive disorder," 428
paraphimosis, 108
paraplegia, 412
parenting
  of adolescents, 283
  anxiety concerning, 276
  by gays and lesbians, 257
  love and, 323–324
  relationship satisfaction and, 354–355
  same-sex and other-sex couples and,
    354–355
Parents, Families, and Friends of Lesbians
    and Gays (PFLAG), 254
PAR-L (Policy, Action, Research List), 33
partialism, 379
participant observation, 45
partnered sexual activity, 372–378
  intimate partner violence, 467–469
  sexual assault and, 456–457
Party for Neighbourly Love, Freedom, and
    Diversity (PNVD), 429
passion, love and, 319
Passionate Love Scale (PLS), 321
patriarchy, 9
  feminist critique of, 22
pederasty, 8, 477
pedophilic disorder, 428–429. *See also* child
    sexual abuse
  assessment and treatment, 434–435
  incidence and prevalence, 367
"peeping Toms," 425–426
peer relationships, 275–277
  adolescence and, 282–283
pelvic cancer, 410
"pelvic hyperemia," 16
pelvic inflammatory disease, 169, 202
penectomy, 231, 411
penile bruising, 107

penile plethysmography, 434
penile strain gauge, 41–42
penis, 92
  cancer of, 109
  disorder of, 106–107
  evolution of, 92
  internal structure, 93
  root, 94
  size, male anxiety concerning, 93
Penis Size and Enlargement (Griffen), 93
penitents, 12
perfect use, birth control, 157
performance fears, 390
The Perfumed Garden, 480
perimenopause, 79
perimetrium, 62–63
perineum, females, 61
perpetrators, 444
  characteristics of, 446–447
persistent sexual arousal syndrome, 399
personality disorders, child sexual abuse and,
    464
Perversion for Profit (film), 490
Peyronie's disease, 107
phalloplasty, 231
  sexual developmental anomalies, 103
phallus, 7
  historic images of, 476–480
"phantom orgasm," 412
phenylethylamine, 333
pheromones, 323
Philosophy in the Bedroom (Sade), 382
phimosis, 108
photography, sexual imagery and, 478–479
photoplethysmograph, 41–42
physiological arousal theory, 322–323
physiology
  in adolescence, 277–278
  aging and, 407–408
  in infants and children, 271–277
  sexual functioning and, 391
  sexual orientation and, 245
pin-up girls, 482–483
placebo pills, 167
placenta, 124, 144
placenta previa, 145
Plain Facts for Young and Old (Kellogg), 369
Plan B emergency contraception, 180–181
Planned Parenthood, 155
plateau phase, 114, 117–119
platonic relations, 9
play, in animals, 275
Playboy magazine, 21, 40–41, 483
Pneumocystis carinii pneumonia
    (PCP), 210
  discovery of, 191
police, reporting sexual assault to, 459
politics
  pornography and, 488–491
  sex research and, 21, 35–36
polyamorist, 346–347
polyandry, 351

polycystic ovarian syndrome (PCOS), 82
polyfidelity, 351–352
polygamous marriage, 351–352
polygamy, 10
  in Canada, 18
  in United States, 20
polygynandry, 351–352
polygyny, 351
polyvictimization, 468–469
Pompeii, erotic art found in, 476–477
popular culture, HIV/AIDS in, 215
pornography, 476
  censorship and, 487–491
  child pornography, 488
  in film, 484–485
  harm principle and, 490–491
  in history, 476–478
  politics of, 488–491
  social theory and, 493
  transgender films and, 485
possessiveness, love and, 333–334
postcoital drip, 160–161
postpartum depression, 147
postpartum parenthood, 146–148
postpartum psychological changes, 146–147
postpartum psychosis, 147
post-traumatic stress disorder (PTSD), 78
  child sexual abuse and, 464
  sexual assault and, 454–455
power
  pornography and, 490
  sexuality and, 444
  sociological theory on sexual assault and, 448
pre-eclampsia, 140
pregnancy
  abortion and, 186
  in adolescence, 6, 187, 283–285
  childbirth and, 140–144
  congenital syphilis and, 199
  drugs and alcohol in, 135
  due date, 126
  early signs of, 124–126
  exercise and nutrition in, 134–135
  fathers and, 134
  health care during, 134–137
  in males, 125
  in older and single women, 136–139, 141
  prenatal period, 132–134
  problems during, 137–140
  sex during, 137
  sexually transmitted infections and, 195–
    196
  testing, 126
  weight gain in, 135
pregnancy-associated plasma protein
    (PAPP-A), 139
prehistoric times, sexual imagery in, 476
preimplantation genetic diagnosis (PGD), 127,
    130
premarital sex
  Christianity and, 12–14
  extramarital sex as, 346

premature birth, 144
premature early ejaculation, 401–402
premenstrual dysmorphic disorder (PMDD), 78
premenstrual syndrome (PMS), 77–78
prenatal development, 132–134
    females, 66–70
    males, 100–101
    sexual differentiation in, 220–221
prenatal testing
    birth defects, 138–139
    sex selection and, 127
prepuce, 58
Pretty Baby (film), 479
priapism, 106–107
primary amenorrhea, 76–77
primary sexual problem, 391
probability sampling, 39–40
probiotics, 201–202
pro-choice supporters, 183
prodromal phase, 203
progesterone, 69
    menstruation and, 70
    oral contraceptives and, 167
progestin hormones, oral contraceptives and, 167, 172–173
progestin-only birth control methods, 172
    emergency contraception, 180
prolactin, 65, 70
pro-life supporter, 182
propinquity, 326
prostaglandins, 186, 398
prostatectomy, 411
prostate gland, 99
    cancer, 109–110, 410–411
prostate-specific antigen (PSA), 109–110
prosthesis implantation, 398
prostitution
    clients of, 493–497
    in Enlightenment and Victorian eras, 15
    female prostitutes, 493–494
    history of, 491–492
    male prostitutes, 494–496
    organizing by prostitutes, 497
    rights for sex workers, 494
    sexual assault and, 457
    social policy and, 497
    social theory concerning, 492–493
    transgender prostitutes, 495
proteins, sexual reproduction, 66–67
Protestantism, sexuality and, 14
pseudocyesis, 125–126
psychoanalysis, 29
    paraphilia, 422
psychoanalytic theory, 28–29, 48
    sexual orientation and, 245–246
psychogenic drugs, 397
psychology of sex, 38
    ejaculatory disorders and, 402–403
    erectile dysfunction and, 397
    mental illness and, 412–413
    sexual assault and, 455–457

    sexual functioning and, 390–391
    sexual pain and, 404–405
psychopathia sexualis, 37–38
Psychopathia Sexualis (Krafft-Ebing), 34, 37–38, 379, 382, 431, 480
psychosexual development, 29
    in adolescence, 278–279
    in early childhood, 271–272
    in middle childhood and preadolescence, 274
psychotherapy, sex offenders, 434–435
psychotropic medications, 391
puberty
    females, 73–74
    males, 104–105
    preadolescence and, 273–274
pubic lice, 196–197
pubococcygeus muscle, 404
pulp fiction, sexual imagery in, 481–482
punishment concept of disease, 193
Puritan ethic, sexuality and, 20
Purity and Danger (Douglas), 490

Q

quadraplegia, 412
quadrupeds, 7
queer, 240
    theory, 23, 33–34, 48
questionnaires, in sex research, 45
question statements, 299
Qur'an, 13

R

race
    adolescence and, 282
    HIV/AIDS and, 209
    homosexuality and, 263–264
    lesbianism and, 262
    oral sex and, 374–375
    prostitution and, 494
    sexual assault attitudes and, 449–450
    sexuality and, 20–23
    sexually transmitted infections and, 194–195
radiation, 84–85
radical mastectomy, 84
radical prostatectomy, 110
radioimmunoassay (RIA), 126
"rainbow parties," 374
random sampling, 41
rape
    athletes and, 453–454
    on campus, 452–454
    coping with, 459–461
    corrective rape, 253, 450–451
    cultural differences concerning, 450–452
    effects of, 454–457
    feminist critique of, 22–23
    gender and, 448, 449
    perpetrator characteristics, 446–447
    pornography and, 491

    sex scandals and, 436–439
    sexual assault as, 444–445
    sexual fantasies about, 367
    sexual sadism and, 428
    in South Africa, 450–451
    theories concerning, 447–449
rape trauma syndrome, 454–455
rapex (anti-rape condom), 450
rapist psychopathology, 447–448
Reality Vaginal Pouch, 161–162
rear-entry position, 378
receptivity, 332
recurrent respiratory papillomatosis, 205
Red Light Center, 371
Red Lights on the Prairies (Gray), 492
Reformation, sexuality in, 14
refractory stage, 120
Regina v. Butler, 487
Relationship Rating Scale (RRS), 321
reliability, in sex research, 44, 47–48
religion
    abortion and, 183–184
    adolescence and, 277, 282–283
    circumcision and, 95
    consanguineous marriages and, 353
    contraceptive use and, 155–156
    homosexuality and, 249–250, 264–265
    sexuality and, 9, 12–14, 32
Renaissance
    sexual imagery in, 477–478
    sexuality in, 14
reparative therapy, 247
repression, 29
reproductive system
    females, 56–65
    fertility and, 120
    health of, in females, 81–87
    males, 92–99
resolution phase, 114, 118, 120
retrograde ejaculation, 402
revascularization, 398
reverse transcriptase, 208
Rh incompatibility, 139
RhoGam, 139
rhythm method, 176
risk factors, breast cancer, 85–86
RISUG (reversible inhibition of sperm under guidance), 181
robotics
    cybersex and, 371–372
    sex research and, 51–52
Rockefeller Foundation, 35
rohypnol, 447
role repertoire, 325
Roman culture
    homosexuality in, 248
    sexual imagery in, 476–477
    sexuality in, 9
romantic love, 317
    companionate love *vs.,* 317–318
Royal Canadian Mounted Police, 420
RU-486, 185–186

S

sadism, 382. *See also* sexual sadism disorder
safe sex practices, 383–384
    HIV/AIDS and, 215
    oral sex as, 374–378
    sexually transmitted infection and, 193–194
St. Augustine, 12, 418
St. Jerome, 12
St. Paul, 12, 418
Same-Sex Marriage (Lahey & Alderson), 297
same-sex marriages, 240. *See also* civil unions
    in Canada, 348–349
    communication in, 297, 301
    early Christianity and, 12–13
    pregnancy and, 128–129, 138, 141
    in United States, 349
same-sex relationships
    in adolescence, 282
    communication and, 296–297, 301
    current trends in, 347–349
    intimate partner violence in, 468
    lifestyle issues and, 256–258
    other-sex relationships and, 348
    parenting and, 257, 354–355
    peer relationships, 276–277
    prevalence measurements of, 241–242
    sexuality in, 348
    in United States, 20–23
samples of convenience, 47
sati ritual, 9
satr al-'awra (modesty), 13
scabies, 196–197
schema, 226
schizophrenia, 413
scrotoplasty, 231
scrotum, 95–96
Seasonale (oral contraceptive), 78
Seasonique oral contraceptive, 78
secondary amenorrhea, 76–77
secondary sexual characteristics, 101
    transgender and, 230–232
secondary sexual problem, 391
The Second Sex (Beauvoir), 22
second-trimester surgical abortion, 185
self-actualization, 31
self-disclosure, 307
self-image
    communication and, 306–307
    jealousy and, 333
selfing behaviour, 71
self-love, 332
semen, 92
    cultural and historical attitudes concerning, 7–15, 156
    diet and, 99
semenarche, 273–274
seminal vesicles, 99
seminiferous tubules, 97–98
semirigid rods, 185, 398

seniors
    homosexuality and, 257–258
    marriage and, 344
    sexual activity in, 235
    sexual assault of, 456
sensate focus, 397
The Sensuous Woman (Garrity), 21
sequential bisexuality, 263
seven-year itch, 356
sex, 66
    gender and, 220
Sex and Germs (Patton), 207
Sex and the Single Girl (Brown), 21
sex chromosomes, 67
sex crimes
    against children, 429
    sexual assault, 444–461
sex development, variations in, 220
sex education
    abstinence-only approaches, 211
    in Canada, 4, 6, 286–292
    for children and adolescence, 274, 286–292
    effects and results, 287–290
    future challenges in, 290–292
    global trends in, 291
    HIV/AIDS and, 215
    in India, 10
    on sexual assault, 453–454
    sexual harassment prevention and, 470
sex flush, 117
sex hormones, 70
sex hormone therapy, transsexuals, 231–232
Sex Offender Information Registration Act, 420
sex offenders, 419–420, 434–435, 444
    characteristics of, 446–447
    child sexual abusers, 464–466
    treatment of, 461
sexologists, 5
    research by, 36–38
    in United States, 21
sexology, 33
Sex Professionals of Canada (SPOC), 496–497
sex reassignment surgery (SRS), 229–232
    in Iran, 228
sex research
    in Canada, 43–44
    cross-cultural research, 49–50
    early research, 34–35
    future issues in, 50–52
    global trends in, 49–51
    Internet and, 46, 50
    methods and issues in, 44–46
    obstacles to, 35
    politics and, 35–36
    problems and issues, 47–48
    recent U.S. trends in, 42–43
    sexology researchers in, 36–38
    in United States, 21, 38–42
sex scandals, 436–439
sex selection, myths about, 126–127
The Sex Technique in Marriage (Hutton), 374

sex therapy, 395
    erectile dysfunction, 397
    sex offenders, 434–435
sex tourism, 494
sex toys, 369–370
sex typing, 227
sexual abuse
    in Catholic Church, 437–439
    of children, 461–466
    in institutions, 413
    pedophilia, 428–429
sexual activity
    in adolescence, 280–285
    of Canadian college students, 362–363
    cultural and religious attitudes about, 7–15
    cybersex, 305, 370–372
    decisions about, 4–5
    fetishistic activity, 379–381
    historical images of, 476–480
    HIV/AIDS and, 208–209
    illness and, 409–413
    masturbation, 368–370
    menstruation and, 79
    non-marital, 340
    oral sex, 373–376
    outside marriage, 345–346
    partnered activity, 372–378
    for same-sex partners, 256–258
    in seniors, 235
    sexual assault effect on, 455
    unconventional sexual behaviour, 379–383
    vaginal intercourse, 376–378
sexual addiction, 432–433
sexual arousal disorders, 393, 395–399
sexual assault, 444
    alcohol and, 453
    among animals, 444
    athletes and, 453–454
    attitudes and cultural variations concerning, 449–452
    on campus, 452–454
    coping with, 459–461
    cultural differences concerning, 450–452
    effects of, 454–457
    lesbians and bisexuals and, 456
    male victims of, 457–458
    of men by men, 458
    of men by women, 458
    myths about, 446
    older women, 456
    partners reactions to, 457
    pornography linked to, 490–491
    of prostitutes, 457
    reporting of, 459–461
    statistics on, 445–446
    theories concerning, 444–445, 447–449
    women with disabilities, 456–457
sexual assault crisis centres, 453
Sexual Behavior in the 1970s (Hunt), 40–41
Sexual Behavior in the Human Female (Kinsey), 39
Sexual Behavior in the Human Male (Kinsey), 39

sexual behaviour, judgment of, 419–420
sexual blame avoidance, 367
sexual cognitions, 365
sexual communication, 306–309
sexual contact
    in adolescence, 280–281
    in middle childhood and preadolescence,
        274–275
sexual crusaders, 21–22
sexual desirability, 367
sexual desire disorders, 392–395
sexual deviation, 418
sexual differentiation
    case study, 221
    in prenatal development, 220–221
sexual experience, 367
sexual experimentation, 241
sexual fantasies, 365–367
    cybersex and, 371–372
    necrophilic fantasy, 432
sexual functioning, 390–391
    aging and, 407–413
    child sexual abuse and disorders of, 464
    disorders of, 395–405
    sexual assault and, 455–457
sexual harassment, 469–470
sexual health
    education for children about, 286–292
    in females, 81–87
    historical concepts concerning, 20–21
    sexual functioning challenges and, 389–391
sexual imagery. *See also* pornography
    in films, 483–485
    in history, 476–480
    in media, 480–487
    orientalism and imperialism and, 478
    in pulp fiction, 481–482
    television and, 485–487
sexual incompatibility, 375
sexual interest disorders, 393
sexual inversion, 418
sexuality, 4
    abnormal sexual expression and, 418–420
    in ancient Asia, 9–10
    in ancient civilizations, 7–11
    biological clock phenomenon and, 136
    in Canadian history, 17–18
    in childhood, 270–277
    communication and, 296–298
    current attitudes concerning, 5–6
    during Enlightenment and Victorian
        eras, 15
    in infants and toddlers, 271–272
    love and, 332–334
    media and, 5–6, 480–487
    medical education concerning, 21
    in men's locker room, 328
    in middle childhood and
        preadolescence, 274
    in middle childhood to preteens, 273–277
    for new parents, 147–148
    in non-human primates, 7–11

parental anxiety concerning, 276
    in Reformation, 14
    religion and, 9, 12–14
    relationships and, 275–277
    in Renaissance, 14
    theories about, 28–34
    in same-sex relationships, 348
    on television, 485–487
    in U.S. history, 20–23
Sexuality Information and Education Council
    of Canada (SIECCAN), 4, 286–290, 362
The Sexual Life of the Child, 37
sexually transmitted infections (STIs), 4, 192
    in adolescence, 285
    in animals, 205
    bacterial infections, 197–202
    birth control and pregnancy and, 195–196
    Canadian college students and risk of,
        362–363
    cervical barriers and, 163–165
    circumcision and, 95
    condom use and, 159–161
    demographic risk factors, 194–195
    ectoparasitic infections, 196–197
    history of, 192–193
    HIV/AIDS, 207–215
    incidence and prevalence, 192
    safe sex practices and, 193–194
    social exclusion and, 33
    in United States, 21
    viral infections, 202–207
sexual masochism disorder, 428
sexual mental diseases, 34
sexual orientation
    behaviourist theory and, 247
    biological theories, 243–245
    birth order and, 244–245
    communication and, 302
    definitions, 240–241
    developmental theories, 245–247
    differences in, 243–247
    intimacy and, 328–329
    models of, 240–241
    pheromones and, 323
    physiology, 245
    prevalence measurements, 241–242
    sexual fantasies and, 367
    sexually transmitted infection risk and,
        193–195
sexual pain problems, 404–405
sexual perversion, 418
Sexual Politics (Millet), 22
Sexual Preference (Weinberg and WIlliams), 41
sexual reproduction, females, 66–67
sexual response, 114
    research on, 114–120
sexual response cycle, 114–120
    in men, 118–120
    in women, 114–118
sexual revolutions, 21–22
sexual sadism disorder, 428
sexual terminology, 309

sex work. *See also* prostitution
    clients of, 493–497, 496–497
    organizing by prostitutes in, 497
    social theory and, 492–493
    strippers, 495–496
Shaker movement, celibacy and, 20
Sharia law
    divorce and, 355
    sexuality and, 13–14
shoe fetishes, 421, 424, 430
shunga (Japanese erotic art), 477
sibling relationships, 277
    incest and, 462
sickle cell disease, 138
side-by-side sexual position, 377–378
side rear-entry position, 378
silent rape reaction, 456
simian immunodeficiency virus (SIV), 208
simple mastectomy, 410
The Sissy Boy Syndrome (Greene), 247
situational erotica, fetishism and, 380–381
situational orgasmic disorder, 400
situational sexual problem, 391
16 and Pregnant (television show), 6
slavery, sexuality and, 20
sleep, sexual dysfunction and, 408
smoking
    in mothers, semen volume in males and, 105
    pregnancy and, 135–136
    sexual function and, 408
socialization, 225
    cross-cultural gender differences, 300–301
    homosexuality and, 256–258
    throughout life span, 234–236
social learning theory, 30, 48
    gender and, 225
    sexuality in media and, 486
social networking, 304–306
    sexuality and, 6
The Social Integration of Peers and Queers
    (Reiss), 495
Society and the Healthy Homosexual
    (Weinberg), 259
sociological theory, 32, 48, 448
    paraphilia and, 422, 424
    sexual orientation and, 247–248
    sex work and, 492–493
A Solemn Appeal (White), 369
sonography, 132
sororal polygyny, 351
South Africa, sexual entitlement and rape in,
    450–451
South America, HIV/AIDS in, 215–216
soy products, sperm count and, 97
Spanish fly, 394
speculum, 81
speech quantity, 300
sperm
    competition and, 92
    sex determination and, 67
    stress and production of, 96
    toxins and, 97